Europe in the Twentieth Century

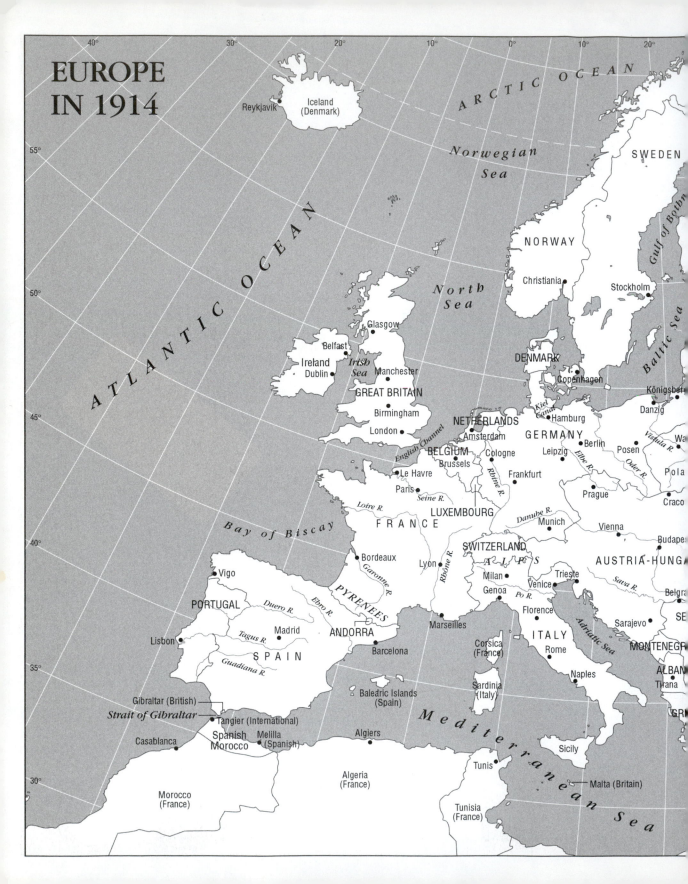

Europe in the Twentieth Century

2005 Update

Fourth Edition

ROBERT O. PAXTON

Columbia University

AUSTRALIA • CANADA • MEXICO • SINGAPORE • SPAIN
UNITED KINGDOM • UNITED STATES

THOMSON
✳
™
WADSWORTH

Publisher: *Clark Baxter*

Assistant Editor: *Paul Massicotte*

Editorial Assistant: *Richard Yoder*

Marketing Manager: *Lori Grebe-Cook*

Marketing Assistant: *Mary Ho*

Advertising Project Manager: *Stacey Purviance*

Project Manager, Editorial Production:
Jennifer Klos

Print Buyer: *Lisa Claudeanos*

Permissions Editor: *Kiely Sexton*

Production Service: *Stratford Publishing Services*

Cover Image: *Alberto Giacometti "Falling Man" 1950 © 2001 Artists Rights Society (ARS), New York/ADAGP Paris*

Text and Cover Printer: *Webcom*

Compositor: *Stratford Publishing Services*

Printed in Canada

2 3 4 5 6 7   08 07 06 05

For more information about our products, contact us at:
Thomson Learning Academic Resource Center
1-800-423-0563

For permission to use material from this text or product, submit a request online at **http://www.thomsonrights.com.**
Web: http://www.thomsonrights.com

Any additional questions about permissions can be submitted by email to **thomsonrights@thomson.com.**

Library of Congress Control Number: 2001088996
ISBN: 0-534-60632-6

Thomson Wadsworth
10 Davis Drive
Belmont, CA 94002-3098
USA

Asia
Thomson Learning
5 Shenton Way #01-01
UIC Building
Singapore 068808

Australia/New Zealand
Thomson Learning
102 Dodds Street
Southbank, Victoria 3006
Australia

Canada
Nelson
1120 Birchmount Road
Toronto, Ontario M1K 5G4
Canada

Europe/Middle East/Africa
Thomson Learning
High Holborn House
50/51 Bedford Row
London WC1R 4LR
United Kingdom

Latin America
Thomson Learning
Seneca, 53
Colonia Polanco
11560 Mexico D.F.
Mexico

Spain/Portugal
Paraninfo
Calle Magallanes, 25
28015 Madrid, Spain

Contents

Preface   xix

1   Europe at Zenith, 1914   1

Europe and the World   2
European Traders, Travelers, and Investors   2
Imperialism   4
European Artists and Scientists   7
European Landscapes: Urban and Rural   7
Life in the City   8
Life in Peasant Europe   9
The Rich and the Poor   10
Class and Social Rank   10
The Poor   12
The Rich   13
The Middle Class   14
Upward Mobility   17
Women and Families   18
Having Fewer Children   18
Women's Place   19
Political Systems and Mass Movements   21
The Monarchy   21
The Role of Parliaments   22
The Socialist Movement   24
Nationalism   26
Inherited Creeds   27
Liberalism   27
Conservatism   30
Organized Religion   31
Toward a New Consciousness   32
The Revolution in Science   32
The Revolution in Art and Thought   33
The Reaction to Cultural Revolution   37
Suggestions for Further Reading   38

2   The Coming of War   43

The July Crisis of 1914   44
The Balkans: Declining Empires and Rising Nationalities   45
Germany's "Blank Check"   50

Austria's Ultimatum to Serbia   52

Escalation: From Local War to Continental War   53

Russia's Mobilization   53

France's Intentions   54

Germany Declares War   55

The Schlieffen Plan   56

Britain Joins In   57

A Longer View of the Causes of War   60

Sovereignty and a Nation's Honor   61

Imperialist Considerations   61

Internal Dissent   62

The Alliance System   63

The War Machines   64

The Exercise of Choice   64

Suggestions for Further Reading   65

3   **The Marne and After, 1914–1917   69**

War Fever   69

A Dilemma for the Socialists   71

War and Social Peace   72

The First Battle of the Marne   73

The Eastern Front   75

Tannenberg and the Masurian Lakes, 1914   75

The Austrian Fronts, 1914–1915   76

The Search for a Breakthrough in the West   77

Assaults "Over the Top"   78

Major Offensives: Verdun, the Somme, the Champagne   79

New Weapons   82

The Widening War   84

The War at Sea   86

The United States Enters the War   87

Suggestions for Further Reading   88

4   **The Impact of Total War   91**

Adjusting to a War of Attrition   92

War Governments: A Comparative Look   93

Great Britain   93

France   95

Germany   97

Russia   99

Austria-Hungary   100

Italy   102

The Social Impact   102

The Status of Women   103

The Status of Organized Labor   104

Social Cleavage   105

The Economic Impact   106
   War Profiteers   106
   The Effects of Inflation   107
The Impact on Internal Order   108
   Strike Activity   108
   Liberal and Socialist War Critiques   109
   Police Power   111
   Control of Public Opinion   112
The Intellectual Impact   113
Suggestions for Further Reading   116

5   Revolution, 1917–1920   119
The Russian Revolutions, 1917   120
   The "February Revolution"   120
   Provisional Government and the Soviets   121
   The "October Revolution"   125
The Bolshevik Regime   127
   Lenin's "Peace, Land, and Bread"   127
   The Establishment of a New Autocracy   129
   Civil War   131
Revolutionary Stirrings in Western Europe, 1917   134
The German Revolution, 1918–1919   136
   Steps toward Revolution   136
   The Socialist Struggle for Power   137
   The Failure of the Social Revolution   138
The Dissolution of Austria-Hungary, 1918–1919   141
   The Breakdown of Dynastic Loyalties   142
   Nation-Building in the Successor States   143
   The Béla Kun Regime   145
Britain, France, Italy: The Unrest of 1919–1920   146
Aftermath and Results   149
   Success and Failure: A Comparative Look   149
   The Third International and the Division of the European Left   150
Suggestions for Further Reading   153

6   The Paris Peace Settlement   157
The Setting: Ideals, Interests, and Ideology   158
   War Aims   158
   The "Fourteen Points"   158
   Wartime Treaties and Promises   159
   National Interests of the Great Powers   161
   Fear of Bolshevism   163
The Settlement   164
The League of Nations Covenant   164
The Western European Settlement   167
   The Attempt to Separate the Rhineland   168

Territorial Changes   168
"Demilitarization" of Germany   168
Reparations   170
The Eastern European Settlement   172
Territorial Changes   172
Frontier Problems   173
Discrimination among Nationalities   178
The Eastern European Settlement Assessed   180
Applying the Peace Settlement   181
The Years of Coercion, 1919–1924   183
The Years of Conciliation, 1924–1929   186
The Locarno Era: The Dawes Plan and the Locarno Treaty   187
The Failure of Disarmament   191
A New Diplomacy?   193
Public Involvement   194
The Communist Threat   196
Diplomatic Machinery   196
Suggestions for Further Reading   197

7   Revolution against Revolution: Fascism   201
Fascism in Italy   202
Mussolini: From Syndicalism to Fascism   202
Early Fascism   204
Fascism's New Course   204
Governmental Crisis   205
The "March on Rome"   207
Mussolini Assumes Personal Rule   208
National Socialism in Germany   210
Postwar Antirevolutionary Vigilantism   211
The Emergence of Hitler   212
The Nazi Party   212
The "Beer Hall *Putsch*," 1923   213
Counterrevolution in Hungary   214
A Closer Look at Fascism   217
The Meaning of Fascism   217
The Roots of Fascism   219
Suggestions for Further Reading   224

8   "Normalcy": Europe in the 1920s   227
A Return to "Normalcy"   228
Neoliberal Economics: Dismantling War Government   228
Neoliberal Politics: Broadening Parliamentary Democracy   229
Britain   231
A Three-Way Party System   231
The First Labour Government, 1924   232
Return to Conservative "Normalcy"   233

France   236
    The *Cartel des Gauches*   236
    Poincaré: Return to "Normalcy"   238
Weimar Germany   239
    Burdens on the Weimar Republic   239
    The "Weimar Coalition"   241
    The "Great Coalition"   243
Eastern Europe   245
    Rural Predominance and Agrarian Discontent   246
    The Problem of National Minorities   249
The Iberian Peninsula   250
Fascist Italy   252
Revolutionary Russia in a Stabilized World   254
    Challenges to the Bolshevik Regime   254
    The "Industrialization Debate"   255
    The Consolidation of Political Dictatorship   256
    The Rise of Stalin   257
A Fragile Stability: Neoliberalism Assessed   259
Suggestions for Further Reading   260

9   Mass Culture and High Culture between the Wars   263
Mass Culture: The Age of Radio and Movies   264
    The Technological Basis for Mass Media   264
    The Creation of Mass Audiences   265
    The Political Uses of Radio and Movies   266
    Control of the Mass Media   267
    The Role of Advertising   268
The New Leisure   269
    Organized Recreation   270
    Sports   271
    Travel   272
The Effects of Mass Culture and Leisure   273
High Culture Between the Wars   276
    Experimental Aesthetic Values   277
    New Concerns   279
The Settings of Interwar Culture   282
    Social Status of Artists   282
    The Search for a Mass Audience   284
    The Academic and Scholarly Worlds   286
    Opposition to the Experimental Arts   288
Suggestions for Further Reading   290

10   The Depression and Its Effects, 1929–1936   293
The Origins and Course of the Great Depression   296
    Domestic Crisis   296
    International Financial Crisis   297

Depression Remedies   298
  Liberal Economics   299
  Socialist Economics   299
  New Economic Solutions   300
  The Call for "Return to the Soil"   301
Depression Politics in the Liberal States   301
  The Scandinavian Countries   301
  Britain   302
  France   306
  Weimar Germany   309
Depression Politics in the Authoritarian States   311
  Nazi Germany   311
  Corporatist Italy   314
  The Soviet Union's "Second Revolution"   316
Conclusion   319
Suggestions for Further Reading   319

11   **The Authoritarian 1930s and the Spread of Fascism   323**
Germany: National Socialism in Power   324
  The Revival of Nazism, 1929–1932   324
  The End of Weimar: Presidential Government, 1930–1933   327
  Revolution after Power, 1933–1939   331
Clerical Authoritarianism   335
  Portugal: Salazar   337
  Christian Social Austria: Dollfuss and Schuschnigg   338
  Spain: Franco and the Falange   340
Fascism in Eastern Europe   340
  Hungary and Bulgaria   341
  Romania   341
Fascist Minorities in Western Europe   343
  France   343
  Britain   345
  The Low Countries and Scandinavia   348
The Appeal of Fascism   349
Suggestions for Further Reading   350

12   **The Popular Front Era, 1934–1939   355**
From "Class against Class" to Popular Front   356
  The Communist Policy of "Class against Class," 1928–1934   357
  Reversal of Comintern Policy, 1934   359
  The Liberal Reaction   360
  The Socialist Reaction   361
The Popular Front in France   362
  The Formation of Léon Blum's Government   363
  The French New Deal   364
Spain: Republic, Revolution, and Civil War   368

The Creation of the Second Republic   368
Political Phases of the Republic   369
The Civil War   372
European Intellectuals and the Popular Front   374
The European Left after the Popular Front   376
Suggestions for Further Reading   379

13   The Paris Peace Settlement Dismantled:
Aggression and Appeasement, 1933–1939   381

Hitler's First Moves   381
Setback in Austria   382
First Violations of the Versailles Treaty   384
The Remilitarization of the Rhineland, March 1936   384
Italy Shifts Sides   387
The Ethiopian Conquest   387
Break with the West   388
Alliance Patterns   389
Hitler's Designs in the East   390
Lebensraum for the Master Race   391
Economic Considerations   391
Anschluß: Test Case of Nazi Aims   392
Czechoslovakia and Appeasement, 1938   393
Czechoslovakia's Precarious Position   393
Appeasement   394
Mounting Crisis in Czechoslovakia   397
The Munich Settlement   398
The Alternative of War   400
The Polish Crisis, 1939: Descent into War   402
Appeasement Abandoned   402
The Nazi-Soviet Pact   403
The Origins of the Second World War   406
Suggestions for Further Reading   408

14   Hitler's Europe: Conquest, Collaboration, and Resistance, 1939–1942   411

The Nature of the Conflict in 1939   412
War in the East, 1939–1940   414
Blitzkrieg in Poland   414
Russian Gains in Eastern Europe, 1939–1940   414
War in the West, 1940   415
The Fall of France   416
The Battle of Britain   418
War in the East, 1941–1942   421
Blitzkrieg in the Balkans   422
Attack on the Soviet Union   422
Hitler's "New Order"   424
Nazi War Economy   426

Occupation Policy   427
The SS Empire   428
The Murder of the Jews   428
Collaboration   431
Ideological Collaboration   431
Collaboration for National and Economic Interests   432
Passive Acquiescence   433
Resistance   435
Resistance outside Germany   436
Resistance within Germany   438
The Military Impact of the Resistance   440
The Intellectual Impact of the Resistance   441
Suggestions for Further Reading   444

15   From Hot War to Cold War, 1942–1949   449
American Hegemony in the West   450
Planning the Second Front   451
Diversionary Second Fronts: North Africa and Italy   453
D-Day and the Assault on Germany   454
Soviet Hegemony in the East   457
Soviet Survival, 1941–1943   457
Soviet Advance to the West   461
The Big Three and the Future of Europe   461
Gathering Political Implications   462
The Teheran Conference, November 1943   463
Soviet Moves in the Balkans   464
The Yalta Conference, February 1945   465
The Potsdam Conference, July 1945   469
Origins of the Cold War   470
Soviet Peace Aims   471
American Peace Aims   472
Seeds of Antagonism   475
First Battlegrounds of the Cold War   476
Poland   476
Germany   478
A World in Two Blocs, 1947–1949   481
Suggestions for Further Reading   486

16   Ruin and Reconstruction, 1945–1953   489
The Work of Reconstruction   492
New Leaders and Parties   492
Economic Recovery and Social Change   495
The Labour Government in Britain, 1945–1951   497
The Beveridge Report: "Full Employment"   497
The British Welfare State   498
Economic Maladjustment   499
The French Fourth Republic   500

The Search for Leadership   500
Nationalization and Planning   502
Postwar Italy   503
The Contest for Political Power   503
Reconstruction   505
The Two Germanies   505
Separate Statehood   506
The West German "Miracle"   507
Reconstruction and Orthodoxy in the Soviet Union   508
Suggestions for Further Reading   510

17   The Soviet Bloc from Stalin to Khrushchev   513
The Soviet Union: From Repression to De-Stalinization   513
Eastern Europe, 1945–1953: The Successor States as Soviet Satellites   515
National Front Regimes, 1945–1947   516
Degrees of Soviet Control   518
Soviet Crackdown in Eastern Europe   520
Peoples' Democracies   521
Forced Collectivization   522
The Struggle for Power in the USSR, 1953–1957   522
"De-Stalinization" and the "Thaw," 1956–1964   523
Eastern Europe: Thaw and Rebellion, 1953–1956   526
The Fall of Khrushchev, 1964   529
Suggestions for Further Reading   530

18   Europe in the Cold War: Between the Superpowers, 1947–1961   533
Europe under the Mushroom Cloud   534
Western Europe: Cold War Politics at Home and Abroad   535
The Isolation of Communist Parties   535
Division of the European Left   537
Centrist and Conservative Governments   538
Colonial Wars   540
Western Europe: The Movement for Union   543
Architects of European Union   544
Pressures for Union   545
Union for Defense: The Creation of NATO   546
Problems of European Unity   546
Attempted Political Union: The Council of Europe   548
Economic Union: The European Coal and Steel Community
and the Common Market   549
Soviet Ripostes in Eastern Europe   552
Suggestions for Further Reading   554

**19   The "New Europe": Consumer Societies and Mass
Culture in the West, 1953–1973   557**
Consumer Societies   559
Distribution of Wealth   560

Social Mobility   563
Politics in Consumer Societies, 1953–1968   565
    The "End of Ideology"   565
    Consensus Politics   566
Mass Culture and High Culture in the "New Europe"   568
    Popular Culture   568
    The Fine Arts   569
    Religious Revival   571
    Scientific Achievements   573
Discontent in Consumer Societies: 1968 and After   574
    Student Discontent   574
    Worker Discontents   577
    The New Feminism and Women's Liberation   578
    The Descent into Terrorism   579
Suggestions for Further Reading   580

20   Cold War Détente: Stirrings of Independence, 1962–1975   583
The Cold War: From Thaw to Détente   584
Polycentrism in the Communist World   586
    The Sino-Soviet Split   586
    National Communism in Eastern Europe   588
Gaullism and the Western "Third Force"   589
The Common Market Redirected   592
The United States and Europe as Economic Rivals   595
Rival Versions of Détente   598
Suggestions for Further Reading   605

21   The Soviet Bloc in the Brezhnev Era   607
Soviet Problems   608
Troubled Eastern Europe: From the Czechoslovak Springtime
    to the Brezhnev Doctrine, 1968–1985   611
    Discontent in Eastern Europe   611
    The Czechoslovak Springtime of 1968   612
    Poland: Unrest and Solidarity   615
    Hungary: The "Goulash Communism" of János Kádár   616
    The German Democratic Republic: Industrial Power and
        Omnipresent Police   617
    Romania, Yugoslavia, Bulgaria: Tyranny and Nationalism   617
Brezhnev's Legacy: Stagnation and Missiles   618
Suggestions for Further Reading   621

22   Western Europe, 1973–1989: Postindustrial Society and "Stagflation"   623
Economic Strains: Oil, Jobs, and Trade   624
    A "Postindustrial" Society?   626
    Immigrants and the New Right   626
Welfare States under Stress   629

Northern Europe: Conservative Revivals   629
Mediterranean Europe: The Left in Power, but Transformed   633
The European Community in Recession   641
Intellectual and Spiritual Certainties Challenged   643
The End of an Era: Moderation and Lowered Expectations   645
Suggestions for Further Reading   646

23   The Revolution of 1989 and After   649
The Gorbachev Experiment, 1985–1991   650
Falling Dominos: Eastern Europe in 1989   651
Reunifying Germany, Ending the Cold War   654
The Collapse of the Soviet Union   656
The Morning After   659
Russia in Trouble   659
Creating Democracy, Inventing the Market in Eastern Europe   664
The New Germany   666
The Yugoslav Civil War   668
Western European Responses to the Revolution of 1989   673
European Union: Between Deepening and Widening   673
Western Europe: Far Right and "New Middle"   676
Suggestions for Further Reading   679

Epilogue   Europe and the United States Since 9/11   681

Credits   683

Index   685

Preface

Europe is the foreign region that Americans are likely to think they know best. It is the origin of more than 70 percent of our citizens. It is the overseas continent most often visited by American tourists. The society, economy, and culture of the United States began as offshoots of Europe, so that an American dealing with European counterparts in business, the arts, or government is likely to take common presumptions for granted.

Yet, while recognizably kin, Europeans live in a profoundly different world. They are conscious of a far longer history than Americans, a past marked by more ups and downs. Europeans are more likely to be aware of the transience of empire and the ambiguity of humanity's efforts to improve itself and the world. They have inherited a more complicated hierarchy of social ranks and classes, a more formal intellectual tradition, and more overtly ideological politics than Americans. Sooner or later one will encounter an educated European convinced that while he can easily understand rootless, straightforward, homogeneous America, Americans have too little historical sense or cultural sophistication to fathom complex Europe. Like most caricatures, that view contains a germ of truth.

I believe that Americans can best acquire a sensitive appreciation of Europe by giving some thought to the past experience of Europeans. *Europe in the Twentieth Century,* 2005 Update Fourth Edition, provides an introduction to their experience since 1914. Those ninety years were clamorous with war, revolution, ethnic conflict, and economic crisis. During that time social ranking, the cultural climate, popular attitudes, and Europeans' consciousness of their place in the world all changed at a dizzying rate.

Historians nowadays pay more attention than before to matters outside the familiar realm of war, diplomacy, and politics. Social mobility, family relationships, deep-seated popular values, and the lives of ordinary women and men are more frequent subjects for serious historical inquiry than they were forty years ago. These concerns are reflected on many pages of this book. Even so, the traditional matters of war, revolution, economy, and struggles over liberty and authority still occupy a central place here. It could not be otherwise without distorting Europeans' experience in the violent century just past.

I have tried to present the essential core of the subject, the major themes of public and private life in Europe since 1914, without excessive detail. I hope that readers will be tempted to deepen their knowledge by exploring the riches of more specialized scholarly works and of European literature and the arts as listed in the updated Suggestions for Further Reading at the end of each chapter. If this introductory textbook makes these works more accessible and more fun, my efforts will have been worthwhile.

Many people helped me along the way to the creation of this updated edition and the editions that came before it. Through their valuable comments, the following scholars helped guide the direction this edition has taken. I heartily thank Jerry H. Brookshire (Middle Tennessee State University), Albert S. Lindemann (University of California at Santa Barbara), Alexis E. Pogorelskin (University of Minnesota at Duluth), and John D. Treadway (University of Richmond). Any errors and shortcomings of the final text are, of course, my own.

In addition, I would like to thank the people at Thomson Wadsworth for their help in bringing out this book: Clark Baxter, publisher; Paul Massicotte, assistant editor; Richard Yoder, editorial assistant; and Jennifer Klos, production project manager. Thank you all.

Map Contents

Europe in 1914   ii
Ethnic/Linguistic Composition of Austria-Hungary, 1914   47
Balkan Conflicts, 1878–1914   48
Original Schlieffen Plan   57
World War I: The Fronts   85
Peace Settlements in Europe, 1919–1920   165
Mandates under the League of Nations   166
Destruction of the Empires   174
European Nationality Problems, 1919–1939   176
Franco-German Security Issues, 1920–1940   189
Eastern Europe   390
Hitler's Europe, 1942   425
Defeat of the Axis, 1942–1945   451
Eastern and Western Fronts at Time
    of the Yalta Conference, February 1945   467
Russia in the Twentieth Century   472
Territorial Adjustments after the Second World War, 1945   474
Germany after Two Wars   482
Expulsion of Germans from Central Europe, 1945–1947   491
Cold War Europe in the 1950s   547
Common Market and COMECON   552
Cold War Europe, 1985   585
Conflicts in the Former Yugoslavia   669
Europe in 2001   720

The upper class at leisure: the beach at Villerville, photographed in 1908 by the French photographer Jacques Henri Lartigue.

1

Europe at Zenith, 1914

Europeans who took stock of themselves as the twentieth century opened were aware that their continent played a very special role in the world, a role out of all proportion to its size. A dense, highly skilled population; massive industrial productivity; a culture that rewarded creative novelty; and a near monopoly of modern military force: These qualities gave Europeans a commanding position on the globe in 1914. Europeans thought of themselves as "the civilized world"; and insofar as other peoples were increasingly influenced by European ways of doing things, the future seemed to promise the eventual Europeanization of the world.

In 1914, there were proportionally more Europeans in the world than ever before, or since.[1] The population explosion that erupts in Asia, Africa, and Latin

---

[1]Europeans constituted 25 percent of the world's population on 7 percent of the earth's surface in 1914. Thereafter, their share of the world's people began to drop. By 2000 only 12 percent of the world's people were Europeans, as compared to 61 percent Asians, 13 percent Africans, 8 percent North Americans, and 6 percent South Americans.

America today began in Europe around the year 1750. After having grown a mere 3 percent from 1650 to 1750, the European population then more than doubled: from 188 million in 1800 to 401 million in 1900. It spilled over into the rest of the world, sending, by 1900, 1 million emigrants a year to new settlements, chiefly in the Americas and Asiatic Russia. Along with them went another mass of "temporary emigrants": the missionaries, soldiers, teachers, and entrepreneurs who were setting the stamp of Europe on the face of the rest of the world. By 1914 there were 100 million persons of European origin in North America and 40 million in Latin America, and there were smaller outpost populations in the European colonies of Africa, Asia, and the Pacific.

EUROPE AND THE WORLD

It was not through their numbers, however, but through their dynamism that Europeans dominated the world in 1914. "While the major part of the globe remained fixed in its customs," wrote the French poet and essayist Paul Valéry, "this little cape on the Asiatic continent . . . set itself clearly apart from the rest."

> Wherever the European spirit prevails, one sees the maximum of needs, the maximum of work, the maximum of capital, the maximum of production, the maximum of ambition, the maximum of power, the maximum of modification of external nature, and the maximum of communications and exchanges.[2]

During the nineteenth century Europeans had become the first people on earth to alter their physical environment almost beyond recognition. They substituted the frenetic rhythms of steam-driven factories, huge cities, and rail travel for the slow seasons of agriculture, the routine of village life, and the pace of a person on foot. In 1914, despite the recent upsurge of Japan and the United States as industrial powers, Europe still retained a decisive economic lead. Europe produced 56 percent of the world's coal (although the United States alone produced another 38 percent of it) and 60 percent of the world's iron and steel (against a United States share of 32 percent). Europe accounted for 62 percent of the world's exports (whereas the United States accounted for 14 percent). To be a European meant to be living in the world's first industrial complex: the oldest in terms of time and still the first in rank.

European Traders, Travelers, and Investors

The rest of the world was being increasingly drawn into a single world economy with Europe at its hub. Wherever goods were traded by means other than simple barter, European mercantile practices came into play. The international gold standard, according to which governments promised to exchange their currencies

---

[2]Paul Valéry, "Caractères de l'esprit européen," *La Revue universelle,* vol. 18, no. 8 (July 1, 1924), pp. 133, 142.

freely for gold at a fixed rate, made it easy to settle commercial accounts for goods sold in one currency but paid for in another. International accounts for companies all over the world were usually settled in London. London had evolved into the de facto capital of a stable, unified world-trading system, because the British pound had been freely convertible into gold since 1821 (most other advanced countries had followed Britain in adopting the gold standard after 1870) and because British clearinghouses, insurance brokers, and shipping agents were the largest, cheapest, and most experienced in the world. In 1914, London handled the clearing of 70 percent of American companies' foreign accounts. And British firms owned 70 percent of the world's shipping.

Freer international trade was the capstone of this "classical-liberal" system. For a brief period, from 1860 to 1879, the world's major trading nations imposed almost no tariffs on foreign goods, and other kinds of restrictions on trade virtually vanished. Never had the movement of people and goods from one country to another been subject to so little government regulation.

The British economist John Maynard Keynes looked back from the 1920s with nostalgia on this prewar London-centered world economy. He recalled that

> the inhabitant of London could order by telephone, sipping his morning tea in bed, the various products of the whole earth, in such quantity as he might see fit, and reasonably expect their early delivery upon his doorstep; he could at the same moment and by the same means adventure his wealth in the natural resources and new enterprises of any quarter of the world, and share, without exertion or even trouble, in their prospective fruits and advantages; or he could decide to couple the security of his fortunes with the good faith of the townspeople of any substantial municipality in any continent that his fancy or information might recommend.
>
> He could secure forthwith, if he wished it, cheap and comfortable means of transit to any country or climate without passport or other formality, could despatch his servant to the neighborhood office of a bank for such supply of the precious metals as might seem convenient, and could proceed abroad to foreign quarters, without knowledge of their religion, language, or customs, bearing coined wealth upon his person, and would consider himself greatly aggrieved and much surprised at the least interference. But, most important of all, he regarded this state of affairs as normal, certain, and permanent, and any deviation from it as aberrant, scandalous, and avoidable.[3]

Dynamic Europeans were not content merely to trade with and travel to the rest of the world. They also invested their money there. In 1914, Europe was the source of 83 percent of the world's foreign investments, in both developed and underdeveloped areas: Canadian mines, American railroads, South American electric companies, Senegalese groundnut plantations, Egyptian cotton farms, South African gold mines, Shanghai trading companies, and the like. Of the Latin American countries, only Chile owned its railroads in 1914. Even the new American giant, the United States, was deeply in debt to European investors. On the eve of the First

---

[3]John Maynard Keynes, *The Economic Consequences of the Peace* (New York, 1920), p. 12. These varied opportunities were open, of course, only to the wealthy.

World War, European investments in the United States totaled nearly $7 billion, whereas United States investments in Europe totaled a mere tenth of that figure.[4]

Imperialism

Could Europeans trade, travel, or invest abroad in full confidence, however, unless they had some means of forcing local governments to protect them and their property? In the case of the modernized states, diplomatic pressure might be enough to protect European business and travel. Many British traders and investors were content in the mid-nineteenth century with what has been called "informal empire," or "free-trade imperialism." The more the Europeans' energies overflowed into underdeveloped regions, however, the more risks they ran from bandits, hostile populations, and the whims of local rulers. In underdeveloped regions, Europeans chose increasingly in the late nineteenth century to safeguard their access to markets, raw materials, and returns on their investments by seizing outright political and military control.

European imperialism—the acquisition of empires—was not new to the late nineteenth century. Europeans had begun establishing outposts at the edges of the world's oceans as early as the fifteenth century.[5] They had set up lucrative mines and

The glory of empire. Lord Curzon, viceroy of India, and Lady Curzon among Indian notables at the turn of the century.

[4]*The Cambridge Economic History of the United States,* vol. II (Cambridge, Mass., 2000), pp. 749, 787.

[5]The first European colony of modern times was Ceuta, an outpost on the northern coast of present-day Morocco. It was founded in 1402, partly for booty and partly for the religious purpose of making contact with Prester John, the legendary Christian emperor and priest, whose kingdom was believed to lie beyond the Moslem world—that is, in Ethiopia.

trading posts in Latin America and Asia in the sixteenth and seventeenth centuries. They had forced foreign rulers to grant "capitulations"—the right of European citizens to be ruled by their own laws—in enclaves like Shanghai and in whole regions like the Ottoman Empire. But all these efforts seemed insignificant compared with the enterprise of the late nineteenth century: the direct seizure of immense tracts of land around the world. Between the 1850s and 1911 the Europeans carved into colonies almost the entire underdeveloped world. They parceled among themselves all of Africa except Liberia and Ethiopia. The French completed their conquest of Indochina in the 1880s. After 1897 Europeans began staking out spheres of influence in China. By 1914 Britain had an empire 140 times its own size; Belgium, an empire 80 times its size; Holland, 60 times; and France 20 times. Russia established itself as a major Pacific Ocean power with the completion of the Trans-Siberian Railroad (1891–1903). Germany, which entered the competition late, in 1885, made up for the relatively restricted empire it had obtained in East and Southwest Africa and on the China coast with investments in the less-developed parts of Europe and with the hasty construction of a powerful fleet after 1900. Only Japan managed to stem the European tide, by adopting European industrial techniques with such success that the "capitulations" granted to foreign traders in 1858 could be revoked in 1894.

The explanation of the gigantic burst of energy that was late-nineteenth-century European imperialism is a central historical controversy. Some historians believe that imperialism was primarily a cultural phenomenon: the zeal of missionaries for converts, of engineers for new rivers to bridge, and of soldiers for glory. In Indochina, it was certainly Catholic missionaries who called for the help of the French navy; and it was the naval officers who, in turn, exceeded their instructions and established French control in Indochina between the 1850s and the 1880s.

Other students of imperialism are convinced that economic drives were far more fundamental. They point to the French occupation of Tunisia in 1881, when French bondholders were faced with the loss of their assets, and to the British occupation of Egypt in 1882, when European investors could no longer collect interest on their loans to the spendthrift ruler of Egypt, Khedive Ismail. Some colonies were almost purely commercial propositions: Sir George Goldie's United African Company of 1879 spread the British presence into what is today Nigeria. The Italian conquest of Libya from the Ottoman Empire in 1911 promised land to its overpopulated south as well as glory.

Explanations of imperialism based on simple trade or settlement are not fully satisfying. For one thing, the territories acquired in the rush from 1885 to 1914 were rarely suitable for European settlement. Furthermore, the imperialist powers traded more with one another than with their colonies. The economic interpretation of imperialism rests on a far more basic judgment of capitalism's inherent faults. A British liberal economist, John A. Hobson, angered by the British war in South Africa, the Boer War (1899–1902), first attributed imperialism in a systematic way to contradictions in capitalism. Hobson suggested that low wages and the maldistribution of wealth left European workers with such low purchasing power that capitalists could escape periodic depression only by a search for richer markets and higher investment returns overseas.[6]

[6]John A. Hobson, *Imperialism, A Study* (London, 1902).

The Russian Marxist V. I. Lenin pushed the arguments of Hobson much further in *Imperialism: The Highest Stage of Capitalism* (1917). Lenin believed that capitalists must turn to monopoly when their rates of profit fall in the face of competition and ever more expensive technology. When the monopolies scramble for the last overseas opportunities, the capitalist states inevitably go to war and, sooner or later, destroy one another in a conflict like the one that raged while Lenin was writing. Lenin seriously underestimated the extent to which capital continued to be invested in the advanced countries, even during the imperialist rush of 1885 to 1914. Nevertheless, no interpretation of imperialism can fail to assign some role to economic aims.

Once begun, for whatever combination of motives, imperial expansion tended to take on a self-sustaining momentum as the last available territories were snapped up. Contemplating this escalation of imperialism in the 1880s and 1890s, Ronald Robinson and John Gallagher maintained that strategic considerations were uppermost in the British government's decisions to occupy Egypt. According to this account, the British took control of Egypt in 1882 in order to protect their stake in India. The very existence of a colony, in other words, created the strategic necessity for controlling access to it.[7] Critics of this theory have not failed to point out that the British were in India in the first place for reasons largely, if not wholly, economic. In any event, by 1914 the net result of imperialism was a world in which the Western powers had established themselves competitively on every continent. After the American Robert Peary had reached the North Pole in 1908 and after Roald Amundsen had raised the Norwegian flag at the South Pole in 1911, no corner of the earth had escaped the impress of imperialist energies in some form.

The Europeans were able to defend their world empires in 1914 because of their near monopoly of modern military force. Colonial armies, officered by Europeans and equipped by means of an ingenious technology, made short work of Oriental potentates, Muslim kingdoms, and African tribes. It was almost unheard of for native forces to gain more than a temporary advantage over the Europeans. The defeat of an Italian force by Ethiopians at Adowa in 1896 was the outstanding exception. The British imperial poet Rudyard Kipling could afford to be magnanimous to the hard-fighting Sudanese warriors:

> An', 'ere's to you, Fuzzy-Wuzzy, . . .
> For you broke a British square.[8]

For, so far, the British had never failed to get what they wanted in the end.

The rising industrial powers outside Europe did not even attempt to build armed forces on a European scale. For example, the primary function of the United States' armed forces in the 1880s was simply to subdue the last of the Indian resisters. At that time, the great land armies of France, Germany, Austria-Hungary, and Russia had no equals on earth except one another. Thus, it was with a shock of premonition that many Europeans watched the United States wrest a colonial empire from Spain in 1898 and saw Japan defeat Russia in 1905.

[7]Ronald Robinson and John Gallagher, *Africa and the Victorians* (London, 1967).

[8]Rudyard Kipling, *Ballads and Barrack Room Ballads* (London, 1892), p. 150.

European Artists and Scientists

European influence in the world was by no means entirely material. European arts and sciences were as much a lodestar to the rest of the world as European commerce and technical skill. The Americans who traveled abroad in Henry James's novels did so not to see quaint sights but to acquire European polish and learning. No American physicist or chemist expected to excel in his field without European study. Hundreds of Americans studied medicine each year in Germany, even after such American universities as Johns Hopkins in the 1870s introduced the Ph.D. degree and graduate seminars modeled on German university practice. So it was not mere ritual politeness that led the Harvard philosopher William James to open his lectures at Edinburgh in 1901 on "The Varieties of Religious Experience" by saying:

> To us Americans, the experience of receiving instruction from the living voice, as well as from the books, of European scholars is very familiar. . . . It seems the natural thing for us to listen while Europeans talk. The contrary habit, of talking while the Europeans listen, we have not yet acquired; and in him who first makes the adventure it begets a certain sense of apology being due for so presumptuous an act.[9]

EUROPEAN LANDSCAPES: URBAN AND RURAL

Europe was the most urban of the continents by 1914. Northern and Western Europe, the first region to shift a majority of its working population from agriculture to industry, was also the first region in which a majority of the population lived in towns and cities. Although the total population soared, the rural portion of it remained stable or even declined: The excess was pouring into cities and towns.

Between 1800 and 1900, the number of European cities with populations over 100,000 increased from 22 to 120. The fastest growing cities and towns were the newer, industrial ones (the population of Essen in Germany, for example, expanded by thirty times between 1800 and 1900). But, even the populations of the pre-industrial capitals—Paris, London, Vienna—expanded by three or four times in the course of the nineteenth century. In 1848, only London and Paris contained more than 1 million inhabitants; in 1914, six European cities had more than 1 million inhabitants, compared with three in the United States, three in Asia, and two in Latin America. By the 1990s, even though only two European cities (London and Moscow) remained among the Asian and Latin American giants on the list of the world's twenty-five greatest cities, Europe remained the most urbanized continent. Seventy-four percent of its population lived in cities— and even more in England, Germany, and the Low Countries, a proportion reached elsewhere only in North America.[10] To be a European meant to live in or near great cities. These cold facts, however, are less important than the social and intellectual impacts of urban living.

[9]William James, *The Varieties of Religious Experience* (New York, 1958), p. 21.

[10]Stanley D. Baum and Jack F. Williams, eds., *Cities in the World,* 2nd ed. (New York, 1993), pp. 13, 19.

Life in the City

Cities were among the most glorious of European creations and, at the same time, among the most squalid. Since medieval times, the cities of Europe had attracted lavish concentrations of money, power, and artistic expression, as well as pestilential slums. The Industrial Revolution poured more crowds into these slums, added miles of hastily built tenements, and overlaid it all with smoke and grime. In 1857, Charles Dickens described a "debilitated old house" in London that

> wrapped in its mantle of soot, and leaning heavily on the crutches that had partaken of its decay and worn out with it, never knew a healthy or cheerful interval. . . . You should alike find rain, hail, frost, and thaw lingering in that dismal enclosure, when they had vanished from other places; and as to snow, you should see it there for weeks, long after it had changed from yellow to black, slowly weeping away its grimy life.[11]

Nineteenth-century builders also contributed to those parts of European cities that were centers of elegance and spectacle. Unlike their predecessors, who had carefully designed the public spaces in imperial Paris, in ecclesiastical Rome, and in Venice and Florence, the nineteenth-century city-builders operated—in ways proper to the century of middle-class prosperity—with a maximum of speculative real estate development and a minimum of planning, except to locate the new wealthy quarters west, or upwind, of the old city centers. Among the more carefully planned projects were the new *grands boulevards* of Paris, cut through the slums by Napoleon III in the 1850s and 1860s. Beginning in 1858, the old city walls of Vienna were torn down and replaced by the broad *Ringstrasse,* with its opera and elegant cafés. Among the least planned were Berlin's great new commercial avenues like the *Kurfürstendamm* and its highly profitable villa developments in the former pine woods and potato fields west of the capital.

No wonder the Europeans' reaction to their cities at the opening of the twentieth century was ambivalent. On the one hand, critics of the cities pointed not only to the obvious squalor of urban slums but to the climate of human indifference and the loss of purpose and meaning that blighted so many urban lives. It is striking how frequently the theme of moving to the city occurs in nineteenth-century novels and how badly the fictitious urban immigrants fared. The prototype was perhaps Julien Sorel in Stendhal's *The Red and the Black* (1831). Increasingly calculated love affairs led him finally to Paris and to execution for having tried to kill his mistress. Many Europeans among the millions who moved into towns and cities did indeed find moral decadence and loneliness as well as physical misery. Although social critics deplored urban poverty, conservatives attacked cities as warrens of uprooted cosmopolitan civilization. The heroes of Maurice Barrès's French novel *The Uprooted* (1897) lost their moral bearings in Paris and committed murder. Writing during the First World War, the German social commentator Oswald Spengler lamented that

> in place of a type-true people, born of and grown in the soil, there is a new sort of nomad, cohering unstably in fluid masses, the parasitical city-dweller, traditionless, utterly

[11]Charles Dickens, *Little Dorritt* (1857).

matter-of-fact, religionless, clever, unfruitful, deeply contemptuous of the countryman and especially that highest form of countryman, the country gentleman.[12]

In the midst of its magnificence the city seemed to many a human wasteland:

> Unreal City,
> Under the brown fog of a winter dawn,
> A crowd flowed over London Bridge, so many,
> I had not thought death had undone so many.
> Sighs, short and infrequent, were exhaled,
> And each man fixed his eyes before his feet.[13]

On the other hand, European cities were still irresistible magnets as the twentieth century opened. The largest crowd that had ever visited a single display, nearly 51 million persons—more than the total population of France—went to the Paris World's Fair during 1900. Millions were still moving into the cities. The ambitious moved because cities offered far wider opportunities for wealth and fame than the countryside. The rural poor moved because a bad job was better than none. Those in trouble moved for the city's anonymity. The artistically creative praised the variety and excitement of cities, as their predecessor Charles Baudelaire had done in the 1860s, as places of both "multitude and solitude," a "spree of vitality," an inebriating world of "feverish joys" where the soul could "give itself utterly, with all its poetry and charity, to the unexpectedly emergent, to the passing unknown."[14] Much of European creativity could not be imagined without the environment of towns and cities.

Life in Peasant Europe

A traveler crossing the Elbe River into Eastern Europe entered a world radically different from the efficient commercial farms and urbanized majorities of Western and Northern Europe. Vast aristocratic estates, inefficiently cultivated by a population of landless laborers, stretched beyond the horizon. The Radziwills owned 500,000 acres in Poland; the Esterházys, 750,000 acres in Hungary. Four thousand great proprietors owned about one-third of Hungary in 1895.[15] The Russian nobility and gentry, even after large losses of land to middle-class purchasers in the late nineteenth century, still owned about 14 percent of the land; the imperial family by itself owned another 1 percent of that vast country.[16] The same was true in Southern Europe. Southern Italy and southern Spain were dominated by enormous estates, or *latifundia*. About 2 percent of the population owned 66.5 percent of the

---

[12]Oswald Spengler, *The Decline of the West,* vol. 1 (New York, 1926), p. 107.

[13]T. S. Eliot, "The Waste Land," in *Collected Poems, 1909–1962* (New York, 1970), p. 55.

[14]Charles Baudelaire, "Petits Poèmes en prose," in *Œuvres completes,* vol. 2, ed. Jacques Crépet (Paris, 1924), p. 163.

[15]C. A. Macartney, *The Habsburg Empire, 1790–1918* (New York, 1969), p. 713.

[16]Geroid Tanquary Robinson, *Rural Russia under the Old Regime* (New York, 1932), p. 268.

land in the southern Spanish province of Andalusia.[17] Small gentry and new middle-class rich imitated the lifestyles of the greatest landowners as well as they could. Landowners exercised social and economic sway in their regions far beyond the power that came from holding local political office.

Agriculture was grossly inefficient in Eastern and Southern Europe in 1914. One-third of Russian peasant holdings still lacked steel ploughs. The ancient three-crop rotation system still kept large areas of land fallow. At the turn of the century, Russian peasants produced about 8.9 bushels of spring wheat per acre, whereas German peasants produced 27.5, and English farmers, 35.4.[18] Vast tracts of land in Andalusia were set aside as bull-raising farms or hunting preserves. With many hands devoted to seasonal tasks without the use of modern tools, the huge rural population in Eastern and Southern Europe was underemployed. Peasants were desperate for some land of their own. In Western and Northern Europe, where independent family farms were the rule, peasant proprietors were a conservative counterweight to urban and labor unrest in the late nineteenth century. In Eastern and Southern Europe, however, a mass of land-hungry peasants formed a powder keg of unrest and anger on the eve of the First World War.

Finally, in Mediterranean Europe and the Balkans, the residents of remote hill villages practiced a primitive, subsistence agriculture almost beyond the reach of modern markets and the modern state. Here, peasants often owned some land, although their pockets of rocky, terraced hillside could not really sustain them. Others paid tribute to rapacious small landlords. The physician and painter Carlo Levi, an urban northern Italian exiled to a hill village in southern Italy by Mussolini's fascist regime, later wrote that Christian civilization itself, everything that had happened since Greek times, seemed to him to have never penetrated up beyond the last market town.[19] Other timelessly ancient hill villages survived in the Balkans, as described in the Yugoslav writer Milovan Djilas's recollections of his home town in Montenegro, *Land without Justice* (1958). Only after 1945 were the last of these relics of subsistence economy drawn into the larger society.

THE RICH AND THE POOR

Class and Social Rank

Society was highly stratified in Europe in 1914. Even after a century of middle-class expansion and hesitant steps toward political democracy, social distances remained very great. They were also quite visible. A European's social position was instantly evident in his clothes, size, complexion, and subtle traits of posture. Manual laborers on the Continent usually wore cloth caps or berets and blue smocks over rough trousers; married lower-class women, especially those in the south and east, were usually dressed in rough black dresses and shawls. Wooden clogs were the common

---

[17]Edward E. Malefakis, *Agrarian Reform and Peasant Revolution in Spain* (New Haven, CT, 1970), p. 29.

[18]Robinson, p. 130.

[19]Carlo Levi, *Christ Stopped at Eboli* (New York, 1947).

© BBC Hulton Picture Library / Liaison Agency

Watching a horse race at Ascot before the First World War. Hats and positions mark social classes very clearly. The upper class, in top hats, stand in carriages; middle-class men appear in bowlers and straw hats. Working-class men, standing on the ground, wear cloth caps.

footwear of the rural poor. Although body size had begun to increase with better nutrition in the late nineteenth century, poor men, even in England, averaged three inches shorter than the wealthy.[20] Hard work and dangerous machinery left their marks on mutilated bodies. Sun-darkened faces and necks were still a caste mark of poverty, not a badge of leisure. A British officer, watching troops bathing in a river during the First World War, is supposed to have turned in astonishment to a fellow officer with the remark, "I had no idea their bodies were so white."

Smell and voice completed the outward marks distinguishing the lower classes. George Bernard Shaw's comedy *Pygmalion* (1900) turns on the relation of accent and class. As Shaw remarked in the play's preface, "It is impossible for an Englishman to open his mouth without making some other Englishman despise him." The idly rich linguist Henry Higgins and his friend Colonel Pickering find Eliza Doolittle, a cockney flower girl, at the Covent Garden open market in London. "You see this creature with her kerbstone English," says Higgins, "the English that will keep her in the gutter to the end of her days. Well, sir, in three months I could pass that girl off as a duchess at an ambassador's garden party. I could even get her a place as a lady's maid or a shop assistant, which requires better English."

[20]Emanuel Le Roy Ladurie dates the "end of the anthropological 'Old Regime'" at around 1860, when the visible "proletariat" of diminutive Europeans began to disappear and average height began to rise from around five feet to the nearer six feet of today. (*Annales: économies, sociétés, civilisations* [July–October 1972], p. 1234.)

The social gradations in England so easily mocked by Shaw in 1900 were nevertheless quite real. Society was even more stratified in Eastern and Southern Europe, where only a small middle class in the rare market towns stood between the landed aristocracy and the peasants.

The Poor

Most Europeans were poor in 1914. But the standard of living was at least higher than it had been in the past. Northern and Western Europe (along with its extension in North America) was the first region on earth where a majority of the population could expect to be able to earn a bit more than what was needed for bare survival. Elsewhere in the world, unremitting labor for all one's days merely kept one alive, but not for long and not in good health.

Historians still argue about whether workers' living standards went up or down with the introduction of the first factories in the early nineteenth century, but real wages certainly rose substantially in the late nineteenth century. Purchasing power almost doubled in England, France, and Germany between 1880 and 1914. By that time, bread and potatoes were often supplemented by meat on working families' tables.[21] Many workers could afford simple factory-made clothes, and there was even a little left over in many a family's budget for beer—the café being the main recreation available after the normal fifty-to-sixty-hour workweek.

The nineteenth century's massive increase in both agricultural and industrial productivity shifted the most urgent problem from quantity of production to distribution of the product. Since Europeans now produced some surplus, a new era was at hand, an era in which all citizens could demand a share in that surplus as rightfully theirs.

Despite the Europeans' very real material progress in the generations before 1914, dire poverty was still widespread in even the richest regions in 1914. The best information comes from the English provincial city of York, where Seebohm Rowntree devoted a lifetime to gathering precise data on the way his fellow citizens lived. The indefatigable Rowntree, conducting a house-to-house survey in 1899, found that nearly 28 percent of the inhabitants of York lived in such irreducible want that "total earnings were insufficient to obtain the minimum necessaries for the maintenance of merely physical efficiency."[22] A similar study of London at about the same time showed that 30.7 percent of its residents lived in poverty.

In plain words, in the richest city of the richest country in the world, in about 1900, nearly one-third of the people felt acute hunger, slept in their clothes for warmth, and looked forward only to death in a charity hospital or on the street and a pauper's burial in an unmarked grave. On the Continent, poverty was no less widespread in the most prosperous areas—northern France, the Low Countries,

---

[21]John Burnett, *Plenty and Want: A Social History of Diet in England from 1815 to the Present* (London, 1966).

[22]Seebohm Rowntree, *Poverty* (London, 1901), pp. 86, 117. Rowntree also conducted a follow-up study in the depression year of 1936 and, in 1951, when he was eighty years old, a study of life under the welfare state. He found 31 percent living in poverty in York in 1936, although its cause had shifted from low wages to unemployment. The big breakthrough came after the Second World War. The 3 percent in poverty in York in 1951 were all aged. See chapter 19, p. 562.

western Germany—than it was in England. In the more backward areas of Eastern and Southern Europe, bare subsistence or less was still the lot of the majority. In 1900, for example, the average life expectancy was under thirty-five years in the Balkans and in Spain.[23]

Even those wage earners who lived above the bare subsistence level had to endure the most inescapable quality of working-class life: permanent insecurity. Social-welfare arrangements were only in their infancy. Germany led the way, after 1883, with compulsory state-run health- and retirement-insurance plans. France followed, far more tentatively, with voluntary social-insurance arrangements in the 1890s. In Britain, the Liberal Party under the leadership of David Lloyd George replaced the trade unions' voluntary insurance schemes with a national, compulsory health- and unemployment-insurance system in 1911. Even so, many of the poor were not covered, notably the self-employed, agricultural workers, and domestics. Most working families had known poverty before and expected to know it again: Illness, accidents, drunkenness, gambling, death of the principal wage earner filled most ordinary working lives with uncertainty.

The Rich

The distance from poor to rich was planetary. In the same year that the fictitious Professor Higgins met Eliza Doolittle selling flowers at Covent Garden, the real landlord of the Covent Garden market, the Duke of Bedford, is supposed to have received £15,000 in rent for that property alone.[24] The guests who gathered every weekend in the great country houses or shooting lodges of England or Andalusia or Hungary took for granted the care given them by the hundreds of servants who unpacked their bags and stood behind each of them at dinner. In that era before income tax, the most prodigal social display was possible. Count Robert de Montesquiou, the model for the Count de Charlus in Marcel Proust's *Remembrance of Things Past* (1913–1927), held a musical gala in Paris in the early 1900s. He had rooms massed with roses and aigrettes, and he placed a Wagnerian soprano "in a cloud of grey irises with a poinsettia here and there to remind us of the fire-theme." One of the guests, Countess Greffulhe, appeared "in a dress embroidered with golden lilies; a string of pearls, twisted in her hair, fell to her waist. She was going on to dine with the Queen of England."[25]

The very rich belonged, technically speaking, to one of two classes: the aristocracy or the upper middle class. Inherited noble title still mattered in the Europe of 1914. The great majority of those large landowners who monopolized social, economic, and political power in Eastern and Southern Europe were titled aristocrats. On his Hungarian estate, a Prince Esterházy was virtually royal. The Prussian aristocracy, concentrated on great estates east of the Elbe, enjoyed almost total control

[23]P. Guillaume and J. P. Poussou, *Démographie historique* (Paris, 1970), p. 341.

[24]About $75,000 at 1900 exchange rates. Of course, the Duke of Bedford also owned many other properties, including great expanses of farmland.

[25]Philippe Jullian, *Prince of Aesthetes: Count Robert de Montesquiou* (New York, 1965), pp. 198–200.

of the officer corps and public administration in the state that dominated the German Empire. Even in urban-industrial England, every prime minister until 1902, except Disraeli and Gladstone, had been a peer.

Only in France and Italy was aristocratic title seriously diminished as a key to political power. The French revolutions of 1789, 1830, and 1848 had abolished the legal (although not the social) distinctions of birth, so that aristocrats were subject to the same laws and restricted to the same political rights as other citizens. The number of nobles in the two French houses of parliament declined from nearly one-third of the total in 1871 to a mere handful in 1914.[26] The unification of Italy, from 1859 to 1871, had swept away the local kingdoms and the ruling houses to which the aristocrats had been attached, thereby diminishing their political roles. But even in France and Italy, aristocrats were still accorded enormous social deference; and, although no longer powerful in electoral politics, they remained strong in the army, the Church, and diplomacy.

The wealthiest industrial and commercial tycoons were equal or superior to the aristocrats in everything except hereditary title. Traditionally, the possessors of great new fortunes did their best to acquire landed estates, aristocratic manners, and, eventually, a noble title itself for their children or grandchildren, if not for themselves. By 1900, however, many of the very wealthy had become less interested in buying their way into the aristocracy. As income from agriculture underwent a relative decline in the late nineteenth century, title more often needed wealth than wealth needed title. To recoup their fortunes, some aristocrats married American heiresses: Lord Randolph Churchill, Winston Churchill's father, married Jennie Jerome of New York; the French Count Boni de Castellane married the daughter of the American railroad entrepreneur Jay Gould. By 1900 the titled and untitled wealthy merged for every practical purpose, except, perhaps, that of inviting each other to dinner.

The Middle Class

Between the few very rich and the many poor lay the broad middle class. In its upper reaches, the European middle class was composed of comfortably established business and professional men, about whose smug self-confidence and intellectual narrowness the English novelist Arnold Bennett complained:

> Their assured, curt voices, their clothes, the similarity of manners, all show that they belong to a caste, and that the caste has been successful in the struggle for life.[27]

In early-twentieth-century literature, the supreme example is the solid Lübeck merchant family whose rise and decline over several generations are described in Thomas Mann's novel *Buddenbrooks* (1902). The creators of the Buddenbrooks firm

---

[26]Mattei Dogan, "Political Ascent in a Class Society," in Dwaine Marvick, ed., *Political Decision Makers* (New York, 1961), pp. 71, 73.

[27]Quoted in Peter Laslett, *The World We Have Lost* (New York, 1984), p. 258.

were sober, hard-working men, careful with their money, confident of its value, contemptuous of the frivolous, spendthrift ways of the aristocracy as much as of the coarse ways of the poor. Their highest aim was to instruct their sons in love of the family business. "I pray to God that I shall be able to turn over the business to you in its present state," old Johann Buddenbrook wrote to his son. "Work, pray, and save."

Middle-class European lifestyles were intended to display respectability. Propriety was more highly valued than gaudy display, which was more characteristic of the *nouveau riche* or of the frivolous nobleman. The stiffness of clothing, the formality of meals, and the elaborate rituals of entertaining and leaving calling cards were expensive and painful ways of demonstrating to the outside world that one knew the proprieties and could afford to maintain them. Early-twentieth-century novels of family life are filled with the "ceremonies of respectability," such as the savage description of Victorian child-rearing in Samuel Butler's *The Way of All Flesh* (1903), whose young hero was "taught to kneel . . . before he could well crawl."

Below the solid upper middle class ranged a large population that struggled, at the edge of insecurity, to keep up as many of the outward signs of respectability as it could. Shopkeepers, some rising skilled workers, and marginal professional men clung to middle-class values and signs, even though the gnawing knowledge that one bad break could send them into poverty dogged their lives, just as it did the lives of the wage earners.

The exact size of the European middle class in 1914 is impossible to measure because of that group's shadowy edges. At the top, the middle class merged into the aristocracy; at the bottom, it merged into the working class. By reputation, the nineteenth century had been the century of middle-class triumph, and it would be easy to assume that by 1914 most residents of the more prosperous nations of Europe fell into this category. But if we consider only those who were established in a secure middle-class status and exclude those who merely aped its lifestyles from below, the European middle class was still a minority in 1914.

The situation in England illustrates this point. One measure of the solid middle class in England was the payment of income tax.[28] The rate before 1914 was 5 percent on income over £150;[29] only about 300,000 persons (1 Englishman in 170) paid income tax, and they grumbled about it. Not all these households could afford the outward signs of middle-class life without struggling. From what we know of the distribution of wealth in England in 1914, some 120,000 households owned about two-thirds of the nation's capital wealth: the real estate and investments that made up the country's capital stock. Among them were perhaps 40,000 landowners who owned 27 of the 34 million acres in the country. At the other end of the scale, about two-thirds of the English population disposed of only 5 percent of the national wealth.[30]

Another measure of the solid middle class was the employment of servants. In 1901, those employed in domestic service formed the largest occupational group in

[28]First levied in England to pay for the Napoleonic wars, the income tax was widely adopted in Europe in the late 1880s and early 1890s. By 1910, only France, the United States, Belgium, and Hungary had not yet levied taxes on income. The United States adopted a national income tax in 1913. The First World War, or its immediate aftermath, brought the income tax to all modern states.

[29]About $750 at 1914 exchange rates.

[30]Laslett, p. 261.

England, larger than mining, engineering, or agriculture, if both men and women are counted. Among working women, domestic service was by far the major occupation, employing about 1.5 million of the 4 million English women who worked for wages.[31] Harold Macmillan, Conservative prime minister of Britain in the late 1950s, recalled his childhood home, the home of a prosperous but austerely Methodist publisher, as one without frills; but there were still seven servants.[32] Further down the scale, marginally middle-class families struggled to keep one servant, for the woman who scrubbed and cooked alone for her family without the aid of gas or electric appliances inevitably looked and felt lower class. The Marx family, exiled in London, barely scraped by in two rooms in Soho, with occasional income from Karl Marx's articles for the New York *Tribune* and with help from his friend Friedrich Engels. Even at the edge of poverty, however, the Marxes still had their faithful servant, Frau Demuth.

The ultimate sign of the solid middle class was something less measurable: the extent to which one could control one's life. The French novelist Roger Vailland's penetrating *The Law* (1957), although actually set in a primitive southern Italian village after the Second World War, is a timeless essay on the meaning of class. Vailland's characters know that status is not simply a matter of wealth but of everyday human relations, of who "makes law" for others, who calls the tune. In Vailland's village no one "makes law" for the decayed nobleman Don Cesare. The aggressive entrepreneur Matteo Brigante subjects most of the villagers to his will, while he is humiliated by a few more independent than he. The rest of the villagers live, by and large, in a state of perpetual humiliation from which they do not have the money, nor the wit, nor the will to free themselves.

Most Europeans were too habituated to certain fundamental constraints—family obligations, sexual roles, and conformity to national styles and religious values—to notice how those constraints controlled their lives. And an increasing proportion of Europeans were subject to decisions made by large companies or bureaucracies. The number of independent artisans had declined by 1900 to the irreducible 10 percent or so of carpenters, plumbers, and the like that has persisted through the twentieth century. Factory workers had become the most rapidly growing element of European populations in the late nineteenth century until their numbers leveled off around 1900 to the approximately one-third of the population that they represented until late in the twentieth century. Their place as the fastest growing element at the turn of the century was taken by white-collar workers: clerical employees; workers in distribution, sales, and communications; and lower-level civil servants, such as teachers and postmen. Although many white-collar workers struggled to maintain a middle-class appearance, their lives were also subject to the decisions of others and to the dimly understood forces of the marketplace or of society.

It is an error, therefore, to believe that after a century of the "rise of the middle class" a majority of Europeans were established as independent middle-class men and women. Peter Laslett estimates that in England, the most highly developed urban and

[31]Ibid., p. 273.

[32]Harold Macmillan, *The Winds of Change* (London, 1966), p. 39.

industrial region of Europe, only about 20 to 30 percent of the population could be called solidly middle class. An Englishman who was born within that charmed circle, or who reached it by his own efforts, could well reflect with Winston Churchill that, "lapped in the accumulated treasure of the long past, the old world in its sunset was fair to see."[33] Outside that charmed circle lay a penumbra of those who struggled to imitate it. And then came the poor majority. If we extend the same analysis to the Continent, we would find rather similar social hierarchies in the most highly urbanized and industrialized regions: northern France, the Low Countries, western Germany, Sweden, and perhaps northern Italy. Further east and south, the middle class was restricted to a meager few merchants and moneylenders in the sparse market towns; here, the aristocrats and the peasant mass confronted each other across even sharper and steeper social gradations.

Upward Mobility

How easily might a European move from one level to another in one lifetime? Clearly, European classes were not castes. One's lifelong social position was not immutably set by birth. Whereas inherited title and upper-class birth still lent enormous social prestige, wealth already counted for more, and that could be attained in a lifetime, given luck and will. However, the way up was narrowing. Studies of successful French businessmen show that more of them had risen out of the artisan ranks in the early stages of industrialization before 1850, than was the case at the end of the nineteenth century, when it took more capital to launch a big enterprise. It was highly exceptional for a European to climb or marry into a higher class in one generation: Moves upward usually took several generations. Most Europeans in 1914 could expect to finish out their days in about the same social position as they had begun.

A move upward, moreover, could involve very painful personal experiences of isolation and rejection. In *Howard's End* (1910), E. M. Forster's novel about the workings of class distinctions in England, young Leonard Bast

> stood at the extreme verge of gentility. He was not in the abyss, but he could see it, and at times people whom he knew had dropped into it. . . . Had he lived some centuries ago, in the brightly colored civilizations of the past, he would have had a definite status, his rank and income would have corresponded. But in his day the angel of Democracy had arisen, enshadowing the classes with leathern wings, and proclaiming: "All men are equal—all men, that is to say, who possess umbrellas." And so he was obliged to assert gentility.[34]

Bast's rather crude efforts to acquire "culture" and the misguided attempts of two wealthy young women to assist his social ascent destroyed him. The women suffered only slightly. The moral seemed to be, "There's never any great risk, as long as you have money."

---

[33]Winston Churchill, *The World Crisis, 1911–1914* (London, 1923), p. 199.

[34]E. M. Forster, *Howard's End* (New York, 1954), pp. 45–46, 60.

WOMEN AND FAMILIES

Having Fewer Children

Europe at the turn of the twentieth century had passed one of the major turning points in social history: the "demographic transition," or the "fertility transition." In its simplest terms, this was the trend toward small families.

Traditional societies may pass through several demographic stages. In the first, population is kept approximately stable because very high birth rates are balanced by very high death rates. In the second stage, improved health conditions and better food supplies diminish the death rate, and population soars. Northern and Western Europe reached this stage in the seventeenth, eighteenth, and early nineteenth centuries (and the Third World reached it after World War II).

In the third stage, birth rates decline, and population again levels off. This began to happen in Europe in the nineteenth century, as parents began to see the advantages of having fewer children.[35] In the first place, there was less reason to have many babies because improved living conditions meant that most of one's children could survive, an experience previously unknown. Second, children became expensive. Although more children may have meant more income on the farm, factory workers discovered, after limitations had been imposed on child labor, that more children only meant higher expenses for food and clothing. And as public education became widespread, the cost of education made children even more expensive. The lower middle class found that a "respectable" middle-class lifestyle would be easier to reach with fewer children. Finally, the state's assumption of care of the aged dispelled the notion that one must have many children to support one's old age.

The choice to have fewer children first became widespread soon after 1800 in the French middle and lower middle class: the first people in the world to practice birth control on a massive scale. Smaller families became more common in England, Germany, and Scandinavia in the 1870s and after. The trend toward smaller families did not correspond clearly to religious teaching, for it was nominally Catholic France that had led the way. Nor did it correspond to the availability of birth-control devices. Some means of preventing births had long been known, especially late marriage and *coitus interruptus.* Modern industry and medical knowledge made more effective devices available: The diaphragm and rubber condoms were manufactured in the late nineteenth century. But, before cheap latex condoms were developed in the 1930s, such devices were too expensive for most people.[36] The important change, even so, was not a technical one but a change in values. The possibility of attaining a middle-class existence now seemed within the grasp of many more families, provided they had fewer children.

As a result of this major shift in social attitudes, the birth rate in Northern and Western Europe declined by one-half over the forty years after 1890. European

---

[35]There is no guarantee that societies will enter this third stage. Where industrial and commercial developments are weak, and where children are sources of income and prestige and are subject to high mortality, parents have strong incentives to have many children. Population in such societies will continue to outstrip productivity.

[36]The pill, which had important social effects both because it was inexpensive and because it was taken at the woman's initiative, was a development of the 1960s.

populations as a whole leveled off. For example, Danish women born between 1840 and 1844 had an average of 4.4 children, with 60 percent of their fertility occurring after the age of thirty; Danish women born between 1905 and 1909 had an average of 2.25 children, with 60 percent of them being born before the women were thirty.[37] Similar changes were taking place in all the modernized nations of Europe.

This shift in social attitudes has been called "one of the outstanding events of modern times,"[38] and it was working itself out through all the social institutions in Europe during the years covered by this book.

One traditional means of birth control in Europe had been late marriage. Many women in nineteenth-century Europe either married late or not at all; unmarried women were at their most numerous in nineteenth-century European societies, and not just in such novels as Jane Austen's *Pride and Prejudice* (1813). Married women, by contrast, continued to bear children late in life, as long as large families remained desirable. The changes at the turn of the century were manifold. People began to marry younger in Europe in the twentieth century, and women bore their children earlier in life; at the same time, their life expectancy was longer. The previously mentioned Danish women born between 1905 and 1909 could expect to live to the age of sixty-eight, whereas their predecessors born between 1840 and 1844 lived only an average of forty-seven years. Having finished childbearing at around the age of thirty, many of these modern women yearned to lead interesting and constructive lives in other ways.

Women's Place

Men were still absolute rulers of their households, however. The Napoleonic Code, which was the law not only in France but in many other European countries that had modernized their statute books in the nineteenth century, reinforced this traditional authority of the husband and father. Wives could not own property by themselves, make decisions concerning the domicile or the education of their children, or testify in court against their husbands. The father in the German upper-middle-class household in which the sociologist Max Weber grew up was probably no more authoritarian than most. Perhaps more than most, however, Weber's mother chafed against her husband's authority after her last child entered school in 1886, because much of the family's wealth came from her dowry and yet she could not use it on the charities in which she wanted to express her Calvinist personality.

> Thus, in the fifth decade of her life, Helene [Weber], in accordance with the tradition of these circles, had at her disposal neither a fixed household allowance nor a special sum for her personal needs. Rather, with her expense books . . . she must request what she needs for the house and for herself from case to case. She is thus subject to continual control and—equally typically under this regimen—to the frequent criticism and amazement

[37]I. C. Mattiessen, "Replacement for Generations of Danish Females, 1840/44–1920/24," in D. V. Glass and Roger Revelle, eds., *Population and Social Change* (London, 1972), p. 203.

[38]Ibid., p. 199.

of her husband at the great expenditure, whose inevitability he cannot really judge. Since over half the family income flows from her own estate, she experiences this situation as increasingly contradictory and burdensome.[39]

By all that we can learn of working-class life in this period, the father's authority was, if anything, more absolute the further one descended in the social scale. A young Englishman later recalled the lifestyle of his grandparents at the end of the nineteenth century. The grandfather, a boot and shoe worker, seems to have been somewhat more harsh and less provident than many English working-class men, but the deference of his wife, who bore eleven children in fourteen years, was probably not exceptional.

The womenfolk had always danced a most slavish attendance upon their men. In the house the men did nothing. They were not expected to carry the coal or to chop sticks or to carry the dustbin through the house to be placed on the pavement for collection. . . . When Edwin came home from work his chair had to be vacated immediately. He would throw down his kit-bag and coat on the floor for her to pick up and without a word he would sit down and lift each boot in turn for her to undo the laces and pull them off,

© BBC Hulton Picture Library / Liaison Agency

Suffragettes being arrested during a demonstration at Buckingham Palace, May 21, 1914.

[39]Arthur Mitzman, *The Iron Cage* (New York, 1970), p. 45.

resting his foot as he did so on the darned and faded pinafore that she always wore in the house. . . . When he died, the attention which he had received all his life devolved upon the only male then living at home.[40]

Women's roles began to change first in political terms in the years before 1914. Since women could already vote in New Zealand (1893), Australia (1902), Finland (1906), and Norway (1913), as well as in some American states such as Wyoming (1869), women's suffrage was already on the agenda. The issue was most energetically pressed in England, where between 1910 and 1914 the determined Mrs. Emmeline Pankhurst, her daughters, and her followers conducted demonstrations for the vote that led to hundreds of arrests and at least one death. The electoral barrier did not break down in England and Germany until after the First World War, however, and even later in France (1944), Italy (1946), Switzerland (1971), and Portugal (1976).

As for the question of women's rights in employment and within the family, the great increase in women's labor during the First World War was only the beginning of a long evolution in Europe toward the expectation that women might lead more independent lives. A much more profound shift of values had to take place before the French Napoleonic Code, for example, could be revised in the 1960s to give full juridical equality to married women.

POLITICAL SYSTEMS AND MASS MOVEMENTS

The basic European political unit in 1914 was the sovereign nation-state. Sovereignty—a political concept developed in sixteenth-century Europe to justify absolute monarchy against the claims of feudal nobles and the Church—was that quality of a state that sprang from a single source of power within and accepted no legal sanctions from without. Sovereignty stood in opposition to the medieval notion that all earthly authority is answerable to a universal divine, or natural, law. Even when the absolute authority of a prince had been replaced by popular sovereignty, it was axiomatic in 1914 that a state was the final judge of its own interests and that it dealt with other states in accordance with those interests. Even though states might accept some international agreements in pre-1914 Europe for their own convenience (for example, international postal conventions, the Red Cross, the rules of war, and the voluntary international arbitration machinery set up at the Hague Conference of 1899), they were still a law unto themselves in their dealings with one another. Those states that commanded sufficient power to prevent any outside intervention in their affairs, in fact as well as in theory, were considered Great Powers. In 1914, the Great Powers included Britain, France, Germany, Russia, Austria-Hungary, and perhaps Italy, but no longer Spain or the Ottoman Empire.

The Monarchy

Most European states were monarchies in 1914. Among the Great Powers, only France was a republic. Spain, which experimented briefly with a republic in 1873, reestablished the monarchy in 1875. Throughout the nineteenth century, newly

[40]Jeremy Seabrook, *The Unprivileged* (London, 1967), pp. 17–18.

independent states had tended to call in some unemployed German princeling to express national unity beyond the reach of any faction: Prince Leopold of Saxe-Coburg for Belgium in 1830; Otto of Bavaria for Greece in 1832 (and a Danish prince when Otto was deposed in 1862); Charles of Hohenzollern-Sigmaringen to become the Romanian King Carol in 1881; Alexander of Battenberg, followed by Ferdinand of Saxe-Coburg for Bulgaria in 1879 and 1886, and so forth.

Outright republicanism was an exceptionally radical political position everywhere outside France and Switzerland up to 1914. In England, the royal house was more sincerely beloved under Victoria and Edward VII than it had been under George IV or William IV earlier in the nineteenth century. Most Italian liberals accepted the Piedmontese royal house that had unified Italy, and almost all German liberals accepted the Prussian Hohenzollerns as emperors of the proud new German Reich. To be republican in the empires of Austria-Hungary and Russia up to 1914 was to be revolutionary.

Although monarchy seemed an unquestioned fixture of most European states, great and small, it was equally accepted in 1914 that it should have constitutional limitations. Here too, a gradation flowed from west to east. In Britain, Scandinavia, and the Low Countries the king reigned but did not rule; in Italy, Germany, and Eastern Europe limitations on royal authority were both newer and narrower. In 1914, it was clear that Kaiser Wilhelm II of Germany, Emperor Franz Josef of Austria-Hungary, and Tsar Nicholas II of Russia still personally had the last word on national policy.

Even in these empires, however, there was a persistent trend toward some degree of constitutional limitation. The German Empire's *Reichstag* (parliament) had decisive budgetary power in many realms, although it had lost the all-important struggle to obtain control over the military budget in 1886 and 1887. Prime ministers of the Habsburg Empire, as in the German Empire, had to obtain the consent of parliaments in Austria and Hungary for their internal policies. Even the autocrat of all the Russias was obliged to establish a parliament (Duma) after the revolution of 1905. Limited though its authority was, the Duma did have legislative powers, and its consent was required to appropriate funds other than those for the military budget and the emperor's own purse. These developments encouraged Russian constitutional liberals like Pavel Miliukov and reformist socialists like Aleksandr Kerensky to believe that their country would eventually be governed like the Western European constitutional monarchies.

For Miliukov and Kerensky, and for European constitutional liberals in general, the political issue in 1914 was still the issue first posed clearly by the French Revolution of 1789: how to replace hereditary authority with careers open to talent. Constitutional liberals in prewar Europe looked to a parliament on the British model as the best instrument to curb hereditary powers.

The Role of Parliaments

Parliaments were being transformed by two parallel developments in the generation before the First World War. First, as states expanded their activities into new social and economic fields, parliaments simply had more to do. With an increase in the scope and complexity of legislation, members of parliaments became less dilet-tantish, and annual sessions took up a greater part of the year. The British House of Commons, for example, which sat an average 116 days a year in the mid-nineteenth century, was sitting an average 146 days a year on the eve of the First World War.

Second, more Europeans were receiving the right to vote for members of their parliaments. Britain had extended the vote to most adult males in 1884. Universal male suffrage had been established in France in 1848, and was effectively exercised after 1871. It was adopted by Belgium in 1893, Spain in 1890, Norway in 1898, Sweden and Austria in 1907, and Italy in 1912.[41]

This development lagged in Central and Eastern Europe. Although the German *Reichstag* was elected by all adult males from the time of the Reich's creation in 1871, members of the powerful upper house, the *Bundesrat,* were appointed. And Prussia, by far the biggest and most powerful state in the German federal system, did not join the lesser German states in granting universal manhood suffrage for state governments. Prussia maintained a three-class voting system that allowed the wealthiest handful of citizens, those who paid the top one-third of the taxes, to elect one-third of the deputies. Hungary and most of the Balkan states had limited suffrage until the First World War. The Russian Empire seemed to be taking steps backward in the decade before 1914. The electoral law that permitted nearly all adult males to vote for the first and second Dumas in 1905 and 1906 was drastically curtailed for the elections of the third and fourth Dumas in 1907 and 1912. But liberal optimists could consider these temporary eddies in an inevitable tide of constitutional government.

In most of Europe, directly elected lower houses gained ground against less democratically chosen upper houses. After the office of Life Senator was abolished in 1884, for example, all French Senators were elected. The most striking victory was won by the British House of Commons over the House of Lords. When the Lords opposed the welfare provisions in the Liberal leader Lloyd George's budget in 1909, they emerged from the conflict shorn of their absolute veto over bills passed by the Commons.

There were other, subtler but no less important, expansions of popular control over legislatures, such as the spread of the secret ballot and salaried parliament seats. The Australian, or secret, ballot provided envelopes and private voting booths for voters. Its introduction in France in 1913 reduced the pervasive influence of local "notables" over their lesser neighbors in political matters. The provision of a salary of £400 per year for all members of the British House of Commons in 1911 made it possible for men without private incomes to serve in that body, long one of the most gentry-dominated European parliaments.

The progress of parliamentary institutions in European politics was still very uneven in 1914. The persistent growth of such institutions made it possible to assume that the trend of the future lay in the direction of broader electoral democracy. But vigorous counterattacks came from both old autocrats and new nationalists. Efforts to broaden the Prussian three-class voting system met with the most resolute opposition of the Kaiser, as well as of many German liberals who had been

---

[41]See p. 21 for the right of women to vote.

converted by Bismarck's successes into believing that a strong state was more important than civil liberties. "What good would social reforms do us," said the German liberal Friedrich Naumann, "if the Cossacks come?"[42] The Austrian parliament had been paralyzed off and on since 1899 by demonstrations begun by Czech and German deputies over the extension of minority language rights in the schools and courtrooms of the multinational empire. The Russian Tsar was successfully rolling back the reforms he had been obliged to grant in 1905. In retrospect, it looks as if the decade before the First World War was not the dawn but the twilight of parliamentary regimes, the last moment before the economic complexities of the postwar years replaced parliaments with bureaucratic planners and before nationalist passion for state "efficiency" replaced them with dictators.

The Socialist Movement

Social justice and economic rights emerged as new and pressing issues alongside the constitutional ones before the First World War. Grim conditions in early factories and among the urban artisans they displaced had helped provoke insurrectionary outbursts in 1848 and in the Paris Commune of 1871. During the generation before the First World War, however, pressures for fundamental change in the capitalistic economic system were more sustained, for they came from new permanent institutions: labor unions and socialist parties.

Trade unions—fraternities of skilled workers who banded together to protect their craft—had broadened into labor unions made up of whole industrial populations in the late nineteenth century. Although many governments had ceased to forbid the existence of labor unions (Britain in 1825; France in 1884), their rapid growth in both numbers and permanent cadres after the 1890s alarmed middle-class liberals as well as conservatives. By 1914 British and German unions had over 2 million members, or about 30 percent of the male labor force. German unions far exceeded those of other countries in wealth and the size of their permanent staffs, which grew ten times—from 290 to 2,867—between 1900 and 1914. French unions, which had organized less than 6 percent of the French work force and had far smaller strike funds, made up in militancy what they lacked in organization. The French government used the army repeatedly to help control major strikes from 1906 to 1909.

New socialist parties made use of broadening voting rights to bring the mass of wage earners into politics independently, as a class. The influence of Karl Marx, who had died in 1883, became predominant among organized factory workers by the 1890s (except in Britain), displacing liberal and Catholic reformers and supplanting earlier spontaneous insurrectionary strategies for changing the economic system. Marx's followers after the 1890s interpreted his strategy as the conquest of European democracies through the sheer numbers of the growing and voting proletariat. Their program did not seem futile in 1914. The German Social Democratic Party with 110 seats and one-third of the votes cast in the elections of 1912, was the

[42]James J. Sheehan, *The Career of Lujo Brentano* (Chicago, 1968), p. 148.

© Roger Viollet

A socialist rally in France, addressed in 1913 by the leading figure of the French socialist movement, Jean Jaurès.

largest single party in the *Reichstag*. That was only the most conspicuous success of the socialist electoral strategy. The French Socialist Party elected 103 of the 602 deputies in 1914, with about 1.5 million votes. The British Labour Party won 29 seats out of 670 in the elections of 1906; the Austrian Social Democrats won 87 out of 516 in 1907; and at their high-water point in the second Duma of 1906, the Russian Social Revolutionaries (agrarian revolutionaries) and Social Democrats (Marxists) together held 103 out of 520 seats.

The impact of electoral socialism on European politics on the eve of war in 1914 was immense. In some cases, when socialists and liberal reformers joined forces, important social reforms were legislated. In England, Labour and Liberal votes combined in 1911 to enact a worker's insurance program. But for many liberals as well as conservatives, the rapid growth of Marxist parties lit up the political sky with the lightning flashes of a coming storm. In the German *Reichstag,* the huge Social Democratic delegation refused to stand for the traditional cheer of *"Kaiser hoch!"*

and the kaiser spoke quite openly of their leaders as enemies of the nation *(Reichs-feinde)*. The outbreak of the war in 1914 interrupted a gathering battle as to whether European liberals, who had traditionally put all their faith in the creation of parliamentary institutions, would let those institutions be captured by Marxists.

Nationalism

Nationalism stirred more hearts in Europe in 1914, including those of many workers, than did socialism. The idea of popular sovereignty led very easily to the notion that the people should be not only sovereign but also enthusiastic citizens. In Western Europe after 1789, emotional loyalty to the nation supported the consolidation of large, homogeneous nation-states. The fervent citizen-armies of the French Revolution had been only the first spectacular example of nationalism ranged against the traditional internationalism of aristocrats and the clergy. Spreading outward from France, nationalism had aroused the dispersed German- and Italian-speaking peoples of Europe to create nation-states in the mid-nineteenth century where there had been only petty principalities before. The young Italian Fabrizio in Stendhal's novel *The Charterhouse of Parma* (1839) wanted to join Napoleon on the battlefield because he thought the emperor represented the triumph of great nations over backward provinces like the Duchy of Parma. The revolutionaries in Germany in 1848 felt the same contempt for the three-dozen small German states that had survived Napoleon's campaigns.

After the unifications of Germany and Italy, by 1871, universal education and mass communication gave both new and old states in Western Europe the means to make citizens more homogeneous and more loyal. Western European states typically used universal education to extirpate regional dialects as well as to teach patriotism. The Bretons, Basques, Welsh, and speakers of Provençal and of various German dialects were absorbed into larger communities; maps showing Europe divided into large areas of unshaded primary colors reflected, not inaccurately, this growing cultural homogeneity. Uprooted populations of the new cities, in need of some kind of emotional attachment, responded warmly to parades and patriotic speeches. Thus by 1914 nationalism tended to reinforce the homogeneity of the Great Powers in Western Europe.

In Eastern Europe, by contrast, nationalism threatened to break up existing states: the polyglot empires of Austria-Hungary, Russia, and Ottoman Turkey. As long-submerged peoples—like the Czechs, Poles, and Hungarians—as well as other ethnic groups that had never formed their own states—like the Slovaks, Slovenes, Albanians, and South Slavs—rediscovered the worth of their own languages and cultures, the trend toward a single state language was reversed. The Czech historian František Palacký, for example, had felt compelled to begin publishing his pioneering history of the Czech people, *History of Bohemia*, in 1836 in German, the language of learning throughout Eastern Europe. Only in 1848 was the publication of a Czech version begun. Such rediscovered national loyalties generated separatist movements. By 1913, the Ottoman Empire had lost all but a few square miles of its European holdings to new nationalities: the Greeks, Albanians, Bulgarians, and

Romanians. The multinational Habsburg Empire conceded special status to the Hungarians in 1867 by creating a "dual monarchy" in which Emperor Franz Josef governed simultaneously as emperor of Austria and king of Hungary, with the two states administering their own internal matters. After that one great national concession, however, Hungarian intransigence prevented similar concessions to the other major Habsburg subject nationalities: the Czechs, Poles, and South Slavs. This refusal only sharpened the thirst of these peoples for national autonomy, and eventually drove them beyond autonomy to demands for total independence during the First World War.

The dominant nationalities of the threatened empires responded with heightened ethnic feelings of their own. Pan-Germans dreamed of uniting all German-speaking peoples of Eastern Europe within the Reich. Pan-Slavs in Russia reasserted their ancient traditions against Western teaching and dreamed of uniting all Slavs under the tutelage of Holy Mother Russia; pan-Slavs in the Balkans wanted both unity and independence. Pan-Turanians, who tried to modernize the failing Ottoman Empire in 1908, wanted to recover all the original Turkish lands in central Asia and unite them under a revivified Ottoman rule.

Far from reinforcing existing states, therefore, Eastern European nationalism eroded or even replaced the dynastic loyalty that had united the multinational empires. A mounting tide of ethnic separatism marked nineteenth-century Eastern Europe: the Greek war of independence from Turkey in the 1820s; Polish risings against Russia in 1848 and 1863; insurrection against Turkey by Bulgarians, Romanians, and South Slavs in 1875–1878; and the Balkan Wars of 1912 to 1913. Other ethnic minorities clamored for independence. Under these conditions, more parliamentary democracy within the multinational empires only gave these boiling ethnic pressures more scope to express themselves, as when Czech and German deputies paralyzed the Austrian Parliament over school languages in 1899.

INHERITED CREEDS

Liberalism

At the opening of the twentieth century, a great many Europeans—mostly members of the middle class or aspirants to it—took for granted the values of nineteenth-century liberalism.[43] Liberal thought was first formulated by the French *philosophes* of the late eighteenth century and the progressive rationalists of the early nineteenth century. But by 1900 their heroic battles had long been over, and all that remained was a pervasive set of assumptions that many middle-class Europeans felt were self-evident.

The first assumption was that the world was fully knowable. The universe was an orderly material system operating according to laws whose detailed workings were being uncovered, bit by bit, by scientists. This point of view had been dramatized by

---

[43]Current American usage of the word *liberal* to refer loosely to the far left may create confusion. In this book, the word *liberal* refers to the faith in progress, individualism, and *laissez-faire* that permeated the European middle class when the twentieth century opened.

the discovery of Sir Isaac Newton (1642–1727) that the same gravitational laws accounted for both the fall of an apple and the orbits of the planets; it had been popularized in the eighteenth century by *philosophes* like Voltaire. The evident progress of science gave that point of view further currency in the nineteenth century.

A second assumption was that human beings were by nature capable of fully understanding this orderly universe. Human beings possessed a fixed, innate quality called "reason," which, when liberated by education from the dark bondage of superstition, could recognize an objective truth on which all men, if properly instructed, would agree. As the British liberal philosopher John Stuart Mill wrote in *On Liberty* (1859):

> There is, on the whole, a preponderance among mankind of rational opinions and rational conduct . . . owing to a quality of the human mind, . . . namely that his errors are corrigible. He is capable of rectifying his mistakes, by discussion and experience. . . . Wrong opinions and practices gradually yield to fact and argument. . . . If the lists are kept open, we may hope that if there be a better truth, it will be found when the human mind is capable of receiving it.[44]

Mill died in 1873, but his cautious hope that free discussion would lead to higher truth was widely taken for granted in 1900.

From these two axioms of liberal thought flowed the corollaries of liberal practice. The basic liberal weapon was schooling. Its fundamental duty was to free all persons from religious superstitions and inherited social distinctions that blocked the full development of reason's capacities—hence, the European middle class's drive for universal, secular, and free primary instruction in the late nineteenth century. Free and obligatory primary schooling had been achieved in Western Europe by the 1880s and was accepted as a goal even in tsarist Russia by 1913, although large areas of illiteracy remained there, as well as in Spain, Italy, and the Balkans.

Once an individual's reason had been set free by education, that person became a *citizen,* to use the term devised in the French Revolution to express the common membership of equally rational human beings in a free society. Citizens could be expected to share in political decisions without becoming playthings of demagoguery or prejudice—hence, the gradual conversion of European liberals to universal manhood suffrage during the nineteenth century, as literacy became more widespread. A citizen in an ideal liberal state also enjoyed equal status before the law and equal opportunity to enter the career best suited to his or her talents. It followed that a society of citizens would be naturally harmonious and that the state would need only a bare minimum of machinery to ensure order. It must be noted that for many liberals, citizenship belonged to the public sphere, hence to the masculine world; women's place was in the private sphere of household and family.[45]

In the economic realm, liberals assumed that reasonable persons would serve their own enlightened self-interest in a way so attuned to natural harmony that all of society would benefit. "Economic man," the business subspecies of rational man, if left free

---

[44]John Stuart Mill, *On Liberty,* ed. R. B. McCallum (Oxford, England, 1948), pp. 17–18.

[45]Some liberals, such as John Stuart Mill, did not believe that a women's place was limited to the private sphere. See his *The Subjugation of Women* (1869).

from clumsy state interference, would produce an ever-better product at an ever-lower price, thereby serving the community as well as himself. Temporary maladjustments in employment, wages, or prices would settle themselves, as if by an "invisible hand," to use the phrase dear to liberal economist Adam Smith (1723–1790) and his nineteenth-century successors. This classical-liberal economy was, of course, nowhere in practice in 1914 Europe, not least because businessmen wanted state protection from foreign competition and from organized workers. But liberal economists still fought against tariffs and business cartels in 1914, convinced that a self-adjusting, worldwide free-trade system was the most efficient way to cheap abundance.

The conspicuous successes of science and technology in the nineteenth century, the rapid spread of literacy, the expansion of political liberties, and unprecedented economic growth encouraged hopes of indefinite progress toward human perfectibility. The French poet Victor Hugo wrote in 1859, after watching the ascent of a balloon, that it represented "the great élan of progress toward the heavens."

> Toward the divine, pure future, toward virtue,
> Toward beckoning science,
> Toward the end of evil, toward generous forgiveness,
> Toward abundance, peace and laughter, and a happy Mankind.[46]

Hugo's poem suggested that human mastery of the air would replace the old "diversity of languages, of reason, of laws, of customs," with a new, twentieth-century world of human harmony. The conquest of "so much sky would abolish the Nations." As late as 1895, the French scientist Marcellin Berthelot could still proclaim his faith in the nineteenth century's positivist dream that the certainties of science would be extended to every aspect of human knowledge, bringing with them not only material but ethical improvement. "The universal triumph of science will assure to mankind the most possible happiness and morality."[47]

But by the time that Europeans had actually begun to master the air (the Frenchman Louis Blériot flew across the English Channel in 1909, only six years after the first brief airplane flight at Kitty Hawk), Victor Hugo's vision of human harmony through flight was already highly dubious. Science seemed as likely to favor the war-makers as the peacemakers, or as likely to permit human beings to become slack and decadent as "happy and moral," which were the two futures promised in H. G. Wells's most popular science fiction novels, *The War of the Worlds* (1898) and *The Time Machine* (1895). The American essayist Henry Adams, visiting the machinery exhibits at the Paris World's Fair of 1900, wrote that he

> would sit by the hour over the great dynamos watching them run noiselessly and smoothly as planets and asking them—with infinite courtesy—where the Hell they are going. They are marvelous. The Gods are not in it. Chiefly the Germans. . . . I can already see that the fellow who gets to 1930 will wish he hadn't.[48]

[46]Victor Hugo, "Le Vingtième Siècle: pleine mer; plein ciel," in *La Légende des siècles* (1859).

[47]Marcellin Berthelot, "Science et Morale," *Revue de Paris* (February 1, 1895), p. 469.

[48]Henry Adams, *The Education of Henry Adams* (Boston, 1918), p. 379, and *Selected Letters*, ed. Newton Arvin (New York, 1951), p. 220.

Such forebodings, however, were still the exception as the new century opened. The French philosopher Jean-Paul Sartre recalled in childlike terms (Sartre was nine years old in 1914) the hopeful view of human destiny that he had absorbed from his grandfather on the eve of the First World War.

> There had been kings, emperors. They were very, very wicked. They had been driven out; everything was happening for the best.[49]

It was not only children who absorbed the liberal confidence in reason and progress in 1914. The Cambridge mathematician and philosopher Bertrand Russell, who was forty-two years old in 1914 and reputed to have the keenest skeptical mind in England, later recalled that "we all felt convinced that nineteenth-century progress would continue, and that we ourselves would be able to contribute something of value."[50] In the words of a more recent Cambridge graduate, Leonard Woolf:

> The main difference in the world before 1914 from the world after 1914 was in the sense of security and the growing belief that it was a supremely good thing for people to be communally and individually happy. . . . It seemed as though human beings might really be on the brink of becoming civilized.[51]

Conservatism

Conservatism was the accepted value system of kings, aristocrats, most priests, and many of their lesser supporters. European conservatives were pessimistic about human nature. They believed that "depraved" humanity was best guided by its natural leaders. Not all conservatives still believed that natural leaders were provided by God; a growing number of secular conservatives argued that natural leaders had been provided by history. Human society, in their view, was the product of a long, evolutionary process. Its parts fit together like a living biological organism, according to the favorite conservative analogy. To hack away at the limbs of that social organism in the name of some abstract principle was, according to conservatives, worse than a crime: It was pointless folly.

It should not be imagined that European conservatism at the beginning of the twentieth century was merely a pale nostalgia for things medieval. Modern conservatism began as a vigorous counterattack against the French Revolution of 1789. By 1914, the threat of socialism and of social revolution (as in France in 1871 and Russia in 1905) had been added to the older threat of democracy and of the abolition of all inherited status.

Modern conservatism had undergone a vigorous rebirth shortly before 1914. A new generation of conservative propagandists and organizers moved conservatism out of the *châteaux* and pulpits and into the streets. They adapted it to the age of mass politics by adding a number of mass enthusiasms—nationalism, anticapitalism, and anti-Semitism—to the older values of social hierarchy, the organic inter-

---

[49]Jean-Paul Sartre, *The Words* (New York, 1966), p. 15.

[50]Alan Wood, *Bertrand Russell, The Passionate Skeptic* (London, 1957), p. 31.

[51]Leonard Woolf, *Beginning Again* (London, 1964), pp. 36, 44.

pretation of society, and the teachings of religion. Although more traditional conservatism reigned in the villages and castles of peasant-aristocratic Eastern and Southern Europe, new conservative leaders appeared in two capitals—Paris and Vienna—where liberal values had been undermined by national decline, fear of socialism, and concern about cultural decadence.

In Paris, Charles Maurras's *Action française* movement was traditionally conservative in its call for a return to monarchy and the Church as the only way to arrest France's alleged slothful decline under the Third Republic. But Maurras also struck a number of new notes. His was a call to action, with high value placed on athletic vigor, and even violence, in life and in politics. His strong-arm squad, the *Camelots du roi,* made up of university students and disgruntled members of the lower middle class, beat up liberal professors and broke up leftist meetings. Maurras appealed to shopkeepers threatened by debt and modern competition with a blend of anti-Semitism and a selective anticapitalism aimed at banks and department stores. His militant nationalism was designed to paper over class conflict with a single mass enthusiasm. The *Action française* was a genuine innovation in the way in which it brought together traditional conservatives and frightened former liberals in a movement that was most conspicuous for what it was against: national disunity, social conflict, and cultural decadence.

Georg von Schönerer's German-National movement in Vienna came out of the animosities on the borderlands of Eastern Europe, where German-speaking peoples found their old preeminence challenged by the rise of Slavic nationalism and socialist claims. Schönerer, the son of a liberal aristocrat, scoffed at his father's formulas for moderate constitutional monarchy. Unlike traditional conservatives, however, he had little faith in the existing social hierarchies under which the Habsburg Empire was slowly drifting into decay. With the sharp aggressiveness characteristic of the new right, Schönerer mobilized students, shopkeepers, and fervent nationalists around a new populist, anti-Semitic demagoguery in the 1880s.[52] The influence of Schönerer was still vivid in Vienna in the early 1900s, when a young art student named Adolf Hitler was living a marginal existence there.

Organized Religion

Most Europeans still professed a religious creed in 1914. Organized religion, however, was certainly weaker than it had been two generations earlier. In the villages, credulity had diminished with the spread of schooling and migration into cities. A widespread positivism, the belief that science would continue to find material explanations for everything, made the cultural climate inhospitable to the claims of religious faith.

No great religious thinkers were able to breast the tide of positivism in the nineteenth century. Among the educated, organized religion had not yet recovered from such humiliations as the public debate between the brilliant Darwinian protagonist Thomas Henry Huxley and Bishop Samuel Wilberforce of Oxford in the 1860s. The Bishop of Oxford thought he had demolished Huxley by asking whether

[52]This new right will be discussed more thoroughly when its fascist offspring is examined in chapter 7.

"it was through his grandfather or his grandmother that he claimed his descent from a monkey"; but it was clearly Huxley who won the day.

The main buttresses of organized religion at the opening of the twentieth century were reduced to social backwardness and social conformity. Religious practice remained fairly vigorous in those villages least penetrated by modernist ideas, and among the middle class that had renounced the skepticism of its fathers and flocked to church as a manifestation of respectability and support for the social order. The churches of Europe emerged as a mainstay of the social order, which did them little good among the resentful poor. The Orthodox Church of Russia was headed by the tsar's appointee, the Procurator of the Holy Synod, and received most of its funds from the state. The Catholic Church, strongest in Southern Europe and the Rhineland, was international, but its social doctrines lent vigorous support to established authority. The Protestant state churches (such as the Church of England and the Lutheran churches in Germany and Scandinavia) functioned primarily as arenas for a weekly display of social correctness by the upper class.

TOWARD A NEW CONCIOUSNESS

The inherited creeds discussed above were the commonplace assumptions of many ordinary, educated Europeans in 1914. Intellectuals, however, began to reject these commonplaces as early as the mid-nineteenth century. At that early stage, challenges came mostly from isolated individuals: the religious anguish of the Danish theologian Sören Kierkegaard, the self-scrutinizing sensitivity of the French poet Charles Baudelaire, and the scorn of the German philosopher Friedrich Nietzsche for the flabby mediocrity of contemporary liberal and Christian values. These lone seekers did not begin to be appreciated until the 1890s. After 1900, intellectual rejection of nineteenth-century ways of understanding human experience swelled into broad movements. By 1914, nothing less than revolutions were underway in science, aesthetic vision, and basic beliefs about the place of reason in human affairs.

The Revolution in Science

In contrast to the easily grasped technical triumphs of the nineteenth century, the most striking scientific achievements of the new century were both difficult to understand and disquieting.

Physicists' assumptions about the very nature of matter were challenged as the twentieth century opened. Like Democritus in 490 B.C., nineteenth-century physicists had supposed that matter was composed of irreducible material particles, or atoms. The accidental discovery of X-rays by the German physicist Wilhelm Röntgen in 1895 set off a train of investigations of their properties; the results were difficult to reconcile with earlier assumptions. The British physicist J. J. Thomson discovered in 1897 that when X-rays were passed through a gas, they dislodged tiny electrically charged particles that left traces on a photographic plate. The uniformity of these particles under various strengths of radiation suggested to Thomson that they must be component parts of the atoms of gas. Subsequent researchers called these particles "electrons." It became clear that atoms were not irreducible, but were whole worlds in themselves. These discoveries opened the entirely new field of atomic physics.

At about the same time, the German physicist Max Planck, unable to account by conventional mechanical calculations for the way energy was distributed along the spectrum of radiant heat, proposed the hypothesis in 1900 that energy was not a continuous flow but a periodic emission of packets of energy, or quanta. His quantum theory turned out to have far wider applications than Planck had anticipated. Most importantly, it cleared away many difficulties in explaining the results of experiments in atomic physics. By applying quantum theory to the internal structure of the atom, Thomson's coworker Ernest Rutherford (1911) and the Danish physicist Niels Bohr (1913) were able to work out a model of the way electrons whirled about the proton within an atom of matter like a miniature solar system.

For a time, the Newtonian solar system remained a persuasive analogy for describing the movement of subatomic particles. But Bohr continually found puzzling indications of randomness. In 1928, the German physicist Werner Heisenberg proposed the theory that atomic structures were "indeterminate." Since physicists had to work with instruments that were moving relatively to the subatomic movements being studied, Heisenberg reasoned, it was impossible for them to measure the position of electrons without distorting their speed or to measure their speed without distorting their position.

Heisenberg's indeterminancy theory presented the world with a universe far different from the comfortable regularities of the Newtonian system. Physicists were now explaining the universe in terms of statistical probabilities rather than mechanical certainties. The physicist's intuition and something akin to an aesthetic flair became essential to the elegant mathematical language with which the universe was interpreted, a language incompatible with the kind of material certainty science had once seemed to embody.

The indeterminancy theory was deeply influenced by the work of Albert Einstein on relativity. Einstein was puzzled by late-nineteenth-century experiments that showed that the velocity of light was constant in whatever direction it was emitted. Either the earth was not moving, or the universe was not uniform. In his special theory of relativity (1905) and his general theory of relativity (1916), Einstein showed mathematically that absolute space and time could not exist in any straightforward mechanical sense. The observed behavior of light could be accounted for only on the hypothesis of curved space, and of space and time as relative to each other and forming a single continuum. Einstein received notoriety in 1919 when the Royal Astronomical Society proved during a solar eclipse that light rays were, indeed, curved when passing through the sun's magnetic field. This widely publicized experiment gave relativity theory much public attention, which Einstein had never sought. Many people leaped to conclusions that the universe could be understood only in subjective terms and that there were no certainties in science.

The Revolution in Art and Thought

No less far-reaching than the revolution in physics was the revolution in aesthetics taking place in the decade before 1914. The two revolutions were not entirely unrelated.

Wassily Kandinsky, a Russian living in Munich, wrote that it was when he learned there were particles smaller than atoms that he began to rethink the whole nature of reality in the arts. He claimed to have made the first purely abstract painting in 1910: a water-color composed of colored areas crisscrossed by lines. Although experimental artists had been arbitrarily distorting nature in order to heighten effects since the time of Vincent van Gogh (1853–1890), Paul Gauguin (1848–1903), and Paul Cézanne (1839–1906), Kandinsky wanted to create an art of pure inwardness without reference to external nature. Kandinsky's book *Concerning the Spiritual in Art* (1912) was the first justification for pure abstraction: the abolition of any representational element at all.

Painting, for Kandinsky, was communication from the painter's soul through the feelings aroused by color and shape. He believed that the painter's emotions could be transmitted to the colors and forms on the canvas, which "call forth a basically similar emotion in the soul of the spectator." Kandinsky thought that of all the arts painting should most resemble music, the art form that attempts least to represent anything else, and in which the composer is free to express himself directly in the language of rhythm and melody. For Kandinsky, colors, like sounds, had emotional values: yellow, for example, was a "strident trumpet blast." Painting was "color music."[53]

Kandinsky and his friends of the *Brücke* (bridge) and *Blaue Reiter* (blue rider) schools in Munich created one of the main prewar modern-art movements in Europe—expressionism, the attempt to transmit strongly charged feelings by violent color and subject matter, arbitrary distortion, and abstract form.

Wassily Kandinsky (1866–1944), *Improvisation No. 30 (On a Warlike Theme)* **(1913). One of the first to paint entirely abstractly, Kandinsky believed that shapes and colors were as effective as music in communicating feelings directly—in this case, his foreboding of war.**

[53]Wassily Kandinsky, *Concerning the Spiritual in Art,* trans. Michael Sadleir et al. (New York, 1947), pp. 23, 46.

Paris was the other center of aesthetic experiment before the First World War. There the *Fauves* (their nickname referred to their wild colors) set out in 1905 to smash the "slickness of over-refined art" through paintings of violent color and distorted forms. The better known of the *Fauves,* such as Henri Matisse (1869–1954), still retained some representational elements in their work, but their arbitrary use of flat, unmodeled areas of brilliant color carried them much farther from observed nature than their impressionist predecessors whose dappled canvases had been an attempt to present light scientifically.

Another major artistic innovation in pre-1914 Paris was cubism, practiced by, among others, the Frenchman Georges Braque (1882–1963) and the Spaniard Pablo Picasso (1881–1973). Cubism was still a way of representing nature, but it was nature utterly transformed by the painter's inner eye. Since all painting is a distortion by which depth is represented on a flat surface, the cubists chose to emphasize that distortion by presenting objects or human bodies seen simultaneously from many angles and arbitrarily rearranged by the artist.

The futurist movement, although it produced artistic work of less-enduring interest, also contributed to the climate of artistic ferment in prewar Paris. The Futurist Manifesto of 1909, the work of two Italians, Filippo Marinetti and Umberto Boccioni, called for a new aesthetic of violence and speed to replace stale, academic culture: "A speeding automobile is more beautiful than the Winged Victory of Samothrace." The futurists wanted to burn libraries and museums; they exalted war and the "subordination of women."

Despite their highly individual differences, the artistic rebels of the last decade before 1914 shared a number of common values. They broke completely with the artistic tradition begun in the Western world during the Renaissance and maintained to some degree even by the impressionists of the late nineteenth century, that the business of art was to represent a universally understood external nature. In so doing, the dissident painters also broke with the very idea of learned technique, of artistic skills transmitted by teachers. Artistic expression became totally subjective; as such, it was without universally applicable standards.

Now that each artist's private creative drives took precedence over learned techniques, the sources of creativity became a matter of heightened interest. European artists were inclined to seek inspiration in childhood spontaneity or primitive feeling, outside the realms of reason and learning. Gauguin had urged painters to go beyond the horse in the Parthenon friezes to a child's rocking horse for inspiration. An exhibit of African masks in Paris in 1905 had a profound effect on the *Fauves* and the cubists, and the Munich expressionists studied primitive art in ethnographic museums. Since art was no longer a learned skill, it was now theoretically open to nonbourgeois Europeans for the first time. The customs collector Henri Rousseau (1844–1910) was hardly proletarian, nor was he genuinely naive, but the childlike vision of his paintings delighted those who looked for an unacademic vision.

It was not only European artists who were rediscovering subjective realities as the twentieth century opened. The French philosopher Henri Bergson (1859–1941), for example, had broken with the mathematical and mechanistic interests of his youth while puzzling about the nature of time. The irreconcilable difference between the physicist's *measured* time and each individual's subjective experience of the *duration* of time so struck the young Bergson that he spent the rest of his career as professor of philosophy working out the importance of intuition in human thought. Bergson argued that a whole realm of reality, of which the duration of time was merely one example, could only be known by direct, sympathetic comprehension or intuition. It could not be known directly by the symbolic language of mathematics or physics.

Bergson began lecturing in Paris in 1897 and won an enthusiastic following of students after the publication of *Creative Evolution* in 1907. His later lectures, exalting the human "vital impulses" *(élan vital)* that came "gushing out unceasingly . . . from an immense reservoir of life" and his mystical allusions to immortality won him a society audience. Ultimately, Bergson's influence was felt in the return of some French intellectuals to religion before 1914, and in the subtle probing of time and memory in Marcel Proust's *Remembrance of Things Past,* the first volume of which was published in 1913.

The most seminal thinker in the "recovery of the unconscious"[54] at the beginning of the twentieth century was unquestionably Sigmund Freud. Freud began practicing medicine in Vienna in the 1880s as a neurologist; his training had led him to treat the nervous system in physiological and even mechanistic terms. Cases of mental illness that seemed to have no physiological basis were then attracting the attention of some of Freud's colleagues, one of whom successfully treated several cases with hypnosis. In 1892, Freud worked on the case of Fräulein Elizabeth von R., who had shown no progress under hypnosis. In treating her, Freud experimented with the technique of getting the patient to recall the remote incidents behind her troubles by intense concentration and free association while lying on a couch with her eyes closed, a process Freud called "psychical analysis." During the 1890s, Freud became convinced from his clinical practice that much mental illness could be traced back to repressed childhood sexual traumas. He believed that such illnesses could be treated by intense sessions of what he now called "psychoanalysis." In psychoanalysis, the patient recalled past experiences by free association, and the doctor took note of the ways in which the patient resisted revealing the most sensitive points and "transferred" his emotions to less-charged substitute issues.

Confident that a powerful unconscious mental life could be studied and treated scientifically, Freud subjected himself to psychoanalysis, through which he discovered his own inner resentments of his father. Freud also studied the importance of dreams and of what we now call "Freudian slips" in language, as clues to the mind's unconscious life. His book *The Interpretation of Dreams* (1899) used dramatic analogies such as the Oedipus legend to illustrate the unconscious sexual jealousy and rivalry Freud perceived between sons and fathers, and to reveal how dependent conscious rational thought is on the unconscious mental life.

Freud's two central discoveries—the force of the unconscious mental life and the importance of childhood sexuality to personality development—arose simply from attempts to understand and treat mental illness. The wider impact of his work had to await the passing of a generation and the revelations of human irrationality in the First World War. In time, it became clear that Freud had made obsolete the notions that reason controls the behavior of at least the educated portion of mankind, and that humans are fully aware of why they do what they do.

[54]The phrase is the heading of chapter 4 of H. Stuart Hughes's classic survey of European culture at the turn of the twentieth century, *Consciousness and Society* (New York, 1958).

The Reaction to Cultural Revolution

The people and the movements singled out for discussion here were still only dissident minorities in 1914. They aroused violent animosity then, and established intellectual institutions had the power to shut them out. Public opinion was much less tolerant of innovation in the arts and in thought in 1914 than it has been since the total victory of the modernists. Moreover, intellectual life was much more rigidly institutionalized in Europe before 1914 than it has been since.

In Paris, for example, the *École des Beaux Arts* had a virtual monopoly of formal instruction in painting, sculpture, and architecture, and its instructors were appointed by the Ministry of Education. As late as 1881, the state exercised control over the Society of French Artists, which showed a selection of approved new paintings each year at its annual *Salon*. But even after the French state granted greater freedom of association, the official *Salon* rejected anything that did not conform to the derivative classicism still taught in the schools. Experimental artists had to show their works separately, at the *Salon des indépendants* (after 1884) or the *Salon d'automne* (after 1903), and they depended for support on friends and on a few adventurous purchasers.

The arts were even more tightly in the hands of conservatives in England. The classicist Lord Leighton, who insisted that art was the "representation of objects visible and tangible to the painter," ran the Royal Academy of Arts for nearly half a century, until 1893. The staff of the Royal Academy, consisting of forty "academicians" who chose their own successors, monopolized art instruction until the Slade School of Fine Arts was founded at the end of the century in the University of London. Experimental artists in Berlin and Vienna faced the same obstacles to being seen and appreciated; they formed "secession" showings when the established art shows were closed to them. No wonder modernism in the arts rejected the very idea of learned technique and perpetuation of historic styles.

Museums, whose very founding principle in the nineteenth century had been awe before the classics, were also closed to experimenters as a source of moral or material support. Many of those in power, both liberal and conservative, were shocked by a "cultural decadence" in modernism that seemed to threaten morals as well as good taste. The German Kaiser Wilhelm II dismissed the director of the Berlin Fine Arts Museum in 1908 for having dared to purchase some works of modern painting. The German empress blocked the production of Richard Strauss's naturalistic opera *Salome* (1905). She also prevented the opening of his *Der Rosenkavalier* (1911) in Berlin, although that opera's wistful treatment of a middle-aged flirtation was hardly daring, even at that time.

Scientists enjoyed more autonomy in their university laboratories, although Einstein had to do his early work outside the university establishment while employed as an examiner of patent applications in Bern, Switzerland. Even after Einstein received the recognition of a university research appointment in Berlin, popularized notions of what he had done were attacked as Jewish cultural depravity in the 1920s. Freud was never accepted by his colleagues in Vienna.

The cultural revolutions of the generation before 1914 had nevertheless succeeded in putting in place the main elements of a new consciousness that was to become much more commonly accepted after the First World War. We are so close to their achievements today, and their experimentation was so individualistic and variegated, that cultural life on the eve of 1914 may seem only a kind of brilliant intellectual pinwheel, without precise meaning. We can single out the main threads, however. A new aesthetic of personal sensibility had replaced the more objective aesthetic of representing external nature. Human consciousness was revealed as possessing unknown depths, and the place of reason in it had been called into question. Nature itself seemed susceptible to interpretation only by the most subjective hypotheses. It was what historian Carl Schorske has called a "great revaluation":

> The primacy of reason in man, the rational structure of nature, and the meaningfulness of history were all brought before the bar of personal psychological experience for judgment.[55]

This revaluation was not achieved without considerable cost. Those who shared in the new consciousness gave up the support of both tradition and any sense of integrated wholeness. They were subject to the loneliness and anxiety of being adrift in a meaningless universe. There remained only the heightened excitement of private artistic experience or piecemeal scientific discovery to cling to. As the French poet Charles Baudelaire had said earlier, "The intoxication of Art is the best thing of all for veiling the terrors of the Pit; . . . genius can play a part at the edge of the tomb with a joy that prevents it from seeing the tomb."[56]

The explorers of the new consciousness had no ready defenses against finding the same excitement in violence or cruelty that they found in artistic experience, as they were about to discover in the global war then brewing. Some people in the comfortable middle-class Europe of 1914 half hoped for some kind of apocalyptic wave of violence that would sweep away dull, bourgeois mediocrity. In the summer of 1913, the young English novelist D. H. Lawrence wrote to friends:

> My religion is a belief in the blood, the flesh, as being wiser than the intellect. We can go wrong in our minds. But what the blood feels and believes and says is always true.[57]

SUGGESTIONS FOR FURTHER READING[58]

Mark Mazower, *Dark Continent: Europe's Twentieth Century** (1999), assesses a troubled time powerfully. Roger Munting and B. A. Holderness, *Crisis, Recovery and War: An Economic History* of Continental Europe, 1918–1945 (1991), and Gerald Ambrosius and William H. Hubbard, *A Social and Economic History of Twentieth Century Europe** (1989), examine the eco-

---

[55]Carl E. Schorske, "The Idea of the City in European Thought," in Oscar Handlin, ed., *The Historian and the City* (Cambridge, MA, 1963), p. 109.

[56]Baudelaire, pp. 94–95.

[57]*The Portable D. H. Lawrence*, ed. Diana Trilling (New York, 1947), p. 563. It is only fair to add that Lawrence, married to a German woman, remained a pacifist during the war.

[58]Suggestions for further reading appear at the end of each chapter. These are limited to some basic recent works and durable classics readily available in English. Many of them contain fuller, more specialized bibliographies. Books available in paperback are marked with an asterisk (*).

nomic and social underpinnings. Geoffrey Barraclough, *An Introduction to Contemporary History* (1968, reprint ed. 1991), frames the novelty of the twentieth century, as do Norman Stone, *Europe Transformed, 1878–1919,*[*] 2nd ed. (1999), and the Dutch nonconformist Marxist Jan Romein, *The Watershed of Two Eras* (1976).

Good surveys of individual European countries in the twentieth century include, for Britain, Robert K. Webb, *Modern England,*[*] 2nd ed. (1990); Peter Clarke, *Hope and Glory: Britain, 1900–1990,*[*] 2nd ed. (2004); H. C. Matthew and Kenneth O. Morgan, *The Oxford History of Britain,* vol. 5, *The Modern Age,*[*] 2nd ed. (2001); and Keith Robbins, *The Eclipse of a Great Power: Modern Britain, 1870–1992,*[*] 2nd ed. (1994). George Dangerfield, *The Strange Death of Liberal England* (1935, reprint ed. 1997), remains a lively account of domestic strains on the eve of the war.

Gordon Wright, *France in Modern Times,*[*] 5th ed. (1995), is a superior text. The *Cambridge History of Modern France* is the best multivolume work; the volume by Madeleine Rebérioux covers the early Third Republic. Theodore Zeldin, *France 1848–1945,*[*] 2 vols. (1981, reprint ed. 1993), contains brilliant though idiosyncratic essays on private as well as public life. Maurice Agulhon, *The French Republic, 1879–1992*[*] (1995), is masterful.

Gordon Craig, *Germany, 1866–1945* (1980) and *The Germans*[*] (1991), are the fruit of a lifetime of scholarship. For the eve of 1914, use Volker Berghahn, *Imperial Germany, 1871–1914*[*] (1994). Alexander Gerschenkron, *Bread and Democracy in Germany,*[*] with foreword by C. S. Maier (1943, reprint ed. 1989), is a classic. These works see German history as divergent from the Western liberal norm. Geoff Eley, *From Unification to Nazism: Reinterpreting the German Past* (1985), rejects this "special path" interpretation. The debate is scrutinized in Richard J. Evans, *Rethinking German History: Nineteenth Century Germany and the Origins of the Third Reich*[*] (2003).

Martin Clark, *Modern Italy, 1871–1995,*[*] 2nd ed. (1996), is the best introduction. Raymond Carr, ed., *Spain: A History* (2000), is an up-to-date account. Gerald Brenan, *The Spanish Labyrinth*[*] (1950, reprint ed. 1990), is a scintillating essay. David Birmingham, *History of Portugal*[*] (1995) is the latest survey. Kenneth Maxwell, *The Making of Portugese Democracy*[*] (1997) is illuminating.

T. K. Derry, *A History of Scandinavia*[*] (2000), and Byron J. Nordstrom, *Scandinavia Since 1500*[*] (2000) are good introductions to the Nordic countries.

The conservative scholar Richard Pipes has written an authoritative study of late imperial Russia, *Russia under the Old Regime*[*] (1997). Nicholas V. Riasanovsky, *A History of Russia,* 6th ed. (1999), is a lucid text. Robert Service, *A History of Modern Russia from Nicholas II to Putin*[*] (2003), provides a densely packed narrative.

R. J. Crampton, *Eastern Europe in the Twentieth Century and After*[*] (1997), introduces the region. For Austria-Hungary, C. A. Macartney, *The Habsburg Empire, 1790–1918* (1969), is a classic. See also Robert A. Kann, *A History of the Habsburg Empire, 1526–1918*[*] (1974), and Jean Berenger, *A History of the Habsburg Empire: 1700–1918*[*] (1997). Mark Mazower, *The Balkans: A Short History*[*] (2000), is the most recent scholarly survey. See also Barbara Jelavich, *Modern Austria: Empire to Republic, 1800–1986*[*] (1987). C. A. Macartney, *October Fifteenth: A History of*

Modern Hungary (1956), remains authoritative, though Jörg K. Hoensch, *A History of Modern Hungary, 1867–1986,*[*] 2nd ed. (1994), and Peter F. Sugar, *A History of Hungary*[*] (1994), are more recent. Norman Davies, *God's Playground: A History of Poland,*[*] 2nd ed. (2004), is passionately engaged as is Josef Korbel, *Twentieth-Century Czechoslovakia: The Meanings of Its History* (1977). Victor S. Mamatey and Radomir Luza, eds., *A History of the Czechoslovak Republic, 1918–1914* (1972), is admirably balanced. See also H. Gordon Skilling, *Czechoslovakia, 1918–1988*[*] (1991). Keith Hitchens, *Rumania, 1866–1947* (1994), Stephen Fischer-Galati, *Rumania*[*] (2003), and R. J. Crampton, *A Short History of Bulgaria*[*] (1997), are standard. Peter F. Sugar and Ivo Lederer, eds., *Nationalism in Eastern Europe*[*] (1994), takes a long perspective.

Guido de Ruggiero, *The History of European Liberalism* (1927, various eds.), is a twilight look back at nineteenth-century liberalism. Richard Bellamy, *Rethinking Liberalism*[*] (2000), and Peter Gay, *Liberalism* (2004), take new looks at liberalism's twentieth-century manifestations.

The best introduction to European conservative thought is Jerry Z. Muller, *Conservatism: An Anthology of Social and Political Thought from David Hume to the Present*[*] (1997). For conservative parties and movements, Hans Rogger and Eugen Weber, eds., *The European Right* (1966), remains basic.

The most substantial recent work on democratic socialism is Geoff Ely, *The Left and the Struggle for Democracy in Europe, 1850–2000*[*] (2002). Albert S. Lindemann, *A History of European Socialism*[*] (1983), and the scintillating Donald Sassoon, *One Hundred Years of Socialism*[*] (1998), are more general surveys.

Excellent introductions to women in European history are Georges Duby, Michelle Perrot, and Françoise Thébaud, eds., *History of Women in the West*, vol. 5: *A Cultural Identity in the Twentieth Century*[*] (1996); Renate Bridenthal, Claudia Koonz, and Susan Stuard, *Becoming Visible: Women in European History,*[*] 3rd ed. (1998); Bonnie Anderson and Judith Zinsser, *A History of Their Own,*[*] vol. 2, (revised ed., 2000); and Bonnie G. Smith, *Changing Lives: Women in European History since 1700*[*] (1989).

David S. Landes, *Unbound Prometheus*[*] (1969), is the classic account of European technological development. See also Patrice Higonnet et al., *Favorites of Fortune*[*] (1995). An up-to-date introduction to European demography is Massimo Livi-Bacci, *The Populations of Europe: A History*[*] (2000).

Eric Hobsbawm, *Nations and Nationalism since 1780,*[*] 2nd ed., (1992), is a stimulating brief introduction. See also Benedict Anderson, *Imagined Communities*[*] (1991), and Ernest Gellner, *Nationalism*[*] (1997).

Among many works on European colonial expansion, see V. G. Kiernan, *Colonial Empires and Armies 1815–1960* (1998), Daniel R. Headrick, *Tools of Empire*[*] (1981), and Wolfgang Mommsen, *Theories of Imperialism*[*] (1982).

Peter Paret, Gordon A. Craig, and Felix Gilbert, eds., *Makers of Modern Strategy from Machiavelli to the Nuclear Age*[*] (revised ed. 1986), is the basic work on military thought. Industrialized warfare is considered in Timothy Travers and Christon Archer, eds., *Men at War: Politics, Technology, and Innovation in the Twentieth Century*[*] (1982).

H. Stuart Hughes, *Consciousness and Society*[*] (reprint 2002), is indispensable for the prewar revolutions in the social sciences and psychology. A superior study of intellectual ferment at the opening of the century is Carl E. Schorske, *Fin-de-Siècle Vienna*[*] (1980). Peter Gay, *Freud: A Life for Our Time*[*] (1989), is outstanding. See also the stimulating *The Culture of Time and Space, 1883–1918*[*] (revised ed. 2003) by Stephen Kern.

An accessible history of science for this century is Gerard Piel, *The Age of Science: What Scientists Learned in the Twentieth Century*[*] (2001). See also Abraham Pais, *Genius of Science: A Portrait of Twentieth Century Physicists*[*] (2000). Biographies of Marie Curie, Nobel Prize winner in both physics and chemistry, are by Françoise Giroud (1986) and Susan Quinn (1995). For biology, see Jan Sapp. *Genesis: The Evolution of Biology*[*] (2003).

Raymond Williams, *The Country and the City*[*] (reprint 1985), explores literary and artistic reactions to urbanization. See also Paul M. Hohenburg and Lynn Hollen Lees, *The Making of Urban Europe, 1000–1950* (1985).

A standard history of the Christian churches is Kenneth Scott Latourette, *Christianity in a Revolutionary Age*, 5 vols. (1958–1963, reprint ed. 1973). Routledge's series *Christianity and Society in the Modern World* (1987–) applies modern social history to religion, and already includes several volumes on modern Europe. See more briefly René Rémond, *Religion and Society in Modern Europe*[*] (1999), and Martin Conway, *Catholic Politics in Europe, 1918–1945*[*] (1997). H. H. Ben Sasson, ed., *A History of the Jewish People* (1976), contains an outstanding section on the modern era by Shmuel Ettinger.

Good introductions to twentieth-century art include Nikos Stangos, *Concepts of Modern Art,*[*] 3rd ed. (1994), and George H. Hamilton, *Painting and Sculpture in Europe, 1880–1940,*[*] 6th ed. (1989). Theda Shapiro, *Painters and Politics: The European Avantgarde and Society, 1900–1925* (1976), does not supplant the classic Arnold Hauser, *The Social History of Art*, vol. 4, *Naturalism, Impressionism, and the Film Age*[*] (reprint ed. 1985). William J. R. Curtis, *Modern Architecture since 1900*[*] (1997), is a standard introduction.

Additional Internet links related to this chapter are available on the Europe in the 20th Century Web site: http://www.history.wadsworth.com/paxton04.

You can also explore images, interactive timelines, and maps related to this chapter on our Western Civilization Resource Center: http://history.wadsworth.com.

The heir to the Habsburg throne, the Archduke Franz Ferdinand, and his wife start out on their fatal ride in Sarajevo, June 28, 1914.

2

The Coming of War

"**I**t seemed as though human beings might really be on the brink of becoming civilized," the British social critic Leonard Woolf remembered having felt before the First World War.[1] The Great War—as many Europeans still call it, even after the Second World War—put an end to such facile illusions. Europe, the most prosperous and sophisticated civilization on earth, failed to avoid war in 1914. The four-year struggle that followed was the bitterest, bloodiest, and costliest war in Europe since the Thirty Years' War (1618–1648). And since the same participants fought again in 1939 after a shaky armed truce of twenty years, twentieth-century Europe could be said to have had its own thirty years' war.[2]

The First World War snuffed out a whole generation of young men and destroyed many of Europe's treasures. It so distorted the world economy that sustained

[1]Leonard Woolf, *Beginning Again* (London, 1964), p. 44.

[2]Mark Mazower, *Dark Continent: Europe's Twentieth Century* (New York, 1999).

prosperity returned only in the 1960s. And it destroyed European primacy. Unable to dominate one another alone, the Great Powers called in an outside Great Power, the United States, and lost sovereign control over their own destinies, perhaps forever.

No one in Europe had expected in 1914 that such a dark age was at hand. To be sure, many Europeans had feared war during periodic international crises that seemed to grow more ominous in the new century. The most frightening of these crises had been confrontations between France and Germany over control of Morocco in 1905 and again in 1911. It was reassuring, however, that the Great Powers appeared determined to settle such confrontations by diplomatic negotiation after some ritual saber rattling. When lesser European states went to war among themselves, as in the two Balkan wars of 1912 and 1913, the Great Powers showed their determination to work together to keep such wars localized, in the nineteenth-century diplomatic tradition of the Concert of Europe.

If war did come, Europeans, touched by liberal optimism, believed that modern weapons would make it quick and decisive. Long wars, like long sieges, were supposed to have disappeared along with medieval weaponry. The Hundred Years' War of the fourteenth century had been followed by the Thirty Years' War of the seventeenth century. The twenty-three-year Napoleonic wars (1792–1815) had been followed by short, decisive campaigns that made maximum use of rapid railway movement. The Prussian wars against Denmark (1864), Austria (1866), and France (1870–1871) seemed to reinforce the hope that science and complex technology made quick knockout blows possible and long wars impossible to sustain. The kind of war that many Europeans feared in 1905 and in 1911 bore little resemblance to the horrors of the war they finally got from 1914 to 1918.

That catastrophe called into doubt the validity of what modern Europeans had accomplished. This shock to Europe's self-confidence accounts for the passion with which the search for the causes of the First World War has been pursued ever since. The emotions of war first produced highly personal explanations, like the "hang the kaiser" sentiment widespread in Britain in 1918. Later, with access to the governments' secret papers, historians developed more sophisticated explanations that we will consider at the end of this chapter. The whole European achievement is placed on trial when one considers the outbreak of the First World War.

THE JULY CRISIS OF 1914

It is necessary first to distinguish between the Austro-Serbian war, which began the confrontation in July 1914, and the subsequent escalation that brought in all the Great Powers. European statesmen had successfully contained local confrontations like this one several times in the recent past.

The crisis began with a political assassination, an act that has not usually led to war. A nineteen-year-old student, Gavrilo Princip, shot and killed the Archduke Franz Ferdinand and his wife on June 28, 1914, in Sarajevo, where the archduke was on an inspection tour of the province of Bosnia. The nephew of the Habsburg Emperor Franz Josef, Ferdinand was heir to the throne. At first glance, it looked like a purely internal matter: An Austro-Hungarian subject had killed the Habsburg heir

Gernsheim Collection, Harry Ransome Humanities Research Center, The University of Texas at Austin

The Bosnian Serb student, Gavrilo Princip, seized by police moments after he shot the heir to the Habsburg throne, the Archduke Franz Ferdinand, and his wife at Sarajevo, June 28, 1914.

on Austro-Hungarian territory. Princip, however, was a Bosnian Serb passionately committed to the ideal of freezing those South Slavic peoples living under Habsburg rule and uniting them with the Kingdom of Serbia, the only independent South Slav state. The South Slavs of Bosnia and Herzegovina had freed themselves from crumbling Turkish rule in 1876–1878, only to fall under Austro-Hungarian control. Princip had been armed and trained by the Black Hand, a terrorist group working underground, from bases in Serbia, for the independence of all the South Slav peoples.

The heart of the matter, then, was how directly the Kingdom of Serbia had abetted Princip's act. For the first month, from the assassination on June 28 to the Russian mobilization on July 29, the crisis revolved around Austro-Hungarian efforts to prove Serbian complicity and punish the Serbs for it. But to understand that conflict it is necessary to look at its Balkan roots.

The Balkans: Declining Empires and Rising Nationalities

The Balkan area was unique in Europe in 1914 for the complexity of its patchwork of national identities and the unsettled status of its boundaries. At the beginning of the nineteenth century, three broad empires—Austria-Hungary, Imperial Russia, and Ottoman Turkey—blanketed all southeastern Europe. They governed a passive citizenry by remote authority, leaving each locality free to speak its own language and practice its own customs and religion. This pattern of governance was altogether contrary to that emerging in western Europe, with its active citizenries made homogeneous by universal literacy and national education. The history of the Balkans since 1815 is structured around the decline of the three empires and the long and still unfinished struggle to put a new pattern of governance into place. Generally, the intellectuals and political leaders of the emerging independent Balkan peoples took the homogeneous states of western Europe as their model, a model tragically ill-adapted to the inextricable mixture of languages, customs, and religions left by the empires' tolerance.

The Ottoman Empire, which had stood at the very gates of Vienna in the 1680s but had become by the nineteenth century "the sick man of Europe," was the first to lose its grip. One Balkan province after another asserted its national autonomy or independence from the Turks: local autonomy for Serbia in 1817 and for Wallachia and Moldavia in 1829; independence for Greece in 1832; full independence for Serbia, and for Wallachia and Moldavia (united to form Romania) in 1878; local autonomy for Bulgaria in 1878 and independence in 1908.

Independence for the subject peoples of the Ottoman Empire, a good thing according to western liberal values, had profoundly destabilizing effects in the Balkans, however. For one thing, the two adjacent empires, Austria-Hungary and Russia, could not remain uninvolved. They abetted the Ottoman breakup in hopes of acquiring new protégés, new trading partners, or even new territory. This set them on a collision course with each other. Neither could afford to let the other predominate. Russian aid to the Bulgarian war for independence (1875–1878) opened forty years of smoldering confrontation with Austria-Hungary in the Balkans. The other Great Powers, led by Bismarck's Germany, worked to neutralize this conflict by balancing gains. The Congress of Berlin in 1878 trimmed back Russia's new client state in Bulgaria and compensated Austria-Hungary with powerful indirect influence in the Kingdom of Serbia and the right to administer a semiautonomous Bosnia and Herzegovina. Imperial ambitions could be tempered, it seemed, by patient diplomacy in which all the Great Powers worked together to deny Balkan hegemony to any one of them.

Independence for the Ottoman Empire's subject peoples was further destabilizing because it threatened the other two multinational empires from within. Both Austria-Hungary and Russia had much to fear from ethnic revivals. Russia ruled over restless Polish-speaking areas in the north, over large Ukrainian- and Turkish-speaking regions, and over Bessarabia, the region just east of the mouth of the Danube that Russia had seized from the Turks in 1812 and that the Romanians now claimed on grounds of national identity. The nationalist challenge to Russia was a pinprick, however, compared to the nationalist threat to Austria-Hungary's very existence. The southeastern half of Hungary, Transylvania, contained a large Romanian population; the southwestern tip of Hungary was inhabited by Croats, and the north by Slovaks. In Austria, an apprehensive German population maintained a precarious dominance over Czechs and Poles in the north, and over

Croats, Serbs, and other South Slavic people in the south. Austro-Hungarian internal politics in the late nineteenth century was a delicate balancing act in which the Hungarian Magyars ruthlessly controlled their minorities and the Austrian Germans sought allies in one or another nationality against the rest. It was not enough for the Austro-Hungarians to keep the Russians out of their kindred Slavic areas in the Balkans. Austro-Hungarian survival depended on muting all national independence movements. Blocking Serbian expansion on Austria–Hungary's southern border became a priority task in Vienna.

Serbia was the only Balkan nation to threaten a Great Power vitally. Following a change of dynasties in Serbia in 1903, the aggressive Serbian leader Nicholas Pašić adopted an openly anti-Austrian policy. The Austro-Hungarian government retaliated with tariff barriers against the main Serbian exports, pigs and plum brandy, in what has been called the "Pig War." More dangerously, the Serbs could or would do little to stop the activities of an anti-Austrian secret society, the Black Hand. Serbia had become after 1903 "a jackal snapping at the Austro-Hungarian Achilles heel."

The Austrian foreign minister, Baron Alois von Aehrenthal, became convinced that unless Austria decided to "grasp the nettle and make a final end to the pan-Slav

ETHNIC/LINGUISTIC COMPOSITION OF AUSTRIA-HUNGARY, 1914

dream" the Austro-Hungarian Empire would continue to "sink miserably step by step."[3] Aehrenthal's first move to block future Serbian growth was to begin a railroad southward to the Aegean that would cut Serbia off from other Slavic areas and from the Adriatic Sea. When this kind of "informal empire" seemed insufficient, Aehrenthal decided in 1908 to annex Bosnia and Herzegovina outright so that they could never become part of a greater South Slav state. The moment seemed propitious, for Russia had just been humiliated in the Russo-Japanese War of 1905, and Turkey was too preoccupied with domestic reform under the Young Turk movement even to protest Bulgarian accession to full independence in 1908.

Aehrenthal negotiated the annexation of Bosnia-Herzegovina with the Russian foreign minister, Alexander Izvolsky, in advance. In the most careful secrecy, the two foreign ministers agreed that in exchange for Russian acquiescence to the annexation the Austro-Hungarian Empire would support Russia's acquisition of the right to move warships through the Straits at Constantinople. Before Izvolsky had finished negotiating his new Straits rights with the other Great Powers, however, Aehrenthal announced the annexation of Bosnia-Herzegovina. Unable to achieve his side of the bargain, Izvolsky felt betrayed. "The dirty Jew has deceived me," Izvolsky cried to the German chancellor, Prince Bernhard von Bülow, in Berlin where he

BALKAN CONFLICTS,
1878–1914

[3]Wayne S. Vucinich, *Serbia between East and West* (Stanford, Calif., 1954), p. 229; Sidney B. Fay, *The Origins of the World War*, vol. 1 (New York, 1929), p. 395.

heard the news. "He lied to me, he bamboozled me, that frightful Jew."[4] Izvolsky's desire to bring Russia to war with Austria over Bosnia-Herzegovina was blocked mainly by a private German threat to release the information that Izvolsky had agreed to the deal earlier in secret. After the Bosnian humiliation of 1908, no Russian statesman could afford to appear to yield an inch to Austria-Hungary.

Imperial ambitions and imperial fears were not the only destabilizing aspect of the Balkan transformations. The newly independent Balkan states themselves did not form unified nation states. The ethnic map of the Balkans was too variegated for that. Ethnic identities in the Balkans were not based on physical differences—everyone looked more or less alike—but on language, culture and religion. They were "imagined communities," in the celebrated phrase of anthropologist Benedict Anderson, but no less passionately felt. The region contained dozens of languages, and language was the chief bearer of new identities. Religiously, a rough line from north to south (crosscutting the national frontiers) separated Roman Catholics in the Western Balkans (with their Latin alphabet) from the Orthodox (Cyrillic alphabet) in the east. Some populations in Bosnia and Albania had adopted the Muslim religion of the Ottoman rulers.

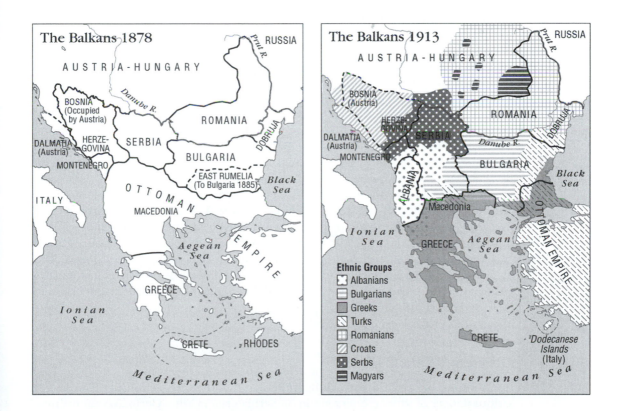

[4]Bernhard von Bülow, *Memoirs*, vol. 2 (Boston, 1931–1932), p. 440. Aehrenthal was not Jewish.

The better-educated and better organized communities set themselves up as western-style homogeneous states, only to discover that they contained intractable minorities, while remnants of their own kin remained outside. The dominant nationalities were tempted to absorb or to expel their minorities, and to expand in order to incorporate their separated kinspeople.

In 1912, Serbia took advantage of an insurrection of Albanian peoples in Macedonia to join its neighbors—Greece, Montenegro, and Bulgaria—in a lightning war of aggression to take Macedonia from the Ottoman Empire. This First Balkan War profited the aggressors handsomely in the spoils of Macedonia, but Austria-Hungary's insistence that an independent Albania be set up blocked Serbian access to the Adriatic Sea once again. Within a few months, the victors of the First Balkan War were quarreling over the spoils. Taking advantage of a Bulgarian general's unauthorized attack on Serbian and Greek positions, Serbia, Greece, and Montenegro, now joined by Romania and Turkey, forced Bulgaria to give up some territory in the Second Balkan War. These struggles were accompanied by the sort of massacres that the world learned in the 1990s to call "ethnic cleansing."

The unedifying Balkan wars of 1912 and 1913 may have lulled Europeans into thinking that since the Great Powers had kept these two conflicts localized by cooperating within the informal "Concert of Europe," they could keep Balkan conflicts localized indefinitely. In Vienna, however, the Balkan wars proved to an alarmed Austro-Hungarian leadership that no further successes must be allowed Serbia, "that viper's nest."

It was in circumstances of narrowed tolerance between Austria-Hungary and Serbia, on the one hand, and between Russia and Austria-Hungary, on the other, that young Princip assassinated the Habsburg heir in Sarajevo in June 1914.

The Austro-Hungarian government had no conclusive proof that the Serbian government knew of the plans of Princip and his helpers. Even today, the most one can say is that some members of the Serbian cabinet and the military command were aware of a number of terrorist plots and that the Serbian government had little zeal and even less power to stop them. In any event, the government in Vienna seized on the assassination as "the moment . . . to render Serbia innocuous once and for all by a display of force."[5] For men like the Austro-Hungarian army's chief of staff, General Franz Conrad von Hötzendorf, who had been urging a preventive war against Serbia since 1908, it was time to put aside such half-way measures as the "pig war," the Aegean railroad, and the creation of an independent Albania. The Habsburg government decided to wage a punitive war directly on Serbia. The Austro-Hungarian leaders bear the heavy responsibility of having made the first decision to go to war in July 1914.

Germany's "Blank Check"

It was important to the Austro-Hungarian plan that this war be limited. There was a serious danger of Russian intervention on Serbia's side. Only a German counterthreat

---

[5]Austrian foreign minister, Count Leopold Berchtold, quoted in Fay, vol. 2, p. 228. Among Habsburg leaders, only the Hungarian prime minister, Count Tisza, made temporary objections to the idea of a war with Serbia on the ground that the Habsburg Empire contained too many Slavs already.

could neutralize the Russians. On July 5, therefore, Aehrenthal's successor as Austro-Hungarian foreign minister, Count Leopold Berchtold, sent a top career diplomat to Berlin to give Kaiser Wilhelm II a personal letter from Emperor Franz Josef urging German support of the Austrian project that Serbia "be destroyed as a power factor." The net of involvements had already begun to ensnare other Great Powers.

The German government had previously helped restrain the Austrians. This time, however, Kaiser Wilhelm granted the Habsburg Empire what has been commonly called a "blank check." He assured Berchtold's envoy that Austria-Hungary could count on Germany's "full support" even "should a war between Austria-Hungary and Russia be unavoidable."[6] Furthermore, in the following days, the German imperial chancellor, Theobald von Bethmann Hollweg, and other German officials actively goaded the Austrians to action with remarks about proving themselves a Great Power and remaining an ally worthy of the German Empire. The working papers of the German government captured after the Second World War show beyond doubt that the kaiser and his chancellor wanted a local Austro-Serbian war to reverse the decline of Germany's only ally. How fully they perceived and accepted the risks of a wider war is the key issue in the debate over the German "blank check" of July 5, 1914.

According to the German state papers of July 1914 that survive, the German leaders knew that Russia might intervene if Austria made war on Serbia. Evidently both civilian and military leaders regarded that possibility as an acceptable risk for Germany. Russia might be only bluffing, and it could be counterbluffed. Impressed by signs of internal unrest in Russia following the Revolution of 1905, the kaiser thought that the Russian government would be unable to wage war. The German leaders also had to take into account the Franco-Russian Alliance, formed in 1891 and tightened since then. The Germans could doubt that France would intervene, since the French had not come automatically to the aid of the Russians either in the Russo-Japanese War of 1905 or in the Bosnian annexation crisis of 1908.

The German leaders seemed to have believed that whatever risks were involved were more than counterbalanced by possible strategic gains. The kaiser was obsessed with the belief that Germany had been "encircled," a word that recurs in his papers. The opportunity offered itself in July 1914 to prove that Germany and Austria could break out of the ring and "to make Austria preponderant in the Balkans at the expense of Russia," as the kaiser wrote in the margin of one of his papers.[7] His army chief of staff, General Helmut von Moltke, nephew of the general who had defeated the French in 1870, assured him that even if the worst happened, Germany was in a better position to fight both Russia and France in 1914 than would be the case later. By 1917 the Russian rearmament program of 1908 would be completed and France would have adjusted to the new three-year military service law of 1913. Some of Moltke's statements lend themselves to the interpretation that he wanted a preventive war against Russia and France while there was still time. At the very least, his advice made the risks of war seem acceptable considering the possible gains. As German leaders saw their strategic position in July 1914, they had to act vigorously to assert their growing world power or reconcile themselves to eventual decline.

[6]Imanuel Geiss, *July 1914* (New York, 1967), p. 77.

[7]Fritz Fischer, *Germany's Aims in the First World War* (New York, 1967), p. 67.

Austria's Ultimatum to Serbia

Their backs stiffened by German prodding through the middle weeks of July, the Austro-Hungarian leaders set about making a public case for Serbian guilt. They prepared an ultimatum quite consciously designed to make demands that Serbia could not accept. Once Serbia rejected the ultimatum, Austria-Hungary would have justification for military action. While Europe returned to midsummer tranquility, and the kaiser departed on a yachting vacation off Norway, this time bomb was being slowly prepared in Vienna. There was no hurry, for the Austrians had decided not to present the ultimatum until July 23, to avoid coinciding with the state visit to St. Petersburg of French President Raymond Poincaré and Prime Minister René Viviani. The timing shows that the Austrians knew they were going to the brink.

The "timed note," as the ultimatum was prudently called, accused Serbia of being "guilty" of "tolerating . . . criminal dealings" of subversion and separatism within the Habsburg lands, which obliged Austria to take on "the duty . . . to put an end to such doings which are constantly threatening the peace of the monarchy."[8] There followed ten demands, some of them merely requiring Serbia to suppress anti-Austrian movements and punish the guilty parties. Other demands were far less compatible with Serbian sovereignty. Austria insisted that Serbia dismiss officials and army officers of Austrian choice, and that Austrian officials take part in the investigation of a conspiracy in Serbia leading up to the assassination. Unconditional acceptance of all demands was required within forty-eight hours. This ultimatum was delivered in Belgrade at 6:00 P.M. on July 23 by an Austrian ambassador who was already packing in anticipation of Serbian rejection.

The Serbian reply, delivered just before the deadline on July 25, was masterfully drafted to arouse European sympathy. The Serbs rejected out of hand only the demand for Austrian participation in the investigation within Serbia. Their replies to the other demands were conciliatory. The Serbian army was mobilized, however.

Despite signs of slackening will in Vienna at the end of July, the Austro-Hungarian ambassador in Belgrade adhered to the plan and broke relations with Serbia on receiving its reply. The German chancellor and foreign minister did their best to keep alive the "spirit of Sarajevo," although they were eager to keep Austria's punitive action localized.

The last week of July was a testing time for traditional Great Power diplomacy. The Great Powers had managed to prevent war between Austria and Russia over Bosnia in 1908, and they had localized the Balkan wars of 1912 and 1913. This crisis, however, was neither a Great Power confrontation, as in 1908, nor a war among lesser states, as in 1912 and 1913. This was an attempt by one Great Power, supported by another, to reduce decisively the power of a small neighbor. That kind of conflict was much more difficult for the other Great Powers to stop.

The British government proposed a mediation that would forestall any military action between Austria and Serbia. But the Germans blocked all efforts at

---

[8]Geiss, Document No. 37, pp. 143–144.

conciliation: They wanted a local war, not peace at any price. This time, localization, as the British diplomat Arthur Nicolson pointed out, meant "holding the ring while Austria quietly strangles Serbia"[9] without intervention by Russia on Serbia's behalf.

On July 28, the Austro-Hungarian Empire declared war on Serbia. The Austrian army shelled Belgrade on July 29. For the first time since 1878, a Great Power was at war on the European Continent. Would the other Great Powers inexorably be drawn in?

ESCALATION: FROM LOCAL WAR TO CONTINENTAL WAR

Austria and Germany had wanted the Austro-Serbian war to remain localized, another Balkan war. But military alliances and Great Power rivalries threatened from the beginning to widen the conflict.[10] Germany prodded its ally Austria-Hungary to seize the opportunity for major gains in the Balkans. Russia, determined to prevent further Austrian aggrandizement, drew confidence from a mutual defense treaty with France. France, in turn, had informal defense agreements with Britain. But alliances are not always honored, and it was not yet clear whether other Great Powers would be drawn into actual fighting. The degree of escalation depended on the diplomatic skills of statesmen who were working to prevent it, their access to information and control over their own complex military machines, and their perception of the unfolding choices between fighting and humiliation.

Russia's Mobilization

Russia was the Great Power most immediately affected by the news of the Austrian ultimatum to Serbia, for Russia could not accept another humiliation like Bosnia in 1908. After that crisis Russia had launched a massive rearmament program designed to bring its army to 2.2 million men. Izvolsky, who had borne the brunt of the humiliation, had been removed as foreign minister and named ambassador to allied France. His successor, Sergei Sazonov, was particularly sensitive to charges of weakness by Russian pan-Slav patriots. In July 1914, exhilarated as well as exhausted by the toasts and speeches of the state visit by French President Poincaré, Sazonov was in no state to deal calmly with the Austro-Serbian situation. The Russian government could barely restrain itself from ordering partial mobilization against Austria on learning the terms of the ultimatum to Serbia on July 24. Russia rushed to arms when Austria declared war on Serbia on July 28. Austrian assurances to the Russians that they planned no permanent annexation of Serbian territory only

---

[9]Fay, vol. 2, p. 355.

[10]European Great Power alliances in 1914: The Central Powers—Germany and Austria-Hungary—allied since 1879, were more loosely tied to Italy since 1882 in the Triple Alliance. The Allies, or the Entente Powers—France and Russia—were allied since 1891; France was linked to Britain by the Entente cordiale of 1904.

showed how determined the Austrians were to complete their punitive expedition. At 11:00 A.M. on July 29, the four Russian military districts fronting Austria-Hungary were mobilized.

With this partial mobilization of the Russian army, military technology first exerted decisive pressure on the unfolding crisis. The preparation of a modern mass army for action had become a feat of prodigious complexity. It took minute planning to recall millions of reservists, to get them to the proper units along with supplies and equipment, and to move these massive assemblages of men and matériel by railroad to the front. Last-minute changes in mobilization plans threatened to throw the whole procedure awry. Improvisation could be fatal. One had to follow the plan or become hopelessly snarled.

The Russian general staff had worked out mobilization plans according to purely technical considerations, without taking into account the diplomatic implications of their elaborate timetables and emplacements. They had arranged for simultaneous mobilization against Germany and Austria. The generals assured Sazonov and the tsar that a partial mobilization against Austria alone would throw the whole army into chaos. Furthermore, it was notorious that the creaking Russian military bureaucracy needed a head start to match Germany. If full mobilization were not ordered soon, Russia would never be ready to parry a possible German attack.

Faced with these technical rigidities, the reluctant tsar ordered full mobilization later in the day of July 29. Just before midnight he revoked his order after receiving a warning telegram addressed to "Nicky" from his cousin "Willy" in Berlin.[11] After frantic appeals by the generals and Sazonov, he reinstated full mobilization on the morning of July 30, lest possible war with Germany be lost in advance. A second Great Power had committed itself irrevocably to a war stance.

France's Intentions

The French role in Russia's decision to mobilize is still controversial. The crucial point is whether the French, as Russia's only continental ally,[12] encouraged Russian belligerence in the hopes that a European war might permit them to recover the provinces of Alsace and Lorraine, lost to Germany in 1871. As we have seen, French president Poincaré and Prime Minister Viviani had been in St. Petersburg on a state visit just before the Austrian demands on Serbia became known. The ritual toasts and parades of the visit no doubt stimulated Russian faith in the Franco-Russian Alliance at that crucial moment. Moreover, the two chief leaders of France were insulated from any direct role in events from July 23 until July 29, when the battleship France finally returned them home. In their absence, Justice Minister Jean-Baptiste Bienvenu-Martin was both inexperienced and uninfluential as acting head of government. These accidents left an unusually large amount of responsibility in

---

[11]The tsar's great-grandmother was a Prussian princess. The kaiser was even more closely related to the Tsarina Alexandra; both were grandchildren of British Queen Victoria.

[12]Although Russia and Great Britain had resolved all existing differences in 1907, no formal alliance existed between them.

the hands of the French ambassador to St. Petersburg, Maurice Paléologue. Apparently without precise instructions from Paris, Ambassador Paléologue allowed his enthusiasm for Russian court life and the excitement of the recent state visit to warp his judgment. He effusively promised Sazonov unconditional French support. At the same time, he failed to inform his own government of the ramifications of Russian mobilization on both the German and Austrian frontiers, a failure that prevented the French government from understanding the full implications of its support.

As an ardent patriot and a native of lost Lorraine, President Poincaré has been suspected of wanting war in order to regain his native province. Only circumstantial evidence supports this allegation. After his return to Paris on July 29, the French government urged caution while assuring Russian Ambassador Izvolsky that "France is ready to fulfill all the obligations of her alliance."[13] The treaty obligations required only that France come to Russia's aid in case of German attack or of Austrian attack supported by Germany. Heretofore, the French had carefully withheld support from Russia's Balkan adventures, as in the 1908 Bosnian crisis. They feared that to stand aside once more while Russia underwent another Balkan humiliation would end the Franco-Russian Alliance and leave France facing Germany alone.

The French government also was coming under pressure from the technical requirements of its own army. General Joseph Joffre, commander in chief of the French armies, warned the government that unless French troops were put on a war footing with sufficient lead time, he would be unable to defend France against German attack. On July 30, therefore, the French "covering force"—the first-line frontier troops—was mobilized, although it was held six miles behind the frontier to avoid provocation. However little French leaders contemplated a preventive war, they were determined not to be caught again as they had been caught in 1870, lacking allies and mobilizing too late.

Germany Declares War

The news of general Russian mobilization late on July 30 presented the German government with a military emergency and gave the generals a dominant voice in what followed. General Moltke was not placated by Russian Foreign Minister Sazonov's assurances that general Russian mobilization did not mean that any Russian troops would cross the frontier. Moltke was keenly aware of the deadline German mobilization must meet in order to catch up with the Russians. He told his government that noon on July 31 was the latest the army could wait and still be assured of matching the Russian mobilization.

The military machines now began to set their own timing on decisions, and it was therefore of little importance that some German statesmen were beginning to recoil before the general war they had so cavalierly risked earlier. Returning from his Norwegian cruise on July 28, Kaiser Wilhelm had finally read the Serbian reply to Austria and had decided that "the grounds for war had now fallen away." At the last moment, Berlin proposed that the Austrian armies "halt in Belgrade" and

[13]Geiss, Document No. 148, pp. 312–313.

merely hold Serbian territory as a bargaining counter. Sazonov held out the promise that the Russians would cancel mobilization in return for Austrian withdrawal from Serbia. Austria, for its part, was willing to accept mediation and to promise not to annex any Serbian territory, but unwilling to renounce its punitive operation altogether.

All these last-minute proposals, like the four-power mediation constantly urged by the British foreign secretary, had one flaw: They offered peace only at the cost of leaving the gradual Austrian decline in the Balkans unchecked by the kind of conspicuous success both Germans and Austrians had looked forward to after July 5. The decisive opinion offered in Berlin late on July 31 was General Moltke's, and it resulted in a German ultimatum to Russia. Germany gave the Russians twelve hours to renounce all military preparations against Austria and Germany. When the ultimatum expired the next day, Germany declared war on Russia at 5:00 P.M. on August 1.

The major question now was whether the French could stand aside if Germany and Russia fought in the east. There is every reason to think that Poincaré and Viviani were supported by public opinion in their determination to accept war rather than isolation from Russia or further German success. France did not feel responsible for war, wrote the centrist mass-circulation daily *Le Matin* on the morning of August 1, but "if it comes, we shall meet it with high hopes. We are convinced that it will bring us the restitutions which are our right."

The Schlieffen Plan

The question of whether France would stand aside was a purely academic one on August 1, for German military planners had decided long ago that the road to St. Petersburg ran through Paris. Assuming that the Franco-Russian Alliance was rigid, the German military planners helped to make it more so by arranging to attack the French first. General Alfred von Schlieffen, German chief of staff from 1891 to 1905, had responded to the Franco-Russian Alliance by shaping all his plans to fit a two-front war. Schlieffen reasoned that France, which could mobilize more quickly than Russia, could be defeated in six weeks by throwing almost the entire German army westward in a curving sweep of the scythe through Holland and Belgium into western France, while only a few covering units held the eastern front. Then the more numerous but slower Russians could be dealt with at leisure by the whole German army.

Although Schlieffen's successor, General Moltke, reduced the scope of the wheeling maneuver in order to leave Holland neutral, he did not abandon the essential pattern of the Schlieffen Plan. When the German twelve-hour ultimatum was dispatched to Russia late on July 31, the German generals had to assume that Paris would be their first target. Moltke could not wait to learn about French intentions before deciding which way to move his forces, for improvising on the Schlieffen Plan risked throwing the whole German war machine into confusion. So a simultaneous ultimatum went out to Paris on July 31: France must declare its neutrality within eighteen hours.

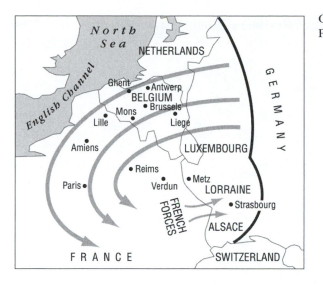

ORIGINAL SCHLIEFFEN
PLAN

French code-breakers learned that the Germans intended to demand the frontier fortresses of Toul and Verdun as surety for France's neutrality. Whatever doubts might have been felt in Paris about Russian general mobilization now disappeared. The French government declared general mobilization on the afternoon of August 1, without awaiting news of German general mobilization, which was announced at about the same time. Claiming for public consumption that French troops had violated the frontier in several places, Germany declared war on August 3. By assuming that war with France was inevitable, the German authorities had helped make it so.

Britain Joins In

There were several reasons why Britain might have considered Germany an enemy in 1914. Germany's enormous warship construction program since 1898 had required Britain to construct a powerful new class of battleships, Dreadnoughts, in order to keep control of the seas. The kaiser's support for Boer independence from the British in South Africa in 1896 and commercial rivalry in the Near East, China, and Latin America had greatly sharpened the British public's awareness of Germany as an enemy. Finally, Britain had been engaged in joint military planning with France since 1905 and had settled all differences with France's ally Russia in 1907.

But no hard and fast agreements obliged the British to aid either France or Russia in case of a war with Germany. And, in fact, in 1914 British–German relations were more cordial than they had been at any time in the recent past. In that very June, Britain and Germany had agreed to cooperate in the completion of the Berlin-to-Baghdad Railway, heretofore a major focus of imperial and commercial rivalry. A British naval unit was visiting the German base at Kiel when the news broke of the Austrian ultimatum to Serbia. Wilhelm II's brother was assured by his cousin and fellow yachtsman, King George V, that England wished to remain

The last meeting of Kaiser Wilhelm II of Germany (left) and King George V of Britain, before the First World War. The two monarchs, both grandsons of Britain's Queen Victoria, are seen here on a family occasion, preparing to review the garrison at the royal palace at Potsdam before the marriage of Kaiser Wilhelm's daughter in 1913. As usual, the Kaiser has taken pains to hide his withered left arm.

neutral. It is characteristic of Wilhelm's view of the world that he based his tough policy on those royal words long after they had been contradicted by such underlings as foreign ministers and ambassadors.

The British foreign secretary, Sir Edward Grey, has been blamed for not using British power more decisively to stave off conflict. It has been suggested that if he had warned Germany sooner that Britain could not stand aside if France were attacked, the kaiser would have assessed the risks far more soberly in mid-July. To Grey's credit, he high-mindedly thought that any threat to make war only made war that much more likely. But having failed to give Germany a clear warning until July 29 that Britain would not remain neutral if France were drawn in, as the French urged, Grey also refused to bring pressure on Russia to demobilize, as the Germans urged. Instead, Grey devoted all his energies to a futile effort to arrange Great Power mediation of the Austro-Serbian dispute. During July he made four mediation proposals, all of which were doomed by German insistence that the conflict be "localized," that is, allowed to take place without Russian intervention. The French could not lend warm support to Grey's attempts at conciliation for fear of casting doubt in St. Petersburg on the reliability of their support as allies.

When events began to move rapidly in late July, the British government found itself thrust into the very position that it had hoped to avoid through its mediation efforts. It had to decide how to respond if the French were drawn into the war. British independence from continental allies had greatly diminished in the decade before 1914. The German naval challenge had led to a fateful British decision in 1912 to concentrate British naval forces in the English Channel, leaving the Mediterranean to be controlled by the French navy. Henceforth, British mastery of the seas depended on a friendly France to assure access to India and to the Middle Eastern oil on which the British Navy was now dependent, having begun to convert from coal to oil in 1911. Even Britain had been forced by the cost of the early-twentieth-century armaments race to count on allies.

Sir Eyre Crowe, a senior career diplomat in the British Foreign Office, drew up a memorandum on July 25 outlining very clearly the alternatives for British world power. If Russia and France were determined to take up the gauntlet, Crowe argued, it would be fatal for Britain to stand aside. If Germany and Austria won, there would be no French fleet; Germany would occupy the channel coast; and "what would be the position of a friendless England?" If France and Russia won without British support, "what would then be their attitude toward England? What about India and the Mediterranean?"[14] There had never been any real possibility of British neutrality if Germany went to war with France, and the stubborn belief of the kaiser and of Chancellor Bethmann Hollweg in British neutrality was one of the most fatal blunders of the July crisis.

Crowe's reasoning shows why the last-minute German offer not to use naval units against the French channel coast failed to work its expected relief in London. It also shows that the British did not really go to war over a mere "scrap of paper," the Belgian Neutrality Treaty of 1839, as Bethmann Hollweg furiously charged on learning

---

[14]G. P. Gooch and Harold Tempersley, eds., *British Documents on the Origins of the World War*, vol. 11 (London, 1926), p. 101.

that his plan for a localized war was exploding into a continental war. It is true that a German ultimatum to Belgium on August 2 united British public opinion behind a dreaded war more effectively than Crowe's brand of geopolitical reasoning could have done. But British statesmen clearly understood well before August 2 that the real issue was not Belgian neutrality and the sanctity of treaties but the place of the British Empire in the world.

Britain declared war on an amazed Germany at 11:00 A.M. on August 4, after the expiration of an ultimatum demanding German withdrawal from Belgium.

Of the major European powers, only Italy stood aside from the conflict. Although formally linked to Germany by treaty since 1882, and informally linked by major economic investments, Italy had drawn more closely into the French economic sphere in the early twentieth century. More importantly, Italian national ambitions centered on the upper Adriatic Sea and its Balkan shores, areas once ruled by the independent Republic of Venice. These ambitions naturally threw Italy increasingly into conflict with Austrian interests in the years before 1914. In July and August 1914, therefore, Italian treaty links to Germany counted for less than potential gains from an Austrian defeat. For the moment, Italy remained neutral.

With that exception, all the European Great Powers were at war on August 4, 1914, for the first time since 1815, in a way no one would have believed possible only a month before.

A LONGER VIEW OF THE CAUSES OF WAR

We have looked at close range at that hectic week of accelerating crisis that led from the announcement of Austria's demands on Serbia on July 24 to the declarations of war from August 1 to 4. From that perspective, one sees flawed and fallible men struggling to understand the rush of events and to take the right steps on short notice. From that perspective, it is tempting to place responsibility on individual personalities or on individual failures to make diplomacy work. For none of the Great Powers got what their leaders wanted in July and August 1914. Germany and Austria did not get their therapeutic local war for Balkan advantage; the Russians did not get their limited war against Austria; the Germans did not get British neutrality in their war with France and Russia; the French and the British could not maintain the status quo that was probably the preference of a majority of their people. The diplomacy of July and August 1914 makes a tale of almost unmitigated failure. Was the First World War, then, a tragic accident, the result of human error that interrupted the course of an otherwise promising civilization?

From a longer point of view, it seems unlikely that so massive a calamity could flow from so ephemeral a cause. It is often argued that inherent flaws in liberal, capitalist society made a general European war unavoidable, sooner or later. The system of sovereign states provided no outside tribunal to settle differences, and rising ethnic nationalism made those differences more intractable. Moreover, imperialist rivalry among capitalist powers and increasing class conflict within capitalist societies made war an attractive choice for European leaders. According to these determinist positions, even if the Great Powers had scraped through the Austro-Serbian crisis as they had earlier crises, a major war was unavoidable in the long run within the existing system.

Sovereignty and a Nation's Honor

The system of sovereign states in Europe and the world allowed for no recourse to a higher tribunal for arbitration or mediation when any two states were on a collision course. Since the sovereign nation-state was accepted as the ultimate human authority, its welfare became a supreme value. "In vital questions, and those of honor," wrote the kaiser in the margin of a memorandum submitted to him, "one does not consult with others."[15] European statesmen considered the state morally as well as legally sovereign; war was an acceptable course of action to save a state from decline, in the view of all but a tiny minority of pacifists in Europe in 1914.

All the European leaders knew recent examples in which restraint had produced national humiliation: Russia in the Bosnian crisis of 1908, Germany in the second Moroccan crisis in 1911, and Austria in the Balkan wars. All of them knew other recent cases in which going to the brink had saved national honor, as in the case of France in the second Moroccan crisis of 1911. A continent crowded with sovereign nations that recognized no higher interest than the state's success seemed bound to be jostled into a major war sooner or later.

Imperialist Considerations

The sharpened commercial and colonial rivalries of the Great Powers made war inevitable, in the opinion of some. Lenin's *Imperialism: The Highest Stage of Capitalism* (1917), for example, argued that as capitalism ripened into monopoly, profits would decline. Therefore, European monopolies would seek higher rates of yield outside their own countries in a worldwide race for profits that was bound to lead to war.

No one can deny the importance of colonial and commercial rivalries in statesmen's calculations of July and August 1914. The German historian Fritz Fischer has shown how frustrations in German commercial expansion eastward and southward in Europe contributed to the German leaders' sense of encirclement in 1914. If they did not build the Berlin-to-Baghdad Railway, someone else would. General Friedrich von Bernhardi's 1912 essay on Germany's choice—"World Power or Decline"—measured "world power" in cultural and commercial terms as well as in military terms.[16]

The two clearest instances in which colonial-commercial rivalry sharpened conflict between eventual belligerents of 1914 were the Moroccan crises of 1905 and

---

[15]Geiss, p. 184.

[16]Friedrich von Bernhardi, *Deutschland und der nächste Krieg* (1912), summarized in Fischer, pp. 34–35.

1911, and the German–British naval race. Both France and Germany had substantial investments in Morocco in the early twentieth century. Germany's deliberate challenge in 1905 to growing French political and military power there clearly heightened French nationalism and military expenditure in the following years. The second clash over Morocco in 1911, in which combined British and French pressure forced the Germans to back down, led General Moltke to write in his memoirs that another such display of weakness would make him despair of the future of the German Reich. The German–British naval race forced the British to admit that even their new fleet of Dreadnoughts could not guarantee access to the British Empire without French help. The web of economic interest and military calculation was tightening in the years before 1914.

It would be a mistake, however, to regard commercial and colonial rivalries as solely determining an inevitable war in 1914. German and British commercial interests recognized that they were each other's best trading partners and that trade prospers best in peace, as they proved by agreeing to the joint construction of the Berlin-to-Baghdad Railway in June 1914. London merchants and bankers were opposed to war during the July crisis. Colonial rivalries did not necessarily determine the alignments of 1914. After all, bitter colonial rivalries had pitted Britain against France in Africa and the Near East, and Britain against Russia in Iran and Afghanistan. Britain and Germany had cooperated in central and North Africa and in the Far East, while even France and Germany had avoided colonial rivalry between 1871 and 1905. Indeed, it was the Russian turn away from colonial interests in the Far East after losing a war to Japan in 1905 that dangerously heightened rivalries in the Balkans and within Europe itself.

Internal Dissent

Did the breath of revolution at home stir some European statesmen to a more bellicose posture abroad? Internal strife certainly rose sharply in a number of European states on the eve of 1914. In France, strikes had reached unprecedented proportions from 1906 to 1909, and after conservatives had succeeded in 1913 in increasing military service to three years, the elections of 1914 threw the whole issue open again by returning a left plurality. The German Social Democrats had become the largest party in the Reichstag in 1912, and the Prussian three-class voting system was under bitter attack. The Italian "Red Week" of June 1914 was the bloodiest strike wave in that country's history. As for Austria-Hungary, where the insoluble problem of dissident ethnic minorities festered beneath the brilliant surface of Viennese culture, wits said that its situation was desperate but not serious. The Russian tsar, aristocrats, and conservatives watched in constant dread for a new revolution following the unsuccessful uprising of 1905. Even Great Britain, that citadel of calm gradualism, was shaken in 1913 and 1914 by three different movements that took their anger into the streets: the mass protests for women's suffrage; the strike wave that was about to culminate in a general strike in August 1914; and, on the right, the army officers and English landowners in Ulster (Northern

Ireland) who threatened civil war rather than accept the new laws providing for Irish Home Rule.

The important point is not whether these states were actually nearing a revolutionary situation in 1914, but whether national leaders thought so and what they proposed to do about it. Some statesmen, both liberal and conservative, feared that the dislocations of a war would "mean a state of things worse than that of 1848."[17] But even the conviction that war would heighten the revolutionary danger may have encouraged the kaiser to believe that the Russians would not dare fight Austria. Other statesmen, mostly conservative, believed that the jingoistic nationalism stimulated by a successful foreign war or warlike bluff was the most effective remedy for internal dissent. Some Austrian leaders believed in "mastering internal troubles by prosecuting an active foreign policy."[18] Russian Foreign Minister Sazonov told the tsar that "unless he yielded to the popular demand and unsheathed the sword on Serbia's behalf, he would run the risk of revolution and perhaps the loss of his throne."[19]

Only the most determinist of historians would suggest that capitalism's late stages must inevitably produce conservative efforts to distract class conflict by external war. Nor is there a clear case of any European statesman manufacturing a national emergency for purely internal purposes. What can be said, however, is that when an international emergency was thrust on them, some European statesmen took risks more willingly in the belief that foreign success could only strengthen the ruling circle at home. At the very least, they knew that international humiliation produced revolution, as in Russia when revolution followed defeat at the hands of the Japanese in 1905. Even the British Liberal Prime Minister Herbert Asquith found some consolation as he contemplated "the most dangerous situation of the last forty years" in the Balkans on July 26: "It may incidentally have the effect of throwing into the background the lurid picture of civil war in Ulster."[20]

The Alliance System

Other serious defects in the European system had developed in the past generation to narrow the choices open to leaders in 1914. Both the Franco-Russian and the Austro-German alliances had been made more binding in the years before the war. It was not the firmer language of the alliance treaties that was dangerous, however, for the Great Powers had not felt obliged in practice to support their allies under any condition contrary to their own interests. France had not given the Russians assurances of help during the Bosnian crisis of 1908, for example. What was dangerous was the growing sense among the Great Powers that their security depended

[17]Sir Edward Grey, quoted in Arno J. Mayer, "Domestic Causes of the First World War," in Leonard Krieger and Fritz Stern, eds., *The Responsibility of Power* (New York, 1967), p. 321.

[18]Prince Karl von Lichnowsky, the German ambassador to London, opposing that remedy, quoted in ibid., p. 320.

[19]Quoted in Hans Rogger, "Russia in 1914," *Journal of Contemporary History,* vol. 3 (1966), p. 243.

[20]Quoted in Cameron Hazlehurst, *Politicians at War* (New York, 1971), p. 32.

on the continued power of an ally. Unlike Bismarck before 1890, who had maintained good relations with both Russia and Austria, the German rulers after 1890 committed themselves to Austria and Italy in the Triple Alliance. As ties with Italy grew slack, the German leaders felt quite alone with Austria-Hungary by 1914, and bound to that empire's uncertain fate. France had no possibility of holding its own against the more numerous Germans without Russian support; if the Russians went to the brink against Germany, the French could not risk future isolation by giving an impression of doubtful support. Even Britain, unfettered by any explicit military obligations, could not imagine a secure future without a strong and friendly France. Increasingly, powerful weapons having made them all more vulnerable, the Great Powers had to support their allies even when those allies took risks.

The War Machines

The industrialization of war also narrowed the statesmen's choices in 1914. European war machines had not only doubled in size between 1890 and 1914, raising military expenditures to the unprecedented level of nearly 5 percent of national income,[21] but they had also become enormously complex. The use of railroads in war since the 1860s put a new premium on speed, without reducing the older emphasis on numbers. Millions of reservists and vast quantities of artillery, ammunition, and supplies had to be moved in a few hours by a rail network that first had to be diverted from its normal commercial uses. Mobilization had to be begun early enough to meet dangers that were still only potential, although the very act of mobilization provoked others to mobilize. Moreover, existing plans had to be followed whether or not they fit the current crisis, since improvisation was likely to produce chaos.

It has been noted how these technical requirements forced diplomacy out of control in the cases of general Russian mobilization on July 30, the German commitment to the Schlieffen Plan, and the early mobilization of the French "covering force" on July 30. Even in Britain, First Lord of the Admiralty Winston Churchill took the exceptional step of not dispersing the fleet from its usual summer maneuvers in July. The fear of being caught unprepared in the railroad age was sharper than the fear of slipping uncontrollably into overreaction.

The Exercise of Choice

We have seen how many features of the European state, economic, and military systems and the perfervid nationalisms of 1914 narrowed statesmen's choices. So

---

[21]Military expenditures during the pre-1914 arms race, although greater than they had ever been before, were still comparatively modest by current standards. The Great Powers spent nearly 10 percent of national income on arms in 1937. The Super Powers' armaments expenditures reached 13 to 15 percent of the gross national product in the Cold War of the 1950s. (Quincy Wright, *A Study of War*, 2nd ed. [Chicago, 1964], pp. 667–672; Charles J. Hitch and Roland N. McKean, *The Economics of Defense in the Nuclear Age* [Cambridge, Mass., 1965], pp. 37, 98.)

much more was involved in the failures of July and August 1914 than mere miscalculation, fatigue, or haste. However, most historians would feel uncomfortable if such emphasis were placed on predetermining conditions for war in 1914 that the free choices of European leaders were ignored. Historians should be as interested in the exercise of choice as in the conditions that limit choice. In July and August 1914, the Austrian leaders chose to punish Serbia for matters going far beyond the assassination of a royal heir. The German kaiser and chancellor supported Austria in a local war in order to reassert German vitality. The Russians had resolved as early as 1908 to forbid any further successes to Austria. French and British leaders decided, as the British foreign minister told the House of Commons on August 3, that "if we are engaged in war, we shall suffer but little more than we shall suffer even if we stand aside."[22]

These choices, it must be realized, were not simple selections between pure states of "peace" or "war." Decisions were made, step-by-step, between acceptable increments of war risk and unacceptable increments of risk of national humiliation, isolation, or decline. At each stage, the war risk seemed all the more acceptable because no European in 1914 had the faintest idea what sort of war the Great Powers could wage in the twentieth century. The length, fanaticism, and violence of what was to come were beyond human imagining as the first eager troops rushed to the front.

SUGGESTIONS FOR FURTHER READING

James Joll, *The Origins of the First World War,*[*] 2nd ed. (1999), is a masterful discussion. Laurence Lafore, *The Long Fuse*[*] (2nd ed. 1997), analyzes lucidly the political and diplomatic background in Central Europe. See also Joachim Remak, *The Origins of World War I, 1871–1914,*[*] 2nd ed. (1994). Enlightening articles are collected in Samuel R. Williamson Jr. et al., *Soldiers, Statesmen and July 1914: Civil-Military Relations and the Origins of the Great War*[*] (2000), and in Richard Evans and Hartmut Pogge von Strandman, eds., *The Coming of the First World War* (1990). James Joll, *The Unspoken Assumptions* (1968), is a classic evaluation of the values that influenced the leaders' decisions. Marc Trachtenberg challenges the view that military machines spun out of control in 1914 in a seminal article, Chapter 2 of his collected essays, *History and Strategy*[*] (1991).

Among more detailed treatments, the Italian newspaper editor Luigi Albertini's *Origins of the War of 1914,* 3 vols. (1952–1957, reprint ed. 2003), provides an incomparable sweep of narrative detail, thorough on Balkan conditions and favorable to the Entente side. Despite new evidence revealed after the Second World War, the great monuments of the interwar "war guilt" controversy are still impressive. Sidney B. Fay, *The Origins of the World War,* 2 vols. (1928), shifts much of the blame from Germany to Serbia and Russia.

---

[22]Zara S. Steiner, *Britain and the Origins of the First World War* (New York, 1977), p. 210.

Bernadotte E. Schmitt, *The Coming of War* (1930), is more critical of the Central Powers.

Paul M. Kennedy, *The Rise of the Anglo-German Antagonism, 1860–1914*[*] (1988), studies public opinion on both sides. Robert Wohl, *The Generation of 1914*[*] (1979), evokes popular feelings on the eve of the war.

In the 1960s, Fritz Fischer, *Germany's Aims in the First World War* (1967), found his own country primarily responsible for war in 1914. He responded to a storm of criticism with *World Power or Decline* (1974), and *War of Illusions: German Policies from 1911 to 1914* (1975). One of Fischer's students, Imanuel Geiss, prepared a volume of documents with commentary, *July 1914* (1967), where the Fischer version can be followed in detail. H. W. Koch, ed., *The Origins of the First World War*[*] (revised ed. 1991), assembles readings on the Fischer debate.

Volker R. Berghahn, *Germany and the Approach of War, 1914,*[*] 2nd ed. (1993), offers the latest scholarly synthesis, largely validating Fischer's charges. It is one of a series in which the role of each Great Power is assessed: Zara S. Steiner, *Britain and the Origins of the First World War,*[*] 2nd ed. (2003), and similar titles for Austria-Hungary by Samuel R. Williamson Jr. (1991), Russia by D. C. B. Lieven (1984), Italy by R. J. B. Bosworth (1983), and France by John F. V. Keiger (1984). Keiger's book, and Gerd Krumeich, ed., *Armaments and Politics in France on the Eve of the First World War*[*] (1987), revive some French responsibility, the latter showing the influence of domestic politics on military doctrine. Douglas Porch gives a sympathetic account of the French officers' struggles with politicians in *The March to the Marne*[*] (reprint 2003).

Samuel R. Williamson Jr. examines the Entente's military planning in *The Politics of Grand Strategy: Britain and France Prepare for War, 1904–1914*[*] (1969, reprint ed. 1990). Jack Snyder, *The Ideology of the Offensive*[*] (1984), examines the assumptions behind French strategic planning. See generally Steven E. Miller, Sean M. Lynn-Jones, and Stephen Van Evera, *Military Strategy and the Origins of the First World War* (revised ed. 1991).

German military preparations are examined by Gerhard Ritter, *The Schlieffen Plan* (1958, reprint ed. 1979) and *The Sword and the Scepter: The Problem of Militarism in Germany,* vol. 2, *1890–1914* (1970), and by the much more critical Gordon A. Craig, *The Politics of the Prussian Army, 1640–1945*[*] (1955, reprint ed. 1964).

Vladimir Dedijer, *The Road to Sarajevo* (1966), defends the idealism of Princip and his comrades, and examines the help Serbian officials gave to their assassination plans.

Arno Mayer examines the resort to war as a diversion from social unrest at home in "Internal Crisis and War since 1870," in Charles Bertrand, ed., *Revolutionary Situations in Europe* (1977), and further explores the background to this issue in *The Persistence of the Old Regime* (1980).

Some of the main protagonists are examined in Konrad Jarausch, *The Enigmatic Chancellor: Bethmann Hollweg and the Hubris of Imperial Germany* (1972), F. H. Hinsley, ed., *British Foreign Policy Under Sir Edward Grey* (1977), and John F. W. Keiger, *Raymond Poincaré*[*] (1997).

Arthur J. Marder's sweeping *From the Dreadnought to Scapa Flow: The Royal Navy in the Fisher Era, 1904–1919,* 5 vols. (1961–1970, reprint ed. 1978), is still basic for the British navy. Jonathan Steinberg, *Yesterday's Deter-*

rent: Tirpitz and the Birth of the German Battle Fleet (1968, reprint ed. 1993), considers the German navy in strategic terms. The Weimar radical Eckhart Kehr's pioneering analysis of German naval rearmament as class defense may be sampled in his *Economic Interests, Militarism, and Foreign Policy* (1977).

Additional Internet links related to this chapter are available on the Europe in the 20th Century Web site: http://www.history.wadsworth.com/paxton04.

You can also explore images, interactive timelines, and maps related to this chapter on our Western Civilization Resource Center: http://history.wadsworth.com.

Jubilant Berlin civilians escort their soldiers to the train, August 1914. Note the civilian at the far right who has traded his straw hat for a soldier's rifle and helmet.

3
The Marne and After, 1914–1917

During the first days of August 1914, more than 5 million young European men responded almost without opposition to military call-up. Many of them boarded the troop trains with genuine enthusiasm. The bands, banners, and young women with flowers were not mere window dressing. Popular animosities were already enflamed enough, and they were soon fanned by government propaganda and by nationalist intellectuals.

WAR FEVER

Each government had been remarkably successful in portraying the other side as the aggressor. The English poet Robert Graves, who had German uncles and a German middle name, recalled being persecuted in high school around 1910 because "German" meant "dirty German." "It meant 'cheap, shoddy goods competing with our sterling industries.' It also meant military menace, Prussianism, useless philosophy, tedious scholarship, loving music, and sabre-rattling."[1] When the war broke out, German shops were damaged in London, German music was dropped from orchestra programs, and German sauerkraut was renamed "liberty cabbage." Stories of atrocities in Belgium, culminating in the German execution of the English nurse Edith Cavell in October 1915, fed those hatreds.

On the German side, many people felt they were defending virile German *Kultur* against the sly, mercantile English and the decadent Slavs and French. The German economist Werner Sombart, who had called himself socialist not long before, explained the war to his fellow citizens in 1915 as a contest between materialism and idealism, between British "Merchants" and German "Heroes:"

> That is why, for us, who are imbued with militarism, the war is holy, the most sacred thing on earth.[2]

Most Frenchmen went to war convinced that they were defending humanitarian liberty against the booted Prussians. Only one major French public figure, novelist Romain Rolland, tried to keep his pacifist, internationalist values intact—"above the melee." He felt he could do so only by moving to Switzerland. All the ethnic groups of the troubled Austro-Hungarian Empire except some South Slavs and Czechs rallied with enthusiasm to the war against tsarist Russia. Even Russians, deep in the throes of near-revolution in the summer of 1914, turned away from strikes and domestic opposition in August to face a common enemy. For every Russian who took part in the enthusiastic parades before the tsar's palace as the war began, there were probably many who merely accepted war sullenly. But the degree of popular enthusiasm surprised even the Russian rulers.

Beyond the national enmities and the arguments of national defense against aggressors, a feeling of release from bourgeois restraints gave war a positive allure for some soldiers. The draftees in Jules Romains's novel *Verdun* (1940) felt that "they were setting off for a noisy, bustling, rough sort of holiday, a real schoolboy expedition." The mediocre old world had been too full of "brittle things" that had to be tended politely.

> Here was a chance to live care-free for a while and irresponsibly to stretch the limbs in an orgy of crude action with never a thought for the brittle things that might be broken. Life would be better for some such "primitive" cure, for relapsing into simpler ways, for losing touch with the manners of refinement.[3]

Romain Rolland had been troubled as early as 1912 that "the children of the nation who had never seen war except in books had no difficulty in endowing it with beauty. Weary of peace and ideas, they hymned the anvil of battle on which, with bloody fists, action would one day new-forge the power of France."[4]

[1]Robert Graves, *Goodbye to All That* (London, 1960), p. 38.

[2]Werner Sombart, *Händler und Helden* (Munich, 1915), p. 88.

[3]Jules Romains, *Verdun* (New York, 1940), pp. 4–5.

[4]Romain Rolland, *Jean Christophe*, Book 3, trans. Gilbert Cannan (New York, 1913), p. 458.

Exultation was all the easier in August 1914 because everyone believed that the war would be short. Every European conflict since 1815 had been decided in a few weeks. The growing complexity of military machines and of civilian economies suggested that a modern society could not support the cost of large-scale destruction for very long. The German chief of staff, General Alfred von Schlieffen, wrote in 1909 that a long war had become "impossible in an age when the existence of the nation is founded upon the uninterrupted continuation of trade and industry."[5] The French economist Paul Leroy-Beaulieu proved mathematically that a war in Europe could not last more than six months. The British Admiralty had stocked only a six-months' supply of naval fuel oil. Most of the soldiers who boarded troop trains in August 1914 were certain that they would be home by Christmas.

A Dilemma for the Socialists

The patriotic surge of August 1914 confronted the European left with decisions of excruciating difficulty. The socialist parties of Europe had been planning during the decade before 1914 to call a general work stoppage in the event of an outbreak of the imperialist war that Marxist analysis had taught them to expect. The Workers' International,[6] the worldwide association of socialist parties in which the European socialists were dominant, had placed war prevention high on its agenda since 1904. The Moroccan crises of 1905 and 1911, the Bosnian crisis of 1908, and the Balkan wars of 1912 and 1913, lent an urgent note to their plans. When the European governments began to rush to the brink of war in 1914, the permanent bureau of the International held a special meeting in Brussels on July 29, and the German Social Democratic leader Hermann Müller came to Paris on July 30 to confer with his fellow socialists in France. The European armies and police forces prepared to arrest socialist leaders in case mobilization was opposed by a general strike.

The war at hand in August 1914, however, resembled none of the hypothetical wars against which the International had laid its plans. Each European socialist party became convinced that its own country was the victim of aggression and that its enemy's victory would set socialism back. The German Social Democratic Party, the largest party in Germany and the most elaborately organized socialist party in the world, decided that German socialism was threatened by the danger of

the victory of Russian despotism, which has stained itself with the blood of the best of its own people. Our task is to ward off this danger, to safeguard the culture and independence of our own country.[7]

The German trade unions decided on August 2 to call off their anticipated strike, and the Social Democratic Party leaders voted 78 to 14 to support the German government. In the *Reichstag*, the Social Democratic deputies joined in a unanimous

---

[5]Gerhard A. Ritter, *The Schlieffen Plan* (New York, 1958), p. 47.

[6]Technically, the Second International, founded in 1889, since the First International had broken down in 1874 in a dispute between followers of Marx and Bakunin.

[7]Speech of German Social Democratic leader Hugo Haase, August 4, 1914, before the *Reichstag*.

approval of special war appropriations on August 4. In France, the trade unions had decided against a strike as early as July 31. From Paris, the victory of autocratic Germany seemed a greater threat to French socialists than anything their own government was likely to do to them. The only socialist parliamentary votes against war appropriations in Europe were two Social Democratic nays in Serbia and the walkout of fourteen Russian Social Democrats, both reformists and revolutionaries (Bolsheviks), and of eleven members of Aleksandr Kerensky's reformist Labor Party. The Italian socialists largely approved their government's decision to stay out of the war, a course that spared them the difficult choices their European colleagues had been forced to make. No general strikes materialized in any belligerent country.

War and Social Peace

With hindsight, some critics have accused the European socialist leaders of betraying their followers at the crucial moment in August 1914. In fact, most European workers were no less convinced of the duty to fight reactionary aggressors than were the socialist leaders. In France, where the general staff had predicted that 13 percent

© Hulton Picture Library

Volunteers flock to a British recruiting office in 1915, before the introduction of the draft.

of draftees would refuse the call, there was a refusal rate of only 1.5 percent, and the government decided not to arrest the socialist leaders whose names appeared on its secret list, "Carnet B." The British case was even more striking. Labour Party leaders Ramsay MacDonald and Philip Snowden, who opposed British entry into the war, were disavowed by the rank and file on August 5 and forced to resign.

Nor was there any relation between revolutionary fervor and pacifism in 1914 among socialist leaders. Pacifism was as strong a minority current in the British Liberal Party as in the Labour Party. On the Continent, reformists like the German Eduard Bernstein were pacifist in 1914, whereas the most militant support for the war came from the ranks of revolutionary syndicalists like the French journalist Gustave Hervé and the Italian Benito Mussolini, men who by temperament welcomed violent solutions.

Assured of the support of most of its working class, every European belligerent entered the war in a mood of enthusiastic national unity. French politicians proclaimed a *union sacrée,* a sacred union of Frenchmen around the flag. Kaiser Wilhelm II announced that he perceived no more enemies within the state; foreign war had created domestic peace (*Burgfrieden,* the internal truce of a besieged fortress). The embittered Russian factory workers and peasantry were the acid test of patriotic union. They ended strikes at the beginning of August, obeyed the draft call more or less without incident, and expressed little discernible opposition through the first months of the war. Internal harmony would never again be as complete as it was in August 1914.

THE FIRST BATTLE OF THE MARNE

On August 4, eager German armies crossed the Belgian frontier, and Moltke's modified version of the Schlieffen Plan began to be executed. Five hundred trains a day ran up to the Belgian border. The Germans threw seven of their eight armies into a vast encircling movement designed to knock France out of the war in one blow. Delayed by the Belgians' stubborn defense of their fortresses, by August 18 the Germans were sweeping in a great arc toward Paris.

As the German planners had hoped, the French army launched the bulk of its forces eastward in an effort to recapture Alsace-Lorraine. This opening campaign of the First World War was, in a sense, the last gesture of chivalric soldiery against the impersonal efficiency of mechanized warfare. The French troops, brightly clad in red trousers and blue tunics and led by young Saint-Cyr military school graduates who had taken an oath to wear their parade-ground headgear and white gloves in the first charge, were decimated by artillery and machine-gun fire. The French offensive gained no permanent ground, leaving the lost provinces to be recaptured only in the last days of the war. More importantly, the French headlong rush toward the Rhine played into the hands of Schlieffen's successors, who hoped to enfold as many French troops as possible into the pocket of their wheeling forces.

By early September, the Germans had approached Paris at the Marne River and the French government had fled for Bordeaux. Schlieffen's dream of a lightning decision in the west appeared close to realization. Then came the French–British

© New York Times

A color guard of cadets at the French military academy at Saint-Cyr, in the white gloves and plumed shakos in which they fought in 1914.

counterattack from September 6 to 10, which has become known as the First Battle of the Marne. It was one of the great deliverances of history.

General Joseph Joffre, a phlegmatic French commander whose legendary appetite and sound sleep during the German advance helped steady French nerves, coolly waited for the moment to strike back. The German advance created its own problems. Some units covered twenty to thirty miles a day on foot and outstripped their artillery and supplies in the effort to draw the immense trap shut. Moltke, ill and indecisive, could keep only distant contact with his army commanders; communications were made even more difficult by the distances that the mounted couriers of the day had to cover. Finally, under General Alexander von Kluck, commander of the outermost wing, the German First Army exposed two vulnerable spots to the watchful Joffre. In accordance with Moltke's retrenched version of the Schlieffen Plan, Kluck wheeled east of Paris, exposing his flank to the French forces in Paris that were now left outside the trap. Next, when he turned part of his army to face the danger from Paris, he opened a gap between his own force and the next German army to the east. On September 6, the French reserves in Paris were rushed out in the city's entire taxi fleet to attack Kluck's exposed flank; meanwhile, the first units of the British Expeditionary Force pushed cautiously into the gap between Kluck and the German Second Army. By September 10, the Germans had fallen back along the Marne, and Paris was saved.

It is true that Joffre was unable to turn this pause into a full German retreat. Indeed, neither army was able to dislodge the other from the trenches that both now began to dig for shelter. Instead, each tried to outflank the other in a series of "end runs" that moved ever more westward and northward until they reached the coast, a movement that is usually misnamed "the race to the sea." By mid-October, the line of combat stretched from the Belgian North Sea coast to the borders of Switzerland along 300 miles of trenches defended by fast-firing weapons and earthworks. They were locked in that tactical immobility where they would remain for the next four years. As historian A. J. P. Taylor noted, "The machine gun and the spade had changed the course of European history."[8]

The First Battle of the Marne set the conditions that prevailed on the major front for the rest of the war. First of all, it ended the expectation that the troops would be home by Christmas. Because the war would be a long one, the home fronts would be inexorably drawn into the business of making war. Furthermore, it meant that the rest of the war in the west would be dominated by the search for a way to break through the crust of trenches and restore the decisive war of movement. That search was eventually to bring the whole world into the war. And it was to produce the brutalizing horrors of trench warfare in which boredom alternated with carnage.

At the Marne, it was neither France nor Germany that had been defeated but prewar European society, which now had to be transformed into one vast war-making machine.

THE EASTERN FRONT

The long eastern front never bogged down in trench warfare. But the resulting war of movement was no more decisive and no less costly in life than in the west. The Germans had expected to contain the slowly mobilizing Russians with one-eighth of their armed forces while knocking France out of the war; the Austrians, similarly, had hoped to annihilate the Serbs before any serious threat arose on the Russian front. Neither expectation was realized, and the Russians were able to advance into East Prussia and Austrian Poland (the province of Galicia) in the opening weeks of the war. These successes were only temporary, however.

Tannenberg and the Masurian Lakes, 1914

The victory denied the Germans on the Marne was won in East Prussia. There, during the same weeks, the outnumbered Germans brought off a daring maneuver by separating two Russian armies and defeating them one at a time, the first one at Tannenberg on August 30, and the second one at the Masurian Lakes on September 15. General Paul von Hindenburg and his chief of staff, General Erich Ludendorff, made themselves formidable reputations. Germany was heartened to fight on harder than ever, and the Russians never again seriously menaced German territory in the north.

---

[8]A. J. P. Taylor, *The Struggle for Mastery in Europe, 1848–1914* (Oxford, England, 1954), p. 531.

Süddeutscher Verlag, Munich

General Paul von Hindenburg watches the battle of Tannenberg through a field periscope, 1914. Generals Erich Ludendorff (second from right) and Max Hoffman (right) stand by.

The Austrian Fronts, 1914–1915

The Austrians, meanwhile, were dealing less successfully with a two-front war. General Conrad von Hötzendorf was obliged to draw off his best troops from the Serbian front to meet an unexpectedly strong Russian showing in Galicia. The result was losses on both fronts. The Russians took all of Galicia in 1914 and threatened the Hungarian Plain across the Carpathian Mountains. By December 1914 on the southern front, the Serbs had thrown Austrian troops off Serbian soil twice after very hard fighting. In May 1915, Italy joined the war on the Entente side[9] and opened an additional southern front against Austria-Hungary. The punitive expedition against Serbia with which Austria had begun the war was now swallowed up in a far graver struggle for Austro-Hungarian survival.

In 1915, the Germans came to the aid of their allies in the east. Since the stalemate on the western front seemed to offer no opportunity for a decisive thrust, Hindenburg and Ludendorff used their new prestige to extract reinforcements from the High Command. A fresh German–Austrian force battered an opening in the Russian line in Galicia on May 2, 1915, initiating one of the great retreats of Russian history. Demoralized and short of ammunition, the tsar's armies reeled back out of Galicia 300 miles into Russian territory, until winter finally terminated operations. Less spectacular than

[9]See below, p. 84–86.

the losses of 1812 and 1941, the great Russian retreat of 1915 nevertheless cost European Russia 15 percent of its territory, 10 percent of its railroads, 30 percent of its industries, and nearly 20 percent of its population. The Russian army's casualties are said to have amounted to 2.5 million killed, wounded, or captured.

Austria's threat from the south, meanwhile, became more urgent when in April 1915 a British–French expeditionary force landed at Gallipoli, at the tip of the peninsula south of Constantinople, in an effort to force the Straits (map, p. 85). That landing was one of the most controversial operations of the war. In the opinion of its supporters, such as First Lord of the Admiralty Winston Churchill, putting a force ashore at the southern entrance to the Straits had the combined advantages of answering the Russian appeal for relief from attack by Turkey (newly allied with Germany) and bypassing the stalemated western front with a daring naval maneuver. It replaced brute force with mobility. In the opinion of its opponents, such as French General Joffre, it drained precious forces from the major front where decision would eventually be reached by piling mass on mass. In the end, the combined British and French force failed to fight its way out of the rocky peninsula of Gallipoli, and never came close to forcing the Straits and putting Turkey out of the war.

The Central Powers acquired a decisive advantage when Bulgaria, impressed by German successes in Russia, and no less thirsty for territorial gain at Serbian expense than in 1875 or 1912, agreed in September 1915 to join Germany and Austria-Hungary in a final attack on Serbia. The Allied response of transferring most of the Gallipoli contingent to the Greek port of Salonika did not redress the balance, and in fact led to the entrapment of a considerable Allied force there for most of the rest of the war.

Taken from both front and flank, the Serbian army was forced into an agonizing retreat through the defiles of the Albanian mountains to the Adriatic Sea, where some 100,000 survivors were picked up by Allied ships. It has been estimated that Serbia lost one-sixth of its population to battle, epidemic, and famine in the course of this campaign. Serbia had been amply punished for the murder of the Archduke Franz Ferdinand, but the South Slav idea was no less militant for all that.

Early in 1916, the new German chief of staff, Erich von Falkenhayn, turned his main attention back to the western front. Conrad Von Hötzendorf was now left to follow his own plan of a major offensive against Italy. The most important result of his campaign in the Trentino in June 1916 was to leave the Russian front covered so thinly that Alexei Brusilov, the most capable Russian general in that war, was able to rout the Austrians and recover much of the Galician ground lost in 1915. Brusilov received no help from other Russian armies to the north, however, and shortages of ammunition kept him from exploiting his skillful breach into Hungary. It was the final spurt of energy from the Russian war machine and the last great campaign of the war on the eastern front.

THE SEARCH FOR A BREAKTHROUGH IN THE WEST

The post-Marne stalemate in the west was a tactical novelty to which political and military leaders adapted only slowly. Moltke and Falkenhayn, no less than the

French commanders Joffre and Ferdinand Foch, had been schooled in the war of movement and maneuver. British commanders, like John French and Douglas Haig, had been cavalry generals in the Boer War. After the Marne, the war in the west was an attempt to get back to the familiar tactics of movement. All the military staffs, prodded by an impatient and uncomprehending public opinion, tried for the next three years to "break the crust."

Assaults "Over the Top"

The basic problem in making an assault was how to open a gap in the opposing line in the face of machine-gun fire, and then pour enough men and equipment through the gap to turn the exposed flanks. It was tempting to try to solve the problem with sheer mass: with numbers of men and quantities of artillery shells.

At first, the belligerents sent every available man to the front. The French even stripped essential armaments plants of their manpower for the anticipated decisive blow. The numbers of men in battle had been enormously increased by European population growth, the principle of universal military service, and the tactics of trying to strike a decisive first blow. Waterloo (1815) had been fought by 170,000 men; Sedan (1870) by 300,000. The First Battle of the Marne involved over 1 million men. But the firepower of artillery, modern rifles, and particularly the machine gun reduced these masses of men to crouching behind earthworks.

AP / Wide World Photos

A German photograph illustrates three reasons why battle casualties ran far higher in the First World War than in earlier wars: artillery-scarred trenches, poison gas, and the machine gun.

The trenches that had been hastily dug in 1914 developed into elaborate systems of defense, doubled or tripled in depth, and reinforced by concrete machine-gun emplacements. Command posts were housed in dugouts, which might be more or less dry, as well as secure from all but direct hits. The connecting trenches, however, were too rat-infested and muddy for the rough wood flooring to give much comfort. Above all, there was always a risk of being picked off by a sniper or a random mortar shot, even between offensives. "The front is a cage in which we must await fearfully whatever may happen," wrote the German war veteran Erich Maria Remarque in his novel *All Quiet on the Western Front* (1929). "We lie under the network of arching shells and live in a suspense of uncertainty. Over us Chance hovers."[10] In front of the trenches were systems of barbed wire, often thirty yards wide and three to five feet high, laced to iron stakes and trestles. And in front of that, "no man's land," the space between enemy lines, where patrols operated silently at night and where each side waited to see the enemy surge forward.

The assault "over the top" under these conditions required a massive preliminary softening up by artillery. Consumption of shells ran beyond any prewar staff officer's wildest imagining. The French general staff had expected to expend about 13,000 shells a day. In the first days of the war, they actually used 120,000 shells a day. In 1916, the British used one gun for every twenty yards on a fourteen-mile front and 1.5 million shells to prepare for the Somme campaign. In April 1917, the French offensive in the Champagne was prepared by firing 6 million shells on a twenty-mile front. The problem with this method of "softening up" was that each artillery barrage warned the enemy of the location of the next offensive in time to reinforce the stunned and battered defenders. The result was generally an expensive but sterile engagement with only a few square yards of advance to show for high casualties. "Still the little piece of convulsed earth on which we lie is held. We have yielded no more than a few hundred yards of it as a prize to the enemy. But on every yard there lies a dead man."[11]

The assaults of 1915 on the western front were inconclusive. Even at Ypres, in Belgian Flanders, where the Germans first used chlorine gas on April 22, they were prevented from following up their success because their reserves had been moved to the major eastern offensive. On neither side had impatient politicians or generals learned to solve the problem of stalemate other than by ever increasing masses of shells and men. Even greater trench battles were mounted in 1916 and early 1917. The most significant of these, which forever marked the First World War as the utter limit of human endurance, were the German offensive at Verdun in 1916, the British campaign on the Somme in 1916, and the quixotic offensive of the French General Robert Nivelle in the Champagne in April 1917. Here the tragic futility of trench warfare reached its climax.

Major Offensives: Verdun, the Somme, the Champagne

At the end of 1915, after brilliant gains on the eastern front, Moltke's successor, Falkenhayn, proposed to reopen the campaign in the west with a plan calculated to

---

[10]Erich Maria Remarque, *All Quiet on the Western Front* (New York, 1966), p. 63.

[11]Ibid., p. 84.

increase the French casualty rate. If the Germans singled out a French position that "touched national honor and pride," he wrote in a December 1915 memorandum to the kaiser, the French would defend it at all cost. "If they do so, they will bleed to death." The target chosen was the fortress city of Verdun: strategically, the vital hinge where the front turned southward along the Meuse River (map, p. 85); morally, a historic strongpoint whose loss would cripple French spirit.

On February 21, 1916, the Germans began a massive artillery barrage designed to obliterate the French trenches protecting Verdun. Joffre took the challenge, and for the next ten months the two sides shelled, took, lost, and retook a few square miles of heavily fortified terrain. General Philippe Pétain, the elderly local commander who had been slated for an early retirement until he showed his methodical coolness in the first battles, held on with a grim determination that was the climax of French military effort in this century. *"Ils ne passeront pas"* (They shall not pass) was his laconic instruction to his troops. For ten months, the bottle-shaped salient of Verdun was supplied under shellfire along a single narrow road by a continuous truck convoy, bringing shells in and wounded out. Week after week the ground was dug and redug by millions of shells. Jules Romains's novel *Verdun* describes an officer stumbling across a corpse on leaving his dugout and then noticing that it was wearing a different uniform than the one he had stumbled across a few hours earlier.

In the end, the Germans did not pass, but the cost was staggering. Those who escaped with their lives were often maimed physically and mentally with what the French sardonically called "Poincaré tattoos." More than 400,000 on both sides did not escape with their lives. Falkenhayn had had his way, with one major amendment: The German army had been bled just as grievously as the French. This greatest of all First World War battles had consumed the young men of a medium-sized town each morning and afternoon for ten months.

The British turn came in July 1916 with the Somme campaign. It was designed to relieve the pressure on the French at Verdun and to achieve the elusive breakthrough by sheer mass. Poet Robert Graves was told by his colonel to forget the trenches and prepare for the war of movement that would follow when the British cavalry got behind the German trenches.[12] Sir Douglas Haig prepared the classic piercing operation. A ferocious artillery barrage of eight days' duration was supposed to open the way for three cavalry divisions to pass through. When the charge came, one-half of the men and three-quarters of the officers were either killed or wounded. The British gained a mere 120 square miles for 400,000 casualties, and the cavalry could never go into action. "For every yard of the 16-mile front from Gommecourt to Montauban there were two British casualties."[13]

As 1917 began, the quest for a decisive battle led the French cabinet to replace Joffre as commander in chief with the more flamboyant Robert Nivelle, a glib cavalry general who had been successful in some local advances at Verdun. Nivelle promised to "break the crust" once and for all with a grand offensive in the Champagne. The Nivelle offensive, which aroused the highest hopes beforehand in Paris

---

[12]Graves, p. 146.

[13]Martin Middlebrook, *The First Day on the Somme: 1 July 1916* (New York, 1972), p. 245.

© Hulton Picture Library

French soldiers crouching in a trench during shelling at Verdun, 1916. The stiff body at the right may date from earlier fighting, for the dead often went unburied.

and the deepest despondency afterward, was tactically no different from Haig's Somme offensive of the previous summer. The results were even poorer, for Hindenburg and Ludendorff, who had replaced the now discredited Falkenhayn, quietly withdrew the German line a few miles before Nivelle began his artillery preparation in April 1917. After another minor gain at great cost, the French army's morale began to crack.

As in the preceding year, British forces tried to divert the Germans in this emergency by attacking northward along the North Sea coast in Flanders. The usual week of artillery preparation opened the dikes, so that men and machines floundered for three indecisive months in the mud around Passchendaele and Ypres. The British strategist Basil H. Liddell-Hart tells of a staff officer who burst into tears on seeing the area later, exclaiming, "My God, did we send men to fight in that?"[14] At the price of 240,000 men, Haig gained fifty square miles and a reputation as a callous squanderer of human life.

New Weapons

Inevitably, the search for a breakthrough led to ideas other than ever more violent assaults "over the top." Modern technology was applied to the problem of restoring offense to an equal footing with defense. The British introduced the first tank on September 15, 1916, near the end of the Somme campaign, in an attempt to give mobility and protection to men attacking a fortified trench position. After a dubious beginning, tanks finally became effective in the campaigns of 1918. The

British soldiers, blinded by gas near Béthune, in northern France, during the final German offensive of April 1918, lead each other toward an advanced dressing station.

[14]Basil H. Liddell-Hart, *The Real War, 1914–1918* (Boston, 1930), p. 337.

© Three Lions Collection / Liaison Agency

To escape the stalemate of trench warfare, military planners devised new weapons such as tanks, poison gas, and airplanes. Here a bomb has been released by hand from a German biplane, an early hint of the way bombers would level cities in the next war.

Germans first used deadly chlorine gas at Ypres in April 1915[15] and the flame thrower at Verdun in February 1916.

The most dramatic new weapon was the airplane. Initially, aircraft were used for observation and artillery ranging. When it became necessary to protect spotter planes from enemy aircraft, air combat took on a life of its own. In October 1915,

[15]Although the French experimented ineffectually in 1914 with shells containing tear gas, the German Army was the first to employ mortal gas, which they drifted downwind onto enemy lines. See the conclusive work of a Swiss scholar, Olivier Lepick, *La Grande guerre chimique, 1914–1918* (Paris, 1998).

the Dutch designer A. H. G. Fokker developed machine guns that were synchronized to fire between the propeller blades. With that invention began a brilliant period of individual air duels. Youthful aces like the German "Red Baron," Manfred von Richthofen, the Frenchman Georges Guynemer, and the Englishman Albert Ball were revered by their publics for what seemed the ultimate in personal daring.

Improved aircraft also increased each side's capacity to bomb the enemy's cities. The lighter-than-air German dirigibles that threw panic into British cities in 1916 had actually been quite vulnerable because they were so easy to shoot down. By 1918, more effective bombing planes were in use against London (1,414 persons were killed by bombs in England during the war) and to a lesser extent in France and Germany (746 Germans were killed by bombs). In this way the widening net of the war began to ensnare civilians far behind the lines in the sufferings of combat.

THE WIDENING WAR

Both sides tried to break the stalemate by drawing new allies into the war. Turkey had come under German military and commercial influence before the war. It became for all practical purposes a belligerent on August 10, 1914, when the German cruisers Goeben and Breslau, fleeing from British warships in the Mediterranean, received refuge in the supposedly neutral Dardanelles. On October 29, these ships, formally purchased by Turkey but under the command of German officers, shelled the Russian Black Sea ports of Odessa and Sevastopol. When Russia declared war on Turkey on November 2, Britain and France soon followed suit.

The Turkish sultan declared a holy war against the infidel and launched a double offensive: One army attacked through the Caucasus toward the Russian oil fields of Baku and, at least in the proclamations of its general, toward India; the other moved on the Suez Canal. The Entente not only found itself blocked from sea contact with Russia but saw its colonial holdings threatened. It was at this point that the British and French reacted with the landing at Gallipoli in April 1915. After Bulgaria's entry into the war on the Central Powers' side and Serbia's defeat in October 1915, the Allies considered the peninsula untenable and withdrew from Gallipoli in January 1916. The only remnant of the abandoned Balkan front was the Entente force that was bottled up at the Greek port of Salonika.

Farther south, Britain moved energetically to stave off the threat to its Middle Eastern position. The tough "Anzacs"—the Australia–New Zealand Army Corps—sufficiently reinforced British units in Egypt to hold off a German–Turkish assault on the Suez Canal in February 1915. The kaiser's dreams of Egyptian and Indian revolts against the British were disappointed. The British were able to mobilize Arab nationalism against the Ottoman Empire by extending vague promises of independence to the sherif of Mecca. And a British–Indian force was brought to the head of the Persian Gulf to block any enemy advance through Mesopotamia (present-day Iraq) toward the oil installations at Abadan (present-day Iran). The war was taking the whole world for its theater.

The Allies also successfully outbid the Central Powers in the effort to bring Italy into the war. Italy had declared its neutrality on August 3, 1914, thereby greatly

WORLD WAR I: THE FRONTS

easing the Allied naval position in the Mediterranean. As the stalemate developed in the west, however, Italian participation in the war became more desirable to both sides. Although Italy had signed treaties with Germany and Austria-Hungary in 1882, the Entente could better gratify Italian ambitions in the Austrian alpine and Adriatic regions. Italian Foreign Minister Sidney Sonnino signed the secret Treaty of London with Britain and France on April 26, 1915. In exchange for declaring war on the Central Powers, Italy was to receive important gains in the Alps (the Italian-speaking Trentino and part of the German-speaking Tirol up to the Brenner Pass), the head of the Adriatic Sea, the Dodecanese Islands, and the south coast of Turkey, as well as compensation in Africa if Britain and France made gains there. The Holy See was to be excluded from eventual peace negotiations. Romania, finally, was brought into the war on the Allied side on August 18, 1916, by the promise of the rich plain of Transylvania, where both Hungarians and Romanians lived (map, p. 49). In the short run, the opening of additional fronts against Austria was immensely important to the eastern front, where, as we have seen, it helped the Brusilov offensive of 1916. By 1917, however, Allied reinforcements had to be sent to Italy, and the western front remained deadlocked.

THE WAR AT SEA

The combatants sought at sea the decision denied them on land. From the first hours of war, Britain and France used their naval superiority to destroy German warships. The heavy German cruisers *Scharnhorst* and *Gneisenau,* which had caused concern in Britain by sinking a British naval force off Chile, were finally run down and sunk by a superior British force off the Falklands in December 1914, and the *Dresden* was sunk off Chile in March 1915. There remained no effective obstacles to an Allied blockade of Germany and Austria-Hungary. It was expected that the Central Powers would be unable to sustain a long, modern war without imports from overseas.

In retaliation, Germany used its submarine fleet to impose a counter-blockade. On February 4, 1915, the German government declared the area around Britain, Ireland, and northern France a war zone within which any ship, even neutral, would be torpedoed without warning. Although there were too few U-boats to interfere seriously with shipping to the British Isles, the sinking of some passenger ships had the effect of creating a strong current of prowar opinion in the United States. This was especially true after the Cunard liner *Lusitania* was sunk off the southern coast of Ireland on May 7, 1915, with a loss of nearly 2,000 lives, some of them American. The following September, German submarine action in the Atlantic was restricted in order to avoid further complications with Washington.

Throughout the first two years of the war, the British and German battle fleets had avoided contact. The British maintained their blockade from afar, whereas the Germans were reluctant to engage their smaller force. Early in 1916, Admiral Reinhard Scheer, commander of the German High Seas Fleet, proposed to bait the British Grand Fleet into an all-out battle that might change the whole balance of sea power and, with it, the outcome of the war. The result was the Battle of Jutland, the one major naval battle of the war and the last involving the maneuvering of battleships to fire their fifteen-inch guns without the intervention of aircraft or submarines. Churchill nostalgically called it "the culminating manifestation of naval force in the history of the world."

The battle actually worked no strategic change in the war. Scheer sent Admiral Franz von Hipper with five cruisers off the Norwegian coast in order to draw Admiral John Jellicoe and the British Dreadnoughts out of the naval base of Scapa Flow in Scotland. Scheer then poised his main fleet to intercept them. Throughout two days of maneuvering west of Denmark, May 30 to June 2, the opposing fleets damaged each other without ever decisively bringing the other into position to be demolished. Scheer, conscious of his inferiority, kept drawing away, and Jellicoe, nervous about torpedo attacks, failed to seize the opportunity to cut Scheer off from his home port. In the end, the British suffered somewhat heavier losses, but the relative strengths of the two navies remained the same. Neither side tried to engage the other directly again until 1918, and the Dreadnoughts remained a deterrent rather than an offensive weapon for the rest of the war.

For Germany, it was tempting to resort once again to submarine warfare to evade British control of the sea's surface. By the end of 1916, Hindenburg and Ludendorff, now in supreme command of the German military forces, had convinced the kaiser that the advantages of unrestricted submarine warfare outweighed the disadvantages. Germany needed relief from growing internal strain, the aid from the United States to Britain had to be diminished, and the possibility of the United States intervening effectively in the European combat was only slight. On February 1, 1917, German submarines were ordered to sink all merchantmen on sight. Losses to British shipping, which had mounted from a monthly average of 51,000 tons in 1914 to 103,000 tons in 1916, now climbed to over 300,000 tons in February 1917 and more than 400,000 tons in June 1917. Only the adoption of the convoy system kept the British Atlantic lifeline functioning.

THE UNITED STATES ENTERS THE WAR

The announcement of unrestricted submarine warfare led the United States to break off diplomatic relations with Germany on February 3, 1917. The forces that had tended to keep the United States neutral were gradually falling away: The antagonism of Washington to British blockade measures was now totally overshadowed by the German sinking of Allied and neutral ships; American doubts about the Entente's war aims were diminished by the replacement of the tsar's autocracy with a democratic regime in Russia in February 1917, which the United States recognized on March 20; the financial and industrial stake of the United States in the war effort of Britain and France had grown to enormous proportions, while Germany, the first to borrow from the United States in 1914, was prevented by the blockade from drawing on American economic power.

Finally, what remained of isolationist sentiment was dispelled by the British Admiralty's decipherment of the so-called Zimmermann Note, instructions from the German Secretary of State for Foreign Affairs Arthur Zimmermann to the German minister in Mexico City to offer German support for the Mexican recovery of Texas, New Mexico, and Arizona in case of war between Germany and the United States. Publication of this document in the American press on March 1, 1917, prepared all but a few ardent isolationists and some German Americans for war on the Entente side. President Wilson's war message to Congress on April 2 led to a joint resolution of Congress, passed on April 6 by a vote of 465 to 56, to join the Entente as an "Associated Power."

The war had become a worldwide conflict. Moreover, the effort to hammer a way out of the stalemate inevitably drew the belligerents into more and more total war.

The inhuman sufferings of the fighting front were soon followed by severe home-front privations and dislocations. The war of 1914 to 1918 is still justly called the Great War, if for no other reason than the profound changes it wrought in European society.

SUGGESTIONS FOR FURTHER READING

John Keegan, *The First World War*[*] (1999) is a superlative study. Hew Strachan, ed., *World War I: A History*[*] (1999) joins excellent brief studies of particular aspects with vivid illustrations. Martin Gilbert, *First World War* (1994), stresses soldiers' experiences. Spencer C. Tucker, *The Great War, 1914–1918* (1998) is precise on armaments and technology, including naval. Brian Bond, ed., *The First World War and British Military History* (1991), reflects on changing interpretations and reputations. Niall Ferguson, *The Pity of War: Explaining World War I*[*] (1998) asks heretically why the soldiers fought, and whether it was worth it.

Basil H. Liddell-Hart, the great theoretician of indirect strategy and tank warfare, blamed Haig for useless slaughter in *Reputations Ten Years After* (reprint ed. 1977). John Terraine, in numerous works such as *The Great War*[*] (1998) and *The Real War*[*] (1963), and Corelli Barnett in *The Swordbearers: Supreme Command in the First World War* (1975), tried to redeem Haig and the British leadership. The fiftieth anniversary produced best-sellers that stressed the blindness of commanders and the absurdity of the bloodletting, such as A. J. P. Taylor, *The First World War* (1963), and Barbara Tuchman, *The Guns of August*[*] (1962, reprint ed. 1994). These debates are deepened and updated by Timothy Travers in *The Killing Ground: The British Army,* the Western Front, and the Emergence of Modern Warfare[*] (1987).

Mechanization gets attention in Timothy Travers, *How the War Was Won: Command and Technology in the British Army on the Western Front, 1917–1918* (1992).

Norman Stone, *The Eastern Front,*[*] 2nd ed. (1998), is the best account of the war's other main sector. See Alan Moorhead, *Gallipoli*[*] (1956, reprint ed. 1994), for the Dardanelles expedition. Alistair Horne, *The Price of Glory*[*] (1978, reprint ed. 2001), recounts the carnage of Verdun with indignation.

Works by Gerhard Ritter and Gordon Craig cited at the end of chapter 2 discuss the emergence of military rule in Germany. Jere Clemens King, *Generals and Politicians* (1952, reprint ed. 1971), treats conflicts between government and high command in France. Maurice Hankey, *The Supreme Command, 1914–1918,* 2 vols. (1961), published the minutes of the British Commmitee of Imperial Defense.

Arthur Marder is the uncontested authority on the British navy and on naval warfare in 1914–1918. See *From the Dreadnought to Scapa Flow* (1965).

A major recent trend has been an interest in common soldiers' experiences. The chapter on the Somme in John Keegan, *The Face of Battle*[*] (1983), makes trench warfare palpable. Martin Middlebrook, *The First Day on the Somme*[*] (1971, reprint ed. 2003), used soldiers' recollections. Tony Ashworth, *Trench Warfare, 1914–1918: The Live and Let-Live System,* 2nd ed. (2000), reveals soldiers' informal truces. See also Eric J. Leed, *No Man's Land: Combat and Identity in World War I* (1979). Leonard V. Smith, *Between Mutiny and Obedience* (1994), reconsiders the French army mutinies within a broader discussion of how military discipline was negotiated between commanders and front-line soldiers.

The horrors endured by ordinary soldiers inspired a richer literature in the First World War than in the Second. Paul Fussell, *The Great War and Modern Memory** (1975, revised ed. 2000), explores the ironic contrast between heroic literature and the grim reality of combat. Samuel Hynes, *A War Imagined: The First World War and British Culture* (1992), examines the war's cultural impact more broadly. These works have no real counterpart for other belligerent countries. Modris Eksteins, *Rites of Spring: The Great War and the Birth of the Modern Age,** reprint ed. (2000), draws parallels between aesthetic and military violence.

Major war novels include Erich Maria Remarque, *All Quiet on the Western Front* (1929, reprint ed. 2003); Henri Barbusse, *Under Fire* (1917, reprint ed. 2003); Jules Romains, *Verdun* (1938, reprint ed. 2003); and Arnold Zweig, *The Case of Sergeant Grisha** (1928, reprint ed. 2002). Personal reminiscences of outstanding merit include Edmund Blunden, *Undertones of War** (1928, reprint ed. 2003); Vera Brittain, *Testament of Youth** (1933, reprint ed. 1994), complemented now by her diary, *Chronicle of Youth: Vera Brittain's Great War Diary, 1913–1917** (2003); Ernst Jünger, *Storm of Steel** (1929, reprint ed. 2003)—one of the few to find beauty in it; Robert Graves, *Goodbye to All That** (1929, reprint ed. 2000); and Siegfried Sassoon, *Memoirs of a Fox-Hunting Man* (1928, reprint ed. 2002).

Additional Internet links related to this chapter are available on the Europe in the 20th Century Web site: http://www.history.wadsworth.com/paxton04.

You can also explore images, interactive timelines, and maps related to this chapter on our Western Civilization Resource Center: http://history.wadsworth.com.

The bones of thousands of unidentifiable French and German soldiers were entombed in this tower at the edge of a French military cemetery at Verdun. The "ossuaire" (charnel-house) of Verdun came to symbolize the terrible human cost of World War I.

4

The Impact of Total War

The Battle of the Marne proved that no one Great Power could finish off another at one blow with the military technology of 1914. Yet the alternative of an immediate compromise peace remained unthinkable to all but a handful of European pacifists. The French had foreign troops on their soil; the Germans had tasted gain. After the Marne, the war could neither be won quickly nor ended quickly.

Those Europeans who thought about warfare before 1914 had been certain that advanced European societies could not support long wars. In a sense they were right. The societies could not support a long war *unchanged,* but they had to endure one anyway. The First World War became total war, or what the German General Erich Ludendorff later called "totalitarian war."[1] It left no aspect of European civilization untouched. It utterly transformed European governments, economies, and societies. "Everywhere in the world was heard the sound of things breaking," wrote

[1] Erich Ludendorff, *The Nation at War,* trans. A. S. Rappoport (London, 1936), p. 9.

a regretful liberal, the British author and diplomat John Buchan. The war, said Trotsky, "was a furious pogrom of human culture."[2]

Total war worked its effects on multiple levels. Materially, total war demanded the marshaling of unprecedented quantities of young men, steel and explosives for them to hurl at one another, and a steady stream of basic supplies to support both. In political terms, because the material effort required allocating people and resources away from their accustomed uses, the state had to take on extensive new powers. All of this imposed such unequal burdens on the populations that the belligerent states had to find new ways to persuade people to accept sacrifices. They had to organize opinion too. Such concentration of energy and thought required nothing less than an unannounced revolution.

ADJUSTING TO A WAR OF ATTRITION

After the Marne, each side could only wear the other down. A war of attrition among advanced industrial societies was something altogether outside historic experience, and in 1914 it remained to be seen how fully their large populations and vast productive capacities could be devoted to mutual destruction without leaving cities hungry and factories dark.

Every belligerent's advance planning for war had proved hopelessly inadequate. The British army had expected to mobilize 100,000 men in the event of a European war; during the war they mobilized 3 million. France eventually called up 8 million men, or 62.7 percent of all males between eighteen and forty (about 20 percent of the total population). State budgets underwent the same sort of distortion. The French budget swelled from about 5 billion francs in 1913 to 190 billion francs in 1918. By then debt service alone—the interest paid to those who had bought war bonds—amounted to 7 billion francs. By that time, the purchasing power of the franc was only about one-sixth of what it had been before the war. With such fundamental matters as human employment and the value of money distorted beyond recognition, governments found their prewar precedents useless.

After the first two months of war, therefore, the belligerent governments were forced to abandon most of their preconceptions about managing warfare and improvise. The French, for example, had expected the civilian economy to more or less hold its breath while everyone who could carry a rifle was sent to meet the more numerous Germans in one decisive battle. They even closed down war plants in order to send their workers to the front. By the end of 1914, the unexpected rate of battlefield consumption and the prospect of a long war forced them to reopen the plants and to allocate men (and women) between the battle front and what began to be called the home front. The challenge of total war went beyond merely marshaling unprecedented quantities of soldiers, money, and supplies. Whole civilian populations had to be kept fed, clothed, productive, and docile. Civilian production and consumption would have to be as minutely regulated as the army itself. A whole new range of human organization had to be conceived and put into operation.

[2]John Buchan, *The King's Grace* (London, 1935), p. 161; Leon Trotsky, *Terrorism and Communism* (New York, 1921), p. 17.

Some of the belligerent states rose to this challenge. Others did not. Those that did not were states already divided by social and ethnic conflict, especially the multinational empires: Austria-Hungary, the Ottoman Empire, and tsarist Russia. Bureaucratic tradition, autocratic authority, large population, and geographic size did not give these states the advantages one might have expected in a more traditional war. Success in the First World War depended more on industrial productivity—the ability to turn out masses of war matériel—and on the kind of internal cohesion and integration that equipped populations to endure the strains and accept the unequal privations of total war. While the empires revealed the hollowness of their authoritarian power, Great Britain rose best to the challenge, followed by republican France. In all fairness, it should be observed that Britain did not endure battles on its own soil. And it might be fairer still to call Britain least unsuccessful rather than most successful, for Britain never fully recovered from the effects of the First World War.

WAR GOVERNMENTS: A COMPARATIVE LOOK

No belligerent state established the full reach of war government at one stroke. There was too much to be unlearned and too many piecemeal expedients to be tried and rejected. No two belligerent states adapted in the same way, for the challenge laid bare their very different qualities and capacities.

Great Britain

When the war began, Britain had been governed for eight years by the Liberal Party. The Liberals had won the election of 1906 on a platform of free trade, and their commitment to a minimum of state interference in economic and social matters had been only slightly breached by the "peoples' budget" of 1909, with its income and inheritance taxes, and by the National Insurance Act of 1911. The orthodox liberal viewpoint of 1914 was expressed by Lord Runciman, a great shipowner and head of the Board of Trade, who said, "No government action can overcome economic laws, and any interference with those laws must end in disaster."[3] Harrods department store launched a popular slogan by placing a newspaper ad reading "Business as usual." Prime Minister Herbert Asquith, a cautious man with diminished zeal after eight years in office, left the various ministries to run things as they wished. The result was that Britain sent the largest volunteer army in modern history to France supported by uncoordinated administration at home.

The British government backed into wartime controls pragmatically under the pressure of circumstances, without any clear decision of principle. Some resources had to be placed at once under government control. Britain's private railway companies were run by a government committee and guaranteed profits at the same rate as in 1913. Sugar, most of which had come from Germany and Austria before

---

[3]A. J. P. Taylor, *English History, 1914–1945* (Oxford, England, 1965), p. 15.

the war, was now traded exclusively by the government. Commodities that were left to free-market operations went up in price. The government then began surreptitiously to influence the wheat market, went on to direct control of food products, and by 1918 instituted food rationing.

Rent controls were imposed in Glasgow in 1915, where labor unrest was high, and gradually spread to the rest of the kingdom. In South Wales, where labor-management conflicts seemed insoluble, the government nationalized the coal mines for the duration of the war, guaranteeing the prewar level of profits to the owners. The free trader Reginald McKenna, Chancellor of the Exchequer in 1915, quietly introduced the "McKenna Duties" on automobiles, moving pictures, clocks, and other "luxury" imports—the first violation of the "holy writ of free trade" since repeal of the Corn Laws (grain tariff) in 1846—primarily to save shipping space and foreign exchange rather than to return Britain to protectionism.

The most pressing need was the production of a flood of munitions. Rumors that the British Expeditionary Force was hindered by a shortage of shells shook confidence in the Liberal cabinet's capacity to run the war. Asquith sought to create a broader nonpartisan regime in May 1915 by bringing into the cabinet several Conservatives and the leader of the Labour Party, Arthur Henderson—the first Labour parliamentarian to hold ministerial office in Britain. The major innovation of the new government was the creation of a Ministry of Munitions under David Lloyd George in July 1915.

Lloyd George, a native of the radical nonconformist mining country of South Wales, which has produced a number of dramatic political figures in modern British history, was the most striking British leader between Benjamin Disraeli and Winston Churchill. He brought his mercurial temperament, a boundless energy, a zest for political infighting, and a complete absence of any preconceived notions to an agency that would eventually extend its tentacles into every cranny of the economy. He was, as George Dangerfield said, a "one-man Welsh revolution."[4]

The business of spending millions of pounds quickly to get private industry to produce war matériel led, necessarily, to control of profits, allocation of manpower and resources, and increasing regulation of the whole economy. Lloyd George did not hold back. In sheer size, his office grew from what had been the Army Contracts Office with 20 clerks in 1914 to a vast bureaucracy in 1918 of 65,000 clerks overseeing the work of 3 million men and women employed in munitions plants. The Ministry of Munitions made more important innovations than size, however. Lloyd George pushed through the Munitions of War Act in May 1915. It empowered the ministry to take over war plants directly in cases where the manufacturer refused the government's terms, which were: to limit profits, to resolve all labor disputes by arbitration, and to tie workers to essential jobs by forbidding the employment of any without a "leaving certificate" from the last employer. In practice if not in principle, the Ministry of Munitions moved the British government into as nearly total a planned and managed economy as technology could provide.

Conscription, the draft, was the government's major step into regulating private life—and death. Sufficient volunteers appeared in the patriotic surge of 1914 and

---

[4]George Dangerfield, *The Strange Death of Liberal England* (London, 1935), p. 19.

1915, and indeed the British Army of 1 million men was the largest volunteer force in modern history. But volunteer service was both inequitable and insufficient for a situation in which a skilled worker might be more urgently needed in his factory than at the front. In January 1916, the government adopted compulsory military service. This great leap in governmental power aroused fierce opposition, even among fervent supporters of the war. The government provided for hearings, therefore, for those who objected on grounds of conscience. Eventually there were about 16,000 "conscientious objectors," all but about 1,500 of whom accepted some form of alternate national service.

Compulsory military service opened up more jobs for women. There were already over 2 million poor women in the labor force. It was the independent wage-earning middle-class woman who broke most markedly with Victorian practice, and who sent the female labor force up to 3 million.

Lloyd George took over from the cautious Asquith as prime minister in December 1916. Britain had found its war leader. This nonconformist from the radical wing of the Liberal Party, who had bitterly opposed the Boer War and who had made England's greatest peacetime assault on the property holder's pocketbook with the peoples' budget of 1909, presided over Britain's evolution into a wartime omnicompetent state. In retrospect, it was a remarkably successful unplanned experiment in planning. Britain paid for more of the war effort by taxation (the income tax went up to an unprecedented 30 percent of income) than any other belligerent, and less by inflation. The sacrifices of war were probably borne less inequitably in Britain than in any other belligerent nation.

France

War government evolved in France in a similarly piecemeal fashion. As noted earlier, munitions plants had been closed down at the beginning of the war and their workers sent to the front in the expectation of a short conflict. Only after the Marne did it become apparent that one must fight and manufacture at the same time. France had a long tradition of compulsory military service; extending that principle to the home front was the first recognition of the necessities of total war.

The regulation of commodities followed more slowly. In October 1915, the government assumed authority to requisition grain at fixed prices, an authority extended in 1916 to sugar, eggs, and milk. In 1917, the Ministry of Food Supply was created, and finally, in June 1918, ration cards were issued for bread and sugar. Even agriculturally rich France had been forced to adopt the same kind of regulations as the food-importing island of Britain.

French war production suffered under special disabilities. The early German successes had cut off the richest industrial parts of the country. The ten occupied northern and eastern departments included the areas where three-quarters of French coal and four-fifths of French iron and steel had been produced. That vast German bite into French wealth had two effects: It made a compromise peace all but inconceivable, and it made war supply that much more difficult. The French could not stop fighting, and yet they could not win without help.

In several respects, war government in France developed less successfully than in England. One problem was financing the war. Whereas the British had had an income tax since 1842, the French still bitterly opposed it. (Lloyd George had decisively defeated the House of Lords between 1909 and 1911 when they opposed funding social services with graduated income taxation.) The French parliament, dominated by provincial small-property interests, had rejected income taxes in favor of sales taxes and government borrowing since the late nineteenth century. As a result, the French government managed to pay only one-fifth of the costs of war from 1914 to 1918 by taxation. To raise the rest, it sold war bonds and printed currency, two steps that prepared grave postwar economic burdens for the French: a crushing load of debt owed to French middle-class bondholders, and runaway inflation.

Civil–military relations also proved more troublesome in France than in England. There was never any doubt about civilian control in England, and when war government found its leader he was a civilian and a radical democrat as well, Lloyd George. The French army, as befits a major land power, had a stronger tradition of military autonomy. Under the republic, the officer corps, strongly marked by conservative and even monarchist sympathies, had maintained a tacit agreement with the republican government that they would leave each other alone. This worked fairly well, except when the army tried to conceal a flagrant legal miscarriage, as in the Dreyfus Affair at the turn of the century. Even Frenchmen of impeccable republican convictions felt in 1914 that civilians should stand aside while the army fought the war. The commander in chief, General Joffre, assumed almost feudal authority over national defense in the fall of 1914, with the understanding that national defense was something separate from the rest of the nation and that the emergency would soon be over. When, after the First Battle of the Marne, it became apparent that the war could be waged only by mobilizing the entire nation, the question of who was the ultimate authority became a thorny one.

That question was finally decided in favor of a civilian authority, in keeping with the French republican tradition, but not before damaging squabbles had taken place during the first three years of the war. The French parliament gradually reasserted its right to oversee the conduct of the war, through the army committees of the Senate and Chamber, and at the end of 1916, weary of Joffre's inability to break out of the post-Marne stalemate, a majority of deputies forced the government to sack him. The decline of military independence was accentuated when Joffre's successor, the ebullient General Robert Nivelle, failed to gain any ground with his widely heralded mass attack in May 1917. The army mutinies that followed seemed to threaten collapse.

French war government finally found its leader at the end of 1917 in Georges Clemenceau. "War is too important to be left to generals," he said. Like Lloyd George, he not only was a civilian, he came from the left of center politically. A crusty old atheist democrat, trained as a doctor, Clemenceau had been a permanent one-man opposition in parliament for most of his life. He had already emerged as a tough administrator in his first prime ministry from 1906 to 1909, when he used the army to smash strikes. Now, in 1917, he brought that combination of surly toughness and left-wing nationalism in the French Jacobin tradition to the administration of the war. When asked in the parliament what his new government's program would be, he replied with four words instead of the usual long policy speech: *"Je fais la guerre!"* (I make war!) Despite that claim, Clemenceau's remedies were more political than technical. He cracked down on defeatists, jailing or silencing those who dared speak for a compromise peace while Germans were still on French soil. Under his authority, France moved into total war government, like the other belligerents.

Germany

German war government, by contrast with that in Britain and France, was consolidated under military authority. Germany's lack of self-sufficiency in food and in some strategic materials made organization especially urgent. The general staff became the dominant force in war government, in keeping with the traditional autonomy of the German military under the sole command of the kaiser.

Two popular military heroes emerged as virtual dictators of the German war effort: General Paul von Hindenburg, as chief of the general staff, and General Erich Ludendorff, as quartermaster-general (the traditional Prussian title of the deputy chief of staff). Hindenburg, a Junker aristocrat, and Ludendorff, one of the few commoners to reach the top of the Prussian officer corps, had become popular idols by winning the one outstanding victory of the first years of the war: the rout of the Russians in the battles of Tannenberg and the Masurian Lakes in the fall of 1914. After the bloody stalemate of Verdun in 1916 had discredited General Falkenhayn, Hindenburg and Ludendorff were put in charge by the kaiser on August 29, 1916. They emerged by 1918 more powerful than the kaiser himself.

What Ludendorff called "war socialism" *(Kriegssozialismus)* was already apparent by 1916. Since the Schlieffen Plan had promised a quick knockout blow of France and then Russia, there had been no prewar plans for organizing the economy and society for a long struggle. The German army had about six months' supply of essential materials in 1914. Production was disrupted as skilled workers were called away to the army. Faced with a long war and inadequate resources, Germany moved more completely than the other belligerents into organizing the home front.

The first major war agency drew on advanced business methods. Walther Rathenau, head of the German General Electric Company *(AEG, Allgemeine Elektrizitäts-Gesellschaft)* was called to reorganize the Raw Materials Section of the army staff. A prophet of technocracy as well as a successful businessman, Rathenau now had a chance to apply on a national scale his ideas of reconciling privately owned business with economic planning. Rathenau grouped the companies in each branch of production into War Raw Materials Corporations, not unlike the cartels that some industries—coal, steel—had formed on their own before the war. Each corporation then bought raw materials and allocated them to the most efficient producers for the most necessary products. In practice, large concerns were likely to be favored over small ones (which did not displease an apostle of industrial efficiency like Rathenau), and, in the urgency of the moment, there was no way to limit exorbitant war profits. From the purely technical point of view, however, the German war machine was very effectively supplied when Rathenau handed over this agency to his successor, an army officer, in 1915.

The War Food Administration, founded in May 1916 under popular pressure, was far less successful. It did operate under extremely difficult conditions, for Germany had produced only 80 percent of its food supply before the war, and food production declined still further during the war because of shortages of farm workers, horses, and nitrogen for fertilizer. Hungry city dwellers demanded measures to compel peasants to relinquish their hoards or to stop the black market. In the winter of 1916–1917, potatoes gave way to turnips as the main food of the poor. The average caloric intake of Germans dropped almost to 1,000 calories per day. Eventually, 750,000 Germans died of hunger. Scarcity of food and city–country antagonisms served to sharpen the sense of class cleavage and of inequitable burdens in wartime Germany.

When Hindenburg and Ludendorff took charge in August 1916, they adopted a system of total personnel mobilization. The Auxiliary Service Law of December 2, 1916, obliged all males between the ages of seventeen and sixty to work in the war economy. One motive, of course, was maximum production; another motive was to control the rising murmurs of discontent and the powerful leverage that the war was giving to labor. The guiding spirit of this project was General Wilhelm Groener, a military technocrat who had excelled in the organization of the railroads. Groener insisted that labor unions be brought into the regional boards that regulated employment. Although this innovation was highly distasteful to conservative industrialists, it permitted Groener to use the unions to help keep social peace while giving them for the first time a legitimate share in government regulation.

After the "turnip winter," the German government tried to reconcile the civilian population to its bitter sufferings. Much effort went into patriotic propaganda devices like the gigantic wooden statues of Field Marshal Hindenburg around which war bond rallies were held. But the gratification of military conquests on the stalemated western front was denied the German propagandists. Nor did it help much any more to promise territorial gains in the Low Countries and Eastern Europe, and the German-dominated *Mitteleuropa* (Middle Europe) to which most German business and military leaders still aspired. An increasing number of Germans wanted to be assured that they were suffering for something more than the privileges and advantages of a few. They were attracted to the possibilities of a German democracy and to "peace without annexations or contributions," a concept to which the new democratic regime in Russia after March 1917 gave much publicity.

Chancellor Bethmann Hollweg tried to revive flagging spirits by getting Kaiser Wilhelm to promise an end to the hated three-class voting system in Prussia after the war. That step only angered Hindenburg and Ludendorff and did little to head off a growing movement in the German parliament for a statement rejecting any war aims of annexation on behalf of the German people. On July 14, 1917, Hindenburg and Ludendorff persuaded the kaiser to replace Chancellor Bethmann Hollweg with a colorless bureaucrat who had never held high public office, Georg Michaelis. The civilian government's weakness in the face of growing military authority was now obvious. Although the moderate parliamentary left (Social Democrats, Progressive Party, Catholic Center) presented its "Peace Resolution" on

July 19, 1917, this appeal for a "peace of understanding and reconciliation among peoples" had no effect on a government now wholly dominated by the annexationist German general staff.

By 1918, Germany had moved far not only toward a fully militarized war government but toward a highly bureaucratized war economy in which expert civil servants allocated resources and men and manipulated economic life, not always to the pleasure of industrialists and labor unions.

Russia

Imperial Russia, a genuine Great Power up to 1914, was soon overwhelmed by the demands of twentieth-century total war. Such a war quickly revealed the disadvantages of being both backward and autocratic. Faced with crippling shortages of matériel from the beginning, the only possible Russian strategy was to swamp the enemy with sheer numbers. But only some soldiers even had a rifle; the others were told to pick one up from the dead.[5] The shortage of Russian artillery shells was largely responsible for German advances in 1915, and for Brusilov's failure to hold the gains of his offensive into Austrian Galicia in the summer of 1916. Under these embittering conditions, to mobilize masses of men meant to radicalize them.

All the belligerents faced shortages, of course. In the Russian case, however, the creaking bureaucracy was incapable of taking steps toward more effective administration. Nicholas assumed personal command of the armed forces, for which he had neither training nor capacity. Domestic policies were left under the control of the tsarina, an ignorant, high-strung German princess. The tsarina became dependent on an Orthodox monk, Grigori Rasputin, a peasant visionary given to gargantuan excesses who claimed he could heal her hemophiliac son. Scurrilous rumors about the imperial family, along with misgovernment, weakened popular reverence for the tsar.

Under such conditions, war agencies emerged parallel to the government or against it, rather than within it. The government itself lapsed into paralysis. While the military went its own way, well-meaning public figures tried to regulate the home front. The Union of Zemstvos and Towns, for example, a body of local government officials intended to look after refugees, assumed larger functions. Leading industrialists had to persuade the regime to let them form military-industrial committees.

It was impossible to mobilize allegiance in a country whose leaders still refused even to grant the vote to its middle class. The Duma (parliament) had been elected on a narrower and narrower franchise since its hopeful beginnings in 1905, and only 9,500 of Moscow's 1.5 million residents could vote for their city council by 1914. The aged bureaucrat who served as prime minister, the seventy-five-year-old Ivan Goremykin, was incapable of grasping the necessity for internal concessions. "First of all," he told the Council of Ministers on September 2, 1915, "we must conclude the war instead of occupying oneself with reforms. There will be enough time

---

[5]Orlando Figes, *A People's Tragedy* (New York, 1997), p. 262.

Popperfoto

Tsar Nicholas II, holding an icon, blesses Russian troops in 1915. Nicholas was the only European monarch who felt he had to assume direct military command himself.

for that after we chase out the Germans."[6] Such benighted government meant that discontent festered among privileged Russians and the educated as well as among workers, soldiers, and peasants. It was a group of aristocrats, including a royal prince, who murdered Rasputin in 1916. The conservatives and constitutional monarchists who dominated the Duma found themselves forced to oppose the tsar even to obtain effective administration of the war.

Austria-Hungary

The Habsburg Empire suffered more than any other belligerent from ethnic centrifugal forces. Of each one hundred soldiers mobilized by Austria-Hungary in August 1914, twenty-five spoke German as their mother tongue; twenty-three spoke Magyar (Hungarian); thirteen spoke Czech; nine, Serbo-Croat; eight, Polish; eight, Ukrainian; seven, Romanian; five, Slovak; three, Slovene; and one, Italian. As wartime propaganda heightened national self-consciousness and spread the idea of self-determination, the national minorities became restless. Britain, France, and even Germany could conciliate their populations with promises of expanded

[6]Michael Cherniavsky, ed., *Prologue to Revolution: Notes of A. N. Iakhontov on the Secret Meetings of the Council of Ministers, 1915* (New York, 1967), pp. 6n, 226.

suffrage and a more democratic society, or by the integration of labor unions into government agencies, but the Habsburgs could not make concessions to ethnic sep- aratists without dissolving the empire altogether.

The outpouring of dynastic loyalty in July and August 1914 had never been unan- imous and finally proved ephemeral. The adversities of a long, general war—so unlike the short, local war for which Austrian leaders had hoped—soon awakened the ethnic animosities that had preoccupied Austro-Hungarian politics since the late nineteenth century. Wartime passions only heightened the intransigence with which the dominant German and Magyar peoples had blocked any further linguis- tic or political decentralization in favor of Poles, Czechs, Romanians, or South Slavs. As a result, the general staff could no longer send troops to any front with the assurance that Slavic soldiers, for example, would fight resolutely against Russians or Serbs.

Such ethnic complications only added to the troubles of a war government already hindered by dualism. The two halves of the Austro-Hungarian Empire com- peted for food and blocked the formation of efficient unitary wartime agencies. Nor was the traditional Habsburg bureaucracy an asset to war government. The new agencies thrown together pragmatically by the British, French, and Germans faced fewer entrenched rivalries. The Habsburg state was too decentralized to wage war effectively but not decentralized enough to satisfy its populations.

Low industrial productivity was another liability for the Habsburg lands. One unit had only enough uniforms for its soldiers in the front line; the men in reserve wore just underwear.[7] Unscrupulous contractors outfitted the army with paper- soled boots. The allied blockade cut off essential imports. The reduction of the flour allowance in Vienna from 200 grams per day to 160 provoked a general strike in January 1918.

The Habsburg case shows how ineffective political autocracy was in waging total war. Since there was no way to mobilize public opinion without raising the national- ities issue, the Austrian prime minister Count Karl Sturgkh attempted to govern without it. Although the Hungarian parliament met during the war, the Austrian *Reichsrat* did not, for fear of giving a platform to dissident Social Democrats, Czechs, and Poles. The *Reichsrat* building was converted into a military hospital. The Aus- trian parliament was finally convened in May 1917, after the young Social Democrat intellectual Friedrich Adler had assassinated Count Sturgkh in October 1916 with a cry of "Down with Absolutism! We want peace!" But it was too late. Separatist feel- ings had ripened beyond the point where Austria-Hungary could resolve the dilemma of finding popular support for war government by any means short of dis- solving the empire itself.

When the old Emperor Franz Josef died at the age of eighty-six in November 1916 after a reign of sixty-eight years, the last link holding these disparate peoples together snapped. His great-nephew and heir, Karl, understood that the war would destroy his dynasty. At the very end of 1916 he put out secret peace feelers through President Woodrow Wilson, the pope, and other possible mediators. The new Habs- burg emperor's known wish for a compromise peace cost him the loyalty of the last

---

[7]C. A. Macartney, *The Habsburg Empire, 1790–1918* (New York, 1969), p. 830.

of his faithful peoples, the ethnic Germans. They now looked to Berlin to carry the war on to the triumph of Germandom throughout central Europe. The Austro-Hungarian Empire withered from within before it was decisively beaten from without.

Italy

Unlike the other major belligerents who had entered the war in patriotic exaltation in August 1914, the Italian government entered the war late (May 1915) in a spirit of bargain rather than of crusade. King Victor Emmanuel III, Prime Minister Antonio Salandra, and Foreign Minister Sidney Sonnino joined the Entente side in the belief that war would be both short and advantageous. A noisy minority of nationalists, including futurist Filippo Marinetti, young syndicalist revolutionary Benito Mussolini, and poet Gabriele D'Annunzio, had demonstrated for war on the streets of Rome. They were convinced that violence would energize an Italy that seemed to slumber since the nineteenth-century battles for unification. "Friends, it is no longer time for talk but for action," D'Annunzio shouted to a crowd of 100,000 from a hotel balcony in Rome on May 12, 1915. "If it is a crime to incite citizens to violence, I shall boast of this crime."[8] The majority of Italians were never enthusiastic about the war, however. The two largest mass organizations in Italy, the Socialist Party and the Catholic Church, opposed it. So did Italy's leading prewar centrist political leader, Giovanni Giolitti. There was no honeymoon period of national unity in Italy to mask the impact of war.

Italy organized to meet the demands of total war less successfully than the other Entente states, Britain and France. For one thing, Italy was no match industrially for the northern and western Great Powers. Shortages were especially difficult to deal with in a country whose south had never been well integrated into the national economy and society. No less than 38 percent of Italians were still illiterate in 1914, making efficient war government difficult to organize. Without effective governmental controls, the powerful distortions of war production and consumption affected Italians both harshly and with extreme inequity. Inflation reduced the real wages of workers in the war plants of Turin and Milan by 27 percent in 1917. When campaigns went badly in the rough eastern Alps where the Italian armies fought the Austrians, Italian regional and social animosities turned into hard anger.

THE SOCIAL IMPACT

No European society could attempt to channel all its resources into total war without undergoing profound change. At first glance, the intense common effort seemed likely to make European societies more uniform and egalitarian. Death itself was the greatest leveler. Every belligerent had some form of compulsory military service, and European aristocracies probably lost a higher proportion of their sons in the hard-hit junior officer ranks than did the middle classes. Wartime scarcities made

---

[8]Quoted in John Woodhouse, *Gabriele D'Annunzio: Defiant Archangel* (Oxford, England, 1998), p. 291.

ostentation, idleness, and luxury bad form. In the euphoria of 1914 it was possible to believe that "warfare releases a devotion and an unconditional community of sacrifice"[9] that would transform each nation into a true family. The British Liberal leader Lloyd George rejoiced on September 19, 1914, that "all classes, high and low, are shedding themselves of selfishness. . . . It is bringing a new outlook to all classes. . . . We can see for the first time the fundamental things that matter in life, and that have been obscured from our vision by the tropical growth of prosperity."[10]

Clothing was a harbinger of a more homogeneous, simplified lifestyle. During the war, dress became much more utilitarian and informal. Europeans would never again drape themselves in such a profusion of bustles, stays, trains, and plumes. Uniforms led the way. The bright blue-and-red prewar French infantry uniforms, which made such good targets for machine-gun fire in 1914, had not been changed during the first months of war because the general staff was convinced that the war would be over before they could do so. Soon, however, every army was in utilitarian khaki. Meanwhile, women's skirts rose above the ankle for good.

The Status of Women

The war transformed the lives of women, too, and not only as wives, daughters, and consumers. As combat drained male labor away, women were needed in war production. Poor women had always worked in the fields or as domestics, of course, but even in factories where they had worked before, as in textile mills, they now replaced men in more skilled assignments. They even worked in heavy industry. By 1918 women workers in the Krupp armaments firm in Germany had increased from 2,000 to 28,000, and in the German machine industry in general from 75,000 in 1913 to nearly 500,000 in 1918. A third of all French munitions workers were female by 1918.[11] After the war, although the surviving soldiers often took their old jobs back from women, women no longer seemed out of place in a wider range of work.

The war changed the lives of middle-class women most. It gave them access to a variety of jobs previously held largely by men, such as office work and teaching. It became acceptable for young, employed, single middle-class women to have their own apartments, to go out without chaperones, and even to smoke in public. Young women not only shortened their skirts but bobbed their hair, and appeared for tennis in trousers. Marie Stopes's 1918 guides to birth control, *Married Love* and *Wise Parenthood*, became best-sellers in England and in 1921 Stopes opened the first English birth control clinic. The heroine of Victor Margueritte's novel *La Garçonne* (*The Bachelor Girl*, 1922) has an interesting job, bobs her hair, plays sports, and expects no less sexual freedom than her fiancé. It sold a million copies in France by 1929. Such "emancipated women" aroused a backlash that fascist movements could

---

[9]Max Weber quoted in Arthur B. Mitzman, *The Iron Cage* (New York, 1970), p. 211.

[10]David Lloyd George, *The Great War* (London, 1914), p. 14.

[11]Gail Braybon, "Women, War and Work," in Hew Strahan, ed., *World War I: A History* (Oxford, England, 1998), p. 152. Women were not yet called into military service, however.

After all able-bodied men except the most irreplaceable technicians had been sent to the front, thousands of women were recruited to work in war production. These British women are gauging shells.

later exploit. On the other hand, as we will see in chapter 8, most countries could no longer exclude women from the vote. In 1919, Lady Astor was elected to the British House of Commons, the first woman to be seated in a European parliament.[12]

The Status of Organized Labor

The war also led to decisive changes in the power and legal status of labor unions. The right of workers to organize went back only a half-century on the Continent (1869 in north Germany; 1884 in France); up to 1914, employers struggled to keep union organizers out of their plants, and armed force was commonly used against strikers. But workers' almost universal rallying to their national flags in 1914 opened the way for wider acceptance of unions, just as it did for the inclusion of reformist socialist politicians in wartime governments. The French socialists Marcel Sembat and Jules Guesde entered the Viviani government in August 1914; Arthur

---

[12]Women had been permitted to join political parties and associations in Germany only since 1908.

Henderson joined the Asquith cabinet in May 1915; John Hodge and George Barnes joined the Lloyd George cabinet in December 1916.

It was less by the parliamentary route than by the bureaucratic route, however, that organized labor was integrated into the most highly organized war governments. Only a short war was possible without union cooperation. When it became necessary to cajole longer hours and higher productivity out of war workers and to prevent free movement of skilled workers away from vital jobs, it became essential to consult with union leaders.

A bargain was struck in Britain, France, and Germany between unions and government. In general, unions accepted a temporary cessation of strikes and harsher work rules in exchange for a de facto integration into public administration. In Britain, these arrangements were worked out in a conference at the Treasury Department in March 1915. Labor consented in the "Treasury Agreement"[13] to the proposal that war workers relax union restrictions on work rules and renounce strikes for the duration of the war in favor of arbitration; in return, labor representatives were named to the National Labour Advisory Committee, and the government undertook to control the industrialists' profits.

Trade union integration went furthest in German military-bureaucratic "war socialism." General Groener, against some opposition from conservative industrialists, forced the inclusion of union representatives in labor committees at the factory level and in regional food and labor committees. This "reform from above" brought greatly increased prestige and membership to the German trade unions, which grew from 967,000 in 1916 to 1,107,000 in 1917. At the end of the war, in the Stinnes-Legien Agreement between representatives of industry and labor, the first German official collective bargaining arrangements were concluded. France, too, followed up its wartime experience by giving legal force to collective bargaining in 1920. Labor leaders found, however, that the integration of unions into war government was a two-edged sword. They had purchased a public role for unions at the cost of having to act more often as the managers of labor than as the adversaries of capital. Many of the rank and file had rejected this bargain by 1918.

Social Cleavage

In some ways, the war was a leveler—for women and for labor, for example. But in other ways, the long war sharpened social cleavages and conflicts. One such cleavage was caused by the unequal apportionment of the risk of death. Although total war meant total mobilization of human labor, not everyone was sent to the trenches. Skilled workers were more vitally needed in war plants. And some with connections managed to secure safe assignments at headquarters. It became clear after the war that two groups had paid the highest blood tax: unskilled workers and junior officers. French peasants made up a larger proportion of the war dead than of the general population. The casualty rate among British junior officers,

---

[13]The miners' unions rejected the Treasury Agreement; under the War Munitions Act of 1915, the mines were nationalized for the duration of the war.

often highly talented and motivated young men, was three times the overall casualty rate. Of the class of 1914 at Saint-Cyr, the French military academy, 63 percent
did not survive the war. The survivors, many of them mutilated, shared a blend of
pride and bitterness that they had endured more than the lot of ordinary men.
This "mystique of the trenches" created a resentful solidarity among front-line veterans, who felt a special mission to keep watch over the nations that they had
saved.

The conflict of generations was also widened by the war. Veterans' disillusion fed
on anger at the older generation that had sent them to the front. The villain of the
greatest First World War novel, Erich Maria Remarque's *All Quiet on the Western
Front,* was not the Allied enemy in the opposite trenches but the soldiers' earlier
spiritual guides, such as the schoolteacher Kantorek, who had sent them off full of
patriotic slogans.

> The first bombardment showed us our mistake, and under it the world as they had taught
> it to us broke in pieces.[14]

THE ECONOMIC IMPACT

The inequitable apportionment of wartime suffering was also felt in economic matters; at one end were those who profited from the war and at the other, those who
suffered the very unequal effects of inflation.

War Profiteers

The possibilities for profit in war manufacture were enormous, and war profiteers
were a public scandal. Fictional new rich, like Frederic Haverkamp, the manufacturer of shoddy boots in Jules Romains's *Verdun,* had numerous factual counterparts. It was rare, however, for governments to interfere with major firms, as
happened when the German military took over the Daimler motor car works for
padding costs on war production contracts.[15]

More subtle was the way in which war government favored large, concentrated
industries over smaller ones. On the Continent, especially, the cartelization of industry was substantially increased. In Germany, for example, Walther Rathenau's War
Raw Materials Corporations allocated scarce materials to selected companies. Since
the largest firms dominated these corporations, they were favored even beyond the
natural stimulus of wartime boom profits. Nonessential firms, which tended to be
small, were simply closed down when coal and other resources became too scarce.
The war was also a stimulus toward grouping companies into larger firms. In 1916
the leading German chemical manufacturers pooled their resources to form the
new combine that became the great postwar chemical giant, I. G. Farben.

---

[14]Erich Maria Remarque, *All Quiet on the Western Front* (New York, 1966), p. 12.

[15]Bernard Bellon, *Mercedes in Peace and War* (New York, 1990), pp. 102–111.

The Effects of Inflation

Inflation worked the most pervasive economic and social effect of all. As war budgets rose to astronomical figures, war economies ran at white heat. Massive demand forced round-the-clock production of war matériel, causing shortages of many consumer goods. Virtually every able-bodied person was employed. This combination of high demand, scarcity, and full employment sent prices soaring, even in the least mismanaged war economies. No belligerent country avoided some degree of inflation. In Britain, a pound sterling bought in 1919 about one-third of what it had bought in 1914. French prices approximately doubled during the war, and worse inflation was yet to come in the 1920s. Inflation rates were even higher in the other belligerents; in Germany, as we shall see in chapter 6, the mark simply ceased to have any value at all at the end of 1923.

The effects of inflation are unequal. Some suffer and some benefit. Skilled workers in strategic industries in Western Europe found that their wages just about kept up with prices, or even surged ahead of them. The unskilled and workers in nonstrategic industries lagged behind. Such disparities in wages among different industries stirred new animosities. Only in Britain did most workers' real incomes keep abreast of prices. A higher proportion of the British national income went, temporarily, to the working class.[16] On the Continent, wages also rose, but wage earners had less real purchasing power at the end of the war than at the beginning. The French cost of living stood in 1917 at an index figure of 180 (100 in 1914), while wages stood at only 170. German workers slipped a bit in real purchasing power, with workers in war industries faring far better than workers in the civilian sector. Even those wage-earning families whose standard of living kept pace with inflation suffered constant short-term grievances as they shopped for ever more expensive food.

The bitterest sufferers from inflation were those members of the middle class dependent on fixed incomes. The incomes of old people on pensions, of the marginal middle class living on small dividends or interest, and of many professional people remained about the same while prices doubled or tripled. Such people fell into genuine material poverty that offended their sense of status. These "new poor" clung to a shabby gentility by repairing old clothes, eking out the food budget with rhubarb grown in the back garden, and giving up everything but the outward show of respectability. The middle class, wrote the English poet Stephen Spender, resembled dancers suspended in midair after the ballroom floor had been knocked away, "miraculously able to pretend that they were still dancing."[17]

Inflation did not just lower these people's standard of living; it radically changed their relative position in society. A host of clerks, lesser civil servants, teachers, clergymen, and small shopkeepers now earned less than many skilled laborers. Some members of the marginal middle class found this indignity harder to endure than reduced comforts and amenities. "I go in the gallery [inexpensive seat] to the cinema," complained an English country doctor's wife. "My charwoman goes in the stalls [best seat]."[18]

[16]Trevor O. Lloyd, *Empire, Welfare State, Europe: English History 1906–1992*, 4th ed. (Oxford, England, 1993), pp. 63, 100.

[17]Stephen Spender, *World within World* (London, 1951), p. 2.

[18]C. F. G. Masterman, *England after the War* (London, 1923), p. 105.

To make matters still more bitter for the "new poor," some great fortunes were built during the wartime and postwar inflation. Those able to borrow could repay their debts in devalued currency earned by the borrowed funds. Some industrialists expanded their plants under the twin stimuli of war contracts and borrowed capital; shortly after the war, the German entrepreneur Hugo Stinnes built an immense business empire by taking advantage of inflation.

The animosities and social divisions bred by the First World War rested less on the amount of wartime suffering than on its unevenness. The cry of "no more war" quickly led to a cry for basic changes in the economic, social, and intellectual system that had produced such a war and had apportioned its burdens so inequitably.

THE IMPACT ON INTERNAL ORDER

The patriotic fervor so widespread in 1914 suggested that war really did reduce internal conflict within belligerent nations, at least in the short run. That unified enthusiasm, however, was unable to survive long years of unequal privations without hope of victory.

Strike Activity

One good measure of growing disaffection in the belligerent countries is strike figures. Strike activity had reached the highest levels so far throughout Europe in the years just before 1914. There had been over 1,500 different work stoppages in France in 1910, the peak prewar year; more than 1 million British workmen had been on strike at some time or another in 1912; there had been more than 3,000 work stoppages in Germany in 1910. Labor relations had been unusually tense in some areas in the summer of 1914, with a bitter transport strike in Dublin, the "Red Week" of early June 1914 in Italy, and widespread strikes in St. Petersburg in July. Then, abruptly, there were hardly any strikes at all during the first year of war enthusiasm. Ten work stoppages involving 4,159 people occurred in St. Petersburg during the rest of 1914. Only 98 work stoppages took place in France throughout 1915, and only 137 in Germany.

The revival of strike activity in 1916 shows that social peace was already wearing thin. Work stoppages and the number of people on strike in France quadrupled in 1916 as compared with 1915. The first major internal disorder in wartime Germany was a three-day walkout of 50,000 Berlin workers in May 1916 to protest the arrest of the pacifist Karl Liebknecht during an illegal May Day demonstration. Two regions of intense labor militancy became active in Britain: the mining areas of South Wales, and the shipbuilding areas along the Clyde River in Scotland downstream from Glasgow, where religious nonconformity, a sense of ethnic distinctness from the English, and a tight-knit worker community provided inhospitable terrain for war government. The South Wales and Clydeside workers rejected the compromises of their union leadership and went out on strikes led by grassroots organizers at the plant level—shop stewards.

AP / Wide World Photos

After the Dublin "Easter Rebellion" of April 1916, fifteen Irish nationalist leaders were executed and thousands were jailed. Here a group of prisoners is marched along a Dublin quay by British soldiers.

Ireland, where bitter controversy over Home Rule had been overtaken by the war, erupted in open revolution. Leaders of the Irish independence movement, Sinn Fein, hoping for aid from Germany, seized government buildings in Dublin on Easter Day, April 24, 1916. The British put down the Easter Rebellion in a week of bloody fighting and executed its leaders.

Liberal and Socialist War Critiques

Opposition to the war had been reduced in August 1914 to a few isolated dissenters. By 1916 organized oppositions began to work actively for a compromise peace.

Roughly speaking, there were two schools of opposition in the belligerent countries: liberal and socialist. The liberal critique of the war rested on assumptions of nineteenth-century democratic internationalists like the Englishman John Bright (an opponent of the Crimean War in the 1850s), who had argued that wars resulted from the selfish ambitions of kings, aristocrats, and heads of state against the wishes of the peaceable mass of humanity. The liberal solution was twofold: the expansion of democratic control at home over foreign policy, and the replacement of "international anarchy"[19] with a system of international law. The main prewar monuments to this approach were the Hague conferences of 1899 and 1907, which drafted rules governing the conduct of warfare and the treatment of prisoners of war and set up the International Court of Arbitration.

Despite the blow given the liberals' assumptions by popular jingoism in 1914, the movement remained alive, especially in Britain. The Labour and Liberal politicians who had opposed war joined to form the Union of Democratic Control in December 1914. Its members advocated an immediate negotiated peace, "open diplomacy" under watchful democratic eyes, and a "League of Nations"[20] to apply international law to the relations among sovereign states. In Germany, a coalition of Social Democratic, Progressive, and Center (Catholic) deputies in the *Reichstag* passed a resolution in July 1917 calling for a peace without annexations. They worked from assumptions similar to the British opposition, but with far less public impact.

The socialist critique of the war rested on Marxist theory, which attributes war to capitalist competition. It made no sense to Marxists to work for an end to the current war without also attempting to overthrow the economic system that, by their diagnosis, would cause others like it.

Marxist antiwar groups were stronger on the Continent than in Britain. The British Independent Labour Party (ILP) of Ramsay MacDonald and Philip Snowden remained allied to Liberals in the Union of Democratic Control. In Germany, however, where the Social Democratic Party (SPD) had unanimously voted for war credits in August 1914, eighteen dissidents left the party during 1916 and formed the Independent Socialist Party (USPD) in March 1917, dedicated to an immediate negotiated peace and domestic revolution. It was more difficult for French socialists, on whose soil stood German troops, to break the *union sacrée* of 1914. Even so, by the time of the December 1916 national congress of the French Socialist Party (SFIO), the party's pacifist wing had risen to almost equal strength with the faction devoted to supporting the war effort. Russian socialists had never taken part in war government, and a majority of Italian socialists opposed the war from the beginning.

These internationalist minorities naturally sought to revive their prewar foreign contacts. The old machinery of the socialist Second International,[21] however, was jammed by the antagonism between the prowar majorities of the French and German socialist parties. Socialists of neutral countries—Switzerland, Sweden, and, up to April 1915, Italy—worked together with Russian *émigrés* like Lenin in Switzerland and Trotsky in Paris to organize unofficial international socialist meetings. The first meeting of European socialists across the battle lines was the Zimmerwald Conference in Switzerland in September 1915. The group was small; one delegate commented wryly that all the internationalist socialists in Europe could be driven to the meeting place in four carriages.[22] Moreover, the delegates were irreconcilably

---

[19]The phrase comes from G. Lowes Dickinson, a Cambridge political scientist and a prominent British pacifist.

[20]Another phrase coined by G. Lowes Dickinson.

[21]See chapter 3, p. 71.

[22]Robert Wohl, *French Communism in the Making, 1914–1924* (Stanford, Calif., 1966), p. 66.

divided between a majority (twenty-three votes) who wanted only to oppose annexationist war aims, and a minority (seven votes) who wanted to use the wartime tensions as a lever for revolution, or, as Lenin put it, to convert the war into civil war. By the time the next conference met, at Kienthal in Switzerland in April 1916, the socialist antiwar movement had become far larger. Governments found it necessary to take notice and refuse passports to their citizens who planned to attend.

In 1917, war morale cracked wide open in all the belligerent countries. As the war approached its third anniversary without any sign of end, populations stirred restlessly. It was the year of the French army mutinies, the "Peace Resolution" of the German *Reichstag,* the secret peace feelers of the Austro-Hungarian monarchy, and the climax of agitation in the shop stewards' movement in Clydeside in Scotland. The Russian Revolution of 1917 was only the greatest of a whole series of shocks to the old regimes of 1914.[23]

Police Power

War governments responded to opposition with extensions of the police power. Authoritarian regimes like that of tsarist Russia had always depended on the use of force and fear. But now even the parliamentary regimes felt required to expand police powers and embark on state control of public opinion.

Emergency police powers were given wide scope in England in August 1914 by the Defence of the Realm Act (DORA). DORA authorized the public authorities to arrest and punish dissidents under martial law if necessary. It was under this act that the leaders of the Irish Easter Rebellion of 1916 were executed. DORA, subsequently extended in later acts, also empowered the British authorities to suspend newspapers and to intervene in such sacrosanct aspects of an Englishman's private life as the use of lights at home, food consumption, and bar hours.

Police powers tended to grow as the war dragged on and as opposition to it increased. This trend was especially marked in France, where public authority had been relatively lenient at the beginning. The sharp rise of strikes, the army mutinies in May and June of 1917, and increasing talk of a negotiated peace raised doubts whether the French war effort could go on. The selection of the tough prewar strikebreaker Georges Clemenceau as prime minister on November 16, 1917, signified that a majority of French political leaders wanted to continue the war even at the cost of less internal liberty. Clemenceau carried out that mandate. He cracked down ruthlessly on anyone suspected of supporting a compromise peace. Minister of the Interior Louis Malvy, who since 1914 had been lenient on suspects, was charged with treason and sentenced to five years' exile. Former Prime Minister Joseph Caillaux, who had publicly advocated a compromise peace, was imprisoned for two years awaiting trial on treason charges. Several antiwar newspaper editors were jailed, and Paul Bolo, editor of an antiwar newspaper believed to be receiving German subsidies, was executed. After the war, many of these treason charges turned out to be the result of war hysteria or calculated political opportunism. They

[23]See chapter 5, pp. 120–127.

revealed the extent to which the wartime suspension of civil liberties could be accepted, even in libertarian France.

Control of Public Opinion

Expanded police powers extended also to the control of information and opinion. Its negative form, the censorship of newspapers and personal mail, was already established practice. Governments normally invoked the extra powers given them in an emergency to prevent disclosure of military secrets and the airing of opinions judged dangerous for the war effort. Positive forms of opinion control were a more genuine innovation of the First World War. All the belligerent governments resorted to what the French historian Elie Halévy later called "the organization of enthusiasm." The governments' efforts to influence their citizens' opinions were one sign for Halévy that the First World War had inaugurated an "era of tyrannies."[24]

At the beginning, governments hardly needed to fan public feeling. In the East End of London, for example, women organized "white feather" patrols to brand

This British recruiting poster tried to arouse shame in able-bodied men who did not volunteer for military service.

Imperial War Museum

Daddy, what did YOU do in the Great War?

---

[24]Elie Halévy, *The Era of Tyrannies,* trans. R. K. Webb (Garden City, N.Y., 1965), p. 266.

young men still in civilian clothes with a symbol of cowardice. Later, governments had to stimulate flagging enthusiasm. Wartime posters achieved a new level of effectiveness. Two British masterpieces before the imposition of the draft in England helped put public pressure on young men to volunteer. In one of these, the war minister, Lord Kitchener, points directly at the viewer over the slogan, "Britain needs you." In another, a little girl asks her father, "Daddy, what did you do in the Great War?"

Clemenceau freely used his power as French prime minister to draft journalists or defer them in exchange for favorable news coverage. The German general staff used labor leaders to run an "enlightenment program" in war plants. Late in the war, the German right adopted a more sophisticated tactic: They formed a new mass party, the Fatherland Party, backed by secret army funds and devoted to propaganda for war discipline and eventual territorial expansion for Germany. By 1918, the Fatherland Party was larger than the Social Democratic Party. German conservative nationalists were skillfully appropriating the mass party techniques invented by the left.

THE INTELLECTUAL IMPACT

Four years of holocaust completely smashed the optimistic liberal-rationalist clichés of the average European of 1914. The most "advanced" quarter of the earth had redescended of its own volition into barbarism. Where was progress? Where reason? The effect was to make the avant-garde criticisms and mockeries of pre-1914 Europe much more acceptable to the general population.

One can follow the loss of illusions and the emergence of a hard new anger in wartime poetry. Poets, like almost everyone else, had gone to war in 1914 believing in heroism. British poet Rupert Brooke exulted in the virile lessons of war:

> Now, God be thanked Who has matched us with His hour,
> And caught our youth, and wakened us from sleeping,
> With hand made sure, clear eye, and sharpened power,
> To turn, as swimmers into cleanness leaping,
> Glad from a world grown old and weary,
> Leave the sick hearts that honor could not move,
> And half-men, and their dirty songs and dreary,
> And all the little emptiness of love.[25]

In France, Charles Péguy, a curious socialist mystic, wrote in 1913:

> Blessed are they who died in great battles
> Stretched out on the ground in the face of God . . .
> Blessed are they who died in a just war
> Blessed is the wheat that is ripe and the wheat
> that is gathered in sheaves.[26]

[25]Rupert Brooke, "1914. Peace," in *The Poetical Works of Rupert Brooke,* ed. Geoffrey Keynes (London, 1946), p. 19.

[26]Charles Peguy, "Blessed are . . .," in *Basic Verities: Prose and Poetry,* trans. Ann Green and Julien Green (New York, 1943), pp. 275–277.

Péguy was killed in 1914, and Brooke died in 1915, so one can only imagine the hardening and embittering impact of trench warfare on them. The British poet Wilfred Owen, who was not killed until 1918, was transformed from a rather pallid romantic versifier into a powerful denouncer of those who had sent young men off to war. In "Dulce et Decorum Est" (1917) he mocked "the old lie" that it was good to die for one's country, after giving a searing description of a gassed soldier coughing out his lungs. Another poem paraphrased the story of Abraham, ready to sacrifice his son Isaac on God's command. Unlike the biblical Abraham, however, Wilfred Owen's Abraham ignores the angel who directs him to "slay the lamb of pride instead."

> But the old man would not, and slew his son
> And half the seed of Europe, one by one.[27]

The anger of these soldier-poets was directed not against the enemy but against the fathers. The real enemy was the old society that had made it hard to avoid war, and the old values that had held that war "sharpened" a man rather than debased him. The First World War produced a whole literature of repudiation. Erich Maria Remarque's *All Quiet on the Western Front*, as noted earlier, made the patriotic schoolteacher the real villain. *Eminent Victorians* (1918) by the British conscientious objector Lytton Strachey derided the whole preceding generation through belittling biographies of some of its leaders.

The war experience did not itself produce new art forms or styles. It acted largely to make the harshest themes and the grimmest or most mocking forms of expression of prewar intellectual life seem more appropriate, and to foster experiments in opposition to the dominant values of contemporary Europe.

Prewar fascination with the absurd and the subconscious seemed much more timely after years of bloodletting. The Dada movement elevated mockery to a minor art form with a series of shocking stunts designed to ridicule stuffy bourgeois culture. Dada (an ostentatiously meaningless name) was founded in Zürich in 1916 by the young Romanian poet Tristan Tzara and spread by the end of the war to Paris, Berlin, and New York. Dada artists enraged audiences by having ten poets read their work simultaneously to the sound of bells, or by displaying a perfect copy of the *Mona Lisa* improved with a moustache. Marcel Duchamp entered a toilet bowl labeled "fountain" in a sculpture exhibit in New York in 1917. Beyond promoting mere pranks by comfortably bourgeois intellectuals, the dadaists announced a serious goal of liberation from conformity and from the false aura of awe surrounding past art. Dadaism advocated the "necessary destruction" of the old world. "After the carnage, we keep only the hope of a purified humanity."[28]

Wartime experiences also prepared the way for the more important surrealist movement of the 1920s. André Breton, a young medical student assigned during the war to a psychiatric hospital in France, had ample opportunity to discover in

---

[27]Wilfred Owen, "Dulce et Decorum Est," and "The Parable of The Old Man and The Young," in *The Collected Poems of Wilfred Owen*, ed. C. Day Lewis (New York, 1964), pp. 42, 55. The first title refers to a verse from an ode by the Latin poet Horace, which Owen had learned at school: It is right and good to die for one's country.

[28]Dada Manifesto (1918) in Maurice Nadeau, *Histoire du surréalisme* (Paris, 1964), chapter 3.

shell shock cases the power of the unconscious and the importance of Freud's work. Fascinated by magic and dreams, Breton abandoned medicine to devote himself to a literature that would liberate the unconscious genius from the restraints not merely of bourgeois art styles but of "any control exercised by reason."[29] "We live still under the reign of logic," declared Breton. He sought to set free the inner genius by such devices as "automatic writing," in which one sets down words in free association. Breton began with Dada but moved beyond it toward the founding of surrealism when he experimented with automatic writing in *Les Champs Magnétiques* (*Magnetic Fields,* 1920).

The early part of the war deeply gratified the fascination with speed, violence, and the machine, as manifested in the work of the Italian poet Filippo Marinetti, the artist Umberto Boccioni, and others of the prewar futurist movement. Marinetti was arrested while demonstrating in the streets of Rome in favor of Italian entry into the war during the spring of 1915.

Although the leaders of these movements quarreled among themselves, they shared a resolute "modernist" contempt for all academic styles in the arts, a hatred for bourgeois culture (more violent in word than in deed), and a commitment to the free expression of individual genius. All these feelings were given an additional dosage of violence and anger by the horrors of the wartime experience.

A mood of desolation and emptiness prevailed at the end of a war in which such enormous sacrifice had accomplished so little. "My senses are charred," Wilfred Owen wrote to his fellow British poet Siegfried Sassoon on October 10, 1918, shortly before Owen was killed. A soldier next to him had been shot in the head, and the corpse had soaked Owen with its blood. "I shall feel again as soon as I dare, but now I must not."[30] Beneath the surface playfulness of Dada lay a similar feeling of emptiness. Far from being mere nonsense, the surrealist Breton's automatic writing turned out to be a powerful evocation of desolation. The most famous single declaration of the spiritual emptiness felt by so many at the end of the war was T. S. Eliot's poem "The Hollow Men" (1925). We know now that its despair was the product of personal difficulties, but its closing lines were immediately seized on to speak for the postwar generation:

> This is the way the world ends
> This is the way the world ends
> This is the way the world ends
> Not with a bang but a whimper.[31]

It was not yet clear at the end of the First World War where such wartime angers would be focused. If these intellectuals drifted into politics, it was bound to be anti-bourgeois politics. In the end, Marinetti went over to Mussolini, his fellow advocate of war for Italy in 1915. The surrealists André Breton and Louis Aragon thought that the Bolshevik Revolution in Russia was opening the way for the liberation of

---

[29]First Surrealist Manifesto (1924) in André Breton, *Manifestoes of Surrealism,* trans. Richard Seaver and Helen R. Lane (Ann Arbor, Mich., 1986), p. 26.

[30]Wilfred Owen, *Collected Letters* (Oxford, England, 1967), p. 581.

[31]T. S. Eliot, "The Hollow Men," in *Collected Poems, 1909–1962* (New York, 1970), p. 82.

creative genius. They joined the new French Communist Party. The reactions of young intellectuals to wartime experience showed that however widely they disagreed among themselves, they were likely to join whatever postwar movement seemed to cut with the sharpest knife.

SUGGESTIONS FOR FURTHER READING

Jay Winter, Geoffrey Parker, and Mary R. Harbeck, eds., *The Great War and the Twentieth Century* (2001), takes a fresh look at the war's wider implications. Roger Chickering and Stig Förster, eds., *Great War, Total War: Combat and Mobilization on the Western Front** (2000) assesses total war on both sides. John Horne, ed., *State, Society, and Mobilization in Eruope during the First World War** (2002), examines how populations were made willing to accept sacrifice. Extensive treatment of the economic and social dimensions of the war in all the major belligerent countries is contained in the many volumes edited in the 1920s and 1930s for the Carnegie Endowment for International Peace by James T. Shotwell, *Economic and Social History of the World War.* This series often provides the fullest information available. The classic essay by Elie Halévy, *The Era of Tyrannies* (1966), is still suggestive for the permanent legacy of war government. The most penetrating study of any single war government is Gerald D. Feldman, *Army, Industry, and Labor in Germany, 1914–1918** (revised ed. 1992), supplemented by his *Iron and Steel in the German Inflation, 1916–1923* (1977). The same author's *The Great Disorder: Politics, Economics, and Society in the German Inflation, 1914–1924** (1997) is the most thorough account of any one country's wartime economic management. See also Roger Chickering, *Imperial Ger-*

*many and the Great War, 1914–1918,** 2nd ed. (2004). Leonard V. Smith, Stéphane Audoin-Rouzeau, and Annette Becker, *France and the Great War** (2003), is the best account of the war's effects on France.

Marc Ferro, *The Great War, 1914–1918,** 2nd ed. (2003), takes a fresh look at the war as a social phenomenon. Excellent on the Great War's social and cultural impact are Richard Wall and Jay Winter, eds., *The Upheaval of War** (2004); Franz Coetzee and Marilyn Shevin-Coetzee, eds., *Authority, Identity, and the Social History of the Great War* (1995); and Margaret R. Higonnet et al., eds., *Behind the Lines: Gender and the Two World Wars** (1989). How the war was remembered and commemorated is the subject of Jay Winter, *Sites of Memory, Sites of Mourning,** and Jay Winter and Immanuel Sivan, eds., *War and Remembrance in the Twentieth Century* (1999).

The fatal division of Italy by the war is vividly portrayed in Paul Corner, *Fascism in Ferrara* (1975). See, more generally, Christopher Seton-Watson, *Italy from Liberalism to Fascism, 1870–1925* (1967).

The social impact of the war on Britain is best treated by Jay Winter, *The Great War and the British People* (1986). Ross McKibbin, *Classes and Cultures in England, 1918–1951** (1998) is a wide-ranging social and cultural history. Still useful are the relevant parts of Samuel H. Beer, *Modern British Politics:*

Parties and Pressure Groups in the Collectivist Age (1982), and Bentley B. Gilbert, *British Social Policy, 1914–1939* (1970).

For the war's impact on women, see Margaret R. Higonnet, ed., *Lines of Fire: Women Writers of World War I** (1997).

On the collapse of the Russian state under war pressures, Allan K. Wildman, *The End of the Russian Imperial Army* (1980), is instructive. István Deák, *Beyond Nationalism: A Social and Political History of the Habsburg Officer Corps, 1848–1918** (1990), reveals the enduring strength of imperial loyalty. See also Robert A. Kann et al., *The Habsburg Empire in World War I* (1977).

Additional Internet links related to this chapter are available on the Europe in the 20th Century Web site: http://www.history.wadsworth.com/paxton04.

You can also explore images, interactive timelines, and maps related to this chapter on our Western Civilization Resource Center: http://history.wadsworth.com.

Demonstrators against the Kerensky government being shot down in Petrograd, July 1917.

5
Revolution, 1917–1920

By 1917, protracted war was producing revolutionary strains in all the belligerent countries. Every war regime faltered in 1917. Some of them, such as Clemenceau's France and the Germany of Hindenburg and Ludendorff, were able to cajole or force their peoples to endure another year of struggle. Others, most conspicuously Austria-Hungary and Russia, could no longer contain the pressures of war weariness, social conflict, and national separatism. The two Russian revolutions of 1917 were merely the most explosive examples of discontent that affected all of Europe. At one time or another between 1917 and 1920, the red flag flew from the Clydeside of western Scotland to Siberia. It remained flying only in Russia. Those nearly universal revolutionary pressures and their relatively localized success are the subject of this chapter.

THE RUSSIAN REVOLUTIONS, 1917

Tsarist Russia was particularly vulnerable to worker unrest. As newcomers to industrialization, its workers were peasant stock undergoing their first generation of factory discipline, the stage of greatest turbulence in every experience of industrialization. That turbulence, moreover, had unusual leverage, for the new Russian industrial plants were highly concentrated in a few major cities. And the dark memories of the frustrated Revolution of 1905 poisoned Russian efforts at patriotic union.

Russia, like the other belligerents, might have survived worker discontent if the tsarist regime had enjoyed the support of any other major element of the population. But the middle classes and liberal aristocrats chafed at the revocation of even the timid democratic concessions of 1905; many of them still awaited Russia's version of the French Revolution of 1789, the replacement of divine right autocracy by constitutional monarchy. Even conservative aristocrats were enraged at the bumbling and sycophancy that insulated the tsar and tsarina from efficient advisers. Finally, combat opened the eyes of the tsar's last naively faithful supporters, the peasantry. Russia went to war superior to its enemies in only one resource: sheer masses of men. The tsar threw the peasant mass of his people at German steel. Ill-equipped and poorly led, the Russian soldiers underwent the most wasting campaigns of any army in the first years of the war. By the spring of 1917, up to 1,850,000 Russian soldiers had been killed and far larger numbers wounded or captured.[1] The tsar mobilized the mass of his subjects into uniform only to see them radicalized. Under such conditions, what needs explaining is how the regime survived as long as it did.

The "February Revolution"

Some historians have argued that the tsarist system was on the verge of revolution even in 1914, only to be granted two more years' respite by the injection of wartime patriotism. Others, to the contrary, feel that the dislocations and strains of war were fatal to a regime that might have reformed itself without war.[2] No one questions, however, that the first outburst came not from a planned revolution but from a spontaneous eruption of mass anger. Women began it, with demonstrations over the lack of bread and coal in the Russian capital of Petrograd[3] that began on March 8, 1917 (February 23 by the old Julian calendar still in use in Russia). The mass support for these demonstrations that welled up from a hungry and disgusted population took every political leader by surprise, even the socialists.

At first, these demonstrations seemed no more serious to the regime than similar unrest in other belligerent countries. The tsar ordered unquestioning repression. The death of forty demonstrators on March 11, when troops fired into a crowd,

---

[1] Allan K. Wildman, *The End of the Russian Imperial Army* (Princeton, NJ, 1980), p. 96, 41n.

[2] Leopold Haimson has argued the first view most trenchantly; Richard Pipes may serve as an example of the second. See the bibliography at the end of this chapter for these and other perspectives.

[3] The Germanic name of St. Petersburg had been Russified at the beginning of the war.

simply solidified the people in their anger. The tsar's regime was fatally stricken when the troops sent to rout the demonstrators fraternized with them instead. Tsarist officials found that their ability to have orders obeyed simply evaporated.

Refusing an imperial order to disband, the Duma (parliament) stepped into the vacuum and named a provisional government on March 12 from among its party leaders. The dominant group in this legislature, elected by increasingly restricted suffrage since the creation of the Duma had been forced on the tsar in 1905, would have preferred a constitutional monarchy. But even such constitutional monarchists as Professor Pavel Miliukov, the new foreign minister, came to see that only a totally new regime had any chance of restoring public order. They persuaded the tsar to yield to the inevitable. He abdicated on March 12, naming Prince George Lvov, the Duma's choice, to be prime minister.[4] Prince Lvov was a respected but ineffectual constitutional monarchist who had headed the Union of Zemstvos and Towns.

Provisional Government and the Soviets

It was relatively easy to form a provisional government; to have its authority accepted and its orders obeyed was more difficult. The Provisional Government sprang from a legislature that had become less and less representative since its beginnings in the Revolution of 1905. In a country 80 percent peasant, it was a parliament of gentry, middle-class professional men, businessmen, and intellectuals. In essence, the Provisional Government's challenge was whether Russia's small liberal elite could succeed where the tsarist autocracy had failed: Could it gird a backward and weary country to go on with the war effort?

That challenge was vastly complicated by the existence of another power in the land, the soviets. *Soviet* is simply the Russian word for council or committee. In 1917, the memory was still fresh of the 1905 St. Petersburg soviet, the steering committee of militant workers formed to guide the general strike of that year. A new Petrograd soviet sprang into being spontaneously in March 1917, led by workers' leaders who had already participated in a joint regulatory agency, the War Industries Committee. The executive committee of the Petrograd soviet, sitting day and night in a girls' school, the Smolny Institute, as a permanent town meeting open to the public, became a sounding board for mass feelings in the capital. More importantly, it issued its own orders and had some sway over hundreds of similar soviets springing up in army units, other factory towns, and even in the countryside. When an all-Russian congress of soviets met in Petrograd on April 11, it brought together workers' delegates from 138 local soviets and soldiers' delegates from 7 armies, 13 rear units, and 26 frontline units.[5]

Whereas the Provisional Government was dominated by liberals, most soviet members were socialists of one school or another. One important current was composed of Social Democrats, Marxists who believed that a growing proletariat of industrial wage

---

[4]The tsar and the rest of the imperial family were subsequently put to death by their guards during the night of July 16, 1918, at Ekaterinburg, when it seemed likely that they might be rescued by counterrevolutionary troops.

[5]William Henry Chamberlin, *The Russian Revolution,* vol. 1 (New York, 1935), p. 112.

earners would eventually succeed in replacing privately owned factories, farms, and stores with collectivized production and distribution. Most Russian Social Democrats, heavily influenced by Western European parliamentary socialism, believed that backward Russia would not be ripe for socialism until industry had become as predominant in the Russian economy as it was already in Britain and Germany. In the meantime, they urged Russia along the path already taken by the West, convinced that if they helped the middle class achieve industrial growth and constitutional reform in Russia, the eventual socialist stage would be brought that much nearer. These reformist Social Democrats, known as Mensheviks, wanted to form a mass electoral socialist party on the Western model.

A vigorous but small faction of Russian Social Democrats, the Bolsheviks,[6] agreed on orthodox Marxist goals but disagreed vehemently that electoral politics was the proper means to achieve them for Russia. Their exiled leader was Vladimir Ulianov (known by his underground name of V. I. Lenin), a public school official's son who had been radicalized at the age of seventeen when his older brother was implicated in an assassination attempt on Tsar Alexander III and executed in 1887. Lenin dismissed parliamentary tactics as incompatible with revolutionary organization and discipline. He believed that even before the proletariat was ready, its "vanguard" should form a tightly disciplined party of dedicated professional revolutionaries, fit for surviving tsarist police methods and for seizing any revolutionary opportunity that presented itself.

The most numerous socialists in the soviets were not Marxists at all but agrarians who believed that Russian peasants should follow their own non-Western path to socialism by expropriating the great estates and establishing a rural democracy on the basis of traditional village councils. These Socialist Revolutionaries, or SRs, were as impatient as the Bolsheviks for immediate revolutionary social and economic change. Unlike Lenin, however, they placed their hopes in peasants rather than urban workers, they were skeptical of disciplined organizations, and they were attracted to tactics of individual violence.

The nine months between the "February Revolution" and the second revolution in November 1917 (October, by the Russian calendar) are often summarized as a competition between two potential governments—the gentry and professional men of the Provisional Government on the one hand, and the radical lawyers and journalists with their worker and peasant following in the soviets on the other. We must qualify this neat picture, however, by pointing out that even the soviets fell far behind the spontaneous urges of city crowds and landless peasants. The first land seizures began in March, and army desertions swelled from a trickle to a flood after the Provisional Government attempted one more military offensive, the Brusilov offensive of July 1917. One's sense of the revolution is complete only if one looks beneath the organizations struggling for power at the summit to see millions of Russian farm laborers taking over estates and hundreds of thousands of soldiers walking away from the front.

---

[6]The word *Bolshevik* means simply "majority" in Russian. At a time when all Russian Social Democrats were either underground or in exile, the Bolsheviks had won a majority in a 1903 convention of exiles in Brussels and London. Subsequently, although the reformist minority (*Mensheviks*) of 1903 grew larger than the Bolsheviks after a Russian parliament was established in 1905, the two factions kept their original nicknames.

The Provisional Government was not completely without resources. It was immediately recognized and welcomed by the Western Allies who expected a new democratic regime to fight more effectively than the decrepit tsardom. It had the support of educated and skilled professional and business people. Its leaders were not without talent and idealism. They enacted such sweeping reforms as universal suffrage and the eight-hour day. They established civil equality for all citizens: Jews were no longer required to live in the regions of the Ukraine and Poland called the "Pale of Settlement"; Polish independence was recognized. The Provisional Government promised that royal and monastic lands would be confiscated and redistributed. It summoned a constitutional convention to meet in the fall of 1917. Not least, it initially enjoyed explicit support from the soviets. Even Lenin, whose return from Switzerland in a sealed train was secretly arranged by the Germans in April 1917 in hopes of further disorganizing the Russian war effort, called Russia "the freest country in the world."[7]

Lenin's arrival at Petrograd's Finland Station, a favorite scene in later Soviet iconography, opened a genuinely new phase of the revolution. Lenin's "April theses" (April 20, 1917) challenged the orthodox Marxist interpretation of the revolution. He argued that Russia was ripe to move at once beyond a bourgeois revolution toward socialism. Furthermore, Lenin presented a clear alternative program to the Provisional Government's mixture of democracy, eventual land reform, and continued war: immediate peace, land, and bread. He proposed to transfer "all power to the soviets," even though the Bolsheviks were still a minority in the councils.

From July 16 to 18, 1917, the Petrograd crowd, still inadequately fed and opposed to the renewed military offensive, rose against the Provisional Government. The demonstrations were spontaneous, but Lenin supported them publicly in order to keep the Bolsheviks from being left behind. The Provisional Government still had enough military force to crush the demonstrators, killing 200 people, and Lenin had to flee to Finland disguised as a locomotive fireman. The July Days showed that Lenin's hope of overthrowing the Provisional Government was still premature.

Only four months later, however, in November 1917, the Provisional Government was swept away almost as easily as tsardom had been swept away the previous February, and with fewer casualties than in July. Although its composition had shifted steadily leftward, the Provisional Government never caught up with the leftward course of mass opinion. Those constitutional liberals around Pavel Miliukov who wanted Russia to claim all its territorial war aims, such as the Straits of Constantinople, went out in May. Prince Lvov resigned after the July Days. By the fall of 1917, there were ten socialist ministers and six nonsocialist ones, with Aleksandr Kerensky, the only man of even the moderate left in the first Provisional Government, now as prime minister. The Provisional Government's reforms always fell behind rising expectations. The promise that the constitutional convention would eventually redistribute royal and monastic lands, for example, seemed irrelevant when peasants were already seizing land for themselves.

Continuing the war, above all, caught the Provisional Government between two irreconcilable demands. On the one hand, a unilateral peace was unthinkable to

---

[7]Quoted in Robert V. Daniels, *Red October: The Bolshevik Revolution of 1917* (Boston, 1984), p. 4.

most politically sophisticated Russians as long as German and Austrian troops had overrun part of Russian soil. Even a Bolshevik could agree that

> when an army faces an army, it would be the most insane policy to suggest to one of these armies to lay down its arms and go home. This would not be a policy of peace but a policy of slavery, which would be rejected with disgust by a free people.[8]

On the other hand, the Provisional Government had neither the skill nor the force to move enough men and matériel to wage war effectively. Lenin realized sooner than anyone else that merely to feed the population would require the Provisional Government to tamper with private property far more extensively than it was prepared to do. Caught in this dilemma, Kerensky ordered the offensive under General Brusilov in July, only to find that this action triggered the final dissolution of the army. The Provisional Government could make neither peace nor war.

If parliamentary government could not solve Russia's problems in 1917, perhaps a military dictatorship could. That solution also was attempted and proven unworkable

Document Illustration

Aleksandr Kerensky, last head of the Provisional Government in Russia, studying a map shortly before the Bolshevik Revolution, November 1917.

[8]Lev Kamenev, in *Pravda,* March 17, 1917. See Edward Hallett Carr, *The Bolshevik Revolution, 1917–1923,* vol. 1 (London, 1950), p. 75.

in 1917. General Lavr Kornilov tried to move troops into Petrograd to crush the rival power of the soviets in September. Kerensky's share in the "Kornilov affair" is probably forever clouded in mystery. The general's supporters asserted that it was Kerensky who asked for help; Kerensky claimed that his intentions had been misunderstood, and that he soon learned that Kornilov planned to sweep away democracy as well as the soviets. In any event, when Kornilov's troops began to move toward the capital, Kerensky turned for support to the left, his enemies of the July Days. He released some Bolsheviks from prison and distributed arms to volunteer units raised by the Petrograd soviet, the "Red Guards." The refusal of prosoviet railroad workers to transport Kornilov's equipment and the fraternization of his troops with Red Guards prevented Kornilov from even reaching Petrograd.

Kerensky thus thwarted a military takeover, but at the price of making his Provisional Government dependent on the soviets. As the desire for peace at any price spread rapidly within the soviets in the fall of 1917, Kerensky was left carrying on the hated war without any reliable sources of support.

The "October Revolution"

When Lenin returned secretly from Finland on October 20, he believed that the situation had been transformed in two significant ways since July. Within Russia, his Bolshevik group had become a majority in the Petrograd and Moscow soviets. Outside Russia, reports of unrest in the German High Seas Fleet at Kiel convinced Lenin that a worldwide revolution was at hand. Lenin argued day and night to convince his fellow Bolshevik leaders that "we are on the threshold of a world proletarian revolution."[9] To let that moment pass, Lenin maintained, would be the ultimate betrayal of Europe's war-weary poor.

Lenin's eloquence met formidable opposition. He expected nothing else from the Mensheviks, who continued to support Kerensky against him. But there was substantial opposition even among Lenin's "old Bolshevik" colleagues. Lev Kamenev had been convinced by the bloody repression of the July Days that any Bolshevik insurrection would be premature. The Bolsheviks would be decimated and their historic chance lost. Their opportunity, argued Kamenev and other old Bolsheviks like Grigori Zinoviev, lay in awaiting the impending constitutional convention and fulfilling the role of militant opposition within a broader democratic regime. It would be wiser to grow within a democracy until the time was ripe than to attempt a premature *coup* and provoke counterrevolution. At the rate things were going, Kamenev contended, the time would be ripe soon.

Away with these "constitutional illusions," Lenin retorted. With passionate conviction, he built up a majority within the Bolshevik Central Committee in favor of immediate insurrection against the Provisional Government without waiting for the constitutional convention. He drew to his side Leon Trotsky, a brilliant young former Menshevik who had once opposed the "barracks regime" of the Bolshevik Party

---

[9]Quoted in Daniels, p. 60. Lenin does not seem to have known about the French Army mutinies of May and June 1917, which might have strengthened his case.

organization, but who had been radicalized by opposition to the war. Other Bolsheviks acquiesced because they feared that Kerensky was about to make a preemptive move against the soviets. A number of militant agrarian revolutionaries (SRs), less committed to awaiting the historically ripe moment than many proper Marxists, also sided with Lenin.

This group turned the Petrograd soviet into a base for Lenin's attempt to seize the central power. This was to be no spontaneous street demonstration by the hungry as in March and in July. "Insurrection is an art,"[10] although it must have broad popular support to succeed. Lenin and Trotsky formed a Military Revolutionary Committee of the Petrograd soviet on October 22 and 23 to plan the seizure of the principal government and communications centers of Petrograd.

© Bettmann / CORBIS

Bolsheviks charge on the Winter Palace, headquarters of the Provisional Government, Petrograd, November 9, 1917 (reconstituted by filmmaker Sergei Eisenstein).

[10]Lenin, quoted in Robert Service, *Lenin: A Political Life* (Bloomington, Ind., 1991), vol. 2, p. 253.

The Bolshevik forces acted in the night of November 9 (October 25, old style, hence "October Revolution"). They had the support of most soldiers of the Petrograd garrison, who had been angered at Kerensky's attempts to send them to the front. The garrison's support meant easy Bolshevik access to weapons. The sailors of the naval base at Kronstadt, who had always been radical, moved the cruiser *Aurora* up the Neva River to command the Winter Palace, seat of the Provisional Government. Unable to raise military support from outside the city, the Provisional Government began to defend the Winter Palace with military school cadets and a unit of 140 young middle-class women that Kerensky had formed earlier in an effort to shame Russian men into military service. Late in the night, when the *Aurora* had fired a few rounds (mostly blanks), these forces melted away, and the Provisional Government collapsed almost without bloodshed. Kerensky escaped from the city, and, when he was unable to muster enough troops to retake Petrograd, he went into hiding. He fled overseas in the summer of 1918.

THE BOLSHEVIK REGIME

It still remained for Lenin and his supporters to extend their control over Petrograd to the rest of Russia. It was a formidable task, which was not complete until after three more years and a bloody civil war, exacerbated by foreign intervention. That was a much greater achievement than overthrowing the moribund Provisional Government. In a sense, power in Russia had been up for grabs for nearly a year. It had eluded the tsar, constitutional monarchists, democrats, and moderate socialists. Lenin deserves to be known as a consummate revolutionary tactician, but even more as a regime builder. He was the first Russian who managed to ride and govern the whirlwind unleashed in March 1917.

He accomplished this, to be sure, at enormous cost not only to his original program but to his people. He promised Russians peace, land, and bread. Under him, they had civil war, famine, and dictatorial rule by a single party. But almost alone among historical revolutionary leaders he succeeded in keeping permanently in power those whom the crest of revolution had carried to the top.

Lenin's "Peace, Land, and Bread"

Land redistribution was Lenin's major trump card. By any normal head count, the SRs, or agrarian revolutionaries, stood closest to the mass aspirations of the land-hungry Russian rural population. Lenin's first step was to appropriate the SR program, while avoiding their inner divisions over how to apply it. In principle, as a good Marxist, he declared the land nationalized and turned its further distribution over to local rural soviets, which were supposed to keep the large estates unified as "model farms." In practice, he simply gave free rein to the peasants who were already seizing the land. Thenceforth, Lenin's regime was invulnerable to any force that seemed likely to try to restore the old landlords.

The promise of peace was more difficult to realize than that of land, for a separate peace with Germany meant accepting such humiliating terms that even

© Liaison Agency

Lenin addresses a crowd in Petrograd in 1917. To the right of the podium is Leon Trotsky. Trotsky was airbrushed out of this picture by the censors in the version used by Stalin's propagandists later, after Trotsky was eliminated.

leading Bolsheviks like Trotsky and Nikolai Bukharin wanted to pursue a "revolutionary war." It also meant acquiescing to the secession from the former Russian Empire of many non-Russian peoples, for whom revolution implied national independence.

In order to obtain peace, the Bolshevik leaders accepted harsh German terms on March 15, 1918. The Treaty of Brest-Litovsk recognized German conquests and detached eastern Poland, the Ukraine, Finland, and the Baltic provinces from Russia and levied a large indemnity on the Russians. Not until 1940 was Stalin, with Hitler's help, able to recover most of the 1914 frontier. For the moment, Lenin silenced his opposition by promising that the spreading world revolution would soon make this treaty obsolete.[11] But even this "revolutionary defeatism" did not bring peace to Russia, for anti-Bolshevik Russians, aided by Allied troops, began to attack the Soviet regime in the fall of 1918.

The promise of bread proved the most difficult of all. Giving free rein to peasant land hunger meant, as Lenin's less pragmatic Marxist critics like Rosa Luxemburg perceived, creation of a mass of small landholders jealously guarding their crops from the city. Peasant hoarding, combined with the civil war that broke out in late 1918, followed by poor harvests, led to years of food shortages and some periods of mass starvation, as in 1921.

---

[11]Lenin did unilaterally denounce the Treaty of Brest-Litovsk when revolution broke out in Germany in November 1918, but it was the successor states (the states that succeeded Austria-Hungary) and not Russia that gained the disputed ground at the Peace Conference. See chapter 6, pp. 172–181.

Refugee children during the famine in Russia, October 1921.

The Establishment of a New Autocracy

The Bolshevik Revolution produced neither the wider European revolution that Lenin expected, nor the new day of liberty that many of his followers expected. We shall discuss that first surprise later in this chapter; the second surprise needs fuller discussion here.

During 1917, the Russian people "threw themselves into a veritable orgy of democracy, carrying it far beyond their Western mentors into practically every area of life. . . . Power cascaded down like water from a broken dam, to every town and province, to every village and regiment, to every mob and every committee that would receive it."[12] In addition to the political councils, or soviets, that sprang up in Russian towns and villages, groups of soldiers formed committees in army units to elect their own officers, and groups of workers organized factory councils in the face of the frightened owners' attempts to lock them out.

This profusion of unplanned, often clumsy, grassroots initiatives was replaced by centralized state administration under one party during 1918 and 1919 as the Bolsheviks consolidated their power. The soldiers' councils gave way to traditionally commanded troops. The factory councils gave way to centralized agencies and trade unions controlled from above. Loose association with the non-Russian border peoples was replaced by centralization under Russian domination thinly disguised as a federal state. This was the system known as War Communism that Lenin established in Russia by 1919.

[12]Daniels, p. 4.

© Hulton Picture Library

Why did the promised liberty turn so quickly into dictatorship after the Bolshevik Revolution? One standard answer has been the authoritarian character of Leninist political theory. From the time of the split in the Russian Social Democratic Party in 1903, Lenin's followers were partisans of tightly disciplined party organization as opposed to those other Marxists who preferred to work more openly through a parliamentary party. The Leninist Party's proven effectiveness in November 1917, and the necessity afterward of governing as a minority only heightened the importance of the party structure in Lenin's eyes.

The absence of any established tradition of self-government in Russia certainly hindered the germination of democratic institutions in 1918 and 1919. When the old autocracy was swept away, it exposed a void that the chattering profusion of local councils was ill-equipped to fill. Lenin's party was available to fill the vacuum.

The Bolsheviks never pretended to run their regime democratically. Universal suffrage in Russia under the conditions of 1917 could produce only some kind of rural small landholder majority. The Bolsheviks wanted a dictatorship of the proletariat, or working class. If the Russian proletariat was still a minority, that anomaly would soon seem inconsequential when the world proletarian revolution spread from Russia to the more urban, industrialized states of Western Europe. Weighed against the possibility of the ultimate liberation of working people outside Russia, the necessity to govern against a majority in Russia seemed a small matter to Lenin and his followers.

Therefore the Bolsheviks dissolved the Constituent Assembly after its first day, when that body, summoned by the Provisional Government and eagerly awaited by Russian democrats, finally met in January 1918. As expected, Russia's first historic exercise of universal suffrage had produced an agrarian majority. The Constituent Assembly contained 420 agrarian revolutionaries (SRs), as against 225 Bolsheviks. For a time, Lenin governed in coalition with the left wing of the SRs. They broke in June 1918. The left-wing SRs, already opposed to the humiliating peace with Germany, resented Lenin's revival of central state administration. From that time until 1990, Russia was governed by dictatorial one-party rule.

There were also good pragmatic reasons for a new autocracy in Russia in 1918. One was the simple necessity to produce. Factory committees did not have the knowledge to revive production nor always much interest in it. They resisted all outside efforts to coordinate their work with others. The intensely revolutionary railroad workers, for example, took over and operated the lines but "for a long period set all external authority at defiance."[13] At issue was whether the new regime should limit itself to the coordination of the factory committees' local efforts or whether it should actually direct Russian industry in centralized fashion from above.

Lenin believed that the process of "trustification"[14] of industry, which capitalism had begun and which the war had intensified, must be carried through as the basis of a socialist economy. Each branch of industry, therefore, was not only nationalized

[13]Carr, vol. 2, p. 71.

[14]Ibid., p. 176.

but centralized into a single state trust. By the end of 1919, some ninety of these state trusts had been organized, all answering to a Supreme Council of National Economy at the top. The metallurgical industry, to take one example, was relatively easy to organize in this way since it had been highly concentrated before the war. By March 1918, it had been brought under a single state agency with a staff of 750, and its workers subjected to strict labor discipline through an official trade union. It did little good for partisans of the recent experiments in workers' control to object that "the masses are being cut off from living creative power in all branches of our national economy."[15] Lenin was convinced that socialist production could only be built on centralized organization.

Civil War

Leninist dictatorship was also a response to civil war. The Bolshevik regime had to fight for its life—against the armed opposition of anti-Bolshevik "white" armies ("white" as opposed to "red"), against border nationalities that declared their independence from Russia, against the intervention of Allied troops, and against the passive resistance of the peasants who kept up a "green revolution" to counter the "red revolution" that requisitioned their grain to feed the cities. The Red Army was engaged in active fighting on every Russian border at some time between 1918 and the end of 1920. At times, Bolshevik authority was reduced to the old Russian heartland. In the end, the Bolshevik regime survived to establish its rule over all the former Russian Empire except the western lands lost to Poland, Czechoslovakia, Romania, and the Baltic States. But during the struggle the regime had been transformed into a bureaucratic, one-party, centralized state. And it emerged from the civil war deeply marked by hostility to the Allied powers that had actively supported its opponents.

Allied intervention began as an attempt to keep the eastern front in action against the Germans. Even during the Kerensky period, as early as July 1917, the Western Allies sought ways to bolster the eastern front. The Bolsheviks' public quest for a separate peace after November 1917 was a serious blow to the British and French, who could never quite rid themselves of the suspicion that Lenin was a German agent. They foresaw the Germans moving all their troops to the west for a one-front, knockout blow. Some Western policymakers maintained contact with the Bolsheviks at first, in the hope that they would eventually reject the harsh German terms and fight on. Bolshevik acceptance of the German terms at Brest-Litovsk in March 1918, however, strengthened the case in Britain and France for intervention. The decision was made in June 1918 when the Germans, now freed in the east, broke through the Allied trenches and advanced to within thirty-seven miles of Paris, the closest since the First Battle of the Marne.

The British and French sent about 24,000 men to the northern Russian ports of Murmansk and Archangel in June 1918 to secure Allied supplies, to prevent German

---

[15]Ibid., p. 97.

and Bolshevik troops (still believed to be secret allies) from joining forces there, and "to make it safe for [anti-Bolshevik] Russian forces to come together in organized bodies in the north."[16] At about the same time, in Siberia, some 40,000 Czech troops (mostly former Austro-Hungarian soldiers captured by the Russians and now eager to fight on for Czech independence) revolted against the shaky local Bolshevik authorities and seized the Trans-Siberian Railroad in order to get out to the western front.

President Wilson, abruptly dropping his earlier reluctance to intervene in Russia, proposed a joint Japanese–American landing at Vladivostok to support the Czechs. The Japanese, who had stationed a few troops at Vladivostok as early as December 1917, now eagerly rushed in 72,000 more, far beyond the figures agreed on with Wilson. The American contingent there numbered about 7,000. In addition, early in the winter of 1918–1919, two British divisions were stationed on the oil-rich Russo-Turkish frontier, beyond the Caucasus, to hold the railroad line from Batum on the Black Sea to Baku on the Caspian. A French division, a French naval squadron, and a small Greek contingent were landed at Odessa, on the Black Sea coast of the Ukraine. In all, over 100,000 troops of fourteen countries—mostly Japanese, British, American, and French—were stationed at one time or another around the edges of Bolshevik territory.

Collections of The New York Public Library, Astor, Lenox, and Tilden Foundations

American soldiers in Vladivostok, 1918, marching in a parade organized to celebrate the arrival of the American expeditionary troops on Siberian soil.

[16]President Wilson's instructions, quoted in George F. Kennan, *The Decision to Intervene*, vol. 2 (Princeton, N.J., 1958), p. 418. At first reluctant, Wilson sent 5,500 United States troops to join them only in September.

The Allies' first intention had been to keep the Germans from filling the vacuum left by the Bolsheviks' separate peace. When the general armistice of November 11, 1918, made that purpose irrelevant, the Allied forces in Russia assumed a much more openly anti-Bolshevik function. Those forces were never very large or well equipped, and they never took direct combat roles in the developing Russian civil war. Nor were they ever united around any common Allied strategy in Russia. They gave moral and material encouragement to the anti-Bolshevik "white" Russian forces, however, and to secessionist border nationalities. Soviet Russians were always taught—with much justification—that the Allied governments did their best to bring the Bolshevik experiment down.

Civil war raged in Russia for more than two years. At one point or another between November 1918 and the end of 1920, anti-Bolshevik Russian armies supported by the Allies controlled broad sweeps of Russian territory, first in Siberia, then in the Ukraine, and finally along the Black Sea coast.

The main threat in 1920 came from Poland. In the spring, the new Polish state set out to conquer parts of Lithuania, western White Russia, and the Ukraine that were not ethnically Polish but had belonged to the medieval Kingdom of Poland at its height. After initial Polish successes, a young Bolshevik commander, Mikhail Tukhachevsky, drove the Poles back to the very gates of Warsaw. For a moment, Lenin believed that his defeat of Poland might set off the long-awaited revolution in Western Europe on which his ultimate survival in Russia seemed to depend. Aided by French supplies and advisors, however, the Poles managed to push back their borders somewhat east of the ethnic frontier. The Peace of Riga in March 1921 established these borders, which remained until 1939.

The anti-Bolshevik armies had experienced officers and trained soldiers on their side. They failed to defeat the untrained Bolshevik forces, however, partly because they took the offensive one by one, without any coordination. The Red Army, meanwhile, benefited from the talent for military organization revealed by the Bolshevik Commissar of War Leon Trotsky. The Bolsheviks were aided by fighting on interior lines, and by the anti-Bolsheviks' lack of popular appeal in the countryside. Despite their widespread passive resistance to Bolshevik control, Russian peasants were even less eager to help the "whites," who threatened to restore the landlords.

Early Bolshevik support for the independence of all the minority nationalities was a casualty of the civil war. The dissolution of the old Russian Empire into new revolutionary nations was acceptable to Lenin only on the premise of the worldwide revolution that he had believed was at hand. If a revolutionary regime survived only in Russia, the border nationalities became possible avenues for counterrevolution.

The Ukraine was a major lesson. In November 1917, the Ukrainian nationalists had taken the Bolshevik revolution as a signal to assume the home rule that the Provisional Government, no less than the tsars, had denied them. The Treaty of Brest-Litovsk in March 1918 detached the Ukraine from Russia and made it an independent state under German supervision. At the defeat of Germany in November 1918, a pro-Allied Menshevik socialist regime governed the still independent Ukraine, which now became a base for Allied anti-Bolshevik movements. When the Bolsheviks retook the Ukraine, first from the "white" Russian General Anton

Denikin in 1919 and then from the Poles in 1920, there was no further Bolshevik tolerance for Ukrainian self-determination.

After winning the civil war, the Bolshevik regime also reestablished direct control over separatist areas in the Caucasus: Georgia, Russian Armenia, and Azerbaijan. In December 1922, the Union of Soviet Socialist Republics was organized as a federal but unitary state. Its constituent parts (Russia, White Russia, the Ukraine, Transcaucasia, and—after 1925—a number of smaller ethnic regions like Uzbekistan, Turkestan, and Kazakstan) possessed substantial autonomy on paper, but the real power lay with the victorious central regime in the new capital of Moscow.

REVOLUTIONARY STIRRINGS IN WESTERN EUROPE, 1917

The news from Russia rang like a fire bell through the other belligerent countries in 1917. Some observers, especially in France, believed for a time that a democratic Russia would fight with heightened patriotic energies, as the citizens of the French Republic had done after 1792. But for those disheartened Europeans who were dreading the fourth winter of the war, Russian developments made it possible to think seriously for the first time about a compromise peace. They also were an object lesson in how easily autocracy could be overthrown. In fact, the Russian experience suggested that peace would not be possible until regimes had been changed. The Bolsheviks deliberately called serious attention to the question of war aims. In November 1917, they published the texts of secret treaties that the tsar had concluded in 1914 and 1915 providing for territorial gains for Russia and France in the event of victory. These revelations suggested that Europeans had been dying and starving for the dynastic or commercial advantages of a few.

As we have seen, all the belligerents' war efforts reached their nadir during 1917. In Italy, forty-one persons were killed during the summer in a bread riot in Turin. Both Pope Benedict XV and Italian socialists called for a compromise peace. When relief on the Russian front permitted, the Austrian army gave the Italians their most stunning defeat of the war at Caporetto in October 1917. They threatened to break out into the Po Valley. Morale was saved from a complete collapse only when the Italian army finally stopped the Austrians on the Piave River, just north of Venice.

In France, the front-line armies themselves threatened to come apart in May and June 1917. That spring, after the Nivelle offensive[17] had once more squandered thousands of lives in exchange for a few yards of terrain, reserve units refused to move up to the offensive. In addition to individual desertions, there were collective acts of mutiny. Some groups of soldiers commandeered trains and steamed for Paris. More than half of the 129 French divisions were affected, and 49 of them were probably unfit for action for several weeks. Although most of the agitation was directed specifically against the tactics of the mass offensive, the French general staff was tempted to believe that repression of antiwar opinion was the best remedy for the mutinies.

The Germans were unaware that parts of the French line lay virtually open in May and June 1917, but even if they had known, they were preoccupied with

---

[17]See chapter 3, pp. 80–81.

problems of their own. Sailors' demonstrations over food and living conditions affected the pent-up German fleet during that same summer. German internal politics in the summer of 1917 were dominated by efforts to assert parliamentary influence over war government and to renounce territorial aims in the July "Peace Resolution." The Germans' major ally, Austria-Hungary, was openly seeking a compromise peace in 1917.

Surmounting the 1917 slump required a mixture of force and persuasion from each war government. Public war weariness and Lenin's revelation of the secret treaties obliged the Allied governments to explain their war aims more clearly. Why, after all, should their populations sacrifice their property and their sons indefinitely for the rulers' glory or for secret territorial deals? Now that the United States had entered the war, President Woodrow Wilson took the Allied lead in explaining the better world of democracy, national independence, and permanent peace that the ultimate defeat of the Central Powers would make possible. As for France, less needed to be said about war aims as long as German troops occupied part of the country. Confident that the vocal advocates of a compromise peace would remain a minority, Clemenceau resolutely jailed his opponents and closed their newspapers after he assumed the prime ministry in November 1917. Even when a renewed German attack was expected in the spring of 1918, Clemenceau kept four cavalry divisions in reserve for possible internal use.

The German solution to the 1917 unrest was both autocratic and expansionist. With the support of the kaiser and of nationalist opinion, Field Marshal Hindenburg and General Ludendorff proposed to exploit Russian weakness in a final effort toward an expansionist victory. By straining every nerve, the Germans would be rewarded with territory in both east and west. At home, this meant silencing the parliamentary opposition that had renounced annexationist war aims in the summer of 1917. The kaiser's support was one element in the generals' success. By persuading him to replace Bethmann Hollweg as chancellor with the inexperienced and docile Michaelis,[18] they reduced parliamentary majorities to a cipher. The other element in their success was the extent to which German centrists, even some of those who had voted for the "Peace Resolution," welcomed the major German gains in the east obtained in the Treaty of Brest-Litovsk in March 1918. The victory over Russia convinced most German leaders to support the generals' gamble on a final major offensive in the west in 1918.

General Ludendorff's all-out attack in the west in March 1918 came nearer to breaking through into a decisive war of movement than any campaign since the First Battle of the Marne. Highly conscious of the political dimension of modern warfare, Ludendorff struck at the British first, on the theory that the French would send their reserves to the British sector only reluctantly. Then if a gap opened between the two armies, he planned to strike for Paris. Five successive German offensives between March and July 1918 pushed the Allied front back nearly forty miles. German troops were at the Marne again, only thirty-seven miles from Paris. But Ludendorff was never able to open the decisive gap he sought. The Allies united their command under the French General Ferdinand Foch and were heartened by

---

[18]See chapter 4, p. 98.

the American troops' arrival. It was the Allies who opened a hole in the overextended German line on July 18, in the Second Battle of the Marne. Having exhausted his reserves, Ludendorff could not prevent the initiative from passing for good into Allied hands. After July 1918, they advanced steadily toward the German frontier.

Ludendorff had made several serious errors. Determined to maintain enough troops in the east to hold the Germans' new territorial gains there, he failed to assemble sufficient force on the western front. He overestimated the exhausted Germans' willingness to fight on for territorial expansion. He underestimated the psychic and material impact of United States participation (over 2 million men by August 1918). Above all, by staking everything on a decisive expansionist campaign, he ruled out the more modest alternative of a fallback position on a defensive line to cover the German border during the negotiation of a compromise peace. When Ludendorff finally turned to a defensive strategy, no reserves of men or morale were left to support it.

THE GERMAN REVOLUTION, 1918–1919

It was General Ludendorff himself who announced to his stunned government on September 29, 1918, that the German army could not contain the Allied breakthrough and that the only way to defend German soil in the west was to make an immediate peace. In the next few weeks, he forced his incredulous government to ask President Wilson for a peace settlement based on the Fourteen Points,[19] and then was dismissed by the kaiser when he refused to accept the conditions the Allies imposed. Since Ludendorff himself helped spread the legend after the war that the German army had been "stabbed in the back" by revolutionaries at home, his initiatives in the first steps to an armistice must be emphasized.

Steps toward Revolution

When President Wilson refused to deal with the "arbitrary power" that had ruled Germany up to 1918, Ludendorff supported the resurrection of the parliamentary form of government that he had pushed aside in 1917. It suited him that civilian authorities should bear the responsibilities of defeat. He is supposed to have said, "They [the parliamentarians] made this soup. Now let them eat it." In this way the first steps of a German revolution, a constitutional revolution, came down from above. Prince Max of Baden, a moderate member of one of the German grand ducal families, was made chancellor. He accomplished at last the two reforms that German reformists had sought in vain under the prewar monarchy: the responsibility of the chancellor to a parliamentary majority instead of to the kaiser, and an end to the three-class voting system in the state of Prussia. But it was too late to head off with overdue reforms the anger and frustration of the German people.

[19]See chapter 6, pp. 158–159.

The next step toward revolution in Germany came from below. It came this time from the armed forces. Ludendorff had changed his mind by late October in favor of continued fighting to hold the richest mining regions of Alsace-Lorraine. Although Ludendorff was forced out of the army command by Prince Max, the kaiser aroused suspicions that he opposed an armistice by moving from Berlin to army headquarters on October 29. When units of the German High Seas Fleet at Kiel were ordered to put to sea to engage the British in a last major battle, the crews mutinied. The sailors' refusal to obey orders spread to the naval base ashore at Kiel on November 4, where sailors' councils were formed. From there the movement spread to the formation of soldiers' and workers' councils in military supply depots and war plants. Ludendorff had led Germans to believe in March 1918 that one final effort could win the war. When another war winter loomed in October 1918, the last links of loyalty that had bound German soldiers and civilians to extraordinary sacrifices simply snapped.

In early November the mass movement for peace took on revolutionary proportions. The federal German Empire seemed about to tear apart when the Kingdom of Bavaria tried to negotiate a separate peace on November 7. The antiwar parliamentary socialist Kurt Eisner led workers and the army garrison in Munich in an uprising that expelled the last Wittelsbach king; he then opened peace negotiations with the Allies. On the morning of November 9 thousands of Berlin workers went into the streets to demonstrate for peace. When it proved impossible to find reliable troops to move against them, the senior army commanders themselves—Generals Hindenburg and Groener, Ludendorff's successor—persuaded Wilhelm II to abdicate as king of Prussia and emperor of Germany before the collapse of all authority affected even the officers' ability to march their troops home.

The Socialist Struggle for Power

As in Russia a year earlier, the question in Germany on November 9, 1918, was who could pick up the pieces of a disintegrating nation. Along with the kaiser and the army command, much of the German parliamentary center had been compromised by its support for a war of territorial expansion rather than defense in 1918. The most important organized opposition was the German Socialist Party, and its leaders now stepped to the fore.

But which German socialists would prevail? The once highly organized German Social Democratic Party (SPD) was passionately divided over all that had happened in August 1914 and after. A majority clung to its prewar reformist tendencies. They wanted to set up a parliamentary republic first, within which they believed social democracy would germinate. The SPD majority was deeply discredited on the left, however, by its support for war credits in 1914. The minority, which had seceded in 1916 to form the Independent Social Democratic Party (USPD) in support of immediate compromise peace, was pulled in two ways in November 1918. Some members wanted to restore unity with the majority in this hour of peace and opportunity. Others were drawn to a small but militant antiparliamentary left, which demanded immediate social revolution through the soldiers', sailors', and workers' councils, on the Russian model. This movement, led by Karl Liebknecht and Rosa Luxemburg, called itself "Spartacus" after the Roman gladiator-revolutionary of the first century B.C.

These two tendencies produced two parallel authorities in Germany at the end of 1918. At 2:00 P.M. on November 9, Philip Scheidemann of the SPD majority proclaimed a parliamentary republic from a window of the Reichstag building. At 4:00 P.M., Karl Liebknecht declared a revolutionary socialist republic from a window of the royal palace, now held by delegations of the soldiers' and workers' councils. On the reformist side emerged a provisional executive of six "peoples' commissars," elected by the Berlin soldiers' and workers' councils on November 10 but composed of majority SPD and reformist USPD leaders. Its dominant personality was Friedrich Ebert, a saddlemaker turned SPD functionary. A career devoted to the creation of the SPD's first paid permanent staff in the early 1900s predisposed Ebert to orderly administration. On the revolutionary side were the Spartacists in the councils, who wanted to bypass a constitutional assembly and proceed directly to workers' control of a socialist state through the German equivalent of soviets.

This conflict of parallel authorities was resolved during the winter of 1918–1919 in the opposite direction from the Russian case. In Russia, Lenin's Bolsheviks had come to control the Petrograd soviet by the end of August 1917. The German soldiers' and workers' councils remained primarily in the hands of followers of the majority SPD. When an all-German congress of soldiers' and workers' councils was held in December 1918, only 10 of the 488 delegates were Spartacists. No less than the majority SPD leadership, the councils called for political democracy first. They supported the provisional executive's call for a constitutional assembly to be elected in January 1919.

As for the Spartacists, Rosa Luxemburg rejected Lenin's strategy of firm party control, preferring spontaneity in revolution and direct worker control after revolution. Thus the Spartacists deprived themselves of one of Lenin's decisive advantages—a disciplined party structure. More importantly, there was no massive popular ground swell to bolster the Spartacists. Ebert preempted the mass peace movement by concluding on November 11, 1918, the armistice that Prince Max had already prepared. No immense land-hungry mass was burning manor houses and seizing estates in Germany. Of Lenin's three great issues—peace, land, and bread—only bread was seriously lacking in Germany in the winter of 1918–1919, and Ebert could blame that on the Allied blockade.

The Failure of the Social Revolution

During December 1918 and January 1919, the German social revolution was liquidated by two simultaneous processes: failure to seize power from below and repression from above. From below, militants among the soldiers' and workers' councils simply failed to take over the decisive political and economic institutions. The way in which the professional state administration and the traditional ruling families reestablished control of local government during the weeks following November 9, 1918, has been revealingly studied in the old port city of Hamburg.[20] The councils

---

[20]Richard A. Comfort, *Revolutionary Hamburg: Labor Politics in the Early Weimar Republic* (Stanford, Calif., 1966).

attempted to govern the city, but in the very act of trying to revive administration they found they needed tax revenues. The old merchant families, which had long dominated the Hamburg senate, offered the councils financial support in return for moderation. For lack of other leadership, the Hamburg soldiers' council fell into the hands of an energetic career officer. The reformist trade unions and SPD officials of Hamburg retained the loyalty of many workers. Thus normal administration revived in Hamburg. The same quiet return to normalcy occurred in many German localities. Social and governmental structure had not dissolved in Germany as it had in Russia in 1917. Only very briefly was there any power vacuum at the grassroots level.

At the top, the provisional executive repressed the Spartacists with the ferocity of sectarian warfare. Friedrich Ebert clearly feared the Spartacists and the radical minority in the soldiers' and workers' council movement more than he feared the German Empire's traditional state services and officer corps. During the few days when German institutions were genuinely malleable, Ebert turned his attention to restoring order instead of achieving basic social change. In a celebrated telephone conversation with General Groener on November 9, he agreed to leave intact the authority of the Imperial Officer Corps (all sworn to personal loyalty to the kaiser) in exchange for the High Command's help in controlling the soldiers' and workers' councils.

AKG London

Spartacists fire from behind a makeshift barricade of rolls of newsprint, Berlin, January 1919.

The decisive test came in early January 1919. When Ebert removed the Berlin police chief who had been installed by the councils, demonstrators began occupying public buildings. Karl Liebknecht and Rosa Luxemburg, who had just transformed the Spartacus movement into a new German Communist Party on December 30, 1918, felt they had to assume leadership, even though they feared that the time was not ripe for a seizure of power. Ebert was determined to crush these rivals to the reformist socialists' control. Having failed to set up an armed force directly loyal to the new regime, however, Ebert was obliged to rely on General Groener and the Imperial Officer Corps and on antirevolutionary volunteers known as *Freikorps* (free corps), which the officers had quietly formed to keep order while the regular army was being demobilized. Although the SPD minister of defense, Gustav Noske, was nominally in charge of keeping order, it was the *Freikorps,* steeped in front fighters' brutality and animosity toward workers, who actually broke up the Spartacist demonstrations. Officers murdered Luxemburg and Liebknecht while transferring them from one prison to another.

Hundreds were killed in Berlin in this Spartacist uprising, and a thousand in a second revolt in March. Noske said, "Somebody has to be the bloodhound," and thus earned the epithet of "the bloodhound of Kiel." Ebert was secure but at the price of the left's bitter resentment and of the surviving independence of the old Imperial Officer Corps.

Restoring administration also meant arresting regional separatism. The revolutionary movement had gone furthest in the former Kingdom of Bavaria, which had never been fully reconciled to Prussian domination of the German Empire. When the new Bavarian socialist leader Kurt Eisner was assassinated in February 1919, his fellow reformist socialists were unable to hold the state together. During the week of April 7, 1919, members of a revolutionary workers' council and a group of intellectuals including the playwright Ernst Toller formed a communist republic in Munich. Again, Ebert in Berlin had no weapon except the army and the *Freikorps.* The destruction of the Munich communist republic by the *Freikorps* was savage. Although the majority socialists were restored to nominal power there, real power lay with the army and *Freikorps.* Ebert was unable to keep Bavaria within the German republic without delivering it over to his own enemies.

On the surface, Germany had accomplished its democratic revolution. The constitutional assembly elected in January 1919 met in Weimar, a provincial capital far removed from Prussian pomp, to found a parliamentary republic that would replace the German Empire's narrow oligarchy with true popular sovereignty. The Weimar Republic seemed to embody the most carefully planned democratic institutions, including women's suffrage. But in his eagerness to restore normal government in 1918 and 1919, Ebert had allowed the traditional bureaucracy, the imperial army, and the oligarchy of great corporations and Prussian estates to survive untouched. The Weimar Constitution was imposed upon the old imperial society, without making significant structural changes in it. The republic had come into being over the bodies of some of its natural supporters. It also bore the stigma of having to accept a harsh peace from the Allies. The nationalists, who hated the Weimar Republic for that, had plenty of leverage thereafter with which to fight it. It would be hard to defend the Weimar Republic from its internal enemies.

THE DISSOLUTION OF AUSTRIA-HUNGARY, 1918–1919

The Habsburg Empire perished in the war it had provoked. The very nationalism that the imperial regime had tried to stifle by making war on Serbia in July 1914 was greatly magnified by the war, until by 1918 the various component peoples simply went their own way. The monarchy's authority evaporated. Within the borders of the old empire, the revolutionary impulses of the war's last days were largely absorbed in the enterprise of carving successor states out of the former ethnic parts.

After the disillusioning later history of these successor states, the victors of the First World War, and especially United States President Woodrow Wilson, have frequently been accused of sacrificing a useful federal system in the Danube basin to the principle of national self-determination. In reality, the old monarchy could no more have been put together again in 1918 than Humpty Dumpty. Even without the war, one wonders how much longer dynastic loyalty could have held that linguistic patchwork together. One of the more optimistic of the monarchy's historians thinks that "in 1914 the future of the monarchy was at best problematical."[21]

Those who believe the old empire was salvageable rest their case on dreams of greater federal autonomy. Habsburg federalists proposed to grant the most vocal unsatisfied minorities, the Czechs and South Slavs, the same local self-rule already enjoyed by the Germans of Austria, the Magyars of Hungary, and, to a more limited extent, the Poles of Galicia and the Croats with their own parliament *(Sabor)* in Hungary. The heir to the throne himself, Archduke Franz Ferdinand, was sympathetic to this approach.

Evolution toward a federal solution was blocked, however. Neither Czechs nor South Slavs could be satisfied without lands taken from both halves of the dual monarchy, Austria and Hungary.[22] The Hungarians held a veto over any such compromises. Ever since the first "compromise" of 1867 had elevated the Kingdom of Hungary to parity with the Empire of Austria in a dual monarchy, no further compromise had been possible since it would have to take place at the Magyars' expense. No new ethnic groups could be satisfied without alienating those already satisfied. Having moved toward a federal solution by becoming a dual monarchy, Austria-Hungary was blocked from moving on to becoming a triple or quadruple one. Even if the Central Powers had won the First World War, the problem of absorbing more Poles from, say, Russian Poland into a new Habsburg Kingdom of Poland in a triple monarchy, would have fatally unbalanced the empire's delicate ethnic standoff of 1914.[23]

It is difficult to avoid an air of fatality in any detailed account of the wartime evolution of the Habsburgs' subjects from federalist goals to goals of outright independence. Through 1916, it must be admitted, dynastic loyalties still showed astonishing vitality. Many Polish nationalists supported the Austro-Hungarian cause because they still thought that defeat of Tsarist Russia with its large Polish minority

---

[21]C. A. Macartney, *The Habsburg Empire, 1790–1918* (New York, 1969), p. 810.

[22]See maps, p. 47 and inside front cover.

[23]Lewis Namier, "The Downfall of the Habsburg Monarchy," in *Vanished Supremacies* (New York, 1958), p. 127.

offered the best chance of reconstituting the Polish national state, as a Habsburg Kingdom of Poland. The Catholic Croats were loyal, and even the most advanced Czech nationalists were still either federalists or discreetly silent. The Czecho-Slovak National Council, set up in early 1915 in Paris by a professor from Prague, Thomas G. Masaryk, had as yet little direct influence at home. The same can be said for the Yugoslav Committee established in London in May 1915.

The Breakdown of Dynastic Loyalties

The first major change in the attitude of the Habsburg minorities followed the entry into the war of additional states whose ethnic brothers lived within the Austro-Hungarian realm. The Italian declaration of war on Austria-Hungary on May 23, 1915, and the Romanian declaration in August 1916, won two Habsburg minorities over to the Allied cause: the Italians along the Adriatic coast, and the Romanians of Transylvania. This meant that an Allied victory must now entail territorial losses for Austria-Hungary. Then, at the end of 1916, Emperor Franz Josef died at the age of eighty-six, snapping a personal link on which the empire depended. Even more influential was the Russian Revolution of February 1917. Now the Poles could perceive more hope for a revived national state on Allied terms than on German-Habsburg terms.

The Bolshevik "October Revolution" in 1917 had a mixed effect on Habsburg solidarity. In the short run, by taking the pressure off the eastern front, the Bolsheviks allowed the Austro-Hungarians to turn all their resources to defeating the Italians at Caporetto. In the long run, however, the Bolsheviks brought home to the war-weary Habsburg subjects how fragile an ancient autocracy was, and gave them an object lesson in self-determination.

War weariness in the Habsburg Empire, therefore, took the form of ethnic polarization. Not only did the minorities come to despair of Habsburg federalism, the dominant German and Hungarian nationalities became even less willing to grant concessions. The first wartime meeting of the Austrian parliament *(Reichsrat)* on May 20, 1917, only gave a public forum to demands for extensive ethnic autonomy. The Czech and South Slav delegates called for "a federal state of free national states with equal rights."

When the imperial government tried to buy off secessionist feelings in 1918 with promises of cultural autonomy that might have been welcomed before 1914, it was too late. Furthermore, the last Habsburg struggles exposed the final flaw: the disaffection of the dominant national elites, German and Magyar. When the young Emperor Karl's secret peace feelers to the Allies were revealed to the world by Clemenceau in the spring of 1918, many German nationalists decided that Habsburg dynastic interests (peace) diverged from German national interests (victory for Berlin). Magyar leaders became even more disaffected with a dynasty that threatened to buy off the minorities with concessions at Hungarian expense.

These developments show that the Allies were not the principal agents in the destruction of the Habsburg Empire. They hastened its dissolution, however, by propaganda for independence of subject peoples in 1918. During the early years of the war the British and French, allied to multinational and autocratic Russia, had said nothing about self-determination. The Russian Revolution, combined with American entry into the war, put democratic reform forward as a major Allied war aim. Woodrow Wilson favored some kind of federal solution for Austria-Hungary in his Fourteen Points speech given in January 1918; later the Allies supported the full independence of subject peoples. In June 1918, the United States promised the South Slavs "complete freedom," even though there were difficulties with Italian claims to the lands at the head of the Adriatic. During the summer, the Allies recognized the full sovereignty of the Polish and Czech national committees located in Paris.

The end came, militarily, in October 1918. An Allied army, mostly French, moving north from Greece forced Bulgaria out of the war at the end of September 1918. Bulgaria's request for an armistice on September 26 opened the Habsburg forces to a threat from the south. At the same time, the Italians began a new campaign at the end of October and defeated the Austrians at Vittorio Veneto. When the Habsburg regime asked for an armistice on November 4, much of its territory was already under the control of de facto Polish, Czech, and South Slav governments.

Nation-Building in the Successor States

Would national successions lead to social revolution? Eastern Europe, at the Soviet borders, was in chaos. Like Russia, much of Eastern Europe had a huge land-hungry peasantry. Seizure of the great estates seemed likely to provide revolutionary fuel. Starving urban workers and land-grabbing peasants might well mix the same brew as in the Russia of 1917.

In all the emerging successor states except one, however, Social Democrats and peasant (or agrarian) parties, rather than Bolsheviks, managed to harness these discontents. Potential class conflicts were neutralized among many Eastern European peoples by ethnic pride and by the excitement of creating or reviving a nation. Ethnic revival aroused strong emotions among the poor as well as in the educated middle classes of Eastern Europe, contrary to Karl Marx's assertion in 1848 that workers have no country. Socialist leaders were well aware before 1914 that international working-class solidarity faced exceptional obstacles in the Austro-Hungarian climate of sharpening ethnic identity. German skilled workers excluded Czechs from their trade unions in Bohemia, for example, while across the frontier in Polish-speaking parts of the German Empire, patriotic Polish workers withdrew from the socialist party (SPD) to form their own Polish Social Democratic Party in 1903. The Austrian socialist intellectual Otto Bauer[24] warned that independence for every ethnic group, however small, was a retrograde step unless it followed the creation of an international socialist world economy. His views carried little weight with ordinary workers, however, among whom nationalism was a more vital loyalty

[24]Otto Bauer's *Die Nationalitätenfrage und die Sozialdemokratie* (Vienna, 1907) was the most notable "Austro-Marxist" effort to find a place for nationalism within the Marxist values of world economic system and class loyalty.

than socialism. When the chance for ethnic self-determination came in 1918, workers danced in the streets of Prague, Warsaw, and Belgrade alongside the nationalist middle class.

Peasants, too, could submerge their revolutionary energies in nation-building in many parts of the Habsburg lands. In Czechoslovakia, for example, where the big landlords were mostly German in the Czech areas and mostly Hungarian in the Slovak areas, expropriation of estates seemed more a national than a class act.

The passions for change and reform in Eastern Europe were channeled mostly into the heady excitement of building new nations that would be reformist and democratic but not socially revolutionary. This was true of most of the successor states, whether they were new states (Czechoslovakia, Yugoslavia), expanded nineteenth-century states (Romania), or revived long-eclipsed states (Poland).

The major exception was Hungary, where national independence brought no satisfaction. The Magyar leaders decided in 1918 that they could better defend their historic borders as a separate state than as one subject to the frantic last-minute ethnic reorganization proposed by Emperor Karl. Hungarian independence thus began as a conservative reaction to preserve the Magyar predominance and the limited suffrage of the old Kingdom of Hungary. The wartime Magyar leaders declared their independence of all but the personal Habsburg tie on October 16. But they were unable to reach a separate armistice through President Wilson without internal reforms. On October 31, therefore, they handed over power to Count Mihály Károlyi, a maverick reformist aristocrat who had led the small

Document Illustration

A demonstration in the streets of Budapest during the establishment of the national-democratic regime in October 1918.

wartime pacifist opposition. Károlyi declared Hungary an independent republic on November 16.

Károlyi's October Republic rested on the calculation that the Allies would reward a new, democratic Hungary, as long as it accepted the universal suffrage and minority language rights the old oligarchy had always resisted, by maintaining the historic Hungarian borders. That calculation was mistaken. The Allied commander in southeastern Europe, the French General Franchet d'Esperey, did not prevent Hungary's new neighbors from seizing territories. Romanian armies advanced into the rich grain-growing plain of Transylvania, where a majority of the peasants spoke Romanian. The Slovaks joined the new Czechoslovak state that had been proclaimed on October 21. The South Slavs of both Austria and Hungary formed the Kingdom of Serbs, Croats, and Slovenes (later Yugoslavia) on October 29.

Since the Allies, particularly the French, who had the only Allied armed force in the area, favored Romania and Czechoslovakia as building blocks of the new Eastern Europe, Károlyi could not keep Hungary intact by dealing with the Allies. Instead, the Allies treated Károlyi's Hungary as a defeated enemy. When General Franchet d'Esperey ordered Hungarian troops on March 20, 1919, to withdraw behind a line that Hungarians feared would be the new border, Károlyi abandoned power. It was grasped by Béla Kun, a Hungarian journalist who had been in Moscow in 1917 and who returned now to lead the Hungarian Bolshevik movement. Kun managed to gain command of the rising tide of strikes and demonstrations in hungry Budapest during the spring of 1919. There was no other alternative to the left of Count Károlyi, for the Hungarian Social Democrats had been a major component of the October Republic.

The Béla Kun Regime

Béla Kun's soviet regime governed in Budapest for 133 days, from March 20 to August 1, 1919. It was the only soviet regime of Eastern Europe between Munich and Moscow and the longest-lived soviet government outside Russia. It controlled Budapest and those parts of the countryside not occupied by Romanian troops, the French, or the counterrevolutionary Hungarian movement that soon formed in southern Hungary under Allied protection.[25]

Kun tried to establish socialism immediately in Hungary, assisted by the Marxist philosopher and minister of culture, Georg Lukács, and by earthier figures such as Minister of the Interior Tibor Szamuelly, whose "Red Terror" produced about fifty deaths. Rumors of a much larger figure terrified the Hungarian upper classes. Kun's decisive enemies in agrarian Hungary were not bourgeois, however, but peasants. Unlike the Russian soviet regime, the Budapest soviet alienated the peasantry from the very beginning. Less pragmatic than Lenin, Kun nationalized the great estates rather than distribute them to small landholders. Furthermore, caught in the classic city–country conflict of any urban regime short of food, he paid for the crops he requisitioned in inflated paper currency. The countryside responded with

[25]See chapter 7, pp. 214–217.

the traditional peasant reactions of hoarding and crop destruction. Kun was unable to deliver peace, land, or bread.

Some Hungarian patriots had supported Kun's regime, believing that Russian aid would help preserve Hungary's historic frontiers against the Allies. Kun's Russian gamble worked no better than Károlyi's Allied gamble. Lenin was occupied at home with civil war and Allied intervention. The Allies saw the Budapest soviet as an unacceptable extension of Bolshevism westward, since it helped inspire the Munich soviet, a revolutionary uprising in Austria, and widespread simultaneous strikes in Italy and France. The French therefore encouraged the Romanian army to advance into Hungary. It captured Budapest in early August 1919. Kun fled. Since the Social Democrats and constitutional republicans had been discredited earlier in the October Republic, Hungary was delivered over to the reactionary former commander in chief of the Austro-Hungarian navy, Admiral Miklós Horthy. His "White Terror" took twice as many lives as had Szamuelly's "Red Terror" in the preceding spring.[26]

BRITAIN, FRANCE, ITALY: THE UNREST OF 1919–1920

The postwar revolutionary wave was not limited to throwing out defeated regimes. Accumulated war weariness and social bitterness burst out even in the victorious countries. Wartime resentments there were compounded by postwar unemployment as demobilization began. In Britain, the traditional "red" areas, especially the Clydeside area of Scotland, experimented with workers' councils under the wartime rebel shop-steward leadership. British workers, led by Ernest Bevin's dockers, struck against ships carrying supplies to anti-Bolsheviks in Russia. In France, an extensive general strike on May 1, 1919, and a somewhat smaller one in May 1920 marked the historic high-water mark of the syndicalist tactic of sponsoring one great insurrectionary day. There was considerable labor militancy even in the United States, culminating in the Seattle general strike of 1920. Italy came close to real social dissolution in the months following the war. It came closer perhaps even than Germany, where most revolutionary pressures were more easily channeled into mere constitutional democratization.

Postwar yearnings for fundamental change took a more irrepressible form in Italy than in the other victor nations because, first of all, few Italians felt any sense of victory. Italy's limited territorial gains, compared with its wartime dreams of control over the whole Adriatic area and southern Asia Minor, seemed a poor recompense for the war's cost in men, effort, and material. Second, ineffective war government had sharpened social conflict in Italy. In a nation already divided between an industrial north and a virtually feudal south, social antagonisms were too raw to bear wartime pressures well. Third, Italy suffered the worst inflation of any victor power. The cost of living quadrupled during the war, with wages trailing behind, and then doubled again in the two immediate postwar years. To make matters worse, wartime regimes had encouraged postwar hopes. Premier Antonio

---

[26]See chapter 7, pp. 216–217.

Salandra had promised in 1916 that returning veterans would receive land. At the war's end, three virulent protest movements—industrial strikes, agrarian land seizures, and nationalist demonstrations—carried Italy to the brink of revolution.

The strike movement of 1919 and 1920 exceeded anything in prior Italian experience. Whereas an average of 200,000 Italian workmen had gone out on strike each year in the immediate prewar decade, five times that many (about 1 million) went out on strike in 1919 and six times that many (about 1.2 million) in 1920. About 320 persons were killed in 140 clashes between police and demonstrators between April 1919 and September 1920.

One strike motive was support for the Soviet Union against Western intervention. A general strike was called for July 19 and 20, 1919, after the Italian government had extended diplomatic recognition to the "White" Russian opponents of Lenin's regime. A more immediate spur was the rapid rise in the cost of living, which soon outran all wage settlements. Worker-elected factory councils, which had acquired a kind of unofficial existence under war government, now claimed a larger role in plant management and a future position as Italian soviets.

The northern industrial cities of Milan and Turin were the centers of worker militancy. In Milan, long negotiations over wages between factory owners and the leading metalworkers' union (FIOM) were sharpened by worker slowdowns. The exasperated employers locked the workers out of the Alfa-Romeo automobile works on August 30, 1920. In response, FIOM occupied all the factories in the Milan area, then in Turin, and eventually in fifty-nine cities. Some 500,000 strikers were involved. Factory councils maintained production in the plants as a demonstration of the soviet principle, under the intellectual leadership of Antonio Gramsci of Turin, the chief theoretician of communism in modern Italy.

The occupation of the factories in August and September 1920 was the end, rather than the beginning, of the workers' revolutionary wave in postwar Italy. Premier Giovanni Giolitti understood far more clearly than the factory owners that the workers did not know what to do next. He insisted on negotiation rather than the use of armed force. After three weeks, the workers, their élan broken, evacuated the factories on the basis of a quite traditional wage raise and an essentially meaningless recognition of the principle of workers' councils that was soon forgotten.

Meanwhile, a wave of land seizures during 1919 frightened rural farm and estate owners. Wartime promises of land to veterans coincided with long-felt peasant resentments against the owners of uncultivated great estates and hunting preserves. In the spring of 1919, bands of rural day laborers and sharecroppers simply occupied fallow lands in many parts of Italy, as they had done in many earlier periods of unrest. The innovation of 1919, however, was the degree of organized support that these land seizures received. Veterans' movements, radical Catholic movements *(Popolari)* in the south and in Lombardy and Tuscany, and socialist agricultural labor unions in the traditionally "red" rural areas around Bologna, all provided organized support for rural militants. In some areas, the landless marched out to fallow lands with bands and banners to dig and plough, encouraged by legislative proposals to grant squatter's rights on uncultivated lands. Farm laborers were organized for wage settlements and for "estate councils," the counterpart of factory councils. Little land actually changed hands by force in the north, although some did in the center and south. In the north, however, many landowners found they could no longer hire farm labor except on the terms demanded by socialist and Catholic rural unions and peasant cooperatives.

The third kind of postwar direct-action movement was the nationalist seizure of territories claimed by Italy but denied it at the Paris Peace Conference. When the Habsburg Empire disintegrated, Italian troops established themselves further east around the head of the Adriatic than wartime promises had provided for; notably, they occupied the port of Fiume (or Rijeka, as the Yugoslavs called it). The Peace Conference's orders for the withdrawal of Italian forces led to angry protests in Italy. The bombastic poet and war hero Gabriele D'Annunzio led 8,000 volunteers, mostly war veterans, to seize the area in September 1919. While the Italian government played for time, D'Annunzio set up the "Republic of Carnaro," which displayed many of the themes and postures of later fascism on a comic-opera scale. Neither rhetoric nor appeals to Lenin and the Sinn Fein could save him, however, when the Italian government reached agreement with the Yugoslavs to make Fiume an international free city. Italian troops expelled D'Annunzio's legionnaires in December 1920. But the incident established a lasting resentment among many veterans and a precedent of nationalist direct action to trouble later Italian politics.

Postwar insurrectionary pressures were clearly diminishing in Italy by the fall of 1920. In retrospect, the impression of imminent revolution was misleading. It is true that the great majority of organized Italian socialists were committed to revolution and supported the position known as "maximalism": They refused any alliances with "bourgeois parties" and assumed a revolutionary posture, flying the red flag rather than the tricolor in areas they controlled and encouraging worker intransigence.[27] As good Social Democrats, however, they expected to gain political power by winning an electoral majority. Moreover, the socialist movement was divided into three factions: the strictly Marxist "maximalists"; a "reformist" minority, powerful in the trade unions, that wanted to form alliances with liberals against the right; and a small abstentionist minority that wanted to have nothing to do with electoral politics. The maximalists, who controlled the party machinery, divorced themselves from the most widespread popular movement for change by condemning the land seizures as a petty bourgeois movement toward small property. The land seizures, in their turn, were divided among socialist, radical Catholic *(Popolari),* and veterans' leadership.

After the collapse of the occupation of the factories in September 1920, dispirited workingmen abandoned unions, whose membership declined rapidly. The beginnings of postwar unemployment further weakened the will and the bargaining position of what was left of organized labor. Electorally, Marxist parties fell away from their high point of November 1919 (156 seats out of 508 in the national legislature), losing 18 seats in the election of May 1921. The revolutionary surge had passed, but the panic it provoked in the Italian middle and upper classes had only begun, as we shall see in a subsequent chapter on the rise of fascism.

[27]Under the guidance of the maximalists, led by Giacinto Serrati, the Italian Socialist Party was the only major Western European socialist party to join the Third International en bloc in October 1919.

AFTERMATH AND RESULTS

By late 1920, the tide of revolution was receding everywhere in Europe. In Germany in 1923, two socialist-communist coalition state governments in Saxony and Thuringia and an abortive uprising in Hamburg were the last remnants of insurrection. Even before then, it was apparent that Soviet Russia, instead of becoming the trigger for revolution in the more advanced countries, as Marxists had anticipated, had survived alone as a socialist regime.

Success and Failure: A Comparative Look

Why had the revolutionary pressures generated by the war produced a new regime in Russia and nowhere else? The question has not ceased to reverberate through the rest of this century. Marxists and counterrevolutionaries alike have based their plans since 1923 on their respective analyses of this unexpected turn of events.

A few conclusions seem obvious. Losing a major war always proved fatal; indeed, no modern European regime has survived even the loss of a minor war in which the population felt that national prestige was deeply involved.[28] However, the converse was not true. Being on the winning side was not enough to assure social stability, as Italy's postwar social explosion showed.

It appears that relatively homogeneous societies in industrially advanced countries with a tradition of democratic institutions, such as Britain and France, withstood the social pressures of total war far better than less homogeneous, less industrialized, more autocratic societies. Certainly, revolutionary pressures were greater in Southern and Eastern Europe than in Western Europe. This observation has had profound repercussions among the theoreticians of revolution. Marxist thinkers, who had held earlier that socialist revolution could not succeed in a backward country like Russia without simultaneous revolution in Western Europe, had to admit in 1919 that revolution had broken out first in agrarian Russia, Hungary, and Bavaria. As Trotsky noted: "History has moved along the line of least resistance. The revolutionary epoch has made its incursion through the least barricaded gates."[29]

Even if revolutions begin at the "weak link" of established society, that still does not explain why one succeeded in the face of armed counterattack whereas others quickly collapsed.

Revolutionary pressures certainly carried further against autocratic regimes because there was a broader coalition of discontent. Governments that still denied elementary political liberties faced many layers of challenge, ranging from liberal aristocrats and middle-class liberals to socialists. The old regime in Russia was swept away in the first instance by all of these oppositions combined. The German monarchy, too, was destroyed by simultaneous democratic and social revolutions. The Germans stopped short at constitutional change, however, so still other factors must be sought to explain successful social revolution.

[28]Consider the French Fourth Republic, overthrown in 1958 after losing Indochina and failing to hold Algeria.

[29]Leon Trotsky, "Reflections on the Course of the Proletarian Revolution," in Isaac Deutscher, *The Prophet Armed: Trotsky, 1879–1921* (New York, 1965), p. 455.

One of the most important preconditions of successful revolution was the existence of a land-hungry peasant mass. Most of industrially advanced Europe had few people on the land (as in England) or had many small family farms (as in France). When urban unrest appeared in such societies, the countryside was inert, if not actually hostile to workers' demands. That had been the lesson of nineteenth-century Western European revolutions, too. But where urban demonstrations have coincided with a tidal wave of land seizures of large estates, it has usually proved impossible to resist these twin forces. France in 1789, Russia in 1917, China in 1948, and Cuba in 1958 all vouch for this observation. The areas of strongest revolutionary stress after the First World War fit rather well, although not perfectly, with areas of simultaneous urban discontent and rural land seizures.

Among socialists, the land issue had been an awkward one. If the peasants were granted their own land, they then became small farmers and a bulwark of the status quo, as in France. That is the reason for Marx's bitter denunciation of peasant conservatism in 1848. Thereafter, socialists remained divided on the land question. Reformist socialists in small farming areas, like Jean Jaurès in France and Georg von Vollmar in Bavaria, accepted the necessity of wooing small family farmers as the only way to get rural votes; Rosa Luxemburg, by contrast, considered such tactics a sellout to rural property-holding conservatism and insisted on the goal of nationalizing rather than distributing land.

That debate had its echoes in the years 1917 to 1921. Lenin, always more concerned for power than dogmatic purity, officially "nationalized" the land but in fact acquiesced in its direct seizure by peasants. Thereafter, he was largely immune from any counterrevolutionary movement, however well armed or financed, that threatened to restore the old landlords' property. By contrast, the Budapest soviet of Béla Kun attempted to transfer land directly from estates to state farms. His city-based regime foundered, in part, on peasant animosity to his orthodox socialist land policy.

Nationalism also affected revolutionary regimes' chances of survival. As a general rule, revolutionary regimes that offended national pride were quickly swept aside. In Hungary, both Count Károlyi and Béla Kun paid dearly for their inability to keep the Romanians from taking Transylvania. The Bavarian soviet threatened to divide Germany into minor states. On the other hand, those Eastern European successor states that gratified national feelings—Poland, Czechoslovakia, Romania, and Yugoslavia—satisfied their peoples' clamorings even without substantial social change or impressive economic success. The Russian case was more complicated, for the humiliating Treaty of Brest-Litovsk drove even some Bolsheviks into opposition. During the civil war, however, the Bolshevik regime drew added strength from its claim that Leon Trotsky's Red Army was effectively defending the national soil against foreign intervention.

The Third International and the Division of the European Left

Lenin remained convinced throughout 1920 that the Russian Revolution would trigger socialist revolutions in the more industrialized countries. He did his best to encourage them. In March 1919, optimistic over the situation in Hungary and

Germany, he summoned the socialists of the world to Moscow to form a new global organization. It was called the Communist International, or Third International, to distinguish it from the prewar socialist leadership of the Second International (formed in 1889), which had, in Lenin's eyes, made fatal compromises with middle-class patriotism and parliamentarism.

The first response to Lenin's appeal among Western European socialists was enthusiastic. The thirst for renewed unity on the left was intense. The Second International was in general disrepute because of its failure to stop war in 1914 and because of the participation of many of its leaders in wartime governments. The first socialist regime in history held power in Russia, and Western European socialists were eager to prevent their governments from crushing it. If the great moment were really at hand, to hold back would be treasonous. The Italian, Norwegian, and Bulgarian socialist parties adhered en masse in 1919 to Lenin's new International, and the parties of Germany, France, and Britain sent sympathetic observers.

Lenin did not want general support or sympathy, however. He wanted committed followers who would emulate the Russian Bolsheviks by forcing revolution on the more cautious parliamentary socialists through the will and discipline of a committed minority. Lenin set stringent conditions for admission to the Third International at its second congress in July 1920. Convinced that Russian success in the war with Poland would soon carry revolution into Germany, Lenin demanded that all candidate parties assent to Twenty-One Points. Would-be member parties must purge their reformist elements, restructure themselves "in the most centralized fashion," support the "Soviet Republics" *(sic)* in their fight against foreign intervention, prepare for a violent seizure of power, and fight by all possible means the rival power of reformist Social Democrats.

Lenin's provocative challenge and the Western European socialists' ambiguous response divided the European left passionately and permanently after 1920. The feasibility of revolution divided them. Whereas Lenin was convinced that world revolution was at hand, many Western European socialists were reluctant to gamble away their previous gains for an uncertain outcome. The cost in liberty and in material comfort of a Leninist seizure of power also divided them. Up to 1914, the German SPD, with its elaborate legal organization, its massive electoral success, and its vision of widening human freedom, had been the preeminent model for other socialists. In 1917, Lenin had introduced a rival model, incompatible with the values of many Social Democrats but incontestably more successful than the SPD in seizing power. Most Social Democrats still preferred to achieve socialism under conditions that would not require dictatorship. Leninists accused them of sabotaging an historic opportunity. The breach remained intensely bitter for two generations.

Every mass socialist movement outside Soviet Russia was split in 1920 and 1921. Lenin accepted no partial adherence to the Twenty-One Points. He specified by name the reformist leaders whom each party must purge, along with their followers. The British Labour Party and some powerful Social Democratic parties, such as the Austrian and the Swedish, lost only a fraction of their members to the Third International. After Lenin rejected the enthusiastic adherence of Serrati's Italian "maximalists" unless they would purge their own ranks of reformists, only about one-third of them finally joined the new Italian Communist Party in January 1921.

On Christmas Day 1920, a majority of the French SFIO voted to accept the Twenty-One Points, taking the party machinery and newspaper *(Humanité)* with them. The old German SPD had been split over the war since 1914, but even that ardent Spartacist Rosa Luxemburg had, before her death, questioned the applicability of Lenin's methods to Western Europe. Only about one-third of the Independent Social Democrats (USPD), went over to the Third International in December 1920. The rest returned to the majority SPD fold or left the movement in disillusion.

Even these moderate successes of the Third International were further weakened as the revolutionary perspective faded in Western Europe after 1920. As the Russian leaders attempted to bring Western European Communist parties under tighter Bolshevik control from Moscow in the 1920s, they discovered that Lenin had recruited enthusiasts for immediate revolution but not disciplined followers. The largest new Communist party in the West, in France, was filled with anarcho-syndicalists who had always opposed parliamentary socialism but who dropped away from communism as soon as its centralized governance became clear. The Norwegian Labour Party, which had rushed eagerly into the Third International in 1919, withdrew in 1923. So there remained in the West minority Communist parties and larger Social Democratic parties, frozen in permanent opposition to each other around the issue of whether revolution had been possible in 1919 and 1920.

One more result of the revolutionary movements after 1917 became clear only later. Even as the revolutionary pressures subsided, a panicky reaction to them began. Many frightened middle-class Europeans began abandoning the nineteenth-century liberalism of their fathers for some stronger bulwarks against revolutionary socialism. We shall look more closely at those fascist bulwarks in chapter 7, after first examining the peace settlement of 1919.

SUGGESTIONS FOR FURTHER READING

Sheila Fitzpatrick, *The Russian Revolution, 1917–1932,*[*] 2nd ed. (2001), is a brilliant short introduction from a perspective of qualified sympathy. Richard Stites, *Revolutionary Dreams: Utopian Passion and Experimental Life in the Russian Revolution*[*] (1989), recalls some of the idealistic ferment that marked the early days. Most new work on the Russian revolution is darkened by the harshness and ultimate failure of the regime it produced. The compelling narrative of Orlando Figes, *A People's Tragedy: Revolution, 1891–1924*[*] (1997), asks how social revolution degenerated into dictatorship. Martin Malia argues in *The Soviet Tragedy*[*] (1994) that the Soviet enterprise was doomed to end as murderous totalitarianism because it was based on a fatal intellectual project, first expressed by Rousseau and developed to extremes by Bolshevism, to realize utopia by force. Richard Pipes in many works, most recently *A Concise History of the Russian Revolution*[*] (1996) and *The Unknown Lenin: From the Secret Archives*[*] (1999), places the blame squarely on the personal cruelty and vindictiveness of Lenin.

The opening of Soviet archives has provided grist for such harsh reassessments. Dmitri Volkogonov, a disillusioned former Leninist, was well placed as head of Soviet military archives to reveal Lenin's dictatorial and vengeful side in *Lenin: A New Biography*[*] (1996), but so narrowly personal a focus misses much. The same author's *Autopsy for an Empire: The Seven Leaders Who Built the Soviet Regime*[*] (1998) and his *Trotsky, the Eternal Revolutionary* (1996) are anecdotal. Robert V. Daniels's readable *Red October* (1967, reprint ed. 1984) emphasizes Lenin's seizure of opportunities. Robert Service, *Lenin: A Biography* (2002), is the most recent and most balanced biography. See also Service's *The Russian Revolution, 1900–1929,*[*] 3rd ed. (1999). Edward Acton, Vladimir I. Cherniaev, and William G. Rosenberg, *A Critical Companion to the Russian Revolution*[*] (1997) presents a rich cross-fertilization of current Russian and Western scholarship. Orlando Figes and Boris Kolonitskii, *Interpreting the Russian Revolution: The Language and Symbols of 1917* (1999) brilliantly explores evolving meanings.

Among participants' accounts, the American radical John Reed's *Ten Days That Shook the World* (1919, reprint ed. 2002) and the hesitant Bolshevik N. N. Sukhanov's *The Russian Revolution* (1955) are classics. William Henry Chamberlin, the *Christian Science Monitor*'s correspondent in Russia, still captures the grand sweep of events in *The Russian Revolution,* 2 vols. (1935, reprint ed. 1992).

The shipwreck of Bolshevism has reawakened interest in other options. Richard Pipes (see work cited at the end of chapter 1) finds potential reform in imperial Russia. Leopold Haimson, in "The Problem of Social Stability in Urban Russia, 1905–1917," *Slavic Review,* vol. 23, no. 4 (Dec. 1964), and vol. 24, no. 1 (March 1965), argued influentially that social polarization and political blockage had already fatally compromised the old regime. See also Haimson, *The Making of Three Revolutionaries** (1988, new ed. 2004).

Other revolutionary currents opposed to Bolshevism are treated by Paul Avrich, *Kronstadt 1921* (1970, reprint ed. 1991); Robert V. Daniels, *The Conscience of a Revolution: Communist Opposition in Soviet Russia* (1988); William G. Rosenberg, *Liberals in the Russian Revolution: The Constitutional Democratic Party, 1917–1921* (1974); and Oliver H. Radkey, *The Agrarian Foes of Bolshevism* (1958), on the Socialist Revolutionary Party.

A rich literature since the 1970s on the social history of the revolution from below includes Diane Koenker, *Moscow Workers and the 1917 Revolution* (1981), and *Strikes and Revolution in Russia, 1917* (1991); Victoria Bonnell, *Roots of Rebellion: Workers' Politics and Organizations in Saint Petersburg and Moscow* (1983); William Husband, *Revolution in the Factory: The Birth of the Soviet Textile Industry, 1917–1920* (1990); and Stephen A. Smith, *Red Petrograd** (1985). Ronald G. Suny, *The Baku Commune* (1972), takes a rare look outside the main cities. Diane Koenker et al., *Party, State, and Society in the Russian Civil War** (1989) examines the civil war in a fresh social perspective.

Theodore H. Von Laue's *Why Lenin? Why Stalin? Why Gorbachev? Rise and Fall of the Soviet System,** 3rd. ed. (1997), employs a long-term modernization perspective. E. H. Carr's multivolume *History of Soviet Russia* (1950–1978), continued by R. W. Davies, is the great monument of sympathetic Western scholarship.

The longest-lived Soviet regime outside Russia is examined in Ivan Völgyes,

ed., *Hungary in Revolution 1918–1919* (1971); Rodolph Tökés, *Béla Kun and the Hungarian Soviet Republic* (1967); Gyorgy Borsanyi, *The Life of a Communist Revolutionary: Béla Kun* (1993); and Miklos Molnar, *From Béla Kun to János Kádar: Seventy Years of Hungarian Communism* (1990).

Charles Bertrand, ed., *Revolutionary Situations in Europe* (1977), includes thoughtful essays about other places. Francis L. Carsten, *Revolution in Central Europe* (1972), is a narrative account of Germany and Austria.

The German revolution was intensely studied in the 1960s. See A. J. Ryder, *The German Revolution of 1918* (1967); Richard A. Comfort, *Revolutionary Hamburg* (1966); Allan Mitchell, *Revolution in Bavaria* (1965); Werner T. Angress, *Stillborn Revolution: The Communist Bid for Power in Germany 1921–1923* (1963, reprint ed. 1972); and J. P. Nettl, *Rosa Luxemburg*, abbreviated. ed. (1989).

Italian Socialist maximalism and the strike wave of 1920 also aroused interest after 1968. See Paolo Spriano, *The Occupation of the Factories: Italy 1920* (1975); John A. Davis, ed., *Gramsci and Italy's Passive Revolution* (1979); Martin Clark, *Antonio Gramsci and the Revolution That Failed* (1977); and Gwynn A. Williams, *Proletarian Order: Antonio Gramsci, Factory Councils, and the Origins of Italian Communism* (1975). James Hinton, *The First Shop Stewards' Movement*, 2nd ed. (1977), takes a sympathetic look at Clydeside radicalism in Britain.

In addition to the general works on the Habsburg Empire cited at the end of chapter 1, see Z. A. B. Zeman, *The Break-up of the Hapsburg Empire, 1914–1918* (1961, reprint ed. 1971), the very detailed Arthur G. May, *The*

Passing of the Habsburg Monarchy 1914–1918, 2 vols. (1966), and Leo Valiani, *The End of Austria-Hungary* (1973). The essay by Lewis B. Namier, "The Downfall of the Habsburg Monarchy," reprinted in his *Vanished Supremacies* (1958, reprint ed. 1977), is as penetrating as when it was first written in 1920.

Additional Internet links related to this chapter are available on the Europe in the 20th Century Web site: http://www.history.wadsworth.com/paxton04.

You can also explore images, interactive timelines, and maps related to this chapter on our Western Civilization Resource Center: http://history.wadsworth.com.

The celebration in Paris on the signing of the Treaty of Versailles.

6

The Paris Peace Settlement

The Allied leaders met in Paris from January through June 1919 to draft peace terms.[1] But the Paris Peace Conference could not simply impose the victors' will on the vanquished. The peace conference faced a more complicated agenda. It would have to create a new kind of international order to replace the four great empires—the German, the Russian, the Austro-Hungarian, and the Ottoman—that had previously structured Central Europe, the Balkans, and the Near East. It would have to satisfy expectations that this "war to end wars"[2] could be concluded with a worldwide settlement so just that it would be permanent. Wartime emotions, heightened by propaganda, made justice hard to locate, however. Whereas Allied nationalists

---

[1]Principal authority over the conference rested in the Council of Four: President Woodrow Wilson of the United States; Prime Minister David Lloyd George of Great Britain; Premier Georges Clemenceau of France; and Prime Minister Vittorio Emanuele Orlando of Italy. For Asian issues, they included Prince Kimmochi Saïonji of Japan, now first formally recognized as a Great Power. Many other states and nationalities were also represented.

[2]H. G. Wells launched this influential slogan in *The Daily News* on August 14, 1914, to help justify the war in British opinion.

blamed the kaiser for the war and called for his trial, many Germans refused to believe they had really been beaten.

Three sets of pragmatic considerations, too, weighed on the deliberations: prior treaties and agreements that the Allies had made with one another and with other peoples during the war; the victors' strategic and economic interests; and their desire to contain the revolutionary regimes spreading in Central Europe in the spring of 1919. In the end, the idealistic language of the peace treaties jarred badly with the interests and deals reflected in their actual terms.

THE SETTING: IDEALS, INTERESTS, AND IDEOLOGY

War Aims

By gradual steps, the war had shifted from a quarrel over national interests to a crusade for freedom and national independence. At the beginning, the Entente could hardly claim to represent such principles better than the Central Powers, since it included tsarist Russia. But the first Russian revolution of February 1917 allowed the Allied populations to believe they were fighting for democracy.

All belligerent governments had persuaded their peoples to endure the long war effort by massive propaganda campaigns. Entente populations had been told of German aggression and atrocities in Belgium. The German internal opposition was mollified by promises to abolish the old three-class voting system in Prussia.[3] Returning British veterans were promised "a land fit for heroes" by Prime Minister David Lloyd George. War governments thus made an implicit bargain with their citizens: Give all for victory, and a better world will follow.

The Bolshevik Revolution of October 1917 brought the issue of war aims to the fore. Announcing that Russia was laying down arms, Lenin urged all peoples to force their rulers to end a war whose aims were solely "to decide which of the strong and healthy nations should dominate the weak ones."[4] To illustrate these accusations, the new Bolshevik Commissar for Foreign Affairs, Leon Trotsky, opened the safes in the deserted Russian foreign ministry and published the wartime secret treaties. In this way, Europeans first learned what deals had been reached by secret diplomacy: that the Russians were fighting in order to annex Galicia from the Austrians and the Straits from the Turks; that France had received promises of Russian support for its reconquest of Alsace-Lorraine; that Italy expected to expand around the head of the Adriatic Sea and into the Alps. Lacking other weapons, the Bolsheviks sought to end the war at once by exposing all the belligerents' expansionist goals to their war-weary populations.

The "Fourteen Points"

President Wilson tried to recapture the propaganda initiative from Lenin. Wilson shifted the war aims debate away from Lenin's appeal for immediate peace to the

[3]See chapter 1, p. 23.

[4]V. I. Lenin, "Decree on Peace, October 26, 1917," in Selected Works, vol. 6 (New York, 1936), p. 401.

good peace that could follow Allied victory. Speaking to the United States Congress in the traditional State of the Union address on January 8, 1918, he outlined in "Fourteen Points" a lasting, just peace that would warrant persevering on to victory. Several declarations of principle later in 1918 completed the Wilsonian vision of eventual peace. Its basic principles were "open covenants of peace, openly arrived at" to replace secret diplomacy; freedom of commerce and trade; reduction of armaments; "readjustment" of colonial empires so that the interests of indigenous populations should have "equal weight" with those of the imperial powers; self-determination of peoples so that nations could have rulers of their choosing and frontiers corresponding as fully as possible to national lines; and, finally, the formation of a "general association of nations" to keep the peace and guarantee the safety of "great and small states alike."

While a few Europeans on both sides shared Lenin's vision of immediate peace through revolution, a majority on the Allied side placed almost religious hopes in Wilson's vision of the just peace that could follow victory. In Britain, Wilson's ascendancy lent further influence to such liberal war critics as the Union of Democratic Control. Wilson's assumptions coincided with theirs: that democracies based on the nationality principle were more peaceable than autocracies; that diplomats would keep the peace if subjected to public scrutiny; and that if national aspirations were granted, there would be no future grounds for war. Wilson's views also made him a prophet elsewhere in Europe; he seemed to crystallize unformed but fervent hopes for a release from the old order that had produced the First World War. As Wilson toured parts of Europe on his way to Paris, he was thronged by adulatory crowds, especially in Italy. Most concretely, it was to Wilson that the Germans had turned for an armistice, which they asked to be based on the Fourteen Points. The liberal critique of the war emerged, then, as the dominant intellectual influence on the making of the peace. But there were also practical considerations.

Wartime Treaties and Promises

First came the wartime "secret treaties" to complicate the work of the peacemakers. As the war had settled into stalemate in the fall of 1914, the Allied governments had tried to solidify and enlarge their alliance by making secret promises. Partly to help prevent a Russian separate peace, Britain and France agreed in March and April 1915 that after an Allied victory Russia should control Constantinople and the Straits in return for Russian acceptance of British aims in Egypt and French aims in Alsace-Lorraine. The Treaty of London, signed on April 26, 1915, held out rich promises to Italy in exchange for Italian entry into the war on the Allied side.[5] Romania had been promised Transylvania. But since Romania had made a separate peace with Germany on May 7, 1918, that promise could be considered lapsed.

During most of the war the Allies had threatened only to amputate territory from the Central Powers, not to destroy them. At the end of the war, however, they also made promises to minority peoples within the great multinational empires, and thus contributed to the revolutionary pressures of nationalism within them.

---

[5]See chapter 3, pp. 84–85.

The Poles were the first stateless people to receive public Allied support for postwar national independence. As long as Russia remained in the war on the Allied side, many Poles, such as the socialist-nationalist leader Josef Pilsudski, had seen more promise for statehood in a German victory. The Germans had announced in November 1916 their intention of making former Russian Poland an independent kingdom. When Russia left the war in the spring of 1918, however, the Allies made a unified Polish national state—comprised of German Poland, Austrian Poland, and Russian Poland—a public war aim. An "independent Poland" with access to the sea was Point 13 of Wilson's Fourteen Points of January 1918.

The Allies recognized the independence of other Habsburg subjects in the summer of 1918. The Czecho-Slovak National Council in Paris, profiting from the anti-Bolshevik activities of the Czech Legion in Siberia, was recognized as a de facto government. Although the Allies declined to choose an official spokesman for all South Slavs from among the Serbian government in Belgrade, the Yugoslav Committee in London, and the Yugoslav National Council in Zagreb, they accepted the goal of a single South Slav state. By the end of October 1918, the Austro-Hungarian Empire had simply ceased to count outside the German and Hungarian areas, as the subject peoples took local administration into their own hands. Thus the Peace Conference was confronted in 1919 not only with Allied promises but with a series of *faits accomplis* by which the many nationalities had asserted their aspirations.

The peoples of another great multinational empire—Ottoman Turkey, which had been drawn into the war by German influence in November 1914—were the object of particularly vague and contradictory promises that returned to haunt the Peace Conference. One set of promises was the result of British efforts to encourage Arab separatism as a weapon against the Turks and a buffer around the Suez Canal. First, they supported guerrilla operations among the Bedouin along the Hijaz Railway in what is today Saudi Arabia.[6] British officials led one of the main Arab families, the Hashemites, to expect British support for an independent Arab kingdom in the Near East if the Arabs helped destroy the Ottoman Empire. Simultaneously, the Sykes-Picot Agreement of May 1916 allocated between Britain and France future colonial spheres of influence in the Near East—in irreconcilable conflict with the very notion of an independent Arab state. By this understanding, the French were to have predominant influence along the northeastern Mediterranean Coast and inland (Syria, the Lebanon) whereas the British were to exercise control in the Tigris-Euphrates Valley (present-day Iraq) and in the Jordan Valley (present-day Israel and Jordan). Finally, the British government agreed in the Balfour Declaration of November 1917 to "look with favor" on the creation of a Jewish "national home" in Palestine, thus encouraging Zionist hopes at potential variance with both other sets of understandings.

The bearers of all these wartime promises attempted to cash them in at the Peace Conference. The national committees of Czechoslovakia and Poland, already recognized as governments, were there. So was Prince Faisal of the Hashemite family, with Colonel T. E. Lawrence, in order to argue for an Arab kingdom in the Middle

---

[6]A highly romanticized account of this action by its British leader, T. E. Lawrence, was the source of a great postwar legend. See T. E. Lawrence, *The Seven Pillars of Wisdom* (London, 1935).

East. Chaim Weizmann, a chemist from Manchester, lobbied for the Zionist ideal of a Jewish national homeland. W. E. B. DuBois organized the first Pan-African Congress on the fringes of the conference. But it was obvious that the secret treaties and the national hopes of the war years were going to meet with very unequal recognition at the Peace Conference. The Czechs, for example, had used their segment of the old Habsburg armed force and local bureaucracy to establish their own de facto state even before the armistice; the Arabs, by contrast, had only their dreams.

Even if the victorious Great Powers had chosen to honor all their promises, it was not within their power to do so. Some of them were simply unfulfillable. There was no way, for example, to draw a Poland that was both ethnically predominantly Polish and still had access to the sea, as President Wilson had recommended. Some agreements, as in the case of the Middle East, were contradictory. Moreover, the earlier "secret treaties" with previously existing states dated from a time when the war was still being waged for dynastic and national interests. Those agreements shifted frontiers with cavalier disregard for ethnic identities and popular self-determination. The emergence of the war aims issue as a major ingredient of propaganda for restless and war-weary peoples, and the intense popular longing for a change in world politics along the lines advocated in the liberal critique of the war, made this kind of territorial deal unacceptable. It was far more difficult in 1919 to bargain away tracts of land without regard to their inhabitants' feelings than it had been in 1915.

National Interests of the Great Powers

A second set of considerations that shaped the Peace Conference's work was the national and strategic self-interest of the principal victors. Georges Clemenceau, in particular, represented France with keen awareness that his people had borne the brunt of the Allied war effort and must bear the brunt of enforcing the peace terms on the continent of Europe. He was determined that the peace terms should favor French security.

The French understood only too well that their influence in 1918 as the main Continental Great Power was artificial and transitory: Their war effort had nearly collapsed in May 1917 and in July 1918. And in the longer run, they were haunted by the growing industrial and demographic imbalance between 60 million Germans and 40 million Frenchmen. The French predominance of 1918 rested on the simultaneous eclipse of Germany and Russia, a state of affairs virtually unprecedented in the history of Great Power rivalries in modern Europe. French troops provided the vast bulk of armed forces not only on Germany's western frontier but in Eastern Europe as well. Theirs was the main force between Germany and Russia, and French military advisors assisted in the capitals of many Eastern European successor states. It was tempting to try to transform this temporary military superiority into a permanent system of dykes and barriers behind which the decline of Germany and Russia might become permanent.

A major thread running through the Peace Conference was Clemenceau's stubborn campaign for firm guarantees of French security. An even more intransigent

© Liaison Agency

French Premier Georges Clemenceau, United States President Woodrow Wilson, and British Prime Minister David Lloyd George (left to right) leave the Versailles Palace after signing the treaty with Germany, June 1919.

French nationalist group battled for detachment of the Rhineland from Germany so that the Rhine River could serve as a military frontier. But Clemenceau was able to assert his authority over this group, and in fact profited by opposing it. By renouncing claims to a separate Rhineland, Clemenceau could refuse to make other concessions. French security interests remained a major criterion for deciding which of the various nationalities would be favored in the postwar system.

Clemenceau was not the only Great Power spokesman to pursue national interests at the conference. The French charged the British with wishing to revive Germany as a "balance" against the victorious French and as a trading partner. Indeed, there is some evidence to support the charge. British national interest favored a self-enforcing nonpunitive peace and rapid economic revival. The British economist John Maynard Keynes stressed the economic importance of a healthy Germany to the European economy in his best-seller *The Economic Consequences of the Peace* (1919). David Lloyd George supported President Wilson in opposing the French projects for a separate Rhineland. The British also tried to obtain an active role in former German colonies in Africa and in the Middle Eastern territories "liberated" from the Ottoman Turks.

President Wilson did not hesitate to fight for United States interests. The Polish constituency in America provided him with good domestic political reasons for supporting Polish claims beyond their ethnic limits. And such Wilsonian principles as the "absolute freedom of navigation upon the seas . . . alike in peace and in war" (Point 2 of the Fourteen Points) and removal of barriers to international trade

(Point 3) were helpful to a rising commercial power. President Wilson also was forced by mounting Senate opposition to have a phrase inserted in the League of Nations Covenant (Article 21) explicitly asserting that the League did not supersede "regional understandings like the Monroe Doctrine."

Fear of Bolshevism

The third set of pragmatic considerations that influenced the Peace Conference was alarm about spreading revolution. Indeed, during the Cold War, some historians perceived Versailles as the first step in the containment of communism.[7] The conference did, in fact, devote much time and energy to the wave of revolutions apparently sweeping Europe in the spring of 1919, and to the question of how to deal with the new Soviet regime in Russia.

The Allies did not at first require the German armies to withdraw from former Russian territories in the east, even though the armistice terms demanded it. German troops remained in the Ukraine and in former Russian Poland until February 1919. They held some vital railroad lines in the Baltic region until the new governments of Estonia, Latvia, and Lithuania could assure their own stability in the summer of 1919. Thus, eight months after the armistice, a *Freikorps* of some 30,000 German volunteers under General Rüdiger von der Goltz was still on a war footing in the fluid borderlands of Eastern Europe, acting as de facto allies of the Western powers against the Bolsheviks.

This help did not win the Germans the role some of them hoped for, however, as the counterbalance to Russia. Instead, the Allies set up a *cordon sanitaire* of Eastern states whose function was to apply counterweight to both Germany and Soviet Russia. The new Poland spread beyond its ethnic frontiers to the east as well as to the west, especially after the French helped Poland in the Russo-Polish War of 1920 and 1921. The new Czechoslovakia extended eastward to include Ruthenian people, closely related to Ukrainians. Romania acquired two ethnically related but mixed areas: Bessarabia from former Russian territory and Transylvania from Hungary. These states were meant to keep both Bolsheviks and Germans bottled up within smaller frontiers.

The Peace Conference leaders' anti-Bolshevism was strong enough to make them forget their commitment to democracy in an emergency. In Hungary, the Allies imposed no effective restraint when the Romanians advanced into Budapest in August 1919 and expelled not only Béla Kun but the moderate socialists who tried to govern after him. The Allies were willing to negotiate the Hungarian peace settlement with the Hungarian officers who took charge when the Romanians withdrew, men of the right without sympathy for any Wilsonian principle except anti-Bolshevism.

It will not do, of course, to make anti-Bolshevism the predominant motive in Paris. Four years of anti-German propaganda could not be forgotten in a moment,

---

[7]Arno J. Mayer, *The Politics and Diplomacy of Peacemaking, Containment and Counterrevolution at Versailles, 1918–1919* (New York, 1968).

especially by the French. Many conservatives thought at first that the Bolsheviks were simply German agents. In January 1919, the French *Action française* journalist Jacques Bainville rejoiced in the Spartacist uprising in Berlin, predicting that a soviet Germany would be weak and fragmented. Premier Clemenceau always waved away German warnings that a harsh peace would spread Bolshevism. Fear of Bolshevism did not win an easier peace for Germany nor produce as rapid a thaw with the Germans as in 1947 to 1949.

THE SETTLEMENT

The terms finally produced by the Peace Conference are known collectively as the peace settlement of Paris. Actually, there were five separate treaties, one with each of the defeated states. Each bears the name of the palace near Paris where the formal signing ceremony took place. The first and most important was the Treaty of Versailles, with Germany, signed on June 28, 1919, in the Hall of Mirrors in that vast palace. Terms were reached with Austria in the Treaty of Saint Germain of September 10, 1919, and with Hungary in the Treaty of the Trianon on June 4, 1920, after the destruction of Béla Kun's soviet regime. The Treaty of Neuilly with Bulgaria was signed on November 27, 1919. Last of all, delayed by the rise of a Turkish nationalist movement under Mustafa Kemal, was the Treaty of Sèvres with Turkey on August 10, 1920.

THE LEAGUE OF NATIONS COVENANT

It was President Wilson who insisted that the first business of the conference be the establishment of a permanent peacekeeping organization, a League of Nations. Strong popular sentiment for basic changes in the way international relations were conducted stood behind this proposal, and Wilson, the first president of the United States to visit Europe while in office, invested all his personal prestige in it.

The principle of a League of Nations was unanimously adopted on January 25, 1919. Drafting the exact terms of the League Covenant took up much of the early months of that year. As finally adopted on April 28, the League of Nations Covenant created a general assembly of all member states[8] and a council consisting of the five Great Powers plus four other nations elected by the general assembly. The League members agreed to "respect and preserve" the territorial integrity of all members— that is, to maintain national boundaries as they existed after the First World War. In case of disputes, the members of the League bound themselves to submit to arbitration, judicial award, or enquiry by the League council, and they agreed not to go to war until three months after such steps had been completed. If any League member went to war in spite of these rules, the others were bound to take "sanctions" against that member in the form of blockade or even military action (Article 16).

---

[8]Forty-two wartime allies and neutrals were invited to join at first. Germany was admitted in 1926, and the Soviet Union joined in 1934.

PEACE SETTLEMENTS IN EUROPE, 1919–1920

Territories lost by:
- Germany
- Bulgaria
- Austria-Hungary
- Russia
- Plebiscite areas
- Demilitarized Rhineland zone of Allied occupation

The League, however, was not sovereign. It had no military force of its own, and it could not take action without unanimous consent of the council.

The League Covenant contained a number of other important general provisions. The colonies and overseas territories of the defeated nations were not awarded directly to the victors, as in the past, but placed under the "tutelage" of the League, if they were "not yet able to stand by themselves under the strenuous conditions of the modern world" (Article 22). The "tutelage" was to be exercised by one of the "advanced" nations under mandate from the League of Nations, to which the mandatory power was supposed to report each year.

The Covenant set up three classes of mandates, graded according to European conceptions of how "advanced" toward possible independence each territory was.

MANDATES UNDER THE LEAGUE
OF NATIONS

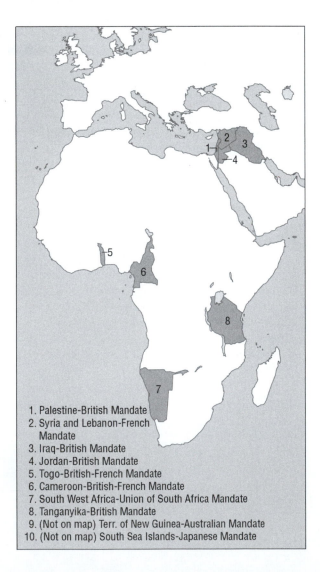

1. Palestine-British Mandate
2. Syria and Lebanon-French
   Mandate
3. Iraq-British Mandate
4. Jordan-British Mandate
5. Togo-British-French Mandate
6. Cameroon-British-French Mandate
7. South West Africa-Union of South Africa Mandate
8. Tanganyika-British Mandate
9. (Not on map) Terr. of New Guinea-Australian Mandate
10. (Not on map) South Sea Islands-Japanese Mandate

Class A mandates were newly liberated peoples expected to reach eventual independence, such as the non-Turkish parts of the former Ottoman Empire. In a settlement closer to the Sykes-Picot Agreement than to the British promises to the Arabs, Syria and the Lebanon were mandated to France, the Tigris-Euphrates Valley and Palestine to Britain. Class B mandates consisted of former German colonies in Africa whose peoples were not expected to accede to independence within the foreseeable future, but which the treatymakers preferred not to have simply absorbed into the existing African empires. Most of Tanganyika (present-day Tanzania) was mandated to Britain, except for parts adjacent to the Congo, which Belgium was to administer. The German West African colonies of Togo and the Cameroons were divided between Britain and France as mandatory powers. Class C mandates consisted of former German possessions that were to pass directly under the laws of the mandatory power. South Africa obtained former German Southwest Africa under this provision, an arrangement that lasted until it received independence as Namibia in 1990. The German Pacific holdings north of the equator went to Japan; those south of the equator went to Australia and New Zealand.

Despite their obligation to administer these territories under League of Nations scrutiny, the mandatory powers tended to assimilate class B and class C mandates into the existing colonial system. Only one class A mandate had attained full sovereignty twenty years later when the Second World War broke out, Britain having accepted independence for Iraq in 1932.

The League Covenant also called for general disarmament (Article 8). Further, the Minorities Commission of the conference promoted a series of treaties between the League and some member states with large national or religious minorities, guaranteeing those minorities protection against discrimination. An International Labor Office was established to report on conditions of work and wages. Finally, a number of specialized agencies were created to deal with medical, humanitarian, and legal matters. In their modest way, these specialized agencies were the most lasting part of the League machinery.

Because the conference spent much of its early months drafting the covenant, more time was left for territorial settlements to be prejudiced by *faits accomplis*. Wilson was willing to make compromises in the territorial settlements to ensure the League's acceptance, however, for he believed that any faults in the treaties could be remedied later if the League functioned properly.

THE WESTERN EUROPEAN SETTLEMENT

Wilson's Fourteen Points entered directly into the Franco-German settlement, for it was on their basis that Prince Max of Baden had appealed for an armistice in October 1918. Only two points dealt with Western Europe specifically. Point 7 required that Belgium, the first victim, be "evacuated and restored." France, according to Point 8, should not only have its invaded territory freed and "restored," but the "wrong done to France in 1871" should be undone by the restoration to France of Alsace-Lorraine. The Western European settlement was more complicated than this, however, because of more pragmatic considerations.

The Attempt to Separate the Rhineland

The fact that Germany was militarily defeated, however late and unexpectedly, put the French army in a position to shape the settlement by direct action. The armistice terms of November 11, 1918, drafted by the French inter-Allied commander in chief, Marshal Ferdinand Foch, with an eye for later, more permanent arrangements, authorized the Allied armies (largely French) to advance to the Rhine, to occupy three bridgeheads across it—at Mainz, Koblenz, and Cologne—and to establish a neutral zone on the other side of the Rhine.

Established on the Rhine, French officials worked directly to detach that area from Germany, although it is not clear with what authority they did so. They found some German Rhinelanders willing to cooperate. Hans Adam Dorten, former district attorney of Dusseldorf and spokesman for the Dusseldorf Industrialists' Club, prepared a Rhineland Constituent Assembly in February 1919. He had the support of some who thought they would be spared harsh peace terms, a few industrialists who wanted ties with France rather than with the socialist regime in Berlin or the soviet regime briefly in power in Bavaria, and Catholics who resented the domination of Protestant Prussia (including the young Catholic mayor of Cologne, Konrad Adenauer, who was to become West Germany's first chancellor thirty years later).

Marshal Foch went over Clemenceau's head to lobby in the conference for a separate Rhineland. But separatism was only a minority current in the German Rhineland, and Lloyd George and Wilson strenuously opposed a territorial settlement that threatened to create another cause for future revenge. The French delegate himself, Georges Clemenceau, overrode his determined military associate on this matter.

Territorial Changes

Actual territorial changes in Western Europe, therefore, were relatively limited. It was obvious that Alsace-Lorraine, which Louis XIV had conquered in the seventeenth century and which had remained French until the Germans took it in the Franco-Prussian War of 1870, would be returned wholly to France, despite some areas of Germanic dialect. The border communities of Eupen, Malmédy, and Moresnet were transferred to Belgium, the first victim in the west. Plebiscites were arranged for border areas taken from Denmark in 1864. The coal mines of the Saar, just across the border north of Lorraine, were placed in the possession of France for fifteen years as "compensation for the destruction of the coal mines in the north of France," after which the Saar population could vote on its national status. (It voted overwhelmingly to remain German when the plebiscite was held in 1935.) The territorial changes in the west left the map of Western Europe still recognizable to a European of 1914.

"Demilitarization" of Germany

Since France had failed to obtain the separation of the Rhineland, the conference tried to set up a physical barrier against future German military movement westward.

A British soldier patrols the Rhine, with the spires of Cologne Cathedral in the background. Allied forces were supposed to remain in occupation of the left bank of the Rhine for fifteen years after the signature of the Treaty of Versailles. The Americans handed their sector (Koblenz) over to the French in January 1923. The British evacuated the Cologne sector in December 1925. The French evacuated their sector (Mainz) five years early, in June 1930, as agreed in the negotiation of the Young Plan.

All German territory west of the Rhine and a strip fifty kilometers wide (about thirty miles) east of the Rhine were demilitarized in perpetuity. German military forces were excluded forever from those parts of German soil. This "demilitarized zone" was intended to hinder a surprise German attack westward, while facilitating French movement east in case France wanted to rescue an eastern ally. The Allied troops occupying the west bank of the Rhine would remain there for fifteen years. Furthermore, it was agreed that the United States and Great Britain would extend treaties of guarantee to France by which they would aid France in the event of a German attack.

Beyond that, the settlement attempted to end Germany's military power. The German general staff was dissolved. The German navy was limited to no more than six battleships of 10,000 tons each, six light cruisers, and twelve destroyers. Germany was forbidden to manufacture or possess submarines, military aircraft, heavy artillery, tanks, and poison gas. The German army was limited to 100,000 volunteers, required to serve for twelve years each so that Germany could not rebuild a large reserve of short-term recruits.

Reparations

The Allies tried to make Germany pay for the war. Victors had always extracted wealth from the vanquished, first as booty, and then as punitive fines. After Napoleon's final defeat in 1815, the victors had levied an indemnity of 700 million francs, about one-half the French annual peacetime budget; it was paid off in five years. After the Franco-German War of 1870–1871, France had to pay 5 billion francs to Germany; that took only four years. The "reparations" demanded of Germany after the First World War were not only far larger than any previous amount, but they also came clothed in a language of moral recrimination. "The aggression of Germany and her allies" had caused the war, asserted the famous Article 231 of the Treaty of Versailles, and so Germany should "make compensation for all damage done to the civilian population of the Allied and Associated Powers and to their property" (Article 232).

The demand for reparations grew in the emotions of the war's end. Woodrow Wilson's Fourteen Points had spoken only vaguely of "restoring" the invaded parts of Belgium and France. When the Germans tried to make the Fourteen Points the basis of armistice negotiations in October 1918, the British and French, not overly enthusiastic about all of Wilson's aspirations, agreed to accept them only with the added demand that Germany make compensation for "all damage done to the civilian population of the Allies and their property by the aggression of Germany."[9] In the "khaki election" of December 1918, Lloyd George demagogically promised the British public that the Germans would pay the costs of the war and reconstruction. Contrary to legend, French officials were no harsher, but newspapers fanned hopes that "Germany will pay."

Behind this moral claim lay a hard-headed political calculation. No belligerent state had paid for all the costs of the war by taxation. All had borrowed immense

The reparations problem, as seen by a British cartoonist in 1923.

PASSING THE BUCK.

Historical Pictures

[9]Memorandum of Observation by the Allied Governments, November 5, 1918.

sums by selling bonds, the principal and interest of which would have to be repaid after the war. They had also issued floods of additional currency to cover wartime budget deficits. The resulting inflation meant that the bondholders would eventually be paid back in money that bought less—if anything at all. Default was also possible, although that would make it harder to borrow again. Either way, the purchasers of war bonds would end up paying for the war by losing their investment. Governments hesitated to antagonize their property-holders to that extent. In addition, vast sums were needed to repair war-damaged buildings, bridges, railroads, and mines, and to restore shell-strewn farmland to productivity. No government would find it easy to raise taxes to pay for all that.

A further complication was war debts. Both Britain and France owed large sums to the United States, whereas France owed additional war debts to Britain. Although the United States advocated moderation in imposing a reparations bill (without actually participating in the work of the Reparations Commission), it adamantly refused throughout the 1920s to consider waiving any part of these war debts. Without collecting reparations from Germany, however, Britain and France could hardly pay what they owed the United States.

The Peace Conference was unable to agree on a reparations figure low enough for the Germans or high enough for the British and French. It left that problem to the Reparations Commission. In the meantime, Germany was supposed to start paying a preliminary 1 billion marks, plus deliveries of coal to compensate the French for mines that were flooded during the German retreat. The Reparations Commission, consisting of representatives of Britain, France, Belgium, Italy, and Serbia, labored through seven conferences in various European resorts before finally agreeing in April 1921 on the sum of 132 billion gold marks ($33 billion, over twice the prewar German national income), payable in yearly installments of 2 billion gold marks, plus 26 percent of the value of German exports.[10]

No postwar German government believed it could accept such a burden on future generations and survive, but neither could a French government that failed to collect reparations survive. In March 1921, even before the final bill had been presented, French troops were sent to occupy three cities in the Ruhr industrial area—Dusseldorf, Ruhrort, and Duisburg—when it was charged that the Germans had fallen behind in deliveries in kind.

The payments posed enormous problems. Even assuming German willingness to pay, it was not simply a matter of raising the necessary sum each year by taxes or borrowing. The money had to be transferred into foreign currencies, that is, the German government had to buy the necessary francs or pounds for marks. Transfer on such a scale was not technically impossible, however, as some claimed at the time.[11] One solution was for Germany to earn much more foreign exchange by increasing its exports, but the Allies did not intend to finance reparations by buying German exports. Another partial solution was to pay a larger proportion in kind— paying in goods and materials to replace similar goods and materials destroyed in

[10]The proposed schedule of payments would have actually transferred less to the Allies, perhaps 108 billion marks. See Marc Trachtenberg, *Reparations in World Politics* (New York, 1980), pp. 210–211. The Germans made some payments in 1919–1922, perhaps 13 billion gold marks, but estimates differ for both technical and partisan reasons.

[11]Ibid., pp. 77–84, 342.

"Hands off the Ruhr!" This poster illustrates the adoption of nationalist themes by the German far left during the French occupation of the Ruhr in 1923.

International Institute of Social History, Amsterdam

Hände weg vom Ruhrgebiet!

the war—and in fact the brilliant German Jewish industrialist and technocrat, Foreign Minister Walther Rathenau, worked out such an agreement in 1922. French industrialists disliked payments in kind, however, and Rathenau was assassinated soon after by German anti-Semitic nationalists for making such a concession. The solution adopted was to haggle and wrangle while the mark declined in value. Germany's runaway inflation had begun long before the first reparations payments were made, the result of wartime deficit spending, continued easy credit after the war, and the speculative purchase of gold and foreign exchange by wealthy Germans. Rather than adopt the internal austerity measures that might have stabilized the mark, German bankers and government financial experts blamed inflation solely on reparations payments. In this way they used the sufferings of inflation victims to bring further pressure on the Allies.

THE EASTERN EUROPEAN SETTLEMENT

Territorial Changes

While minor adjustments were being made in the ancient Franco-German frontier in the west, the map of Eastern Europe was being entirely redrawn. The Paris Peace

Conference presided over the most extensive revision of frontiers in modern European history except for the Vienna Conference of 1815, and, unlike the Vienna settlement, it enlarged the number of states in Europe instead of diminishing them. The proud empires that had controlled Eastern Europe had been destroyed. The German borders were pulled back hundreds of miles westward, giving up much of Silesia and East Prussia. The Russian border remained far east of the 1914 frontier, where imperial Germany had imposed it in the Treaty of Brest-Litovsk,[12] for the Western Allies were happy to accept the anti-Bolshevik consequences of German victory in the east. The Austro-Hungarian Empire disappeared from the map altogether. New nation-states took the place of parts of these three empires in the north and center: Finland, Latvia, Estonia, Lithuania, Poland, Czechoslovakia, Austria, and Hungary. In the Balkans, Romania gained territory from Hungary, Russia, and Bulgaria, while Serbia—where the war had begun—became the root stock of a large new South Slav state, the Kingdom of Serbs, Croats, and Slovenes, called Yugoslavia after 1929.

The principle on which the makers of postwar Eastern Europe claimed to base their work was the self-determination of nations, as promised in President Wilson's Fourteen Points and subsequent statements. Practice did not always fit principle. Even more than the Western European settlement, the postwar settlement in Eastern Europe was influenced by the national interests of the victors, prior commitments, *faits accomplis* by Eastern European national movements, and the noncommunist states' desire to keep Bolshevik Russia at bay.

Frontier Problems

The application of the principle of self-determination was complicated in Eastern Europe by the absence of neat ethnic frontiers. In the west, states had been consolidated prior to the appearance of mass nationalism. Their central governments had subsequently been able to impose a single language and national loyalty on the varied peoples within their borders through education and common experience. In Eastern Europe, national consciousness grew up in the nineteenth century around folk languages and religions, at cross purposes with existing state frontiers or economic relations. Forming new states along national lines in Eastern Europe would have been easy if an ethnic, linguistic or religious map had revealed neat borders. That state of affairs was rare enough along the relatively stable borders of Western Europe; it was rarer still in Eastern Europe. The "clearly recognizable lines of nationality" of President Wilson's Point 9 often clashed with the "historically established lines of allegiance and nationality" of Point 11.

The case of Teschen, a small mining area claimed by both the new Poland and the new Czechoslovakia, shows how intractable some border issues were. Although not part of Bohemia proper, Teschen had been ruled for 500 years by the kings of Bohemia. "Historically established lines of allegiance" suggested that it pass with

---

[12]The Soviet regime managed to recover some of the territory lost at Brest-Litovsk during 1919–1921, and recovered most of the rest of tsarist territories during the Second World War.

DESTRUCTION OF THE EMPIRES

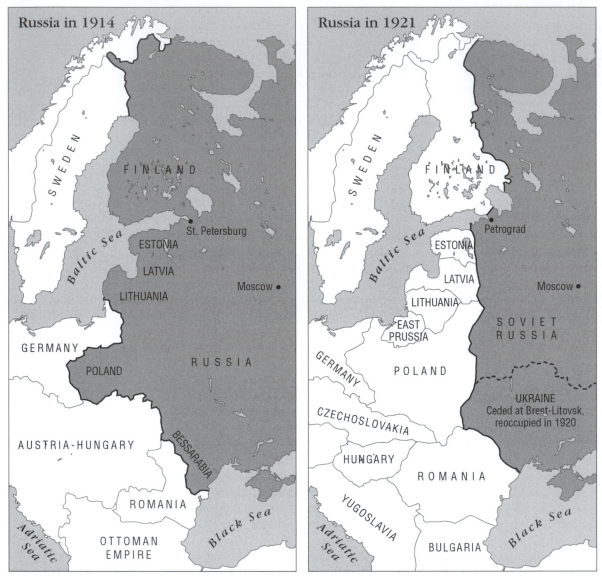

Bohemia to the new Czechoslovakia. The 1910 census, however, reported that 56 percent of the inhabitants of Teschen were Polish-speaking; 26 percent, Czech-speaking; and 18 percent, German-speaking. The principle of national self-determination thus seemed to favor the Poles, even though ethnic and linguistic censuses were notoriously uncertain. They arbitrarily assigned speakers of interme-diate Czech-Polish dialects to one side or the other and overlooked the frequency of bilingualism. To introduce a third criterion, the Teschen area was economically linked to the banks and markets of Vienna. Vienna, however, was being reduced

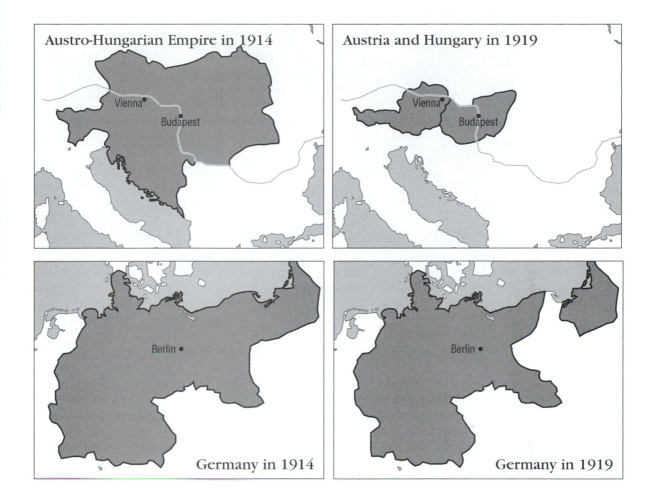

from an imperial capital and regional center to merely the capital of the small nation of Austria.

Since history, language, and economic links gave conflicting answers to the question of Teschen's proper national identity, the solution was left to the traditional means of international politics: force or bargaining. The Versailles settlement split Teschen approximately in two. That judgment of Solomon satisfied no one. The Poles and Czechs fought over Teschen in 1919 and 1920. Later, in 1938, when the Czechs were preoccupied with Hitler's claims to the German-speaking Sudetenland, the Poles simply stepped in and took the rest of Teschen by force.

The list of frontier problems in Eastern Europe complicated by national self-determination was endless. In much of Eastern Europe, cities and commercial and industrial life had developed under strong German influence, while local ethnic groups prevailed in the countryside. For example, industrial development in Silesia

European Nationality Problems, 1919–1939

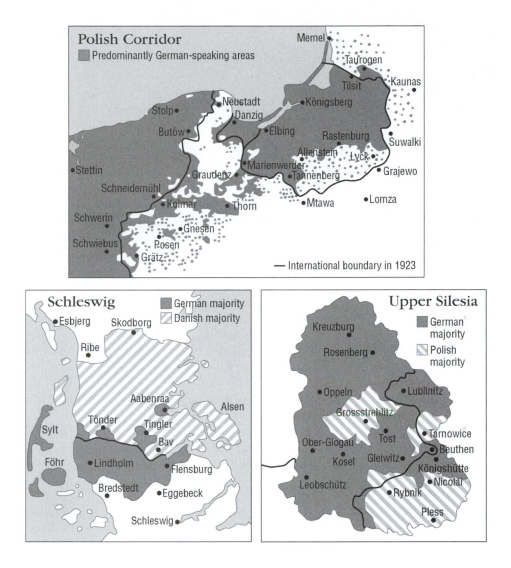

Polish Corridor

☐ Predominantly German-speaking areas

Memel
Taurogen
Tilsit
Kaunas
Königsberg
Neustadt
Stolp
Danzig
Butöw
Elbing
Rastenburg
Allenstein
Suwalki
Marienwerder
Lyck
Stettin
Graudenz
Tannenberg
Grajewo
Schneidemühl
Mtawa
Lomza
Kolmar
Thorn
Schwerin
Gnesen
Schwiebus
Posen
Grätz

— International boundary in 1923

Schleswig

☐ German majority
▨ Danish majority

Esbjerg
Skodborg
Ribe
Aabenraa
Alsen
Sylt
Tönder
Tingler
Bav
Föhr
Lindholm
Flensburg
Bredstedt
Eggebeck
Schleswig

Upper Silesia

☐ German majority
▨ Polish majority

Kreuzburg
Rosenberg
Oppeln
Lublinitz
Grossstrehlitz
Ober-Glogau
Tost
Tarnowice
Kosel
Gleiwitz
Beuthen
Leobschütz
Königshütte
Nicolai
Rybnik
Pless

took place in the nineteenth century, after Prussia had seized that Polish-speaking region from Austria in 1742. The entrepreneurs and merchants were German, and many Silesian Polish families were assimilated into German culture as they became miners or workers in new industries. The peasantry, however, remained Polish. How could Silesia find a single national identity in 1919? How could homogeneous national units be mapped where town and country spoke different languages? A similar problem arose with the promise to Poland of access to the sea. The largely German port city of Danzig was imbedded in a region of Polish peasantry.

The task of recomposing Eastern Europe on the basis of a separate state for each nationality—so appealing from afar—revealed all sorts of ugly complications as the delegates to the Paris Peace Conference consulted their maps and listened to the experts and the spokesmen for the nationalities. An Eastern Europe of independent nations, drawn to the satisfaction of every claimant, was probably beyond human wisdom in 1919, even if the Versailles peacemakers had been totally free from any other kinds of considerations. Other considerations had a major influence on the settlement, however.

Discrimination among Nationalities

To begin, not all nationalities in Eastern Europe received equal recognition. Those whose national consciousness had been reborn in the nineteenth century—Poles and Czechs—had already won strong emotional acceptance in Western Europe from the days of Frédéric Chopin and the poet Adam Mickiewicz in the 1840s. Others, such as the Croats or Slovaks, were only beginning to arrive at national or linguistic self-consciousness. Still others, such as the Slovenes, had hardly begun to claim to be a separate people. In any event, where would the process of atomization end if the speakers of every local dialect developed a fierce separatist consciousness?

Eastern European nationalities also differed in the services they had rendered the Allies during the war. Although Poles had fought on both sides at the beginning, the fall of tsarist Russia brought the strongest force, Marshal Josef Pilsudski's Polish Legion, into action against Germany at the end. Czechs taken prisoner on the Russian front formed a pro-Allied army in Russia in 1918. "Gallant Serbia" had been the Central Powers' first victim. Although independent Romania had joined the war on the Allied side in 1916, it was defeated and signed a separate peace in May 1918. Did Romania still deserve the advantages promised in 1916 by the Allies? On the other side of the ledger stood Austria and Hungary, which had made war against Serbia in the first place, and Bulgaria, whose king had dragged it reluctantly into the war on the Central Powers' side. Hungary was doubly damned by having formed a soviet in May 1919, at the very moment its borders were on the drafting boards in Paris.

France had the largest stake in discriminating among favored and disfavored nationalities in Eastern Europe. French diplomacy and armed forces were more active in Eastern Europe than those of any other Great Power. As the chief land power of the Continent, principal victim and principal rival of Germany, France desired strong allies on Germany's eastern frontiers. Such allies would permit the French to continue their strategy of threatening a resurgent Germany with a two-front war. Because France's major Eastern ally since 1892, Russia, was now materially weak and politically hostile, French security planners built instead on maximum satisfaction for Poland, Czechoslovakia, Yugoslavia, and Romania. If these states were made as strong as possible, even at the expense of some valid nationality claims, French security needs would be doubly served, against Germany and against Bolshevik Russia.

With tacit Allied acceptance and even support, the favored Eastern European nationalities embarked in the closing days of the war on a round of "claim-jumping"

Escorted by Czech veterans in the various uniforms in which they had participated in the First World War, Thomas Masaryk enters Prague in 1919 to assume the presidency of the Czechoslovak republic.

in which they established a de facto military presence in disputed areas. On October 6, 1918, the South Slavs set up the National Committee of Serbs, Croats, and Slovenes, to establish sovereignty in the former South Slavic areas of the Habsburg Empire. The Czech national committee set itself up in Prague as a government in October 1918; in January 1919 it was fighting with Polish forces over Teschen. The Poles, remembering the vast medieval Kingdom of Poland, attempted from 1919 to 1921 to conquer parts of Lithuania and the Ukraine to form a Great Confederation. The Romanians, who had taken Bessarabia from the Soviet Russians in 1918, went on in July 1919 to seize Transylvania and other territories from Hungary. Thus before the Peace Conference opened and while it sat, future boundaries were set by direct action in Eastern Europe, with Allied, and especially French, complicity.

At the conference, France took the lead in favoring a strong Poland, Czechoslovakia, Romania, and Yugoslavia. Clemenceau pressed for Polish expansion in Silesia and right up to the Baltic in a corridor of clearly Germanic population. Lloyd George, worried about creating future ethnic trouble spots, forced the conference to provide for plebiscites in Silesia and for the separate status of German-speaking Danzig as a free city. As for Czechoslovakia, the French supported the integral inclusion of historic Bohemia despite large numbers of Germans along the western border, and prevented any consideration of a separate Slovakia. The spokesman for Slovak separatism, the Catholic priest Father Andrej Hlinka, was hustled out of Paris by French police. The same treatment was accorded Stjepan Radić, the spokesman for a separate Croatia instead of a great Yugoslavia. The largest possible Romanian claims were also supported at the conference.

The Eastern European Settlement Assessed

The new map of Eastern Europe was thus the product of compromises between principle—the self-determination of nations, a goal only partly realizable at best in that ethnic patchwork—and the immediate national interests of the victors. Far from building on a permanent foundation of satisfied nationality, the Paris peace settlement rested on a temporary circumstance: the unprecedented eclipse of the two powers that had traditionally disputed predominance over Eastern Europe—Germany and Russia. Neither of these proud peoples was about to accept diminution for long. Such contested borders could subsist only if propped up from outside. Since Britain and the United States were unwilling to do that, France was left with a potential burden far beyond its capacities to handle.

The settlement left numerous local grievances that a renascent Germany and Russia would be able to exploit. The nations of Eastern Europe were divided after 1919 between gratified states and revisionist states. The first included a large Poland, created at the expense not only of Germany and Russia but also of Lithuania; a large Czechoslovakia, whose Slovak eastern half felt subordinate to the dominant Czechs; an enlarged Romania which had grown at the expense of Russia and, even more, Hungary; and a large Kingdom of Serbs, Croats, and Slovenes—renamed Yugoslavia in 1929—whose very distinct constituent peoples had been thrust temporarily together by their common opposition to the Habsburg Monarchy. These fortunate countries looked to France to help preserve the status quo.

Conversely, other states were eager to overturn an unfavorable settlement: the truncated remnant of Hungary, shrunk by two-thirds; the German-speaking rump of Austria; a diminished Bulgaria. There were also peoples whose claim to found nation-states had been denied, such as the Slovaks and Croats. These revisionists looked for powerful allies to help them change the peace settlement. Many Austrians dreamed of union with Germany, expressly forbidden by the peace terms. No Hungarian regime could survive without seeking revision of the Treaty of the Trianon. Admiral Miklós Horthy, Hungary's strong man between the wars, emerged from isolation first in 1927 with ties to Mussolini, and later looked to Hitler for support. Bulgarians thought their Russian cousins might help them revise the Treaty of Neuilly.

Eastern European instability was further increased by the presence of national minorities in every one of the new states, especially in the gratified ones. The new Poland contained 7.5 million Germans, concentrated around Danzig and in the parts of Silesia it had won in the 1921 plebiscite. As for Czechoslovakia, although its later president Eduard Beneš liked to call it an "Eastern European Switzerland," it more resembled a miniature Habsburg Monarchy. Nearly one quarter of its population, 3 out of 13 million, was German, mostly concentrated along the western border of Bohemia (the Sudetenland). The Slovak perception of second-class citizenship created another potential division. For a time, Czechoslovakia was the most democratic and prosperous of the new states. Then the Depression and Hitler's agitation pulled the nationalities apart, so that by 1938 the Sudeten Germans' secessionist efforts would bring Europe to the brink of war.[13] The Slovaks

---

[13]See chapter 13, pp. 397–398.

were to seize their opportunity to secede in 1939.[14] The Croats were to form their own state when Hitler invaded Yugoslavia in 1941.[15]

One more problem was the effect of the new national boundaries on the Eastern European economy. Once a single trading and financial unit, the Austro-Hungarian Empire consisted now of seven independent states, each with its own frontiers, customs inspectors, and commercial regulations. New economic channels had to be opened. For example, the Slovak iron miners, who had shipped their ore to Budapest under the old regime, now redirected their sales to Prague. In more prosperous times, these dislocations might have been quickly overcome, but now the strains of new statehood were soon compounded by the first signs of depression: the decline of agricultural prices of the late 1920s. The new states consequently erected ever-higher protectionist barriers against one another. The old Empire began to look good in retrospect, but dreams of a renewed Danubian free-trade area proved impossible to realize.

The Wilsonian ideal presumed that the self-determination of nations would automatically produce a world of democratic and peaceable peoples. That proved a misplaced hope in Eastern Europe. The new states were deeply divided by class and ethnicity. In all but Czechoslovakia, the economies were still largely agrarian, with extensive estates and land-hungry peasants. Except for Czechoslovakia, the strains of internal conflict and faltering economies made democracy unworkable. By the 1930s, if not sooner, the new states fell into the hands of strong men or authoritarian monarchs, with the acquiescence of Western Allies more fearful of Bolshevism than eager for social reform. The question was not whether the Eastern European frontiers of 1919 would change, but when; and whether these changes would be made by force, entailing the risk of another European war.

APPLYING THE PEACE SETTLEMENT

The work of the Paris Peace Conference did not end when the five treaties had been signed. It took years of effort to establish new frontiers, run plebiscites in disputed areas, oversee disarmament, and set up the League of Nations. The peace settlement was not self-enforcing. The German government accepted the Treaty of Versailles only under protest, after the Allies prolonged their economic blockade and threatened to occupy Berlin. The German chancellor, Social Democrat Philip Scheidemann, declared in May 1919 that "the hand should wither" that signed such terms.[16] Even the Catholic internationalist Matthias Erzberger, who finally formed a government willing to sign the treaty, struggled to amend it.[17]

In Eastern Europe peoples continued to fight over their frontiers. Even after settlement of the Polish–Russian War in 1921,[18] Polish irregulars held the city of Vilna,

[14]See chapter 13, p. 399–400.

[15]See chapter 14, p. 432.

[16]Klaus Epstein, *Matthias Erzberger and the Dilemma of German Democracy* (Princeton, N.J., 1959), p. 304.

[17]Erzberger was assassinated in 1921 by two former officers who were later treated as heroes.

[18]See chapter 5, p. 133.

which the Peace Conference had awarded to Lithuania. Poles also fought with Czechs over Teschen until July 1920, and they contested the outcome of the plebiscite in Upper Silesia. Austrians and Hungarians fought over the Burgenland, a border area near Vienna, until late in 1921. After Yugoslavia was awarded the Adriatic port of Fiume, Italian nationalist volunteers occupied it by force in 1919 and 1922; Italy finally annexed it in 1924. A Turkish nationalist movement under the army officer Mustapha Kemal (later known as Atatürk) rejected the treaty terms that the Sultan had accepted, overthrew the Sultan, defeated a Greek army supported by the Allies, and won control over all of Anatolia by 1923.

The letter of the treaties, therefore, often mattered less than the spirit with which they were interpreted and enforced. According to one interpretation, the peace terms were meant to produce a self-regulating world of satisfied, democratic nations linked by free cultural and economic exchange. According to another quite legitimate reading, the treaties were meant to guarantee to the victors the permanence of what they had won by the sacrifice of their men in the trenches.

France had taken this latter view during the negotiations, and postwar developments left France effectively in charge of enforcing the settlement. First the United States withdrew from any active role in European security matters. Woodrow Wilson lost control of both houses of Congress in the midterm elections of November 1918 to Republicans distrustful of entangling overseas alliances. In November 1919, the Senate refused to ratify the Treaty of Versailles and the League Covenant without conditions which the president—now ill—was unwilling to accept. The American turn to political isolationism was confirmed by the election of Republican Warren G. Harding as president in November 1920. Although British Prime Minister David Lloyd George enlarged his wartime coalition in the "khaki election" of November 1918, the "hang the kaiser" nationalism aroused by that election was soon transformed in British public opinion into a reluctance to be drawn into any kind of Continental entanglement.

France also followed the trend toward conservatism and nationalism. A new Chamber of Deputies elected in November 1919 was the most conservative since 1871. It contained so many war veterans that it was dubbed the "horizon-blue Chamber," in reference to the color of army dress uniforms. Until the next election, in 1924, the French parliament supported its government's vigilant enforcement of the peace terms, high military readiness, and alliances with Eastern European states against a revived Germany. Prime Minister Raymond Poincaré (1922–1924) came to personify this spirit. A strong-willed lawyer from traditionally nationalist Lorraine, Poincaré was said to "know everything and understand nothing."[19] He construed the treaties with a strict legalism, backed with the force of his character, and the prestige of having been president of France during the war (1913–1920).

Thus, the first five years after the Peace Conference were years of coercion. France, supported more or less grudgingly by some of its wartime allies, attempted

---

[19]This popular jibe contrasted him to his main political rival of the 1920s, the conciliator Aristide Briand, who "understood everything and knew nothing."

to preserve its 1919 eminence by force. After 1924, the weary French and Germans accepted a degree of accommodation, and there followed five years of conciliation.

The Years of Coercion, 1919–1924

France had emerged from the First World War with the most powerful land army in the world. Its apparent hegemony was fragile, however. Victory had been possible in 1918 only with Allied aid, at a price in men and matériel that could never be spent a second time. Germany was still larger than France, and would soon be outproducing French goods and babies. Russia no longer served as a natural counter-weight to the east. The failure of the United States Senate to ratify the Treaty of Versailles meant the lapse of simultaneous treaties that had provided for automatic United States and British aid in case of German attack. No British government would provide a similar guarantee alone. French leaders felt betrayed by this, for they had moderated their demands on Germany in return for this promise of outside support.

French governments after 1919 tried to make up for the deficiencies of their position by two strategies: a single-handed application of the punitive features of the peace settlement, and alliances with those new states in Eastern Europe that had the most to lose by any challenge to the peace terms.

The Eastern alliances were meant to replace the Franco-Russian Treaty that had been the mainstay of French security from Germany between 1892 and 1914. Three of the new states that France had favored in the peace negotiations—Czechoslovakia, Romania, and Yugoslavia—formed the Little Entente in 1921. France concluded military alliances with them and strengthened their mutual cultural and economic ties. Poland was the other essential cog in the French alliance system, for it had more to lose from German and Russian revival than any other new state. French officers had helped Poland stave off Soviet armies in 1920, and French diplomats helped Poland obtain generous solutions to border disputes: the mining and industrial areas of Upper Silesia from Germany, and the city of Vilna from Lithuania. In 1921 Poland and France concluded a treaty of mutual assistance in which each promised to aid the other in case of attack.

France's network of Eastern European clients was a poor substitute for the pre-war Franco-Russian Alliance. The only successor state with a strong industrial base was Czechoslovakia. But the Czechs and Poles were opposed over Teschen. The Little Entente was really directed more against Hungary than against Germany. And even though Romania was tied to France by having a romance language, it had more to lose by Russian revival than by German revival. The Eastern alliances actually complicated France's interwar foreign policy and security problems more than they resolved them.

France's revival of alliance politics also helped push the two main outsider nations—Weimar Germany and Soviet Russia—into each others' arms. While the European states, including Germany and Russia, were meeting at Genoa in April 1922 to discuss world economic problems and to try to get the Soviet Union to repay tsarist debts to them, German Foreign Minister Walther Rathenau and Soviet

© Bettmann / CORBIS

French troops occupy the Ruhr, 1923.

Foreign Minister George Chicherin slipped off to nearby Rapallo and signed a treaty establishing diplomatic relations and promising not to make any economic demands on each other. There were no secret military clauses, but soon thereafter General Hans von Seeckt was working out secret arrangements whereby the USSR manufactured arms for Germany and trained German soldiers clandestinely. The Treaty of Rapallo was a bombshell. It was the first step outside the Paris peace settlement toward an opposing alignment: France and the Little Entente on one side, Germany and the Soviet Union on the other.

The high point of unilateral enforcement was the French military occupation of the Ruhr in January 1923. Convinced that the Germans were falling behind in the coal shipments required as part of reparations payments, Poincaré sent a technical mission, protected by two army divisions, to Essen, headquarters of the German Coal Syndicate, with orders to expedite coal deliveries. The German authorities simply withdrew. Their passive resistance required the French to send in thousands of engineers, administrators, and railroad men plus five army divisions.

In the short term, Poincaré got his coal but at a very high price. One cost was the paroxysm of anger and disorder that shook Germany in 1923. Although most residents of the Ruhr obeyed their government's order of passive resistance, acts of sabotage led to armed clashes. In the most serious of these, thirteen Germans were killed. The German Communist Party revived in the Ruhr, and shared power in coalition governments in the central German states of Thuringia and Saxony. In November, Hitler entered the German political scene with his abortive "beer hall *Putsch*" in Munich.

Another cost was economic disruption. The German mark, already weakened by years of wartime and postwar inflation, now plummeted out of control, as the government recklessly printed money to pay workers and enterprises practicing passive resistance. Prices leapt upward by the hour in summer 1923. The inflationary spiral exceeded anything known before. On April 25, 1923, a family of four already needed 463,000 marks to buy the necessities of life for four weeks. By June 6, it needed 981,000 marks; by August 14, 84,000,000.[20] At the worst, in autumn 1923, prices were doubling or tripling every week.[21] Anyone in Germany with savings or investments lost them. This epoch-making evaporation of wealth poisoned the German economic and financial climate for years afterward.

During the runaway German inflation of 1923, banknotes quickly lost their value. Here a newspaper vendor collects her money in a laundry basket.

© 2000 Stock Montage, Inc.

[20]Gerald D. Feldman, *The Great Disorder: Politics, Economics, and Society in the German Inflation, 1914–1924* (New York, 1993), p. 673.

[21]Barry Eichengreen, *Golden Fetters: The Gold Standard and the Great Depression, 1919–1939* (Oxford, England, 1992), p. 125.

France suffered financially too. The franc had already lost half of its purchasing power and exchange value during the war because of huge budget deficits. In 1923, the expense and anxiety of the Ruhr occupation, accompanied by the realization that the promised German reparations would never close the French budget gap, provoked an international sell-off of the franc and exacerbated a new surge of inflation. When financial stability was finally restored in 1928, the franc had only about one-fifth of its prewar purchasing power. Although some wage-earners kept pace with inflation, anyone with a fixed income was impoverished. Frenchmen with prewar savings or pensions, or those who had bought war bonds, bitterly concluded that they—instead of the promised German reparations—had paid for the war after all with the loss of their savings.

Poincaré paid a further price in loss of international support. Forgetting the vengefulness of their 1918 "khaki election," much of British opinion now shared the view of John Maynard Keynes in his best-seller *The Economic Consequences of the Peace* (1919), which blamed French vindictiveness for blocking European economic recovery. The British government abstained conspicuously from the Ruhr occupation. The Belgians sent token forces and Mussolini's Italy gave Poincaré at least moral support. But it became clear that if France tried to extract its pound of flesh from Germany by force, it would stand alone.

The Years of Conciliation, 1924–1929

Mutual exhaustion opened the way to more conciliatory times. The French discovered they could not coerce Germany alone. The Germans learned that their passive resistance was self-destructive. Out of this negative balance grew a normalization of international relations in Europe in the later 1920s.

As Germany teetered on the brink of chaos, all the major parties that supported the infant Weimar Republic, from the Social Democrats on the left to the Peoples' Party on the center right, banded together in August 1923 in a "Great Coalition" to deal with the emergency. Peoples' Party leader Gustav Stresemann became the new chancellor (prime minister). Stresemann's success in ending the crisis made him the outstanding figure in German politics and in European diplomacy until his death in 1929.

Although Stresemann's own government lasted only three months (August–November 1923), it was a decisive "hundred days." He ordered an end to passive resistance, issued a stable new German currency, blocked a Communist uprising in Hamburg and the "Hitler *Putsch*" in Munich,[22] and made overtures for an understanding with France. As foreign minister in all succeeding governments until his death nearly six years later, Stresemann led Germany into a new foreign policy of "fulfillment" *(Erfüllung)*.

Stresemann attempted to negotiate gradual changes in the Versailles system while carrying out its provisions. His new German foreign policy has received varying assessments. At the time, and even more in retrospect when Germany was under Hitler,

---

[22]See chapter 7, pp. 213–214.

Stresemann seemed the very model of international conciliation. He was awarded the Nobel Peace Prize in 1926. After the Second World War, however, the discovery of his private papers produced a harsh reassessment. It was clear that, even though Stresemann was willing to live with Germany's western frontiers, he never accepted the eastern frontiers. One key document in Stresemann's papers was a secret memorandum of September 7, 1925, to the exiled crown prince of Prussia, in which Stresemann set out a kind of timetable for dismantling the Versailles system: first, resolution of the reparations issue; then, the protection of Germans outside the national frontiers; finally, the rectification of the eastern borders—regaining Danzig, the Polish Corridor, and parts of Upper Silesia; revising the frontier with Czechoslovakia; and perhaps eventually uniting with Austria. Stresemann thought all this could be achieved by cautious but ever more forceful steps. "First we must get the throttler from our throat"; then Germany could seek more active goals by "being crafty" *(finassieren)*.

Stresemann never had time to carry out his grand design, but his private papers reveal him as a determined revisionist who sought many of the changes that Hitler achieved in the late 1930s, including expansion beyond Germany's 1914 borders in the east. Any comparison with Hitler must, of course, stress the total absence in Stresemann of territorial aims outside German-speaking areas, of overt racialist doctrines, or of Hitler's evident need to display force in his victories.

The Locarno Era: The Dawes Plan and the Locarno Treaty

The new climate was reflected in elections in Britain and France at the turn of 1923–1924. Both countries' voters repudiated the hard-liners who had come to power in 1918–1919.[23] Ramsay MacDonald, Britain's first Labour prime minister, and a new French leadership from the center left, premier Edouard Herriot and Foreign Minister Aristide Briand, responded eagerly to Stresemann's offers of "fulfillment." Briand, who remained in charge of French foreign policy under various governments from April 1925 until his death in January 1932, came to personify the "years of conciliation" as Poincaré had personified the "years of coercion." Where Poincaré had been dry and legalistic, Briand was warm and effusive. His emotional speeches at the League of Nations in the late 1920s won him a worldwide reputation as the "apostle of peace." On closer inspection, Briand actually conceded very little in private negotiation, needing as he did to retain the confidence of a nationalistic parliamentary majority.

At this point, Stresemann's first priority was reparations. That, after all, was the immediate issue behind the Ruhr crisis of 1923 that brought him to power. By November 1923, Poincaré himself was willing to accept the appointment of an international commission to review the whole question and to move reparations from the realm of moral censure to the more realistic realm of economic capacity. Charles G. Dawes, an American financier and later vice president of the United States under Calvin Coolidge, headed a commission that produced a new plan for reparations in London in July and August 1924.

[23]See chapter 8, pp. 232–233, 236–238.

The Dawes Plan was meant to put reparations on a businesslike footing. To begin, German payments must be based not on Allied moral indignation or even on Allied reconstruction needs but on German capacity to pay. The funds were to be raised in Germany by new taxes and by income from the railroads, which were placed under international supervision. The transfer of the marks into foreign currencies was to be carefully regulated in order to avoid damaging the mark on international exchanges. Finally, the Dawes Plan recognized the need for a respite. Payments were to begin at a low level, assisted at first by foreign loans (the "Dawes loans"). Only by 1928 and 1929 would the payments reach the full 2 billion marks per year. Then another settlement must be agreed on, for the Dawes Commission had refused to set any total figure. In practice, the Dawes Plan worked smoothly. The new German currency was firmly stabilized, and foreign loans flowed into the reviving German business community to such a point that they outweighed the reparations payments going out.[24]

The diplomatic deadlock provoked by the French occupation of the Ruhr began to loosen when German Foreign Minister Stresemann proposed a mutual Franco-German agreement not to violate the Rhine frontier. Briand and the British Conservative Foreign Secretary Austen Chamberlain, committed like most of his countrymen to more conciliatory relations with Germany, took up Stresemann's proposal with alacrity. They met at the Swiss resort of Locarno, on Lake Maggiore, in October 1925 and concluded the Locarno Agreements, which launched a new era of European international relaxation.

The heart of the Locarno Agreements was a Franco-German promise to maintain the Rhine frontier as the Treaty of Versailles had settled it. France and Germany recognized their common border as legitimate. Britain and Italy promised to intervene if either France or Germany tried to send an army across that frontier, or if Germany sent troops into the demilitarized areas of the Rhineland. The German eastern frontiers were not guaranteed in the same way. To make that omission less threatening, Germany subsequently signed arbitration treaties with Poland and Czechoslovakia. And just to make sure, France strengthened its ties with the Little Entente states by making even more binding treaties of mutual assistance among them in case of a German attack.

Each participant yielded something and gained something in the Locarno Agreements. Germany renounced any attempt to regain Alsace-Lorraine by force, or to remilitarize the Rhineland unilaterally. Those acts were far beyond Germany's military capacity for years to come anyway, given the embryonic state of its clandestine rearmament. In return, Stresemann won separation of the issue of the eastern frontiers from the western, was assured of French support for German admission to the League of Nations (1926), and persuaded France to begin withdrawing occupation troops from the Rhineland, a process that was completed in 1930 rather than 1935 and that effectively halted French efforts to detach that area from Germany.

France renounced the possibility of direct armed intervention in Germany, as had been attempted several times from 1920 to 1923. Those efforts had proven

---

[24]Germany paid $2 billion in reparations in 1924–1929 (about 3 percent of GNP by 1928). Barry Eichengreen, *Golden Fetters,* p. 224. Foreign loans to German businesses and local governments in 1924–1929 totaled $3 billion. William McNeil, *American Money and the Weimar Republic* (New York, 1986), p. 292.

FRANCO-GERMAN SECURITY ISSUES, 1920–1940

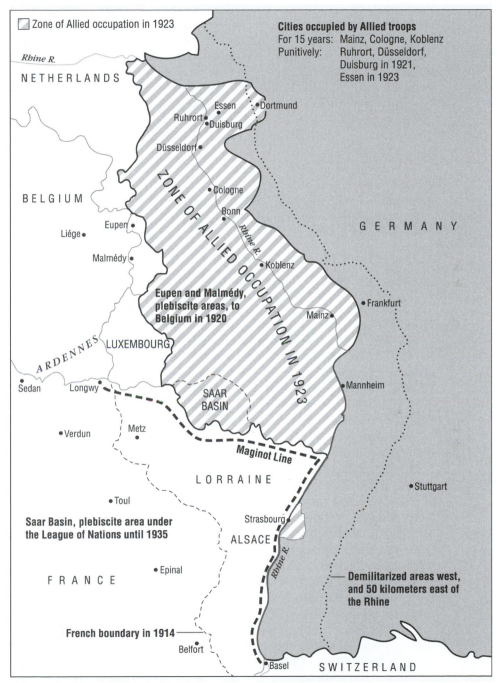

counterproductive anyway, as had French efforts to promote separatist sentiment in the Rhineland. In addition, the French accepted Germany as an equal diplomatic interlocutor, as symbolized by its entry into the League, and withdrew by 1930 the troops that were supposed to occupy the Rhineland until 1935. Briand also tacitly accepted a less-settled status for the eastern frontiers. Of course, as long as the Rhineland remained empty of German troops in perpetuity, as was explicitly stated in the Locarno Agreements, France could still bring an effective threat to bear on Germany from the west in case Germany menaced Poland or Czechoslovakia.

Britain renounced its isolation and participated for the first time since 1919 in a Continental guarantee. That pledge was limited to Western Europe, however, and it applied equally to Germany and to France, so that the British public, exasperated by French intransigence, would have less fear of being dragged into a war by France. Thus, the Locarno Agreements relieved the French pressures for a British treaty of assistance that both Briand and Poincaré had sought in vain.

The most significant feature of the Locarno Agreements was the spirit of hope they had awakened in Europe. When the accords were concluded on October 16, 1925,

> Austen Chamberlain, the British Foreign Secretary, trembled and wept with joy, as did the French Foreign Minister, Aristide Briand. Benito Mussolini kissed Mrs. Chamberlain's hands. Bands played, members of the assembled crowd danced in the square. . . . The next day the headlines in the New York *Times* read, "France and Germany Ban War Forever," and those in the London *Times* declared, "Peace at Last."[25]

It was for that spirit, rather than for the concrete terms of the agreements, that Stresemann and Briand were jointly awarded the Nobel Peace Prize in 1926.

In this heady mood, the major European states, the United States, and Japan concluded the Kellogg-Briand Pact on August 27, 1928.[26] The signatories promised to "renounce war as an instrument of national policy," although no means of enforcing this promise were included in the pact.

On closer inspection, the Locarno spirit was far too optimistic. It rested on a transient balance struck briefly between French and German force. France had publicly revealed its inability to coerce Germany alone. Britain had publicly revealed its unwillingness to help France do so. Germany's clandestine rearmament had hardly begun, despite some Soviet assistance, yet any clear-sighted person could foresee the disparity of potential force between 60 million Germans and 40 million Frenchmen. Everything depended on Briand's gamble that concessions would disarm the Germans "morally" and that moderation would reconcile them to Versailles where force had failed.

Those hopes were not realized. The follow-up after Locarno was slow and grudging, for Briand was under constant pressure from his centrist majority. Moreover, Briand was a careless diplomat who promised more in his generous oratory than he could actually deliver. Stresemann, for his part, was never able to persuade German

---

[25]Jon Jacobson, *Locarno Diplomacy: Germany and the West, 1925–1929* (Princeton, N.J., 1972), p. 3.

[26]Frank B. Kellogg was the United States secretary of state.

Seated from left to right are Gustav Stresemann, Sir Austen Chamberlain, Aristide Briand, and German diplomat Karl von Schubert, in Geneva for a League of Nations meeting in September 1926.

nationalists that the French concessions really amounted to anything compared with the immense humiliation of Versailles.

When the temporary reparations arrangements of the Dawes Plan expired in 1929, a storm of German nationalist opposition arose over the successor plan worked out by the American businessman Owen D. Young. The Young Plan removed Allied tutelage from the German economy, but it provided for continued reparations payments to 1988. The howl of resentment over the Young Plan helped revive the Nazi Party in the summer of 1929, even before the onset of the depression.

The Failure of Disarmament

The Locarno spirit did not suffice to make disarmament possible. The League of Nations Covenant, borrowing the exact language of Wilson's Fourteen Points (Point 4), had called for "the reduction of national armaments to the lowest point consistent with national safety" (Article 8). The Treaty of Versailles had stripped

Germany of armed force as a "first step" toward a general reduction of armaments; Germany had promised to observe those limitations on the understanding that other states would also disarm. The World Disarmament Conference promised in 1919 was not seriously prepared for until 1927 and did not actually meet until February 1932, when it was already far too late. In the meantime, no government had felt confident enough of its national security to entrust its survival to anything except its own armed force.

With respect to land armies, the basic problems were the disparity between German and French military potentials, and the difficulty of verifying any artificial ceiling placed on German military power. The experience of German clandestine rearmament in the 1920s had shown that outside inspection teams could do very little to impose artificial limitations on the armaments of a recalcitrant government that was backed by its public. The Allied Control Commission filed two long reports, one on January 5, 1925, and the other on January 31, 1927, stating that Germany "had never disarmed, had never had the intention of disarming, and for seven years had done everything in her power to deceive" the foreign inspectors.

Even if one accepts the later opinion of the British strategist Major Basil H. Liddell-Hart that the practical effects of German clandestine rearmament were "overrated,"[27] and that well into the 1930s the German army was no match for the French, the long-term implications were clear then. The view from Paris was that Germany would eventually gravitate back toward a position of equality or better with the French, and given the resentments bred by Versailles, it would attack as soon as the chances of success became more or less even. French fears were greatly magnified by solitude; neither the United States nor Britain had been willing to conclude a bilateral defense pact with France. The French believed that general disarmament would make Germany more likely, not less, to commit aggression. As a result, France continued to spend a higher percentage of its national income on armaments in the late 1920s than any other European state except Soviet Russia.[28]

Beginning in 1929, successive French governments, from right to moderate left, appropriated huge sums for the construction of the Maginot Line, a vast network of underground fortresses and armored turrets whose overlapping fields of fire were impassable to anything known in 1918. When completed at the end of 1935, the Maginot Line extended along the Franco-German frontier from the Swiss border north to the Ardennes Forest, at the Franco-Belgian border, and public opinion was urging the government, against military advice, to extend this steel womb all the way to the English Channel.

From 1927 until 1932 the Disarmament Preparatory Commission worked on preliminary drafts for an agreement. The German demands centered on equality of armament, which in practice meant leveling upward. When a Soviet delegate joined the commission in 1928, he urged the immediate liquidation of all armed forces. All Allied proposals foundered on unstated French assumptions that French survival

---

[27]Basil H. Liddell-Hart, *The German Generals Talk* (New York, 1948), pp. 13–14.

[28]Figures for 1929: Russian military expenditures, 5.3 percent of national income; French, 4.5 percent; Italian, 4.4 percent; Japanese, 4.3 percent; British, 2.5 percent; American, 1.1 percent; German, 1 percent. When all states' military expenditures soared in the 1930s, France slipped to fifth place. (Quincy Wright, *A Study of War* [Chicago, 1941], pp. 670–671.)

depended on having a larger ground force than Germany. It was as the Spanish diplomat Salvador de Madariaga said in his parable of the disarmament conference of the animals: The lion proposed the abolition of all weapons except claws and teeth; the eagle, all weapons except beaks and talons; and so on.

When the World Disarmament Conference actually opened in Geneva in February 1932, the moment for agreement had long passed. The opening day of the conference was postponed by news of the Japanese bombing of Shanghai. The German delegation left the conference between July and September 1932, until the French accepted the principle of equality within a system of collective security. Hitler's delegate left the conference for good in October 1933. Indeed, as long as no larger sovereignty than the nation-state functioned in Europe and as long as each state subordinated disarmament to its own definition of "the lowest point consistent with national safety," it was difficult to imagine any effective reduction of armaments in Europe by treaty.

Naval disarmament offered more hopeful signs of progress in the 1920s than disarmament of land forces. That was because naval forces were easier to inspect, the conferences were held sooner after the end of the war, and the Franco-German conflict was less directly involved. The Washington Naval Conference of 1921 and 1922 managed to agree on ratios of tonnage in capital ships (battleships, aircraft carriers) among the five main naval powers as follows: the United States and Britain, 5; Japan, 3; France and Italy, 1.75. But the conference failed to deal with smaller ships, such as submarines, destroyers, and cruisers. When that effort was made at Geneva in 1927, it uncovered heated controversy between Britain and the United States and between France and Italy; neither Britain nor France accepted parity in cruisers with its Washington Naval Conference partner. A final attempt to settle naval force limits at the London Naval Conference of 1930 did produce agreed ratios for all types of ships on the part of Britain, the United States, and Japan (France and Italy refused to be bound by any such agreements), but the overriding importance of national self-reliance was made clear in the famous "Escalator Clause": Any nation that felt threatened by a nonsignatory power could unilaterally go beyond the agreed limits. In the world of 1930 and after, all nations felt threatened, and the whole enterprise of disarmament by conference failed by trying to alleviate symptoms rather than fundamental causes of that insecurity.

A NEW DIPLOMACY?

The peace settlement of 1919 was framed in a climate of hope that "open covenants of peace openly arrived at" might replace the old international power politics. "After that, there shall be no private international understandings of any kind but diplomacy shall proceed always frankly and in the public view" (Point 1 of Woodrow Wilson's Fourteen Points). Neither President Wilson nor any other statesman actually dealt with other states this way, of course, but the dream of a "new diplomacy" was very widespread. The British diplomat Harold Nicolson remembered going off to the Paris Peace Conference as a young man eager to undo the "mistakes" that "the reactionary . . . aristocrats" had made in previous peace conferences.

> We were journeying to Paris not merely to liquidate the war, but to found a New Order in Europe. We were preparing not peace only, but Eternal Peace. There was about us the halo of some divine mission.[29]

Reality was far soberer. Governments continued to deal with each other in secret, and the interest of states (as perceived by each, of course) continued to be the driving force of international relations. Foreign relations had nevertheless been profoundly and permanently altered by the First World War.

Public Involvement

Although statesmen continued to negotiate in secret, foreign affairs became a more and more public matter between the wars. Before 1914, it was still uncommon for foreign relations to become a major political issue in peacetime.[30] Occasionally political oppositions formed around foreign and colonial policy, as they did in Britain during the Boer War (1899–1902) and in France at the time of the secret diplomacy of the second Moroccan crisis of 1911, but executive branches remained in full control of foreign policy. Even in parliamentary systems, the deputies' powers of review of treaties were incomplete. No one believed, for example, that a parliament could declare a past treaty invalid. As often as not, the executive authorities themselves injected issues of foreign and colonial grandeur into partisan politics in order to strengthen their position. German Chancellor Bernhard von Bülow won an enlarged government majority in the so-called Hottentot election of 1907. Von Bülow appealed for unlimited executive freedom to conduct foreign policy and colonial expansion among the African Hottentots or anywhere else the government chose, without the "unendurable meddling"[31] of parliament. As von Bülow hoped, his patriotic appeals helped reduce the anticolonial Social Democrats' representation from eighty-one seats to forty-three.

The passions of the First World War aroused public sensitivity and emotion concerning foreign policy. During the last year of the war, Wilson and Lenin heightened expectations with a propaganda duel about war aims and programs for reordering the world. The great gathering of world leaders in Paris in 1919 made the ensuing world system seem more man-made and less a natural inheritance than before. Thus, the subsequent disillusions about that system brought blame to political leaders, and elections turned more and more frequently on foreign policy issues. Aristide Briand lost office as prime minister and foreign minister in 1922 for seeming too compliant toward England and was narrowly limited after Locarno in the concessions he could offer Germany. The elections of 1924 turned partly on foreign affairs in both France and England. Hitler's immediate predecessors struggled to

[29]Harold Nicolson, *Peacemaking, 1919* (London, 1935), p. 25.

[30]One exception was the Turkish slaughter of rebellious Bulgarians in 1876 and the ensuing war between Russia and Turkey, which involved British public emotions for the first time in daily newspaper accounts of a distant war. The word *jingoism* entered the language from a British patriotic song of 1878: "We don't want to fight, but, by jingo, if we do, we've got the men, we've got the ships, we've got the money too."

[31]Quoted in Carl E. Schorske, *German Social Democracy, 1905–1917* (Cambridge, Mass., 1955), p. 60.

Bildarchiv der Österreichische Nationalbibliothek / Picture Archives of the Austrian National Library

The defeated people suffered intensely from hunger and cold in the winter of 1918–1919. The Austrians cut down the Vienna Woods for fuel, and the middle class as well as the poor were reduced to carrying firewood.

win electoral support through foreign policy successes. In 1935, to look a decade ahead, British and French governments fell because they seemed to acquiesce in the Italian conquest of Ethiopia, and in the late 1930s the reaction to Hitler's expansionism was the dominant preoccupation of politics. Sustained public emotional involvement in foreign policy was not the guarantee of peace that the Wilsonians had expected, for public opinion turned out to be more jingoistic than rulers had been, and weak governments catered to that jingoism.

One major reason for public emotion over foreign relations was economic. Almost every European was touched in his pocket by international affairs in ways that seemed all the more frightening for being uncontrollable and beyond comprehension. Most Frenchmen knew that rising prices and decline of the franc in the 1920s were somehow tied to war debts to America and the failure of Germany to pay full reparations. Most Germans felt that the implacable Allied victors had somehow destroyed the mark in 1923. Most Englishmen were aware of the fact that the great coal and textile industries, the foundations of the British Empire, were somehow worth less in the postwar world and that Britain was now in debt to its offspring America. Popular emotions were closely tied to foreign affairs after 1918 because the purchasing power of one's money and the value of one's property were now more buffeted about by international fluctuations and influences than ever before.

The Communist Threat

Foreign relations took on a more ideological tone, too, now that the communist movement controlled the machinery of a state. World communist parties intervened in interstate relations on two levels: through traditional diplomacy and through revolutionary parties. As a sovereign state, the Soviet Union sought normal diplomatic relations with other states after the expected world revolution had failed to materialize. Weimar Germany was the first major state to exchange ambassadors with the Soviet Union at Rapallo in 1922. Britain and France and most other countries followed suit in 1924.[32] The Japanese evacuated their last holdings in Siberia in 1925 and recognized the new regime. As the British Liberal politician Lloyd George said, one trades even with cannibals. Leaders on both sides recognized that even though the Bolshevik Revolution stood little chance in the 1920s of spreading outside Russia, the Communist Party was in firm control there. The Soviet Union practiced its conventional interstate diplomacy in the 1920s under George Chicherin, a veteran tsarist diplomat but a Menshevik, or reformist socialist, by conviction.

Simultaneously, however, the Soviet Union was the major force in the Comintern,[33] the global organization of pro-Soviet Marxist parties formed by Lenin in 1919 in the expectation of imminent world revolution and led through the 1920s by the old Bolshevik Grigori Zinoviev. Agents of the Comintern worked within foreign states to strengthen communist internal opposition. The Comintern's influence over Soviet foreign policy diminished through the 1920s as the exercise of state power in Russia and the protection of the homeland of communism came to prevail over the promotion of world revolution. Nevertheless the noncommunist states' relations with the Soviet Union were always complicated by this ambiguous dual diplomacy. Allegations of Comintern activity in Britain brought about defeat of the Labour Party in 1924 and suspension of diplomatic relations with the Soviet Union. The British election of 1924 revealed how sensitive an issue the unofficial foreign activities of communist parties remained.

Diplomatic Machinery

Optimists hoped that the League of Nations would provide effective machinery for resolving international disputes. But it was no world government. Before the League could act against an aggressor, the council must first vote unanimously that aggression had been committed. Then member states must contribute forces to act

---

[32]The United States did not exchange ambassadors with the Soviet Union until after the election of Franklin D. Roosevelt in 1932, although there had been aid missions during the famine of 1921 and 1922, and some United States firms had negotiated contracts with the Soviet government.

[33]The Communist International, or Third International. See chapter 5, pp. 150–152.

in the League's name. At best, the League could only do what its most powerful members agreed to do.

The internationalists elected to power in France and Britain in 1924, Herriot, Briand, and Ramsay MacDonald, tried to give more teeth to the League of Nations peacekeeping machinery. The League charter left unspecified how to define aggression or agree to act against it. MacDonald and Herriot proposed an arbitration device, by which any party to a dispute who refused arbitration would automatically be deemed an aggressor and thus subject to sanctions by other members of the League. This proposal, known as the Geneva Protocol, was the most significant attempt between the world wars to replace traditional power politics with some kind of legal procedure for the resolution of international disputes. It was never adopted; Conservatives who returned to power in British elections in September 1924 rejected it.

The League helped solve a half-dozen minor border disputes in the 1920s in cases where the major powers concurred. It became less a victors' coalition and more a family of nations when Germany (1926) and then Russia (1934) were admitted. But the United States never joined, a near-fatal blow. Its greatest successes were the promotion of international cooperation in matters like public health and communications. Its failure to do anything about the Japanese invasion of Manchuria in 1931 dealt it a major humiliation, and its inability to halt aggression by a large state was confirmed in 1934–1935 when Italy invaded Ethiopia.

Thus, between the world wars, international relations remained in the hands of sovereign states, much as before. Only now there were many more of them. And the European states could be powerfully affected by distant powers such as Japan and the United States. As a result, the affairs of Europe were less under the control of the Great Powers than before. The new nation-states of Eastern Europe generated at least as many international problems as the dynasties they had replaced. The loser states of 1920, Germany and Russia at their head, looked for opportunities to regain their temporarily eclipsed power. So the settlement of 1919, far from ushering in a time of peace, merely suspended temporarily what has been called Europe's second Thirty Years' War (1914–1945).

SUGGESTIONS FOR FURTHER READING

Margaret Olwen MacMillan, *Paris 1919: Six Months That Changed the World*[*] (2002), is lively and thoughtful. Alan Sharp, *The Versailles Settlement: Peacemaking in Paris, 1919*[*] (1991), remains an acute brief introduction. The latest scholarship is reviewed in Manfred F. Boemeke, Gerald D. Feldman, and Elizabeth Glasser, *The Treaty of Versailles: A Reassessment after 75 Years* (1998). David Stevenson, *The First World War and International Politics*[*] (1991), provides a long-range international perspective.

The massive H. W. V. Temperley, ed., *History of the Peace Conference of Paris*, 6 vols. (1920–1924), is still useful. It needs to be counterbalanced by the French perspective in André Tardieu, *The Truth about the Treaty* (1921), and by David Lloyd George, *The Truth about the Peace Treaties* (1938).

The negotiations may be followed in Arthur Link, ed., *The Deliberations of the Council of Four* (1992), and more completely in the notes of the secretary to the British Delegation, Sir Maurice Hankey, published by the U.S. Department of State, *Foreign Relations of the United States,* "The Paris Peace Conference, 1919," vols. 3–5 (1943–1946).

Harold Nicolson, *Peacemaking, 1919,* new ed. (2001), remains the most evocative of participants' memoirs. John Maynard Keynes's criticism in *The Economic Consequences of the Peace* (1919, reprint ed. 2004) was criticized in turn by Etienne Mantoux, *The Carthaginian Peace, or the Economic Consequences of Mr. Keynes*[*] (1946, reprint ed. 1999).

The impact of war aims and wartime promises on the peace settlement is explored in V. H. Rothwell, *British War Aims and Peace Diplomacy, 1914–1918* (1971), and David Stevenson, *French War Aims against Germany, 1914–1919* (1982). Klaus Epstein treated the struggle within Germany over accepting the peace terms in *Matthias Erzberger and the Dilemma of German Democracy* (1959, reprint ed. 1971).

Among accounts of individual governments recent enough to have used the archives, see Erik Goldstein, *Winning the Peace: British Diplomatic Strategy, Peace Planning, and the Paris Peace Conference 1916–1920* (1991); Sally Marks, *Innocent Abroad: Belgium and the Paris Peace Conference of 1919* (1981); Kay Lundgreen-Nielson, *The Polish Problem at the Paris Peace Conference* (1979); and Marian Kent, *The Great Powers and the End of the Ottoman Empire,*[*] 2nd ed. (1996). Seth P. Tillman, *Anglo-American Relations at the Paris Peace Conference of 1919* (1961, reprint ed. 2003), is still useful. For Italy, refer to H. James Burgwyn, *The Legend of the Mutilated Victory: Italy, the Great War, and the Paris Peace Conference* (1993), and for the South Slavs to Ivo Lederer, *Yugoslavia at the Paris Peace Conference* (1966).

Still essential for the eastern settlement is John W. Wheeler-Bennett, *Brest-Litovsk: The Forgotten Peace, March 1918* (revised ed. 1971). Arno J. Mayer has directed attention to the role played in the peace settlement by anti-Bolshevism in *Wilson vs. Lenin: Political Origins of the New Diplomacy 1917–1918* (1959, reprint ed. 1964) and *The Politics and Diplomacy of Peace-Making* (1967).

Good biographies of Clemenceau in English are Donald R. Watson, *Georges Clemenceau: A Political Biography* (1976), and Gregor Dallas's more personal *At the Heart of a Tiger* (1993). For Lloyd George, in addition to the monumental biography by John Grigg, see Bentley B. Gilbert, *David Lloyd Georqe: A Political Life* (1992), and the brief introduction by Chris Wrigley, *Lloyd George*[*] (1990). Woodrow Wilson is scrutinized without indulgence by the German scholar Klaus Schwabe in *Woodrow Wilson, Revolutionary Germany and Peacemaking, 1918–1919* (1985), by Arthur Walworth, *Wilson and His Peacemakers* (1986), and more favorably in many volumes by Arthur Link, including *Woodrow Wilson: Revolution, War, and Peace*[*] (1985).

Lorna S. Jaffe, *The Decision to Disarm Germany* (1985), is good on disarmament. James F. Willis, *Prologue to Nuremburg: The Politics and Diplomacy of Punishing War Criminals of the First World War* (1982), treats the first war crimes jurisdiction.

Good on international relations in the 1920s are Sally Marks, *The Illusion of*

Peace: Europe's International Relations, 1918–1933, 2nd ed (2003), and Jon Jacobson, *Locarno Diplomacy* (1972). In the absence of a good biography of Briand, Jacobson shows him convincingly in action. Walter McDougall, *France's Rhineland Diplomacy, 1914–1924* (1978), is basic for Poincaré's hard line. Stephen A. Schuker, *The End of French Predominance in Europe** (1988), gives the essential economic-financial background to France's inability to enforce its peace.

German foreign policy in the 1920s is synonymous with the career of Gustav Stresemann. Hans W. Gatzke revealed Stresemann's revisionist aims in *Stresemann and the Rearmament of Germany* (1954). The latest scholarly treatment of Soviet foreign policy in the 1920s is Jon Jacobson, *When the Soviet Union Entered World Politics** (1994).

Michael C. Howard, *The Continental Commitment* (1989), caps a rich literature on the dilemmas of British foreign policy after 1918. The French alliances in the east are scrutinized by Piotr Wandycz in *France and Her Eastern Allies, 1915–1919* (1974), and *The Twilight of France's Eastern Alliances, 1926–1936** (1988). Anna Cienciala, *From Versailles to Locarno: Keys to Polish Foreign Policy, 1919–1925* (1984), is a valuable monograph.

Gerald D. Feldman, *The Great Disorder: Politics, Economics, and Society in the German Inflation** (1997), is the fullest examination of postwar inflation's impact on any one country. William C. McNeil, *American Money and the Weimar Republic* (1986), is basic for the economic dimension of the German "fulfillment" policy.

The reparations debate is continued in Robert E. Bunselmeyer, *The Cost of the War of 1914–1918: British Economic War Aims and the Origins of Reparations* (1975); Marc Trachtenberg, *Reparations in World Politics* (1980), more lenient towards France than most; and Bruce Kent, *The Spoils of War** (1989).

F. S. Northedge, *The League of Nations: Its Life and Times, 1920–1946* (1986), is a solid survey; F. P. Walters, *A History of the League of Nations,* 2 vols., (1952), remains an indispensable inside view by a member of the League secretariat. See also George Egerton, *Great Britain and the Creation of the League of Nations* (1979).

Additional Internet links related to this chapter are available on the Europe in the 20th Century Web site: http://www.history.wadsworth.com/paxton04.

You can also explore images, interactive timelines, and maps related to this chapter on our Western Civilization Resource Center: http://history.wadsworth.com.

Members of the Fascist boys' movement, the *Figli della Lupa* (Roman Wolf's Cubs), parading with miniature rifles before Benito Mussolini in the Roman forum on the twentieth anniversary of the Italian entry into the First World War, May 1935.

7

Revolution against Revolution: Fascism

The revolutionary wave in Europe after 1917 generated a counterrevolutionary response at once. But postwar counterrevolution did not mean the return to religion and to social deference with which nineteenth-century traditional conservatives had tried to meet revolutionary threats. There was a new name—fascism—and behind it, a new reality. Fascism put together mass movements, nationalism, antisocialism, and antiliberal values in largely unforeseen ways.

Mass politics had entered European history in the nineteenth century on the left. The values of nineteenth-century middle- and lower-middle-class Europeans tended to be liberal: They invested great hopes in the ballot box; in universal, secular, public education; and in the self-determination of nations. In the 1890s, many working-class and lower-middle-class Europeans became attracted to the new socialist parties. Their electoral success enabled Karl Marx's collaborator and successor, Friedrich Engels, to believe in 1895 that "we shall conquer the greater part of the middle strata of society, petty bourgeois and small peasants, and grow into the decisive power in the land."[1] The broadening of citizen participation in politics, as the middle and lower classes expanded, seemed to promise an indefinite progression of European mass politics toward the left. Nineteenth-century conservatives, with some exceptions, had preferred a passive citizenry. A European familiar with the political landscape up to 1890, suddenly transplanted to a mass rally of the 1920s or 1930s in which an aroused crowd bayed its approval of a uniformed leader's harangue against socialists, intellectuals, foreigners, and Jews, might have believed himself on another planet.

With the advantages of hindsight, it is possible to see a number of ways in which fascism was prepared by late-nineteenth-century developments. We shall look back to these precursors later in this chapter. But first, to recapture the sense of newness and urgency with which fascist movements sprang up in the disorder of postwar Europe, it seems best to take a close look at the movement that provided the name, Italian fascism, and at two important similar movements of the years 1919 to 1923 in Germany and Hungary.

FASCISM IN ITALY

Many Italians were disillusioned at the close of the First World War by the costs of an inconclusive victory, and after the armistice they bitterly confronted one another over social and national issues.[2] The strikes and factory occupations of 1919 and 1920 and the land seizures of 1919 seemed to be leading toward an Italian socialist revolution. Meanwhile, Gabriele D'Annunzio's seizure of Fiume in 1919 suggested to militant nationalists that they could shove aside a faltering state and get what they wanted by direct action. In that chaos was born Benito Mussolini's Fascist movement.

Mussolini: From Syndicalism to Fascism

When asked to define fascism, Mussolini liked to say, "I am Fascism." So it is appropriate to begin with a look at the leader himself. He was born in the traditionally volatile *Romagna* region, northeast of Rome, to a schoolteacher and an anarchist blacksmith, who named him after the Mexican revolutionary Benito Juarez. Unlike his German imitator Hitler, Mussolini achieved some prewar status. He was a leading figure on the Italian left before he was thirty. He became editor of the Socialist Party newspaper *Avanti! (Forward!)* at the end of 1912, and quadrupled its readership to 100,000 over the next two years. In 1913, he was elected to the city council of Milan, Italy's largest industrial city.

---

[1]Friedrich Engels's 1895 introduction to Karl Marx, *The Class Struggles in France, 1848–1850* (New York, 1964).

[2]See chapter 5, pp. 146–148.

By political persuasion and temperament, Mussolini was syndicalist rather than socialist. Syndicalism was an individualistic, antiauthoritarian movement of revolt endemic to rural artisans, agricultural laborers, railroad workers, and miners, in France, Italy, and Spain. Syndicalists were bitterly hostile not only to parliamentary, reformist socialists but also to the Marxist strategy of attempting to take over the state. They wanted to dissolve the state, not take it over. Their strategy rested on bringing down the whole immoral world of property with one apocalyptic "great day," a mass general strike. Then they would replace the state, not with another authority as previous revolutionists (from the Jacobins to Lenin) had done, but with a free community in which the only organizations would be workers' associations *(syndicats)* exchanging goods and services among themselves. Syndicalism's inchoate, millenarian revolutionism was deeply rooted in the *Romagna,* and as a student the young Mussolini further steeped himself in the French syndicalist Georges Sorel's cult of action, in a vulgarized Nietzschean exaltation of will, and in Bergsonian faith in intuition. It was actually easier for a syndicalist to pass to the far right than to subside into moderation, and through a lifetime of political metamorphoses, Mussolini never lost his impatient contempt for parliaments and his intransigent activism.

Mussolini was named editor of *Avanti!* in December 1912, after Italian syndicalists won control of the Italian Socialist Party machinery from parliamentary socialists, some of whom had discredited themselves by supporting the Italian conquest of Libya. He was expelled from the party two years later, however, when, in a characteristic about-face, he urged Italian entry into the First World War on the Allied side. Mussolini had become a "national syndicalist." War seemed to his impatient temperament a more revolutionary state than passive neutrality. His new prowar newspaper, *Il Popolo d'Italia,* got money from France, although this seems to have come afterward as reward rather than beforehand as bribe, as sometimes alleged.

In 1918, Mussolini was one of millions of veterans finding their way in the dislocations of demobilization. Since he had seen some front-line service, and had been wounded accidentally but painfully when a shell exploded during trench mortar practice (he dramatized this as "forty-four wounds" by counting every fragment), his *Popolo d'Italia* had some claim to speak for veterans. With the peace settlement at hand, Mussolini joined the annexationist chorus, calling Italy a "proletarian nation" that must expropriate the colonies of rich nations. His social criticism reflected the veterans' bitterness at war profiteers, pacifists, and the comfortable. Mussolini thought that the floating mass of veterans could be harnessed to a movement that would be both left and nationalist.

> The bourgeois revolution of 1789—which was revolution and war in one—opened the gates of the world to the bourgeoisie. . . . The present revolution, which is also a war, seems to open the gates of the future to the masses, who have served their hard apprenticeship of blood and death in the trenches.[3]

---

[3] *Il Popolo d'Italia,* March 1919, quoted in Christopher Seton-Watson, *Italy from Liberalism to Fascism, 1870–1925* (London, 1967), p. 517.

Early Fascism

The first *fasci*[4] were formed on March 23, 1919, when Mussolini gathered 145 friends in an upstairs room in Milan. There were a number of old syndicalist faithfuls who had shared his prowar attitudes in 1914, to whom were added veterans especially oriented toward chauvinism and direct action, such as the former *arditi* (commandos). The Milan *arditi* had their headquarters in the home of the futurist intellectual Filippo Marinetti, whose adulation of speed and violence helped set the tone.[5]

The fascist program, which was drafted by the prowar syndicalist Alceste De Ambris, mixed nationalism and social radicalism with impatient yearning to sweep away flabby prewar institutions. It demanded just rewards for Italian victory—acquisition of the lands in the Alps and along the Dalmatian coast that Italian nationalists called *Italia irredenta,* "unredeemed Italy." It also called for a constituent assembly, the vote for women, abolition of the Senate, a tax on capital, an eight-hour day in industry, workers' share in control of factories, confiscation of Church property, and a redistribution of land for peasants. The Italian Socialist Party, from which Mussolini had been expelled in 1914, was attacked with a special loathing proper to a syndicalist renegade. Mussolini now joined nationalist war veterans in denouncing socialist moderation on Italian war aims as "renunciation," or betrayal of the soldiers.

Deeds spoke even louder than the caustic words of the *Popolo d'Italia.* Mussolini and Marinetti disrupted a socialist meeting at La Scala Opera House in Milan on January 11, 1919, and in April a group of *arditi* led by Marinetti sacked and burned the editorial offices of *Avanti!* Still, Mussolini supported workers' demands at the grassroots and publicly backed several sit-down strikes in which the workers themselves carried on production. It was not yet clear in 1919 whether fascism was meant to be a rival to socialism on the left or its enemy on the right.

Early fascism's blend of radicalism and nationalism failed to gain many recruits in 1919. As an independent candidate for parliament from Milan in November 1919, running on a program that mixed antiliberalism and antisocialism with attacks on big business, Mussolini got fewer than 5,000 votes out of 270,000. Less than a thousand members remained active in the *fasci* at the end of 1919.

Fascism's New Course

It was the near civil war of 1919 and 1920 that set fascism on a new course and made its fortunes. Mussolini found that his group's physical attacks on socialists aroused more interest and more support than his radical language. The strikes and land seizures of 1919 had created genuine panic among the factory- and landowners. The turning point came with the workers' occupation of factories in Turin and Milan in August and September 1920.[6] Although Prime Minister Giovanni Giolitti

---

[4]*Fasci Italiani de Combattimento. Fascio* was simply a Latinate word for "bundle," or, by extension to politics, a closely knit band, unlike a party. Its usage had been largely left wing, as in the Sicilian anarchist *Fasci dei lavoratori* of 1894.

[5]See chapter 1, p. 35, and chapter 4, p. 115.

[6]See chapter 5, pp. 146–148.

had successfully waited it out, so that the "factory council" movement burned itself out quickly, his unhurried calm had heightened the panicky owners' conviction that the liberal state could not save them. After the threat to their property had begun to subside, the owners of factories and big farms began to take matters into their own hands. To help them, they called on Mussolini's direct-action bands, the *squadristi*.

Mussolini had organized his *squadristi* in the supernationalistic Adriatic frontier territories. They saw their first action in Trieste in July 1920, where they sacked the headquarters of a Slovene nationalist association. It was a simple matter to switch from beating Slavs to beating socialists. Moreover, the *squadristi* received money from the landowners and industrialists for this purpose, as well as trucks and equipment from the army. Through late 1920 and 1921, they exercised their war-learned brutalities on Italian socialists.

The *squadristi* were most active in the small towns and country villages of northeastern Italy, where local landowners used them to break up farm laborers' unions and cooperatives. Their "punitive expeditions" set off at night in borrowed trucks manned by nationalist veterans, the unemployed, and sons of threatened landowners. At their destination, they beat socialist or left-Catholic organizers, often administering a near lethal dose of castor oil, or shaving off half a moustache. There were some fatalities, but mostly the *squadristi* attacked the offices, presses, or pride of their enemies. During the first six months of 1921, Mussolini's toughs destroyed twenty-five cooperative apartment houses, fifty-nine local labor clubhouses, eighty-five cooperatives, thirty-four headquarters of agricultural workers' unions, fifty-one political party headquarters, ten printing works, and six newspaper offices, mostly in rural north-central Italy.

Although Mussolini denied that the Fascists had become "watchdogs of capitalism," some of the economic radicals and revolutionary syndicalists of the first days dropped away. Their places were taken by a horde of frankly right-wing newcomers. Membership in the *fasci* mounted to 30,000 in 1920 and to ten times that, 300,000, by the end of 1922.

Governmental Crisis

Premier Giolitti tried to practice on the burgeoning Fascist movement the same coopting strategy that had worked with the reformist left in the course of his long parliamentary career. Giolitti believed that, like the factory occupations in 1920, fascism would lose its vehemence with time and experience. He drew Mussolini into an electoral coalition with his Liberal Party and the Nationalists. In Italy's second postwar election on May 15, 1921, Giolitti's National Bloc won 105 seats out of a total of 535, of which Mussolini and the Fascists had 35. At first, Giolitti had reason to believe that he had tamed fascism and yoked it to his parliamentary coalition. Mussolini had already acceded to Giolitti's compromise over Fiume in 1920, and the Fascists had done nothing when Italian troops forced D'Annunzio's volunteers to give up the city. During 1921, Mussolini also made some attempt to curb the *squadristi.* That movement was almost beyond his control, however, and the local militants repeatedly forced Mussolini's hand by undertaking more raids.

At the same time, the parliamentary monarchy was proving incapable of governing postwar Italy. Postwar ministries had been unable to maintain law and order against either the revolutionary left or the vigilante right. The 1921 elections made things even worse by returning a parliament with no possible coherent majority. The center liberal and democratic parties had no majority by themselves. Socialists, with 123 seats, refused to participate in any bourgeois ministry. The most important newcomer on the Italian political scene was the left Catholic *Popolari* Party of Don Luigi Sturzo, with 108 seats. But their demands for social reforms like land redistribution made coalition with Giolitti's Liberals impossible. And although some of Sturzo's followers were more radical than some socialists, the Church–state issue blocked any coalition between the *Popolari* and the anticlerical left. Giolitti, the personification of prewar centrist coalition politics, found no stable majority and left office in June 1921 for good at the age of seventy-nine.

For the next fourteen months, Italians endured a lingering governmental crisis, while postwar internal problems went unsolved. Demobilization and the end of wartime production had thrown Italy into economic depression. Rising unemployment and the defeats of 1919 and 1920 left Italian workers bitter and apathetic. Resentments seethed among returning veterans and a middle class pinched by inflation and fearful of revolution. Italians looking to the government for salvation saw only an unedifying round of fruitless coalition-mending among parliamentary factions. No government at all could be formed during the first three weeks of February 1922, the longest ministerial crisis up to that time in Italy. After August 1922, there was only a caretaker ministry under a colorless Giolitti lieutenant, Luigi Facta, who governed without a majority.

The *squadristi* helped make Italy ungovernable during 1922. Local Fascists in northeastern Italy had now developed their own momentum of "punitive expeditions." The local leaders, called *ras* after Ethiopian feudal chieftains, resented Mussolini's attempts to curb their activities from his seat in parliament. Encouraged by local conservatives and army commanders, they now took over entire towns, expelling socialist or Communist mayors and councils. In May 1922, Italo Balbo, one of the most brutal of the *ras,* mobilized 50,000 unemployed in a "fascist strike" that held the town hall of Ferrara for a week until the local prefect had promised to hire them all on public works projects. At the end of May, he did the same with the Communist city government of Bologna. In July, Fascists took over Rimini, Cremona, and Ravenna, and in August, briefly, Milan. By the early fall of 1922, Fascists had become the de facto local government in parts of northern Italy.

The concentration of early Fascist power in north-central and northeastern Italy (Emilia, Tuscany, Romagna) is significant. It follows rather closely the region of maximum revolutionary agitation and conservative backlash in 1919 and 1920, especially areas where landowners' authority was threatened, as in the Po Valley. Such workers' strongholds as Turin remained closed to Fascist influence, and the underdeveloped south was almost untouched by it. Where it was strong, however, fascism exposed the incapacity of the Italian government to have its orders carried out.

The "March on Rome"

Mussolini, struggling to remain in control of his followers, heightened the governmental crisis by talking vaguely but incessantly about a "march on Rome." He suggested that, just as the *squadristi* had marched on Ferrara and other cities to clear out leftists, they would march on the capital to clear out incompetents. The Fascist Congress of October 1922 in Naples (marking the movement's penetration of the south) went beyond talk. A high command of four Fascist leaders—*quadrumvirs* in the grandiose Latinisms that the movement relished—laid plans for three Fascist columns to converge on Rome during the night of October 27–28. The *quadrumvirs* reflected Fascism's following: Italo Balbo, former officer of Alpine troops and *ras* of Ferrara, stood for disgruntled veterans. Michele Bianchi had been a revolutionary syndicalist; he stood for fascism's roots in the antiparliamentary left. General Emilio De Bono came from the regular army. Cesare De Vecchi, the organizer of fascism in Piedmont, was an avowed monarchist who stood for fascism's later recruits among traditional conservatives disillusioned by liberal monarchy.

It was not by a "march on Rome," however, that Mussolini became prime minister of Italy on October 30. He arrived by sleeping car from Milan, after King Victor Emmanuel III had asked him to form a government in due constitutional form. The

Brown Brothers

Mussolini and his *quadrumvirs* march in Rome, October 31, 1922. From left to right are Michele Bianchi, Italo Balbo, Mussolini, Cesare De Vecchi, and General De Bono.

"march on Rome" was a threat, not a *coup d'état*. The threat exposed Prime Minister Facta's dependence on dubious army support for survival. Rather than test that support, the king asked Mussolini himself to take over the task of maintaining order. The Fascist columns did not conquer Rome by force. Police stopped all but about 9,000, who reached the city gates shoddily dressed and poorly armed, dispirited in a steady rain. About 20,000 paraded in the city only after Mussolini was in office.

How had this marginal agitator of 1919 become the head of the Italian government in October 1922? Mussolini's success was due partly to the absence of alternatives. A resolutely anti-Fascist government was possible only on condition that the socialists and the Catholic *Popolari* submerge their differences over religion. Only at the last minute, when it was too late, did the reformist socialists express a willingness to participate in an anti-Fascist coalition, but this act split their party. The centrist leaders capable of forming an effective coalition preferred to coopt Mussolini rather than block him. In October 1922, Giolitti was busy behind the scenes directing one more combination to include Fascists in a new ministry, but he offered Mussolini only a few seats, and he negotiated with pre-1914 slowness. Mussolini was encouraged to hold out for more by the fact that wartime Prime Minister Antonio Salandra was simultaneously bargaining with him to bring the Fascists into a more frankly conservative coalition.

Mussolini's bedraggled *squadristi* might have been kept out of Rome had Prime Minister Facta and the king acted resolutely against them. There is good reason to think that the army would have obeyed an order by the king to disperse the *squadristi*, whatever the private feelings of many officers. The king bears a heavy responsibility for refusing to test the army's obedience. Nervous about reports that his cousin, the Duke of Aosta, was maneuvering for the crown with Fascist support, Victor Emmanuel refused to countersign Facta's decree of martial law on the morning of October 28. Instead, after Mussolini had refused one more request to join a Salandra government, the king appealed directly to Mussolini, who was anxiously waiting in the Milan offices of his newspaper. Mussolini arrived in Rome on the morning of October 30, and began forming his ministry.

Technically, Mussolini had become the prime minister of Italy according to constitutional form. In another sense, however, Mussolini had come to power by force. He had helped to make normal government impossible in 1921 and 1922, until the political leaders of Italy bought him off. Moreover, he had made a violent antisocialist weapon available to those groups in Italy—industrialists, landowners, army officers, and police—who wanted to smash socialism at all cost. By the time the *squadristi* had seized a number of northern and central towns, it would have taken force to exclude the Fascists from power.

Mussolini Assumes Personal Rule

It was not clear in October 1922 whether Mussolini would govern by force or whether he would be "transformed," according to Giolitti's term, into just another parliamentary coalition-monger.

Mussolini's costume when he stepped from the train reflected that ambiguity. His Fascist black shirt contrasted incongruously with formal white spats. "Your

Fascist blackshirts burn socialist literature following the "march on Rome," November 1922.

Majesty," he said to the king, "will you forgive my black shirt? I just came from the battle, fortunately bloodless."[7] The new cabinet also reflected its mixed origins. It was a coalition of Fascists with the center and right. Although there were only four Fascists among fourteen ministers, the Fascists held the key posts. Mussolini himself was interior minister (who controls the national police in most European countries) as well as foreign minister and prime minister. Three other Fascists held the ministries of justice, liberated territories, and finance. There were even two reformist Social Democrats in the cabinet, and the eminent conservative Salandra represented the regime at the League of Nations. Behind this coalition, however, stood the restless *squadristi,* who began to talk of a "second revolution."

How this mixture of elements would sort itself out remained an open question for the next two years. Mussolini's external appearances reassured those who hoped for just another centrist ministry a bit firmer than the last. He dressed in the formal attire traditional for prime ministers and instituted no startling innovations. The brutal side showed only in the Corfu Incident. When an Italian general and some officers inspecting the Greek-Albanian border were assassinated on Greek territory in August 1923, Mussolini bombarded the Greek island of Corfu and occupied it until the Greeks were forced to apologize and pay an indemnity. Elsewhere, Italian

[7]Simonetta Falasca-Zamponi, *Fascist Spectacle: The Aesthetics of Power in Mussolini's Italy* (Berkeley, Calif., 1997), p. 195.

foreign policy gave the impression of moderation, especially when the differences with Yugoslavia over Fiume were settled by treaty in January 1924.

Internally, the major change was the Acerbo Election Law.[8] This election gimmick awarded two-thirds of the seats in the lower house of parliament to the party that received the largest number of votes (provided it was over 25 percent) and then distributed the rest among the other parties by proportional representation. It was approved by 235 votes to 139 (mostly socialist and communist) in a chamber that included only 35 Fascists. Clearly, the center and right parties still chose order over electoral democracy, even if the Fascists were the chief gainers. With the machinery of government in their hands, Mussolini's coalition slate won 374 out of 535 seats in the elections of April 1924, of whom 275 were Fascists. It was the last quasi-normal election in Italy for twenty years.

Another brutal act of *squadrismo* soon forced Mussolini to choose between personal rule or defeat. On June 10, 1924, Mussolini's most articulate critic, the parliamentary socialist leader Giacomo Matteotti, was abducted and murdered by five Fascist thugs on the payroll of Mussolini's press secretary, Cesare Rossi. Although there is no proof that Mussolini had directly ordered the killing, Matteotti's murder brought into the open the major issue of whether Mussolini was capable of even controlling the violence he had unleashed. Some centrist supporters of Mussolini broke with him, and the opposition began to revive. For some months, Mussolini was disoriented and uncertain, exposing the vacillator under his tough mask.

Prodded by the *ras,* Mussolini eventually saw that he must assume total power or lose the power he had. He spoke to the Chamber in a new, defiant mood on January 3, 1925: "We wish to make the nation fascist." At the same time, he unleashed the *squadristi* and ordered a police crackdown on the growing liberal and socialist opposition. A series of decrees transformed Italy from a parliamentary monarchy into a one-party dictatorship. By the end of 1926 all parties except the Fascists had been dissolved; the death penalty, abolished in 1890, had been restored; controls had been imposed on the press and local government; and Mussolini seemed on his way toward the "second revolution" for which his more impatient followers had clamored.

NATIONAL SOCIALISM IN GERMANY

In Germany, defeat had followed the military triumphs of the spring of 1918 with dizzying suddenness. The German Empire had been overthrown, the kaiser exiled, and a new republic created whose ability to protect German property, German values, and German borders was doubted by conservatives and nationalists. The victors were busy carving off great slices of former German territory. The German Communist Party was preparing further revolutionary steps. The Allied blockade made food scarcer than ever in the months following the armistice. Prices and unemployment were rising. Humiliation, hunger, and fear were the daily companions of many Germans during 1919 and 1920.

It was under these conditions in September 1919 that Corporal Adolf Hitler, working for army intelligence in Munich, encountered a "German Workers' Party"

---

[8]Named for its sponsor, the Fascist deputy Giacomo Acerbo.

that was trying to unite veterans and working men around a nationalistic but economically radical program. Liking what he found there, Hitler joined up.

Postwar Antirevolutionary Vigilantism

Munich had become a gathering spot for radical right fringe groups and angry nationalists by September 1919. The revolutionary pendulum had swung farthest to the left in Munich with the Soviet Republic of April 1919, and then far to the right with that brief regime's destruction by the army and General Franz Ritter von Epp's *Freikorps* in early May 1919. The armed forces restored power, for the moment, to the moderate Social Democrats who had governed in Bavaria since November 1918. Many of the officers, however, had only contempt for the new republic, which was bowing to the Treaty of Versailles.

The *Freikorps* were even more passionate and less disciplined in their hatred of the republic. As noted earlier, the general staff had created these volunteer units to help control Berlin in December 1918, with the acquiescence of Social Democrats like Friedrich Ebert and Gustav Noske, who dominated the provisional government.[9] There was no difficulty finding *Freikorps* volunteers among the unemployed and among the swollen numbers of demobilized officers now adrift. The *Freikorps'* experience in putting down workers' uprisings in Berlin, Leipzig, and Munich in the spring of 1919 sharpened their antisocialist edge, and those who held the Baltic frontiers against the Russian Bolsheviks in 1919 and 1920 identified antisocialism with defense of the national territory. The *Freikorps* mixed together a poisonous brew of attitudes drawn from the young middle-class antibourgeois style of the prewar German hiking clubs *(Wandervögel)*, the wartime hardening of the "front fighters," and the postwar crusade to save Germandom on the Baltic or in the streets of cities held by revolutionaries.

These armed enemies of the infant Weimar Republic could not destroy it by a frontal attack. They tried to do so in the "Kapp *Putsch*" of March 1920. When the republic attempted to demobilize some of the *Freikorps* units, one unit, the Erhardt Brigade, which had helped "clean up" Munich in May 1919, rebelled and marched into Berlin wearing its swastika symbol. Powerful antirepublican officers and civil servants, such as Wolfgang Kapp, a Prussian official who had helped found the Fatherland Party in 1917, hoped to use Erhardt's men to unseat the government. When the army commander in chief, General Hans von Seeckt, refused to divide the army by ordering it into action against the Erhardt Brigade, the government left Berlin to the mutineers. Kapp's attempt to form a new government failed, however, when enough civil servants refused to carry out his orders and when the most widespread workers' general strike of modern German history paralyzed the economy. After four days, Kapp gave up, and the Weimar Republic resumed its functions in Berlin.

In Munich, the local army command now pushed aside the Social Democratic Bavarian state government and installed a more amenable nationalist state government under Gustav von Kahr, a conservative supporter of Bavarian autonomy. In the climate of the early Weimar Republic, "autonomy" meant not carrying out the

---

[9]See chapter 5, p. 140.

federal government's efforts to control the insurrectionary right in the early 1920s. Those efforts were meager enough, for the republic's leaders had chosen to leave the reconstruction of the German army under the Versailles restrictions to General von Seeckt, whose political "neutrality" in March 1920 had opened Berlin to the Erhardt Brigade. In Munich, the army did not even pretend to be neutral.

The Emergence of Hitler

The army command in Munich set up political instruction programs to guard its soldiers against subversive propaganda. One of the instructors was Corporal Adolf Hitler. Hitler was the son of an Austrian customs official, a moody, solitary youth who had spent his early twenties in Vienna failing to get into art school, soaking up the German nationalism and anti-Semitism of the Vienna crowd, and feeling sorry for himself. Gifts from his mother and eventually a small inheritance kept him from real want, although he chose to describe his Vienna years later in his autobiography *Mein Kampf* (1925) as a misunderstood young artist's struggle against poverty and subversive anti-German ideas. The outbreak of the First World War found him in Munich, where he had emigrated to avoid the Austrian draft. In 1914, Hitler volunteered in the Bavarian army. The war gave him the first real fulfillment of his life. He served four years as a runner carrying messages between the headquarters and the front and was wounded twice. He was awarded the Iron Cross First Class, rare for a corporal. Hospitalized with temporary blindness from gas in 1918, he reacted to the defeat with hallucinations that he claimed summoned him to save Germany.

The Second Army's Political Department in Munich ordered Hitler in 1919 to investigate the German Workers' Party as an undercover agent. The party had been founded in Munich in March 1918 by a locksmith eager to win his fellow workers from socialism to nationalism. Hitler joined the movement with card number 555, came to dominate it, and in April 1920 dropped his army job to spend full time with the party. He changed its name to National Socialist German Workers' Party.[10] Hitler's oratory gave the party new dynamism and drew many new members from the same sources as the *Freikorps*. He bought a newspaper, the *Völkischer Beobachter (Peoples' Observer)*.[11] The party's paramilitary direct-action squad, the *Sturmabteilung* (SA), or storm troopers, fought socialists in the streets and kept up the *Freikorps* tradition of the chosen band sworn to a single leader.

The Nazi Party

Hitler's new party was only one of the nationalist anti-Semitic direct-action groups that flourished in Germany after 1919. But it was more successful than the others. Hitler managed to recruit a social cross-section, one of the hallmarks of a fascist

---

[10]NSDAP, *National-sozialistische Deutsche Arbeiterpartei*, or "Nazi" Party for short.

[11]The German adjective *völkisch* is imperfectly translated as "peoples'." It refers to one's own ethnic stock in both racial and cultural terms, a meaning developed in nineteenth-century German nationalist writing.

movement. In addition to the small craftsmen who started the movement, there was support from the highly placed and the wealthy. Hitler enjoyed support from politically minded army officers, such as Captain Ernst Röhm and General Ritter von Epp, the *Freikorps* leader who had "liberated" Munich from the soviet in May 1919. Half the purchase money for the *Völkischer Beobachter* came from them, as well as useful protection and publicity. Other wealthy supporters were two women, Hélène Bechstein (the piano-manufacturing family) and Elsa Bruckmann (publishing), whom Hitler had met through Putzi Hanfstaengl, a Harvard-educated art dealer's heir and Munich café intellectual. There were drifting veterans, such as Captain Hermann Göring, the much-decorated fighter pilot who had succeeded Baron Manfred von Richthofen as commander of Germany's most famous fighter squadron and who was now unemployed and taking drugs. And there were ethnic Germans from the lost eastern borderlands, such as Alfred Rosenberg from the Baltic.

The Nazi Party's program was set forth in Twenty-Five Points, adopted in February 1920 when the party was still a small movement of artisans and craftsmen. Its content was a mixture of ardent nationalism, anti-Semitism, and anticapitalism. The program called for the abrogation of the Versailles Treaty and union with Austria in a Greater Germany, that is, a state larger than 1914 Germany. Jews were to be excluded from citizenship and office. The anticapitalism of the Twenty-Five Points, for which Hitler's predecessors in the German Workers' Party were responsible, was not socialist in the sense of opposing private property or calling for socialist revolution. It was rather an assertion of the little people's grievances against their creditors and the rich. It called for abolition of unearned income, confiscation of war profits, nationalization of trusts, and regulation of the profits of large corporations. The Nazis proposed to "communalize" department stores in order to rent out their premises to groups of small tradespeople. They called for land reform, prevention of land speculation, and expropriation of land "for communal purposes."

The Twenty-Five Points were more noteworthy as an expression of lower-middle-class grievances than as a guide to later Nazi action. Once in power, a decade later, Hitler pursued quite different social policies. Even at the beginning, however, the Nazis put more stress on the techniques of mass mobilization than on programs. Mass parades and assemblies may have entered European politics on the left, but the Nazis turned them into an art form in the service of nationalism, antisocialism, and anti-Semitism. Uniforms, banners, and night rallies by torchlight touched many German emotions. The party openly mocked the Weimar Republic's efforts to control public order, as in the parade of 800 SA men in Coburg in October 1922 in defiance of a ban on demonstrations. SA actions against socialist meetings gratified hatreds directly or vicariously, and provided publicity even in the hostile parts of the press.

The "Beer Hall *Putsch*," 1923

The German political climate grew stormy again in 1923. The French had occupied the Ruhr, the Communist Party attempted to take power in Hamburg, and the currency inflated out of sight. Despair and scorn for the Weimar Republic pushed a

Hitler and his fellow conspirators in the Munich "beer hall *Putsch*" during their trial for high treason, February 24, 1924. General Erich Ludendorff is at the center next to Hitler, and Captain Ernst Röhm, commander of the SA, is second from right.

tide of support toward the Nazis. General Ludendorff, the First World War commander, now stood at Hitler's side at rallies. Buoyed by such support, Hitler decided to force the nationalist state government of Bavaria to serve as his base for overthrowing the Weimar Republic. Invading a meeting in the Munich *Bürgerbräukeller* (a large beer hall) on November 8, 1923, the Nazis seized the Bavarian Governor Gustav von Kahr and senior local army and police officials and forced them to pledge public support to Hitler's appeal for a national revolution. Although Kahr and the others repudiated Hitler as soon as they were set free, Captain Ernst Röhm and his SA men succeeded in occupying the Bavarian War Ministry with the complicity of army officers. Hitler led a march on other government buildings on November 9, confident that the presence beside him of General Ludendorff would neutralize the army and police units guarding them. The army commanders in Bavaria supported legal authority, however, and when Hitler and Ludendorff approached the government's barricades at the head of their column, the police fired. Sixteen Nazis and four policemen were killed. Hitler was arrested, and although he made use of his trial as a public platform ("I wanted to become the destroyer of Marxism"), he was sent to prison.

During 1924, the Weimar Republic managed to stabilize itself, and the tensions and vigilantism of 1923 diminished. Nazism seemed to be in decline. But the ingredients it contained were still latent in German society and values, ready to be summoned forth in the event of any future crisis.

COUNTERREVOLUTION IN HUNGARY

Hungary, too, was ripe for a mass, anti-Marxist, nationalist movement after the First World War. Proportionally, Hungary was the greatest territorial loser of the war.

Once a ruling state lording it over minorities of Slovaks, Romanians, and South Slavs, Hungary was now a starveling remnant barely one-third its prewar size. Three million Magyars were now themselves minority subjects in Romania, Yugoslavia, and Czechoslovakia. Every political movement, from Marxist to royalist rejected the Treaty of the Trianon (Hungary's part of the Paris peace settlement) and called for national restoration. Nearly every Hungarian was revisionist and nationalist. Their response to Hungary's postwar status was the slogan *Nem, nem, soha* (no, no, never).

The British historian A. J. P. Taylor had some reason for calling Hungary "the first breeding ground of fascism."[12] Postwar events had poisoned liberal values in Hungary, for the October Republic of Count Mihály Károlyi, even more than the Weimar Republic for German nationalists, spelled national humiliation and social disorder.[13] The soviet regime set up in 1919 gave a nasty fright to the ruling gentry and aristocracy, who had always enjoyed the most one-sided land distribution in Europe outside of Romania and southern Spain.[14] The desperately land-hungry peasants hated "communists and gentlemen" equally.[15] A large uprooted and frightened mass of demobilized army officers and of Hungarian officials expelled from the lost two-thirds of the kingdom, further swelled by business and professional people bankrupted by territorial amputation and postwar economic dislocation, built up both anti-Semitic and anti-Marxist sentiments. They resented the extremely large role of Jews in Hungarian banking and commerce,[16] as well as Béla Kun's soviet regime.

Postwar Hungary was formed in counterrevolution. Even during the October Republic of 1918, before Kun's 133-day soviet regime, demobilized officers and uprooted civil servants were forming secret societies devoted to replacing Western ideas with "Hungarianism," a vague mixture of racist and hierarchical social ideas expressed in romantic neomedieval language. The town of Szeged, on the southern border and behind the protection of French armies, was the center of these movements. From here sprang the "circle of the twelve captains," antiliberal young army officers who furnished part of the interwar Hungarian leadership. They soon formed such underground activist groups as the Awakening Hungarians or the EKSZ (Etelköz Association), which claimed to be an imitation of early Hungarian tribal society, complete with an oath to seven tribal chiefs and commitment to "a great, Christian, and racially pure Hungary."

The most eminent personage at Szeged was Admiral Miklós Horthy, the last commander in chief of the Austro-Hungarian navy. But the most dynamic figure was one of the "twelve captains," Captain Gyula Gömbös, who organized a volunteer anti-Bolshevik army under Horthy's command. Gömbös, born to a schoolteacher

---

[12]A. J. P. Taylor, "Introduction," in Mihály Károlyi, *Memoirs: Faith without Illusion* (New York, 1957), p. 7.

[13]See chapter 5, pp. 144–145.

[14]C. A. Macartney, *The Habsburg Empire, 1790–1918* (New York, 1969), pp. 713, 716. About four thousand great families owned about a third of the arable land in prewar Hungary.

[15]Istvan Deák, "Hungary," in Hans Rogger and Eugen Weber, eds., *The European Right* (Los Angeles, 1965), p. 385.

[16]"In 1910, 21.8 percent of salaried employees in industry, 54.0 percent of self-employed traders, and 85.0 percent of the self-employed persons in banking and finance were Jews." (ibid., p. 368.)

and a farmer's daughter in a German-speaking district, stood outside the gentry families who had traditionally ruled Hungary, and even outside a fully Hungarian cultural inheritance. He compensated for this, however, by the vehemence of his opposition to the Paris peace settlement, his devotion to Hungarian cultural revival, and his attacks on Marxism as "a destructive heresy foisted on simple workers by self-seeking international Jews."[17]

Gömbös was already calling himself a national socialist in 1919: national, in his determination to restore Hungarian values and frontiers to what he imagined was their historic right; socialist, in his proposal to expropriate international financiers to make jobs for Hungarian workers and expropriate great estates to give land to Hungarian peasants. Unlike the Hungarian gentry, Gömbös had no use for the Habsburg ruling house. He was later to block all attempts to restore the last Austro-Hungarian Emperor, Karl, as king of Hungary during the 1920s, and when he became prime minister in 1932, Gömbös formed the first cabinet in modern Hungarian history that contained no aristocrats. Gömbös's Party of Racial Defense became a rallying point for demobilized junior officers, angry nationalists, and anti-Semitic lower-level civil servants and businessmen. He drew inspiration after 1922 from Mussolini's platform style and was in touch with Hitler as early as 1923.

Another Hungarian counterrevolutionary center in 1919 was Vienna, where an anti-Bolshevik Committee was formed under Count Istvan Bethlen, a great landowner from the Calvinist aristocracy of eastern Hungary. Bethlen spoke for a

Admiral Miklós Horthy, regent of Hungary, 1919–1944.

© UPI / Bettmann / CORBIS

[17]Quoted in Eugen Weber, *The Varieties of Fascism* (New York, 1964), p. 90.

more aristocratic, tolerant, and cultivated milieu of great landowners who were more sympathetic than Gömbös to the limited parliamentary traditions of the late-nineteenth-century ruling families of Hungary.

From these two counterrevolutionary centers—Szeged and Vienna—came the forces that occupied Budapest after the Romanians had driven Béla Kun out on August 1, 1919. The retaking of Budapest was accompanied by a "White Terror" that took the lives of a thousand persons more or less indiscriminately identified as socialists or Jews. Admiral Horthy began a landlocked second career as "regent" of a Hungarian monarchy whose throne was vacant.

The predominant influence at first lay with the "racialist dynamism and the anti-Red fury" of Szeged secret societies and young "captains." By 1921, however, the social fever had diminished. Horthy made Count Bethlen prime minister. Although the Bethlen regime was free from the more strident anti-Semitism and mysticism of the Szeged officers, it tried to restore gentry rule. Bethlen reduced eligible voters to 27 percent of the population, for example, and restored public balloting in the rural precincts so that landlords could know how their peasants voted. He permitted labor unions to function again in cities, but this bargain forbade them to try to organize agricultural workers. A form of oligarchic parliamentarism thus took over from the Szeged groups for the rest of the 1920s.

A CLOSER LOOK AT FASCISM

The three groups examined above—Italian fascism, German National Socialism, and the Hungarian captains—were not the only popular, violence-prone, antiliberal, and anti-Marxist movements active in Europe at the end of the war. There were many smaller, less successful examples. The Frenchman Georges Valois broke with the monarchist Catholic *Action française* after the war, in hopes of drawing French workers away from Marxism with a more radical "national socialism." His *Faisceau* was an attempt to adapt the Italian *fascio,* or band of brothers, directly to French conditions. A longer lasting French movement was *Jeunesses patriotes* (Patriotic Youth), a direct-action squad of nationalist students and veterans, founded in 1924 by the champagne manufacturer Pierre Taittinger. The Romanian student Corneliu Codreanu's National-Christian Socialism of 1920 was devoted to strikebreaking, the disruption of liberal professors' classes, and a campaign to restrict the number of Jews in Romanian universities and professions. Such movements were widespread, novel, and important. What did they stand for, and how did they come about?

The Meaning of Fascism

Fascism was not simply the far right. The terms *right* and *left* were first applied to politics during the French Revolution.[18] They belong to the political vocabulary of nineteenth-century struggles over popular sovereignty, individual liberties, and

---

[18]In the converted riding stable used for the National Assembly of 1789, seats were arranged in the shape of a fan, rather than facing each other as in the chapel long used by the British parliament. The French king's supporters fell into the habit of sitting on the speaker's right, his opponents on the speaker's left.

property. With fascist movements, we find ourselves in a strange landscape where familiar signposts like right and left do not give very precise directions.

Much about the early fascist movements seemed insurrectionary and hostile to traditional rightist conservatism. Like the left, fascism was a mass movement. Its marching ranks wearing identically colored shirts, its plebeian leaders full of contempt for kings and aristocrats, its strident rallies, and its appeals to action, were worlds away from the hereditary hierarchies and deferential, passive lower orders that traditional conservatives longed for. No one would mistake Captain Gömbös for the polished Count Bethlen, or Mussolini for an Italian aristocrat or wealthy industrialist. Many fascists were hostile to the Church (although less so in Scandinavia, Romania, and Hungary).

Early fascist platforms called their movements "national syndicalist" or "national socialist," and leveled bitter attacks on international capitalism, department stores, banks, and, in some cases, on large land holdings. They recruited ex-syndicalists who hated the Socialist Party, young bourgeois who hated their parents' complacency, veterans who hated those who had sent them to war and then failed to give them jobs, intellectuals who hated modern mass culture, men who feared the new independent women, and struggling shopkeepers or petty officials who feared social decline. Because they wanted radical change in the way things were headed, fascists have often been considered revolutionaries. "National Socialism," wrote Hermann Rauschning, a former Nazi leader in Danzig who broke with the party, "is an unquestionably genuine revolutionary movement in the sense of the 'mass rising' dreamed of by Anarchists and Communists."[19] This revolution was aimless, Rauschning thought, except in terms of grasping and consolidating power, but it was no less destructive of the status quo.

On the one hand, the anticapitalist and antibourgeois rhetoric would appear to make the fascists opposed to the right. On the other hand, all fascist movements without exception saw Marxism as the enemy and flabby liberalism as the enemy's main accomplice. Fascist violence was directed against socialist and left-Catholic parties and unions and against ethnic "enemies." The regimes that fascists wished to overthrow were the ineffective liberal or reformist regimes that they judged inadequate to maintain national power, jobs, and order.

Anticapitalist and antibourgeois rhetoric, moreover, was not universal to fascist movements, and it was always a selective anticapitalism they preached. Their grievances were those of a middle class squeezed by inflation and caught between growing capitalist corporations and growing trade unions. When they called for the nationalization of the banks to which they were indebted to "break the capital-interest yoke" (Point 11 of the Nazi Twenty-Five Points), they wanted easy credit and low interest for their small businesses, not socialism. When they called for the nationalization of the trusts whose competition threatened them, they wanted to protect small property, not abolish property. Their call for an organized economy meant the dissolution of independent trade unions, not the end of free enterprise. Despite the antibourgeois rhetoric of some of its intellectuals, fascism wanted a revolution to protect the middle class, not to install the proletariat in power. "Things must change if they are going to remain the same," said the young heir in Giuseppe de Lampedusa's novel of Sicilian society, *The Leopard* (1956).

[19]Hermann Rauschning, *Revolution of Nihilism* (New York, 1939), p. 19.

In any event, fascist rhetoric was much less important than fascist practice. The one fascist movement to gain power in the 1920s, Italian fascism, did so with the aid and complicity of traditional conservatives. Once in power, it forgot its early rhetoric and came to terms with king, aristocracy, Church, and business (as we shall see in more detail in chapter 8). German National Socialism made similar alliances to reach power. To claim, as have some Marxists, that fascism was merely a device created by capitalists for the dual purpose of beating back Marxism and overcoming economic strains, is to underestimate the popular roots of fascist movements.[20] But it is difficult to deny that fascists and traditional conservatives often struck up fruitful alliances. Fascism belongs on the right clearly enough, but it was a new right.

The proper placement of fascism on a right-left scale is further complicated by its claim to cut across class lines. Fascists promised to cancel out the class struggle in a fervent national reconciliation. That was one of its appeals to the traditional right. That claim was not altogether spurious. Although the middle class provided the most recruits, fascism did indeed attract some workers, mostly those outside the pervasive socialist culture of the European working class: patriotic antisocialists, the youthful unemployed, and the unorganized poor in areas like Eastern Europe and southern Italy, where workers had never received the attentions of a mass movement.

In some ways, youth distinguishes fascism better than does class or political ideology. Fascism tapped the rebellion of the young outsiders who had come of age in the trenches of war or in the street demonstrations and unemployment lines of the immediate postwar days. Mussolini's *squadristi* marched off singing *Giovinezza* (Youth). Captain Gömbös was thirty-three in 1920; Codreanu was twenty; Hitler thirty-one.

Fascism leaves behind the nineteenth-century world in which middle- and lower-middle-class Europeans were usually liberal. In times of emergency, such as economic depression, national defeat, or inadequate access to political redress, middle-class Europeans had tended to polarize toward the left, as in the revolutions of 1848. In fascist movements, lower-middle-class Europeans moved toward a radical antisocialist, antiliberal authoritarianism. They found wanting the predominantly liberal or socialist values of their fathers. This is the larger historical transformation that students of fascism must examine.

The Roots of Fascism

Although fascism in its fully developed form burst on the world only after the shocks of the First World War and the Bolshevik Revolution, it is possible to discern a number of ways in which the terrain had been prepared in the late nineteenth century.

A first step was some conservatives' acceptance of mass politics. In the mid-nineteenth century, activist authoritarians like the French Emperor Napoleon III and the German Chancellor Otto von Bismarck adopted universal manhood suffrage as a tactic for recruiting mass support over the heads of the upper-class liberal parliamentary opposition.

---

[20]Serious Marxist interpreters of fascism have avoided this error. See Nicos Poulantzas, *Fascism and Dictatorship* (London and New York, 1974).

The Catholic Church, too, accepted the necessity for mass politics and began to make its peace with anticlerical liberals who were sufficiently antisocialist. In the days of Pope Pius IX (1846–1878), the main enemies of the Church had been the new, militantly anticlerical French Republic, which took public education out of the Church's hands in the 1880s, and the new, unified Kingdom of Italy, which had seized Church lands in 1870. Pope Leo XIII (1878–1903) nudged French Catholics toward acceptance of the French Third Republic in the 1890s. Leo's successor, Pius X (1903–1914), made an even more conspicuous departure in 1904 when he authorized Italian Catholics to vote in cases where their ballots could block a socialist candidate. It was the first Italian election since 1870 in which Catholics had been permitted by the Church to take part. The clerical issue was not dead, as a bitter squabble over separation of Church and state in France in 1905 proved. But it was one of the nineteenth-century divisions whose significance was becoming eclipsed by the growing power of socialism. By the end of the nineteenth century, many European conservatives preferred to adapt to mass politics rather than follow the traditional conservative aim of trying to keep the masses out of politics.

This tactic made sense, of course, only if mass support for conservative interests was forthcoming. There were signs at the end of the nineteenth century of the exhaustion of liberalism as the political voice of the European middle and lower middle classes. On the political level, as socialist parties began winning substantial numbers of parliamentary seats through manhood suffrage in the 1890s,[21] some middle-class Europeans began having second thoughts about the efficacy of parliamentary democracy. On the economic level, many middle-class Europeans felt no love for a *laissez-faire*, free-market economy that pinched them between increasingly organized capitalists and increasingly organized labor. Small property, the individual shop or craft, had been the chief lower-middle-class route to independence. But such property came under permanent pressure in the late nineteenth century: Small shops suffered from the competition of new forms of retailing through chains and department stores as much as craftsmen suffered from industrial competition. These pressures were intensified during periods of cyclical business depression such as the 1880s.

The resentments of small-business owners and craftsmen could not be expressed well through existing parties, either Marxist or liberal. Liberal political economists still resisted state intervention in the economy. Marxists opposed all private property in production and commerce, while advocating continued industrialization as the necessary preparation for the next stage of socialist, collectivized abundance. Middle-class opponents of *laissez-faire* capitalism were groping confusedly before the war for some "middle way" or "third way,"[22] neither liberal nor Marxist. Only something new seemed able to protect small property from both big business and big labor. That was the kind of new formula that Charles Maurras was already putting together in the *Action française* movement of the early 1900s. One of his precocious campaigns, for example, attacked a dairy chain that threatened the livelihood of small grocers.

---

[21]The number of French socialist deputies increased from twelve to forty-one in the election of 1893; the German Social Democratic Party's voters grew from 763,128 in 1887 to 3,010,771 in 1903, or from 10.1 percent to 31.7 percent of the total vote.

[22]These phrases recur in the political discussions of the 1920s and 1930s. See chapter 10, pp. 300–301.

While the independent lower middle class slowly and painfully contracted in Europe before the First World War, the salaried lower middle class grew rapidly, providing another potential mass clientele for fascism. Karl Marx had expected industrial progress to produce an ever larger proletariat. Instead, the proportion of factory workers in Northern and Western Europe leveled off at around one-third of the total populations in the 1890s. Although the absolute numbers of industrial workers continued to increase, their relative numbers were kept down by enormous increases in the lower middle class, or what has been called the tertiary sector of the economy: white-collar employees, clerical workers, workers in sales and distribution, and lesser civil servants. These groups constituted the fastest growing segment of the population of industrialized and urbanized European countries in the twentieth century. Although they worked for wages like any factory worker, many white-collar employees clung to some sign of middle-class respectability. The German or Austrian petty civil servant, black suit worn shiny at the elbows, briefcase containing only a lunchtime salami, is, like many caricatures, close to reality. This new middle class supported democracy as long as it promised them security or progress. In a crisis, however, they were terrified of dropping into the proletariat. Although many of them hated their bosses, they hesitated to become socialist, which meant accepting proletarian status. The European lower middle class had supplied mass recruits for the revolutionary barricades of 1848; they supplied even more mass recruits for the fascist right in the twentieth century.

The exhaustion of liberalism was apparent also on the intellectual plane before the war. This did not mean the victory of liberalism's old enemies. By the end of the nineteenth century, traditional conservatives' challenge to liberalism in the name of faith and the divine right of hereditary authority was no longer taken very seriously. The important change was a dissipation of liberal confidence in human progress and the universality of human reason within liberalism's former stronghold, the educated middle class. An earlier chapter examined the many levels—the visual arts, philosophy, psychology, and science—in which nineteenth-century liberal assumptions were being challenged.[23] Some of the challengers themselves, such as the futurist Marinetti, joined enthusiastically into the cult of action and the contempt for liberal values that Mussolini's fascism offered.

Other Europeans were prepared more subtly and indirectly for fascism by the disintegration of a familiar liberal psychic universe. Some felt a sense of foreboding at the century's end. Some felt revulsion at the ugliness of urban, industrial society, at the shrill destructiveness of intellectuals, at a perceived decline of male dominance, and at the self-indulgence of bourgeois individualism. They were frightened by a feeling that Europe was decadent. The fear of decadence easily turned into a cosmic historical pessimism. Maurras's Frenchmen could measure the decline of their nation's prestige under the flabby Third Republic; Italians looked back to a vanished Roman Empire; Georg von Schönerer's Austrian-Germans saw their people being swallowed up in a sea of Slavs and Jews. They sought a remedy in a kind of spiritual revival in which racial purity, mass fervor, virile toughness, national unity, and authoritarian rule reinforced one another.

---

[23]See chapter 1, pp. 32–38.

The generous nationalism of the early nineteenth century, which envisioned the self-determining nations as a future happy family, had become much more closed and exclusive in the late nineteenth century. At the same time, the concept of race gained greater currency. Liberal intellectuals had put uppermost those qualities of all humanity that united people across the artificial barriers of title and rank, but the explorers, travelers, geographers, and anthropologists of expanding nineteenth-century Europe rediscovered humanity's diversity, most of which they attributed to race. Racial thinking spread among less-educated Europeans in the form of anti-Semitism. Efforts by the Russian tsars to "Russify" all their minorities after the 1880s helped stimulate popular passions against the Jews concentrated in the Pale of western Russia and Poland, to which they were restricted by law. Pogroms, attacks on Jewish shops and settlements, caused thousands of deaths after the 1880s; the most vicious single pogrom before the war was the murder of over 300 Jews in Odessa, in October 1905, while the authorities stood by. The emigration of Orthodox Jews from Russia aroused antagonism to these outsiders in Western Europe in the 1890s. Medieval Christian hostility to Jews was now reinforced by notions of racial difference and the fear that Jews weakened the homogeneity of any nation that harbored them.

All the ingredients of fascism were thus present before 1914. The First World War was the catalyst of fascism rather than its creator. In a number of different ways at once, the war experience magnified and fused these disparate elements. The war so discredited the entire prewar European order, particularly among the young, that the search for a "new way" took on new urgency among all those unwilling to accept the Soviet model for change. The war also revealed depths of human evil and irrationality that confirmed the prewar critique of liberal assumptions.

The war multiplied fascism's potential clientele. A whole generation had gone off to war, and some of these young men had returned hardened with a "front fighter" mentality and embittered by the "steel bath" of the First World War. Italo Balbo, Mussolini's future associate, recalled that

> when I returned from the war—just like so many others—I hated politics and politicians, who, in my opinion, had betrayed the hopes of soldiers, reducing Italy to a shameful peace and to a systematic humiliation Italians who maintained the cult of heroes. To struggle, to fight in order to return to the land of Giolitti, who made a merchandise of every ideal? No. Rather deny everything, destroy everything, in order to renew everything from the foundations.[24]

These veterans, unassimilable into peacetime drudgery, sought ways to keep alive the hard, pure masculine camaraderie of the trenches. By themselves they would have merely created marginal street gangs. A mass clientele was provided, however, by wartime social change: Dislocations threatened the status of whole masses of formerly secure members of the middle class. The workers' rise frightened the status conscious, and the enormous impetus given to industrial concentration by total war frightened the small-business owner. But the major engine of dislocation for the middle classes was inflation.

---

[24]Quoted in Herman Finer, *Mussolini's Italy* (London, 1935), p. 139.

Wartime price rises did not stop in 1918. In France, after a brief postwar stabilization, the franc fell on international exchanges during the years 1924 to 1926 to a fraction of its prewar value. When the franc was stabilized in 1928 at one-fifth of its prewar international exchange value, the French middle class, whose savings were now worth only twenty centimes for every prewar franc saved, felt they had paid a disproportionate share of war damages. Inflation was still worse in Italy, and far worse in the truncated remnants of Austria-Hungary. In Austria, in July 1919, it cost about 2,500 crowns to buy a month's supply of food for a family of four; in July 1922 it cost 297,000 crowns.[25] In Germany the currency simply ceased to buy anything in the runaway inflation of 1923. Anyone with a fixed income was reduced to charity, and the underpinnings of middle-class independence—savings, investments, and annuities—were simply wiped out.

The final catalyst to fascism was the threat of revolutionary socialism. A map of emerging fascism fits the map of revolutionary emergency in 1919 and 1920 fairly

Hitler's vehement speeches and parades by his uniformed SA appealed to embittered veterans, anti-communists, extreme nationalists, and the unemployed, though the Nazi movement remained small until 1929. Here he returns the salute of one of his followers in the town of Weimar, 1926. Party Secretary Rudolf Hess is just behind Hitler's left elbow, and Captain Hermann Göring is partly hidden by SA chief Ernst Röhm, saluting, at the front of Hitler's Mercedes.

[25]Charles A. Gulick, *Austria from Habsburg to Hitler,* vol. 1 (Los Angeles, 1948), p. 153.

well, although not perfectly. Some Europeans still put their faith in traditional conservatism. After the intense labor strife of 1917 to 1920 in Spain, a military dictatorship under General Primo de Rivera governed the country without any fascist trappings under the ultimate authority of King Alfonso XIII. The Portuguese Republic was overthrown in 1926 by a military junta without any clear program except disgust with party politics. The victor nations of Britain and France resolved their postwar problems within their existing parliamentary framework. By 1923, only one European nation—Italy—had a regime of the new style, and although some other Europeans imitated the uniforms, the colored shirts, the rhetoric, and the tone of fascism, it was not certain how widely it would spread.

Fascism remained available, however, for future emergencies. If faced with disintegration of the economy in depression or inflation, disintegration of the culture in modern decadence, and disintegration of the nation in class struggle, frightened Europeans might well turn to a forcible integration of economy, culture, and classes within a fascist state.

SUGGESTIONS FOR FURTHER READING

Robert O. Paxton, *The Anatomy of Fascism* (2004), shows how fascism worked. Stanley G. Payne, *A History of Fascism, 1919–1945*[*] (1996), is the best-informed descriptive survey. Hans Rogger and Eugen Weber, eds., *The European Right* (1965), has not been superseded for background. Kevin Passmore, *Fascism: A Very Short Introduction*[*] (2002), is probing but assumes knowledge.

Given the leader's central role in fascism, biographies are crucial. Ian Kershaw, *Hitler, 1889–1936 Hubris,*[*] and *Hitler 1937–1945 Nemesis* (2000), are now best on the man and his public. One can still consult Alan Bullock, *Hitler: A Study in Tyranny*[*] (revised ed. 1962, reprint ed. 1999), the same author's *Hitler and Stalin: Parallel Lives,*[*] 2nd ed. (1998), or Joachim Fest, *Hitler*[*] (revised ed. 2002). Ron Rosenbaum, *Explaining Hitler*[*] (1998) examines efforts to penetrate Hitler's inner life. R. J. B. Bosworth, *Mussolini*[*] (2003), is the most complete recent biography. Mussolini's main Italian biographer is discussed in Borden

W. Painter Jr., "Renzo De Felice and the Historiography of Italian Fascism," *American Historical Review,* vol., 95: no. 2 (Apr. 1990), pp. 391–405.

Adrian Lyttelton, *The Seizure of Power: Fascism in Italy, 1919–1929,* 2nd. ed. (2003), is the most penetrating analysis of Mussolini's rise; it presumes background knowledge, which may be obtained in Martin Clark (see chapter 1) or the useful brief introduction by Alexander De Grand, *Italian Fascism,*[*] 3rd ed. (2000). John Whittam, *Fascist Italy*[*] (1995), and Martin Blinkhorn, *Mussolini and Fascist Italy,*[*] 2nd ed. (1994), are also good short summaries. R. J. B. Bosworth, *The Italian Dictatorship: Problems and Perspectives in the Interpretation of Mussolini and Fascism*[*] (1998) is a valuable if idiosyncratic introduction to debates. Angelo Tasca, *The Rise of Italian Fascism* (1928), the keen observations of an ex-Communist exile, remains a classic. Paul Corner, *Fascism in Ferrara* (1975), is an illuminating local study of how conservative, agrarian fascism succeeded while radical, urban fascism failed. Frank Snowden, *The Fascist Revolution in Tuscany, 1919–1922** (1990), the same author's *Violence and the Great Estates in the South of Italy: Apulia, 1900–1914** (1986), Anthony Cardoza, *Agrarian Elites and Italian Fascism: The Province of Bologna, 1901–1926* (1982), and Alice Kelikian, *Town and Country under Fascism: The Transformation of Brescia, 1915–1926* (1986), are good local studies.

Anthony J. Nicholls, *Weimar and the Rise of Hitler,** 3rd ed. (1991), is a helpful introduction. Richard J. Evans, *The Coming of The Third Reich** (2004), is a masterful synthesis. Harold J. Gordon Jr., *Hitler and the Beer Hall Putsch* (1972), explores Hitler's first bid for power. Valuable articles on the growth of Nazism in the later 1920s are collected in Richard Bessel and E. J. Feuchtwanger, eds., *Social Change and Political Development in the Weimar Republic* (1981).

The various national fascist movements are explored deeply in Stein U. Larsen et al., eds., *Who Were the Fascists?* (1980), along with some probing essays on fascism in general. Walter Laqueur, *Fascism: A Reader's Guide* (1978), is still a useful guide to debates about generic fascism. Stuart Woolf, ed., *Fascism in Europe* (1981), gathers excellent studies of particular cases. There are brief sketches of the various European fascist movements and excerpts from their propaganda in Eugen Weber, *The Varieties of Fascism** (1982).

The beginnings of Hungarian fascism are suggestively introduced by Istvan Deák in Hans Rogger and Eugen Weber, eds., *The European Right* (1965), and colorfully elaborated (along with the early Romanian fascists) in M. Nagy-Talavera, *The Greenshirts and the Others* (1970). There are summary accounts in Peter F. Sugar, ed., *Native Fascism in the Successor States* (1971). Francis L. Carsten, *Fascist Movements in Austria from Schönerer to Hitler* (1977), is a useful introduction.

Efforts to locate deeper roots of fascism vary profoundly. Roger Griffin, ed., *International Fascism: Theories, Causes, and the New Consensus** (1998), defines fascism as an ideology of national regeneration and samples many other approaches. Zeev Sternhell attributes fascism to antimaterialist and nationalist renegades within the French and Italian left. See *The Birth of Fascist Ideology** (1994), among other works. For right-wing intellectual and cultural roots of Nazism, see Fritz Stern, *The Politics of Cultural Despair** (1961); Jeffrey Herf, *Reactionary Modernism** (1986); and George Mosse, *The Crisis of German Ideology** (1964, reprint ed. 1998). Early Fascism's links with aesthetic modernism are explored by Walter L. Adamson, *Avant-Garde Florence: From Modernism to Fascism* (1993). Marxist explanations of fascism as the defensive reaction of beleaguered capitalism are presented by David Beetham, ed., *Marxists in Face of Fascism* (1983).

Additional Internet links related to this chapter are available on the Europe in the 20th Century Web site: http://www.history.wadsworth.com/paxton04.

You can also explore images, interactive timelines, and maps related to this chapter on our Western Civilization Resource Center: http://history.wadsworth.com.

British Conservative leader Stanley Baldwin: Prime Minister 1923, 1924–1929, 1935–1937.

8

"Normalcy": Europe in the 1920s

Only in the mid-1920s could Europeans begin to feel "the full sunshine of peace."[1] Then tensions relaxed, and a period of calm and prosperity followed in the late 1920s. Internationally, the bitter confrontations of the early years of the decade, such as the French occupation of the Ruhr, were replaced by the Locarno spirit. In domestic politics, the surges of both revolution and counterrevolution subsided, and the parliamentary states settled down into the alternation of more moderate left and right. Wartime controls were dismantled, and reconstruction began to cover up the outward signs of war. In Western Europe, at least, booming prosperity carried production figures back to 1914 levels. The war's loosening of social restraints, compounded by the indulgence of deferred desires, lent these boom years of the late 1920s a glitter of brash vulgarity.

[1]Robert Graves and Alan Hodge, *The Long Week-End: A Social History of Great Britain, 1918–1939* (London, 1940), p. 113.

A RETURN TO "NORMALCY"

United States president Warren Harding's term for this period was a "return to normalcy." But what was "normal" for Europe after four years of total war, followed by another four years of postwar turmoil? In the late 1920s, the moderate center-left and center-right coalitions that dominated public life in Western European parliamentary regimes revived the values of late-nineteenth-century liberalism: broadened parliamentary democracy, individual liberties, and a market economy based on private enterprise and operating under a bare minimum of state intervention. Since the liberal Western states Britain and France had won the war, had restrained revolution, and had then recovered the highest living standards in Europe, those values tended to seem "normal" to many Europeans in the late 1920s. The question still to be answered was how adequately these "normal" nineteenth-century liberal values fit the postwar world.

Neoliberal Economics: Dismantling War Government

No one expected to maintain the fever-pitch effort or the stringent controls of war government indefinitely. Once military demobilization had been completed and internal order was assured, the various war boards and regulations began to be dissolved. By 1922, wartime agencies had been almost entirely dismantled, outside the Soviet Union. Liberal values held that economic and social decisions are best made in a free market, and "normalcy" meant the fullest possible return to that state of affairs. European liberals thought of wartime economic management as distasteful emergency expedients. "We want to get on with our business," said the British Tory Lord Inchcape, and

> not spend our time arguing with Government clerks, dancing attendance at the Board of Trade, appearing before committees, wheedling Consuls for permission to import what we need, throwing open our books, bills, and invoices to inspectors from Whitehall, and going through all the worry and expense to justify every transaction . . . to some official inquisitor.[2]

Even in states with the least tradition of state intervention, however, it was clear that the old world could not be fully restored. One small but revealing example was the passport. In 1914, Europeans had traveled freely throughout the Continent except in the Russian and Ottoman empires. After 1918, all European states required travelers to carry passports.

Restoring a pure *laissez-faire* economy would have been even more difficult than restoring unrestricted travel, for no European economy had been left to the free play of market forces even before 1914. All European states except that preeminent trading nation, Britain, had protected domestic industry by tariffs or other trade restrictions after the 1880s. Internally, governments had intervened to protect firms against their workers, and had been far more vigilant against combinations of

---

[2]Paul Barton Johnson, *Land Fit for Heroes: The Planning of British Reconstruction, 1916–1919* (Chicago, 1968), p. 451.

workers than against combinations of employers. Virtually all governments had begun to supervise working hours and conditions and to support health- and retirement-insurance plans. In Britain, Lloyd George had promised a postwar "land fit for heroes." How could this promise be kept by letting everything seek its own level?

In fact, no European liberal proposed to restore a mythical pure *laissez-faire* economy in Europe, nor would either businessmen or organized labor have accepted such aims. The liberals hoped to restore as much as possible of the economic freedom that businessmen had enjoyed before the war within a world financial, trading, and banking system resembling that of 1914. The clearest sign of these intentions was the reestablishment of the international gold standard, first in England in 1925 and subsequently in most European states outside the Soviet Union.

But even in its most booming prosperity the European economy of the late 1920s could only be a distorted imitation of that of 1914. For one thing, the war had vastly increased the scale and power of organizations in the economy. Business cartels, already present before the war, had emerged vastly strengthened by war government, especially on the Continent. In the 1920s, international cartels regulated the sales of iron, steel, oil, chemicals, and other major industrial products in Europe. At the same time, labor unions enrolled a higher proportion of industrial workers than before the war, and they had participated in centralized economic decisions under war government. Under such conditions, a liberal economic policy amounted to arbitrating among powerful organized interests.

The international economy was also permanently changed by the effects of war. The reinstitution of the gold standard did not restore a smoothly functioning medium of international trade. Postwar inflation had made currencies fluctuate wildly in relation to one another, and speculators stood ready to profit by these swings and to accentuate them by large purchases and sales of currency. Above all, the burden of reparations and war debts interfered with international trade and exchange. Germany owed money to Britain and France; France owed money to Britain and the United States; Britain owed money to the United States. United States loans to Germany in the late 1920s made the whole circuit possible. If anything happened to the economy of the United States, the whole delicate structure of the neoliberal international payments system would come tumbling down.

Neoliberal Politics: Broadening Parliamentary Democracy

Normalcy in politics meant a hastening of the late-nineteenth-century march toward universal suffrage, parliamentary regimes, and republics.

For the first time, republics became the rule in Europe. Before the war, only one Great Power, France, had been a republic. War and revolution swept away four great thrones (the Hohenzollern, the Habsburg, the Romanov, and the Ottoman) as well as some lesser ones, such as the Bavarian and (temporarily, from 1924 to 1935) the Greek. After the war, only Great Britain and Italy, among major states, remained monarchies. Most monarchies were now small states, as in the Low Countries and Scandinavia. Only one of the Eastern European creations was a monarchy: Yugoslavia.

The creation of new regimes provided a field day for constitution makers. New constitutions frequently took the western victors as examples; they often combined French parliamentary structures with a popularly elected president on the American model. The most important state to draft a new parliamentary constitution was Germany. The Weimar Constitution of August 1919 was supposed to embody the best legal scholarship and parliamentary experience. Drafted by a liberal Berlin law professor, Hugo Preuss, assisted by sociologist Max Weber and others, the Weimar Constitution was meant to move German politics firmly onto a democratic path and at the same time strengthen the central power over the individual German states. A president, popularly elected to serve seven years, designated the chancellor, whose cabinet must have the support of a majority in the popularly elected chamber *(Reichstag)*. An upper house *(Reichsrat)* of delegates of the states could delay but not block legislation. In order to provide the most mathematically equal weighting to each citizen's vote, the Weimar drafters experimented with proportional representation, by which every political party received seats in the legislature in proportion to its share of the total popular vote.

The vote was significantly widened in the postwar constitutions. Wartime pressures had forced even the German Empire to promise in 1917 to end the Prussian three-class voting system. More women received voting rights in Europe just after the First World War than in any other comparable period until the next wave of new constitutions in 1946. Before the war, women in Europe had been permitted to vote only in Finland (1906) and Norway (1913).[3] In 1918, Britain introduced virtually universal manhood suffrage and the vote for women over thirty; younger women were enfranchised in 1928. In the postwar period, women got the vote in Weimar Germany, three successor states (Poland, Czechoslovakia, and Austria), the Low Countries, Scandinavia, and Spain (1931). Women could not yet vote in Italy, Switzerland, France, or Portugal. And women occupied important political roles between the wars only in Britain and the Soviet Union.

The leveling effects of the war were apparent in postwar politics. Socialist parties, including some members of genuine working-class background, shared power in the parliamentary democracies. The new president of Weimar Germany, Social Democrat Friedrich Ebert, had been a saddlemaker's apprentice. The first British Labour government members of 1924 debated heatedly among themselves about the proper clothing to wear for the ritual call on King George V. Eventually they decided on the traditional tailcoats. One war later, the Labour leaders of 1945 were to call on George VI in street clothes.

The three major parliamentary democracies of Western Europe—Britain, France, and Germany—settled into centrist coalitions by the mid-1920s. During the late 1920s, these regimes gave an outward impression of governmental stability and consensus.

Postwar normalcy meant not only the attempt to restore liberal politics and economics in Northern and Western Europe but the urge to spread them to the rest of the Continent. Parliamentary institutions could not be effectively transplanted to

---

[3]Women could also vote in New Zealand (1893), Australia (1902), and twelve western states of the United States before 1914. See Renate Bridenthal and Claudia Koonz, *Becoming Visible: Women in European History,* 2nd. ed., (New York, 1987), p. 474.

Eastern and Southern European areas, however, where large parts of the population were illiterate peasants and where nationalities clashed.

BRITAIN

The highly personal government of wartime leader David Lloyd George had continued after the armistice, fortified by the "khaki election" of December 1918. But in late 1922, Conservative Party leaders, confident of their strength in the country and chafing under Lloyd George's one-man rule and taste for governmental activism, withdrew from the six-year-old coalition. The collapse of Lloyd George's personal majority marked a return to more traditional party politics in Britain.

A Three-Way Party System

As the election of November 1922 showed, however, British party politics no longer resembled the nineteenth-century alternation of Liberals and Conservatives. While the Conservatives won a large majority, the balance of power shifted within the opposition, and Labour emerged as the second most powerful party of the kingdom. The Liberal Party, the proud successor of eighteenth-century Whigs and nineteenth-century reformers like Grey, Peel, and Gladstone, slipped to third place.[4] For the moment, since many British voters were doubtful of Labour's capacity to govern, the Liberal Party held on to a balancing share of the electorate. The British parliamentary system, which had evolved in the rivalry of two parties, functioned as a three-party system throughout the interwar period.

On one level, the Liberal decline could be attributed to the vagaries of politics. The Liberal Party had split twice in two generations: once in the 1890s over the question of Irish independence, and again between followers of Asquith and Lloyd George during the First World War. On a more profound level, however, the Liberal decline suggested that the party's values of political democracy and economic *laissez-faire* offered a diminishing prospect of coping with the social and economic challenges Britain had confronted since 1914. The British economy's nineteenth-century staples, coal and textiles, were no longer very profitable, and much of its cushion of foreign investment had been liquidated during the war. Social expectations had been raised by the experiment of war government, while the British capacity to earn had been deeply eroded. The Liberal Party was destined to shrink to a mere splinter by the 1940s, one war later.

The Conservative ministers who succeeded Lloyd George from 1922 to 1924 wanted Britain to "get on with its own work, with the minimum of interference at home and of disturbance abroad."[5] This was a reasonable program for normalcy. The major innovation of the postwar Conservatives was their full commitment as a

---

[4]Electoral results, November 1922: Conservatives, 345 seats; Labour, 142 seats; Liberals, 117 seats.

[5]Electoral program of Prime Minister Bonar Law, 1922, quoted in A. J. P. Taylor, *English History, 1914–1945* (Oxford, England, 1965), p. 196.

party to protective tariffs in recognition of British industry's diminished competitive advantage in the postwar world. Some individual Conservatives had advocated special trade privileges for the empire before 1914, and wartime trade controls had set a precedent. But when Conservatives chose to fight the elections of 1923 on the issue of tariff protection, it was the first time since 1846 that a major British party had advocated peacetime tariffs in an election. In the hostile economic jungle of the postwar world, Conservatives had abandoned the trade principles of most nineteenth-century British leaders. Both Liberals and Labour supported free trade, however, and their combined majority in the elections of December 1923 provided an unambiguous mandate for it.[6] A return to free trade could also be considered a vote for normalcy, since Britain's nineteenth-century economic supremacy had been bound up with it.

The First Labour Government, 1924

Although Labour had reinforced its position as the largest party of the opposition, neither the Liberals nor Labour enjoyed a majority by itself after the election. Instead of joining in a coalition, the Liberal Party leader, former Prime Minister Asquith, decided to allow the Labour Party its first taste of governing responsibility—and perhaps enough leeway to discredit itself. Thus, with Liberal Party support, the Labour leader Ramsay MacDonald was able to form the first nominally socialist government in Britain in January 1924.

Some English people feared Labour would nationalize "everything including women."[7] A few hoped for a revolutionary socialist regime. MacDonald's government fulfilled neither the fears nor the hopes it aroused. Although MacDonald had helped found the more radical Independent Labour Party in the 1890s and had been among the handful of outspoken British pacifists during the First World War, he had no intention of trying to impose socialism on Britain. Nor had he the power to do so. His government depended on Liberal votes for its majority. His cabinet included a number of recruits from the Liberal Party, but only one wartime radical from the Clydeside industrial area, John Wheatley. The Wheatley Housing Act, which launched the construction of municipal housing at controlled rents, was the one genuine domestic innovation of the period. Aside from that first peacetime experiment in business–government cooperation and social planning, the Mac-Donald government did more to adapt politicians of genuine working-class background (MacDonald himself was the illegitimate son of a Scottish sharecropper) to the mainstream than vice versa. "It's a lum hat [top hat] government like a' the rest," one disillusioned British workman is supposed to have said.

The MacDonald government was more a reaffirmation of economic liberalism and the continued dismantling of wartime controls than a turn to the left. No doubt this was what most of the electorate wanted. MacDonald effectively established the legitimacy of Labour as a governing party and enormously widened access to the British political elite. That was no mean achievement.

[6]Electoral results, December 1923: Conservative, 258; Labour, 191; Liberal, 158.

[7]Graves and Hodge, p. 76.

In any event, the first Labour government was brief. It fell ten months later over personal matters: "Gentleman Mac" had been accused of accepting an expensive limousine and of shelving the prosecution of a communist newspaper. In the ensuing election of October 1924, the Conservatives focused on the alleged dangerous radicalism of MacDonald's foreign policy, including recognition of the Soviet Union. The conservative press produced a letter from Comintern Chairman Grigori Zinoviev advising British Communists on ways to undermine British capitalism. MacDonald was accused of being dangerously "soft" on subversive activities. The Zinoviev letter is now known to have been forged by a Polish anti-Bolshevik, although the British editors who used it probably thought it was genuine. It was enough to help defeat Labour, although the Liberal Party suffered even more heavily in the climate of political polarization that the letter created.

Return to Conservative "Normalcy"

The election of 1924 brought back to power the Conservative leader Stanley Baldwin, who personified the British version of normalcy in the late 1920s. Baldwin was a cabinet member from 1924 to 1937, except for the period of the second Labour government (1929–1931), and was prime minister during 1923, 1924 to 1929, and 1935 to 1937, one of the longest spans of political power in modern British history.

Stanley Baldwin went to some pains to present himself as moderate rather than conservative. Photographers and cartoonists pictured this wealthy steel manufacturer's son as a solid yeoman of Old England, a ruddy-faced taciturn man walking the fields and admiring his pigs, puffing a pipe, waving aside intellectuals, and speaking a bluff, frank common sense. He was the first British prime minister to address cabinet members by their first names, and the first to make effective political use of the radio. He prided himself on good relations with Labour. He helped establish a pragmatic, middle-class style in the British Conservative Party that supplanted forever the aristocratic manner of the previous generation of Tory leaders such as Lord Salisbury and Lord Curzon, who is said to have called Baldwin "a man of the utmost insignificance." On closer inspection, Baldwin turns out to have been a shrewd parliamentary tactician and a man of quite fixed economic orthodoxy. He helped steer England back to a hollow reconstruction of pre-1914 financial and business arrangements.

The most noteworthy single step in British neoliberalism was the return to the international gold standard. The two fixed poles of nineteenth-century world trade had been the free interchangeability of all major currencies with gold and the role of London as world financial capital. But the gold standard had been suspended by wartime currency controls, while London had been separated from part of its clientele, disrupted by the war effort, and permanently weakened by the loss of British investment overseas during the war. To the economically orthodox, return to the gold standard and the revival of London went hand in hand.

Winston Churchill, Baldwin's Chancellor of the Exchequer, announced the end of the wartime suspension of the gold standard in his budget speech of April 1925. Henceforth, the pound was freely convertible anywhere in the world to gold. It was not a classic gold standard, for gold coins no longer circulated freely in domestic transactions in England. But it gave the illusion that the old world was restored and that the last of the war's effects had vanished.

Britain's return to the gold standard probably hampered the nation's search for renewed prosperity in the late 1920s. For one thing, it made British goods more expensive on the world market, since Churchill had insisted on returning to 1914 exchange rates, which overvalued the pound in relation to the dollar.[8] A more fundamental criticism was that whereas the prewar free exchange of pounds for gold had rested on a large British surplus in international accounts and large gold holdings, the postwar London gold market rested on a weakened economy. Gold was supplemented by holdings of reserves in foreign exchange, such as marks or dollars, which could be quickly withdrawn in case of trouble. That fragile system came crashing down in 1929–1931, damaging the British economy far more severely than a less grandiose financial restoration in 1925 would have.

Normalcy did nothing for the British workingman's standard of living in the 1920s. The basic adjustments that Britain had to make to a changed place in the world economy were made more difficult by the high price of British goods abroad on the gold standard. The mainstays of the British export trade—coal and textiles—were stagnating. British exports never made up for the wartime loss of overseas investments. Even worse, unemployment in Britain never dropped below a shocking 10 percent throughout the interwar period, even in the most prosperous years of the late 1920s. Stanley Baldwin's solution to Britain's economic troubles was nothing if not frank. "All the workers in this country," he said in a speech on July 30, 1925, "have got to take reductions in wages to help put industry on its feet."[9]

The coal industry provided the most serious challenge to Baldwin's hope for Britain's return to normalcy. Rich coal mines close to the sea had been a major stimulus to British commercial and industrial preeminence in the nineteenth century, and the mines were still the largest single employer in Britain. In the 1920s, however, there was a world glut of coal. The British mines competed especially poorly, for their markets had been interrupted during the war, their equipment was outdated, and their management was fragmented among many marginal companies. The mine owners believed that wage cuts were their only way back to the world market; the miners adamantly refused to work for less than they had been receiving.[10] A government-appointed commission, headed by Herbert Samuel, tried unsuccessfully to persuade the mine owners to rationalize, consolidate, and modernize their mines in return for government assistance in negotiating lower wages. When negotiations deadlocked, the miners went out on strike at the beginning of May 1926.

The miners' grievances were the principal fuel for the General Strike of 1926, the tensest moment of class conflict in modern Britain between the "hands off Russia" strikes of 1919 and 1920 and the energy crisis of the winter of 1973–1974. The

---

[8] In *The Economic Consequences of Mr. Churchill* (1925), John Maynard Keynes charged that the pound was overvalued by 10 percent as compared with 1914. Indeed, British exports never returned to the 1914 level in the 1920s.

[9] Quoted in Taylor, p. 239.

[10] The least skilled mineworkers in the hardest hit region were asked to accept a wage cut from 78s per week to 45s 10d (from about $19 to about $12 at contemporary exchange rates), with hours cut to six per day.

Gernsheim Collection, Harry Ransom Humanities Research Center, The University of Texas at Austin

Opponents of the General Strike of May 1926 in England organized makeshift transportation to get to work.

striking miners were joined by very nearly all organized labor in the fullest demonstration of union solidarity in British history. Close to 4 million workers were out on the peak day, May 13. The general council of the Trades Union Congress (TUC) accepted a compromise after nine days (government enforcement of the modernization advocated in the Samuel report in exchange for any lowering of wages), but some of the rank and file continued the strike. Many miners were starved back to work, at lower wages, only six months later.

The British General Strike of 1926 seems in retrospect an end rather than a beginning. Its leaders had intended all along to use the strike as a lever for negotiation, not as a revolutionary step. The TUC even used the term *national strike* rather than the old syndicalist term *general strike,* with its intimations of replacing the state by workers' associations. Unlike the strikes in the Clydeside area just after the war, there was no mention during the 1926 strike of soviets or strike committees assuming governmental functions. Although there were some acts of violence on both sides as well as organized strikebreaking by the government and by university students, there were no deaths. All this gives the lie to hysterical fears of "microbes of Bolshevism" published in the conservative press at the time, and to dire predictions by hard-liner Winston Churchill that the strike could "only end in the overthrow of Parliamentary Government or its decisive victory."[11]

The results of the General Strike, on the government side, were a new law in 1927 outlawing sympathy strikes and the rupture of trade and diplomatic relations with the Soviet Union, which some Conservatives accused of having contributed relief funds to the miners. On the TUC side, the British union movement eventually recovered its losses in funds and membership; its commitment to collective bargaining within the existing British social system was actually strengthened. At the level of the individual miners and their families, the bitterness and suffering had no chronicler.

In the later 1920s, Britain appeared peaceful and prosperous. But the external trappings of normalcy barely concealed the inadequate adjustment Britain had made to its diminished world economic position.

FRANCE

After the Poincaré government's hard line toward Germany had been discredited by the occupation of the Ruhr, the French electorate gave a majority to a moderate left coalition in the elections of May 1924. The *cartel des gauches* was an electoral alliance of the two main parliamentary left parties in France, Radicals and reformist Socialists.

The *Cartel des Gauches*

This coalition warrants close examination, for it provides the key to the apparent labyrinth of Third Republic politics in interwar France. American readers, used to a more cautious political vocabulary, are likely to be misled by the flaming labels given Latin parties. The French Radical Party was the lineal descendant of genuine radicals of the 1860s Second Empire: partisans of universal suffrage, parliamentary primacy over the executive, free universal secondary education, the disestablishment of the Catholic Church, and the replacement of professional armies by militia. Although some Radicals had favored an income tax in the 1890s, the party generally disapproved of state intervention in the economy. By 1905, with the separation of Church and state in France, the Radical program had been virtually fulfilled. The Radical Party remained as the main political expression of the "little man" in France: anticlerical, egalitarian in political terms, *laissez-faire* in economic terms, sentimental about the French Revolution, ready to defend the republic if it seemed threatened by bishops, generals, or aristocrats. (All European Catholic countries had similar anticlerical, democratic, small-property parties.)

[11]Martin Gilbert, *Winston S. Churchill,* vol. V, 1922–1939 (London, 1976), p. 154.

The other half of the *cartel des gauches* was the French Socialist Party (SFIO, or French Section of the [Second] Workers' International). This was the remaining remnant of French parliamentary socialism after a majority of Socialists voted in 1920 to join the Third International (Comintern). The SFIO was well on its way back to becoming the other main parliamentary party on the French left by 1924. Although nominally committed to Marxist socialism and the eventual workers' revolution, the SFIO placed a high value on the survival of the parliamentary republic as a first step toward these goals. French Socialists were willing to cooperate at election time with the Radicals in order to prevent a right-wing victory, but they were unwilling to take part in a "bourgeois" government until they had an electoral majority of their own and could enact socialist laws.

The basis of the alliance, then, was defense of the Third Republic against clerical or monarchist enemies on the right, not a common social policy. It was a 1924 reincarnation of the Radical–Socialist alliance that had formed at the turn of the century over the Dreyfus affair (1899–1906), when it seemed that clericals and army officers were willing to violate the constitution rather than admit that a military court had erred in sentencing the Jewish Captain Alfred Dreyfus on a trumped-up charge of treason. Such an alliance worked best at election time, when the danger of splitting the left vote was uppermost in the politicians' minds. Both Radicals and Socialists promised to support whichever of their candidates was ahead in a run-off.[12] This practice of "republican discipline" returned reformist left majorities to parliament in three of the five French elections between the wars (1924, 1932, and 1936).

Once elected, however, Radical and SFIO deputies had trouble cooperating in a positive governmental program. They could agree on political liberties, freer education, anticlericalism, and antimilitarism. But if economic issues arose, the Radicals' small-property bias clashed fundamentally with the SFIO's Marxism. Between elections, therefore, the pivotal Radical Party tended to turn back toward center coalitions. The resulting incoherency of majorities was a major ingredient of what the American political scientist Stanley Hoffmann has called the "stalemate" of the Third Republic, an immobile political system that was the counterpart of the cautious economy and low birth rate that prevailed in France.

The election of the *cartel des gauches* in May 1924 permits us to see this political stalemate at work. The new prime minister was Edouard Herriot, leader of the Radical Party between the wars and the personification of the nonsocialist left in the later Third Republic. Herriot was a man of good qualities, a humanist author (he wrote a number of books, including biographies of Beethoven and Madame De Staël), active in providing municipal social services when he was mayor of Lyon, genuinely concerned about political liberties, a consummate parliamentary bargainer. His enormous physical bulk testified to his pleasure in the cafés and restaurants of Lyon and Paris.

Herriot's accomplishments as French premier (June 1924–April 1925) reveal the areas in which the *cartel des gauches* was capable of decisive action. We have already

---

[12]French electoral practice, as is proper in a multiparty political system, provides for a run-off in the likely event that no candidate gets 50 percent or more of the votes in the first election.

seen Herriot's contribution to international conciliation, along with Ramsay Mac-Donald and Gustav Stresemann in 1924.[13] He extended diplomatic recognition to the Soviet Union and began to withdraw it from the Holy See. French laws removing clerical influence from the public schools were extended to Alsace-Lorraine (which had not been part of France when those laws were passed in the 1880s). Steps were taken toward democratizing the elitist French public high schools. Antimilitarism, anticlericalism, enlargement of individual opportunity through education—that was the common ground on which French Radicals and Socialists felt happy.[14]

Unfortunately, the major problems faced by the *cartel des gauches* were economic and financial. France had expected to pay its war debts with German reparations. German reparations were also expected to cover the enormous costs of postwar reconstruction, which were causing the French budget to continue to run at a deficit. Herriot's liquidation of the Ruhr occupation, however, showed that France was probably never going to squeeze much money out of Germany. Inflation had run rampant since the end of wartime economic controls. French conservatives, distrustful of Herriot, lost confidence in the international value of the franc. Holders of francs began selling them for gold and other currencies, creating a "run on the franc." At the same time, the financial community and the Bank of France put pressure on Herriot to balance the budget. Eventually the Bank of France refused to lend current operating sums to the government.

Herriot and the Radical Party always claimed that conservative financiers had erected a "wall of money" against the republic. It was typical Radical rhetoric, the "little man's" suspicion of great economic powers. There is no doubt that conservative hostility to Herriot contributed to the run on the franc. But the real problem lay in the French people's years of refusal to support the expenses of war and reconstruction by taxation and in the Radicals' horror of state regulation. As in Britain in 1924, the move to the left meant less governmental intervention, not more. Wartime controls were an unpleasant memory. Aside from proposing steeper income taxes, the French Socialists had no interest in government intervention within capitalism. The Radicals preferred to let the economy regulate itself. So Herriot held back from the higher taxes and currency control that might have helped balance the budget and stabilize the franc.

After Herriot's fall in April 1925, seven ministries followed within fifteen months. While the Radicals felt their way toward a more centrist coalition without the Socialists, inflation soared, and the franc declined on the world's money markets to about one-tenth of its prewar value.

Poincaré: Return to "Normalcy"

France finally found its normalcy of the late 1920s in the austere person of Raymond Poincaré. Poincaré, repudiated in 1924 for occupying the Ruhr, returned in

---

[13]See chapter 6, pp. 187–191.

[14]The SFIO did not hold cabinet positions in this "bourgeois" government but contributed essential votes to its parliamentary majority.

1926 as a kind of national financial savior. His personal probity and dour legalism provided emotional reassurance to a people frightened at seeing their savings evaporate in a never-ending inflationary spiral. Even before Poincaré did anything, investors began buying francs back, and the recovery began. Mostly by that emotional reassurance, and in part by the traditional conservative remedies of governmental parsimony and careful management, Poincaré was able to nurse the franc back to one-fifth of its prewar international value in 1928. At that point he returned to the international gold standard. The "Napoleon franc" had endured unchanged from 1807 to 1914 as a firm economic rock on which the French middle class had built in serenity. Then it had been shaken by the war and destroyed by postwar inflation. Now that it was replaced by the "Poincaré franc" in 1928, the middle class could begin to glimpse the revival of a stable world. The war had been paid for out of their savings, however, and even during the historic high level of prosperity reached in 1929, there remained tender spots on French middle-class consciousness. The franc must never be touched again. And France must never again embark on another war, so costly in gold and blood.

The Poincaré government, one of the longest "reigns" of any Third Republic premier (July 1926–July 1929), embodied the French version of the late 1920s normalcy. The presence of Aristide Briand, the man of Locarno, at the Foreign Ministry assured that Poincaré's hard line of 1922 to 1924 had been replaced by conciliation and the end of dangerous foreign confrontations. At home, the return to the gold standard and balanced budgets seemed a reassuring return to the economic verities. Wartime controls and scarcities and postwar turmoil seemed things of the past.

WEIMAR GERMANY

The Weimar Republic was, outwardly, a dramatic departure for Germany. The very decision to draft the new constitution during the summer of 1919 in Weimar, the town of Goethe, rather than in Berlin, was itself a powerful symbolic gesture. Berlin had been the garrison city of the Hohenzollern kings of Prussia; it had become the Red city of Rosa Luxemburg, Karl Liebknecht, and the Spartacists. At Weimar, the liberal ideals of the nineteenth century seemed to reach belated fulfillment. These ideals had been deflected in Germany during the 1860s and 1870s, when a majority of German liberals chose to overlook Bismarck's subversion of the parliamentary system in their enthusiasm for German unification and military victories. A German liberal like the historian Friedrich Meinecke could now hope that in the regime created at Weimar the German "men of culture" (*Kulturmenschen*) had won the upper hand over the German "men of power" (*Machtmenschen*) at long last.[15]

Burdens of the Weimar Republic

The Weimar Republic was burdened from the beginning by almost crushing liabilities. The constitution no doubt had its faults; the proportional representation system,

[15]Friedrich Meinecke, *The German Catastrophe*, trans. Sidney B. Fay (Cambridge, Mass., 1950), pp. 27–29.

for example, magnified the country's divisions in a multiparty parliament. But a reasonably harmonious national community can govern itself well, despite flawed constitutional arrangements. The Weimar regime faced far more fundamental problems. It was indelibly imprinted for many Germans with the stain of defeat, for it was the regime that had accepted the *Diktat* of Versailles in the summer of 1919. In the eyes of many German nationalists, the left had first stabbed the German army in the back by revolution in November 1918 and had then been rewarded with political power. At the same time, the incomplete character of the German revolution of 1918 and 1919[16] had left most of the Weimar Republic's enemies intact: the officer corps, the aristocracy, leaders of powerful business cartels, nationalist and monarchist movements unreconciled to the overthrow of the imperial regime and Germany's reduced status.

Organizations had grown larger and more influential at all levels of public life in Germany during the war. The cartels of German heavy industry, while not in agreement among themselves on everything, worked together against Weimar labor policies. Trade unions, with increased membership, dealt directly with business. The traditional two legislative houses and cabinet of ministers set up by the Weimar Constitution could never adequately control these organizations. Moreover, the Weimar Republic lacked deeply rooted values on which to build, since it had not germinated naturally out of a successful middle-class resistance to authority during the previous generations. "The authoritarian state had fallen into eclipse, but the wonted traditions, attitudes, and institutions that had been formed in reference to it gradually resumed their accustomed sway."[17]

To make matters worse, the Weimar Republic was forced to assume responsibility for allocating the material burdens of a lost war. Even the victorious nations had trouble taxing their populations for the costs of reconstruction and of increased social services. Efforts of the Weimar Republic to institute broader progressive income taxes were doubly resented because, as nationalists charged, some of the money went to pay hated reparations to the Allies.

The Weimar Republic, then, passed through exceptional turmoil and class antagonism up through 1923. Even after it had crushed its own revolutionary left in January through May 1919, accepted the Treaty of Versailles unconditionally under threat of invasion in June 1919, and survived the occupation of Berlin by *Freikorps* in the Kapp *Putsch* of March 1920,[18] the new German republic had to face still more conflicts. The details of the peace settlement, applied under duress, continually opened raw wounds. French troops occupied Ruhr cities in the spring of 1919 and again in March 1921 to enforce their interpretation of the treaties. Settling other borders in Silesia and Schleswig-Holstein provoked conflict until 1922. Workers in the Ruhr, with the support of Spartacists, went out on insurrectionary strikes in the spring of 1920. The purchasing power of the German mark lost ground steadily. The nationalist state government of Bavaria went its own way, protecting and encouraging the remnants of the *Freikorps* and militant nationalist groups like

---

[16]See chapter 5, pp. 138–140.

[17]Leonard Krieger, *The German Idea of Freedom* (Boston, 1957), p. 465.

[18]See chapter 7, p. 211.

Hitler's German National Socialist Workers' Party. Assassinations punctuated political life. Matthias Erzberger, leader of the Catholic Center Party, who had proposed the Peace Resolution of 1917, had led in accepting the Versailles settlement, and had proposed progressive income taxation, was murdered by nationalists in August 1921. Walther Rathenau, who as foreign minister in 1922 had tried to negotiate a compromise reparations settlement, was murdered in June 1922. At this point, the worst was still to come—the occupation of the Ruhr in 1923 and total collapse of the mark.

Eventually, in the late 1920s, the Weimar Republic settled into relatively stable years. Even then, however, parliamentary government never had the wide acceptance it enjoyed in England or France, nor did the Weimar institutions work in the ways their creators had expected. In Weimar Germany military and economic organizations held vast power outside parliamentary control and liberal values had no deep historical legitimacy.

The "Weimar Coalition"

No coherent political majority emerged to deal with these manifold problems within the Weimar constitutional machinery. The "Weimar Coalition" of Social Democrats, Democrats, and Center Party members that had written the constitution might have been expected to run the government. These parties had received about two-thirds of the votes when the constituent assembly was elected in January 1919, and that assembly had prudently extended its life as the first parliament of the Weimar Republic after the constitution had been adopted. Social Democrat Friedrich Ebert had been named first president of the republic (1919–1925) by the constituent assembly. When the "Weimar Coalition" was tested in the first parliamentary elections in June 1920, however, its popular vote fell to about 40 percent.

Each party of the "Weimar Coalition" was precluded in some fundamental way from serving as the basis of a broad parliamentary majority. The Social Democrats proclaimed themselves a Marxist workers' party, but they had been stained with workers' blood when they prevented the constitutional revolution of 1918 and 1919 from turning into a social revolution. The Democratic Party remained a small group of liberal intellectuals around Hugo Preuss, the drafter of the Weimar Constitution, most of whose potential middle-class following still preferred nationalist success to liberal principle. The Center Party was a Catholic confessional group rather than either a class party or an ideological party; its following ranged from constitutionalists like Matthias Erzberger to conservatives. Although the "Weimar Coalition" parties came close to winning an electoral majority in 1928, they never again after the election of June 1920 could run by themselves the machinery they had created.

Every Weimar government after 1920 was able to form a majority only by drawing some support from elements of the center and right that were at best provisionally tolerant of the Weimar Constitution. The new People's Party, based on former National Liberals with close ties to business and led by Gustav Stresemann, captured about 15 percent of the electorate in 1920. So did the German National People's Party (DNVP), a regrouping of nationalists and monarchists. The People's

President Friedrich Ebert of Germany reviews police forces on the fifth anniversary of the Weimar Constitution, August 1924.

Party accepted the parliamentary republic as Germany's most feasible instrument for regaining world power. The DNVP's acceptance of parliamentary participation was far more conditional than that of the People's Party. They participated only in order to work for a more authoritarian system. In times of crisis, the Communists and Nationalists (DNVP) drew even more support away from the fragmented center. At such times, the Weimar center resembled a candle burning at both ends.

President Ebert, a scrupulous observer of the constitution, made no attempt to assure the continued power of his Social Democrats in the face of the poor electoral results but instead chose new chancellors from the moderate center of the legislature. Even so, the trend was not so much toward the middle parties as it was toward nonparty rule by technicians. After two brief ministries of the Catholic Center Party had failed either to reach a more satisfactory settlement with the Versailles powers or to stop the galloping inflation that was reducing the mark to worthless paper, the head of the Hamburg-America shipping line, Wilhelm Cuno, was asked to form a government of nonparty technical experts in November 1922. Cuno was not even a member of the *Reichstag*. The pattern was established of turning to presidential authority and technical expertise to fill the void of a parliamentary majority.

Another pattern was set as the regime focused its chief preoccupations on foreign and economic issues. The possibility of internal changes that would liberalize German social institutions like the army, the civil service, and universities to match the new democratic constitution had vanished with the election of June 1920, if not earlier. German governments henceforth succeeded or failed according to their success in coping with foreign affairs and the economy.

These two issues came to the crisis point in 1923, the year of the French occupation of the Ruhr and the collapse of the mark. In that year the Weimar Republic faced its gravest challenge of the decade. Chancellor Cuno's policy of passive resistance against the French in the Ruhr only helped bring the economy to a standstill. Both Communists and Nationalists battled the French and made a hero of Leo Schlageter, a young *Freikorps* veteran executed by the French for having sabotaged a rail line near Düsseldorf. Encouraged by rising strike activity and widespread dissatisfaction with the soaring cost of living, the German Communist Party attempted a revolutionary uprising in October. In the states of Saxony and Thuringia, governed by dissident Social Democrats and Communists, revolutionaries recruited popular militia, or "proletarian hundreds." At the other extreme, Adolf Hitler, taking a lesson from Mussolini, attempted to launch a nationalist revolution in Munich with the "beer hall *Putsch.*" German central authority was imperiled at the same time as the mark lost its power to buy anything; the very fabric of life seemed to be coming apart.

The "Great Coalition"

In March 1920, the Kapp Putsch had been thwarted by a general strike of the trade unions, and political authority had been restored by the "Weimar Coalition." In late 1923, by contrast, the republic was saved by three conservatives, who worked principally outside the parliamentary framework and who remained dominant figures in the stable Weimar regime of the later 1920s: the political leader Gustav Stresemann, the German army commander General Hans von Seeckt, and the financial expert Hjalmar Schacht.

The dominant political figure was Gustav Stresemann. Stresemann was a beer wholesaler's son who had succeeded in business and in centrist politics under the empire. A supporter of German expansion during the war, Stresemann was deeply shocked by the revolution of 1918 and skeptical of the new republic. But his humble origins, his realism, and his taste for stability made him even more hostile to the aristocrats and officers of the intransigent right. Offended by the nationalist follies of the Kapp *Putsch* and the assassinations of Erzberger and Rathenau, Stresemann gradually brought his People's Party into positive support of the Weimar Constitution as a lesser evil. Contemporaries called him a *Vernunftrepublikaner,* a republican of the mind but not of the heart.

As the crisis deepened in August 1923, Stresemann pieced together a parliamentary majority committed to saving the Weimar Republic from both the right and the left. He joined the People's Party to the "Weimar Coalition" of Social Democrats, Democrats, and Center Party to form a "Great Coalition." We have already seen his decisive contribution as Foreign Minister to international conciliation.[19] Stresemann's Great Coalition (August–November 1923) was equally decisive in preserving

[19]See chapter 6, pp. 187–191.

the Weimar Constitution within Germany. But the inclusion of such contradictory parties in the Great Coalition was a source of weakness as well as strength. When Stresemann proved far more resolute in expelling the Communist ministers from the state governments of Saxony and Thuringia than in forcing the nationalist state government of Bavaria to apply the law to the far right, at least until Hitler's beer hall *Putsch* on November 8, the Social Democrats went into opposition for the first time. Centrist coalitions governed Germany for the next four years without them. Stresemann had saved the republic, but he had helped take it permanently out of the hands of the "Weimar Coalition."

It was to General Hans von Seeckt, rather than to parliament, that Stresemann had to turn to beat back insurrectionary movements on both extremes. Seeckt, commander of the German army from 1920 to 1926, had worked more or less within the Versailles limitations to make his 100,000-man force a unified, high-quality body of potential future leaders, even more socially conservative and insulated from government control than the old imperial army.[20] Seeckt's priorities were the unity of the German state and the unity of the army. He was willing to use the army to defend the republic as long as the republic promoted those two values. The Communist–Social Democrat state governments formed in October in Saxony and Thuringia threatened central government authority as well as property. The local army commander acted to defend both when he occupied the two state capitals (Dresden and Weimar) and deposed the state governments in October and November. To meet the threat of Bavarian separatism posed by Hitler's Munich *Putsch,* Seeckt was entrusted with full dictatorial power on November 8 under Article 48 of the constitution, the emergency presidential power article. Fortunately for Seeckt, the local Bavarian conservatives crushed the *Putsch* without the need for using federal army force against Hitler's most famous accomplice, the war hero General Ludendorff. At the same time, police and navy units crushed the last Communist uprising of Weimar Germany, in the port city of Hamburg, on October 23. The republic had been saved but at the price of greater centralization and a more autonomous army.

The other emergency that Stresemann had to deal with was runaway inflation. On November 12, Stresemann appointed the banker and economist Hjalmar Horace Greeley Schacht as currency commissioner. Schacht simply started over with a new currency, the *Rentenmark,* each of which was worth 1 trillion marks. The "miracle of the *Rentenmark,*" for which Schacht took full credit, consisted in two achievements that were as much psychological as economic. Because not enough gold and foreign exchange were deposited in German banks to back the new currency, Schacht backed it with an unexchangeable medium, a mortgage on all the land, industries, and commerce of Germany. Then he kept the new currency stable by stringently limiting the amount available for the government to spend and for firms to borrow. When the Dawes Plan loans began to flow into Germany in 1924,[21]

---

[20]Almost every other officer in the Weimar officer corps was the son of an officer compared with every fourth in the imperial officer corps; one officer in five was a nobleman in 1920, one in four in 1932. There were fewer Social Democrats in the small Weimar army than there had been in the imperial army. (Hajo Holborn, *A History of Modern Germany, 1840–1945* [New York, 1969], pp. 586–587.)

[21]See chapter 6, p. 188.

Schacht was able to shift to a gold-based currency, the *Reichsmark,* which remained stable until the Great Depression.

It has been said: "The Inflation was the real German Revolution."[22] Unlike the political revolution of 1918 and 1919, it changed economic and social relationships. It reduced many middle-class people to scrubbing their own floors. Such people would follow any savior in the event of another economic crisis. Schacht's tight new deflationary economy forced marginal enterprises out of business. Only large firms that rationalized and modernized production profited by the German economic boom of the late 1920s. New cartels and trusts were formed. The United Steel combine (*Vereinigte Stahlwerke,* 1926), which grouped many of the coal, iron, and steel interests, produced about one-half of German steel. The great Krupp empire produced most of the rest. The chemical and dye trust (*Interessengemeinschaft Farbenindustrie A. G.,* or *I. G. Farben,* 1925) was the largest corporation on the European Continent.

Thus, the Weimar Republic emerged from the brink of destruction in 1923 into a period of calm. Politically, it continued to move to the right. When President Ebert died in 1925, the old Social Democrat was replaced by the Prussian war hero Field Marshal Paul von Hindenburg. Other presidential candidates together received more than a majority of votes, but the Communist candidate, Ernst Thälmann, drew off decisive votes from the centrist republican candidate, Wilhelm Marx, a striking instance of the consequences of a divided left. Government majorities stepped one more notch to the right in 1927 by including members of the German Nationalist Party (DNVP), whose press and local leaders continued to call for the replacement of the republic by either a king or a dictator. The left gained in the 1928 elections, but the new Social Democratic chancellor, Hermann Müller, could govern only with a "Great Coalition."

With the economy booming, the political fever chart did fall. The assassinations of the early period now ceased, and the paramilitary street gangs of angry veterans and authoritarians were less conspicuous. Following his failed *Putsch,* Hitler sat in the Landsberg prison writing his political credo, *Mein Kampf* (1925). Individual liberties were more or less assured, and Berlin rivaled Paris as a cosmopolitan center of artistic experimentation. The Weimar Republic was surviving, but its parliamentary façade barely concealed an autonomous, authoritarian officer corps, dominant big business combines, and a technocratic civil service with no real commitment to political liberties. If the parliamentary regime failed in either foreign or economic affairs, these powerful bodies would shove it aside in favor of something more effective.

EASTERN EUROPE

The new states of Eastern Europe, like Germany, were the scene of constitution-making on the liberal model after the First World War. Strong liberal influence was only to be expected. The new regimes were the product of three simultaneous liberal victories: the victory of the Western parliamentary powers—Great Britain and

---

[22]Godfrey Scheele, *The Weimar Republic* (London, 1946), p. 77.

France—over the autocratic Central Powers; the victory of national independence movements over the multinational dynasties of Germany, Austria-Hungary, and Russia; and the victory of middle- and upper-class interests over the Bolshevik movement in Eastern Europe in 1919 and 1920.

National independence went hand in hand with parliamentary democracy in the political climate of the 1920s. The new states (Austria, Poland, Czechoslovakia) were republics, with the exception of Yugoslavia, or the Kingdom of Serbs, Croats, and Slovenes, as it was known until 1929. The preexisting kingdoms of Romania and Bulgaria adopted new parliamentary constitutions in the early 1920s, whereas Hungary remained a regency without a king and Greece became a republic (temporarily) in 1924. The new constitutions drew largely on French, British, and American political practice. The electorate was far broader than before; the limited suffrage of Hungary was the major exception.

It seemed, on paper at least, that the decade of the 1920s was the high point of political democracy in Eastern Europe. Liberal politics and economics, however, were being transplanted into alien soil. Western parliamentary systems had evolved gradually through long and painful conflicts between divine right monarchy and an alliance of the gentry with a large, growing middle class. In Eastern Europe, by contrast, liberal values had been espoused by nationalist intellectuals without a broad social base. There was no substantial middle class in Eastern Europe. The region was overwhelmingly rural. Commercial and professional people in many parts of Eastern Europe, such as Poland, Hungary, and Romania, were often German or Jewish and hence on uneasy terms with the national movements that had created the successor states. Only among the Czechs was there a large, national middle class with liberal traditions.

The problems of new states further complicated matters for the infant parliamentary systems of Eastern Europe. Indigenous leadership was inexperienced, and the great majority of the rural population had never been drawn into sustained involvement in national political life. As much as three-quarters of the population were still illiterate in parts of the Balkans. Under these conditions, politics was bound to remain the preserve of a few. The inclusion of obligatory voting in some new Eastern European constitutions was less an expression of advanced ideas of political participation than of fear of a passive citizenry.

Economic dislocation imposed another severe burden. New frontiers abruptly cut off many Eastern Europeans from the cities with which they had customarily traded. There was massive demand for land reform and for the development of basic transportation resources. Inflation was nearly as disastrous as in Germany. Under such conditions, *laissez-faire* economics made no sense.

The liberal experiments in Eastern Europe had to come to terms with two fundamental features of the region: peasant predominance and ethnic diversity. Regimes stood or fell in Eastern Europe during much of the first half of the twentieth century by their handling of the issues of agriculture and nationality.

Rural Predominance and Agrarian Discontent

Most Eastern Europeans still worked on the land at the end of the war. The proportion of the total population engaged directly in farming or herding reached almost

80 percent in Bulgaria and Yugoslavia; it was over 60 percent in Romania, Poland, and Hungary. The agrarian proportion fell only to half in the region's most industrialized state, Czechoslovakia. (At the same time, by contrast, that proportion was less than 20 percent in Britain.) Moreover, as has been noted, much of the land was owned by great landlords. Latifundia (huge estates) dominated the countryside in Poland, Hungary, and Romania to a degree matched in Western Europe only by southern Spain. Since there were few urban or industrial outlets for a growing population, massive underemployment and land hunger festered among the mounting number of day laborers and subsistence farmers on small holdings.

Direct, violent peasant action seemed likely. An assault by Romanian peasants on manor houses and Jewish moneylenders in 1907, the bloodiest peasant uprising in modern European history, had been a first warning. Its suppression had cost 10,000 peasant lives. Massive land seizures by the Russian peasantry in 1917 and 1918 set an almost irresistible example nearby. Eastern European rulers knew that some form of land redistribution was almost inevitable in the early 1920s; the main question was what form it would take.

Béla Kun's Budapest soviet had proposed revolutionary land redistribution in the spring of 1919, but Kun's orthodox insistence on collectivizing large estates appealed less to the Eastern European peasantry than Lenin's more flexible acquiescence in land redistribution among individual peasants. In any event, a revolutionary solution had been blocked by the crushing of Béla Kun's regime in the summer of 1919. Henceforth, Eastern European land reform was in the hands of the middle- and upper-class leaders of the successor states. Their approach to land reform, supported by liberal intellectuals and a few progressive landlords as well as many peasants, aimed at a substantial increase in the number of independent family farms. This would be accomplished by redistributing to family farmers expropriated crown lands, foreign estates, and excess land purchased from estates above a maximum permissible size.

Every Eastern European successor state redistributed some land in this fashion in the early 1920s. The change was fairly substantial in Czechoslovakia and Romania, where many landlords were foreign. In Romania, between 1920 and 1941, 13,000,000 acres were distributed to 1,400,000 peasants, leaving only 13 percent of the arable land in estates larger than 220 acres.[23] Bulgaria was unique in having widespread small holdings and almost no aristocracy to begin with, but it broadened its family farm base still further under the agrarian regime of Alexander Stamboliski (1919–1923). Stamboliski set an upper limit of 75 acres on Bulgarian rural property holdings, and by 1934 only 1 percent of the country's farms and 6 percent of its total land area were in units larger than that. Elsewhere, land reform was much more grudging. In many cases, newly independent peasants, heavily mortgaged and suffering declining agricultural prices in the later 1920s, sold out again to larger landlords. The Radziwill estates in Poland still amounted to 200,000 acres in 1937. Nor did mere redistribution solve basic rural problems of overpopulation and inefficient farming methods.

Widened suffrage in predominantly rural countries opened up political opportunities for farmers' parties. Agrarian, peasant, or smallholders' parties (to use the

---

[23]Keith Hitchens, *Rumania 1866–1947* (Oxford, England, 1994), p. 351.

most common names), dedicated to serving the interests of the small landowner, held a major position in the parliaments of Eastern Europe, whereas they were largely absent from Western European party systems. A Smallholders' Party emerged in the first Hungarian elections in 1919 as the largest single party, although it was eventually overshadowed by the counterrevolutionary elements discussed in chapter 7. The Peasant Party of Wincenty Witos dominated Polish ministries between 1923 and 1926. Stjepan Radić's Croatian Peasant Party was the largest political party in the new kingdom of Serbs, Croats, and Slovenes (later Yugoslavia) during the 1920s. But the most striking peasant leader was Alexander Stamboliski, head of the Bulgarian Peasant Union.

Stamboliski ran Bulgaria as a virtual agrarian dictatorship from 1919 until his assassination in 1923. He loathed the urban middle-class "parasites" who kept the peasants in debt, and he had contempt for industrial workers who, he believed, were narrowed by repetitious mechanical work.

> I don't like these workers with the narrow ideas of the West; they have little culture. . . . With peasants it is different—In the peasant are the seeds of a fully developed human personality. . . . The experience of the peasant assures him an incontestable advantage over the worker for nature, who is his master, took it upon herself to round off his education.[24]

Convinced that productivity, virtue, and wisdom reside close to the soil, Stamboliski looked forward to a peasant democracy in which bankers and bureaucrats would disappear.

Stamboliski was the only Eastern European peasant politician who almost had enough power to bring such a democracy about. The Bulgarian rural mass gave him close to an absolute majority—112 seats out of 236 in the *Sobranie,* or Bulgarian parliament. The Communist Party, also strong in the villages, was second with 50 seats. In addition to limiting the size of rural property holdings and making it difficult for city dwellers to own them, Stamboliski slanted taxation heavily against urban middle-class taxpayers and placed tight controls on law and banking. His private army of Orange Guards beat up his enemies and broke strikes. He founded a "Green International" to unify peasant landholders' interests throughout Eastern Europe against the collectivist "Red International."

Stamboliski came to a brutal end in the style of his own Orange Guards' forays. He had frightened the urban middle class, offended both nationalists and Communists by siding with the Allies in international matters, and antagonized the Macedonian minority by accepting good-neighborly relations with Yugoslavia. While the Communists stood aside, Stamboliski was overthrown by a reserve officers' *coup* in 1923. He was then captured by a Macedonian terrorist band, who cut off his hands before beheading him.

The Bulgarian experience suggested that even the most uniform peasant population in Eastern Europe could not govern a state in opposition to the towns and the army. The peasant parties had sufficient numbers to complicate parliamentary life but not enough strength to provide a coherent political program. They were

---

[24]Quoted in Joseph Rothschild, *The Communist Party of Bulgaria* (New York, 1959), p. 87.

unified only by a vague antiurban populism, the notion that cities corrupt and that peasants should liberate themselves from the domination of bankers and merchants. Beyond that, they were pulled in contradictory directions. Some peasant leaders, like the Croatian populist Stjepan Radić, favored radical agrarian reform and joined the Third International. Others, like Stamboliski, defended small landholders against Marxist collectivists. This lack of political cohesiveness reflected the conflicting interests of rural populations, divided among landless laborers, owners of dwarf plots, family farmers, and landlords. Moreover, peasant politicians were often inexperienced; they were soon tempted to conform with the style of urban politicians, for which their constituents then despised them. The peasant parties of Eastern Europe deprived urban liberal politicians of a governing majority without providing a workable alternative.

Even more fundamentally, the strength of Eastern European peasant parties, it could be argued, made it more difficult to overcome social backwardness. In the long run, one could imagine a prosperous Eastern Europe built either on efficient, highly productive agriculture, as in Denmark, or on the absorption of excess rural population in growing industry. What Eastern Europe got in the 1920s was a dense population that remained on the land, a plethora of inefficient small farms, and slow industrialization. All the Eastern European countries were especially vulnerable later, during the Great Depression, when world farm prices dropped and their main livelihood was destroyed.

The Problem of National Minorities

The other major problem in governing the successor states in the 1920s was unresolved national aspirations. The defeated states, especially Hungary, chafed in resentment. The victor states contained large unassimilated ethnic minorities, the price paid for the construction of a large Czechoslovakia, Romania, and Poland in 1918 and 1919.

The South Slavs were a striking example of the fate of new parliamentary regimes confronted with intractable nationality divisions. None of the component parts of the Kingdom of Serbs, Croats, and Slovenes was large enough to dominate the others, nor could they cooperate without friction. After the defeat of their common Habsburg enemy, the Serbs (Orthodox religion, Serbo-Croatian language, Cyrillic alphabet), Croats (Catholic religion, Serbo-Croatian language, Roman alphabet), and Slovenes (Catholic religion, Slovenian language, Roman alphabet) found little to unite them. The new kingdom's decentralized federal system exaggerated the divisions. Since the Croatian leader Stjepan Radić had turned to the Third International, separatism was overlaid with a Bolshevik threat. King Alexander abolished the constitution in January 1929, replaced the ethnically based federal districts with a centralized authority, and renamed the kingdom Yugoslavia, thereby "solving" in one blow the problems of revolution, local separatism, and governmental instability. His autocracy solved nothing, however, as the Ustasha, the extreme wing of Croatian separatism, assassinated him in Marseilles on October 9, 1934, during a state visit to France.

Many other Eastern European states had already taken the same authoritarian route. King Boris of Bulgaria named a conservative politician to run that country by police power after the murder of Stamboliski in 1923. King Carol II of Romania, who had lived in voluntary exile since 1925, returned in 1930 to resume the throne and active rule. Most striking of all was the military *coup* by which Marshal Josef Pilsudski took over the Polish government from the agrarian Prime Minister Witos in May 1926.

The Polish constitution of 1921 had vested power in a cabinet responsible to a parliamentary majority. But that majority was so fragmented among no less than fifty-nine parties (including thirty-three groups representing ethnic minorities) that fourteen ministries succeeded one another in the eight years between November 1918 and May 1926. Witos's agrarians and the urban liberal groups, who had the most to gain by the success of a parliamentary regime, could form no coherent center. Without effective administration, the Polish economy had difficulty adjusting to unity. Silesians who had traded with Berlin, Galicians who had traded with Vienna, and eastern Poles who had been oriented toward Russian economic life, all redirected their economic activities slowly and painfully around Warsaw.

The parliamentary regime gradually fell into popular contempt. Marshal Pilsudski, an old patriot-socialist who had led Polish legions against the Russians in the First World War, had the support of both the trade unions and the army in his *coup* in May 1926. After assuming power, Pilsudski founded a single national movement, the Nonpartisan Bloc for Cooperation with the Government. Its function was to promote the national "moral renovation" *(sanacja)* that had been so lacking in the squabbling of parties.

In new nations that desperately needed unity and administrative stability, the parliamentary regimes of the 1920s had won a reputation for inefficiency, corruption, and factious divisiveness. Parliamentary institutions that survived the 1920s were replaced by authoritarian regimes during the 1930s. Only Czechoslovakia functioned as a parliamentary republic throughout the interwar period. The Czechs, alone among Eastern European peoples, had a substantial indigenous middle class and a highly developed liberal tradition. Having inherited an important part of the industrial base of the old Austrian Empire, Czechoslovakia experienced less maladjustment and inflation while establishing economic life within the new borders than did the other successor states. The Czechs managed to sidetrack the grievances of the Slovak and German minorities within a centralized administration. Above it all presided the person of Thomas Masaryk. Until his death in 1935, Masaryk held together a parliamentary center of reformist socialists, agrarians, and Catholics by the sheer force of his character, in what the French historian Maurice Baumont called a "dictatorship of respect."[25]

THE IBERIAN PENINSULA

As in Eastern Europe, lackluster parliamentary regimes in both Spain and Portugal could not survive the 1920s. Like Eastern Europeans, the Iberian populations were

[25]Maurice Baumont, *La Faillite de la paix: De Rethondes à Stresa* (Paris, 1951), p. 439.

overwhelmingly rural, predominantly illiterate, still deeply anchored in traditional village routines, and powerfully influenced by local landlords and clergy. Agriculture was inefficient as well. For example, although three-quarters of the Portuguese people lived in the countryside, Portugal had trouble producing a sufficient basic bread supply.

The Iberian countries differed in important ways from Eastern Europe, of course, but not in ways conducive to the success of liberal institutions. Instead of being new successor states struggling to launch an administration and an economy within new frontiers, Spain and Portugal were old decayed empires run by entrenched political clienteles and a top-heavy bureaucracy. The Catholic Church was far more pervasive in Spain and Portugal than was any one clergy in Eastern Europe outside of Catholic Poland, but the Iberian populations were not thereby any more homogeneous. Urban–rural antagonisms, conflicts of interest between a small landholding north and a latifundist south, and especially bitter cultural divisions among Basques, Catalans, and the dominant Aragon-Castille heartland of Spain, obstructed formation of the basic consensus necessary for functioning electoral politics. Finally, neither the parliamentary monarchy of Spain nor the Portuguese Republic of 1910 enjoyed even the brief euphoria of nation building with which the successor states began. Liberal institutions had been implanted in the Iberian Peninsula in the late nineteenth century on the model of dominant north western Europe. They bore the blame for wartime and postwar dislocations, whether the regime remained neutral in the war, as did Spain, or participated in it, as did Portugal on the Allied side after 1916. During the 1920s, both countries slipped back into the nineteenth-century tradition of military *pronunciamientos (coups)*. Officer groups took over both governments with promises of social order and regeneration.

In Spain, the industrial boom and inflation accompanying the First World War had magnified social tensions in the principal industrial areas, culturally distinct Catalonia (Barcelona), and the Basque region. The strikes that began in 1917 and continued from 1919 to 1923 combined familiar ingredients of church burning, calls for Catalan autonomy, and the rhetoric of revolutionary general strikes, which talked more of contesting power than ameliorating working conditions. Their scale, however, was unprecedented, and they were accompanied by anarchist peasant risings in the south. Soviet influence was much in evidence; one peasant leader in Andalusia changed his name from Cordon to Cordoniev. Colonial defeats in 1921 by Moroccan guerrillas were simply the last straw for Spain, long haunted by the decline of its empire. With the approval of King Alfonso XIII, General Miguel Primo de Rivera led a military *coup* in September 1923.

Primo de Rivera swept away the "old politicians," whom he blamed with simplistic military bluntness for Spain's decline, and set up a one-man rule that lasted until 1930. Primo was no mere Spanish reactionary, however. He established arbitration committees of labor and management, in which some reformist trade unions took part. He surrounded himself with technical experts committed to economic modernization and he greatly expanded Spanish road and electrical systems. *La Dictadura* was a modernizing dictatorship, determined to bring labor into peaceful participation with the more progressive sectors of the economy. But Primo de

Rivera made enemies among reactionaries and big business as well as among republicans and the intransigent left. When the Spanish economy began to suffer from the depression in 1930, King Alfonso XIII withdrew his confidence rather than go down with a failing military junta. Primo went into exile in France in January 1930 and died there shortly thereafter.

The Portuguese Republic of 1910 had never achieved either political stability or financial probity. Since its political base was a relatively narrow stratum of freethinking commercial and professional people in the cities of Lisbon and Porto, and since its chief accomplishment was anticlericalism (separation of Church and state, legalization of divorce, an end to the educational monopoly of the Catholic University of Coimbra), the republic depended on the passivity of the rural population and the acquiescence of the bureaucracy and the army. Participation in the First World War on the British side (where most of Portugal's trade was transacted), ran the country deeply into debt, setting off a disastrous inflation that damaged the republic's own supporters the most. General strikes were declared in 1919, 1920, and 1921, but by the mid-1920s an eight-hour day was widespread, and workers' purchasing power was no lower than it had been in 1914. By then, bitterness was most widespread in the middle classes. Upper civil servants (including army officers) found that inflation and government economies had eroded their real purchasing power to half of what it had been in 1914.

These conditions were easy to blame on the republic's constitution of 1911, which gave primacy to a parliament whose inner circle of liberal politicians traded cabinet seats among themselves. Portugal had no less than forty-five ministries during the sixteen years following the overthrow of the monarchy in 1910, and fifteen elections (in which nearly half the electorate did not bother to participate).

Opposition to the republic was centered in the army and among Catholic professors at Coimbra, who were deeply influenced by the "integral nationalism" of the French "new right" theorist Charles Maurras.[26] In 1926, the countryside remained passive while a group of officers seized power. By the year 1928, an ascetic professor of economics at Coimbra, Antonio de Oliveira Salazar, had emerged as the strong man of the regime; he was the only person capable of balancing Portugal's precarious finances. First as minister of finance and after 1932 as premier, Salazar dominated the government until he was incapacitated by a stroke in 1968. His dictatorship was the most hermetically closed and longest-lived clerical authoritarian regime of modern Europe.

FASCIST ITALY

In his rebound from momentary immobility after the murder of Matteotti, Mussolini had gone on in 1925 and 1926 to lay the basis for a one-party dictatorship in Italy. There were two ways open to him. He could initiate the "second revolution" called for by the more radical Fascists; or he could make his peace with the principal nonparliamentary institutions of conservative Italy—monarchy, Church, and

[26]See chapter 1, p. 31.

army. The first route involved an ill-defined program of sweeping away all the worn-out institutions of prefascist Italy, including the monarchy. The old governing elites of Italy would be replaced wholesale with *squadristi,* the angry young anticlerical, antisocialist veterans who had ejected the town governments from northern cities in 1922. When Roberto Farinacci, a former socialist railwayman and toughest of the *squadristi* who had become boss *(ras)* of Cremona when the Fascists took the town over in 1922, became Fascist Party secretary in February 1925, it looked as though Mussolini was headed down that route.

In April 1926, however, Mussolini removed Farinacci from office. Thereafter, he quietly reduced the power of the party that had helped bring him to power, and he made his peace with the status quo. The most striking step was his accord with the Catholic Church. The Church had never recognized united Italy after that secular state had seized papal lands in the 1860s. In the Lateran Pact of 1929 Mussolini's Italy recognized papal sovereignty in miniature in Vatican City and made other concessions (such as agreeing to abolish divorce except under the most stringent conditions) that not even the most conservative leader of prefascist Italy could have made. In return, the papacy declared its differences with the Italian state at an end and urged the faithful to support the regime. The pact endured until February 1984, when the first socialist premier of the postwar republic abrogated most of Mussolini's concessions.

In the late 1920s, fascist Italy slipped into a normalcy of its own. The state continued to be a one-party dictatorship, but it ruled in partnership with the institutions and groups that had brought the Fascists to power in 1922. Nonfascist elements—the monarchy, the Church, the army—retained their autonomous

Gernsheim Collection, Ransom Humanities Research Center, University of Texas at Austin

Mussolini and Cardinal Gasparri, Papal Secretary of State (third from right), sign the Lateran Pact on February 11, 1929, making peace after fifty-nine years of conflict between the papacy and the Italian state and establishing the pope as temporal ruler of the Vatican City.

authority. Big business achieved a form of unofficial self-regulation under the developing corporatist system.[27] All these elements accepted Mussolini's political rule, and the fascist stage effects that went with it, as long as Mussolini was able to assure internal order and prosperity.

REVOLUTIONARY RUSSIA IN A STABILIZED WORLD

The civil war was over in Russia when Trotsky's Red Army defeated the last two counterrevolutionary offensives in Poland and in the Crimea at the end of 1920. Sheer survival in the face of internal and external opposition had been an extraordinary achievement for the Bolshevik regime. The country was in desperate straits, however.

Challenges to the Bolshevik Regime

Industrial output in 1921 was down to about one-fifth of what it had been in 1913. The temporary expedient of War Communism, which had called for full collectivization of productive capacity, could not get production started again amidst the wreckage of war. The most important obstacles were lack of raw materials, transportation chaos, and the absence of technical and managerial skills. War Communism made conditions even worse in the countryside. Forced requisitions had provoked the age-old peasant reactions of hoarding, consuming at home, and the willful destruction of livestock. Drought was added to these problems. Between 1913 and 1921, Russia had been transformed from a major exporter of grain to a country that could not feed itself.

The cities stood half-empty in 1921. Massive starvation, epidemics of typhus, and fighting took more lives between 1918 and 1921—perhaps 20 million—than losses in the First World War and the relatively bloodless 1917 revolution put together. One Bolshevik declared in 1921 that the economic collapse was "unparalleled in the history of humanity."[28]

Most alarming for the Bolsheviks was the massive disaffection that began to spread among their most enthusiastic supporters. Peasant bands defied authority. There were 118 peasant disorders in February 1921 alone. At the end of February, a strike wave swept Petrograd. Opposition came to a head on March 1 with an uprising of sailors at the Kronstadt naval base in Petrograd harbor; this was the very unit whose guns had covered the Bolshevik seizure of the Winter Palace in October 1917. The Kronstadt sailors proclaimed a "third revolution"[29] of "freely elected soviets" against the "commissarocracy" of Lenin's War Communism. The Kronstadt rising was crushed by a 35,000-man Red Army force, but at the cost of immense loss of

---

[27]See chapter 10, pp. 314–315 for a fuller discussion of corporatism in practice in Italy.

[28]Quoted in Paul Avrich, *Kronstadt 1921* (Princeton, N.J., 1970), p. 8.

[29]The "bourgeois" revolution of February 1917 had been the first, and the Bolshevik Revolution of October 1917 was the second.

life. Moreover, the danger signals could not be ignored. The revolt had been spontaneous, even though some anti-Bolshevik exiles had tried unsuccessfully to aid it once it had broken out. Similar resentments were expressed in the underground Workers' Truth Movement. As a leading Bolshevik, Nikolai Bukharin, said in March 1921, "Now the Republic hangs by a hair."[30]

Lenin responded to these challenges in March 1921 by replacing War Communism with the New Economic Policy (NEP). Under NEP, grain requisitions were replaced by limited deliveries to the state, and peasants were eventually allowed to market their surpluses freely. About 75 percent of retail trade, as well as a large number of small craft enterprises, slipped back into private hands. The state, however, retained what Lenin called the "commanding heights" of the economy: heavy industry, wholesale commerce, banking, and transport. During 1922, the revived market and a good growing season produced enough food, and normal life became possible in Russia.

It was at this point, in May 1922, that Lenin suffered the first of a series of strokes; in January 1924 he died. No clear line of succession had been provided for. The ensuing struggle for power was not merely a personal rivalry for ascendancy over party and country. The most fundamental and vital issues of how to build the first socialist regime in history were at stake. What would the new regime be like and what would be its first normal steps, now that the crisis out of which it had been born had lost its immediacy?

The situation facing the Russian Bolsheviks at Lenin's death was one for which neither Marxist theory nor practical experience had prepared them. There was no sign of the workers' revolution in more advanced countries, which all Russian Marxists deemed essential for the survival of socialism in backward Russia. The last spark of postwar disorder in Europe flickered out with the crushing of the Hamburg uprising of October 1923. The Russian Bolshevik regime would have to adapt to a world in which capitalism had stabilized itself (around liberal institutions in advanced northern and Western Europe and under authoritarian regimes in more agrarian Eastern and southern Europe). Under these conditions, could the Russian Bolsheviks progress toward "socialism in one country," and in a largely preindustrial country at that?

The "Industrialization Debate"

The Bolsheviks believed that progress toward socialism was possible only through the development of a large base of industrial workers in a country like Russia, or through the support of companion Communist regimes in countries that already had such a base. Since further revolution abroad seemed precluded after 1923, the problem was how to build a large industrial base in their own country.

A "left" group, led by War Commissar Leon Trotsky joined later by Comintern chairman Grigori Zinoviev and Lev Kamenev, chairman of the Moscow soviet, proposed a return to the "heroic" stance of 1917 both at home and abroad. Abroad,

[30]Stephen F. Cohen, *Bukharin and the Bolshevik Revolution* (New York, 1973), p. 106.

the left group wanted to continue revolutionary pressures; they would carry these pressures into Asia if Europe proved totally unresponsive. At home, they held that the "dictatorship of industry" was the only possible route to socialism. This meant squeezing a maximum of development capital out of the one Russian group capable of producing excess wealth—the peasantry.

Before 1914, agricultural export had been the chief earner of foreign exchange, and tsarist Russian industrial development had been built, in a sense, on peasant backs.[31] The left proposed to continue to pump the surplus productive capacity of the peasants into industrial growth by setting food prices low and the prices of manufactured goods high, spread apart like the blades of a scissors. During the early years of NEP, peasants had complained of a "scissors crisis" of just this sort; the Bolshevik left wanted to continue and even accentuate that pressure. The left strategy consisted of self-financing rapid industrialization by wringing wealth out of the great majority of Russians, the farmers who had benefited from the land redistribution of 1917 and 1918, especially the middle-class farmers, or "kulaks," who now threatened to create a powerful agrarian middle class.

A "right" group, led by Nikolai Bukharin, argued that socialist industrialization with the cooperation of a satisfied peasantry was not only possible but preferable. Like the left, Bukharin thought that Russia must industrialize to develop socialism and that the resources must come from within. Unlike the left, he thought that those resources would be generated much more quickly if peasants producing for the market were allowed to profit and thus swell their own purchasing power for industrial goods. After all, Bukharin argued, peasants were "the huge majority on our planet."[32] If Bolshevik Russia showed the way to cooperation between peasants and industrial workers, socialism could bypass the stabilized West and spread naturally through the rest of the world. Bukharin had endured exile like the others; nevertheless, he maintained an open manner and a preference for conciliation that his admirers believe could have produced a socialist but uncoercive state in Russia.

Neither side in the great "industrialization debate" of the 1920s advocated returning to a bourgeois regime and a multiparty government to await the inevitable ripening of a revolutionary proletariat in Russia or elsewhere. Both sides were determined to dig in and defend socialism in Russia from being reabsorbed into the prosperous liberal economic sphere of the West. Both saw the necessity of financing Russian industrialization from within. Those decisions made political dictatorship necessary, regardless of whether the Bolshevik left or right won the day.

The Consolidation of Political Dictatorship

In the 1920s, even fewer Russians were urban wage earners than before the dislocations of the Revolution; only a minority of that minority were convinced and reliable Bolsheviks. For example, in the Smolensk District, a rural region in western Russia with a population of about 2.3 million, there were only 5,416 Communist

---

[31]Grain composed 62 percent of Russian exports in 1900.

[32]Cohen, p. 168.

Party members in 1924, mostly in the city of Smolensk itself.[33] Under such conditions, the regime could survive only through firm bureaucratic control under the sole political direction of the Communist Party. The "dictatorship of the proletariat" would have to be exercised on the proletariat's behalf by a minority party.

Lenin never had any doubts about the necessity for one-party rule during postrevolutionary consolidation. In 1919, he had written that the soviets, "which according to their program were organs of government by the workers, are in fact only organs of government for the workers by the most advanced sections of the proletariat, but not by the working masses themselves."[34] It could not be otherwise in Lenin's opinion, as long as the mass of workers had not acquired a communist culture. In the meantime, "the Party's proletarian policy is not made by the rank and file, but by the immense and undivided authority of the tiny section that might be called the Party's Old Guard."[35]

Up to 1921, civil war and revival of production had required the Bolshevik leaders to adopt a high degree of bureaucratic centralization. The loosening of market controls for small enterprises under NEP, however, did not lead to the loosening of political control. Lenin had made the decision in March and April 1921 to forbid the existence of factions in the party and to give the party's Central Committee the power to exclude those who publicly opposed the committee's policy. Thus the relaxations of NEP did nothing to restore any of the free communitarian self-government that the soviet movement had seemed to promise at the beginning.

Toward the end of his life Lenin began to worry about the nature of party rule. He spoke about the danger of that handful of "the best Communists" being submerged in the "alien culture" of a mass of short-sighted bureaucrats.

> Take the case of Moscow: 4,700 Communist leaders and an enormous mass of bureaucrats. Who is leading and who is being led? I very much doubt if it can be said that the Communists are leading. I think it can be said that they are being led.[36]

As long as Lenin lived, his personal ascendancy kept power in the hands of the Old Bolsheviks who made up the party's Central Committee. After his death, however, the full-time administrative personnel of the party—the Political Bureau (Politburo) of the Central Committee and its permanent Secretariat—gradually assumed more and more control over running the state.

The Rise of Stalin

This tendency favored the rise of Josef Stalin, the party secretary since 1922 and perhaps the only Old Bolshevik of truly lower-class origin. Stalin was born Josef Djugashvili, the son of a shoemaker and the grandson of serfs, in the trans-Caucasus

---

[33]Merle Fainsod, *Smolensk under Soviet Rule* (Cambridge, Mass., 1958), pp. 17, 44.

[34]Moshe Lewin, *Lenin's Last Struggle* (New York, 1968), p. 6.

[35]Ibid., p. 12.

[36]Ibid., p. 10.

province of Georgia. After dropping out of theological seminary, he was drawn into the Bolshevik movement around 1900 and undertook such clandestine activities as bank raids for party funds. It was then that he adopted his underground name, which means "man of steel." Hardened in tsarist prisons and Siberian exile, Stalin had none of the broader culture of his colleagues, most of whom had passed years of exile in Western Europe. There is no certain proof to the allegations that he had acted as a double agent for the tsarist secret police. What is certain is that Stalin's strategic position as party secretary, coupled with his toughness, coincided with the growing ascendancy of a hard new generation of officials who had been bred not in the exile movements of the Old Bolsheviks but in the struggles since 1917. Easily overriding the warnings against his "rudeness" and rigidity contained in Lenin's testament, Stalin seized the initiative.

Stalin sided firmly with Bukharin in the "industrialization debate." The NEP concessions to peasant trade were broadened, and agricultural production rose again toward 1913 levels. As the left Bolsheviks lost vote after vote in the Central Committee, they were expelled one by one from positions of power. Trotsky, who had created and exhorted the Red Army, was removed from the War Commissariat in 1925. Zinoviev was dismissed as Comintern chairman after the failure of a communist uprising in Bulgaria in 1925 whose main achievement was the dynamiting of Sofia Cathedral. The Old Bolsheviks' bases of independent authority, such as Kamenev's control of the Moscow party organization and Zinoviev's in Petrograd (renamed

The former seminarian turned revolutionary Josef Djugashvili, known to his Bolshevik comrades as Stalin, "man of steel," at age 38 in 1917.

© Liaison Agency

Leningrad after Lenin's death), were gradually replaced by centralized party control. The Fifteenth Party Congress in December 1927 finally condemned all "deviation from the Party line" as decided by Stalin. In 1929 Trotsky was forced into exile, where he wrote about "the revolution betrayed" and the "substitution" of party for proletariat. Stalin had emerged as the preeminent leader of Soviet Russia. Russia had become, said one disgruntled Old Bolshevik, "the dictatorship of the Secretariat."[37]

The Soviet Union thus adjusted to a nonrevolutionary world in the late 1920s and stabilized around a combination of NEP economics and one-party bureaucratic political control. It was a period of some material improvement, although industrial production and livestock breeding remained below 1913 levels. The literacy rate rose rapidly, and the excitement of this vast social experiment released powerful literary and artistic energies. Under Minister of Culture Anatole Lunacharsky, architecture, theater, poetry, and the arts in general flourished brilliantly. The great beneficiaries of the period were 100 million peasants, whose 25 million family farms were more numerous and freer than ever before or since in Russian history. The questions raised in the "industrialization debate" remained, however. Could the Soviet Union avoid stagnation if its economy continued to be dominated by small peasantry?

A FRAGILE STABILITY: NEOLIBERALISM ASSESSED

By comparison with the past and with what was to come, Europe in the late 1920s seemed stable and prosperous. Northern and Western Europe flourished, and even Eastern Europe's economies improved. When the British historian A. J. P. Taylor referred to the late 1920s in his country as "the years of gold,"[38] however, his definition was two-edged. The international gold standard had been restored, but the rest of the nineteenth-century liberal vision had not automatically returned with it. Unemployment, for example, never dropped below 10 percent. Much of the gold of those years was the dross of garish pleasure-seeking in the "roaring twenties."

The attempt to restore or expand liberal Europe on the Continent had been only a qualified success. Parliamentary systems had not worked in Eastern and Southern Europe, where agrarians predominated and nationalities clashed. Even the prosperous populations of France and Germany were scarred by their recent experiences with inflation: Their loyalties to neoliberal regimes would last only as long as they assured economic stability.

For the moment, many Europeans could afford to sing and dance to the new American jazz and enjoy the novelties of movies and more widespread automobiles. It was a neoliberal illusion, however, to believe that the relative prosperity of the late 1920s could endure simply by letting things alone. The Great Depression was to bring that illusion to an end.

[37]Boris Souvarine, quoted in Cohen, p. 214.

[38]Taylor, pp. 227ff.

SUGGESTIONS FOR FURTHER READING

The effort to restore "normalcy" is given a stimulating analysis by Charles S. Maier, *Recasting Bourgeois Europe*[*] (1974). See also Dan P. Silverman, *Reconstructing Europe after the Great War* (1982).

Barry Eichengreen, *Golden Fetters: The Gold Standard and the Great Depression, 1919–1939*[*] (1996), is the best starting point for economic policies in the 1920s.

Karen Barkey and Mark Von Hagen, eds., *After Empire: Multiethnic Societies and Nation-Building: The Soviet Union and the Russian, Ottoman, and Habsburg Empires*[*] (1997), address the challenge of replacing multinational empires with unified nation states.

For individual European states in the 1920s, in addition to works mentioned in the bibliography to chapter 1, see the following:

Britain: Along with the works of Marwick, Beer, and Gilbert cited in the bibliography to chapter 4, see Peter Clarke, *Hope and Glory: Britain in the Twentieth Century*[*] (1997). Robert Graves, *The Long Week-End* (1940, reprint ed. 2004), is a brilliant personal reflection.

France: The volume by Philippe Bernard in the *Cambridge History of Modern France* is a useful introduction.

Germany: In addition to works mentioned in the bibliography to chapter 7, see Hans Mommsen, *The Rise and Fall of Weimar Democracy*[*] (1996), Richard Bessel, *Weimar Germany, 1918–1933*[*] (2001), and Eberhard Kolb, *The Weimar Republic*[*] (1993). Detlev Peukert, *Weimar Germany: The Crisis of Classical Modernity*[*] (1993), explores antimodernist reactions brilliantly. Weimar intellectual life is assessed in Anson Rabinbach, *In the Shadow of Catastrophe: German Intellectuals between Apocalypse and Enlightenment* (1997). Major biographies include Jonathan Wright, *Gustav Stresemann: Weimar's Greatest Statesman* (2002), David Felix, *Walther Rathenau and the Weimar Republic: The Politics of Reparations* (1971), and John A. Leopold, *Alfred Hugenberg: The Radical Nationalist Campaign against the Weimar Republic* (1977).

The Republic's relationship with the army is studied in Francis L. Carsten, *The Reichswehr and Politics, 1918–1933* (1966), and Gaines Post Jr., *The Civil-Military Fabric of Weimar Foreign Policy* (1973), in addition to the works of Craig and Ritter listed at the end of chapter 2.

Italy: Adrian Lyttelton, *The Seizure of Power,* 2nd ed. (2003), is essential for fascist Italy up to 1929, though it presumes background knowledge. See also Alan Cassels, *Mussolini's Early Diplomacy* (1970), and Claudio F. Segrè, *Italo Balbo: A Fascist Life*[*] (1987). Fascist attempts to shape Italian life are examined deeply by Victoria De Grazia in *The Culture of Consent* (1981) and *How Fascism Ruled Women*[*] (1991) and surveyed more broadly in Edward Tannenbaum, *The Fascist Experience* (1972). Mussolini's accord with the Church is explored by John F. Pollard, *The Vatican and Italian Fascism* (1985), and by Richard A. Webster, *Cross and Fasces* (1960). The keen contemporary observations of Gaetano Salvemini, *Under the Axe of Fascism* (1936, reprint ed. 1970), and Herman Finer, *Mussolini's Italy,* 2nd ed. (1935), have not lost their punch. The articles in Roland Sarti, *The Ax Within: Italian Fascism in Action* (1974), are still valuable.

Spain: Shlomo Ben-Ami, *Fascism from Above: The Dictatorship of Primo de Rivera in Spain, 1921–1930* (1983), studies a failed modernizing dictatorship.

Austria: Barbara Jelavich, *Modern Austria: Empire and Republic*[*] (1987), is the place to begin. Klemens von Klemperer, *Ignaz Seipel: Christian Statesman in a Time of Crisis* (1972), defends the Christian Social leader. Charles A. Gulick, *Austria from Habsburg to Hitler,* 2 vols. (1948, reprint ed. 1981), contains rich detail.

The Soviet Union: Sheila Fitzpatrick, *The Russian Revolution, 1917–1932,*[*] 2nd ed. (2001), is helpful for the 1920s. Stephen F. Cohen, *Bukharin and the Bolshevik Revolution: A Political Biography 1888–1938*[*] (revised ed. 1980), is essential for the industrialization debate. Important new monographs include Sheila Fitzpatrick et al., eds., *Russia in the Era of NEP*[*] (1991), and Mark Von Hagen, *Soldiers in the Proletarian Dictatorship. The Red Army and the Soviet Socialist State, 1917–1930*[*] (1990). Sheila Fitzpatrick, *The Commissariat of Enlightenment: Soviet Organization of Education and the Arts under Lunacharsky, October 1917–1921,*[*] new ed. (2002), treats cultural policy before Stalin imposed conformity.

Scholars are beginning to draw on newly opened Soviet archives, but no startling revelations have emerged about Stalin himself. New Russian biographies have tended to be trivially personal. The most historically useful of them is Dmitri Volkogonov's *Stalin: Triumph and Tragedy*[*] (1996). The author, head of Soviet military archives, attributed harsh policies to Stalin's personality in this book and only later traced systemic faults to Lenin. Robert Conquest, *Stalin: Breaker of Nations*[*] (1992), indicts the dictator. See also Adam Ulam, *Stalin*[*] (revised ed. 1989). Robert C. Tucker, *Stalin as Revolutionary, 1879–1929*[*] (1973, reprint ed. 1992) remains an interesting psychological portrait.

The standard account of how one-party rule was consolidated in the Soviet Union is Jerry F. Hough and Merle Fainsod, *How the Soviet Union Is Governed* (1979). Fainsod used local party archives captured by the Germans in 1941 in *Smolensk under Soviet Rule* (1958) to reveal Communist administration at the grassroots. R. W. Davies, *Soviet Economic Development from Lenin to Khrushchev*[*] (1998), provides an authoritative brief account. See also Alec Nove, *An Economic History of the Soviet Union* (1993).

For East Central Europe in the 1920s, use Joseph Rothschild, *East Central Europe Between the World Wars*[*] (revised ed. 1992), and Michael C. Kaser, *Economic History of Eastern Europe,* vol. 1 (1986). Classics among older monographs include Joseph Rothschild, *Pilsudski's Coup d'Etat* (1966); Henry L. Roberts, *Rumania: Political Problems of an Agrarian State* (1951, reprint ed. 1969); and John D. Bell, *Peasants in Power: Alexander Stamboliski and the Bulgarian Agrarian National Union, 1899–1923* (1977).

Additional Internet links related to this chapter are available on the Europe in the 20th Century Web site: http://www.history.wadsworth.com/paxton04.

You can also explore images, interactive timelines, and maps related to this chapter on our Western Civilization Resource Center: http://history.wadsworth.com.

Fernand Léger, *The City*, 1919.

9

Mass Culture and High Culture between the Wars

The 1920s summon up images of the brilliant triumph of modernism in the arts: Picasso painting in Paris and Kandinsky in Weimar; Stravinsky composing in Paris and Schoenberg in Vienna; the functionalist buildings of Gropius and Le Corbusier. Closer inspection shows that the vigorous new generation of the 1920s was only working out the implications of the great prewar shift in high cultural values.[1] The primary achievement of these artists in the interwar years was to bring the avant-garde of prewar Europe into the mainstream of high culture. The more significant and profound changes were taking place in mass culture. It was the mass dissemination of commercialized popular entertainment that most radically transformed the culture of Europeans between the wars.

[1]See chapter 1, pp. 32–36.

MASS CULTURE: THE AGE OF RADIO AND MOVIES

Two new forms of communication in the 1920s enabled the famous and the powerful to address millions of persons at once for the first time: radio and motion pictures. In one bound, Europeans left behind an era when a person could speak to groups only if they were within physical earshot. Even the massive propaganda efforts during the war had been largely limited to the printed word, to the artistry of posters, or to the voices of speakers physically present. Not until the end of the war were the possibilities of movie newsreels being realized; radio was still at the infant stage of occasional broadcasts by amateurs.

The Technological Basis for Mass Media

Public radio broadcasting was made possible by a quickening stream of nineteenth-century inventions in communications. The first major step had been the telegraph, which permitted virtually instantaneous transmission of coded messages wherever lines had been strung. With the opening of a line from England to Australia in 1872, the telegraph net was almost worldwide. At the same time, the early telephone permitted voice transmission along lines. Rapid communications acquired real flexibility, however, only with liberation from transmission wires. In 1901, an Italian engineer, Guglielmo Marconi, managed to send messages by "wireless" radio waves from England to Canada. Subsequent improvements, especially the development of the vacuum tube in the United States after 1906, made it possible to broadcast the human voice, instead of just coded messages, reliably by wireless transmission.

So far, these transmissions had linked individuals. The major breakthrough of the 1920s was the capacity to broadcast simultaneously to large numbers of people. The first radio broadcasts were one-time transmissions, such as the concert by soprano Nellie Melba from London on June 16, 1920, or the report of the United States presidential election results from Pittsburgh, which scooped the press in November 1920. During 1921 and 1922, permanent broadcasting facilities were established in the United States, Europe, and Japan, and receiving sets began to be mass-produced. The Age of Radio was at hand. When the BBC (British Broadcasting Corporation) was reorganized as a public corporation in 1926, there were 2,178,259 radio receivers in the United Kingdom. At the end of the 1930s, there were 9 million—nearly three out of four British households owned a radio. By 1938 Germany had more than 9 million receivers; France, more than 4 million; Russia, 4.5 million (for a much larger population); and Czechoslovakia, Sweden, and the Netherlands each had more than 1 million.[2]

An imposing radio set now jostled with the piano and the potted *aspidistra* plant for a conspicuous place in every middle-class living room, and the European consumer boasted of the number of tubes in his set in the same vein as he boasted of the cylinders of his car. Radio sets began to spread to working-class homes as well.

[2]Asa Briggs, *The History of Broadcasting in the United Kingdom* (Oxford, England, 1961–1970), vol. 1, p. 12; vol. 2, p. 6; vol. 3, p. 737. Italy and Belgium followed with slightly fewer than 1 million receivers in 1938.

In the 1930s, the cheapest German set, which the propaganda-conscious Nazi regime encouraged its people to buy, cost thirty-five marks, or about one week's average wage.[3] After furniture and a bicycle, a radio was the next major purchase for many a settled working-class family in Europe.

The technical basis for motion pictures had been developed in the 1890s as an adjunct to vaudeville and music hall entertainment. The early short action and trick reels soon gave way to multireel films with a story line. *The Great Train Robbery* (1903), one of the first films with a plot, lasted a full eight minutes and enjoyed tremendous success. The Italian-made *Quo Vadis* (1912) ran for two hours, and the way was open for the cinema to draw on the theatrical tradition as a conscious art form. But it was after the First World War that motion pictures became the most important medium of popular culture. In Britain, where moviegoing was most widespread, there were 18–19 million weekly attendances in a country of 50 million persons throughout the 1930s. British movie attendance reached a peak of 30 million a week in 1946 before giving ground to television; one third of the whole population went to the movies once a week.[4] Figures were not much lower on the Continent.

The Creation of Mass Audiences

Radio and motion pictures created simultaneous mass audiences on a national and even international scale for the first time. One would have to go back to the invention of movable type to find a threshold of equivalent importance in the transmission of culture. The mass audience in itself was not a total novelty, strictly speaking, thanks to the spread of literacy and cheap printing in the nineteenth century. Alfred Harmsworth, later Lord Northcliffe, had begun a commercial revolution in the newspaper industry in the 1890s by selling his papers at or below cost and shifting his revenues from selling papers to selling advertisements. He found that businesses were willing to pay large sums to buy display advertisements designed to appeal to a mass readership. His *Evening News* and *Daily Mail* were the first halfpenny papers in London and the first in Europe to reach the unprecedented circulation figure of 500,000.

The spread of newspapers beyond the elite was a gradual process, however. Only after 1910 did more than half the adult British population read one of the Sunday papers, which generally emphasized crimes, sports, and sensational fiction. More than half read a daily paper only after 1920.[5] Continental newspapers between the wars reached, if anything, a more traditionally elite audience. Prestigious dailies like the Paris *Le Temps* preferred to draw revenue from secret government funds than from large display advertising. By contrast, radio and the movies very rapidly became majority pastimes. Moreover, radio and the movies, unlike the printed word, could provide a mass audience with the immediate impact of experience. Early audiences shrank back as the speeding locomotive approached the bound

[3]Richard Grunberger, *The Twelve-Year Reich* (New York, 1971), p. 401.

[4]Ross McKibbin, *Classes and Cultures: England 1918–1951* (Oxford, England, 1998), pp. 419–420.

[5]Raymond Williams, *Communication*, 2nd ed. (London, 1966), p. 29.

"All Germany listens to the Führer on the people's radio receiver." Governments quickly learned the power of radio, and the Nazi regime subsidized the production of inexpensive sets like this one, capable of receiving only German stations.

Bundes-archiv

heroine in *The Perils of Pauline* with the same involuntary reaction shown by later audiences as they gripped their seats during the roller coaster ride in the first of the "three-dimensional" (3–D) films of the 1950s.

The Political Uses of Radio and Movies

Political figures turned to the radio early, and it was quickly apparent that some of them were much more effective at the microphone than others. The learned discourses carefully drafted by nineteenth-century parliamentarians had far less impact over a radio than they had in a room full of other parliamentarians or read the next day in the *Journal des débats*. At the radio microphone, two very different styles proved to be successful. The friendly simple chat was perfected by the stolid British Conservative leader Stanley Baldwin, who managed to project old-fashioned rural common sense as if speaking "with his feet on your fender" (fireside). Baldwin was more effective on the radio than the greater public orators of the time like Lloyd George, whose rhetoric seemed strained without the face and hands in view. The other style that worked on radio was the impassioned harangue that hammered away on a few simple slogans, as perfected by Mussolini and Hitler. Although Hitler did not neglect dramatic personal appearances, where he materialized quickly in an airplane or a high-powered Mercedes, he was so convinced of the importance of radio that he delivered no less than fifty radio speeches during his first year in power. His propaganda minister, Josef Goebbels, also a master of the fevered radio harangue, lent state support to the production of inexpensive radios and organized group listening in youth camps, factories, and barracks. As a result, Germany seems to have had the densest radio coverage in Europe: 16 million out of 23 million households were equipped with radios by 1942. Britain came in second place. Because Italy had far fewer radios, it was a less fruitful terrain for Mussolini, but he used radio effectively and organized group listening. Among the high points of political radio between the wars were Mussolini's broadcast announcements on October 2, 1935, that he had decided to invade Ethiopia and on the night of May 9, 1936, proclaiming victory. Mussolini's broadcasts were punctuated over the radio by the braying of hundreds of thousands of people below his balcony:

> Officers! Non-commissioned officers! Soldiers of all the armed forces of the state in Africa and Italy! Blackshirts of the Revolution! Italians in the Fatherland and in the world! Listen!
>
> With the decisions that in a few moments you will learn . . . a great event is accomplished: Today, 9 May, of the fourteenth year of the Fascist era, the fate of Ethiopia is sealed. . . .
>
> The Italian people has created the empire with its blood. It will fecundate it with its work and defend it against anyone with its arms. . . .
>
> Will you be worthy of it? (Crowd: "Yes!")[6]

Radio thus reduced the effectiveness of traditional oratory and increased the importance of both personality and rhetorical style in European politics.

Politicians also quickly realized the propaganda potential of movies. The fascist regimes carefully controlled the content of newsreels, although newsreels in all countries were characterized by the stentorian voice, the simplified sentiment, the short take, and the emphasis on individual exploits (whether in sports or war) and on "human interest." Hitler engaged a young woman filmmaker, Leni Riefenstahl, to film the Nazi party rally at Nuremberg in 1934 and the 1936 Olympics. In her film of the party rally, *The Triumph of the Will* (1934), aerial views of Nuremberg through steeply banked cumulus clouds close in on stunning shots of tight ranks of marchers and ceremonial ritual; the film remains a stirring and troubling visual experience.

Control of the Mass Media

A central political problem was who should control the mass media. Radio broadcasting required some kind of international regulation, if only to prevent several broadcasters from interrupting one another on the same frequency. Beyond that

[6]*Scritti e discorsi di Benito Mussolini*, vol. X (Milan, 1936), pp. 117–119.

essential technical coordination, three basic forms of control developed. The United States, Latin America, and Japan left broadcasting entirely in the hands of companies whose revenue came from advertisements. No European state, liberal or collectivist, accepted purely commercial sponsorship. In the 1920s, most Continental states, including France and Weimar Germany as well as fascist Italy and communist Russia, placed radio broadcasting under some form of direct government control. A third form of control was represented by the BBC, a public monopoly run by its own board and financed by an annual license fee paid by each radio owner. The first general director of the BBC, the strong-minded Scotsman John Reith, firmly established the dual tradition of intellectual uplift and political neutrality that made the BBC the most independent of all noncommercial radio systems. Although the BBC was sometimes accused of blandness, it successfully avoided the major pitfalls of the other systems: the crass commercialism of the American pattern and the abuses of government propaganda in the Continental pattern. The way each country controlled radio was doubly important, for the even more pervasive medium of television settled naturally into the same patterns after 1945.[7]

Except for the subsidized party-oriented films of the Nazi and fascist regimes and the Soviet Union's tight control over all films, motion pictures were an almost entirely commercial proposition. Indeed, most films shown in Europe between the wars were not only commercial products; they were American. Although French and Italian filmmakers had led the way before 1914 in producing long features, their momentum had been halted during the war because the nitrocellulose used for film was needed for explosives. This pause allowed United States filmmakers to dominate the industry with their silent films in the 1920s. The coming of "talkies" at the end of the decade tended to limit the audiences to single-language groups and give Continental filmmakers a new impetus in the 1930s. The British government, however, felt obliged to impose quotas of home-produced films on British movie houses when American films had absorbed 90 percent of the market.

Newspapers were commercially controlled in most of Europe, outside the party press of Nazi Germany, fascist Italy, and the Soviet Union.[8] Newspapers were also changing in character and falling into the hands of large press empires. European dailies continued the commercial revolution begun in England by Lord Northcliffe in the 1890s. Between the wars, major dailies like the *Daily Express* and the *Petit Parisien* reached circulation figures of around 2 million through the formula of lively prose, extensive advertising, and low price per copy.

The Role of Advertising

Radio, the movies, and the popular press made it possible to inundate whole populations with skillful and aggressive commercial salesmanship to a degree hardly

---

[7]No European radio system conformed absolutely to one pattern of control. French national radio accepted advertising until 1935, and even after that French listeners could hear commercial radio from Luxemburg and Monaco. The British government authorized an independent (commercial) television network in 1955, and France did so in 1982.

[8]Party newspapers, especially on the left, competed with the blander commercial dailies in the liberal states. Large "nonpolitical" commercial dailies survived in fascist Germany and Italy. Only the Soviet Union had a party press monopoly.

imagined before 1914. Advertising was an ancient medium, and it had grown rapidly with the development of large newspaper displays after the 1890s. Between the wars, however, it grew so dramatically in size and in kind as to dwarf what had gone before.

Most great daily newspapers between the wars drew from one-half to three-quarters of their revenues from advertising.[9] To entice the advertisers, publishers had to keep circulation high by pandering to popular tastes for sports, crime reporting, and sentimental fiction as well as simplified, chauvinist news coverage. In each major city, two or three large sensationalist dailies, usually owned by one of the large press empires, dominated the advertising market and forced smaller papers out of business. Sometimes a serious newspaper like the London *Times* (circulation, 225,000) survived by promising advertisers access to the most educated and influential minority. On the Continent, where commercial evolution was less advanced, some dailies like the Paris *Le Temps* preserved an old-fashioned seriousness without display advertising by receiving secret subsidies from its own and foreign governments hoping to obtain favorable news coverage. Radio gave advertising a whole new dimension. Professional advertising agencies learned to apply psychology to taste shaping. Total advertising expenditure grew prodigiously. In England, it expanded from about £26 million per year before the war to £96 million in 1938; this was close to 2 percent of the national income,[10] far more than what was spent on either scientific research or the fine arts. At its best, advertising drew on good modern design and helped elevate the taste of popular culture. At its worst, European advertising encouraged frivolous buying by those who could not afford it; and, in the case of untested medicines, it could be positively dangerous.

THE NEW LEISURE

Popular mass culture went hand in hand with the leisure to enjoy it. When the nineteenth century ended, leisure time was still for the most part the preserve of the wealthy. Second- and third-generation business families had only recently emerged from the abstemious habits and long working hours needed to accumulate capital at the beginnings of industrialization. By the 1890s, many factory workers were working only a ten-hour day, although rural workers still stumbled from sleep to toil and back to sleep according to the rhythms of the sun, just as most factory workers had done in the early stages of the Industrial Revolution. A few workers, such as miners in France, enjoyed eight-hour work days even before 1914. At the end of the First World War, the eight-hour day became quite general for office and factory workers in Northern and Western Europe. In 1936 the French government set the work week at forty hours. For the first time in the history of work, men and women wage earners had as many waking hours for their own amusement as they spent on the job.

[9]Williams, p. 27.

[10]Ralph Harris and Arthur Selden, *Advertising and the Public* (London, 1962), pp. 39–42. The proportion of national income spent on advertising was slightly higher in the United States than in Britain, and slightly lower on the Continent.

Early legislation limiting working hours had usually been intended to preserve the health and productivity of the worker. After the war, a new conception of leisure as a positive human right made itself widely felt. The healthy fulfillment of each citizen's individual qualities in leisure-time recreation began to be a concern of governments.

Along with the forty-hour workweek, the French government provided in 1936 for two weeks' vacation with pay for all employees of firms larger than family shops. In August 1936, then, millions of ordinary Frenchmen found themselves blinking their eyes unaccustomed to midday-sunshine, with two weeks free to be used as they wished, without having to be sick or injured to receive time off. Many French workers could not afford to go anywhere at that time, but the way was open for the human tide of campers, cyclists, hikers, and tourists who now regularly inundate the beaches and mountains of Europe.

Organized Recreation

Totalitarian regimes were not satisfied merely to leave their citizens the rich delight of free time. Every moment must be filled with useful—and nonpolitical—activity. "Their leisure hours were a danger-spot for the whole nation," wrote an Italian Fascist spokesman of his fellow citizens in 1925.[11] In that year, the Fascist regime swallowed up every autonomous leisure-time organization, from mandolin societies to football clubs, into a vast national recreation agency: the *Operaio Nazionale Dopolavoro*.

The *Dopolavoro* (afterwork) was charged with corralling the supposed willfully individualistic Italian workers into mass recreational activities that would make them docile citizens and good soldiers. Zealous officials published statistics showing how many million Italians had been marched to museums, parks, beaches, operas, and sports matches each year, to the point where a scornful refugee, Gaetano Salvemini, predicted that

> the number of kisses exchanged under the auspices of the Dopolavoro . . . will soon be counted, and the staggering total will be attributed to the genius of Mussolini.[12]

Viewed more realistically, only about 2 million out of 12 million Italian workers could be persuaded or coerced into joining *Dopolavoro* activities, and rural and village workers were inevitably less accessible to a distant bureaucracy. In many areas of southern Italy, however, the *Dopolavoro* was the first agency to step between the villagers and their virtually feudal superiors. Fascist recreation was one of the first steps toward a fuller mobilization of Italian citizens into modern mass culture.

After 1933, Hitler copied the *Dopolavoro* in his *Kraft durch Freude* (strength through joy) movement. Although workers' cruises to Madeira and Norway were widely publicized, only about one worker out of twenty actually enjoyed such a privilege. But

---

[11]Quoted in Gaetano Salvemini, *Under the Axe of Fascism* (New York, 1936), p. 334.
[12]Ibid.

Verlag

"Strength Through Joy," the Nazi recreation agency, gave wide publicity to the special vacations it provided for a few chosen workers, such as this cruise to Madeira in 1935.

the regime did invest great sums in promoting and organizing sports and mass recreation in ways designed to spread enthusiasm, inculcate discipline, and induce workers to forget that real wages were lower than in 1929.

The Soviet state also assumed responsibility for leisure-time activities. The *Komsomol* (Young Communist League) organized summer camps and promoted sports, and the regime turned the villas and hunting lodges of the aristocracy into vacation centers. In practice, however, the enormous strains of rapid land collectivization and factory development after 1929 left little surplus of either resources or free time for widespread leisure and recreation.

Sports

Professional sports was the leisure-time activity that most Europeans enjoyed between the wars. Games like association football (soccer) had been transformed from spontaneous play into systematic contests in the nineteenth century, with formal rules and a network of permanent teams (the Football Association in England,

1854). Lower-class professional players began to supplant middle- and upper-class amateurs in public sports contests. Association football spread to the Continent and to Latin America before the First World War, in conscious imitation of the British: The football team in Milano even used the English name of its own town in its team title, A. C. Milan. The game became a mass spectator sport in the twentieth century, and the establishment of World Cup contests in 1930 sharpened the nationalist fervor that surrounded it.

The 1920s and 1930s were the great era of stadium building both in Europe and in the United States. Whereas the first modern stadiums, such as the one built in Athens in 1896, had held 50,000 to 60,000 spectators, the great football stadiums built after 1918 held crowds approaching the size of the armies at Waterloo. The Lenin Stadium in Moscow held 103,000; Wembley Stadium in north London, 126,000. The great stadium built in Berlin for the 1936 Olympics held 140,000, and the *Sportspalast* built the following year in Nuremberg held 225,000. The biggest stadium in the world was the Strahav Stadium in Prague (1934), designed for gymnastics and track meets, which could hold 240,000 spectators.

The enormous sums bet on association football were some measure of the public's infatuation with the game. It is estimated that the total wagered in the football pools in England in the 1934–1935 season was about £20 million (nearly $100 million at contemporary exchange rates), and that the figure doubled in 1936; extra postmen had to be put on duty in working-class neighborhoods every Monday and Tuesday, when the wagers for the following weekend's matches were sent in.[13] The amount bet on horse racing was still bigger. These mass-attended sports far outweighed in popularity the more traditional upper-class amateur sports of Rugby football, tennis, and cricket.

Bicycle racing was always more fanatically popular on the Continent than in England. Following the bicycle craze of the 1890s when the machine was new, a number of celebrated long-distance bicycle races absorbed vast advertising money and popular enthusiasm between the wars. The Tour de France, a bicycle race that attracted Belgian and Italian cyclists as well as French, went on for ten days or so. The Berlin bicycle race tied up the city for six days.

Travel

With leisure, travel also became more accessible to masses of people. Great technical breakthroughs revolutionized the pace of travel. Most important was the conquest of the air. Once the basic techniques of flight had been mastered, progress was very rapid. The Wright brothers had kept a heavier-than-air machine aloft for three minutes across the dunes at Kitty Hawk, North Carolina, in 1903. Just six years later the Frenchman Louis Blériot flew across the English Channel in thirty-seven minutes. Military use of aircraft during the war enormously increased both speed and distance, so that at the war's end Europe and the world were ready for civilian air travel.

[13]Robert Graves and Alan Hodge, *The Long Week-End: A Social History of Great Britain, 1918–1939* (London, 1940), pp. 383–384.

In 1919, the British flyers John Alcock and Arthur Brown first flew the Atlantic nonstop,[14] and in the same year the first regular international airmail service was begun, linking Paris and London. Passenger service followed almost at once. By 1934, an Englishman could reach Australia in four days by air, a trip that took weeks by ship. The only comparable acceleration in travel had been the application of steam to travel in the 1830–1870 period.[15] Air travel was even more liberating, however, for air passengers (and bombers) could reach any point on earth across both geographical and political frontiers without the need for a continuous path or waterway.

Only the wealthy or adventurous traveled by air between the wars, of course. But the average traveler could now supplement the train with buses and private cars. Many traveled by bicycle. Hiking, too, became very widespread among European youth in the 1930s. Germany, with its long tradition of scouting and hiking in the pre-war *Wandervögel* movement, was the center of knapsack traveling among the young. This was combined with the cult of outdoor toughness that the Nazi regime liked to contrast with liberal, bourgeois flabbiness. Every year several young Germans fell to their deaths on the sheer north wall of the Eigerwand in Switzerland, trying to prove themselves and their ideology against the mountain. The knapsacking cult was not limited to Germany. The youth hostels movement spread in France and elsewhere in the 1930s. Even some Frenchmen equated tramping youth with an antiliberal toughening: "The France of camping out will vanquish the France of the *apéritif* and the Party Congress," wrote the right-wing novelist Drieu La Rochelle in 1937.[16]

However they traveled and under whatever ideological sign, ordinary Europeans had much more chance of moving about than their parents and grandparents. The business of catering to leisure had been completely transformed. Lavish nineteenth-century resorts like the mountain springs of Marienbad, Bad Godesberg, and Vichy, where the wealthy gathered to "take the waters," were being jostled by more plebeian holiday camps. Crowds built up on beaches like the one at Brighton, where the prince regent had first popularized sea bathing in the 1820s. The giant liners that took first-class passengers across the Atlantic in the comfort of a luxury hotel now passed *Kraft durch Freude* ships on their way to Madeira and *Dopolavoro* cruises to Majorca. The ease with which news, styles, and people traveled around the earth had much to do with spreading an international popular culture after 1918.

THE EFFECTS OF MASS CULTURE AND LEISURE

The cumulative effects of mass leisure and a newly self-confident and economically powerful popular culture are still a subject of debate. One major effect clearly was to increase the homogeneity of national populations, a process that had begun in

[14]The significance of Lindbergh's exploit of 1927, surrounded by much more publicity, was that he made the flight alone.

[15]The opening of the U.S. transcontinental railroad in 1869 cut travel time across the United States from four weeks by horse to four days, a seven-fold reduction in time. Propeller-driven airliners cut train time in the 1940s about ten-fold.

[16]*L'Emancipation nationale*, August 20, 1937.

the nineteenth century. The popular press and radio transmitted the tastes and spoken accents of Paris or Berlin or London or Rome to the remotest villages of the Auvergne or Bavaria or Northumberland or Calabria. Deep-rooted local cultures retreated at a faster rate before national cultures; in turn, national ways of life were influenced more and more by an international consumer culture. The heroine of Thomas Hardy's novel *Tess of the D'Urbervilles* (1891) had felt as though moving from one valley to another was the equivalent of changing countries; the time was not too distant when only the elderly would retain traces of local accents and customs.

The process of homogeneity was hastened by cheaper, more uniform manufactured clothing. Europeans of the 1920s were perhaps the last generation whose class status and even employment could be told at a glance by dress. Rayon, the first widely used synthetic fabric, was already becoming a commonplace during the 1920s.[17] Rayon blurred the ancient line between those who could afford silk and those who could not.

Some observers felt that more homogeneous populations were a sign of fruitful egalitarianism. If the visible marks of class—the blue smock, the cloth cap, the different accent—were diminished, might not the old "two nations" about which Disraeli had warned in the 1840s at last be merging into that single body of citizens about which democrats had dreamed since the French Revolution?

Some of the techniques used to mobilize the classes and local minorities into a common citizenry, however, aroused worries about manipulation. Youth groups, organized recreation, and the pageantry of parades and rallies were only the most spectacular examples of the ways by which totalitarian governments attempted to mold citizens. The techniques of mass political manipulation were also developed in liberal states. An early example was the Budget League in England in 1909, a group established to arouse public opinion in favor of Lloyd George's Liberal Party budget reforms. It was a pioneer in the use of press releases, mass meetings, and publicity in British politics.[18] Organized opinion making during the war vastly increased each government's experience in manipulating its citizenry. It seems likely that the vast machinery of persuasion set up by advertisers and promoters in the popular culture also worked to mold a citizenry that was prepared to march to a single command. That command might not come from a government; it might come from a sponsor commanding the public to buy a new product, or it might come from a deep popular emotion, such as anti-Semitism. Many Europeans focused concern about their manipulability on an evil conveniently labeled "Americanization," for much of the content of popular entertainment—jazz, escapist movies—came from the United States, and the techniques of advertising and publicity seemed more highly developed there.[19]

A more homogeneous citizenry meant the disappearance of an older, more localized, orally transmitted popular culture. To some cultivated Europeans, that

---

[17]The word *rayon* was first used in 1924. First commercial production began in 1891, but remained small until the First World War. British production grew twenty-five fold between 1913 and 1929.

[18]Cameron Hazelhurst, "Asquith as Prime Minister," *English Historical Review,* vol. 85, no. 336 (July 1970).

[19]See, for example, Georges Duhamel, *America the Menace* (Boston, 1931).

culture seemed vastly superior to the commercial mass culture, with its appeal to the lowest common denominator and its artificially stimulated wants and curiosities. Richard Hoggart, a British intellectual of working-class origin, reflected with some bitterness on the disappearance of the values of his grandparents' generation between the wars:

> The world of club-singing is being gradually replaced by that of typical radio dance-music and crooning, television cabaret and commercial-radio variety. The uniform national type which the popular papers help to produce is writ even larger in the uniform international type which the film studios of Hollywood present. The old forms of class culture are in danger of being replaced by a poorer kind of classless, or by what I was led earlier to describe as "graceless," culture, and this is to be regretted.[20]

Other European intellectuals were more worried about mass culture's inroads on elite values than on the old customs. There had always been "popular culture," of course, as long as there had been ballads, folk dances, and tales handed down outside schools and the literary world. Highly educated Europeans had generally ignored it, for it made few converts outside its own class. What was frightening to these intellectuals was the material power and dynamism of the new mass culture and its ability to wean away with facile pleasures the elite young who were supposed to carry on the arts and sciences. Who would learn Greek and mathematics, and who would advance physics if middle-class European students joined the masses at the movies? The young Jean-Paul Sartre and his mother slipped off to the movies despite his scholarly grandfather's displeasure.

> We blindly entered a century without tradition, a century that was to contrast strongly with the others by its bad manners, and the new art (the cinema), the art of the common man, foreshadowed our barbarism. Born in a den of thieves, officially classified as a travelling show, it had popular ways that shocked serious people. It was an amusement for women and children.[21]

The Spanish philosopher José Ortega y Gasset provided one of the most widely read warnings against mass culture in *The Revolt of the Masses* (1930). Already predisposed by the pessimism of the Spanish Generation of 1898 to reflect on Spain's decadence and decline, Ortega was convinced that European civilization, that fragile creation of exceptional men, would be trampled by "mass men," heedless seekers of instant gratification, unwilling either to master civilized creativity themselves or to submit to those who were civilized. Although he was a self-professed "democrat" and an opponent of both fascism and bolshevism, Ortega spoke for many who intimated that they would accept strong measures to preserve elite culture from the brute force of mass commercial culture.

Oswald Spengler put some of the same concerns into a more specifically German context in a best-seller of 1919, *The Decline of the West*. Spengler's book is best remembered for its view of the inevitable rise and fall of cultures. In keeping with a

---

[20]Richard Hoggart, *The Uses of Literacy* (London, 1957), p. 280.

[21]Jean-Paul Sartre, *The Words* (New York, 1966), p. 118.

tradition of German nationalist writing, Spengler feared that "Culture" (deep-rooted German traditions as distinct from those of Western Europe) was being overwhelmed by "Civilization" (the more cosmopolitan, commercialized mass culture that Spengler identified with liberal Western Europe). Spengler foresaw an emerging "World City," a faceless, cosmopolitan anthill within which the national cultures (including the virile, spiritual values of Germanness) would be submerged and lost. One can recognize a form of attack on mass culture here, distorted by the passions of Germany's defeat in 1918 and by the nationalist assertion of the distinctness and superiority of German traditions. Down the road that Spengler took was an intellectual acceptance of dictatorship if dictatorship was necessary to save German values from cosmopolitan mass values.

There were several problems with this point of view. One was that ordinary Europeans, left to their own choices, enthusiastically embraced the new popular culture. Radio, movies, and the popular styles flourished mightily. The other problem was that the high culture itself was abandoning tradition with alacrity and embarking in the 1920s on a period of rich and raucous experiment.

HIGH CULTURE BETWEEN THE WARS

On the surface, 1920s culture has a reputation for glitter, brash vitality, and novelty. Indeed, there was a wide variety of artistic and literary events whose main common ingredient was a strenuous effort to be new: the first performance in Berlin in 1925 of the opera *Wozzeck,* Alban Berg's powerful union of serial music and expressionist drama; the triumph of the opening night of Bertolt Brecht and Kurt Weill's jazz play *The Threepenny Opera* (Berlin, 1928); Darius Milhaud's jazz ballet *La Création du Monde* (Paris, 1923), with sets by the cubist painter Fernand Léger; the extraordinary assemblage of talent, including Walter Gropius and Paul Klee, teaching and designing at the Bauhaus in Weimar.

The high culture of the 1920s did not innovate, however, in basic aesthetic terms. The artistic leaders in that decade simply continued to work out the implications of the great aesthetic revolution of the turn of the century. More importantly, they brought the isolated experiments of the pre-1914 avant-garde into the mainstream. In Peter Gay's terms, the prewar "outsiders" had become "insiders."[22]

How did the prewar avant-garde culture become acceptable, even fashionable, in the 1920s? First, the horrors of global war had made the language of primitivism, subjective irrationality, and violence seem far more appropriate to an interpretation of the world. Second, the revolutionary impulse at the war's end heightened impatience with the status quo, in the arts as elsewhere. "There is a new spirit," said the young Swiss architect and city planner Le Corbusier in 1923. "[We need a] revision of values: If there is no revolution in architecture, there will be social revolution."[23] Third, young people, caught up in a generational conflict at the end of the war, had a strong sense of their mission to reject and reshape the values of their elders, who

[22]Peter Gay, *Weimar Culture: The Outsider as Insider* (New York, 1968).

[23]C. E. Jeannerret-Gris (Le Corbusier), *Towards a New Architecture* (London, 1931), p. 89.

had put them in the trenches. Finally, the prosperity of the 1920s revived as enemies and targets "all those who long for a return to philistinism and the glorious time when it was only necessary to make money and accompany a decent digestion with a pious upward glance."[24]

The twentieth century long preserved a basic aesthetic unity. An explanation for that is apparent when one contemplates the long lives of the great pre-1914 pioneers: The *Fauve* painter Henri Matisse lived productively until 1954; Picasso until 1973; the musical pioneer Igor Stravinsky lived until 1972, actively composing almost to the end. Among the founders of functionalist architecture, Le Corbusier lived until 1965; Walter Gropius and Ludwig Mies van der Rohe until 1969. No wonder their successors seemed to be mostly derivative, the lesser practitioners of arts invented by more formidable predecessors. No wonder that most of the artistic idioms of the 1920s still seem modern eighty years later.

Experimental Aesthetic Values

A few experimental painters had already renounced before 1914 the aesthetic assignment of the Renaissance—to portray nature and human nature—and were establishing new aesthetic values. Most postwar painters took up these values, which indeed were still being worked out far into the twentieth century. As Paul Klee, one of the more articulate of painters, put it in lectures at the Bauhaus in 1923, artists no longer attached "such intense importance to natural form . . . but more value to the powers that do the forming." Klee imagined a dialogue with one of those tiresome laymen who "always looks for his favorite subject" in a picture:

> Layman: "But that isn't a bit like uncle." The artist, if his nerve is disciplined, thinks to himself: "To Hell with uncle. I must get on with my building. This new brick is a little too heavy and to my mind puts too much weight on the left. I must add a good-sized counterweight to the right to restore the equilibrium."[25]

The artist "must distort," insisted Klee, "for therein is nature reborn."[26] In his emphasis on "building" a painting and on "composition," Klee, like many interwar painters, carried forward the prewar cubists' experiments with form and structure. Few interwar painters were as playful and articulate as Klee, but they nearly unanimously rejected any obligation to be either photographic or conventionally beautiful.

Purified, simplified form for its own sake was a new aesthetic basis for other arts as well. The musical avant-garde had partially broken with key and harmony before 1914. Then, in 1924, the Viennese composer Arnold Schoenberg published a piano suite in which he perfected an altogether different musical idiom: the twelve-tone or serial system, in which the composer arranged twelve tones in a series that then became the building block of the composition, in place of a conventional scale.

---

[24]Harry Kessler, *In the Twenties, The Diaries of Harry Kessler* (New York, 1971), p. 267.

[25]Paul Klee, *On Modern Art* (London, 1948), p. 19.

[26]Ibid., p. 29.

Together with his pupils Alban Berg and Anton Webern, Schoenberg took music into whole new realms, although few of their contemporaries could follow these innovators with pleasure.

Many architects completed the prewar rejection of ornament in favor of a severe style subordinated to functional needs and the aesthetics of simple mass and balance. Le Corbusier turned for guidance to the engineer, whose only aesthetic was thought to be the natural harmony derived from simple utility. "The Engineer's aesthetic and Architecture are two things that march together and follow one from the other."[27] After praising the functional elegance of grain silos, automobiles, airplanes, and other machines, Le Corbusier insisted that "a house is a machine for living in."[28] He designed mass-produced houses of reinforced concrete with long horizontal windows and flexible interior spaces to express the functional simplicity with which people should live. Cities, he said, should be towers among gardens and playing fields, with living, playing, and transportation carried on at different levels.[29]

A machine aesthetic permeated a number of artistic fields in the 1920s. Arthur Honegger's railroad composition, *Pacific 231* (1924), is only the most celebrated of a number of efforts to enrich the musical vocabulary with industrial sounds, most of which are simply dated curiosities today. Some painters, like the Frenchman Fernand Léger, applied cubism to the exploration of industrial shapes. More important than these superficial influences on mere subject matter was the discovery of a fundamental kinship between the simple elegance of a machine and artistic expression. Members of the Bauhaus community tried to bring good design to everyday objects like furniture and household utensils. They wanted to unite aesthetics and material considerations into a "social art" whose combination of beauty and efficiency would restore wholeness to everyday life.

Functionalism, good social organization, and delight in purified form, then, were aesthetic values carried forward in the 1920s from the prewar avant-garde. Another major taproot of modernism was the expression of feeling, heightened if necessary by distortion, emphatic techniques, harsh flat colors, and morbid subject matter. The *Fauves* had replaced modeling with flat, bright color for shock effect as early as 1905 in Paris; the German expressionists applied their neo-Gothic morbidity, distortion, and heightened emotion to all the arts before 1914.[30] The expression of heightened feeling and emotion by artistic distortion was still a major characteristic of modernism in the 1920s.

The theater and the new art of motion pictures lent themselves particularly well to expressionist purposes. Films were ideally suited to a powerful evocation of horror and mystery through calculated distortion, as was proved by the masterpiece of German expressionist filmmaking, *The Cabinet of Dr. Caligari* (1919). A high point of expressionist drama was Alban Berg's opera *Wozzeck*—a melodramatic tale of a soldier driven to murder his mistress by a mysterious inner terror heightened by the taunts of others about her unfaithfulness.

[27]Le Corbusier, p. 1.

[28]Ibid., p. 15.

[29]Ibid., p. 57.

[30]See chapter 1, pp. 33–35.

The Museum of Modern Art / Film Still Archives

A shot from *The Cabinet of Dr. Caligari* (1919), a striking example of expressionist film-making in Germany.

New Concerns

Whether purity of form or power of expression was their main purpose, the modern artistic movements of the 1920s shared a number of new concerns. All the intellectual leaders rejected "art," in the sense of traditional or learned techniques invested with exaggerated awe by a social elite. The modern arts were intensely personal acts of self-expression, and those who cared to respond did so on their own emotional terms. With few exceptions, the modern artists "did" rather than "talked." They were better at denouncing dead tradition and the philistines than at explaining what they wanted to do. Their creations would have to speak for themselves.

All the interwar art forms plunged yet deeper into the subjectivity that had appeared before the war. War and revolution heightened Europeans' fascination with the human unconscious, sometimes in very direct ways. We have already seen how his work with shell-shocked soldiers in 1917 had awakened André Breton's curiosity about expressions of deep unconscious feelings in the arts.[31] His surrealist movement (1924) tried automatic writing, in which the author was supposed to produce whatever words were suggested by some mysterious inner prompting. It glorified the "divine madness" of those reaches of the unconscious that the arts had

[31]See chapter 4, pp. 114–115.

hitherto ignored. Later, surrealist painters, such as the Belgian René Magritte and the Spaniard Salvador Dali, placed highly realistic details in grotesque imaginary landscapes in playful yet disturbing explorations of the depths of the human psyche.

In addition to Breton's automatic writing, other new literary techniques reflected the growing interest in the unconscious. Marcel Proust probed the workings of memory and of social status in the multivolume novel *À la recherche du temps perdu (Remembrance of Things Past)*. Although his first volume had gone unnoticed in 1913, the next volume won a major French literary prize in 1921. And there was the "stream of consciousness" technique, by which the reader was brought directly into the mind of a character with all his or her disconnected ramblings, free association of banalities and profundities, and suggestive, half-understood allusions. The most masterful of the "stream of consciousness" writers was the Irish exile James Joyce, whose *Ulysses* was published in 1922.

Sigmund Freud was perhaps the single most influential thinker in interwar intellectual life. Freud had established his two principal points before the war: that our conscious reasoning is to some extent rationalization of unconscious desires and conflicts; and that sexual conflict, often in infancy, is the principal source of mental illness. Freud continued to refine his work after the war, adding the famous threefold analysis of the personality: the id, or unconscious; the ego, or drive for self-preservation; and the superego, or Freudian equivalent of conscience. Freud also undertook after the war an interpretation of human history and society. In *Civilization and Its Discontents* (1929) he argued that some form of sexual repression was a necessary precondition of group living and cultural development. The overall thrust of Freud's writing was somewhat pessimistic and determinist, strongly suggesting that every individual's personality elements were at war with one another and with the surrounding culture. The best one could hope for was a certain mitigation of the pain by psychoanalytically assisted "adjustment."

Freud's scientific influence spread after the war because of wartime experiences with battlefield emotional disorders. Outside Freud's Vienna, important centers of psychoanalysis grew up in Berlin, London, and New York. His influence among ordinary people, however, was of a different kind, for his name became associated with a prurient exploitation of youthful postwar hedonism. The notions that sexual repression was harmful and that salvation came through free sexual expression were closer to Freud's heretical student Wilhelm Reich than to the master himself. Freud did not know whether to be angry or amused when the Hollywood producer Samuel Goldwyn offered him $100,000 in 1925 to serve as consultant for a series of films on the variants of love.[32]

Human sexuality was treated far more explicitly and centrally in the arts after the war than before. Even the late-nineteenth-century naturalistic French novelist, Émile Zola, whose sexual frankness had resulted in censorship and lawsuits, had described lust and sexual violence as merely unpleasant and discrete aspects of human ugliness. For some interwar writers, sexuality was not only more pervasive but more sanctified; it was an expression of humanity's most fundamental energies

---

[32]Ernest Jones, *The Life and Work of Sigmund Freud,* ed. and abridged, Lionel Trilling and Stephen Marcus (London, 1961), p. 566.

Pablo Picasso, *Igor Stravinsky,* **1920.**

and passions. The British novelist D. H. Lawrence frankly reveled in the pagan enjoyment of instinct. His novels contrasted the effete, repressed upper classes with vigorous primitives who "thought with their blood."

The vitality of primitive creative instincts was accepted without argument by most interwar artists. The whole point of self-expression in the arts was to bypass the thin-blooded conformism of learned art and the academies. Just as Picasso and Matisse had found inspiration in African masks in 1905 and the German expressionist Ludwig Kirchner in sculptures from the Pacific in 1904, the interwar artists continued to look for deep sources of vigor and certainty, whether in their own unconscious, in the work of children, or in the arts of the happily "uncivilized" peoples of the world. Study of primitive art in ethnographic museums or through travel had become an essential part of a painter's experience; Kandinsky referred to the "shattering impression that the ethnographic museum made on me."[33]

The search for primitive roots was especially pronounced among the Russian exiles who contributed so much to Western European intellectual life after 1917. The composer Igor Stravinsky turned away from the lush romanticism of his first

[33]Quoted in Frank Whitford, *Expressionism* (London, 1970), p. 180.

compositions toward simplicity, clarity, and ritual. His *Weddings* (*Les noces,* 1923) recalled folk rituals in music of great strength and hypnotic repetition; in subsequent revisions he made his orchestration leaner and purer as if in a continuing effort to return to the simplest verity. The painter Marc Chagall created his own fanciful world of the people of his native village in the Jewish Pale of Russia.

On any scale—imagination, individuality, or vigor—the postwar years rank among the most brilliantly expressive. To understand cultural climates more fully, however, we need to know more about their settings.

THE SETTINGS OF INTERWAR CULTURE

Sophisticated cultural expressions were restricted, for the most part, to large cities. Two European centers stood out for the brilliance of their cultural life: Paris and (until 1933) Weimar Germany. Paris had attracted an international artist community before 1914, when it had been the freest republican capital in the world and the center of intense experimentation in the visual arts: Picasso had come from Spain, van Gogh from Holland, Sergei Diaghilev from Russia, among others. Paris, then, was a natural setting for the flowering of avant-garde art. After 1918, Americans joined the European artists, and the introduction of jazz, together with the new spare literary style of American expatriate writers like Hemingway, marked the first time that the United States had been a contributor to rather than a borrower of European cultural expression.

Germany was different. Its cultural flowering followed a revolution, so that the triumph of new forms of expression was accompanied by the entry of the prewar "outsiders" into positions of influence and authority. They found jobs and patrons under the Weimar Republic. The architect Gropius and the painters Klee and Kandinsky, among others, taught at the state-subsidized Bauhaus; Alban Berg found a wealthy patron, Alma Mahler Werfel, to pay for producing his opera *Wozzeck.* The prewar experimenters thus found a stage and a voice. But the revolution that brought the Weimar Republic into being ultimately failed, and the old conformities were soon powerful again. The experience of having once been "outsiders" and the tenuousness of their victory gave German artists a stridency and combativeness that fit well with the political and economic uncertainties of the time.

Social Status of Artists

As in the late nineteenth century, most artists and intellectuals were bourgeois. And as in the late nineteenth century, they were rebels against their own upbringing. Nothing had diminished their scorn for middle-class values and their rage at authority and conformity. Some of their artistic expressions took the form of playful mockery. Klee's *Twittering Machine* (1922) revealed delight in pure form as well as in ridiculing the sanctimoniousness of "serious art." The French composers who called themselves "The Six" drew on the musical games and foolery of their master,

Paul Klee, *Three White Bellflowers* (1920). Klee, who taught at the Bauhaus and painted nature and geometrical subjects with only a hint of representation, wanted his painting to communicate by form and structure.

Copyright Nimatallah / Art Resource, NY / © 2002 Artists Rights Society (ARS), New York / VVG Bild-Kunst, Bonn

Erik Satie. The predominant tone, however, especially in Berlin, was an insecure, angry scorn. Count Harry Kessler wondered why his friend George Grosz devoted "his art exclusively to the depiction of the repulsiveness of bourgeois philistinism." Kessler decided that Grosz was a wounded idealist whose sensitivity had been turned "outrageously brutal" by his "fanatical hatred" for everything in modern German life that was authoritarian, crassly materialist, and self-satisfied.[34]

There were signs of change in the class position of artists after the war. A few working-class painters and writers achieved major successes in the arts, which now required less formal training: D. H. Lawrence, from a coal mining family of the English Midlands, is a major example.

[34]Kessler, p. 64.

The Search for a Mass Audience

Artists reached out for popular audiences after the First World War. Few artists accepted the notion of the arts as ornament for royal or ecclesiastical patrons, or even as delectation for a narrow circle of sophisticated initiates in the manner of some late-nineteenth-century aesthetes. To attract a wider audience some interwar artists drew enthusiastically on popular culture, not only on disappearing folk culture as in Chagall's paintings or Stravinsky's compositions, but on the new mass culture. Kurt Weill, at first a struggling composer of difficult chamber music, eventually found his métier in composing jazz rhythms and spare, angular, bittersweet music for Bertolt Brecht's antibourgeois satires *The Threepenny Opera* and *The Rise and Fall of the City of Mahagonny* (1930). Francis Poulenc, best-known of the French "Six," also worked jazz into much of his lean antiromantic composition of the 1920s. And, of course, film was rapidly seized on for artistic experimentation.

The more radical among postwar artists regarded the arts as a medium for transforming society. Even before the war, the first expressionists had established a group studio in the poorest neighborhood of Dresden rather than set up the customary individual studios in middle-class neighborhoods or in the country: "As youth, we carry the future with us, and want to establish the freedom of life and movement in opposition to the entrenched older forces."[35] George Grosz, a savagely antibourgeois artist, told a friend in 1919 that he wanted to become "the German Hogarth, deliberately realistic and didactic; to preach, improve, and reform. . . . He loathes painting and the pointlessness of painting as practiced so far."[36] The Bauhaus in Germany was the outstanding example of using the arts as instruments for transforming society. Its classes, according to Walter Gropius, "would enable the coming generation to achieve the reunion of all forms of creative work and become the architects of a new civilization."[37]

The theater lent itself especially well to the efforts of postwar artists to affect a vast popular audience. Berlin, with its rich dramatic tradition and its state-supported theaters, was a center of stage experimentation designed to involve a wider audience in the theatrical experience. The director Max Reinhardt transformed the plays of Aeschylus and Shakespeare into stunning displays using revolving stages and spectacular lighting. Reinhardt abolished the curtain and traditional naturalistic sets in order to bring the audience more intimately into the spectacle. More political was Leopold Jessner, a Social Democratic director designated by the new German republic to run the Berlin State Theater. His 1919 production of Schiller's *William Tell* presented the tyrant Gessler as a German general with rouged cheeks and covered with medals; Tell himself was thinly disguised as a defender of the German Revolution of 1918. Most radical of all was Erwin Piscator, who began his Berlin career as a director by presenting plays to workers on picket lines during the 1918 and 1919 strikes. Piscator expected to find a large proletarian audience for experimental drama with a strong political message heightened by techniques like

[35]*Die Brücke* Manifesto, 1905.

[36]Kessler, p. 64.

[37]Quoted in Gay, p. 99.

newsreels and slides interspersed with the play and fast-moving short scenes on a stage free of naturalistic sets. According to his widow, Piscator meant to present "plays of active protest, a deliberate J'Accuse; a reportage and montage; a warning, history marching on; political satire, morality plays and court trials, purposefully shocking."[38] Piscator had Walter Gropius design a flexible theater-in-the-round for his concept of total theater, but he never managed to raise the money to build it.

The possibility of creating a new humanity through cultural revolution seemed greatest in Russia. Leon Trotsky predicted in 1923 that under communism

> man will become immeasurably stronger, wiser, and subtler; his body will become more harmonized, his movements more rhythmic, his voice more musical. The forms of life will become dynamically dramatic. The average human type will rise to the heights of an Aristotle, a Goethe, or a Marx. And above this range new peaks will rise.[39]

Trotsky and Lenin, both men of broad cultivation, opposed the attempts of some Bolsheviks to sweep away everything except proletarian culture. Although a number of intellectuals chose exile, those that remained enjoyed a relatively open atmosphere in the 1920s. Many of them were stimulated to rich creativity. Sergei Eisenstein developed stunning camera techniques in his epic films of the Bolshevik Revolution. Vladimir Tatlin developed a "constructivist" architecture that rejected surface ornament in favor of functional buildings, garden cities, and monuments derived from the industrial forms he thought appropriate to a socialist society. The poet Vladimir Mayakovsky declaimed rough-hewn verses that exalted the revolution.

> Fall in and prepare to march!
> No time now to talk or trifle.
> Silence, you orators!
> The word is with you,
> Comrade Rifle!
> We have lived long enough by laws
> Of which Adam and Eve made the draft.
> Stable history's poor old horse!
> Left!
> Left!
> Left![40]

The Russian theater experienced a golden age like that of Weimar Berlin. While Konstantin Stanislavsky continued to train his actors at the Moscow Art Theater in the method of close psychological identification with their parts, his pupil Vsevelod Meyerhold carried out an "October revolution of the theater" with stylized sets and actors trained in mechanical gestures. He arranged seats freely in his theater and issued tickets at random to soldiers and workers. As late as 1929, Meyerhold was allowed to produce a play as critical of the Soviet bureaucracy as Mayakovsky's *The Bedbug* (1928).

---

[38]Quoted in Otto Friedrich, *Before the Deluge: A Portrait of Berlin in the 1920s* (New York, 1972), p. 255.

[39]Leon Trotsky, *Literature and Revolution* (New York, 1957), p. 256.

[40]Vladimir Mayakovsky, "Left March," trans. C. M. Bowra, in C. M. Bowra, ed., *Second Book of Russian Verse* (London, 1948), p. 131.

Whether in Paris, Berlin, or Moscow, the postwar artists' and intellectuals' desire to assemble a mass audience and transform it was doomed to frustration. The artists would do everything to spread their message except renounce individual self-expression in favor of the stale, conformist aesthetics that mass taste still preferred. There is a pathetic note in Klee's concession in his 1923 Bauhaus lectures. All that was lacking in the community begun at the Bauhaus, Klee said, was an audience: "We seek a people."[41]

The Academic and Scholarly Worlds

The modern arts not only found no mass audience between the wars; they had little effect on the academic and learned worlds. Higher education was relatively unchanged by the postwar revolutionary urges, at least outside the Soviet Union. Education beyond elementary school was still directed to a small elite carefully selected on the basis of excellence in classical education. In France, the superb *lycées* (public high schools) required fees until 1930; the prestigious British "public schools" were in fact costly private institutions, while the inferior public secondary schools required fees of all but a few winners of scholarships. Even among those who could afford the fees, admission was limited to those who had excelled in written and oral examinations on classical subjects. Admission was by merit, of course, but lower-class children were deprived of the home environment needed for scholarly excellence in the classics. The day of widespread, free secondary education was far in the future, one of the basic social changes of the post-1945 reconstruction.

Beyond the elite secondary schools, the universities were an even more confined world of specialists. In the French *lycée* system, more than half the students—already a small elite—were expected to fail the rigorous *baccalauréat* examinations that gave entry to universities and professional schools. The struggle to replace Latin and Greek with modern languages and philosophy was already underway at the universities, but technical education was still considered inferior in European school systems. It was outside the classroom, and partly in protest against their narrow classical education, that secondary school and university students associated themselves with the new art forms. No wonder the modern artists looked for popular audiences and appropriated elements of popular culture. They scorned the academic world, which more than returned that scorn.

As knowledge increased, the learned world fragmented more and more into specialization. That community of craftsmen sought by the Bauhaus was far removed from the reality of learned specialists in the sciences and scholarly professions.

The prewar revolution in physics begun by Rutherford, Bohr, Planck, and Einstein was carried further between the wars. The indeterminacy theory (1926–1927) of the German physicist Werner Heisenberg completed the overthrow of classical physics. Heisenberg's predecessors had shown that atomic structure was based on force fields or electric charges rather than on particles of matter, but they had tended to argue, by analogy with the Newtonian solar system, that subatomic

[41]Klee, p. 55.

elements were organized within the atom somewhat like planets around a sun. Heisenberg found that any particular electron could be located only within a range of probabilities, as the observer influenced the observation. Hence its location was indeterminate.

Only a handful of Europeans were capable of really understanding these theories. Indeed the difficulty that readers—and writers—of textbooks still today encounter in trying to make sense of the subtle mathematical language of modern physics is a reminder of the increasingly closed compartments into which knowledge became divided in the twentieth century. No single physical scientist between the wars had as much impact on public attitudes as Charles Darwin, for instance, had had in the late nineteenth century. Albert Einstein was clearly the nearest parallel after 1918, but Einstein had more notoriety than genuine cultural influence.

Einstein's special theory of relativity (1905) had suggested that gravity has an effect on light waves in space; since the speed of light is constant, that effect could be true only if space and time were relative to each observer's place in a universe of flux. When a solar eclipse in 1919 enabled British astronomers to verify that light waves were indeed affected by gravitational fields, headlines proclaimed that the "relativity" of time and space had been proven. Einstein's name became a household word, much to the bemusement of that modest, self-deprecating scientist. "Relativism" came to lend a supposed scientific support to subjectivism in other areas of culture between the wars. Popularizers of science like Sir Arthur Eddington, whose *Nature of the Physical Universe* (1930) was widely read, suggested that physics no longer conflicted with spiritual beliefs.

As for the scientists themselves, the area of Heisenbergian uncertainty within the application of hypotheses to experimental cases in atomic physics did not lessen their sense that each successive hypothesis came nearer to explaining every aspect of the universe in terms of scientific knowledge. The early-twentieth-century revolution in physics quietly prepared the way for the next generation's revolutions in the study of crystals, solid-state physics, molecular particles, and the living cell.

The other fields of scholarly knowledge were no more clearly understood outside a narrow circle of specialists. The gap between popular Freudianism and psychoanalysis has already been noted. Major advances made in other areas of study had little popular impact. Sociology had been established as an academic discipline only at the end of the nineteenth century. It was profoundly influenced by the German Max Weber, who wanted to supplement (but not replace) Marx's emphasis on economic causation in social development with other kinds of social force—the growth of bureaucracy, religion, and what he called "charismatic leadership." The assumptions and field techniques of the young science of anthropology were decisively influenced by Bronislaw Malinowski, a Polish scholar working in England.

Philosophy developed in divergent directions in England and on the Continent. English philosophy, under the influence of the Viennese Ludwig Wittgenstein, rejected speculation on metaphysical issues in favor of the careful analysis of the logic of concrete statements. On the Continent, metaphysics was renewed by Edmund Husserl (1859–1938) and his student Martin Heidegger (1889–1976). Husserl tried to ground human knowledge in the direct experience of phenomena. Heidegger devoted this "phenomenology" to exploring the phenomena of Being and Time (1929). For Heidegger, life was a struggle between authentic existence, with its pains of anxiety and conscience, and mere living among modern gadgetry. His enthusiastic Nazism in 1933 tarnished but did not destroy his influence as a philosopher.

These very different worlds—the artistic, the academic, and the scholarly—went their ways between the wars, affecting mass culture only in the case of a few notorious individuals. The artistic world in particular found notoriety enough with its scandalous novelties, but not the new popular base that many artists had hoped to find. Hence the feverish experimentation of the 1920s was highly vulnerable to its enemies.

Opposition to the Experimental Arts

The experimental arts did not fail to arouse savage antagonism. They were connected, especially in Germany, with the revolution of 1918 and the installation of "democrats, Jews, and other outsiders"[42] in cultural and academic realms heretofore reserved for an older elite. Worse still, the new arts and sciences positively gloried in trampling on established values. Many of the more celebrated opening nights, particularly in Berlin, were occasions for fistfights between the supporters of the new arts and nationalist, traditionalist action squads. Two irreconcilable conceptions of cultural life clashed head on: the sacred duty of self-expression to the limits of one's creativity and the idea of the arts as a heritage of values that must be transmitted to the otherwise unruly young.

One of the roots of fascism was the panic among many traditionalist Europeans at what they feared was a tidal wave of degeneracy and decadence in the arts and sciences. When the Hungarian officers destroyed Béla Kun's Budapest soviet in August 1919, one of their first acts was to close down the offices of Freud's most active disciple, Sandor Ferenczi. The Nazis in Germany specialized in breaking up artistic performances that seemed to threaten the German state or the racial purity of traditional *Kultur.* The objects of their displeasure ranged from the film based on Remarque's novel *All Quiet on the Western Front* to expressionist plays to psychoanalysis. In 1929, the Nazi pseudophilosopher Alfred Rosenberg founded the Militant League for German Culture. In and out of power, the Nazis won supporters by promising "to substitute a 'German' art and an eternal art" for the cosmopolitan "modern art" that tried to "reduce art to the level of fashions in dress, with the motto 'every year something fresh'—Impressionism, Futurism, Cubism, perhaps also Dadaism." That was the crowd-pleasing mockery used effectively by a one-time art student, Adolf Hitler. As he dedicated the House of German Art in Munich on July 18, 1937, containing an exhibition of "decadent" art presented for public ridicule, Hitler made these further remarks:

> As in politics, so in German art-life: we are determined to make a clean sweep of phrases. Ability is the necessary qualification if an artist wishes his work to be exhibited here. . . .

---

[42]The phrase is Gustav Meyer's, a Jewish historian who failed to get a post as professor in Germany until the republic was established. See Gay, p. 88.

The influence of Jews was paramount and through their control of the press they were able to intimidate those who desired to champion "the normal sound intelligence and instinct of men." . . . From the pictures sent in for exhibition it is clear that there really are men who on principle feel meadows to be blue, the heavens green, clouds sulphur yellow—or as they perhaps prefer to say, "experience" them thus. I need not ask whether they really do see or feel things in this way, but in the name of the German people I have only to prevent these pitiable unfortunates who clearly suffer from defects of vision from attempting with violence to persuade contemporaries by their chatter that these faults of observation are indeed realities, or from presenting them as "Art." . . . The artist does not create for the artist; he creates for the people and we will see to it that henceforth the people will be called in to judge its art. . . . The people regarded this art as the outcome of an impudent or unashamed arrogance or of a simply shocking lack of skill . . . which might have been produced by untalented children of from eight to ten years old . . . this art-stammer . . . which might have been made by a man of the Stone Age."[43]

Nazi Germany was not the only society in which the arts were subordinated to the inculcation of "useful" social values in the 1930s. As Stalin consolidated his grip on the Soviet Union in the late 1920s, the heady artistic experimentation of the early years of the decade became suspect as an excess of bourgeois individualism. Stanislavsky was removed as director of the Moscow Art Theater in 1928, and Anatole Lunacharsky was dismissed as commissar of education in 1929. Mayakovsky, tormented by personal troubles as well as disillusioned by the regime, committed suicide in 1930. Eisenstein was ordered to change his film *The General Line* in the same year. Meyerhold disappeared in the purges of the late 1930s. All writers were required to join the National Union of Writers in 1934. At the same time, the party congress approved the doctrine that all art should express "socialist realism," a numbing conformity to nineteenth-century pictorial style that would be devoted to the propaganda services of the regime.

No one has explained why both Hitler and Stalin tried to impose commonplace nineteenth-century art styles on their subjects in what professed to be revolutionary regimes. But it is clear that the burst of artistic and scientific energies of the 1920s had not won the popular support that might have saved them from persecution in the 1930s.

[43]Quoted in George L. Mosse, *Nazi Culture* (New York, 1966), pp. 11–15.

SUGGESTIONS FOR FURTHER READING

The most penetrating study of the social and political context of culture in any interwar European state is Peter Gay, *Weimar Culture: The Outsider as Insider** (1970, reprint ed. 2003). See also the informative studies of French social thinkers between the wars in H. Stuart Hughes, *The Obstructed Path: French Social Thought in the Years of Desperation, 1930–1960** (reprint ed. 2001). Robert Graves, *The Long Week-End** (1940, reprint ed. 2004), is a lively look at British popular culture between the wars.

The best study of mass communications in any European state is Asa Briggs, *The BBC: The First Fifty Years* (1985). See also Briggs's comprehensive *The History of Broadcasting in the United Kingdom,* 4 vols. (1961–1979, reprint ed. 1995). There is nothing comparable in English about the more statist continental radio and television systems.

David A. Cook, *A History of Narrative Film,** 4th ed. (2004), and Thomas W. Bohn and Richard L. Stromgren, *Light and Shadows: A History of Motion Pictures,** 3rd ed. (1987), cover European film well. See also Pierre Sorlin, *European Cinema, European Societies** (1991), and the same author's *Italian National Cinema, 1896–1996** (1996). On the mass media generally, see the brief introductions by Ken Ward, *Mass Communications and the Modern World** (1989) and Pierre Sorlin, *Mass-Media** (1994).

On state management of culture in the USSR, Sheila Fitzpatrick, *The Commissariat of Enlightenment: Soviet Organization of Education and the Arts under Lunacharsky** (1970, new ed. 2002), is basic. See also Richard Stites, *Russian Popular Culture: Entertainment and Society since 1900** (1992), and Orlando Figes, *Natasha's Dance: A Cultural History of Russia** (2003).

Victoria De Grazia, *The Culture of Consent** (1981, reprint ed. 2002), is important for Italian fascism's manipulation of leisure activities. Paul Brooker, *The Faces of Fraternalism* (1991), discusses the manufacture of consensus in Germany and Italy. A model monograph on Nazi arts policy is Barbara Miller Lane, *Architecture and Politics in Germany, 1918–1945** (1985).

The emergence of leisure time is explored in Rudy Koshar, ed., *Histories of Leisure** (2002), and James Walvin, *Leisure and Society, 1830–1950* (1978), and examined more closely in John K. Walton and James Walvin, eds., *Leisure Time in Britain, 1780–1939* (1988). The significance of leisure time is analyzed by Gareth Stedman Jones in "Class Expression versus Social Control: A Critique of Recent Trends in the Social History of Leisure," in G. Stedman Jones, *Languages of Class* (1983). John Hargreaves, *Sport, Power, and Culture** (1986), studies the most important leisure time activity in Britain. See also Jeffrey Hill, *Sport, Leisure and Culture in Twentieth Century Britain** (2002), and Claire Langhamer, *Women's Leisure in England, 1920–1960* (2001).

A layman's introduction to twentieth century science through its main practitioners is Abraham Pais, *The Genius of Science: A Portrait Gallery* (2000). Major developments in physics between the wars are treated by Barbara Cline, *Men Who Made a New Physics: Physicists and the Quantum Theory*[*] (1987); Abraham Pais, *Niels Bohr's Times*[*] (1994), Jeremy Bernstein, *Quantum Profiles* (1990), David M. Cassidy, *Uncertainty: The Life and Science of Werner Heisenberg* (1993), and Laurie M. Brown et al., *Twentieth Century Physics* (1995), in addition to works mentioned at the end of Chapter 1.

Additional Internet links related to this chapter are available on the Europe in the 20th Century Web site: http://www.history.wadsworth.com/paxton04.

You can also explore images, interactive timelines, and maps related to this chapter on our Western Civilization Resource Center: http://history.wadsworth.com.

Unemployed Germans without enough money for a room pay a few pennies for several hours' sleep "on the line" in a Hamburg flophouse.

10

The Depression and Its Effects, 1929–1936

In the late 1920s, many Europeans expected a future of peace and broadening prosperity. After 1929, however, millions of them could not find work, even though they might be strong and skillful. Millions of Europeans were ill clad, even though the factories that could produce needed clothing lay idle. Many went hungry, while farmers destroyed crops they could not sell. Maddened by their impotence in the face of these absurdities, most Europeans were sunk in despair or swept by rage. These were some of the effects of the Great Depression.

A depression is a prolonged slowdown in buying and selling: Businesses are unable to sell all they produce. Stocks pile up, despite competitive price-cutting. Firms increasingly lay off workers or go out of business altogether. Since the unemployed, in turn, can buy nothing, sales decline still further. More firms close, and banks that have lent them money can no longer cover all their deposits. Savings are swept away in bank failures. The sufferings are uneven. As prices fall, those who still have jobs or who spend cash reserves can live comfortably. For the rest, there is only demoralizing helplessness. Businessmen go bankrupt; professional people lose their clients; millions of salaried people lose their jobs and can find no way to support themselves and their families.

Europeans had known depression before 1929. But never before had there been unemployment on such a great scale, or so deep a business decline. Nor had European leaders seemed so helpless. The depression of 1929 completely outran previous experience. The American economist Wesley Clair Mitchell, in a classic work on the business cycle, had written that depressed economies normally begin to recover in the first or second year, because lower prices encourage more buying.[1] Two years after the crash of 1929, however, the world economy plunged still further down in a wave of bank failures. At the very time that the public was coming to expect more of governments, government performance had never been more ineffectual.

At the worst point of the Great Depression, in 1932, one Englishman in four was on the dole, whereas in Germany two out of five were unemployed. There were over 6 million unemployed in Germany in 1932, about 12 million in the United States. Industrial production dropped by 47 percent in the United States between 1929 and 1932, by 44 percent in Germany, and by 37 percent in the world, excluding the Soviet Union.[2]

© Hulton Picture Library

British miners looking for work. This queue was at the Labour Exchange in Wigan.

[1]Wesley Clair Mitchell, *The Business Cycle* (Berkeley, Calif., 1913), p. 565.

[2]Barry Eichengreen, *Golden Fetters: The Gold Standard and the Great Depression, 1919–1939* (New York and Oxford, England, 1992), pp. 258–259.

These statistics tell us little about the depression's impact on individual people. For that, we may turn to the arts. The 1930s were a brilliant period for mordant social criticism in novels, essays, and the theater (painting, among the visual arts, had largely relinquished the role of social criticism to photography and film). The emphasis shifted away from the private self-expression of the 1920s toward social concerns. The fiction, essays, and drama of the 1930s often speak with the authentic voices of the angry and bewildered. For the wounds of the depression were not merely physical want. They were the psychic wounds of humiliating helplessness among willing workers unable to provide for their families; there were sharpened and polarized social antagonisms and the search for a savior. All these concerns permeate the art of the 1930s.

The waitress Jenny, in *The Threepenny Opera* (1928) of the German playwright Bertolt Brecht and the composer Kurt Weill, has a bitter daydream: A "pirate ship with fifty cannon" comes into the harbor, and she dreams that the pirate chief asks her whom she wants killed. Jenny orders all the townsmen killed and goes off with the pirates. In real life, however, she is still waiting on tables and scrubbing floors. There are satirical attacks on the depersonalizing machine in films like René Clair's *À nous la liberté* (1931) and Charlie Chaplin's *Modern Times* (1936). There is the desperate, jobless salesclerk in the German novelist Hans Fallada's *Little Man, What Now?* (1932). The British writer George Orwell reflects on life and social distinctions in an English coal mining town. At one point, Orwell describes the "scramble for coal" in which poor families glean fragments of coal from the mine tailings.

> That scene stays in my mind as one of my pictures of Lancashire: the dumpy, shawled women, with their sacking aprons and their heavy black clogs, kneeling in the cindery mud and the bitter wind searching for tiny chips of coal. . . . In winter they are almost desperate for fuel; it is more important almost than food. Meanwhile, all round, as far as the eye can see are the slag-heaps and hoisting gear of collieries, and not one of those collieries can sell all the coal it is capable of producing.[3]

That very juxtaposition of poor people in desperate material want and companies unable to sell the goods they produced aroused profound questioning in Europe. The very values that had seemed the formula for success in the 1920s now seemed touched with a curse. National self-determination had appeared a lofty ideal, but it had helped cut Europe up into economically inefficient units. The end of wartime regulation had been welcomed as a return to normalcy, but it had left the European economy a jungle. Return to the gold standard had seemed a self-evident improvement, but it had kept prices and unemployment high.

It was the whole nineteenth-century liberal ideal of a self-regulating market economy that went bankrupt in 1929. Those ideas came to be regarded as not only absurd but positively evil after 1929. No regime could survive that could not provide its citizens with a way to earn a living. This concrete problem made the depression a "crisis of liberalism." The search for something better dominated European affairs in the 1930s and challenged Europe as profoundly as the First World War had done. Whoever could solve the economic riddles of the 1930s would have Europe at his feet.

[3]George Orwell, *The Road to Wigan Pier* (London, 1937), p. 95.

THE ORIGINS AND COURSE OF THE GREAT DEPRESSION

The Great Depression is commonly traced back to the collapse of the New York stock market in October 1929 with its repercussions in international finance. Well before the crash, however, there were signs of a downturn in domestic economies. It is probably helpful at this point to make a distinction between two aspects of the depression: domestic economic difficulty and the international financial panic set off by Wall Street in 1929. Before the 1929 stock market crash, buying and selling were already slowing down, beginning with depressed world prices for agricultural goods and coal and later affecting all commodities as the depression deepened. After the 1929 crash, panic movements of gold and currency undermined banks and made nations struggle to maintain the international value of their currencies.

The two matters were closely interrelated, of course, and to separate them, even for purposes of discussion, is somewhat artificial. For example, rapid withdrawal of American capital from Germany in 1929 had much to do with the business slowdown there; in turn, weakening business activity within each of the countries undermined the solvency of banks and national currencies in international markets, especially in agrarian Eastern Europe. The point of separating these two aspects is to observe that it was the international side of the depression that governments set out to remedy, rather than attempting to stimulate the domestic economy. Indeed, those governments that threw their budgets into deficit in the effort to create new jobs or assist the unemployed promptly provoked international speculation against their own currencies.

Domestic Crisis

Like an earlier long depression in the 1880s, when American and Russian wheat first appeared on world markets and pushed farm incomes down in Europe, the Great Depression began with declining agricultural prices in the mid-1920s. The First World War had encouraged a large increase in farm production. In response to high wartime prices, about 33 million additional acres had been put to the plow in the United States, Canada, Argentina, and Australia. After the war, this acreage produced more grain than existing markets could easily absorb. Furthermore, by 1930 it cost 60 percent less to ship wheat from Vancouver to the mouth of the Rhine than it cost to move wheat by rail from Budapest to Berlin. The world agricultural price index, at 226 in 1919, dropped to 134 by 1929.

Because agrarian parties were important to the politics of the successor states in Eastern Europe, the farmers' plight quickly translated itself into political instability. Moreover, each of the numerous small states in Eastern Europe had already begun before 1929 to shut out foreign agricultural competition. The resort to tariffs in central Europe was the first major flight from liberal economic ideals. Germany restored farm tariffs in 1925, the Czechs renounced their agreement to buy Hungarian wheat in 1929, and so on. The former free-trade area of the Habsburg Empire was by now a collection of small, competing economic units.

A calamity similar to that of European agriculture also afflicted coal mining between the wars. Coal had been the fuel of the early Industrial Revolution.

England, in particular, had built an empire partly on the export of coal. After the war, however, coal sales were never again as profitable as before 1914. The war relocated trade patterns, some of them toward the United States. And the global demand for coal rose more slowly after the war, due in part to competing new sources of power: oil and hydroelectricity. British coal never recovered its prewar position, and that helps explain why unemployment in Britain never fell below 10 percent of the work force between the wars. The coal industry, like agriculture, was in depression even before 1929.

International Financial Crisis

The international financial arrangements of Europe after the First World War constituted a house of cards. Like the prewar system, the international finance system artificially reconstructed after the war could be criticized for its tacit acceptance of business cycles as regulating devices. But the postwar system contained three additional flaws. First, it restored to the British pound its prewar role as the main international currency of exchange at a time when the British economy no longer had its prewar power. Second, there was the distorting effect of reparations. The Germans were expected to pay large sums to France, Britain, and Belgium until the end of the twentieth century, outside the normal exchanges of commerce; since 1924 the Germans had made reparations payments by borrowing from the United States. Finally, there was the question of the war debts that France and Belgium owed Britain and that all three owed the United States. A major feature of these arrangements was the close dependence of the whole financial structure on United States bank loans to Germany. Under the Dawes Plan, the equivalent of 23 billion marks went into Germany in the form of American purchases of municipal bonds or loans to industry, while nearly 8 billion marks had come out as reparations.

In 1928 and 1929, however, American credit was pulled out of Germany and attracted back to the higher profits available in the booming New York stock market. The German credit structure was badly shaken by this withdrawal of funds. Then, after the New York market crashed in October 1929, many American speculators who were caught short quickly pulled the rest of their capital out of Germany and other European investments. In this way, the depressing effect of the Wall Street slump was transmitted to Europe. That effect was compounded by the sharp decline in United States purchases from Europe after October 1929.

The international position of German and central European banks was further undermined by the withdrawal of foreign funds, mostly American, in the years following the Wall Street crash. In the first seven months of 1931, 2 billion marks were pulled out of Germany alone by American and British creditors, who needed the money at home or were losing confidence in the safety of their German investments.

The news on May 11, 1931, that Austria's largest deposit bank, the *Credit-Anstalt* in Vienna had gone broke, triggered a four-month international financial crisis that ended only when the British pound was devalued and untied from gold the following September. It was to be expected that the first major bank failure of the European depression should occur in Vienna. All the elements of depression converged there when the long decline in Eastern European farm incomes coincided with the erection of trade and financial barriers. The financial establishments of Vienna, once a regional capital, had been forced to constrict their fields of activity more and more to tiny Austria.

Efforts by other European financial centers to prop up the *Credit-Anstalt* did not succeed. Individual investors and speculators withdrew their funds from Austrian banks as quickly as possible to avoid losing them, and moved them from country to country looking for safety. This began an epidemic of bank runs wherever rumors suggested that currencies were about to be devalued or banks to fail. The situation was further complicated by international rivalries and pressure politics. The French, for example, did not help the *Credit-Anstalt* at first because they were trying to bring pressure on Austria to abandon a proposed German-Austrian customs union, which the French regarded as a violation of the Treaty of Versailles.

The crisis in Austria cast suspicion next on the stability of the closely related German banks. When a decline appeared in the German government's weekly statement of foreign exchange and gold reserves in early July 1931, a run on the mark was set off. German and foreign holders of marks tried to sell them for gold or for what they believed to be safer currencies before it was too late. The moratorium on all payments of reparations and war debts announced by United States president Herbert Hoover on July 6 could not stem the tide. In August, Germany was forced to "freeze" foreign credits, that is, refuse to transfer marks held by foreigners into foreign currencies.

London now remained the largest free gold market in Europe, and speculators eager for the safety of gold tried to sell as many pounds for gold in London as possible. British banks were obliged to sell gold to anyone with pounds who wanted to buy gold, but they had been seriously weakened by the "freezing" of that part of their assets that remained deposited in Germany and Austria. When it became impossible to sell any more gold without calling the exchange value of the pound into question, the British government was forced, on September 19, 1931, to "go off the gold standard" and refuse to sell gold freely for pounds. The postwar effort to reestablish a world international banking system based on gold had collapsed forever.

Losses suffered in this banking crisis that constituted a second phase of the depression pushed business activity down even further in the various domestic economies. Furthermore, the adoption of currency restrictions and the absence of any one standard of exchange made foreign trade much more complicated and uncertain. By 1932, the European economies were limping along at half or a little more of their 1929 level of activity.

DEPRESSION REMEDIES

The Great Depression confronted European leaders with their greatest challenge since the First World War. Several different remedies were available in contemporary economic thought. These had different political constituencies and proposed to lay the burdens on different shoulders. But no remedy could claim final wisdom, for this was a totally new experience.

Liberal Economics

Classical, or orthodox, liberal economics was the conventional wisdom. In this view, the root problem was malfunction of the international monetary system. Solutions, therefore, must deal with the international monetary system. If a country's currency came under speculative pressure, the way to stop a "run" on the currency was to balance the government's budget, thereby proving to the world the solidity and responsibility of its economy. Currency fluctuations reflected loss of confidence, the classical liberals believed, and they were best cured by restoring confidence among the bankers, financiers, and speculators of the world. To shut oneself off from the international money market would simply make everyone poorer. The second part of the classical remedy concerned world trade. A declining economy was best revived by becoming more competitive in world markets. One good way to become more competitive was to cut prices by lowering wages. This was to the ultimate benefit of workers, so ran the classical argument, for one could sell more and thus eventually return more workers to work.

These solutions were called "deflation": lowering government expenditures in order to balance the budget and lowering the costs of products in order to sell more. A government that intervened to stimulate employment or pay unemployment benefits, thereby incurring a budgetary deficit, only made matters worse by preserving inefficient sectors of the economy and pricing its goods out of the world market. The healthiest cure came out of market self-adjustment. Thus the classicists subordinated immediate domestic welfare to the imperatives of international monetary stability.

Classical liberal economics had many supporters in 1929. It was the position of a majority of bankers, professional economists, academics, and government experts. Most politicians shared the same assumptions in a less scholarly form. These views served the interests of exporters, bondholders, and other powerful business leaders. Tradition also favored this view, for up to 1931 modern governments never restricted foreign currency transactions during peacetime.

The classicists faced one overwhelming difficulty, however. A brief deflation might be politically possible, but to cut government expenditure and to lower wages for a long period would raise a growing howl of misery. The howl would be all the more insistent since the experiments of war government had made people familiar with the possibilities of government social action. A long-term deflation was probably possible only if governments were allowed to stifle dissent. Deflation, in other words, required authoritarian rule. Thus the liberal economic solution worked only with illiberal politics.

Socialist Economics

Socialists, like liberals, saw the depression as a result of overproduction. But they drew the opposite conclusion. What was produced could not be consumed under capitalism because the profit system skimmed off the value that workers created, leaving them with a subsistence wage—hence, underconsumption. The only meaningful solution was massive change in the ownership of factories and farms. Once the workers owned the means of production and received the full value of their labor, they would be able to buy more, and there could be no such thing as over-production. From such a perspective, the technicalities of world monetary exchanges were irrelevant nuisances. The only solution to depression, socialists argued, was to end the capitalist system with its inherent contradictions.

The socialists were not remotely ready to seize power, however. Indeed, the effect of unemployment was to weaken unions, diminish organized militancy, and lessen the effect of the strike weapon. Socialists had never given much thought to short-term partial remedies short of revolution, so that where they shared power (as in Germany and England), they had nothing to offer except, perhaps, tax reform. The British Labour Party, in fact, was militantly orthodox in its immediate economic solutions.

New Economic Solutions

Yet another strand of social thought was the attempt to find a "middle way" between discredited liberalism and Marxism. Like the liberals, seekers for this middle way wanted to preserve the property relations of capitalism. But they regarded the liberal global monetary system and the self-regulated market economy as hopeless anachronisms. Like socialists, they thought the heart of the problem was undercon-sumption, and they put domestic welfare ahead of international monetary stability. Their ultimate aim, however, was to maintain existing property, not abolish it. Their first priority was to revive the domestic economy, if necessary by a radical dose of state intervention of the sort pioneered during the First World War. If the budget deficits incurred in subsidizing full employment unleashed the international speculators against one's currency, then it would be necessary to impose currency restrictions. A country should secede from the world economy, if necessary, and develop a planned, managed prosperity within a closed national economy.

Partisans of the "middle way" formed no school, professed no orthodoxy, and followed no one leader. We refer here to those varied and disparate Europeans who rejected both liberal capitalism and international socialism, and whose quest for solutions led them to two fundamental points agreed on by most innovators in the 1930s: Economies must be planned to some degree and prosperity managed, and depression solutions must put national prosperity before international liquidity. The most famous "middle way" thinker in the Anglo-Saxon world was the British economist John Maynard Keynes, whose major innovations in consumer-based state economic management are discussed more fully later in this chapter. Some hereti-cal socialists also reacted to the depression with a similar emphasis on planning and on national solutions. The Belgian Henri de Man and the French neosocialist Mar-cel Déat advocated thoroughgoing economic planning in cooperation with the middle class, and within national units. The depression turned these socialists into "national socialists."

A "middle way" much favored by businessmen was corporatism. Corporatists pro-posed to organize each branch of the economy into a nationwide corporation empowered to settle prices, regulate production to meet demand, and deal with labor relations. Some corporatists proposed to include workers' representatives alongside management in these planning bodies, on the theory that the "class struggle" would be submerged in the common interest shared by capital and labor in the prosperity of each branch of industry. Other corporatists wished to elevate existing cartels and trusts into national agencies, thus, in effect, turning the economy over to self-regulation by organized business. The ideas of corporatism predated the depression, but the corporatist experiments of Mussolini aroused considerable interest among European businessmen, and they will be considered more closely in the discussion of the depression in Italy.

The Call for "Return to the Soil"

One last social nostrum was revived by the depression. Some publicists and intellectuals, mostly innocent of economics, proposed a "return to the soil." A number of European thinkers had long found the city immoral; after 1929 they added that it was unworkable. A stable, healthy society could be restored only where people produced true wealth from the soil or at the workbench, instead of making transient, speculative wealth from the stock market. Such nostalgic cries helped discredit the existing regimes in Europe, but while the proponents of a return to the soil helped fascism to come to power in some countries, they were unable to impose their views on fascist regimes once in power.

This was the range of intellectual perspectives available to the European governments as they tried to come to grips with the depression.

DEPRESSION POLITICS IN THE LIBERAL STATES

The Scandinavian Countries

Only the Scandinavian countries won comparatively high marks in the 1930s for coping with the depression without either stagnation or dictatorship. Naturally the Scandinavian economies, which were highly dependent on foreign trade, suffered severely in the depression, and unemployment exceeded 20 percent for a time. But the difficulties were mitigated to some degree by a homogeneous population; rich resources in dairy products, fisheries, and iron ore; the absence of international conflicts; and coherent political majorities. Reformist Social Democratic parties came to power in Denmark (1929), Sweden (1932), and Norway (1935) and governed, sometimes with coalition support from farmers' parties and liberals, for the next forty years. Scandinavian Social Democrats were able to build on deeply rooted traditions of public social service and a strong cooperative movement.

In Sweden, to take the largest and most prosperous example, cooperatives expanded in the 1930s until about half the population belonged to some consumer or producer cooperative association. No businesses were nationalized, but cooperatives enlarged their share of the market by buying in bulk and offering low prices until they accounted for 12 percent of retail trade. Producer cooperatives affected only about 2 percent of production, but advocates of the cooperative movement maintain that private producers kept prices low for fear of stimulating further inroads by cooperatives. An early form of the welfare state in the 1930s took shape in such areas as free prenatal care, social insurance, and garden cities. Sweden was not exempt from difficulties with high tax rates and growing rates of alcoholism and divorce. But the Swedish economy returned to predepression levels sooner than most; by 1939 Sweden enjoyed a greater rise in real wages since 1900 than any other European country.

Britain

For reasons quite unconnected with the onset of the depression, Britain's second Labour government (May 1929–August 1931) was in power when the crisis came. But that did not presage any attempt to remedy the depression by redistribution of property. Both Prime Minister Ramsay MacDonald and Chancellor of the Exchequer Philip Snowden were reformist to the core and thus opposed to immediate collectivization by force. And although the Labour Party had emerged as the largest British party for the first time in the elections of May 1929, it did not have an absolute majority.[4] The government depended on Liberal votes.

The main problem, however, was that Labour spokesmen had no intellectual alternative to classical liberal economics in the short run. All their economic thought had gone into the socialism of a distant future, not into immediate remedies within the existing system. Moreover, planning seemed an affront to Labour's sacred free trade, a prop to the existing system, and a step toward authoritarianism.

The new Chancellor of the Exchequer was one of those genuine proletarians who set the British Labour Party apart from the more intellectual middle-class socialist leaders of the Continent. Politically, Philip Snowden came from the left of his party; he had been a pacifist during the First World War. At the same time, Snowden, the son of a weaver, was steeped in a devout chapel-going puritanism and defense of free trade against Tory protectionist schemes. He identified free trade with cheap bread for the poor. Completely lacking any economic training, Snowden was convinced that government's main economic precepts should be thrift and probity. Crippled in a childhood bicycle accident, Snowden had transcended both pain and poverty in a long climb up the ranks of the Labour Party. His pinched, intense face gave some clue to the evangelical fervor with which he held to the economic virtues.

When the economy began to falter in late 1929, Snowden and the cabinet increased public works and unemployment benefits, while bringing the budget into balance with a steeper income tax. The rise in government spending and the decline in tax receipts caused by unemployment, however, created an unbridgeable gap between the two sides of the government's ledgers. Since Liberal votes prevented further tax increases, Snowden had to borrow, that is, sell bonds, in order to maintain unemployment benefits.

---

[4]Labour, 287 seats; Conservatives, 261 seats; Liberals, 59 seats.

A middle-class victim of unemployment in Britain, 1930.

I KNOW 3 TRADES
I SPEAK 3 LANGUAGES
FOUGHT FOR 3 YEARS
HAVE 3 CHILDREN
AND NO WORK FOR
3 MONTHS
BUT I ONLY WANT
ONE JOB

© Hulton Pictures Library

The banking crisis in London in July 1931 fed on the lack of confidence that bankers and investors felt for a Labour government. They brought pressure on the government to reduce unemployment benefits in order to keep the budget in balance. When the Bank of England sought to stem the run on the pound by borrowing from Paris and New York, the American investment firm of J. P. Morgan and Company replied that it could not lend any more to the Bank of England unless the Labour government cut its expenditures.

Morgan's answer on August 23 put the choice very clearly between those measures that would improve domestic living standards and those that would save the pound. Saving the pound meant cutting unemployment relief. MacDonald and Snowden accepted the classical diagnosis and prepared a 10 percent cut in the "dole." About half the cabinet refused to go along, however, and the second and last interwar Labour government resigned on August 24.

It was replaced by the National Government (1931–1935), a nonparty coalition of leading individuals joined to remedy the depression crisis by deflation. Ramsay MacDonald retained the post of prime minister, flanked now by Conservative leader Stanley Baldwin. Labour opinion thereafter regarded "Gentleman Mac" as a traitor, along with Philip Snowden, who also remained in the cabinet.

Investors and speculators continued to sell pounds for gold, despite the cut in relief. Indeed, the government's efforts to reduce costs only made things worse. Sailors demonstrated against pay cuts in the British home fleet at Invergordon, Scotland, in what became known as the "Invergordon Mutiny." Because "mutiny" in the British fleet sounded like Gibraltar sinking, the run on the pound became an unstemmable flood. On September 19, 1931, the National Government took Britain off the international gold standard. Individuals were no longer permitted to buy gold for pounds. Furthermore, the pound was allowed to sink about a third in international exchange value.

The National Government's backing now became frankly conservative. The elections of October 27, 1931, gave the Tories over 60 percent of the vote, the highest majority in British electoral history, and ushered in an era of Conservative predominance that was to last until 1945.

Having lost its battle to save the pound on the world market, the National Government might have been expected to take bold action to stimulate employment, but it did not. Devaluation of the pound, of course, made British goods cheaper on the world market for a time. Housing construction was spurred by lower costs and by Labour's Wheatley Act of 1924 and a slum clearance act of the 1930s. Several very advanced steel mills were also constructed in this period. By and large, however, the National Government followed a policy of protectionism and cutting back production. Protective tariffs, defeated so roundly at the polls in the 1920s, became government policy for the first time in peacetime in nearly a century. The Import Duties Act of 1932 imposed a 10 percent duty on all goods except those produced in the empire ("imperial preference") and a few free items. Factory owners were allowed to replace competition with planned production levels in order to keep prices up. The Labour government had already accepted this expedient for the outdated and vastly overextended British coal industry; under the National Government, restrictive practices became generalized in other ailing traditional industries such as shipbuilding and iron and steel.

Thus the British economy slowly revived in the 1930s more by a gradual turn in the business cycle, aided by devaluation and de facto cartelization, than by any significant rise in purchasing power or employment.

In retrospect, the existing British party structure simply failed to provide alternatives to classical depression remedies. Those few people with theoretical or practical alternatives to offer were outsiders. Sir Oswald Mosley, a wealthy thirty-three-year-old convert to Labour who had a minor office but major ambitions in the Labour cabinet, produced a memorandum in the spring of 1930 that attracted attention in the party left.

Mosley assigned first priority to alleviating unemployment and then let other policy matters fall into place around a "living wage policy." Unemployment would be ended by increasing purchasing power, permitting earlier retirement on good pensions, and forcing up productivity. This required public planning and management of production, as well as deficit spending. Those departures from accepted government practice would shock investors and speculators, of course, so the British economy would have to be insulated from international financial pressures; that is, it must be national rather than international. These heresies left older and more orthodox Labour leaders like Chancellor of the Exchequer Snowden aghast. Mosley's rejection by Labour leaders in 1930 points up the inability of that generation to tear itself free from the perspectives of liberal economists.

The better-known outsider was John Maynard Keynes. When the depression struck, the Cambridge economist was only beginning to refine his new doctrine,

Sharp divisions in social class were evident during the depression years. Here, local boys watch two Eton students outside Lords cricket grounds in London at the 1937 Eton v. Harrow match.

which was published in 1936 as *General Theory of Employment, Interest, and Money.* Keynes, too, gave top priority at this point in his life to a solution to unemployment. But unlike that impatient pragmatist Mosely, Keynes's major contribution was to provide a whole new theoretical framework within which to refute classical remedies. The orthodox looked on unemployment as the result of overproduction; from such a perspective, raising wages would only make conditions worse. Keynes argued that the level of unemployment depended on insufficient demand. Demand could be increased by increasing the money supply, stimulating production by public works, and making society's distribution of wealth more equal. Such policies, of course, demanded two things: accurate data and a high level of government intervention. Keynes pioneered in the calculation of aggregate demand, which once known, could be influenced. Keynes's impact was destined to be overwhelming on the Second World War generation; it was minimal during the depression.

Still other outsiders advocated the nationalization of all or part of British productive capacity. Some of them, like G. D. H. Cole, an Oxford professor of politics and historian of the labor movement, were on the intellectual fringes of the Labour Party. The intellectuals had little influence, however, with the Labour Party leadership or with the rank and file, mostly trade union members.

In short, none of the advocates of planning or nationalization had any organized political force behind them. The intellectual perspectives of those who had such force—Labour, Liberal, and Conservative—allowed them to contemplate no way of dealing with the depression except to let the economy revive by itself, which it began to do by the end of 1934.

France

The depression came late to France. For the first two years, Paris remained a haven for gold, which had fled from German and British banking systems. French social commentators praised their country's cautious, small firms and numerous independent peasants who had avoided the boom and bust of more dynamic economies. By 1932, however, the French economy had settled into a deep slump that then lasted longer than elsewhere. Even in 1938, French production was not back to 1929 levels.

The depression was never the cataclysm in France that it was elsewhere. There was no spectacular run on the franc, no awesome crash of world role as in the British devaluation of 1931; the regime was not swept away as it was in Germany. Official unemployment figures never exceeded about 600,000. That figure greatly understated the reality, however, for it did not reflect the many Frenchmen underemployed on family farms or in small shops. In any case, the depression in France was more a slow, demoralizing rot than a major upheaval.

Several conditions made it worse than it might have been. French public opinion resisted with a passion any governmental tampering with the international value of the franc. Even within classical economics, a timely devaluation of the franc would have helped stimulate exports. But French small savers and investors had been so traumatized by the inflation of 1924 to 1928 that they clung fervently to the Poincaré franc. Most French politicians declined to incur public wrath by touching it in the 1930s. That devaluation in a depression was altogether different from inflation made no difference to public opinion.

More adventurous economic policies were even farther than devaluation from political feasibility. There was no possible majority support for projects of job creation or economic planning. Most French socialists rejected planning under existing property relationships as a mere prop to capitalism and an authoritarian step backward. Only a minority of socialists were more interested in reviving production than in equalizing distribution in the economy; they recognized that planning required working within a national framework insulated from the world economy by tariffs and currency control. Some of these minority socialists seceded to form a new "neosocialist party" in 1933, whose most conspicuous leader was Marcel Déat. Déat, like Oswald Mosley, was to follow the implications of his heresy all the way to national socialism.

On the right, among businessmen, industrialists, high civil servants, and professors of law, there was great enthusiasm for corporatism. But it was the center-left that won both the 1932 and 1936 elections. And even though the Radical Party drifted back toward the center after elections, especially on economic issues, the

Radicals did not support the corporatists' proposal that organized business regulate the economy. Like the small peasants and shopkeepers whom they represented, the Radicals believed only in applying their personal economic values of thrift and prudence to the state: Spend no more than you take in, and put the savings in a sock. Thus the French Third Republic dealt with the depression by a policy of budget cutting and deflation.

Governmental instability tended to compound the effects of the depression. As in the inflation years of the mid-1920s, economic emergency made the French party system incoherent. The parliamentary elections of 1932 were won by a center-left coalition similar to the *cartel des gauches* of 1924 (Radicals, Socialists, and smaller reformist parties). Once again the two main partners—Radicals and Socialists— found their incompatibilities widened by an economic challenge. It had been effective during the election to stress unifying issues like Catholic and military threats to the republic. But as the depression deepened after 1932, divisive matters such as tax increases or regulation of foreign exchange were brought to the top of the agenda.

The premier who emerged from the electoral victory of 1932 was that stalwart leader of the French Radical Party, Edouard Herriot.[5] Herriot was thrust into a situation for which his literary background and parliamentary skills had not prepared him. French investors and speculators, prejudiced against even a moderate left government, sold francs for gold in expectation of a decline in the international value of the franc. It was a self-fulfilling prophecy; the franc declined after 1933. Unwilling to invoke exchange controls, Herriot could do little but try to balance the budget and to display confidence by continuing to pay war debts to the United States. That gesture cost him his parliamentary majority. Herriot was followed by five governments in the next fourteen months. Meanwhile, the economy drifted downward.

By 1934, the Radicals had drawn away from their Socialist election partners over economic policy, and a Radical-Center coalition was the only possible majority. Premier Pierre Laval (June 1935–January 1936) vigorously applied deflationary measures during this period. Laval was an innkeeper's son from the southern hill country of the Auvergne who had worked his way up by combining politics, business, and a law practice. After winning his first major case, the defense of some workmen charged with blowing up a power line, Laval won election to parliament from a Paris suburb as a Socialist. Once in politics, however, he gravitated to the center and became wealthy by canny investments helped along, it was suspected, by political influence.

Laval had the superb self-confidence of a self-made man, without any economic knowledge. Deciding that the budget had to be balanced in a declining economy, Laval ruthlessly cut wages paid by the state by 10 percent and tried to roll back wages paid by private industry. To ease the wage earners' lot, he also tried to reduce rents and prices. But although Laval deserved very high marks for vigor, he earned low marks for results. The deflationary remedy of 1935 further slowed the French economy at a time when other countries were beginning to revive. It also swung the electorate sharply to the left for the elections of 1936.

[5]See chapter 8, pp. 237–238.

The elections of May 1936 brought to power the Popular Front, an electoral coalition of the left that included the Communist Party for the first time in French history, as well as those more habitual electoral allies, the Radicals and Socialists. Because the startling innovation of Communist participation in reformist parliamentary politics resulted more from Stalin's desire for alliances against Hitler than from the depression, the Popular Front is discussed more fully in a subsequent chapter on the antifascist alliances of the 1930s.[6] But Premier Léon Blum (June 1936–June 1937) must be included in this consideration of depression politics, for of all Western European parliamentary leaders he made the boldest attempt to find an alternative to deflation within the context of a middle-class democracy. Reversing the wage-cutting of his predecessors, Blum tried to remedy the depression by an increase in general purchasing power.

Leader of the French Socialist Party (SFIO) since 1920, Léon Blum became premier of France in 1936 in an atmosphere of mingled jubilation and panic. The Popular Front's electoral victory was accompanied by the most massive work stoppage between the strike waves of 1919–1920 and 1947–1948, a general strike surpassed only once in French history, in May and June 1968. In retrospect, we know that the workmen and department store clerks who occupied the premises and sometimes danced in them were celebrating Blum's victory. The strikes were a grassroots release of steam after years of pent-up resentment at deflationary wage cuts; they were not a concerted effort to expropriate property. Trade union leaders struggled to channel the movement into traditional wages and hours negotiations. At the time, however, it looked very much like revolution to French conservatives already unsettled at the prospect of France's first Jewish socialist premier.

The crisis atmosphere helped Blum accomplish major changes quickly. The terrified French manufacturers' association turned to Blum as to their only port in the storm. In an all-night session at his official residence, Blum brought the manufacturers' association and the trade union leaders together on a settlement providing raises of up to 15 percent, as well as belated recognition by employers of workers' rights to join unions without being fired and of the right of unions to negotiate collective contracts on behalf of their members. In the next few days, Blum pushed through parliament a forty-hour week and two-week vacations with pay for all salaried employees except those of the smallest shops. Finally, he increased public spending, including armaments.

In other ways, the crisis atmosphere made the Popular Front's economic life more difficult. French savers and investors had learned under the *cartel des gauches* in 1924 and 1925 to associate leftist governments with financial instability. They were especially adamant against a devaluation of the franc, a perfectly orthodox measure that would have stimulated French exports. Even though Blum promised publicly not to devalue or impose exchange controls and tried not to alarm the business community, large-scale speculation against the franc set in. Eventually, the government was forced to devalue under heavy international pressure. Blum thus lost middle-class support at home without gaining any of the trade benefits that an early voluntary devaluation might have achieved.

[6]See chapter 12, pp. 362–368.

In the end, Blum's government did not succeed in reviving the depressed French economy. The forty-hour week, designed in part to spread employment more widely, was interpreted rigidly to mean that plants operated only one forty-hour shift each week. Wages were raised more for social reasons than as a Keynesian increase in purchasing power, and inflation soon reduced their capacity to stimulate declining demand. By 1938, French industrial production was still below that of 1929.

Weimar Germany

The depression swept the British Labour Party out of power until 1945, and it reduced the French Third Republic to its weakest and most divided condition since its founding. In Germany, the depression brought the whole Weimar Republic down.

The German republic had entered the crisis with a socialist chancellor, Hermann Müller, an old trade union leader from the prewar years. Müller had governed since 1928 at the head of the Great Coalition, a broad alliance of no fewer than five parties that accepted the republic, ranging from moderate right to moderate left. It now took five parties to constitute a parliamentary majority. No coherent socialist majority was possible as long as Social Democrats and Communists continued to be so bitterly divided by the split of 1914 to 1917; and no coherent conservative majority was possible while the nationalist parties rejected the very idea of a republic and even partial "fulfillment" of the Versailles settlement.

As long as the major issues remained foreign policy and the survival of the republic, the Great Coalition could find reason to cooperate in a program of international "fulfillment." When the central issues became economic, there was no common ground. The appearance of urgent economic issues in late 1929 pulled the Great Coalition's majority apart.

The precise issue on which the Great Coalition splintered was a classic example of depression alternatives: Should unemployment benefits be reduced in order to balance the budget? Or should they be maintained or increased in order to keep up purchasing power? The economic decline of late 1929 hit Germany quickly and sharply, and the fund for unemployment benefits was soon exhausted. The options were to support unemployment benefits from other government sources (such as the *Osthilfe*, the relief fund for Prussian agriculture), or to raise more taxes, or to reduce unemployment benefits. The first two of these options were politically impossible: President Hindenburg was deeply committed to the *Osthilfe*, and the German people would not support a tax increase. When the German government approached the New York investment bank of Dillon, Read for a loan to cover immediate governing expenses, they were told that American lenders could have no confidence in a government that did not balance its budget. Since the German economy desperately needed to reassure its American creditors (who were withdrawing funds anyway in the aftermath of the crash in New York), the government decided to balance the budget by reducing unemployment benefits. This decision angered the German trade unions, which forced the Social Democratic deputies to withdraw their support from the government. Müller's government resigned on March 27, 1930. One could argue that the Weimar Republic's parliamentary system actually ceased to function at that point. Henceforth there was no way to build a majority around any one depression remedy: deficit spending or classical budget-balancing.

For nearly the next three years, Germany was governed without any parliamentary majority. President Hindenburg used the authority granted by the Weimar Constitution (Article 48) to govern by decree in case of emergency. During most of that time (March 1930–June 1932), Hindenburg conferred his powers on Heinrich Brüning as chancellor.

Brüning was a Catholic Center Party politician who had served as executive secretary to the German Catholic trade union organization. That administrative experience commended him to Hindenburg, as did Brüning's reserve officer commission. For over two years the cold, precise administrator was able to persuade the aged field marshal to legitimize his actions by use of Article 48.

Brüning, who never doubted the validity of classical economic liberalism, used presidential powers for two interlocking policies. First, he attempted to cure the domestic economic crisis by deflation: He took vigorous government action to cut prices, wages, and state expenditure in order to stem the flight of foreign capital from Germany. A series of decrees cut civil servants' salaries by 12 to 16 percent, reduced unemployment benefits twice, and ordered wages lowered to the level of January 1, 1927. Although Brüning tried to compensate by ordering a lowering of rents and prices, it was of course easier for the government to roll back wages than prices. He was hated afterward as the "hunger chancellor."

The second half of Brüning's strategy was dramatic foreign success. Since deflation was painful to all except creditors, the chancellor hoped to assuage public discontent and undercut rising nationalist competition by bringing off two striking diplomatic moves. He planned a customs union with Austria (a country forbidden by the Versailles settlement to form any kind of political tie with Germany), and he campaigned for German parity in armaments.

The net result of Brüning's twin strategy was the opposite of his hopes. The vigorous government deflationary efforts only accentuated the economic downturn. Unemployment figures soared until they reached 6 million in 1932. Abroad, both of his grandstand plays were frustrated. France, in what was to be its last vigorous defense of the Versailles terms, fought the Austro-German customs union as a violation of the treaty. The Bank of France brought pressure to bear by withholding assistance to Viennese banks, thereby helping to permit the collapse of the *Credit-Anstalt* in May 1931 and setting off the European banking crisis.[7] Nor would France hear of arms parity for Germany just at the moment when the European disarmament conference was about to open.

Without dramatic foreign successes, Brüning was more and more dependent on presidential decree powers to carry out an unpopular domestic policy. Nevertheless, he hoped to return from presidential to parliamentary government. Strongly

---

[7] It is no longer certain that the French actually made things worse by withdrawing funds from the *Credit-Anstalt,* as is usually charged.

antisocialist, Brüning saw more hope in wooing the nationalists (including the growing National Socialists) into a new parliamentary majority than in trying to revive a Great Coalition that included the Social Democrats.

Believing a new nationalist majority could be elected, Brüning dissolved the dormant *Reichstag* in September 1930 and called for new elections. The result made parliamentary government even less possible. The anger and frustration generated by the depression had strongly polarized the electorate. The Nazi Party was the most spectacular gainer, jumping from 12 seats to 107. Communists also gained, at the expense of Social Democrats. Except for Brüning's own Catholic Center Party, all the moderate and liberal parties lost to the extremes. Most disquieting of all, Nazism and communism were particularly attractive to new and young voters. Brüning had proven that the Weimar Constitution was incapable, even under presidential emergency authority, of success either at home or abroad.

Brüning himself, a stiff, formal man in public, was incapable of building a following. The British novelist Christopher Isherwood has described the chancellor at a public meeting:

> His gestures were sharp and admonitory; his spectacles gleamed emotion in the limelight. His voice quivered with dry academic passion.[8]

"Every week," wrote Isherwood, "there were new emergency decrees. Brüning's weary episcopal voice issued commands to the shopkeepers and was not obeyed."[9] In June 1932, President Hindenburg, at the age of eighty-three, easily influenced by gossip from his immediate associates, abruptly withdrew his support from Brüning, whom he now suddenly suspected of dangerous radicalism because the chancellor wished to investigate reported fraud in the administration of agricultural relief (*Osthilfe*) funds.

Baron Franz von Papen, a Catholic aristocrat with close friends in the president's own circle, became the new chancellor. Papen's efforts to appropriate the Nazi following belong to the next chapter. Under Papen, however, the Weimar Republic unquestionably became an authoritarian state without pretense of constitutional rule. Parliamentary government in Germany was destroyed by its inability to deal with the depression several years before Hitler came to power.

DEPRESSION POLITICS IN THE AUTHORITARIAN STATES

Nazi Germany

After Adolf Hitler assumed power in Germany in January 1933,[10] the new Nazi regime adopted economic policies totally different from the deflation of Brüning. The results seemed nothing less than a miracle. Germany was transformed from the

---

[8]Christopher Isherwood, *Berlin Stories* (London, 1935), p. 85.

[9]Ibid., p. 88.

[10]Hitler's assumption of power and his new regime are treated in chapter 11, pp. 324–335.

country hardest hit by the depression in 1932 to the frightening giant of 1938. Unemployment dropped from 6 million in 1932 to 164,000 by 1936. After 1936, Germany imported foreign workers to fill a labor shortage.

This economic "miracle" was accomplished by policies as far removed from the return-to-the-soil jargon of Nazi intellectuals as they were from the nostrums of classical liberalism. There were basically three interrelated steps: Vast deficit spending on public works stimulated employment; the ensuing inflation then required state control of prices and wages; and the German economy had to be sealed off from the world banking and monetary system to insulate the mark from international speculation. Hjalmar Schacht, who had restored the German currency on neoliberal lines in 1923 and 1924, now adjusted his thinking to become chief financial and economic planner of a managed economy closer to the economic control of the First World War than to any liberal model.

The first step required a great surge of government expenditure. Since rearmament was still theoretically forbidden by the Treaty of Versailles, the most conspicuous early project was a network of four-lane superhighways, the *Autobahnen*. After open rearmament began in 1935, military spending rose to 60 percent of the budget by 1938, or 21 percent of the gross national product.[11]

In a free-market situation, this full-throttle rearmament would have triggered another inflation. Building on the precedents of the war, the government organized all branches of industry and agriculture into cartels, set prices, regulated wages through officials of the Labor Ministry (trustees of labor), and allocated raw materials. Owners were no longer free to make individual business decisions, but to many that seemed a small price to pay for order and prosperity. Furthermore, labor unions were dissolved and wage disputes handled by civil servants.

A major obstacle to such measures in a liberal economy was their expected impact on the international value of the country's currency and on foreign trade. The Nazi solution was autarky, or economic self-sufficiency. Trade had fallen sharply anyway as a result of the depression, and the partisans of autarky were happy to leave exports at less than half and imports at little more than a third of the 1928 level, even in 1938.[12] The German economy was supposed to become self-sufficient in agriculture and invent synthetic substitutes for materials it could not produce.

Major steps toward isolating the German economy were taken in 1936 with the announcement of a Four-Year Plan. Schacht, who wanted to expand foreign trade now that the economy was reviving, lost control over economic policy to Hermann Göring, head of the Plan. The Reich began to produce several very expensive synthetics: Buna, which cost seven times as much as natural rubber, and synthetic oil. Steel was also produced expensively with low-quality ore in the Hermann Göring Works.

---

[11]These rates of military spending were comparable to those of the United States in the late 1960s, but they were unprecedented in peacetime before the 1930s.

[12]Willi A. Boelcke, *Deutschland als Welthandelsmacht* (Stuttgart, Germany, 1994), p. 37.

The dynamism of the German economy by 1938 was an object of fear and wonder in the struggling liberal countries. Unlike them, Germany had full employment, growth, and stability—at the price of individual liberties. It had smashed trade unions and organized the economy into cartels. As in liberal capitalism, owners of farms and factories continued to own them, although they had renounced some liberty of economic decision (including the unwanted liberty to make wrong economic decisions). Unlike the situation in liberal capitalism, however, the owners were subject to a planned and managed economy, in which they contended with civil servants for predominance. Some observers tended to lump this experiment with communism as two faces of a single totalitarianism, but it must be remembered that in Hitler's Germany there was no expropriation of owners of farms and factories.

Who profited from the new German dynamism? By 1938, the real purchasing power of German wage earners had risen to the levels of 1913 and 1929, years of maximum pre-Nazi prosperity. Deprived of the strike weapon, however, German workers failed to keep pace with the enormous growth in national production. Compared with 1929, wages and salaries made up a smaller share of the national income; profits in trade and industry a larger share.[13] Even so, after the Weimar nightmare, most German wage earners were reconciled by full employment and nationalist excitement.

Small farmers and the middle class, who had supported the Nazis most enthusiastically, continued their long, slow decline compared with bigger enterprises. Production was oriented away from consumer goods, and savings were funneled off into the great projects of the regime. For example, small savers poured 285 million marks into advance down payments on Ferdinand Porsche's brilliantly designed cheap "peoples' car," only to find when Volkswagens began to roll off the assembly line in 1939 that they all went to the army. But most middle-class Germans were too enthusiastic over the destruction of socialism and over revived German power to object.

Big business leaders grumbled at having to share the costs of such expensive projects as the Hermann Göring steel mill, and some great speculative fortunes were lost. Big armaments concerns like Krupp steel and *I. G. Farben* chemicals, into whose growth the nation's energies and savings were channeled, were clearly the principal gainers from the Nazi economic miracle.

The most important decisions affecting the Nazi economic system were not taken solely on their economic merits, however. The political aims of the regime took precedence over mere economic efficacy. The decision to seek autarky was motivated in large part by the desire to overcome the material shortages that had condemned the German Empire during the war. That decision forced the German people to pay for expensive substitutes and to consume lower quality goods (such as ersatz coffee). The drive for autarky made territorial expansion more attractive for the Nazi leaders, who coveted the wheat and oil of Eastern Europe, but did not want to depend on trade to get them. For those political aims the German people were eventually to pay very dearly indeed.

---

[13]Harold James, *The German Slump: Politics and Economics, 1924–1936* (Oxford, England, 1986), p. 416.

Corporatist Italy

Despite the serious difficulties of modern industry in the north of Italy, the depression gave the appearance of being less cataclysmic in Italy than in other countries. Unemployment was easily concealed in Italy's backward south and in its numerous small shops. Immense publicity was given to "progressive" projects like the draining of the Pontine Marshes for settlement,[14] and to the famous trains that ran on time. And Italy seemed to be free of social discontent. The system that was alleged to produce these combined boons of progress, efficiency, and order was called corporatism. Since corporatism was widely praised and imitated in the 1930s, it deserves more than passing mention here.

Corporatism was not Mussolini's idea. Intellectually, it derived from several attempts in the late nineteenth century to discover a solution to worker misery that would be neither liberal nor Marxist. Catholic social thinkers made one such attempt. They contrasted the atomized city world, easily whipped up into artificial class alignments by demagogues, with an organic society in which natural groupings, such as families, villages, or crafts, lived and worked in harmony. Pope Leo XIII's encyclical *Rerum Novarum* (1891) castigated liberal capitalism for its impersonal economic ties and its heartless exploitation, proposing instead the application of Christian charity to the economy and a revival of organic social groups.

Another intellectual root was syndicalism, the revolutionary labor union movement that was powerful in southern Europe. The syndicalists' basic unit of action was the *syndicat,* or labor union, organized by factory or village rather than by craft or skill. When the "great day" of the revolutionary general strike came, each *syndicat* would simply seize its factory or village. Together they would abolish the state. Thereafter, the workers would run things themselves, with the *syndicats* as the only remaining organizations in a free society.

Despite their profound differences, Catholic organic social thought and revolutionary syndicalism had some elements in common. Both distrusted parliamentary and electoral action; both preferred local "natural" groupings to the centralized bureaucratic state. People from both traditions would be able to cooperate in an anti-Marxist, antiparliamentarian reconstruction of the social order.

Corporatism had pragmatic roots as well as intellectual ones. Cartels were widely used in highly concentrated industries for bringing a whole branch of production together to limit free competition in the marketplace. The experience of managed economies during the war, although too bureaucratic for most industrialists' tastes in good times, revealed the possibilities of regulation as a remedy for distorted economies in bad times.

Drawing from all these sources, corporatists proposed to regroup each branch of industry, agriculture, and commerce in its own syndicate, or corporation. Each of these could then regulate its own affairs: allocating resources, dividing up the market, rationalizing production, and replacing the liberal free market with planned, managed economic activity. The main questions, of course, were who would run the corporations and whom their decisions would favor. The answers to those questions were not immediately apparent when Mussolini assumed office in 1922.

---

[14]Only 19,000 families were actually settled there.

One of Mussolini's first associates was the former syndicalist Edmondo Rossoni, an IWW (International Workers of the World) organizer among Italian immigrants in New Jersey before he joined Mussolini. Rossoni began to apply corporatism as a form of updated syndicalism: Workers and managers would cooperate in the new corporations around a goal of higher productivity. Expanded production, rather than a revolutionary redistribution of property, now seemed to Rossoni the solution to poverty. Businessmen could agree with that, but they were alarmed by the way Rossoni promised a direct role in economic management to active Fascist worker associations. By 1928 Mussolini had removed Rossoni from influence.

Businessmen and big landowners had contributed money to Mussolini, and the *Duce* had apparently promised a group of industrialists headed by Alberto Pirelli, the tire manufacturer, before the March on Rome in 1922 that he meant to "reestablish discipline particularly within the factories and that no outlandish experiments would be carried out."[15] By the late 1920s it was clear that Mussolini intended to develop the same kind of pragmatic working relations with industrial and agricultural leaders as he was establishing with other traditional Italian power blocs, including king, army, and pope. The Fascist regime talked less and less of corporatism while quietly shifting economic influence from Fascist ideologues like Rossoni and from state agencies to the Italian businessmen's association, the General Confederation of Italian Industry (CGII).

When Italian businesses began to suffer after 1929, however, Mussolini devised on paper a system of economic organization that was called "corporatist" for public effect. A National Council of Corporations was set up in 1930, within which twenty-two different branches of industry and trade were organized into "corporations" by 1934. In 1939, the lower house of the Chamber of Deputies was transformed into a Chamber of Corporations, designed to transfer representation from the discredited liberal system of elected citizens to spokesmen for "organic" economic interests. Although Fascist propaganda boasted about its harmonization of "natural" interests within corporatism, the whole machinery was in fact staffed by the CGII. Workers were not only excluded from these organizations but also had long since lost the right to strike.

The most lasting monument to what corporatism meant in practice in fascist Italy was the IRI (Institute for Industrial Reconstruction). When some important Italian businesses approached bankruptcy as the depression worsened, the IRI was established in January 1933 to lend them money. By the time the IRI was made permanent in 1937, the government's loans had evolved into a controlling interest in Italian steel, heavy machinery, shipping, electricity, and telephones. In this way, the Fascist regime rescued unprofitable sectors of the Italian economy by what amounted to partial nationalization. Even then, however, civil servants had little role in so-called corporatism. Organized business continued to manage the cartelized economy very much on its own terms. Wages remained low, and production failed to gain very much. Fascism permitted Italian businessmen to ride out the depression freed from meddling bureaucracy, independent trade unions, and responsibility for unprofitable sectors of the economy.

[15]Roland Sarti, *Fascism and the Industrial Leadership in Italy, 1919–1940* (Berkeley, Calif., 1971), p. 37.

The Soviet Union's "Second Revolution"

By 1927, the Bukharin policy of slow, steady economic growth based on the productivity of a satisfied small peasantry had yielded disappointing results.[16] The disruptions of war Communism and the Civil War and the division of farms into small plots lowered output. Russia's peasants produced mostly for themselves. The world's first socialist state was in danger of becoming economically becalmed in a sea of 25 million small family farms. Now all-powerful at the head of the Russian Communist Party and freed from the left opposition of the earlier 1920s, Stalin turned on Bukharin in December 1927 and adopted the left's economic policy of stimulating industry through the profits extracted from collectivized farms.

Stalin's first intention was to collectivize only the lands of the wealthier kulaks, the larger farmers who employed wage labor and accounted for perhaps 14 percent of Russia's farms. Their collectivization was widely resisted, however. Whole rural communities, including the poorest peasants, responded with the traditional weapons of hoarding crops and slaughtering livestock. In reaction to this unexpectedly strong resistance, and convinced by the Wall Street crash that the era of "capitalist stabilization" had ended, Stalin and his party bureaucracy sharply escalated their program. Close to half of all peasant households—10 million families—were forced into collectives by March 1930. When agricultural production subsequently plummeted, Stalin called a temporary halt on the grounds that Russia was "dizzy with success," but there was no way to proceed but forward. By 1934, Russia's 25 million family farms had been combined into 250,000 collectives. Not only was grain production far lower than in 1928, but the slaughter of livestock was so widespread that 1928 levels in meat production were recovered only in the 1950s, a quarter century later. Stalin himself admitted years later to British Prime Minister Winston Churchill that 10 million peasants died in the artificially imposed famine of 1932 and 1933,[17] and the figure may have been higher.

As a companion piece to the collectivization of farms, Stalin launched the First Five-year Plan to stimulate Soviet industrial production. The First Five-Year Plan, to run from October 1928 through 1933, was the most important internal decision of Stalin's career. It was a virtual economic revolution, this time from above, and it sealed Russia off from the world economy in an effort to build "socialism in one country." Since the wealth necessary for a crash program of industrial investment could come only from expropriating a resisting peasantry, the plan engendered a far harsher authoritarian control than anything seen in the relatively open mid-1920s. The Soviet example offered rapid industrial growth and full employment at a time when capitalist Europe could offer neither, but it did so at the price of renewed starvation, tens of millions of deaths, and eventually an unspeakably harsh system of labor camps and political purges.

The economic changes in Russia after 1929 constituted a more profound revolution than that of 1917. The ancient ways of Russian village life, where the vast bulk of the population still lived, were completely transformed. The Soviet Union was on

---

[16]See chapter 8, pp. 256, 258.

[17]Winston Churchill, *History of the Second World War: The Hinge of Fate* (London, 1950), p. 498.

Illustrated London News Picture Library

A group of kulaks (peasants prosperous enough to employ others) is deported from a Russian village during the first stages of land collectivization, 1930. The banners read, "The kulak class must be eliminated."

its way to becoming an urban, industrial nation within one generation. It is incorrect to suppose that Russia had no significant industry before the five-year plans began; Russia ranked fifth in gross national product in 1929. Just twenty years later, however, it stood second, behind only the United States. The wealth skimmed off the land by requisition from the rural collectives was poured into the construction of factories, dams, and entire new cities. By 1937, heavy industrial production had increased by three to six times (depending on whose statistics are used) since 1928. A new city such as Magnitogorsk could grow from a population of zero to 250,000 in a few years. The Soviet Union advanced from fifteenth to third place in the production of electrical power during the time of the first three five-year plans (1928–1941). Regardless of whether one accepts the Soviet figures of an annual growth rate of 20 percent a year in overall production, or the more cautious Western figures of 14 percent a year, the effects were astonishing to a world sunk in depression.

Stalin's "great change" was possible only because the party bureaucracy had been strengthened under his sole command. That iron rule was made even more necessary by the chaos that accompanied forced collectivization and the discipline needed in new industry. Factory workers were no longer permitted to change jobs. A regime of low wages, speeded-up production, and steeply differentiated piece rates in industry was sweetened by propaganda and praise for sacrifice for the new socialist state. Aleksei Stakhanov, a coal miner in the Donetz Basin who exceeded his quota by 1,400 percent in 1935, became a model for other workers to emulate. "Stakhanovites" were paid in praise rather than in consumer goods, however, and the Soviet economy under the five-year plans bore no relation to a consumer economy on Keynesian lines.

The rigors of forced collectivization and industrialization were harsh enough in themselves. Even harsher was the treatment of peasant resisters, industrial misfits, and political opponents, who swelled the populations of forced labor camps in Siberia in the early 1930s. But the worst was yet to come in the great purges of 1936 to 1938, a product of Stalin's own paranoid temperament coupled with his drive for sole control of decision making.

Until 1934, the weight of political repression had fallen on old tsarist personnel and those who obstructed the new course. On December 1, 1934, the Communist Party secretary in Leningrad, Sergei Kirov, was assassinated, and the left opposition was officially accused of the act. Revelations in the de-Stalinization speech by Nikita Khrushchev in 1956 make it appear that Stalin himself may have arranged Kirov's execution in order to remove a rival. What is certain is that the assassination was followed by an ascending spiral of denunciations and arrests as virtually the entire remaining Old Bolshevik leadership, as well as all those suspected of supporting it, was decimated. The most astonishing aspect of the great purge was the series of show trials in which many Bolshevik leaders confessed to various crimes of treason before being shot. The left opposition leaders Kamenev and Zinoviev were tried in 1936; sixteen other eminent Bolsheviks in 1937, including Marshal Mikhail Tukhachevsky, who had defeated the Poles in 1920; and another twenty-one, including Bukharin, in 1938.

At lower levels an orgy of denunciation and spy-mania engulfed the party, the state apparatus, and ordinary citizens. The purge was particularly severe among senior army officers, diplomats, and others who could be shown to have had foreign contacts (including contacts with foreign communists). It is likely that 7 million Russians, including many party members, perished in the great purge. Twenty million more joined that world of prisoners and outcasts that the novelist Aleksandr Solzhenitsyn (who was later one of them) described as "the mysterious and terrible country of 'Gulag' . . . with its own social system, its written and unwritten laws, its population, its customs, its rulers, and its subjects."[18]

The poisoning of Soviet Russian life by the purges of the late 1930s has aroused passionate controversy. For some sympathetic Western observers at the time, the Old Bolsheviks' confessions proved that the Soviet experiment was indeed under fascist and capitalist attack and was forced to depart from judicial norms in order to protect itself. It seems likely today that the confessions were extorted, if not by physical torture, at least by promises to spare the wives and children of the accused. Other Western observers concluded that despotism had always been inherent in Lenin's concept of a vanguard party exercising dictatorship in the name of a backward proletariat. Still other Westerners, such as George Kennan, attributed the purges to Stalin's own paranoia.

---

[18]Aleksandr Solzhenitsyn, *The Gulag Archipelago, 1918–1956,* trans. Thomas P. Whitney (New York, 1974); Robert Conquest, *The Great Terror: A Reassessment* (New York, 1990), p. 487.

The most interesting debate about Stalinist rule broke out within the Soviet Union. Nikita Khrushchev opened a Pandora's box of criticisms of Stalin at the Twentieth Party Congress in 1956. The Soviet historian Roy Medvedev argued that Lenin's imperfect but promising beginning was perverted by Stalinism, a personal aberration that built on elements present in party rule but which was not inevitable. Solzhenitsyn came to believe that Lenin had erred fatally in trying to create socialism in an underindustrialized country, and that Stalin simply "followed in Lenin's footsteps."[19]

Whatever its proper explanation, the Stalinist blood bath made the Soviet economic achievement considerably less attractive after 1936. The British Labour Party intellectuals Beatrice and Sidney Webb had referred to the Soviet Union in 1935 as "a new civilization." Another Western journalist called the 1930s Russia's "iron age."[20] It was that, in two senses of the term: an extraordinary achievement in heavy industrial production and a descent into barbarism.

CONCLUSION

Governments dealt with the challenges of the depression with widely varying success. The authoritarian regimes expanded their industrial power and kept order despite low wages. The liberal regimes sank ever deeper into unemployment as they tried deflation and lapsed into internal social conflict. Liberal politics and liberal economics were completely discredited. From the vantage point of the bread lines and soup kitchens of London, Paris, or republican Berlin, either communist Russia or fascist Italy looked like greener pastures, according to one's predilection. Then when Nazi Germany grew into the industrial and military giant of the Continent by the mid-1930s, the comparative impression of decadent liberalism and burgeoning authoritarianism grew even stronger.

The British novelist E. M. Forster later summed up the air of doubt and lassitude felt in the major liberal states with the title of his volume of essays, *Two Cheers for Democracy*. The liberal states were deprived by their depression remedies of both the material and moral means and the will to oppose the dictators resolutely. In the 1930s, fascism seemed the wave of the future.

SUGGESTIONS FOR FURTHER READING

David C. Large, *Between Two Fires: Europe's Path in the 1930s** (1991), is a lively narrative relevant to chapters 10–14. Charles H. Feinstein et al., *The European Economy Between the Wars** (1997), provides the best new introduction, with an excellent guide to more specialized reading. Patricia Clavin, *The Great Depression in Europe, 1929–1939** (2001) is clear and nontechnical. Barry Eichengreen, *Golden Fetters: The Gold Standard and the Great*

[19]Ibid.

[20]William Henry Chamberlin, *Russia's Iron Age* (Boston, 1934).

Depression, 1919–1939* (1996), argues that the return to the gold standard in a world altered by World War I made the depression worse. Peter Temin, *Lessons from the Great Depression** (1989), takes a similar position. Charles P. Kindleberger, *The World in the Depression, 1929–1939,** (revised ed. 1986), attributes the depression's severity to the absence of a hegemonic economic center such as the City of London had provided before 1914. Harold James, *The End of Globalization: Lessons from the Great Depression* (2001), sees the slump as a flight from free exchange. Gilbert Ziebura, *World Economy and World Politics, 1924–1931* (1990), looks for policy errors and structural faults behind the Great Depression.

Robert Skidelsky's great biography of John Maynard Keynes (3 vols., 1994–2001*) is summarized in *Keynes** (1996). See also D. E. Moggridge, *Maynard Keynes: An Economist's Biography* (1992). Peter Clarke, *The Keynesian Revolution in the Making* (1989), shows how Keynes's theoretical work was shaped by contemporary policy issues in Britain, and Peter A. Hall, ed., *The Political Power of Economic Ideas: Keynesianism across Nations* (1989), examines its application.

The emergence of welfare states is explored in Peter Flora and Arnold J. Heidenheimer, eds., *The Development of Welfare States in Europe and America** (1981). Peter Baldwin, *The Politics of Social Solidarity** (1992), explains the origins of the welfare state in the farmer-labor-middle-class coalition of Scandinavia before and after World War I. Marquis Childs, *Sweden, The Middle Way* (1936, reprint ed. 1961), advocated cooperativist solutions widely admired in the 1930s; he fol-

lowed up with *The Middle Way on Trial* (1984).

Good studies of individual nations at grips with the depression include Robert Skidelsky, *Politicians and the Slump* (reprint ed. 1994), for Britain; Julian Jackson, *The Politics of Depression in France, 1932–1936** (reprint ed. 2002); and Harold James, *The German Slump: Politics and Economics* (1987). Still useful is Karl Hardach, *The Political Economy of Germany in the Twentieth Century** (1980). There is lively detail in Eugen Weber, *Hollow Years: France in the 1930s** (1996). Works by Marwick, Beer, and Gilbert cited at the end of chapter 4 are also useful for Britain in the Depression. Roland Sarti, *Fascism and the Industrial Elite in Italy, 1919–1940* (1971), successfully de-mythologizes corporatism, as does Frederick Hugh Adler, *Italian Industrialists from Liberalism to Fascism* (1995).

George Orwell, *The Road to Wigan Pier** (1937, reprint ed. 2001), is a justly famous essay on a coal-mining town in the English Midlands during the Depression, by a middle-class intellectual acutely aware of his temptation to condescend to the poor. Hans Fallada, *Little Man, What Now?** (1933, reprint ed. 1992), and Christopher Isherwood, *Berlin Stories** (1935, reprint ed. 1979), are among the most enduring depression fiction, one employing pathos, the other satire to portray the desperate middle class in Berlin just before Hitler.

R. J. Overy, *The Nazi Economic Recovery, 1932–1938,** 2nd ed. (1996), briefly introduces the issues and literature. Avraham Barkai, *Nazi Economics* (1990), explores the origins of the Nazis' job-creation program. The most penetrating analysis of the fascist states' depression remedies is chapter

2 of Charles S. Maier, *In Search of Stability** (1988).

For the depression in East Central Europe, consult Michael Kaser and E. A. Radice, *The Economic History of Eastern Europe, 1919–1975,* 3 vols. (1986–1987).

Stalin's reduction of the peasantry to a "second serfdom" is explored from below by Sheila Fitzpatrick in *Stalin's Peasants: Resistance and Survival in the Russian Village After Collectivization* (1994), Lynne Viola, *Peasant Rebels under Stalin** (1996), and also by Viola, *Contending with Stalinism** (2002). Authentic Soviet economic achievements are distinguished from propaganda in R. W. Davies, *Soviet Economic Development from Lenin to Khrushchev** (1998). Recent looks at the social impact of the five-year plans include William G. Rosenberg, *Social Dimensions of Soviet Industrialization* (1993), Donald Filtzer, *Soviet Workers and Stalinist Industrialization, The Formation of Modern Soviet Production Relations, 1929–1941* (1986), and Lewis H. Siegelbaum, ed., *Making Workers Soviet: Power, Class, and Identity** (1998).

Robert C. Tucker, *Stalin in Power: The Revolution from Above, 1929–1941** (1992), studies the transformations of the 1930s through the dictator's personality. See also the biographies of Stalin cited at the end of chapter 8. Robert C. Tucker, ed., *Stalinism** (new ed. 1998), contains illuminating discussions of the meaning of Stalin's dictatorship. Sheila Fitzpatrick draws on new Russian scholarship in *Stalinism: A Reader** (1999). Chris Ward, *Stalin's Russia,** 2nd ed. (1999) surveys the debates. The "revisionists," for whom Soviet society was complex and its achievements not only negative, restate their case in Nick Lampert and Gabor T. Rittersporn, eds., *Stalinism: Its Nature and Aftermath* (1993), and in Alec Nove, *The Stalin Phenomenon* (1993).

The debate over the appalling human cost of this "second revolution" has been sharpened by the opening of Soviet archives. Robert Conquest's harsh conclusions about Stalin's purges are updated in *Harvest of Sorrow: Soviet Collectivization and the Terror-Famine** (2002). His "revisionist" critics have adjusted their figures to newly accessible archives and seek explanations broader than the dictator's whim. See most recently J. Arch Getty, *The Road to Terror: Stalin and the Self-Destruction of the Bolsheviks, 1932–1939** (1999). Sheila Fitzpatrick examines ordinary people during the purges in *Everyday Stalinism** (1999).

Powerful memoirs about the experience of Stalin's Terror are Eugenia Ginzburg, *Journey into the Whirlwind** (1967, reprint ed. 1997), and Nadezhda Mandelstam, *Hope Against Hope** (1970, reprint ed. 1999). Arthur Koestler, *Darkness at Noon** (1941, reprint ed. 1987), is the classic novel of the purge, based loosely on the trial of Bukharin.

Additional Internet links related to this chapter are available on the Europe in the 20th Century Web site: http://www.history.wadsworth.com/paxton04.

You can also explore images, interactive timelines, and maps related to this chapter on our Western Civilization Resource Center: http://history.wadsworth.com.

Hitler addresses the *Reichstag*, 1933. Göring presides, behind.

11

The Authoritarian 1930s and the Spread of Fascism

Make way for the "new man, the fascist man, the man of the twentieth century," and "We are the pioneers that head the column of the future"[1]—for a time, these claims by young fascists of the 1930s seemed on the verge of fulfillment. Whereas in the 1920s only one regime, Italy, could be called fascist, in the 1930s it was joined by Nazi Germany, and clerical regimes influenced by fascism ruled in Austria, Portugal, and, after 1939, Spain. The trend toward authoritarian regimes in Eastern Europe was completed in the 1930s (with the exception of Czechoslovakia). For a time in 1934 it looked as if fascist movements might overthrow the French Republic. Small but vociferous fascist movements were active in Britain, the Low Countries, and Scandinavia. Although not all these movements or regimes adopted the dictatorship, the guided economies, the anti-Semitism, and the unbridled dynamism of Italian Fascism and German Nazism, much of the political tone and style of the 1930s were influenced by apparent fascist successes.

[1]Corneliu Codreanu and Anton Adriaan Mussert, Romanian and Dutch fascists.

Fascism seemed the wave of the future; the liberal regimes, by contrast, seemed old and tired. Liberal Europe, complained the Austrian socialist leader Otto Bauer, was "bewitched" by the apparent mechanical efficiency of fascist states where "the trains ran on time."[2]

GERMANY: NATIONAL SOCIALISM IN POWER

The Revival of Nazism, 1929–1932

Even before the great crash of 1929, the Nazi party had begun to reemerge from its mid-1920s obscurity. The passions aroused by debate over the Young Plan (1928–1929), which set reparations payments over many years to come, gave Hitler his best platform since the French occupation of the Ruhr in 1923. It was the depression of 1929, however, that really opened the way for Hitler by reviving fear of revolution and exposing the fecklessness of the Weimar Republic.

As we have seen, the deteriorating economy had made a parliamentary majority impossible in the Weimar Republic after March 1930.[3] The *Reichstag* election of September 14, 1930, only proved how radically the electorate had been polarized: Nazis increased their seats from 12 to 107, and the German Communist Party rose from 54 to 77 seats. These trends continued in the *Reichstag* election of July 1932, when the Nazis replaced the Social Democrats as the largest party in Germany by winning 230 seats.

Hitler's mass electoral following provides a rough guide to the social dislocations of depression-ridden Germany. Hitler's supporters included declining small farmers, distressed shopkeepers, minor civil servants suffering from wage cuts, embittered nationalists, and frightened conservatives seeking some strong medicine against Germany's apparently headlong rush into an atomized, rootless, disorderly society.

The Nazis scored their greatest successes in Protestant agricultural areas. Schleswig-Holstein, a region of small independent dairy and beef cattle farmers, was the only German state to give Hitler's party an absolute majority before the Nazis took power. Farmers there had become violently hostile to the Weimar regime. The tariff of 1925 had failed to protect them against frozen meat imports from the British Empire, whereas it had made imported feed grains more expensive.[4] When the world agricultural depression began around 1927, the number of farms and herds seized for unpaid debts rose sharply. Farmers felt they were victims of "interest slavery." The Schleswig-Holstein farmers felt little confidence in their government, for their region had been annexed by Prussia in the war of 1866. Their way of life, it seemed to them, was being swallowed up by the faceless, godless, urban society of Social-Democratic Prussia and its great decadent capital city of

[2]Otto Bauer, *Zwischen zwei Weltkriegen?* (Bratislava, Czechoslovakia, 1936), p. 135.

[3]See chapter 10, pp. 309–311.

[4]A British firm received a concession for a frozen meat–importing facility at Altona, near Hamburg, in the 1920s.

Berlin. Convinced that their existing political leaders, hopelessly enmeshed in Weimar republican deal-making, could do nothing to alleviate their predicament, the Schleswig-Holstein farmers flocked first to a local peasant party strongly impregnated with national socialist attitudes, and eventually to the National Socialist Party itself. This local example of small independent farmers switching precipitously from middle-class Weimar parties to Nazism is only the most conspicuous case, and the one most fully studied.[5] Similar cases could be found among other Protestant small farmers, equally maddened by debt, concerned about their vanishing way of life, and resentful against workers, unions, and cities.

No constituency in Germany gave the Nazis less than 20 percent of the vote in July 1932. This showing included the cities, even though Social Democratic political machines were powerfully entrenched there.[6] The Nazi Party did well in upper-class neighborhoods, but the vulnerable lower middle class—retail merchants, artisans, lower civil servants, and those on the bottom rungs of the independent professions—were the most susceptible to Nazi recruitment. In their view, the Weimar Republic neglected them. Whereas the workers had their unions and welfare legislation, the lower middle class felt isolated and helpless in the depression. The Marxist parties had no appeal to these Germans, who clung to their middle-class status. The established upper-class elites excited their envy or resentment more than their admiration. For the threadbare *petit bourgeois,* the National Socialists' two-pronged attack on socialism and big finance touched responsive chords.

At the end of Hans Fallada's novel *Little Man, What Now?* (1932), it is not clear whether the protagonist will turn to the far left or far right after losing his job with a heartless department store. This new proletarian's bitter sense of loss of status is complete when callous bourgeois elbow him off the sidewalk on his way home. Since the Marxist parties appealed only to those ready to accept working-class status, Nazism was the only protest movement open to the desperate of all the other social classes; hence, its growth from 2.6 percent of the vote in 1928 to 18.3 percent in September 1930, and again to 37.3 percent in July 1932.

Hitler's violent anticommunism and his mass electoral following among Germany's rural and urban middle class attracted the attention of the German elite. At first, Hitler had seemed boorish and offensive to many upper-class Germans. But he fought the Marxists more rigorously than anyone else, and after his vote-getting capacity had been demonstrated, Germany's leaders rushed to try to enlist that power for their own purposes.

German intellectual leaders had already helped prepare the way. As early as the Napoleonic wars, nationalist professors had tried to arouse patriotic pride in German *Kultur* as distinguished from the invaders' values of liberty, equality, and fraternity. During the nineteenth century, anti-Semitism and intellectual rejection of Western liberal rationalism grew more pervasive. At the beginning of the twentieth century, a mood of cultural pessimism was widespread among German intellectuals.

---

[5]Rudolf Heberle, *From Democracy to Nazism. A Regional Case Study of Political Parties in Germany* (1945; reprint ed., Baton Rouge, La., 1970).

[6]The lowest votes were in Social-Democratic Berlin, Catholic Cologne, and rural Catholic lower Bavaria.

They called for a redeemer who would save German blood, soil, and idealism from the corruptions of ugly factory cities, flabby bourgeois, and rootless aliens. Although few major German intellectuals actually gave the uncouth Nazis their personal support during the movement's growth, they had helped make Nazi propaganda themes acceptable.

Business leaders' aid to Hitler has been much debated. Fritz Thyssen, heir to the powerful *Vereinigte Stahlwerke,* for example, gave Hitler substantial sums. After Hitler's electoral success in 1930 aroused greater interest in him, prestigious big business groups such as the Düsseldorf Industry Club helped confer respectability on him by inviting him to speak. On such occasions Hitler stressed his movement's antisocialism and disavowed the anticapitalist rhetoric of some of his associates. It is not true, however, that German big business paid for Hitler's success. Hitler's best source of funds was ticket sales to party rallies. Business leaders contributed more money to safer centrist and conservative leaders like Franz von Papen. Their decisive contribution came in January 1933, when they accepted Hitler's entry into the government on the understanding that the government would be dominated by traditional conservatives.

The older nationalist movements tried hard to attract Hitler into their ranks. They had more money than Hitler, but he had mass popular backing. Hoping to make Hitler a vassal rather than a rival, Alfred Hugenberg, a former Krupp director who became head of the German National People's Party (DNVP) in 1928, attempted to make common cause with Hitler in the fight over the Young Plan in 1929.

Chancellor Brüning himself also tried to enlist Hitler's support. He needed it, for his deflationary depression remedies had made widespread enemies. Brüning's economic policies were too unpopular to allow him to form any parliamentary majority with the existing parties. He had to govern either by presidential decree or by finding some new form of mass backing. Deflation, in other words, could be carried out only by force or cajolery: Hitler's mass following and his shock troops were vital to either attempt.

Buoyed by their ascending influence, Hitler and his followers added all they could to the atmosphere of crisis in which they flourished. They gave an impression of tough vigor unmatched by anyone except the less numerous German Communists, and an impression of anti-Marxist violence far beyond that of any other force on the right. The brown-shirted SA (stormtroopers, *Sturmabteilungen*) held mass rallies, broke up leftist protest demonstrations and offices, and fought pitched battles with Marxists in the streets. In one small town, the subject of William Sheridan Allen's *The Nazi Seizure of Power: The Experience of a Single German Town* (1984), there were no less than thirty-seven political street fights between 1930 and 1933, of which four were general melees. This figure does not include the number of times that political rallies were forbidden without leading to violence, or the number of times that the state police had to be called in to supplement the local force. The atmosphere of incipient chaos led many conservative Germans to blame the unemployed for causing the disorder, the left for encouraging it, and the Weimar Republic for failing to prevent it. For such persons, Hitler's strong-arm tactics offered the hope of bringing all three to heel.

The End of Weimar: Presidential Government, 1930–1933

Parliamentary government had ceased to function normally according to the Weimar Constitution with the collapse of Chancellor Hermann Müller's majority on March 27, 1930.[7] It was not clear for some time what would replace it.

One possibility was a pure socialist ministry. The Social Democrats, after all, remained the largest German party in Weimar's third legislature, having won about 30 percent of the popular vote in 1928; together with the German Communist Party, Marxists had received just over 40 percent of the popular vote (compared with the Nazis' 2.6 percent). This possibility was only theoretical, however. Socialists and Communists had been bitterly divided since 1917. Moreover, a minority cabinet had to depend on the president's power to promulgate laws directly, without a parliamentary majority, in case of emergency. And since the death of the moderate Social Democratic President Friedrich Ebert in 1925, the president had been the far more conservative Marshal Paul von Hindenburg.

A second possibility was renewed recourse to elections to produce a coherent majority of left, center, or right. The German public did, in fact, endure a veritable orgy of balloting between 1930 and 1933: three *Reichstag* elections (September 1930, July 1932, November 1932) and a two-stage presidential election (March 1932), plus many state elections. No coherent majority emerged in the crosscurrents of depression politics and national politics, although Nazis replaced Social Democrats as the largest single party in July 1932, and the moderate parties nearly vanished. In the meantime, many Germans simply became disillusioned with the electoral process.

The course actually followed after March 1930 was a compromise that pleased no one. While continuing to seek a majority in frequent elections, a series of conservative chancellors who had President Hindenburg's personal confidence exercised presidential government, calling on the president to countersign their decrees under Article 48. Three chancellors in turn governed this way between 1930 and January 1933: Heinrich Brüning (March 1930–July 1932); Baron Franz von Papen (July–December 1932); and General Kurt von Schleicher (December 1932–January 1933). This situation obviously gave a great deal of power to the aging and impressionable field marshal. German history from 1930 to 1933 is a story of personal intrigue for the president's confidence. And it is a story that helps explain how far from inevitable was Hitler's accession to the office of chancellor and how large was the immediate responsibility of a handful of men.

Chancellor Brüning, as we have seen, was forced back on the president's support after his only electoral effort, the *Reichstag* elections of September 14, 1930, gave the Nazis the opportunity to display their popular appeal. Although the Social Democrats offered not to oppose the government, in a noble but self-defeating gesture of loyalty to the Weimar system, Brüning's memoirs make it clear that he wanted above all to draw the Nazi following into a new Catholic-nationalist majority.[8] Fearful of further elections, however, he continued his twin program of deflation at home and intransigence abroad with the president's support. The failure of

---

[7]See chapter 10, pp. 309–310.

[8]Heinrich Brüning, *Memoiren, 1918–1934* (Stuttgart, Germany, 1970), p. 461.

A Nazi electoral poster: "Women! Millions of men are without work. Millions of children are without a future. Save the German family! Vote for Adolf Hitler!"

Katherine Young

both left him totally dependent on Hindenburg's friendship, and the old man's opinions were increasingly subject to influence from a few close associates. They persuaded him in May 1932 to replace Brüning with someone more willing to harness the Nazi movement to conservative purposes.

Hindenburg then named as chancellor Baron Franz von Papen, a Catholic nobleman of good social connections and reactionary convictions. Papen put together a "ministry of barons" (senior army officers and top civil servants) with almost no support in parliament. Papen began his ministry with two acts of conspicuous favor to the far right. On June 16, he cancelled a ban on the Nazi SA that Brüning had imposed in April, thereby restoring to Hitler the possibility of mastering the street. In the ensuing brawls between Nazi and left demonstrators, 103 people were killed and hundreds wounded in a few weeks.[9] The disorder gave Papen the excuse to destroy the last remaining stronghold of the democratic left. On July 20, drawing on presidential emergency powers, Papen expelled from office the duly-elected state government of Prussia, a coalition of Social Democrats and Centrists, and put the state police under army orders. Then Papen called a new *Reichstag* election for July 31, 1932. Nazi support grew from 18 to 37 percent of the popular vote.

[9]Ian Kershaw, *Hitler 1886–1936: Hubris* (New York, 1999), p. 368.

Hitler now made a direct bid to President Hindenburg for office. The interview went badly. Hindenburg later remarked that "the corporal" was an odd sort who might be fit for, at most, the Ministry of Posts.[10] Angered by the old man's brusque discourtesy, Hitler insisted on the office of chancellor or nothing. Papen believed that he could electioneer the Nazis to death and then draw their following into his own machine. The elections of November 6, 1932, seemed to confirm his strategy. The Nazis were left exhausted and deeply in debt as they suffered their first electoral decline (from 37 percent to 33 percent). Papen, however, still had no parliamentary majority to show for his efforts.

Here personal intrigue reached its most decisive point. Papen proposed to use the president's powers to suspend elections and install a nonparliamentary regime, frankly contrary to the Weimar Constitution. But General Kurt von Schleicher, Hindenburg's closest military associate, convinced the president that the army would not be able to handle the likely civil disorders. Schleicher proposed one more try at a parliamentary majority. He would detach the "left" Nazi Gregor Strasser and his following from Hitler and form a coalition extending all the way to trade union officials on the left: a last echo of the army–union cooperation under military government from 1916 to 1918.[11] Schleicher replaced Papen as chancellor on December 2, 1932, and started to work on this byzantine coalition.

The outraged Papen was able to rally a coalition of his own—all of Schleicher's enemies. Hitler, worried by the apparent downturn of his fortunes since the November elections and eager to halt the defection of Strasser, now expressed his willingness to work with Papen rather than rule alone. Prominent businessmen, upset at Schleicher's efforts to bring trade unionists into the government, turned their support to Papen. When Schleicher's scheme came apart as trade unionists and moderate party leaders refused to participate, Papen's new coalition was ready. He proposed that Hitler be made chancellor, Papen himself vice chancellor, and the nationalist leader Hugenberg minister of finance, a combination too full of mutual distrust to have come together unless threatened with exclusion by Schleicher.

Hindenburg was persuaded that the Papen plan might achieve what successive chancellors had sought since 1930. A Hitler-Papen-Hugenberg coalition government offered a chance to obtain a parliamentary majority excluding the Social Democrats and Communists, to keep the Nazis in line by absorbing their leaders within a reassuring conservative coalition, and to escape from the improvisation of presidential government. On January 30, 1933, Hindenburg received Hitler and made "the corporal" chancellor of the German Reich.

Responsibilities for bringing Hitler to power are widely shared. The voters who awarded him the largest proportion of electoral strength gave him his basic leverage. When that electoral strength failed to reach absolute majority and began to recede in November 1932, however, President Hindenburg and the intriguers around him saved Hitler in the effort to harness Nazi street and electoral power to their own purposes. Businessmen, army officers, and other conservatives were willing to acquiesce in any coalition that would keep the Marxists out of office.

---

[10]Alan Bullock, *A Study of Tyranny,* 2nd ed. (New York, 1962), p. 187.

[11]See chapter 4, p. 98. Schleicher had worked with General Groener.

The new German Chancellor Adolf Hitler, Vice Chancellor Franz von Papen (left), and Propaganda Chief Joseph Goebbels *(right)* **at a youth ceremony in May 1933.**

Although at least 63 percent of the electorate voted for non-Nazi parties through November 1932, the opposition failed to make use of its numerical majority. The moderate parties were more willing to form coalitions with the Nazis than with the Marxists. The German Communists, convinced that Hitler represented the last stage of dying capitalism, actually cooperated with the Nazis in a recall petition against the Social Democratic–Center Prussian state government in the spring of 1932 and in a Berlin transit strike in November. They reserved their bitterest enmity for the Social Democrats, whom they called "social fascists" for being content to practice politics as usual in a time of crisis. Social Democrats, in fact, did just that. Whereas they had thwarted the Kapp *Putsch* of 1920 with massive strike movements, they made no similar effort against such flagrant illegalities as Papen's expulsion of the Prussian state government in July 1932.

Hitler neither seized power nor was brought to power by some inevitable fate of German history. He was given a temporary prominence by large numbers of voters, brought into office by a backstairs conspiracy, and, finally, acquiesced in by the majority of average non-Nazi citizens.

Revolution after Power, 1933–1939

What did it mean to have Adolf Hitler as chancellor of the German Reich? The conservative politicians, senior officers, and high bureaucrats around Hindenburg thought they had at last escaped from improvised presidential government by making use of Hitler's mass following. Hitler, however, expected to make use of the office to consolidate his still limited power. Hitler's interpretation proved correct. If there was a Nazi revolution, it took place after he had become chancellor, not before.

Hitler worked to heighten the impression that a Communist conspiracy was at work and that only the Nazis could deal with it effectively. His opportunity came with the burning of the *Reichstag* building in Berlin on the night of February 27–28, 1933. It is no longer thought that the Nazis hired the mentally retarded young Dutch Communist, Marinus van der Lubbe, who set the fires.[12] The Nazis really believed that a Communist uprising had begun. Much of the German public shared that hysteria and raised no objection to the mass arrests and show trial of Communist leaders that followed. A decree February 28 suspended rights of speech and assembly (for good, as it turned out) "as a defensive measure against Communist acts of violence."

Hitler's backers within the establishment had hoped that he could provide a way out of the electoral deadlock that had dogged German politics since 1930. But even with all the resources of the state at their command, as well as the calculated violence of the SA, Hitler's candidates could not obtain an absolute majority of the votes. In the elections of March 5, 1933, the Nazis won 288 seats, just short of 44 percent of the popular vote. The Catholic Center held firm, and the Social Democrats

---

[12]Fritz Tobias, *The Reichstag Fire,* trans. Arnold J. Pomeranz (New York, 1963), argued that van der Lubbe did in fact burn down the Reichstag building on his own, a conclusion supported by later investigation. Hans Mommsen, "The Reichstag Fire and Its Political Consequences," in Hajo Holborn, ed., *Republic to Reich: The Making of the Nazi Revolution* (New York, 1972). The issue is still debated.

© CORBIS

The Nazi party rally at Nuremberg in November 1934 was designed for the new medium of film. The brilliant documentary that Leni Riefenstahl made of it, *The Triumph of the Will*, sought to make the world forget the "night of the long knives" of the previous June and perceive all Germans as united behind the Führer.

and Communists shared almost a third of the popular vote. The electoral route had still not given anyone an unquestioned mandate.

Hitler then proposed an enabling act empowering him as chancellor to promulgate laws on his own authority for the next four years. The Nazis, Hugenberg's Nationalists, and the Catholic Center Party provided the necessary two-thirds vote for this change in the constitution. Only the Social Democrats, twelve of whose deputies were already in prison, voted against the proposal; the Communist deputies were already in prison. That vote of 441 to 92, on March 23, 1933, freed Hitler from the presidential countersignature as well as from the *Reichstag*, while in the nation at large, the impression of impending communist revolution freed Hitler from any genuine opposition from German moderates. The stage was set for Hitler to grasp all the reins of power.

There followed a process that German historians call *Gleichschaltung*, a useful word without an exact English equivalent that means "leveling" or "bringing into line." Step-by-step, all public agencies and all traditional bodies that had formerly enjoyed great autonomy in Germany—army, churches, bureaucratic corps—were brought into line over the following four years by a mixture of threat and reward.

Hitler never bothered to replace the Weimar Constitution with a Nazi charter. Nevertheless, he made decisive changes in German public order. Various parties were either outlawed (Communists, Socialists) or persuaded to dissolve (Center, Nationalists) until on July 14, 1933, the National Socialist Party was declared the only legal party. The political autonomy of the federal states, which even Bismarck had not dared touch, was curtailed by appointing governors *(Statthalter)* to replace elected state governments and by abolishing the German upper house or *Reichsrat,* which had represented the states. Thus, Germany became for the first time a centralized rather than a federal state. Finally, with the death of President Hindenburg in August 1934, Hitler absorbed that office and eliminated any possible rivalry from above.

Racial laws put Nazi anti-Semitism into effect. As early as April 1933, all "non-Aryan" members of the civil service were excluded from public office. The far-reaching Nuremberg Decrees of September 1935 deprived Jews of citizenship and forbade intermarriage with "Aryans." Quotas were set in the professions. Following the assassination of a German diplomat in Paris by a Jew in November 1938, the Nazis went on a rampage intended to force Jews to sell or abandon their property

© Hulton Deutsch Collection / CORBIS

German President Hindenburg with his new Chancellor Adolf Hitler in 1933. The President's death the following year left Hitler with unchallenged power.

© Bettmann / CORBIS

In the night of November 9–10, 1938, Nazi mobs went on a rampage of arson, destruction, and murder directed against the Jews of Germany. In this Berlin street scene, strollers pass one of the thousands of smashed Jewish shops with its glass fragments that gave the incident its name of *"Kristallnacht,"* the night of broken glass.

and emigrate. SA men smashed 7,500 Jewish store fronts, burned over 200 synagogues, and killed 91 persons throughout Germany during the night of November 9, the *Kristallnacht* (night of broken glass). In addition to being denied insurance on the damage, the German Jews were assessed a fine of 1 billion marks, and 20,000 of them were herded into concentration camps.

Hitler also tried to turn the churches into instruments of state policy. The Protestant churches, attended by many Nazi supporters and lacking any single center as a focus for opposition, were particularly susceptible to Nazi influence. Hitler united the various state-supported Lutheran churches into a single German Evangelical Church under governmental authority; opposition leaders, such as Pastor Martin Niemöller, were imprisoned. The Catholic Church, unified and led from abroad, was less subject to Nazi control. But it was eager enough to safeguard the Catholic school system in Germany to sign a concordat with Germany in July 1933 forbidding priests to take part in politics and giving the Nazi regime a say in naming bishops.

The diplomatic corps and the army were among the last German groups to be brought into line. When Foreign Minister Baron Konstantin von Neurath turned sixty-five years in February 1938, he was replaced by a party stalwart, Joachim von Ribbentrop, marking the party's intrusion into a function traditionally reserved for career diplomats. At the same time, leaders of the army—Minister of War General Werner von Blomberg and Chief of Staff General Werner von Fritsch—were removed under spurious accusations of sexual irregularities.

Finally, as we have seen, the German economy was whipped into intense activity by public-works and rearmament projects under centralized state direction.[13] Despite Nazi propaganda favoring peasants and craftsmen, Germany had more great industrial concerns and more crowded cities by 1939, and fewer small farmers and artisans than in 1933.

This revolution after power was not the "second revolution" that some Nazi ideologues had hoped for. Gottfried Feder had wanted to curb big business in favor of small business. Ernst Röhm had wanted to sweep away the old elites and replace them with new Nazi men; in particular, he wanted to replace the traditional officer corps with a mass army based on his SA Brown Shirts. Even as he brought German institutions into line with the party, however, Hitler also brought party mavericks into line with the real sources of power: big business, bureaucracy, and the army. He did this by murder. During the chilling "night of the long knives," on June 30, 1934, hand-picked squads raided homes and apartments and took an estimated 150 to 200 people off to their deaths: Röhm and much of the SA Leadership; Schleicher, who had tried to block the way in 1932; and the radical Nazi Gregor Strasser, who had wanted to accept a cabinet post from Schleicher. Thereafter, Hitler had no opposition within the party.

As for opposition from the general citizenry, it was effectively muted. Opposition still smacked of communism, and the penalties were severe. Above all, Hitler's mounting economic and strategic successes stilled criticism.

By 1939, Germany had been transformed from a pariah into the state most feared in Europe. But Hitler's *Gleichschaltung* had not really turned Germany into one well-oiled war machine. It is now known that the regime was kept running in many cases by carefully nurtured rivalries. The party encroached on the domain of professional civil servants; the army resented Hitler's growing private armed force, the *Schutzstaffel*, or SS; and so on. The capstone of *Gleichschaltung*, therefore, was the creation of an outward impression of monolithic efficiency through Joseph Goebbels's propaganda services and the efforts of an increasingly arbitrary police.

CLERICAL AUTHORITARIANISM

The antiliberal swing of the 1930s took on a special tone in Catholic Europe. It was no accident that only the Catholic Center Party, among moderate constitutional parties of the Weimar Republic, retained its electorate during the polarizing elections of 1930 to 1933. European Catholics, who had for the most part never accepted the individualistic, anticlerical tenets of nineteenth-century liberalism, had their own forms of antiliberal politics to which Catholic electors remained loyal after 1929 as before.

[13]See chapter 10, pp. 311–313.

In the late nineteenth century, the Catholic Church had struggled to defend itself against the effects of liberalism: the idea of separation of Church and state; the individualist notion that each person is master of his own conscience; the replacement of priests with laymen as schoolteachers when education became free, public, and compulsory. It was republican France and the new constitutional monarchy of Italy that transgressed most actively in these regards: Italy had conquered Rome and the Papal States in 1870; France had made education both public and secular in the 1880s and had separated Church and state in 1905.

The mainstream of Catholic social and political thought, therefore, remained hostile to constitutional liberalism and individualism. Even Pope Leo XIII, who was finally willing to permit French and Italian Catholics to participate in republican electoral politics, advocated a hierarchical, organic view of social rights and obligations in *Rerum Novarum* (1891), the Catholic Church's first formal pronouncement "on the condition of workers." In the ordered hierarchy of a good society, according to Leo XIII, each class enjoyed rights and exercised duties commensurate with its station: Workers owed their employers respect and obedience; employers owed their workers respect and humane treatment. Some more radical Catholic social thinkers attacked capitalism itself for its callous disregard for workers. But they did not think private property should be abolished. It should be purified by a moral regeneration in which Christian employers would treat their employees as wards.

The depression encouraged the revival of Catholic criticisms of unbridled liberal capitalism. In his encyclical *Quadragesimo Anno* (1931),[14] Pope Pius XI outlined a model economic and social system in accord with "the natural law, or rather, God's will manifested by it." Property is legitimate, he argued, and "man is born to labor as the bird to fly." But capital had grasped "excessive advantages," leaving the workers a "bare minimum" under the "Liberalistic tenets of the so-called Manchester School." Worse still, free competition had produced "immense power and despotic economic domination . . . concentrated in the hands of a few." Capital and labor alike must be subordinated to the good of the whole community. Free competition must be limited, workers must receive a "just wage" sufficient to "overcome" the proletarian condition, and owners should receive a "just share only of the fruits of production."

The pope admitted that only the constituted authorities could perform this work of social reconstruction. The best system, he thought, was corporatism. The state should grant virtual monopoly status to "Syndical or corporative organizations" that included representatives of workers and employers in the same trade or profession. These then would administer all matters of common interest; strikes and lockouts would be forbidden. The advantages were "peaceful collaboration of the classes, repression of socialist organizations and efforts," and defense of "the peace and tranquility of human society . . . against the forces of revolution."

Followers of Pope Pius XI's socioeconomic views insisted on their distance from Hitlerian National Socialism. They rejected Nazism's atheism, its cult of action for

---

[14]The official English title reads, in part, "Encyclical letter . . . on Reconstructing the Social Order and Perfecting it Conformably to the Precepts of the Gospel." The opening Latin words *Quadragesimo anno* refer to the fortieth anniversary of Leo XIII's social encyclical *Rerum Novarum* (1891).

its own sake, its frank acceptance of state power. They longed for an organic society in which "natural" groupings would run society in harmony and without great extremes of wealth and poverty. Like Nazism, however, they subordinated individuals to the good of the whole and pointed to socialism as the main enemy. They helped pave the way to acceptability for authoritarian regimes in Catholic countries.

Portugal: Salazar

The Portuguese Republic had been swept away by a military *coup* in 1926, before the depression; it had lasted only sixteen years. Antonio Oliveira Salazar, the military junta's finance minister, emerged as the strong man of the regime in the 1930s. He was content to leave the presidency to generals, but as premier (1932–1969) he actually ran Portugal in his own style.

Salazar was a Catholic Integralist.[15] As such, he considered the rights of individuals subordinate to the needs of the group, and longed for a hierarchical society in which each person knew his place and kept it. Commitment to stable order, deep philosophic doubt about the possibility of human progress, and piety marked Salazar's regime.

Salazar had abandoned theological seminary for the study of economics. As a student leader of young conservatives at the University of Coimbra, he drew his values from Charles Maurras's *Action française* movement. He entered the government in 1928 when as Professor of Economics at the University of Coimbra he was called on to get the new military junta out of financial difficulties. Salazar was a strictly orthodox economist. A balanced budget was sacrosanct to him. He simply cut spending to fit income, paid off the national debt, and froze Portugal for twenty years in an almost immobile state of economic backwardness. In 1934, the total value of industrial production in Portugal was only one-fifth that of agriculture. It was not until the first Development Plan of 1953 to 1958 that Salazar actively promoted industrial development, with its concomitant need for outside capital and its risks of social disorder.

Politically, Salazar sought a similar immobilism. The Constitution of 1933 retained the nonparty Chamber together with the Chamber of Corporations, but no opposition candidates were permitted, and the premier was responsible only to the president. Strikes were forbidden; married women were not permitted to hold jobs. This regime kept Portugal politically somnolent until an opposition candidate ran for president in 1958. In 1959, Salazar abolished presidential elections.

In 1936, the regime took on some of the external trappings of fascism. An obligatory youth movement, the green-shirted *Mocidade Portuguesa,* enrolled all youth from seven to fourteen. The paramilitary Portuguese Legion used the Roman salute. Tight censorship and strict police control restricted civil liberties in the name of order. The regime was now called the New State (*Estado Novo*).

[15]See chapter 8, p. 252.

At root, however, Salazar's regime was more conservative than fascist. Salazar himself, an austere bachelor, shunned public appearances and did nothing to mobilize fervent masses. He quietly broke the National Syndicalist movement that attempted to found a more dogmatic fascist party in 1933 and 1934. Salazar chose immobility rather than adventure, safety rather than dynamism. In his quest for security, he even sacrificed economic growth for the preservation of Integralist Christian corporatist values and a stable society.

Christian Social Austria: Dollfuss and Schuschnigg

Post-Versailles Austria was a hydrocephalic monster. Its huge head, the former Habsburg imperial capital of Vienna with its 2 million worldly inhabitants, was mismatched with the tiny body of the German parts of the former empire, some 4 million upper Austrians, mostly alpine farmers. The one solution longed for by almost every Austrian in 1919, union *(Anschluß)* with Germany, was forbidden by the Treaty of Saint Germain, Austria's part of the peace settlement. Economic activity within cramped new borders got underway only with the support of substantial Allied loans, which forced the Austrian state budget to stringent economies. Under such conditions, it is hardly surprising that parliamentary politics never worked in the infant Austrian Republic.

Austrian politics in the 1920s was a deadlock between two irreconcilable forces. A formidably solid Social Democratic Party, fortified with its own armed paramilitary force *(Schutzbund),* governed Vienna. Less weakened by the Socialist-Communist split than most Western Marxist parties, the Austrian Social Democrats remained both large and intransigent during the 1920s under the leadership of the scholarly Otto Bauer. Austria's loose federal structure gave the party large powers in Vienna, where it created an elaborate social-welfare program including immense public housing projects like the 1,500-family Karl-Marx-Hof. On the anti-Marxist side was the Christian Social Party, which united most of the Catholic population of the rest of Austria, fearful of "Red Vienna." It was led by an austere priest and professor of theology, Father Ignaz Seipel, who struck outside observers as a figure transplanted from the Counter-Reformation.[16] Also on the anti-Marxist side was another paramilitary force, the Home Guard *(Heimwehr),* a loose collection of local militias formed just after the First World War to fight against revolution and against possible incursions from neighboring successor states. Neither the Social Democrats nor the Christian Social Party could capture more than about 45 percent of the votes, although Father Seipel managed to govern for most of the time between 1923 and 1927, with the aid of Protestant anti-Marxists and a small Peasant Party. At best, the two antagonistic blocs eyed each other sullenly. At worst, they fought it out. On Black Friday, July 15, 1927, demonstrations got out of hand in Vienna. The Hall of Justice was burned, and eighty-seven persons were killed during uncontrolled police revenge.

This unpromising situation was seriously aggravated by two additional factors after 1930. The shaky Austrian economy was especially susceptible to the depression.

---

[16]He was, in fact, of modest origin: son of a cabdriver.

As has been noted, the failure of a great Vienna bank, the *Credit-Anstalt,* set off the European banking crisis of the summer of 1931. Further, anti-Marxist activists were increasingly swallowed up in a burgeoning Nazi movement spreading from Bavaria. With the parliament deadlocked in an almost even split, some kind of authoritarian regime seemed inevitable. The issue became an international one in Austria, because no solution was possible without outside help. The Nazis sought help from Hitler; the Christian Social Party turned to Mussolini.

The Christian Social dictatorship of Chancellor Engelbert Dollfuss (1933–1934) combined a Catholic, corporatist authoritarianism at home with a foreign policy of independence from Germany supported by Italy. Dollfuss, whose small stature (4 ft. 11 in.) was more than compensated for by his rashness, thought he could govern by "a single party, whose common bases will be the defense of Austrian independence and the corporative organization of the State."[17]

Dollfuss dissolved the deadlocked parliament in March 1933. Then he began to construct a new regime, which he claimed would be the first in the world based on the 1931 papal encyclical *Quadragesimo Anno.* Only a single party, the Fatherland Front, was allowed to function. Dollfuss reduced the independence of the Social Democratic city government of Vienna, and placed restrictions on socialist newspapers and organizations. The death penalty, abolished in 1919, was restored. The *Heimwehr* provided shock troops for the regime. The government tolerated anti-Semitism. A concordat gave the Catholic Church the major role in public education. The new constitution, finally issued in May 1934, replaced "exaggerated parliamentarism" with a series of corporative councils, most of whose members were appointed.

The Social Democratic Party found its activities more and more constricted. Finally, determined not to repeat the German Social Democrats' passivity in the face of Hitler, the Austrian left acted. After *Heimwehr* units had invaded a Social Democratic headquarters in Linz and seized some weapons, the Social Democrats decided to call out the *Schutzbund* in Vienna and begin a general strike. Dollfuss retaliated with military force, including an artillery shelling of the Karl-Marx-Hof apartment complex on February 12, 1934. That day 193 civilians were killed and 128 among the government forces. The Social Democratic newspapers and organizations were then outlawed.

Dollfuss insisted that his regime was not fascist. To guard against being swallowed up in an atheist, statist German dictatorship, the Christian Social regime even forbade Nazi Party activities in Austria. In March 1934, Dollfuss negotiated an alliance with Mussolini and with Julius Gömbös, the authoritarian prime minister of Hungary, to aid him in this policy. When a Nazi band assassinated Dollfuss on July 25, 1934, and attempted to install a Nazi regime, Italian armed forces on maneuvers in the Alps gathered at the Brenner Pass while loyal *Heimwehr* units regained control for Dollfuss's associate, Kurt Schuschnigg. In many ways, Austria under Dollfuss and his successor Schuschnigg (1934–1938) bore resemblances to Nazi Germany during the same period. Their sharpest difference was the Austrian regime's commitment to separate existence. The clerical authoritarian Austrians,

[17]Quoted by French Minister to Austria Gabriel Puaux, September 15, 1933. *Documents diplomatiques français, 1932–1939,* Ire série, vol. 4, p. 367.

aided by the Fascist Mussolini, thus administered a far more striking blow to Hitler in 1934 than did any of the liberal states at any time during the 1930s.

Spain: Franco and the Falange

The military revolt against the legal government of republican Spain in 1936 and the subsequent three-year civil war will be discussed in chapter 12, on the Popular Front era. But this account of the European turn toward authoritarianism in the 1930s is not complete without a brief look at Franco's Spain.

The dictatorship of General Francisco Franco (1939–1975) was the only interwar authoritarian regime to take power by military conquest. Franco and his followers invaded Spain from Spanish Morocco in July 1936. With the support of most of the professional army and the acquiescence of conservatives and most of the clergy, they fought their way across Spain until the republican forces were finally defeated in 1939.

Unlike Hitler and Mussolini, therefore, Franco did not owe any of his power in Spain to a mass fascist movement. The *Falange,* a fascist-styled group founded by José Antonio Primo de Rivera, the son of the "dictator" of 1923 to 1930, contributed little to Franco's success and assumed only a marginal role in the new regime. Franco was a pragmatically conservative professional officer, bitterly opposed to the republic's antimilitarism and anticlericalism, its incipient socialism, and the leeway it gave Catalan separatism. He was more hostile to Freemasons than to Jews. The new regime favored landowners, businessmen, and the clergy without being as dependent on any of them as they were dependent on it. Like Salazar, Franco chose immobilism rather than expansion and so survived the Second World War.

FASCISM IN EASTERN EUROPE

Conditions were ripe for fascism in Eastern Europe in the 1930s. Ethnic antagonisms remained virulent in each country. Unsatisfied national minorities—Germans in the Polish Corridor and in the Czech Sudetenland, Slovaks in eastern Czechoslovakia, Croats in northwestern Yugoslavia—turned naturally to those arch enemies of the postwar settlement, Hitler and Mussolini. Dominant national groups, threatened by internal secession movements, looked around for authoritarian routes to national unity.

Since Eastern Europe was heavily agricultural, the worldwide collapse of farm prices in the late 1920s drove governments and citizens to bankruptcy. Bankers and merchants foreclosed on family farms. Because nowhere else in the world did Jews compose so high a proportion of bankers and merchants, anti-Semitism became a convenient shorthand for rural resentments against cities and against "the modern world." The land-hungry Eastern European peasants, attracted to Lenin a decade earlier, looked to new saviors after witnessing the results of Stalin's forcible land collectivization.

Eastern European parliamentary regimes offered no solution to these catastrophes. Their agrarian parties were powerless to stop the collapse of farm prices alone, and their liberal parties were narrowly based on urban professionals. Parliamentarism came to seem an alien implantation. Some Eastern Europeans rediscovered the charms of more or less fictitious "historic" traditions of authoritarian rule and ethnic purity.

All these encouragements to fascism were reinforced by a profound shift in Great Power positions in Eastern Europe in the 1930s. On every level—economic, military, and cultural—the French preeminence of the 1920s gave way to rising Italian and German influence. Successor states that had absorbed Russian soil in 1918 looked for stronger anti-Soviet bulwarks than the French army, entrenched behind its Maginot Line. And the German economic boom after 1933 shifted the focus of Eastern European trade and finance away from the sagging French economy.

Hungary and Bulgaria

It was only to be expected that the main losers of the postwar settlement—Hungary and Bulgaria—would be drawn to the most vigorous anti-Versailles powers. Hungary, too, had experienced Bolshevik revolution in 1919; and among its bankers and merchants was an especially high proportion of Jews on whom rural resentment was focused. Admiral Miklós Horthy, who had guided the counterrevolutionary victory in Hungary in 1919, continued to rule as "regent" through the Second World War. The upper-class parliamentarism of the 1920s vanished, however, with the appointment of General Julius Gömbös—an admirer of Mussolini and Hitler—as an authoritarian prime minister (1932–1936). He strengthened ties with Mussolini and established an alliance with Dollfuss. An overtly fascist movement, the Arrow Cross, advocated more violent solutions, but Hungary remained in the hands of the counterrevolutionary traditionalists when Gömbös died in 1936.

The same was true of Bulgaria. Under King Boris III there was virtual authoritarian rule after 1934, when the parliament was dispensed with altogether for several years. But Boris successfully blocked more radical right movements, such as IMRO, the Macedonian nationalist-terrorist organization.

Romania

A surprising development was the appearance of the most original, spectacular, and successful of the interwar fascist movements in Eastern Europe in a "victor" state, Romania. This was Corneliu Codreanu's Legion of the Archangel Michael and its strong-arm squad, the Iron Guard.

Even though Romania had been doubled in size and power by the Versailles settlement, that did not solve pressing internal problems. The nation was four-fifths peasant, suffering from vast rural overpopulation on tiny family plots. The merchant and professional classes were very largely Jewish; in Bucharest, anti-Semites claimed, 11,000 out of 14,000 employees of banks and commercial establishments were Jewish. Peasants in debt thought of their creditors or of large landholding syndicates as Jewish whether they were or not. Romania's expansion had exposed the state to new perils, for it had acquired the mouth of the Danube (Bessarabia) from Russia, which wanted it back. Hence, even though there was no internal Marxist threat (the Communist Party was very small after the first years, and in 1937 Socialists received only 0.8 percent of the vote), the external Marxist threat was very real. Finally, there was no effective political solution to any of these difficulties. When universal suffrage was first introduced in Romania in 1919, it was natural to assume that a peasant party would receive an automatic majority. In fact, the prewar elite managed to hold on through the Liberal Party, which was in power for ten of the sixteen years after the First World War. And even when the Agrarian Party spent some years in power, it could not solve Romania's problems. Meanwhile, the depression was beginning to affect farm prices. Romanians with grievances were forced to look outside the political system for redress.

Codreanu, son of a schoolteacher, managed to harness these discontents in an extraordinary movement. He began by organizing students, an alienated group without enough jobs to look forward to: Their main demand was the imposition of quotas on Jewish admissions to the universities. The other main component was discontented, small family farmers, mostly in the poorest areas of northeastern Romania (Moldavia) where the middle class was largely Jewish and which earlier politicians had ignored. He welded these two groups together around religion, anti-Semitism, hatred of cities, and rejection of modern liberal society. Codreanu's legion was the most outwardly religious of all fascist movements: Legionnaries, led by Orthodox clergy carrying icons, were sent into remote villages with songs and costumes to win rural converts. Codreanu himself wore traditional Moldavian peasant dress.

The Iron Guard was a religious fraternity organized in cells (nests) whose members had sworn a blood oath to poverty, duty, and, if need be, murder on behalf of a purified Romania. Codreanu had begun his party activity with the assassination of a local police official. Political murder became virtually a way of life for the Iron Guard. Legionaries killed eleven public officials in the 1930s.

Codreanu's party was no mere fringe movement. Its 16 percent of the popular vote in 1937 made it the third largest party behind the Liberals and Agrarians. Rather than continue with parliamentary government, however, King Carol II tried to beat the legion at its own game. In 1938, he suspended the constitution, imposed authoritarian rule, and jailed the legion's leaders. Codreanu and others were "killed while trying to escape," according to the official account.

The king's experiment failed, partly because Romania's problems in the 1930s were insoluble. A more immediate reason for failure was the country's vulnerability to a whole ring of neighbors (Russia, Bulgaria, Hungary) that had lost land to Romania in the postwar settlement. When representatives of Hitler and Stalin negotiated a new partition of Eastern Europe in August 1939, there was no power to which Romania could turn to defend its swollen 1919 frontiers. A year later, after Hitler's defeat of Poland and France, the Russians demanded and received not only Bessarabia but other territories that had never been Russian. In September 1940, under German and Italian pressure, the Romanians had to give up much of Transylvania to Hungary and return to Bulgaria territories won in 1913. Altogether, Romania lost one-third of its territory. King Carol was forced to abdicate.

General Ion Antonescu, a professional officer with Iron Guard sympathies, ruled after September 1940 as "conducator" (the Romanian equivalent of *Führer*) with the aid of Horia Sima, Codreanu's successor as guard chief. Thus the Iron Guard finally reached political power. Pressing for a "second revolution," guard members committed mass murders of Jews and imprisoned former political leaders. But since Hitler and Antonescu wanted order more than fervor at this point, the "conducator" had the army crush the Iron Guard in three days of bloody fighting in Bucharest in January 1941. Thereafter, Antonescu ruled as an outright military dictator without fascist ideological trappings.

The Iron Guard was the only fascist movement in Eastern Europe that actually ruled without direct German occupation, and its moment of power lasted only four months. Considering the virulence of Eastern European fascism, its relative failure may seem surprising. The social structure was partly responsible. In Eastern Europe, fascist movements drew on a massive distressed peasantry but only a rather small distressed middle class, and it was the older elites that remained in power. That is the chief reason for the fascists' relative lack of success. Even before 1929, Eastern European states had turned to authoritarian officers or revived monarchies. Thus, the work of "saving society" had already been performed by conservatives before the fascist revival of the 1930s. The Eastern European fascist movements appeared late on the scene, often as rivals or even enemies of more traditional authoritarian regimes. To the end, therefore, these fascist movements retained an anti-establishment tone; scholars who have specialized in the study of Eastern European peasant fascism, such as as Eugen Weber, stress its revolutionary character. By and large, Eastern European fascist movements remained sectarian minorities.

FASCIST MINORITIES IN WESTERN EUROPE

Fascism also remained a minority movement in the deeply rooted constitutional regimes of Western Europe. Even there, however, it colored and influenced the more moderate center-right groups struggling to retain their supporters.

France

France had the most vigorous fascist minority in Western Europe. That was to be expected for a number of reasons. First, Frenchmen had become conscious as early as the 1890s of their country's decline from the greatest world power of the seventeenth century to the stagnant and sometimes unedifying Third Republic. Those who blamed the decline on bourgeois softness and the rise of the left had already rallied to Charles Maurras's *Action française* before the First World War.[18] The ambiguity of France's victory in 1918 contributed to the sense of decline. It had been possible only with powerful allies and, even then, at a cost that could never be

---

[18]See chapter 1, p. 31.

repeated without fatally weakening the French population. Second, the French middle class had suffered severely from inflation, and France was preeminently a nation of small, independent proprietors. Finally, in a country with a rich revolutionary tradition, the overwhelming commitment of French industrial workers to militant Marxism seemed a threat both to the wealthy and to many small, independent Frenchmen, nominally partisans of the "Great Revolution" of 1789. Under these conditions, movements that promised national revival, order, economic stability, and authority were endemic in French political life between the wars. They were relatively inconspicuous when things went well for the republic; when things went badly, they became a serious alternative.

Things did go badly for the French Republic in the 1930s. It proved totally incapable of dealing with the depression, and with the menace posed as Germany slipped its Versailles chains to become even more aggressive than in 1914. Veterans who charged that the republic had lost in useless palaver what the soldiers had won in the trenches joined their rage with that of the unemployed and those whose salaries or pensions had been cut by classical depression remedies.[19] Finally, the inclusion of Communists in the Popular Front electoral alliance of 1936, coupled with the spontaneous sit-down strike that accompanied the Popular Front's electoral victory, sent a wave of fear through French conservatives. These developments brought many recruits to French fascism.

The largest of the new movements, claiming nearly 1 million members, was the *Croix de feu*,[20] headed by a retired colonel with monarchist connections, François de La Rocque. Much smaller but more outspokenly profascist was the *Parti populaire français* of Jacques Doriot, former leader of the French Communist youth movement. When Doriot was expelled from the Communist Party in 1934 for premature espousal of a Popular Front strategy, he ricocheted from the far left to the far right. A magnetic personality, Doriot was so deeply entrenched as mayor of the working-class Paris suburb of Saint-Denis that he brought that following over with him into anticommunist authoritarian nationalism, which also attracted ardent middle-class reactionaries disillusioned with the rather cautious La Rocque. Another French fascist movement that derived from the French left grew out of a youthful revolt against the financial orthodoxy of the French Socialist Party (SFIO). Marcel Déat and other reformist socialists broke with the SFIO in 1932 over their desire to participate in a bourgeois government. Déat then went on to preach a nationalist rather than internationalist socialist solution to the depression in his neosocialist movement. In addition, there emerged a number of anti-Semitic groups and right-wing action squads, such as the blue-shirted *Solidarité française* financed by the perfume manufacturer François Coty. All these movements called themselves leagues, to distinguish themselves clearly from "corrupt" parties.

The climax of French fascism between the wars came on the night of February 6, 1934, when a number of right-wing leagues combined in a massive demonstration against the Chamber of Deputies. The immediate pretext was a moral crusade against the part played by some of the deputies in the Stavisky affair, a case involving

---

[19]See chapter 10, pp. 306–309.

[20]The name comes from its origins as a veterans' movement restricted to soldiers who had won the Croix de guerre under fire; that is, front-line veterans. It has nothing to do with the "fiery cross" of the Ku Klux Klan.

cover-up of fraud by a Jewish promoter, Alexander Stavisky. But behind that crusade lay the pent-up exasperation of veterans, nationalists, sufferers in the depression, and all those who associated France's troubles in the 1930s with inadequate public authority. Premier Edouard Daladier called out armed police to keep the crowd out of the parliament buildings, and in the ensuing fight thousands were injured and sixteen persons killed, the bloodiest street fighting in Paris between the Commune of 1871 and the liberation of 1944. Daladier resigned the next day, even though he still had a majority of votes in parliament. A former president of the republic, Gaston Doumergue, put together a nonparty cabinet of national unity, ranging from Radicals on the center-left to the parliamentary right and including such extraparliamentary figures as the World War I hero Marshal Pétain as Minister of War. Thus, the fascist leagues had been able to shift the government from the moderate left to a nonparty emergency regime.

In the long run, however, French fascists were unable to gain power by their own devices. Although their tone became much more shrill after the left electoral successes of May 1936 and the subsequent strike wave, they were clearly on the defensive and unable (or unwilling) to take action when the Popular Front government outlawed all paramilitary forces in June 1936. Since the scheduled elections of 1940 were overtaken by the war, it is impossible to give any precise measure of the electoral support for the legal parties that La Rocque and Doriot created after suppression of their action squads. All that can be said is that the French fascist critique of the Third Republic's inefficacy and decadence helped sweep away the republic and all its works after the defeat of June 1940, and it strongly colored the French regime that replaced the republic after the armistice.

Why did French fascism remain a minority movement in the 1930s? Nationalists were too traditionally anti-German to copy German models for French revival. France had, after all, been nominally victorious in the First World War and thereafter less disastrously affected by subsequent economic catastrophes than Germany. French grandeur continued to be associated with the revolutionary traditions of 1789, rather than with the conservative opposition to them. Finally, the division of the French fascist movements and the absence of any one exceptional leader made coordinated efforts difficult. The riots of February 6, 1934, helped arouse the old cry of republican defense more fully than any event since the Dreyfus affair, and the French fascist leagues never achieved another such peak of activity until the German occupation in June 1940.

Britain

The only significant fascist movement in interwar Britain grew out of the frustrations of the depression, which hit Britain more disastrously than any other nation except Germany and the United States. While unemployment was reaching 20 percent of the labor force, no party had any convincing solution to offer.

The Labour government's rejection of Sir Oswald Mosley's bold and original plans for stimulating purchasing power[21] in 1930 convinced Mosley that the Labour

---

[21]See chapter 10, p. 304.

© Hulton Getty / Liaison Agency

Sir Oswald Mosley returns the salute of blackshirted militants of the British Union of Fascists in London, 1936.

Party was a bunch of worthless weaklings, "a Salvation Army that took to its heels on the day of Judgment." He endeavored to transcend the existing party deadlock by founding the New Party in March 1931, but this effort only convinced him that any parliamentary combination was a hopeless instrument for radical change. The New Party won no seats in the election of September 1931, and its original recruits of young Labour leftists (John Strachey, Aneurin Bevan) soon quit in protest over Mosley's anti-Soviet attitude and his hiring of strong-arm squads to protect him from hostile Labourites.

In October 1932, Mosley founded the British Union of Fascists (BUF). His starting point, as in his Labour days, was a bold and decisive remedy for unemployment. That led him to other far-reaching proposals. A "living wage policy" was impossible, of course, with the "old gang of present parliamentarism," left and right. Mosley proposed a "modern" regime "capable of rising to new tasks,"[22] in which a Chamber of Corporations would manage the economy, and a parliament, composed of representatives of various economic interests, would have only consultative powers.

[22]Oswald Mosley, *Greater Britain* (London, 1932), pp. 16, 156.

The king would name the prime minister after consultation with a National Council of Fascists; the prime minister's work would be ratified by plebiscites every five years. Mosley turned current economic priorities upside down, giving domestic measures against unemployment precedence over concern for international financial stability. Hence, he attacked "international finance capital" and talked of nationalizing the banks. Although he opposed the international capitalists of London, he based his hopes for British economic revival on "national" capitalism, which, he insisted, had common interests with the workingman. Both would benefit by Britain's turning its back on Europe and developing the empire under a system of imperial preference. With this last proposal, Mosley resembled the pro-empire right of prewar days. But his political techniques had not been seen in Britain before. BUF mass meetings were marked by black-shirted guards and floodlit black flags. Mosley insisted on the "dynamic" and "modern" character of fascism.

The high point of Mosley's popularity came in 1934, when the *Daily Mail* published an editorial headlined, "Hurrah for the Blackshirts!"[23] Party membership was estimated to reach 20,000. Mosley's only genuine mass following, however, emerged in the proletarian East End of London, where he struck a responsive chord with his contempt for parliamentary Labour and, later, with his anti-Semitism. His Black Shirts switched from beating up Labour Party members to beating up unassimilated Eastern European Jews who had settled in the East End of London before the war.

These tactics produced widespread revulsion in England, and in 1936 the Tory government outlawed uniformed groups and tightened police measures against parades and rallies. But the BUF's decline after 1934 stemmed from more fundamental causes. Tory electoral victories in 1931 and 1935 reassured most British conservatives that Stanley Baldwin was safeguard enough, as did the modest revival of prosperity that Britain enjoyed despite Baldwin's inactivity. Britain had not suffered military defeat, and parliamentary government was closely associated with British images of national greatness. Mosley's BUF had been founded before Hitler came to power, and growing anti-German sentiment lessened his appeal to the British middle class. After 1936, Mosley, a declining star at the age of thirty-eight, was reduced to Jew-baiting in the East End of London, a scurrilous end for a man of his brilliant but wayward talents. In the end, the far right was less successful in interwar Britain than it had been in a previous crisis, the battle over Irish Home Rule from 1910 to 1914.

British fascism is an interesting phenomenon, not only because of Mosley's stature (he was one of few European fascist leaders who achieved eminence before becoming fascist) but also because its original motive force was economic crisis rather than cultural despair or military defeat. Above all, British fascism revealed the vigor of reaction against liberal parliamentarism and free-trade capitalism in the 1930s, even in their homeland. Although the overtly fascist BUF became a marginal sect, the traditional parties were also subtly drawn away from liberal values. They accepted the necessity of protective tariffs, state-regulated business cartels, and other types of public economic management that had still been anathema ten years earlier.

---

[23]*Daily Mail*, January 8, 1934.

The Low Countries and Scandinavia

Flemish resentment against the French-speaking Walloons' dominance of bina-tional Belgium was by far the most active unresolved nationality issue in Continen-tal Western Europe between the wars. It was only natural that Flemish nationalists, for whom the established Belgian parties (Catholic, Liberal, Socialist) offered no redress, should turn in the 1930s to antiparliamentary mass movements with fascist trappings. Various Flemish movements united to form the *Vlaamsch Nationaal Ver-bond* (Flemish National Union) in 1933, led by a former schoolmaster, Staf de Clercq, and supported in part by German money. The VNV had a genuine mass fol-lowing in rural Flemish districts; it received 13 percent of the vote in the four north-ern provinces in 1936 and 15 percent in 1939. Its main rival was the fervent uniformed squad of young men known as *Verdinasos* or *Dinasos* (a contraction of *Ver-bond van Dietsche Nationaalsolidaristen,* Band of Dutch-speaking National Solidarists) led by a young lawyer, Joris Van Severen, with special appeal to veterans and stu-dents. Van Severen advocated the reunion of all Flemish (Dutch) peoples in mod-ern Holland, Belgium, and Luxemburg in an expanded Netherlands as powerful as that of the seventeenth century.

The most successful antiparliamentary mass movement in the Low Countries—indeed, perhaps the biggest for a brief time in all Western Europe—was not based on nationalist resentments, however. Léon Degrelle's Rexist movement in Belgium tapped a protean ground swell of disgust with parliamentary politics in 1935 and 1936 and seemed capable, for a moment, of replacing the old parties with one new mass party. Degrelle emerged as a militant in the Belgian Catholic Youth Move-ment; he was in charge of its publishing house, called "Rex" (after *Christus Rex,* Christ the King). In November 1935, at the age of twenty-nine, he launched a cam-paign to displace the stuffy leadership of the Catholic Party, as well as of the Liberal and Socialist parties. Promising to sweep clean with a "new broom," Degrelle unleashed a kind of emotional binge against slack and corrupt parliamentarism. His followers demonstrated with brooms in front of party headquarters, and they packed political rallies shouting *"Rex vaincra"* (Rex will win).

The movement mobilized crowds in a way unknown to staid Belgian parliamen-tary politics. Its Catholic, monarchist, corporative authoritarianism owed much to Degrelle's former idol, Charles Maurras. His followers were the young, the previ-ously apolitical, and a host of rural and small-town folk easily aroused against "high finance," corrupt cities, and Marxism ("Rex or Moscow" was a leading slogan). Although the depression was passing, its ravages were clearly a factor in Rexist popularity. Mussolini sent secret funds to the Rexists and allowed Degrelle to use Italian radio beamed to Belgium.

The elections of May 1936 gave Rexist candidates 11.5 percent of the total vote (21 out of 202 seats). Votes ran as high as 29 percent in rural French-speak-ing districts, but Degrelle also had some following in the Flemish districts of northern Belgium. The showdown came in a parliamentary by-election in early 1937 in which Degrelle himself was a candidate. He proclaimed that if he won his seat, a general election would then have to be called. The existing parties united around the future Prime Minister Paul Van Zeeland as Degrelle's opponent. After the Catholic primate of Belgium condemned Rexism as a "danger for the country and for the Church," Degrelle was held to 20 percent of the vote against Van Zeeland's 80 percent. This broke the spell, for a movement whose main asset was the promise of a victorious new style of politics could not survive any interruption of its climb. Brief as its heyday was, however, Rexism revealed how deep the inarticulate frustration with parliamentary regimes ran in postdepression Western Europe.

In Protestant Holland, fascism was a more secular affair than Degrelle's Catholic Integralism, but there were common themes of authority, anti-Marxism, national regeneration, and the "new man." The immediate spur to Dutch fascism was a naval mutiny aboard the warship *Seven Provinces* in Dutch Indonesia in 1931. Profiting by this shock to the social and imperial order, a waterworks engineer, Anton Adriaan Mussert, founded the National-Socialist League (NSB). Mussert received almost 8 percent of the vote in elections of April 1935, with the proportion reaching 20 percent in Protestant small-farming areas in the southwest. The NSB was then the fifth largest party in Holland. The stability of Dutch parliamentary monarchy, recovery from the depression, and growing fears of Nazi Germany hurt Mussert's movement, and in spite of the slogan "Mussert or Moscow" his electoral toll dropped in 1937.

Even relatively stable Scandinavia had its fascist movements, although there, too, they remained noisy minorities. The most conspicuous of these was the Norwegian movement of Vidkun Quisling, whose last name became a synonym for collaboration after the German occupation of Norway in 1940. Quisling was a professional army officer (like Franco, Mosley, and the Hungarian Julius Gömbös). As Norwegian military attaché to St. Petersburg, he had actually witnessed the Bolshevik Revolution and its aftermath, when he participated in international food relief in the Crimea. After entering Norwegian politics in the Agrarian Party, Quisling became defense minister in 1931, a position that he lost in a controversy surrounding his use of troops against strikers. Quisling then founded the *Nasjonal Samling* (National League) in May 1933. His following remained small, for Norway had no sensitive nationality problem, and Quisling failed to generate excitement over recovering Greenland and Iceland from Denmark. Furthermore, even though the Norwegian Socialists had been the only Scandinavian Socialist party to join the Third International in 1919, the Norwegian left posed no revolutionary threat in the 1930s. The special stamp of Quisling's fascism, beyond a vague anti-Marxism and ritual attacks on "Anglo-Jewish finance capital," was the leader's taste for evoking ancient Norse grandeur and Nordic racial solidarity. The movement was important mainly for assembling a few elements on which the Nazis would try to build wartime collaboration after 1940.

THE APPEAL OF FASCISM

At the worst moment of the depression, when Mussolini was still the only fascist in power, former Liberal Prime Minister David Lloyd George stood up in the British

House of Commons and contrasted the "courage" and "positive force" of the Duce to the faltering hesitations of the democracies.[24] During the 1930s, similar doubts about the European liberal tradition swelled to a roar.

Fascism caught up the refugees from a liberal system that no longer appeared to work. Liberalism seemed to provide neither a living nor security. Some of these ideological refugees could turn to Marxism, but that step required one to identify with the proletariat and to accept the Soviet Union as a model. Thus, Marxism's growth in the 1930s had inherent limits. Fascism offered something to every kind of discontent; indeed, its very denial of class was one of its major assets. To the threatened elites, the authority of fascism offered an immediate end to class struggles and a managed economy without ruinous competition. To a desperate lower middle class, fascism offered security and a chance to bring organized labor to heel. To embittered nationalists, it offered national unity and glory. To the jobless, it offered jobs.

It will not do, of course, to assess fascism's appeal solely in terms of economic and social interest. In ways still only partly understood, fascism offered all sorts of psychological gratifications: for some, the reassurance of belonging; for some, the thrill of authorized vicarious brutality, for still others a defense against godless, materialist Marxism.[25]

At bottom, the authoritarian regimes seemed simply to work better than liberal regimes in the 1930s. The appeals of success evaporated, of course, when fascism was defeated in 1945. The outer trappings of fascism have therefore fallen into disrepute. That does not preclude the possibility, however, of similar future reactions by frightened and insecure middle and upper classes.

SUGGESTIONS FOR FURTHER READING

How Hitler reached office is studied most recently by Henry A. Turner Jr., who shows in *Hitler's Thirty Days to Power* (1997) that it was not inevitable but the result of choices by top German leaders. Refer also to the biographies of Hitler listed at the end of chapter 7.

On the local level, William Sheridan Allen, *The Nazi Seizure of Power: The Experience of a Single Town* (1984, reprint ed. 1995), is a compelling narrative of Nazi success at the grassroots. Other good local studies include Jeremy Noakes on Lower Saxony (1971), Geoffrey Pridham on Bavaria

(1973), Johnpeter Horst Grill on Baden (1983), and David C. Large, *Where Ghosts Walked: Munich's Road to the Third Reich* (1997). Rudolf Heberle, *From Democracy to Nazism* (1945; reprint ed. 1970), is a pioneer study of the only German state to give Hitler an absolute majority before 1933, Schleswig-Holstein.

Hitler's constituency has been intensely studied. Richard Hamilton, *Who Voted for Hitler?* (1982), argues that the upper middle class supported him as well as the lower middle class. Thomas Childers, *The Nazi Voter: The Social Foundations of Fascism in Germany, 1919–*

[24]Speech of 22 December 1932, quoted in Renzo De Felice, *Mussolini il duce. I. Gli anni del consenso* (Torino, Italy, 1974), p. 101n.

[25]See *"L'enfance d'un chef,"* Jean-Paul Sartre's short story of a self-doubting adolescent boy who enjoys the tough pose of a fascist youth gang. Jean-Paul Sartre, *Le Mur* (Paris, 1939), pp. 145–241.

*1933** (1984), analyzes the electorate most precisely. See also Childers, *The Formation of the Nazi Constituency* (1986). Peter Fritzsche, *Germans into Nazis** (1999) evokes the hope and excitement (more than the hatred) that brought recruits to Nazism.

Michael Burleigh, *The Third Reich: A New History** (2000), evokes brilliantly the sordid reality of Nazi Germany. Ian Kershaw, *The Nazi Dictatorship: Problems and Perspectives of Interpretation,** 4th ed. (2000), reviews interpretations of the Nazi regime with authority. Karl Dietrich Bracher, *The German Dictatorship** (1970), remains important as the authoritative synthesis of the prevailing interpretation of a generation ago, which focused centrally on the dictator's authority. Hans Mommsen, *The Third Reich between Vision and Reality: New Perspectives on German History, 1918–1945** (2000), reflects the current generation's emphasis on interactions between German society and Nazism. Allen Mitchell, *The Nazi Revolution: Hitler's Dictatorship and the German Nation,** 4th ed. (1997), is an excellent general introduction. See also Michael Burleigh, *Confronting the Nazi Past: New Debates on Modern German History** (1996). Jeremy Noakes and Geoffrey Pridham, eds., *Nazism: 1919–1945,** 4 vols. (2001), present an outstanding document collection with enlightening commentary.

Martin Broszat, *The Hitler State** (1981, reprint ed. 1989), portrays Nazi Germany as a "polyocracy" in which rival agencies competed for Hitler's favor, as does the influential work of Hans Mommsen (see above). Dietrich Orlow, *The History of the Nazi Party*, 2 vols. (1969–1973), describes evolving political structures. David Schoenbaum, *Hitler's Social Revolution** (1980, reprint ed. 1997), shows how the Nazi regime, breaking Hitler's promises to farmers and the lower middle class, made Germany more urban and industrial. The classic essay by Ralf Dahrendorf, *Society and Democracy in Germany* (1968, reprint ed. 1993), suggests further that the destructions of the Nazi era cleared the ground for postwar democracy. Pierre Ayçoberry, *The Social History of the Third Reich** (2000) contests some standard views. Important interpretative articles appear in David Crew, ed., *Nazism and German Society** (1994), Thomas Childers and Jane Caplan, eds., *Reevaluating the Third Reich** (1993) and Moshe Lewin, ed., *Stalinism and Nazism: Dictatorships in Comparison** (1997). The articles in Peter Stachura, ed., *The Shaping of the Nazi State* (1978), have not lost their interest.

Useful biographies of Nazi leaders include Ralf Georg Reuth, *Goebbels** (1994), Richard Overy, *Goering, The Iron Man** (2000), Michael Bloch, *Ribbentrop* (1992), and works on Himmler by Richard Breitman (2004*) and Peter Padfield (2001*). Joachim Fest provides short sketches in *The Face of the Third Reich** (1999).

New biomedical and gender studies cast harsh light on the nature of Nazism. See Atina Grossmann, *Reforming Sex: The German Movement for Birth Control and Abortion Reform* (1995); Michael Burleigh and Wolfgang Wippermann, *The Racial State* (1991); Götz Aly, *Cleansing the Fatherland: Nazi Medicine and Racial Hygiene** (1994); and Michael Burleigh, *Death and Deliverance: Euthanasia in Germany, c. 1900–1945** (new ed. 2002).

The German officer corps is accused of yielding to Hitler by John W. Wheeler-Bennett, *Nemesis of Power: The German Army in Politics*, 2nd ed. (2003), and by Gordon Craig's work cited at the end of chapter 2. The most recent treatment of the army in Nazi Germany is Klaus-Jürgen Müller, *Army, Politics, and Society in Germany, 1933–1945* (1987).

The controversial relations between German business and Hitler have been most soundly treated for the period before Hitler came to power by Henry A. Turner Jr., *German Big Business and the Rise of Hitler* (1984). For the period after 1933, two model studies examine individual firms: Peter Hayes, *Industry and Ideology,*[*] 2nd ed (2001), on I. G. Farben; and Bernard Bellon's unsparing *Mercedes in Peace and War*[*] (1990). See also Dan P. Silverman, *Hitler's Economy: Nazi Work Creation Programs, 1933–1936* (1999). Best on labor is Tim Mason, *Social Policy in the Third Reich*[*] (1995). See also Mason's collected essays, *Nazism, Fascism, and the Working Class*[*] (1995). The German judiciary gets attention from Michael Stolleis, *The Law under the Swastika* (1998), Ingo Muller, *Hitler's Justice* (1991), and H. W. Koch, *In the Name of the Volk: Political Justice in Hitler's Germany* (1997).

The growing Nazi terror machine is treated most authoritatively by Eric A. Johnson, *Nazi Terror: The Gestapo, Jews, and Ordinary Germans*[*] (2000), which shows both the extent and the limits of citizen support for it. The public's help to the police (by denunciations) has been measured by Robert Gellately in *The Gestapo and German Society*[*] (1990), and in *Backing Hitler: Consent and Coercion in Nazi Germany*[*] (2002). Helmut Krausnick et al.,

Anatomy of the SS State (1968), the legal brief prepared for the prosecution of the Auschwitz extermination camp staff, is still fascinating.

The life of ordinary people under Nazism is explored in Richard Bessel, *Life in the Third Reich*[*] (1987), and Detlev Peukert, *Inside Nazi Germany: Continuity, Opposition, and Racism in Ordinary Life* (1987). The intimate view of daily life by Victor Klemperer, a Jew who survived, in *I Will Bear Witness,*[*] 2 vols. (1999–2000) is haunting. Ian Kershaw, *Popular Opinion and Public Dissent in the Third Reich: Bavaria, 1933–1945*[*] (1985) and the same author's *The "Hitler Myth": Image and Reality in the Third Reich*[*] (1989), are the most reliable examinations of public opinion under Nazism. See Renate Bridenthal et al., *When Biology Became Destiny: Women in Weimar and Nazi Germany*[*] (1989), for gender issues.

Saul Friedländer, *Nazi Germany and the Jews,*[*] vol. 1, 1933–1939 (1997), is now the basic treatment of Nazi anti-Semitism. Karl A. Schleunes, *The Twisted Road to Auschwitz*[*] (1970, reprint ed. 1990), sees anti-Semitism developing in Nazi Germany by fits and starts. Lucy Dawidowicz, *The War against the Jews*[*] (1986), sees extermination as Hitler's design from the beginning. The necessary link to medicine and public health is made by Götz Aly, *Final Solution: Nazi Population Policy and the Murder of European Jews*[*] (1999). More works on the Final Solution are discussed after chapter 14.

For fascist movements outside Germany, the suggestions made at the end of chapter 7 are mostly relevant for the 1930s also. Significant monographs on individual countries include Robert Skidelsky, *Sir Oswald*

Mosley (1975); Richard C. Thurlow, *Fascism in Britain** (1998); Robert Soucy, *French Fascism: The First Wave, 1924–1933* (1986), and *French Fascism: The Second Wave, 1933–1939** (1997); Zeev Sternhell, *Neither Right nor Left: Fascist Ideology in France** (1996); Oddvar K. Hoidal, *Quisling: A Study of Treason* (1989); Hans V. Dall, *Quisling: A Study in Treachery* (1999); Lawrence D. Stokes, "Anton Mussert and the NSB," *History*, vol. 56, no. 188 (Oct. 1971); and Miklos Lacko, *Arrow Cross Men, National Socialists, 1935–1944* (1969).

Richard A. H. Robinson, *The Origins of Franco's Spain* (1970), examines the Spanish right before 1936. Stanley G. Payne, *Fascism in Spain, 1923–1977** (1999), makes clear the *Falange*'s minor role. The fullest biography of Franco is by Paul Preston (1994), and a good survey of his regime is Stanley G. Payne, *The Franco Regime* (1994, reprint ed. 2000). For Portugal, the place to begin is Antonio Costa Pinto, *Salazar's Dictatorship and European Fascism** (1996).

Martin Kitchen, *The Coming of Austrian Fascism* (1980), gives useful background to the establishment of the authoritarian state in February 1934. See also Francis L. Carsten, *Fascist Movements in Austria from Schönerer to Hitler* (1977). For Austrian opinion, see Evan Burr Bukey, *Hitler's Austria: Popular Sentiment in the Nazi Era, 1938–1945** (2000).

Additional Internet links related to this chapter are available on the Europe in the 20th Century Web site: http://www.history.wadsworth.com/paxton04.

You can also explore images, interactive timelines, and maps related to this chapter on our Western Civilization Resource Center: http://history.wadsworth.com.

Poorly equipped Spanish Republican volunteers surrender to Nationalist troops in the Somosierra Pass during the fight for Madrid in 1936.

12

The Popular Front Era, 1934–1939

In 1933, Daniel Guérin, a young French left intellectual, toured Germany by bicycle gathering material for articles in the French socialist newspaper, *Le populaire*. He reported what he saw in a mood of mingled fear and awe:

> By bicycle, across Germany, I pedaled as though through a ruined city, and I drew up the bleak inventory. The worker colossus, Social Democracy, Communist Party, unions with millions of members, collapsed or were swept away like a house of cards. Their banners, newspapers, posters, and books burned on bonfires in the town squares. Their members peopled concentration camps. Their sumptuous headquarters flew the swastika. I was present at a twilight of the gods.[1]

After the destruction of socialism in Italy, Germany, and Austria, where would the fascists strike next? Would the democracies of Europe and European socialist parties

[1]Daniel Guérin, *Front populaire: Révolution manquée,* 2nd ed. (Paris, 1970), p. 57.

and trade unions be picked off one by one by fascism's apparently inexorable advance? Did fascism's opponents hate each other more than they feared fascism? The anxious search for answers to these questions produced the Popular Front of the 1930s.

The Popular Front was an alliance of Marxists and democrats against a common fascist enemy. It rested on two fundamental assumptions: that fascism was so urgent a threat that impeding its advance took precedence over everything else; and that the best means of blocking fascism was a broad coalition around the defense of political liberties rather than a narrow coalition around either liberal or socialist goals. In order to agree on those assumptions, the diverse elements of the European left had to make major changes in outlook and strategy. Marxists had to subordinate their social program to the defense of middle-class democracies; democrats had to suspend their distrust of Marxists. Within the Marxist camp, Social Democrats and Communists had to forget fifteen years of bitter recriminations over blame for the failure of Western revolutions from 1917 to 1923. No wonder such an alliance was awkward, slow, and difficult to achieve.

A Popular Front had been unthinkable in the 1920s, when the possibility of social revolution had been the uppermost issue for the European left. It became unthinkable again later during the Cold War. The Popular Front was possible only in the 1930s and the resistance years during the Second World War, for it was a child of the depression and of the fears aroused by the conquests of Hitler and Mussolini. Even then, Popular Front coalitions were successfully formed only here and there in nonfascist Europe: in France, Spain, and among German and Italian exiles.

For its participants, the Popular Front was an experience of fervent commitment: "the 1848 of the 20th century."[2] It meant the reconciliation of the left, divided since 1917. It meant a possible turn of the tide against fascism, and a chance to do something other than wring hands as Hitler and Mussolini advanced. For committed revolutionaries, however, the Popular Front meant selling out to another flabby political alliance. For conservatives and many frightened democrats, the Popular Front meant opening the doors of Western Europe to communism. Those controversies lay at the center of public life and intellectual activity in the liberal regimes from the 1930s to the 1950s. They gave those decades their character of passionate engagement in a struggle to determine whether democrats, Marxists, or fascists would control the world.

FROM "CLASS AGAINST CLASS" TO POPULAR FRONT

The Popular Front was a grassroots enthusiasm before the organized parties worked their way around to accepting it. Its first signs appeared in France in February 1934. During the night of February 6, powerful antiparliamentary leagues fought with police in what looked then like an attempt to overthrow the French Republic. That night, French Communists also demonstrated against the bourgeois

---

[2]Stephen Spender, *World within World* (London, 1951), p. 187.

republic—separately but in parallel fashion. A significant shift took place during the next few days, however. Paris sections of the Communist Party agreed to take part—although still separately—in a great parade against fascism, organized by noncommunist trade unions and the main parties of the parliamentary left, Socialists and Radicals (small-property democrats). As the two columns turned together into a broad avenue in the Paris suburb of Vincennes, they fused, with shouts of "Unity! Unity!" At the head of what now became a single column, the Communist leader Maurice Thorez linked arms with the Socialist leader Léon Blum and the recently resigned Radical premier, Edouard Daladier. Hundreds of thousands of Parisians remembered that day of February 12 as one of reconciliation and a new beginning for the French Republic.

But there remained a period of difficult transition before the Communist, Socialist, and democratic party leaders of France and the rest of nonfascist Europe could overcome years of mutual animosity.

The Communist Policy of "Class against Class," 1928–1934

Communist parties had to make the largest leap to accept a Popular Front coalition, for they had been ordered at the Sixth Comintern Congress (1928) into a position of hardened intransigence against reformist socialists. Like most of Stalin's major decisions, this one remains wrapped in some obscurity. It was probably partly a reaction to foreign disappointments. During the period of liberal and capitalist stabilization after 1924, the dwindling Communist parties of the world had accepted some degree of cooperation with the reformist left in Western Europe and with national liberation movements overseas. This tactic had not been very fruitful. In Britain, for example, Communist support for the General Strike of 1926 had done nothing to improve the party's marginal position there. It had only helped prod the Conservatives into breaking diplomatic and trade relations with the Soviet Union in 1927. Far more damaging was the fiasco of cooperation with the nationalist Kuomintang Party in its attacks on Western capitalist concessions in China. Stalin was deeply shaken when nationalist General Chiang Kai-shek turned on the Chinese Communists and their Russian advisors in April 1927 and massacred a large number of them, driving the rest into the interior.

Stalin's hard line abroad also fit with the sharp left turn of Russian internal policy. It was illogical to permit Communists abroad to accommodate themselves to capitalist stabilization at a time when the Russian population was straining to carry out a "second revolution" of collectivization and industrialization.[3] Some of Stalin's critics have accused him of forcing foreign Communists into the same "ultraleftism" out of "meaningless mimicry,"[4] without regard for local parties' tactical needs. It seems likely that Stalin knew little about foreign Communist parties and cared only for their perfect conformity to Russian requirements.

[3]See chapter 10, pp. 316–319.

[4]Isaac Deutscher, *Stalin: A Political Biography,* 2nd ed. (New York, 1967), p. 404. This compelling biography is strongly colored by sympathy for Trotsky.

Comintern intransigence reflected Stalin's assertion in December 1927 that capitalism was entering a "third period," a time of sharpened contradictions and intensified disorder.[5] The world depression of 1929 added plausibility to the view that the overthrow of capitalism was once more possible. In that case, workers must not be sidetracked into the defense of democracy. According to the Comintern view, democracy and fascism were merely different forms of a single reality, governments devoted to the defense of bourgeois property and the rescue of capitalism. Indeed, Stalin singled out the Western democracies as Soviet Russia's most dangerous enemies. Italy was still the only example of a fascist state. Britain and France had been the creators of the Paris peace system, the promoters of armed intervention in Russia in 1919 and 1920, and the chief bulwark of capitalist stabilization. There is some evidence that Stalin feared renewed military intervention by Britain and France in the late 1920s.

In the Comintern perspective, the proper course for workers in the "third period" was heightened class struggle, aligning all workers against all members of the middle class, whether democrats or fascists, in an attitude of "class against class." Stalin viewed the efforts of Western European Social Democrats to defend democracy as treason to the workers' cause. Social Democrats, he claimed, were propping up capitalism and lulling workers into nonrevolutionary stances in a revolutionary time. "Objectively," Stalin had written in 1924, "Social Democracy is the moderate wing of fascism. . . . They are not antipodes but twins."[6] It was a position to which he returned after 1928. Social Democrats and reformist trade unions were the principal support of bourgeois democracy and the principal obstacle to the overthrow of capitalism. They must be destroyed.

In the French elections of 1928, for example, Communists competed with Socialists for established Socialist seats. The Communist leader Jacques Duclos defeated Socialist leader Léon Blum for the Paris seat Blum had held since 1920. French Socialists could complain that "class against class" cost them twenty-two seats (including the seat of Karl Marx's grandson Jean Longuet) in cases in which a Socialist had been leading in the first ballot only to have a Communist remain in the run-off and throw the election to a united right-wing candidacy.[7] The French Communist poet Louis Aragon gave the clearest literary expression of "class against class" politics in his poem "Red Front" (1931):

> Fire on Léon Blum . . .
> Fire on the trained bears of social democracy[8]

In Germany, Hitler's ascent was but one more confirmation for Stalin that capitalism was grasping for desperate remedies. The correct policy for German Communists, from Stalin's point of view in 1932 and 1933, was to heighten the tension, help widen political polarization, attack Social Democrats as "social fascists," and count

---

[5]The revolutionary years of 1917 to 1923 were alleged to form a "first period," followed by a "second period" of capitalist stabilization in the mid-1920s.

[6]Deutscher, pp. 406–407.

[7]Georges Lefranc, *Le Mouvement socialiste sous la troisième République* (Paris, 1963), p. 275.

[8]Louis Aragon, "Red Front," in Maurice Nadeau, *History of Surrealism,* trans. Richard Howard (New York, 1965), p. 288.

on the next swing of the pendulum to bring revolution. That analysis was not shaken by Hitler's success in taking power in 1933, for Communists could believe that the pendulum would swing again. Stalin was not totally wrong. Communism did succeed Nazism in at least part of Germany, but Stalin had not expected that process to take twelve painful years and a world war.

Germany was important to Russian national interests, whoever its leader. Since the Treaty of Rapallo in 1922, a revisionist Germany had been Russia's natural ally against the Versailles victors. Therefore Stalin did not renounce the Russo-German pact of neutrality and friendship of 1926 when Hitler came to power. Indeed, he renewed it in May 1933 and so became the first ruler to conclude a diplomatic agreement with Hitler. The secret training and arms production in Russia for the German army continued through 1934. Behind a smoke screen of hostile rhetoric, the two states maintained practical working relations. As late as the Seventeenth Communist Party Congress in January 1934, Stalin was still stating publicly that "fascism is not the issue," that the Soviet Union enjoyed the "best relations" with Italy, and that the Soviet Union was still an opponent of the Paris peace settlement. Dimitri Manuilski, the party secretary-general, told the conference that "the destruction of Social Democracy is one of the most essential conditions for hastening the growth of the revolutionary crisis."[9]

Reversal of Comintern Policy, 1934

The change came some time in the late spring of 1934. For several months there had been straws in the wind. Soviet diplomats expressed great concern to Western diplomats in late 1933 about Japanese expansion in Manchuria, a sign that Stalin was beginning to worry about a two-front war. In late 1933 and early 1934 the Soviet government made inquiries about French technical assistance to the Soviet air force, and in early 1934 about possible Soviet membership in the League of Nations. By June 1934, a united front with democrats had become the official policy of the French Communist Party, obviously with official approval from Moscow.

Stalin's reassessment was a sweeping one. He renounced revolution as a real possibility in the rest of Europe. Defense of the Soviet state took precedence over class warfare abroad, and Germany was now seen as the chief threat to the Soviet state. The democracies, in this changed perspective, became the most promising military allies in case of war with Germany. The democracies' crisis was no longer something to foster, and the Social Democrats or reformist Socialists were no longer "social fascists." Stalin's aim was now to seek the widest possible alliance against Germany on pragmatic military grounds.

In September 1934, the Soviet Union joined the League of Nations. Late in 1934, the Soviet foreign minister, Maxim Litvinov, was one of the main proponents of an "eastern Locarno," a multinational guarantee of Germany's Versailles frontiers in the east to match the guarantees of the western frontiers settled in 1925. When that

---

[9]*Rundschau*, the Comintern newspaper, February 20, 1934, quoted in Julius Braunthal, *History of the International*, vol. 2 (London, 1967), p. 423.

project was thwarted by German and Polish opposition, the Soviet Union concluded mutual security treaties with France and Czechoslovakia in which each partner promised to help the other in case of German attack. The new policy was made official at the Seventh World Congress of the Communist International (Comintern) in Moscow in the summer of 1935. The delegates were told that the main task of workers was to unite in defense of democracy against fascism.

At the time of the signing of the Franco-Soviet Pact in May 1935, Stalin himself gave a striking confirmation of the Popular Front. French foreign minister Pierre Laval returned from Moscow authorized to announce that Stalin "understood and fully supported" French policies of national defense. This constituted a communist accolade to the French army, chief bulwark of Versailles, against whose appropriations French Communists had voted since the party's creation. Stalin's statement served notice that the Popular Front was at bottom a military alliance against Hitler and that all dreams of social progress evoked by the reunion of the European lefts must take second place.

Because of its military nature, Stalin meant for the Popular Front to extend as far as possible into the democratic center. There had been united fronts between Socialists and Communists before; this was to be a "peoples' front," including middle-class democrats (Liberal and Radical parties) and even conservatives[10] who were willing to oppose fascism actively.

The Liberal Reaction

The Popular Front idea divided democrats in Western Europe. There was virtually no sympathy for it among British Liberals, or even among British Labour. On the Continent, many erstwhile political liberals disapproved of an alliance including Communists. Most of those Continental democrats who responded warmly to the idea were members of Radical parties.

Radical parties were no longer "radical," in any contemporary sense, in interwar Europe. They had been radically committed to the nineteenth-century struggles for universal suffrage, universal free public schools, separation of Church and state, and curbs on professional armies. Vigorous anticlericalism kept them militant after their other goals had been achieved, so that Radical parties flourished far longer with a keener sense of left-wing identity in Catholic countries (France during the Dreyfus Affair, Italy under Giolitti, Spain in the Republic of 1931) than among Protestant Liberals in England or Germany. In social and economic terms, Radicals were defenders of the independent small man: shopkeepers, family farmers, village lawyers, and schoolteachers. They were in fundamental disagreement with Marxists over property: whereas Marxists wanted to replace private property with collective property, Radicals wanted to give every citizen a chance to own property. But since the Popular Front muted these social questions, the issues that aroused the Radicals' traditional libertarianism came to the fore in the face of fascism. Against Mussolini, Hitler, and their allies, Radicals rallied to their ingrained individualism and the defense of freedom of thought and expression.

[10]The French Communist leader Maurice Thorez, in a speech on April 17, 1936, extended a fraternal hand to Catholics, war veterans, and all those "oppressed by the same cares" who wanted to "save the country from ruin."

Radicalism was dead in Italy, but Radicals in France and Spain responded to the fascist advance by reviving the cry they used against kings and churches: "no enemies to the left." Although Edouard Herriot and Edouard Daladier battled for control of the French Radical Party in the "war of the two Edouards," they agreed in seeing the new fascist leagues as the revival of the old enemy: counterrevolution, powerful priests and officers, and the authoritarian state. Moreover, the sufferings of French small-property owners during the depression had heightened many Radicals' willingness to accept vigorous, if limited, social reforms. Similar attitudes were found in Spain, where Manuel Azaña, journalist and president of a Madrid literary club (the *Ataneo*), militant anticlerical and proponent of civilian control over the military, was to be the Popular Front prime minister. Such democrats responded readily to the Communist proposal of a broad alliance against fascism that played down social questions.

The Socialist Reaction

Without the Socialists, a Communist–Radical understanding would be meaningless. But the bitterness between Socialists and Communists was not easy to overcome. There were both old and new wounds: the ancient reformist-revolutionist quarrel; the resentment against those who had carried Socialists over to national patriotism in 1914; the antagonisms created during the splits of 1919 to 1921; and the policy of "class against class" after 1928.

While Communists had accused Socialists of not being revolutionary enough, Socialists had accused Communists of introducing an alien and retrograde authoritarianism into the advanced socialist movements of the West. Communist attacks on German Social Democrats as "social fascists" had been the last straw. The Austrian Social Democrat Friedrich Adler, leader of the Second (Socialist) International, accused Communists of regarding the destruction of democracy as a condition for achieving socialism and following tactics "which led to the hell of fascism" because they felt that "the only way to the socialist paradise leads through this hell."[11] Socialists were also reluctant to agree to a common program that included so little social change. They wanted to be reassured of the Popular Front's commitment to social reforms, and, even more, of the willingness of Communists to cooperate with the existing socialist leadership. Socialists could well be skeptical of united fronts, which heretofore had often meant uniting from the base—to draw off the socialist following from its leaders, or "to pluck the socialist goose" *(plumer la volaille),* as the phrase went. In the end, however, the emergency presented by fascist advances and grassroots enthusiasm for the Popular Front overcame many socialist leaders' hesitations.

Popular Fronts were not created everywhere in democratic Europe. In general, they were formed where the fascist threat seemed paramount, as among the German and Italian exiles, and where large Marxist parties coexisted with anticlerical Radicals, as in Catholic France and Spain. In England, Labour was not only anti-Communist but anti-Liberal after the disastrous coalitions of 1924 and 1929 to

---

[11]Quoted in Braunthal, vol. 2, p. 399. Friedrich Adler was not necessarily always opposed to violent action; he had personally assassinated the Austrian Prime Minister, Karl Stürgkh, in 1916.

1931. The few left-wing Labour intellectuals who advocated a Popular Front alliance with the tiny Communist Party found no following among the trade union rank and file. The strong Social Democratic parties of the Low Countries and Scandinavia expressed little interest in reconciliation with small Communist parties there. In Sweden, Social Democrats had governed on their own since 1931, and in Norway since 1935. The only Communist Party surviving in Eastern Europe, the Czech Communist Party, had not been accepted by the pronational Social Democrats because of its opposition to the very principle of a Czechoslovak state up to 1935.

Where Popular Front coalitions were successfully established, they released a fervent enthusiasm among politicians, rank and file, and intellectuals. Popular Front supporters believed that at last the natural numbers of antifascists would exert their due weight. The painful divisions of the European left seemed healed, and at last something constructive could be done to stop the advancing fascist monster.

THE POPULAR FRONT IN FRANCE

France was a logical place for the most prominent Popular Front experiment. The antiparliamentary demonstrations of February 6, 1934, had made France seem next on the fascist list. Drawn up on the opposite side were the Socialists and Communists, the two largest Marxist parties remaining in Western Europe after the destruction of those in Italy, Germany, and Austria. Whereas part of the French middle class saw in fascism the only route to both grandeur and safety, special features of the French political tradition made other middle-class French citizens favor a Popular Front. The French had fought a great popular war against the kings of Europe under Jacobin[12] leadership in 1793; in 1936, a new Jacobin appeal against a new form of counterrevolution aroused positive emotions. The Jacobin tradition permitted French citizens to be both left and nationalist in the defense of republican liberties. Anticlericalism also kept many middle-class French receptive to the left. More immediately, Pierre Laval's harsh deflationary depression remedies of 1935[13] turned many a French pensioner, war veteran, and lower civil servant toward the left. In France, the Marxist parties could win middle-class allies by stressing nationalism, defense of political liberties, and economic revival.

Even so, a Popular Front was difficult to construct. It was hard for Socialist and Communist leaders to forget fifteen years of fratricidal mudslinging. The two Marxist parties also had different priorities. French Socialists wanted to seek immediate social changes, including some nationalization of industry and more steeply graduated taxes. French Communists wanted to help defend the Soviet Union by forming the widest possible coalition against Nazi Germany, including small-property Radicals and Catholic democrats, even if this meant limiting the Popular Front to the defense of political liberties against fascism. In the end, the rising specter of mass

---

[12]The revolutionary democrats in France during the French Revolution were called Jacobins because they held their meetings in a convent of an order named the Jacobin friars.

[13]See chapter 10, p. 307.

support for Colonel de La Rocque's protofascist *Croix de feu,* which threatened to become the largest French party by the time of the elections of 1936, overrode all hesitations. The Popular Front alliance was sealed with a Bastille Day parade on July 14, 1935, in which the Socialist, Communist, and Radical leaders—Léon Blum, Maurice Thorez, and Edouard Daladier—linked arms before more than a million jubilant Parisians in the traditional setting of Jacobin unity, the *Place de la Bastille.*

The Formation of Léon Blum's Government

The election of May 1936 was the most significant in interwar France. The Popular Front candidates won a small increase in total votes (57 percent, compared with 54 percent for the same parties separately in 1932) but an overwhelming victory in parliamentary seats: 386 out of 608, a gain of 40 seats since 1932. Few French voters had changed their minds; the two-stage electoral system simply favored the most united coalition. Communists and Socialists did not compete with one another in the run-off as they had before. The parliamentary strength of the Popular Front was, therefore, artificially greater than its actual electoral strength, a disproportion that led to exaggerated fears on the right, exaggerated expectations on the left, and exaggerated disappointment within the Popular Front over what accomplishments were eventually possible.

The elections also produced a realignment within the French left. Communist seats increased from eleven to seventy-two, the most important advance the party made in France until the first elections after the liberation in 1945. The Radicals, who had formed the largest party in France before the First World War, now fell behind the Socialists for the first time. They began at once to have second thoughts about the Popular Front.

Since the French Socialist Party emerged as the leading party of the victorious coalition, its leader, Léon Blum, became premier of France on June 5, 1936. He was the first Socialist and the first Jew to hold that office.

Blum, the son of a prosperous Parisian wholesaler of silk ribbon, had distinguished himself in two careers before turning to politics. In his twenties, at the turn of the century, he was already a prominent avant-garde literary critic and essayist. He also spent a quarter century as a judge in the *Conseil d'état,* France's highest court of administrative law, where citizens' disputes with government agencies were adjudicated. The Dreyfus Affair drew him into socialist politics, along with so many other intellectuals of his generation. But Blum could not imagine socialism without political liberty. When the majority of French Socialists joined Lenin's Third International in 1920, Blum led the minority who refused to accept the Bolshevik formulas of centralized party authority, secrecy, and purges. Blum's party recovered to become the largest in France by 1936, and Blum himself assumed the mantle of Jean Jaurès as the leading French democratic Socialist of the first half of the century.

This slender, ascetic, refined intellectual seemed an anomaly as head of a working-class party. Blum's reedy voice spelled out all the theoretical pros and cons of each policy with the elegance he had once displayed in his avant-garde essays and the

French socialist leader Léon Blum (right) with British Labour Party leader Clement Attlee in front of the House of Commons in London, May 1939.

analytical rigor he had employed in his legal briefs. He never swayed audiences in the manner of the ebullient Jaurès. Blum was vilified and beloved in his own time. The right attacked him as a "subtle Talmudist" who had no business governing an "ancient Gallo-Roman" people."[14] Nationalist demonstrators beat him in the street in February 1936; in his seventies, he survived a German concentration camp. On his own left, he was accused of insufficient revolutionary will. Blum nonetheless won a devoted following by his earnest commitment to humanitarian ideals and the open honesty with which he evaluated in public his agonizing choices.

The 1936 election seemed to promise a new direction in European affairs. At a time when no democracy had worked well since 1929, a major European state had turned resolutely toward social democracy combined with parliamentary practice. Europeans watched the results to see whether the democracies had discovered a new lease on life.

The French New Deal

Blum's year in power, from June 1936 to June 1937, is sometimes referred to as the French New Deal. Unlike United States president Franklin D. Roosevelt, however,

---

[14]The Catholic nationalist Xavier Vallat in the Chamber of Deputies, June 5, 1936.

France, mass strikes of May and June 1936. The placard identifies the boss as "one of the thieves."

Blum had neither overwhelming electoral support, a fixed term of office, broad executive powers, or comparative freedom from international complications.

Blum took office in an atmosphere bordering on civil war, amid exalted hopes and exaggerated fears. More than 2 million French workers were out on strike—or rather in, for the tactic of sit-down strikes in factories spread like a grass fire, beyond any capacity of the union leadership to control it. Some of them believed, like the exiled Russian revolutionary Leon Trotsky, that "the French Revolution had begun." At the other political pole, another 2 million French belonged to antiparliamentary leagues like La Rocque's *parti social français.* Even the moderately conservative press, such as the staid *Le Temps,* referred to the Popular Front as "revolutionary" despite its quite modest program.

On June 7, Blum met all night with union leaders and terrified industrialists in his official residence, the Matignon Palace, and arbitrated a nonrevolutionary settlement to the strike wave. The Matignon Agreements recognized collective bargaining, the right of labor to organize, and a 15 percent wage increase.

Extensive change in the French social system was not part of the Popular Front's mandate. The coalition depended on muting social questions in order to form the largest possible antifascist alliance. Léon Blum, with his characteristically scrupulous distinctions, reminded his socialist followers that the Popular Front was an "exercise of power within the framework of existing institutions and . . . the present constitution"[15] rather than a revolutionary "conquest of power" for the pursuit of radical change.

Nevertheless, Blum's Popular Front tried to address three major issues: social inequality, the depression, and the rising tide of fascism. The rush of legislation in the Popular Front government's first weeks produced some social reforms that changed the lives of millions of French people and that no subsequent government, even under German occupation in the Second World War, dared repeal. Most important of these was the two-week vacation with pay for employees of all except small family enterprises. With this act the French government first recognized leisure as a basic social right; the massive movement of French families to the sea and the mountains in August remains the most substantial monument to Blum's humanitarian vision. Blum's government also intervened more directly in labor–management relations than any of its predecessors. In addition to the Matignon Agreements of June 1936, a new law of June 24 promoted collective bargaining and provided for the election of workers' representatives in larger factories. Blum also gave three minor cabinet posts to women, the first to hold political office in France. Though limited in scope, the Popular Front's social reforms constituted its most lasting contribution.

Blum's government dealt less successfully with the depression. His policy of replacing deflation with "reflation" and stimulating the economy by increased purchasing power[16] looked more promising than the previous "deflation." In application, however, these remedies were vitiated by awkward circumstances, internal resistance, and the government's own hesitancy. The forty-hour week, however desirable in social terms, was applied in ways that reduced production. Exports continued to fall, for French prices rose faster than production, and Blum hesitated to take the one measure that would most stimulate exports—devaluation of the franc—because of popular sensitivity about monetary fluctuations. As the French balance of payments worsened, French investors and speculators—no friends of the Popular Front under any circumstances—started a flow of francs out of the country by buying gold and foreign currencies. Unwilling to impose exchange controls, the government was forced by these pressures to devalue the franc in September 1936, under conditions that brought no gain in foreign trade. By 1938, production was still lower than the level of 1929, and price rises had absorbed the wage gains of the summer of 1936.

The fight against fascism was the Popular Front's chief reason for existence; yet it became its chief obstacle to survival. Blum's government, less committed to a balanced budget than its predecessors, began the first significant rearmament of

---

[15]Joel Colton, *Léon Blum: Humanist in Politics,* 2nd ed. (New York, 1987), p. 137.

[16]See chapter 10, pp. 308–309.

France against the German menace. A left government that strengthened the army remained a left government in conservative eyes, however. In a curious reversal of foreign policy, many conservatives began to regard Hitler as a bulwark against communism and a war to stop Hitler as "Stalin's War," which would simultaneously let the Russians into Europe and unleash revolution at home, as in 1917. Polarization in French foreign affairs made every potential ally politically unacceptable to some important section of French opinion.

The only plausible counterweight to a revived Germany was Russia, even weakened by forced collectivization and purges. Indeed, the old Franco-Russian Alliance of 1892 to 1917 began to be revived before Blum came to power, when Laval visited Stalin and signed a mutual defense agreement in May 1935. When that treaty came before parliament for confirmation in February 1936, however, bitter opposition nearly defeated it. Blum did nothing with this treaty, claiming later that the army had been opposed to it. The only other potential counterweight to Germany, fascist Italy, had already broken irrevocably with the democracies in 1935 over the Ethiopian War,[17] although the French right never ceased blaming Blum for not trying to reopen contacts with Mussolini. The Eastern European successor states, the basis of France's alliance system against Germany in the 1920s, were drifting into the more dynamic German economic orbit; in any case, the French army was incapable of coming to the aid of any of them after Germany reoccupied the Rhineland in March 1936. After that event, the Belgians ended their defensive arrangements with the French in the summer of 1936 and declared their neutrality. The Popular Front had set out to oppose Hitler's spread by military and diplomatic means, but it was left with a partly disaffected army and a single ally, Britain, which, in turn, was committed to a policy of noninterference on the Continent.

The antifascist stance of the Popular Front was challenged in its very first days by the outbreak of the Spanish Civil War. Dissident Spanish generals and the Spanish Moroccan Legion rebelled against the Spanish republican government on July 18, 1936. Spain had also been governed by a Popular Front coalition since February, and Blum was eager to aid a sister regime. The situation seemed straightforward. A legitimate Spanish government was asking for French arms in order to defeat a military uprising, and France had every reason to want to avoid facing yet another fascist regime on a third frontier.

Aid to republican Spain aroused such furious opposition from Blum's own moderate coalition partners, the Radicals, and from the British government, however, that Blum felt unable to offer more than a little clandestine aid. Given the power of fascist leagues in France, Blum also feared that direct French participation in the Spanish struggle would spread civil war to France.

Blum resigned himself to the more cautious policy of trying to stop all outside aid to either side, in the hope that republican Spain would survive if Germany and Italy were prevented from aiding the insurgents. He cooperated with England and other European states in setting up a Non-Intervention Commission to block all arms imports into Spain. The result was a leaky blockade through which the Spanish Republic received less aid (mostly from the Soviet Union) than the Spanish

---

[17]See chapter 13, pp. 387–389.

insurgents received from Germany and Italy. Blum wound up facing total war in Spain anyway and passionate controversy at home. Conservatives accused the government of tolerating clandestine aid to Spanish "Reds" and predicted the spread of civil war to France; the left demonstrated for greater aid to Spain. During a clash between a right-wing league and Communist demonstrators in the Paris suburb of Clichy on March 16, 1937, police killed six Popular Front supporters. The regime seemed to be devouring its own children. The Popular Front, formed to combat fascism, found itself curbing those who wanted to fight fascism in Spain.

Financial strains had already forced Blum to declare a "pause" in February 1937. In an effort to persuade rather than coerce French financiers and industrialists, he restored the free market in gold, appointed a group of orthodox financial advisors, and announced an end to wage raises until the economy could catch its breath. As real wages lost ground again in the spring of 1937, and as discontent grew among the Popular Front's left over nonintervention in Spain, Blum was caught in precisely the situation that he had warned against when defining the concept of "exercise of power." He had committed the French Socialists to the responsibilities of office without being able to avoid compromise policies that were abhorrent to the party's rank and file. When the Senate refused in June 1937 to vote full powers to Blum to deal with the worsening economic situation, Blum took the occasion to resign.

Technically, the French Popular Front coalition continued to hold office until November 1938 under more moderate Radical leaders, interspersed with another brief Blum ministry in the spring of 1938. But the original hopes had vanished in that first winter. The Socialist Party's more intransigent wing believed, as its leader Marceau Pivert said, that "everything is possible," despite the basic conservatism of France's small-property majority. A fanatical right wing invented monstrous fantasies about the scrupulous Blum, portraying him as an immigrant revolutionary whose real name was Karfunkelstein. With limited elbow room between these extremes, Blum proceded with perhaps excessive caution, preferring to persuade rather than coerce the hostile business community. In its brief life, the French New Deal left France more polarized than ever, ill-equipped to make difficult decisions to cure the depression or resist Nazi expansion.

SPAIN: REPUBLIC, REVOLUTION, AND CIVIL WAR

Spain was the only other European country in which a Popular Front coalition held power. A Popular Front coalition won the elections of February 1936 and tried to defend the recently founded Second Republic against the insurgent generals who rose against it in July 1936.

The Creation of the Second Republic

The Second Spanish Republic (1931–1939) was not created by a revolution; it simply filled a vacuum. The authoritarian regime of General Primo de Rivera (1923–1930) had not made the monarchy any stronger. When municipal elections in April 1931 revealed widespread disaffection for the monarchy, King Alfonso XIII left the country rather than risk a struggle in which he was not sure of military and police support.

Into the vacuum rushed a number of competing claimants for power. These claimants were far more diverse than those in France, for Spain was a far less homogeneous country. At the top, there were an entrenched aristocracy, a deeply conservative Catholic hierarchy, an army still smarting from its defeats by the United States in 1898 and by Moroccan tribesmen in 1921, an ancient tradition of political bossism, and intellectuals brooding over Spain's long decline since the sixteenth century. At the bottom was a poverty-stricken and largely illiterate population. Most of Spain was agricultural. Small peasant plots predominated in northern Spain, whereas in southern Spain (Andalusia) less than 2 percent of the population owned 66.5 percent of the land.[18] Spain was not wholly preindustrial, however. There were two very vigorous islands of industrial activity. Catalonia, with its great industrial city of Barcelona, was Spain's most economically advanced area. The Basque country in the north contained the leading coal and iron mining areas. Since both of these regions had separate languages and a strong sense of cultural distinctness, industry only aggravated Spain's lack of national integration.

It was not easy to find an electoral majority capable of speaking for such diverse interests. Nevertheless, when King Alfonso XIII left in 1931, a coalition of democrats and reformist socialists provided Spain with a parliamentary constitution modeled on the French and Weimar examples (at a time when both countries were having trouble coping with depression strains themselves). A single chamber (*Cortes*), elected by all adult men and women, held the preponderant power in this "republic of workers of all categories." The president's powers were carefully limited, in reaction against Primo de Rivera and Alfonso XIII.

Political Phases of the Republic

The short-lived Spanish Republic passed through three distinct political periods. An anticlerical, antimilitarist intellectual, Manuel Azaña, was prime minister during the "red biennium," from October 1931 until just before the elections of November 1933. Those elections gave 40 percent of the seats to conservatives and only 20 percent to the various lefts (the anarchists had counseled abstention), and so a center-right coalition governed during the "black biennium" (1934–1936). A Popular Front coalition then won control of the legislature in the elections of February 1936.

Quite independently of these political phases, massive extraparliamentary currents carried Spain along beyond the control of politicians. Submerged popular resentments broke to the surface of public life. Anticlericals burned or took over hundreds of churches and convents in May 1931 and some scattered ones later.[19]

---

[18]Edward E. Malefakis, *Agrarian Reform and Peasant Revolution in Spain: Origins of the Civil War* (New Haven, Conn., 1970), p. 29.

[19]Terrified bishops believed that 20,000 churches were burned and tombs desecrated. On this controversial issue, I have accepted the figures of Burnett Bolloten, *The Spanish Civil War: Revolution and Counter-Revolution* (Chapel Hill, N.C., 1991), p. 51.

Agrarian rebellion, expressed since the 1880s in a popular anarchism as distrustful of parliamentary reform as it was hostile to the landlords, led to land seizures and communal uprisings among Andalusian farm laborers. Fearful conservatives grew increasingly willing to accept some authoritarian solution to disorder. It is probably fair to say that none of the successive governments of the republic after 1931, including the Popular Front, ever managed to contain all these forces.

The first phase of the republic (1931–1933) was most important for the enemies it made. Prime Minister Azaña's majority was radical in the late-nineteenth-century European meaning of the word: It considered universal suffrage and education to be the most important reforms, and the Catholic Church and professional officers to be the most important threats to democracy. Azaña's government dissolved the Jesuit order, curtailed sharply the liberty of religious orders to engage in teaching and in business, and ordered Catholic private schools closed by the beginning of the school year of 1933. Divorce was permitted and women voted for the first time in Spain. Azaña took steps to reduce the surplus of officers in the Spanish army, to cut military service to one year, and to abolish the army staff college—the pride and joy of Spain's most rapidly rising young general, Francisco Franco. Catalonia received a large measure of provincial autonomy. Land reform was the most obvious social need. The Azaña government forced through a law for the redistribution of some of the largest tracts of uncultivated latifundia, but the legal provisions were so complicated that only about 40,000 peasants were resettled, many of them only temporarily.[20] While social unrest continued to rise, Catholics and many officers aligned themselves against the republic.

What Spanish republicans call the "black biennium" began with conservative victories at the polls in November 1933. For over two years, governments were headed by a coalition of centrist republicans who depended for their majority on the CEDA (Confederation of Autonomous Right Parties), a new Catholic Party that was now the largest in Spain. José Maria Gil Robles, the young dynamic CEDA leader, refused to recognize that the republic had any legitimacy except as "the regime of the moment." When several CEDA deputies were given cabinet posts in October 1934, the coal miners of the region of Asturias revolted to protest this threat to the republic, as well as their depression sufferings. Spanish Moroccan Foreign Legionnaires, under General Franco, suppressed the Asturias resistance bloodily. The clerical associates of Gil Robles proceeded to undo much of Azaña's anticlerical and antimilitarist legislation; they restored the death penalty, abolished Catalonian autonomy, and stopped coeducation in state schools.

From the end of 1934, the Spanish government maintained an official "state of alarm," which permitted the suspension of civil liberties. Thousands of Spaniards were in prison; thousands more contemplated direct action. As the elections of February 1936 approached, Spaniards increasingly classified themselves according to hatreds. Each camp nourished its own horror stories: nuns raped by miners; miners tortured by Foreign Legionnaires. Those who felt that a revolution had already begun in the anarchist villages of Andalusia, in the mines of Asturias, and in

[20]Malefakis, p. 281.

separatist Catalonia, threw their support to conservatives, or to Franco's Foreign Legionnaires, or to José Antonio Primo de Rivera's *Falange*. Those who believed that clericals and reactionaires had goaded peasants and miners to desperate action in order to crush them prepared a massive electoral turnout for the Popular Front.

The Spanish Popular Front resembled the French one only in general outline: an antifascist electoral coalition of democrats, socialists, and the revolutionary left. As such, it conformed to a larger European pattern. Adapted to Spanish conditions, however, the Popular Front was transformed. It faced a domestic political spectrum far more polarized than in any northern European country. And the mix of the various lefts was quite unique. The Communist Party was a marginal movement in Spain, with 20,000 members; it won only sixteen seats in 1936. The heart of the Spanish left was anarchist and syndicalist. The peasants' anarchist counterculture, with its own tradition of spontaneous uprisings, was intractable to organization or control by formal parties. The largest unions were syndicalist, fervent believers in general strike tactics and skeptical of parliamentary action. In 1936,

Universal Pictorial Press

General Francisco Franco takes the oath as Supreme Head of the insurgent "Nationalist Government" in Burgos, in northern Spain, which he made his capital in October 1936.

the Spanish Socialists, under the leadership of the genuinely proletarian stonecutter Francisco Largo Caballero, rushed toward the left to keep up with the rank and file unionists. Even more than in France, the Popular Front in Spain consisted of the combined efforts of democrats and Communists to subject Socialists, syndicalists, and anarchists to political discipline in the name of a worldwide struggle against fascism.

Manuel Azaña became prime minister again after the Popular Front electoral victory of February 1936 (the anarchists had voted this time). The Popular Front's efforts seem petty against the forces that began to move then. Despite energetic land reform that resulted in the settlement of 111,000 peasants on new lands in three months, peasants ceased to work for their landlords and began seizing lands in the most extensive strike wave in Spanish history.[21] During the same spring, senior army officers drew up plans to seize power. In a private plane lent by a British admirer, Franco flew to Morocco from the Canary Islands, where Azaña had exiled him. The generals gave the signal to invade from Spanish Morocco on July 18, 1936, and with the aid of transport planes lent by Mussolini, began ferrying Foreign Legionnaires across the Straits of Gibraltar to Andalusia. The Spanish Civil War had begun.

The Civil War

It took three years and at least 500,000 deaths for the insurgents to fight their way to conquest of a brutalized Spain.[22] Neither side was strong enough to carry a speedy victory, nor weak enough to lose heart early. The insurgents could rely on most of the army, on money and arms and men from Italy and Germany, and on broad middle- and upper-class backing in the agricultural areas of Spain. They began with a solid foothold in Andalusia and along the Portuguese frontier to the province of Galicia in northwestern Spain. The Popular Front's assets included a good part of the Spanish air force and navy, volunteers from abroad, aid from the Soviet Union and Mexico, and mass support in the industrial areas, the capital, and the east coast. The insurgents could feed themselves and mount massive military campaigns; the Popular Front could produce more goods and rely on more of the population, but it had to improvise its military actions.

The focus of the first year of fighting was the capital city, Madrid. The insurgents advanced on the city with a formidable military force in four columns and expected help from a "fifth column" of sympathizers within the city. A makeshift but fervent Popular Front force unexpectedly held Madrid, however, showing what a determined popular militia could do in an urban setting.

The insurgents then drew on fascist Europe for help. The Anglo-French Non-Intervention Commission kept more foreign aid from the government than from the insurgents. Between December 1936 and April 1937, the Italians sent 100,000

[21]Malefakis, p. 365.

[22]Hugh Thomas, *The Spanish Civil War,* revised ed., (London, 1986), p. 926.

troops (70,000 Italians and 30,000 North African colonial soldiers) to Spain. In November 1936, the Germans sent the Condor Legion air units, manned by about 6,000 men, along with some artillery and tanks. Even so, the insurgents still could not succeed in driving on Madrid. When an Italian tank division was decimated by republican planes in mountain passes at Guadalajara in March 1937, jubilant Spanish republicans renamed the Italian CTV (Corps of Voluntary Troops) *¿Cuándo Te Vas?* (When are you leaving?).

Organizing the Popular Front for war posed a choice between spontaneity and discipline. The passions and necessities of war pushed the republic rapidly to the left, but which left would call the tune, anarcho-syndicalists or communists? The syndicalist workers of Catalonia, once again grasping provincial autonomy, seized factories and ran them by workers' committees, and set up rural cooperatives. The syndicalist POUM (*Partido Obrero de Unificación Marxista*, Workers' Party of Marxist Unity) insisted it was initiating the libertarian society of the future. The Communists called these steps "infantile leftism," quoting Lenin, and argued that hasty internal social changes would rupture the common front against fascism. They charged that the workers' committees produced less war matériel than the previous owners.

The Communists won, not only because war production put a greater premium on efficiency than on liberty, but also because the Soviet Union provided the only substantial outside aid to the republic. The Russians sent about 400 trucks, 50 planes, 100 tanks, 400 pilots and tank drivers, and a number of senior military advisors before "nonintervention" agreements closed the ports in late 1936. As Russian advisers increased in influence, the Communist Party in Spain ceased to be a marginal element of the Spanish left; it became a mass party for the first time. Communist opposition to hasty social change made itself felt. In August 1937, for example, public worship was restored in the republican zones. Far more importantly, the Communist-dominated police in Catalonia arrested the POUM leaders and closed its offices in June 1937.[23] The Communists may have imposed some discipline on the Spanish Popular Front, but they divided and weakened its popular base.

In the meantime, the better-equipped insurgents turned away from Madrid after the first year and nibbled at the republic's other strongholds. First they pierced northward to the Bay of Biscay, causing British businessmen with extensive mining and banking interests there to wish to do business with Franco. Then they cut the republican areas in half by following the Ebro River down to the Mediterranean coast in late 1938. After that, it was only a mopping-up process. As thousands of refugees streamed into France from Catalonia, the European democracies debated whether to recognize the Franco regime. They did so in February 1939. With the fall of Madrid on March 28, the civil war came to an end.

The Spanish Civil War had been fought with passionate intensity on both sides. The Popular Front's efforts caught the imagination of intellectuals and the left

---

[23]The best-known English-language memoir of the Spanish Civil War, the British volunteer George Orwell's *Homage to Catalonia* (London, 1938), takes its tone of bitter disillusionment from his personal friendship with POUM leaders and his rage at Stalin's destruction of the POUM's revolutionary experiments.

British cartoonist David Low took a skeptical view of Franco's independence of his Axis supporters in 1939, when Britain and France were considering recognizing the new Spanish regime. Here Franco tells Chamberlain and Daladier, "Honest, Mister, there's nobody here but us Spaniards."

throughout the world; some 40,000 volunteers came to aid the Spanish Republic at one time or another. From the insurgent side, the operation was partly a reenactment of the wars of unification of the fifteenth and sixteenth centuries, with aristocratic Castile reconquering the Catalans and Andalusians, and partly a transplant of colonial war methods to the homeland, with the Spanish Legionnaires' cry of *¡Viva la muerte!* (Long live death!). In its brutality, the Spanish Civil War was a foretaste of the Second World War, as exemplified by the Condor Legion's bombing of the Basque market town of Guernica on market day, April 26, 1937, and on the other side, by the murder of twelve bishops and perhaps as many as 13 percent of the parish clergy. In its exaltation, it was a last crusade, burning out most of the fervor before the more dogged great war to come.

EUROPEAN INTELLECTUALS AND THE POPULAR FRONT

The depression and the rise of fascism turned European intellectual life away from the self-expression of the 1920s to the social activism of the 1930s. A few intellectuals were drawn to fascism's promises of camaraderie, action, and "defense of Western values" against decadence. The vast majority of European writers and artists, however, enlisted in the enthusiasms of the Popular Front. Even painting, the most thoroughly private of the arts in the 1920s, produced important works of antifascist propaganda, such as Picasso's *Guernica* (1937).

The manifest bankruptcy of liberalism in the 1930s sent some intellectuals searching for new values. The only possible movement, according to the British writer Stephen Spender, was "forward from liberalism." Spender argued that whereas nineteenth-century liberalism at its best had represented an "active will toward political justice,"[24] that same goal could now only be pursued within communism. He was willing to accept the necessity of fighting and of temporary coercion in order to reach a new classless society in which the highest goals of forerunners like John Stuart Mill could be truly realized. Spender believed the arts would be more creative in such a society. A half-educated democracy that evolved out of contemporary liberalism would produce only the "mob rule of tastelessness." Spender clearly shared Trotsky's prediction of 1923 that "the average human type will rise to the heights of an Aristotle, a Goethe, or a Marx."[25] As intellectuals seeking the best route to personal liberty and artistic creativity, Spender and his like were drawn to an alliance with communism in the 1930s rather than to a conversion to it.

Others became true converts. One should not take too literally the self-criticism of ex-converts like Arthur Koestler, who later attributed the appeal of communism to intellectuals of the 1930s to a psychological craving for a disciple–master relationship, and to the deep satisfaction afforded by a closed system with unassailable answers to all questions.[26] Nevertheless, discipline and self-sacrifice clearly attracted some sensitive younger middle-class intellectuals who rejected the condescension and self-indulgence of their elders' individualistic games of protest (such as surrealism) in the 1920s. A young French philosophy student, Paul Nizan, for example, found in the Communist Party "a framework of order, duty, and discipline within which the individual could channel his sense of revolt while avoiding self-love."[27]

The Popular Front posed problems, of course, for its intellectual admirers. One problem was the manifest coercion and drab conformity of the Soviet Union in the 1930s, to which was added the international reaction to the purge trials. Spender could mitigate his doubts about these matters by arguing that the Russian experience had been perverted by its difficult birth and encircling enemies, not by innate faults. Another problem was the justification of violence. But after the fate suffered by the passive German left in 1933, it became easier to renounce the pacifism of the postwar generation. As the crusade against fascism in Spain took shape, the possibility of sharing in a just war proved attractive to many intellectuals.

---

[24]Stephen Spender, *Forward from Liberalism* (London, 1937), p. 189.

[25]See chapter 9, p. 285.

[26]See, for example, Arthur Koestler's contribution to the collection of statements of renunciation of communism, Richard Crossman, ed., *The God That Failed* (New York, 1959).

[27]David Caute, *Communism and the French Intellectuals, 1914–1960* (New York, 1964), p. 95.

The Spanish Civil War drew intellectuals into active commitment as did no other twentieth-century crisis. Robert Graves thought that no foreign issue had so divided educated British opinion since the French Revolution.[28] The division, however, was one-sided. A poll taken in England in 1937 turned up only five British intellectuals publicly in favor of the insurgents (including Evelyn Waugh and the South African poet Roy Campbell). Another sixteen (including T. S. Eliot and Ezra Pound) were neutral, and a round one hundred were in favor of the Spanish Republic. A number of scholars and writers left their desks to fight in Spain, impelled by an emotional commitment unknown to either world war. The First World War had been fought under dehumanized conditions by blind masses; the Second World War was fought at a distance by machines. It seemed that the Spanish Civil War was fought by individual heroes, especially among volunteers on the republican side who were drawn by the illusion of doing something direct and personal to defeat fascism. The volunteers included a number of remarkable individuals: the French novelist André Malraux, who flew fighter planes for the Popular Front; John Cornford, Charles Darwin's great-grandson, a brilliant student at Cambridge and a communist organizer, who died in Spain on his twenty-first birthday; the Cambridge scientist J. B. S. Haldane and his wife, who were first drawn in by the enlistment of their sixteen-year-old son in the International Brigade and who eventually became leading British Communists. Whether communist or not, the intellectuals among the international volunteers were torn between spontaneity and discipline, between the critical nuances of intellectual judgment and the clear commitment of action. Not a few of them emerged disillusioned. In André Malraux's Spanish war novel, *Man's Hope* (1937), the "lyric illusion" with which the volunteers began is slowly eroded by the increasing mechanization of the war and doubts that the victory of either side will make much difference in social justice. At the end, "the age of parties" has arrived.

> What worries me the most is to see how much, in any war, each one takes after his enemy, whether he wants to or not.[29]

THE EUROPEAN LEFT AFTER THE POPULAR FRONT

The Popular Front was dead before 1939. In Spain, it had been conquered by a military insurrection. In France, the alliance came apart from within. The Radical Party, disquieted by Socialist and Communist gains in the 1936 election, was the first partner of the French coalition to grow dubious. The Communist Party, which had no cabinet seat except a hypothetical "ministry of the masses," criticized the government bitterly for its inaction in Spain and its economic failures. The Socialists, committed by the "exercise of power" to the compromises and disillusionments

[28]Robert Graves and Alan Hodge, *The Long Week-End: A Social History of Great Britain, 1918–1939* (London, 1940), p. 337.
[29]André Malraux, *L'Espoir* (Paris, 1963), p. 494.

of office, suffered more and more from internal rifts. The Popular Front alliance was officially dissolved when Radicals supported strike-breaking measures in November 1938, but its spirit had been broken long before that.

It is easy to see, in retrospect, that the Popular Front had been an incongruous alliance. Its common denominator was antifascism. But how best to oppose fascism aroused passionate discord. Military preparedness, one obvious solution, flew in the face of the left's traditional pacifism. The other taproot of the Popular Front was the depression, and in this case there was no broader consensus about remedies. Piecemeal reforms seemed worse than nothing to revolutionaries, whereas a Marxist remedy promised to drive away the middle class and all hopes of a majority.

The divisions left by the Popular Front seemed to doom the left in its familiar Western European forms, democratic and socialist, to a position of permanent minority status. One of the partners, however, made striking gains. In France, the Communist Party consolidated Marxism's hold on factory workers, dating from the end of the nineteenth century, and extended it among farm laborers and intellectuals. After 1936, the Communist Party never fell below 15 percent in a French parliamentary election until 1981. Its very gains, however, increased doubts and reservations among the other Popular Front partners, parliamentary socialists and democrats. Moreover, Marxism had come close to exhausting its potential recruiting ground. Contrary to Marx's own expectations, it was not workers but clerks and lower civil servants who had become the fastest growing elements of the European populations. Marxism appealed forthrightly to one class, the working class, which turned out to have leveled off at about one-third of the population. Marxism was to hold on until the 1980s to its recruits in Western Europe, but at the cost of becoming an isolated enclave in European political life. After the Popular Front, a party capable of being both proletarian and majoritarian began to seem a contradiction in terms.

These developments were to be interrupted by the Second World War. For a time, the Popular Front was revived in the resistance movements of occupied Europe. In the long run, however, the problems raised by the Popular Front have still not been worked out today. Are electoral majorities of the left that are both democratic and social-reformist increasingly unworkable in industrialized Europe? Does the political future lie with other majorities?

In the short run, the Popular Front left a quite disproportionate legacy of fear among conservatives. Many Europeans began to prefer fascism to the left: "Better Hitler than Blum." Although conservatives had traditionally supported national glory and national defense, they feared being dragged into "Stalin's War" by the antifascist crusade of the left.

As for Stalin himself, he could well judge by 1938 that the Popular Front had done nothing to insure the safety of the Soviet Union. It had produced no reliable military allies on Germany's western frontier. The purge trials that reached their peak in 1936 and 1937 were one sign of Stalin's deepening distrust of outside influences. Among the Soviet leaders who disappeared were all those who had served in Spain.

Hitler had a freer hand than ever by 1938. The Popular Front had left Britain and France cool to each other and the Soviet Union cool to both. The remaining democratic countries were worried about the internal expansion of Marxism and fearful that a renewed war would plunge them into revolution. The disillusioned Austrian exile Arthur Koestler could later describe the Popular Front, "with drums and fanfares, advancing from defeat to defeat."[30]

[30]Arthur Koestler, *The Invisible Writing* (London, 1954), p. 188.

SUGGESTIONS FOR FURTHER READING

The general works on the European left cited in the bibliography to chapter 1 contain discussions of the Popular Front era. Martin S. Alexander and Helen Graham, eds., *The French and Spanish Popular Fronts: Comparative Perspectives*[*] (2002), compare political developments instructively.

Sympathetic biographies of Léon Blum by Joel Colton (2nd ed., 1987[*]) and Jean Lacouture (1982[*]) provide an excellent introduction to the French Popular Front experience. The best general account in English is Julian Jackson, *The Popular Front in France: Defending Democracy* (1990). Eugen Weber, *Hollow Years: France in the 1930s*[*] (1996), has vivid detail. See more generally Anthony Adamthwaite, *Grandeur and Misery: France's Bid for Power in Europe, 1914–1940*[*] (1995).

Anson Rabinbach, *The Crisis of Austrian Socialism: From Red Vienna to the Civil War, 1927–1934* (1983), asks why socialism was so easily crushed in Vienna in 1934.

Hugh Thomas, *The Spanish Civil War*[*] (revised ed. 1994), is still the most gripping narrative. Helen Graham, *The Spanish Civil War*[*] (2004) is a brief introduction. Burnett Bolloten, *The Spanish Civil War* (1991), is the exhaustive life's work of a journalist and collector of archives, who finds as much to blame in the excesses of the left as of the right. Gabriel Jackson, *A Concise History of the Spanish Civil War*[*] (1980), blames the generals. George Esenwein and Adrian Schubert analyze the background in *Spain at War: The Spanish Civil War in Context, 1931–1939* (1995). Among many works by Paul Preston, see *The Coming of the Spanish Civil War*,[*] 2nd ed. (1994), and *The Politics of Revenge: Fascism and the Military in Twentieth Century Spain*[*] (1995). Particularly relevant for the Spanish Popular Front are Stanley G. Payne, *Spain's First Democracy: The Second Republic, 1931–1936*[*] (1993) and Gabriel Jackson, *The Spanish Republic and the Civil War, 1931–1919*[*] (1965), sympathetic to the moderate left.

R. Dan Richardson, *Comintern Army* (1981), studies the International Brigades in Spain largely in terms of Soviet aims. More personal is Peter Stansky and William Abraham, *Journey to the Frontier: Two Roads to the Spanish Civil War*[*] (1966), a moving account of two British students killed in Spain.

David Caute, *The Fellow Travellers*[*] (revised ed. 1988), explains the attractions of the Communist Party to intellectuals during the Popular Front era. Arthur Koestler, *Arrow in the Blue* (1952) and *The Invisible Writing* (1954), are classic memoirs by a Popular Front intellectual. Koestler and others later recounted their fascination and subsequent disillusionment with communism in the classic *The God that Failed*[*] (1982). Franz Borkenau, *World Communism: A History of the Communist International* (1962), the work of a disillusioned former Communist official, is still revealing. Julius Braunthal, *History of the International*, 3 vols. (1967–1971), is an informative work by a former official of the Second (socialist) International.

Additional Internet links related to this chapter are available on the Europe in the 20th Century Web site: http://www.history.wadsworth.com/paxton04.

You can also explore images, interactive timelines, and maps related to this chapter on our Western Civilization Resource Center: http://history.wadsworth.com

Mussolini and Hitler, 1937.

13

The Paris Peace Settlement Dismantled: Aggression and Appeasement, 1933–1939

The Paris peace settlement, still largely intact in 1929, had been virtually swept away by 1939. It was not a self-enforcing system. The attempt to fence in a wounded and resentful Germany could last no longer than Germany's neighbors were willing and able to maintain that fence by force. Before the outbreak of the Second World War on September 3, 1939, Germany had already made substantial territorial gains in the east, far exceeding its 1914 frontiers in Austria and parts of Czechoslovakia. The dismantling of the Paris settlement had two complementary aspects: increasingly militant German pressures on the one hand, and a divided and demoralized First World War victor coalition on the other.

HITLER'S FIRST MOVES

There was no overnight change in German foreign policy when Hitler became chancellor of the German Reich on January 30, 1933. For the moment, Hitler reserved his lightning thrusts for the internal work of *Gleichschaltung:* bringing German institutions into line. He was still an upstart, uncertain of his power. The vice chancellor, Franz von Papen, expected to dominate the government. Marshal Hindenburg remained president. Bureaucracy, army, church, and professional diplomats all remained independent, to be brought only gradually under Hitler's control.

Although Foreign Minister Konstantin von Neurath assured foreign diplomats in February 1933 that the presence of old-line officials like himself in the new government was a guarantee that "no experiments in foreign policy were to be tried," and that "Hitler was proving reasonable,"[1] that did not mean that a majority of Germans did not desire revision of the Treaty of Versailles. When Hitler's campaign for revision reached demonic intensity in 1938 and 1939, traditional career officials, far from restraining him, for the most part fell into line. Even Hitler's predecessors, Stresemann and Brüning, had worked for revisions of the Versailles settlement; the army had quietly circumvented its provisions by clandestine training and arms manufacture in the Soviet Union; neither had admitted the legitimacy of the eastern frontiers of 1919. But in 1933, the French army was still clearly master of the field, despite the beginnings of secret German rearmament; the depression had affected Germany far more disastrously than France.

Hitler's first steps, therefore, were cautious. When he withdrew from the League of Nations and the Disarmament Conference in October 1933, it was only after shrewdly proposing general measures that exposed the other powers' unwillingness to disarm down to the German level. His vigorous campaign for a pro-German plebiscite in the Saar in January 1935[2] was accompanied by a promise that he had no other claims on France, thus seeming to renounce Alsace-Lorraine. He concluded a mutual pact of nonaggression with Poland in January 1934, a state that he had vowed in *Mein Kampf* to destroy.[3] He continued to renew agreements with the Soviet Union until 1935. Up until 1936, Hitler portrayed himself in public speeches as a veteran of the trenches who hated war above all things.

Setback in Austria

Impatient violence showed only in Hitler's early dealings with Austria, his birthplace. An *Anschluß* (union) between Germany and German-speaking Austria had been blocked before 1918 by the inclusion of Austria in the multinational Habsburg Empire. Now that the empire was broken up, Hitler was determined to bring Austria into the Reich. The main obstacles were Article 80 of the Treaty of Versailles and the Christian Social authoritarian regime of Engelbert Dollfuss, which was creating a

---

[1]Quoted in Jürgen Gehl, *Austria, Germany, and the Anschluss, 1931–1938* (Oxford, England, 1963), p. 90.

[2]In 1920, this rich coal region had been placed under French administration for fifteen years, after which the population would decide whether to be part of France or Germany. It voted overwhelmingly in 1935 to be restored to Germany.

[3]Hitler wrote an autobiographical work, *Mein Kampf,* in prison after the Munich *Putsch.* He wrote another book in 1928 on foreign policy, which remained unpublished until 1961.

Austrian Chancellor Engelbert Dollfuss with members of his cabinet. After Nazis murdered Dollfuss in July 1934, Kurt Schuschnigg, far left, succeeded him and continued the doomed effort to keep Austria independent.

new sense of separate identity for Austrians.[4] Hitler could assume, however, that the western democracies had no love for Dollfuss, who had shelled the Austrian Social Democrats into submission in February 1934. Moreover, the Austrian branch of the Nazi Party was growing rapidly among Austrians who wanted union with a reviving Greater Germany. Even so, Hitler seems to have meant to rely on indirect means. In May 1934, he closed off German tourist traffic to Austria, a serious blow to the Austrian economy, and permitted his ministers to talk openly about Austria's future destiny as part of Germany. He acquiesced in a *coup* planned by the Austrian Nazis, who misled him about their support in the Austrian army. On July 25, 1934, a Nazi band seized the chancellery and radio stations in Vienna. In the ensuing scuffle, Chancellor Dollfuss was shot and left to bleed to death on the sofa in his office.

As it turned out, it was not the western Allies but Mussolini who gave Hitler his severest foreign setback of the 1930s. Mussolini had a large stake in Austrian independence, an important element in Italian influence in the Danube basin. He mobilized 100,000 men on the Brenner Pass while the Italian-supported *Heimwehr*

[4]See chapter 11, pp. 338–340.

recovered control for Dollfuss's successor, Kurt Schuschnigg. Hitler was obliged to disavow the failed Austrian *coup* and agree to the separation of the Austrian and German sections of the Nazi Party. The *Anschluß* seemed postponed indefinitely.

First Violations of the Versailles Treaty

Hitler openly repudiated major provisions of the Versailles Treaty only after two years in power. In the first of his famous Saturday surprises, on March 9, 1935, Hitler announced the formation of a German air force. A week later he declared that Germany was reinstituting the draft to form an army of thirty-six divisions (500,000 men).

The reaction of the Allies was hostile but muted, for they had not fulfilled the postwar disarmament provisions either. The British and French prime ministers met with Mussolini at the Italian lakeside resort of Stresa. The "Stresa Front's" agreement to use military force if necessary to maintain the existing political structure of Europe seemed the beginning of a powerful anti-Hitler alliance. But Mussolini was already chasing after an African empire in Ethiopia, and a few months after Stresa, in June 1935, the British and German governments announced a naval agreement whereby the Germans could rebuild a fleet up to one-third the size of the British navy. It was clear that no one was prepared to enforce the letter of the Versailles system; the way was open to whatever new arrangements could be worked out by pressure and negotiation.

THE REMILITARIZATION OF THE RHINELAND, MARCH 1936

On the morning of March 7, 1936, Hitler sent a division of 10,000 men to the Rhine and a battalion of about 1,000 men across the river in each of three places: Düsseldorf, Cologne, and Mainz. That act remilitarized the Rhineland. It thereby broke down the main security barrier that the Versailles system had erected on Germany's western frontier.

The Treaty of Versailles had forbidden Germany to place any soldiers or military installations in a broad band of German territory: all land west of the Rhine, and a strip fifty kilometers (thirty miles) wide along the east bank of the Rhine. That highly artificial restriction on German sovereignty served two purposes: to expose any German military build-up against France at an early stage, and to permit easy French invasion of Germany in case the Germans attacked France's allies in the east. The remilitarization of the Rhineland was a crucial turning point in the power shift within Europe in the 1930s from the Allies to Germany, and in the march toward the Second World War. Perhaps the most familiar cliché about interwar European international relations is that the Allies missed their best chance of stopping Hitler in failing to act decisively at this point.

The Allies faced two alternatives. On the one hand, they could admit Germany's sovereign right to move troops anywhere within its frontiers, and thus quietly aban-

Bayerische Staatsbibliothek München

German infantry cross the Rhine on the Hohenzollern Bridge at Cologne, March 7, 1936. This act, and similar crossings by small detachments at Mainz and Düsseldorf, signaled Hitler's repudiation of the clause of the Treaty of Versailles that demilitarized in perpetuity the left bank of the Rhine.

don an unusual and outdated security arrangement. After all, the few troops that Hitler had moved into the Rhineland were clearly not intended to invade any foreign territory. As the London *Times* commented, the Germans were only "going into their own back garden." In fact, in the preceding months, British and French diplomats had secretly discussed this alternative, although it was rather a different matter to negotiate such a relaxation mutually than to accede to a unilateral act of defiance.

On the other hand, the Allies had abundant justification for immediate armed counteraction. Article 44 of the Treaty of Versailles had made clear this provision's importance, declaring that any violation of the demilitarized Rhineland "in any manner" was a hostile act. In the Locarno Pact of 1925,[5] Germany had explicitly accepted these terms once again and recognized the Allies' right to maintain them by force, if necessary, as an "exercise of the legitimate right of self defense." France had sufficient legal authority to act, alone or with the other signatories of Locarno.

[5]See chapter 6, pp. 188–191.

There was some political justification for a French reaction, too, since the demilitarized Rhineland had itself been a lesser substitute for French plans for a separate state there. The French had accepted a compromise only when promised an Anglo-American mutual defense treaty, which had never materialized. Once the Rhineland barrier was down and German troops stood on the frontiers of Alsace-Lorraine, nothing would be left of the security arrangements of 1919. With these considerations in mind, French Prime Minister Albert Sarrault made a ringing declaration on French radio on March 8 that "we will not let Strasbourg[6] fall within German cannon range." French military staffs began planning the seizure of the Saar and Luxembourg as a "bargaining counter," and, alternatively, planned for a military operation deep into the Rhineland.

In the end, France merely lodged a protest with the League of Nations. There were technical obstacles to a military riposte: The French army had been reorganized in a fashion that required it to move all at once, including mobilization of reserves, or not at all. No mobile force was available for immediate, limited action. Even if one had existed, moreover, the political obstacles were even greater. Mobilization of reserves would have been political suicide in March 1935, on the eve of elections. The Ruhr occupation of 1923 had not been an encouraging precedent. Economically, France was in the trough of the depression: Austerity budgets limited military preparation, and the economy's effects on morale were severe. Morale was further reduced by the "hollow years," the years beginning in 1935 when the reduced birth rate of 1917 and 1918 produced only half as many draftable eighteen-year-olds as usual. It was a time to reflect on the human wastage of war. The Versailles structure had been designed to block an all-out German military onslaught. Few in France were ready to wage war over a largely symbolic German troop movement within Germany.

Even fewer in Britain were ready to support an active French response. Since 1919, British governments had consistently opposed the more vigorous French security measures. British public opinion, still influenced by John Maynard Keynes's *The Economic Consequences of the Peace,* tended to regard the French as militaristic and unreasonable. The French have frequently charged that Britain vetoed the necessary action in 1936. It is clear now that the decision not to act was made in Paris, but the certainty of Britain's opposition made that decision easier to make.

In retrospect, the popular cliché of the last, lost opportunity in 1936 to stop Hitler can be seen to rest on several false assumptions. One assumption is that the token German forces had orders to withdraw at the slightest sign of opposition, a notion based on the testimony of General Alfred Jodl at the postwar Nuremberg trials. A closer look at captured German documents shows that the units had orders to resist. Another assumption is that the German opposition to Hitler would have overthrown him from within at his first serious setback, but this seems doubtful in view of the German public's patriotic response to later crises. A French riposte would probably have led to significant fighting, in which the French would have been labeled the more conspicuous aggressor. What would the French have done after seizing parts of German territory, which they had the physical power to do?

---

[6]The capital of newly regained Alsace.

Would internal opposition have been stronger on the Allied side than on the German side?

All these legitimate speculations call for serious thought about the use of force in maintaining a treaty system over long periods, particularly when some parties to the treaty have significant doubts about its legitimacy. It has been common to draw lessons from the Rhineland crisis of 1936 about the virtues of early force against challengers to the status quo. The character of Hitler and his later triumphs have made it easier to defend this case than it perhaps should be. The Rhineland crisis needs careful thought in a wider perspective, one that would consider the validity of the Versailles arrangements, the precedent of the Ruhr invasion of 1923, and their share in Hitler's coming to power. The case for 1936 as a "lost opportunity" to overthrow him by force from outside remains unproven.

ITALY SHIFTS SIDES

Despite Italian conflicts of interest with the French and British in the Mediterranean, Fascist Italy remained, at least until 1935, in an anti-German position. Well into the 1930s, Mussolini hoped to fulfill old Italian nationalist dreams of succeeding the Habsburgs as the principal power in the Danube basin and around the Adriatic Sea. These ambitions made Germany the principal rival. As leader of the prowar socialists in 1915, the young Mussolini had helped push Italy into war against Germany. Mussolini had supported the French occupation of the Ruhr in 1923, had been one of the guarantors of the Locarno Agreements in 1925, and during the attempted takeover of Austria in July 1934 had administered the only international public humiliation to Hitler of the whole interwar period. As late as April 1935, he was host to the Allied conference at Stresa protesting German rearmament. By the time of the Rhineland crisis of March 1936, however, he had moved out of the German containment camp for good.

The Ethiopian Conquest

Dreams of imperial expansion in Africa were the main reason for this policy shift. Mussolini became his own foreign minister in 1932 and replaced career diplomats with Fascists in important foreign policy posts. At first there was a burst of activity in the European area. In June 1933, Mussolini initiated the Four-Power Pact, an attempt to establish a directorate that would rule European affairs, in which Italy would share an equal role with Britain, France, and Germany. The Four-Power Pact never really led to anything, and growing German vigor in the north suggested doubts about future Italian possibilities on the Continent. Furthermore, the Fascist regime was undergoing an internal crisis of confidence in 1933 and 1934. A new generation of Italians was coming of age without direct experience of the "heroic" days of 1922. The aging Fascist leadership seemed to them to offer little more than the liberal parliamentary monarchy it had replaced ten years earlier. The depression affected Italian employment and morale far more than appeared on the official façade. Corporatism was revealed more and more clearly to be self-regulation by sub-sidized big business. Without other means of assuring social solidarity and of attract-ing youth, fascism's best way out was aggressive expansion.

In late 1933 or early 1934, Mussolini began to study the possibility of taking Ethiopia. Ethiopia was both a logical and an emotional choice: It lay inland from Italy's East African possessions of Eritrea and Italian Somaliland, it was the one major African region still uncontrolled by Europeans, and it was the scene of an Italian defeat in 1896 (Adowa) that Italian nationalists would delight in avenging. The attempted Nazi *coup* in Austria in July 1934 seems to have convinced Mussolini that he had to act quickly before the start of a new European war. By August 1934, foreign diplomats in Italy were already reporting the beginning of military prepara-tions.[7]

A skirmish in December 1934 at Walwal—a desert waterhole in disputed frontier territory between Italian Somaliland and Ethiopia—served as the public pretext for Mussolini's planned invasion. Intense diplomatic bargaining among Italy, France, and Britain only convinced Mussolini that he would meet no effective European obstruction. Italian troops invaded Ethiopia in October 1935. Although the Ethiopian troops fought more stubbornly than anyone in Italy had anticipated, they were no match for Italian aircraft and poison gas. Mussolini proclaimed King Victor Emmanuel III emperor of Ethiopia in May 1936.

Break with the West

Mussolini seems to have expected to mend his fences with Britain and France after conquering Ethiopia, but that conquest's repercussions were much too violent for that. When Ethiopian Emperor Haile Selassie appealed to the League of Nations for help in October 1935, he became a heroic symbol to European democratic opinion. It was forgotten that Ethiopia had been admitted to the League in 1923 only on Italian insistence, and that Britain and France had voted against entry because Ethiopia still practiced slavery. Although a powerful groundswell of demo-cratic opinion urged active League sanctions against Italy in 1935, diplomatic pru-dence suggested that Mussolini should not be permanently lost as a potential ally against Hitler. In the end, Britain and France settled somewhere between rigor and compromise and suffered the disadvantages of both. They pursued what the British Foreign Minister Sir Samuel Hoare called "a double line of approach."[8] In an effort to take some action without actually antagonizing Italy, the League adopted an arms embargo and a limitation on loans and credits to Italy and imports from Italy. That was enough to arouse patriotic resentment in Italy without taking the one step—stopping shipments of oil to Italy—that would actually have hampered the campaign in Ethiopia.

---

[7]*Foreign Relations of the United States, 1934*, vol. 2, p. 754, quoted in George W. Baer, *The Coming of the Italian-Ethiopian War* (Cambridge, Mass., 1967), p. 42.

[8]Samuel Hoare, *Nine Troubled Years* (London, 1953), p. 168.

Meanwhile, diplomats tried to arrange a solution behind the scenes that would recognize a predominant Italian role in Ethiopia without condoning outright Italian conquest. The French and British foreign ministers, Pierre Laval and Sir Samuel Hoare, drafted a plan in December 1935 to end the fighting on these terms, only to have it leak out to an outraged public opinion, especially in Britain, where exposure of the plan ended Hoare's public career. Italian preponderance in Ethiopia was attained by arms rather than by negotiation, and the breach between Britain and France and Mussolini was never healed.

That breach was widened in July 1936 when Mussolini supplied essential military assistance to General Francisco Franco's revolt against the Spanish Republic. Eventually 70,000 Italian "volunteers" were fighting for Franco. It was now the turn of French public opinion to become inflamed, for a fascist Spain would nearly complete the ring of hostile dictatorships around republican France.

Mussolini solidified his new alignment by sending his foreign minister and son-in-law, Count Galeazzo Ciano, to visit Hitler in October 1936. On November 1, 1936, Mussolini first referred publicly to a Rome–Berlin "Axis" as the new focus of European alignments.

Alliance Patterns

Mussolini's shift in 1935 and 1936 had grave consequences for Europe. It threatened France with a two-front war, and it aligned European powers on the basis of ideology rather than of interest. Since it was still possible that Mussolini might return to an anti-German coalition, the hope of luring him back by concessions continued to tempt some British and French leaders until 1940. From 1935 on, in effect, two patterns of anti-Hitler alliance competed for attention. Anglo-French conservatives tried to revive the "Stresa Front" with Italy or even Mussolini's project of a four-power directorate—a coalition of the anti-Soviet powers of Europe, both dictatorships and republics, perhaps even including Germany, to settle Europe's affairs among themselves. The other pattern was an alliance with the Soviet Union as the only force capable of bringing serious pressure on Germany.

British and French leaders engaged in both kinds of anti-Hitler alliances at various times after 1936. The British, in particular, offered concessions to Mussolini: a "Gentleman's Agreement" in April 1938 to respect the status quo in the Mediterranean and the Red Sea, including British recognition of Italy's empire in Ethiopia. The alternate alliance with the Soviet Union seemed to have the upper hand during the Popular Front ministries in France in 1936 and 1937, and briefly in the spring of 1938, when the French government resumed aid to the Spanish republicans. But the two patterns were too strongly ideological to be either combined or pursued to the end. An alliance with Italy seemed to sanction fascism; with Russia, communism. One could not combine the two alliance patterns, and either of them alone was ideologically divisive.

As for Mussolini, he clung more and more to the Axis. Although he told Hitler he could not engage in a European war before 1943, he allowed himself to be drawn into a military pact with Germany in May 1939, the "Pact of Steel."

HITLER'S DESIGNS IN THE EAST

Hitler's moves of 1935 and 1936 had essentially aimed to restore full sovereignty within the German frontiers of 1919 through rearmament and remilitarization of the Rhineland. The next moves, those of 1938 and 1939, exceeded the frontiers of 1919 with Austria, Czechoslovakia, and Poland. These far more ambitious steps took the Third Reich not only back to the 1914 eastern frontiers of the Second Reich but beyond them, and even beyond areas of ethnic German settlement. What led Hitler to reach so far?

EASTERN EUROPE

Lebensraum **for the Master Race**

Hitler had talked about expanding the German frontiers all his adult life. *Mein Kampf* (1925–1926) had made clear a set of racialist ideals that were to govern his choices to the end. He had never intended a mere return to the eastern frontiers of 1914, the undeclared aim of his Weimar predecessors, Stresemann and Brüning. Hitler intended to assemble the whole German *Volk*[9] in one nation, including his homeland Austria and the other Germanic parts of the former Habsburg Empire. Beyond that, he meant to give the superior German *Volk* sufficient "living space" *(Lebensraum)* by taking it from "inferior" Slavic peoples to the east. Renouncing, at least temporarily, the Second Reich's interests in the west and in a colonial empire, Hitler intended his Third Reich to establish good relations with "Germanic" Britain, leave France isolated, and develop a vast German agrarian colony in Poland and the Ukraine.

The program outlined in *Mein Kampf* was never carried out in detail, of course. The agreement with Britain proved impossible, and Hitler did indeed return to western conquests and to overseas colonial projects. But he never abandoned the ideological priorities; they were responsible for his fatal choice of invading Russia in 1941 rather than pursuing a Mediterranean strategy.

Economic Considerations

Another interpretation of Hitler's motives in 1938 and 1939 rests on economic considerations. The brilliant Nazi success in restoring full employment by 1935 had been based on massive public spending, sealing German currency off from international fluctuations, and maintaining low wages by political authority. The major problem in the mid-1930s was what to do next. The recurrence of either inflation or domestic disorder would destroy the regime, and it was not certain that simply continuing those early economic measures indefinitely could avoid one or both disasters.

The chief architect of Germany's economic "miracle" after 1933, Finance Minister Hjalmar Schacht, held that Germany could not remain economically isolated in the long run. The only way to overcome Germany's basic raw material shortages, Schacht believed, was to revive foreign trade, which was feasible within the improved economic circumstances of 1936. Reichsmarschall Hermann Göring, however, advocated autarky, or economic self-sufficiency. Göring reflected Hitler's views, and he was named head of the Four-Year Plan organization, in September 1936, to develop self-sufficiency. The decision for autarky committed Germany to developing its own low-grade iron ore and expensive substitutes for oil and rubber. Under these conditions, full employment and social stability may have seemed possible only through territorial expansion: to obtain the oil and wheat of Eastern Europe, and to compensate austerity with the glory of conquest. In any event, autarky showed that Hitler had chosen guns over butter.

---

[9]People, in a racial sense.

Anschluß: Test Case of Nazi Aims

According to yet another interpretation of Nazi aims, Hitler was simply a master pragmatist, seizing opportunities as they presented themselves. Such an opportunity was clearly at hand at the beginning of 1938. Italian involvement in Ethiopia freed Hitler from his main rival in Austria; the way was open for another attempt at *Anschluß.*

After Chancellor Dollfuss's murder in the failed *coup* of 1934, his associate and successor Kurt Schuschnigg attempted to keep Austria independent by balancing off rival forces. On the one hand, there was the home militia *(Heimwehr)* under Prince Ernst Rüdiger von Starhemberg, Mussolini's main support in Austria; on the other hand, there was the Austrian Nazi Party, temporarily set back by its failure in July 1934. Germany's growing strength and the desire of many Austrians to escape from the petty nationhood left to them by the Paris peace settlement soon revived the illegal Austrian branch of the Nazi Party. When it became apparent that Italian interests had shifted elsewhere with the conquest of Ethiopia, Schuschnigg was forced to contend with the Austrian Nazis without outside help. At the end of 1937, he tried to divide the pro-*Anschluß* forces by bringing into the government one of their more respectable leaders, the lawyer Arthur Seyss-Inquart, while cracking down on illegal Nazi activities in Austria.

These steps provided the background for the famous meeting between Hitler and Schuschnigg on February 12, 1938, at Berchtesgaden, Hitler's alpine retreat. On the basis of Schuschnigg's own account of the three-hour browbeating he received from Hitler, it was long assumed that Hitler was treacherously preparing armed forces behind Schuschnigg's back. In fact, Hitler decided to send German troops into Austria only several weeks later, in a spur-of-the-moment decision that lends weight to the opportunistic interpretation of Hitler's expansionist moves. At Berchtesgaden, Hitler had assumed he was making sufficient progress through indirect pressure: Schuschnigg agreed to appoint the pro-*Anschluß* Seyss-Inquart to the vital position of Minister of the Interior, with its control of the police.

Hitler decided on armed action when Schuschnigg suddenly announced on March 9 that he would put the question of Austrian independence to a plebiscite on the following Sunday, March 13. If a majority of Austrians voted for independence, Hitler's hopes for *Anschluß* by indirect means would suffer another long postponement. The next day, March 10, Hitler ordered troops to prepare for movement into Austria. Late on March 11 he gave the signal to move. By then, Schuschnigg had agreed to cancel the plebiscite, but Göring engineered a fictitious request from the new Minister of the Interior, Seyss-Inquart, for German intervention to "preserve order." At the same time Mussolini assured Hitler that he now had no objections to *Anschluß.* Hitler's response over the telephone to his representative in Rome shows his nervous excitement and relief:

PRINCE PHILIP OF HESSE I have just come back from the Palazzo Venezia. The duce accepted
　　the whole thing in a very friendly manner. He sends you his regards. . . .
HITLER Then please tell Mussolini I will never forget him for this.
PRINCE PHILIP Yes.
HITLER Never, never, never, whatever happens. . . . As soon as the Austrian affair is settled, I
　　shall be ready to go with him, through thick and thin, no matter what happens.
PRINCE PHILIP Yes, my Führer.

HITLER Listen, I shall make any agreement—I am no longer in fear of the terrible position which would have existed militarily in case we had got into a conflict. You may tell him that I thank him ever so much; never, never shall I forget.

PRINCE PHILIP Yes, my Führer.

HITLER I will never forget, whatever may happen. If he should ever need any help or be in any danger, he can be convinced that I shall stick by him, whatever may happen, even if the whole world were against him.

PRINCE PHILIP Yes, my Führer.[10]

At dawn on March 12, German troops marched into Austria. Hitler received a tumultuous welcome in his hometown, Linz, and in Vienna, the city of his adolescent quests. Although many German tanks and trucks broke down along the highway to Vienna, there was neither time nor resources for an opposition to form. Abroad, it was accepted that the *Anschluß* was probably supported by a majority of Austrians, which made it a belated exercise in Wilsonian self-determination. No European power was prepared to use force against a *fait accompli,* and a popular one at that. Hitler's Germany had expanded into territory that had never been part of the old Reich. Germany was now a nation of 80 million people.

CZECHOSLOVAKIA AND APPEASEMENT, 1938

Successful *Anschluß* with Austria called all of Germany's other eastern frontiers into question. Hitler had acquired a new sense of assurance. German-speaking populations in Czechoslovakia and Poland began to clamor for protection. Europe passed through one border crisis after another for eighteen months until the Second World War began on September 3, 1939.

Czechoslovakia's Precarious Position

On the post-Anschluß map, Czechoslovakia now looked like a man with his head in a lion's jaws. The ring of mountain defenses on the German border could now be turned from the south through Austria. Worse still, the new state suffered from nationality problems. The large Czechoslovak state created in 1919 with French support was not so much a triumph of self-determination for Czechs as a smaller copy of the Habsburg Empire. Alongside 7.25 million Czechs were 5 million Slovaks, not all of whom were reconciled to union with dominant Czechs; 750,000 Magyars, 500,000 Ruthenians, and 90,000 Poles remained conscious of linguistic and cultural distinctness. Some 3.25 million Germans lived in the Sudetenland, along the German and Austrian borders. It was from the Sudetenland that Georg von Schönerer had come, the founder of the pan-German movement that had influenced Hitler as a drifting youth in Vienna.[11] Although a law in 1920 permitted the use of minority languages in schools and law courts where a minority surpassed

---

[10]Quoted in Alan Bullock, *Hitler: A Study in Tyranny,* 2nd ed. (New York, 1962), p. 432.

[11]See chapter 1, p. 31.

20 percent of the population, there continued to be much resentment over the language of schooling and over alleged discrimination against minorities in the public services. To make matters worse, the depression hit hardest in German-speaking cities. The overall unemployment rate was about 25 percent, but Germans complained that they were laid off before Czechs. Czechoslovakia had seemed the most successful democracy among the Eastern European successor states, but depression and resurgent nationalism began to threaten its very existence. Small wonder that President Eduard Beneš and the dominant Czech parties were adamant against the idea of plebiscites among the other nationalities. Any concession seemed likely to open the floodgates of massive secession.

Czechoslovakia was made of flammable material, and Hitler blew vigorously on the sparks. He encouraged the nationalist demonstrations led by Konrad Henlein, a physical education teacher in a German-language high school in the Sudetenland, who had emerged as the leading spokesman for German ethnic identity there. Soon after the *Anschluß*, Hitler received Henlein at Berchtesgaden and encouraged him to escalate his demands steadily beyond whatever the Czechs were willing to accept. "We must always demand so much that we can never be satisfied."[12]

Appeasement

Rising tensions in Czechoslovakia made some dramatic new German gain there likely. We must now look closely at the British and French responses to this prospect, for their solution to the Czech crisis was the high point of the policy known as "appeasement." The errors of appeasement at that time were so firmly impressed on those leaders who reached adulthood in the 1930s that they spent the 1950s and 1960s reacting in the opposite fashion to international crises: for example, Anthony Eden against the Egyptians at Suez in 1956; United States policymakers against the Viet Cong in 1965. Since it has been the most influential negative lesson for a whole generation of Western leaders, it is important to understand appeasement in the 1930s.

One notion to dismiss is that the appeasers of Hitler in Britain and France were sympathetic to Hitler's ideas or methods. The dominant figure in the appeasement policy was Neville Chamberlain, who succeeded Stanley Baldwin as prime minister and foreign minister of England in May 1937. Chamberlain came from the progressive wing of the Conservative Party, from a tradition of municipal social services in Birmingham where both he and his father had been mayor. As Minister of Health in 1931, he was the strongest Tory spokesman for government measures of social welfare and an ancestor of the welfare-state Tories of the following generation. He occupied the other extreme of the party from men like Winston Churchill, who was much more interested in world grandeur and not unsympathetic to Franco and Mussolini. Chamberlain's letters to his sister, the best guide to his way of thinking, are full of a fastidious distaste for Hitler and Nazism, befitting a rather austere Unitarian

[12]*Documents on German Foreign Policy, 1933–1945*, series D, vol. 2, no. 107, pp. 197–198.

reformer: "Is it not positively horrible to think that the fate of hundreds of millions of persons depends on one man, and he is half mad."[13]

Appeasement was neither a policy of drift nor an absence of policy. Chamberlain, on the contrary, was an activist in foreign policy. A post-Wilsonian idealist who distrusted professional diplomats, he was convinced by his own successes in labor–management relations that he could do better himself with face-to-face contact. In addition to his own "summit diplomacy," Chamberlain was inclined to rely on other amateurs, such as the shipping magnate Lord Runciman, for delicate diplomatic missions.

Appeasement was Chamberlain's energetic and calculated effort to locate the sources of Germany's frustrations and then to "remove the danger spots one by one"[14] by bargaining instead of letting them spin out of control, as in 1914. *To appease,* before 1938, was simply a noncontroversial verb meaning "to lessen friction and conflict." In that sense, the policy led by Chamberlain and accepted by the French had its reasonable side. Only later, after that policy had failed to keep Europe from plunging once more into war, did the word become an epithet.

Appeasement rested on a number of assumptions. Perhaps its basic foundation was the conviction among the survivors of the First World War that Europe could not survive another such bloodletting. Every French town had its *monument aux morts* with its long list of the dead; no British village was without its war memorial. Even tiny villages displayed prodigious lists of casualties. Mutilated war veterans were conspicuous reminders, as was the arrival of the "hollow years" in the 1930s. Added to this were science-fiction conceptions of the next war, with its aerial bombardments and poison gas. Millions of deaths were predicted, and imaginations ran riot about the fate of London or Paris as larger Guernicas, or even Berlin: German populations had to be reassured in the late 1930s that they were safe from aerial bombardment.[15] On the Allied side, a growing consciousness of inferiority in armaments made hearts sink even lower at the prospect of war.

Appeasement rested, further, on several less-explicit suppositions. Nazism, the appeasers believed, was a political disease caused by the Versailles Treaty. Once the worst irritants were removed, the fever and swelling would go down. Many British, in particular, accepted the validity of some of the German grievances at the hands of an arrogant and bellicose France in 1919. Although the German tone was truculent, the changes demanded up into 1938 did not extend beyond the apparently enthusiastic union of German-speaking peoples in Eastern Europe; the most shocking internal excesses were still to come (the arson and murder of Jews in the *Kristallnacht* of November 1938, for example). The appeasers assumed that Hitler would prefer a peaceable negotiation of issues to forcible settlement, and that he would raise only a finite number of such issues. Chamberlain, therefore, tried to explain to Hitler that he could win substantial revision of the Versailles system by negotiation if he would just lower his voice.

---

[13] Quoted in Keith Feiling, *The Life of Neville Chamberlain* (London, 1946), p. 357.

[14] Quoted in ibid., p. 351.

[15] *Illustrierter Beobachter,* August 24, 1939, pp. 1316–1318.

Finally, and least explicitly of all, appeasement rested on domestic considerations of internal order. At the most elementary level, the appeasers assumed that a new war would lead to another round of revolutions like those of 1917. They had no stomach for another bout with the social tensions of total war. Regardless of how distasteful his manners or his regime were, Hitler was a barrier to Bolshevik expansion into central Europe. Two of Chamberlain's associates—Lord Halifax and Sir Horace Wilson—praised Hitler to his face in 1938 for his "great services" to the defense of European civilization from the Bolsheviks. Geoffrey Dawson, editor of the most authoritative conservative newspaper in England, the London *Times,* was "certainly influenced," says his biographer, "by the thought that Nazi Germany served as a barrier to the spread of Communism."[16] Chamberlain's predecessor Stanley Baldwin said, "If Hitler moves east, I shall not break my heart."[17]

The curious effect of these assumptions was to align the proponents of military action and the proponents of peace in the Western democracies in 1938 and 1939 in unexpected camps. The proponents of military action admired Léon Blum's Popular Front in France, advocated more active alliance with the Soviet Union, and favored more vigorous aid to republican Spain. They drew on traditionally pacifist elements of the European left. The proponents of appeasement hoped to woo Mussolini away from the Axis, and offered substantial concessions to Hitler in the effort to avoid a war that could only benefit the revolutionary left. They began to regard a war to block Hitler as "Stalin's War." They drew on elements of the traditional admirers of armies and empires. This crossover of traditional foreign policy preferences helped to make any concerted policy toward Hitler on the part of Britain and France nationally divisive.

Working from the presumptions underlying appeasement, Neville Chamberlain set out even before the *Anschluß* to replace Stanley Baldwin's passivity with an active policy of finding and resolving conflicts with Hitler before they could become crises. He took the initiative, not waiting for Hitler's thrusts. In November 1937, he sent Lord Halifax to attend a fox hunt with Reichsmarschall Göring, whose many titles included that of Master of the German Hunt. Halifax's mission was to assure the German leaders privately about

> questions arising out of the Versailles settlement which were capable of causing trouble if they were unwisely settled—Danzig, Austria, Czechoslovakia—on all these matters we were not necessarily concerned to stand for the status quo as of today, but we were very much concerned to secure the avoidance of such treatment of them as would be likely to cause trouble.[18]

In other words, the British government was ready to negotiate adjustments in Germany's eastern frontiers if the changes could be carried out peaceably.

The British government continued this approach after the *Anschluß* when in the spring of 1938 pressures began to build around Czechoslovakia. French Premier

---

[16]J. E. Wrench, *Geoffrey Dawson and Our Times* (London, 1955), p. 376.

[17]Robert Keith Middlemas and John Barnes, *Baldwin* (London, 1969), p. 947.

[18]Andrew Roberts, *"The Holy Fox:" A Biography of Lord Halifax* (London, 1991), p. 71

Léon Blum, whose government was already bound to Czechoslovakia by a mutual defense treaty since 1924, proposed in March 1938 that Britain and France issue a joint statement guaranteeing the existing Czech borders. But the British government continued to refuse any commitments east of the Rhine, as it had done since 1919. Lord Halifax, now foreign minister, gave the reply: "Quite frankly, the moment is unfavorable, and our plans, both for offense and defense, are not sufficiently advanced."[19] After Blum left office again in April 1938, his successors—Prime Minister Edouard Daladier and Foreign Minister Georges Bonnet—left foreign policy initiatives to Chamberlain.

Mounting Crisis in Czechoslovakia

Technically speaking, the quarrel was an internal matter between the Czechoslovak government and its German-speaking minority in the Sudetenland. Konrad Henlein presented an ambitious list of demands in April 1938. The Karlsbad Program, as it was called, demanded internal autonomy for German-speaking areas, reparations to the German minority for all their sufferings since 1918, and full liberty for Germans to express "the ideology of Germans." The Czechoslovak government countered with plans to liberalize the Nationalities Statute of 1920 to some degree. A war scare over the weekend of May 20 and 21, however, showed how easily these internal tensions might bring all the principal states of Europe into conflict. Claiming that the Germans were amassing troops on the frontier, the Czechoslovaks mobilized their army on May 20. The French and Russian governments publicly affirmed their treaty commitments to Czechoslovakia, and Lord Halifax warned that Britain could not be guaranteed to stand aside if the Germans intervened in Czechoslovakia. Hitler was forced to deny publicly any aggressive intentions toward the Czechs.

After the war scare, positions hardened on all sides. Hitler seems to have decided not only to get his revenge on the Czechs but to do so by force, regardless of the possibilities of negotiation that might arise. He issued military orders on May 30 stating his "unalterable intention to smash Czechoslovakia by military action in the near future," whenever "a convenient apparent excuse and adequate political justification"[20] could be found. Czech president Beneš stiffened his resolve not to yield to German force. The Allies, and particularly Neville Chamberlain, resolved not to be led to the brink of war again by Czechoslovak intransigence. A senior British diplomat in Berlin suggested to a German official that if the German government would confidentially make known its wishes in the Sudetenland, the British government would force the Czechs to accept them.[21] When Czechoslovak concessions to the German minority were slow, the British ambassador to Germany, Sir Nevile Henderson, thought in July 1938 that it was time to give the Czechs "a real twist of the screw."[22]

---

[19]*Documents on British Foreign Policy, 1919–1939*, series 3, vol. 1, no. 107, p. 87.

[20]*Documents on German Foreign Policy, 1933–1945*, series D, vol. 2, no. 221, p. 358.

[21]Ibid., no. 151.

[22]*Documents on British Foreign Policy*, series 3, vol. 1, no. 512, p. 590.

Tension mounted sharply again in September 1938. Following an impassioned speech by Hitler at the Nuremberg Party Rally on September 12, rioting broke out in the Sudetenland, whereupon the Czechoslovak government declared martial law. Henlein fled into Germany and organized a *Freikorps* for raids across the border. Signs increased of a German armed intervention. At the end of September, it seemed so certain that war would break out that armed forces were being mobilized in Britain and France, and schoolchildren were being evacuated from London.

The Munich Settlement

Neville Chamberlain now took the initiative to force a solution on Czechoslovakia that would satisfy Hitler and thus avert war. Boarding an airplane for the first time in his sixty-nine years, the British prime minister flew to Germany three times in fourteen days: to Hitler's mountain retreat at Berchtesgaden on September 15, to the Rhine resort town of Godesberg on September 22, and then to Munich on September 29. There it was agreed to buy Hitler off with immediate transfer of the Sudetenland from Czechoslovakia to Germany. The whole negotiation is known as the Munich settlement—virtually a synonym for appeasement.

At Berchtesgaden on September 15, Hitler delivered a tirade on alleged Czechoslovak atrocities against Germans in the Sudetenland. Chamberlain believed that only a border adjustment could prevent war. He accepted "the principle of the detachment of the Sudeten areas"—more than the mere autonomy Konrad Henlein had demanded a few months earlier and more than Hitler had publicly demanded up to that time.

Chamberlain and French Premier Daladier then had to force President Beneš to accept this territorial cession. It was this task that engendered the guilt feelings that clung forever after to the Munich settlement in Britain and France. Beneš held out until 5:00 P.M. on September 21, yielding only after the British and French governments had threatened to abandon Czechoslovakia to its fate. Thinking the crisis was over, Chamberlain flew to Godesberg to give Hitler the news on September 22. Chamberlain had not yet grasped that Hitler did not want a peaceful compromise, even one that granted all his territorial demands. He was astonished at Hitler's reply to his good news: *"Das geht nicht mehr."* (That won't do any more.) The proposed cession of the Sudetenland must now take place within three days, and German troops must enter the ceded areas at once.

Chamberlain returned to London believing that his mission had failed. The British fleet was mobilized on September 27; French troops manned the newly completed Maginot Line for the first time. Trenches were dug and gas masks issued in London. For a few days horrified Europeans expected at any moment to hear the first bombs fall on their cities.

Frantic last-minute negotiations continued nevertheless. Mussolini proposed a four-power conference.[23] Although Hitler later complained he was cheated of his

---

[23]Britain, France, Germany, and Italy. Czechoslovakia and the Soviet Union were excluded from the Munich Conference.

© Hulton Getty / Liaison Agency

September 30, 1938: Neville Chamberlain returns to London after signing the Munich settlement. Chamberlain is showing the paper with the terms—signed by Hitler—to the crowd upon his arrival at Heston Airport.

march into Prague, he agreed to negotiate the details of the Sudetenland cession rather than take it by force. Hitler's letter agreeing to discuss the matter once again was delivered while Chamberlain was addressing the House of Commons at 8:30 P.M. on September 28 about this "horrible, incredible" situation that had arisen "because of a quarrel in a faraway country between people of whom we know nothing."

At Munich on September 29, Hitler obtained almost everything he had demanded in his ultimatum to Chamberlain at Godesberg. The Sudetenland was transferred to Germany, of which it had never been part. All Sudeten areas with populations more than 50 percent German were transferred at once. Plebiscites were to be held in other areas with large German minorities (they were, in fact, never held). In addition to 2,825,000 Germans, some 800,000 Czechs were thus forcibly shifted into Germany in what claimed to be an exercise in national self-determination. Hitler agreed to respect the sovereignty of the rest of Czechoslovakia. Both Chamberlain and Daladier were mobbed by deliriously joyful crowds on their return. In the very short run, the Munich settlement was a success. There was no war in September 1938.

In the longer run, the Munich settlement accomplished none of the goals that the appeasement policy had been intended to achieve. It did not preserve the rest of Czechoslovakia. Poland and Hungary demanded and received parts of Czechoslovakia that contained their fellow nationals; then, exploiting unrest among Slovaks who showed renewed interest in separation from the Czechs, Hitler himself

Mary Evans Picture Library

German troops enter Prague, 15 March 1939, received by glum-faced crowds and a few Nazi salutes.

broke the agreement six months later. German troops moved into Prague on March 15, 1939. The Czech areas became the "Protectorate of Bohemia-Moravia," and the Slovak areas were set up as an independent nation. In the long run, settlement did not prevent war either. It further divided a potential anti-Hitler alliance by excluding the Soviet Union from an active role in the Czechoslovak crisis. The Munich settlement has had no defenders, either on moral or pragmatic grounds.

The Alternative of War

The alternative to appeasement in 1938 was to stand ready to support Czechoslovakia by military force. France was bound to come to the Czechs' aid by a 1924 treaty, part of the French security system in Eastern Europe. The Soviet Union was bound by a 1935 treaty to come to the Czechs' aid if the French did so. If the Czechs held firm and went to war to retain the German-speaking Sudetenland, the play of alliances would bring France and then the Soviet Union into a widening European conflict against Germany. In short, the alternative was a preventive war against Hitler by France and perhaps Britain, alongside the Soviet Union, to preserve one of the national anomalies of the Paris peace settlement.

The heart of the matter was what the Soviets meant to do. Would Stalin help capitalist Britain and France defend Czechoslovakia? Soviet Foreign Minister Maxim Litvinov stated publicly as early as March 17, 1938, that his country was ready to "participate in collective actions" to "stop the further development of aggression."

On September 2, Litvinov proposed an appeal to the League of Nations and a joint British-French-Soviet "statement of intention" to protect Czechoslovakia. The main problem with Soviet military intervention was that Soviet troops or aircraft would have to cross Polish or Romanian soil to reach Czechoslovakia. Although Poland was adamantly opposed to the passage of Soviet forces, there is some evidence that the Romanian government was willing to allow Soviet passage if the League of Nations voted for sanctions against Germany. Another problem was that Stalin's purge trials were in the process of eliminating more than half of the Soviet officer corps. Some evidence has been uncovered in Russian archives that Soviet forces were placed on alert, but they were never called upon to aid the Czechs.

What is clear is that the British and French governments wanted no part of a preventive war fought alongside the Soviet Union. Western suspicion of communist intentions in European affairs was at its height after two years of the Spanish Civil War. After the Soviet proposal of March 17, Lord Halifax wrote the British ambassador in France that "we did not think it had any great value."[24] Chamberlain referred to the Soviet Union as that "more than half Asian" nation. The French government was eager to avoid a situation in which its treaty obligations would come into effect. For both Western governments, almost any concession was preferable to "Stalin's War."

Since the Second World War, there has been much speculation that if the other European states had supported Czechoslovakia in 1938, the internal German opposition to Hitler would have overthrown him. The appeal of this possibility is evident: It rests on the chance that Czechoslovakia could have been defended without war, that Hitler could have been removed from within, and that the Soviet Union would not have been brought into the heart of Europe by the Second World War, if only Britain and France had shown more courage in September 1938. Indeed, many German generals were alarmed by the prospect of war in 1938, a war for which they expected to be ready only in 1943. Chief of the General Staff General Ludwig Beck even resigned over the Czech crisis. But since other generals took no action, most of our knowledge of their intentions rests on postwar memoirs. Even if we accept their recollected intentions at face value, their chances of rallying many other German officers and bureaucrats to disobedience during a time of international crisis were extremely small. In any event, the appeasers were sure at the time that they would have to fight to keep the Sudetenland Czech, and that they declined to do.

It may well be that an effort to save Czechoslovakia by force in September 1938 would have divided the Western powers and the Soviet Union more than it would have divided Germany. Revulsion against another war spread not only among the fearful conservatives but among the traditionally pacifist left. Even Léon Blum had to admit his "sense of deliverance."[25] A vast majority of Western Europeans backed appeasement in September 1938.

The appeasement policy failed both to save the rest of Czechoslovakia and to avoid war in the 1930s. That point is obvious to everyone now. All the assumptions were wrong in Hitler's case. That does not mean, of course, that the appeasers'

---

[24]*Documents on British Foreign Policy, 1919–1939*, series 3, vol. 1, no. 109, p. 88.

[25]Quoted in *Le populaire*, October 1, 1938.

basic aim of locating grievances and attempting to negotiate them rather than responding automatically by force to every challenge to the status quo should not be applied to other cases and at other times.

THE POLISH CRISIS, 1939: DESCENT INTO WAR

It was soon clear that Poland was next. No other part of the eastern settlement of 1919 was as offensive to German public opinion as the Polish frontiers. The Polish Corridor cut East Prussia off from the rest of Germany; the population of Danzig, a free city under League of Nations supervision, was mostly German; and Poland controlled German minorities in rich Silesia. In the spring of 1939, German Foreign Minister Joachim von Ribbentrop demanded that Poland return Danzig to Germany and permit a road-rail route across the corridor; in exchange Germany would offer some form of common defense against the Soviet Union. Hitler seems at this stage to have expected mere adjustments of the Polish-German frontiers without war, although Hitler's style of alternating between reason and force makes his intentions at any one point difficult to fathom. The Polish Foreign Minister Colonel Josef Beck was ready to profit by Hitler's aggressions when he could; for example, Poland had seized the disputed area of Teschen from the Czechs soon after Munich. But Beck intended to balance between Germany and the Soviet Union rather than commit Poland to the protection of either giant neighbor.

Appeasement Abandoned

The decisive change came from England and France. Angered and disillusioned that Hitler had mocked the Munich settlement by dismembering the rest of Czechoslovakia in March 1939 and alarmed by strident German propaganda attacks on Poland, Neville Chamberlain announced publicly in the House of Commons on March 31 that England and France would bring Poland "all the support in their power" if Polish independence were "clearly threatened." Here was the firm Continental commitment that the British had resisted since 1919. The British government had extended to Poland the guarantee denied the more easily defended Czechoslovakia a year earlier. Neville Chamberlain himself had abandoned appeasement.

   This Anglo-French guarantee to Poland has become a hotly disputed step in the path to the Second World War. According to the conventional wisdom, the Western democracies should have done this from the start. But the guarantee raises legitimate questions. Some Polish-German frontier adjustment was not unreasonable. Did a righteously indignant Chamberlain, enraged by Hitler's betrayal of the Munich settlement, seek to block any chance for a second Munich over Poland at the cost of leaving unexplored the possibility for negotiated settlement? Did he inject a new rigidity into this new European crisis?

   Did he commit Europe to a global war by deciding that it was inevitable, with the same evangelical fervor with which he had earlier decided that all problems were negotiable? Was the guarantee a "provocative" act[26] that only hardened Polish obstinacy and goaded Hitler into a forceful solution he had not wanted?

One's feelings about a lost opportunity for negotiation over Danzig in 1939 depend on one's sense of Hitler's intentions. Whatever his interest in a negotiated settlement earlier, by the end of May 1939 Hitler had clearly decided that "successes can no longer be attained without the shedding of blood. . . . There is no question of sparing Poland and we are left with the decision: to attack Poland at the first suitable opportunity. . . . There will be war."[27] The war he seems to have wanted, however, was meant to be both local and short. For that purpose he needed to divide Poland from its Anglo-French guarantors. By claiming in public to want only Danzig and the right of German transit across the corridor, he hoped to make the Poles appear the intransigent party and raise resentment against them in London and Paris. Then he could deal with Poland alone, without a general war.

Hitler could still believe that the Anglo-French guarantee was not serious. The British army was unprepared. A groundswell of French opinion did not want to "die for Danzig." Above all, what force could Britain and France actually bring to bear on the defense of distant Poland? As tension mounted over Danzig in 1939, other parties became the crucial actors on each side: the Soviet Union and Italy.

The Nazi-Soviet Pact

The Anglo-French guarantee to Poland could not be applied effectively without Soviet help. The French could attack western Germany, of course, but they would have little time to act before Poland had been defeated—even assuming there was anyone in France who wanted to make such an attack in 1939. A Soviet alliance was the obvious way to confront Hitler with the two-front menace of 1914. The British and French governments, however, were lukewarm at best. In addition to their basic distaste for the Soviet regime, they suspected Stalin's motives (was he trying to involve Hitler in a war in the west?) and doubted the capability of his recently purged officer corps. Might not an alliance with Stalin make war more likely than less? Nevertheless, British and French representatives did negotiate all spring and summer with the Soviets over a possible three-power security treaty. On August 22, 1939, however, like a bombshell, came the astonishing announcement that German Foreign Minister Ribbentrop was in Moscow to sign an agreement: the Nazi–Soviet Pact.

The British and French governments have often been accused of throwing away potential Soviet help against Hitler out of ideological distaste, or even of scheming to encourage Hitler to move east. They settled the Czech affair without Soviet participation at Munich in September 1938; they rejected Soviet Foreign Minister Litvinov's proposals for a three-power treaty in April 1939; they sent minor figures by slow boat to negotiate a more limited security treaty in Moscow. The difficulties

---

[26]Basil H. Liddell-Hart, *Memoirs*, vol. 2 (London, 1965), pp. 214, 217, 255. These questions were first raised in vigorous form in A. J. P. Taylor, *The Origins of the Second World War* (London, 1961), chapters 10 and 11.

[27]*Documents on German Foreign Policy, 1933–1945*, series D, vol. 6, no. 433, pp. 574–580.

Elated by their deal, Stalin and German Foreign Minister Joachim von Ribbentrop shake hands after the signing of The Nazi–Soviet Pact on August 23, 1939. Eight days later, German armies invaded Poland.

were genuine, however. Soviet troops could not attack Hitler without crossing Poland or aid Czechoslovakia without crossing Romania. The British and French refused to impose Soviet entry rights on Poland and Romania, and they were suspicious that Stalin meant to use his proposal to combat "indirect aggression" in the Baltic States (Latvia, Estonia, Lithuania) as a pretext for taking them over. At bottom, however, the decisive fact in the signing of a Nazi-Soviet Pact was that Hitler could offer something to Stalin that the Western democracies could not.

German–Soviet contacts (not counting the military arrangements of the early years) went back to the revival of economic negotiations in early spring 1939. The German economic negotiator dropped some broad hints to the Soviets in April, and on May 3 Stalin fired his "pro-League" (and Jewish) Foreign Minister Litvinov. Hitler decided in May to explore seriously the possibility of obtaining Soviet neutrality.

The negotiations began in earnest only when the urgency with which German diplomats pressed for a decision in August 1939 made the Russians aware that Hitler was about to invade Poland. With that knowledge, Stalin's choice was clear. To join the Allies meant going to war over Poland; Hitler offered neutrality. Furthermore, Hitler offered the Soviets the opportunity to expand in the Baltic region, eastern Poland, and Bessarabia. Skirmishes with the Japanese on the Manchurian border in 1938–1939 made Hitler's olive branch all the more welcome. In short, the Allies offered "war without gain"; Hitler offered "gain without war."[28] Stalin made the obvious opportunistic choice in the Nazi–Soviet Pact.

The Nazi–Soviet Pact in itself was simply an agreement for each side to remain neutral in case the other became involved in a war with other nations. Attached to it, however, was a secret protocol providing for the division of Eastern Europe into spheres of influence. "In the event of a territorial and political rearrangement," Soviet Russia was to get Finland; the Baltic States of Estonia, Latvia, and most of Lithuania; the eastern third of Poland; and Bessarabia, the area northeast of the Danube mouth awarded to Romania in 1918. Germany would get the rest of Poland and Lithuania.

Hitler now hastened his invasion plans. Assured of a free hand from Stalin, he needed only British acquiescence and Mussolini's support to make his short war against Poland absolutely safe. He offered to guarantee the British Empire in exchange for neutrality. Chamberlain, however, ostentatiously signed the promised Anglo-Polish guarantee on August 25. Eager to avoid Sir Edward Grey's error in 1914 of failing to tell Germany what England would do if Belgium were invaded, Chamberlain assured Hitler in both a public announcement and a personal letter that England would declare war if Germany threatened Polish independence. Mussolini regretfully told Hitler that he would have to stand aside because his country was unprepared for war. Hitler cancelled his war orders and for five days he seemed to go along with Mussolini's mediation proposals and Chamberlain's efforts to promote a direct Polish–German negotiation. The Poles refused to be drawn into another Munich, which Hitler quite likely did not want. Convinced that Chamberlain was bluffing, he ordered the invasion to begin September 1. Indeed, he judged correctly how deeply the British and French dreaded another war. They did not

[28]Christopher Thorne, *The Approach of War, 1938–1939* (London, 1967), p. 137.

declare war on Germany until September 3, two days after the invasion began. Europeans entered the Second World War with sinking hearts, without any of the enthusiasm of 1914.

THE ORIGINS OF THE SECOND WORLD WAR

There has been much less dispute about the causes of the Second World War than of the First. The war of September 1939 has been almost universally considered Hitler's war, far more the willful act of one man than an overcharged diplomatic-military-economic system spinning out of control as in 1914.

In the case of the Second World War the historians have generally agreed with the propagandists. Twenty years after 1914, "revisionist" historians in the Allied countries had thoroughly discredited the Allied propagandists' version of sole German war guilt. That debate about 1914 forced attention away from personal and national "guilt" toward underlying problems of alliance diplomacy, economic rivalry, popular nationalism, and uncontrolled military planning.

Twenty-five years after 1939, only one "revisionist" account of the outbreak of the Second World War had appeared in the Allied countries,[29] and serious sequels followed only in the 1990s. Moreover, that "revisionist" work actually focused the debate even more clearly on the leaders' personalities and decisions. Opening the German archives produced more evidence of Hitler's personal role; as for German survivors and historians, they have been delighted to unload all responsibility on a single set of shoulders. It may well be that Hitler's own cravings for violent solutions were the indispensable "proximate cause" of the war: no Hitler, no war.

There is a larger view, however, according to which both wars reflect fundamental shortcomings of a brilliant but flawed civilization that could not settle its differences without periodic blood baths. Nothing in the 1919 settlement had changed the basic division of Europe (and the world) into separate sovereign states that recognized no higher authority than national interest. Experiments with a League of Nations and a more public diplomacy had proved no more successful in averting war than the rival alliance systems and the secret dynastic diplomacy of the years before 1914; if anything, they were less successful. Some would argue that until the state system is replaced by a world government, there can be no lasting peace. Even that solution, however, assuming that it has the remotest chance of realization, leaves the way open for civil war or local conflicts.

Neither had the efforts at Versailles to recognize national aspirations and spread democracy in Europe impeded the resort to war. Indeed, the very conception of national or ethnic identity lay at the root of the Eastern European border quarrels that Hitler had exploited. And democratic regimes reflected popular passions for triumph and revenge no less readily than authoritarian ones. Despite the manifest failure of the policy of national self-determination as applied from 1919 to 1939 to create a stable Europe, the same pattern continued to spread in the world after 1945.

[29]A. J. P. Taylor, *Origins.*

Some would argue that economic failure was the fundamental reason for Europe's return to war in 1939. Clearly the depression of the 1930s, the most severe Europe had ever endured, had much to do with Hitler's ascent to power and the inability of his neighbors to stop him. Marxists would put the case more fundamentally: that a depression was inevitable to a ripe capitalist system at some point and that when domestic profit rates began to fall, the capitalist powers would eventually go to war over the spoils of the rest of the world. That interpretation of war, however, is clouded by the fact that Marxist states (for example, the Soviet Union and China) have also fought among themselves.

It may be that no human groups have altogether avoided war for long. The novelty of the European experience may be not its near suicide twice in thirty years on the battlefield, but the spreading belief in Europe since 1914 that war is unnatural and avoidable.

SUGGESTIONS FOR FURTHER READING

Recent introductions to this subject include R. J. Overy, *The Road to War: The Origins of World War II** (2nd ed. 1998); P. M. H. Bell, *The Origins of the Second World War,* 2nd ed. (1997); Robert Boyce, *Origins of World War II** (2003); Victor Rothwell, *The Origins of the Second World War** (2001); and Anthony Adamthwaite, *The Making of the Second World War,* 2nd ed. (1989). Gordon A. Craig and Felix Gilbert, eds., *The Diplomats, 1919–1939** (revised ed. 1994) continues to be indispensable here. Patrick Finney, ed., *Origins of the Second World War** (1997) reprints outstanding articles.

The origins of the Second World War have been less controversial than those of the First. Sixty years after the event, A. J. P. Taylor, *Origins of the Second World War,* 2nd ed. (1966, reprint ed. 1996), remains the most fundamental challenge to orthodoxy. Taylor argued that Hitler was a pragmatist whose goals resembled those of Stresemann and Bismarck, and that the British and French helped bring about war over Poland in 1939. The passionate controversy aroused by Taylor's book may be followed in Gordon Martel, ed., *The Origins of the Second World War Reconsidered: A. J. P. Taylor and the Historians,* 2nd ed. (1999).

The issue of continuity between Hitler and his predecessors, raised by Taylor, has continued to concern others. Klaus Hildebrand, *The Foreign Policy of the Third Reich** (new ed. 1992), is lucid on this point and others. Edward W. Bennett, *German Rearmament and the West, 1932–1933* (1979), shows that Hitler's arrival made little immediate change in clandestine rearmament.

Nevertheless Hitler remains at the center of the story. Gerhard L. Weinberg, *The Foreign Policy of Hitler's Germany,* 2 vols. (reprint ed. 1998), is based on minute examination of captured German documents. Norman Rich, *Hitler's War Aims,* 2 vols. (new ed. 1992), weighs ideology against pragmatism in Hitler's moves. Eberhard Jäckel, *Hitler's World View: A Blueprint for Power** (1990), gives more weight to ideology. Richard Overy, *Goering: The Iron Man* (1984), and Wilhelm Deist, *The Wehrmacht and German Rearmament* (1981), are important for rearmament.

The immense literature on appeasement is briefly introduced in Keith Robbins, *Appeasement,* 2nd ed. (1997), and more fully in Frank McDonough, *Hitler, Chamberlain and Appeasement** (2002), and in Maurice Cowling, *The Impact of Hitler** (1977, reprint ed. 1995). Gaines Post Jr., *Dilemmas of Appeasement: British Deterrence and Defense* (1993), broadens the issue beyond that of the leaders' moral courage to the economic and military factors that limited their options. That broadening was already begun by Wolfgang J. Mommsen and Lothar Kettenacker, eds., *The Fascist Challenge and the Policy of Appeasement, 1937–1940* (1978), and by Williamson Murray, *The Change in the European Balance of Power, 1938–1939* (1984). All these works center on Britain; Maya Latynski, ed., *Reappraising the Munich Pact: Continental Perspectives** (1992), widens the canvas to include other powers.

Stalin's version of appeasement and *realpolitik* is now elucidated, using Soviet archives, in Bernd Wegner, ed., *From Peace to War: Germany, Soviet Russia, and the World, 1939–1941* (1997), and Hugh Ragsdale, *The Soviets, the Munich Crisis, and the Coming of World War II* (2004). See also Geoffrey Roberts, *The Soviet Union and the Origins of the Second World War** (1995). Adam B. Ulam, *Expansion and Coexistence: Soviet Foreign Policy, 1917–1993*, 2nd ed. (1993), is still useful.

David E. Kaiser, *Economic Diplomacy and the Origins of the Second World War* (1980), provides the vital economic context. Ernest R. May, ed., *Knowing One's Enemies: Intelligence Assessment before the Two World Wars* (1984), adds a further dimension.

Well-informed recent studies of other major powers' foreign policies include Anthony Adamthwaite, *Grandeur and Misery: France's Bid for Power, 1914–1940** (1995); Nicole Jordan, *The Popular Front and Central Europe: The Dilemmas of French Impotence, 1918–1940* (new ed. 2002); Robert J. Young, *France and the Origins of the Second World War** (1996); Richard Davis, *Anglo-French Relations before World War II: Appeasement and Crisis* (2001); John F. Coverdale, *Italian Intervention in the Spanish Civil War* (1975); Denis Mack Smith, *Mussolini's Roman Empire* (1976); Robert Mallett, *Mussolini and the Origins of the Second World War** (2003); and MacGregor Knox, *Mussolini Unleashed** (1986). Anita J. Prazmowska, *Eastern Europe and the Origins of the Second World War,** exposes active policy initiatives by the successor states.

For particular crises, Stephen A. Schuker, "France and the Remilitarization of the Rhineland, 1936," in the Finney volume mentioned at the head of this section, doubts that a French military response was feasible then. Jurgen Gehl, *Austria, Germany, and the Anschluss* (1979) shows Hitler as opportunist. Telford Taylor's massive *Munich: The Price of Peace* (1979) restates the Churchillian position that the Western powers missed their best chance to stop Hitler in Czechoslovakia. Igor Lukes and Erik Goldstein, eds., *The Munich Crisis 1938: Prelude to World War II* (1999), draws on new eastern sources. John Charmley, *Chamberlain and the Lost Peace* (1990), tries to make a case for a negotiated settlement (assuming Hitler would accept one). A balance is struck by R. A. C. Parker, *Chamberlain and Appeasement** (1993).

The opening of military archives now permits the study of military planning and presuppositions. In addition to the works on the German army cited at the end of chapter 11, see Donald Cameron Watt, *Too Serious a Business: European Armed Forces and the Approach of the Second World War** (1992); the Gaines Post work cited above; Robert J. Young, *In Command of France: French Foreign Policy and Military Planning, 1933–1940* (1978); Martin Alexander, *The Republic in Danger: Gen. Maurice Gamelin and the Politics of French Defense* (1992); and B. J. C. McKercher and Roch Legault, eds., *Military Planning and the Origins of the Second World War in Europe* (2000).

Additional Internet links related to this chapter are available on the Europe in the 20th Century Web site: http://www. history.wadsworth.com/paxton04.

You can also explore images, interactive timelines, and maps related to this chapter on our Western Civilization Resource Center: http://history. wadsworth.com

A *Panzer* unit moves up on the eastern front, 1941. Troops and supplies are motorized in order to keep up with the Mark II tank, at right. In *Blitzkrieg, Panzer* units supported by *Stuka* dive bombers broke through enemy defenses, followed by slower moving horse-drawn units to consolidate the gain.

14

Hitler's Europe: Conquest, Collaboration, and Resistance, 1939–1942

Hitler was genuinely surprised when his war against Poland turned out to be a general European war. But he was not overly alarmed. His Third Reich seemed to have solved the problem that had destroyed Kaiser Wilhelm II's Second Reich: how to expand in Europe without facing a two-front war. His armies were overwhelmingly superior to the Poles. The only potential rival to the east, the Soviet Union, was ready to join him in the spoils. His western enemies were obviously reluctant to fight. Free to reverse the timing forced on his 1914 predecessors, Hitler could deal with Poland first, and then move the bulk of his forces west to deal with France at his leisure, if that was even necessary. Hitler wrote to Mussolini on August 26, 1939:

> As Germany, thanks to her agreement with Russia, will have all her forces free in the East after the defeat of Poland . . . I do not shrink from solving the Eastern question even at the risk of complications in the West.[1]

[1]Quoted in Alan Bullock, *Hitler: A Study in Tyranny*, 2nd ed. (New York, 1962), p. 538.

THE NATURE OF THE CONFLICT IN 1939

The success of Hitler's calculation depended on speed. He had not solved his predecessors' problem of insufficient resources for a long war of attrition. Germany's efforts toward self-sufficiency through exploiting low-grade German iron ores and producing ersatz rubber and oil had only narrowed the gap. For any extended war, Germany would be dependent on iron ore from Sweden, oil from Romania and the Soviet Union, and grain from the east. Diplomacy might keep these resources flowing for a time, but their supply remained uncertain for a long war. To win, Hitler must win quickly.

German army logistics experts, fearful of another long war, thought that Germany must shift over its entire productive capacity for war matériel, a process that could not be completed before 1943. Hitler decided instead on a strategy of *Blitzkrieg* (lightning war). By simply stockpiling enough supplies and armaments for one decisive strike against a surprised enemy, he thought he could not only win his immediate objectives but capture enough supplies and armaments to make up for his losses. This approach had the added advantage of sparing German civilians the pains (and the resentments) of a war economy. Hitler had decided simply to sidestep Germany's economic shortcomings, not solve them from within.

Germany entered war in 1939, therefore, superbly equipped for rapid thrusts but quite unprepared for an extended war. There was no long-range bomber in the German arsenal. The German navy had only fifty-seven submarines, of which just eighteen were designated for the high seas.[2] This deliberate shortage of what had been Germany's chief maritime weapon after 1917 was a sign that Hitler did not expect war with Britain. Although rationing and wage-price controls were instituted, the German economy put no more resources into war production in 1939 and 1940 than it had in the years 1936 to 1939. Consumer goods continued to be produced, superhighways built (not always for strategic purposes), and as late as 1942, marble was still being imported for Hitler's grandiose building projects in Berlin.

Hitler's combined enemies were his superior in both numbers and resources. Poland, France, and Britain together had 120 million people to Hitler's 80 million. They held undisputed control of the seas and, with them, access to the world's strategic resources. Despite the Neutrality Acts of the United States, Franklin Roosevelt's "cash and carry" policy (sale of goods to any belligerent who could pay cash and transport them from American shores) gave France and Britain a virtual monopoly of American productive capacity, unlike the situation under American neutrality between 1914 and 1917. The Allies could defeat Hitler, then, under two conditions: first, if they could stave off that initial lightning thrust, and then proceed gradually to choke off the German economy by blockade and peripheral encirclement. No other strategies were open to the Allies. Their depression remedies had prevented the construction of powerful offensive forces, and public opinion would make a preemptive strike difficult, even if they had been equipped for one. Everything depended on the effectiveness of their defensive preparations and on their material and emotional readiness to sustain another prolonged war.

---

[2]Holger Herwig, *Politics of Frustration: The United States in German Naval Planning, 1889–1941* (Boston, 1976), pp. 198, 200.

The Allies were not hopelessly ill-equipped for their strategic position. The French navy alone was far larger than the German; the British and French navies together could control both the Atlantic and the Mediterranean. The British were more advanced in heavy bomber design, and their light Mosquito bomber, so fast that it could dispense with defensive armament, could reach Berlin. On the ground, the French Maginot Line effectively closed the Rhine frontier from Switzerland to the Ardennes hills, at the French-Belgian border; indeed the Germans never overran it directly.

Taking the defensive position imposed grave disadvantages on the Allies, however. Although France and Britain had excellent prototypes of fighter aircraft and tanks, they had not put the latest models into mass production for fear of stockpiling equipment that might become obsolete before a war began. And they had to cover all fronts, not knowing where the Axis would strike. Graver still was the problem of morale. Hitler also belonged to the generation of the First World War, and he had reason to judge that the Allied populations would not support the one strategy open to them, another long war of attrition. Especially not after several tastes of *Blitzkrieg*.

In sharp contrast to the naive enthusiasm of 1914, the European populations of 1939 faced war with deepening gloom. Even in Germany, crowds watched in stony silence as the troops passed by. Europeans had come to expect that the next war would involve the massive bombing of cities and the use of poison gas. There had been foretastes of the one in Spain and the other in Ethiopia.

Psychological warfare contributed to this sense of alarm. On the battlefield, *Blitzkrieg* made calculated use of surprise and terror. The *Stuka* dive bomber, although rather slow and vulnerable, was equipped with sirens to terrify opposing ground forces. The Germans parachuted mannequins behind enemy lines to great effect. Their use of commandos dressed in Polish and Dutch uniforms lent credence to exaggerated rumors of "fifth columns." On the home front, both sides managed their own populations' opinions with great care and aimed propaganda broadcasts at the opposing populations.

The terrors aroused by the prospect of war in 1939 were closely tied to the general expectations that science and technology would dominate it. In fact, however, the war began with weapons that were recognizable derivatives of those of 1918. The only important exception was radar, a British invention that allowed them to win the air war of 1940. In technological matters, the advantage lay less with conceptions of *Blitzkrieg,* which depended on stockpiled weapons, than with the long sustained efforts, the larger resources, and the total war economies of the Allies. Anti-Semitism probably set German science back. Although the Berlin chemist Otto Hahn was the first to achieve fission of a uranium nucleus in 1939, his chief assistant, the brilliant woman physicist Lise Meitner, and other leading Jewish scientists were forced into exile, where they helped the Allies develop atomic weapons. But the chief blame for the stagnation of German nuclear physics was the government's decision to invest in missile technology instead. Shortage of fuel explains the German failure to exploit their engineers' development of the world's first jet aircraft, the Messerschmidt 262, at the very end of the war.

When the war began in 1939, it was not clear who would win. It was clear, however, that the war would wreak even more terror and havoc on European civilians than the last one.

WAR IN THE EAST, 1939–1940

Blitzkrieg in Poland

The Polish campaign of September 1939 provided Europe's first good look at *Blitzkrieg*. Propaganda helped open the way. Hitler denounced the terrible sufferings of Germans who had been forced to live "under a people of inferior cultural value."[3] At the end of August, he staged a phony raid on a German frontier post by SS troops disguised in Polish uniforms; they left a dead concentration camp inmate in a Polish uniform as proof of Polish "aggression." Even as his armies assembled, Hitler dangled hopes of negotiation, which persuaded the British and French to force the Poles to postpone mobilization for another twenty-four hours. At dawn on September 1, German forces invaded Poland.

The main weapon was the *Panzer* division. It was not so much the numerical superiority of Germany's sixty-three divisions to Poland's forty as it was the presence of six *Panzer* divisions that completely disrupted the Polish defenses. A *Panzer* division was a self-contained striking force led by 300 or so tanks and accompanied by supporting forces and supplies capable of moving along at the same speed. A screen of fighter aircraft flew overhead, while *Stuka* dive bombers demoralized and destroyed opposition just ahead of the tanks. After the *Panzers* had secured an opening in the enemy defenses, they moved on, leaving behind more conventional units with horse-drawn equipment to hold the newly gained ground. The flat, open Polish terrain was ideal for fast tank warfare.

Although Britain and France were explicitly committed to come to Poland's defense immediately by air and by the sixteenth day with ground troops, there was only a minor French advance into the Saar on September 8. Further attacks were cancelled when it had obviously become too late to help. Without foreign aid, it was only a matter of time before Poland gave way. Despite vigorous efforts to reassemble a shattered defense, Warsaw fell on September 27, and the last Polish holdouts surrendered on October 2.

Russian Gains in Eastern Europe, 1939–1940

Stalin was no less surprised than anyone else by the speed of the German advance in Eastern Europe. Nervous about German armies reaching the Soviet frontiers and anxious to assure his share of territory as promised by the secret protocol of August 23,[4] he rushed troops west into Poland on September 17. In the end he gained more territory than the Germans. A further division of territory was arranged in a second Ribbentrop visit to Moscow at the end of September, and Germany and Russia again shared a common border, as they had from 1815 to 1914.[5]

Stalin found this an opportune moment to improve his western defensive frontiers. He concluded treaties of mutual assistance with Latvia, Estonia, and Lithuania,

[3]Bullock, pp. 551–552.

[4]See chapter 13, p. 405.

[5]Stalin rejected Hitler's original plan of a rump client state around Warsaw.

obtaining the right to station Soviet troops in the latter country. (Lithuania had grasped the opportunity to reannex Vilna, taken by the Poles in 1920.)

Stalin then demanded that the Finns give up the Vyborg area, at the head of the Gulf of Finland, where the frontier was only twenty miles from Leningrad. When negotiations proved fruitless, the Soviets renounced their 1932 nonaggression pact with Finland and, without declaring war, invaded Finland on November 30, 1939. The ensuing "winter war" was surprisingly difficult for the Russians. The rest of the world (including Mussolini, bitterly affronted by the Nazi-Soviet Pact, which threatened Italy's Balkan interests) cheered for the "brave little Finns," while the Russians incurred more casualties than there were troops in the Finnish army. The poor Russian performance confirmed Western suspicions that the Soviet army had been fatally weakened by the purges. By concentrating overwhelming force, the Soviets were finally able to force the Finns to surrender Vyborg on March 12, 1940.

Stalin recouped most of the rest of Russia's 1917 losses in the summer of 1940, while Hitler was preoccupied in the west. He seized the three Baltic States—Latvia, Estonia, and Lithuania—in June and incorporated them in August as member republics of the Soviet Union. On June 26 Stalin demanded that Romania cede Bessarabia, which had been Russian before the First World War, and Bukovina, which had not. By these steps, Russia had gained more than it had lost in 1917 at the mouth of the Danube, had recovered a large portion of former tsarist territory in Poland, and had advanced beyond tsarist frontiers in Finland.[6] Stalin may have anticipated an eventual break with Hitler, for which his defensive position was now improved. For the moment, however, he fulfilled the terms of the Nazi–Soviet Pact scrupulously, supplying Germany with vitally needed materials, especially oil and grain.

WAR IN THE WEST, 1940

When Hitler publicly offered peace to Britain and France on October 6, 1939, Chamberlain and Daladier did not even inquire about the terms, although there were numerous partisans of a compromise settlement in both countries. In any event, Hitler had already ordered plans drawn up for action in the west. An immediate campaign was delayed by the onset of autumn, so a period of waiting ensued, ironically known as the "phony war," during which the French and British troops lost whatever fighting edge they might have had.

While waiting, the French and British governments discussed possible offensive strategies. They believed a direct preemptive assault across the Rhine was impossible both materially and politically (no one wanted to provoke the bombing of Paris and London); attrition and encirclement seemed more appropriate to the Allied position. A blockade was set up against Germany, although the Soviet Union and Italy (which still imported British coal, as the British hoped to keep Mussolini neutral) were gigantic leaks in the system. Other plans were directed with more alacrity against Hitler's Soviet ally than against Hitler himself. The French considered

[6]Finland had been an autonomous grand duchy under the Russian tsar from 1809 to 1917.

opening a Balkan front and bombing the Russian oil fields in the Caucasus. During the Russo-Finnish "winter war," an Anglo–French force was prepared to help the Finns. After the Finns were beaten, this plan was shifted to an attempt to cut off the main summer route for shipment of Swedish iron ore to Germany along the coast of Norway.

Hitler forestalled this plan with his second lightning stroke of the war, a daring seizure of Denmark and Norway on April 9, 1940. Denmark fell in a few hours, with thirteen Danish casualties. Norway offered more serious resistance to the thinly stretched German parachutists and seaborne troops, however. The Franco-British forces that had been prepared for action there landed in the north (Narvik) in an attempt to help push the Germans back out. The great German western offensive of May 10 cut this effort short.

The Fall of France

The German attack on France and the Low Countries that began May 10 followed a daring but risky plan worked out by General Fritz Erich von Manstein, perhaps the most brilliant German tactician of the war. Instead of following the 1914 Schlieffen Plan route through coastal Belgium and Holland, Manstein proposed to thrust the main striking force—ten *Panzer* divisions—through the deeply wooded Ardennes hills to come out at the weakest point in the French defense system, at Sedan, north of the end of the Maginot Line. The French had believed the terrain was too rough for a major attack at this point.

The French and British had anticipated a repetition of the Schlieffen Plan. They planned to move their most modern units north into Belgium and Holland to confront the Germans as far away as possible from the French industrial zones of the northeast. But since Belgium and Holland remained adamantly neutral for fear of provoking a German attack, this complicated move and the junction with Belgian and Dutch defense lines could begin only after a German invasion. This Allied maneuver, in the French historian Henri Michel's fine metaphor, was like a great tree pulling up its roots, making it all the easier to topple. Furthermore, it showed that the Franco-British sense of the pace of mechanized warfare was hopelessly out of step with the speed of *Panzer* divisions. They expected to move whole armies more than one hundred miles north to head off German armies that had already begun to move with a shorter distance to cover.

General Guderian's ten *Panzer* divisions drove through the Ardennes as scheduled, over a road system so narrow that one army "head" had reached the Meuse River while its "tail" stretched back east of the Rhine. What followed was a brilliant exercise in *Blitzkrieg*. Since the Ardennes offensive was not preceded by a long artillery barrage as in the First World War, the French continued for three days to think that the simultaneous advance of a conventional German army into Belgium was the main attack. By May 13, two days ahead of schedule, Guderian had crossed the poorly defended Meuse at Sedan and was driving across open country toward the English Channel, threatening to cut off the cream of the Allied forces in Belgium.

The chief risk in Manstein's plan was that the fast *Panzer* divisions would extend a long salient out across northern France that could then be pinched off by simultaneous Allied attacks from north and south before the slower regular German troops could fill in. That was indeed the plan of the Allied commander in chief, the French General Maurice Gamelin, and of his successor after May 19, General Maxime Weygand. There were moments of alarm at German headquarters when General Guderian, ignoring orders to consolidate, plunged ahead despite the vacuum opening up behind.

The fall of France is to be understood in the failure to pinch off Guderian's exposed salient in northern France immediately after May 13. Here was an opportunity for another Battle of the Marne, and the justification for arguing that Hitler's victory in France was not a foregone conclusion.

The French defeat has commonly been attributed to a combination of insufficient matériel and poor morale. In fact, the 94 French divisions, plus 10 British, 8 Dutch, and 22 Belgian divisions, were not hopelessly mismatched against Germany's 134 divisions. The Allies were superior in artillery, and they had about an equal number of tanks, a few of which were technically superior to the German tanks. Their most damaging shortages were in communications, anti-aircraft artillery, and planes for close support and reconnaissance. The Allies' chief problem was in the way their forces were used. Basing their strategy on lessons learned in winning the First World War, the French, in particular, distributed their tanks among infantry units rather than in armored divisions. The one British and four French armored divisions (one under Colonel Charles de Gaulle, the main French proponent of tank warfare) were thrown piecemeal into the line, always one jump behind the speeding German tanks.

Another major problem was time. The Allies never adjusted to the new pace of war. Without adequate communications, it was impossible to plan the point of attack and then assemble units there before the opportunity to strike had passed. The Battle of France from the French side was a bit like one of those slow motion nightmares. French soldiers fought bravely enough to suffer casualties at First World War rates, but there were never enough of them ready at any one point to interrupt the *Panzer* advance.

A final serious problem was Allied disunity. As noted, the Dutch and Belgians refused to run the risk of joint preparations before the German invasion actually began. The British Expeditionary Force under Lord Gort, fearful of being encircled in Belgium, began falling back toward the Channel ports after a tentative advance on Guderian's salient to his south, an action that the French have never forgiven.

Under these conditions, the planned simultaneous counterattack from north and south on the *Panzer* salient produced only some uncoordinated local attacks. The Germans reached the English Channel at Dunkirk at the end of May, cutting off the best Allied units to the north. A heroic armada of small boats helped the British navy evacuate 200,000 British and 130,000 French troops from Dunkirk in the first days of June, but they had to leave all their equipment on the beach.

After this, little chance remained for the French to reorganize a new defensive line against a German move southward into the heart of France. Prime Minister

On the beach at Dunkirk, May 30, 1940, troops of the retreating British Expeditionary Force await evacuation by ships, fishing boats, pleasure crafts, and even sailing boats.

© Hulton Getty

Paul Reynaud and others wanted to fight on with British help and evacuate the government to North Africa if necessary. But a growing peace movement formed around First World War hero Marshal Pétain, joined by the commander in chief himself, General Weygand. They argued that social revolution might break out in France without some remaining civil and military authority, that the French had suffered all they could, and that the British had abandoned them at Dunkirk. Pétain formed a new government when Reynaud resigned on June 16 and negotiated an armistice. It provided that only northern France and the coast would be occupied. The French government agreed to demobilize, to keep its citizens from continuing any acts of war against Germany at home or abroad, and to "collaborate" with the German occupying authority. France, the greatest military power on the Continent only ten years before, had been reduced to surrender in a bare six weeks.

The Battle of Britain

The French armistice left the British alone and exposed. The British Isles were defended only by the disarmed remnant of the Expeditionary Force taken off the beaches at Dunkirk, plus veterans armed with hunting shotguns who were hastily assembled as a home guard, the navy, and the still untried Royal Air Force. Germany faced them with eighty divisions on the Channel coast and an opening on the

Atlantic for its submarines. After what he had done to the better-prepared French, Hitler expected the British to come to terms.

Instead, the British rallied to the leadership of Winston Churchill, who replaced Chamberlain as prime minister on May 10. Churchill, a brilliant but wayward man whose impetuous rashness ill fitted him for peacetime politics, now found the words and the spirit to unite his country around a supreme war effort. When the French request for an armistice became known Churchill said, on June 18, that Britain would fight on, "if necessary alone, if necessary for years," so that if the British Empire lasted a thousand years, men would still say, "this was their finest hour." He stirred pride in going on alone, relishing "the honor to be the sole champion of the liberties of all of Europe," when "we stood alone and all the world wondered." He aimed at nothing less than "victory—victory at all costs . . . victory, however long and hard the road may be," even though the cost would be unremitting "blood, toil, tears, and sweat."[7]

In fact, the cost turned out to be nothing less than the empire and Britain's world role, for the logic of Churchill's (and Hitler's) policy of war to the finish eventually shifted the decisive role to two emerging superpowers outside Europe: the United States and the Soviet Union. In that larger sense, Churchill was a failure. More immediately, however, the resolution, verve, and style with which he mobilized Britain for the supreme effort made him one of the giants of the century. His

[7]Churchill speeches in the House of Commons, May 13, June 18, and November 5, 1940.

spirit certainly won over public opinion in 1940. When the Independent Labour Party proposed peace negotiations in December 1940, the House of Commons rejected the idea 341 to 4. The British braced for Hitler's onslaught with an almost exhilarated determination.

British intransigence left Hitler with several options. One was a frontal assault on Britain, the last western holdout. This is what the German army and air force expected. A second option was an oblique strategy of encirclement. Axis forces could control the western Mediterranean and North Africa via Gibraltar, exploiting the cooperation of Franco and Pétain; or they could control the eastern Mediterranean and Suez via the Balkans or Italian Libya. Either way, the British stood to lose their empire, their oil, and their morale. This choice, supported by Admiral Erich Raeder and the German navy, looks in retrospect like Hitler's best chance of winning outright hegemony in Western Europe. The third possibility was a return to *Lebensraum,* expansion in the east. No one except Hitler thought seriously about this choice, for although the oil and grain of Eastern Europe would become essential in a long war, to attack the Soviet Union without first reducing Britain was to choose deliberately a two-front war.

Hitler's astounding successes in May and June 1940 left him genuinely undecided about the next step. Through the summer and fall of 1940 he kept all these possibilities alive. At the beginning, however, he went ahead with plans for the first of the options outlined above.

Frontal assault on the British Isles, against the superior British navy, required air superiority at the very least. Indeed, encouraged by Reichsmarschall Göring, commander of the air force, Hitler seems to have believed that he could break the British will by air attacks alone. While the German navy gathered landing craft on the Channel coast, the *Luftwaffe* began the Battle of Britain. This contest for control of the skies over England became the greatest air battle of the war. The Germans could reach southeastern England with light bombers and fighter cover from airfields in France. If the Germans had continued their initial tactic of bombing British airfields, they might have won local control of the air. Instead, they switched on September 7, 1940, to bombing London. This came about after one German pilot had bombed London, against orders, on August 24. When the British responded with night bombing of German cities on August 25, Hitler and Göring let the desire for vengeance triumph over sound tactics.

London was bombed every night from September 7 to November 2. Although 15,000 people died in London in these raids and although thousands of buildings were destroyed, including the House of Commons on May 10, 1941, the London population bedded down in cellars and subway stations and stoically endured their sufferings. Well before November, however, a decisive point had been passed. British radar and superior communications, the excellent Spitfire and Hurricane fighter aircraft, and the advantage of fighting close to home bases allowed the Royal Air Force to inflict a heavy margin of loss on the Germans. While London soaked up bombs, British aircraft factories increased their output. On September 17, 1940, Hitler postponed the invasion for the winter—and, in fact, for good. The British could not yet know the danger of invasion had passed, for the bombing went on into 1941. But Hitler had already changed his mind.

Londoners spending the night in a subway station during the *blitz***, October 1940.**

In October and November Hitler toyed with the second option, the Mediterranean. He visited Franco and Pétain. Both wanted neutrality. Pétain's government at Vichy,[8] war weary and embittered by Churchill's first actions (the British bombarded the French Mediterranean Fleet in Algeria on July 3, killing over 1,200 French sailors, to keep it out of German hands) was eager for cooperation with Germany in a new Continental system. The French price was a generous peace settlement, but Hitler wanted to avenge 1918. Soon, however, alarmed by Stalin's moves in June 1940, he began to study possible German moves east.

WAR IN THE EAST, 1941–1942

On December 18, 1940, Hitler issued orders for the preparation of Operation Barbarossa, the invasion of the Soviet Union. That decision may have been the turning point of the war, Hitler's fatal mistake. He voluntarily chose a two-front war, insisting that Russia must be defeated even before Britain. Hitler evidently expected that the Communist regime would crack under pressure and that he could capture all the oil and grain he needed for a long war.

---

[8]Vichy is a health resort in the south-central mountains of France where the French government was located "temporarily" during the occupation.

Blitzkrieg in the Balkans

The attack on the Soviet Union was preceded by one more stunning display of *Blitzkrieg,* this time in the Balkans. Mussolini, who had entered the war in the last stages of the French campaign (June 10, 1940), asserted his independence by invading Greece in October 1940. The Greeks not only pushed the Italian forces back into Albania, but brought in a British force the following March. Hitler was forced to come to Mussolini's rescue to prevent his proposed invasion of the Soviet Union from being threatened by an Allied front on the Balkan flank. When the Yugoslav government agreed to assist Hitler and Mussolini, a military revolt in that country overthrew the regime, and the new government prepared to side with the Allies. German armies struck southward on April 6, overrunning both Yugoslavia and Greece and seizing the island of Crete in a daring paratroop operation on May 20.

At the same time, the Germans sent weapons to an Arab nationalist rebellion in Iraq, where the British had reestablished bases in their former mandated territory. German use of the Vichy French colony of Syria as a staging area for supporting the Iraqi rebels obliged the thinly stretched British to occupy Syria as well in June 1941, aided by Free French forces. Hitler also sent General Erwin Rommel's tank force to Libya to reinforce the Italians there. If Hitler had continued his conquest of the eastern Mediterranean along these lines in the summer of 1941, the British Empire might well have been cut in two at Suez. Instead, he persisted with Operation Barbarossa.

Attack on the Soviet Union

Hitler invaded the Soviet Union in the early hours of June 22, 1941, with his most massive force so far—175 divisions.[9] It was the mightiest operation of his career.

At first Hitler seemed justified in his gamble on speedy success in Russia. Things looked dark indeed for the Soviet Union in the first months. Unlike the situation in 1914, the Germans were not preoccupied with another front in the west. Only Britain remained at war with Hitler there, and British resources were fully devoted to defending the home island and the lifeline to India. Moreover, the Russians were unprepared. Perhaps, as Khrushchev was to charge in 1956, Stalin had failed to fortify his frontier in order to avoid provoking Hitler. He may have clung to the hope (not unlike Neville Chamberlain in 1938) that Hitler would be satisfied with his acquisition of most of Poland in 1940. Whatever his reasons, Stalin had scrupulously kept up his side of the Nazi–Soviet Pact, delivering grain and oil to the very last. He had also disregarded several foreign warnings of an imminent German attack.

The German invasion of June 22 threw the unprepared Soviet forces into confusion. Instead of withdrawing to some defensible line, the Soviet command lost masses of troops in piecemeal defense. Furthermore, civilians in some areas—notably the Ukraine—welcomed the Germans as liberators. It had been only ten

---

[9]He had pitted 134 divisions against the French, British, Dutch, and Belgians in May 1940.

As German forces advanced on Moscow in July 1941, the Soviet regime mobilized its entire population in the national defense effort. Here Moscow women dig antitank ditches outside the capital.

years since the rural rebellions against collectivization and only four years since the liquidation of over half the officer corps in the purges. Stalin himself did not even speak on the radio for two weeks. While the rest of the government evacuated Moscow, he remained for a last-ditch defense of the capital. During the anti-Stalin revisionism of the late 1950s, Marshal Georgi Zhukov claimed that Stalin actually expected defeat. By November 1941, Hitler had penetrated deeper into Russia than had Napoleon: to the outskirts of Leningrad in the north, into the very suburbs of Moscow in the center, and to the Don River in the south.

Hitler had not, however, achieved the lightning victory essential to his plans. The logic of *Blitzkrieg* required the smaller, less naturally endowed Germany to defeat the Soviet Union at once, without lapsing into a long war of attrition favorable to the larger combatant. By November 1941, the Germans had reached deep into the vast Russian spaces without managing to grasp a vital organ. German troops, unequipped for winter fighting, were now dangerously overextended. Time, space, winter, and the natural weight of Soviet resources were on Stalin's side.

The first Russian counteroffensive at the end of November 1941 recaptured the city of Rostov-on-Don. This was a major psychological victory, for it was the first conspicuous German military reversal on the ground since the war had begun in September 1939. Then in December General Georgi Zhukov counterattacked in front of Moscow. Many German commanders wanted to pull their shivering armies back to avoid a winter encirclement. Hitler refused any retreat, and sacked a field marshal and thirty-five corps and divisional commanders to get his way. The German soldiers' ability to cling to their advanced positions fortified his contempt for his generals and his rejection of tactical withdrawals.[10]

Soviet survival during that first winter was the eastern front's equivalent of the Battle of Britain. *Blitzkrieg* had failed, and the Russians had forced Hitler to face a long war against an opponent with greater resources. The German threat was far from ended, however. Two more German summer advances followed, succeeded by Russian winter recoveries. The great German advance of the summer of 1942, focused this time on the south, penetrated even deeper than in 1941. German armies reached the lower Volga River at Stalingrad (map, p. 451), almost to the Caspian Sea. In late 1942, they held more Russian soil than any other foreign army in history.

HITLER'S "NEW ORDER"

At the end of 1942, Hitler had put together by conquest and by alliance a Continental empire without parallel in European history. The directly occupied areas extended from the Atlantic coast of France, the Low Countries, and Norway east to Leningrad, the approaches to Moscow, the Volga River, and deep into the Caucasus region, approaching the Caspian Sea. From Norway and Denmark in the north, the directly occupied areas extended south through the Balkans to Greece and Crete, while the German army helped the Italians in Libya in an attempt to overrun the Suez Canal.

Around the rim of these directly occupied areas lay a ring of more or less cooperative or allied states. Italy, having abandoned Danubian interests for Ethiopian ones, had been publicly allied with Germany since November 1936 and a belligerent since June 10, 1940. Admiral Miklós Horthy's Hungary had been gratified by the acquisition in 1939 and 1940 of much of the disputed territories lost in 1918 to its new neighbors—Czechoslovakia, Yugoslavia, and Romania. Romania, under General Ion Antonescu, hoped to make up for losing Transylvania to Hungary by joining Hitler's attack on the Soviet Union. Independent Slovakia and Croatia had been established for grateful minorities in what had been Czechoslovakia and Yugoslavia. Marshal Karl Gustav Mannerheim's Finland received German help against another possible Soviet attack. In Western Europe, the French regime of Marshal Pétain controlled from its capital at Vichy the unoccupied southern third of France and most of the French African empire in a state of cooperative neutrality. Spain was friendly, even though Franco had refused to help the Germans take Gibraltar in 1940. Sweden was officially neutral, but 10 million tons of Swedish iron ore supplied the German war machine each year. Only Portugal (doctrinally sympathetic to Germany but economically tied to England) and Switzerland (engaged in profitable financial dealings with both sides) claimed to be neutral in Continental Europe in late 1942.

A "New Order" began to take shape in Europe. At a minimum, the New Order meant an expanded Germany surrounded by a common market of client states,

---

[10]Alan Clark, *Barbarossa: The Russo-German Conflict, 1941–1945* (London, 1996), pp. 177–178, 182, 187.

forming a Great Economic Unit *(Großwirtschaftsraum)* in which German economic influence would supplant Anglo-French economic influence. The German frontiers were restored to the 1914 borders in the west (chiefly by reannexing Alsace-Lorraine from France) and extended beyond them in the east (Austria, Bohemia-Moravia, part of Poland). In the wake of the armies, German industrialists completed their economic conquest of Eastern Europe and the Balkans, obtaining former French shares in Balkan mining concerns, the great Czech Skoda armaments factories, and control of Romanian oil. German farmers were settled on "abandoned" farms in Poland and northeastern France, and eventual massive settlement of German farmers was planned in Russia. Jewish businesses and art collections were confiscated.

At a maximum, the New Order meant fulfilling the fantastic dreams spun around Hitler's table late at night, when traditional German conceptions of *Mitteleuropa* and eastern expansion were escalated to new heights by success and overt racism. The Führer talked of absorbing the Low Countries or of reviving ancient Brittany and Burgundy at the expense of France. As for the Soviet Union: "This Russian desert, we shall populate it. . . . We'll take away its character of an Asiatic steppe, we'll Europeanize it. . . . There's only one duty: to Germanize this country by the immigration of Germans and to look upon the natives as Redskins."[11]

Nazi War Economy

In early 1942, Hitler's Europe began to feel the economic effects of the shift from *Blitzkrieg* to a long war of attrition. The Nazi economy of the late 1930s had already devoted a higher proportion of the national budget to strategic and military purposes than any other state in peacetime.[12] According to *Blitzkrieg* tactics, accumulated resources would make possible short, sharp thrusts that would, in turn, recover their costs in booty. It would not be necessary to divert more resources away from the civilian economy. At the beginning of 1942, Germany was far less mobilized than Britain. Consumer goods production was still only 3 percent below peacetime levels; as late as April 1942, most German armaments factories still operated on only one shift a day.

Two developments in December 1941 forced Germany to mobilize more systematically for war in early 1942: The Russian campaign bogged down, and the United States entered the war. Fritz Todt, minister of armaments and munitions, began setting up centralized agencies for allocating more resources to the war effort in the spring of 1942. After Todt's death in an airplane crash, his more famous successor, Albert Speer, managed to more than triple German armaments production between the spring of 1942 and July 1944. German populations began to know privation then, as well as a mounting rhythm of Allied bombing raids. Even so, the German civilian economy was never as fully subordinated to the war effort as the British. The Nazis were more reluctant to mobilize German women for war work, for example, than were the British.

Increased war efforts forced the Nazi system to reveal its very essence. The early ideological commitment to defense of the small farmer and shopkeeper (long observed mostly in the breach) was now cast to the winds. Under Albert Speer's Central Planning Committee, staffed by business executives from the great companies

---

[11]*Hitler's Table Talk, 1941–1944* (London, 1953), pp. 68–69. Conversation of October 17, 1941.

[12]The military and strategic spending of the United States and the Soviet Union during the Cold War was to reach roughly the same proportions of the national budget as the German spending did then.

and cartels, war resources and labor were allocated to the largest and most efficient plants. Industry, agriculture, and retail trade were all concentrated in fewer hands. Occupation policy began to be shaped more and more by race ideology.

Occupation Policy

The apportionment of burdens in the New Order rested on the Nazi concept of Germans as the "master race" and others, especially Jews, Slavs, and Mediterranean peoples, as inferior. Hitler's Europe could be self-sustaining in a long war if enough resources were squeezed out of subject peoples. Huge financial contributions were exacted from the occupied nations in the guise of "occupation costs." France, for example, transferred 58 percent of its tax receipts to Germany during the war. Within the occupied countries, the Germans also collected war materials, melted down statues and church bells for scrap, and requisitioned vast quantities of food. Occupied peoples were explicitly meant to have less to eat than Germans.

The treatment of Poles showed racially inspired occupation policy in action. A decree of October 26, 1939, subjected all Polish men and women from eighteen to sixty years of age to "compulsory public labor." By 1942, more than 1 million of them had been brought to Germany to work on farms, in mines, and in heavy construction. While their lands were settled by German farmers, Polish workers in Germany were maintained at a bare subsistence level, forced to wear a violet *P* on their clothes, and segregated from social contacts with Germans. Editorials exhorted Germans to treat the Poles as "inferior to each German comrade on his farm or in his factory. Be just, as Germans have always been, but never forget that you are a member of the master race!"[13] The penalty for Polish men who had sexual relations with German women was death.

After June 1941, Russian prisoners of war became Germany's main source of heavy labor. But the Reich worked or starved 4 out of 5 million of them to death. This forced the Germans to start drawing labor from the western occupied areas, mainly the Low Countries and France, in 1942. Late in the war, the largest national contingent among foreign workers in Germany was French.

The treatment of occupied peoples varied widely, according to a mixture of racial prejudice and opportunity. The treatment of Slavic peoples was particularly harsh. Even though the Germans could have won Ukrainian allies by restoring family farms there, German desires for immediate deliveries of grain and future settlement led to self-defeating brutalities.[14] Despite the eagerness of many Frenchmen to end their long conflict with Germany, the Germans refused offers of cooperation from this "mongrelized" people and treated collaborationist France no less harshly than the fully occupied areas of Western Europe. Nordic occupied people like the Dutch and Norwegians, workers and farmers in Bohemia-Moravia, and farmers in

---

[13]William L. Shirer, *Berlin Diary* (New York, 1941), p. 513.

[14]"In the face of these tasks," said Erich Koch, German governor [*Gauleiter*] of the Ukraine, "feeding the civilian population [in the Ukraine] is a matter of the utmost indifference." (Alexander Dallin, *German Rule in Russia, 1941–1945: A Study in Occupation Policies,* 2nd ed. [New York, 1981], p. 345.)

the dairy regions of Denmark, had a relatively easy time of it at first. But the screws tightened everywhere after 1942. Many Europeans suffered severe shortages of food, clothing, and shelter, in addition to the humiliation of defeat and the grief of lost relatives.

The SS Empire

Contrary to Western impressions at the time, the Nazi war machine was not a monolith of perfect efficiency. Below the single authority of Hitler, agencies and cliques competed for power and influence. Among these rival factions the agencies of police and terror became increasingly powerful. Chief among these was the black-shirted paramilitary party force, the SS *(Schutzstaffel)* of Heinrich Himmler, which became a virtual "state within a state." The SS did not limit itself to filling and running the network of concentration camps. It recruited front-line fighting units, the *Waffen-SS*. It even competed with German businessmen, for whom some SS leaders still felt the anticapitalist contempt characteristic of early Nazism, in setting up business enterprises in occupied Russia. The SS, with its cult of blood, seemed to be the ultimate expression of the Nazi system under pressure. As the SS grew in power, especially in the eastern war zones, its racial doctrines became more compelling than military need or economic advantage.

The Murder of the Jews

Nothing done within Hitler's Europe matches in horror the Nazis' systematic killing of all Jews within their reach—men, women, and children—and their effort to eliminate the very traces of Jewish culture from Europe.

From his student days in Vienna, Hitler had been obsessed by Jews as a menace to Germandom. Since he perceived that menace in racial terms, the conversion or assimilation that earlier religious anti-Semites had seen as the solution were insufficient for him. For Hitler, the least visible, most assimilated Jews were the greatest danger of all. Thus his form of anti-Semitism was potentially murderous from the beginning. However, anti-Jewish measures instigated by the Nazis escalated only gradually through the 1930s, with pauses (such as in 1936 for the Olympic Games). The goal in that early period seemed to be segregation of Jews within German society.[15] Segregation reached its climax in September 1941 when Jews were required to sew a yellow star on their outer clothing.

Nazi zealots had by then already escalated to a new stage: expulsion. The absorption of Austria in 1938 provided the first occasion. A young SS officer, Adolf Eichmann, distinguished himself by devising a profitable system of selling emigration papers to wealthy Austrian Jews, with part of the proceeds going to cover the costs of expelling the rest. After the war began, the Nazis started dumping German Jews into newly conquered territory. Some favored Jews, such as war veterans, were resettled in

[15]See chapter 11, pp. 333–334.

a "model" ghetto near Prague, Theresienstadt. Outlets for expulsion grew ever fewer, however, as the war spread. Proposed resettlement areas like Madagascar were now out of German reach. Wealthy neutrals like the United States were conspicuously reluctant to open their doors to hundreds of thousands of central European Jews. Anyway, by the end of 1941, they were no longer neutral.

Hitler's invasion of the Soviet Union was a further turning point. It soon brought him millions more unwanted Jews, along with vast new spaces in which to deal with them. The Russian front, where the Nazis already practiced a war of extermination against "Bolsheviks," provided a laboratory for mass killing techniques. Special "intervention squads" *(Einsatzgruppen)* accompanied the German attack forces with orders to liquidate Communist Party officials and Jews. When mass shooting proved inefficient and troubling to German regular soldiers' morale, the *Einsatzgruppen* devised mobile vans into which engine exhaust could be pumped. A further refinement was Zyklon-B gas, an insecticide turned against humans in Hitler's program of euthanasia for the mentally ill in 1939. It was used next against "subhuman" Slavic prisoners, and finally against Jews.

Late in 1941, probably in December, the ultimate threshold was crossed. The sporadic killings of Jews that had accompanied military operations were now regularized into something without human precedent: the systematic extermination by industrial methods of an entire people. According to one theory, it was local zealots on the scene, competing for the Führer's approval, who devised the killing factories in order to deal with local problems of crowding and supply in territories newly conquered from the Soviet Union. A more familiar "intentionalist" theory holds that Hitler personally decided to begin the "Final Solution." A major difficulty with this view is that no trace of a written order by Hitler survives in the Nazi archives.

The probable date of December 1941 helps clarify the immediate motives that prompted the decision to turn sporadic killings into total extermination. More than the opportunity opened by the conquest of vast territories in the east or the vexing problems of administering them and their flood of Slavic and Jewish refugees, it was rage at having failed to defeat the Soviets by *Blitzkrieg* before winter and at the entry of the "Jewish" United States into what had become a global conflict. Hitler's guiding role is clear in documents that show how he diverted precious resources from crucial battles to the extermination of the Jews. It is also clear that large numbers of German officials and their collaborators of many nationalities assisted with this immense and hideous project. Many bystanders knew what was going on.

By the spring of 1942, extermination camps—factories designed for killing large numbers of human beings—had been built on former Polish soil, in the area without national identity but under SS control known as the *"Gouvernement General."*

The largest of these killing centers, a collection of camps and factories known collectively as Auschwitz, about thirty miles west of Cracow, Poland, contained branches of Krupp steel and I. G. Farben chemicals, crude dormitories, killing installations where the Zyklon-B gas was pumped through what appeared to be showers, and crematoria. As each trainload of deportees arrived, the able-bodied were held aside for a few months' exhausting labor while the sick, the old, women and children were sent at once to "the showers." More than one father, faced with this choice, unwittingly sent his teenaged son off with his mother or grandparents for what he thought was an easier fate.

After killing had reached industrial proportions on the eastern front, the Nazi leaders extended it to occupied Western Europe. Reinhard Heydrich, deputy chief of the SS, warned that, if any escaped, "natural selection" under hardship would produce "the germ cell of a new Jewish revival."[16] The SS officer Adolf Eichmann now organized the systematic gathering and transport of the Jews of Western Europe to Auschwitz and other killing centers in former Polish territory. The system worked best where Jews were already concentrated, as in the Vichy French internment camps or in Amsterdam. In Eastern Europe, the Jewish population was packed into a

Netherlands Institute for War Documentation

Nazi officers oversee Dutch Jews being loaded aboard freight cars for shipment to extermination camps.

[16]Reinhard Heydrich, deputy chief of the SS, at the Wannsee Conference of January 20, 1942, quoted in Martin Gilbert, *The Holocaust* (New York, 1985), p. 282.

handful of official ghettos that were ostensibly permanent communities (the extermination was a closely guarded secret) but were actually only way stations to the killing centers. The Jewish community leaders of these ghettos faced excruciating choices, and in some cases let themselves be drawn into the selection of victims.

In some cases, younger and more militant Jews revolted against what they now understood was happening. In the most celebrated instance, the Nazis encountered armed resistance when they began the third massive round-up in a year in the Warsaw ghetto on April 19, 1943, the first day of Passover. Burning and dynamiting their way block by block, the SS lost up to 700 killed or wounded and killed about 50,000 dug-in Jews, who used Molotov cocktails and home-made grenades. SS General Jürgen Stroop finished his work by dynamiting the Warsaw synagogue on May 16 and wired to Himmler, "The Warsaw ghetto is no more."[17]

Deportations to the extermination camps continued to the very end, though western collaborationists such as the Vichy French assisted less by mid-1943 and the Hungarians tried to block them in summer 1944. Word reached the west in conflicting forms, and even Jewish organizations found the stories hard to believe. No effective aid arrived from outside. The Allies declined to use military resources by bombing the rail line to Auschwitz, for example.

There had been ethnic violence in the past, and the Nazis included other groups such as gypsies in their exterminating frenzy. But never had such methodical organization gone into exterminating a people as the Nazis invested in the killing of the Jews. By 1945, more than 5 million Jews had been killed, two-thirds of the Jewish population of prewar Europe.

COLLABORATION

Ideological Collaboration

Hitler's New Order was able to draw on the cooperation of a number of non-Germans in the occupied areas of Europe. The most notorious of these were ideological collaborators who sympathized with fascist doctrines: profascist intellectuals and leaders of prewar fascist groups. For some intellectuals, such as the French novelists Pierre Drieu la Rochelle and Robert Brasillach, the defeat of the "decadent" democratic regime of their own country was little enough price to pay for a "virile" dynamic new Europe. Some of the prewar fascist leaders outside Germany looked forward to leading roles in the new Europe. For others, however, nationalism was still important, and a few even resisted the German occupation.

The ideological collaborators were more noisy than important. It was primarily Hitler who limited them to a minor role. He always preferred to work through established leaders in occupied countries than to give power to local fascist chiefs who might have pretensions about partnership and who could not always keep order. Thus he dealt with Marshal Pétain in France rather than with the French fascists (some of whom later fought in the resistance); with Admiral Horthy in Hungary rather than with the Arrow-Cross leader Ferenc Szálasy, who came to power

[17]*The Stroop Report: "The Jewish Quarter of Warsaw Is No More!"* facsimile edition, trans. and annotated by Sybil Milton (New York, 1979).

only in October 1944, when the Russians were already pouring into Hungary; with General Antonescu in Romania, who crushed the fascist Iron Guard in 1941. The Dutch fascist leader Anton Adriaan Mussert was given only a figurehead role in 1942; the Norwegian fascist Vidkun Quisling was shunted aside by German military commanders in April 1940 and assumed mere shadow power in February 1942.

Ideological collaboration received an important boost with Hitler's invasion of the Soviet Union on June 22, 1941. From that point on, anticommunism was Hitler's most telling propaganda device. Hitler's propaganda chief Joseph Goebbels could argue that whatever discomforts occupied Europe might be suffering under Hitler would be worse if the Russians conquered Europe. From this perspective, Hitler seemed the last remaining bulwark against Bolshevism, while the Allies' bullheaded insistence on invading Europe from the west was only helping Stalin. Eventually some 500,000 non-German Europeans fought the Russians in the volunteer foreign divisions of the *Waffen-SS*. East Europeans, such as Baltic peoples and Croatians fighting for their national independence, made up the largest number, but there were also 50,000 Dutchmen, 40,000 Belgians (about evenly divided between Flemish and French-speaking Walloons), 20,000 Frenchmen, about 6,000 Danes, and another 6,000 Norwegians.[18] Behind these volunteers stood millions of less committed Europeans who nevertheless shared the same basic priorities: some kind of accommodation with the New Europe, whose harshest phase would end with a German-imposed peace, rather than an Allied victory that would let the Russians in.

Collaboration for National and Economic Interests

The New Europe appealed to interests as well as ideology. The stepchild nationalities of 1918 at last had a chance to reshuffle the map of Eastern Europe. Hungary retrieved Transylvania from Romania and regained other borderlands from what had been Czechoslovakia and Yugoslavia. Admiral Horthy sent troops to assist the German conquest of Russia. Romania contributed thirty divisions to the invasion of Russia, hoping to make up east of the Danube and even in the Crimea the equivalent of what had been lost to Hungary. Two peoples who did not achieve statehood in 1918—Slovaks and Croats—now had their revenge against the formerly dominant Czechs and Serbs. The Slovak national leader, Father Andrej Hlinka, had been denied a hearing at Versailles; his successor, Monsignor Joseph Tiso (the Slovak Peoples' Party was strongly Catholic) now headed an independent Slovakia. Ante Pavelič, who had led the Croat liberation movement (*Ustasha*) from exile in Italy since 1929, now headed an independent Croatia and applied the *Ustasha*'s terrorist methods to Serbs, Jews, and gypsies.[19]

---

[18]George H. Stein, *The Waffen-SS* (Ithaca, N.Y., 1966), pp. 138–139. Not all volunteers volunteered "voluntarily"; some foreign labor in Germany enlisted in the *Waffen-SS* as a lesser evil, and some Eastern Europeans were more or less forcibly recruited.

[19]Serb historians claim "genocide," with a death rate of Serbs within Croatia reaching one in six; Croat historians, such as the later Croatian president Franjo Tudjman, rejected the charge. Aleksa Djilas, *The Contested Country* (Cambridge, Mass., 1991), p. 127.

Hitler's Europe served economic as well as national interests. Some industrialists outside Germany received lucrative orders for war matériel, especially after 1943 when Albert Speer reversed the policy of bringing labor to the Reich in favor of dispersing production throughout occupied Europe. The new French aluminum industry, for example, produced more under the German occupation than before the war (although most French industries fared less well). These industrialists were also liberated from the trade union movement, and some among them dreamed of a postwar Europe fully cartelized and united against the rising American giant. French industrialist François Lehideux, for example, the Vichy French Minister of Industrial Production and nephew of the automobile magnate Louis Renault, tried to plan a postwar Franco-German-Italian automaking giant that would dominate the world market in opposition to the "American bloc."

Some farmers also prospered in a world desperately short of food, especially in such highly productive dairy regions as Normandy, Denmark, and parts of Bohemia-Moravia. Since the official food ration was little above starvation level, a vast black market sprang up for items like eggs and cheese, which were almost literally worth their weight in gold.

Passive Acquiescence

The true mass basis of collaboration was mere passive acquiescence. Some peoples, of course, had no choice. For Poles or Ukrainians, the occupation was so harsh that any voluntary impulse to seek a place in Hitler's New Europe was soon crushed. Occupied peoples who could lead more normal lives faced more ambiguous choices.

France had the most uncertain choices of all, which makes it the most interesting case for discovering who collaborated and who did not. Loyalties were uniquely divided in France after 1940 between two claimants to legitimate authority: the collaborationist French state of Marshal Pétain at Vichy and the Free French in London under General Charles de Gaulle. Other occupied peoples had less difficulty deciding where legitimate authority lay. The Dutch Queen Wilhelmina and the Dutch government in exile in London had the support of most of their people; so did the Norwegian ministers in exile in London under King Haakon VII. Although the Belgian cabinet went to London, King Leopold III elected to declare himself a prisoner with his army and ceased all governmental function. The Danish regime stayed in place, and the seventy-year-old King Christian X, a popular monarch of simple tastes, rode out in the streets of Copenhagen daily on horseback. Whatever their location, these governments had two features in common: They kept legitimate authority unified; and they refused to legislate under German occupation, limiting their activity to basic administrative services.

In France legitimacy was not only divided; the Vichy regime actively tried to replace the Third Republic with a corporative, authoritarian state. Underlying the French division was the intensity of prewar social conflict during the Popular Front, the bitter discredit into which the Third Republic had been thrown by losing the war, and the yearning of many Frenchmen to be spared another blood bath like that of the First World War. Under the aged Marshal Pétain, the hero of the First World War battle of Verdun, Vichy France tried to reach a compromise peace with Hitler and to make a place for itself in the New Europe. Conservative leaders, out of power between the wars, attempted to create a "National Revival" even while German troops still occupied the northern half of France. They abolished parliament and trade unions, passed anti-Semitic legislation, favored the Catholic Church, and set up a corporative economic system operated, in practice, by executives of big companies. For French conservatives, the German defeat of the Third Republic was an opportunity to reverse what they regarded as fifty years of democratic "decadence."

A majority of Frenchmen trusted Marshal Pétain as a national hero and were relieved to be out of the war. General de Gaulle's Free French, by contrast, seemed to offer only renewed fighting (for England's profit, it appeared) and, after 1941, indirect help for Stalin and his French Communist minions. The normal course in France, at least through 1942, was to carry out "business as usual." Was this collaboration? Did delivering the mail or teaching school in Pétain's regime constitute aid to France's German enemies? After the war, the treason trials of the liberation held

© Archive Photos / Liaison Agency

Marshal Philippe Pétain, head of the new French government at Vichy, makes his collaborationist policy official in a meeting with Hitler at Montoire, in occupied central France, on October 24, 1940.

that collaboration consisted of going out of one's way to help the occupying power, such as holding a policy-making position or exceeding mere duty in helping the Germans. On these terms, about 38,000 Frenchmen were imprisoned after the war for collaboration, close to 1,600 were executed, and nearly 50,000 were deprived of voting rights.[20] But others who had acquiesced provided the climate in which more active support of Hitler's Europe became legitimized. By choosing to participate in the New Europe, the Vichy regime had tainted the most everyday acts of its citizens with de facto collaboration.

As Hitler's chances of victory waned, many Europeans gained renewed hope in an Allied victory. Many others, however, still feared the social consequences of renewed fighting in the west, which could only bring Stalin into Europe. By this logic, many Europeans not overtly sympathetic to fascism continued to wish for a compromise peace until 1944.

RESISTANCE

Nazi domination confronted Hitler's opponents in Europe with an agonizing question: Should they suffer in resignation, or should they take action against unjust authority? Action posed both practical and ethical problems. What action was possible against a tyranny both limitless and popular? What responsibility did each individual bear for opposing evil in the world and for the kind of acts with which he or she opposed it? In the absence of any lawful forms of dissent, did moral ends justify acts usually considered criminal—even killing people?

There were compelling reasons for acquiescence, the easiest and commonest course. The full brutality of German occupation was not revealed all at once, particularly in Western Europe, Bohemia-Moravia, and Scandinavia, where the early occupation was comparatively mild. Moreover, many could feel no hope of change until after the war's turning point. The Nazi's most bestial acts had no precedent, so that many Jews, for example, had gone passively to their deaths, unaware of their destiny. Finally, even when these horrors began to be known, those Europeans less immediately threatened felt strong inhibitions against violent acts in the name of a higher morality. Had not the Nazis themselves justified their attacks on Weimar legality in just this way? Might not a violent resistance simply replace tyranny with anarchy?

Above all, resistance was dangerous. It meant exposing one's family and neighbors to reprisals and running personal risks of death or, even worse, torture. A resister had to renounce comfort, routine, safety, and even conventional morality. That is why active resisters were few, and why they were often outsiders: young, single people without attachments; enemies of the regime who had no choice; old street fighters from both nationalist and revolutionary ranks.

---

[20]Henry Rousso, "L'Epuration en France: Une histoire inachevée," *Vingtième siècle: Revue d'histoire*, no. 33 (January–March 1992), p. 102.

In spite of all these obstacles, resistance movements appeared in occupied Europe and even in Germany itself. Active resisters were those who committed overt acts punishable by the authorities, and not those who expressed mere disapproval, or dissented silently, or even worked with calculated inefficiency. Overt acts ran a wide gamut, from writing or distributing subversive tracts and scrawling anti-regime slogans on walls, through gathering intelligence information for the Allies and sheltering enemies of the regime, to outright acts of sabotage and assassination. All such acts required a decision to break the law and incur grave risks.

Few in number, often isolated, and harassed by a vigilant and merciless authority, the European resisters rarely had direct military significance. But they captured the world's imagination with their bravery. The men and women who underwent danger together in the name of a new Europe after Hitler created a special fraternity, one that frequently threw together prewar opponents like priests and communists. Their intellectual leaders helped shape postwar Europe and raised major moral issues about individual responsibility and the legitimacy of opposition to unjust authority.

Resistance outside Germany

The European resistance varied greatly in time and place. In the early days of the war, there was neither hope nor (except in Poland) unbearable provocation. The early resistance leaders were mostly conservatives, nationalists, and officers like the Free French leader Charles de Gaulle. Their conception of the resistance was gathering intelligence for the Allies and preparing clandestine forces to assist an eventual Allied landing in Europe. As long as the Nazi–Soviet Pact remained in force, European Communists, with the strongest underground organization in Europe, were devoted to pacifism rather than resistance. The Comintern's instructions ordered European workers to take no part in this "imperialist war." To be sure, the party regarded Hitler and his collaborators as evil. But in a return to the "class against class" intransigence of 1928 to 1934, it argued that Hitler's enemies, the city of London and its vassals, were identical to Hitler in class terms. Workers would not benefit by the victory of either. "Neither cholera nor the plague," read illegal Communist handbills in occupied Paris in early 1941: that is, neither Pétain nor de Gaulle, neither Hitler nor Churchill. Down with the imperialist war. Frenchmen should not die for the capitalists. French Soviets to power. Long live peace.[21] Workers in Europe were urged to establish good relations with German workers and with the neutral Soviet Union and to work for immediate peace. This position was intensely uncomfortable for many European Communists, both then and since. The party subsequently has been able to point with pride to some workers who disobeyed its orders, such as the French coal miners who struck in May 1941.

The first major turning point in the European resistance, then, came with the German invasion of the Soviet Union on June 22, 1941. The European Communist

[21]A. Rossi (Angelo Tasca), *La Guerre des papillons* (Paris, 1954), pp. 37–53 and appendices.

underground immediately swung with relief and enthusiasm into direct action against Hitler. There was a sudden rise in sabotage and assassination in the occupied countries. Well organized and manned by dedicated and committed fighters, the Communist movement was better prepared, both materially and morally, than other groups to attract the most vigorous and active resisters. The European resistance now became a renewed Popular Front: a coalition of all antifascists in a satisfying unity of action for national liberation. As the French Communist poet Louis Aragon wrote with relief, "My party has given me back the French flag."[22]

The second major turning point is less precisely dated but no less significant. In late 1942 and early 1943, the possibility of German defeat became apparent; simultaneously, the Germans began extorting more booty from the occupied areas. This was a particularly striking shift for Western Europe, which up to that time had suffered more in pride than in body. But now young men began to be drafted in France, Holland, and Belgium to work in German factories. Food rations were diminished. Massive deportation of Jews from Western Europe to the crematoria

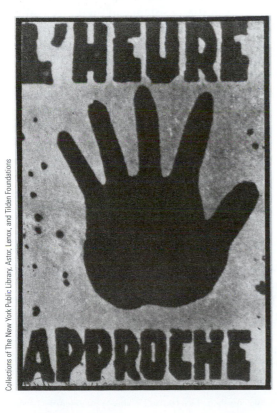

"The hour is coming." A crude but effective resistance sticker on a wall in Belgium, as D-Day drew near.

[22]Louis Aragon, "Du poète à son parti," in Claude Roy, ed., *Aragon* (Paris, 1962), p. 164.

began in the summer of 1942, the first issue on which the Catholic clergy in Western Europe took a public position against the occupation authorities. At this point the French *maquis*[23] appeared: resistance encampments in remote areas peopled by those who were fleeing the labor draft or deportation; they lived on local support while preparing to aid an Allied invasion. Thus, at the beginning of 1943, there was an increase in both hope and anger, along with wider community acceptance of resistance acts. The European resistance had acquired a mass base.

Resistance was not uniform throughout occupied Europe, of course. Its strength depended on opportunity and the extent of animosity. Temptations to acquiesce to the Germans were greater in relatively comfortable occupied areas like Denmark and Bohemia-Moravia or in half-occupied France. Resistance was ineffectual in states at the other extreme, like Poland, whose citizens were threatened with annihilation. The open terrain in Poland, moreover, could not protect the resistance fighters as did the French central hills, the Alps, and the mountains of Yugoslavia. The most suitable areas for resistance lay between the extremes, in places where hope was possible and shelter available.

Resistance also varied with the legal sanction given it by legitimate governments. Governments in exile that were recognized by almost all their citizens as legitimate and that fought alongside the British justified internal resistance in their own countries; the Dutch and Norwegian monarchs and governments in London were examples. In France, by contrast, the existence of rival regimes claiming legitimacy made the right path much more difficult to find. Almost all French people longed to be delivered from the harsh German occupation. But it was not until the Allied invasion of June 1944 had proved capable of driving the Germans out rapidly, without another stalemate trench campaign as in 1914 to 1918, that a majority of the French decided that General de Gaulle's path of armed liberation was more promising than Marshal Pétain's path of negotiated cooperation. Before then, postwar figures suggest that about 2 percent of French adults took the heroic risks required of active resistance; perhaps as many as 10 percent read the clandestine press. At least that many fervently supported the Pétain regime to the end.[24]

Resistance within Germany

Resistance within Germany faced special hazards and limitations. Resistance in the occupied countries could appeal to nationalism as well as to moral principle and self-interest. The German resistance, by contrast, was accused of stabbing its own country in the back, especially after the war began. Strong national traditions of political discipline were reinforced by the genuine mass fervor aroused by Hitler's successes. A hostile public opinion exposed the German resisters more relentlessly to the attention of the police and SS than in the occupied countries.

---

[23] *Maquis* is a Corsican word for scrubby Mediterranean hillside brush in which outlaws hid and, by extension, the bands of outlaws themselves.

[24] Robert O. Paxton, *Vichy France: Old Guard and New Order,* 2nd ed. (New York, 2000), p. 294.

The German resistance was also deeply fragmented among mutually hostile groups on the left and right. These groups lacked a goal of national liberation to unite them and a strong common liberal tradition. The left had a potential mass following but no means of penetrating the army or bureaucracy. The conservative resistance had some chance of recruiting helpers in the army and bureaucracy but no mass following.

A majority of Germans had voted against Hitler as late as March 1933, and some continued to oppose him. The left—Social Democrats, Communists, and trade unionists—formed the largest potential opposition. But the German left missed its last opportunity for concerted action in 1932 and 1933. Social Democrats and trade unionists remained committed to legal means against even lawless opponents; Communists clung to the belief that Hitler's destruction of the Weimar Republic only brought a German "Red October" that much closer; and the two factions regarded each other as the principal enemy. The German left's institutions were closed down in the first weeks of the regime and its leaders arrested or driven underground and abroad. Prison or death awaited anyone who attempted to reorganize socialist parties or trade unions. The great mass of Germans, including some workers, were "Nazified" by the economic and international successes of the regime. Eventually, the Social Democrats and Communists formed some important resistance movements, such as the "Red Orchestra" group rounded up in August 1942. The Nazi regime kept the German left under constant surveillance, however, and the main measure of what might have become a mass left opposition was the hundreds of thousands of Germans held after 1933 in the concentration camps.

The churches were the next most important potential source of resistance in Germany. Although German Protestants were too fragmented and too imbued with the Lutheran tradition of state loyalty to offer concerted opposition, Nazi efforts to found a new "German Christian" church—the "SA of Jesus Christ"—produced a Protestant opposition in the Confessional Church, led by such men as Pastor Martin Niemöller, former U-boat captain in the First World War and opponent of the Weimar Republic. The Catholic Church concluded a concordat with Hitler in 1933, in which it agreed to abolish the Center Party and to abstain from political action in exchange for the survival of parochial schools and parish organizations. By 1939 the papacy and the German clerical hierarchy had expressed open opposition to particular features of the regime, including its militant secularism, racism, and the policy of euthanasia.[25] Notwithstanding the courageous opposition of many Christians, the churches worked more for their own autonomy within the regime than for an end to the regime.

Before the war began, some conservatives opposed the Nazi regime on religious or humanitarian principles. Generally, they retreated into private disgruntlement, or they formed secret discussion groups, such as Count Helmut von Moltke's Kreisau Circle, which laid plans for an integrated new Europe, without international rivalries, to come into existence after others should have brought about

---

[25]See the 1937 papal encyclical *Mit brennender Sorge* (With Burning Concern).

Hitler's end. The possibility that Hitler would stumble into defeat, however, galvanized some of the military and bureaucratic opposition into action.

One high point of this opposition was 1938, when Hitler seemed to be driving a still unprepared Germany into war with both Russia and the West. It has been asserted since the war that Hitler's military and bureaucratic opponents planned to overthrow him at the moment he attempted to declare war. The chief of staff, General Ludwig Beck, did in fact resign in August 1938 in disagreement with Hitler's ambitions. But the postwar claim of some German officers and high civil servants that Neville Chamberlain's concessions at Munich undercut and neutralized their plan to overthrow Hitler must be regarded with some caution. When war did break out under more favorable circumstances in September 1939, patriotic reflexes overrode any significant opposition from army or bureaucratic quarters. Furthermore, the conservative opposition had no mass following; it remained elitist and authoritarian, a continuation in some ways of the anti-Weimar movements of the 1920s. The final obstruction to their action was the narrow range of acts open to the conservatives: Without a mass basis, only a *coup d'état* or an assassination could bring about their aim—an authoritarian and powerful Germany without Hitler—and such means were repugnant to them.

When the war began to appear lost in 1943 and 1944 and the threat of a Bolshevized Europe took shape, the conservative opposition overcame its scruples. An assassination attempt in March 1943 failed. On July 20, 1944, Colonel Count Klaus Schenk von Stauffenberg set off a bomb during a briefing in Hitler's headquarters at Rastenburg, near the Russian front. Hitler was only shaken and temporarily deafened. The conspirators, who had meant to close down the concentration camps, abolish the SS, and seek a separate peace with the West, were shot or hung up on meat hooks to die. Only military defeat from the outside would finally bring Hitler down, and all Germany with him.

The Military Impact of the Resistance

The military outcome of the war was influenced only marginally by the European resistance. The impact of the resistance was probably greater in Eastern than in Western Europe. Partisan bands behind the German lines in Russia seriously interfered with transportation and security and required the diversion of some German troops from the front.

Yugoslavia provided the most militarily effective resistance in Europe. When Yugoslavia was overrun by the Germans in April 1941, the army did not disband; it took to the hills. The rugged Yugoslav terrain was never under secure German control. As the two sides settled down into stalemate, however, General Draša Mikhailović's "Chetniks" tended to establish de facto truces with the German occupying forces. When the Communists entered the war, a more active resistance movement was created by a Croatian Communist, Josip Broz, better known as Tito. The Yugoslav case posed the issue of two possible resistance strategies: immediate action, with all its risks of reprisals and greater short-term suffering, or a more cautious policy of awaiting the arrival of superior Allied forces. British observers who parachuted in to meet Tito sent back reports of his activism that persuaded the Allies to shift their financial and material aid from Mikhailović to Tito. In the end, Tito's forces held down ten German divisions. He emerged as the unrivaled postwar leader of Yugoslavia, less divided ethnically than between the wars and committed to a new leadership combining communism and nationalism.

The resistance did not decisively affect the military outcome in Western Europe. Resistance organizations there did provide essential information on German military installations, and they helped delay German troop movements during the Allied invasion of Normandy on D-Day, June 6, 1944. The real significance of the resistance in the West, however, was the intellectual and spiritual renewal that it stimulated.

The Intellectual Impact of the Resistance

Resistance meant thought as well as action. Depression, fascism, and war—the second European fratricide in twenty-five years—all demanded an unsparing criticism of the European experience and hard thought about the new Europe that should be built after Hitler:

> After the Resistance, after the economic, social and political Revolution that each one of us bears within him . . . what republic? What democracy?[26]

Although resistance intellectuals came from widely varied backgrounds from Catholic to communist, the enormity of Europe's self-destruction and the risks of clandestine writing and speaking imposed some common characteristics on them. The nature of the enemy identified the resistance firmly with the left after the Soviet Union entered the war in June 1941. The resistance intellectuals rejected prewar Europe almost universally; virtually no one worked to resurrect interwar conditions. Because the totality of the crisis demanded profound change, they prepared nothing less than a transformation of European politics, society, and economy. Most resistance thinkers supported a return to parliamentary democracy, but a system purified of the fumbling and corruption attributed to interwar parliaments. They called for a more open and egalitarian access to schools, jobs, and honors. They rejected the notion of a self-regulating market, blamed now for the depression; but unlike the prewar left, resistance economists accepted some degree of planning and state intervention within mixed economies. (These wartime hopes will be examined more fully in the next chapter.)

A major resistance innovation was the ferment produced in the European churches. Although no Christian denomination entered the resistance en bloc, many younger priests and pastors went beyond the mere struggle for religious

---

[26]The French resistance leaflet "Après," no. 2 (July 1943), quoted in Henri Michel and Boris Mirkine-Guetzévitch, *Les idées politiques et sociales de la résistance* (Paris, 1954), p. 87.

autonomy to an active social and political commitment. The churches' previous positions on obedience to secular authority and on socioeconomic issues were challenged as never before. A major Catholic innovation was the worker-priests who exchanged their cassocks for overalls and shared directly in the labor experience. The worker-priest experiment began with ministry to drafted French factory workers in German munitions plants and thus drew in part on Vichy roots as well as on the resistance; in both cases, the worker-priests insisted on breaking decisively with the middle-class existence of the conventional priesthood.

The question of whether to commit unlawful acts against an unjust authority posed serious moral problems for priests and pastors. Every standard precept called for submission to the state. Pastor Dietrich Bonhoeffer, a young German Protestant seminary professor, has made perhaps the profoundest impression on Christian ethical thinking since the war. Bonhoeffer was a follower of the Swiss theologian Karl Barth, who had criticized modern liberal theology as too human-centered and optimistic. The actions of the Nazi regime reinforced Barth's attack on the more facile forms of liberal "social Gospel" theology, calling renewed attention to the depths of human evil and awakening doubts about the reality of social progress on earth. Instead of drawing quietistic conclusions from this, however, Bonhoeffer insisted that Christians should not live separate lives of mere piety but should share fully in the secular world as imitators of Christ. Bonhoeffer was convinced that only the defeat of his country could produce the necessary collective penance and start the church out afresh in Germany, stripped of its surface piety and its property. Bonhoeffer was in touch with the conspirators of July 20, 1944, and was one of four clergymen executed after that assassination attempt on Hitler.

The most important secular ethic to come out of the resistance was existentialism. Its main figure, the French philosopher Jean-Paul Sartre, had avoided political commitment in the 1930s. He had worked on philosophical problems of being and knowing, under the influence of the German phenomenologists Edmund Husserl and Martin Heidegger. The descent into war forced Sartre to realize that no one could be free, not even a philosopher, unless he accepted an active responsibility for the state of the world. Otherwise, decisions of life and death would be made for him by others. How should a person act, however, if, like Sartre, he could believe neither in God, nor in immutable moral laws, nor in a predetermined human nature? Sartre found a philosophy of action in his earlier philosophy of existence. An individual's existence, Sartre thought, was the only certainty. What each person made of his existence was a matter of free choice. "Choices are possible in one direction or another; what is not possible is not to choose." The individual of good faith accepted this burden of choice and "engaged" himself in the situation around him, acting according to his own "project" of what the world should be, conscious that his "act engages all humanity." The individual of bad faith ignored his responsibility and freedom, blaming others for the state of the world; but such a person had made his choice no less than the first.[27]

A simplified existentialism, ignoring the great complexity and subtlety of Sartre's philosophical work, became a kind of fad among resistance intellectuals by the end

[27]Jean-Paul Sartre, *L'Existentialisme est un humanisme* (Paris, 1945), pp. 27, 73.

of the war. In fact, Sartre had put his finger on the agony of choice experienced by active resisters. The consequences of one's acts were exposed with brutal clarity in a situation in which one might be tortured, and where "one word sufficed to provide ten, a hundred arrests. This total responsibility in total solitude, is it not the clearest revelation of our freedom?"[28] In Sartre's terms, the resistance was a "Republic of Silence" in which solitary, free men and women engaged their lives and the lives of others by deliberate acts of moral choice.

[28]Jean-Paul Sartre, "Le République du silence," printed clandestinely in 1944, reprinted in Sartre, *Situations, III* (Paris, 1949), p. 13.

SUGGESTIONS FOR FURTHER READING

Gerhard L. Weinberg, *A World at Arms*[*] (1994), is a superb global treatment of the war. Martin Gilbert, *The Second World War*[*] (1995), is more impressionistic. John Keegan, *Second World War*[*] (1990), is authoritative for the campaigns. Richard Overy, *Why the Allies Won*[*] (1997), is a masterful analysis of moral, psychological, intellectual, and material resources. Williamson Murray and Allan R. Millett, *A War to Be Won: Fighting the Second World War, 1937–1945* (2000) is vivid and precise about the battles. John Keegan, *The Battle for History: Refighting World War II*[*] (1996), reviews debates. Clive Ponting, *Armageddon: The Second World War* (1995), examines particular themes revealingly.

The fall of France is made less inevitable by Ernest R. May, *Strange Victory: Hitler's Conquest of France* (2000). The works on French military preparation listed at the end of chapter 13 are still useful here. Jeffery A. Gunsburg, *Divided and Conquered* (1979), blames poor Franco-British coordination. Don W. Alexander, "Repercussions of the Breda Variant," *French Historical Studies,* vol. 8, no. 3 (Spring 1974), blames the rash French advance into Holland. French and German air forces are precisely evaluated by Lee Kennett, "German Air Superiority in the Westfeldzug of 1940," in F. X. J. Homer and Larry D. Wilcox, eds., *Germany and Europe in the Era of the Two World Wars* (1986), pp. 141–156. Marc Bloch evokes unforgettably the atmosphere in *Strange Defeat*[*] (1946, reprint ed. 1999). Eleanor M. Gates, *The End of the Affair: The Collapse of the Franco-British Alliance, 1939–1940* (1981), documents the failure of interallied cooperation in 1940.

The Battle of Britain is vividly recounted in Patrick Bishop, *Fighter Boys*[*] (2004). Richard Overy, *The Air War, 1939–1945* (1981), and Max Hastings, *The Battle of Britain*[*] (2001), are more scholarly.

The heroic image of Churchill is presented most faithfully by official biographer Martin Gilbert and by John Lukacs, *Five Days in London: May 1940*[*] (1999). Gilbert's multivolume biography is condensed into one as *Churchill: A Life*[*] (1995). After a half century, revisionists have begun to attack Churchill. The most iconoclastic are John Charmley, *Churchill: The End of Glory*[*] (1993), who thinks Churchill's refusal of a compromise peace cost Britain its empire and world power, and Clive Ponting, *Churchill* (1994) and *1940: Myth and Reality* (1990), who sees confusion and mismanagement. More balanced assessments are Robert Blake and Wm. Roger Louis, eds., *Churchill*[*] (1996); Norman Rose, *Churchill: The Unruly Giant* (1995); and Sheila Lawlor, *Churchill and the Politics of War 1940–1941*[*] (1994).

Authoritative for Germany is the multivolume series, Wilhelm Deist et al., *Germany and the Second World War* (1990–). Percy Ernst Schramm based his classic work on Hitler as strategist, *Hitler: The Man and the Military Leader*[*] (reprint ed. 1999), on his war council minutes. The latest in a long series of works on Hitler's relations with the German high command, Geoffrey P. Megargee's scholarly *Inside Hitler's High*

Command (2000), gives the officers high marks for technical competence and low marks for strategic understanding. For the German air war, see Williamson Murray, *Strategy for Defeat: The Luftwaffe, 1933–1945*[*] (1996). Norman Rich, *Hitler's War Aims,* 2 vols. (new ed. 1992), is still useful here.

The Eastern front, where the decisive land battles were fought, is treated most authoritatively, from both German and Russian sources, in Rolf-Dieter Müller and Gerd R. Uebershär, *Hitler's War in the East*[*] (1997). Alan Clark, *Barbarossa: The Russo-German Conflict*[*] (reprint ed. 2001), is a lively account. See also Earl F. Ziemke, *Moscow to Stalingrad: Decision in the East* (1987), and John Erickson's exhaustive *The Road to Stalingrad*[*] (reprint ed. 2003). Omer Bartov shows in *The Eastern Front, 1941–1945: German Troops and the Barbarization of Warfare,*[*] 2nd ed. (2001) and *Hitler's Army*[*] (1996) that the army was as brutal as the SS on the eastern front.

Mussolini's role in the war is best recounted in MacGregor Knox, *Mussolini Unleashed* (1982), *Hitler's Italian Allies* (2000), and *Common Destiny: Dictatorship, Foreign Policy, and War in Fascist Italy and Nazi Germany* (2000). The other end of the story is in F. W. Deakin, *Brutal Friendship: Mussolini, Hitler, and the Fall of Italian Fascism*[*] (reprint ed. 2002).

Stephen W. Roskill, *The War at Sea, 1939–1945,* 3 vols. (1952–1961, reprint ed. 1994), the official history, is basic for the British side. For the U.S. side, see Samuel Eliot Morison, *History of U.S. Naval Operations in World War II* (1947–1962, condensed ed. 2003[*]).

Alan S. Milward, *War, Economy and Society* (1977, reprint ed. 1993), is an excellent introduction to the war's social and economic aspects. The usual view that Hitler planned short, limited military actions *(Blitzkrieg)* rather than total war is challenged by R. J. Overy, *War and Economy in the Third Reich*[*] (1995).

The murder of the Jews is the subject of an immense literature. Master syntheses include Raul Hilberg, *The Destruction of the European Jews,* 3 vols. (3rd ed. 2003), based on a lifetime's study of Nazi archives, and Leni Yahil, *The Holocaust: The Fate of European Jewry*[*] (1990), who worked more with the Jewish documents. Martin Gilbert, *Holocaust: A History of the Jews of Europe during the Second World War*[*] (1987), stresses individual experiences. Deborah Dwork and Robert Jan Van Pelt, *Holocaust: A History*[*] (2002), combine a broad canvas with personal details. See also works on Nazi anti-Semitism listed at the end of chapter 11. Historical debates are reviewed in Michael R. Marrus, *The Holocaust in History,*[*] 2nd ed. (2002); Michael Berenbaum and Abraham J. Peck, *The Holocaust and History: The Known, the Unknown, the Disputed, and the Reexamined*[*] (new ed. 2002); Yehuda Bauer, *Rethinking the Holocaust* (2000); Omer Bartov, *Holocaust Origins, Implementation, and Aftermath*[*] (2000); and Donald L. Niewyk, *The Holocaust: Problems and Perspectives of Interpretation,*[*] 3rd ed. (2002).

Daniel J. Goldhagen dramatically highlighted the unrepentant sadism of the perpetrators in *Hitler's Willing Executioners: Ordinary Germans and the Holocaust*[*] (1997) but recklessly blamed German national character (many perpetrators were not German).

Christopher Browning deals expertly with the absence of a Hitler order and other problems of command, motivation, and timing in many works, including *Ordinary Men: Reserve Police Battalion 101 and the Final Solution in Poland** (new ed. 2001); *The Path to Genocide: Essays on Launching the Final Solution* (1992); *Nazi Policy, Jewish Workers, German Killers** (2000); and especially his masterful *Origins of the Final Solution* (2004). Jonathan Steinberg, *All or Nothing: The Axis and the Holocaust** (1994), looks at Italian help and obstruction. Philippe Burrin, *Hitler and the Jews: The Genesis of the Holocaust** (1998), dates the final decision to late 1941, with Hitler's rage at the failure of his armies to conquer Moscow before winter. Geoff Eley, *The "Goldhagen Effect": History, Memory, Fascism: Facing the German Past* (2000), reconsiders efforts to come to terms with guilt.

Alexander Dallin, *German Rule in Russia, 1941–1945,* 2nd ed. (1981), is a particularly revealing monograph about Nazi occupation priorities. Other occupation regimes and collaborationist responses are treated in Louis de Jong, *The Netherlands and Nazi Germany* (1990); Robert O. Paxton, *Vichy France: Old Guard and New Order,** 2nd ed. (2000); John Sweets, *Choices in Vichy France** (1994); Philippe Burrin, *France under the Germans** (1998); Alan S. Milward, *The New Order and the French Ecoomy* (reprint ed. 1993); Oddvar K. Hoidal, *Quisling: A Study of Treason* (1989); Hans Fredrick Dahl, *Quisling: A Study in Treachery* (1999); Vojtech Mastny, *The Czechs under Nazi Rule* (1971); and Mark Mazower, *Inside Hitler's Greece** (1995). Martin Conway's study of ideological collaborationists, *Collabo-*

ration in Belgium: Léon Degrelle and the Rexist Movement (1993), needs to be supplemented by John Gillingham's study of the more pragmatic collaboration of businessmen, *Belgian Business in the Nazi New Order* (1977).

Peter Hoffmann, *The German Resistance to Hitler** (1988), is a condensed version of his exhaustive *History of the German Resistance,** 3rd ed. (1996); despite its title, it concerns almost entirely the conservative resistance, as do Joachim Fest, *Plotting Hitler's Demise: The Story of the German Resistance** (1997) and Theodore S. Hamerow, *On the Road to the Wolf's Lair: German Resistance to Hitler** (1997). Much less has been written in English about the left-wing and exile resistance, but L. E. Hill, "Towards a New History of German Resistance to Hitler," *Central European History,* vol. 14, no. 4 (December 1981), tries to redress the balance. Klemens von Klemperer, *The German Resistance against Hitler: The Search for Allies Abroad, 1938–1945** (1993), deplores Western unresponsiveness. Francis R. Nicosia and Lawrence D. Stokes, *Germans against Nazism: Non-conformity, Opposition and Resistance in the Third Reich* (1992), looks at more diverse kinds of nonconformity, as do David C. Large, ed., *Contending with Hitler: Varieties of German Resistance to the Third Reich** (1994), and Hans Mommsen, *Alternatives to Hitler: German Resistance Under the Third Reich* (2003). There are probing essays and case studies in Michael Geyer and John Boyer, eds., *Resistance against the Third Reich** (1994).

Various types of resistance in German-occupied Europe are analyzed in Jacques Semelin, *Unarmed against Hitler** (1993); Henri Michel, *The*

Shadow War (1972); and Jorgen Haestrup, *Europe Ablaze: An Analysis of the History of the European Resistance (1939–1945)* (1978). Alan Milward applies cost-benefit analysis to the resistance in Stephen Hawes and Ralph White, eds., *Resistance in Europe 1939–1945* (1975). James D. Wilkinson, *The Intellectual Resistance in Europe* (1981), treats antifascist intellectuals in France, Germany, and Italy.

Charles Delzell, *Mussolini's Enemies* (1961), is still basic for the resistance in Italy. See also Philip Cooke, ed., *The Italian Resistance: An Anthology** (1998). Most thoughtful in English on the French resistance is H. Roderick Kedward, *Resistance in Vichy France* (1978) and *In Search of the Maquis** (1993). For the two most enduring anti-Hitler leaders, see Walter R. Roberts, *Tito, Mihailović and the Allies, 1941–1945** (1987), and Jean Lacouture's massive biography of General De Gaulle. Among many other shorter biogra-

phies of De Gaulle, see Julian Jackson, *De Gaulle** (2003), and Charles G. Cogan, *Charles De Gaulle: A Brief Biography with Documents** (1996). De Gaulle's own trenchant words have no equal: *The Complete War Memoirs of Charles De Gaulle,** 3 vols. (reprint ed. 1998). Recent work on women in the resistance includes Margaret Collins Weitz, *Sisters in the Resistance: How Women Fought to Free France, 1940–1945** (1998), and Dorothee Von Meding, *Courageous Hearts: Women and the Anti-Hitler Plot of 1944* (1997).

Additional Internet links related to this chapter are available on the Europe in the 20th Century Web site: http://www.history.wadsworth.com/paxton04.

You can also explore images, interactive timelines, and maps related to this chapter on our Western Civilization Resource Center: http://history.wadsworth.com

D-Day: American troops wade through the surf and heavy German machine gun fire to the beach in Normandy on the morning of June 6, 1944.

15

From Hot War to Cold War, 1942–1949

Adolf Hitler lost the military initiative during the winter of 1942–1943. After that turning point, even though the Nazi war machine was still capable of savage short thrusts, Hitler found himself obliged to respond to Allied initiatives rather than surprise the world as before with his own audacious moves. The war was far from over, of course. The Allies disagreed sharply among themselves over the strategy best suited to force Germany to unconditional surrender. Over two years of bitter fighting remained before that surrender on May 7, 1945. Nevertheless, by 1943 it was the Allies who chose the time and place of most battles. With that advantage, they gradually overwhelmed the Third Reich with their superior resources.

The military initiative that the Allies regained passed out of the hands of the former Great Powers that had dominated European affairs since the rise of modern states. Even in the First World War, one group of European nations had managed to defeat another only by turning outside Europe for help. The renewed European conflict that broke out in 1939 was even more quickly transformed into a world war with the involvement of Japan (openly allied with the Axis in September 1940), Russia (June 1941), and the United States (December 1941). The Second World War demanded greater resources than the traditional European Great Powers, states of 50 million people or so, could provide. Only superpowers, industrialized states of nearer 200 million people, now commanded enough resources under a single political authority to determine the outcome of wars. Hitler's Europe was the first of these superpowers. The United States and the Soviet Union rose to the challenge as the only states capable of defeating Hitler. In the process, basic decision making about the future of Europe was shifted away from Berlin, London, and Paris to two new capitals: Washington and Moscow. Europe's last civil war cost Europe her autonomy.

AMERICAN HEGEMONY IN THE WEST

In 1940, the United States lagged far behind European states in military power. Its army was smaller than the Belgian army. But behind that modest military façade was an immense economic potential. When the United States entered the war in December 1941, more than two years after the fighting had begun in Europe, American productivity and manpower thrust the country into a growing domination over the Western European partners of the alliance.

One factor in American hegemony was economic. Even more quickly than in the First World War, the United States became the arsenal of the alliance against Germany. American productive power quadrupled under the stimulus of war production for the alliance, while European productive power was being wrecked by wear and military action. Massive purchases of armaments in the United States forced the anti-Hitler nations once again to liquidate their reserves of gold, foreign exchange, and overseas investments. This occurred despite President Franklin Roosevelt's attempt, even before the United States entered the war, to assist Hitler's enemies to purchase supplies in the United States without exhausting their credit and dislocating the world economy with war debts as in 1914 to 1918. The Lend-Lease Act of March 1941 empowered him to lend war matériel to friendly nations in exchange for leases to military bases. Eventually $43 billion in war matériel was supplied to the anti-Hitler coalition in this fashion. But this aid was a mere palliative. Europe spent its accumulated riches, while the United States supplanted Europe as the productive center of the Western world.

The other factor in American hegemony was strategic. Allied strategists were determined not to accept a negotiated settlement with Germany this time. They were resolved to force Hitler to nothing less than unconditional surrender. As early as August 1941 Roosevelt met with British Prime Minister Churchill, aboard the cruiser *Augusta* off Newfoundland, to spell out their ultimate aims in the Atlantic Charter: to seek no territory for themselves, but to create a world in which people could choose their own form of government and live in freedom and security. These aims could be achieved only after "the final destruction of Nazi tyranny." The principles of the Atlantic Charter helped rally anti-Hitler Europeans to the effort of the second total war in a quarter century. But they could not be realized without opening a second front somewhere in Hitler's Fortress Europe and fighting through to Berlin, an enterprise that would require concentrations of force beyond the reach of any powers except the United States and the Soviet Union.

Planning the Second Front

The Japanese attack on Pearl Harbor, on December 7, 1941, brought the United States into the war. Churchill went to Washington at once to begin military planning with Roosevelt. Their meeting in January 1942, code-named Arcadia, was the

DEFEAT OF THE AXIS, 1942–1945

first of a long series of personal conferences in which the Allied statesmen tried to reconcile their interests around a common strategy. American military planners joined their British counterparts in the Combined Chiefs of Staff Committee. Initially, Churchill, a seasoned war leader, got his way. Roosevelt agreed to a "Europe first" strategy according to which Allied forces would concentrate on defeating Hitler before concentrating on Japan. Twenty-four other nations (including the Soviet Union and China) joined with the British and Americans on New Year's Day, 1942, in a United Nations Declaration subscribing to the principles of the Atlantic Charter and pledging their "full resources" to "complete victory over their enemies." Thus the Allies' commitment to unconditional surrender and an assault on Fortress Europe was reaffirmed.

The time and place of that assault remained to be decided, however. This became the central theme of Anglo-American wartime relations over the next three years, a period during which the preponderance of influence gradually slipped from Churchill's London to Roosevelt's Washington. Although the two partners were agreed on fundamentals—the priority of Europe and the necessity of a second front—British and American strategic conceptions reflected their different national experiences and capacities.

Churchill was inclined to feel for soft spots around the edges of Hitler's Europe. The British and French had spent their time during the "phony war" of the winter of 1939–1940 looking for openings in Scandinavia or the Balkans as an alternative to a frontal assault across the Rhine. After France was knocked out of the war, Churchill's long imperial experience made him acutely conscious of British interests in the Mediterranean. Moreover, those who had seen battle on the western front in the First World War and during 1940 were understandably reluctant to embark once more on a rash and perhaps premature frontal assault. "The British," wrote United States Secretary of War Henry Stimson in his diary in 1943, "are haunted by shadows of Passchendaele and Dunkirk."[1] These influences made Churchill give priority to securing the Mediterranean Sea and, once the immediate threat to Egypt and the Suez Canal was reduced by an Allied landing in North Africa in November 1942, to exploring feasible invasion routes up through southern Europe.

Some have claimed that Churchill, steeped in the history and practice of European power politics, tried from the beginning to fit strategy to political aims by moving the Anglo-American second front to a point from which the Western Allies might beat the Russians to control Eastern Europe. In fact, until 1944 Churchill was more nervous about Russian defeat or a separate Russian peace than about Russian conquest of Europe. But there is no question that Churchill was highly sensitive to the second front's political implications for postwar British power.

The Americans concentrated on a frontal assault on Germany with what some British commentators have regarded as a kind of frontier crudity. The Americans tended to see the issue as a technical one of accumulating the necessary force for

---

[1]Passchendaele, a town in Belgium, was the site of particularly bloody and futile British attacks in November 1917; Dunkirk was the city on the French Channel coast from whose beaches the British Expeditionary Force was rescued by a flotilla of boats in June 1940.

an overwhelming knockout blow. "Realist" critics of American foreign policy, such as George Kennan, have charged also that American policy makers naively refused to admit that every strategy contained political implications; they wanted to believe that Americans were rising above European power politics by making "pure" military decisions. Suspicious of the imperial motives lurking behind Churchill's plans for Mediterranean and southern European landings, the Americans preferred to gather a massive force for the earliest possible frontal assault on the Channel coast. At bottom, there remained a Wilsonian vision of the United States, unsullied by "immoral" political calculations, straightening out wicked Europe again with one massive military blow. After a clean decision, the Americans hoped to leave European peacekeeping to a future United Nations organization.

The history of the second front in Western Europe consists of a gradual evolution toward American strategic conceptions along with American material preponderance. The Soviet Union hastened this evolution by Stalin's desperate need for relief from the one-front war he waged against Germany from June 1941 until D-Day, June 6, 1944, when an Anglo-American force finally came ashore in Normandy. Reeling under the full German onslaught, Stalin made insistent demands for an immediate Allied second front in Western Europe. Indeed, the alliance depended on first preventing Russian defeat and then, after that threat became less immediate, persuading the dubious and resentful Stalin that the landing was being prepared for the earliest time that it could be accomplished successfully.

Diversionary Second Fronts: North Africa and Italy

At the beginning of 1942, the tottering Russians needed some kind of diversionary second front in Western Europe. An American proposal to launch a cross-Channel assault despite all risks, if the Russian situation became desperate, was set aside in favor of a more Churchillian strategy, a probe toward a weaker flank. Operation TORCH, the first Anglo-American initiative of the war, landed troops in North Africa and opened up the Mediterranean Sea.

Up to the end of 1942, Germany and Italy had threatened to shut the Allies completely out of the Mediterranean. At the western entrance, two neutrals determined to remain in Hitler's good graces—Franco's Spain and Vichy French Morocco—stood watch over the Straits of Gibraltar. At the eastern entrance, a brilliant German general, Erwin Rommel, whose troops had been reinforcing the Italians in Libya since 1941, twice pushed eastward to within 100 miles of the Suez Canal. During the night of November 8, 1942, however, an American force with some British support landed in three places in French Morocco and Algeria. The best efforts of the poorly equipped Vichy French troops to keep North Africa out of Allied–Axis contention could not prevent Allied capture of those two colonies. Then, assisted by those French ready to return to war, the Allies advanced eastward into Tunisia. From there, Rommel's *Afrika Korps* could be taken from behind. Allied access to the Mediterranean was thereby assured, and southern Europe lay open to Allied thrusts from the sea.

TORCH has been sharply criticized as an attack on a potentially friendly neutral, but the move made much sense. It was psychologically important for the United

States to take some conspicuous but successful initiative as early as possible. Vichy French North Africa, neutral and thinly defended, was an area into which inexperienced American troops could move quickly, successfully, and usefully. The main disappointment in TORCH was that delays in obtaining French cooperation in Morocco and Algeria gave the Axis time to reinforce Tunisia. The rest of North Africa, therefore, did not fall into Allied hands until May 1943.

After the defeat of Rommel's *Afrika Korps,* the central issue was what to do next with the Allied forces concentrated in North Africa. Stalin refused to admit that TORCH had reduced any pressure on the eastern front, despite Churchill's efforts at persuasion. Over dinner in the Kremlin in August 1942, Churchill had attempted to convince Stalin of the advantages of a peripheral strategy. Drawing a crocodile on the tablecloth, he had pointed to the "soft belly." After TORCH, Churchill proposed that the Allies move north against the next weak link—Italy—and strike at the "underbelly" of the Axis.[2]

Roosevelt accepted Churchill's idea at the Casablanca Conference of January 1943. In public, the Casablanca Conference produced a ringing affirmation that the Allies would accept nothing less than Axis unconditional surrender. In private, Anglo-American military planners were more cautious. German submarine successes against Allied supply ships continued to rise to their highest levels of the war in the spring of 1943. In March 1943 alone, more than 1 million tons of Allied shipping sank in the North Atlantic, about twice as much as shipyards could replace in the same length of time. The business of assembling enough men and matériel in Britain to blast an entry into Europe was proving a more massive task than anyone had foreseen in 1942. The only way to make any move at all in 1943 was to delay the cross-Channel invasion another year, disappoint Stalin once more, and attack Italy.

On July 10, 1943, British and American forces landed in Sicily. At first, the Italian campaign promised to yield enormous dividends. On July 25, Mussolini was overthrown in a *coup d'état* led by the former chief of staff of the army, Marshal Pietro Badoglio. The *coup* was supported by the king and those members of the Fascist Grand Council who preferred to capitulate to the Allies than see Italy become a battleground. But before arrangements could be made for a rapid Allied advance into the Italian vacuum, the Germans rushed in major reinforcements, rescued Mussolini in a daring light-plane operation, and turned Italy into an occupied country. Allied forces could not cross from Sicily to the Italian mainland until September 2. Thereafter, assisted by Free French and Polish forces, they inched forward through rough terrain tenaciously defended by the Germans. In the end, the Italian campaign brought the miseries of protracted war to Italy without opening an easy route into central Europe for the Allies.

D-Day and the Assault on Germany

The long-awaited second front was finally opened in Western Europe with an immense amphibious landing on the Normandy coast on June 6, 1944, D-Day. Even

---

[2]Winston Churchill, *The Hinge of Fate* (New York, 1950), pp. 430–434, and Robert S. Sherwood, *Roosevelt and Hopkins* (New York, 1948), p. 674.

A shattered Mussolini with the German commando that rescued him in September 1943 after his overthrow and imprisonment by King Victor Emmanuel and Marshal Pietro Badoglio in July. Mussolini then set up the Italian Social Republic at Salò, under German protection in northern Italy, until he was captured and killed by partisans in April 1945.

at that late date, landing troops from the rough English Channel onto a steep coast bristling with fortifications involved enormous risks. Aside from the sheer mass of their forces, the Allies were aided by elaborate counterintelligence, including false signals and a dummy army in Britain, that persuaded the Germans to expect the landings on the flat plains of northern France. Convinced that the Normandy landing was a feint, Hitler held several tank divisions in northern France too long to throw the landing forces back in their first vulnerable days. During that time, the Allies managed to construct two artificial harbors out of old ships and floating concrete caissons ("Mulberries"). The Allies then proceeded to make the most of American productive capacity. In the first 100 days after D-Day, 2.2 million men, 450,000 vehicles, and 4 million tons of supplies went ashore through the Mulberries and the port of Cherbourg, captured on June 27. Even so, it was early August before Allied forces could fight their way out of the Normandy hedgerow country into the open plains of western France.

In the final assault on the German heartland, American production and strategic and tactical thinking assumed clear predominance on the western front. Whereas Churchill wanted the Allied troops in Italy to invade central Europe through a pass at the east end of the Alps (the Ljubljana Gap, in Yugoslavia), the Americans insisted on taking troops out of Italy for a supplementary landing in southern France on August 15, 1944. This move reflected American uncertainty in Normandy as well as hostility to Churchill's supposed schemes for protecting British spheres of influence in Eastern Europe, an enterprise that Washington feared would require protracted occupation duties and political complications at the end of the war.

After D-Day, an American general, Dwight D. Eisenhower, commanded all Allied forces—American, British, and French. Eisenhower's preference for advance on a broad front, cautiously supported by thorough buildup of supplies, prevailed over the more audacious proposals for a concentrated strike deep into Germany sug-

Ullstein Bilderdienst

A stunned German family is helped by a home guard after an Allied bombing raid on Mannheim.

gested by the senior British commander, General Bernard Law Montgomery, and by an American general, George S. Patton. In the British view, Eisenhower followed the "strategy of an elephant leaning on an obstacle to crush it."[3] Eisenhower and the American chief of staff, George C. Marshall, were particularly opposed to Churchill's suggestions that the Anglo-American forces capture Berlin and Prague before the Russians. According to American thinking, such proposals injected political considerations into what should be a purely military enterprise. Eisenhower told Marshall, "I shall not attempt any move I deem militarily unwise merely to gain a political prize unless I receive specific orders from the Combined Chiefs of Staff." No such orders came, for General Marshall wrote, "Personally . . . I would be loath to hazard American lives for purely political purposes."[4]

The Allied advance was delayed still further by the Battle of the Bulge, a massive German counterattack westward into Luxembourg and Belgium that took place during Christmas 1944. When bad weather prevented the Allies from using their air superiority, it looked for a moment as though the Germans might break through to the Channel again. Even after the German "Bulge" was hammered back, it was not until March 7, 1945, that American soldiers, dashing across a railroad bridge at Remagen as German defenders tried to dynamite it, secured a way across the Rhine.

SOVIET HEGEMONY IN THE EAST

While the United States was emerging as the dominant partner of the Anglo-American alliance, the Soviet Union was becoming the other great superpower of postwar Europe. That prospect seemed much less evident in 1941 than it does in retrospect. Although Soviet economic growth had been impressive in the 1930s, foreign public opinion had been much more strongly impressed by the social costs of collectivizing the farms and, above all, by the purges that decimated the country's leaders. These impressions of a Soviet Union tottering at the brink of internal dissolution were reinforced by Stalin's choice of neutrality over the risk of war with Hitler in August 1939 and by the poor showing the Russians made against the Finns in the Winter War of 1939–1940. Hitler calculated in June 1941 that the Soviet Union would fall apart under the blows of his invasion, and Western observers feared the same result. The Joint Intelligence Committee in London estimated that Hitler would be in Moscow within six weeks.[5]

Soviet Survival, 1941–1943

The battles that followed Hitler's invasion of Russia were the most gigantic of the war. The Soviets assembled 3 million men for the defense of Moscow in late 1941, for example, and would later send 6,000 tanks against the Germans in the Battle of Kursk-Orel in July 1943. In a sense, the Soviets played in the Second World War the

[3]London *Economist,* quoted in Diane Shaver Clemens, *Yalta* (New York, 1970), p. 99.

[4]Dwight D. Eisenhower, telegram of May 1, 1945, and George C. Marshall, telegram of April 28, 1945, quoted in Forrest C. Pogue, *George C. Marshall: Organizer of Victory, 1943–1945* (New York, 1973), p. 573.

[5]Sherwood, pp. 304, 327.

Novosti Press Agency

The battle of Stalingrad, November 1942. Soviet troops hold part of the city in yard-by-yard desperate combat.

role of the French in the First World War. They endured the most massive battles on their own soil, suffered the largest loss of life (perhaps 18 million dead), and claimed the leading postwar role on the Continent. With justification, the Russians have looked on the eastern front as the main theater of the Second World War.

It was at Stalingrad at the end of 1942 that the Soviets were able to turn the tide. In November, a German army advanced into the very streets of Stalingrad, the principal city of the lower Volga River and gateway to the oil-rich Caucasus region. If they broke through, the Germans would consolidate their hold on half the Soviet supply of oil and wheat. Instead, Soviet troops clung to Stalingrad, street by street and house by house, while the Soviet command launched encircling counterattacks under the cover of oncoming winter. When Hitler refused to allow the surrounded German force in Stalingrad even the slightest strategic retreat, the entire sixth army (twenty-two divisions, whose 500,000 men had been reduced to 80,000 by casualties) was taken prisoner along with its commander, Field Marshal Friedrich Paulus, on February 2, 1943. It was the first time in history that a German field marshal had been captured in battle. During the same weeks, at the northern end of the eastern front, on the Baltic Sea, Soviet troops managed to open a precarious supply route into Leningrad, which had been tightly ringed by German forces for 506 days, the longest siege ever endured by a modern city.[6]

The Germans pushed forward once again on several fronts in the spring of 1943, but the Soviets were able to gain their first summer victory in the great tank battle of Kursk-Orel in July 1943. The grim endurance phase of the Russo-German war had come to an end. From the summer of 1943 on, the Soviets began the relentless advance that brought them to the 1939 Polish frontier by February 1944. From there they entered central Europe just as the Western Allies were landing on the

[6]Leningrad remained under German shellfire for more than another year, although the period of most severe starvation was over. (Harrison Salisbury, *The 900 Days: The Siege of Leningrad* [New York, 1969], pp. 550, 567.)

French coast. With the elimination of Germany and Japan in 1945, for the first time no major powers stood across Soviet paths to the sea to the east and west.

What had brought the Soviet Union to this position? How had it survived? Three major Soviet achievements stand out: industrial reconstruction, mass public support, and the emergence of new officer talent. Soviet survival seems to have been more a product of internal resources than of outside assistance in the form of Western aid and Hitler's errors.

A major difficulty had been presented by the German occupation of the most productive areas of the Soviet Union. Forty percent of the Soviet population and perhaps 75 percent of its productive capacity lay in the occupied western border areas. The Soviets moved whole populations eastward and built 1,360 factories in new industrial centers east of the Urals. The Soviet economy emerged strengthened, in the long run, from newly tooled, more evenly spread urban-industrial development.

The enormous population of the Soviet Union was an asset only if the Soviet leaders managed to keep it united and willing to undergo the greatest sacrifices of any Allied nation. Stalin drew on deep nationalist feelings for this purpose. Reviewing the customary parade on the anniversary of the Bolshevik Revolution in November 1941, this time with German armies in the suburbs of Moscow, Stalin invoked "our great ancestors," including those of tsarist Russia. The portraits of the tsarist generals who had fought Napoleon, Alexander Souvarov and Mikhail Kutuzov, hung in Stalin's office.[7] In 1938, film director Sergei Eisenstein and composer Sergei Prokofiev had joined to create a brilliant film, *Alexander Nevsky*, evoking the thirteenth-century defense against the Teutonic knights. Rather than a war to defend the homeland of communism, the war against Hitler became the Great Patriotic War, as all Soviet writers referred to it afterward.

The brutality of the German occupation helped prevent collaboration by disgruntled Soviet populations. Instead of attempting to garner support from Soviet peasants in the occupied areas, the Germans tried to extort a maximum amount of grain from them and threatened to displace them with German settlers. The result was passive resistance to the Germans by the same peasants who had resisted Soviet collectivization a decade before. In late 1941, the Germans got less grain from direct exploitation of their occupied areas of the Soviet Union than they had been getting under the Nazi–Soviet Pact in early 1941.[8] Some Soviet dissidents were willing to collaborate with the Germans, such as General Andrei Vlasov, who tried to form an anti-Communist army among Soviet prisoners of war. But they were never given much independence by the Nazis, who considered them all Slavic *Untermenschen* (subhumans).

The mass of Soviet citizenry rallied to the defense of Soviet soil, whatever their attitudes toward Stalin's regime. One measure of the Soviet population's solidarity was Leningrad's endurance of ghastly suffering during its year-and-a-half siege. Starvation and disease reduced the population from 4 million to 2.5 million. Another sign of the regime's viability under pressure was the emergence of a new generation of talented officers only a few years after more than half the officer corps had been

---

[7]Seweryn Bialer, *Stalin and His Generals* (New York, 1969), p. 516.

[8]Alexander Dallin, *German Rule in Russia, 1941–1945: A Study in Occupation Policies,* 2nd ed. (New York, 1981), p. 369.

Leningrad during the siege, 1942. A couple is dragging a body down Nevsky Prospect on a sled.

purged. Georgi Zhukov, for example, the defender of Moscow in 1941, rose from colonel to marshal in three years.

Outside assistance also helped the Soviet Union survive and then turn the tide. At the time Hitler launched his Operation Barbarossa in 1941, Churchill, still enduring Britain's "darkest hour," threw off his traditional anticommunism and offered alliance to Stalin within hours. After November 1941 the United States included the Soviet Union in its shipment of lend-lease supplies. Even so, such outside assistance seems to have been only a marginal factor in Stalin's success. Western aid was limited by harsh conditions along two available routes: through Iran, and by ship around Arctic Norway to the northern Soviet ports of Murmansk and Archangel. This northern sea route, limited by ice part of the year, had to be suspended in 1942 and again in 1943 after heavy losses to German air and submarine attacks. Although Western material aid was more substantial than the Soviets have wanted to admit,[9] that aid was effective only because internal Soviet resiliency in fighting Hitler almost alone for three years made it usable. It also helped that Japan remained inactive on the Manchurian border.

Hitler's mistakes contributed another form of outside assistance. Hitler's decision to invade the Soviet Union seems in retrospect a fatal act of overreaching. Once launched, however, the eastern campaign had to succeed quickly or lapse into a long war of attrition in which the immense Soviet Union had long-term advantages. Hitler's

[9]About $9.5 billion out of a total of $43 billion in lend-lease went to the Soviet Union. The Soviets estimate that 5 percent of their vital supplies came from the West; the United States estimates about 15 percent. The single most important item was 425,000 American trucks.

judgment that the Soviet Union would collapse under pressure was ideologically distorted. Moreover, the opportunity to strike a knockout blow in 1941 was diminished by a late start, on June 22, 1941, following spring diversions into Yugoslavia, Greece, and Crete. Surviving German generals have blamed Hitler for advancing into the Soviet Union on a broad front rather than striking directly at Moscow and then, by diverting forces from the Moscow front in mid-July 1941 to the rich oil and grain areas of the south, permitting Zhukov to organize the defense of Moscow in November. By then, the Germans were suffering from their lack of winter equipment.

Hitler's errors as a defensive strategist are more widely agreed on than his possible mistakes as an offensive strategist. His refusal to make a tactical withdrawal from Moscow in November 1941, as some of his generals advised, was probably correct. But his failure to draw back from Stalingrad in November 1942 cost him an entire army. The same dogged refusal to shorten his defensive lines in 1943 probably helped the Soviets break through into their final advance to the west. Even Hitler's most obvious errors are not the major explanation for Soviet success, however. Once the Soviet Union survived its first winter of German assault, the Soviet leaders acquired a far larger margin of possible error. When the war of attrition set in, the smallest errors on the German side were fatal ones.

Soviet Advance to the West

By the time the Allies were finally landing at the western edge of Hitler's Europe, in June 1944, Soviet forces had been advancing relentlessly to the west for nearly a year, since their breakthrough in July 1943. In the winter of 1943–1944 they recaptured most of their 1939 territory. In the spring of 1944 they reached their 1914 frontiers in the interwar Baltic States and in Poland. Then, from August to November 1944, halting their advance in Poland, they turned to the south and broke through into the Danube Valley in Romania and Hungary, farther west than any Soviet troops had stood since the Napoleonic wars. In January 1945, the Soviets resumed their advance into Poland. When the Allied leaders met at Yalta in February 1945, the Western Allies were still bogged down on the far side of the Rhine, while the Soviets were within 100 miles of Berlin. The postwar settlement was already being shaped by the respective positions of the Allied armies.

THE BIG THREE AND THE FUTURE OF EUROPE

In the early years of the Second World War, when the central issue of the anti-Hitler coalition was the survival of Britain and the Soviet Union, the exact configuration of postwar Europe seemed a distant and academic issue to Americans. President Roosevelt and his Secretary of State Cordell Hull shrank from premature political commitments that recalled the unhappy precedent of the encumbering secret treaties of the First World War. As long as possible, the American leaders attempted to confine wartime diplomacy to "military" matters, as if these decisions in themselves had no political implications.

Insofar as they made overtly "political" agreements in those early years, the American leaders limited themselves to broad statements of principle—the Atlantic Charter of August 14, 1941, for example—and to committing all the Allies to a projected new international organization—the United Nations—within which postwar political issues could be worked out in a climate of cooperation. The Americans were determined to do Woodrow Wilson's work right this time.

When Soviet Foreign Minister V. M. Molotov tried to get his new American and British allies to recognize the Soviet Union's 1941 frontiers (and thus its 1939 and 1940 gains with Hitler's help), he was forced to settle in May 1942 for a purely military alliance. The first major wartime Allied leaders' conference at Casablanca, Morocco, in January 1943,[10] limited itself to immediate military decisions and to establishing the principle of accepting nothing less than Axis unconditional surrender. Meanwhile, the future of Europe continued to be shaped informally in the battlefield.

Gathering Political Implications

The political implications of the unfolding military campaigns could no longer be held in abeyance after the summer of 1943. The Soviets had begun their drive to the west. One of the Axis partners, Italy, had withdrawn from the war, not by unconditional surrender, but by secret negotiations between some of Mussolini's dissident associates and the Anglo-American leaders, negotiations in which the Soviet Union had played no part. Another German ally, Romania, was sending peace-feeler signals to the West. Stalin was deeply suspicious about delays in opening the second front in the west, about the suspension of Allied convoys to Murmansk, and about the postwar plans of the firmly anti-Communist Polish government in exile in London. An Allied political conference could no longer be deferred.

The foreign ministers of the United States, Britain, and the Soviet Union met in Moscow in October 1943—the first political conference of the main Allied powers.[11] The conference's outcome was an uneasy compromise between simple matters of general principle and thorny matters of future boundaries and regimes. Secretary of State Hull guided the conference resolutely onto the high ground of principle. Most public attention was fixed on the Declaration of General Security reaffirming the determination of the anti-Hitler allies to resolve their postwar problems cooperatively in a United Nations Organization. In more concrete matters, the foreign ministers restated their resolution to force Hitler to unconditional surrender to be followed by the military occupation of Germany, a complete purge of all Nazi officials, and the total demobilization of Germany's armed forces. The foreign ministers set up a permanent working group—the European Advisory Commission—to draft more specific terms of the postwar settlement. Thus, the Soviets had been brought into participation in postwar planning before any of the major policy questions had been settled. As Secretary of State Hull saw it, that

---

[10]Roosevelt, Churchill, and the French leaders de Gaulle and Giraud; Stalin was invited but declined to leave his command post.

[11]China was also represented.

success justified skirting the tougher issues—postwar frontiers and spheres of influence in Central and Eastern Europe.

The Teheran Conference, November 1943

None of these issues, of course, could be solved without the personal assent of Joseph Stalin. The Anglo-American leaders wanted to draw Stalin more fully into confident participation in the United Nations in advance of the actual postwar settlement. In addition, Stalin clearly needed to be reassured about plans for a second front, while the Western leaders needed to be reassured that Stalin would remain in the coalition to the end, even against Japan. Roosevelt, who seems to have believed that he was more capable than diplomats of charming Stalin into a more open partnership, energetically promoted a personal meeting of the three heads of state. He suggested a number of midway points for a conference, including a warship in the Bering Strait. Stalin finally agreed to come no further than the Iranian capital of Teheran, where Soviet troops could help maintain tight security.

Stalin, Churchill, and Roosevelt met in the large walled garden of the Soviet Embassy in Teheran for three days at the end of November 1943. Never before had wartime leaders traveled halfway around the globe to confer on strategy and the future shape of the world. As for Stalin, it was his only trip outside Russia except for a congress of exiled Soviet socialists in London in 1903 and the Potsdam Conference in July 1945.

Over long state banquets in the evening, the three leaders sized one another up and talked expansively about the future of Europe. Churchill and Stalin needled each other with evident relish. In this relaxed mood and with Soviet and Anglo-American armies still far from German soil, it was easy to agree generally on harsh punishment for the Nazis. The other leaders raised no objection when Stalin declared that 50,000 to 100,000 Nazis would have to be executed after the war. Even Churchill, who was later to work for a united Germany as a counterweight to Soviet expansion in Europe, agreed with the others that Germany should be partitioned. But there were also glimpses of future differences. Roosevelt found that he was closer to Stalin than to Churchill on some issues, such as the future disposition of European overseas empires. The Polish question already seemed too sensitive to touch, even before the Soviet armies had reached Polish soil. Roosevelt refused to discuss it; 6 or 7 million Polish Americans, he told Stalin, would vote in the American presidential elections of 1944. Churchill, however, saw no objection to recognizing the 1940 Polish-Soviet frontier in the east provided that an independent Poland were compensated at German expense in the west. With three matches on the tablecloth, he illustrated how all the Polish frontiers could be moved westward, like a "closing left" maneuver on a parade ground.

In retrospect, those conversations sounded to one Cold War observer like "a flourish of knives over the body of Europe."[12] But no concrete frontier settlements were reached. The Americans still preferred to leave what Hull called "that Pandora's Box

---

[12]Herbert Feis, *Churchill, Roosevelt, and Stalin: The War They Waged and the Peace They Sought* (Princeton, N.J., 1957), p. 275.

of infinite troubles" to the happier future when the Soviets would be fully integrated into a United Nations. Stalin said that he had "no desire to speak at the present time about any Soviet desires, but when the time comes, we will speak."[13]

Stalin seemed primarily interested in military plans. The second front in the west, promised him in 1942, had still not been opened in 1943. Churchill, more anxious than ever about the cost of a frontal assault into France, was profuse with eastern Mediterranean plans: opening up the Black Sea, giving aid to Yugoslavia, or sending a force north through the Ljubljana Gap at the head of the Adriatic Sea into the Danube Basin, to "extend our right hand along the Danube."[14] Roosevelt and Stalin overrode his eloquence. The invasion of Western Europe (code-named operation OVERLORD), so many times deferred, was now firmly set for May 1, 1944.

That decision—the major concrete result of Teheran—meant that Soviet and Western armies would divide Europe along a north-south line, roughly in the middle. Later, from a Cold War perspective, that looked like "Stalin's supreme triumph":[15] a military division of Europe in which Anglo-American influence was kept out of the Balkans and Eastern Europe. Those long-term implications may have been less clear at the end of 1943, when the Soviets had still not yet recaptured their 1941 frontiers. Churchill never denied that the English Channel coast must become the main western theater of war, a point the Germans were soon to reinforce by launching a new generation of rocket bombs—V2s—on London from occupied Holland. Moreover, the craggy Balkans were not an easy route into Eastern Europe for the Anglo-American troops; General Marshall later growled drily that the "soft underbelly had chrome-steel sideboards."[16] Above all, Roosevelt shrank from projects that might involve the United States in postwar troop duty in Europe. After Teheran, it was clear that all Eastern Europe and the Balkans would be liberated by the Soviets.

Soviet Moves in the Balkans

The Soviet armies began to do just that in the year following the Teheran Conference. They crossed the old Polish frontiers in January 1944. When the Anglo-American forces landed on the French coast on June 6, 1944, as planned, Stalin kept his promise to conduct a simultaneous offensive toward Warsaw that would prevent Hitler from shifting troops to the west. Then, in August 1944 the Soviet armies stopped short of Warsaw for five months, even though the city rose against its German occupiers in anticipation of liberation. The main Soviet advance shifted south, where the surrender of Romania on August 23, 1944, and Bulgaria on August 26, 1944, opened the way to the Balkans. During September and October 1944, Soviet armies took the lower Danube basin, up to the gates of Budapest, the

[13]U.S., Department of State, *The Conferences at Cairo and Teheran* (Washington, D.C., 1961), p. 555.

[14]Feis, p. 229.

[15]Isaac Deutscher, *Stalin: A Political Biography,* 2nd ed. (New York, 1967), p. 508.

[16]Quoted in Pogue, p. 415. Marshall used these words in an interview in 1956.

capital of Hungary. By November 1944, Soviet armies occupied Balkan territory far beyond the wildest dreams of imperial Russia.

Churchill was determined to pin Stalin down to a concrete agreement on future spheres of influence in the Balkans, without United States assent if necessary. He flew to Moscow on October 9, 1944. With armies advancing against Hitler from both east and west, the conversation was easy and expansive. After dinner Churchill said, "Let us settle our affairs in the Balkans." He proposed a frank division of influence, with the Soviet Union predominant in Romania and Bulgaria, Britain predominant in Greece, and a "fifty-fifty" division in Yugoslavia and Hungary. Stalin quickly agreed, putting a large blue pencil mark on Churchill's scrap of paper.

The Yalta Conference, February 1945

Nothing, of course, was official without Roosevelt's agreement. The "Big Three" met again in February 1945, in the former Livadia Palace of Tsar Nicholas II at the Soviet Black Sea resort of Yalta. At the time, with victory approaching, the Yalta Conference seemed one more celebration of growing Allied cooperation and harmony, the "dawn of the new day we had all been praying for and talking about for so many years."[17] But later, in the highly charged Cold War climate of the 1950s, the view was widespread that Roosevelt, through careless negotiation, ill health (he died two months later), or outright treason within his staff,[18] simply handed over Eastern and Central Europe to Stalin at Yalta. Yalta seemed "the high point of Soviet diplomatic success and correspondingly the low point of American appeasement."[19]

A soberer examination shows that the major lines of postwar influence in Europe had already been drawn by the Allied armies. At the time the three leaders met in Yalta, the Anglo–American armies were still west of the Rhine, recovering from the Battle of the Bulge, while the Soviet armies were within 100 miles of Berlin. In any event, a war devoted to Germany's destruction could hardly fail to enhance the power of Germany's main eastern neighbor.

Another problem was that while Roosevelt could offer Stalin relatively little in February 1945, he had much to ask. The United States military leaders wanted Soviet help against Japan "at the earliest possible date."[20] When two atomic bombs subsequently brought Japanese surrender a mere three months after Germany surrendered, it was difficult to remember how formidable the Japanese had still seemed at the time of Yalta. American military planners expected to lose as many as

---

[17]Harry Hopkins, quoted in Clemens, pp. 279–280.

[18]Alger Hiss, the State Department officer responsible for drawing up United States proposals at the Yalta Conference for the future United Nations organization, was accused in 1948 by members of the House Un-American Activities Committee of having given secret documents to Communist agents, in what became the most celebrated Cold War trial in the United States. When he denied the charges, Hiss was convicted of perjury.

[19]William Chamberlin, quoted in Clemens, p. 280.

[20]U.S. Department of State, *Foreign Relations of the United States: The Conferences at Malta and Yalta* (Washington, D.C., 1955), pp. 388ff. General Douglas MacArthur, commander of United States forces in the Pacific, denied in the later atmosphere of the Cold War that he had asked for Soviet help against Japan.

© Hulton Getty / Liaison Agency

The Big Three—Churchill, Roosevelt, and Stalin—on the patio of the Livadia Palace at Yalta, February 1945. Roosevelt died two months later.

1 million men in another D-Day, an amphibious landing in the Japanese home islands. Roosevelt therefore agreed to an expanded Soviet role in the Far East— possession of Sakhalin and the Kurile Islands, a share in postwar influence in Korea, and support in negotiating two warm-water ports and railroad rights in Manchuria with the Chinese—in return for a promise of Soviet military assistance against Japan and of American air bases in Siberia.

The establishment of the United Nations was a major American preoccupation at Yalta. Roosevelt knew that American public opinion would not permit him to commit troops to Europe for any length of time after Germany's defeat. Along with Secretary of State Hull, he wanted to draw the Big Three into a postwar international organization before particular postwar issues could divide them into opposing camps. Through the United Nations, he hoped to achieve a self-enforcing peace settlement that would not require American troops, as well as an open world without spheres of influence in which American enterprise could work freely. To American staff members of the Yalta delegation, imperial Britain seemed a more immediate threat to this prospect than Soviet Russia. They were afraid that a British attempt to set up spheres of influence in Europe would provoke the Soviets to do the same. The resulting conflicts might well produce "a war which we could not win."[21] The British and French empires also seemed obstacles to the future open world Roosevelt envisioned, and he talked freely to Stalin of dissolving the old European empires in Asia.

Roosevelt and the American delegation spent much more time pinning down the details of the future United Nations than on resolving immediate problems in Poland and Germany. Their design for the organization was heavily weighted with members friendly or subordinate to the United States, and it provided for the right of veto over any actions taken against the wishes of any one of the Big Three, a procedure necessary for ratification by the United States Senate and gladly accepted by Stalin and Churchill. Stalin accepted the rest of the design, without showing much interest, after a compromise had been reached on Poland and after the addition of two Soviet states—the Ukraine and Byelorussia—as voting members. Churchill

EASTERN AND WESTERN FRONTS AT TIME OF YALTA CONFERENCE, FEBRUARY 1945

[21]Admiral William D. Leahy, quoted in ibid., p. 108.

accepted the rest after being promised that the trusteeship provisions for United Nations supervision of former colonies would apply to "not one scrap of British Territory."

The immediate issues of Germany and Eastern Europe were treated much less conclusively. Differences among the Allies were beginning to emerge. The Big Three reaffirmed their agreement that Germany must surrender unconditionally, be disarmed, and be denazified. Occupation zones were allocated. France was brought in to occupy one zone at the insistence of Churchill, who foresaw Britain left alone facing Russia in Europe. But was Germany to be dismembered, or administered as a single unit? With Churchill now doubtful about the effects of an atomized central Europe, the question was left unanswered. No agreement could be reached on reparations either. Stalin, supported by Roosevelt, proposed that a total of $20 billion in reparations from Germany, plus forced labor, be drawn from all the occupation zones; Russia would get half of this total. Churchill found these plans excessive. These unsettled issues were to cause much grief later on.

The Yalta compromises on Eastern Europe attempted to reconcile two irreconcilable goals: that nations be governed by truly democratic regimes and at the same

National Archives 111-SC-207118

American and Russian officers dance with Red Army girls following a dinner celebrating the meeting of the two armies at Torgau, Germany, April 25, 1945. Note spelling of *Amerikan* on the Russians' banner.

time remain friendly with the Soviet Union. Agreement was possible only if this fundamental contradiction were glossed over. The Soviets had tried to predetermine the Polish settlement by recognizing a hand-picked government in the areas already occupied by Soviet troops. The Anglo-American leaders got Stalin to accept the "reorganization" of this new government to include some pro-Western Poles, and to promise future elections. Elsewhere in Eastern Europe, three-power Allied control commissions were to oversee the establishment of new governments. In the absence of any western troops there, however, the Anglo-American members eventually found the authority of these commissions to be ephemeral.

At Yalta, hospitality and the euphoria of approaching victory covered over the latent conflicts. Three months later, when Hitler committed suicide on April 30, 1945, and the remnants of his army surrendered on May 7, the linchpin of the anti-Hitler alliance was removed. The Big Three met one last time in July 1945 in Potsdam, a posh suburb of Berlin, the very capital of the country they had defeated.

The Potsdam Conference, July 1945

Much had changed since Yalta. Roosevelt had died on April 12. The unknown and inexperienced vice president, a former senator from Missouri, Harry S Truman, was just getting his bearings when the Potsdam Conference began on July 17. Winston Churchill, voted out of office in a general election during the conference, was replaced by the Labour leader, Clement Attlee. None of the old conviviality of Teheran and Yalta brightened this meeting. Immediate decisions on the future of Europe could no longer be set aside in favor of more congenial discussions of military progress. Germany and its satellites had been defeated; now they had to be administered.

One more major change had occurred. The day before the Potsdam Conference opened, the first of three experimental atomic bombs was successfully exploded in the New Mexico desert at Alamagordo. Truman was informed immediately:

> The test was successful beyond the most optimistic expectations of anyone. . . . For a brief period there was a lightning effect within a radius of twenty miles equal to several suns at midday; a huge ball of fire was formed which lasted for several seconds. This ball mushroomed and rose to a height of over 10,000 feet before it dimmed. The light from the explosion was seen clearly at Albuquerque, Santa Fe, Silver City, El Paso and other points generally to about 180 miles away. The sound was heard to the same distance in a few instances but generally to about 100 miles. Only a few windows were broken although one was some 125 miles away. . . . Dr. Kistiakowsky . . . threw his arms around Dr. Oppenheimer and embraced him with shouts of glee. . . . All seemed to feel that they had been present at the birth of a new age.[22]

The other two bombs could now be dropped on Japan. The British chief of staff saw the implications at once: "It was no longer necessary for the Soviets to come into

---

[22]General L. R. Groves, "Memorandum for the Secretary of War," July 18, 1945, Potsdam Document No. 1305. This letter was read directly to Truman and Churchill at Potsdam; Stalin was given only brief information about a new bomb, but he knew already.

the Japanese war. . . . Furthermore we now had something in our hands which would redress the balance with the Soviets."[23]

Whether the Alamagordo explosion itself stiffened Truman in the Potsdam negotiations, as the American New Left historian Gar Alperovitz claimed in his *Atomic Diplomacy* (1965), is a hotly disputed point. In any case, it is difficult to imagine leaders of such different social systems finding much common ground in discussions of the political, social, and economic structure of postwar Europe. Agreements at Potsdam were largely limited to reaffirming previous general understandings: that Germany should be demilitarized, denazified, and its leaders brought before the International War Crimes Tribunal. Positive new arrangements could be agreed on only by phrasing them in ambiguous terms that the two sides soon interpreted in their own way.

Both sides already felt that the other had violated earlier agreements. For example, Truman no longer supported the reparations arrangements that Roosevelt had accepted at Yalta. Under a new arrangement, the Soviets could draw reparations only from their own zone, along with 25 percent of the "unnecessary" capital equipment of the Western zones—a formula bound to lead to different interpretations. The Soviets had added only two pro-Western ministers to the Polish government, which they now ceased to call "provisional." Each side had a long list of alleged acts of bad faith by the other.

The two victorious superpowers now eyed each other across the rubble.

ORIGINS OF THE COLD WAR

Several burning issues had to be settled at once at the war's end in the summer of 1945. Those that could not be settled by agreement were settled by fait accompli. Time had run out on the use of wartime camaraderie to smooth over these issues. The Allies' attention had turned from the relatively technical business of defeating Hitler's Europe to the overtly political business of installing Hitler's successors. Who would become the presidents, governors, or mayors of the liberated territories? What form of government should be set up? Who owned the properties there? Who would make these decisions? Did each Allied power have the right to impose regimes of its own choosing in the areas liberated by its blood? If the liberated populations had any choice in the matter, how would their opinions be ascertained?

At bottom lay a basic question no one dared ask publicly: Were United States and Soviet aims in postwar Europe fundamentally irreconcilable? To each side, its own peace aims seemed reasonable, even self-evident; only an ally of bad faith could object to them. Europe, of course, was only one part of a world stage on which the superpowers now calculated their interests, but it was a central part. Europe's future depended in large measure on how Washington and Moscow got along with each other.

---

[23]Field Marshal Lord Alanbrooke, *War Diaries, 1939–1945* (London, 2001), entry of July 23, 1945, p. 709.

Soviet Peace Aims

Stalin's aims in Europe in 1945 were at the heart of the matter. The Soviet Union had obviously transformed its world power position. How did the Soviet leaders intend to use that power? During the Cold War, many Americans assumed that Stalin's aims were constant and insatiable. From this perspective, whatever limits Stalin accepted in 1945 were those forced on him by countervailing power. Stalin's aims no doubt grew during the Cold War, but a good case can be made for the view that initially they were limited and largely defensive. The security of the Soviet state rather than the spread of Communist regimes far and wide seems to have had first priority in 1945.

No one challenged the Soviet intention to regain some former Russian soil lost to the Japanese in 1905, to the Germans in 1918, and to the successor states in 1919 and 1920. Some of Stalin's western frontier claims were less extensive than those tsarist Russia had asked its Allies to approve in 1914 to 1917, when it had wanted to annex the Dardanelles and expected to keep its broad Polish lands. In other places the new western frontiers ran along those of 1914 (such as much of the frontier with Romania). In some places (at Memel on the Baltic, and in Galicia, Ruthenia, and Bukovina in the Carpathian Mountains) the new Soviet frontiers lay west of any pre-war Russian territory. In the Far East, Stalin regained approximately the frontiers Russia had prior to its defeat by Japan in 1905. By and large, Stalin avenged the humiliations of Tsushima, Brest-Litovsk, and Versailles and reestablished the frontiers of tsarist Russia at its height.[24]

Around those frontiers Stalin seemed to be working for contiguous rings of friendly states. Some of those adjoining states had made war on the Soviet Union alongside the Germans after 1941: Romania, Hungary, and Finland; other adjoining states, such as Poland, had been invasion routes into Russia for centuries. Romania and Finland had to give up territory. Poland was moved bodily westward. Czechoslovakia lost its easternmost extremity, Trans-Carpathian Ruthenia. And Stalin insisted, above all, that "friendly" governments rule these border states.

One problem with these arrangements was that regaining part of the tsarist frontiers required snuffing out the national independence of some of the successor states carved out of Eastern Europe in 1918 and 1919: most conspicuously, the Baltic nations of Lithuania, Latvia, and Estonia. Another crucial problem was the nature of the "friendly" governments that Stalin demanded on his frontiers. Could they be freely elected, pluralistic regimes open to Western trade and travel and still "friendly" on Stalin's terms? Must they be communist to be "friendly"?

Outside the immediately contiguous states, Stalin appears to have accepted the spheres of influence that he and Churchill had so easily agreed to after dinner on October 9, 1944.[25] In Greece, he allowed the British to settle the civil war between communist and pro-Western groups in their own favor. In Western Europe, up to 1947, Stalin ordered local Communist parties to work within democratically elected

---

[24]See maps pp. 472–473. Finland had been an independent duchy under the tsar's personal rule between 1809 and 1914. The Ruthenians of the newly acquired Trans-Carpathian region spoke a language close to Ukrainian. Even here, therefore, Soviet claims were not entirely without basis.

[25]See this chapter, p. 465.

RUSSIA IN THE TWENTIETH CENTURY

1914

Popular Fronts. He accepted Chiang Kai-shek without question as the legitimate ruler of China. Suspicious as always of distant Communist parties not under his direct control, Stalin seems to have given no orders for revolution abroad.

American Peace Aims

Most Americans are accustomed to think that the United States wanted nothing in postwar Europe except the peaceful self-government that would come naturally unless the superpowers interfered. In this spirit, American armed forces were

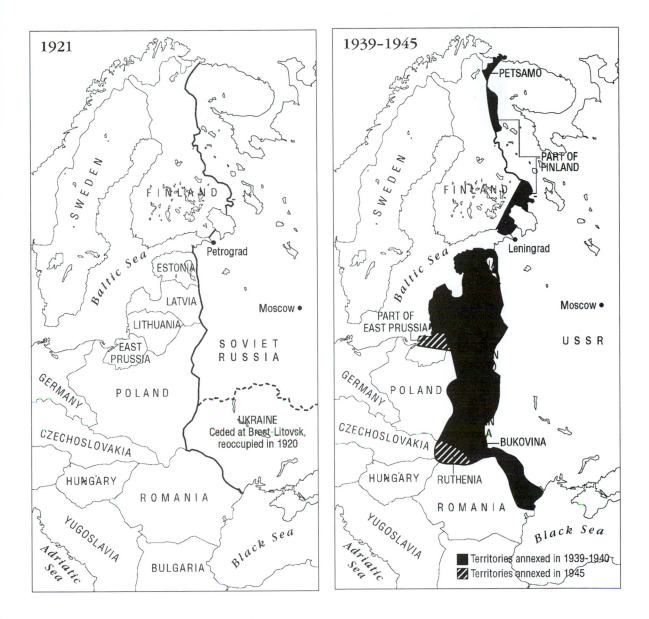

reduced from 3.5 million to 500,000 within less than ten months at the end of the war. But there was a design for Europe, and the world, reflected in American statements and actions: a world without barriers to trade and investment; an open, pluralistic world, favorable to American economic penetration as well as in keeping with American emotional preferences. These goals resembled earlier Open Door policies in China, extended now to the whole world. Stalin's conception of closed spheres of influence was anathema to these goals.

American peace aims in Europe come into sharper relief when contrasted with the aims of allied Western democracies, especially Britain and France. One conflict

TERRITORIAL ADJUSTMENTS AFTER THE SECOND WORLD WAR, 1945

concerned colonies. Roosevelt spoke frankly at Yalta and elsewhere about his hopes of seeing the European colonies in Asia replaced by trusteeships. At that stage, for example, American officials in China enjoyed good relations with the exiled Vietnamese nationalist leader, Ho Chi Minh. The French claimed, not illogically, that the Americans simply wanted to replace French economic presence in Indochina with their own.

The United States and its Western European allies also disagreed on the economic conditions of recovery. Postwar British and French governments assumed that restoration of the prewar economy was impossible without extensive government control. The United States, by contrast, insisted that Britain lift currency controls and return the pound to free international trading in 1947 as a condition for receiving an American loan. It is now almost universally agreed that this step was premature. The pound rapidly declined on its reappearance in a free world currency market. Despite British efforts to cut their consumption of imported goods (including food) to a bare minimum, the pound had to be devalued from \$4.03 to \$2.80 in September 1949. Since much food and material for reconstruction had to be imported from the United States, scarce dollars acquired very high values in European currencies. It became inexpensive for American tourists to travel in Europe and for American firms to buy up European branches. The dollar reigned supreme in Europe after 1945, encountering its first difficulties only in the late 1960s, when long years of American spending in Europe began to produce large trade deficits with revived European economies.

These conflicts of interest between the United States and the Western European democracies suggest that American peace aims after 1945 included, at least implicitly, the creation of an open world economy, in which the dollar was the strongest currency and in which American firms could operate most freely. American power was sufficient to get its way over the objections of former Great Powers like Britain and France. The Soviet Union, however, was strong enough to set up its own immense sphere of influence from which American investors, traders, and tourists were excluded.

Seeds of Antagonism

Economic conflict coincided with the ideological clash between capitalism and communism. If the Soviet sphere of influence had been merely authoritarian, one could still have expected United States–Russian friction like the Open Door conflict among the United States and Britain and Germany over China at the opening of the century. Ideological suspicions made the United States–Soviet clash of interests assume the emotional dimensions of a crusade. Each side came to believe that an aggressive enemy wanted to extinguish its whole way of life. Soviet leaders increasingly told their people after 1945 that the capitalist powers, led by the United States, were encircling them. The American people increasingly came to believe that the Communist bloc, led by the Soviet Union, was trying to overthrow every free-enterprise regime in the world by subversion. Encirclement and subversion: These twin specters took on reality as the acts of each side seemed to confirm suspicions.

For example, the Soviets viewed America's return to armament in 1947, coupled with its creation of a worldwide system of military bases and alliances, as confirmation of an ever tightening capitalist encirclement. These growing, self-fulfilling suspicions slipped easily into old grooves of ideological conflict dating back to 1917. In that sense, the Cold War was one more installment in a long history of revolution versus containment going back to Lenin and Woodrow Wilson.

Who struck the first blow in the Cold War, and where? The possible answers differ as widely as interpretations of the Cold War itself. From the Soviet point of view, the capitalist powers first showed their determination to crush the Soviet regime with their military intervention of 1919 and 1920.[26] Stalin's suspicions of the West were never entirely allayed during the war. When the Western allies excluded him from the secret surrender negotiations with Italy in July 1943, Stalin could well assume that each liberating army was arranging matters to its own tastes. Stalin followed the same course with the Romanian and Bulgarian surrenders in August 1944; he subsequently felt aggrieved that the Western allies wanted to interfere in the regimes of states bordering the Soviet Union. In May 1945 President Truman cut off lend-lease aid so abruptly that ships already bound for Soviet ports were called back. At Potsdam, Truman seemed to the Soviets to have hardened the American position on German reparations since Yalta.

From the American point of view, the first unmistakable sign of Stalin's apparent aim to impose Communist regimes on countries liberated by the Red Army came just before the Yalta Conference, in January 1945, when Stalin unilaterally recognized his hand-picked Communist Lublin Committee as the legitimate government of Poland. Even more alarming were hints that Communists would foment insurrections after the war even beyond the range of the Red Army. The first of these was the mutiny in the Greek naval units at Alexandria, Egypt, on April 4, 1944, and the uprisings in Athens in December 1944. These events suggested to some Western Europeans and Americans that Communist aims went far beyond mere security for the Soviet Union to revolutionary change throughout Europe and the world. Even before the German surrender at Reims on May 7, 1945, therefore, both sides regarded each other with mutual distrust.

FIRST BATTLEGROUNDS OF THE COLD WAR

Poland

No question aroused more distrust and bitterness among the Allies at the end of the war than the future of Poland. The Polish issue is an ideal case for observing in detail how conflicting interests between the Soviets and the Western Allies generated a spiral of mutual suspicion and antagonism.

Poland's frontiers were part of the problem. This issue went back to the re-creation of Poland at the Paris Peace Conference. The experts had drafted a proposed Russian-Polish frontier in 1919, the Curzon Line, which conformed roughly to lin-

---

[26]See chapter 5, pp. 131–133.

guistic frontiers. After the Soviet–Polish war of 1920, however, the Allied powers agreed to an expanded Poland whose frontier, 150 miles east of the proposed Curzon Line, included many Ukrainians and White Russians.[27] Stalin watched for his first opportunity to rectify a Soviet-Polish frontier that many, even outside the Soviet Union, could regard as a violation of national self-determination. His first chance came with the Nazi–Soviet Pact of August 1939, with its secret clauses in which Hitler agreed to Soviet aims in Eastern Europe.

When Germany defeated Poland in September 1939, Stalin quickly moved into the eastern part, up to approximately the Curzon Line. Later, when Stalin was fighting against Hitler, he tried to persuade his new British and American allies to recognize his 1939 gain. They refused to make any firm frontier settlements as long as the war continued. The Curzon Line was not unreasonable on either ethnic or historic terms, however, and a Poland moved bodily westward was better from the Western point of view than no Poland at all. At the Teheran Conference in November 1943, therefore, both Churchill and Roosevelt led Stalin to believe that a Poland stretching from the Curzon Line in the east westward to the Oder and Neisse rivers, including some former German territory in the west, was a reasonable basis for discussion.[28]

Behind the territorial question lay a political one: What kind of regime would govern Poland? The Western Allies regarded the Polish government in exile in London as the legitimate future government. The London Poles and their leader, General Wladyslaw Sikorski, were remnants of the Polish army along with middle-class political leaders who had escaped to the West. They had useful contacts with the internal resistance, and a Polish army under General Wladyslaw Anders was giving assistance to the British in the Middle East and later in Italy. The London Poles (like many Poles at home) were determined not to relinquish an inch of their swollen 1921 frontiers. Indeed, some of the London Poles had dreams of an even greater Poland that would take advantage of a mutually exhausted Germany and Russia. They shared the anti-Soviet feelings of the Polish army, now made even sharper by the Soviet annexation of the eastern territories with Hitler's help in 1939. Thus, General Sikorski and the London Poles were both a help and a potential embarrassment to the wartime coalition.

Stalin considered the London Poles both hostile and expansionist, the heirs of the Polish leaders who had fought the Soviets in 1920. He found his opportunity to break with them over the Katyn Massacre. In April 1943 the Germans announced the discovery of the bodies of 10,000 Polish officers in a mass grave in the Katyn Forest, near Smolensk, Russia, and claimed that the Soviets had executed them in 1940. The London Poles called for an international investigation. Stalin was enraged—he reverted often to the claim that the London Poles were working for the Nazis—and refused to have anything more to do with Sikorski.[29]

---

[27]See chapter 5, p. 133.

[28]Roosevelt did not know that there was an eastern Neisse River and a western Neisse River; the Soviets claimed they meant the western Neisse. Roosevelt refused any public discussion of this question for fear of offending Polish-American voters in the 1944 election.

[29]The Soviet government admitted in 1990 that Stalin ordered the execution of these officers during the Soviet occupation of eastern Poland from 1939 to 1941.

Instead, the Soviet government recognized a group of Polish Communist refugees in Moscow as the legitimate government of Poland—a Poland that remained west of the Curzon Line, to be sure. When Soviet armies reached Poland in July 1944, the pro-Soviet Poles set up a provisional government in the liberated town of Lublin.

There remained a substantial independent force in Poland: the Home Army, a resistance unit under officers of the former Polish army, loyal to the London Poles, and supported from Britain. As the Soviet army approached Warsaw in August 1944, the Home Army rose against the Germans in anticipation of Soviet aid. But instead of rushing into Warsaw to join forces with the Home Army, the Soviet army stopped outside the city on the other side of the Vistula River. For two months the Home Army held out alone against the Germans, while Western efforts to airdrop supplies were hampered by Soviet refusals to allow the planes to land behind Soviet lines. After sixty-three desperate days, the last of the Polish Home Army was liquidated. Westerners have been convinced that Stalin knowingly allowed the Germans to wipe out his main rivals for future control of Poland. There is some evidence, however, that the Soviet army was devoting all its resources to the advance into Hungary. In any event, the results left the Lublin Poles in sole control of liberated Poland, under the Red Army. Stalin extended official diplomatic recognition to the Lublin Committee just before going to Yalta in January 1945.

At the Yalta Conference the Western allies tried to trade territorial concessions for political concessions. They recognized the Curzon Line in the east, and the right of the Poles to "administer" former German soil up to the Oder-Neisse rivers in the west as compensation, while awaiting a future more definite settlement. In exchange, they insisted that the Lublin Committee be expanded to include some representatives of the London Poles and that free elections be held in Poland. Stalin no doubt deeply resented his Western allies' insistence on dealing with Poles who represented for him the expansionist Poland of 1919 to 1921. Moreover, at Potsdam President Truman went beyond the Yalta agreements in calling for a "new" Polish government rather than merely a "reorganized" one.

Stalin included only two London Poles in the Polish government, and by the time elections were finally held in January 1947 all businesses employing more than fifty persons had been nationalized, and police action had been taken against the middle-class parties. Stalin had gotten his way, but not before his suspicions were confirmed that the West wanted an anti-Soviet buffer government in Poland; the West, in its turn, felt that Stalin had reneged on the Yalta terms regarding Poland.

Germany

Germany was the other main arena of Cold War conflict in Europe in 1945. It was against Germany that the American–Soviet alliance had formed; it was in Germany, at the village of Torgau along the Elbe River, that American and Soviet soldiers had first met and grasped hands on April 25, 1945; it was the future of Germany that would test and then break the alliance.

Allied determination to accept nothing less than unconditional German surrender had decided some matters about the future of Germany in advance. This time, unlike 1918, Germany would be entirely occupied by its victors, and it would be

German civilians are forced by United States soldiers to view the bodies of Jewish women who starved during a 300-mile march, April 1945. Many Germans believed that such atrocities were invented by the Allies for propaganda purposes.

US Army Photograph / National Archives

administered by the victors rather than by indigenous German officials. Beyond that, however, two major decisions remained to be made about how the occupation of Germany would work. Should the emphasis of occupation policy fall on retribution or rehabilitation? And should Germany be dismembered or occupied as a single unit? The details of occupation zones, reparations, and the machinery of interallied cooperation in Germany depended on these two major questions.

All of Hitler's enemies in 1945 wanted to prevent the resurgence of an armed, expansive Germany. Russia, Stalin said, could not afford to fight the Germans once in every generation, and his Western allies readily agreed. How to prevent that revival was more controversial. Early in the war, a number of dismemberment schemes had been drawn up in the West. President Roosevelt's Treasury Secretary Henry Morgenthau proposed to split Germany into a half-dozen small states with primarily agrarian economies. Churchill suggested separating Prussia from the rest of Germany and creating a new Catholic south Germany centered on Vienna. By the war's end, however, the British began to resist the fragmentation of Central Europe in order to pit a counterweight against the Soviet Union. At Yalta, Churchill held out against the dismemberment plans of Roosevelt and Stalin. The Yalta decision was ambiguous: Germany was to be "dismembered" in some unspecified way, but a single unified Allied Control Commission was supposed to coordinate the policies of the four occupation zones (now including France).

In fact, the opposite happened. Germany was never formally dismembered; indeed, no formal peace terms for Germany could ever be agreed on. Instead, the various occupation zones went their own way in a de facto dismemberment.

Divergent economic aims soon set the occupation zones on irreconcilable paths. While all the Allies still agreed on dismantling German armed forces and war production, and attempted, more or less clumsily, to denazify German society with new education schemes and purges of personnel, they differed sharply about Germany's economic future. Britain and the United States wanted to restore peacetime productivity as quickly as possible; the Soviet Union and France wanted to extract a maximum of German wealth and labor to rebuild their ravaged countries.

Calvin B. Hoover, chief economic advisor in the American zone, pointed out as early as December 1945, that, without the recovery of German industry, the United States would have to feed and supply Germany and Europe for a long time. Other local American officials observed that economic chaos would help spread communism in Europe. American occupation authorities promoted German industrial exports that would make Germany self-sufficient, help rebuild all of Europe, and make it immune to communism. Wartime punitive schemes like the Morgenthau Plan seemed simply irrelevant to those involved in the immediate tasks of feeding and sheltering a prostrate Europe. Meanwhile, in the Soviet zone, the Soviets were dismantling the German industrial system and beginning the breakup of the great East Elbian estates, but Western occupation authorities found that they were systematically excluded from finding out what was going on there.

Reparations produced the most immediate friction. It had been agreed at the Yalta Conference that Germany must pay reparations to those who suffered war damage. President Roosevelt accepted Stalin's figures as a basis for discussion: $20 billion, of which half would go to the Soviets. Stalin expected to collect reparations from the whole of Germany in two forms: a share of the whole existing German industrial plant and a share of current production. At Potsdam, in July 1945, President Truman drew back from the Yalta position. The Soviets were cut back to 25 percent of "unneeded" industrial equipment in the Western zones and to a share of current production from their zone only. That formula was impossible to apply. What was "unneeded" industrial plant in the Western zones depended on one's opinion of the proper standard of industrial production for the Germans. The Soviet leaders felt justified in demanding their full pound of flesh from all the occupation zones of Germany because that had been agreed to at Yalta, because much of Germany's wealth lay in the west, because Russia had borne the brunt of the land war, and because the alternative was to seek economic aid for Soviet reconstruction directly from the United States, aid that might well be tied to political conditions. From the American point of view, the Soviets were simply stripping Germany of the means to live in a free enterprise world. In May 1946, General Lucius Clay closed the American zone to any further Soviet extraction of reparations.

Thereafter, all general discussions of the German question broke down over the reparations issue and the irreconcilable aims for the German economic future that it entailed. Meetings of the four Allied foreign ministers in Moscow in March and April 1947 and in London in November and December 1947 ended in openly hostile disagreement over German peace terms. Meanwhile, the two sides went their separate ways in the day-to-day administration of the zones. In early 1947, the Americans and British merged their two zones in a new economic unit ("Bizonia") and set 1936 levels as their goals for German production. Local German representatives were given increased responsibility. The Soviets countered with an Economic Council in their zone and the beginnings of German political life with the German Peoples' Congress for Unity and a Just Peace. In February 1948, the three Western occupying powers agreed to proceed toward a separate constitution for revived German political authority in the west. In response to this, the Soviets walked out of the Allied Control Commission on March 20, 1948. Even the pretense of a united four-power occupation had come to an end.

A direct confrontation ensued in the summer of 1948. The immediate cause was again economic policy, the key to each side's aims for the German future. When a new currency was issued for the now united western zones in June 1948, it circulated in Berlin at much more favorable rates than the eastern zone's currency. The city of Berlin, under its own four-power arrangement, was buried deep within the eastern zone. The Soviets faced a choice of either allowing Berlin to become an outpost of the reviving West German economy or sealing it off. They blocked all Western traffic to Berlin. The Allies responded to the blockade with an airlift. For the next 324 days, hundreds of planes ferried the necessities of life to Berlin from the West, averaging 8,000 tons per day. General Clay reflected the tone of the now open East–West conflict:

> When Berlin falls, western Germany will be next. . . . If we withdraw, our position in Europe is threatened. If America does not understand this now, does not know that the issue is cast, then it never will and Communism will run rampant.[30]

Although the successful airlift forced the Soviets to back down in May 1949, the Berlin crisis had hastened the formation of two Germanies. Each side called for union, but on its own terms. Unable to get its own terms, each side built a bastion on that part of Germany that it controlled. The western Federal Republic of Germany became a sovereign state in September 1949. The eastern German Democratic Republic came into existence the following month.

A WORLD IN TWO BLOCS, 1947–1949

As early as March 1946, former British Prime Minister Winston Churchill lent his gift for phrasemaking to the opening East–West conflict in Europe:

> From Stettin in the Baltic to Trieste in the Adriatic, an iron curtain has descended across the continent.[31]

[30]Lucius D. Clay, *Decision in Europe* (Garden City, N.Y., 1950), p. 361.
[31]Excerpt from a speech given at Westminister College, Fulton, Missouri, March 6, 1946.

GERMANY AFTER TWO WARS

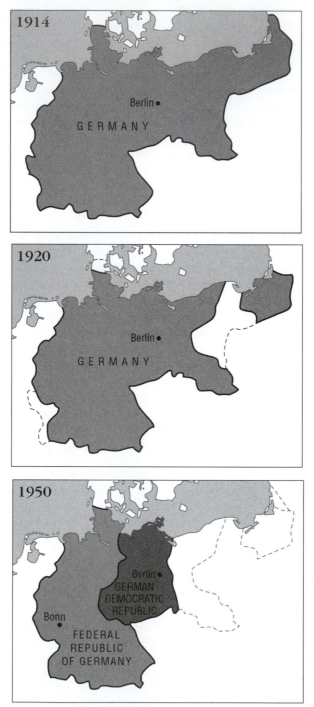

Western observers were already deeply disturbed by their exclusion from any role in the states bordering on the Soviet Union (Poland, Romania, Bulgaria) and from those self-liberated states with powerful Communist movements (Yugoslavia, Albania). American policy had carried forward into peacetime the basic assumption that, as Roosevelt warned Stalin in a telegram in October 1944, "there is in this global war literally no question, either military or political, in which the United States is not interested."[32] Stalin, who observed that the Soviet Union had equally little to say in the occupation policies applied to Italy and Japan, worked on quite different premises.

> This war is not as in the past; whoever occupies a territory also imposes his own system. Everyone imposes his own system as far as his armies can reach. It cannot be otherwise.[33]

While the West could do nothing about Eastern Europe short of marching in a new army, the southern frontiers of Soviet influence were much more fluid. The three areas of contention there from 1945 to 1947 were Iran and the two states at the approaches to the Black Sea, Turkey and Greece. Emerging conflicts in these areas led the United States to create a new policy of military alliances and worldwide armed intervention to support its postwar ideal of "one world," a global Open Door accessible to American trade and influence.

Soviet and British troops had been stationed in Iran since 1941 to counter German influence. In 1946, the Soviets sponsored independence movements among northern border minorities, the Kurds and Azerbaijanis, and demanded a share in Iranian oil rights. With British support and a favorable United Nations resolution behind it, the Iranian government repressed the border nationalities and then cancelled the draft oil contract, while Stalin decided not to press the issue.

Turkey controlled passage from the Black Sea to the Mediterranean, and the Soviet government brought pressure to bear on the Turkish government to revise the Treaty of Montreux (1936) by which the Turks could close the Straits to warships in time of war, thereby sealing the Soviets up in the Black Sea. The Turks refused, again with British support.

The British were also deeply involved in the extremely bitter civil war between the Greek royal government and Communist movements spawned by the wartime resistance. Although Stalin had given the Greek Communists little support at the beginning (apparently honoring his understanding with Churchill of October 1944), important aid began to come from Greece's neighbor, Communist Yugoslavia.

In the spring of 1947, beset by worldwide commitments and dwindling resources, the British passed all these responsibilities to the United States. On March 12, President Truman laid down new principles of American foreign policy

[32]Sherwood, p. 834.

[33]Quoted in Milovan Djilas, *Conversations with Stalin,* trans. Michael B. Petrovich (New York, 1962), p. 114.

in a message to Congress asking for emergency appropriations to aid Turkey and Greece:

> I believe that it must be the policy of the United States to support free people who are resisting attempted subjugation by armed minorities or by outside pressures.[34]

Although Congress voted funds only for the specific purpose of aiding Greece and Turkey, the Truman Doctrine committed the United States publicly to intervene in any area in the world that threatened to come under Communist control.

The economic counterpart to this new active American involvement was the Marshall Plan, a sweeping program of economic aid to Europe announced by Secretary of State George C. Marshall in a commencement speech at Harvard in June 1947. The United States offered substantial sums of money for restoring European prosperity—both East and West—on condition that the European recipient states join together to plan its most effective use. The American aim, Marshall said, was "the revival of a working economy in the world so as to permit the emergence of political and social conditions in which free institutions can exist."

From a Soviet point of view, Marshall Plan aid seemed likely to draw any nation that received it into the American economic orbit. When Czechoslovakia agreed to participate, and Poland and Hungary appeared interested, the Soviet Union stepped in and blocked them. Over the next four years, the United States contributed $12 billion for the European Recovery Program, all of which went to Western Europe. The Soviet reaction had helped solidify the division of Europe into two closed camps.

Looking at the world in 1947, Stalin could see that Soviet aspirations had been checked in the south and that his experiment with multiparty regimes under Communist supervision in a ring of "friendly" states on the western borders[35] did not afford iron-clad security. The desire of some Eastern European states to affiliate with the Marshall Plan revealed the Western economies' powers of attraction. And the vagaries of multiparty systems left open the possibility of Communist electoral setbacks. In late 1947 and early 1948, therefore, Stalin cracked down hard on Eastern Europe. He replaced the multiparty regimes with full Communist control in all the areas he could influence.

The assumption of outright Communist power in Czechoslovakia in February 1948 may have been Stalin's defensive response to the prospect of serious Communist losses in forthcoming elections. But the "Prague *coup*" did more than any other single act to convince the West that Stalin's expansionist appetite was insatiable. The independence of Czechoslovakia was a tender point for all who remembered the West's betrayal at Munich in 1938. Czechoslovakia's President Eduard Beneš had aroused cautious optimism in the West by his success between 1945 and 1948 in trading off subordination in foreign policy to the Soviet Union against an internal political system that provided some degree of personal freedom and electoral

---

[34]Harry S Truman, *Memoirs* (Garden City, N.Y., 1956), vol. 2, p. 106.

[35]The evolution from multiparty National Fronts in Eastern Europe in 1946 to outright Communist control by 1948 is explored more fully in chapter 17, pp. 515–522.

expression. When Stalin brought that compromise to an end, he persuaded most Westerners that no compromise was possible with him.

The establishment of full Communist control in Hungary during the summer of 1948 and the Berlin Blockade of June 1948 confirmed Western alarm. The response was a military alliance against the Soviet Union. The North Atlantic Treaty Organization of twelve Western states (1949) faced 200 Soviet divisions in Eastern Europe, later organized into the Warsaw Pact (1955). The real strength of these two alliances, however, lay with the two superpowers who faced each other as mortal enemies. Europe, split in two, seemed likely to become their battleground.

SUGGESTIONS FOR FURTHER READING

For growing U.S. influence over Allied strategy, Forrest C. Pogue's official history, *The Supreme Command** (reprint ed. 2003), and his *George C. Marshall: Organizer of Victory, 1943–1945* (1973), are still basic. The British equivalent is J. R. M. Butler, et al., *Grand Strategy* (1957–1972). Winston S. Churchill, *The Second World War,* 6 vols. (1948–1953), presents the British leader's own epic vision (but see the works about him cited at the end of the previous chapter). In addition to the Schramm work on Hitler as strategist cited at the end of chapter 14, see Ronald Lewin's suggestive *Hitler's Mistakes** (1987).

John Keegan, *Six Armies in Normandy,** (revised ed. 2001), treats various national forces after D-Day with verve and empathy. David Eisenhower, *Eisenhower at War, 1943–1945* (1991), reviews fairly the dispute between his grandfather and Montgomery over the proposed dash for Berlin. Stephen E. Ambrose defends Ike in his authorized biography, *Eisenhower: Soldier and President** (reprint ed. 2003). The British point of view is laid out in Field Marshal Lord Alanbrooke, *War Diaries, 1939–1945** (2003), and powerfully defended in Chester Wilmot, *Struggle for Europe** (1952, reprint ed. 1998).

Impressively informed and balanced are Russell F. Weigley, *Eisenhower's Lieutenants: The Campaign of France and Germany** (reprint ed. 1990), and Max Hastings, *Overlord: D-Day and the Battle for Normandy 1944** (reprint ed. 1999). For a soldier's point of view, see Paul Fussell, *The Boys' Crusade: The American Infantry in Northwestern Europe, 1944–1945* (2003).

For the decisive Soviet victories in the East, in addition to works cited at the end of chapter 14, see Earl F. Ziemke, *Stalingrad to Berlin* (1968, reprint ed. 2003), and John Erickson, *The Road to Berlin** (1983, reprint ed. 2003). Christopher Duffy, *Red Storm on the Reich** (2000), recalls German suffering, a bit one-sidedly.

The main innovation in recent military history is assessing the importance to Allied victory of access to German codes, kept secret until the 1970s. F. H. Hinsley, *British Intelligence in the Second World War,* 5 vols. (1979–1988), is the most scholarly treatment. See also Ronald Lewin, *Ultra Goes to War** (2001), and David Kahn, *Seizing the Enigma* (1997). Wladyslaw Kozaczuk, *Enigma* (1984), adds the essential Polish and French contributions.

Lloyd C. Gardner, *Spheres of Influence** (1994), gives an up-to-date overview of international relations between Munich and Yalta. See also Keith Sainsbury, *The Turning Point** (1985), on the Moscow, Cairo, and Teheran conferences, and the same author's *Churchill and Roosevelt at War* (1994). See also Jon Meacham, *Franklin and Winston: An Intimate Portrait of an Epic Friendship* (2003).

The Cold War has produced long and bitter disputes. The first generation focused on charges that Roosevelt had conceded too much to Stalin. William H. McNeill, *America, Britain, and Russia: Their Cooperation and Conflict* (1953, reprint ed. 1987), refuted them. The view that Stalin's "thrusts" provoked a legitimate reaction from peaceful Americans was embodied in its most scholarly form in the many works of a State Department economist, Herbert Feis: *Churchill, Roosevelt, Stalin: The War They Waged and the Peace They Sought,** 2nd ed. (reprint ed.

2003), *Between War and Peace: The Potsdam Conference** (reprint ed. 2003), and *From Trust to Terror: The Onset of the Cold War, 1945–1951* (1970). A new round began in the late 1960s when "revisionist" historians claimed that the United States pursued a self-interested agenda, and at times struck the first blows. William Appleman Williams, *The Tragedy of American Diplomacy,** 2nd ed. (1972, reprint ed. 1994); Gabriel Kolko, *The Politics of War* (1968, reprint ed. 1990); and Gabriel Kolko and Joyce Kolko, *The Limits of Power* (1972), all stressed the active American economic agenda.

John L. Gaddis, *The United States and the Origins of the Cold War, 1941–1947** (1972, new ed. 2001), reconsidered much of the documentation of American foreign policy in the light of the revisionists' charges, but accepted few of their conclusions. Walter Lafeber, *America, Russia, and the Cold War,** 9th ed. (2002), is more sympathetic to revisionism. A valuable overall assessment is Daniel Yergin, *Shattered Peace: The Origins of the Cold War and the National Security State,** (revised ed. 1990). Robert J. McMahon and Thomas G. Paterson, eds., *The Origins of the Cold War,** 4th ed. (1998), reviews the debates. Martin McCauley, *Origins of the Cold War,** 3rd ed. (2003), is a useful brief introduction. Odd Arne Westad, ed., *Reviewing the Cold War** (2000), provides an illuminating international perspective, as does Melvyn Leffler and David S. Painter, *Origins of the Cold War: An International History** (1994).

The Soviet side is being rewritten from Russian archives. The authoritative Vladislav Zuboc and Constantin Pleshakov, *Inside the Kremlin's Cold War** (1996), argues that Stalin started the Cold War and the Americans continued it. See also Vojtech Mastny, *Russia's Road to the Cold War* (1979) and *The Cold War and Soviet Insecurity: The Stalin Years** (1996).

Additional Internet links related to this chapter are available on the Europe in the 20th Century Web site: http://www.history.wadsworth.com/paxton04.

You can also explore images, interactive timelines, and maps related to this chapter on our Western Civilization Resource Center: http://history.wadsworth.com

Street scene in Warsaw, April 1946.

16
Ruin and Reconstruction, 1945–1953

Europe in 1945 was an even more desolate landscape than it had been in 1918. Although proportionally fewer soldiers had died in Europe during the faster moving Second World War, civilians had suffered far more bitterly. Strategic bombing and the sweep of motorized armies turned cities into major battlefields. More English civilians than soldiers were killed between June 1940 and September 1941 during the Battle of Britain.[1] At least 35,000 Germans perished in the firebombing of Dresden on February 13, 1945, the most civilians killed in any single action of the European war.[2] The Soviet Union suffered the highest casualty rate of all the belligerents, perhaps 7 million civilians and 11 million soldiers killed. In all, 18 million

---

[1]A. J. P. Taylor, *English History, 1914–1945* (Oxford, England, 1965), p. 502.

[2]Götz Bergander, *Dresden im Luftkrieg* (Cologne, Germany, 1977), p. 268. The atomic bombing of Hiroshima killed 78,000.

European noncombatants died from bombing, shelling, disease, malnutrition, over-work, and outright genocide between 1939 and 1945.

In September 1945, the American diplomat George Kennan passed through the ruins of the Finnish city of Vyborg, which had been fought over twice since 1939.

> The onetime modern Finnish town of Vyborg . . . was, so far as I could see, devoid of habitation. . . . I left the train in early morning when it stopped at the Vyborg station and roamed about among the ruins of the place. While I was doing this it began to rain heavily. I took refuge from the rain in what had been the doorway of a fine modern department store, now gutted and wrecked. Not having seen a living being on my entire walk, I was surprised, standing there in the doorway, to hear a noise behind me. Looking around, I discovered that I was sharing the shelter of the doorway with a goat. The two of us, it seemed, were for the moment the sole inhabitants of this once thriving modern city.[3]

Similar scenes of urban desolation were spread across Europe from downtown London to Stalingrad.

Food remained scarce through 1947. The war-ravaged soil brought forth a little over half its prewar crop in 1946. Livestock had been killed off, and fertilizer was nonexistent. To make matters worse, the winter of 1946–1947 was the coldest in fifty years. Hunger was most severe in Eastern Europe. Soon after the war, doctors in a Vienna hospital were reported to be getting "unsweetened coffee, a very thin soup, and bread. Less than 500 calories in all."[4] The French ration allowed Parisians three more slices of bread per day in 1946 than the Nazis had granted in 1942.[5]

Production and marketing were too disrupted to give useful jobs to those Europeans who wanted to work. In many parts of Europe, the black market was more lucrative than honest labor, and barter brought more than money. The dwarf hero of Günter Grass's novel *The Tin Drum* (1959) sold his mother's ruby necklace for "a real leather briefcase and twelve cartons of Lucky Strikes, a fortune." His employer, the tombstone carver, would provide his clients "a plain but good-sized stone of Grenzheim shell lime" for five sacks of potatoes.

Runaway inflation, as in the years after the First World War, discouraged saving and pauperized those members of the middle class who depended on past savings. The most prestigious French literary prize, the Goncourt Prize, of 5,000 francs, had been worth $1,000 when it was created in 1903. In 1953, the same number of francs was worth $14.29.

Political and moral dislocations added to the turmoil. Some members of resistance movements, including a few last-minute adherents, wreaked vengeance on former collaborators. Homeless youths who had known nothing but violence in their short lives formed gangs in the ruined cities. The uncertainty of the future, in both the Western and Soviet-dominated areas, discouraged purposeful activity.

---

[3]George F. Kennan, *Memoirs: 1925–1950* (New York, 1967), p. 280.

[4]George Orwell, *In Front of Your Nose* (New York, 1968), p. 83.

[5]Janet Flanner, *Paris Journal, 1944–1965* (New York, 1965), p. 51.

EXPULSION OF GERMANS FROM CENTRAL EUROPE, 1945–1947

The most desperate Europeans of all were the nearly 11 million destitute wanderers, "displaced persons" or "DPs" in the impersonal jargon of the relief agencies. These uprooted people included liberated prisoners of war, Jews who had survived the extermination camps, the forced laborers that had been taken from all over Europe to work in German factories, and most numerous of all, those who had fled before the advance of the Soviet armies. It took more than a decade for such agencies as UNRRA (United Nations Relief and Rehabilitation Agency) to repatriate or resettle all the refugees of five years of war. The last DP camps were closed in the early 1960s.

Vast exchanges of populations swelled the numbers of the uprooted. Instead of trying to fit borders to nationality as at Paris in 1919, the victorious powers fit nationality to borders. Almost 20 million Europeans were moved out of disputed frontier areas in the postwar settlement: 12 million Germans were expelled from ancestral homes in the Sudetenland, Silesia, and the lands east of the Oder-Neisse rivers destined to become Polish; 6.5 million people were moved to fit new borders between Russia and its western neighbors, Poland and Czechoslovakia.[6] The result, wrote Arnold Toynbee, "was to cancel the ethnic effects of a thousand years of German, Polish and Lithuanian conquest and colonization and to restore the ethnic map to something like the *status quo ante* A.D. 1200."[7]

[6]Joseph R. Schechtman, *Postwar Population Transfers in Europe, 1945–1955* (Philadelphia, 1962), p. 363.

[7]Arnold Toynbee and Veronica M. Toynbee, eds., *The Realignment of Europe* (Oxford, England, 1955), p. 7.

THE WORK OF RECONSTRUCTION

A prodigious work of reconstruction was necessary before most Europeans could even be assured of the basic necessities of life. But reconstruction did not mean simply restoring Europe to its condition before 1939 or 1933. The depression of the 1930s, no less than the war, had discredited the self-regulating liberal market, *laissez-faire* politics, and the international anarchy of competitive sovereign states. Even if it had not, the ruin and scarcities caused by the war obliged war government to continue into the indefinite future. By both conviction and necessity, liberated Europe began to rebuild along new lines of socialist or mixed economies and state intervention in the public welfare.

New Leaders and Parties

Europe's old leadership was leavened by new leaders and new parties. The purge of Hitler's allies and collaborators opened up more places than had been normal after earlier, less ideological wars. In France, nearly 125,000 collaboration cases were heard before special courts after the liberation; more than 1,500 persons were executed and thousands sentenced to prison. Even though Holland, Denmark, and Norway had long since abolished the death penalty, they restored it for a few dozen top collaborators, including the Dutch and Norwegian fascist leaders Anton Adriaan Mussert and Vidkun Quisling. Several Western countries imprisoned an even larger proportion of their populations for collaboration than did the French: 60 per 10,000 in Norway, 55 in Belgium, 50 in Holland, and 12 in France. That part of the prewar Western European leadership that had collaborated with Hitler was in disgrace. Not even those prewar leaders who had led the Allies to victory were guaranteed leadership roles after the liberation. The indomitable Churchill was voted out of office in the election of July 26, 1945, even while he was conferring with Truman and Stalin at Potsdam.

Into the vacancies stepped a new generation of resistance leaders, new parties, and a greatly strengthened Socialist and Communist left. The resistance contributed fewer important figures than might have been expected from the movement's vigor and popularity. Only two active resistance commanders played major roles in their countries after the liberation: France's General Charles de Gaulle and Yugoslavia's Marshal Tito. De Gaulle headed the provisional government of liberated France until January 1946 and then returned to power in 1958 during the crisis of the Algerian War and served as president of a Fifth French Republic until 1969. Josip Broz, alias Marshal Tito, a former metal worker who commanded the Communist resistance in Yugoslavia, the Partisans, ruled that country almost without contest for thirty-six years until his death in 1980. Elsewhere the most successful underground fighters did not always thrive in postwar politics, and other resistance veterans, especially the intellectuals, preferred to return to their chosen occupations. The resistance was more significant for the climate it created in 1945 than for its leaders: it provided a union of Catholic, communist, socialist, and liberal anti-Nazis determined to create a new Europe, socially just and free from the threat of war.

Josip Broz, better known as Marshal Tito, was one of the few Resistance leaders to play the main role in his country's postwar reconstruction. Shown here as the partisans' leader in 1944, Tito ruled Communist but independent Yugoslavia absolutely until his death in 1980.

The most important new parties on the Continent were progressive Catholic parties, usually called Christian Democrats. The war and the fascist experience had profoundly transformed Catholicism in Europe. An older generation willing to accept any allies, even fascists, against Godless communism, was discredited, and a younger generation of progressive Catholic resistance veterans came forward. Combining traditional paternalism with the economic and social radicalism of the resistance, some of the new Catholic leaders tried to free the Church from too close an identification with capitalism. Christian Democrat leaders were also in the forefront of the European unity movement after the war, in part out of genuine internationalism, in part as a response to what some saw as the Soviet danger.

As religion-based rather than class-based parties, Christian Democrats ran up very large numbers of votes in the Catholic areas of liberated Europe after 1945. They appealed to Catholics of both the working class and the middle class. For want of alternatives, many conservatives also voted for them. Women's suffrage in France and Italy (1946) helped swell the totals. In Germany a special situation was created by the Communist grip on the old Protestant regions. Whereas Protestant Prussia had dominated the old Reich, the Catholic Rhineland and Bavaria dominated postwar West German politics.

Under Konrad Adenauer, who had been mayor of Cologne in the 1920s and who had been interned under Hitler, the Christian Democrats governed in Germany from 1949 to 1969.[8] The Italian Christian Democrats, led first by Alcide De Gasperi, dominated every government of Italy from November 1945 to April 1993, and provided every prime minister until 1981. The French Catholic left (*Mouvement républicain populaire,* MRP) comprised the largest party in France briefly in 1946 and remained powerful until the early 1950s.

The other dominant postwar parties in Continental Europe came from the Marxist left, both socialist and communist. Their major roles in the resistance prepared the way for a new Popular Front era of broad left cooperation. After the German invasion of the Soviet Union in June 1941, Communists had enjoyed particular success in the resistance; they were well equipped for clandestine activity and prepared to submerge the call of revolution within the broader appeal of national liberation. The Italian Communist Party became the largest in the West; it grew from about 10,000 underground members in 1943 to 400,000 members in 1944 and to 2 million members in 1947. The Communists were the largest party in France at one point in 1945, and their vote total never fell much below 25 percent until 1958. The reformist left, rather than the Communist left, was strengthened in West Germany and Britain. In the Western-occupied zones of Germany, the Communist Party drew only 5.7 percent of the vote in 1949; it was eventually outlawed by Adenauer in 1956. In Britain, the Labour Party maintained its traditional grasp on the British left. In Eastern Europe, Communist parties flourished under Russian encouragement. Socialists remained mass parties in most of liberated Europe, but they were constricted by more active competitors to the right and left.

Despite the Marxist resurgence, Western Europe was not at the brink of social revolution in 1945, as it had been from 1918 to 1920. Perhaps the most urgent revolutionary drives had spent themselves in Europe after the First World War: the overthrow of the last traditional autocracies, the national independence movements of Eastern Europe, and land seizures by desperate peasants. However, the desire for social change was strong, and the resistance emerged from underground in some parts of Europe with the material capacity to take power and in a climate approaching social revolution: in northern Italy, some parts of the southern French hill country, and in Brussels, which experienced general strikes immediately after the Germans withdrew. But only in Yugoslavia and Albania, out of the reach of both Russian and Allied armies, did the resistance lead directly to social revolution.

The major difference from the previous postwar period was the Soviet Union's rejection of the revolutionary course in 1945. By all evidence, Stalin valued Russian security more than social revolution then. Apparently on order, the Communist resistance units in Western Europe stacked their arms. All Western European Communist parties participated in reformist regimes until 1947. Eastern European Communists also worked with reformist parties in National Fronts under Russian occupation until 1947. The Western Allies stood ready, of course, to throttle social revolution wherever it showed itself within their reach (as Britain did in Greece in

[8]Under Adenauer's successors after 1963.

1944), but they were never seriously challenged. There were no new waves of soldiers', sailors', and workers' councils on this second armistice day.

Economic Recovery and Social Change

Europeans faced daunting tasks of reconstruction in 1945. It was easy to suppose that they would not enjoy normal life for many decades, and perhaps never again experience the serene comforts of the privileged before 1914. As late as 1953, an American journalist aroused curiosity by suggesting that Europe was beginning to show signs of "fire in the ashes."[9] But by the mid-1950s, it was evident that Western Europe, at least, had entered a period of unprecedented economic growth and social innovation.

After the bitter 1930s, few Europeans wanted simply to restore prewar economic and social arrangements. War had left the social clay soft for modeling, and they set about to reshape states and societies. Almost none believed that a free market could regulate an economy both justly and effectively in peacetime. Most believed that some degree of governmental direction and planning was a permanent necessity. Moreover, virtually all European governments now accepted the basic assumptions of the welfare state that health, housing, education, a job, and a living income for all citizens were part of their normal responsibilities. Now that most European women could vote (except in some Swiss cantons and Portugal), some began to think beyond that agenda. Simone de Beauvoir opened new horizons in *The Second Sex* (1947) by arguing that gender roles and identities are social constructions, making it possible to imagine far greater autonomy and independence for women.

Europe's economic dynamism had survived even the Second World War. To be sure, many former European markets and resources in Latin America, Africa, and the Pacific had slipped into United States hands, and European businessmen surveying the wreckage of their continent could hardly expect to compete soon with the new Western colossus. In Eastern Europe, reparations to Russia and the diversion of old trade patterns to the Soviet bloc imposed additional burdens. The very destruction of war, however, offered opportunities to rebuild with the latest technology. The skills and imagination of these sophisticated peoples were intact. Refugees offered cheap and willing labor. The European birth rate was rising, a sign of revived hope and a stimulus to buying.

Marshall Plan aid from the United States further stimulated the pace of recovery in Western Europe. Over seven years, from 1947 to 1954, the European Recovery Program poured $12 billion into the sixteen participating nations. This aid amounted to $29 for each inhabitant of West Germany, $33 per capita for Italy, $72 for France, $77 for England, and $104 for Austria. At American insistence, the aid was funneled through an international agency, the Organization for European Economic Cooperation (OEEC), which attempted to encourage rational planning on a continent-wide basis within the open world market that American policymakers sought. Their more immediate aim was to jump-start economic growth, for Americans were sure that

[9]Theodore H. White, *Fire in the Ashes* (New York, 1953).

hopeless poverty bred revolution and aided communism. The Marshall Plan was clearly intended to serve the interests of the United States, but it just as clearly served the material interests of those Western Europeans who began to prosper again in the early 1950s.

Even critics of the Marshall Plan do not deny its share in Western European economic revival. The direct injection of capital funds for reconstruction in a temporarily dislocated but advanced region had far more effect than similar aid to underdeveloped regions. "The Marshall Plan had worked because the Europeans had the technical know-how and capital resources to turn every dollar of American aid into six dollars of capital formation."[10]

Critics, however, have charged the Marshall Plan with subordinating Western Europe to the American economy. That subordination, of course, was the result of far wider forces. While Europe was economically prostrate, the necessity of importing food, fuel, and manufactured goods (mostly from the United States) produced an enormous dollar gap: Europeans had to spend more dollars to import necessities than they could earn by selling goods to Americans. That explained the great scarcity of dollars in European hands and the very high value of dollars in exchange for pounds, francs, marks, or lire. In the long run, no doubt, economic recovery helped prepare the way for greater European independence; in the short run, however, it widened the dollar gap, since revived prosperity only promoted more imports from the United States.

During the depression of the 1930s or under fascist autarky, such disparities in currency values would have been taken care of by trade restrictions, barter devices, and currency controls. After 1945 the Americans, supported by liberal European economists, were determined to avoid such closed monetary regimes. The Bretton Woods Agreement of July 1944 was the cornerstone of the postwar monetary order. The forty-four participating nations committed themselves, for the first time, to an institutionalized system of fixed currency exchange rates coupled with the freest possible trade and currency exchange, with an International Monetary Fund (IMF)[11] standing by to smooth over temporary maladjustments in international monetary exchange by loans and grants. These "administered" exchange rates were an attempt to achieve the commercial freedom of the nineteenth-century gold standard without the dangers of that system's cyclical fluctuations in a highly distorted postwar world economy.

Although the Bretton Woods system established no official reserve currency, unofficially the dollar played a gargantuan role in world monetary affairs. Individual Americans could live better than kings in Europe. They casually bought up centuries' accumulations of silver and art. American firms could purchase European subsidiaries with ease, threatening the independence of European economies. American economic power made it more difficult for European governments to

---

[10]Walter La Feber, *America, Russia, and the Cold War, 1945–1992*, 7th ed., (New York, 1993), pp. 176–177.

[11]The IMF is an international fund intended to provide temporary support to currencies under heavy selling pressure in international exchanges and thus avoid forced devaluations, such as that of the pound in 1931. It began operating in 1946 with assets of $8.5 billion, 25 percent supplied by the United States, and kept non-Communist currencies convertible at fixed rates, by periodic support or devaluation, until the early 1970s.

oppose American policies, such as German rearmament, or resist repeated devaluations of the pound, the franc, or the lira to keep the open economy going.

The Soviet Union declined to participate in the Bretton Woods system. And, as noted in the preceding chapter, when some of its Eastern European clients (Poland, Hungary, and Czechoslovakia) showed interest in the Marshall Plan, the Soviet leaders began in 1947 to install one-party regimes and tie the Eastern European economies more tightly to Russia. A basic minimum of prosperity came to Eastern Europe only in the 1960s. Thus, the reconstruction of Europe took place under conditions that widened the differences between East and West.

THE LABOUR GOVERNMENT IN BRITAIN, 1945–1951

The prewar order was rejected in Britain no less than on the Continent, even though Britain had experienced no occupation, resistance, or armed liberation, and the doggedly respectable Labour Party had retained firm control of the British left. Even in the best years between the wars, no fewer than 10 percent of British workers had been unable to find jobs, leaving nearly 2 million families in despair. British citizens voted against a return to prewar arrangements in July 1945 when they gave the Labour Party its first outright majority in history. That Clement Attlee, former professor at the London School of Economics and a scholarly reformist, replaced Churchill in the very moment of Churchill's war triumph showed how decisively the British public refused the domestic status quo.

The Beveridge Report: "Full Employment"

Persistent unemployment had been the shame of twentieth-century Britain. "Full Employment in a Free Society," the title of Sir William Beveridge's[12] February 1943 report on postwar social security arrangements, helped set priorities for the Labour government of 1945 to 1951. Even for a free-trade economist like Beveridge, the "unplanned market economy" stood condemned for "its failure to generate sufficient steady demand for its products." The experience of two wars had shown that unemployment vanished when the state set up "unlimited demand for a compelling common purpose." On these pragmatic grounds, Beveridge (following Keynes) proposed that the state accept its responsibility even in peacetime to generate sufficient purchasing power to keep everyone employed.

Putting full employment first thrust new obligations on the Labour government. In domestic policy, the state undertook to forecast what level private investment was likely to attain and then make sufficient public outlay to close the foreseen employment gap, even if the budget did not balance. In international economic policy, this meant standing the depression policy of both Labour and the Conservatives on its head. Instead of mollifying international bankers and thwarting currency speculators with balanced budgets and reduced social services, the welfare state resolved to

[12]Beveridge was the director of the London School of Economics.

attain full employment and then take whatever measures (currency control, devaluation) might be necessary on the international money market.

In Beveridge's terms, full employment could be assured "in a free society," without all the compulsions of a war economy or a totalitarian regime. A majority of Labour Party members, the trade union mass more fully than the intellectual wing, accepted Beveridge's view that it was "sufficient to . . . socialize demand" and not necessary to "socialize production. . . . The need for socialism has not yet been demonstrated."[13] State control of part of the economy would provide sufficient leverage over the rest.

Therefore, the Labour government limited its nationalization to the permanently ailing coal industry and some basic commodities like steel and transportation, plus a few service enterprises (some public restaurants, a few breweries). Eighty percent of British industry remained in private hands. Considering the extent to which even the Conservatives had brought such ailing businesses as coal and steel under government coordination between the wars, Labour's limited nationalization was a relatively minor departure.

The British Welfare State

The most sweeping Labour innovations provided basic social services to all British subjects on the principle of universal right rather than according to need. This was intended to remove the traditional stigma of charity from public services. After 1948 the National Health Service provided medical care free to everyone in Britain who wished to use it. Health Minister Aneurin Bevan nationalized hospitals but left doctors free to practice privately if they wished. By 1950, 95 percent of the British public went to doctors enrolled in the National Health Service. Social security arrangements dating back to Lloyd George were rounded out with family assistance. The British welfare state also built on several major wartime reforms. The English Education Act of 1944 made some form of secondary education available to all, although an examination taken after grade school (the "eleven-plus examination") channeled students into technical or classical secondary schools in a way that tended to perpetuate class distinctions. The Town and Country Planning Act of 1943 gave the government power to set aside green space and prevent speculation in land values distorted by the anticipated post-*blitz* housing shortage.

The cost of these new programs was met in part by very steep income and inheritance taxes. Between 1938 and 1949, taxes increased fourfold. In 1938, 7,000 persons had admitted to annual incomes after taxes of over £6,000 (about $30,000 at the time); in 1947 and 1948 there were only 70 incomes this large.[14] The very wealthy could still thrive by spending capital, and businessmen quickly learned expense-account living, but the spread of wealth in Britain was narrowed for a time. The nobleman who opened his ancestral home to tourists at two shillings a visit became a familiar feature of postwar England.

[13]William H. Beveridge, *Full Employment in a Free Society* (New York, 1945), pp. 21, 28–30, 37.

[14]Arthur Marwick, *Britain in the Century of Total War* (Boston, 1968), p. 359.

Economic Maladjustment

Britain's immediate postwar years were a time of almost unending crisis. This was less the result of Labour's social policies than of painful adjustment to Britain's fundamentally changed place in the world. This small island's economic hegemony in the nineteenth century had owed much to temporary preeminence in coal, textiles, shipping, and finance. Even before 1914, other countries were catching up with Britain and even passing it by leapfrogging technological stages. The First World War had liquidated much of Britain's nineteenth-century accumulation of overseas investment; the Second World War had reduced it still further. After 1945, the British economy struggled with almost permanent deficits in international accounts. In a country that had to import much of its food, fuel, and raw materials and that no longer drew much income from overseas investments, the slightest slack in production or the slightest release of consumer buying threw imports ahead of exports.

Under these conditions, British recovery depended on getting the British people to work as hard as possible and consume as little as possible. Even basic foods like bread continued to be rationed for years; British consumers could not buy butter and sugar freely until 1954. While writing his novel *1984* on the Scottish island of Jura in the fall of 1947, George Orwell wrote a friend that he was gathering wood and peat to eke out his small hoard of coal for the "pretty bleak" winter he expected.[15] The official British policy was called "austerity," and for the British who endured those grim years, austerity was indelibly associated with the severe black-coated figure and dour expression of Chancellor of the Exchequer Sir Stafford Cripps, a Labour Party intellectual of upper-middle-class origin from the party's left wing.

British recovery was complicated by some unnecessary burdens. The record winter cold of 1946–1947 required spending precious foreign exchange to import coal; it was a case literally of "carrying coals to Newcastle." Since a majority of Labour leaders were reluctant to withdraw from those parts of Britain's overseas possessions outside India and the Middle East, heavy military expenditures (especially after the Korean War began in 1950) diverted funds away from productive investment. Finally, when the United States forced Britain to restore the pound to free international trading in 1947, trade deficits and heavy speculation against the pound caused a devaluation in 1949. Although British exporters could sell their goods more cheaply, imports became more expensive, one of the costs of belonging to the American economic sphere.

The British people had freely consented to sacrifices when the enemy was Hitler. Sacrifices were harder to extract against that less discernible enemy, economic maladjustment. Strikes, notably of dockworkers in 1949, put the Labour government in the awkward position of opposing union demands. The more radical wing of the Labour Party, led by the intransigent and blunt-spoken Welshman Aneurin Bevan, broke with the government in 1950 over the restoration of partial medical fees (for eyeglasses and false teeth) and over defense expenditures that "dragged" Britain, Bevan said, "behind the wheels of American diplomacy."[16]

[15]Orwell, p. 376.

[16]Michael Foot, *Aneurin Bevan: A Biography* (London, 1997), p. 421.

The opposition Conservatives also attacked Labour unmercifully for alleged mismanagement of the nationalized industries. How was it possible, for example, that coal-exporting England had had to import coal in the winter of 1946–1947? The notorious inefficiency of the coal industry before the war, however, makes it unlikely that the Conservatives would have dealt more successfully with the insoluble problems confronting Britain after 1945. In any event, when the Conservatives won the election of October 1951, they returned only steel and road transport (the only profit-making industries that Labour had nationalized) to private ownership. Coal and railroads remained nationalized. Welfare provisions remained intact, although more medical fees were instituted in 1957. The British Conservatives accepted the major elements of the welfare state, adding only a dash of state planning for greater productivity.

THE FRENCH FOURTH REPUBLIC

Liberated France had even less desire than Britain to return to the ways of the discredited 1930s. The French people voted almost 20 to 1 in a referendum in October 1945 against reviving the prewar Third Republic, which had failed both to remedy the depression and to stop Hitler. The new Fourth Republic (1946–1958) had to satisfy a number of French aspirations after the liberation: It must be a parliamentary republic, in reaffirmation of French libertarian values against the hated collaborationist Vichy state, but it must be more efficient and more socially progressive than the Third Republic had been. Efficiency, freedom, and social welfare would be difficult goals to reconcile even without the wreckage left by four years of occupation and the bitter divisions left by collaboration and resistance. Creating the Fourth Republic was even more complicated by the search for a new leadership among the varied groups that had cooperated in the liberation of France.

The Search for Leadership

The preeminent French liberation leader was General Charles de Gaulle. That austere, brilliant, aloof officer had pursued since June 1940 the mission of personifying an invisible French grandeur. As the head of the Free French in London, de Gaulle had insisted that eternal France had been only temporarily eclipsed by defeat and that the collaborationist Vichy regime (despite its superficial marks of legality) forfeited its legitimacy for lack of independence. Almost alone at first, he took comfort in the certainty of his convictions. His stand as an advocate of armored warfare in the French army before the war had been lonely but correct; he believed he was still correct, although alone in London, in June 1940. Gradually he imposed his leadership on one after another of the elements of the French resistance. He waged his most difficult battle against his American and British allies, who tried to treat him as a subordinate instead of as the embodiment of France.

By a combination of luck, skill, and inflexibility, de Gaulle outdistanced all potential rivals for power during the liberation of France. He could ignore the

© Robert Capa / Magnum

The Free French leader, General Charles de Gaulle, walks down the Champs-Elysées the day after the surrender of the German general commanding the Paris garrison, August 26, 1944. De Gaulle soon withdrew as postwar French leader, frustrated by partisan squabbling, but returned to create the Fifth Republic in 1958 and served as its president until 1969.

Americans' interest in resurrecting some Third Republic stalwarts, such as Edouard Herriot. He could not ignore the dream of some *maquis* units to assume control over the regions they helped liberate. De Gaulle sent handpicked senior civil servants—Commissioners of the Republic—into major towns as the German and Vichy officials withdrew. Thus, he forestalled local takeovers by either the *maquis* or American military administrators, although, in the same process, he also assured the continuity of France's centralized professional administrative system.

His moral authority equaled in French history only by that of the first Napoleon, de Gaulle presided over the French provisional government in 1945, while an elected constituent assembly drafted the basic charter of the new republic. In January 1946, however, General de Gaulle abruptly resigned as head of the provisional government, disgusted by the revival of party bickering and of civilian meddling in army affairs. The assembly produced a Fourth Republic all too similar to the Third, in which parliament had its way against a weak executive. De Gaulle issued occasional declarations that indicated he still hoped to replace multiparty parliamentarism with a stronger executive.

The fighters of the resistance also played a small role in the new republic. Expertise and experience were needed to assure the transition from Vichy to the Fourth Republic. Except for the most conspicuous collaborators, the bureaucracy remained substantially intact. Resistance personnel were largely shunted to the sidelines because of their inexperience or distaste for politics.

The Fourth Republic, therefore, was created by three political parties and run by the traditional bureaucracy. The revived Third Republic Marxist parties—Communists and Socialists—and the French version of the Christian Democratic parties of Catholic Western Europe, the MRP, continued their cooperation born in the resistance. These three parties divided the French vote about equally among them and governed France in a three-way coalition *(tripartisme)* until 1947.

The constitution of the Fourth Republic combined the preferences of these three parties. A parliamentary regime like the Third Republic, the Fourth Republic placed even more weight in the Chamber of Deputies. Voting for party lists rather than individual candidates gave more power to political parties. The president had largely ceremonial functions, while the prime minister, reluctant by tradition to use the power of dissolution, had no influence over the Chamber except the promise of cabinet seats in the government coalition of the moment. The multiparty parliament of the Fourth Republic did not generate the forceful political leadership that French citizens had wanted after the war. In its twelve years of existence, the Fourth Republic had twenty-six cabinets, all coalitions. Would-be prime ministers sometimes spent weeks piecing together a coalition, in a prolonged "crisis" during which France had no effective government at all.

Nationalization and Planning

The three parties took a number of major steps toward creating a mixed economy and a welfare state even before the Fourth Republic's constitution was drawn up. Nationalization went further in France than in England. The French railroads were already public (as in all Continental countries), while the aviation and armaments industries had been partially nationalized by the Popular Front. Added to these after the war were the Bank of France, the largest insurance companies, coal, steel, electricity, and gas. The Renault automobile firm was nationalized while Louis Renault awaited trial for having built tanks for the Germans. Because he died before his trial, the company remained in public hands. As the purge impulse waned, other major firms that had produced matériel for the Germans during the occupation remained private. There were no further nationalizations after 1946 until the Socialists came to power in 1981.

The Fourth Republic extended social services further than had been possible under the Third Republic with its small-town, small-property majority. The social security system, created in 1931, now included universal medical insurance. Concerned by its low birth rate, France granted larger family allocations (begun in 1939) than most Western countries.

The major economic innovation of postwar France was the adoption of planning. As in Britain, the economy was mixed; most productive capacity remained in private hands, but the state could now use its important nationalized sector to influence the rest. A new planning agency, the *Commissariat du Plan,* was created by executive decree, a reflection of the increasing role given to nonelected experts and the diminishing ability of parliament to deal with complex economic questions. Under Jean Monnet, the *Commissariat* launched a vigorous program to modernize French productive capacity, which had been debilitated by years of neglect during the depression and by German pillage. Mere replacement did not satisfy the energetic Monnet and his expert staff. They wanted to make the French economy dynamic. Beyond overseeing the state's share of the economy, the *Commissariat* could apply "indicative" (but not "coercive") planning to the whole economy by setting goals, providing accurate economic forecasts, inhibiting investment in mere gimmickry, and providing incentives for investment in needed sectors, such as automobiles and chemicals. According to Monnet's gospel, "Productivity is not a state of affairs; it is a state of mind."[17] French businessmen, who had long preferred some degree of state-aided coordination over cutthroat competition, participated, as did government experts and representatives of trade unions. By the end of the First Plan (1947–1952) French gross national product was 14 percent higher than it had been in 1938.

Tripartisme became a casualty of the Cold War when the Communists were forced out of the government in May 1947. The national elections of 1951 revived moderate and conservative parties. Thereafter, the Fourth Republic was governed by centrist coalitions as in the Third Republic. But state welfare and planning had become permanent features of French life. As the private sector prospered, the planning agency simply became more "indicative," and the state continued to encourage growth industries.

POSTWAR ITALY

Italy faced reconstruction under special circumstances. As the battleground of a long, bitterly contested land campaign (1943–1945), Italy had suffered more war damage than any other Western nation except Germany. Italy was also a defeated enemy. The Peace Treaty of 1947 gave somewhat less recognition than many Italians had hoped to the fact that Marshal Badoglio and King Victor Emmanuel III had removed Mussolini from power in July 1943 and had shifted to support of the Allies. The Peace Treaty stripped Italy of its African and Aegean empires, and transferred Fiume and its hinterland to Yugoslavia.[18]

The Contest for Political Power

It was certain that the new regime in postwar Italy would be antifascist. Two very different antifascist groups had some claim on power, however. In the expanding Allied-controlled areas of the south, the revived parties of prefascist Italy, under the temporary government of Mussolini's former associate Marshal Badoglio, expected

[17]République française. Commissariat-général du Plan de modernisation et d'équipement, *Rapport général sur le premier plan* (Paris, 1946), p. 6.

[18]The fate of the other contested port, Trieste, was not finally settled until 1954, when it was restored to full Italian sovereignty under the new conditions of the Cold War.

to restore parliamentary monarchy. In the north, armed resistance units and local Committees of Liberation, in which the Communist Party played a large role, exercised de facto control over large areas that they liberated ahead of the Allied armies in the spring of 1945. They expected to transform Italy by social revolution and moral regeneration.

Within a few months of the war's end, it was clear that the resistance movement would have no more say in postwar Italy than anywhere else in Western Europe. The encouragement that the Anglo-American military administration gave to moderate parliamentary parties was only one explanation for the absence of revolutionary change. Many resistance leaders had no political experience and wished only to return to private life. Most importantly, Palmiro Togliatti, the leader of the Italian Communist Party, returned in 1944 from his many years of exile in Moscow with orders to cooperate with the provisional regime in the south, even with Marshal Badoglio. At the end of the war, the Committees of Liberation for the most part gave up their arms as directed by the provisional government.

Italy's first postwar elections in June 1946 produced a constituent assembly in which three parties predominated, not unlike the French political spectrum: Christian Democrats (207), Socialists (115), and Communists (104). Together they drafted a parliamentary constitution similar to that of the 1919 to 1922 period. The major changes were the election of the upper house (formerly appointed), the vote for women, and the dismissal of the royal house. Fifty-four percent of the Italian voters having rejected a continuation of the monarchy in June 1946, Italy became a republic.

The two giants of postwar Italy were the Communist leader, Palmiro Togliatti, and the new leader of the Christian Democrats, Alcide De Gasperi. De Gasperi, a veteran of the Catholic *Popolari* of the 1920s, had passed the war years in more or less open opposition to Mussolini from the shelter of his post as Vatican librarian. In 1945, the Communist Party was far more powerful in Italy than it had been in the years 1919 to 1922. Its leadership of antifascist resistance and its control over the antifascist trade unions at the end of the war made it the largest Communist Party outside areas directly controlled by Soviet armies, with around 2 million members. It regularly won a third of the popular vote and governed some major Italian cities until the late 1980s. When the Communist Party went into opposition at the beginning of the Cold War in 1947,[19] it was De Gasperi who emerged with the predominant power over postwar Italy.

In April 1948, in the first parliamentary elections held under the new constitution, De Gasperi's Christian Democrats won an absolute majority, the first (and so far only) single party majority in modern Italian parliamentary history. The extension of the vote to women in that Catholic country, where women were traditionally more religious than men, probably helped him. As the one alternative to communism, De Gasperi also benefited from political and economic support from the United States and from the Italian clergy. De Gasperi remained prime minister until 1953, and his Christian Democrats continued to be the largest party of the governing coalition until 1993.

[19]See chapter 18, p. 536.

Reconstruction

The reconstruction of postwar Italy took place under the auspices of a Catholic party whose commitment to a free-enterprise economy was strongly colored by social paternalism and corporatism. After a period of disastrous inflation and black-marketeering, the regime used Marshall Plan aid to stabilize an economy relatively free of wartime controls after 1947. By 1957, worker income had risen well above 1938 levels, almost as much by increased welfare payments as by wages. Italian worker families received only an average of 59 percent of their income from wages; the rest came from various forms of welfare payments, the highest proportion in Western Europe.[20] As usual, it was middle-class recipients of civil-service salaries and holders of savings who had suffered most severely as the costs of fascism were liquidated by inflation (the lira was stabilized at about one-fiftieth of its prewar value), but in a country where fascism had just been discredited, they had no leaders to turn to except De Gasperi.

As in all Western European welfare states, private enterprise and government managed the economy together in De Gasperi's Italy. The role of the state was larger in Italy, however, in part through the legacy of Fascist economic institutions. Italy was more openly "neocorporatist" than the other welfare states. The manufacturers association *(Confindustria)*, its personnel unchanged, retained a powerful role in economic management, under an umbrella of benevolent state assistance. The major state holding company of the 1930s—IRI, the Institute for Industrial Reconstruction—continued until its dissolution in 2000 to own a large share of Italian metallurgy, chemicals, shipbuilding, and airlines, whose administration it left to businessmen. Two-fifths of all capital invested in Italy by the early 1960s was channeled through IRI and the state oil company. Only the giant FIAT automobile works remained fully private among major Italian corporations. On the other hand, the workers' factory councils created at the liberation ceased to function.

The major economic problems of postwar Italy were the backwardness of the south and land hunger. Prodded by another wave of land occupations in the south, De Gasperi distributed 1.75 million acres bought (on generous terms) from large uncultivated estates in the south. About 85,000 families were settled as owner-farmers, far fewer than had expected help. The principal social change—the movement of millions of southern Italians to the industrial cities of northern Italy and the rest of Western Europe—had to await the great boom of the 1960s.

THE TWO GERMANIES

As the occupation zones of Germany hardened into de facto partition, the German people could look forward to little better than an animal existence. Weeds grew around the foundations of what had been city blocks; two-thirds of the homes in most larger cities lay in ruins. The first foreign correspondents to enter Berlin were

---

[20]The average Western European working-class family received 63 percent of its income in wages; the British working-class family, 84 percent. (Anthony Sampson, *The Anatomy of Europe* [New York, 1968], p. 358.)

appalled by the stench of corpses buried in mounds of rubble that almost obliterated the traces of former streets.

> Nothing is left in Berlin. There are no homes, no shops, no transportation, no government buildings. Only a few walls. . . . Berlin can now be regarded only as a geographical location heaped with mountainous mounds of debris.[21]

The survivors, their numbers swollen by millions of refugees, camped in exposed corners of basements and hallways. Barter and the black market were the main sources for the necessities of life. The cigarettes an American GI casually gave his German girlfriend could keep her family alive by barter. Only the grotesque seemed adequate to describe the immediate postwar years, such as the misshapen but clairvoyant dwarf hero of Günter Grass's novel *The Tin Drum.*

Separate Statehood

As East and West seized on their parts of Germany as Cold War chess pieces, German national life revived along the tensest frontier of the emerging Cold War. Each side encouraged those German political elements favorable to itself in its own area of control. The result was an accelerated drive toward separate and distorted statehood.

German officials had been put to work in state and city governments from the beginning. The major issues were whether and how a federal German administration would develop and what would be the conditions of economic revival. After the Moscow Conference of spring 1947, the French dropped their objections to central German authority in the west. A central German Economic Council was set up in the British and American zones in May 1947. The Soviets countered with a similar body in the east in June 1947. Central political institutions followed in 1948. The East Germans called a Peoples' Congress on March 18, 1948, the hundredth anniversary of the 1848 revolution, to promote a unified socialist Germany. After the Soviets began to blockade Berlin, a West German constitutional convention met in September 1948. Under the new constitution of the Federal Republic of Germany (May 1949), the first West German government (still subject to the supervision of the occupying powers) took office in September 1949. Under a constitution drawn up in March 1949 by another Peoples' Congress, the (East) German Democratic Republic was created in October 1949.

Two competing Germanies had come into existence. Inevitably, their internal politics were polarized by their Cold War origins. The Soviet hand in the new German Democratic Republic was blatant. Although the unified Social Democratic-Communist movement (Socialist Unity Party, SED) that the Soviets had pushed together did not have a majority in the one free election held in the Russian zone,[22]

---

[21] *New York Herald Tribune,* May 9, 1945, pp. 1, 8.

[22] The results of the local election of October 1946 in the Soviet zone were: Socialist Unity Party, 45 percent; Christian Democratic Party, 24.5 percent; Liberal Party, 24.6 percent.

it had the lion's share of places in the single-list elections held in the new German Democratic Republic. Furthermore, the smaller Communist Party controlled leadership positions and policymaking in the SED even though the Social Democrats were more numerous. The German Democratic Republic was a one-party state whose authority rested on twenty Russian divisions and the Communist Party apparatus under Walter Ulbricht, who had spent the war in Moscow. Ulbricht was to rule East Germany as party secretary from 1945 to 1971.

The Federal Republic of Germany was governed from a new capital at Bonn by the Christian Democrats under Konrad Adenauer and his successors for twenty years, from 1949 to 1969. Adenauer was hardly forced on West Germany by the Allies, since the Christian Democrats won a plurality in free elections in 1949 and improved their position steadily to an outright majority by 1957.[23] The division of Germany did give the Christian Democrats an artificial advantage, however. The Social Democrats, the largest party of the Weimar Republic, were outnumbered in Catholic West Germany. In East Germany, the Social Democrats were forced into the SED and deprived of any national role in their old stronghold, the occupied former capital, Berlin.

The West German "Miracle"

Under the Christian Democrats, West Germany sprang in less than a decade from rubble to the richest economy in Western Europe. The first step in economic recovery was the currency reform of June 20, 1948. On that Sunday, each West German received forty new Deutschmarks in exchange for forty *Reichsmark*s.[24] With that fresh start, West Germans began acting as if buying and selling, saving and investing were worthwhile again. Hoarded goods came out of hiding, and the black market dried up. The West Germans had begun their postwar economic "miracle."

The economic revival was carried out under the direction of Ludwig Erhard, Chancellor Adenauer's economics minister and eventual successor, who applied a more market-oriented policy than the welfare states of Britain and France. Britain and France, having failed to solve the depression of the 1930s with a liberal economy, adopted sweeping measures of state intervention in a mixed economy after 1945. West Germany, having associated twelve years of economic management under the Nazis with scarcity and defeat, chose to release competitive energies by removing most controls and encouraging private enterprise. Erhard called it a *soziale Marktwirtschaft* (social market economy), which one commentator has translated freely as "a free enterprise economy with a social conscience."[25] The heart of the system was incentive. In addition to the inherent incentive of rebuilding the ruins, all sorts of tax rewards were offered for reinvestment by owners and overtime

---

[23]The results of the first federal elections in the western zones in August 1949 were: Christian Democratic Party, 31 percent; Social Democratic Party, 29 percent; Liberal Party, 21 percent; fringe parties, 5 percent; Communist Party, 5.7 percent.

[24]About $10 at the contemporary rate. Additional currency, bank deposits, or other holdings, such as insurance policies or pension holdings, were redeemed eventually at about one-fifteenth of face value.

[25]Alfred Grosser, *Germany in Our Time* (New York, 1971), p. 177.

work by labor. The ultimate incentive was the possibility of riches. Twenty years later, 16,000 Germans admitted to incomes higher than 1 million Deutschmarks per year.[26] The "social conscience" part of the *soziale Marktwirtschaft* appeared in the Bismarckian tradition of state insurance for all paid workers, rather than in the form of wages. Most West Germans accepted low wages and initially high unemployment in exchange for rapid growth and future promise.

The West German economic "miracle" is attributable to a mixture of causes. Energetic and disciplined people were stimulated by the possibilities of rebuilding their country. The Western Allies abandoned their efforts to limit the German economy and to break up its giant economic units. The 12 million refugees from Eastern Europe, a ready source of cheap labor, were more a help than a burden. No investment went into military development or colonial wars. Unexpectedly, the Korean War spurred German machinery exports from 1951 to 1953. Few would attribute the German success solely to free-market policies; indeed, the *soziale Marktwirtschaft* included increasing economic planning and widespread social security measures and public investment. But the West German success began the gradual swing of all Western Europe back toward *laissez-faire* in the 1950s.

The German Democratic Republic, meanwhile, languished in poverty into the 1950s, as the Russians drew reparations totaling an estimated 70 billion marks (at 200 times the rate the Western Allies drew reparations from West Germany after 1945) from that agricultural rump of the old Germany, a region about the size of Ohio. There was as yet little sign of the East German industrial growth of the 1960s. Many of East Germany's skilled young escaped to the West.

Both Walter Ulbricht and Konrad Adenauer governed under constitutions that were meant to be temporary. Both governed longer than Hitler, however. Although the division of Germany was accepted by few Germans, any conceivable form of unification seemed to require the victory of one half of Germany over the other.

RECONSTRUCTION AND ORTHODOXY IN THE SOVIET UNION

The Soviet Union faced a more gigantic reconstruction task than any other belligerent except Germany. At least 18 million people had been killed, and whole regions of western Russia—the most highly developed area before the war—had been devastated by fighting and scorched-earth tactics. Stalin was determined not merely to restore the Soviet economy to its prewar levels but to build an industrial base appropriate to the USSR's new world role as the greatest military force on the Continent and the leader of a group of "friendly" new regimes.

There were two possible ways to proceed. One of them, reconstruction through aid from and trade with the West, probably seemed too costly to Stalin's freedom of political action. In any case, Stalin had been reminded of its limitations by the sudden end of lend-lease in 1945 and the disputes over reparations from the Western occupation zones in Germany. The route chosen was a return to the 1930s policy of

---

[26]More than $260,000; ibid., p. 186.

extracting development capital from the labor of Soviet citizens. Reconstruction from within was eased slightly by the unwilling aid of Eastern Europe and by the labor of German prisoners, but it rested mostly on the willingness of most Soviet citizens to tighten their belts once more. From 1946 to 1950, while housing remained so desperately short that newly married couples lived for years with in-laws in a single room, and while only the barest minimum of consumer goods was being produced, the Soviet leaders poured more capital into investment than they had in the thirteen years following the launching of the First Five-Year Plan in 1928. This accomplishment rested on extracting every possible kopek of surplus value from the labor of both men and women. In a population whose males had been decimated by wars and civil wars, women made up 74 percent of the doctors, 56 percent of agricultural labor, and most of the janitors and street sweepers.[27] The USSR was on its way to creating the industrial basis for a world power position on the backs of a population crammed into small rooms and barely supplied with the basic necessities.

Forced-draft rebuilding from inner resources also implied tighter political control. Diverging reconstruction strategies widened the division in Europe between East and West. Henceforth, we shall have to deal with each half separately.

[27]Dorothy Atkinson, Alexander Dallin, and Gail Warshowsky Lapidus, eds., *Women in Russia* (Stamford, Conn. 1977), pp. 205, 208, 214.

SUGGESTIONS FOR FURTHER READING

William I. Hitchcock, *The Struggle for Europe, 1945–2002* (2003), gives a lively overview. Marc Trachtenberg, *A Constructed Peace: The Making of the European Settlement*[*] (1999), shows the postwar order emerging from compromises. Gordon A. Craig and Francis L. Loewenheim, *The Diplomats, 1939–1979*[*] (1994), reveals much about international relations through its main practitioners.

Michael J. Hogan, *The Marshall Plan: America, Britain, and the Reconstruction of Western Europe* (1989), reviews the American role in European reconstruction. Alan Milward, *The Reconstruction of Western Europe*[*] (1987), finds that U.S. aid had less impact than indigenous resources. John Gillingham, *Coal, Steel and the Rebirth of Europe, 1945–1955*[*] (new ed. 2004), is a good guide to the beginnings of European integration. See also John Gimbel, *The Origins of the Marshall Plan* (1976), Stanley Hoffmann, ed., *The Marshall Plan: A Retrospective* (1984), Martin A. Schain, *The Marshall Plan Fifty Years After* (2001), and Charles S. Maier and Gunter Bischof, eds., *The Marshall Plan and Germany* (1991).

The Bretton Woods system's creation and vicissitudes are authoritatively treated by Harold James, *International Monetary Cooperation since Bretton Woods* (1996). Charles P. Kindleberger, *A Financial History of Western Europe*,[*] 2nd ed. (1993), assumes basic knowledge. Richard N. Gardner, *Sterling-Dollar Diplomacy,* 2nd ed. (1981), is still useful for American postwar financial influence.

Charles S. Maier compared the aftermaths of the two World Wars in a seminal article, "The Two Post-War Eras and Conditions for Stability in Twentieth-Century Western Europe,"

American Historical Review, vol. 86, no 2 (April 1981), reprinted in Maier, *In Search of Stability: Explorations in Historical Political Economy*[*] (1987).

Gosta Esping-Andersen, *The Three Worlds of Welfare Capitalism*[*] (1992), along with works by Peter Baldwin and Peter Flora and Arnold J. Heidenheimer cited at the end of chapter 10, make clear the broad constituency of the postwar European welfare state. See also Douglas Ashford, *The Emergence of the Welfare States* (1987).

How war victims were remembered and portrayed is studied by Pieter Lagrou, *Legacy of the Nazi Occupation: Patriotic Memory and National Recovery in Western Europe, 1945–1965* (2000), a sophisticated example of the new cultural history.

In addition to the works on individual countries cited at the end of chapter 1, the following deal more particularly with the postwar period.

Henry A. Turner Jr., *Germany from Partition to Reunification,*[*] 2nd ed. (1992), and Anthony J. Nicholls, *The Bonn Republic: West German Democracy, 1945–1990*[*] (1997), are excellent introductions. A positive view of West German democracy is detailed in Dennis L. Bark and David R. Gress, *A History of West Germany, 1945–1991,* 2 vols. (1993), whereas J. M. Dennison and Mike Dennis, *The Rise and Fall of the German Democratic Republic, 1945–1990* (2000), and Feiwel Kupferberg, *The Rise and Fall of the German Democratic Republic* (2002), are useful studies of the other side. Occupation and denazification are evoked in Noel Annan, *Changing Enemies: The Defeat and Regeneration of Germany*[*] (1996). Relations between the two Germanies are probed deeply by A. James McAdams,

*Germany Divided** (1993). The most authoritative biography of Adenauer is by Hans-Peter Schwarz, 2 vols. (1995–1997). Ralf Dahrendorf, *Society and Democracy in Germany* (1967, reprint ed. 1993), is a classic reflection on how destructions by Nazism and the war opened spaces for building a democratic political culture. Alfred-Maurice de Zayas, *A Terrible Revenge** (1994), recalls the expulsion of Germans from East-Central Europe after 1945.

The standard work on the postwar British Labour government is Kenneth O. Morgan, *Labour in Power 1945–1951** (1985). See, more generally, his *Britain Since 1945: The People's Peace,** 2nd ed. (2002).

The most complete account of postwar France is Jean-Pierre Rioux, *The Fourth Republic** (1989). Frank Giles, *The Locust Years: The History of the Fourth French Republic, 1946–1958* (1995), is a well-informed political narrative. Best on postwar Italy in any language is Paul Ginsborg, *A History of Contemporary Italy, 1943–1988** (reprint ed. 2003). Donald Sassoon, *Contemporary Italy** (1997), is packed with information.

Helpful for Spain are Stanley G. Payne, *The Franco Regime: 1936–1975* (1987), and Adrian Shubert, *A Social History of Modern Spain* (1990).

Thomas W. Simons Jr., *Eastern Europe in the Postwar World,* 2nd ed. (1993), is a cogent introduction, while Joseph Rothschild and Nancy Wingfield, *Return to Diversity: A Political History of East Central Europe since World War II,** 3rd ed. (1999), is the best longer history. T. Ivan Berend, *Central and Eastern Europe, 1944–1993: Detour from the Periphery to the Periphery* (1999), is best for economic history. See Adam B. Ulam, *The Communists: The Story of Power and Lost Illusions, 1948–1991* (1992), generally for the postwar Soviet Union. Use Mark Pittaway, *Eastern Europe: States and Societies, 1945–2000* (2004), for that region, and Hans Renner, *The History of Czechoslovakia since 1945,** 2nd ed. (1996), for that country.

Additional Internet links related to this chapter are available on the Europe in the 20th Century Web site: http://www.history.wadsworth.com/paxton04.

You can also explore images, interactive timelines, and maps related to this chapter on our Western Civilization Resource Center: http://history.wadsworth.com

Nikita Khrushchev, First Secretary of the Communist Party of the Soviet Union, harangues the United Nations General Assembly on September 23, 1960, at a tense moment in the Cold War. The Soviets had recently downed an American surveillance plane in their own air space, and the UN was intervening in the Congo civil war. Khrushchev demanded an immediate end to all colonial empires, and the replacement of the UN Secretary-General by a triumvirate representing the USSR, the unaligned nations, and the West.

17

The Soviet Bloc from Stalin to Khrushchev

THE SOVIET UNION: FROM REPRESSION TO DE-STALINIZATION

It might have been expected that the end of the war would open new breathing spaces in the Soviet Union's tightly closed society. Quite the contrary happened. A certain ideological relaxation had accompanied the Great Patriotic War. Many Soviet citizens had been exposed to Western contacts, to revived religion, to a resurgence of private farm plots during wartime shortages, and even, in the Western occupied areas, to years of life under non-Communist rule. After the war, the Soviet regime perceived these wartime relaxations as a threat to orthodoxy, compounded by the return of Soviet prisoners of war (some of them against their will) and the need to assimilate new populations in the lands taken from Poland, Czechoslovakia, Romania, and the Baltic States.

Stalin's strategy for reconstruction also required tightened orthodoxy. His chief lieutenant immediately after the war (1946–1948) was Andrei Zhdanov, the party boss of Leningrad during the wartime siege and a particularly narrow-minded representative of that new generation of party functionaries whose careers had consisted more of serving the Soviet state than of opposing tsardom.[1] The Zhdanov decrees of 1946 subordinated all forms of literary and scientific expression to the political needs of the regime.

The arts declined into numbing conformity. The great filmmaker Sergei Eisenstein, whose *Alexander Nevsky* had helped kindle Russian patriotism after 1938, ran into trouble with his striking depiction of a despot's moral decay in *Ivan the Terrible*. The composer Sergei Prokofiev, who had been persuaded to return to Russia from California in the late 1930s, found his work impeded by political criticisms. Many writers were silent. The poet Boris Pasternak earned a living by translations. The most celebrated instance of political interference in science was the power that Trofim Lysenko wielded over biology. Lysenko was an agronomist whose conviction that acquired characteristics could be inherited fit Stalin's faith in the possibility of changing mankind by changing the environment. Lysenko's domination of biology crippled the science of genetics in the Soviet Union for a generation.

Even before the Cold War had taken clear shape in international relations, the Soviet forced labor camps were filled with actual or potential dissidents. There were returning prisoners of war, some of whom were shipped directly from the camps of Hitler to the camps of Stalin. There were ethnic groups that Stalin had dispersed preventively before the Nazi advance, such as the Volga Germans, and others that had collaborated with the invader, such as the Crimean Tartars. And there were young Russians imprisoned for frank wartime speaking. The army Captain Aleksandr Solzhenitsyn, who had been trained as a mathematician before the war, had been arrested in Germany at the war's end for criticizing Stalin in letters to a friend. As he was taken down a long escalator in the Moscow subway, on his way to fourteen years of imprisonment, facing the unknowing looks of those on their way up, he resolved to become a writer to tell his fellow citizens about that other country, the world of prisoners, that was growing so rapidly even in the moment of Soviet triumph.[2] But conditions were to become even harsher in the Cold War before Solzhenitsyn's name would be known to many Soviet citizens.

Growing Cold War tensions tightened the Soviet regime even further. The USSR's burden of industrial reconstruction was made still heavier by full-blast rearmament. Scarce resources were diverted into a mammoth military research and development program which produced an atomic bomb (tested in 1949), a thermonuclear bomb (tested in 1953), the high-performance MIG-15 jet fighter (into service in 1949), and sufficiently powerful missiles to launch the world's first space satellite, *Sputnik* (1957). Stalin's conviction of Western aggressive intentions only heightened his paranoid suspicion, thirst for domination, and penchant for unlimited police control. Soviet citizens lived out Stalin's last years in the shadow of anticipated war and harsh repression.

Lavrenti Beria, head of the secret police, kept even Stalin's colleagues ill at ease. A new purge seemed to be in the offing, and a more overtly anti-Semitic one, when

---

[1]Vladislav Zubok and Constantine Pleshakov, *Inside the Kremlin's Cold War* (Cambridge, Mass., 1996), pp. 8, 115. Zhdanov was twenty-one years old in 1917.

[2]Aleksandr Solzhenitsyn, *The Gulag Archipelago, 1918–1956*, trans. Thomas R. Whitney (New York, 1974), pp. 17–18.

Itar-Tass / Sovfoto

Stalin's successors line up at his funeral, March 6, 1953: from left to right, Molotov, Voroshilov, Beria, Malenkov, Bulganin, Khrushchev, Kaganovich, and Mikoyan.

nine Jewish doctors were arrested in January 1953 on charges of shortening the lives of Soviet officials. Before the "doctors' plot" could ramify, however, Stalin died of a stroke on March 5, 1953. The man who had been more powerful than any tsar was buried beside Lenin in the great mausoleum alongside the Kremlin wall, amidst mass expressions of grief in which several dozen people were trampled to death.

EASTERN EUROPE, 1945–1953: THE SUCCESSOR STATES AS SOVIET SATELLITES

The dominant fact of life in Europe east of the Elbe River after 1945 was the Soviet presence. Two hundred Soviet divisions occupied Eastern Europe, and nothing could be done there against the will of Soviet authorities.

The Eastern European peace settlement of 1919 had meant to fill the void left by the destruction of three great multinational empires—Austro-Hungarian, Ottoman, and Russian—by satisfying each nationality with its own independent state. In practice, however, the successor states had been far from satisfied: their populations ethnically divided, their political systems and their frontiers contested, and their economies closed and backward. Resurgent Germany had established economic dominance over Eastern Europe during the depression and consolidated its hold during the Second World War.

That war replaced Germans with Russians in Eastern Europe. More or less by default, a system evolved by which each power established its influence over the areas that its troops had liberated. However earnestly the Western Allies wanted a say in the affairs of Eastern Europe, they had no physical presence in the area, nor were they inclined to reciprocate with a corresponding Soviet say in the areas they had liberated, such as Italy or Japan. The Western Allies were neither militarily nor morally prepared to challenge the Soviet sphere in Eastern Europe. What was not yet clear in 1945 was how closely the Soviet Union would make those "friendly" states on its borders conform to its own economic and political system.

Eventually, with the exception of Austria, rigid Communist regimes controlled all the countries that Soviet troops had impacted in 1944–1945: Poland, Czechoslovakia, Hungary, Romania, Bulgaria, Yugoslavia,[3] Albania, and East Germany (known after 1949 as the German Democratic Republic). A region of 90 million people, nearly half as populous as the Soviet Union itself, was virtually annexed to the Soviet economic, political, and military system. The Soviets called these countries Peoples' Democracies. Hostile Westerners called them satellites.

National Front Regimes, 1945–1947

At the outset, Stalin did not install one-party Communist regimes. Until late 1947 or early 1948, he permitted non-Communist elements to share power with indigenous Communists. The other mass parties in post-Hitlerian Eastern Europe—Social Democrats and agrarian or peasant parties—exercised a relatively large freedom of action within National Fronts.

No one could expect Eastern Europe to return to interwar conditions. Few would have even wanted such a restoration. The successor states' initial parliamentary systems had almost all turned into autocracies of various sorts, none of them successful. All were discredited, along with much of the ruling classes, by collaboration with the Nazis. This still archaic agricultural region, with its underemployed rural majorities, continued to be stirred by land hunger. What there was of large-scale commerce and industry, much of it foreign-owned and damaged by the war, was riper for nationalization than for a free-market economy, which had never really worked well in that region. Eastern Europe was even readier than Western Europe to jettison its discredited interwar arrangements.

There was no major grassroots revolutionary wave in Eastern Europe in 1945 comparable to that of 1918 to 1920, however. The Russian liberators were not met by spontaneous soviets or workers' and peasants' councils claiming sovereignty for a revolutionary people, except in Yugoslavia and Albania, which were beyond Soviet control. Nor did Stalin try to stimulate anything of the sort. He was interested in controlling his country's western approaches, not a rerun of 1917. Even so, the Soviet authorities did not smother all local aspirations for change. They channeled indigenous ferments in ways beneficial to their control.

Land redistribution was the most revolutionary act of the National Front regimes in Eastern Europe. The case of Romania may serve as an example. The agrarian leader Petru Groza, of the Plowman's Front, was more or less forced on King Michael as prime minister, with Communist support, soon after Romania surrendered. Through a law of March 23, 1945, even before Germany had been defeated, the state expropriated all estates larger than fifty hectares (110 acres), as well as those larger than ten hectares that had not been cultivated for seven years, and the

---

[3]Yugoslavia remained Communist but outside the Soviet sphere after Marshal Tito refused to accept Soviet control over his secret police and army in 1948. Since Yugoslavia had liberated itself without Soviet troops, like Albania, its Communist-led resistance movement carried through a revolutionary seizure of power and assumed one-party rule, unlike the National Front regimes in the Soviet-controlled areas up through 1947. Thus, Yugoslavia stood first to the left of Soviet policy and then to the right.

land of collaborators. Nearly 800,000 peasant families were given about three acres apiece. Although the agrarian reform in Romania in 1919 and 1920 had involved more land (over 1 million peasant families had received an average of nearly nine acres apiece), this step in 1945 seemed to complete the triumph of the small farmer. Throughout Eastern Europe, from Poland to Bulgaria, 3 million peasant families shared about 6 million acres of land in similar acts of expropriation.

In ways reminiscent of Lenin's tactic of giving land to the peasants in 1917, the National Front regimes took over the policies of agrarians and reaped a harvest of peasant followers. This dramatic completion of the post–First World War land reforms was not without its dangers for the Communist parties, however. It created a host of inefficient small plots in a region of low agricultural productivity. The mass of small landholders would vigorously resist any turn toward collectivization. And it prepared fertile ground for the Communists' main rivals, the agrarian parties, who could promise the small landholders long-term security more convincingly than the Communists.

The other main domestic work of the National Fronts in Eastern Europe was nationalization of key sectors of the economy. The local Communist parties supported the old program of their Social Democratic allies within the National Fronts. The nationalization of steel, coal, and the major banks and insurance companies met with little opposition in Eastern Europe, where the major industries and mines had been French and British before becoming German and where the indigenous middle class tended to be small.

Even Czechoslovakia, the only industrialized country in Eastern Europe and one with a substantial indigenous middle class, had no trouble nationalizing a major part of its economy. It had a well-developed trade union movement and powerful Marxist parties. Moreover, many of the country's major industrial owners were foreigners or collaborationist Czechs, some of whom had fled ahead of the Soviet armies. The provisional administration of the first days, in which communist and socialist workers were prominent, installed temporary state administrators over such property. Much de facto nationalization had already taken place, therefore, before the pre-Munich rulers of Czechoslovakia returned after their country's liberation. A presidential decree of October 1945 nationalized all sectors of the economy essential to the national interest (mines, metal production, electric power, armaments works, banks, and insurance companies) as well as all firms that employed more than 120 to 500 workers, depending on the kind of enterprise involved. As in Western Europe, the Czech Social Democrats were more eager for total nationalization than the Czech Communists, who were interested at this stage in maintaining broad political alliances. The National Front settled on nationalizing about three-quarters of Czech industries employing about two-thirds of Czech industrial workers;[4] smaller enterprises and most commerce were left in private hands. Compensation was promised, but when the Communists took power in 1948 it had not yet been paid. The Communists then nationalized all firms with more than fifty workers.

---

[4]Josef Korbel, *The Communist Subversion of Czechoslovakia, 1938–1948: The Failure of Coexistence* (Princeton, N.J., 1959), p. 165.

The National Fronts' agrarian and industrial policies both built on local nationalism. Land reform had a particularly nationalist character in Eastern Europe, because the largely Slavic rural population had long endured the exactions of Germanic and Magyar landlords and creditors. The last of the large German estate owners in Eastern Europe were now swept away in their home nation's defeat, while the Magyar landlords in Romania were reduced to small landholders. Communist parties won friends as the sponsors of this marriage of land hunger and nationalism. The Polish communist Wladyslav Gomulka, later long-term party secretary (1956–1970), was put in charge of settling Polish families on lands vacated by the Germans east of the Oder and Neisse rivers in 1945. In this way, Communist parties in Poland and elsewhere got credit for the "revenge of the Slavs and Romanians against the 'master races.'"[5]

Finally, the National Fronts profited from the immediate postwar surge of antifascist and anti-German feeling. Peoples like the Poles and the Czechs, who expelled millions of Germans from their ancestral homes in 1945, and all who remembered Nazi brutalities better than they could imagine the consequences of Soviet dominance, felt they needed the Russians more than the Russians needed them. The postwar purges helped open the way for new political elites, particularly in former dictatorships and monarchies like Hungary, Romania, and Bulgaria, where leaders and principal businessmen had collaborated with the Nazis. It is doubtful that the National Front regimes of Eastern Europe actually executed more collaborators than did Western European regimes after the liberation,[6] but the vacant leadership positions were more readily occupied by Communists in Soviet-occupied Eastern Europe.

In all these ways, the National Front regimes built on indigenous pressures for change and renovation following the dark night of war and occupation. And after the failure of the successor states to make democracy work between the wars, Eastern Europeans were far less interested in returning to the parliamentary experiments of the 1920s than were the Western Europeans in returning to their own better-established liberties.

Degrees of Soviet Control

Stalin did not treat all the states of Eastern Europe alike, in fact. Soviet control was most direct in the principal border states: Poland, Romania, and Bulgaria. Poland, the key to keeping Germany in check, clearly had the highest priority. We have already seen how Stalin broke with the London Poles as early as 1943 and prepared a Communist provisional government in exile in Moscow. At Yalta and Potsdam, the Western Allies had been able to persuade Stalin to include only two London Poles—including the agrarian leader Stanislaw Mikolajczyk—in the new government. When elections were finally held in January 1947, major industries had

[5]François Fejtö, *Histoire des démocraties populaires* (Paris, 1952), p. 150.

[6]More than 2,000 in Bulgaria; 362 in Czechoslovakia, of whom 250 were Germans; 430 in Hungary. France executed 1,500 to 1,600 collaborators.

already been nationalized and opposition parties were harassed by the police and the Communist Party. Following Communist successes in these elections, Mikolajczyk went into exile in October 1947, and the Polish government could be seen as a Soviet satellite regime. The commander in chief of the Polish armed forces from 1949 to 1956, Marshal Konstantin Rokossovsky, was a Russian officer.

The Soviets also asserted their will forcefully in Romania, which was not only a major border state but one whose armies had invaded the Ukraine in 1941. Although the young King Michael had hastily changed sides in 1944 (and had received the Russian Order of Victory for it), he was obliged to choose his first postwar prime minister from within the National Democratic Front, a coalition of agrarians and Communists. The first elections a year and a half later, in November 1946, were marked by harassment of the opposition (as oppositions had always been harassed in Romanian elections). The Romanians lost eastern and northern territory to the USSR, but having regained Transylvania from Hungary at the Soviets' behest, they continued to need Soviet support.

Bulgaria was the simplest case. This country of small peasant proprietors, so similar to Russia in language, religion, and culture, had felt strong sentimental ties to Russia even in tsarist times. A relatively free election in November 1945 overwhelmingly replaced the monarchy (which had been a passive Axis satellite) with the Fatherland Front, a coalition of Communists and agrarians.

Soviet control remained far looser during this "dualist" period in the less strategically vital Czechoslovakia and Hungary. Czechoslovakia was the exception to every Eastern European rule. It was an industrialized island in the peasant sea of Eastern Europe. It was the one Eastern European nation with a substantial middle class and industrial working class and an experience of political democracy between the wars. Czechoslovakia was the only Eastern European country with a large indigenous Communist Party even before the Second World War. And it was the only one in which prewar leaders were restored to power. During the "dualist" period, the prewar democratic leaders—President Eduard Beneš and Foreign Minister Jan Masaryk—attempted to govern a social democracy with internal political liberty while maintaining close voluntary relations with the Soviet Union in foreign affairs.

As early as December 1943, President Beneš—then in exile in London—visited Moscow and concluded a treaty of alliance and postwar cooperation with Stalin. Beneš told Molotov that in important matters the postwar Czechoslovak government "would always speak and act in a fashion agreeable to . . . the Soviet government."[7] Beneš's deliberate and controversial choice of close cooperation with the Soviet Union was based on his fear of postwar German revival, his disillusion with the failure of England and France to help him in 1938, and a realistic reading of probable postwar power relationships in Eastern Europe.

The USSR later became much more powerful in Eastern Europe than Beneš (or anyone else) had imagined in 1943, but his calculation seemed to work at first. After the Soviets liberated Prague, they permitted the restoration of the prewar

[7]Quoted in Vojtech Mastny, *Russia's Road to the Cold War: Diplomacy, Warfare, and the Politics of Communism, 1941–1945* (New York, 1979), p. 137.

Czechoslovak Republic with its full range of parties and Beneš as president. In return for the cession to the Soviet Union of the eastern tip of his country (whose Ruthenian people spoke a Ukrainian dialect), Beneš had a firm guarantee against future German efforts to regain the Sudetenland, from which he expelled almost the entire German population. At the end of 1945, Soviet troops were withdrawn from Czechoslovakia. In free elections in May 1946 the Communists, building on a strong prewar base, received 38 percent of the vote. Their leader, Klement Gottwald, was the logical choice for prime minister in a coalition cabinet with socialists and Beneš's liberal followers. Beneš's regime was a test of whether it was possible for a relatively open, pluralistic regime to cooperate voluntarily with the Soviet Union as a "friendly" but non-Communist neighbor.

Hungary was an overwhelmingly agricultural country whose upper classes had been deeply implicated in Admiral Horthy's policy of cooperation with the Axis. It was not surprising, then, that in free elections in November 1945—the freest in Hungary's troubled history—the peasant Smallholders' Party received an absolute majority, and the Smallholders' leader, Zoltán Tildy, became prime minister of the new Hungarian Republic. The Communist vote was 17 percent. There seemed to be no effort at that time to tie Hungary to a closed Soviet sphere.

Could these Eastern European dualist regimes, in most of which local Communist parties shared power with other parties under the eye of Soviet army units, be permanent? Would Stalin be satisfied with friendly but pluralist non-Communist neighbors? Given the disruption and chaos of the immediate postwar years, would these mixed regimes be able to surmount problems that their interwar predecessors had failed to cope with except by some form of autocracy?

These questions soon became academic. From summer 1947 into early 1948, Stalin brought all the areas within reach of Soviet soldiers under one-party Communist control.

Soviet Crackdown in Eastern Europe

The first sign of the Soviet crackdown was a concerted attack throughout Eastern Europe on the Communists' main rivals for a mass following, the agrarian parties. In July 1947, the Romanian National Peasant and National Liberal parties were dissolved, and the peasant leader Iuliu Maniu was sentenced to life imprisonment. In the same month the Bulgarian agrarian leader Nikolaj Petkov was brought to trial and executed. In August 1947, elections in Hungary, in which intimidation was widespread, reduced the hold of the majority Smallholders' Party. In October 1947, the Polish agrarian leader Mikolajczyk fled abroad. In September 1947, at a secret meeting in Poland, the Communist Parties of Eastern Europe and the Soviet Union agreed to form an international steering body, the Cominform, successor to the Comintern Stalin had dissolved in 1943. Zhdanov explained to the delegates that its purpose was to confront the new division of the world into two antagonistic "blocs." The final step was changes of regime: King Michael of Romania abdicated at the end of December 1947. The Communists seized power in Czechoslovakia in February 1948. During the six months from late summer 1947 to early 1948, all the National Front, or dualist, regimes were replaced by one-party Communist regimes.

The facts are clear enough. Their meaning is more difficult to interpret. For those who believe that Stalin meant all along to impose Communist regimes on Eastern Europe, the two years from 1945 to 1947 were mere preparation. It seems likely, however, that he cracked down when confronted by two pressures: He needed the wealth of Eastern Europe for reconstruction, and he feared losing control of Eastern Europe unless he governed it more directly. From this point of view, the turning point came with the announcement of the Marshall Plan in June 1947. Czech, Polish, and Hungarian interest in taking part was a warning that the mixed regimes might be tempted to participate in the reviving Western European economy.

The Czech takeover of February 1948 clearly suggests that Stalin feared a decline of his postwar position in Eastern Europe. In early 1948, the non-Communist members of the government proposed to resign in a body and call new elections in which the Communists were unlikely to repeat the 38 percent they had won in 1946. President Beneš received the resignations on February 21, 1948. The Communist Party and trade unions responded by occupying the main government buildings in Prague and preventing the election from taking place. In that sense, the Prague *coup* of February 1948 was a preemptive move designed to keep Czechoslovakia from slipping back into the Western orbit. Beyond that, however, the Communists forced Beneš to form a government dominated by Communists under Gottwald. When Foreign Minister Jan Masaryk was found dead in the courtyard of the Foreign Ministry on March 10, an apparent suicide,[8] and when Beneš died the following September, there were no further barriers to a one-party Communist regime. The Czech *coup* sent shock waves throughout the world, for it persuaded the West that Stalin would tolerate nothing short of outright Communist control of the border states, and it aroused fears of other Communist *coups* in Europe.

Peoples' Democracies

The new Communist regimes in Eastern Europe were called Peoples' Democracies, to distinguish them from the more "advanced" Soviet socialist state. Their constitutions provided for parliamentary forms and guaranteed the usual liberties. In practice, the Communist Party and the security police ran the system. The local Communist parties were brought under direct Soviet control in a series of purges in the late 1940s and early 1950s. A number of prewar local Communist leaders (of whom the most celebrated was the Hungarian László Rajk) and Jewish Communists, such as the Hungarian Anna Pauker, the Czech Rudolph Slanský, and ten other Jewish Communist leaders in Czechoslovakia, were executed after show trials and replaced by Soviet proteges. Only Yugoslavia, which had liberated itself and had no common border with the Soviet Union, preserved a form of national communism separate from the Soviet bloc after 1948, despite Stalin's efforts first to control it and then to eliminate it.

The Eastern European satellites were geared to the economic needs of Soviet reconstruction. This entailed the forced collectivization of small farms after 1948,

[8]There is evidence he was pushed rather than having jumped from the window.

over vigorous peasant protests. Surplus labor was diverted into factory production under a series of five-year plans begun in 1948. Former trade patterns with the West were broken. The Soviet share of Czech trade, for example, increased from 6 percent in 1947 to 27.5 percent in 1950 and to 34.5 percent in 1956. By 1947, Eastern Europe as a whole provided a market for nearly half of Soviet exports and supplied more than a third of Soviet imports. Under commercial treaties among the state trading offices of the Communist bloc countries, the Soviet Union paid low prices for industrial products shipped to Russia, whereas the peoples' democracies paid prices higher than world market levels for raw materials imported from the Soviet Union. These unfavorable terms of trade amounted to forced contributions from the satellite economies to Soviet reconstruction: an amount estimated at $20 billion in all. Such exactions postponed Eastern European recovery and made it a grim and unhappy area long after Western Europe had returned to prosperity.

Forced Collectivization

In one Eastern European country after another after 1947, coercion replaced persuasion in the effort to convert family farms into collectives. The process went furthest in Bulgaria, the closest of the satellites. In one year, 370,000 Bulgarian farms were collectivized. By the end of 1952, 52 percent of the country's arable land was collectivized. The process was slower in Poland, Hungary, and Romania, but the final goal was clear.

The land collectivization, although less violent than it had been in the Soviet Union from 1929 to 1931, did require force and aroused anguished opposition. After initial overt resistance, the peasants adopted the classic strategy of devoting intense care to the one-acre plot authorized for each family's own use while giving lax attention to the collective lands. Low productivity made agriculture the great failure of the Eastern European regimes through the post-war period, as in the Soviet Union. More than half the agricultural productivity of the Polish collective farms, for example, is estimated to have come from the peasants' small private plots.

Without surplus wealth from agriculture, industrial growth had to be financed out of low consumption. The five-year plans adopted by all the Peoples' Democracies after 1949 placed major emphasis on heavy capital goods, so that consumer goods were scarce. The austerity of life was aggravated by the unfavorable terms of trade with the Soviet Union explained just above. Under any social system, of course, predominantly agricultural Eastern Europe would have lagged behind Western Europe in economic growth. But economic subordination to the Soviet Union, engaged in a gigantic effort not only to recover from the war but to surpass the West, imposed an almost unbearably drab and laborious life on the peoples of Eastern Europe.

THE STRUGGLE FOR POWER IN THE USSR, 1953–1957

Stalin's death in 1953 left the USSR in the hands of a "collective leadership," not as a matter of constitutional principle but because no one of Stalin's associates could immediately dominate the others. Behind the collective façade they struggled for power within a governing system in which political succession had hitherto taken place only through usurpations and executions.

Georgi Malenkov, a party functionary of middle-class origins who had run Stalin's personal secretariat, was pushed forward by security chief Beria. As premier, with Beria's support, Malenkov set a new course. He increased the availability of consumer goods for the first time since the war and advocated peaceful coexistence with the West. Coexistence was opposed by hard-liners who believed that tough Communists could survive a nuclear exchange better than soft capitalist consumers, and doubted Malenkov's conclusion that capitalism was probably not doomed.

Beria was the first member of the "collective leadership" to fall. His taste for arbitrary police power united all the others against him. They plotted to arrest him in June 1953 and had him executed soon after, the last victim of his own purges. It was Nikita Khrushchev who eventually muscled aside his colleagues and emerged by 1957 as the principal leader.

Unlike most of Stalin's heirs, Khrushchev rose from real poverty by sheer force of character, intelligence, and will. Son of a peasant turned miner in the Donbass coal-mining region of the Ukraine, the young Nikita could neither read nor write until his twenties. His first wife died in the famine of 1921. A metalworker, then a mine supervisor, Khrushchev rose within the Ukrainian Communist Party organization until in 1938, at 44, he became Party boss there. Responsibility for the Ukraine during the Nazi occupation and liberation campaigns kept him closer than most Soviet leaders to ordinary soldiers and citizens. He loved to spar verbally, with plain people no less than with heads of state. The British journalist Edward Crankshaw recalled him "willing to get mud on his boots," disputing with peasants in the middle of a field about how best to plant potatoes.[9] He once punctuated a speech to the General Assembly of the United Nations by taking off his shoe and pounding on the lectern with it.

Occupying Stalin's old position as party secretary after 1953, Khrushchev first sided with conservatives against Malenkov's proposals for consumer goods and peaceful coexistence. When Malenkov resigned in 1955, Khrushchev then appropriated the ousted premier's policies. In February 1956 he took a startling initiative against the hard-liners by denouncing Stalin's crimes in a closed session of the Twentieth Party Congress.

"De-Stalinization" and the "Thaw," 1956–1964

Khrushchev's secret anti-Stalin speech of 1956 was probably the most influential single utterance in Russia since Lenin addressed the crowd on arriving at Leningrad's Finland Station in April 1917. Although the cruelties of Stalin's purges and deportations (in which Khrushchev had participated fully) were known piecemeal to everyone, their full sweep, plus Khrushchev's new charge against Stalin of

---

[9]Introduction, *Khrushchev Remembers* (Boston, 1990), p. xiii.

incompetence during the German invasion of 1941, were a revelation. The speech's contents soon leaked out, provoking uneasy questioning throughout the USSR. Some students in Stalin's native Georgia demonstrated in his support; a few reformers took heart; most Soviet citizens simply hoped for a better life. In the satellite regimes of Eastern Europe and in foreign Communist parties the speech shook Soviet authority.

After the Hungarian revolt later in 1956,[10] Khrushchev's colleagues tried to remove him. They held a majority in the ruling body, the Presidium (Politburo, in Stalin's day) of the party's Central Committee. By appealing over the Presidium's head to the whole Central Committee, filled with provincial party leaders with whom he was on good terms, the party secretary was able to win a majority vote in June 1957 and exile what he called the "anti-party faction"[11] to minor posts in the provinces. That they were not shot represented progress of a sort. Khrushchev was now the ruler of the Soviet Union. By August 1958, he combined in his own hands the offices of party secretary and premier (Chairman of the Council of Ministers).

Why did Khrushchev shake the whole Soviet edifice by denouncing Stalin, when he himself had faithfully applied Stalin's purges in the Ukraine? He admitted to affection for Stalin; he had even wept at Stalin's death.[12] He could easily have blamed all excesses on the discredited Beria. One possible motive for the speech was to mark a new beginning. Most scholars think that Khrushchev sought to discredit his conservative colleagues by blaming Stalin's evils on them, and thus consolidate his power. It is certain that he was no democrat; he aimed only to "build socialism" by cleansing Leninism of its Stalinist deviations. But he seems to have become genuinely convinced that less arbitrary rule was necessary for Soviet economic performance and international prestige.

Profound changes in Soviet society since Stalin's accession to power meant that the dictator's whim was no longer the best way to control it. Only 10 percent urban in 1920, half of Soviet citizens lived in cities by the late 1950s; once mostly illiterate peasants, they now included a large educated elite of engineers, scientists, and technicians who were loyal to the regime but demanded more scope for professional and personal fulfillment. Stalin's successors were required to bring the Party, the military, and the new managerial elite into voluntary cooperation in order to make the new Soviet superpower work. Nuclear scientists and missile technicians were even harder to bludgeon into creativity than peasants and metalworkers. By some mix of conviction, opportunism, and circumstance, Khrushchev chose to permit a "thaw" in Soviet internal life.

The new Soviet ruler underlined his break with Stalinism by transferring the dictator's body from the Lenin Mausoleum to the Kremlin Wall and by removing Stalin's name and his statues from streets, institutions, and cities. Stalingrad was rebaptized Volgograd. The most welcome aspect of de-Stalinization was the limited intellectual freedom that Khrushchev tolerated. The "thaw" was uneven and halting, however, for Soviet leaders were unaccustomed to criticism and remained

[10]See below, pp. 526–529.

[11]Led by the hard-liners Molotov and Kaganovich, now joined by the demoted technician Malenkov.

[12]*Khrushchev Remembers*, pp. 322–323.

uncertain where to draw the line. On the one hand, the new first secretary understood that it was impossible to return to repression. On the other hand, this peasant autodidact distrusted intellectuals, feared the effects of their debate, and found their artistic experiments fit only "to cover urinals with."[13] But he dealt with them directly and in person, rather than by a policeman's knock on the door.

A symbol of the new freedom was the publication of Vladimir Dudintsev's *Not by Bread Alone* (1957), a rather pedestrian morality tale of an idealistic inventor's frustrations at the hands of bureaucracy. Dudintsev's book had an enormous impact, not for any literary quality, but because of how openly it suggested that progress came from free individuals rather than from the Party. Of more lasting merit was Aleksandr Solzhenitsyn's *One Day in the Life of Ivan Denisovich* (1962), the first literary work to speak openly of Stalin's prison camps. Having uncapped the bottle a little, Khrushchev was appalled by the intellectual ferments that rose from it and attempted to close it again. Boris Pasternak's novel *Dr. Zhivago* (1957), which portrayed the Revolution of 1917 as a disaster for Russia, was published only abroad, and Pasternak was warned that if he went to Stockholm to accept his Nobel Prize in person he would not be allowed to return to the Soviet Union.

Unwilling or unable to manage his country's elite by force alone, Khrushchev had to persuade them at least some of the time. One device was the promise of a less dreary life. He replaced the centralized economic planning system in 1957 with supposedly more flexible regional planning offices in an effort to remove administrative bottlenecks (only to resort again later to central directives). The new Party program of July 1961 promised to complete the Soviet Union's "transition to communism" by 1980 by surpassing the United States in steel, farm products, and other basic commodities. The Soviet leader assured his citizens that they could look forward by 1980 to having apartments of their own, "even newlyweds."

Agriculture was his particular specialty (he had been in charge of Soviet agriculture in Stalin's last days). He kept looking for some panacea to make the collective farms productive. Well aware that Soviet agriculture had never regained the precollectivization levels of 1928,[14] he invested huge sums in one grandiose farm remedy after another. One was the massive adoption of American hybrid corn for animal feed; in the Virgin Lands Project he sent soldiers and students to turn 90 million acres of central Asian steppe to wheat.

Another way to manage the Soviet elite was international prestige. Immediately after Stalin's death, the Soviet leaders had sought reconciliation with Yugoslavia and had met President Eisenhower in the first summit conference of the Cold War era in Geneva in 1955. Once settled in power, however, Khrushchev lashed out aggressively against the West. Between 1958 and 1961, Berlin was the focal point of Soviet pressure in Europe. Harassing Western traffic to Berlin and threatening to transfer Soviet occupation rights in Berlin unilaterally to the East Germans, Khrushchev tried to force the Western occupying powers out of the city. When he

---

[13]Among Khrushchev's more printable words during a surprise visit on December 1, 1962, to a show of modern painting at the Manezh Museum in Moscow. Priscilla Johnson, *Khrushchev and the Arts* (Cambridge, Mass., 1965), p. 103, contains the full text.

[14]As head of Soviet agriculture in 1953, Khrushchev admitted that the USSR still had 3.5 million fewer cows than in 1941, and 9 million fewer than in 1928. (Edward Crankshaw, *Khrushchev's Russia,* 2nd ed. [London, 1962], p. 83.)

failed, he ordered the Berlin Wall built in August 1961. The first Soviet leader since Stalin's failure in China in 1927 to see promise in Third World nationalist leaders, he established close ties with Syria, Egypt, India, and the African state of Guinea. In 1962, he began constructing missile sites in Cuba.[15] His adventurous foreign-policy initiatives and agricultural experiments rested on an absolute conviction that, as he warned the West in November 1956, "we will bury you."

EASTERN EUROPE: THAW AND REBELLION, 1953–1956

Collectivization of farms, factories, and businesses, low wages, scarce and shoddy consumer goods, one-party rule, and intellectual censorship made life bleak in Soviet-dominated Eastern Europe. With no competing parties and with ethnic minorities deprived of any voice along with everyone else, politics in the Communist satellite states were reduced to local reactions to what Moscow wanted. So Stalin's death in 1953 and the experiments of his successors released volatile responses in Eastern Europe.

The first serious disorders within the Peoples' Democracies broke out soon after Stalin's death. Continued efforts to squeeze more productivity out of Eastern European workers aroused resentments that were both economic and nationalist. In Czechoslovakia, where worker morale and productivity were extremely low, the regime attempted to force the population to work harder by confiscating savings in May 1953. The result was a massive demonstration in Pilsen, in which workers displayed pictures of Beneš and Masaryk. The most serious troubles occurred in East Berlin. The government's announcement of new norms for construction workers on June 16, 1953, led to a strike that grew on June 17 into a full-fledged revolt. It had to be put down at the cost of twenty-five dead and some six hundred subsequent executions.

Warned by these events, and in consonance with the promise of more consumer goods in the Soviet Union announced by Stalin's successor Malenkov, most of the Peoples' Democracies announced a new course toward less repressive conditions. Hungarian Premier Imre Nagy (1953–1955) went furthest in the quest for a more relaxed, more national variant of socialism within the Soviet bloc. Nagy announced a halt in land collectivization and permitted some collectives to disband, so that about 70 percent of the farm land in Hungary remained in private hands at the end of 1953. Nagy also diverted more resources into consumer goods. He relaxed police control to the point where Budapest became one of the most outspoken of Eastern European capitals. Nagy said that Hungary must find its own way to socialism, "to cut our coat according to our cloth." When Nagy's model, Malenkov, fell in the Soviet Union, Nagy's enemies, led by Hungarian Party Secretary Mátyás Rákosi, removed him from office.

Khrushchev's de-Stalinization speech of 1956 aroused even more threatening Eastern European reactions. In both Poland and Hungary, Communist intellectuals took the lead in exploring ways to make their regimes more open and more national within the socialist system. In Poland, the former Stalinist poet Adam

---

[15]See pp. 529, 553, 584–586 for fuller discussion of foreign policy.

AP / Wide World Photos

Two East Berlin youths stone a Russian tank during the demonstrations of June 17, 1953.

Wazyk formed the Crooked Circle Club, which soon spread a libertarian, national message. His "Poem for Adults" of August 1956 demanded

> Clear truths
> The bread of liberty,
> And resplendent reason.[16]

Workers in Poznan, Poland, demonstrated in July 1956 carrying banners reading "bread and liberty," and the police and army could not be relied on to use force against them. The Soviet regime accepted the recall to power of Wladyslav Gomulka, who had been out of favor since 1947 for advocating a Polish way to socialism. In what many Poles referred to as "spring in October," Gomulka stopped the collectivization of land, set a more moderate course toward the Church (Poland is the most Catholic country of Eastern Europe), and established himself as the indispensable guarantor until 1970 of a regime that would be both loyal to the Russian alliance and socialist in its own way—peasant and Catholic.

Polish de-Stalinization was carried through peacefully; in Hungary, de-Stalinization led to insurrection followed by harsh repression. The Budapest Communist intellectuals formed the Petöfi Circle, named for a poet of the 1848 revolutions, to

[16]Quoted in François Fejtö, *Histoire des démocraties populaires*, vol. 2 (Paris, 1969), p. 71.

spread their message. Budapest steelworkers led demonstrations for better conditions. When the authorities forbade a demonstration on October 20, 1956, in sympathy for Gomulka's new program in Poland, 200,000 protestors, mostly students, gathered in Budapest chanting Petöfi's verse, "We shall never again be slaves." That night Imre Nagy was recalled to be premier.

Events might have been channeled into something parallel to the Polish compromise, but shots were fired, and the demonstrations became uncontrollable. Soviet flags and Stalin's statue were pulled down in Budapest, revolt spread to the rural collectives, and revolutionary and workers' councils assumed control of some localities. On October 29 it was announced that Soviet troops were being withdrawn. On October 30, 1956, Nagy announced a return to a multiparty system and a coalition government of Communists, Social Democrats, and Smallholders "as in 1945." The following day he announced Hungary's withdrawal from the Warsaw Pact and neutrality. The Soviet leaders, however, unwilling to accept the loss of Hungary and covered by the diversion of international attention to the Suez crisis, withdrew only to prepare the military reconquest of Hungary. Starting November 4, a Soviet armed force including 2,500 tanks spread through Hungary, shelling thousands of buildings in Budapest and killing at least 3,000 Hungarians.[17] An estimated 200,000 refugees, or nearly 2 percent of the total population, fled to the West. A deeply wounded Hungary was restored to firm Communist rule under János Kádár. Nagy and other leaders of the Hungarian "New Course" were subsequently put to death.

AP / Wide World Photos

The great bronze statue of Stalin, tumbled by the crowd in Budapest, November 1956.

[17]Hungarian government statistics, in United Nations, General Assembly, *Report of the Special Committee on the Problem of Hungary*, Supplement 18 (A/3592) (New York, 1957), p. 33. Outside estimates ran as high as 20,000 Hungarians and 7,000 Soviets killed.

The agony of Hungary in November 1956 showed clearly that although the Soviet Union would permit some leeway within the satellite countries, as in Poland, it would go to almost any lengths to preserve the essence of Soviet control of the Socialist bloc. It showed, too, that hopes of United States intervention behind the Iron Curtain were vain. Whatever change was to come in the Peoples' Democracies would have to come by internal evolution.

THE FALL OF KHRUSHCHEV, 1964

Khrushchev was certainly the most interesting of Stalin's successors until Gorbachev, but the qualities of boldness, inquisitiveness, and spontaneous human warmth that fascinated the world also exposed him to spectacular failures.

He was unable to keep his promise of abundance. The Cold War and expensive space and armaments programs postponed any significant shift to consumer goods. Although the USSR maintained its lead in space by orbiting the first man around the earth, Yuri Gagarin, in April 1961,[18] Khrushchev opposed the mass production of private automobiles—"those armchairs on wheels"—for Soviet citizens. Most of his agricultural projects backfired. The Virgin Lands project transformed broad stretches of Central Asia into a dust bowl. The American corn failed to mature so far north. A bad harvest in 1963 made it clear that despite his passion for farming and huge investments, he had not managed to return to the agricultural surpluses of pre-1914 Russia.

As the last romantic "true believer" in world revolution,[19] Khrushchev took foreign adventures that exposed him to high risks and the distrust of his more pragmatic colleagues. It was embarrassingly clear that Khrushchev had had to back down over Cuba in 1962 and that Soviet relations with Germany and China had deteriorated. De-Stalinization and a grudging toleration of artistic expression had shaken authority without satisfying intellectuals.

The very tactics by which Khrushchev had consolidated his authority in 1957 left him vulnerable. Stalin's despotism had been impossible to reproduce. We have seen how Khrushchev overcame the challenge of the "antiparty group" in June 1957, by mobilizing provincial party leaders in the large Central Committee against the inner circle in the Presidium. Once victorious, he was satisfied to demote his rivals rather than kill them.

Thus he established, if not democracy, a form of collegial power. But that permitted politics within the Kremlin. Even Stalin had not ruled entirely alone; his successors needed even more to appease or dominate various ideological camps and institutional interests, from the army and the KGB to collective farm managers. Western "kremlinologists" of the post-Stalin era tried to divine the relative position of rivals and potential successors inside the Kremlin by such signs as the order in

---

[18]The first U.S. astronaut to orbit the earth was John Glenn in February 1962. Even in the late 1980s, despite mounting economic difficulties, the USSR had the world's most powerful missile launchers and succeeded in placing in orbit the world's first manned space station, *Mir. Mir* was used actively by many nations until 2001.

[19]Zubok and Plekhanov, pp. 178, 192–193, 280–281.

which the Soviet leaders stood to watch military parades pass the Lenin Mausoleum.

By 1964, the failures of many of Khrushchev's grand projects and his confrontational style had gathered a coalition of hard-liners and technicians against what they called his "voluntarism" and his "harebrained schemes." This coalition, holding a majority in the Presidium, quietly removed him from power in October 1964. That he could retire to a country *dacha*, receive visitors, and write memoirs that were eventually published in the West showed how far Khrushchev had moved the Soviet political system away from arbitrary violence. But although the new way of choosing Soviet rulers had become less murderous, political succession was now both complex and unforeseeable. In the absence of any written rules, power required affirming authority over an establishment of high party and police officials—the *Nomenklatura*[20]—who had never known any political reality but the management of a one-party dictatorship. Khrushchev's successors would be unable to deal creatively with the USSR's problems within such a straitjacket.

SUGGESTIONS FOR FURTHER READING

Stalin's paranoid last days are grimly described by his daughter Svetlana Alliluyeva in *Twenty Letters to a Friend* (1967), and by Milovan Djilas, *Conversations with Stalin*[*] (1963). Amy Knight, *Beria: Stalin's First Lieutenant*[*] (1993), draws on newly opened Soviet archives. Donald Filtzer, *The Khrushchev Era, 1953–1964*[*] (1996) is a good short introduction. William Taubman, *Khrushchev: The Man and His Era*[*] (2004), is the latest biography. *Khrushchev Remembers: The Glasnost Tapes* (1990) gives partial but fascinating glimpses, and Sergei Khrushchev speaks revealingly about his father in *Nikita Khrushchev and the Creation of a Superpower* (2000). An important work of postCommunist Russian scholarship, Vladislav Zubok and Constantine Pleshakov, *Inside the Kremlin's Cold War*[*] (reprint ed. 2001), includes a penetrating portrait of Khrushchev as the last romantic "true believer." George W. Breslauer, *Khrushchev and Brezhnev as Leaders* (1982), finds that the two leaders' styles differed more than the issues and systems of rule they faced. Geoffrey A. Hosking, *The First Socialist Society: A History of the Soviet Union from Within*,[*] 2nd ed. (1993), examines the workings of the Soviet social system. Moshe Lewin, *The Gorbachev Phenomenon: A Historical Interpretation*,[*] 2nd ed. (1991), though dated in some details, remains essential for the social underpinnings of all Soviet regimes since Stalin. The works on Soviet government cited at the end of chapter 8 are still relevant here.

David Holloway, *Stalin and the Bomb*[*] (1996), shows that Stalin benefited from espionage for the A-bomb but not for the H-bomb and explores the strains and compatibilities between dictatorship and world-class physics; David Joravsky, *The Lysenko Affair*[*] (1970, reprint ed. 1986), does the same for genetics. See also Loren R. Graham, *Science and the Soviet Social Order* (1990).

[20]The term comes from the official list from which high officials and managers were chosen.

The books by Simons and Rothschild suggested after the previous chapter are still basic here. François Fejtö, *History of the Peoples' Democracies* (1971), the still-useful work of a very well informed Hungarian emigré, argues that Stalin tightened control in 1947 out of fear that central Europe was being drawn into the Western orbit. Hugh Seton-Watson, *The East European Revolution,* 3rd ed. (reprint ed. 2003), believes that Stalin meant from the beginning to sovietize it. The important work of Zubok and Pleshakov, cited above, says Hiroshima and the Marshall Plan hardened Stalin.

In addition to the study of postwar Czech history by Hans Renner, mentioned at the end of chapter 16, refer to Karel Kaplan, *The Short March: The Communist Takeover in Czechoslovakia, 1945–1948* (1987). Yugoslavia is examined by Ivo Banac, *The National Question in Yugoslavia** (revised ed. 1988), along with the national histories cited at the end of chapters 1 and 16. Richard West, *Tito and the Rise and Fall of Yugoslavia** (1996), blames refractory Croats, as does Aleksa Djilas, *Contested Country: Yugoslav Unity and Communist Revolution** (1996).

For the two most dramatic examples of East European resistance to Communist rule, one may begin with Klaus Harpprecht, *The East Grman Rising: Seventeenth June 1953* (1979). Useful works on Hungary include Paul E. Zinner, *Revolution in Hungary* (reprint ed. 1977), Bela Kiraly, *The First War between Socialist States: The Hungarian Revolution of 1956 and its Impact* (1984) (the work of a Hungarian general escaped to the West), and Gyorgy Litvan, *The Hungarian Revolution of 1956* (1996). Works on the German Democratic Republic are listed at the end of chapter 16.

Additional Internet links related to this chapter are available on the Europe in the 20th Century Web site: http://www. history.wadsworth.com/paxton04.

You can also explore images, interactive timelines, and maps related to this chapter on our Western Civilization Resource Center: http://history. wadsworth.com

The Berlin Wall, erected in 1961, divided many families. Here a wedding party in West Berlin waves to relatives isolated on the other side.

18

Europe in the Cold War: Between the Superpowers, 1947–1961

By 1947 and 1948, the United States and the Soviet Union had dropped all pretense of trying to continue their wartime alliance. This hardened antagonism between the communist states and the capitalist states produced a new kind of conflict: the Cold War. The availability on both sides of nuclear weapons capable of annihilating the other[1] made war unthinkable; yet each side's claim to universal ideological legitimacy made peace impossible. Under an umbrella of mutual nuclear terror, the two sides grappled with each other by every means short of the war that might obliterate them both.

The Cold War conflict was as bitter as war, without actual armed combat between the principal powers. Its arena was virtually worldwide, even more than the Second

---

[1] The Soviets tested an atomic bomb in September 1949 and announced their possession of thermonuclear weapons in August 1953. One thermonuclear weapon had a force about equal to all the bombs dropped on Germany between 1939 and 1945.

World War. Its techniques included economic penetration, intellectual persuasion, and subversive propaganda as well as more traditional forms of political and military influence. Each side lent military and economic assistance to its allies and dependents. The Soviets supported movements for ethnic separatism and colonial independence in the Western sphere; the Americans broadcast encouragement to dissidents behind the Iron Curtain and supported anti-Communist regimes around the world. Both sides struggled for the upper hand in the emerging new nations of Africa and Asia. The result was an unending series of *coups,* guerrilla warfare, and civil wars with more or less open support from Moscow and Washington. Over it all brooded the possibility that the two rivals would come to direct combat, which must inevitably mean nuclear war.

EUROPE UNDER THE MUSHROOM CLOUD

Europeans had to endure the humiliation of looking on powerlessly as the two giant rivals circled each other. After centuries of confident domination of the world, the Europeans found their fate now dependent on the distant rulers of "upstart nations." For fifteen years or so after the war, the possibility of being incinerated by the side effects of remote power politics haunted every European. As one of the characters in Swiss playwright Max Frisch's *The Chinese Wall* (1946) says:

> A slight whim on the part of the man on the throne, a nervous breakdown, a touch of neurosis, a flame struck by his madness, a moment of impatience on account of indigestion—and the jig is up. Everything! A cloud of yellow or brown ashes boiling up towards the heavens in the shape of a mushroom, a dirty cauliflower—and the rest is silence, radioactive silence.[2]

Europeans' prospects for regaining some control over their destinies looked bleak indeed in the 1950s. Eastern Europeans seemed condemned to indefinite Soviet control. Western European dependence, although less direct, was almost more terrifying. The 200 Soviet divisions could swarm west almost at will unless the Americans intervened. American intervention, however, meant the "massive retaliation" with which Secretary of State John Foster Dulles (1952–1959) threatened a Russian advance with conventional arms in Europe: nuclear annihilation of the European battleground in the guise of saving it. Europeans felt threatened by what Arnold Toynbee called "annihilation without representation."[3] Many Europeans reacted to the situation with a sense of cosmic absurdity or with profound pessimism.

George Orwell, depressed already by the tuberculosis he had contracted in Britain's harsh postwar conditions, wondered in a letter to a friend in December 1947 whether it was worth worrying about the crises of the moment.

> This stupid war is coming off in about 10–20 years, and this country will be blown off the map whatever happens. The only hope is to have a home with a few animals in some place not worth a bomb.

[2]Max Frisch, *The Chinese Wall,* trans. James L. Rosenberg (New York, 1955), p. 28.

[3]Quoted in Hans W. Gatzke, *The Present in Perspective,* 3rd ed. (New York, 1965), p. 181.

A year later he was writing that he hoped his young son would become a farmer. "Of course that may be the only job left after the atom bombs."[4] "Europe is contracting," wrote Janet Flanner from Paris in October 1946. "The USSR and USA areas of influence are expanding. It is as if Europe were slowly entering a new ice age."[5]

After the Berlin Blockade ended in May 1949 with the United States, Britain, and France still grimly holding on to the Western occupation sectors of the city, the Cold War frontiers were frozen in Europe for a generation. Further Soviet gains in the West (assuming that the Soviets really wanted more territory beyond Berlin) were now possible only by outright military action that risked American massive retaliation. The Americans were equally reluctant to disturb the East European status quo, as United States restraint showed during the uprisings in East Berlin (June 1953), Poland (October 1956), and Hungary (October 1956). The high cost of change on both sides locked the two Cold War blocs into a precarious stability.

After 1949, the hottest battleground of the Cold War shifted to Asia. In the Korean War (1950–1953), United States and Communist Chinese forces fought each other to stalemate by conventional arms without either side daring to expand the conflict. Distant though it was, the Korean War affected Europe deeply. Aside from the small European troop contributions to the United Nations force in Korea, the war stimulated European economic growth and led to the rearmament of Germany within a new Western anti-Communist alliance. But that did not diminish Europeans' fear that war might engulf their continent again.

WESTERN EUROPE: COLD WAR POLITICS AT HOME AND ABROAD

The Isolation of Communist Parties

The Cold War split the resistance coalitions that governed liberated Europe after 1945. On the Continent, the tripartite coalitions of communists, socialists, and antifascist Catholics—whose new-found unity in the resistance had been the basis of politics since 1945—did not survive the widening divisions between Communists and anti-Communists. In the spring of 1947, Communist parties went into opposition everywhere in Western Europe. Thereafter, Western European states were governed by centrist or conservative regimes.

Belgium led the way. By March 1947, cooperation between Catholics and Communists had become impossible in the ruling coalition. At that point, Paul-Henri Spaak, an anti-Communist Socialist, formed Belgium's first postwar cabinet of Socialists and Catholics from which Communists were excluded. Spaak was to dominate Belgian politics and the European unity movement for the next generation.

The French Communist Party's departure from the government on May 5, 1947, illustrates how domestic strains and international tensions combined to both push and pull the Western Communist parties into a new isolation. Communist participation in postwar reconstruction had become more and more awkward. "Unite,

---

[4] *The Collected Essays, Letters, and Journalism of George Orwell,* vol. 4 (New York, 1968), pp. 387, 451, 454.

[5] Janet Flanner, *Paris Journal, 1944–1965* (New York, 1965), p. 69.

Work, Struggle!" had been the French Communist Party's slogan during the postwar reconstruction period. Having chosen to participate legally in a nonrevolutionary government, the Communist Party was obliged to share in that government's austerity reconstruction policies. Controlled wages, price inflation, no strikes, and hard work at rebuilding the country were the workingman's lot. In the spring of 1947, a wildcat strike at the state-owned Renault automobile plant in Paris showed the French Communist leaders that they were in danger of being passed on their own left. It was time to return to the purity of opposition.

The French Communist Party leaders could well suppose that they had more to lose than gain from further participation in parliamentary coalitions. Their acceptance of the government's economic austerity program was costing them worker support. And although the Communist Party had been the largest party in France briefly in 1945, the other two parties of the liberation—Socialists and left Catholics (MRP)—were united in their determination to block Communist access to the premiership or to the crucial ministries controlling the army or police.

Foreign pressures also played a role. In the immediate postwar years, French governments had relied on Soviet support for their punitive German policy: They wanted to keep Germany divided and deindustrialized. By the spring of 1947, however, France was getting coal from the British and American occupation zones and had assumed control of the Saar in return for excluding the Soviets from a share in occupation policies in the western zones. With those questions settled, France no longer needed Soviet cooperation in Germany. They did need American economic support during the hardships of the reconstruction years, however, and the United States made no secret of its nervousness about Communist strength in France. In the spring of 1947, Jean Monnet and the prewar French Popular Front leader Léon Blum, recently returned from a German prison camp, went to Washington to seek help for French reconstruction. They obtained the renunciation of French war debts to the United States (thus avoiding the war debts problem of the 1920s), a promise of surplus goods, and a $650 million reconstruction loan. Although Blum and Monnet declared that they had accepted no political conditions, it was obvious to French political leaders that "it is not to a socialist-communist regime that the United States will grant the loan we need."[6]

When on May 5, 1947, the Communist ministers tried to square the circle by voting for wage raises opposed by the government to which they belonged, Premier Paul Ramadier, a Socialist, demanded their resignation.

The break came at almost the same moment in Italy under similar pressures. Many Italian Socialists, however, led by Pietro Nenni, were more determined than French Socialists to avoid a rupture with the Communists. The subsequent split among the Socialists left the new Christian Democratic Party under Alcide De Gasperi as the dominant political force of a coalition excluding Communists and relying on United States financial assistance. De Gasperi had visited the United States in January 1947, where he was put under great pressure to exclude the Communists from the coalition. In May 1947, he succeeded in piecing together a coalition of Christian Democrats, anti-Communist Socialists, and centrists. De Gasperi won an absolute majority in Italy's first postwar legislative elections in April 1948

[6]Left Catholic (MRP) leader P. H. Teitgen, quoted in Jacques Fauvet, *La IVe république* (Paris, 1959), p. 94.

with the support of the United States, the clergy, and all those who regarded him as the only alternative to communism in Italy.

The split affected the powerful Marxist trade union federations of both Italy and France, which divided into Communist and anti-Communist factions at the end of 1947. Secret funds from the American labor movement assisted the formation of *Force ouvrière,* a non-Communist trade union that recruited about 15 percent of French union members as compared with about 40 percent for the Communist CGT *(Confédération générale du travail),* and about 20 percent for the Catholic Unions. In Italy during the 1950s, the United States refused to award manufacturing contracts to Italian firms in which a majority of the workers supported the Communist union, CGIL *(Confederazione Generale Italiana del Lavoro).* For their part, the Communist unions, no longer required to discipline the work force for reconstruction, embarked on a series of insurrectionary strikes in France and Italy in late 1947 and in 1948.

The Cold War division naturally took a different form in Great Britain, where communism had always been marginal and the war had not involved the polarizing experiences of occupation, collaboration, and liberation. Even so, the Labour Party split over national defense policy in the Cold War. A majority of the Labour government, supported by the Trades Union Congress, wanted Britain to continue to play a world military role. After the Korean War broke out, Britain contributed a small force, and Prime Minister Clement Attlee proposed a three-year armament program costing nearly £5 billion. Social services began to be cut. In April 1951, Health Minister Aneurin Bevan and some of his followers, including Harold Wilson, resigned from the government, charging that Britain was being dragged "behind the wheels of American diplomacy" into "the anarchy of American competitive capitalism" by an arms race that would reduce the British standard of living.[7] Divided, the Labour Party lost the October 1951 elections to the Conservatives.

Division of the European Left

The result of these developments, in Britain as on the Continent, was the division of the European left. The Western European Communist parties reverted to a position of hostile isolation as complete as that of the early 1930s. Aside from a few intellectual fellow travelers and such socialists as the followers of Pietro Nenni in Italy, the non-Communist left in Western Europe went out of its way to mark its distance from the Communists. It was a socialist Minister of the Interior, Jules Moch, who crushed the French strike wave of 1947 and 1948. The old leader of the French Socialist Party, Léon Blum, called the French Communists "the foreign nationalist party." His successor, Guy Mollet, declared that the French Communists were not left but east. Arguing in favor of German arms in 1954, Mollet claimed:

> We have to have them, because since the war Russians have kept millions of men under arms, because in the last ten years Russia has destroyed the liberties of so many people, and because all the troubles today come from Russian expansionism.[8]

[7]Michael Foot, *Aneurin Bevan: A Biography,* ed. Brian Brivati (London, 1997), p. 421.
[8]Flanner, p. 260.

In France and Italy, the Communists retained a strong emotional hold on many workers convinced of their permanent exile within a capitalist system; the Communist vote never dropped much below 20 percent. Meanwhile, the French and Italian Socialist parties became increasingly limited to lower civil servants and school teachers. So divided, the left had no chance of electoral victory. By contrast to the rhetorical Marxism of many French and Italian Socialists, the West German Social Democratic Party set out to win an electoral majority by making as broad an appeal as possible to a population in which workers formed a smaller and smaller proportion. In 1959, at the annual party congress at Bad Godesberg, the party that had once been the most powerful Marxist party in the world formally renounced the teachings of Karl Marx. But revived prosperity reduced its appeal. Either way, sectarian or not, the Western European left was generally out of power during the Cold War years.

Cold War divisions posed a painful dilemma for those Western European intellectuals whom the Popular Front, the Spanish Civil War, and the resistance had drawn into action on behalf of a united left. The debate over correct attitudes toward the United States and the Soviet Union in the 1950s was particularly sharp in Paris, where intellectuals held public attention and where they had been deeply influenced by the anti-Hitler resistance and by Marxist thought. The issue was joined in 1950 after a survivor of one of Hitler's concentration camps published an attack on Stalin's concentration camps.[9] Was Stalin the new tyrant against whom European intellectuals should unite? The novelist Albert Camus concluded after much soul-searching that his ultimate loyalty lay with the West because the Soviet Union permitted no personal liberty.

The existentialist philosopher Jean-Paul Sartre was the most important spokesman for the other side. While admitting the existence of evils at that time in the Soviet Union, Sartre could not side with the United States. He was too hostile to the European bourgeoisie for that, and too predisposed by his existentialism, to make major choices in terms of ultimate goals. Despite its transitory evils, the Soviet Union represented for Sartre the ultimate promise of a better life. Sartre did not join the Communist Party, but preserved his individual freedom while supporting Communist causes. Leon Trotsky had called such intellectual outsiders "fellow travelers," and the term became a current epithet for Sartre and like-minded sympathizers.

The Cold War prompted some intellectuals to renounce the political engagement of the 1930s and 1940s altogether. The Irish playwright Samuel Beckett, living in France, achieved an enormous impact with *Waiting for Godot* (1952), in which two tramps face an empty universe with humor and dogged persistence. To pessimist humanists like Beckett, the Cold War world was simply absurd. At best one could find in it an occasional glimpse of redeeming human perseverance.

Centrist and Conservative Governments

Western Europe was governed in the 1950s largely by centrist or conservative parties. This was the Europe of Alcide De Gasperi and his Christian Democrat followers

---

[9]The first of many such articles was "Au secours des déportés dans les camps soviétiques! Un appel de David Rousset aux anciens déportés des camps Nazis," *Le Figaro littéraire*, Nov. 12, 1949.

in Italy; of Konrad Adenauer in Germany; of Churchill, Anthony Eden, and Harold Macmillan in Britain. In France the collapse of the Fourth Republic at the end of the decade brought back to power General Charles de Gaulle with a new constitution that reinforced presidential authority.

Italy continued to be governed through the postwar years by the Christian Democratic Party. Since the Christian Democrats never again won an absolute majority of the seats as they had in 1948, however, Italian politics became a disheartening round of brief coalition governments. After De Gasperi's death in 1954, five governments succeeded one another in as many years. Political strategists continued to piece together Christian Democrat–Liberal coalitions of the center right, refusing to attempt the other alternative of an "opening to the left" offered by Pietro Nenni's left-wing Socialists, who moved away from the Communists after the Hungarian uprising of 1956. Basically, Italian citizens showed relatively little interest in matters other than Italy's rapid economic growth (the fastest in Western Europe) and border disputes with Yugoslavia and Austria. The Christian Democrats solidified their hold with patronage and the help of the Church in elections. In 1959, Italy became the first European nation to permit the United States to base intermediate range ballistic missiles (IRBMs) on its soil.

Germany's aged Konrad Adenauer went on from strength to strength in the 1950s. His Christian Democrats' plurality grew with each election until they achieved an absolute majority in September 1957. The extraordinary prosperity of West Germany's free-enterprise economy spread a self-satisfied glow over the country. The stresses of the Cold War brought West Germany into an active international role more quickly than would have been thought possible at the end of the war. After the Korean War began, West Germany was allowed to join the North Atlantic Treaty Organization (NATO) and was permitted to set up armed forces in 1955.

Those pariahs of Europe, Spain and Portugal, also became respectable allies within the Western anti-Communist alliance in the 1950s. At the end of the war, the United States, Britain, and France had publicly called for Franco's overthrow. By 1953, however, in exchange for the right to build military bases on Spanish soil, the United States extended economic aid to Spain. In 1955, Spain was admitted to the United Nations, although not to NATO. The role of the fascist party, the *Falange,* had never been great under Franco, and it now almost disappeared within a regime of pragmatic technicians, monarchists, and Catholic businessmen (often members of a lay order called *Opus dei*) who presided over the beginnings of rapid economic growth.

Portugal's Salazar had always enjoyed a better press than Franco because he had not been personally involved in the 1926 military *coup* against the Portuguese Republic and because Portugal had provided Allied bases in the Azores during the war. Thus, although flags flew at half-mast in Lisbon following the news of Hitler's death in May 1945, Portugal was a founding member of NATO in 1949. Abandoning his policy of economic stability in the 1950s, Salazar accepted loans from the United States and undertook economic development that heralded the eventual end of Portugal's static, hierarchical society. Although Salazar suffered a disabling stroke in September 1968 at the age of seventy-nine, his authoritarian regime remained intact until 1974, with single-candidate elections and strict control of information.

After their electoral victory of October 1951, the British Tories enjoyed power until 1964, the longest unbroken Conservative rule until Margaret Thatcher.[10] To be sure, this was no reactionary party. British Conservatives under Churchill and his successors (Anthony Eden, 1955–1957; Harold Macmillan, 1957–1963; Sir Alec Douglas-Home, 1963–1964) accepted the main elements of the welfare state. Trucking and steel were denationalized, and additional fees were imposed on medical services in 1957, but on the whole, the Conservatives—especially Macmillan—frankly accepted the mixed economic system created by Labour from 1945 to 1951.

The French Fourth Republic shifted back to the center after conservatives made their first substantial postwar showing in the elections of 1951. Antoine Pinay, premier in 1952 and the first conservative to head a French government after the war, reassured French investors by his very presence, rather like Poincaré in 1926. Pinay reduced French inflation and reestablished a more stable franc on which the postwar economic boom began to build. Although the elections of 1956 gave the French Socialists (SFIO) a strategic position, they could not rule without allies. Refusing Communist support, Socialist Guy Mollet maintained the longest government of the Fourth Republic (sixteen months, February 1956 to June 1957) through the expedient of satisfying the center and right by his vigorous prosecution of the Algerian War.

Colonial Wars

The major European colonial empires were dismantled after the Second World War. By 1962, only the Portuguese still fought to maintain direct rule of overseas possessions. In retrospect, the Italian seizure of Ethiopia in 1935 and 1936 had been the last overt European conquest of overseas territory, and that had been short-lived.

At the close of the First World War powerful independence movements had already arisen in areas like British India, where the lawyer Mohandas K. Gandhi perfected techniques of nonviolent civil disobedience during 1919 and 1920 that forced the British authorities either to make concessions or to appear more harshly repressive than British public opinion would accept. The ideal of national self-determination propagated by the Paris Peace Conference contributed to the growth of national independence movements in the colonies, even though the Versailles settlement actually perpetuated colonial regimes under the mandate system.[11]

Although the German colonies had been distributed among the Allies as mandates, the other colonial powers had relatively little difficulty maintaining their empires throughout the interwar period by means of a mixture of minor concessions to local self-government and of armed force. Iraq, under British mandate, was the only colonial possession to attain independence between the wars (1932). Indeed, the rise of fascism stimulated renewed interest in colonies. Hitler claimed

---

[10]Even the Liberal Party's eclipse following Gladstone's divisive adoption of Home Rule for Ireland gave the Tories briefer periods of rule: from 1886 to 1892, and from 1895 to 1905.

[11]See chapter 6, pp. 166–167.

the return of German colonies, and Mussolini avenged the old Italian defeat at Adowa by the conquest of Ethiopia. Colonies came to seem more important than ever to the British and Free French during the Second World War for recruiting forces and establishing strategic bases. The British and French clearly expected to retain their empires after the war, perhaps with greater local autonomy as dominions, but tied nonetheless to their imperial systems.

Instead, the European empires were almost all swept away in the years between 1945 and 1960. The eclipse of the power of European states during the war destroyed whatever legitimacy their colonial regimes had possessed, and the exhaustion of Britain and France after the war precluded any successful efforts to reestablish that authority. The United States was favorably inclined at the end of the war to colonial self-determination, for reasons of both sentiment and self-interest. The Soviet Union and, after 1948, Communist China, offered support and encouragement to anticolonial revolutions. There emerged in the Third World a generation of skilled guerrilla tacticians and nationalist political leaders who successfully exploited the heightened expectations, the swollen populations, and the land hunger that European contact itself had generated. It was taken for granted that the Class A Mandates held under the League of Nations between the wars would now accede to independence. In this way, the remaining Middle Eastern countries emerged as sovereign states, though not without some rearguard fighting by the French in Syria and Lebanon in May 1945. The Class B and C Mandates in Africa and the Pacific were transferred to trusteeship under the United Nations for what turned out to be in most cases a final fifteen years or so of colonial supervision. The British had realized during the war that they could not rule India. Independence was agreed to in 1946, and amidst dreadful communal violence between Hindus and Muslims, the new states of India and Pakistan came into existence in 1947. The Dutch lost Indonesia after bitter fighting in 1948. No European state had lost a colony to insurrection between 1825 and 1940; none successfully kept a colony by force after 1945.

The Cold War soon amplified every colonial struggle into an arena for superpower competition. The day was now past when a European state could quietly stifle a colonial independence movement while others looked away. As the Soviet Union and, after 1948, Communist China proclaimed that communism was the only route to independence, the United States swung around to support for Europeans' efforts to hang on to overseas possessions.

No European state tried harder to reclaim its empire than France. It was through the colonies, after all, that the Gaullist Free French had advanced toward the liberation of the motherland. The Empire seemed more essential than ever for French revival. France engaged nonstop, but futilely, in one colonial war after another during sixteen years after World War II: first against the Communist-led Vietminh in Indochina (1946–1954), and then against the nationalist FLN *(Front de Libération Nationale)* in Algeria (1954–1961). Before the final French defeat in Indochina at Dien Bien Phu, the United States had reached the point of supplying 80 percent of their matériel. After the French departure in 1954, the United States supplanted France as the main protector of the nonCommunist parts of Indochina: the Republic of South Vietnam, and Laos. This French defeat involved only professional soldiers,

France fought from 1946 to 1954 to keep its colony in Indochina. Although the French Army had locally superior firepower near the coast, as in this picture of the surrender of an inhabitant of the village of Phu Ly, the Vietminh (Vietnamese Communist movement) had greater mobility and control over the population.

but the officers returned from it embittered against the Fourth Republic that had not supported them and the United States that had supplanted them, and eager to use their new-found guerrilla warfare skills not only against future colonial rebels but against their domestic opponents in France as well.

French draftees were mobilized for the war against the Algerian independence movement. In this way, French civilians for the first time shared the French army's frustration at the failure of modern weapons to deal with guerrillas hidden in rocky hills and sympathetic villages. As cases of French atrocities began to be revealed, life in France in the late 1950s was poisoned by bitter division between critics of a cruel, fruitless war and those who saw France defending Western civilization against Communist–Arab barbarism. Army officers and French settlers, frightened that the government was losing Algeria to the FLN through irresolution and division, took matters into their own hands in May 1958. A crowd of settlers invaded government headquarters in Algiers, and officers who were resolved to keep Algeria French at all costs took over from French civilian authorities. They next seized the island of Corsica and threatened to send paratroops to Paris. General de Gaulle announced from retirement that he was ready to save the Republic once more. Unable to get the army or police to obey orders to crush the rebellion, the Fourth Republic gave way, unmourned, to the strong presidency of de Gaulle and a more authoritarian Fifth Republic. The one Cold War change of regime in Western Europe had thus been nationalist and conservative.

The British also poured their dwindling resources into imperial holding operations. In the 1950s, they struggled against oil nationalization in Iran and tried to mediate an intractable civil war between Greeks and Turks on Cyprus. They were successful in crushing a revolt by Chinese in Malaya but only at the price of granting Malayan independence.

One of the most spectacular European military operations in the 1950s was the Suez Campaign of 1956. Britain and France had stepped into the vacuum left by the collapse of the Ottoman Empire in 1918. Arab resentment at seeing their national aspirations thwarted by British mandates over Palestine and Iraq and French mandates over Syria and Lebanon simmered between the wars. It was raised to fever pitch by the Zionists' success in creating a Jewish state in part of Palestine in 1948. A new generation of angry young Arab middle-class leaders, such as the Egyptian Colonel Gamal Abdel Nasser, threw out some of the corrupt pro-Western monarchies of the Middle East and turned to the Soviet Union for aid. Egypt and Syria accepted Soviet arms in 1955. Then, when the United States refused to provide funds to Egypt for a new high dam at Aswan on the Nile, Nasser nationalized the Suez Canal. Britain, France, and Israel devised a joint lightning attack that was supposed to seize the canal and Cairo. When the operation took too long and the Soviets threatened to intervene, the United States brought economic and political pressure on Anthony Eden, Guy Mollet, and Israeli premier David Ben-Gurion to withdraw their forces and accept United Nations mediation.

The Suez Campaign elicited the first public example of converging United States–Soviet will to restrain crises. And it showed Europeans how limited were their prestige and independence, regardless of whether the superpowers got along or whether they quarreled. The humiliation of Suez suggested to some Europeans (such as de Gaulle) that they must take their own destinies back from American hands, and to others that the old European states could accomplish something only by combining their forces.

WESTERN EUROPE: THE MOVEMENT FOR UNION

The ideal of European unity was at flood tide in 1945. Two impulses pushed it forward. One was the vow never again to allow their national rivalries to provoke a war. The other was a keen awareness that, alone, the former Great Powers of Europe no longer had the capacity to act freely on a world stage dominated by superpowers.

There were two possible kinds of response. Europeans could throw themselves into the arms of one superpower to save themselves from the other. Or they could unite their fragmented energies into a larger unit—a united Europe—and become a new superpower in their own right. Europeans did some of both after 1945.

A sense of Continental European identity went back as far as Latin Christendom. After the modern European nation-states had taken shape and had waged repeated wars against one another, periodic proposals appeared for some substitute to the system of competing sovereign states. Satisfied powers proposed international organization to preserve the status quo, from the European federation and arbitration council proposed by the Abbé de Saint-Pierre at the end of the reign of Louis XIV (1713) through Tsar Alexander I's Holy Alliance of 1815 to the 1930 proposal of a United States of Europe by French leaders Herriot and Briand. After the First World War, European businessmen proposed organizing the European economy against American competition. Europeans on the left, from utopians like Saint-Simon to Marxist internationalists, expected revolution to replace warring dynasties and monopolies with a united world of productive workers. The schemes that came closest to realization were those backed by conquest: the spread of the French revolutionary constitution across Europe by Napoleon I, and Hitler's European Economic Sphere *(Großwirtschaftsraum)* organized against the USSR and the Anglo-Americans.

The liberation of 1945 made European union not only current but practicable: The totality of destruction left everything fluid. Left-leaning European resistance movements spoke hopefully of a "European federation, democratic, open to all European peoples including England and the USSR."[12] The conservative anti-Hitler movement in Germany, which had hoped for a separate peace with the Anglo-Americans in time to turn together on the Russians, advocated rather a "Europe unified on the base of Christianity and German predominance, designed to avert Bolshevism."[13]

Architects of European Union

When steps were actually taken toward European union in the late 1940s, the Cold War had so intensified that the anti-Bolshevik motive mingled with the desire to end European fratricide. Many of the architects of a new Europe came from the Catholic Rhineland, the border terrain across which Frenchmen and Germans had been killing each other for centuries. On the French side was Robert Schuman, foreign minister ten times in the four years after 1948. Schuman came from one of those borderland families that had lived under both French and German flags and had seen the horrors of war too often. Schuman himself had been a German officer in the First World War, a French deputy for restored Alsace after 1919, and a founder of the French Christian Democratic Party (MRP) in 1945. Indeed, between Schuman and his colleague George Bidault, the MRP controlled the French Foreign Ministry for the first eight years and twenty ministries of the Fourth Republic.

Further down the Rhine on the German side was Konrad Adenauer, the Catholic mayor of Cologne in the 1920s. As an opponent of Protestant Social Democratic Prussia, Adenauer had been at least marginally involved in plans for an autonomous Rhineland state in the early 1920s. The Nazi regime removed him from office and subjected him to periods of internment. As the German Christian Democrat leader and first chancellor of West Germany after 1949, Adenauer was ready to listen to Schuman, as was the Italian Christian Democrat leader Alcide De Gasperi.

---

[12]Henri Michel and Boris Mirkine-Guetzévitch, *Les Idées politiques et sociales de la Résistance* (Paris, 1954), p. 399.

[13]Ernst Jünger, *L'Appel,* quoted in Flanner, p. 273.

These Christian Democrat architects of European unity were joined by some anti-Communist Socialists, whose traditional internationalism was colored by fear of further Soviet expansion. The Belgian Socialist leader Paul-Henri Spaak, prime minister of his country after 1947, spoke of the "creation of a Europe united economically and politically" as the work to which he gave "the most heart, will, and sustained effort."[14] Spaak was to be the first president of the OEEC, the European organization of recipients of Marshall Plan aid, and later was to be secretary-general of NATO. The British Labour government's foreign secretary, Ernest Bevin, supported cooperation among the non-Communist European nations without accepting his country's full integration into Europe.

European union also found fervent supporters among Western European businessmen and high civil servants. Convinced that the individual European states offered too narrow a scope for economic, technical or social progress, enlightened businessmen like the Frenchman Jean Monnet worked for a unified European economy on the scale of the United States.

Pressures for Union

Economic rationalization and Cold War alarms provided the immediate impetus for Western European union. "Europeans, let us be modest. It is the fear of Stalin and the daring views of [General] Marshall which led us into the right path," wrote Spaak.[15] The United States government, committed to efficiency as well as to prevention of a return to the closed economic nationalisms of the 1930s, required that Marshall Plan funds be funneled through an integrated multinational agency, the Organization for European Economic Cooperation (OEEC), rather than given piecemeal to individual states.

Stalin's acts in 1948 stimulated military alliances in Western Europe. The Czech *coup* of February 1948 and the Berlin Blockade the following summer convinced a number of Western Europeans that the Soviet Union would be more powerful than Germany in the postwar world. Suddenly nothing seemed to stand between the most powerful army on earth and the English Channel. As de Gaulle said in 1947, the Soviet army was "no further from France than two days of a bicycle race." It is difficult to convey vividly enough the dread felt by Western Europeans in the late 1940s that the Soviet armies would march west.

The first Western European responses were traditional military alliances. Britain and France had already concluded a mutual defense agreement, the Treaty of Dunkirk, on March 4, 1947: It provided the firm Continental obligation that the British had steadfastly refused after the First World War. This treaty was directed explicitly against German revival. Immediately after the Czech *coup*, on March 17, 1948, Britain and France joined with the Benelux countries[16] in the Treaty of Brussels to form a common defense system, directed this time at the Soviet threat.

---

[14]Paul-Henri Spaak, *Combats inachevés*, vol. 2 (Paris, 1969), p. 11.

[15]Ibid., p. 12.

[16]Belgium, the Netherlands, and Luxemburg had formed a Customs Union, or free-trade area, in 1944. Although each nation retained its full sovereignty, Benelux regulated the economies of the three members as a unit.

By themselves the Western European nations were no match for the 200 Soviet divisions, the most powerful army in the world. At that time the United States was just beginning to reverse its postwar demobilization. A major shift in Washington was the Senate resolution of June 1948,[17] sponsored by Arthur Vandenberg, Republican of Michigan, who converted from isolationism. The Vandenberg resolution advocated American association with regional collective defense arrangements elsewhere in the world, a striking departure from the rapid American withdrawal of troops in 1918 and 1919 and in 1945 and 1946, and from the political isolationism of the prewar Republican Party.

Union for Defense: The Creation of NATO

Armed with the promise of bipartisan United States support, British Foreign Secretary Ernest Bevin led the way in creating a five-nation defense coordinating command under the Treaty of Brussels. Field Marshal Bernard L. Montgomery, the greatest British commander of the Second World War, set up an international command staff at the palace of Fontainebleau, outside Paris, in the summer of 1948. By then, Bevin and Spaak were exploring the idea of a much broader collective defense arrangement against the Soviet Union. The result was NATO—the North Atlantic Treaty Organization—created on April 4, 1949.

NATO went far beyond the traditional European military alliance. It committed the United States, for the first time, to a long-term military partnership outside the Americas in peacetime. Together with Canada and ten European nations, the United States agreed to a twenty-year alliance in which "an attack upon one" of the members in Europe, North Africa, or North America would be considered an "attack upon all" (Article 5). In pooling their military units under international command, the European members integrated their forces more closely than they had in any previous military alliance. The participants joined not merely in the defense of territory but to "safeguard the freedom, common heritage, and civilization of their peoples" and to bring about the closer integration of the North Atlantic area. At the end of 1950, the Supreme Allied Commander–Europe (SACEUR), American general Dwight Eisenhower, set up his international command at Paris.

Problems of European Unity

Uniting the Western democracies for defense raised two very thorny issues. Who was included in the "free world" (as the phrase soon described it)? Semifascist Portugal was a NATO member from the beginning;[18] Greece and Turkey joined in October 1951; should West Germany be included? And how far should the European nations go in submerging their individual sovereignties in a supranational body?

[17]Only four senators voted against; seventy-nine for.

[18]Spain joined NATO in 1982, confirmed by a referendum in 1986. For military strengths in Europe as of 1984, see chapter 20, p. 602n.18. East Germany merged with West Germany in 1990, and Poland, Hungary, and the Czech Republic joined NATO in 1999 making a total membership of nineteen. Seven more joined in 2004 (p. 676).

COLD WAR EUROPE IN THE 1950s

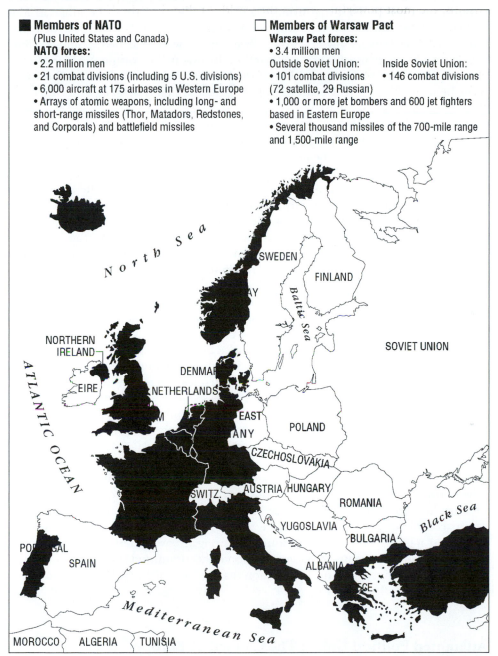

■ Members of NATO
(Plus United States and Canada)
NATO forces:
• 2.2 million men
• 21 combat divisions (including 5 U.S. divisions)
• 6,000 aircraft at 175 airbases in Western Europe
• Arrays of atomic weapons, including long- and
short-range missiles (Thor, Matadors, Redstones,
and Corporals) and battlefield missiles

□ Members of Warsaw Pact
Warsaw Pact forces:
• 3.4 million men
Outside Soviet Union: Inside Soviet Union:
• 101 combat divisions   • 146 combat divisions
(72 satellite, 29 Russian)
• 1,000 or more jet bombers and 600 jet fighters
based in Eastern Europe
• Several thousand missiles of the 700-mile range
and 1,500-mile range

The issue of Germany's role in the anti-Soviet alliance agitated Western European foreign policy from the formation of the Federal German Republic in May 1949 until West Germany's inclusion in NATO in October 1954. The issue of supranational authority was entwined with it. If Germany were rearmed, would German officers then command French or Dutch or British troops within NATO? Should European soldiers be organized by national units or should a genuine European army be formed in which German, French, British, Italian, Belgian, and Dutch soldiers mingled in the same unit?

The French were the most sensitive on both points. A probable majority of French citizens of all political persuasions was opposed to rearming Germans in any form. But partisans of European unity reasoned that since Germany would eventually rearm in some fashion, the best safeguard for the future was to submerge German soldiers in a fully integrated European army. The outbreak of the Korean War in June 1950 made the question urgent, as the United States pressed vigorously for West German rearmament. To block the creation of a separate German army, the French premier René Pleven proposed a truly supranational army, the European Defense Community (EDC). Although Pleven's proposal received support in other European states in 1951 and 1952, the French parliament itself voted EDC down in June 1954. After that, the French got what they least wanted. Not only was Germany rearmed, but a separate German army was recreated only ten years after Hitler's death. Although still forbidden possession of nuclear, biological, and chemical weapons by the terms of its entry into NATO, West Germany was well on its way to assuming major weight in the Western alliance by 1955.

German officials attended their first NATO ministers' meeting in Paris on May 7, 1955, ten years to the day after the German armies' surrender at Reims in 1945. The chief German military representative, who came discreetly dressed in civilian clothes, was General Hans Speidel, a senior officer in the German occupation of France from 1941 to 1943. It seemed, wrote Janet Flanner, "the strangest week since the end of the war, because all that was postwar ended too."[19]

The other thorny issue, still to be resolved, was the supranational nature of the new Europe. Should Europe remain a coalition of sovereign states or should the new European institutions possess authority to make sovereign decisions affecting defense, foreign policy, and finance? NATO units were international only at the senior command level, and the failure of EDC in 1954 determined that Western European nations would not relinquish sovereignty over their individual armed services. Many Europeans remained passionately committed, however, to the creation of supranational political institutions as the basis of a new Western European union.

Attempted Political Union: The Council of Europe

The first attempt to found common political institutions for Europe was a kind of European parliament, the Council of Europe, set up at Strasbourg, France, in May

---

[19]Flanner, p. 272.

1949. In some prointegration quarters, the Council of Europe was regarded as the future legislative branch of a United States of Europe. The British, however, under both Labour and Conservative governments, prevented this and all other bodies to which they belonged from acquiring any independent supranational functions during the 1950s and 1960s. The Labour government of 1945 to 1951, like the Scandinavian socialist governments, remained suspicious of a Continental integration movement dominated by Catholics and technocrats. Moreover, British leaders of both parties felt that any absorption of British sovereignty in a new European state was incompatible with Britain's special role as head of the Commonwealth. Although less imperial minded than the Tories, British Labour was strongly attached to the preferential trading agreements that brought inexpensive food from Canada and New Zealand. British Labour was also insular. Its delegate to the creation of the Council of Europe, William Whiteley, had never before been out of England.

The Council of Europe, therefore, was not the step toward political integration that its first president, Paul-Henri Spaak, and others had hoped. Since its members were not elected directly by European citizens but were delegations of parliamentarians sent by member countries prorated by size (three each for Iceland and Luxemburg; eighteen for France, Germany, Italy, Britain), the council represented governments and political patronage rather than a popular electorate. Its main achievement was the European Convention on Human Rights (1950) and the European Court of Human Rights set up to enforce it. Even though the council eventually included parliamentarians of forty-one nations, its annual meetings at Strasbourg were better known for gastronomy and abstract language than for any independent political force. As the British political scientist Wilfrid Pickles observed, the Council of Europe resembled a real parliament about as much as an adulterous weekend at Brighton resembled marriage: "it offers some of the pleasures but none of the responsibilities."[20]

With the parliamentary route to European integration blocked by the stillborn Council of Europe and the European army route to integration blocked by the failure of the European Defense Community, the movement for European unity would have to follow other paths, and it would have to proceed without Britain. Grand designs for political union from the top came to seem utopian. Instead, supranational institutions took root and grew on the economic level and with limited functions. Partisans of wider European union could take comfort in the hope that as supranational decision making became established in limited economic sectors, the effects of these decisions might spill over into political arenas and bring about an organic growth of common institutions.

Economic Union: The European Coal and Steel Community and the Common Market

The Marshall Plan had prompted the creation of the multinational OEEC in 1947 to disburse the funds. The OEEC was only advisory, however, and could not make

---

[20]Quoted in Howard Bliss, *The Political Development of the European Community: A Documentary Collection* (Waltham, Mass., 1970), p. 5.

policy for its member states. The first step toward a genuine economic supranational institution was the Schuman Plan. French foreign minister Robert Schuman proposed in 1950 that "the entire Franco-German production of coal and steel be placed under a common High Authority," as "the first step in the federation of Europe." In this fashion, war between France and Germany would become "not merely inconceivable but physically impossible." Robert Schuman's daring initiative produced the European Coal and Steel Community (ECSC) of 1951.

The Schuman Plan was a radical departure from other moves toward European unity, both in the completeness of the integration proposed and in the limited sector to be integrated. In that way, it neatly sidestepped the deadlocked debate between federalists and unionists. Since its functions of economic planning were new, it did not amputate precious prerogatives from existing states nor trespass on sensitive areas of military command or political choice. In political terms, it offered a dramatic gain to those Europeans who longed for some way to transcend the old nationalisms. In economic terms, it promised to replace the marginally profitable steel mills and coal mines previously kept going for national purposes with the most efficient exploitation of Western European coal and steel irrespective of national boundaries. For the French, it offered access to Ruhr coal plus some degree of international control over the inevitable but feared German economic recovery. For the Germans, it offered access to Lorraine iron ore plus escape from economic interference by the Allied occupation authorities (still dedicated to "decartelizing" Germany) via a voice in the international management of European coal and steel.

The most striking novelty of the ECSC was its top administrative agency, the High Authority. This executive committee of nine technical experts[21] administered the coal and steel resources of the six member states: France, Germany, Italy, and the Benelux countries. Since they were not subject to electoral control and since they could not be dismissed during their term of office, members of the High Authority enjoyed an important measure of power independent of the member state governments. They could set and regulate prices, levy fees to cover the costs of their operations (a form of taxing power), and encourage or discourage investment for the most efficient use of resources according to purely technical criteria. In the one limited sector in its charge, the High Authority introduced genuine supranational decision making to European institutions.

The European Coal and Steel Community was a success. Coinciding with the beginning of the postwar boom in 1953 and no doubt helping to encourage it, the ECSC acquired a reputation for stimulating economic growth that it would have had difficulty winning under depression conditions. Early success overcame remaining suspicions among both business and labor. At the moment when the merger of state sovereignties was suffering an apparently mortal setback with the defeat of the European Defense Community in the French parliament in 1954, the thriving ECSC pointed the way toward a different mode of unification: sector-by-sector economic integration, followed by spillover into such political realms as wages and social policy.

---

[21]Eight were named by the six participant governments; the ninth was chosen by co-optation by the other eight members.

The European Coal and Steel Community provided the roots for the European Common Market. The Common Market's members were the same: France, Germany, Italy, Belgium, Holland, and Luxembourg, known as "the Six." Its concept of economic integration by sectors was a lesson learned from the ECSC. The immediate impetus for its creation was the European humiliation of the Suez crisis of 1956. The Treaties of Rome (March 25, 1957) united the Six in two agencies: the European Atomic Energy Agency (Euratom) and the European Economic Community (EEC), better known as the Common Market. They went into effect on January 1, 1958, opening a new era of European integration.

The Common Market created within Western Europe a single free-trade area roughly comparable to the United States in size and population (175 million people), within which goods, capital, and workers could move freely. Tariffs between the six members were to be lowered to zero in stages over the following twelve to fifteen years. Since no one member could pursue wage or social security policies, or support farm prices, in a manner substantially different from that of the other partners without distorting trade within the Common Market, the expected spillover effect led the EEC into the business of harmonizing the economic and social policies of the Six. Thus the Common Market was far more than merely a free-trade zone like the European Free Trade Association (EFTA) that the British, Danes, Norwegians, Swedes, Swiss, Austrians, and Portuguese (known as "the Outer Seven") set up by way of response in 1959.

Harmonizing social and economic policy among the Six obviously suggested some kind of supranational authority and the transfer to the EEC of powers usually reserved to sovereign states. Here the EEC went less far than had the European Coal and Steel Community. Its top directing agency, the EEC Executive, resembled the Coal and Steel High Authority in that it was a body of international civil servants whose loyalties tended to be attached to the community as a whole rather than to their country of origin. Overall policies, however, were set by the EEC Council of Ministers who spoke for the member state governments, and a unanimity rule in all important matters gave each member state a veto.

The Common Market took root and flourished. It contributed to, as well as profited from, the unprecedented prosperity of Europe in the 1960s. It met all its economic deadlines ahead of time. The last internal tariffs were abolished in 1968, after ten years instead of the anticipated twelve to fifteen. Trade among the Six grew steeply: Trade between France and Germany, for example, increased by about 40 percent over the first nine years of the EEC. Millions of workers from the backward regions of the Six, such as southern Italy, moved freely to work in France and Germany. A corps of dedicated international civil servants emerged in Brussels to staff the agencies of a new bureaucracy. National animosities abated within the Six to the point where German NATO troops trained on French soil in the middle 1960s almost without public notice. Just over ten years after the Common Market had begun, observers could speak of Western Europe as an "emergent nation."[22]

---

[22]Carl J. Friedrich, *Europe: An Emergent Nation?* (New York, 1969).

COMMON MARKET AND COMECON 1961[23]

SOVIET RIPOSTES IN EASTERN EUROPE

In response to Western European unification movements, the Soviet Union led Eastern Europe into supranational organizations. Its economic counterpart to the Marshall Plan and the OEEC was the Council for Mutual Economic Assistance (popularly known as COMECON), established in January 1949. COMECON organized and facilitated trade among the satellites and with the Soviet Union, mostly by

[23]Britain, Ireland, and Denmark were admitted in 1973 to what had been called since 1967 "The European Community"; Greece was admitted in 1981. Spain and Portugal entered on January 1, 1986. Sweden, Finland, and Austria joined in 1995. Negotiations to expand "The European Union" (the name since 1993) further to the east were advancing slowly in 2001.

barter agreements (in the absence of market prices). It standardized railway gauges and electrical grids and established the "Friendship" pipeline to deliver Soviet oil to Central Europe. But unlike the Common Market, COMECON included its giant neighbor as a member. Thus, it served mainly to hitch the Central European economies to Soviet postwar reconstruction priorities.

Five days after Germany joined NATO, in May 1955, the seven satellites and the Soviet Union signed a twenty-five year mutual defense treaty, the Warsaw Pact. The Soviet Union's domination of the Warsaw Pact was even more complete than the United States domination of NATO, for it served as a cover for outright military repression as in Hungary in 1956 and Czechoslovakia in 1968.

Thus, the continent of Europe was divided between two great opposing military alliances. Neither side dared infringe the other's sphere of influence. In the same month that it formed the Warsaw Pact, the Soviet Union finally agreed to conclude a long-debated peace treaty with Austria. Soviet and Western troops withdrew from that country, which became a neutral buffer between the two blocs.

The Austrian treaty was a sign that by 1955 both sides wanted stability more than gain. The USSR also exchanged ambassadors with West Germany at that time. Similarly, the United States did not intervene in Hungary in 1956. Each side tried to unsettle the other by propaganda. The West's Radio Free Europe beamed jazz and unpleasant truths about the USSR eastwards. The East dangled the prospect of German reunification in exchange for a neutralized Central Europe, as in the Rapacki Plan put forward by the Polish foreign minister in 1957. It found support among Bevanites in England and part of the Continental left, but it was inconceivable without dismantling NATO, which was surely one of its purposes.

Each side tried to solidify its own zone. The United States used its economic and cultural influence against communism in Western Europe; the Federal Republic of Germany banned the Communist Party altogether. Khrushchev, as we have seen, tried to pinch off the Western presence in the four-power enclave of Berlin at the end of the 1950s. When that failed, he had the Berlin Wall built in August 1961. The two camps glowered at each other across the wall, militarily deadlocked: the Soviets stronger in conventional armed forces, the West in nuclear retaliatory power.

It was by producing economic plenty that the Western side was going to prevail over COMECON and the Warsaw Pact. The residents of drab, cheerless East Berlin, looking out over West Berlin's *Kurfürstendamm*, with its brightly lit cafés and traffic jams of Mercedes and Volkswagens, would not postpone the good life forever.

SUGGESTIONS FOR FURTHER READING

Recommended works on the origins of the Cold War are found in the bibliography to chapter 15. For its continuation, see John L. Gaddis, *The Long Peace*[*] (1989), and the valuable chapter "The Berlin Crisis" in Marc Trachtenberg, *History and Strategy*[*] (1991). Charles S. Maier, ed., *The Cold War in Europe,*[*] 3rd ed. (1997), contains stimulating articles on its impact, both domestic and international.

In addition to works noted at the end of chapter 16, the beginnings and course of European integration are surveyed in Derek W. Urwin, *The Community of Europe: A History of European Integration since 1945,*[*] 3rd ed. (2004). Andrew Moravcsik, *The Choice for Europe: Social Purpose and State Power from Messina to Maastricht*[*] (1998), concludes that European integration was pushed forward by the member states. Alan Milward finds similarly in *The European Rescue of the Nation State,* 2nd ed. (2000), that the European states adopted economic integration to further national ends. Jean Monnet's *Memoirs* (1978) reveal the Father of Europe's methods and passion. See also Douglas Brinkley and Clifford Hackett, *Jean Monnet: The Path to European Unity*[*] (1992), and François Duchene, *Jean Monnet: The First Statesman of Interdependence*[*] (1994). John Gillingham, *European Integration: Superstate or New Market Economy?*[*] (2003), argues that the supranationalism of Monnet was a dead end.

For European military integration and German rearmament, see Edward Furdson, *The European Defense Community* (1980). One may still consult F. Roy Willis, *France, Germany, and the New Europe, 1945–1967* (1968), and Robert McGeehan, *The German Rearmament Question*[*] (1971).

Lawrence S. Kaplan is the author of standard works on NATO, for example *NATO and the United States: The Enduring Alliance*[*] (1994) and *The Long Entanglement: The United States and NATO After Fifty Years*[*] (1999). There are interesting essays in Francis H. Heller and John Gillingham, eds., *NATO: The Founding of the Atlantic Alliance and the Integration of Europe* (1992), and, by the same editors, *The United States and the Integration of Europe: Legacies of the Postwar Era* (1996).

In addition to works on Soviet foreign policy by Adam Ulam mentioned earlier, see Alvin Z. Rubinstein, *Soviet Foreign Policy since World War II,* 4th ed. (1991). Soviet military policy is considered by Honoré M. Catudal, *Soviet Nuclear Strategy from Stalin to Gorbachev* (1989); western military policy by Andrew Pierre, *Nuclear Weapons in Europe* (1984) and *The Conventional Defence of Europe* (1986).

For East European economic integration, consult Jenny Brine, *COMECON: The Rise and Fall of an International Socialist Organization* (1992); for military integration, use Robin A. Remington, *Warsaw Pact,*[*] 2nd ed. (1996); and David Holloway and James M. Sharp, eds., *Warsaw Pact: Alliance in Transition?* (1984). Charles Gati, *The Bloc That Failed* (1990), gives their postmortem.

Western–Soviet conflict over Berlin is studied in Robert M. Slusser, *The Berlin Crisis of 1961*[*] (1973), and Honoré M. Catudal, *Kennedy and the Berlin Crisis* (1986).

Recent works on the loss of European empires include M. E. Chamberlin,

Decolonization: The Fall of the European Empires,[*] 2nd ed. (1999); Raymond F. Betts, *Decolonization,*[*] 2nd ed. (2004); and (for Britain) D. A. Low, *Eclipse of Empire*[*] (1993). For Britain's withdrawal from south Asia, one can begin with Judith M. Brown, *Modern India,*[*] 2nd ed. (1994), and Ayesha Jalal, *The Sole Spokesman: Jinnah, the Moslem League, and the Demand for Pakistan*[*] (1994). Africa is treated by John D. Hargreaves, *Decolonization in Africa,*[*] 2nd ed. (1996); David Birmingham, *The Decolonization of Africa*[*] (1995); Henry S. Wilson, *African Decolonization*[*] (1999); and Prosser Gifford and Wm. Roger Louis, *Decolonization and African Independence* (1988). For the French war in Indochina, see Jacques Dalloz, *The War in Indochina* (1990). A gripping work on the Franco-Algerian War, based on materials from both sides, is Alistair Horne, *Savage War of Peace*[*] (reprint ed. 2002); see also John Talbott, *The War without a Name* (1980). Anthony Clayton, *The Wars of French Decolonization*[*] (1995), covers both. Howard M. Sachar, *Europe Leaves the Middle East, 1936–1954* (1972), may be supplemented by Anthony Gorst, *The Suez Crisis*[*] (1997), and Diane B. Kunz, *The Economic Diplomacy of the Suez Crisis*[*] (1991).

Additional Internet links related to this chapter are available on the Europe in the 20th Century Web site: http://www.history.wadsworth.com/paxton04.

You can also explore images, interactive timelines, and maps related to this chapter on our Western Civilization Resource Center: http://history.wadsworth.com

A traffic jam in Rome reflects the joys and frustrations of Western European consumer society.

19

The "New Europe": Consumer Societies and Mass Culture in the West, 1953–1973

After the First World War, Europeans had struggled to regain the prosperity of 1914, that *belle epoque* to which people of property, at least, looked back with nostalgia. In the best years of the late 1920s boom, European production had not far exceeded that of 1914. During the depressed 1930s, production figures had fallen lower. In 1938, only Germany and Russia were producing much more than they had produced in 1914.

After the Second World War, the Western European economies not only recovered those long-sought 1914 levels, they surged ahead to reach the highest levels of prosperity they had ever known. Postwar recovery was completed by about 1953 in most of Western Europe, and the harsh late 1940s began to recede into memory. Then, instead of slackening, the Western European economies took off into sustained growth. By the mid-1960s, production in Italy, Germany, and Holland, for example, was three times the 1914 level. Although the pace of growth slackened at times (as in the brief "recession" of 1966 and 1967 in England and Germany), modern

Europe had never experienced so long a period of growth uninterrupted by depression or financial crisis. Poverty was still very real in southern Italy, the Balkans, and Spain, and the Eastern European economies remained far behind, but there were now whole regions in Europe, such as Scandinavia, where poverty was virtually unknown. The 1914 figures—along with nostalgia for some past *belle epoque*—had become simply irrelevant for Europeans of the 1960s. Riches had never been so great or so widespread.

A quarter century of almost uninterrupted boom by the early 1970s was a phenomenon that the business cycle specialists of the 1930s had not trained economists to interpret. Postwar reconstruction was bound to stimulate the European economies for a time. But economic growth continued long after that immediate impetus had been spent and beyond what past history of boom and bust had permitted anyone to expect. What sustained such long-running growth?

The credit claimed by state planners and Keynesian economists in France, Italy, and England applied less to Germany, where the success of the "Social Market Economy" required some explanation other than state economic intervention. Even there, however, the state increased public investment when German economic growth slowed down alarmingly in the "recession" of 1966 and 1967. Each government's determination to keep employment high had something to do with maintaining the boom.

The increasing speed of technological advance also deserved credit for continued growth. Technical innovation moved much faster from idea to commercial application in the twentieth century, especially after the technological stimulus of the Second World War. It had taken more than a century for the steam engine to evolve from the first sketches to the first practical devices of the eighteenth century; nuclear power, by contrast, went from theory to producing electricity in less than a generation. Similarly, in the electronic field, radio tubes had not gone into mass production until the 1920s, even though Thomas Edison had made a prototype in 1884. By contrast, transistors (1948) and integrated circuits (1958) went into widespread use almost at once in radios and computers.[1] Wider technical education and commercial expectations hastened the application of inventions, which in turn generated new production.

The most decisive changes seem to have occurred in the realm of attitudes. After a long generation of relative stagnation that lasted from 1914 to the early 1950s, Europeans recaptured some of the feverish energy of the Industrial Revolution's beginnings of the late eighteenth and early nineteenth centuries. Governments and businessmen began to value growth more than security. Consumers who snapped up television sets, refrigerators, and automobiles and then replaced them every few years formed what looked like a permanent boom market.

The result was what Andrew Shonfield, a defender of the apparent success of "neocapitalism" in Western Europe in the 1960s, called "supergrowth."[2] Super-

---

[1]These examples come from David S. Landes, *The Unbound Prometheus* (Cambridge, Mass., 1969), pp. 518–519.

[2]Andrew Shonfield, *Modern Capitalism: The Changing Balance of Public and Private Power,* corrected ed. (Oxford, England, 1969).

growth was not simply an expanded version of prewar European economies. It did not resemble the normalcy of the late 1920s. It built on two elements with self-sustaining momentum: high mass consumption, and continued state welfare and planning policies. At first, it was accompanied by an apparent decline in class conflict, but in 1968, student and worker protests revealed new kinds of dissatisfaction appropriate to consumer societies.

CONSUMER SOCIETIES

British rationing, the last vestige of wartime controls in Western Europe, ended in 1954.[3] Until then, no British boy or girl under eighteen had ever known free shopping. The end of fifteen years of scarcity would have produced something of a buying spree under any conditions. Among the young, it was accompanied by new ideas about saving and spending. In the British postwar welfare state no one needed to starve in unemployment or old age, or go without medicine. So, unlike their elders, young workers began to spend what they earned. This pattern was common to much of Europe.

In the early 1950s, an American social anthropologist, Lawrence Wylie, lived with his family for a year in a remote village in southern France. He found the villagers cautious and parsimonious, distrustful of the state and of their neighbors, and conditioned by ages of war and revolution against flaunting their little savings in conspicuous consumption. The men were so pessimistic about renewed war that they would not make any long-term investment.

> Plant an apricot orchard so the Russians and Americans can use it as a battlefield? Thanks, not so dumb.[4]

Then the Wylies returned for a visit in 1961. They found the old women in black shawls beginning to be outnumbered by noisy children and brightly clad young women. The men were now willing to borrow to buy tractors in the expectation that economic growth and political stability could be counted on. Their wives were trying out washing machines.

The demand function of the economy had been transformed. Purchases did not decline when postwar reconstruction had been completed, because welfare states diminished the necessity to save against disaster, because planned economies seemed to reduce the risk of depression, because young people spent more and more, and because rising birth rates produced more young people. Two decades of full employment and rising real wages bred still further confidence.

One prominent sign of that confidence was the spread of installment buying, or purchases on credit. Frugal artisans and close-handed peasants had considered it a calamity in the past when the need for raw materials or seed forced them into debt

---

[3]Rationing continued in some Eastern European countries into the 1960s.

[4]Lawrence Wylie, *Village in the Vaucluse,* 2nd ed. (Cambridge, Mass., 1964), p. 33.

with its attendant ruinous interest and risks of foreclosure by the moneylender. By contrast, postwar Western European consumers embraced new schemes for paying for television sets or automobiles over time. The British, to take one example, purchased goods worth over £400 million "on the never-never" in 1957; the figure had tripled by 1965.[5]

The most coveted consumer goods were television sets and automobiles. Television figures are most accurate for Britain, where the state requires a license for each radio or television receiver. Although nearly 11 million radio licenses were issued in 1947, only 14,500 television licenses were sold. Barely twenty years later, in 1965, the British public bought 13 million television licenses.[6] Once a rich sportsman's toy, the automobile had already reached a large middle-class market in Western Europe between the wars. But the consumer economy truly arrived in the 1960s when the lower middle class and skilled workers, in their turn, stepped up from bicycles to motorcyles and then, increasingly, to inexpensive automobiles. The simple mass-produced Citroën 2CV (*deux chevaux,* or "two horse-power"), a kind of latter-day Model T Ford whose highly sophisticated front-wheel drive and clutchless transmission were planted in an ungainly rudimentary body, enabled millions of French people to own their first car. By the early 1970s, seven French adults in ten owned a car. Other Western European nations whose density of automobiles began to approach that of the United States were Sweden, West Germany, and Britain.[7]

Such goods as refrigerators, washing machines, and alcohol and tobacco also claimed high shares of consumer spending. Food, once the preponderant expenditure of the poor, now accounted for less than 50 percent of personal spending in most Western European countries for the first time. The main public amusement of the 1920s, the cinema, declined in favor of television.

Total production and total national wealth had grown dramatically in all the European nations. By 1967, the national per capita income had reached $2,480 in Switzerland, $2,046 in France, and $2,010 in West Germany as compared with $3,146 in the United States. But these aggregate figures do not tell us all we need to know about how the long Western European boom of the 1950s and 1960s affected society. We must look more closely at the distribution of wealth and at social mobility.

Distribution of Wealth

At the top, new fortunes were made in Western Europe. There was relatively little room for quick wealth in basic industry, unlike the opportunities opened by the early-nineteenth-century Industrial Revolution. Railroads, airlines, and coal mines were state property almost everywhere in Europe, and major steel companies

---

[5]Pauline Gregg, *The Welfare State* (Amherst, Mass., 1969), pp. 240, 350.

[6]François Bédarida, *A Social History of England, 1851–1990* (London, 1991). p. 264.

[7]Motor Vehicles per 1,000 population (1970): United States 532, Sweden 283, West Germany 253, Britain 244, Italy 206, Japan 172. *The New York Times,* April 8, 1973, sec. 1a, p. 8, and *Statistisk Årsbok för Sverige* (Stockholm, 1971), p. 176.

remained in private hands only in West Germany and in post-Labour Britain from 1951 to 1964, at which time the Labour government nationalized steel again. Several of the largest automobile manufacturers (Renault; Volkswagen until 1956) were state firms.

Some of the great European industrial dynasties saw their family firms slip into the hands of managers and technicians. The German metal and armaments firm of Krupp, which had survived Allied prosecution and plans for dismemberment after the Second World War, and had recovered great economic power in West Germany, encountered financial difficulties in 1969 and was put under state-appointed management on behalf of the shareholders. Other European family firms, such as Peugeot automobiles, were forced by competition into larger conglomerates. Of course, many of the industrial dynasties navigated these flood waters of the European boom successfully, such as FIAT's Giovanni Agnelli and the business machine magnate Arrigo Olivetti. The top managers and technicians of the new European enterprises also became wealthy men, although perhaps not on the scale of the heads of the former large family firms.

The new millionaires of postwar consumer societies were usually neither captains of industry in basic commodities nor the managers of huge firms. They were ambitious entrepreneurs in real estate, electric household appliances, mass communications, and entertainment. Some of the most spectacular of these new fortunes flourished in the relatively open market economy of West Germany. Axel Springer found himself at the end of the war with the ruins of his father's small printing shop in Hamburg and an idea: to sell printed schedules for radio programs. With the profits from this modest enterprise and a permit to publish from the Allied occupation authorities, Springer proceeded to build an empire of newspapers and slick magazines that by the 1960s was the fifth largest in the world. His *Bildzeitung*, a popular Sunday photo sheet, had the largest circulation of any European newspaper.

Another spectacular example was Max Grundig, a radio salesman before the war. He assembled a wheelbarrow load of tools in an old courtyard in the Nuremberg suburb of Fürth in 1945 and, with seven helpers, put together the first Grundig radio. This was a simple assemble-it-yourself kit that the public bought eagerly, since old radios had often been confiscated and new ones were rationed. Twenty years later, Grundig owned the largest television factory in Germany, the largest radio factory in Europe, and the largest sound-track factory in the world.

Some fortunes were built around the careers of successful popular musicians like the Beatles. An occasional fortune could be built in partnership with the state, such as Marcel Dassault's success in designing and building civil aircraft for Air France and Mirage fighter bombers for General de Gaulle's nuclear attack force, the *force de frappe*.

At the bottom, there was more disposable wealth than ever before. Even though prices rose almost constantly after the war, average real wages rose ahead of them through the 1950s and 1960s in Western Europe. Even in Great Britain, whose economic performance fell behind that of the Continent, average weekly earnings more than doubled between 1950 and 1961, while retail prices advanced by only about 50 percent.[8] Increased social services, such as free medical care, education, and subsidized public transportation, helped to bring some degree of security and even modest comfort to broad ranges of working people. In Continental Western Europe, an average of 36 percent of working families' income came from various fringe benefits paid by state social welfare agencies; in Italy, that figure was 51 percent.[9] Seebohm Rowntree, who observed social conditions in the British city of York, found soon after the war that only 3 percent of the citizens of York were in real need.[10] All of those were aged, the only group neglected by youth-oriented postwar British society. The institution of the welfare state during and after the war had made the decisive difference.

The last pockets of traditional poverty began to be drawn into the economic mainstream. During the summer of 1973, a Paris museum displayed the recent history of Minot, a village in Burgundy devoted to primitive subsistence agriculture that "could be described as late neolithic" until after the Second World War. Then consumer society broke in with a rush.

> The last horse collar was made in Minot in 1949; the last horse trod its streets in 1968. The old water mill closed down in 1952. The washing machine replaced the wash house—and broke up the community of women—in the nineteen sixties. In 1968, the anthropologists moved in, as into some Amazonian jungle tribe, and in 1973 Minot entered the museum.[11]

The main lever of change in the remaining preindustrial corners of Europe was the movement of young men from Spain, Portugal, southern Italy, and Turkey to the factories of northern Europe. Some 6 million southern Italians moved to northern Italian industrial cities in the 1960s. Foreigners made up 37 percent of the manual labor population of Switzerland by 1967. Although these workers were concentrated in the lowest forms of manual labor, and although there was friction with East Indians in Britain, Algerians in France, and Turks in Germany, some of this "subproletariat" returned home with savings and training and began middle-class lives as, for instance, automobile mechanics or television repairmen.

Wealth remained remarkably concentrated in a few hands in prosperous Western Europe, probably more so than during the enforced egalitarianism of war and reconstruction. British inheritance tax figures in 1971 showed that the top 1.2 percent of persons (about 61,000 individuals) owned 21.44 percent of the total personal wealth in Great Britain, and the top quarter owned about three-quarters of the total personal wealth.[12] Disparity was greater in West Germany, where the top 1.7 percent owned 35 percent of the total wealth. Since those described as

---

[8]Gregg, p. 236.

[9]Anthony Sampson, *Anatomy of Europe* (New York, 1969), p. 238.

[10]As compared to 31 percent in 1936. See chapter 1, p. 12.

[11]*The New York Times,* June 13, 1973, p. 58.

[12]Murray Forsyth, "Property and Property Distribution Policy," *PEP Broadsheet,* no. 528 (July 1971). The top 1.2 percent of Americans owned 33 percent of the total personal wealth and 54 percent of investment assets in 1962, according to a Federal Reserve study.

independent were accumulating wealth faster than those described as dependent (that is, salaried or wage workers), the disparity of wealth was probably widening in the Western Europe of the early 1970s.

Social Mobility

In between the richest and the poorest, the mass of Western Europeans gave evidence of greater homogeneity and easier social mobility. The twentieth-century trend toward fewer outward signs of social distinction was accelerated after the war by informal habits of dress, especially among the young, by inexpensive standardized clothing and by widening access to such status symbols as the automobile. A lower-middle-class European commented to an interviewer that at his job he was a nobody; at the wheel of his car, he felt he was treated with respect.[13]

The two most powerful forces for egalitarianism were education and leisure. Mass primary education had been instituted in the late nineteenth century. Secondary and university systems remained narrowly selective until after the Second World War. By deeply rooted European tradition, secondary schooling had consisted of rigorous training in literary expression based on the classics; it was accessible only to upper-class boys and a few poor boys of exceptional literary talent. After the war there were powerful movements in two complementary directions: toward greater democracy in higher education (including girls) and toward more technical competence in the skills of science, engineering, and business. The first result was an enormous increase of enrollment in secondary schools. The French had abolished fees for state secondary schools by 1933; the British abolished them in 1947. The right of all to a free secondary education up to the age of fifteen was recognized for the first time in British history. The French raised their school-leaving age to sixteen in 1967. Education became the fastest growing item in Western European budgets. The proportion of gross national product devoted to education in Britain rose from 2.8 percent in 1938 to 5.4 percent in 1965, and in France, from 2 percent in 1952 to 4.6 percent in 1965.

But what should be taught in the now crowded secondary schools? Since aptitudes and backgrounds in the schools became less uniform, the standard Western European solution was to divide the curriculum into different tracks: classical and "modern" for the more gifted, and vocational for the less intellectually gifted. In France, the traditional, rigorous *lycées* were supplemented by more egalitarian *collèges d'éducation secondaire,* but it was clear to all that very different degrees of prestige were attached to the different schools, that family background had much to do with the school that one attended, and that the choices made there often committed a student to his or her lifetime social level. High tensions developed around examinations for entry into one school or the other. The "eleven-plus" examination in England was an awesome hurdle, for the entry at eleven years of age into a vocational "secondary modern" school instead of a more prestigious

---

[13] *The New York Times,* April 8, 1973, sec. 1a, p. 8.

"grammar" school might well limit one's future status for good. When the Labour Party returned to power in Britain in 1964, it began phasing out the "eleven-plus" examination and providing for freer transfer among schools as a student's talents developed. Even with modification of this sort, however, Western European secondary schools had clearly become an arena of fierce status pressure among the young.

The experience of mass schooling showed that the children of literate or cultivated parents performed better, from the first classes on, than children of workers or peasants. As schooling became more and more important for jobs in a technical society, few people of poor backgrounds actually advanced far beyond their parents' social standing. A study of top executives in France in 1968 showed that 40 percent of them had been born in Paris, and that three-quarters were sons (none were women) of high-ranking business or professional families; only about 10 percent had come from modest backgrounds. The fact that more than a third had grandparents of modest social position suggested that the narrow path to social advancement was a matter of at least two generations.[14]

Enrollment also increased rapidly in Western European universities. The number of British universities increased from sixteen in 1935 to fifty-two in 1965, and university enrollment from 50,000 to 168,000. University enrollment in France more than tripled in fifteen years after 1950, West German enrollment almost tripled, and Italian enrollment more than doubled. Western European nations sent between 8 percent and 15 percent of the age group twenty to twenty-four to universities in 1965, compared with 3 percent to 5 percent in 1950.[15] The prospects were for continued growth, as university education was nearly free (except for living expenses). Governments subsidized higher education because high skills were an advantage in the race for prosperity. The educational disparity between middle-class and working-class or peasant youths was further accentuated by university admissions, however, and university study was even more clearly geared to access to professions than was secondary-school education.

The spread of leisure was a more genuinely egalitarian development than the spread of education. The establishment of leisure as a right of working people in the 1930s[16] was followed during the postwar boom by major development of leisure travel. As paid vacations became standard among employees, the sheer numbers of those looking for escape to the sea or the mountains climbed prodigiously. Among the West Germans, the most avid foreign travelers in Western Europe, a fifth of the whole population went abroad each year. In 1966, 5.5 million Germans visited Italy alone. Catering to tourists became a big business in itself, as tourism was the largest foreign-exchange earner in Spain, Italy, and Greece. Thinly settled coastal land around the Mediterranean became the object of frantic speculation for hotels, second homes, and campsites. While most tourists carefully preserved their national

---

[14]*Le Monde,* October 1, 1968.

[15]In the United States, 43 percent received some form of higher education at least for a time in 1965.

[16]See chapter 9, pp. 269–271.

and class surroundings in tours or vacation communities, a highly successful French enterprise, the *Club Méditerranée*, built more than forty-five imitation Tahitian villages around the world, where those seeking escape from middle-class conformity could live in mock austerity, using beads for money and enjoying a brief fling without social ostentation or hierarchy.

POLITICS IN CONSUMER SOCIETIES, 1953–1968

The "End of Ideology"

"The affluent society banks the fires of indignation," observed the French political scientist Raymond Aron in 1957.[17] Compared to the reconstructing zeal of the liberation years and to the impassioned divisions of the Cold War, the prosperous late 1950s seemed a time of ideological simmering-down in Europe. Sociologists talked of the "end of ideology."[18]

One could argue that prosperous times and the access of more and more salaried workers to material comfort had merely reduced social frictions for a while. To an extent, that was true. Even at the turn of the century, the German economist Werner Sombart had tried to explain the failure of ideological socialism in the United States in part by sheer abundance: "On the reefs of roast beef and apple pie socialist Utopias of every sort are sent to their doom."[19] Marxists had had no difficulty disposing of this argument by predicting coming depression or a widening disparity between the rich and the rest.

Beyond a mere temporary prosperity, however, it seemed possible in the late 1950s and early 1960s that lasting social, economic, and political changes were in the process of making the "end of ideology" permanent. One important structural change was the faster growth of white-collar than of blue-collar workers as a proportion of the total population. This process, in fact, had begun in the 1890s in the most advanced industrial countries. Factory workers leveled off at about a third of the population, instead of becoming the predicted absolute majority; by contrast, the number of clerical and service workers began growing rapidly. In the 1950s it seemed that white-collar workers might actually outnumber blue-collar workers in advanced industrial countries. The "proletariat" was being replaced by a "salariat."[20] On the theory that white-collar workers were less alienated from middle-class aspirations, some French businesses actually tried to hasten this process in the early 1970s by paying factory workers a monthly salary rather than a weekly wage.

Another element of the "end of ideology" view was a new confidence that planned economies and welfare states had conquered the business cycle. Up to

---

[17]Raymond Aron, *The Opium of the Intellectuals,* trans. Terence Kilmartin (New York, 1962), p. xv.

[18]Daniel Bell, *The End of Ideology: The Exhaustion of Political Ideals in the Fifties* (Glencoe, Ill., 1960). Although Bell applied the phrase mostly to the United States, it is equally apt for Western Europe.

[19]Werner Sombart, *Warum gibt es in den Vereinigten Staaten keinen Sozialismus?* (Tübingen, Germany, 1906), p. 126.

[20]Bell, p. 217. The United States passed this landmark in 1956.

1945, depression and unemployment had discredited the European system as much as war had. If the postwar planners could replace the old boom-and-bust rhythm with steady growth in both productivity and incomes, the gnawing insecurity that had dominated proletarian life even during interludes of prosperity would be vanquished. As the Western European welfare states approached their second decade since 1945 without a serious depression and with virtually full employment, the growing prosperity seemed more than a mere interlude.

A final element in the "end of ideology" position was the discrediting of the vigorous doctrines of earlier times. *Laissez-faire* had been discredited during the Great Depression to the point where even European businessmen rarely talked of the values of individual enterprise. A whole range of Integralist Catholic and racial ideologies (although not nationalism) had been discredited by the defeat of fascism. On the left, the harsh realities of Stalinist practice stripped Marxism of some of its attraction. Even before de-Stalinization began in Moscow, many Western sympathizers were stopped short by Albert Camus's question: "Do you, yes or no, regard the Soviet Union as having fulfilled the revolutionary 'project'?"[21] De-Stalinization hastened this critical reevaluation after 1956, and the Soviet interventions in Hungary (1956) and Czechoslovakia (1968) accelerated it even more. Doubts about collectivism were heightened in Western Europe by the disillusioning experience of partial nationalization. Working for a large state-owned firm resembled all too closely working for a large privately owned firm, in terms of job boredom, low pay, and lack of advancement. But if collectivism did not necessarily bring more personal freedom, it might at least bring higher productivity. Even the promise of more productivity through collectivism was belied, however, when Western European growth rates persistently led Soviet growth rates in the 1960s.

Consensus Politics

The main political mark of the "end of ideology" years was the emergence of a broad consensus around pragmatic, technical management of public affairs for sustained economic growth. Both right and left in Western Europe seemed to agree on the virtues of a mixed economy, the welfare state, and pragmatic planning. Even the Soviet Union seemed to differ mainly on the means to attain the same end: an economy of abundance.

In practice, this consensus was expressed in Western Europe by conservatives in power through the late 1950s and 1960s. In this sense, the "end of ideology" years built on the political triumph of conservatives in Western Europe during the Cold War. Germany continued to be ruled by Konrad Adenauer (1949–1963), followed by his economics minister and the deviser of the German economic "miracle," Ludwig Erhard (1963–1966). In England, the longest-lived Tory government up to that time ruled from 1951 to 1964 under Churchill and his successors. Italy was governed by the Christian Democratic successors of Alcide De Gasperi. France, the one

[21]Albert Camus, letter in *Les Temps modernes,* August 1952.

nation in Western Europe to change its political system substantially in these years, turned to a strong executive under General Charles de Gaulle (1958–1969).

It was less the governments than the oppositions that changed during the "end of ideology" period. The Western European left became more gradualist and pragmatic; in some instances, it shared power with the center. Western European socialists talked less about nationalization after the late 1950s and more about technical problems of planned economic growth, about worker participation in the decisions of a managed economy, about how to reconcile automation with satisfying work, and about the organization of leisure in the welfare state.

The most striking transformation was that of the West German Social Democratic Party (SPD). The first Marxist party of Western Europe (1869) and until 1933 the largest, it was the repository of orthodox Marxist social democracy after the death of Marx and Engels. But the SPD decided at its 1959 annual congress at Bad Godesberg to renounce Marxist doctrine as the party's main guide. "The SPD, which was a party of the working class, is now a party of the whole people." The program described democratic socialism as a set of values rooted in "Christian ethics, humanism, and classic philosophy," and a set of pragmatic political aims designed to "establish a way of life," not to carry out a revolution. The new SPD opposed great concentrations of economic power in either private or state hands; hence, there was less talk of nationalization than of shared, decentralized decision making. "As much competition as possible, as much planning as necessary" for economic abundance was the party's motto. Like the British Labour Party and the Swedish Socialist Party, the new SPD after Bad Godesberg was designed to appeal to a majority of an electorate in which factory workers were only a minority.[22]

In practice, the Bad Godesberg program meant the replacement of the old Social Democratic survivors of Weimar with a new generation of SPD leaders. The indomitable Kurt Schumacher, marked by the First World War and by Hitler's concentration camps with the loss of a leg and an arm, was the last strong representative of Weimar social democracy until his death in 1953. The main new leader was Willy Brandt. As a student, Brandt had left Germany when Hitler came to power and spent hard years in Norway (where he took the name Brandt from an Ibsen play) and in Sweden. In 1957, he was elected mayor of West Berlin where he made his mark more by youth and energy than by doctrine.

In 1966, seven years after the adoption of the Bad Godesberg program and two years after Willy Brandt became leader of the German SPD, the flagging Christian Democrats joined with the SPD in a "Great Coalition" government in which Brandt was foreign minister. It was the first time the German Christian Democrats had shared power with another political party since 1948, and Brandt was the first SPD minister in Germany since 1930.

The British Labour Party, reformist since its beginning, also entered a more pragmatic period with the death in 1960 of the Welsh radical Aneurin Bevan, Labour's gadfly, and with the replacement of Clement Attlee as party leader by the scholarly Hugh Gaitskell, a proponent of a mixed economy run by experts. Indeed, the distinctions

---

[22]SPD Bad Godesberg program, quoted in Alfred Grosser, *Germany in Our Time* (New York, 1971), p. 151.

between the welfare state Toryism of R. A. Butler, the Conservative Chancellor of the Exchequer (1951–1955), and Gaitskell's ideas of a planned mixed economy were so slight that bemused Englishmen simply called both parties' programs "Butskellism." When Gaitskell died prematurely, an Oxford economics professor, Harold Wilson, brought Labour back to power in 1964, after thirteen years of Tory government. Wilson renationalized steel and democratized secondary education, but the main platform of the second postwar Labour government (1964–1970) was scientific and technological contributions to further economic growth.

In Italy, the independent Socialist leader Pietro Nenni, whose determination to cooperate with the Italian Communist Party in 1948 and 1949 had split the Italian Socialists, also evolved toward a more centrist position in the 1960s. When the ruling Christian Democrats proposed an "opening to the left" to broaden their coalition, the Nenni Socialists even participated in the government for a time (1963–1968).

Western European Communist parties found themselves with aging leaders and members, isolated from the rest of the left, and approaching their lowest point since the Second World War. When de Gaulle came to power in June 1958, the French Communist Party retained only 19 percent of the popular vote, its lowest percentage since 1936. Many sympathetic Western intellectuals had cooled to the party since the Soviet invasion of Hungary and the revelations of de-Stalinization in 1956. The years of Cold War passion and intellectual *engagement* that Simone de Beauvoir had described in her prize-winning novel of 1957, *Les Mandarins,* seemed a bygone era by 1965. The new leaders of Europe were no longer *engagé* intellectuals, like de Beauvoir and Sartre, but pragmatic experts, the bright young technicians who designed Europe's high-speed trains and nuclear power plants. The future seemed to hold out a long vista of sustained growth and stability.

MASS CULTURE AND HIGH CULTURE IN THE "NEW EUROPE"

Popular Culture

The young and wage earners with spare cash to spend provided a mass market for an emerging worldwide popular culture in the 1960s. Its modes of transmission were television, cheap transistor radios, recordings, films, and inexpensive international travel. Its content was casual, spontaneous enjoyment of leisure and the senses. Its forms of expression were drawn, for the most part, from American models: jazz and rock music, informal clothing, western movies. This popular culture received wide acceptance in all of Europe, including Eastern Europe where it was officially discouraged. It was the basis of enormous new fortunes. It finished off the remains of traditional regional folk cultures (except for a few artificial nostalgic "folk" songs), further increased the homogeneity of European young people, and widened the gap between the tastes of the young and their elders.

The most celebrated figures in 1960s mass culture were a quartet of young singers from the British port city of Liverpool, The Beatles. Their infectious, relaxed enthusiasm, conveyed by highly expert recordings and publicity, made The Beatles among the best-known personages in the world of the late 1960s. The songs and films they created carried a vaguely antiauthoritarian, antimilitarist, antihierarchial message. They leveled gentle ridicule at a status-conscious middle class, sanctioned the use of consciousness-affecting drugs, and publicized a life of apparently carefree, good-humored hedonism.

It was significant that The Beatles came from working-class backgrounds, from a provincial city outside any of the traditional cultural capitals, and that their art bore almost no relation to traditional high culture. The British historian Eric Hobsbawm claimed that with The Beatles, British culture had become working class.[23] In truth, The Beatles stood less for anything properly British than for an international culture of youth and leisure. It is doubtful that any entertainers had ever before transcended national boundaries so fully. The Beatles enjoyed their first success in a Hamburg nightclub, made films that were dubbed into dozens of languages, and toured the world in person and on records. The British government's recognition of their export value with the award of the Order of the British Empire simply called attention to the anachronism of national cultures and middle-class deference and manners.

The Beatles, of course, were only the most celebrated example of an international phenomenon. The young Muscovites who tried to buy blue jeans from Western tourists showed that the international culture of youth and leisure was more powerful than bureaucracies and national cultural establishments.

The Fine Arts

Totalitarianism and war had grievously damaged artistic creation in Europe. The flight of refugee artists to the New World after 1933, along with American prosperity after 1945, shifted the art market from Paris to New York. American fine arts had grown more self-confident during the eclipse of European arts under Hitler and Stalin. That, combined with the growing influence around the world of American popular music and film, put Europe in America's cultural shadow for the first time. Many Europeans feared what they regarded as a cultural invasion and took measures, such as film quotas, to limit it.

European artists did not make another fundamental aesthetic revolution after the Second World War. They continued for the most part to work the mine of self-expression opened at the beginning of the century. Art historian E. H. Gombrich holds that "no revolution in art has been more successful than that which started before World War I."[24] That revolution had consisted in setting artists free of learned conventions, allowing them to explore every possible medium of self-expression. The variety of subject matter, technique, and medium made it impossible to call any one of them characteristic of the postwar period. What was important was the virtual disappearance of the angry shock that had greeted experiment as

[23]Eric Hobsbawm, *Industry and Empire* (New York, 1968), p. 276.

[24]E. H. Gombrich, *The Story of Art*, 16th ed. (London, 1995), p. 610.

The sculptor Alberto Giacometti with some of his work, 1964.

© Gisele Freund / Photo Researchers

late as 1914, and the universal acceptance of the belief that artistic success was measured in terms of expressing oneself in an original idiom. Even Gombrich, fundamentally sympathetic to the modern arts, could wonder whether the obligation to be "new" had not become the new conformity of the later twentieth century.

European artists did find distinctive personal idioms, however. The horrors of the war had cried out for artistic expression and had helped to revive figurative painting and sculpture about public themes. The sculptor Henry Moore, whose rounded shapes pierced by holes were only barely suggestive of the human body, drew powerful images of the London population huddled in its bomb shelters during the *blitz* of 1941. After the war, some of the giants among European painters and sculptors reworked figurative art in very personal ways to express disturbing, often private emotions.

Balthazar Klossowski (1908–2001), who signed his work Balthus, painted a private vision of mysterious interiors and landscapes, often inhabited by remote but seductive little girls. The Anglo-Irish painter Francis Bacon (1909–1992) transformed photographs or old master portraits into powerful images of human desolation and terror. The Swiss painter and sculptor Alberto Giacometti had already returned in the late 1930s from abstraction to portrayals of the human form; after the war he created hauntingly attenuated and isolated human figures. The English painter Lucian Freud created intimate but disquieting human figures and portraits. More accessible to the public were the German painter Anselm Kieffer's satiric portrayals of Nazism, the war, and postwar desolation.

A similar fragmentation of vision occurred in the novel. The "new novel" of French writers like Alain Robbe-Grillet and Natalie Sarraute focused on concrete details without plot, character development, or a clear sense of the observer's identity. The traditional novel also enjoyed continued vigor in Britain, Italy, and Germany. The German postwar realists still wrote satirical social novels; Heinrich Böll won a Nobel Prize for his *Group Portrait with Lady* (1973), which follows fifty years of the ups and downs of Cologne in the twentieth century through the life of one woman.

Despite the serious inroads television made on the cinema as popular entertainment, films continued to be a vigorous form of artistic expression in the 1960s, one that offered a vision accessible to a wider audience than painting. Paris and Rome were centers of experimental filmmaking in the 1960s. The most provocative works were the savage exposés of empty urban life by Jean-Luc Godard and Michelangelo Antonioni, Luchino Visconti's brooding explorations of decadence, the dark psychological dramas of the Swedish director Ingmar Bergman, and the Catholic-Freudian allegories of the Spaniard Luis Buñuel.

Composers continued their search for new sounds to complete their liberation from tone and harmony. The most important postwar developments did not differ in kind from their interwar predecessors, but the composers did discover new ranges of sound. Electronic music, begun between the wars by Edgard Varèse, was given immense new range by the application of computers and electronic instruments like the Moog synthesizer. Another new trend was the use of silence and of chance in "aleatory" music that the performers improvised according to the composer's general instructions. "Concrete" music shared the fragmented vision of the 1960s with its concentration on individual sounds. The Frenchman Pierre Boulez was the most distinguished exponent of atonal composition, but, as in the other arts, there was abundant room for variety. The German Carl Orff reduced his choral settings to highly ritualized, almost hypnotic repetitions of a few harmonic patterns. The German Karl-Heinz Stockhausen and the Italian Luigi Nono used electronic and atonal music to express their left political position in the late 1960s.

The most accessible of the fine arts was architecture, to which postwar reconstruction and expansion gave great scope. For the most part, the architects of the postwar period continued to develop the main ideas of the period just before and after the First World War. Italian architect Pier Luigi Nervi continued to produce magnificent free forms in concrete; Ludwig Mies van der Rohe and other Bauhaus disciples carried on functionalism; Le Corbusier put some of his thoughts about the social functions of buildings into practice in housing projects in the south of France.

Religious Revival

The churches emerged from the war strengthened by the moral revulsion against Nazism. Even though much of the high culture had been materialistic and at least agnostic for two centuries, there were signs of religious revival.

The death of Pope Pius XII (1939–1958), a cautious, aristocratic administrator, allowed wartime and postwar currents to come to the top. The new pope, John

XXIII (1958–1963), was his predecessor's opposite: a jovial, robust man of peasant origins, who radiated human warmth. Pope John's brief papacy incorporated much of the postwar ferment in a wave of up-dating *(aggiornamento)*. Pope John called the first world Catholic council since 1870 at the Vatican, soon known as "Vatican II" (1962–1965), which authorized the use of local languages rather than Latin in the celebration of mass, approved ecumenical approaches to other Christians, and vested more power in Church councils. Pope John's two major encyclicals, *Mater et Magistra* (1961) and *Pacem in Terris* (1963), emphasized the need for social justice and more worker participation in the decisions that affected them, and called for an end to international conflict.

Pope Paul VI (1963–1978) carried forward the essentials of Pope John's reforms as effectively as a cautious papal administrator shocked by the libertarian 1960s could do. He remained traditionalist on birth control, clerical celibacy, and the ordination of women, positions that gave him difficulties with the Dutch Catholic clergy and others eager for change. The first pope to travel outside Italy since 1809 and the first to board an airplane, Paul VI flew all over the world, despite fatigue and illness, urging social justice and peace. He enlarged the role of Third World clerics in the affairs of the Catholic Church, sought contacts with Protestant leaders, and, despite deep anti-Marxism, he ended the intransigent refusal of an older generation of Eastern European clerics to establish a *modus vivendi* within the people's republics.

Among Protestant theologians, the Second World War had deepened a concern with the pervasiveness of human evil, original sin. The comfortable liberal Protestantism of the late nineteenth century, too submerged in its own petty concerns to resist Nazism, was discredited, along with an easy belief in human moral progress.

There were two possible directions to go from there. For the Swiss theologian Karl Barth, the liberal belief that one could save oneself by reason was a treacherous slope down which one soon slid to believing that people made whatever religion they needed. Barth resisted this train of thought with a vigorous fundamentalism, which reasserted the primacy of revelation and the powerlessness of anyone to save her- or himself without God's grace. Barth had given intellectual and moral leadership to the Protestant opposition to Hitler. Dietrich Bonhoeffer, who was executed by the Nazis in 1944, was the most influential of his German students.

The other path led, like nineteenth-century liberalism, through human reasoning, but, unlike the liberal Protestantism of that century, it was not content with individual piety, the "historical Jesus," and reasoned moral progress. Theologians like Rudolf Bultmann argued that the biblical message had been phrased in older cultural terms that could not be understood in the modern context. Modern Christians must extract the inner meanings from the old biblical myths and apply them to each situation of modern life. For some, such as the British theologian John Robinson, this meant that "God was dead" in the sense that pious Sunday school myths would have to be rephrased in a language suitable for our own day.

Both churches approached each other, the Catholics in an ecumenical broadening and the Protestants in a rediscovery of the importance of liturgy and rite. In both, there was a revival of public worship.

Scientific Achievements

European science recovered only slowly from the effects of depression, war, and "brain drain" to the United States. Western European supranational scientific efforts began to show some results in the 1960s. CERN (The European Center for Nuclear Research) built one of the world's most powerful nuclear accelerators in Switzerland, and ELDO (European Launch Development Organization) developed a heavy rocket-launching device (Ariane) which by 1995 had captured half the world's satellite-launching market. Western European universities were not always well equipped for modern research, however, and a far smaller proportion of the national income was devoted to pure science than in the United States and the Soviet Union. In spite of the disasters of Stalin's meddling in linguistics and genetics, Soviet applied technology scored striking successes in nuclear energy and rocketry, and Russian physics and chemistry were highly creditable.

Whereas physics continued, often brilliantly, to develop the implications of the great leaps made at the beginning of the century, the most profound changes occurred in biology and biochemistry. Study of the basic structure of the proteins that make living cells and of the biochemical structure of genetic elements opened up the possibility of synthesizing living tissue and, beyond that, raised the moral question of how to control experiments modifying living creatures or human personality. The Nobel Prize in Medicine and Physiology in 1962 was given to Sir Francis Crick of Cambridge University along with the American James Watson, for working out the structure of DNA, the basic protein component of genetic material.

The social sciences and philosophy, less dependent than the physical sciences on massive research expenditure, were areas of European brilliance after the Second World War. With the decline of immediate postwar ideologies, there were fewer Europeans who clung to vast overarching philosophical or sociological systems. The logical positivists, followers of Ludwig Wittgenstein and Bertrand Russell, such as the Oxford philosopher A. J. Ayer, shied away from large ethical or metaphysical questions to study with mathematical precision the structure of the logic of individual statements. The same fragmentation, although less deliberate, governed research in the social sciences, which became heavily influenced by American pragmatic, detailed observation. No major figures emerged to take the place of the great masters of social thought who had dominated the earlier generation: Marx, Weber, Freud.

The closest thing to a powerful new influence in the social sciences was structuralism, to which the French anthropologist Claude Lévi-Strauss gave the most sophisticated expression. While teaching in Brazil in the 1930s and in exile in New York from Vichy France in the 1940s, Lévi-Strauss became profoundly moved by the Brazilian Indian tribes that he saw gradually vanishing before the advance of "civilization." Already doubtful of the superiority of that civilization, Lévi-Strauss set out to discover the basic elements of all thought processes among primitive peoples. By analyzing the detailed content of myths about food, cooking, and smoking, Lévi-Strauss thought he could discover and catalogue a finite number of concrete logical processes that were the basic structure of all human thought: pairing, opposites, and the like. His interest was in the structure of thought, not in its history, in attempting to "decipher a code rather than tracing a pedigree."[25] In *The Savage Mind* (1962) he argued that the logical processes of thought of unchanging ("primitive") societies were as complex, and as valid, as those of changing or developing societies. In his most accessible work, *Tristes Tropiques* (1955), Lévi-Strauss mused about the clash of cultures, suggested his doubts about the relative validity of Western civilizations, and maintained that the nature of human thought could best be approached by finding the code of inner logical structure than by tracing a history.

The word *fragmented* has appeared often in this chapter. While Americanized popular culture dominated mass attention, high culture after the Second World War found itself divided among specialists pursuing ever more arcane matters.

In Britain in the 1960s, vigorous debate centered on a celebrated exchange between a scientist, C. P. Snow, and a literary critic, F. W. Leavis. Snow had argued that there were "two cultures," the scientific and the literary, and in its more elementary form, the debate turned around which was superior. In fact, there were many cultures, some inaccessible to even the educated. Europeans had lost not only their assurance of cultural superiority, but their vision of a whole culture.

DISCONTENT IN CONSUMER SOCIETIES: 1968 AND AFTER

The postideological stability forecast in the 1950s and early 1960s turned out to be illusory in 1967–1968. Those were tumultuous years in Western European universities, factories, and streets. Students and workers had often protested in the past. What made 1967–1968 special was the protesters' sweeping rejection of existing society, and their contempt for the narrow workaday agendas of the established Left parties and unions.

Student Discontent

Students, crowded into universities and secondary schools ill prepared for the swollen enrollments that came with prosperity and new social benefits, were the first to rebel. They demonstrated and "sat in" on campuses in Italy, Germany, and France in 1967–1968 for more fundamental issues than their inadequate facilities, however. They denounced the emptiness of consumerism, the conformity of the societies they were preparing to enter, the meaningless work they blamed on capitalism, and European complicity in the United States' war in Vietnam. Their synchrony with American and Japanese students testified to the emergence of a worldwide youth culture. But the European students took social theory more seriously than Americans. Drawing on Mao Tse-tung's "cultural revolution" and Latin American revolutionaries like Che Guevara, they wanted something more spontaneous and antihierarchical than the orthodox Marxism of Europe or even the USSR.

Since alienated young people were a worldwide phenomenon, it would be a mistake to look for purely European explanations. The American anthropologist Mar-

---

[25]George Lichtheim, *Europe in the Twentieth Century* (New York, 1972), p. 180.

garet Mead found an intelligible general explanation in the rapid pace of technological change.[26] She argued that in stable societies the young had believed that
their own lives would resemble the lives of their parents; hence, the parents' experiences provided lessons worth transmitting. Not so in an age in which the condition of life changed beyond recognition within a few years. Whereas it had taken a
generation to assimilate the automobile into public life, the airplane had moved
from plaything to basic transportation in less time, atomic energy had been put to
practical use in two decades, and space travel ceased to arouse wonder in a few
years. Mead believed that in the 1960s young people had simply ceased to believe
that their elders had anything to teach them.[27]

Students occupied an ambiguous social position: Although not yet integrated into
society, they were subject to its pressures in a brutally competitive, career-oriented
educational system; scornful of materialism, they nevertheless saw their future material possibilities being set by examination performance. There were, of course, particular reasons for European student dissent. European universities grew very
rapidly in enrollment in the prosperous 1960s. They left students without faculty
contact or adequate facilities, while sharpening their critical capacities.

These grievances took acute form in European consumer societies. The university students of the late 1960s had known nothing but prosperity. The sufferings in
earlier depressions and wars were so many proofs of their parents' failures, while
the last stages of the Cold War seemed further evidence of incompetence and bad
faith among their elders. Questions about moral responsibility for Nazism and the
crass materialism of the German revival further widened the generation gap in Germany. Many of the particularly powerful hierarchies of German universities were
virtually paralyzed by their tug of war with student radicals between 1967 and 1971.
Italian students, overenrolled tenfold in inadequate facilities and deeply disaffected
from industrial society, battled police and flirted with terrorism.

The most spectacular case was France in May 1968. Troubles began when a
minority of students opposed the French universities' role as selector and producer
of docile technocrats, as "an initiation into bourgeois affairs," and as an old-fashioned
vehicle for "only the acquisition of a cultural heritage" inadequate to keep up with
the "New Industrial Revolution."[28] Priding itself more on spontaneity than doctrine, the group took the name "March 22 Movement"—the date of the first sit-in at
the new, raw campus of Nanterre in suburban Paris, led by a German exchange student, Daniel Cohn-Bendit. The movement won its first mass base when police over-
reacted during a demonstration at the Paris Sorbonne campus on the night of May
11, 1968; 367 persons were wounded and 460 arrested. Encouraged by widespread
public sympathy, the students sought allies in the factories, and some industries
began strikes on May 14 over quite different issues of boring work and inflation. By
late May, 10 million people were on strike in France, the largest social outburst
since May 1936 and a spontaneous one, without the leadership of the communist or
socialist unions.

---

[26]Margaret Mead, *Culture and Commitment: A Study of the Generation Gap* (Garden City, N.Y., 1970).

[27]See chapter 4, p. 114 for an earlier form of conflict between generations.

[28]*Bulletin du mouvement du 22 mars*, April 1968. Statement of the *Syndicat national de l'Enseignement supérieur* (Instructors'
Union), May 1968.

Students confront armed riot police in Paris, near the Sorbonne, in May 1968. Although the students, temporarily allied with striking factory workers, brought their country nearly to a standstill, elections in June gave an absolute majority to the candidates of president Charles de Gaulle's conservative party.

As France became paralyzed by shortages of gas and food, General de Gaulle's regime was thought to be finished when the general disappeared on May 29. It turned out that he had gone secretly to West Germany to assure the loyalty of French army units stationed there. De Gaulle did not need armed force to survive, however, because the wage demands of consumer-oriented workers began to diverge from the more fundamental social criticism of the students. When a majority of the workers finally accepted a large wage raise in early June, the students became isolated. Elections held on June 23 gave de Gaulle the benefit of a backlash of frightened and angry French citizens who had been plunged suddenly from an imperfect but relative abundance into a nightmare of stalled automobiles, food hoarding, and uncongenial youthful lifestyles. For the first time in French history, a single party—the Gaullists—received an absolute majority of parliamentary seats.

The immediate effect of the Paris May, then, was to solidify the status quo. For the moment, most workers seemed to want mere wage raises and most other French people to want mere stability. But the fragility of highly technological consumer societies had been clearly demonstrated. De Gaulle's image had been severely battered, and a year later, at the age of seventy-nine, he left office after a relatively minor constitutional proposal was rejected at the polls.

Worker Discontents

We have seen how student discontent and its repression in France soon helped trigger industrial unrest. The same spillover went even further in Italy. The "hot autumn" of 1969 in Italy saw the biggest strike wave in that country since the factory occupations of September 1920. More than a million and a half workers participated in various forms of strikes, disruptions, and factory occupations, and unrest spread even among hitherto passive service and white-collar workers.

As in France, skilled workers, antagonized by speedups, boring assembly-line work, tight management control, and the spiraling cost of living, started the protests in Italy. They began in July 1969 by rejecting union-negotiated contracts at the Pirelli tire factory in Milan that seemed to them too timid. Bypassing traditional union leadership by forming shop-floor committees, they drew in younger, unskilled workers recently arrived from the south and easily radicalized in their unfamiliar industrial environment. New movements arose such as *Lotta continua* (unceasing struggle), which made far more sweeping demands about more equal pay and workers' control of production than those of the traditional unions and the Communist Party. For a moment, it looked as though an alliance between student radicals and younger workers was going to shake Italian society deeply. By the end of fall 1969, however, traditional union leadership had reasserted itself and most workers accepted a new national contract along traditional wages and hours lines: the 40-hour week universal throughout Italy, a pay increase of 18.3 percent, and wages indexed to the cost of living—the famous *scala mobile*. This wage momentum, locked firmly to price increases after indexing reached 100 percent in 1975, helped produce the highest inflation rates in Europe and revolving-door governments in the 1970s.

The worker movements of 1968–1969 were remarkable for their rejection of traditional union and party leaders, and for their sweeping aspirations. They sought worker control—"autogestion"—because neither the state nor management had answers to their two most frightening insecurities: unemployment and inflation. The most celebrated case of worker management was the Lip watch factory, in Besançon, France, whose workers, faced in 1973 by closure of an unprofitable plant, took over and operated the plant themselves for a year, refusing to sacrifice any workers to efficiency.

Efforts to regulate wages and prices sharpened labor–management tensions to the point where parliamentary institutions could hardly deal with them. British Conservative Prime Minister Edward Heath (1970–1974) tried to freeze wages and prices in November 1972, following the first nationwide coal miners' strike since 1926. Labor tension worsened in 1973. After Britain's first general civil servants' strike and another prolonged miners' stoppage, Heath lost his majority in the elections of 1974. Even Spain, silent as a tomb since the end of the Civil War in 1939, experienced increased linguistic nationalism, labor unrest, and intellectual dissent after the late 1960s.

There were rural tensions as well as urban ones. Economic planners had encouraged the replacement of traditional peasant dwarf holdings by mechanized agribusiness. For the first time, the farm population dropped below a third of the working population in France and approached that level in Italy. Improved productivity generated surpluses, however, and the remaining farmers were pinched between inflated costs of what they had to buy and trailing farm incomes. While the Communist Party had some success organizing declining small farmers in France and Italy (a short-term success but a long-term risk in tying communism to technical backwardness), some market-oriented farmers resorted to direct action in France. They blocked highways with unsellable surplus crops and occupied government offices on several occasions in the late 1960s. The European economies were under strain even before the oil shock of 1973 set off the depression that is the subject of chapter 22.

The New Feminism and Women's Liberation

All Western European women, except the Portuguese and some Swiss, had been allowed to vote since at least the end of the Second World War. But constitutional equality failed to address all women's grievances within consumer society. Moreover, radical women perceived during the protests of 1968 that "we cook while the men talk of revolution." Women's liberation movements—the term came from the United States—spread throughout Western Europe in the early 1970s.

Three kinds of issues fueled this new feminism. Conditions of work remained important, for increasing numbers of wives, including middle-class women, found a second salary necessary to support a family; yet certain professions, and many upper level positions, remained closed to them, and nowhere did women receive equal pay for equal work. Issues of procreation were also discussed more openly than ever before, as many women demanded the right to birth control and abortion. There was, finally, a new frankness among some women about sexual liberation. To the more radical women, traditional opposition parties seemed irrelevant to these issues. What did it accomplish to abolish capitalism, they argued, if the family was still patriarchal? So radical women formed their own movements and published their own periodicals, such as the irreverent *Spare Rib,* produced by a women's collective in London after 1972. It featured a men's page.

Even in Catholic countries, women's protests and petitions helped establish the right to divorce in Italy (1970, upheld by referendum in 1974 despite an active clerical campaign) and the right to abortion in France (1975) and Italy (1978). Ireland was the only European country that still forbade abortion absolutely.

The Descent into Terrorism

The belief that radical social change was at hand, so powerful in 1968, receded during the 1970s. Most radicals had to accept a world that they were not going to be able to transform quickly. A few of them, in frustration, turned to violence. In Germany, Andreas Baader, son of a professor, and Ulrike Meinhof, a journalist, drew a group of like-minded young people of middle-class origins into a series of bank robberies and bomb attacks for which they were sentenced to life imprisonment in 1972. Their cause was taken up by even more violent successors, the Red Army Faction. Between 1970 and 1978, Baader-Meinhof and the Red Army Faction between them killed 28 people, wounded 93, took 162 hostages, and took more than 5 million marks in 35 bank robberies.[29] The sensational kidnapping in October 1977 of Hanns-Martin Schleyer, a Daimler-Benz executive who was president of the German employers' association, culminated in an aircraft hijacking, the murder of Schleyer, and the suicide (or perhaps murder) of Baader and others in their prison cells. These events destroyed any lingering glamour that the Red Army Faction might have retained among all but the most totally disaffected young people.

After 1970 in Italy, the Red Brigades attacked capitalism by beating, kneecapping, or kidnapping its leading representatives. The climax of the movement was the kidnapping in March 1978 and murder fifty-five days later of former Prime Minister Aldo Moro in Rome. Although several dozen more people were killed in the following two years, the Red Brigades were isolated and divided after Moro's murder, and, with the help of inside informers, the Italian police finally dismantled them in 1980.

These perversions of the aspirations of 1968 aroused nearly universal condemnation, and the spirit of contestation turned inward in the later 1970s to artistic experiment, hallucinogens, communes, and "green" ecological activism. In any event, a sea change had occurred in 1973. The oil crisis in that year brought Western European economic growth and full employment to an end, and, with them, the kinds of discontent that accompanied abundance.

---

[29]John Ardagh, *Germany and the Germans* (New York, 1987), p. 424.

SUGGESTIONS FOR FURTHER READING

Frank B. Tipton and Robert Aldrich, *An Economic and Social History of Europe from 1939 to the Present*[*] (1987), provides solid background. There are suggestive observations about consumer society, weighted toward the French experience, in Antoine Prost and Gérard Vincent, eds., *Riddles of Identity in Modern Times,* vol. 5 of *A History of Private Life* (1991). Donald Sassoon, *One Hundred Years of Socialism: The Western European Left in the Twentieth Century*[*] (1998), ranges widely, emphasizing the years after 1945.

The works on economic recovery cited at the end of chapter 16 are still relevant here. A classic defense of Keynesian managed capitalism is Andrew Shonfield, *Modern Capitalism* (1969). The boom years of 1953–1973 are put into perspective in Stephen A. Marglin and Juliet B. Schor, eds., *The Golden Age of Capitalism: Reinterpretation of the Postwar Experience*[*] (1990), and John H. Goldthorpe, "Problems of Political Economy after the Postwar Period," in Charles S. Maier, ed., *Changing Boundaries of the Political*[*] (1987). See also Philip Armstrong, Andrew Glyn, and John Harrison, *Capitalism since 1945*[*] (1991).

Trade-offs between leisure and consumption are explored in Susan Strasser, Charles McGovern, and Matthias Judt, eds., *Getting and Spending: European and American Consumption in the Twentieth Century*[*] (1998), and Gary Cross, *Time and Money: The Making of Consumerist Modernity*[*] (1993). Les Haywood et al., *Understanding Leisure*[*] (1999), includes history. Victoria De Grazia and Ellen Furlough, eds., *The Sex of Things: Gender and Consumption in Historical Perspective*[*] (1996), adds an essential dimension. While Carl Gardner and Julie Sheppard, *Consuming Passion: The Rise of Retail Culture* (1989), treat Britain, they introduce larger issues.

Religion in postwar Europe is examined by Suzanne Berger, "Religious Transformation and the Future of Politics," in Charles S. Maier, ed., *Changing Boundaries of the Political*[*] (1987). Jackson W. Carroll, Wade C. Roof, et al., eds., *The Postwar Generation and the Establishment of Religion* (1995), contains interesting essays.

The books on the welfare state listed at the end of chapter 16 are also useful here.

Anthony Giddens argues in *The Class Structure of Advanced Societies* (1975) that the welfare state consolidated capitalism. For the supposed effects of prosperity on class relations, see John Goldthorpe, *The Affluent Worker: Political Attitudes and Behavior* (1968), and David Lockwood, *The Black-Coated Worker: A Study in Class Consciousness,*[*] 2nd ed. (1989). Richard F. Hamilton, *Affluence and the French Worker in the Fourth Republic* (1967), found that French workers voted according to the political affiliation of their union rather than by income. The classic texts of the "end of ideology" thesis are Daniel Bell, *The End of Ideology*[*] (1960, revised ed. 2000), and Raymond Aron, *Opium of the Intellectuals*[*] (1975, reprint ed. 2001).

Stephen R. Graubard, ed., *The New Europe?* (1964), reflects the optimism about further European integration current in the 1960s; so does Carl J. Friedrich, *Europe: An Emergent New Nation?* (1970).

A number of interesting studies treat the transformation of rural life.

Lawrence Wylie, *Village in the Vaucluse,*[*] 3rd ed. (1974), is justly regarded as a classic. Other fine village studies include Ronald Blythe, *Akenfield*[*] (1980); Pierre-Jakez Hélias, *The Horse of Pride*[*] (1980); Edgar Morin, *The Red and the White: Report from a French Village* (1970); Benjamin R. Barber, *The Death of Communal Liberty: A History of Freedom in a Swiss Mountain Canton*[*] (1974); Julian Pitt-Rivers, *People of the Sierra,*[*] 2nd ed. (1971, reprint ed. 1996); Ruth Behar, *The Present and the Past in a Spanish Village*[*] (1991); and Susan Carol Rogers, *Shaping Modern Times in Rural France: The Transformation and Reproduction of an Aveyronnais Community* (1991). Sidney Tarrow, *Peasant Communism in Southern Italy* (1967), discusses the political radicalism of declining agriculture.

The social conflicts of the late 1960s are analyzed most thoroughly in Robert J. Flanagan, David W. Soskice, and Lloyd Ulman, *Unionism, Economic Stabilization, and Incomes Policies: The European Experience*[*] (1983), and Colin Crouch and Alessandro Pizzorno, eds., *The Resurgence of Class Conflicts in Western Europe since 1968,* 2 vols. (1983). Vivid narratives are David Caute, *Sixty-Eight: The Year of the Barricades*[*] (1988), and

Robert V. Daniels, *Year of the Heroic Guerrilla: World Revolution in 1968*[*] (1989), the latter giving less attention to Europe. For particular countries, see Sidney Tarrow, *Democracy and Disorder: Protest and Politics in Italy, 1965–1975*[*] (1989), and Keith A. Reader and Khursheed Wadia, *The May 1968 Events in France* (1993).

Daniel Wheeler, *Art since Mid-Century: 1945 to the Present*[*] (1991), is a good introduction. For the social history of film in Europe since World War II, see Pierre Sorlin, *European Cinemas, European Societies, 1939–1990*[*] (1991).

Two European intellectuals disappointed by the uses to which working people put their leisure time and consumer power are Ignazio Silone, *Emergency Exit* (1968), and Richard Hoggart, *The Uses of Literacy*[*] (1957, reprint ed. 2001).

Additional Internet links related to this chapter are available on the Europe in the 20th Century Web site: http://www.history.wadsworth.com/paxton04.

You can also explore images, interactive timelines, and maps related to this chapter on our Western Civilization Resource Center: http://history.wadsworth.com

A dramatic moment in West German Chancellor Willy Brandt's *Ostpolitik*. Brandt kneels before the memorial to Jewish victims of the Nazis in Warsaw, December 1970, shortly before West Germany and Poland established diplomatic relations.

20

Cold War Détente: Stirrings of Independence, 1962–1975

After 1962, the European theater of the Cold War returned to a kind of stalemate. The Berlin Wall itself (August 1961), however shocking its construction, came to signify that both sides had learned to accept the Iron Curtain as final. While each would police its own turf vigorously, as the Soviets showed in Czechoslovakia in August 1968, neither expected to advance beyond it. By the late 1960s, the fear of a Soviet march westward had lost most of its urgency. From the late 1960s to about 1975, détente—the traditional French diplomatic term for the relaxation of tensions—became the key word in world politics. Europeans could begin to breathe a little more easily.

Along with relaxation came independent stirrings by members of both blocs. The Communist bloc split in two, as China and the Soviet Union quarreled. Within the Soviet sphere, Eastern European Communists cautiously widened their elbow room. Within the much more collegial Western bloc, the United States found it harder to get its way. In economic terms, the European Community's wealth grew to the point where it became a competitor to the United States and a magnet to Eastern Europe. The "almighty dollar" came under such strain from the Vietnam War that it had to be devalued in 1971 and 1973, and the system of fixed exchange rates set up at Bretton Woods at American behest in 1945 broke down. The European Community took its first steps toward creating its own currency system. The Soviet Union's attainment of nuclear parity some time in the late 1960s called into question the United States' willingness to make a nuclear strike to defend Europe, and the French decided to go their own way with an independent defense policy. Distinctions between the victors and vanquished of World War II grew fainter, as both Germanies joined the United Nations in 1973. As these and other certainties of the immediate postwar years lost their hold, the postwar era came to an end.

THE COLD WAR: FROM THAW TO DÉTENTE

It is artificial to designate one turning point, but the Cuban missile crisis, the hottest moment of the Cold War, did appear to end one era and begin a new one. In October 1962, United States reconnaissance planes discovered that the Soviet Union was installing ballistic missiles in Cuba, as close to Florida as United States missiles in Turkey were to the Soviet frontier. Unlike the Korean War, indeed unlike any Cold War confrontation since the Berlin Airlift of 1948, the Cuban crisis set the armed forces of the two nuclear powers directly against each other, without intermediaries. If either side judged that the other was about to strike first, overreaction could lead to nuclear war.

Despite unclear communication, time pressure, and fatigue, both Soviet premier Khrushchev and United States president Kennedy managed to convey their desire for settlement short of war and to control their own partisans of overreaction. Kennedy postponed the air strike on the missile sites urged by some of his advisors; instead, he adopted the more limited riposte of a naval blockade of Cuba. Khrushchev turned sixteen Cuba-bound Russian ships around in midocean on the strength of a positive American reply to his offer to remove the missiles in exchange for an American agreement not to invade Cuba. The Russians gave up active military presence in Cuba, without insisting on the removal of United States missiles in Turkey in exchange; the Americans accepted the continued existence of communist Cuba as an exception to the Monroe Doctrine. Each side could claim to have won its essential point without going to war.

The Cuban crisis reminded the superpowers that they had more interest in jointly preserving the status quo and their advantageous postwar positions than in precipitating a fatal duel. That awareness had been evident when the United States and the Soviet Union, separately and for their own reasons, had forced the British, French, and Israelis to abandon their occupation of the Suez Canal in October 1956. The next year Communist leaders revived Malenkov's talk of "peaceful coexistence." Representatives of twelve Communist parties, assembled in Moscow for the fortieth anniversary of the Bolshevik Revolution in November 1957, had declared:

COLD WAR EUROPE, 1985

> At the present time the forces of peace have grown to such an extent that there is a real possibility of averting wars. . . . The Communist and Workers' Parties taking part in this meeting declare that the Leninist principle of peaceful coexistence of the two systems, "socialist and capitalist," . . . is the sound basis of the foreign policy of socialist countries and the dependable pillar of peace and friendship among the peoples.[1]

That common interest had been lost from view during Khrushchev's challenges in Berlin, Lebanon, and Southeast Asia from 1958 to 1961. But the sense of relief after going to the brink over Cuba opened the way for more substantial relaxation of tensions than during the 1957 thaw.

In the summer of 1963, Kennedy and Khrushchev signed a partial Nuclear Test Ban Treaty ending all but underground explosions. A telephone "hot line" was installed between the Kremlin and the White House to prevent poor communication from complicating future confrontations. Most importantly for Europeans, the Soviet Union ceased to set deadlines for ending the four-power presence in Berlin and turning Berlin into a free city. To be sure, there was shock and outrage in August 1968 when the Soviet Union crushed the Dubček regime in Czechoslovakia by armed force. Although that action proved Russian determination to maintain its sphere of influence intact, there were no apparent Soviet territorial aims west of the Iron Curtain after the four occupying powers concluded a new agreement in 1971 that settled their rights of access to Berlin.

Superpower negotiations now picked up speed. It has been calculated that no fewer than 58 of all the 105 treaties between the United States and the Soviet Union since resumption of diplomatic relations in 1933 were concluded between 1969 and 1975.[2] Two Strategic Arms Limitation Treaties (SALT, discussed below) tried to limit long-range nuclear weapons. Among the European states, there were armaments reduction talks and agreements to accept the territorial boundaries set by force in 1945. Both sides were eager for more Western trade and investment in the Eastern bloc. The most dramatic symbol of détente was the link-up in space of Soviet and American spacecraft on July 17, 1975, a distant echo of the handshake of American and Soviet soldiers at Torgau, Germany, in April 1945. Europeans could believe they could now stretch their limbs a little in a less threatening world.

POLYCENTRISM IN THE COMMUNIST WORLD

The Sino-Soviet Split

The most striking dissension appeared on the Communist side with the Sino-Soviet split. The Chinese Communists had won their victory of 1948 without Soviet aid, and their leaders had bitter memories of Stalin's withdrawal of support in 1927.[3]

---

[1]Moscow Declaration of November 16, 1957. Quoted in O. Edmund Clubb Jr., *China and Russia: The Great Game* (New York, 1970), p. 442.

[2]Alistair Buchan, "The United States and the Security of Europe," in David S. Landes, ed., *Western Europe: The Trials of Partnership* (Lexington, Mass., 1977), p. 297.

[3]See chapter 12, p. 357.

Economic difficulties and Cold War unity kept these frictions hidden until the late 1950s. Mao Tse-tung even signed the Moscow Declaration of Peaceful Coexistence of November 1957 in person. But as the Chinese began their "great leap forward" into agricultural communes in 1958, and as they engaged in more active military confrontations with the nationalist Chinese on Taiwan, against Soviet advice, they began to enunciate a separate Maoist Communist doctrine.

Mao objected to the ideology of peaceful coexistence and to the Soviets' belief that their model applied to Chinese experience. He proposed a policy of active attacks on imperialism, in which reformist socialists or Third World bourgeois-nationalist states were enemies as dangerous as the great bourgeois states themselves—in other words, a return to the 1928 to 1934 policy of "class against class." Mao also argued that the peasant communism that had produced the Chinese victory of 1948 was as valid as the Russian industrial model, and indeed more applicable to future revolutionary situations—hence, Russia was no longer an example for other Communists. Mao even charged the Soviet Union with "economism"—putting its own economic growth ahead of promoting world revolution.

Behind these doctrinal differences lay Chinese–Russian antagonisms that were practical, territorial, and even nationalist. Mao wanted the Soviets to cease all aid to Third World bourgeois-nationalist states (such as India, with whom China waged a border war in 1962) so that all Soviet economic surplus could be devoted to Chinese needs. Anxious to reassert ancient Chinese influence over central Asia, Mao accused the Russians of having overrun Chinese lands in its nineteenth-century expansion eastward. Mao, finally, expressed national pride in the autonomy of China's own revolutionary pattern and set out to supplant the Soviet Union as the leader of Communist movements in the Third World.

The disagreement was mutual. In July 1960, the Soviet Union withdrew all of its 1,390 technicians from China and suspended its economic aid. Khrushchev's hard line of 1960 and 1961, including the resumption of nuclear testing, was intended as much to threaten as to outflank the Chinese. Up until late 1962 they attacked each other only indirectly. The Chinese denounced the Yugoslavs; the Soviet replies were directed at Albania, China's only European ally. In October and November 1962, however, came both the Russian failure in Cuba and the China-India border war, in which the Soviets continued to supply arms to the Indians. Thereafter, the Soviet Union and China attacked each other openly. Disagreement over the Nuclear Test Ban Treaty of July 1963 broke off all contact between the two. The Chinese accused the Russians of "capitulation to United States imperialism"; Khrushchev charged the Chinese with the "madness" of wanting to unleash a nuclear war that only the Chinese masses would survive. By 1969, their troops were skirmishing in two places on their long border: along the Amur and Ussuri rivers north of Manchuria and on the Sinkiang frontier in central Asia. One encounter cost over 800 casualties. There were rumors that the Soviets had plans to bomb the Chinese nuclear research center, where the Chinese tested their first nuclear bomb in 1964.

The break with China sent a rift through all the Communist parties of the world. European Maoists were always few, although these splinter groups diverted some of the young and the active from Communist parties in Italy and France. Only one European state—Albania—entered wholly into the Maoist camp. More important for Europe was the indirect support given by the Sino-Soviet split to the Eastern European movement toward national communism.

National Communism in Eastern Europe

Just after Khrushchev's denunciation of Stalin in June 1956, the Italian Communist leader Palmiro Togliatti had proposed that world communism become "polycentric":

> The Soviet model cannot and must not any longer be obligatory. . . . The whole system becomes polycentric, and even in the Communist movement itself we can not speak of a single guide.[4]

Khrushchev was obliged to accept publicly the validity of a "multiplicity of forms of socialist development" in an effort at reconciliation with Tito in June 1956. Soviet intervention in Hungary in November 1956, however, revealed the limits of permissible divergence within the Soviet bloc. The Moscow Declaration of November 1957 continued to refer to the Soviet Union as leader of the "socialist camp."

Aided by Chinese attacks on the Soviet right of leadership in the 1960s, tendencies toward nationally independent forms of communism reappeared in Eastern Europe. The two cases of dissidence in 1956, one limited and peaceful (Poland) and the other uncontrolled and crushed (Hungary), had two successors in the 1960s. The Czechoslovak attempt to move rapidly toward political and intellectual freedom within a socialist economy provoked the brutal Soviet invasion of August 21, 1968. But the Romanians followed the opposite course of political autocracy combined with economic independence, with far more success.

Romania, in fact, achieved an extraordinary degree of economic leeway. In 1962 the Eastern European economic organization, COMECON, adopted a division of labor by which some communist nations would produce finished products and others would supply raw materials. As a primarily agricultural state with large oil reserves, Romania foresaw itself condemned by this plan to perpetual economic backwardness. At a COMECON meeting in February 1963, Romania refused to accept the sacrifices demanded of it in the name of a "socialist division of labor"; that is, to renounce its own production of commodities that would compete with the more industrial Czechoslovakia and East Germany.

In 1964, the Romanian leaders publicly declared the independence of all communist nations and the obligation of noninterference in others' affairs, a warning to the Soviet Union to allow Romanian economic development to follow its own course. In the same year, the Romanians sought economic and technical aid from France and the United States. After that, Romania conducted up to a third of its foreign trade with the West and pursued a partly independent foreign policy.

There was nothing politically liberal about Romanian national communism, however. Party Secretary Gheorghe Gheorghiu-Dej (1944–1965) was one of the

---

[4]Palmiro Togliatti, "Nine Questions of Stalinism." Polycentrism was launched in a Togliatti interview in an Italian party publication, *Nuovi Argomenti,* on June 16, 1956. Although Togliatti himself later recanted, polycentrism was irreversible.

strictest of the Eastern European Stalinists; he supported the Soviet Union fully in its struggles with China. His successor, Nicolae Ceausescu (1965–1989), set longevity records among Eastern European leaders by carrying the same split-level policy further. At home, he ran the tightest one-man autocracy in Eastern Europe. Abroad, he stretched independence in foreign policy to the limits of Soviet tolerance. His rejection of COMECON plans for Romania's economy was aided by the fact that Romania was the only Eastern European country independent of Soviet oil. Although nominally a member of the Warsaw Pact, he refused to cooperate in combined operations such as the occupation of Czechoslovakia in 1968 and declined to accept Soviet missiles on his territory in August 1984. In 1969 and 1970, he became the first Eastern European leader to exchange state visits with an American president, Richard Nixon. Alongside Tito, he endorsed Eurocommunist theories of separate roads to socialism while rejecting Eurocommunist political pluralism. His capacity to show some independence of the Soviet Union gratified Romanian national feelings, which little else in that drab dictatorship could gratify.

By 1970, it had long been impossible to talk of a single Communist bloc. Since 1963, there had been at least two blocs: Soviet and Chinese. By the late 1960s, a wide variety of Eastern European Communist regimes had evolved. In Poland and Yugoslavia, about 85 percent of the arable land was in private family farms. Every successive Polish leader had had to come to terms with the bedrock Catholicism of the Poles. Poland, Yugoslavia, and Romania were receiving American economic aid. Albania was in the Chinese camp. Hungary, having learned the limits of dissent in 1956, came to enjoy more access to Western literature and goods under János Kádár's "Goulash Communism" than the Soviet Union, as we will see more fully in the next chapter. The invasion of Czechoslovakia in August 1968 proved that the Soviet Union would use force to retain political dominance, if not economic uniformity. But there was a limit to the number of times the Soviet Union could afford to offend its foreign followers so deeply for any purpose.

By the early 1970s, the challenge for the Eastern European Communist regimes was to find some way of assuring abundance, even through exchanges with the West, without catching what they considered to be the cultural malaise, divisions, and critical spirit of the West.

GAULLISM AND THE WESTERN "THIRD FORCE"

When France emerged in 1962 from eight bitter years of war in Algeria—the last great European colonial war except for the Portuguese in Angola and Mozambique—French president Charles de Gaulle (1958–1969) became free to turn to other matters. De Gaulle, whose consuming passion since the fall of France in 1940 had been the restoration of his country's grandeur, understood that his humiliated army and deeply divided people needed the tonic of great new enterprises. Chafing within the straitjacket imposed on Europe by the Cold War alignment, de Gaulle perceived that a middle-ranking nation had new opportunities for maneuver between and within the loosening blocs, opportunities that were denied to the superpowers themselves. By skillful maneuvering, a middle-ranking nation could exercise power far beyond its physical means.

De Gaulle's first step was to free his officer corps from the effects of nearly twenty years of colonial war by giving the French Army an exciting new task, the development of its own nuclear weapons.

Only Britain and France among Western European states had attempted to build a modern nuclear armed force after the war. The British tested their first atomic bomb in October 1951 and their first nuclear bomb in March 1957. The burden was immense, however, for a country whose economic growth rate fell below that of the Continent. In 1957, the British government renounced all pretense of independent military resources and accepted missiles from the United States. The British defense effort had served mainly to maintain influence with the United States, but it was an effort that required British alignment with American policy. In effect, Britain could not use this force against American wishes.

The French went a separate way, not entirely by choice: The United States refused to provide technical defense information to the French government, deemed less secure than the British. The French Fourth Republic increased independent nuclear research after the Suez crisis, and de Gaulle hastened the program when he returned to power in 1958. The first French atomic bomb was exploded in the Sahara in 1960, and the first thermonuclear weapon in the French Pacific islands in 1968.

De Gaulle did not think a proud country like France would expend the effort to create a major military force unless it had sole authority to give it orders. The British armed force was tied to American policy; all the NATO forces were under the command of integrated staffs and ultimately under an American general, the Supreme Allied Commander–Europe. De Gaulle's rejection of this state of affairs seemed to many observers a kind of archaic nationalism. Nevertheless, his separate path struck a responsive chord in many Europeans outside France as well.

De Gaulle had begun to remove French armed forces from NATO integrated command as early as 1959, when he pulled out the fighter aircraft squadrons and the French Mediterranean fleet. He removed the Atlantic and Channel fleets from NATO command in June 1963, and in 1966 he withdrew all French participation from NATO integrated military structures (while proclaiming that France would remain a member of the Atlantic Alliance). NATO headquarters moved from near Paris to near Brussels in 1966.

While Americans were still reeling from this first NATO defection, de Gaulle extended diplomatic recognition to Communist China (1964) and paid a lavish state visit to Moscow (1966), during which he offered the Russians "détente, entente, and cooperation." His proposals for scientific and technological collaboration were eagerly seized upon by the Soviet leader Brezhnev, though de Gaulle's vision of a "European Europe . . . from the Atlantic to the Urals" was merely waved aside. The geography of that celebrated phrase was somewhat vague, and his hope of loosening the Soviet grip on Eastern Europe seemed chimerical, but de Gaulle was the first major European statesman since the Second World War to show that Europe was prepared to go its own way.

Two grand old men of the New Europe. Former West German chancellor Konrad Adenauer and French president Charles de Gaulle in Paris, 1966.

De Gaulle also sought to develop an independent relationship with the Third World. It was in this period that per capita French foreign aid passed that of the United States, a matter he made much of in a tour through Latin America (1964). In Cambodia in 1966 he denounced the American military intervention in Vietnam. Carried away by the enthusiasm of a French Canadian crowd, he infuriated the federal government in Ottawa by crying "Long live Free Quebec!" (1967). Many Americans concluded that de Gaulle had embarked on an anti-American vendetta.

The impression was heightened by his attacks on "franglais" (American phrases that crept into the French language along with American fads), his efforts to limit American corporations' power in the French economy, and, as we will see below, he took action to weaken the international role of the dollar. De Gaulle aroused more anger in the United States than any European leader outside the Soviet Union since World War II. On occasion, newspaper photographers showed irate Americans pouring good burgundy wine down the drain.

In calmer afterthought, de Gaulle can be seen to have been a subtle player of balance-of-power *Realpolitik* in the European tradition, a tradition often misunderstood by Americans who expected alliances to express friendship more than self-interest. For de Gaulle, keenly aware of the rise and decline of nations throughout history, a nation that had the will to resist decline must seek its national interest by constant struggle on all fronts. Alliances for him were the mere shifting expressions of national interest. De Gaulle always insisted that one element of French interest was Western solidarity, and indeed his strategy took American defense of Western Europe for granted. De Gaulle took pains to reconfirm that aspect of his policy whenever the West seemed threatened. He supported Kennedy during the Berlin and Cuban crises in 1961 and 1962, more firmly than any other Western European statesman, and again during the Soviet occupation of Czechoslovakia in 1968. He always insisted that France had not left NATO, only the integrated military command. When the Soviets were not being aggressive, however, he believed in exploiting the spaces within the decaying Cold War alliance system to maximum advantage. Although his larger visions belonged to a distant future, he united the French population, from nationalist to communist, around renewed French self-confidence and gave France a decade of prosperity and stability such as it had not seen since the nineteenth century. Some American sympathizers, such as Secretary of State Henry Kissinger, felt that de Gaulle did more in this way for Western strength than any number of mere vassals.

De Gaulle was not appreciated by all Europeans, of course. Some of the smaller members of the European Community resented the close cooperation established between de Gaulle and German chancellor Adenauer, beginning with a treaty in 1963 that marked the end of an historic national enmity, as an effort to turn the Common Market into a Franco-German condominium. Those feelings were reinforced when de Gaulle vetoed British entry into the Common Market in 1963 and again in 1967.

A less complex statesman than de Gaulle might have found in the Common Market the ideal vehicle for raising Europe to the status of a third superpower. De Gaulle threw his will and intelligence into a double policy, however, whose inherent contradiction some have seen as a fatal flaw in his effort to shape the future. De Gaulle wanted an independent France in an independent Europe. But Europe must be a *Europe des patries,* he insisted—a federation of the traditional nation-states—and not some faceless new entity whose inhabitants spoke "Esperanto or Volapuk." De Gaulle may thus have caused Europe to miss a prime opportunity to become a real "Third Force."

THE COMMON MARKET REDIRECTED

De Gaulle soon found an opportunity to raise the question of what direction the European integration movement would now take. On the one hand lay the possibility that, having succeeded brilliantly in its initial economic assignment,[5] the European Common Market would make its supranational elements (such as the common

[5]See chapter 18, p. 551.

agricultural policy) the germ cell of a genuine political union. That was the hope of the aged survivors of the European integration movement's heroic days, such as Jean Monnet, and of the growing body of supranational officials, such as Walter Hallstein, president of the Common Market's Commission for the first ten years (1958–1967). Hallstein liked to speak of the Treaty of Rome (1958) as a "constitutional document," the "first chapter of a European constitution."[6] From this point of view, the Common Market should take on not only new functions but new members. For example, it should assume powers of taxation, and it should expand to include Britain and other members of the European Free Trade Association (EFTA) who had changed their minds about European integration.

On the other hand lay the idea of a more limited cooperation among states, for which de Gaulle was the most conspicuous but by no means the only spokesman. Despite his clear aversion to supranationality, de Gaulle did not want to dissolve the Common Market or other European agencies. He wanted to use the Common Market for his own goals: to make powerful again a Europe led by France. Using France's veto power to block any decisions until he got his way, de Gaulle prodded the Common Market in directions favorable to French interests. The Common Market members were forced into the uncomfortable choice of doing things his way or not at all.

As the main agricultural producer of the Six, France insisted that the Common Market absorb French agricultural surpluses. France wanted Common Market overseas development funds directed largely to French Africa. De Gaulle vetoed British entry into the Common Market because British imports of Commonwealth agricultural products were a threat to French agriculture and because he felt that Britain was too closely tied to United States policy. When Hallstein attempted to increase the Common Market's budgetary independence by collecting some customs duties and disbursing agricultural subsidies directly, de Gaulle brought the whole machinery to a halt for seven months, from July 1965 to January 1966. Common Market institutions began to function again only in January 1966, under the "Luxembourg compromise," which in effect gave each member a veto power in cases of vital national interest. The Common Market did not make the scheduled leap to the next stage of supranationality, in which the Commission would have been empowered to take initiatives backed by a mere majority of member states. De Gaulle had blocked it, perhaps to the secret relief of some other member governments.

Nevertheless the Common Market had too much momentum and served too many interests to be destroyed—nor had that been de Gaulle's intention. Its power and legitimacy continued to grow, though now toward a system of consensus among member states. The Commission was not headed by another international official with the Europeanist zeal of a Walter Hallstein for another twenty years. Instead of becoming the executive body of a European political union, the Commission subsided into a planning and administrative staff. Political power gravitated back to the representatives of the member states. At the everyday working level, there was a

[6]European Economic Community, *Bulletin,* no. 7-1967 (July 1967), p. 8.

Council of Permanent Representatives (COREPER, in the acronyms that flourished in Brussels). The various ministers—especially foreign and agriculture ministers—met often with their Common Market colleagues in Councils of Ministers. Finally, after 1969 the heads of government began meeting, and after 1974 their three meetings a year became formalized as the European Council.

On this new federalist track, the Common Market continued to root itself in the everyday life of West Europeans. In 1967, the three European bodies—Common Market, Coal-Steel Community, and Euratom—merged into a single European Community (EC). In 1968, ahead of schedule, the last internal tariffs disappeared. The Community acquired both judicial and taxing power. A body of case law built up around the EC's Court of Justice in Luxembourg, which successfully asserted the primacy of community law over national law in an increasing range of cases. In one instance, the court ruled that whipping schoolboys, still practiced in some British schools, and not contrary to any British law, contravened the Community's Human Rights Code. After 1975, the Community had its own income, drawn partly from external customs duties and partly from a 1 percent value-added tax imposed in all member states. In 1979, the European Monetary System was created (without England and Denmark)—not the single currency that Europeanists had dreamed of but a mechanism for dampening the fluctuations among member currencies. Finally, after 1979 the European Parliament was chosen no longer by the parliaments of member states but directly by the citizens of the states. Although the Parliament's ultimate power was to veto the budget, which it did in 1979 and 1982, it functioned mainly as a European sounding board, and transnational party groups grew up around it in the same way that transnational labor unions and businessmen's associations had grown up around the Commission. At the working level, however, there was little "spillover" from the first supranational regulation of coal and steel through widening circles of the national economies. Industry remained mostly national. The main exceptions were rudimentary space research and more substantial nuclear energy research, aircraft such as the British–French Concorde and the German-French-British-Spanish Airbus, and a few smaller amalgamations such as the German and Belgian photographic film industries.

Now that the EC had been redirected along federal lines, and after de Gaulle's departure from the scene, further geographical expansion became possible. Britain was finally admitted in 1973, reducing its "special relationship" with the United States and turning from the Commonwealth to Europe. This step divided the British public (the Labour Party opposed it), but it was reaffirmed in a 1975 referendum. Ireland and Denmark, whose economies were closely tied to Britain's, joined at the same time. When Greece became a member on January 1, 1981, the Six had become the Ten. Spain and Portugal joined on January 1, 1986. Geographical expansion, however, also meant greater heterogeneity. It moved Western Europe away from any genuine merger as a United States of Europe.

By the 1970s, the EC had become one of the industrial great powers. It was the largest trading unit in the world. Some of its products cut deeply into American industrial supremacy: automobiles, for example. The ubiquitous Volkswagen "Beetle," by itself, accounted for 10 percent of American new car purchases at its peak in the early 1970s. Western European steel production now ran ahead of American levels:

	1959	1971[7]
United States	93 million tons	141 million tons
Europe (the Six plus Britain)	88 million tons	147 million tons

Europe's industrial growth was not merely quantitative. Reconstruction of war-damaged plants permitted Western European industry to start fresh with the latest technology. Such processes as continuously cast steel spread in European firms well before American ones. Western Europe had emerged as a major economic power in its own right, an industrialized region of 175 million highly skilled people, comparable to the superpowers themselves in economic weight.

THE UNITED STATES AND EUROPE AS ECONOMIC RIVALS

It took time for the changed relationship between Europe and the United States to overcome mental habits set in 1945. At that time, the United States had accounted for half the world's productive capacity. Throughout the 1950s, the European economies had struggled against a chronic "dollar gap." Europeans needed desperately to buy food, coal, and machinery from dollar areas at a time when they obtained dollars only from foreign aid, American travel abroad, and the small American imports from Europe. To prevent disastrous declines in their own currencies' relative value, Western European governments had to limit imports and control their citizens' access to dollars. As late as 1955, observers as astute as Raymond Aron could still believe that the economic gap was widening between the United States and Europe.[8]

All that changed in the 1960s. The last direct American aid to Europe, military assistance, had ended in 1956. Americans began buying more from the emerging European giant. By the end of 1970, the United States trade deficit with Europe had risen to over $10 billion per year. Americans had learned in 1945 to think of Europe as a poor relation that needed help. Europeans had learned to look westward toward an America of luxury and progress. Both had assumed that European economic recovery was a matter of mutual interest. During the 1960s, they began to think of each other instead as rivals and competitors.

Economic conflicts between the United States and Western Europe centered on three issues: trade rivalries, the power of multinational firms (still mostly American), and the dollar's stability as the principal international currency.

The "chicken war" of 1963 was the first skirmish in the trade wars that rage today. It was to be expected that agriculture would provoke the first skirmish, for farm products were the most successful common project of the European Community. The EC devoted three-fourths of its budget to agriculture. It developed a system of

[7]Michael Mandelbaum and Daniel Yergin, "Balancing the Power," *Yale Review,* vol. 62, no. 3 (March 1973), p. 324.

[8]Aron, *The Opium of the Intellectuals,* trans. Terence Kilmartin, (New York, 1962) p. 222.

farm price supports that sustained them well above world prices. These were accompanied by import duties that raised the price of farm products of non-EC origin to Community levels. That income, in turn, paid for the subsidies to EC farmers. When this system went into effect for poultry in 1963, American farmers lost a lucrative market. American pressure on Western Europe to resume its imports of American poultry were strong enough to irritate but not strong enough to achieve their goal. Community imports of poultry declined 43 percent between 1963 and 1970, and, by 1982, the EC had been transformed from the world's largest importer of poultry to its largest exporter.

EC farm price supports inevitably produced huge surpluses. Contemplating the "mountains" of butter and "lakes" of wine that accumulated, EC officials devised a system of export subsidies that returned to the farmer the difference between the supported EC price and the lower world price. This permitted European farm exports to become a major competitor on world markets by the late 1970s. The United States, which also subsidized farm products but by different mechanisms, objected strenuously to the way the EC undercut American farm exports to the Third World.

Although Europe had lost the last of its formal empire with full independence for most of Africa between 1957 and 1962, an informal empire gave the EC privileged access to many former colonial areas. Indeed, as European aid, trade, and investment revived in former colonies, more French nationals, for example, were to be found living in such West African states as Senegal and the Ivory Coast than in colonial days. As long as world trade was expanding, the preferential investment and trade arrangements that the EC established with the former colonies of its members—especially the former French colonies in Africa—did not lead to major conflicts with the United States. It was a different matter in contracting world markets after 1973.[9]

The most conspicuous special EC arrangement with the Third World was the Lomé Convention, concluded in 1975 (and renewed regularly until 2000) between the EC and forty-six former colonies in Africa, the Caribbean, and the Pacific. The number of signatories had grown to seventy-one by 2000. Signatories of the Lomé Convention were able to export their products duty-free into the Common Market, without any corresponding requirement to accept European goods in return. In this respect, Lomé was an improvement over the more neocolonialist Yaoundé Convention of 1963, which had linked the EC to former colonies. One of the most innovative sections of the Lomé Convention set up a stabilization fund to maintain steady prices for certain Third World raw products (coffee, sugar, cacao, and the like) whose previous fluctuations had seriously disrupted the development efforts of one-crop countries. This was Europe's main contribution to what came to be called "North-South dialogue" between the developed and less-developed worlds. From the American point of view, however, it was a neocolonial barrier to American trade and hence another source of European–American economic conflict.

The problem of American investments in the Common Market countries was more difficult. As the European market flourished, United States companies established branches within the Six in order to avoid the external tariff. By 1965 the EC Commis-

[9]See chapter 22, p. 623.

sion in Brussels estimated that American branches or subsidiaries accounted for 80 percent of computer production in Europe, 24 percent of automobiles, 15 percent of synthetic rubber, and 10 percent of petrochemicals.[10] The prospect that overseas American firms would become the main beneficiaries of the Common Market boom, controlling vital sectors of the Western European economy, raised an alarm that can be measured by the way in which French journalist Jean-Jacques Servan-Schreiber's *The American Challenge* (1967)[11] became the best seller in French publishing history.

American subsidiaries in Europe were linked to the currency issue. Since 1945, the dollar had been virtually equivalent to gold as a reserve currency to be held by national banking systems. This gold exchange standard, unlike the pre-1914 pure gold standard, meant that European national banks did not have to cash their dollars in for gold, for the dollar was "as good as gold." When the balance of trade changed around 1960, European banking systems and firms began accumulating large dollar reserves. If all these dollar reserves had been presented at Fort Knox for gold at once, the United States would have been unable to continue pouring dollars overseas in military spending, tourist spending, and business investment. In that sense, the dollar was overvalued, and the gold exchange standard permitted American firms to invest more freely in Europe than they could have if all European-held dollars had been redeemed for gold at once.

It was General de Gaulle who first called public attention to the dollar's overvaluation, and who opposed its special privileges. At the beginning of 1965, he advocated returning to a pure gold standard. To prove his point, the French government redeemed several hundred million dollars for gold. As American gold reserves shrank, the International Monetary Fund, the chief regulating office for foreign exchange matters set up at Bretton Woods, tried in 1969 to take pressure off the dollar by creating a new reserve fund, a paper reserve called Special Drawing Rights, and by allowing individuals to buy gold at a floating rate, while the official rate for United States government transactions remained $35 per ounce of gold.

Finally, beginning in May 1971, a massive wave of speculation against the dollar brought the Bretton Woods system of fixed exchange rates to an end.[12] The wild sale of dollars by Swiss bankers (the "gnomes of Zurich"), American speculators, and oil-rich Arabs revealed to the public that the dollar would have to be looked at according to hard facts rather than its postwar mystique. The hard facts were that the annual American trade deficit had reached $10.68 billion in 1970 and was headed higher. The United States government was spending vast sums abroad, particularly for the Vietnam War (1961–1973). Moreover, inflation in the United States, combined with low interest rates there, encouraged American speculators to shift funds to Germany where interest rates were high. In 1970, $6 billion was transferred in this fashion from the United States to Germany. Instability was further increased by the enormous growth of Eurodollars, which had reached $50 billion by 1971, mostly

[10]George Lichtheim, *Europe in the Twentieth Century* (New York, 1972), p. 314.

[11]The book did not, of course, examine only American investments in Europe. It also warned against the power of American technological and management skill on a world level, and urged Europeans to emulate it.

[12]See chapter 16, pp. 496–497.

since 1969. Eurodollars were dollar credits held by Europeans or by American firms doing business in Europe. They were lent to other Europeans or to American branches in a way that multiplied dollar holdings in Europe and added enormously to the mass of speculation. The holders of Eurodollars were tempted to exchange them for German marks when the dollar began to look weak in May 1971. The final hard fact was the dwindling United States gold and foreign currency reserves. The gold reserve had fallen to about $11 billion in May 1971; at that time, there were $20 billion afloat in West Germany alone. If every West German holder of dollars had demanded gold at once, the United States would have been technically bankrupt.

On May 5, 1971, most European central banks, overwhelmed in the rush, simply stopped foreign exchange trading. President Nixon tried to persuade Europe to solve the problem by assuming more NATO defense costs, by lowering EC tariffs, and by buying more United States goods. In August, the United States unilaterally uncoupled the dollar from gold, and then in December devalued the dollar by 8.57 percent. A second devaluation of 10 percent followed in February 1973.

Thereafter, currency exchange rates floated. The dollar's volatility and American unilateralism in monetary matters stimulated an interest already expressed within the Common Market for Europe's own currency system. A first agreement in 1972 to link the European currencies together by permitting fluctuations no greater that 2.25 percent (called "the snake" after the wriggly line traced by the highs and lows of the various European currencies) did not survive the financial turbulence of the 1970s, discussed in chapter 22. A more serious effort in 1979 to link the Common Market members' currencies in a European Monetary System (EMS) proved more durable. The EMS, in effect, committed the European currencies to vary no more than 2.25 percent from a fixed relation to its stablest member, the German Mark. Its members began to accustom themselves to pegging their currencies to the Mark (even when that required high interest rates that slowed economic activity), a process that down the line, in 2002, produced a single European currency.

Western Europe and the United States were capable by the 1970s of inflicting serious economic damage on each other. They dealt with each other carefully, however, knowing that the prosperity of each depended on the prosperity of all. But they pushed and shoved at each other in ways that would not have been dreamed of a decade earlier. The Common Market convicted the United States Continental Can Company of monopoly practices in Europe in 1972; the United States brought suit before the General Agreement on Trade and Tariffs (GATT) against some forms of European agricultural subsidies that damaged American farm exports. Western Europe had now acquired the economic weight to go its own way in the world, a less clearly bipolar world than the one after 1945.

RIVAL VERSIONS OF DÉTENTE

Defense and military strategy was another area in which postwar assumptions of European–American harmony of interests gave way to realizations of conflicting priorities and perspectives. The Cuban missile crisis brought some of these dis-agreements to the surface. Khrushchev had demonstrated his fundamental desire to avoid war, given Soviet military inferiority. At the same time, that awful moment at the brink had showed Europeans that the two superpowers could wager Euro-pean lives in their power gambles without Europeans having any voice in the mat-ter. President Kennedy had sent emissaries to European capitals to "inform" allied leaders of his decisions, not to "consult" with them. Although all of them supported the United States publicly, and none more unhesitatingly than Charles de Gaulle, even the NATO Council was critical of the lack of consultation in a matter that might involve Western Europe in a nuclear war.

Europeans' claim for a voice in Western strategic matters might seem ill justified by the small proportion of their resources they spent on their own defense. That asymmetry of contribution was part of the problem, however. Western Europe's defense against Soviet attack was a "tripwire" detachment of American troops, too small in itself to hold off the Warsaw Pact armies, even as part of combined NATO forces, but sufficient to bring American nuclear force into play.

As long as the American nuclear force had clear superiority, few Europeans doubted that the United States would retaliate with a nuclear attack on the Soviet Union against a Soviet military advance into Western Europe. And according to the American doctrine of "massive retaliation," Russia would be the battleground. Both of these propositions became open to doubt in the 1960s. Massive Soviet armaments expenditures after their Cuban defeat swelled the Soviet arsenal to something approaching parity in missiles, aviation, and submarines with the United States. As the Soviets acquired greater capability to retaliate directly against American cities, Americans began to look for other options. Kennedy's Secretary of Defense Robert McNamara (1961–1968) replaced "massive retaliation" with "graduated deterrence." According to this innovation, American force would be deployed in gradually ascending steps against a Soviet advance. While this new strategy offered more opportunities for the superpowers to stop short of a nuclear holocaust, it had the grave disadvantage in European eyes of making their continent the probable battle-field again. This prospect was all the more daunting when battlefield-level tactical nuclear weapons entered the arsenals of both superpowers in the 1970s. Henry Kissinger, for one, thought that many Europeans saw "graduated deterrence" as a "symptom of growing reluctance of the United States to use nuclear force."[13]

General de Gaulle was the first European leader to express these doubts openly, but not the last. It was one rationale for his perseverance in the construction of an independent nuclear force for France. The United States attempted to promote more coordinated Western defense efforts in several ways, without much success. One way was to meet the apparent Western European desire for a greater voice in the nuclear decision. In March 1963, the United States proposed a Multilateral Nuclear Force (MLF), a flotilla of surface ships manned by NATO crews and fur-nished with American Polaris missiles. Although Britain had already accepted dependence on American missile technology, France opposed the MLF so

---

[13]Henry A. Kissinger, *White House Years* (New York, 1979), p. 391.

adamantly that the idea was dropped in 1964. The other way was constant pressure on European members of NATO to enhance their conventional armed forces. But even the threat of American reduction of its "tripwire" force in Europe, offered in Senator Mike Mansfield's annual amendment to the military appropriations bill, could not persuade Western European states to spend more on conventional armaments when tensions between East and West seemed to be easing.[14]

The SALT[15] agreements took détente another major step beyond what Kennedy and Khrushchev had found possible in the Nuclear Test Ban Treaty of 1963. Years of disarmament talks during the 1960s had failed to reach agreement on limitation of nuclear warheads. The United States demanded nine on-site inspections per year, whereas the Soviet Union would permit only three. While space technology made it easier to detect missile launchers, the technological leap of multiple warheads on a single missile (Multiple Intertargetable Reentry Vehicles, or MIRVs), introduced by the United States in the late 1960s, made the number of warheads almost impossible to verify. The SALT talks broke through by agreeing to focus only on missile launchers. The SALT I treaty, signed by President Nixon and Secretary Brezhnev in Moscow in June 1972, permitted 40 percent more launchers to the USSR than to the United States because the United States had multiple warheads. SALT I further set narrow limits to both sides' development of antiballistic missile defense systems. When that treaty expired in 1977, the two superpowers continued to observe its provisions. Neither wished to incur the blame for interrupting what seemed the irresistible progress of détente. By the time of the second SALT agreement, initialed in Vienna by President Carter and Secretary Brezhnev in 1979 and applied even though never ratified by the United States Senate, the Russians had MIRVs too. This agreement covered additional delivery systems such as long-range bombers and nuclear submarines and set identical limits for MIRVed missiles at 1,200 for each country. By these agreements the superpowers publicly acknowledged and accepted nuclear parity.

The SALT treaties were universally welcomed by Western Europeans as a step away from the war that had never been far from their thoughts since 1945. The welcome was clouded, however, by the way in which the two superpowers had continued to settle the affairs of the world over Europeans' heads. "SALT is the only major East-West transaction that has lacked European participation."[16] On the other hand, the progress of détente encouraged Europeans to move ahead on their own. The more American nuclear protection seemed both uncertain and lethal, and the less the superpowers consulted them, the more Western European leaders were tempted to follow the path blazed by General de Gaulle.

---

[14]Even after a NATO plan of 1978 for annual 3 percent increases in conventional armaments expenditure, defense budgets as percentages of gross domestic product were as follows in 1983: United States, 7.2 percent; Britain, about 5 percent; West Germany, 4.3 percent; France, 4.1 percent; the rest, between 3.3 percent and 2 percent. Though hard to measure, USSR military expenditure is believed never to have fallen below 18 percent of GDP even in the years of détente.

[15]Strategic Arms Limitation Treaty.

[16]John Newhouse, *Cold Dawn: The Story of SALT* (New York, 1973), p. 271.

General de Gaulle's assault on the two-bloc system had been more verbal than real. It was the most dynamic Western European statesman to follow him, West Germany's Social Democratic chancellor Willy Brandt (1969–1974), who made more discernible change in the frozen frontier down the center of Europe.

The very existence of a Social Democratic government in West Germany was a sign that the postwar world had given way to something new. The long domination of West German politics since the war by the Christian Democrats ended with elections in October 1969 and with the decision of the small centrist Free Democrats to switch their support to Willy Brandt's Social Democratic Party (SPD). Although the Free Democrats supported *laissez-faire* economic policies at home, they were willing to work with the SPD for broad relaxation of relations with the communist neighbors. With Brandt as chancellor, the German Social Democrats held power in Germany for the first time since Chancellor Hermann Müller (1928–1930). The SPD–Free Democrat coalition was to govern West Germany from 1969 to 1982.

Brandt, aged fifty-eight in 1969, was in an exceptionally strong position to sweep with a new broom. He had spent the years from 1933 to 1945 in Norway and Sweden, where he participated in underground resistance to Hitler. While there, he became impressed with the pragmatic welfare state social democracy of Scandinavia. As the young mayor of West Berlin after 1957, he showed himself imaginative and energetic. In 1964, he became leader of the German Social Democratic Party and changed it into a pragmatic mass party.[17] As chancellor of a heavily one-sided coalition after October 1969, Brandt enjoyed much more leeway than had Müller in 1928. To be sure, his Free Democrat partners prevented any major social change, but Brandt's priority was *Ostpolitik* (eastern policy): dismantling the wall across central Europe. In this task, he fended off both the student and radical left, who attacked him for working within capitalism, and the Christian Democrats, who were shocked at any deviation from Adenauer's rigid prohibition against dealing with anyone who recognized East Germany.

Brandt's first major breakthrough took place in Moscow, for the Soviet Union held the key to any change in the Eastern European relationship. In any case, the Soviet Union was eager for what Brandt had to offer. The Moscow Treaty of August 1970 provided for mutual recognition of existing frontiers. This was tantamount to West German renunciation of the lost lands east of the Oder-Neisse River, now in Poland, and of such former Germanic territories as the Czech Sudetenland, which Hitler acquired at Munich and which some German nationalists still claimed. This giant step made subsequent treaties with Poland and Czechoslovakia almost anticlimactic. A new era had dawned, however, when a German chancellor could place a wreath on the monument to the Jewish victims of Nazi barbarism in Warsaw, as Brandt did in December 1970. In early 1973, he agreed with the Czech government to renounce the Munich settlement of 1938 and thereby any German claim to the Sudetenland, from which so many German-speaking people had been evicted in 1945.

With East Germany, negotiations went somewhat more awkwardly. When Brandt first met East German chancellor Willi Stoph at Erfurt in March 1970, the East

---

[17]See chapter 19, p. 567.

German crowd surged forward shouting Brandt's name. This demonstration of enthusiasm was highly embarrassing to those who claimed legitimacy for East Germany. The East German leaders, who had built the Berlin Wall only nine years earlier out of fear of the corrosive effect of Western contacts on their people, had second thoughts about détente. But the way seemed more open again after Walter Ulbricht, the wooden first secretary of the East German Socialist Unity Party (SED), retired in 1971 at the age of seventy-seven. Now both Adenauer and Ulbricht, the twin personifications of Cold War rigidity in the two Germanies, were gone.

Even though Ulbricht's successor, Erich Honecker, was an old-line party functionary who also feared Western contacts, progress was made in ways that would have seemed unthinkable earlier. At Christmas 1972, the first major movement of persons across the border took place after eleven years of isolation. Many divided families were reunited as an estimated 500,000 West Germans took advantage of the permission to visit East Germany for up to thirty days. East Germans, however, could still not travel. In June 1973, the two Germanies were admitted simultaneously to the United Nations after their mutual diplomatic recognition. It was the most dramatic negotiated change in European state relations since the Locarno Agreements of 1925.

The way was now open for more general negotiations between the Western and Eastern European countries. The SALT agreements were superpower deals that affected Europe vitally but passively. SALT I was followed by a series of multilateral negotiations in which the European states were actively involved: the thirty-five-nation Conference on Security and Cooperation in Europe (CSCE), which opened in Helsinki, Finland, in November 1972; and the eleven-power talks on Mutual and Balanced Force Reductions (MBFR), which began in Vienna in October 1973.

The force reduction talks in Vienna (MBFR) were designed to make the war fuse in central Europe a little less short. The Russians enjoyed an overwhelming and growing superiority in conventional armament there.[18] As a Soviet military advance westward by conventional forces appeared easier and easier, the delay before the West would have to escalate its tactical nuclear weapons to strategic nuclear weapons in a losing land battle grew shorter and shorter. Whereas Western Europeans wanted to negotiate asymmetrical reductions in such areas of decisive Russian lead such as battle tanks, the Russians insisted on strictly proportional

---

[18]Force levels in 1984:

	Warsaw Pact	NATO
Personnel	4,000,000	2,600,000
Divisions	173 (included 32 Soviet divisions in Eastern Europe)	84 (included 5 U.S. divisions in Western Europe)
Main Battle Tanks	42,500	13,000
Aircraft	7,240	3,000
Intermediate-Range Missiles	c.800 SS-20 missiles (in Western USSR) c.100 SS-20 missiles (in Eastern Europe)	108 Pershing II missiles 464 ground-launched cruise missiles (installed in Western Europe)

reductions that would maintain their advantage. These talks dragged on indecisively into the 1980s, long after the initial détente impulse had died.

The Helsinki Conference (1972–1975), by contrast, was the culminating moment of détente. The Final Act, signed August 1, 1975, by thirty-five participants—thirty-two European states plus Canada and the two superpowers—recognized all the existing borders of Europe and the military alliances of NATO and the Warsaw Pact. The two sides agreed to notify each other of major military exercises. The signatories also called for increased trade and cultural relations between the two blocs and agreed to guarantee human rights and political liberties within their borders. The Soviet Union accepted this part grudgingly. Indeed, the Soviet government spent the next ten years crushing Russian dissidents' efforts to have the Helsinki Final Act applied in their country, and similar movements in the *satellites* such as the Czech Charter 77 movement. But it was the Soviets' payment for what amounted to Western recognition of Soviet hegemony in Eastern Europe.

For, on closer inspection, Willy Brandt's *Ostpolitik* and the Helsinki Final Act were a de facto German peace settlement on the basis of the status quo, the settlement so long deferred since the end of World War II. In effect, the two blocs accepted their current borders. At the same time, the human significance of those borders was being reduced by increased trade and cultural contacts. The West hoped that freer contacts would loosen the Soviet monolith. Brezhnev wanted Western technology, investment capital, and farm products without any cultural contamination.

The opening of the Eastern bloc to Western European and American economic penetration was a silent revolution of the 1970s. Exports from NATO countries to the Soviet Union multiplied sixfold in the course of the decade.[19] In October 1975, President Ford concluded a grain export deal with the Soviet Union that made the United States the main foreign supplier of Russian grain. The Italian government helped build and supervise a FIAT automobile plant in the Soviet Union, in a town that the Russians renamed Tolyatti in honor of the late Italian Communist leader Togliatti. France eagerly marketed electronic technology, such as its color television process, in the Soviet Union. Eastern Europe borrowed heavily in the West to finance the import of advanced equipment, foodstuffs, and consumer goods. The combined foreign debt of the Eastern bloc grew from $19 billion in 1975 to about $62 billion in 1981, of which the largest single creditor was West Germany. The largest debtor was Poland, which owed $28 billion by itself to Western banks.

While Europeans and Americans shared hopes that détente would somehow lessen the threat of nuclear war, the practical effects of détente were to emphasize divergences between Western Europe and the United States. The West had huddled together under the shadow of Stalinism. As the prospect of immediate war receded, disagreements emerged in defense and military matters. Disagreement was even more intense in economic matters, however, and one effect of détente was to shift the focus of attention within the Western alliance from the military to the economic

---

[19] *The New York Times,* January 17, 1982, sec. iv, p. E3.

realm. The possibilities of trade and investment in Eastern Europe and the Soviet Union brought Western European–American economic rivalry into the foreground. This made it harder to cling to the postwar view that American and European economic interests were complementary. The frictions already apparent in good times were to become even sharper when good times came to an end with the oil crisis of 1973.

SUGGESTIONS FOR FURTHER READING

The works on the cold war cited at the end of chapter 18 are fundamental here too. See also John Gaddis, *Russia, the Soviet Union, and the United States,*[*] 2nd ed. (1990).

Raymond Garthoff, *Détente and Confrontation: American-Soviet Relations from Nixon to Reagan*[*] (revised ed. 1994), looks coolly at both sides. Fred Halliday, *The Making of the Second Cold War,* 2nd ed. (1986), considers the United States primarily responsible for the end of détente. Soviet and Western missile strategies are best followed in the works by Honoré M. Catudal and Andrew Pierre cited at the end of chapter 18.

The most authoritative study of de Gaulle's rule is Jean Lacouture, *De Gaulle: The Ruler, 1945–1970* (1992), a sympathetic account based on massive interviewing. In addition to those mentioned at the end of chapter 14, Andrew Shennan, *De Gaulle*[*] (1995), is an up-to-date one-volume biography; see also the penetrating chapters on de Gaulle by Stanley Hoffmann in *Decline or Renewal? France since the 1930s* (1974). Excellent studies of de Gaulle's challenge to American leadership are Edward A. Kolodziej, *French International Policy under de Gaulle and Pompidou* (1974); Michael Harrison, *Reluctant Ally: France and Atlantic Security* (1981); and Philip G. Cerny, *The Politics of Grandeur* (1980). Authoritative for the Fifth French Republic is Serge Berstein, *The Republic of De Gaulle* (1993).

Willy Brandt's agreements with Germany's eastern neighbors are scrutinized by William E. Griffith, *The Ostpolitik of the Federal Republic of Germany* (1978); see also Brandt, *My Life in Politics* (1992). Clay Clemens, *Reluctant Realists: The CDU-CSU and West German Ostpolitik* (1989), provides the sequel. The Franco-German tandem within the European Community is explored by Haig Simonian, *The Privileged Partnership* (1985).

The functioning of the European Economic Community is thoroughly laid out in Helen Wallace and William Wallace, *Policy-Making in the European Community,* 4th ed. (2000), and by other works noted at the end of chapter 23. Paul Taylor, *The Limits of European Integration* (1983), reflects the climate of the period of "Euroscepticism."

For the U.S. side in détente, in addition to Henry Kissinger's memoirs, *White House Years* (1979, reprint ed. 1999), *Years of Upheaval* (1982, reprint ed. 1999), and *Years of Renewal*[*] (1998), Robert D. Schulzinger, *Henry Kissinger: Doctor of Diplomacy*[*] (1989), is the least polemical of several biographies. Walter Isaacson, *Kissinger: A Biography*[*] (1993), has more personal detail. See more generally Richard C. Thornton, *The Nixon Kissinger Years: The Reshaping of American Foreign Policy*[*] (new ed. 2002).

Most complete on the Sino-Soviet rift is Alfred D. Low, *The Sino-Soviet Dispute* (1976), followed by his *Sino-Soviet Confrontation* (1987). Soviet reactions to polycentrism can be studied in works on foreign policy by Adam Ulam and Alvin Z. Rubinstein cited at the end of chapters 16 and 18.

Additional Internet links related to this chapter are available on the Europe in the 20th Century Web site: http://www.history.wadsworth.com/paxton04.

You can also explore images, interactive timelines, and maps related to this chapter on our Western Civilization Resource Center: http://history.wadsworth.com

The annual display of Soviet military might in Moscow on the anniversary of the Bolshevik Revolution, November 10, 1964. Intercontinental ballistic missiles (ICBMs) pass in review in Red Square before First Secretary Leonid Brezhnev and other Soviet leaders standing atop Lenin's tomb (the low, square structure, center right).

21

The Soviet Bloc in the Brezhnev Era

Khrushchev was ousted as first secretary of the Communist Party of the USSR in October 1964 by a palace *coup* led by his heir apparent, Leonid Brezhnev. The new party secretary was a stolid official with narrowly technical training as an engineer and a liking for fast cars and hunting.

It has been customary to stress the contrasts between the ebullient, free-wheeling Khrushchev and the complacent Brezhnev—especially after the latter became nearly immobilized by the illnesses that were to kill him in 1982. Their differences of style were profound. But the two men faced similar problems and addressed them similarly through central party direction. Both had to work within a collegial power structure.

At first, Brezhnev was party secretary only. Gradually establishing his dominance, he became in 1977 chief of state (chairman of the Presidium of the Supreme Soviet) and head of the armed forces, with the rank of marshal. He was the first Soviet leader to combine both the top party office (the seat of real power in Stalin's day) and the hitherto largely ceremonial post of chief of state. But whereas Khrushchev had "led from the front," taking "vital policy decisions and bypassing his colleagues when he deemed it necessary," Brezhnev led "from the middle. If you follow the first course, you can wield more power while you are in office, but your tenure of office is likely to be shorter, for when things go wrong . . . it will be too late to seek the security of collective responsibility."[1] So Brezhnev lasted eighteen years, longer than any other Soviet ruler except Stalin. But grave problems festered unresolved.

One must not blame the immobilism of the Brezhnev years solely on the leader. Collegial rule put the government and administration of the Soviet Union firmly in the grip of a privileged inner circle: the *nomenklatura*, satisfied men who had known only Soviet rule (Brezhnev himself was only eleven in 1917) and who had a vested interest in things as they were. The *nomenklatura* was aging, too. Catapulted into major responsibilities as very young men when Stalin's purges swept away their seniors in the late 1930s, they acquired security of life under Khrushchev and then security of office under Brezhnev.[2] By the 1970s, they had become entrenched seventy-year-olds willing to accept only the most anodine reforms.

SOVIET PROBLEMS

One long-running problem was the poor quality and quantity of consumer goods. Party secretary Brezhnev, whose own garage contained a Rolls-Royce, a Mercedes, a Citroën-Maserati, and a Cadillac, felt none of Khrushchev's purist commitment to deferred gratification while building communism. The Twenty-third Party Congress (March–April 1966) announced for the first time in Soviet history that consumer goods production would rise more rapidly than basic investment in productive capacity.

Brezhnev turned increasingly to Western technology and capital in order to reach this goal. After all, Lenin had done the same. In 1966 he signed major contracts with western firms, including one with Italy's FIAT for a vast automobile plant that was expected to triple Soviet automobile output in the 1970s.

Producing ever more of both guns and butter, however, required the Soviet Union to maintain the economic pace of the 1960s. Nikita Khrushchev's boasts of overtaking the West had been lent credibility by 6 percent annual growth rates, and by the world's first successful voyages into space. In 1971 the USSR surpassed the United States in steel production.[3] After that, however, Soviet productivity stagnated. As Soviet industry reached maturity, only increased labor efficiency or technological breakthroughs would provide further growth. There was little incentive for either, however, in what remained, despite a flirtation with

---

[1] Archie Brown, "The Power of the General Secretary," in T. H. Rigby, Archie Brown, and Peter Reddaway, eds., *Authority, Power, and Policy in the USSR* (London, 1980), pp. 151–152.

[2] Seweryn Bialer, *Stalin's Successors* (Cambridge, England 1980), p. 91.

[3] By the 1980s, Japan was ahead of them both.

Two examples of Soviet bloc immobility, Soviet president Leonid Brezhnev joins East German president Erich Honecker in October 1979 for the thirtieth anniversary of the creation of the German Democratic Republic. Brezhnev presided over the USSR's long stagnation from 1964 to 1985. Honecker ruled from 1971 until his regime crumbled in 1989.

Libermanism,[4] a centrally directed economy. Central planning afflicted the economy with multiple blockages and inefficiencies. Managers learned to fulfill quotas rather than seek efficiency or innovation. Planners remained fixed on yesterday's measures of industrial power: coal and steel. Energy was critically short and computers nonexistent. These shortcomings were compounded by massive cynicism, corruption, and alcoholism. As a favorite Soviet joke had it, "we pretend to work and they pretend to pay us." By the 1980s, total Soviet output would actually have declined except for two growth sectors: oil, whose reserves Soviet economic managers rapidly depleted as a quick economic fix,[5] and vodka. All other kinds of production actually shrank.

[4]Beginning in 1962, the economist Yevsei Liberman proposed introducing limited market mechanisms within socialism. Some prices would be freed, plant managers would receive more autonomy to buy and sell according to market calculations rather than according to the plan, and profits would be distributed within the firm. Entrenched bureaucrats limited these experiments to some isolated plants.

[5]High world prices for the oil and gold they now exported in large quantities gave the Soviets temporary breathing space in the 1980s, and also aided Russian recovery after 1998.

Ecological disaster accompanied economic stagnation. After decades of reckless industrial and agricultural pollution, Soviet public health deteriorated. Life expectancy actually shortened from 66 years to 63 during the 1970s. A massive scheme to grow irrigated cotton around the Aral Sea, for example, caused the world's most extensive ecological catastrophe: the dessication of the sea and the pollution of groundwater that so multiplied illnesses and birth defects that separatist sentiments spread among the Kazakhs and Uzbeks.

In an earlier era, Soviet citizens might have stoically tightened their belts yet again, but Khrushchev had aroused hopes of better living conditions and of a freer society. Three generations of Soviet citizens had sacrificed personal liberty in exchange for the promise of equitably distributed abundance. When they realized that they faced instead an indefinite future of scarce and shoddy goods, made more unbearable by the affluence of top officials, cynicism and corruption spread widely under a façade of Communist conformity. This added a cultural crisis—loss of faith—to the economic and ecological ones.

In the non-Russian areas of the Soviet Union, grievances against ecological damage, shortages, and crude intellectual repression tended to be retranslated into nationalist terms. Non-Russians, particularly in the poorer Central Asian regions, believed Russians enjoyed privileged status throughout the USSR. Increased local linguistic and religious loyalty refuted the Soviet claim to have united this multiethnic empire by creating "the new Soviet man." As early as 1978, the French scholar Hélène Carrère d'Encausse predicted that the Soviet Union would be "incapable of extricating itself from the nationality impasse."[6] Now that we have witnessed its disintegration in 1991, it is hard to remember how rash her prediction seemed then.

Brezhnev tightened the cultural screws, as indeed Khrushchev had already begun to do. But that only made intellectual ferment bubble faster. Young people listened privately to Western popular music and wore jeans; the regime's warnings against Western decadence only made it more attractive. Science, high technology, and artistic creation became ever harder to reconcile with tight intellectual control. The trial in 1965 of two writers, Andrei Sinyavsky and Yuli Daniel, for publishing their work abroad, made it plain that the "thaw" was over. After that, even mainstream intellectuals joined the protesters. Clandestine writings, from poetry to politics, circulated widely in handwritten or crudely typed copies known as *Samizdat*.[7] This was, of course, an improvement over Stalin's day, when dissidents had had to commit poems and texts to memory.[8]

The two most celebrated dissidents of the 1970s espoused quite different values. The physicist Andrei Sakharov, who had directed the successful Soviet nuclear program, warned Brezhnev in a 1970 letter, widely circulated in *Samizdat*, that Soviet science, productivity, and living conditions would fall even further behind the West

---

[6]Hélène Carrère d'Encausse, *Decline of an Empire: The Soviet Socialist Republics in Revolt* (New York, 1979), p. 274.

[7]Literally, "self-publishing," in contrast to Gosizdat, the state publishing house. Julius Telesin, "Inside *Samizdat*," *Encounter,* February 1973, and George Saunders, ed., *Samizdat: Voices of the Soviet Opposition*ʼ (1975).

[8]The great poet Anna Akhmatova would silently write out her work to be memorized by Lydia Chukovskaya (even words spoken aloud in a communal apartment were dangerous), and then the women would burn the compromising paper in an ashtray. See Beth Holmgren, *Women's Works in Stalin's Time* (Bloomington, Ind., 1994), p. 86.

without freer circulation of ideas and more democratic airing of problems.[9] When he went on to espouse the return of the national minorities exiled by Stalin, to oppose the pollution of Lake Baikal, and to assert that nuclear war had become unthinkable since capitalism and socialism were converging anyway, he and his even more outspoken wife, Elena Bonner, were isolated in the provincial town of Gorky under house arrest. By contrast to Sakharov's Westernism, the novelist Aleksandr Solzhenitsyn advocated a return to what he regarded as traditional Slavic values of human responsibility, community solidarity, and spiritual asceticism. In view of his distrust of Western materialism and individualism, it was particularly cruel to exile Solzhenitsyn by force to the West after he published his exposé of Stalin's camps—*The Gulag Archipelago*—in the West in 1974.

The Soviet leaders reacted toughly to these criticisms, especially those that took public form or were smuggled out to be published in the West. It was perhaps progress that prominent dissidents, such as General Pyotr Grigorenko, who demonstrated publicly on behalf of the Tartars who wanted to return to their prewar region, and Roy Medvedev's brother Zhores, a biologist, should be confined to mental institutions rather than simply disappear into the living death of a Siberian labor camp as in Stalin's day. But the Soviet Union under Brezhnev had still not solved the problem of how to provide abundance to its people and how to educate many of them to the highest technical competence without also letting them speak their minds.

TROUBLED EASTERN EUROPE: FROM THE CZECHOSLOVAK SPRINGTIME TO THE BREZHNEV DOCTRINE, 1968–1985

Discontent in Eastern Europe

Eastern Europeans were massively disaffected in the Brezhnev years, though not in the same way as the students of Paris or Milan in 1968. Intellectuals and students in Eastern Europe, as in the Soviet Union, were beginning to reach for basic rights of expression that had long been enjoyed in the West. Frustrated nationalism added to the ferment. Mediocre living conditions angered the most people; these were easily blamed on the Soviet masters. For years, the satellites' economies had been stripped for the benefit of Soviet postwar reconstruction.

By the 1970s, however, the economic balance had shifted. Eastern Europe exported manufactured goods to the USSR, and imported Soviet raw materials—oil in particular. Indeed, by the end of the Brezhnev years, Eastern Europeans enjoyed a higher standard of living than most Soviet citizens. Only one Soviet citizen in forty-six had a car, as compared with one out of eight or nine East Germans or Czechs.[10] But when the Soviets tried to reverse their own economic decline by

---

[9]The text of this letter, also signed by the historian Roy Medvedev and the physicist Valery Turchin, is published in *Sakharov Speaks* (New York, 1974), pp. 115–134.

[10]Marshall I. Goldman, *The USSR in Crisis: The Failure of an Economic System* (New York, 1983), p. 99. The corresponding ratio in the West was one out of three or four.

charging more for oil, the resulting price increases in Eastern Europe could be blamed squarely on Moscow. Those Eastern European satellites who half-opened their economies to Western imports and loans in the 1970s also had to raise consumer prices in order to make repayments and cope with inflating Western prices after the oil shocks.[11] In centrally planned economies, setbacks to rising living standards tended to be blamed, even more than in the West, on the political leaders.

The Czechoslovak Springtime of 1968

The most direct challenge to the Communist regimes of Eastern Europe since 1956 took place in Czechoslovakia in 1968 as a result of a combination of stresses: nationalism, desire for freer expression, and demand for better working conditions.

The Czechoslovak regime of Klement Gottwald (1948–1953) and his successor as first secretary of the Czechoslovak Communist Party, Antonín Novotný (1953–1968), had been the most reliably Stalinist of the peoples' democracies, with the possible exception of Walter Ulbricht's East Germany. Novotný survived the troubles of 1956 and subsequent de-Stalinization with only minor adjustments, such as rehabilitating in 1963 some of the surviving victims of the 1951 and 1952 party purges. In late 1967, however, Novotný simply lost his capacity to have orders obeyed in the face of two obstinate grassroots movements: a desire of the Slovaks for more autonomy and a clamor for greater self-expression among younger intellectuals and officials.

It was striking that effective opposition to Novotný's Stalinism came from the top—from within the younger generation of skilled technicians, state administrators, and intellectuals that the regime itself had produced. In that way, the Czechoslovak crisis reflected a problem common to all the peoples' democracies and the Soviet Union itself. The party operatives who had created the new Communist regimes, mostly men of little education, toughened by the experience of clandestine resistance and postwar revolution in the 1940s, had raised up a younger generation of leaders who had known less struggle and whose training was better suited to the technical progress and managed economic growth of the 1960s. The young scientists, agronomists, journalists, and economists who came of age in the 1960s wanted freer rein to apply their skills in a pragmatic fashion.[12] They were supported from below by workers who resented quotas, norms, steeply graduated piecework wage scales, and distant authority. Such groups wanted, for the most part, to reform rather than abolish the socialist system in Czechoslovakia. It was a majority of the Czech Communist Party's Central Committee that eased Novotný out of the post of party secretary in January 1968 and replaced him with a young spokesman for Slovak autonomy, Alexander Dubček.[13]

Alexander Dubček was no Western liberal. He wanted to make the party more national, more popular, and more responsive without its ceasing to be the only party.

---

[11]The oil crisis of 1973 and subsequent economic difficulties in Western Europe are the subject of the next chapter.

[12]For an analysis of a similar development in the German Democratic Republic, see Peter C. Ludz, *The Changing Party Elite in East Germany* (Cambridge, Mass., 1972).

[13]Novotný remained president until March 1968.

Nor did he have any intention of dismantling the economic structures of socialism. He wanted only to prove that the Czech Communist Party was "capable of exercising political direction by means other than bureaucratic and police methods." The new program of the Czech Communist Party (April 5, 1968) announced a "Czechoslovak way to socialism," reflecting a burgeoning sense of national distinctiveness.

> We engage ourselves in the construction of a new model of socialist society, profoundly democratic, and adapted to Czechoslovak conditions.[14]

Without permitting a legal opposition, the new program authorized the "expression of different points of view" by the parties that had cooperated with the Communists in the National Front of 1945 to 1948: the Social Democrats and the late President Beneš's party, the Socialist National Party. In that sense, part of the "Czechoslovak Spring" harkened back to the immediate postwar pluralist regime voluntarily aligned with the Soviet Union. In other ways, the Dubček experiments tried to break new ground in the organization of work and in the devolution of decision making. Trade unions, youth groups, and other grassroots organizations were encouraged to take an active role in a more decentralized administration.

Dubček's problem was to steer Czechoslovakia between two rising tides. A wave of free debate and discussion swelled up in this traditionally vivacious people that had repressed its intellectual curiosity for twenty years. After censorship was abolished on June 25, 1968, there was no restraining Czech imaginations. Incautious reformers burst into print with suggestions for a multiparty system, national neutrality (withdrawal from the Warsaw Pact), and artistic experiment, all of which went further than Dubček, a convinced if pragmatic Communist, was willing to go. The other tide was the growing alarm of Czechoslovakia's neighbors, especially East Germany and Poland, who watched nervously for the contagion to spread to their populations.

Soviet Party secretary Leonid Brezhnev attempted to put pressure on Dubček, evidently hoping for a compromise along the Gomulka lines of 1956 rather than a repeat of the Hungarian explosion of 1956. Although Soviet troops had been withdrawn from Czechoslovakia in 1945, some units entered the country briefly in June 1968 for Warsaw Pact "maneuvers." Finally, Dubček's determination to proceed with an open Party Congress in September seemed too grave a danger. On August 21, 1968, the Soviets (supported by troops from East Germany, Poland, Hungary, and Bulgaria) moved 500,000 men and several thousand tanks into Czechoslovakia in a smoothly organized airborne operation. The Russians justified the military solution of the Czech challenge with the Brezhnev doctrine of limited national independence among socialist countries: a threat to a socialist regime in any one of them was a threat to all.

Although the Czechs offered no armed opposition (thus avoiding a disaster on the scale of Hungary in 1956), they received the invading soldiers with almost unanimous passive resistance. Briefed to expect West German anti-Communists at work in Czechoslovakia, the Soviets soldiers had no idea how to deal with the "legions of young bluejeaned Czechs sitting in their serried ranks in the roadways, jeering and

---

[14]Alexander Dubček, *Hope Dies Last,* ed. and trans. Jiri Hochman (New York, 1993), p. 334.

A student waves the Czechoslovak flag from atop a Soviet tank in Prague, August 22, 1968.

whistling at the boot-faced troops,"[15] or with the workers who went ahead and held the promised Party Congress secretly in a factory. Dubček was arrested at first, but after President Ludvík Svoboda, a tough-minded old general, refused to cooperate, and no Czech collaborators stepped forward as János Kádár had done in Hungary in 1956, Brezhnev decided to let Dubček govern under close control. A delicate process of gradually tightening repression followed. Dubček was removed from office in September 1969 and expelled from the party in 1970, along with nearly 500 other members. Trials went on through 1972. The Russians clearly preferred an unpopular but obedient communism in Eastern Europe to a popular, nationalist one.

Only seven of the world's ninety Communist parties, outside the five participants, supported the Russian military destruction of Dubček's regime. Most of the Western European Communist parties denounced it publicly. The protests of foreign Communists and the criticism of fellow-traveling intellectuals could be shrugged off as they had been in 1956. This time, however, the Soviet action in Czechoslovakia called attention to dissent at home. Pavel Litvinov, the grandson of Stalin's foreign minister in the 1930s, and several others were arrested for demonstrating in Moscow's Red Square. The difficulties that the Soviet regime had faced with dissident writers and scientists were sharply increased.

---

[15] *The Economist,* August 31, 1968.

Poland: Unrest and Solidarity

Steep food price increases announced just before Christmas 1970 set off the most serious troubles in Poland since 1956. Premier Gomulka, whose regime had begun as a liberalizing compromise in 1956, had governed more and more repressively in the ensuing fourteen years. He even resorted to anti-Semitism to divert popular disgruntlement (20,000 Jews emigrated between 1968 and 1970, leaving almost none). His Christmas 1970 price increases set off demonstrations in the Lenin shipyard in Gdansk (Danzig, before the war) that spread to Szczecin (formerly Stettin) and other Baltic port cities. After three hundred people had been killed in futile efforts to put down the revolts by force, Edward Gierek replaced Gomulka as party secretary. Gierek lowered food prices, scrapped an unpopular wage incentive system, and imported more consumer goods from the West.

Neither carrots nor sticks, however, could maintain stability. The carrots were consumer goods; many of them imported from the West. During the middle 1970s real incomes rose "faster and further than at any time in Polish history."[16] In the absence of any major Polish exports to the West, however, this import-led boom could be paid for only by further borrowing in the West. By the late 1970s, one-third of the revenue from Polish exports went to pay interest to Western banks. Efforts to increase farm production only aroused the resistance of Polish farmers, whom earlier relaxations had placed in control of most of the agricultural land of Poland. When efforts were made to force more of them into cooperative livestock raising, they slaughtered livestock, and meat became even scarcer. Meat price increases on July 1, 1980, set off a new round of demonstrations.

The great strike wave of July and August 1980 was one of the most exhilarating and terrifying times in Polish history. The government was powerless against millions of strikers, for soldiers and police fraternized with them. The Polish Catholic Church, the liveliest symbol of Polish national identity, gave them full support. The demonstrators gained outright control of some work places, such as the shipyards of Gdansk. There they propounded a new vision of socialism in which direct worker control would express both individual liberty and national independence. Thus, as in the Czechoslovak "Spring," Polish workers, led by a canny shipyard electrician named Lech Walesa, developed a challenge not merely to public order but to official ideology.

Both sides walked a tightrope. Walesa did not want to provoke a Soviet armed intervention, and the Russians hoped the Polish regime could solve matters internally. On August 31, 1980, strike leaders and government negotiators reached an agreement by which the union—Solidarity—became the first autonomous workers' organization recognized by a Communist state. The workers, in turn, agreed to recognize the preeminent role of the Communist Party and Poland's existing international agreements (such as COMECON and the Warsaw Pact). Both sides jockeyed for more in a very unstable situation for fifteen months, until the Polish army, under Defense Minister Wojciech Jaruzelski, crushed the union movement and declared martial law on December 13, 1981, in order to keep the Soviets from

---

[16]Archie Brown, "Eastern Europe: 1958, 1978, 1988," *Daedalus,* Winter 1979, p. 156.

Lech Walesa addresses his fellow shipyard workers in Gdansk, Poland, in August 1980. These demonstrations were to grow into the Solidarity labor movement.

doing the same. The conservative nationalism of General Jaruzelsky had throttled the libertarian nationalism of Lech Walesa. Although martial law was relaxed in July 1983, Solidarity remained a major force underground while public attention shifted to the regime's troubles with Western creditors and the Church (a popular pro-Solidarity priest was murdered by police in late 1984). Even though the Soviets had not had to intervene, their model of socialism had lost even more credibility as it became clear that Polish workers accepted it only at the point of a bayonet.

Hungary: The "Goulash Communism" of János Kádár

The most wounded satellite regime in 1956, Hungary under party chief János Kádár gradually became the East European country where small private businesses and intellectuals enjoyed the most freedom. After 1968, a "New Economic Mechanism" permitted enterprises to make their own plans and to choose within limited price ranges. Although Hungarian agriculture was fully collectivized after 1956, peasants could sell part of their own produce. Private retailing spread. The 1970s were difficult, however. Hungary's dependence on Soviet oil and expensive imports from the West, especially West Germany, could not be compensated for by sufficient exports. The Western European recession and inflation and increased Soviet oil prices required belt-tightening in Hungary. In mid-1979 the greatest price increases in thirty years became necessary. Even so, there was no overt opposition. Kádárism still seemed preferable to the agony of 1956. In 1982, economic liberalization began again. Workers were permitted to establish private "works communities" within state enterprises to furnish specialized goods and services. Central planning became only indicative; enterprises could decide most production issues themselves within general guidelines. The effect of this economic decentralization was limited, however, by the domination of most production sectors by huge state monopolies. Nevertheless Kádár's "Goulash Communism" offered a relatively palatable mix of plentiful consumer goods and political passivity.

The German Democratic Republic: Industrial Power and Omnipresent Police

Erich Honecker ruled East Germany as autocratically after 1971 as had Walter Ulbricht before, aided by the highest standard of living in the Eastern Bloc—it claimed to be the world's tenth industrial power—and a ubiquitous secret police network. The infamous STASI (*Staatssicherheitsdienst*) was revealed after the regime's collapse to have kept files on six million of the GDR's sixteen million inhabitants. Its staff of 100,000 was far larger (though less bloody) than the Nazi Gestapo, and its 170,000 informants turned out to have included spouses, friends and dissident intellectuals as well as party faithful. The wall could not keep out West German television, however, nor could it keep discontented East Germans in. Attracted by Western freedom and prosperity, thousands of East Germans tried to scale the Berlin wall or the electrified fence that closed the rural border; dozens of them were killed in the attempt.

Romania, Yugoslavia, Bulgaria: Tyranny and Nationalism

In Romania, the ruler's whim replaced Communist orthodoxy. Nicolai Ceausescu, Party Secretary from 1965 to 1989, lost some of his independence of COMECON and the Warsaw Pact[17] when, having exhausted the Romanian oil fields by 1979, he had to import Soviet oil. But although he gratified Romanian nationalism by harassing Hungarian and German minorities, Ceausescu subjected his people to an ever more megalomaniac regimentation. His grandiose schemes in the 1980s included razing ancient villages and forcing their inhabitants into barracks called "agro-industrial complexes." Whole neighborhoods of the capital city of Bucharest were flattened to make way for extravagant new towers of unannounced purpose. He built a new port city in the ecologically fragile marshes of the mouth of the Danube.

---

[17]See chapter 18, pp. 552–553.

Needing foreign exchange for these follies, he sold most of the nation's food production abroad. All forms of birth control were forbidden. Deliberately induced shortages of food, medicine, and energy—apartments were not supposed to be heated beyond 45 degrees Fahrenheit—went beyond mere discipline. The leader seemed to want to punish his people. Of all Eastern Europeans, Ceausescu's Romanians were most often hungry and ill.

The aging Tito's personal whims ran in more sybaritic directions to fancy uniforms and luxurious palaces on the Dalmatian coast. He was acutely aware that only his personal prestige held together a Yugoslavia made up, according to the popular saying, of "six republics, five nationalities, four languages, three religions, two alphabets and one Tito." When Croatian nationalists demanded more autonomy in the 1970s, Tito cracked down on intellectuals and universities there. Hoping to prepare an orderly succession, he produced a new constitution in 1974 that gave greater independence to the federal states, recognized the Muslims for the first time as a nationality, and set up a revolving collective presidency that was supposed to keep all the fractious peoples represented. It became unworkable under conditions of rising national feeling and economic recession.

When Tito died in 1980, the last major Second World War leader and the longest-serving twentieth-century European ruler, his awkward country had to face the combined strains of recession and revived nationalism. But the worker-run factories, the distinctive feature of Yugoslav communism, were unable to make the hard choices required to cut costs during a slowdown. Falling production made it harder to pay for imports and repay western loans with exports, although the Yugoslavs managed to sell a small car, the Yugo, in the United States between 1985 and 1991. As standards of living declined and the different regions struggled for relative advantage, attachment to the federal state weakened. The more prosperous northern republics, especially Slovenia and Croatia, came to feel that their strong economies were subsidizing the poorer south. The dominant Republic of Serbia was swept by Greater Serbian nationalism, fanned by its president, Slobodan Milošević. Previously a Communist functionary, Milošević discovered a talent for demagogic oratory on June 28, 1989, while addressing the Serbian minority in Kosovo—a particularly tense spot since this hallowed site of a historic Serbian defeat six hundred years earlier was now inhabited by a majority of refractory Albanians. As both communism and Yugoslav federalism lost their hold on most South Slavs, Milošević learned to motivate his own people with the prospect of a Greater Serbia.

Bulgaria was the most docile and untroubled of the satellites, but even there the long-ruling Todor Zhivkov (1954–1989) played with nationalism to help hold his regime together—another ominous foretaste of postCommunist politics. In the 1980s, Bulgaria tried to force its Turkish minority to renounce their family names and take Slavic ones.

BREZHNEV'S LEGACY: STAGNATION AND MISSILES

Brezhnev's gamble—that he could combine high-technology growth with intellectual conformity—required buying silence with either abundance or international prestige. Instead of abundance, as we have seen, Soviet citizens experienced economic stagnation and environmental degradation.

So Brezhnev pursued an aggressive foreign policy. It enjoyed some success. In the SALT I agreement (1972), Nixon, Kissinger, and the United States Senate accepted Soviet parity in armaments as normal; this important concession was confirmed by Carter in SALT II (1979).[18] Having applied the Brezhnev doctrine once in Czechoslovakia (1968), the Soviet leader kept Eastern Europe frozen by merely appearing ready to apply it again. Going even further in the late 1970s, he embarked on a new arms race (which he claimed the United States started).

In 1977, he began updating Soviet intermediate-range ballistic missiles aimed at Western Europe with new 3,000-mile SS-20s, in range of any point on the European continent. Equipped with multiple warheads, these missiles aroused Western fears that the Soviets were ahead in theater nuclear weapons in Europe at a time when approximate parity had already been established in intercontinental weapons. Simultaneously, the Soviet Union continued to intervene in trouble spots in the Third World. It established new areas of influence on the Horn of Africa and, through Cuban intermediaries, in newly independent Angola. On Christmas Day, 1979, it sent troops into Afghanistan where one pro-Soviet faction had deposed another. The United States hastened arms development in response to these actions, first under President Carter and then, even more massively, under President Reagan.

In December 1979, the NATO Council called for the installation of American intermediate range missiles in Western Europe if no United States–Soviet agreement on mutual reductions could be reached. The plan called for 108 Pershing II missile launchers in West Germany to replace obsolete Pershing IA launchers, and 464 ground-launched cruise missiles in Britain, West Germany, Italy, Belgium, and Holland. Although West German Social Democratic chancellor Helmut Schmidt had made the initial proposal and it enjoyed nearly universal government support, the prospect of bigger weapons with shorter fuses on European soil was profoundly disturbing to many Europeans. Disarmament movements became as active in some areas as they had been in the 1950s, when the first ICBMs were installed in Europe— this was the case in Britain, the Low Countries, and Germany, but far less so in France and Italy. On April 1, 1983, in a way recalling the 1950s, protectors formed a fourteen-mile human chain linking Greenham Common, a proposed cruise missile site in England, with two British nuclear weapons research facilities. Very different was the movement in West Germany, where the public had considered itself uninvolved in such matters in the 1950s. At one point, West German proponents of a mutual nuclear arms freeze extended their demonstration into East Germany (whose authorities no doubt hoped to encourage Western unilateral disarmers) where they found East Germans also willing to advocate an arms freeze on both sides—perhaps the first joint demonstration of East and West Germans since the war.

These displays did not prevent the arrival of the first missiles in West Germany, Britain, and Sicily at the end of 1983, when SALT II (1979) limitations on new cruise missiles had expired. The Russians, in turn, installed additional missiles in

---

[18]See chapter 20, p. 600.

East Germany. The protests died down, though no one slept any easier. There had always been conflict between Europeans and the United States over defense policy, but European–American conflicts became far sharper at the government level in the 1980s because they now involved economic rivalries as well as disagreements about armaments. The issue of how to respond to the Soviet Union had acquired an economic dimension during the period of détente. The partisans of increased trade with the Soviet Union (European as well as American) liked to think that trade would hasten an eventual Russian mellowing. Opponents (particularly United States president Reagan) insisted that trade with the Soviet Union only enhanced the Russians' war-making power. This argument erupted into the bitterest European–American quarrel in 1981 over the proposed natural gas pipeline from the Soviet Union to Western Europe. Western Europe, hungry for energy, proposed to buy natural gas from the Soviet Union. The United States government tried to prevent the pipeline's construction. When it ordered European subsidiaries of American companies to block shipment of vital pipeline components, the Europeans protested against what they saw as American interference in their internal economic affairs. They pointed out that America continued to sell grain to the Soviet Union while trying to hinder European–Russian trade. The fact that Europe's staunchest conservatives—British prime minister Margaret Thatcher and German chancellor Helmut Kohl—were the angriest showed how far European and American conceptions of relations with the Soviet Union had diverged.

By 1980, détente seemed dead. Even if few Europeans expected a conventional Soviet invasion any more, the two superpowers still confronted each other, one finger on weapons that could destroy the world, across a wall that still cut Europe in two. As Reagan and Brezhnev set out to outspend each other on national defense, no one could imagine that the Cold War would be over in less than a decade.

The ailing Brezhnev died in November 1982, at seventy-six. Faced with the third succession crisis since Stalin's death, the inner circle of Soviet leadership showed that it had learned to navigate such transitions smoothly. But it was not necessarily equipped to choose the most dynamic leader. Yuri Andropov (party secretary 1982–1984) hardly represented a younger generation, at sixty-eight, nor did his career as head of the Soviet secret police (KGB) augur well for an internal loosening up. The KGB knew better than anyone else, however, the true gravity of Soviet economic and social problems. Many of its younger leaders were eager for major reforms. Andropov set about attacking corruption, alcoholism, and economic blockages from above. When he died in February 1984, instead of anointing the young reformer whom Andropov had promoted, Mikhail Gorbachev, the Presidium chose an elderly Brezhnev crony, Konstantin Chernenko, as First Secretary. Never an innovator and already ill at seventy-two, Chernenko kept the Soviet leadership in suspended animation for thirteen months. His death in March 1985 finally opened the way for Gorbachev. The new First Secretary's colleagues didn't know what they were in for.

SUGGESTIONS FOR FURTHER READING

Moshe Lewin, *The Gorbachev Phenomenon: A Historical Interpretation,*[*] 2nd ed. (1991), though dated in some details, situates all post-Stalin Soviet leaders within a long process of social modernization; see also George Breslauer's comparison of Khrushchev and Brezhnev cited at the end of chapter 17. There is no satisfactory biography of Brezhnev. Edwin Bacon and Mark Sandler, eds., *Brezhnev Reconsidered* (2003), find some good in him, aided by some nostalgic Russians.

The works on Soviet government by Jerry Hough and Merle Fainsod, first cited at the end of chapter 8, and on Soviet society by Geoffrey Hosking, recommended at the end of chapter 17, are still important here. In addition to the general histories of twentieth-century Russia noted at the end of chapter 1, Ronald G. Suny, *The Soviet Experiment*[*] (1999), assesses the whole regime. Marshall I. Goldman, *The USSR in Crisis: The Failure of an Economic System* (1983), is admirably clear and nontechnical on economic stagnation.

Still useful for the Brezhnev era are Archie Brown and Michael Kaser, *The Soviet Union since the Fall of Khrushchev,* 2nd ed. (1978), and its sequel, *Soviet Policy for the 1980s* (1982).

The works of Simons and Rothschild cited at the end of chapter 16 are the place to begin for Eastern Europe. The "Czechoslovak Spring" and Soviet intervention are covered in Jiri Valenta, *Soviet Intervention in Czechoslovakia, 1968*[*] (revised ed. 1991), H. Gordon Skilling, *Czechoslovakia's Interrupted Revolution* (reprint ed. 1992), and in the Renner work cited at the end of chapter 16. For "Goulash Communism," see Rudolf L. Tökés, *Hungary's Negotiated Revolution*[*] (1996); Ivan T. Berend, *Hungarian Economic Reforms, 1953–1988* (1990); and the relevant sections of Miklos Molnar, *From Béla Kun to János Kádár: Seventy Years of Hungarian Communism* (1990). The economist János Kornai offers a rationale for a reformed socialist economy in *The Socialist System: Political Economy of Socialism*[*] (1992).

Abraham Brumberg, ed., *Poland: Genesis of a Revolution*[*] (1983) includes some eye-witness material, as does the vivid reportage of Lawrence Weschler, *The Passion of Poland* (1984). See more recently Timothy Garton Ash, *The Polish Revolution: Solidarity,*[*] 3rd ed. (2002), and Arista M. Cirtautas, *The Polish Solidarity Movement* (1997).

In addition to the works on the German Democratic Republic cited at the end of chapter 16, consult Konrad Jarausch, *Dictatorship as Experience: Toward a Socio-Cultural History of the German Democratic Republic* (1999), and David Childs, *The Stasi* (1996). In addition to works on Yugoslavia recommended at the end of chapter 17, see John R. Lampe, *Yugoslavia as History: Twice There was a Country,*[*] 2nd ed. (2000).

Additional Internet links related to this chapter are available on the Europe in the 20th Century Web site: http://www.history.wadsworth.com/paxton04

You can also explore images, interactive timelines, and maps related to this chapter on our Western Civilization Resource Center: http://history.wadsworth.com

Antinuclear activists form a fourteen-mile chain on April 1, 1983, at Greenham Common, to protest the installation of American missiles in England.

22

Western Europe, 1973–1989: Postindustrial Society and "Stagflation"

Western Europe's apparently limitless postwar economic miracle jolted to a halt with the oil crisis of 1973. On October 17 the cartel of oil-exporting countries—OPEC[1]—raised its oil prices by 70 percent. OPEC's Arab members went even further. In an effort to punish Israel's supporters in the Six-Day War (October 1973), they cut off oil shipments entirely to the United States and to the Netherlands, the one European state that had permitted the shipment of American supplies to Israel across its territory. Although this embargo was relatively brief, the price rises continued. By 1979, oil had reached $30 a barrel, or ten times its 1973 price. Then it jumped again to $34 when the overthrow of the Shah of Iran in January 1979 shut off oil exports

---

[1]OPEC—The Organization of Petroleum-Exporting Countries—consisted of two Latin American states (Venezuela, Ecuador), two sub-Saharan African states (Nigeria, Gabon), Indonesia, Iran, and seven Arab states (Algeria, Libya, Saudi Arabia, the United Arab Emirates, Iraq, Kuwait, and Qatar). It controlled 53 percent of world oil production, and almost all of Western Europe's supply. Formed at the initiative of Venezuela in 1960, OPEC included enough members and enjoyed enough market leverage to begin affecting world prices after 1970.

© Hulton Archive

During the oil crisis of 1973, British motorists "queued up" for limited supplies of "petrol" (gas). According to the sign posted at this filling station, the price had risen to over $7 per gallon.

from that country. By March 1983, however, the combined effects of conservation, alternate sources of energy, and divisions within the cartel loosened OPEC's grip a bit and forced its price down to $29 a barrel, and from there to $15 in 1988.

ECONOMIC STRAINS: OIL, JOBS, AND TRADE

The Western European economies had come to depend increasingly on imported oil during the postwar boom. Oil had supplanted coal as their principal source of energy. Oil's share of Western European energy needs had risen from one-fifth in 1955 to three-fifths by 1972. As the cost of oil multiplied by ten, everything that required energy became much more expensive. Wage earners struggled to obtain higher pay to meet higher food and fuel bills. Since many consumers were purchasing less, however, many workers had to be laid off. The cost of assisting the unemployed soared, just as tax revenues began to fall. Western economies slipped into recession.

After the immediate panic of gasoline famine was more or less resolved in Western Europe, it became apparent that behind the energy crisis lay deeper structural problems. Aging Western European industries had lost some of their earlier technological edge. Their workers enjoyed high pay and extensive social services. Manufacturers in Japan, soon joined by even newer industrial entrepreneurs in Taiwan, South Korea, Brazil, and Mexico, built newer plants and paid their workers less. It was not easy to compete with them by new investment, for Western investment funds were seeking the higher profits available overseas, and Western governments were too fearful of the inflation that now plagued welfare states with full employment to apply massive new stimuli to investment at home. Whole branches of older industries that had led the postwar European boom, such as automobiles and steel, were driven off the world market by lower-priced Asian and Latin American competitors, while whole branches of new technology, such as computers and electronics, failed to receive adequate investment in Europe. A massive shift in world productive capacity seemed to be underway. Europe faced a dismantling of its industrial plant, "dis-industrialization." The confidence of the 1960s was replaced by "Europessimism."

Europe had experienced minor downturns since the Second World War, notably in 1958–1959 and 1966–1967. But the decline that began in the 1970s was the first whose severity and length deserved the name *depression*. Western Europe's proud achievement in keeping unemployment down to 2 and 3 percent since postwar reconstruction began had led its people to believe in permanent full employment. After the second oil shock in 1979 and widespread shutdowns of aging "smoke-stack" industries, unemployment rose in Western Europe as a whole from 4.2 percent of the work force to 10.3 percent in 1983. In 1984, unemployment reached 9.1 percent in relatively healthy West Germany, 12.6 percent in chronically ill Britain, and 17.5 percent in struggling Spain. The young suffered particularly. A fourth of Western European youths under twenty-five had no job in 1983, nearly a third in Holland, Spain, and Italy. In 1983, real purchasing power went down in Western European households for the first time since the postwar boom began.

The new depression was no rerun of the 1930s, however. There was no "crash" as in 1929, and welfare states prevented catastrophic human impact. There was neither the shame of the "dole" nor the soup kitchens of the Great Depression. At the same time, however, the good salaries and benefits enjoyed by Western European workers made Western European manufactured goods too expensive for the world market.

Another difference was inflation. Prices had dropped in the 1930s; in the 1970s, prices were spinning upward at an alarming rate. Modest inflation had in fact been part of the postwar growth pattern. Even before 1973, inflationary pressures had been growing whenever Western European economic planners tried to stimulate growth under conditions of full employment. The surprise after 1973 was that inflation kept growing even when employment and production fell. For one thing, the price of oil kept rising, and that affected the energy costs of all production, including food. Another reason was the welfare state. Social benefits maintained consumer purchasing power even when employment fell. In Britain, inflation reached the astonishing level of 17 percent in 1975. In Italy, it reached an explosive 24 percent in 1980, and was still at 17 percent at the end of 1982. At that rate, prices would double every four years.

This combination of economic stagnation and inflation was something new. The term "stagflation" was soon coined for it. Western European governments were accustomed to taking active measures to restore prosperity. Under conditions of "stagflation," however, the Keynesian recipe of deficit spending to stimulate purchasing power no longer worked. Instead of increasing employment, it increased inflation and threatened overseas sales. The traditional austerity measures to reduce inflation, on the other hand, tended to deepen stagnation. It was demoralizing to find that now, after having come to believe that Keynes had conquered unemployment and the business cycle, no one—neither conservatives nor socialists—knew what to do.

A "Postindustrial" Society?

The apparent permanence of economic maladjustment after 1973, along with the new forms taken by social protest in 1967–1968,[2] led some Western Europeans to believe they had entered a "postindustrial" era:[3] a time when manufacturing was no longer a sure route to jobs or wealth and where services, communications, the media, and entertainment provided higher returns. In this emerging new age, parts of the proud old skilled working class were doomed to sink, along with parts of the middle class, whereas the entrepreneurs and stars of the new fields would grow rich. The poorly educated and unskilled seemed unlikely ever to find meaningful work. As jobs demanded ever more technical skill, education's role as society's selection mechanism became more visible: Schools ushered the favored few up the ladder to professional success and relegated others to an increasingly permanent underclass. In a "postindustrial" era, alienated students, marginal minorities, and a permanently excluded "non-class of non-workers"[4] would take the place of the traditional working class—now both diminished and assimilated—as the troublemakers. Therefore future social conflicts would revolve less around production issues (wages and hours) than around issues of consumption and quality of life (the environment, health, control over the media, the status of women).

Insofar as the problem was merely a shortage of oil, remedies were not hard to find. Britain and Norway discovered major oil fields beneath the North Sea. Both had become net exporters of oil by the end of the 1970s. Holland found abundant natural gas there. France took the lead in nuclear power development. The proportion of French electricity generated by nuclear power rose from 8.4 percent in 1977 to 75 percent by 1990. All of Europe cultivated good relations with Arab oil exporters.

Reviving productivity demanded much more drastic and untested measures, however. Would Western Europe have to sacrifice full employment and the welfare state—the very foundation stones of its postwar social and political stability—on the altar of more competitive production costs? Could aging industries be shut down en bloc and their workers retrained for some new technology? Who could tell in advance which new technology was the right gamble? And who could pay for so vast a redirection of the economy and the attendant social dislocations? Faced with challenges of these dimensions, European leaders of both Left and Right muddled through with austerity and waited for American recovery to lift everyone's boats.

Immigrants and the New Right

Recession hardened Western European attitudes toward immigrants after 1973. During the boom years, most Western European governments and businessmen had eagerly promoted the immigration of cheap labor, to do the menial jobs their own workers now disdained. By 1975 10 percent of the labor force in Western

---

[2]See chapter 19, pp. 574–579.

[3]The American socialist Daniel Bell is usually credited with coining this term. The French sociologist Alain Touraine, reflecting on the student revolt he had witnessed in May 1968, used it already in 1969; see his *The Post-Industrial Society* (New York, 1971).

[4]André Gorz, *Farewell to the Working Class* (London, 1982), pp. 7–8, 71.

Europe was foreign born: 9 percent in West Germany, 11 percent in France, and over 25 percent in Switzerland.[5]

Western Europe had received waves of immigrants before. But whereas most of these had come from Catholic southern Europe (with the notable exception of Jewish refugees from Russia in the 1880s and from central Europe in the 1930s), post–Second World War immigrants increasingly brought profoundly different customs and religions. Germany drew Turks; France was a magnet to its former colonial subjects in North and West Africa and the Antilles; Britain received Indians, Pakistanis, and West Indians from the Commonwealth; and Holland from its former colonies in Indonesia and Surinam, as well as Turkey and Morocco.

Anti-immigrant violence had already appeared before the economy turned down in 1973. The first major alarm bell was the clash of hundreds of British working class youths and West Indian immigrants in Notting Hill, a poor quarter of London, in September 1958. By long British tradition, enacted into law in 1948, immigrants from the Commonwealth enjoyed full rights of citizenship in the "mother country." Instead of the expected Canadians or Australians, however, it was Jamaicans who arrived that year, along with Indians and Pakistanis fleeing the violence that accompanied their independence. When the United States narrowed its quotas in 1952, more Jamaicans went to Britain. Further immigrant waves included Indian merchants fleeing newly independent Kenya in 1968, and Idi Amin's Uganda in 1972. In a series of Immigration Acts passed by both Conservative and Labour governments between 1962 and 1973, the British government limited immigration from the Commonwealth to those with work permits and British ancestry—in effect, a racial criterion. Even this did not satisfy everyone. A Tory renegade, Enoch Powell, rode a groundswell of anti-immigrant feeling after 1968, warning of "rivers of blood" unless the aliens were sent home.

After the economic pinch began in 1973, Western European nationalists accused immigrants of competing for jobs, of burdening an overstrained social security system, and of refusing assimilation into the host culture. Most Western European states took measures to restrict immigration in 1973 to 1974. This did not diminish their foreign-born populations, however. Family members and political refugees could still enter legally; thousands more entered clandestinely. Moreover, no Western European state was willing to expel those foreigners already present.[6]

Thus, supposedly temporary "birds of passage" turned into settled minorities. Many Western Europeans had to learn for the first time to get along with numerous neighbors of radically different cultures and religions. Germany had had its Poles, Britain its Irish; but permanently settled Turkish *Gastarbeiter* in Germany and Pakistani and West Indian neighborhoods in declining British midland towns forced these countries to cope with racial conflict, to learn to live with cultural diversity, and even to adopt a more heterogeneous image of their national identity. France, more accustomed to immigration, had to learn how to bend its assimilationist tradition to

---

[5]Michael J. Piore, *Birds of Passage: Migrant Labor in Industrial Societies* (Cambridge, England, 1979), p. 1.

[6]France, under President Valéry Giscard d'Estaing, came close to forcible repatriation of Algerians in 1978–1980, but was stopped by judicial opposition. West Germany wished to avoid any reminder of Nazi expulsions; it only offered financial incentives to persuade some Turkish workers to go home. Jacqueline Costa-Lascoux and Patrick Weil, *Logiques d'états et immigrations* (Paris, 1992), pp. 62–63.

accommodate the enduring presence of thousands of practicing Muslims. Whether to allow the newcomers to acquire citizenship became an issue: France and Britain did, West Germany did not until the 1990s. Sweden and Holland experimented with local voting rights for resident foreigners.

Despite official efforts to foster racial understanding, frictions multiplied. Xenophobes demanded strong action against immigrants, even their expulsion. One kind of anti-immigrant action was the casual violence of "skinheads": working-class youth gangs who parodied fascist style. More permanent and influential were Far Right political parties, which seized upon anti-immigrant resentment with alacrity.

Far Right parties already existed, of course. Before 1973, Western Europe's Far Right had surfaced sporadically, taking advantage of local issues and clienteles specific to each country. The Federal Republic of Germany, where explicit neo-Nazism was outlawed, had several near-Nazi parties based mostly on those expelled from the lost eastern territories, a diminishing clientele. The most important of these, the National Democratic Party (NPD), peaked in 1969 (stimulated by left-wing student activism) with about 4 percent of the vote. Mussolini's heirs faced no legal restrictions in Italy: Their *Movimento sociale italiano* (MSI) had its best electoral score (8.7 percent) in 1972, in reaction to the "hot autumn" of 1969. Most of their strength was in the backward south. In France, anti-Algerian feeling was sharpened by Algerian independence in 1962, following eight years of bitter war, plus the disorders of 1968. A neofascist group, *Ordre nouveau,* stirred anti-Algerian feelings and provoked street fighting between immigrants and nationalist youths in 1973. Even tolerant Holland found its patience tried when Moluccan activists hijacked a train in 1975; three persons were killed in the ensuing police action.

What was different after 1973 was that the Western European Far Right grew, and that it converged: All its national variants focused intensively on immigrants and their alleged harm (unemployment, cultural dilution, petty crime). The National Front in Britain reached 15 to 20 percent of the vote in some Midlands cities in 1974, only to decline by the late 1970s. The French *Front National* of Jean-Marie Le Pen, with an almost exclusively anti-immigrant program, became the most successful Far Right party in Western Europe in the 1980s. It reached 10 percent of the national vote in 1983 and 14 percent in 1988. In such southern cities as Marseilles where many refugees from French Algeria confronted Algerian immigrants, Le Pen's vote exceeded 20 percent. The German and Austrian Far Right had their greatest success after 1989 as a new wave of refugees arrived from collapsing Communist Eastern Europe, a situation discussed in chapter 23.

These Far Right successes aroused fears of a revival of fascism. Unlike the fascists of the 1930s, however, the Western European Far Right after 1973 rarely attacked the democratic constitutions and welfare capitalism that both conservatives and progressives overwhelmingly accepted in Western Europe. They limited their propaganda mostly to the one issue that worked—immigration. Their electoral results were far below 1930s levels. Nevertheless, they showed that exclusivist nationalism and racial discrimination were no longer taboo in electoral campaigns, for the first time since the defeat of Hitler and Mussolini. Even mainstream political dialogue was shifted a few degrees in their direction.

WELFARE STATES UNDER STRESS

The Welfare State had been the distinctive mark of Western European public policy since the end of the Second World War. Rooted in social Catholicism as much as in socialism and serving middle-class as well as working-class interests, rural as well as urban, it enjoyed broad support from Right to Left. It was much harder to operate in a shrinking economy, however, than in a growing one. Social programs grew costlier just as the money to pay for them grew scarcer. Not only were there more people in need of assistance, inflation was pushing the costs of social programs even higher, especially in countries like Italy where they rode up on automatic cost-of-living indexing. Between 1960 and 1981, according to OECD (Organization for Economic Cooperation and Development) figures, social expenditures rose from 14.5 percent to 26.3 percent of the total output of goods and services in the principal Western European countries, and in West Germany, Sweden, Holland, and Belgium they rose to over 30 percent.[7] Pressures to reduce these costs came from several quarters. Taxpayers grew restive under their burden. Exporters complained that labor costs made sales overseas impossible. Requirements to reduce government expenditure were often a condition of currency-support loans from the International Monetary Fund or foreign creditors.

Northern Europe: Conservative Revivals

Reformist social democratic or labor parties were in power in northern Europe, by and large, when the crisis began. They operated solidly established welfare state systems from well-entrenched political positions, without serious communist rivals. After 1973, they were obliged to grasp at least one of several painful nettles: to reduce social programs, to increase taxation, or to let inflation run unchecked. Their difficulties helped conservatives back to power in a number of cases. Even though these new conservative majorities of the 1970s and 1980s trimmed social programs rather than dismantled them, they openly challenged the welfare state consensus for the first time in thirty years.

Scandinavia

The proud old establishment of Scandinavian social democracy was the first to be shaken. Social Democrats had governed in Sweden since 1932, often in coalition with a small farmers' party, but without interruption. The Nordic welfare systems were the most inclusive in Western Europe. Unlike contributory schemes, as in Britain, where workers and management shared contributions, Nordic welfare systems were financed entirely by tax revenues. Unlike the West German system, they included all citizens, not just "workers." A country like Sweden, without oil resources of its own and competing against other manufacturers of automobiles, aircraft, and

[7] *The New York Times,* February 19, 1984, sec. iv.

industrial machinery, was particularly vulnerable to the kind of structural crisis that began in 1973. Faced with higher taxes and diminished employment, a majority of Swedish voters turned against the Social Democrats in 1974 for the first time in forty-two years. The centrist governments that followed imposed austerity, though they did not radically reorient Swedish social policy. The costs of social programs continued to rise despite cutbacks, Swedish social expenditures reaching 29.8 percent of the gross domestic product by 1980, then the highest figure in Western Europe (Denmark was next with 26.8 percent).[8] In October 1982, Olof Palme returned to power with the Social Democrats, but he, in his turn, was obliged to concentrate on trimming social programs.

Danish voters reacted even more dramatically against high taxes. A new "Progress Party," based on a militant taxpayers' revolt, sprang up and became the second largest party in Denmark in the 1974 elections, after fifty years of more or less steady Social Democratic control. It proposed a radical dismantling of the welfare state and sharp reductions in government spending and taxation. The jailing of its leader, Mogens Glistrup, for tax evasion cut short the Progress Party's rapid rise. It was the Danish Conservative Party, instead, which succeeded in putting together a new coalition in the early 1980s and making more modest cuts in social programs.

West Germany

The West German Social Democrats held on a bit longer, partly because powerful West German industry postponed depression by massive exports of automobiles, machinery, and engineering skills to oil-rich Arab states. Led by the shrewd and popular Helmut Schmidt, after Willy Brandt had to step down following the revelation of a security leak in his office in 1974, they practiced moderate austerity. Some of Schmidt's troubles came from within his own party. Rank-and-file Social Democrats grumbled as unemployment reached figures unknown since the early 1930s and as once-booming Ruhr industrial cities stagnated. Young radicals outside the party protested when Schmidt supported the installation of new American missiles in Western Europe after 1979. Still other troubles came from his centrist coalition partners, the Free Democrats, who objected to deficit spending. They finally overturned the government on that issue in October 1982. It was the first time in the history of the Federal Republic that a government had lost its parliamentary majority between elections. The long reign of the West German Social Democrats (1969–1982) was over.

The Christian Democrats regained power in West Germany under a new leader, the bulky, stolid Helmut Kohl. Kohl cut West German social programs sharply. Pensions declined by 5 to 6 percent in real terms; unemployment benefits fell by about the same amount. Time-off benefits for new mothers declined from $268 a month to $182, and student aid was made reimbursable to the state. But Kohl, like Adenauer and Ludwig Erhard, did not challenge the legitimacy in principle of social programs. A far more surprising continuity was in *Ostpolitik*. Although conservative Christian Democrats had called Willy Brandt's Eastern European settlement

---

[8]Bent Rold Anderson, "Rationality and Irrationality in the Nordic Welfare State," *Daedalus* (Winter 1984), p. 115. In West Germany in 1980, social expenditures amounted to 20.1 percent of the gross national product, in the United States to 18.1 percent, and in France to 15.2 percent.

treason ten years earlier, Chancellor Kohl continued to seek trade and cultural exchange with East Germany.

Britain: Margaret Thatcher's Free-Market Crusade

By far the most flamboyant conservative leader to emerge in northern Europe was the passionate and fearless Margaret Thatcher, who tried in eleven years as Prime Minister (1979–1990) to shake Britain out of what she considered its lethargic dependence on the "nanny state." Mrs. Thatcher had not been given much of a chance when, as an outsider (she was a grocer's daughter trained as an industrial chemist) and as a doctrinaire opponent of big government, she won control of the Conservative Party in 1975. In 1979, aided by six years of ineffectual Labour response to the problems of stagflation, she led the Tories back to power. In office, she cut taxes; privatized the state's share in the oil, air, telecommunications, and automobile industries; slashed aid to education, social programs, and the arts; and refused the customary aid to ailing industries such as steel and coal. When the powerful coal miners' union tried to bring her down by strikes, as they had done with her predecessors, she seized the opportunity to legislate a drastic weakening of unions' powers to raise funds and take action without consulting their membership. Despite the luck of finding North Sea oil, her economic cold bath hurt many victims. Unemployment swelled from 5 percent to nearly 14 percent, by far the worst since the 1930s.

Even so, the "Iron Lady" won reelection in 1983 and again in 1987, to become the longest-serving British prime minister of the twentieth century. She alienated intellectuals more than workers, who liked her plan to let residents of public housing buy their apartments. The decline of inflation from 10 percent to 5 percent restored purchasing power to everyone employed. As her spirit of enterprise took hold, British productivity finally increased. And her cuts in the British welfare state were relatively modest, considering her uncompromising free-market rhetoric. She did not denationalize steel, for example, as the Tories had done in 1951, perhaps because that moribund industry had no takers. Above all, the relish with which Mrs. Thatcher repelled by war the 1982 Argentine seizure of the Falkland Islands struck a popular chord.

But the principal reason for Thatcher's success was the near shipwreck of the British Labour Party that had governed for seventeen of the thirty-four years since the end of the Second World War. It won barely 38 percent of the working class vote in 1983, its worst showing since the 1930s. Labour's burden of responsibility during the crisis-ridden 1970s had broken the party to pieces. When Labour had returned to power in the elections of 1974, Prime Minister Harold Wilson, a former economics professor and a convinced Keynesian from the left of his party, inherited serious inflation from his Conservative predecessor Edward Heath (1970–1974). Under Wilson it spun out of control, reaching 17 percent, a figure unknown in modern British experience. His successor, James Callaghan (1976–1979), tried to apply an "incomes policy": harsh government restrictions on wage raises and on unions' bargaining powers. These efforts brought inflation down to 10 percent, but they snapped the Labour Party in two. Radical union militants recaptured control in 1979, but their leader, Michael Foot, alienated the parliamentary and reformist wings by advocating

**Conservative leader Margaret
Thatcher campaigning,
March 1979.**

AP / Wide World Photos

unilateral nuclear disarmament. To make matters worse for the British Left, a new
reformist center-left party, the Social Democrats, made up mostly of parliamentary
Labour and allied to the vestige of the old Liberal Party, split the Left vote. So Mrs.
Thatcher never needed more than a plurality against a divided opposition, and, in
fact, never exceeded the 44 percent of the popular note she won in 1979.

Mrs. Thatcher's election marked the arrival in British politics of a new generation that had known neither the 1930s nor the war. It marked the end of the postwar "Butskellist" consensus by which the Tories accepted the welfare state and
Labour accepted a largely capitalist economy. She lost no opportunity to shift her
own party away from the paternalist social assistance accepted by most Tories since
Disraeli, hectoring the "wet" Tory Left left as weak and timid. Labour responded
with ideological hardening under Michael Foot. Thatcher was Europe's nearest
equivalent to United States president Ronald Reagan in temperament and ideas.
However, her quarrels with him over the Russian gas pipeline[9] and over the United

⁹See chapter 21, p. 620.

States' invasion of a Commonwealth member, Grenada, without consulting her, showed that not even their personal friendship sufficed to paper over the cracks opening between American and European interests. For this new generation, the wartime alliance was not even a memory.

Mediterranean Europe: The Left in Power, but Transformed

Political responses to the crisis that opened in 1973 were inevitably different in those European countries with large Communist parties. These were located, with the exception of Finland, in Mediterranean Europe. The division of the Left in those countries had placed power in the hands of conservatives, and it was they who had to face the crisis that opened in 1973. Economic strains thus translated into electoral gains for the Left in southern Europe. The Western European Left, however, was being transformed.

Decline of the Soviet Model

As in the 1930s, the powerful Communist parties of the Mediterranean world were eager for political alliances, though circumstances differed profoundly from those of the Popular Front era. The most striking difference was the Soviet model's loss of credibility even within Western European Communist parties. Poor Soviet economic performance was obvious to all, and previously sympathetic westerners were offended by clumsy Soviet efforts to stifle dissent. Brezhnev's psychiatric wards were less final than Stalin's camps, but all the more visible for that. The breaking point for many had been the heavy-handed Russian military intervention in Czechoslovakia in August 1968. Western European Communist parties experimented in the 1970s with their own version of Dubček's "communism with a human face": Eurocommunism.

The Eurocommunists of the 1970s (most of them did not like the word) attempted to reconcile their hope for a communist victory in Western Europe with the distinctive character of Western European life. The Soviet model seemed to them not merely inappropriate but a positive hindrance to success in a highly industrial region with deeply entrenched traditions of political liberty and economic pluralism.

Eurocommunism and Enrico Berlinguer

Eurocommunism's main spokesman was Enrico Berlinguer, the ascetic intellectual secretary general of the Italian Communist Party (1972–1984). Berlinguer's vision of a separate Western path to communism was shaped partly by Italian experience, partly by contemporary observation. He was keenly aware of how the "maximalism" of the Italian Left in 1920 had opened the way to Mussolini. He was also deeply affected, like much of the European Left, by the overthrow in September 1973 of the Allende government in Chile, which had tried to apply radical economic change on the basis of a 36.7 percent share of the electorate. Berlinguer also believed that a viable Western communism required democracy and that democracy was in trouble

Enrico Berlinguer, head of the Italian Communist Party and intellectual leader of Eurocommunism, July 1983.

© Bettmann / CORBIS

in Italy in the 1970s. One party, the Christian Democrats, had held power since November 1945. It was blamed not merely for the current recession but for the corruption and cronyism that immobilized Italian response to the recession. The Catholic culture in which the Christian Democrats' majorities were rooted was also weakening, as shown by a referenda upholding the legality of divorce (1974) and the legalizing of abortion (1978). Yet no alternative majority was in sight. Terrorism by both the Left and the neofascist Right was destabilizing the country. Berlinguer concluded that an alliance with the socialists to seek an outright Left victory would leave Italy polarized and without any potential majority. The ensuing constitutional deadlock would be more likely to profit the extreme Right than the Left, as had happened in 1920–1922.

So Berlinguer sought what he called a "historic compromise" with the left wing of the ruling Christian Democratic Party. He declared that the Italian Communist Party accepted electoral democracy with all its risks, including the possibility of being voted out of office. He accepted Italian membership in the European Community and even in NATO. His party supported firm measures against terrorism on both Left and Right. Invited to speak in Moscow at the sixtieth anniversary of the Bolshevik Revolution in November 1977, he proclaimed that his party would have to accept the rules of pluralist democracy in order to succeed in Italy. Relations worsened with Moscow, and when Berlinguer called the Soviet form of communism "a spent force" after the imposition of martial law in Poland in December 1981,[10] they were virtually broken.

Berlinguer's Eurocommunism appealed to many Italians. He won 34 percent in the parliamentary elections of June 1976, the highest poll attained so far by any

---

[10]*L'Unità*, December 16, 1981. I thank John Alcorn for this reference.

Western Communist Party in a free election. This put him within 4 percent of the slipping Christian Democrats. It was especially useful for Berlinguer's strategy that the party controlled most of Italy's major cities and seven out of sixteen regions by 1976, either alone or in coalition. Its city governments won widespread respect for honesty and efficiency. For a time in 1977–1979, Berlinguer's Communists were part of a shaky governing coalition of "national solidarity," though without cabinet seats, in the face of vehement American opposition.

Berlinguer was followed to varying degrees by other Western Communist leaders. The French Communist Party followed the de-Stalinist path more cautiously, under the earthier leadership of former industrial worker Georges Marchais. Even so, French Communists vigorously denounced Soviet policy in Czechoslovakia. But while Berlinguer sought alliance with his country's Christian Democratic Party (perhaps to split it) against Italian socialists, Marchais signed a "Common Program" with the French Socialist Party in 1977. That put a public stamp on the French Communist Party's gradual renunciation of the "dictatorship of the proletariat" and acceptance of an electoral route into, and out of, power. Even two parties behind the Iron Curtain, in Yugoslavia and Romania, supported Berlinguer's doctrine of separate paths at international Marxist gatherings. The Spanish Communist Party under Santiago Carrillo was closest to Berlinguer, although his Portuguese neighbor, Alvaro Cunhal, rejected Eurocommunism altogether in favor of an intransigent revolutionism.

Eurocommunism did not become the major political force in Western Europe that seemed possible in the 1970s, however. Its social base was shrinking in post-industrial society. Its moderation ran the risk of alienating the old militants without drawing in enough replacements from the center to take their place. In France, Spain, and Portugal it was Socialist parties that came to occupy the strategic center-left and form the pole of an alternate majority.

Without a united Left, it proved harder to find the pole of an alternate majority in Italy. At first the shrinking Christian Democrats coopted more partners in broader centrist coalitions. In June 1981, Giovanni Spadolini, head of the tiny Republican Party, became the first non–Christian Democratic prime minister since 1945, at the head of a coalition in which the Christian Democrats still predominated. The Italian Socialist Party looked like the alternative when its energetic leader Bettino Craxi headed the same coalition as prime minister (postwar Italy's forty-fourth) for a record four years (1983–1987), but it became engulfed in the same corruption scandals that were to bring down the Christian Democrats in 1993. Then some of Berlinguer's heirs would have their turn, as we will see in the next chapter.

All the while, the Italian people, who had seen millennia of history, shrugged politics off as a sideshow and went about their business in the nimble and vigorous enterprises that worked so much better than their state.

Spain and Portugal: From Dictatorship to Democracy

The most radical political changes of the 1970s occurred in Spain and Portugal. The authoritarian dictatorships of Franco and Salazar had lingered on there, like dinosaurs, into the mid-1970s. Precedent suggested that dying dictatorships usually end in revolutionary turmoil, followed by counterrevolutionary response. In both countries, however, political moderation finally prevailed (in Portugal only after an authentic social revolution). Dictatorship had left bad memories, the star of communism was waning, and the European Community exerted a powerful pull toward market economies and open political systems, even in lean years.

The transition to democracy in Spain was gratifyingly tranquil. The dictator of Spain, General Francisco Franco, died in November 1975 at the age of eighty-two. The succession he had prepared for Prince Juan Carlos (grandson of King Alfonso XIII, who had left the throne in 1931)[11] was gladly accepted by the Spanish people, eager to be spared the trauma of another civil war. This general desire for reconciliation was shared by Santiago Carrillo, who returned from exile in France filled with the Eurocommunist spirit, as soon as the Communist Party was legalized in 1977. Spain, he said, took civil liberties seriously after having been deprived of them for so long.

It was not Santiago Carrillo's Communists who were going to fill the post-Franco vacuum, however, as might have been the case in earlier, more polarized days. Two moderate parties, the Democratic Center of Adolfo Suarez and the Socialist Workers' Party of Felipe Gonzáles, were going to preside over the relaunching of political democracy in Spain. Elections in June 1977—the first in forty-one years—gave the first majority to Suarez.

Not that the old demons of civil war were totally dead. Several generals left the government when the Communist Party was legalized. The restoration of autonomy to Catalonia in 1978 stirred further conservative opposition. A new constitution that disestablished the Catholic Church, restored the right of divorce, and legalized strikes was approved by a slender majority in a December 1978 referendum (32 percent abstained). But most conservatives, lacking the international support Franco had enjoyed in the 1930s, understood that to oppose the King was to court something worse. When a group of Civil Guard officers invaded the Spanish parliament and took the members hostage on February 23, 1981, in the expectation of widespread military support, King Juan Carlos was able to extract personal pledges of loyalty from all but one regional army commander. The *coup* collapsed after a tense eighteen hours. Several more officers were arrested in 1982 for a new plot against the regime, but the old tradition of *pronunciamiento* was discredited.

Spanish democracy seemed to have taken firm root when the election of October 1982 transferred power quietly to the reformist Socialists of Felipe Gonzáles. At forty the youngest prime minister in Europe, the pragmatic Gonzáles proved to be a popular and effective leader. In retrospect, it was apparent that the economic development begun in Franco's last years, combined with the arrival of a new generation to political maturity, had quietly created a majority in Spain for moderate politics. Having drawn closer to the rest of Europe in social and economic terms, Spain now joined Europe formally as well. Spain joined NATO in 1982, confirmed by referendum in 1986, excluding nuclear weapons at its own request (as Denmark and Norway had done earlier), and joined the European Community in 1986.

Gonzáles faced a daunting economic assignment, however. His margin for maneuver was narrow, for the Spanish economy had little fat to be trimmed, and

[11]See chapter 12, p. 369.

© Bettmann / CORBIS

Spanish Civil Guard officers take over the parliament chambers, February 23, 1981.

Gonzáles had to tread a very fine line between his electors' claims for social services and the budgetary discipline and industrial restructuring required by EC membership. He survived to 1996 because Spain's benefits from EC trade outweighed the pains of high unemployment.

The Portuguese transition from dictatorship to democracy was much more troubled. Salazar had successfully fended off both the Left and military rivals until his seventy-ninth year, 1968, when he suffered an accidental fall. He lingered in a coma until July 1970. The president (Salazar had governed as prime minister under a figurehead president) named a loyal but moderate law professor, Marcello Caetano, as prime minister. But continuity was much harder to maintain in Portugal than in Spain. There had been no recent civil war in Portugal to teach moderation, whereas the faltering colonial war in Angola and Mozambique had radicalized many officers involved in it. A growing number of Portuguese officers had come to believe that only a profound transformation of their country could end the fruitless war in Africa and bring Portugal into the modern world. If Alvaro Cunhal rejected Eurocommunism, it was partly because radical army officers seemed to offer his Portuguese Communist Party a powerful parallel revolutionary force. In May 1974, a Supreme Revolutionary Council composed of generals and colonels from the Angolan war overthrew Marcello Caetano.

The officers of the Supreme Revolutionary Council imposed major social and political changes on Portugal during 1974 and into 1975. They ended the war and granted independence to Angola and Mozambique. They collectivized the great estates of southern Portugal and replaced them with cooperatives. They delegated extensive powers to elected factory councils.

Radical forces seemed to control Portugal in June 1974 when the procommunist Colonel Vasco Gonçalves became prime minister and the swashbuckling populist Major Otelo de Carvalho created a new army command structure, COPCON, to support him. Over the ensuing year, however, the radicals' grip weakened. They were divided, for even the most radical officers shared power grudgingly with civilian Communists. Elections in April 1975 revealed that a large majority of the Portuguese population, especially the family farmers of the north and the urban middle class, supported the moderate socialists of Mario Soares (40%) or democrats (27%) rather than Communists (12.5%) or the Extreme Right. The radicals overplayed their hand in May 1975 when they occupied a Catholic radio station and a moderate socialist newspaper in Lisbon. Active internal unrest developed, especially in the Catholic small-farm areas of the north, and both Washington and the European Community made their opposition clear. The Gonçalves government was now vulnerable to foreign pressures because, having spent up Salazar's considerable cash reserve, they needed foreign assistance.

In August 1975, the president of Portugal, General Costa Gomes, whose survival skills earned him the nickname "the cork," replaced Gonçalves with a moderate prime minister. When Otelo de Carvalho (now a general) and other radical officers attempted to seize power in a *coup d'état* in November, it was crushed at the cost of five dead. Most military units remained loyal to President Costa Gomez and the moderate government. Revolutionary élan was broken. Cunhal, denounced for "adventurism" by all Western Communist parties except the French, was isolated. Most officers accepted a purge of the "Angolans" and the demotion of the flamboyant Otelo to the rank of major. It was the closest any European state had come since 1948 to a revolutionary seizure of power.

A new constitution in April 1976 (officially the replacement for Salazar's "Estado Novo" of 1933) ostensibly committed Portugal to the achievement of a "socialist society," but it diminished the powers of the Supreme Revolutionary Council. The Council was abolished altogether in 1982. By that time, General Antonio dos Santos Ramalho Eanes, the first president elected under the new constitution (in June 1976 and again in 1980), had provided a steady guiding hand through a dizzying succession of nine ministries between 1976 and 1984. No one political party achieved a majority in four successive elections (1976, 1979, 1980, and 1983). The reformist socialists of Mario Soares led coalitions during 1976 to 1979 and after 1983. Soares quietly trimmed the powers of the factory councils and, in 1977, provided for the return of some confiscated estates to their former owners. Rural cooperatives in the south declined from over two million acres to just over one million by 1984. They struggled for economic survival, often having lost their choicest lands.

The infant Portuguese democracy struggled against severe odds. It faced intransigent reactionaries on one side (a right-wing general had received 40 percent of the presidential vote in 1980) and, on the other side, Cunhal's revolutionary Communists. Cunhal's followers were entrenched in the southern rural cooperatives, and received up to 19 percent of the popular vote. The International Monetary Fund, which had provided essential foreign credits, insisted on austerity measures that offended the government's natural supporters. Socialist leaders in France and Germany urged moderation on their Portuguese colleagues, however, and the prospect of membership in the European Community reinforced their message. Portugal joined the EC in 1986.

France: Mitterrand and the Reformist Left

Power in France passed electorally into the hands of a Socialist-Communist coalition in May 1981 with the election to the presidency of Socialist leader François Mitterrand. Conservatives had governed France in unprecedented prosperity and stability since de Gaulle created the Fifth Republic in 1958. The banker Georges Pompidou (1969–1974) easily won the presidency after de Gaulle's departure, benefiting from a divided Left and backlash against the demonstrations of May 1968. After Pompidou's early death, his Finance Minister Valéry Giscard d'Estaing (1974–1981) barely won presidential election over Mitterrand, as the economy dipped. Giscard d'Estaing began more innovatively than Pompidou. He reduced the voting age to eighteen, introduced a progressive capital gains tax, lowered medical costs for the aged, and, with Françoise Giroud, Europe's first Minister for the Status of Women, improved women's professional status and eased access to abortion. Soon, however, the worsening economy became his principal preoccupation. After 1978, through Prime Minister Raymond Barre, a conservative economics professor, he imposed stringent austerity. That bitter medicine, along with the sense that conservatives had enjoyed power too complacently in France for twenty-three years, gave the presidential election of May 1981 to François Mitterrand.

In a way reminiscent of Blum's Popular Front victory in 1936, Mitterrand's victory aroused jubilation and expectations of better days. And as in 1936, the French Socialist regime was to find it very difficult to carry out radical changes at home within a hostile international economic environment. In another respect, the Mitterrand experiment was the opposite of 1936. This time the Communist Party was the declining partner. It was Mitterrand's main unannounced achievement to reverse the postwar relationship between socialism and communism in France. The Communists now seemed hidebound and stodgy. They dropped to 16 percent in 1981, and continued to drop in by-elections into the early 1980s to an estimated 10 to 12 percent of the popular vote, less than half the size of the thriving young Socialists. In retrospect, Mitterrand's victory could be seen more as a consolidation of the reformist Left in French politics than a revolutionary turn.

Nevertheless, Mitterrand's regime began radically enough, with a double gamble. On the one hand, a Keynesian increase in wages and social benefits was meant to stimulate the economy by promoting a buying spree. On the other hand, sweeping nationalization that raised the state's share in French industry from 15 percent to about 35 percent and in banking from 85 percent to nearly 100 percent was supposed to permit the state to focus investment on future technological winners. This step made France's state economic sector second only to Italy's in Western Europe. It was the sort of expensive gamble that socialists in less wealthy countries— Gonzáles in Spain or Soares in Portugal—could not afford. But it had a consistent rationale, while other European states were muddling through with austerity. It was accompanied by significant civic reforms such as abolition of the death penalty and

AP / Wide World Photos

French Socialist leader François Mitterrand campaigning, February 1978.

greater freedom for the media. Vivacious private FM stations, once unthinkable in centralized France, now sprang up.

Mitterrand's program ran into multiple difficulties. First, the buying spree went mostly into imports. This offered no help to French employment, and it weakened the franc. Already shaken by speculation and panic selling, the French currency lost 50 percent of its international value between 1981 and 1984. Modernizing industries meant closing old ones, and unemployment continued to climb past 9 percent in 1984, the highest since the 1930s. Mitterrand's expensive gamble had depended on a rising American economy; instead, high American interest rates and continued recession damaged the French economy further. Before heavy investment in new technology could show results, France fell deeply into debt.

By March 1983, France could salvage its neo-Keynesian policy only if it imposed exchange controls incompatible with the European Community. Decisively choosing Europe, Mitterrand turned back to an austerity even severer than that of Professor Barre. Naturally, this imposed sacrifices on the government's own supporters and in July 1984, the French Communist Party abandoned an alliance whose main duty was to make the unions swallow austerity. The Right began to recover, assisted by the resentment some French voters felt toward North African and black African immigrants.

In 1986, conservatives returned in force in parliamentary elections and President Mitterrand was forced to share power with a prime minister from the center-right, Jacques Chirac. François Mitterrand's skillful management of this "cohabitation" and economic revival won him reelection to a second seven-year term (1988–1995), and his Socialists regained their parliamentary majority—proving that they had definitively won acceptance as a government party by moving to the center. French politics were now based on the alternation of a moderate Left and Right, but similar priorities—budgetary austerity, a stable currency, openness to trade in Europe and the world—made the two sides almost indistinguishable.

To complete the roster of Socialist victories in Mediterranean Europe, the PASOK (Pan-Hellenic Socialist Movement) of Andreas Papandreou won elections in Greece in October 1981. Papandreou spoke at first of radical social change and of departure from NATO, but he too was soon obliged to turn to austerity measures.

Reformist socialists held power in the early 1980s across much of Mediterranean Europe, quite unlike northern Europe. It was they, rather than the Eurocommunists, who received the assignment of reconciling social change with democracy, and who stepped into the gaps opened by faltering conservative regimes and the disappearing last bastions of 1930s authoritarianism. But they had been transformed by the exercise of power. Their budget balancing and fiscal austerity were hard to distinguish from the policies of the moderate right.

THE EUROPEAN COMMUNITY IN RECESSION

It proved to be much harder to coordinate stagnant or shrinking economies than growing ones. The economic crisis that opened in 1973 did not fail to bring to the surface differences of interest within the European Community that prosperity had managed to paper over earlier.

The first act of the oil crisis showed how fragile European unity was. When the Arab members of OPEC imposed a complete oil boycott on one Community member—the Netherlands—in October 1973, the other members of the Community were very careful not to endanger their own oil supplies by helping the Dutch. Subsequently, the Community opened conversations with the Arab League as one of its first common foreign policy actions, but it was never able to formulate a single energy policy or to act as a unit in energy matters.

Economic contraction soon stimulated protectionism, not only toward the outside world, but within the Community itself. The sharpest conflicts within the Community divided France and Italy over agricultural products. The French government shut off wine imports from Italy in 1978 and was censured by the Community for it. Even though the French government could be brought into line, however, French winegrowers took matters into their own hands. They waylaid Italian wine trucks in the south and overturned or burned them. The same treatment to Spanish fruit and vegetable shipments pointed out how hard it was going to be for France to accept Spanish entrance into the Community.

It was all the harder for the Community to formulate a common depression strategy because the member nations' economies performed so differently. West German exports to oil-rich Arab states kept West Germany prosperous longer than other EC members. By 1979, West German weight had grown in the Community until it accounted for a third of the Nine's entire Gross Domestic Product.[12] Only after 1983, when oil prices fell and the Arab states cut back consumption, did the

[12]Albert Bressand, "The New European Economies," *Daedalus* (Winter 1979), p. 66.

West German economy falter. After 1981, the different economic tack taken by France under the Socialists made the coordination of economic policies even more problematic.

Some voices in the Community proposed a common restructuring of European production, favoring technological innovation and shifting production away from weaker sectors. Others wanted to support each member nation's industry in order to overcome unemployment. The former approach meant a bold expansion of Community functions into industrial planning, redeployment of investment, and major structural change without regard for individual national preferences. It also meant worsening unemployment in some regions and favoring others that were already ahead technologically. The majority easily chose the second option of trying to save employment in each member nation.

Steel and agriculture were the gravest problem areas. Steel plants in the Community were working at only 55 percent of capacity by the early 1980s. The Community did, exceptionally, permit the formation of a Community-wide "crisis cartel," Eurofer, that tried (but failed) to persuade the national companies to reduce their output and rationalize their production according to a Europe-wide steel plan. Eurofer had no enforcement teeth, so each country wound up supplying subsidies to its own steelmakers and using Community subsidies for sales in the world market. Subsidized European steel was thus imported into the United States, for example, at a time when American steelmakers were laying off thousands of workers. In spring 1982, pressure from United States companies and unions led the United States Department of Commerce to find that European steelmakers were subsidizing their sales abroad, a finding which permitted the imposition of import duties and quotas under the United States Trade Act of 1974.

Agriculture came far closer to bringing the Community to deadlock. Major farm countries like France benefited most from high farm supports, while Britain and Germany found themselves paying higher food prices. The issue was further complicated by British insistence that its contribution to the Community budget was too high. Mrs. Thatcher managed to block any further Community business in 1983 and 1984 until her grievance was settled. Only in spring 1984 did the Community take a first step toward lowering food price supports. Its decision to cut milk support by 1 percent provoked outrage in dairy areas such as Normandy. Decidedly, it was harder to redistribute contraction than to coordinate growth.

To be sure, no one proposed to break up the Community. Its institutions continued to function. The European Parliament continued to be elected by direct popular vote after 1979. A few areas of high technology, such as space research and particle physics, were conducted at the Community level. Economic rivalry with the United States and Japan was helping to force industrial agreements among European producers, such as common motor production by Volvo and Citroën-Peugeot. Most members encouraged "national champions" like Siemens, ICI, or Philips, capable of competing with American multinational giants, even though this gave rise to charges that the EC favored big business.

Élan toward supranational development was at a low ebb, however. The Community seemed to have become a setting for resolving disputes among the member states rather than a common agency for dealing with the Depression or with the decline of détente that manifested itself after 1979.

INTELLECTUAL AND SPIRITUAL CERTAINTIES CHALLENGED

Many orthodoxies that had dominated postwar Western European intellectual life weakened after the 1970s. Marxism was particularly discredited. The Cold War had solidified its grip on Continental intellectuals (with the major exceptions of Britain and West Germany). However grim the Eastern bloc looked, many Western European intellectuals resisted being aligned with what they saw as the materialism, the racism, the vulgar mass culture, and the aggressive expansionism of the United States. Détente softened this polarization, and the publication in 1974 of Solzhenitsyn's *Gulag Archipelago* swept away the habitual willingness of many postwar Western European intellectuals to overlook abuses in the Soviet Bloc.[13] Even Left intellectuals, many of whom had quietly distanced themselves from the USSR over Hungary in 1956 or Czechoslovakia in 1968, now attacked the Soviet Union openly as a deformation of socialism rather than its supreme expression. If they did not gravitate to the Right, they now advocated an autonomous "Western Marxism."[14]

The USSR's negative image was not Marxism's only problem in Western Europe, however. In a "postindustrial" society, the skilled factory workers who had provided the core of the organized labor movement diminished; white-collar service employees increased. The shop floor ceased to be the central focus of social issues. Trade Union membership declined in some parts of Western Europe, such as France (15 to 20 percent of wage and salary earners, the lowest level in the twentieth century), and Spain (under 10 percent).[15]

Holding the Marxist agenda of economic and social liberation inadequate, the most celebrated intellectuals of Western Europe after the 1970s took a "linguistic turn."[16] They explored the structures of thought and language that underlay meaning. The French anthropologist Claude Levi-Strauss[17] had argued that language sprang from deep cultural structures. Roland Barthes (1915–1980) pushed structuralism further in a series of playful essays revealing the human construction of meaning within all sorts of communication from advertising to clothing. More subversively, the French "poststructuralist" Jacques Derrida (1930–) began to consider all forms of communication, verbal or not, as entirely social constructions. He and his successors carried "deconstruction" of meaning among texts, subtexts, and intertexts, between *signifier* and *signified,* to the point where the very possibility of communication seemed doubtful.

Michel Foucault (1926–1984) applied deconstruction to history in particularly original ways. Where traditional historians had perceived linear progressions, Foucault looked for breaks: the moment, for example, when the insane began to be incarcerated, as a sign that something deep in the human understanding of mental

---

[13] Tony Judt, *Past Imperfect: French Intellectuals, 1944–1956* (Berkeley, Calif., 1992), is a severe indictment of intellectuals' refusal to admit Soviet abuses.

[14] Perry Anderson, *Considerations on Western Marxism* (London, 1976), criticized Western Marxism for its academicism and its remoteness from authentic struggle but took for granted the inapplicability of Soviet communism to the West.

[15] Guido Baglioni and Colin Crouch, eds., *European Industrial Relations* (London, 1990), pp. 106, 265.

[16] John E. Toews, "Intellectual History after the Linguistic Turn," *American Historical Review* 92:4 (October 1987).

[17] See chapter 19, pp. 573–574.

illness had shifted.[18] Though he was not always able to explain why such shifts occurred, he focused attention firmly on the power of language as an instrument of human domination. Those who are in a position to control language, symbols, and meanings, he insisted, can also control human understanding. His affirmations that knowledge is power and that social behavior—even sexual identity—is socially constructed fascinated some and outraged others.

The leading German social thinker of the second postwar generation, Jürgen Habermas (1929–), made the French poststructuralists seem narrow. He took as his assignment nothing less than an all-inclusive theory of the historical evolution of human society. He too found Marx insufficient, but he took a "social turn" as well as a "linguistic turn."[19] Taking up the broadening of Marx begun in Germany before Hitler by the Frankfurt School, Habermas divided human activity into two: not only work, on which Marx had based everything, but also communication. Hence, Habermas also studied language and meaning, but he was unwilling to do so without attention to the social pressures and interests that shaped them. It is impossible to do justice in one paragraph to the richness of Habermas's work, but one of his concerns may serve as an example: the changing frontiers between private and public space. Looking at the strains European capitalism faced in the 1970s, Habermas (who had been actively involved in the ferment of 1968 in German universities) believed that capitalism's private appropriation of public wealth survived only by the manipulation of such public spaces as universities and the media.

Although the poststructuralists and Habermas had immense intellectual influence (in the case of Derrida, more so in American universities than in Europe), their difficult prose was beyond the average reader. Average Europeans, and especially the young, fell even further under the sway of American films, clothing, and popular music. This aroused despair in many of their elders, and stimulated commercial emulation by some European investors. American and French promoters opened a Disneyland in the suburbs of Paris in 1992 that, after initial difficulties, planted American icons so conspicuously on the French scene that one high-schooler wrote in an exam of the great Renaissance sculptor "Mickey l'Angelo."

The Catholic Church was led after 1978 by its first non-Italian Pope since 1523, John Paul II, formerly Karol Cardinal Wojtyla of Cracow. The new pontiff had already demonstrated his strong will by supporting Solidarity against the Marxist regime in Poland. He became the most widely traveled pope in history, drawing millions of faithful on five continents. He was the first Pope to travel to Islamic countries and the first to enter a synagogue. But his explicit message was not always what his welcomers wanted to hear. While he pleased progressives by denouncing anti-Semitism and blaming the excesses of capitalism alongside those of Marxism, he was adamantly opposed to all forms of birth control and abortion and to the ordination of women. He removed teachers and priests who espoused "liberation theology" or who disagreed with him on family matters. It is possible that John Paul II had more influence outside Europe than within it. For, although he controlled the upper clergy with an iron hand, Catholic populations slipped, like Protestant, into

---

[18]Michel Foucault, *Madness and Civilization: A History of Insanity in the Age of Reason* (New York, 1965).

[19]Thomas McCarthy, *The Cultural Theory of Jürgen Habermas* (Cambridge, Mass., 1978), pp. 22, 91.

indifference. Even in formerly fervent Spain, less than a quarter of those under thirty-five went to mass at least once a month.[20]

The End of an Era: Moderation and Lowered Expectations

By the late 1980s, for all its problems, Western Europe had contained inflation and returned to modest levels of economic growth—2 to 3 percent a year, instead of the 5 to 6 percent of the long postwar boom. But it did so with lowered expectations. The confidence now faded that Keynesian job-creation measures in a mixed economy could infallibly produce permanent full employment. Indeed, the welfare state was coming to seem part of the problem under conditions of sharpened competition from Asia and the Americas. Continued access to world markets and deeper European unification required stable exchange rates and low inflation, so these now took precedence over full employment. Western European governments, even nominally socialist ones, came to acquiesce in unemployment as a permanent ill against which they could offer only palliatives, not a cure. As Communist parties weakened and Socialist parties accepted these new priorities, the postwar goal of full employment quietly slipped lower in governments' social agendas.

It was in that sense that the 1970s marked a real watershed for Western Europe. The recession set off by the oil crisis of 1973–1979 was not just a temporary cycle. The vistas that had opened in the early 1950s of unending economic growth through the production of consumer goods were now closed. Were the welfare state and free trade—the twin pillars on which the postwar Western European boom had been built—even compatible? Was Western European "welfare capitalism" viable in the face of international competition? Did European intellectuals and artists still have something to say to the rest of the world? Could their cultural identities withstand the onslaught of American pop culture and Third World immigrants?

By and large, Western Europeans coped with these lowered expectations and renewed doubts after 1973 without listening to the extremists in their midst. They resisted the appeals of the New Right and lost interest in the communist alternative. They remembered well their parents' bitter experience with extremes of Right and Left; the challenges they faced, to be sure, were less cataclysmic. The radical strivings of the early 1970s had long since burned themselves out. By the end of the 1980s, most Western Europeans faced their piecemeal and halting adaptation to post-industrial society still committed to political democracy, willing to pay taxes in order to minimize the inevitable contractions in social welfare, and open to world trade.

It even became possible to think of getting Europe moving again. Under the pro-European leadership of French president Mitterrand and West German chancellor Kohl, the European Community decided in the Single European Act of February 1986 to eliminate the final barriers to the free movement of goods, people, and services within it by the end of 1992. Also in 1986, the EC and the individual Western European states embarked with the United States and Japan on the "Uruguay Round" of free-trade negotiations sponsored by the GATT (General Agreement on

---

[20]John Hooper, *The New Spaniards* (London, 1995), p. 133.

Tariffs and Trade). Western Europe was still in 1989 the largest trading bloc in the world, and it was trying again to act as a unit. Despite lowered horizons, its distinctive model of welfare and mixed economies had been challenged and trimmed since 1973, but not dismantled.

SUGGESTIONS FOR FURTHER READING

Daniel Yergin, *The Prize*[*] (1993), gives the fullest account of the oil crisis. Robert Skidelsky, ed., *The End of the Keynesian Era* (1977), examines economic policy dilemmas after the slowdown began.

Marglin and Schor, *The Golden Age of Capitalism*, already listed at the end of chapter 19, seeks deeper reasons for lowered European economic performance after 1973, as does R. C. Matthews, ed., *Slower Growth in the Western World* (1982). The nontechnical sections of Michael Bruno and Jeffrey Sachs, *The Economics of Worldwide Stagflation* (1985), are enlightening; see also Robert Z. Lawrence and Charles Schultze, eds., *Barriers to European Growth: A Transatlantic View*[*] (1987). British policy trade-offs are examined closely in Bob Rowthorn and John R. Wells, *Deindustrialization and Free Trade* (1987).

The management of Western European economies is studied by Peter A. Hall, *Governing the Economy: The Politics of State Intervention in Britain and France*[*] (1986). Problems of the European social order are probed by Claus Offe, *Contradictions of the Welfare State*[*] (1984). The difficulties of Sweden, flagship of welfare capitalism, are explored in Barry Bosworth and Alice M. Rivlin, eds., *The Swedish Economy* (1987).

Stephen Castles, *Here for Good: Western Europe's New Ethnic Minorities* (1984), surveys immigrant populations; see also his *Age of Migration*,[*] 3rd ed. (2003). Michael J. Piore, *Birds of Passage: Migrant Labor and Industrial Societies* (1979), analyzes the way they fit into their host economies, while Stephen Castles and Godulka Kosack, *Immigrant Workers and Class Structure in Western Europe*, 2nd ed. (1985), does the same for society. Grete Brochmann, ed., *Mechanisms of Immigration Control: A Comparative Analysis of European Regulation Policies*[*] (1999), examines the changing management of population flows in Europe. Rogers Brubaker, *Citizenship and Nationhood in France and Germany*[*] (1994), is the deepest study of citizenship in two different national traditions.

Debates about social class shifted after 1973 from "the end of ideology" to the effects of stagnation. Examples are Max Haller, ed., *Class Structure in Europe: New Findings from East-West Comparisons of Social Structure and Mobility*[*] (1988), and John H. Goldthorpe et al., *Social Mobility and Class Structure in Modern Britain*,[*] 2nd ed. (1987).

Conflicting strands within the European Left are surveyed in David Childs, *Two Red Flags: European Social Democracy and Soviet Communism Since 1945*[*] (2000). Eurocommunism's moment of optimism is reflected in Howard Machin, ed., *National Communism in Western Europe: A Third Way for Socialism?* (1983); see also Bernard E. Brown, ed., *Eurocommunism and Eurosocialism: The Left Confronts Modernity* (1979).

For labor issues after 1973, see Peter Lang, George Ross et al., *Unions, Change, and Crisis: French and Italian Union Strategies and the Political Economy, 1945–1980* (1984) and *Unions and Economic Crisis: Britain, West Germany, and Sweden* (1984). Jane Jensen and George Ross, *The View from Inside: A French Communist Cell in Crisis* (1984), is a graphic account of a vigorous grassroots Left in trouble.

The revival of a violent extreme Right is treated by Luciano Cheles et al., *The Far Right in Europe,*[*] 2nd ed. (1996); Paul Hainsworth, *The Politics of the Extreme Right*[*] (2000); Piero Ignazi, *Extreme Right Parties in Western Europe* (2003); and Martin Schain, Aristide Zolberg, and Patrick Hossay, *Shadows over Europe* (2002).

Excellent accounts of Spain's transition to democracy are Paul Preston, *The Triumph of Democracy in Spain*[*] (1987); Raymond Carr, *Spain: Dictatorship to Democracy,*[*] 2nd. ed. (1991); and Kenneth Maxwell and Steven Spiegel, *The New Spain: From Isolation to Influence*[*] (1994).

Well-informed on the Portuguese revolution and its taming are Kenneth Maxwell, *The Making of Portuguese Democracy*[*] (1995), and Lawrence S. Graham and Douglas H. Wheeler, eds., *In Search of Modern Portugal: The Revolution and Its Consequences* (1983).

French socialism's shift toward the center is examined in Howard Machin and Vincent Wright, eds., *Economic Policy and Policy-Making under the Mitterrand Presidency, 1981–1984* (1985). The impact of France's socialist presidency is weighed in Julius W. Friend, *The Long Presidency: France in the Mitterrand Years* (1997), and Ronald Tiersky, *François Mitterrand: A Very French President* (2000).

Hugo Young, *One of Us: The Life of Margaret Thatcher,*[*] 2nd ed. (1993), and John Campbell, *Margaret Thatcher,* 2 vols. (2003), are major biographies; see also Thatcher's memoirs, *Downing Street Years*[*] (1995). Her legacy is evaluated briefly in Anthony Selden and Daniel Collings, *Britain under Thatcher*[*] (2000); in Eric J. Evans, *Thatcher and Thatcherism,*[*] 2nd ed. (2004); and at more length in Peter Jenkins, *Mrs. Thatcher's Revolution* (1988).

John Gillingham, *European Integration* (see chapter 18), examines the period of "Europessimism."

Intellectual celebrities of the 1970s are studied by David Macey, *The Lives of Michel Foucault*[*] (1998); James Miller, *The Passion of Michel Foucault*[*] (2000); Marcel Henaff, *Lévi-Strauss and the Making of Structural Anthropology*[*] (1998); Edmund R. Leach, *Claude Lévi–Strauss*[*] (1989); Allan Megill, *Prophets of Extremity: Nietzsche, Heidegger, Foucault, Derrida*[*] (1985); and Christopher Johnson, *Derrida*[*] (1999). Geoffrey Bennington, *Jacques Derrida*[*] (1999), is accompanied by Derrida's own playful commentary casting doubt on the validity of such a work. Helpful for Habermas are Thomas A. McCarthy, *The Critical Theory of Jürgen Habermas*[*] (1981), and Stephen K. White, *The Cambridge Companion to Habermas*[*] (1995); on the impact of these trends on history, see John Toews, "The Linguistic Turn," *American Historical Review,* vol. 92, no. 4 (Oct. 1987).

Additional Internet links related to this chapter are available on the Europe in the 20th Century Web site: http://www.history.wadsworth.com/paxton04

You can also explore images, interactive timelines, and maps related to this chapter on our Western Civilization Resource Center: http://history.wadsworth.com

Personifying *glasnost* **("openness"), a smiling Mikhail Gorbachev with his wife, Raisa, during a reception in the Soviet leader's honor at the United Nations in New York, December 1988.**

23

The Revolution of 1989 and After

During 1989, the world watched in amazement as the communist system faltered in the Soviet Union and its satellites in Eastern Europe slipped free. Even stranger miracles followed. The Communist Party lost its monopoly in the USSR in 1990. And in 1991, the USSR itself ceased to exist, breaking up into fifteen separate republics. The "revolution of 1989" in Central and Eastern Europe and its aftermath brought about the most sweeping changes in European regimes and borders since the First and Second World Wars. Unlike those earlier war-borne transformations, however, these events were largely peaceful. Accompanied by joyous hopes of national independence, democracy, and material abundance, they recalled the 1848 "springtime of the peoples" more than the habitual strife of the twentieth century.

THE GORBACHEV EXPERIMENT, 1985–1991

The peaceful character of communism's collapse in Eastern Europe was due mainly to the reluctance—or incapacity—of the Soviet authorities to intervene. The Soviet governing system itself was losing its grip. As we saw in chapter 21, economic stagnation, environmental pollution, declining public health, and citizens' loss of faith in the regime had posed grave problems that Brezhnev had been unable to address. A year after Gorbachev took the reins, on April 26, 1986, a nuclear power plant exploded at Chernobyl in the Ukraine, killing thirty-one people, forcing about 300,000 to abandon their irradiated homes, and affecting millions more. The Soviet Union's economic, ecological, and management failures had reached the level of national emergency.

The Soviet army's inability, despite a ten-year effort (1979–1989) and heavy casualties, to impose a satellite government in Afghanistan also aroused something akin to a genuine domestic opposition in the USSR. Whereas only a handful of courageous Soviet dissidents had protested the repression in August 1968 of the "Czechoslovak Spring," open disaffection spread among Soviet veterans of the Afghan conflict and bereaved wives and mothers.

The new party secretary undertook daring reforms to deal with these multiple ills. With Gorbachev, only 54, a new generation reached power. The child of successful collective farm managers, a law student and amateur actor at university, Gorbachev had been deeply influenced in 1956, as a young Party official, by Khrushchev's secret anti-Stalin speech. After succeeding as a local official in the Russian south, Gorbachev was brought into the Party leadership as a protégé of Yuri Andropov, the head of the Soviet intelligence agency (KGB), who tried briefly as general secretary in 1982–1984 to impose efficiency from above. What set Gorbachev apart from other reformers, however, was a personal quality of directness and frankness that came as a fresh breeze after years of wooden propaganda. Instead of responding to Soviet decline by either the inertia of Brezhnev or the violence of Stalin, the pragmatic and self-confident Gorbachev proclaimed a new course of "openness" *(glasnost)* and "restructuring" *(perestroika)*.

Openness meant dealing with the Chernobyl disaster without the habitual secrecy, liberating political dissidents such as Andrei Sakharov and Elena Bonner, and permitting more open political debate. It also meant filling in the "blank spaces" in Soviet citizens' understanding of their own history, as Gorbachev promised in an eye-opening speech on the seventieth anniversary of the November 1917 revolution. Thereafter the USSR publicly admitted responsibility for the massacre of thousands of Polish officers in the Katyn Forest in 1940, "discovered" the long-denied secret protocol to the Nazi–Soviet Pact that granted Stalin territorial gains in Eastern Europe, and rehabilitated thousands of Stalin's victims. Nikolai Bukharin, the proponent of a more gradual collectivization of agriculture, whom Stalin had executed after a show trial in 1937,[1] became Gorbachev's model of a more flexible "socialist alternative." The emergence into celebrity of Bukharin's young widow, Anna Larina,[2] from her long nightmare as a "nonperson" epitomized the hopes of the late 1980s.

---

[1] See chapter 8, p. 256; chapter 10, p. 318; chapter 13, p. 403; and chapter 15, p. 477.

[2] See Anna Larina, *This I Cannot Forget: The Memoirs of Nikolai Bukharin's Widow* (New York, 1993).

Restructuring meant authorizing multicandidate elections, shifting some economic decision making to local levels, and permitting a few farms and small businesses to function as cooperatives. A new Congress of Peoples' Deputies that met in May 1989 was the first representative body elected from multiple candidacies in Russia since Lenin dismissed the Constituent Assembly in January 1918. A constitutional amendment in March 1990 entrusted real power to paid deputies, and eliminated the Communist Party's monopoly on political representation. Once the position of party secretary had been the key to power; now Gorbachev created a new executive title, President of the USSR, to which he was elected in March 1990 by the congress.

Gorbachev, however, was neither a democrat nor an economic liberal. He wanted to revitalize the Soviet system, not destroy it. He wanted to transform its passive subjects into responsible citizens, and he thought giving them fuller information and some electoral choice would suffice. He expected the Communist Party to direct these reforms. His first changes, however, shook both political and economic control and released a cascade of experiment and reclamation that ran far beyond what the president wanted. For the moment, his daring and the lack of alternatives kept his head above water.

Abroad, Gorbachev boldly cut costs by abandoning the arms race and by declining to send troops to prop up the Eastern European satellites, as his predecessors had done in 1956 and 1968, at great material and political cost. The new Soviet hands-off policy became evident only gradually, however. In Poland, the underground labor movement Solidarity and General Jaruzelsky's military dictatorship circled each other warily in the late 1980s because neither wanted to provoke Soviet military intervention. Gorbachev urged liberalization on a visit to Prague in April 1987, but he made his repeal of the Brezhnev doctrine explicit only on October 7, 1989, when, on a state visit for the fortieth anniversary of the German Democratic Republic (East Germany), he warned Party Secretary Erich Honecker not to count on Soviet troops. This left the satellite regimes with only two options: to satisfy their restive populations or to keep them in line with their own forces.

During 1989, a dawning awareness of the satellites' vulnerability tempted the Eastern European populations to test their masters' resolve. One after another, at a quickening pace as the example spread, Eastern European Communist rulers hesitated to crush massive demonstrations and found themselves powerless. For letting this happen peacefully, as well as for hastening disarmament and abandoning Cold War animosities, Gorbachev merited the Nobel Peace Prize awarded him in October 1990.

Falling Dominos: Eastern Europe in 1989

At the beginning of 1989, although authority had been shaken in the Soviet Union and in its Eastern European satellites, everyone assumed that inertia and force could prop up the status quo indefinitely. Most citizens of the satellite regimes hoped to gain at most some of the *glasnost* and *perestroika* that Gorbachev had promised Soviet citizens. Before the world's astonished eyes, the satellites all collapsed in the fall of 1989 without (except in Romania) a shot being fired.

What we can now identify as the first falling stone of the landslide was the Polish military dictatorship's decision in January 1989 to accept talks with Solidarity, the illegal labor movement. General Jaruzelsky's martial law of 1981 to 1983 had not worked. Solidarity had survived underground, and strikes and demonstrations against rising food prices had become epidemic. The "round table" talks of spring 1989 won Solidarity the right to present candidates for the senate and a third of the lower house in elections on June 4—the first free elections in Poland since 1939, and anywhere in Eastern Europe since 1948. Solidarity won all but one of the seats opened to public choice. Unable or unwilling to restore martial law, Jaruzelsky gave in and appointed the Catholic editor Tadeusz Mazowiecki, a Solidarity militant, as prime minister. (Solidarity leader Lech Walesa would have to wait for his personal triumph.) Fearful of provoking Soviet intervention, Solidarity in turn supported Jaruzelsky's reelection to the presidency, which left intact for the moment the Warsaw Pact's political and military structures.

It is not surprising that Communist dictatorship cracked first in Poland, for no other Eastern European dissident movement matched Solidarity, with its roots deep in the labor movement and in the Catholic Church. Hungary budged next, for its Communist government had long been experimenting with a mixed economy and even, after Communist reformers ousted János Kádár in May 1988 after thirty-two years as party secretary, with multiple parties and unions. In June 1989, Hungary's new leaders gave a state funeral to the remains of Imre Nagy and other leaders of the 1956 rebellion and moved toward "socialist pluralism."

The Communists' own dismantling of one-party dictatorship in Hungary brought pressure next on the hard-line dictatorship of Erich Honecker in the German Democratic Republic. When the Hungarians cut down part of their barbed wire barrier with Austria in May and opened the frontier on September 10—the first hole in the Iron Curtain—a mounting flood of East Germans, lured by the glitter they could see by turning on West German television, took "vacations" in Hungary and then went West. Tantalized crowds took to the streets of the East German industrial city of Leipzig on October 16 and confronted Honecker with the choice of using force or losing control. That evening, East Germany was moments away from a bloody repression like that of June 17, 1953, in East Berlin. Honecker's subordinates, however, confident of Gorbachev's approval, vetoed the use of force and eased the aging Honecker from office on October 18. In a desperate attempt to stop illegal emigration by making it legal, East German authorities opened the Berlin Wall on November 9. The result was a joyous surge of four million East Germans into West Berlin, most of them for only a few hours of celebration and window-shopping. It was, said a British observer, the "greatest street party in the history of the world."[3] East Germany was obviously sliding out of control.

The movement away from one-party rule now picked up momentum. The Bulgarian Communist Party tried to stem the tide by replacing Todor Zhivkov, absolute ruler of Bulgaria for thirty-five years, with his foreign minister, the younger and more reformist Petur Mladenov, on November 10. In Czechoslovakia, hundreds of thousands of students and others demonstrated in the streets of Prague on Novem-

---

[3]Timothy Garton Ash, *The Magic Lantern: The Revolution of '89 Witnessed in Warsaw, Budapest, Berlin and Prague* (New York, 1990), p. 62

A demonstrator smasher the Berlin Wall as East German border guards look on, November 11, 1989.

ber 17. When Czech television showed police beatings, the crowds swelled beyond control. Civic Forum, a new political movement led by the dissident playwright Václav Havel and other leaders of the Charter 77 civil liberties movement, formed a virtual parallel government in a Prague avant-garde theater, The Magic Lantern. Understanding that only force could keep it in power, but that force alone was powerless, the government brought Civic Forum into a coalition in late November. At the end of December, Havel was elected president and Alexander Dubček, veteran of the Czechoslovak springtime of 1968, became president of parliament. Power had passed so smoothly in Prague that Czechoslovakia's liberation was called "the velvet revolution."

Václav Havel, soon
to be president of
post-Communist
Czechoslovakia, and
Alexander Dubček,
leader of the Prague
Spring of 1968,
celebrate the news
that the Communist
government has
resigned, November
1989.

AP / Wide World Photos

Violence marred the process only in Romania. The macabre autocrat Nicolae
Ceausescu, urged on by his adamant wife, ordered the security police to fire on
demonstrators. The massacre of 4,000 protesters in Timisoara and other cities on
December 17 aroused such revulsion that the army withdrew its support from the
Ceausescus. After the crowd took up some students' hostile chant in the dictator's
presence at a public rally in Bucharest on December 21, the Ceausescus attempted
to flee. They were shot after a military trial on Christmas Day 1989 and their bodies
displayed on television. Except for Maoist Albania, which remained isolated in
almost medieval backwardness until fall 1990, every one of the Eastern European
satellites had abolished one-party Communist rule in the space of six months.

Reunifying Germany, Ending the Cold War

Runaway changes in the Soviet Union and the dismantling of the satellites relaxed
the Cold War's grip on European borders to the point that the last traces of the Second World War could be effaced.

The most urgent business was the groundswell toward German reunification. At
first the Communist reformers who took power in East Germany in October 1989
hoped to prepare a separate socialist and neutral future for their country, a "third
way" between Communist dictatorship and unbridled capitalism. But West German

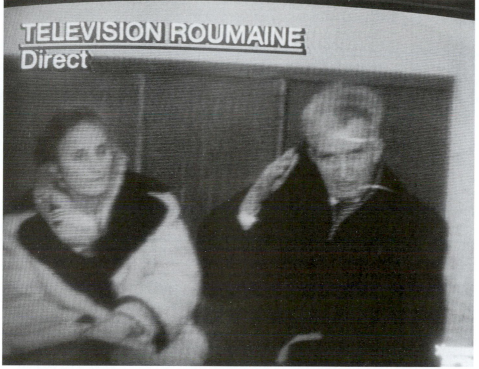

Deposed Romanian president Nicolae Ceaucescu, with his wife, Elena, as seen on Romanian television during his trial, on Christmas Day, 1989. The couple was shot later that day by the Romanian army.

chancellor Helmut Kohl seized the initiative in November with a ten-point plan that, in effect, would absorb East into West, sweetened by the lure of a one-to-one exchange of East German pensions and savings accounts for Western Deutschmarks. East Germans opted overwhelmingly for fusion with West Germany by giving nearly 50 percent of their votes to Christian Democratic candidates in parliamentary elections on March 18, 1990.

Soviet objections to a form of German reunification that amounted to outright annexation by West Germany (and NATO expansion) were bought off by Western promises. In addition to economic aid and agreement that the new Germany would still be denied "ABC" weapons—atomic, biological, and chemical—the 380,000 Soviet troops stationed in East Germany were permitted a delayed withdrawal by gradual phases. Then the four victorious powers of 1945 were ready to sit down with the two Germanies in the "two-plus-four" conferences (May–September 1990) to renounce formally their military occupation rights in Germany. The Western Deutschmark became the currency of all Germany on July 1, 1990, and the two Germanies became a single country under the West German constitution on October 3. When the last Soviet troops left East German soil on August 31, 1994, followed a few days later by the last symbolic U.S., British, and French occupation units in Berlin, the final outward traces of the postwar occupation of Germany had vanished.

Gorbachev could accept German reunification on almost entirely Western terms because it had been preceded by a relaxation of the arms race. Unable to keep up Brezhnev's missile program, Gorbachev accepted Reagan's "zero option" proposal and agreed in a December 1987 Washington summit to the total elimination of land-based intermediate-range missiles. Once the disarmament logjam had been broken, the two superpowers went on to the reduction of conventional weapons, in which the Soviet Union had long enjoyed superiority. Gorbachev was eager to cut military expenses. In a gala meeting in Paris in November 1990, representatives of the USSR, the United States, and twenty-two European states signed an agreement reducing conventional arms dramatically in Europe, as well as recognizing European frontiers as they stood. Although no formal peace treaty had ever ended the Second World War, the Paris Accord of November 1990 closed the books on it.

Then it became possible to begin dismantling the two sides' doomsday machines, their intercontinental ballistic missile (ICBM) arsenals. Presidents Bush and Gorbachev agreed on July 31, 1991 (the START I agreement), to a mutual reduction of ICBMs, about 800 on the Soviet side with more than 5,000 warheads and about 250 with 3,500 warheads on the American side, to reach parity. The Warsaw Pact had already been formally abolished on July 1, 1991. On September 27, 1991, President Bush cancelled the twenty-four-hour ground alert status of American B-52 and B-1 bombers that had been in effect since 1957 and announced a unilateral cut of about 2,400 nuclear weapons. President Gorbachev responded with similar stand-downs. The START II negotiations beginning in 1993 reduced missile armaments still further. For the first time in forty years Soviet and American forces were no longer poised to inflict instant nuclear destruction on each other. The Cold War was over.

The Collapse of the Soviet Union

After the unexpected liberation of the satellites came the unimaginable dissolution of the USSR itself, a superpower that only a few years earlier had made the world tremble. Optimists had expected the Soviet dictatorship to moderate, as new generations of highly trained technicians demanded more personal freedom and consumer goods. But only a dreamer would have foreseen the peaceful disappearance of one of the two Great Powers of the Cold War world. Even so, the USSR ceased to exist as such in December 1991. It was replaced by a Russian Federation ringed by fourteen uneasily independent countries that it had formerly ruled, from the Baltic States to the Turkic peoples of central Asia.

The excitement of Gorbachev's first liberalizations had given way to anxiety and anger as the old economic system was thrown out of gear before something new could replace it. One trouble was that the president could not make up his mind, launching and then canceling some twelve different economic reforms. Given some freedom, producers concentrated on their most rewarding items and certain necessities grew scarce. In 1991, net income fell 17 percent, more than in the United States in any one year of the Great Depression.

Economic dislocation and political fluidity stimulated local nationalisms. These were strongest in the Baltic States, where on the fiftieth anniversary of the Nazi-Soviet pact of August 23, 1939, an estimated 2 million Latvians, Lithuanians, and Estonians formed a human chain along their borders. Lithuania declared its independence (at least in principle) in March 1990, followed in May by the others. All the Baltic States began instituting discriminatory measures against the Russian managerial and military elites that the USSR had installed.

The Baltic States were not the only secessionists, however. Separatist movements and civil wars broke out in several border regions that had known a momentary independence in 1918 to 1920: Georgia, Azerbaijan, Armenia. President Gorbachev sought to hold the USSR together with both carrots and sticks. On the one hand, he withheld vital supplies like oil and raw materials from the Baltics, or even used force, as in Georgia in April 1989 and in Azerbaijan in January 1990, where hundreds of people were killed as Soviet troops recovered control of the capital city of Baku from demonstrators. At the same time, he tried to persuade all the member republics of the USSR to sign Union Treaties establishing a looser federation. By April 1991 he had obtained the agreement of nine republics to the Union Treaties, but the Baltics, Moldova, Armenia, and Georgia held back. Ratification was scheduled for August 1991.

Gorbachev had only meant to make Soviet communism work better. As change spiraled beyond what he could accept, amidst worsening living conditions and secessionism, the beleaguered president lost the initiative. He turned back for support to conservatives. His acquiescence in a bloody action in January 1991 by local Soviet army and KGB leaders to restore control over Lithuania and Latvia, which killed thirteen, cost him the support of progressives without winning back the conservatives.

The initiative now passed to two more single-minded forces. On the one hand, some wanted to go further toward democracy, private property, and a market system. They were led by Boris Yeltsin, the rough-hewn Moscow party leader eager to settle scores with Gorbachev for demoting him from the Politburo in 1987 as too outspoken. Others were nostalgic for the old regime. They blamed Gorbachev for the collapse of the Soviet Empire, growing internal chaos, and declining living standards. The nostalgics began planning a *coup d'état* for August 1991, in time to block the final signature of the Union Treaties.

Boris Yeltsin held several trump cards. He had chosen the Russian Federation as his comeback route. By May 1990 he was president of Russia—first as president of the Russian parliament, and then as president of the Russian Federation, a new office to which he was elected by universal suffrage in June 1991. He thus ruled the richest two-thirds of the Soviet Union as the first popularly elected leader in Russian history.[4] Beyond that, he was popular (Muscovites loved him for taking the bus instead of his official limousine), energetic, and daring. Yeltsin's moment came in August 1991 when Party and army leaders launched their *coup d'état*. Gorbachev was on holiday in the south. It was Yeltsin who mobilized enough proreform army units

---

[4]Gorbachev was never popularly elected. He was chosen president of the USSR by the Congress of Peoples' Deputies.

© Sovfoto / Eastfoto

Boris Yeltsin, president of the Russian Republic (holding paper), stands on a tank to address the crowd in front of the White House, the Parliament building in Moscow, on August 19, 1991. Yeltsin faced down a *coup* by army and Communist Party leaders who wanted to restore centralized party control over the Soviet Union.

and civil authorities in Moscow to defeat the irresolute and incompetent plotters. Some 70,000 citizens defended the Russian parliament's tower in Moscow, the White House, from advancing tanks. Climbing on a stalled tank, Yeltsin proclaimed the "rebirth of Russia" and established an indelible image of raw courage.

The plotters had timed their *coup* so as to forestall Gorbachev's Union Treaties and to restore a centralized USSR. Their failure left the Soviet Union in a state of dissolution. Yeltsin had fought back by dismantling the USSR's power centers within the Russian Republic, starting with the Communist Party. The *coup* also stimulated secession movements. The Baltic States declared full independence on September 6, and heartland regions like the Ukraine and Belarus made movements in the same direction. Russians themselves began to feel that their empire had been a burden. Yeltsin and his economic advisors seem to have believed that the market reforms they planned would work faster if Russia acted alone. They withheld tax receipts from the Union. The fatal blow fell on December 1 when 90 percent of the Ukrainian population, including the Russian-speaking eastern regions, voted for full independence.

Yeltsin now considered the USSR defunct and proceeded on December 21 to negotiate with the heads of the Ukraine and Belarus its replacement by a new Commonwealth of Independent States (CIS). Yeltsin's Russian Republic assumed the international responsibilities and remaining powers of the USSR. Gorbachev resigned on Christmas Day 1991, passing the nuclear weapons codes to Yeltsin. The red hammer and sickle was hauled down from the Kremlin and a new tricolored Russian flag was hoisted in its place. The Soviet Union had ceased to exist.

THE MORNING AFTER

Russia in Trouble

Boris Yeltsin and Russia now faced the multiple challenges that had brought down Gorbachev and the Soviet Union. Yeltsin's most immediate challenge was to reverse the economy's slide. Unlike Gorbachev, Yeltsin believed in private property and the market. In January 1992, his young Finance Minister Yegor Gaidar applied shock therapy. He flung open the market by freeing prices and abolishing subsidies. Becoming prime minister later in 1992, Gaidar launched a vast privatization program that eventually transferred 122,000 enterprises to private ownership. Managers and employees were allotted 51 percent of their enterprises' shares. All Russian citizens received vouchers worth a modest 10,000 rubles (about $25) that they could invest in firms, sell to other investors, or swap for shares in mutual funds. By the end of June 1994, when the vouchers expired, the private sector produced 62 percent of Russian GDP and employed 86 percent of the Russian industrial labor force. There were 40 million Russian shareholders.[5]

But the Russian economy responded less positively than the Polish, Czech, or Hungarian economies to market opportunities. Productivity did not rise to the incentives of vastly higher prices. One problem was many Russians' antipathy for competition and profit. Another was the lack of clear title or protection from rackets. Naturally little foreign or domestic capital was available for start-ups or upgrading. Although retail and restaurants blossomed, big enterprises often went to profiteers, readier to strip assets and expatriate capital than to invest in productivity. These included "red managers" who had made astute use of their reserved shares as well as criminals. Organized crime was estimated to control 40 percent of the economy by 1999. Monopolists excluded competitors by force. The result was what Marshall Goldman calls a "supply-side depression."[6] Without a stream of new goods, prices rose twenty-fold by the end of 1992.

By 1993, anywhere from 30 to 80 percent of Russians were living below the poverty line. In a country where the price of bread had not changed in thirty years, the shock was profound. Widening inequities between the new poor and the new rich aroused sharp bitterness. Among the former were professional people whose salaries did not keep pace with inflation, victims of factory closures, and pensioners, like the widows seen selling their husbands' medals on Moscow street corners. The latter included those managers who had wound up as owners of privatized plants (the cynical called privatization "grabitization"[7]), and new millionaires who flaunted their new wealth in armored limousines, protected by private guards.

---

[5]"Survey: Russia's Silent Revolution," *The Economist* (April 8–14, 1995), pp. 3, 5–6.

[6]Marshall Goldman, *Lost Opportunity: Why Economic Reforms in Russia Have Not Worked* (New York, 1996), p. 21.

[7]Ibid., p. 138. In Russian, *prikhvatizatsiya* instead of *privatizatsiya*.

In the new Russia, the shopwindows were full, but while a few became rich, many once comfortable citizens were reduced to penury.

White-collar crime and petty street crime, theoretically nonexistent under communism, became common. As health care and social services collapsed, life expectancy dropped to 58 years for men. The Russian population actually declined by nearly three million between 1992 and 2000. In the absence of stable money and a framework of business law, many enterprises resorted to barter. A trickle of Western investment and some loans from the IMF helped a bit, but meeting IMF criteria for a balanced budget prevented assistance to the poor and fueled tendencies to blame Western interference for making things worse.

During 1998, Russian economic decline finally seemed to be bottoming out. After a decline of some 53 percent in ten years, production was expected to show its first annual increase. In August, however, side effects of an Asian investment collapse, along with falling world oil prices, forced Russia to default on $40 billion of foreign loans and devalue the ruble by 75 percent. Withdrawal of funds caused bank collapses in which most of the new Russian middle class lost savings and investments. Many Russians, raised to consider all private property illicit, now equated a market economy with impoverishment, corruption, "crony capitalism," physical insecurity, and national humiliation. The Russian economy avoided disaster—there was nothing like the starvation of 1921 or 1931—but no developed country had ever experienced such a drastic evaporation of wealth.

Yeltsin's second challenge was to root an effective and legitimate system of electoral democracy in Russian life. Here, too, although Russia avoided the oft-predicted disasters of dictatorship or anarchy, Yeltsin's record was mixed. In his eight and a half years as president of Russia (1991–1999), he established almost limitless powers for the executive. He treated parliament roughly. Having saved it from the tanks in

Armored forces loyal to Russian president Boris Yeltsin shell the Parliament building in Moscow, occupied by parliamentary leaders who have organized popular demonstrations against Yeltsin's rapid move toward a market economy (October 4, 1993).

August 1991, he assaulted it with tanks in October 1993. The parliament elected in 1990 was dominated by old Communist apparatchiks and managers of former state monopolies. It fought Yeltsin's austerity policies by voting the printing of new money to cover social relief measures and subsidies to inefficient state enterprises that Yeltsin was trying to close down. Yeltsin—in step with the 1990s Thatcherite West and under pressure from the IMF, which controlled his access to Western aid—feared inflation more than unemployment and social dislocation. After a referendum in April 1993 showed public support for him and his market economy, despite the pains of austerity, he dissolved parliament on September 21, 1993. Parliament's leaders, holed up in the White House (the parliament tower in Moscow), sent demonstrators to assault the Moscow city hall and the government's television center. Yeltsin sent tanks against the White House. Some 120 people were killed as the tower's top floors were shelled and burned. Moscow had not seen such violence in its streets since 1905.

Having asserted by force his power to dissolve parliament, Yeltsin issued a new constitution in November 1993 that confirmed a strong presidency with powers exceeding those of his American and French models. Some 60 percent of those voting approved it in a referendum (with 53 percent participating), making Yeltsin feel entitled to govern as he wished. He did not dispense with parliament, however. Two hostile legislatures followed. In the parliamentary elections of December 1993, the neofascist Liberal Democratic Party of Vladimir Zhirinovsky came in first, with nearly 23 percent of the vote. Yeltsin's supporters, split into several parties, together polled only about 30 percent. In the parliamentary elections of December 1995, the Communist Party, whose leader Gennady Zyuganov skillfully kept his intentions veiled, led the pack (21 percent), with Zhirinovsky second. President Yeltsin alternately bullied and ignored these two legislatures. Not until that second legislature had served its term did elections in December 1999 give Yeltsin his own parliamentary base. In the meantime, Yeltsin had confirmed his grip on power by being elected to a second term as president in July 1996 with the help of a media campaign financed by favored businessmen. He had low public approval, but all the other candidates seemed worse.

Although President Yeltsin went through the motions of obtaining parliamentary approval for his prime ministers, they answered only to him and it was he who dismissed them, in an increasingly arbitrary fashion. The longest-serving prime minister was Viktor Chernomyrdin (1992–1998), former head of the state natural gas monopoly and now largest shareholder of the vast private gas monopoly Gazprom. As Yeltsin became immobilized by ill health (he had a quintuple bypass operation in 1996 and was believed to drink heavily), Chernomyrdin established an independent power base among the new business elite. It was apparently to block this emerging rival that Yeltsin dismissed him in March 1998. There followed four prime ministers in the next eighteen months, sometimes unknown young men with backgrounds in police or security work, one of whom served only 82 days.

Within Yeltsin's presidential autocracy, a kind of democracy stumbled along, resting upon a critical press, public debate, and contested elections. The consolidation of presidential authority left little space for either of the two extremes so feared by Western observers in the early 1990s. The Communist Party spoke mostly for the disappearing elderly. The far right, with its poisonous brew of nationalism, religious fundamentalism, monarchist nostalgia, anti-Westernism, and anti-Semitism, grouped around Zhirinovsky and movements like *Pamyat* (memory), lost credibility when Zhirinovsky's ludicrous projects, such as the recovery of Alaska, and Jewish ancestry became public. Russia's gravest political problems were the nearly unchecked nature of presidential power, which a successor might abuse, and the growing political influence of the "oligarchs," the billionaire victors of "grabitization" such as Boris Berezovsky, whose power in the media helped reelect Yeltsin president in 1996.

After economic revival and political legitimacy, the third challenge facing Yeltsin was Russia's relations with the outside world. A major preoccupation was the "near abroad," the ring of newly independent states surrounding Russia that had once been part of the Soviet Union. Yeltsin tried to use Russia's superior energy resources and armaments to give substance to the Commonwealth of Independent States (CIS), but Russia's economic floundering and the power of national feeling kept it a shadow organization. Some of the breakaway republics had great riches in oil and other strategic resources, and three of them—Belarus, the Ukraine, and Kazakhstan—even possessed nuclear weapons whose ownership they disputed with Russia. Some of the new republics fell victim to their own ethnic divisions (bloody civil wars broke out in Armenia, Georgia, and Azerbaijan). Some of the Central Asian republics flirted with their Islamic neighbors, hesitating between secular Turkey and fundamentalist Iran.

Since 25 million Russians now lived in the surrounding "near abroad," the world could expect Russia to exert pressures—or worse—on its neighbors. The cycle of independence and recapture of 1918–1920 seemed likely to repeat itself. Belarus signed a treaty in 1999 promising vaguely to join Russia in a loose confederation. Georgia felt obliged to accept a Russian military presence in return for aid against ethnic secessionists. Matters came to bloody warfare when Yeltsin tried to subdue the Caucasion border province of Chechnya in 1994–1996. The Islamic Chechen guerrillas held out, and the war was unpopular in Russia. A long future of tensions and conflicts around Russia's borders seemed likely.

Farther afield, Yeltsin felt obliged to maintain working relations with the West for economic and financial reasons, despite the expansion of NATO eastward and the suspicion of many Russians that the West was making Russian problems worse.

The new Russian president, Vladimir Putin, former KGB officer, displays his judo skills during a state visit to Japan in September 2000.

Against the wishes of many of his people who considered the Serbs brother Slavs, he offered grudging support to Western efforts to block Slobodan Milošević's Greater Serbia, as we will see below.

As the millennium ended, the intermittently ailing Yeltsin managed one final exploit of will and daring. At midnight on December 31, 1999, he suddenly resigned the presidency, with over a year remaining in his term of office, and named as acting president his last prime minister and protégé, Vladimir Putin. He thus managed to pass on his powers to a chosen successor, whose first act decreed legal immunity for Yeltsin and his family, closely implicated with the "oligarchs."

Putin, a KGB official of only forty-six, was unexpected as head of the Russian Federation. His renewed war in Chechnya was popular, however, and he was elected president in his own right on March 26, 2000. He tightened central administration, improved the legal status of property, and took arbitrary action against certain "oligarchs," mostly those with overly independent-minded TV stations. The economy grew 5 percent a year, aided by high oil prices and a cheap ruble. So even as Russian infrastructure crumbled and most Russians remained poorer than under Brezhnev, and although Putin's visit to President Bush did not prevent NATO expansion to his doorstep, the president was reelected in March 2004 almost without opposition. Democracy and the market were battered but alive in Russia.

Creating Democracy, Inventing the Market in East-Central Europe

In the former satellites the joy of 1989 soon gave way to painful reality. The rotten old structures had fallen easily. But building new constitutional regimes, civil societies, economies, and value systems in the void posed daunting difficulties through the 1990s.

The least painful transition was to electoral democracy. Some leaders of international stature appeared, such as the eloquent Czech president Václav Havel. But the broad coalitions of dissidents that had taken power in 1989 inevitably split up when confronted with the hard choices of governing. The most famous dissident leader of Eastern Europe, Solidarity leader Lech Walesa, did indeed become president of Poland in December 1990, but Solidarity soon thereafter broke in two. Indeed sixty-seven parties contested the October 1991 legislative elections in Poland, forty-five the Hungarian elections of March 1990, and seventy-four the Romanian elections of September 1992.

One common pattern was a rapid loss of popularity by the idealistic but inexperienced new leaders of 1989. Under the shock of unemployment and skyrocketing prices, inconclusive elections, fragmented parties, and weak coalition governments, voters returned former Communists to a majority in freely elected parliaments in Lithuania (1992), Poland (September 1993), and Hungary (spring 1994). Walesa was defeated in the Polish presidential election of November 1995 by a former Communist official turned democrat, Alexander Wasniewski. In Poland and Hungary, these ex-Communists proclaimed themselves converts to democracy and the market, however. At most, they slowed privatization and increased aid to the economic losers.

In another political pattern more common in the Balkans, former Communist officials retained power without interruption, recycling themselves for election as pragmatic nationalists. This was the case in Bulgaria, Romania, Albania, and the component republics of Yugoslavia, such as Croatia, with Franjo Tudjman, and Serbia, with Slobodan Milošević. Here presidential rule, ratified by election but rooted in clientelism and patronage, was the norm.

Far more difficult was the shift from state-run communist economies to market economies. No precedents existed to guide this transition, and the legal, institutional, and cultural underpinnings were missing. In the short run, the immediate impact was a decline of economic activity by up to a third. The USSR and COMECON, Eastern Europe's main customers, were no longer buying, and many of the state behemoths could not compete under free market conditions.

The East-Central European states followed different economic strategies. Poland decided to take the cold plunge into market-driven prices all at once. On January 1, 1990, price controls and subsidies were abolished, and consumers suddenly had to pay much more for formerly subsidized daily necessities. Unemployment and high prices made life very difficult in Poland for two years, but entrepreneurs (Poland already had a private sector) were ready to respond to market needs. Shops soon filled. Poland's economy became the fastest growing in Europe, adding over 6 percent to GDP every year from 1995 to 2000.

Czechoslovakia adopted the ex-communist world's first mass privatization scheme under Prime Minister Václav Klaus (1992–1997), an economist whose model was Margaret Thatcher. While the Polish government hesitated to sell off or break up the state behemoths (whose market share was diminishing anyway), Czechoslovakia transferred 2,000 firms to its citizens in 1992 by issuing each of them vouchers. Most Czechs exchanged these vouchers for mutual funds, mostly organized by banks (which became, in effect, the owners of much of Czech industry). Hungary's economy, already the freest in Eastern Europe, changed more slowly. Its well-established private sector was attractive to foreign lenders, and Hungary attracted nearly half the region's entire foreign investment, over $15 billion by the end of 1998. It, too, grew more that 5 percent each year in the late 1990s.

Other former Communist states hesitated to expose their citizens to the full blast of rising prices and unemployment. The Slovaks, who had long chafed within Czechoslovakia, were persuaded to secede on January 1, 1993, by Vladimir Mečiar, who led separate Slovakia much more slowly toward democracy and the market. Romania and Bulgaria hardly began to establish the legal foundations of property in land and business until the later 1990s. As late as 1997, Bulgaria's rich fruit and vegetable farms lay fallow because of uncertainty about who owned them.

Even in the strongest postCommunist economies in Eastern Europe, losers jostled winners. Unemployment figures hovered around 15 percent in much of the region—hard enough in old democracies, and almost unbearable where unemployment had been unknown (at least in theory). Inflation also remained dangerously high in some Eastern European countries (34 percent in Poland in 1994). Governments ran large deficits, partly because tax revenues were low, partly because politicians felt compelled to aid their poorest citizens.

In the realm of values, the discredit of the ruling ideology left room, as Václav Havel lamented, for "an enormous and dazzling explosion of every imaginable human vice."[8] The democratic idealism of the dissident intellectuals who had led

[8]Václav Havel, *Summer Meditations* (New York, 1992), p. 1.

the fight against Communist autocracy was often replaced among the uneducated by a mere craving for Western material abundance and individual hedonism. If democracy and the market disappointed these hopes in the short term, baser popular passions might take their place. The old ethnic hatreds of pre-1914 Eastern Europe resurfaced, sometimes sharpened by twentieth-century conflicts, and seized upon by desperate leaders looking for a popular cause. Unfortunately, no Eastern European state lacked its national minorities and ethnic tensions. Hungarian Prime Minister Viktor Orban (1998–2002) alarmed his neighbors by allusions to the unity of all Hungarians (some 2 million of whom lived in Romanian Transylvania and another 600,000 in Slovakia). Mečiar's Slovakia discriminated against Hungarians and gypsies.

One difficult decision was whether to forget the misdeeds of the old rulers (as post-Franco–Spain did after 1975) or to subject the former Communist leadership to purges and trials as most liberated countries had done after World War II. Germany went furthest, condemning Honecker and other former East German authorities to prison for having ordered the police to shoot youths who climbed the wall. The *Stasi*'s miles of files were opened, exposing many to the pain of discovering that a spouse or friend had been an informer. Czechoslovakia passed a "lustration" law in 1991, literally exposing to light the actions of former officials, and excluded all former officials from office for five years, without judicial procedure. "Lustration" could backfire, as when Lech Walesa was accused, perhaps maliciously, of having been an informer for the Polish secret police before 1989.

By 2004, no former Communist regime had yet turned to an extremist party or had severely infringed market principles. The number of parties had settled down. The hope that democracy could survive the strains of transition to a market economy seemed well founded. The desire to join the European Union was still the strongest force in favor of persevering in that direction. On May 1, 2004, ten of them had met the requirements to join the European Union, but not without cold feet on both sides, as we will see.

The New Germany

The breathtakingly rapid reunification of the two Germanies changed the face of Europe. Now an outsized economic powerhouse dominated its center. But before Germany's neighbors could decide how to react, Germany itself would have to overcome the gigantic economic, social, and psychological costs of unification. At first, both "Ossies" and "Wessies"—inhabitants of former East and West Germany—tended to accept Chancellor Kohl's assurances that the absorption and rehabilitation of East Germany would be rapid. The Easterners expected to enjoy Western standards of living soon. On December 2, 1990, in the first free elections for all Germans since 1932, the German public rewarded Chancellor Kohl with a triumphant majority for the Christian Democrats and their coalition partners, the Free Democrats.

Instantaneous unification made East German economic problems simultaneously easier and harder than in the rest of the former satellites, however. On the

© Reuters / Bettmann / CORBIS

West German chancellor Helmut Kohl works the crowd in Erfurt, East Germany, on February 20, 1990. Kohl's Christian Democrats did well enough in parliamentary elections in East Germany on March 18 to provide a comfortable majority for Kohl's proposal to simply absorb East Germany into the Federal Republic (West Germany) under the existing West German constitution.

plus side, West Germany was picking up the tab. On the minus side, the East German economy collapsed more utterly than the others. "Ossies" did not want to drive their clunky Trabants any more, and their craving for Western goods was so strong that East German milk had to be trucked to the West and relabeled there for sale in the East. To make matters worse, Kohl's generous offer of parity with the West German Deutschmark made East German products now cost four times their previous price. Under these conditions, most East German enterprises could not sell anything. A liquidation agency, the *Treuhandanstalt*,[9] attempted to sell, close, or restructure some 60,000 public enterprises of the former GDR between 1990 and 1995. Inevitably, many went unsold and had to be shut. Their workers went idle. Thus even the most favored former satellite economy, the only one reunited with wealthy cousins, had to pass through a period of massive unemployment—a form of suffering officially unknown under Communism—before the standard of living could return even to pre-1989 levels.

So East and West Germans had to get to know each other under a double burden. "Ossies," sidelined not only by economic collapse but by the takeover of managerial

[9]Literally, the Trust Department.

positions, teaching, and the media by carpet-bagging "Wessies," felt like second-class citizens in their own country. The sudden disappearance of their security, their status, and even their pride shattered East German self-confidence; in the three years after 1989, the birthrate dropped 60 percent in the ex-GDR, and the marriage rate 65 percent. Westerners, on their side, began to resent the years of heavy taxation needed to rebuild an ungrateful East. Both felt somehow cheated by the unification process.

Three sets of aspirations about Germany were thus frustrated. First thwarted were the hopes of some East Germans for a "third way," combining political freedom with what they saw as the redeeming features of the former GDR: its social services and the prestige it accorded to artists and intellectuals. Second, the lure of Western glitter deceived many who expected instant abundance and who instead faced high unemployment, loss of social protection, and lower wages than in the West. Finally, Germany's neighbors wondered how to keep the emerging new superpower of Central Europe in check. Even so, German voters gave Chancellor Kohl's Christian Democrats another majority in elections in October 1994. Kohl had governed Germany 16 years, longer than Hitler, when the Social Democrats finally managed to beat him in the September 1998 elections by offering more of the same, the "new middle" of Gerhard Schröder. By 2000, Germany, its capital moved back to imperial Berlin, was the third economic power of the world, but unemployment still exceeded 10 percent and the economic, social, and psychological stresses of reunification had not yet been overcome.

The Yugoslav Civil War

East-Central Europe's basket case was Yugoslavia. Some Europeans and Americans considered Yugoslavia hopelessly consumed by ancient hatreds, an interpretation that encouraged hands-off resignation. Ancient hatreds there were, but it was the importation into the Balkans of the modern Western idea that each people must have its own homogeneous state that inspired murderous attempts to impose greater Serbia, greater Croatia, greater Albania, and the like, on the Balkans' human patchwork.

No sooner had Serbian president Slobodan Milošević discovered how effective demagogic nationalism was in a postCommunist world,[10] he began reducing the rights of non-Serbs within Serbia. In 1989, he abolished the semiautonomy previously enjoyed by the Albanian majority in Kosovo and the Hungarian minority in the Vojvodina, and began replacing their police and teachers with Serbs. Croatia and Slovenia responded with more adamant separatism. In March 1991, the Collective Presidency of the Yugoslav Federation lost its quorum when the Serb member and his allies withdrew. Efforts to renegotiate a looser Yugoslav federal system proved impossible, there being no middle ground between Serb centralism and Slovenian and Croation separatism. Croatia and Slovenia declared their independence on June 25, 1991. European leaders tried to withhold diplomatic recognition

---

[10]See chapter 21, p. 618.

CONFLICTS IN THE FORMER YUGOSLAVIA

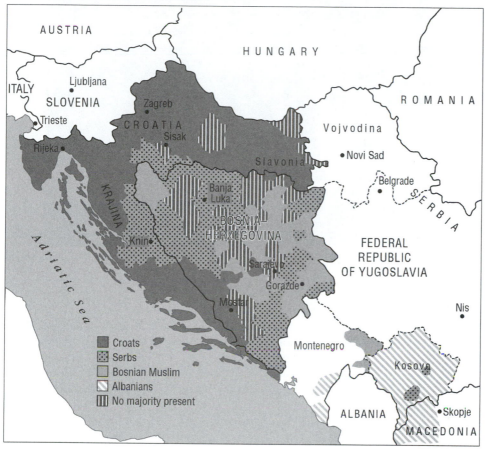

until these breakaway republics included guarantees for minorities in their constitutions, but Germany jumped the gun and promised to recognize the two new states by Christmas 1991—the first muscle-flexing in foreign affairs by the new Germany.

The Serb minorities in newly independent Slovenia and Croatia, supported by the Serb-dominated federal Yugoslav army (the fourth largest in Europe), reacted by taking up arms. Slovenia, the most homogeneous of Yugoslav regions, was able to fend off the federal army. Croatia, whose Serb minority amounted to 12 percent of the population, became engulfed in civil war in July 1991. The Serbs of Croatia turned their enclaves along the southeastern frontier with Bosnia into the "Serbian Republic of Krajina." Serbian president Milošević recognized Krajina (no other state did), and allowed the Yugoslav army to help Krajina's popular militia. Croat nationalists responded in kind. The fighting in Croatia was aimed with particular cruelty at civilians, including shelling by Serb forces of the historic cities of

© Wesley Bocxe / Photo Researchers

War in former Yugoslavia: A soccer field in Sarajevo, the capital of Bosnia, is converted into a cemetery (July 1993).

Dubrovnik and Vukovar. This was, after all, the fourth Croat–Serb war of the twentieth century. Serbs remembered with particular bitterness their slaughter at the hands of pro-Nazi *Ustasha* in independent Croatia during 1941–1944. Croats recalled how Serbia had always dominated the Yugoslav federation. The president of independent Croatia, Franjo Tudjman (1991–1999), had suffered imprisonment in the 1970s for nationalist activity as a history professor. He made matters worse by adopting some *Ustasha* emblems.

When Bosnia, in turn, voted for independence on March 1, 1992, the fighting spread there. The Serbs of Bosnia, around 30 percent of the population, refused to accept a state where Muslims (Slavs converted during Ottoman rule) were a majority. Serb popular militias formed inside Bosnia, assisted by the Serbian government and the Yugoslav federal army. The civil war in Bosnia was particularly vicious, for Bosnia had been the most nationally complex republic and the one where the Yugoslav ideal of a secular, tolerant multiethnic state had been most fully realized in intermarriages and mingled neighborhoods. Each nationality tried to make the regions it controlled uniform by "ethnic cleansing"[11]: systematically expelling members of the "alien" nationality from their homes, gang-raping their women, or even murdering residents in order to convert complex neighborhoods into homogeneous zones. The Bosnian capital city, Sarajevo, the spot where a Bosnian Serb had touched off the First World War, was surrounded by Serb forces, whose artillery lobbed shells into crowded streets on market days from April 1992 to September 1995. By late 1995, an estimated 200,000 persons were dead in ex-Yugoslavia, and more than 3 million refugees had been displaced. Total war had returned to European soil, from which it had supposedly been banished forever in 1945—or even in 1918.

---

[11]This graphic term is inaccurate, for the differences for which the former Yugoslavs killed each other were religious and cultural, not ethnic.

Exposed regularly on television to these pitiless cruelties, the citizens of Europe and the United States wanted to do something. It was not clear, however, how foreign forces might intervene successfully in a war without frontiers, of neighbor against neighbor. At first the United States and the European Union tried to stop the fighting where the combatants stood, and embargoed arms shipments to Bosnia. This solution, however, gave an advantage to the Serbs, who were making most of the gains through 1993 and 1994. By mid-1994, they occupied more than half of Bosnia and a quarter of Croatia. Negotiations for partition pleased no party, all of whom hoped for more.

The United Nations sent a peacekeeping force in early 1992 and set up a half-dozen "safe areas" where threatened civilians could be protected from marauding combatants. These were woefully undermanned, however, as most Western nations were reluctant to commit troops to such a dangerous and ambiguous assignment. When the Bosnian Serbs overran the UN "safe area" of Gorazde in April 1994, the United States authorized the first NATO air strikes against Bosnian Serb positions, over British and French objections (their participants in the UN force were vulnerable). The enraged Bosnian Serbs responded by taking 350 UN soldiers hostage in May 1995, and in July overran the UN "safe area" of Srebrenica, slaughtering some 7,000 men and boys captured there. It was the worst mass killing in Europe since the Second World War.

Anti-Serb forces now received Western help. Croats and Muslims made peace against their common Serb enemy in Bosnia and regained some ground there. A Croat Army rearmed and retrained with American and German complicity wiped out the Serb enclaves of "Krajina" and Western Slavonia in summer 1995, expelling 180,000 Serbs from their homes in southeastern and eastern Croatia. President Tudjman had won his war, and Croatia had become a homogeneous state.

NATO now took over principal responsibility for action in the former Yugoslavia from the faltering forces of the UN and the European Union. It conducted massive air strikes against Bosnian Serb infrastructure as well as military positions in early September 1995. At this point, Milošević opportunistically stopped supporting the Serbs outside his own country and accepted a bargain with the West. He bought his own personal survival in power in Serbia by becoming the essential Serb partner in the shaky peace wrung in November 1995 from reluctant negotiators at Wright-Patterson Air Force Base in Dayton, Ohio. The Dayton agreement forced Bosnian Serbs back into 49 percent of the territory of Bosnia and obliged them to live within a loose Bosnian federal state. Their aspirations to join a Greater Serbia were frustrated for the moment by U.S. and other NATO troops sent to enforce the Dayton agreements. A special UN tribunal indicted seven Croats and forty-five Bosnian Serbs for war crimes, but the most conspicuous ones, including the Bosnian Serb leader Radovan Karadžić and military commander Gen. Ratko Mladić, directly responsible for the Srebrenica masssacre, were sheltered within their community.

After the Dayton Agreement, a lull followed in the ex-Yugoslav cauldron, as all parties preferred an imperfect peace to a renewal of the horrors of war. Nationalist demons had been let loose in Kosovo, however. This southern province of Serbia, site of major Serb religious sites and the epic Battle of *Kosova Polje* (the Field of the Blackbirds) against the Muslims in 1389, had become 90 percent Muslim Albanian by population transfers and natural increase. Deprived of their local autonomy by

© AFP / CORBIS

After crowds in Belgrade forced Slobodan Milošević to accept Vojislav Kostunica's victory in presidential elections in rump Yugoslavia in October 2000, Kostunica greets his supporters.

Milošević in 1989, the Albanian Kosovars abandoned their more pacific leaders and increasingly after 1997 supported the militant Kosovo Liberation Army (KLA). Incidents multiplied, and in summer 1998 Milošević sent the Serbian Army into Kosovo to clear the frontier zone with Albania and stop the flow of arms and volunteers to the KLA. Serb soldiers and volunteers emptied whole villages as they went, turning thousands of Albanian Kosovars into refugees.

In February 1999, Milošević rejected a compromise worked out by Western diplomats (the KLA had accepted disarmament and abandoned independence in exchange for local autonomy and the withdrawal of Serb forces). Instead he stepped up the emptying of Albanian Kosovar villages. Fearful that a flood of refugees would destabilize neighboring Macedonia, Albania, and even Greece, the Western states agreed to military action more quickly than they had in Bosnia. Starting on March 24, 1999, NATO launched guided missiles against a limited number of Serb military targets, confident that Milošević would capitulate as he had in Bosnia. Instead Milošević started expelling the entire Albanian population from Kosovo, blaming the flood of refugees on the West. Unwilling to venture ground troops into such treacherous terrain, NATO attempted to defeat the Serbian Army by escalating air attacks. Although NATO tried to target only strategic sites, excellent Serb air defenses forced its planes to remain above 15,000 feet. Inevitably Serb civilians were killed, upsetting both Russian and Western opinion, as Milošević hoped. As skilled camouflage and dispersal protected Serbian armor from NATO missiles (the Serbs turned their radars on only momentarily in order to avoid detection), NATO felt obliged to take out the Serbian civilian infrastructure. As power plants and bridges were destroyed, the population of Belgrade danced in the streets and sang their defiance of NATO. Only after 78 days, 36,000 guided missile attacks, and the refusal of Russian military aid, did Milošević agree to withdraw his troops from Kosovo and accept a NATO peacekeeping force on June 9, 1999. Although most Serbs still believed their national cause was just, they increasingly recognized that Milošević had ruined the country and corrupted the state. Fragmented opposition groups finally united around the moderate nationalist law professor Vojislav Koštunica for the Yugoslav presidential elections of September 24, 2000. When the official election commission refused to ratify Koštunica's victory and tried to call a run-off election, angry crowds gathered in Belgrade. On October 5 they stormed and burned the parliament and state TV buildings. The defection to Koštunica of important police and army leaders forced Milošević to step down on October 6 as President of Yugoslavia. Local elections in Serbia in December completed the rout of Milošević's party. The rump of Yugoslavia (now reduced to Serbia and an increasingly restive Montenegro) could now begin to recover from Europe's first real war since 1945. On April 1, 2001, the new government arrested Milošević for corruption and abuse of power. On June 28, under Western pressure, it handed him over to the UN Tribunal for the former Yugoslavia in The Hague for trial for crimes against humanity.

WESTERN EUROPEAN RESPONSES TO THE REVOLUTION OF 1989

European Union: Between Deepening and Widening

After 1989, it became possible for the first time since the Second World War to imagine a truly united Europe, no longer walled into two parts. The European Community faced these new opportunities with two perhaps incompatible strategies: deepening the integration of its members into the Community, and widening the membership. The first impulse of EC Commission president Jacques Delors (1985–1995), the most activist Commission president since Walter Hallstein in the 1960s, was to deepen.

The European Single Act of 1986[12] had already proposed bold new agendas: the unimpeded transfer of labor, capital, and services; a single European currency; and a common foreign and military policy. When unimpeded transfer came into effect on January 1, 1993, it became possible for banks, insurance companies, professionals, and craftsmen to market their skills throughout the Community (lawyers, for example, could theoretically move more freely than in the United States, though

---

[12]See chapter 22, p. 645.

linguistic and cultural barriers remained). On that date, the European Community renamed itself the European Union (EU).

French president Mitterrand and German chancellor Kohl wanted to maintain the momentum generated by the 1986 Single Act. With their encouragement, Commission president Delors prepared measures to move the EU forward toward the next stages called for in the Single Act: a single currency, and common defense and foreign policies. The twelve member states were not equally enthusiastic, especially the British. British prime minister Thatcher led the opposition until she was forced, by dissent within her own party over other issues, to step down in November 1990 in her eleventh year of office. Her less abrasive conservative successor, John Major, accepted a limited federalism. After a year of laborious compromise, a convention in the Dutch town of Maastricht hammered out a treaty in December 1991 that promised the most radical revision of the EC since its beginning: a timetable for moves toward a single currency by 1998, proposals to form common foreign and defense policies, increased use of majority voting, and greater parliamentary powers.

It proved surprisingly difficult to have the Maastricht Treaty ratified in the twelve member states. The ratification procedures revealed deep popular opposition to what was perceived as an unresponsive EC bureaucracy in Brussels and growing attachment to national traditions in matters like hunting, brewing, and cheese making, threatened by new European health and environmental standards. The Danes had to vote twice, and the French ratified by a narrow 51 percent. When the Maastricht Treaty finally took effect in November 1993, the limits of the deepening impulse had become clear.

Even so, the EU managed one more prodigious step forward. Almost on schedule, on January 1, 1999, eleven of the EU members fused their currencies into a single European money—the euro. At first, the euro was a "virtual" currency, used only for accounting purposes. Actual bills and coins denominated in euros went into circulation on January 1, 2002, and eleven proud, historic currencies—the franc, the lira, the mark, and so on—went out of circulation a few months later. This bold unifying step had seemed beyond realization at first. Britain and Italy had had to withdraw from the EU's earlier currency structure, the European Monetary System, during a bout of economic recession in September 1992. Aided by a period of growth and the support of businessmen who anticipated huge savings in exchange costs, the member nations managed to reduce their inflation, budgetary deficit, and national debt figures to the low German level (tolerating high levels of unemployment along the way) in order to make currency fusion possible. Thereafter, in most of Western Europe, an area roughly equivalent to the United States in size and wealth, it was no longer necessary to change money for cross-border transactions within the euro area. The eleven euro countries would, however, be unable to stimulate their local economies by single-country devaluations. The creators of the euro had hoped that it would rival the dollar as a currency of deposit and transaction, but investors voted for the dollar during the Internet boom at the end of the twentieth century, and by August 2000 the euro had slipped from $1.17 to $0.87. As the ballooning American budget deficit weakened the dollar, however, it grew to $1.20 by 2004.

Deepening had its limits. In other than monetary and trade respects, the EU remained a loose confederation of sovereign states. The European Council, composed of the national leaders, served increasingly as the Union's motor, while the supranational Commission merely executed its policies, especially under the less visionary presidents Jacques Santer (1995–1999) and Romano Prodi (1999–). Moreover, the fact that four EU members remained outside the euro zone— Britain, Sweden, Denmark, and Finland—meant that the EU now functioned more than ever on multiple levels of completeness.

That flexibility, in turn, made widening easier. Remaining members of the European Free Trade Association (EFTA)—Sweden and Finland (but not Norway, whose oil and natural gas resources permitted independence and whose fishermen and farmers preferred local protection) along with Austria—became members on January 1, 1995, raising EU membership to fifteen.

The economic and political success in the 1990s of many former Soviet satellites made their membership in the EU conceivable. This posed daunting problems, however. Economic assistance costs threatened to be enormous. Members feared waves of job-seekers as their own unemployment rate approached 10 percent. Masses of inefficient Eastern European peasants might swamp the already costly Common Agricultural Program (CAP). One-fifth of the Polish population still works the land, with less than 12 acres apiece.

On the candidates' side, farmers and businessmen feared efficient western producers. Most expected the benefits to outweigh the costs, however. Referenda for union passed in ten candidate states during 2003; the Baltic States of Latvia, Estonia, and Lithuania; Poland; Hungary; the Czech Republic; Slovakia; Slovenia; and the two island states of Malta and Cyprus. While no referendum failed, only 54 percent approved in Malta and 67 percent in Latvia and Estonia. On April 16, 2003, these ten candidates signed a Treaty of Accession with the EU.

How executive positions would be allocated and votes weighted among twenty-five members posed thorny problems. The necessary procedural adjustments were made slowly, with evident reluctance. The Treaty of Amsterdam (May 1, 1999) did little more than expand slightly the powers of the parliament and the Commission President. Quarrels about how voting would be weighted in the Council nearly wrecked the Nice Summit of December 2000. Most embarrassingly, a proposed new "Constitution for Europe," published on July 18, 2003, was shelved in November 2003 after objections by Poland and Spain.

Nevertheless the ten candidates joined the EU on May 1, 2004, before the machinery was ready and with sobering limitations. The existing members can restrict worker immigration from the new members for up to seven years. Aid to farmers starts at one-quarter of old members' levels, rising to parity by 2013. It is second-class membership, widening at the expense of deepening.

Another possible pole around which Europeans might pool their resources was NATO. The disappearance of the USSR might seem to deprive NATO of its very reason for existence. Instead of vanishing, however, NATO expanded, incorporating new members in Eastern Europe, and waging its first full-scale military operation in Kosovo, outside NATO territory, in 1999. Even without communism, the instability of the Russian and Balkan frontiers required Europeans to continue to provide for common security measures. The role of the United States in European security aroused conflicting responses among Europeans. On the one hand, they wanted the United States to continue to bear part of the burden of European defense. On the other hand, American predominance in NATO aroused their desire for greater independence in defense matters. At first the Europeans dusted off the Western European Union (WEU), founded in 1948 and put to use in 1954 to bring West Germany into controlled rearmament, and revived it as the "European pillar" of NATO, a supposedly equal partner to the United States. It was officially as the WEU that European forces took part in the Gulf War in early 1991 and in the blockade of the former Yugoslavia after 1992.

The failure of the European Community and the United Nations to stem the slaughter in Bosnia suggested the need for something stronger. European subordination was underlined still further in 1999 where 70 percent of the aerial bombardment missions in Kosovo were American. Although the Europeans together spent nearly two thirds as much as the United States on defense, they had almost no capacity in "smart" missiles. Their defense suppliers were still almost entirely national, resulting in duplication and technological lag. The EU's response to repeated demonstrations of powerlessness in the Balkans was the creation by the Treaty of Amsterdam of the post of EU High Commissioner for Foreign and Defence Policy, held by the Spaniard Javier Solano, former Secretary-General of NATO. The Europeans also began thinking seriously about adapting their defense industries, heretofore strictly national, to a continental scale. In 2000, French, German, and Spanish aerospace manufactures merged to form the European Aeronautic, Defense and Space Company (EADS), the world's third largest aerospace contractor just behind Boeing-McDonnell-Douglas and Lockheed-Martin. The EU's plan to set up its own European Rapid Reaction Force of 60,000 men by 2003 aroused American concern about diluting NATO.

Expansion of NATO to the east, eagerly sought by Poland and other countries on the volatile Russian border, was approached cautiously as unnecessarily provocative toward Russia. Efforts to reduce tension between NATO and Russia culminated in the creation of the NATO–Russian Council in May 2002, a body designed to keep communication channels open. In the end, Poland, Hungary, and the Czech Republic joined NATO in March 1999 and Yeltsin's Russia, preoccupied with other problems, acquiesced. Putin, similarly, had to swallow the arrival of NATO at his border in March 2004 when the Baltic States, Bulgaria, Romania, Slovakia, and Slovenia joined.

Western Europe: Far Right and "New Middle"

After the year 2000, Western Europe faced the same intractable troubles it had confronted since 1973. One was stubborn unemployment, linked to the high costs of Europe's elaborate social welfare system; the other was immigration.

To the undiminished flood of unskilled laborers from the Mediterranean and Africa lured by the prosperity of Western Europe was added a new stream: refugees from the turmoil of Central and Eastern Europe. The New Right profited by the fears aroused by waves of foreigners. The most disquieting response was those of neo-Nazi skinheads in Britain, Italy, and especially Germany. In Germany, they were responsible for over 2,500 violent incidents and nineteen deaths in 1993, and there was a renewed burst of anti-immigrant violence in 2000, especially in the disgruntled east.

But such actions aroused mass indignation, and Far Right parties grew only where the existing system was perceived as impotent. The German *Republikaner* remained small in Helmut Kohl's Germany, and the French *Front National* split in 1999 in a quarrel over the succession to seventy-year-old Jean-Marie Le Pen, though he bounced back to win 19 percent in the presidential election of 2002.

The most successful far right party was the Austrian Freedom Party, carried by its photogenic leader Jörg Haider to 27 percent of the votes in the parliamentary elections of October 3, 1999, second only to the Social Democrats with 33 percent. When the Freedom Party and the center-right People's Party formed a coalition government in February 2000, the United States and the EU withdrew their ambassadors from Vienna in protest. The Freedom Party was more an anti-immigrant protest movement than overt fascism, though Haider had praised Hitler's full-employment economy and sometimes attended rallies of SS veterans. Haider gave up his party's leadership to let things cool, but remained Governor of Corinthia. Many Austrian voters simply wanted an alternative after thirteen years of a cozy People's Party–Socialist alliance that parceled out patronage between them.

A more blatant case of neofascist participation in government was Italy. The Christian Democrats' unbroken rule of Italy since 1945 was ended by the revelations of massive corruption that emerged in 1992 from a sweeping judicial investigation, triggered by the discovery of party kickbacks in public works contracts in Milan. Because the main opposition party, Craxi's Socialists, was also implicated, no normal political alternation was possible. The vacuum was filled by Silvio Berlusconi, a one-time cruise ship crooner who had become the wealthiest media tycoon in Italy, proprietor of most of Italy's private television channels as well as the Milan soccer team. Forming a new party whose title—*Forza italia*—was a soccer cheer, Berlusconi joined with the National Alliance (direct descendent of the neofascist Italian Social Movement but insisting it was "postfascist") and a protest movement called the Northern League, which expressed mainly northern Italians' unwillingness to keep subsidizing the south. Berlusconi's coalition won a narrow parliamentary majority in the elections in March 1994, and the neofascist National Alliance had seats in his ministry. This disquieting turn toward personalized media politics reflected Italian exhaustion with traditional Christian Democratic dominance. That dominance had remained unbudgeable so long as a powerful Communist Party occupied the principal space on the left. After 1989 the Italian Communist Party split. Leaving behind a little band of irreconcilables, most of Berlinguer's heirs formed a reformist Party of the Democratic Left (PDS), which joined with other parties of the center-left in Italy's first plausible left alternative, the Olive Tree Coalition. When Berlusconi became weakened in his turn by judicial investigations for tax evasion, new elections in April 1996 gave a small majority to the Olive Tree Coalition. The economist Romano Prodi (1996–1998) and PDS leader Massimo d'Alema (1998–2000) led Italy's first left governments—a very pale pink—since 1920. Italians began hoping for a "second republic," in which a regular alternation of coherent majorities might become possible. The parliament, however, dominated by the leaders of small parties, proved unable to pass constitutional revisions that would strengthen the roles of the president and prime minister. In the meantime, the Italian people accepted the necessary budget-trimming to join the euro in 1999, perceiving in the EU the good government that they could not achieve at home. They were so fed up with the old parties of both left and right, however, that on May 13, 2001 they gave a parliamentary majority once again to Berlusconi, despite his far right allies, the multiple legal troubles of his business empire, and the control he would thereby gain over virtually all of Italian television, public as well as private.

As in Italy, much of the Western European Left in postCommunist Europe sought to reposition itself nearer the center. This proved attractive to voters, and after 1998 all the major Western European states (except Spain) had centrist-leaning parties of the Left at their helm. German Social Democratic chancellor Gerhard Schroeder, who defeated the Christian Democrats in September 1998 after sixteen years of Helmut Kohl, called his policy "the New Center"—*die neue Mitte.* British prime minister Tony Blair, who ended Labour's long losing streak of four elections, on May 1, 1997, spoke of "New Labour." Having given up Keynesian deficit spending as inflationary and prevented by the EU common currency from seeking export advantage by currency devaluation, the Western European "new middle" streamlined social welfare programs, cut taxes and government regulation, privatized the public sector, and balanced budgets, much as Margaret Thatcher had done but without her rhetoric.

Even Sweden experimented once again with an alternative to its Social Democrats, who had governed most of the time since 1931. The conservative Carl Bildt tried during 1991–1994 to prune Sweden's enormous budget deficits and restore its industries' competitivity, but lost again to the Social Democrats in 1994, who then did very much the same thing. Only French Socialist prime minister Lionel Jospin (1997–2002) avoided centrist language, but, like the others, he quietly reduced government restrictions and privatized public services. In 2000, the New Left's solutions to Europe's problems of high unemployment and global competition were hard to distinguish from those of conservatives.

Europe was a powerhouse of production and creativity in 2004. It produced over 30 percent of the world's goods. Its standard of living, at least in the North and West, matched America's, and perhaps exceeded it if one considers health, education, low crime rates, and cultural amenities. While 1 American in 163 was in prison, Europe's figure was one-sixth of that. Its scientists had isolated the AIDS virus (French biologist Luc Montagnier at the Institut Pasteur in 1983) and created the World Wide Web (British physicist Tim Berners-Lee at the European Nuclear Research Center near Geneva in 1990).

And yet, ethnic violence and border disputes festered in the Balkans. Democracy and the market were distorted in Russia by corruption and presidential autocracy. Even in the West, growth was inhibited by high social costs, the far right won followers, and unemployment remained high. Europe's future was open, and it deserved America's close attention.

SUGGESTIONS FOR FURTHER READING

Among a multitude of books about Gorbachev, you might start with Martin McCauley, *Gorbachev,*[*] 2nd ed. (2000), and the more analytical Archie Brown, *The Gorbachev Factor*[*] (1997). David Remnick, *Lenin's Tomb*[*] (1994), is a vivid eyewitness narrative.

Leon Aron, *Yeltsin: A Revolutionary Life* (2000), is sympathetic and well-informed. Archie Brown and Lelia Shevtsova introduce political strategies briefly in *Gorbachev, Yeltsin and Putin: Political Leadership in Russia's Transition*[*] (2001), while George W. Breslauer, *Gorbachev and Yeltsin as Leaders*[*] (2002), examines them at more length. See also Michael McFaul, *Russia's Unfinished Revolution: Political Change from Gorbachev to Putin*[*] (2002).

Works on Russia's economic travails have a short shelf life. Among recent works, Marshall I. Goldman, *The Piratization of Russia*[*] (2003), and David Hoffman, *The Oligarchs*[*] (2004), take a dim view, as does Chrystia Freeland's racier *The Sale of the Century*[*] (2000). Andrei Shleifer and Daniel Treisman, *Without a Map: Political Tactics and Economic Reform in Russia*[*] (2002), are more pragmatic. Anders Åslund, *Building Capitalism: The Transformation of the Former Soviet Bloc*[*] (2002), defends shock treatment.

Numerous works on German reunification include Charles S. Maier, *Dissolution: The Crisis of Communism and the End of East Germany*[*] (1999), David Childs, *The Fall of the GDR*[*] (2001), and Elizabeth Pond, *Beyond the Wall: Germany's Road to Unification* (1995). Konrad H. Jarausch, *The Rush to German Unity*[*] (1994), is both an eyewitness account and a historical assessment. Jarausch followed up with *After Unity: Reconfiguring German Identity*[*] (1997).

Imanuel Geiss, *The Question of German Unification, 1806–1995*[*] (1997) takes a long view. Peter H. Merkl, *German Unification in the European Context*[*] (1993), and Harold James, ed., *When the Walls Came Tumbling Down: Reactions to German Reunification*[*] (1992), examine the reactions of Germany's neighbors.

Three outstanding on-the-spot accounts of the transformations of Eastern Europe in 1989 and after are Timothy Garton Ash, *The Magic Lantern*[*] (1990) and *History of the Present* (1999), and Misha Glenny, *The Rebirth of History*[*] (reprint ed. 2001); see also Gale Stokes, *The Walls Came Tumbling Down*[*] (1993). Particular Eastern European transformations are treated in Robin Shepherd, *Czechoslovakia: The Velvet Revolution and Beyond* (2000); Bernard Wheaton and Zdenek Kavan, *The Velvet Revolution: Czechoslovakia, 1988–1991*[*] (1992); Richard F. Staar, ed., *Transition to Democracy in Poland* (1998); Frances Millard, *Politics and Society in Poland* (1999); Anatol Lieven, *The Baltic Revolution*[*] (1994); and, in addition to the Tőkés work noted at the end of chapter 21, Aurel Braun and Zoltan Barany, eds., *Dilemmas of Transition: The Hungarian Experience*[*] (2001).

The political transformations of Eastern Europe are well summarized in Attila Agh, *Emerging Democracies in East Central Europe and the Balkans* (1998), and analyzed in Juan Linz and Alfred Stepan, *Problems of Democratic Transition* (1996). There is more attention to civil society in Claus Offe, *Varieties of Transition: The East European and German Experience*[*] (1996), and Jon Elster, Claus Offe, and Ulrich K. Preuss, *Institutional Design in Post-Communist Societies*[*] (1998). Alexander Motyl et al., *Nations in Transit 2003*[*] (2004), gives a scorecard to 27 postSoviet states. For the Eastern and Central European economies, see Martin Potucek, *Not Only the Market*[*] (2000), and especially the Anders Åslund book mentioned above. John Borneman, *Settling Accounts: Violence, Justice, and Accountability in Post-Socialist Europe*[*] (1997), examines the various ways in which some of the pre-1989 Communist leadership was purged or punished.

Best for Berlusconi's Italy is Paul Ginsborg, *Italy and its Discontents*[*] (2003).

The Yugoslav catastrophe spawned an immense literature. For historical background, see works cited after chapters 17 and 21. Noel Malcolm, *Bosnia: A Short History*[*] (1996); and the same author's *Kosovo: A Short History*[*] (1999). Marcus Tanner, *Croatia: A Nation Forged in War*[*] (1998), and Tim Judah, *The Serbs: History, Myth, and the Destruction of Yugoslavia*[*] (1998), stress ancient grievances. Misha Glenny gives a vivid narrative history in *The Balkans* (2000). Closer examinations of the break-up include Branka Magas and Ivo Zanic, eds., *The War in Croatia and Bosnia-Herzegovina, 1991–1995*[*] (2004); Misha Glenny, *The Fall of Yugoslavia*,[*] 3rd ed. (1997); and Sabrina P. Ramet, *Balkan Babel: The Disintegration of Yugoslavia from the Death of Tito to Ethnic War*,[*] 2nd ed. (1996). More intimate accounts, where protagonists speak for themselves, are Laura Silber and Allan Little, *Yugoslavia: Death of a Nation*[*] (1995), based on a BBC documentary; Roger Cohen, *Hearts Grown Brutal: Sagas of Sarajevo* (1998); and Jasminka Udovicki and James Ridgeway, *Burn This House: The Making and Unmaking of Yugoslavia*[*] (1998). For Kosovo, see Tim Judah, *Kosovo: War and Revenge*,[*] 2nd ed. (2002).

The end of the Cold War permitted the first retrospective looks back. See two works by John Lewis Gaddis, *The United States and the End of the Cold War*[*] (1994), and *We Now Know: Rethinking Cold War History*[*] (1998).

For neo-Nazism in the 1990s, refer again to works cited at the end of chapter 22.

Essential for the transformations of the European Union is George Ross, *Jacques Delors and European Integration*[*] (1995). Andrew Moravcsik examines the European Union's choice of futures in *Centralization or Fragmentation? Europe before the Challenges of Deepening, Diversity, and Democracy*[*] (1998). Recent studies of how the European Union works now include Neill Nugent, *The Government and Politics of the European Union,*[*] 4th ed. (1999); Desmond Dinan, *Ever Closer Union,*[*] 2nd ed. (1999); Helen Wallace, *Making Sense of the New Europe* (2002); Jack Hayward and Anand Menon, eds., *Governing Europe*[*] (2003); and Clive Archer, *Organizing Europe: The Institutions of Integration,* 2nd ed. (1998).

The EU's economic policies since 1992 are most thoroughly examined by John Gillingham, *European Integration 1950–2003: Superstate or New Market Economy?*[*] (2003).

European relations with the United States are assessed in Elizabeth Pond, *Friendly Fire: The Near-Death of the Transatlantic Alliance*[*] (2003). See also Lawrence S. Kaplan, *NATO United, NATO Divided*[*] (2004).

Additional Internet links related to this chapter are available on the Europe in the 20th Century Web site: http://www.history.wadsworth.com/paxton04

You can also explore images, interactive timelines, and maps related to this chapter on our Western Civilization Resource Center: http://history.wadsworth.com

Epilogue

Europe and the
United States
Since 9/11

After the Soviet system collapsed in 1989, Europeans felt free to seek a larger role for their continent. Their relationship with the United States was no longer shaped mainly by the Soviet threat, against which they needed American protection. Uppermost now were the economic rivalries and cultural quarrels that divided them. The European consortium that built Airbus now edged out Boeing with more than half the world's orders for new airliners. The Europeans took their American competitors to court in the World Trade Organization (WTO) over steel tariffs, tax breaks, and other issues, and they often won. Europeans tried to defend their cultural distinctiveness against the blue jeans, rock and rap, and McDonald's that swept over their continent. France, in particular, upheld its subsidies to the arts and quotas on foreign films despite American attempts to open these areas to outside competition.

Notwithstanding these frictions, Europeans reacted with almost universal expressions of solidarity with Americans when nineteen Muslim activists hijacked four airliners on September 11, 2001, and crashed two of them into the World Trade

Center in New York City and one into the Pentagon in Washington, D.C. The usually prickly Paris daily *Le Monde* editorialized, "We are all Americans now." NATO voted for the first time in its history to invoke Article 5 of the North Atlantic Treaty, which required member nations to aid a member that had been attacked. NATO forces played an important role in the U.S.-sponsored military operation against the Taliban and Al Qaeda in Afghanistan in 2002. In 2004, French, German, and other European troops were still on duty there alongside the Americans. Long active against terrorism on their own soil, Europeans cooperated vigorously with the United States in international efforts to track and arrest Al Qaeda militants. The one person charged in an American court in connection with the September 11 attacks had been the subject of warnings by the French police.

This climate changed radically when it became apparent that the United States intended to invade Iraq. France, Germany, and Russia urged the United States to give the UN inspectors more time to complete their work in Iraq before resorting to force. As American forces assembled in the Persian Gulf, Iraqi dictator Saddam Hussein opened his country's military facilities bit by bit to the inspectors, though he never fully cooperated with them. France, Russia, and China threatened to veto an American resolution in the Security Council, declaring the arms inspection process exhausted and authorizing military action. When the United States went ahead with its military operation without UN sanction on March 20, 2003, only Britain, Spain, Italy, and the new East-Central European NATO members assisted. Many European citizens demonstrated against the war, even in the participating countries.

The Iraq War embarrassed the European Union deeply. The EU had failed once again to muster a united military and diplomatic position on an issue of major significance. Its members stood on opposite sides of the question, and exchanged hostile words. The Spanish government was turned out in an election in March 2004 in part because of public hostility to its participation in the Iraq War, and British prime minister Tony Blair—the most important ally of American president George W. Bush on Iraq—encountered serious political difficulty.

Yet the United States and Europe remained indispensable to one another: military allies, principal trading and investment partners, targets of attacks by Islamic fundamentalists, and joint heirs of a rich cultural heritage. European efforts to restore a constructive relationship were receiving some encouragement in Washington, D.C., in 2004.

PHOTO CREDITS

LITERARY CREDITS

INDEX

Abortion rights, 578
Abstract painting, 34. *See also* Painting
Accent, class and, 11
Acerbo Election Law (Italy), 210
Action française, 31, 164, 220, 337, 343
Adams, Henry, 29
Adenauer, Konrad, 168, 494, 507, 508, 539, 591, 630
  consensus politics and, 566
  European union and, 544
Adler, Friedrich, 101, 361
Adowa, 388, 541
  battle at, 6
Advertising
  agencies, 269
  mass communications and, 268–269
  radio and, 268
Aehrenthal, Alois von, 47–48, 51
Aerospace contractors, 676
Aesthetics. *See* Art(s); High culture; Mass culture; specific arts
Afghanistan, Soviet invasion of, 619
Africa
  colonies in, 5
  Ethiopia and, 388
  European trade with, 596
Afrika Korps, 453–454
Age of Radio, 264
Aggression. *See* specific countries and wars
Agnelli, Giovanni, 561
Agrarian Party, in Romania, 342
Agrarian regions. *See also* Rural areas
  discontent in, 246–249
  in Eastern Europe, 516–517
Agrarian revolutionaries (SRs). *See* Socialist Revolutionaries (SRs)
Agriculture. *See also* Farms and farming

in Eastern and Southern Europe, 10
in EC, 642
  Great Depression and, 296
  under Khrushchev, 525
  "return to the soil" and, 301
  U.S.-European rivalry and, 595–596
AIDS virus, 678
Airlift, in Berlin, 481
Airmail service, 273
Airplanes, 29, 83–85
  in First World War, 272–273
Alamagordo, atomic bomb at, 469
Albania and Albanians, 50
  China and, 587
  communism in, 516
  Kosovo and, 671
  Serbia and, 618
Alcock, John, 273
Alexander (Yugoslavia), 249
Alexander I (Russia), 544
Alexander III (Russia), 122
Alexander Nevsky (Eisenstein), 459, 514
Alexander of Battenberg, 22
Alfonso XIII (Spain), 224, 251, 252, 369, 636
Algeria, 453
  immigrants to France from, 628
  independence movement in, 541, 542
Algerian War, France and, 492, 540, 542–543
Allen, William Sheridan, 326
Alliances. *See also* European Union (EU); specific alliances
  in Eastern Europe, 183
  Entente Powers, 53n, 84
  of European Great Powers (1914), 53n
  Franco-Russian, 51, 54
  Italian, 389
  Little Entente, 183
  in 1930s, 389

military, 545
politics of, 183–184
Russia-Great Britain, 54n
Alliance system, before First World War, 63–64
Allied Control Commission, in Germany, 480
Allies (First World War), 84–85. *See also* specific countries
  appeasement and, 394–400
  attack on Russia by, 128, 131–134
  Habsburg dissolution and, 142–143
  in 1918, 135–136
  Rhineland and, 168–169, 384–387
  Second World War and, 406
Allies (Second World War), 412–413, 417. *See also* specific countries
  meetings in 1947, 481
  Stalin and, 476
  United States and, 450–457
  victories by, 449–450
All Quiet on the Western Front (Remarque), 79, 106, 114, 288
Alperovitz, Gar, 470
Alsace-Lorraine, 54, 158, 159
  First World War and, 73
  France and, 386
  Hitler and, 382
  Nazi annexation of, 425
  return to France, 167, 168
Ambris, Alceste De, 204
American Challenge, The (Servan-Schreiber), 597
Amsterdam, Treaty of, 675
Amundsen, Roald, 6
Anatolia, 182
Anders, Wladyslaw, 477
Anderson, Benedict, 49
Andropov, Yuri, 620, 650

Anglo-French Non-Intervention Commission, 367–368, 372–373
Anglo-Polish guarantee, 405
Angola
  Portugal and, 637, 638
  Soviets and, 619
Anschluß, Germany-Austria, 338, 382–384, 392–393, 396
Anthropology, 643
  Lévi-Strauss and, 573–574
Antibourgeois, fascism and, 218
Anticapitalism, 30
  fascism and, 218
Anticlericalism. *See also* Radical parties
  in Portugal, 252
  in Spain, 369–370
Anticolonialism, 540–543
Antifascism, in Eastern Europe, 518
Antinuclear protests, 619, 622
Anti-Semitism, 30, 31, 37
  Hitler's policies of, 333–334
  of Nazis, 212, 213, 428–431
  in Poland, 615, 666
  Rathenau and, 172
  sciences and, 413
  in Vichy France, 434
Antiwar movement, 109–110
  socialist, 110–111
Antonescu, Ion, 343, 424, 432
Antonioni, Michelangelo, 571
Anzacs (Australia-New Zealand Army Corps), 84
Appeasement
  abandonment of, 402–403
  Czechoslovakia and, 394–397
  failure of, 399–400
  foundations of policy, 394–396
  Munich settlement and, 398–400

685

Appeasement *(continued)*
    Western European back-
        ing of, 401–402
Appliances, after Second
    World War, 560
Arab-Israeli wars, Six-Day
    War (1973), 623
Arab League, 641
Arab world. *See also* OPEC
    (Organization of
    Petroleum-Exporting
    Countries)
    European relations with,
        626
    after First World War, 160
    nationalist rebellion in
        Iraq, 422
    Suez Campaign and,
        543
Aragon, Louis, 115, 358, 437
Aral Sea, pollution of, 610
Arcadia meeting, 451–452
Archangel, Russian Civil War
    and, 131–132
Architecture, 276–277
    experimental, 277, 278
    postwar, 571
Ardennes region, 192, 416
Argentina, Falklands seizure
    by, 632
Aristocracy, 13–14
Armed forces. *See also* Military
    in Britain, 74, 94, 95
    colonial, 6
    in France, 96, 590
    in Germany, 98, 169
    of NATO, 539
    revolt in Germany,
        137–140
Armenia, 663
Armistice (1918), 138
Arms and armaments. *See*
    Weapons
Arms race, 619. *See also*
    Nuclear power;
    Weapons; specific
    weapons
    dismantling of arsenals,
        656
Aron, Raymond, 565, 595
Arrow-Cross, 431
Art(s), 7. *See also* Culture;
    Mass culture; Popular
    culture; specific arts
    in Britain, 37

experimental, 277–278,
    279, 288–289
fine arts, 569–571
in First World War,
    114–115
in France, 37
in Great Depression, 295
mass audience for,
    284–286
in 1920s and 1930s,
    276–278, 279
primitive instincts and,
    281–282
reaction to, 37–38
revolution in, 33–35
Russian exiles in,
    281–282
social change through,
    284–285
social status of artists,
    282–283
unconscious and,
    279–280
Artillery. *See also* Weapons
    in First World War, 79
Aryans, in Nazi Germany,
    333
Asia, 5. *See also* specific coun-
    tries
    China and, 587
    Cold War in, 535
    economic competition
        from, 624, 625
Asquith, Herbert, 63, 93, 94, 95
Assassinations, 100, 101, 241
    attempt against Hitler,
        440, 442
    in Soviet Union, 318
Astor, Lady (Nancy Lang-
        horne Witcher), 104
Atatürk. *See* Kemal,
        Mustapha (Atatürk)
Atlantic Alliance, NATO and,
        590
Atlantic Charter, 450, 462
Atlantic Ocean in First World
        War, 86
    in Second World War, 412,
        454
Atom, subatomic particles
        and, 286–287
Atomic bomb, 469–470. *See
        also* Nuclear power
Atomic Diplomacy (Alper-
        ovitz), 470

Atomic physics, 33, 287
    atoms and, 32–33
Atonal music, 571
Attlee, Clement, 497, 537,
    567
    at Potsdam, 469
Audience, mass, 264
Augusta (ship), 450
Auschwitz, 429–430
Austen, Jane, 19
Austria, 246. *See also* Austria-
    Hungary
    Anschluß with Germany,
        338, 382–384,
        392–393
    banking crisis in, 297–298
    Christian Socialism in,
        338–340
    Far Right in, 676–677
    in First World War, 76–77,
        134
    First World War treaty
        with (1919), 164
    German customs union
        with, 310
    Germany and, 55–56
    Hitler and, 212, 382–384
    Italy and, 60
    Nazi Party in, 383
    parliament in, 24
    Social Democrats in, 151
    Soviet peace treaty with,
        553
Austria-Hungary, 27, 44–45.
        See also Austria;
        Balkan region; First
        World War; Hungary;
        Serbia
    dissidents in, 62
    dissolution of (1918-
        1919), 141–146
    end of, 160
    ethnic/linguistic compo-
        sition of, 46–47, 47
        (map)
    before and after First
        World War, 175 (map)
    First World War and, 76,
        93, 100–102, 135
    Franz Ferdinand and, 44
    monarchy in, 22
    nation-states after First
        World War and, 173
    Ottoman Empire and, 46
    Serbia and, 50

ultimatum to Serbia and,
    52–53
Austrian Freedom Party,
    677
Austrian-Germans, fascism
    and, 221
Austro-Hungarian Empire.
    See Austria-Hungary
Austro-Serbian war (1914), 44
Autarky, in Nazi Germany,
    313, 391
Authoritarianism. *See also*
    Fascism; Nazi Ger-
    many
    clerical, 335–340
    in Eastern Europe,
        249–250
    in Germany, 324–335
    in 1930s, 323–350
    in Russia, 131
    in Spain, 340
Autocracy, in Russia,
    129–130
Automatic writing, 279–280
Automobile industry
    "Beetle" sales and,
        594–595
    EC production and, 642
    postwar sales of, 560
    Yugo and, 618
Autonomy, in Germany,
    332–333
Avant-garde
    in arts, 277–278, 279
    in Paris, 282
Avanti! (newspaper), 202,
    204
Axis powers. *See also* Italy;
    Nazi Germany
    creation of, 389
    defeat of, 451 (map)
    Franco and, 374
    Japan and, 450
Ayer, A. J., 573
Azaña, Manuel, 361,
    369–370, 372
Azerbaijan, 483, 657, 663

Baader, Andreas, 579
Baader-Meinhoff, 579
Bacon, Francis, 570
Bad Godesberg, SPD con-
    gress at (1959), 567
Badoglio, Pietro, 454, 455,
    503

Bainville, Jacques, 164

Balbo, Italo, 206, 207, 222

Baldwin, Stanley, 226, 233, 234, 303, 347
  appeasement and, 396
  radio use by, 266–267

Balfour Declaration (1917), 160

Balkan region
  Blitzkrieg in, 422
  conflicts in (1878-1914), 48–49, 71
  in First World War, 84
  nationalities in, 45–50
  peasants in, 10
  politics in, 246, 664
  rivalries in, 62
  Soviets in, 464–465

Balkan Wars (1912-1913), 27, 44, 50, 52

Ball, Albert, 84

Balthus. *See* Klossowski, Balthazar (Balthus)

Baltic region
  after First World War, 163
  independence in, 657, 658
  Soviets and, 405, 415, 458

Bank crisis
  in Great Depression, 294, 297–298
  in London, 303

Bank of England, 303

Banks and banking
  France and, 306
  in Germany, 309
  Great Depression and, 297

Barnes, George, 105

Barre, Raymond, 639

Barrès, Maurice, 8

Barth, Karl, 442, 572

Barthes, Roland, 643

Basque region (Spain), social tensions in, 251

Battle of Britain (1940), 418–421

Battle of the Bulge, 457

Battles. *See* specific battles and wars

Battleships, British, 57

Baudelaire, Charles, 9, 32, 38

Bauer, Otto, 143–144, 338

Bauhaus, 277, 278, 282, 283, 571

Baumont, Maurice, 250

Bavaria, 150. *See also* Germany
  separatism in, 244

BBC, 268

Beatles, The, 568–569

Beauvoir, Simone de, 495, 568

Bechstein, Hélène, 213

Beck, Josef, 402

Beck, Ludwig, 401, 440

Beckett, Samuel, 538

Bedbug, The (Mayakovsky), 285

Bedouin peoples, 160

Beer Hall *Putsch*, 185, 186, 213–214, 243, 244, 245

"Beetle" (Volkswagen), 594–595

Being and Time (Heidegger), 287–288

Belarus, 658, 663

Belgian Neutrality Treaty, 59–60

Belgium
  Battle of the Bulge and, 457
  Cold War and, 535
  collaborators in, 432, 492
  empire of, 5
  fascism in, 348
  after First World War, 168
  in First World War, 73
  German ultimatum to, 60
  neutrality of, 367
  resistance movement in, 437

Bell, Daniel, 626n

Belligerents, in First World War, 158

Benedict XV (Pope), 134

Benelux countries, 545

Beneš Eduard, 180, 394, 397, 484–485, 519, 521, 526
  Munich settlement and, 398

Ben-Gurion, David, 543

Bennett, Arnold, 14

Berchtesgaden, 392, 398

Berchtold, Leopold, 51

Berg, Alban, 276, 278, 282

Bergman, Ingmar, 571

Bergson, Henri, 35–36

Beria, Lavrenti, 514–515, 523

Berlin, 8
  arts in, 284
  bicycle race in, 272
  1936 Olympics in, 272
  Soviets and, 461, 525–526, 586
  Spartacist uprising in, 140
  U.S. peace aims for, 473–475

Berlin airlift, 481

Berlin Blockade, 506, 535

Berlin Fine Arts Museum, 37

Berlinguer, Enrico, 633–635

Berlin-to-Baghdad Railway, 57, 61, 62

Berlin Wall, 526, 532, 583
  destruction of, 652, 653

Berlusconi, Silvio, 677–678

Berners-Lee, Tim, 678

Bernhardi, Friedrich von, 61

Bernstein, Eduard, 73

Berthelot, Marcellin, 29

Bessarabia, 46, 163, 179, 342, 415
  Soviets and, 405

Bethlen, Istvan, 216–217

Bethmann Hollweg, Theobald von, 51, 59–60, 98, 135

Bevan, Aneurin, 346, 498, 499, 537, 553, 567

Beveridge, William, 497

Bevin, Ernest, 146
  European Union, 545

Bianchi, Michele, 207

Bicycles
  racing and, 272
  travel and, 273

Bidault, Georges, 544

Bienvenue-Martin, Jean-Baptiste, 54

Big Three
  future of Europe and, 461–470
  at Teheran, 463–464
  at Yalta, 465–469

Bildt, Carl, 678

Bildzeitung, 561

Biochemistry, 573

Biology, 573
  Lysenko and, 514

Birth control, 18–19, 103

Birth rate, decline in, 18–19

Bismarck, Otto von, 46
  fascism and, 219

Black biennium (Spain), 370

Black Friday (1927), in Vienna, 338

Black Hand terrorists, 45, 47

Black Sea region
  Allies and, 464
  in First World War, 84
  after Second World War, 483

Blackshirts (fascists), in Italy, 209

Blair, Tony, 678, 682

"Blank check," Germany, Austria-Hungary, and, 51

Blaue Reiter school, 34

Blériot, Louis, 29, 272

Blitzkrieg (lightning war), 410, 412, 413
  in Balkans, 422
  Battle of Britain and, 420–421
  fall of France and, 416–417
  against Soviet Union, 423

Blockade, in Spanish Civil War, 367–368

Blocs
  Communist, 589
  after Second World War, 481–485
  Soviet, 513–530, 607–620
  split in Communist, 583–584

Blomberg, Werner von, 335

Blue-collar workers, 565

Blum, Léon, 308–309, 358, 536, 537
  Czechoslovakia and, 397, 401
  government of, 362–368

Boccioni, Umberto, 35, 115

Boers
  Boer War and, 5, 194
  Britain, Germany, and, 57

Bohemia, Teschen and, 173–175

Bohr, Niels, 33

Böll, Heinrich, 571

Bolo, Paul, 111

Bolshevik Revolution. *See* Russian Revolutions (1917)

Bolsheviks, 122. *See also* Russia; Soviet Union
   challenges to, 254–255
   civil war and, 131–134
   fear of, 163–164
   meaning of term, 122n
   nation-building after First World War and, 143–145
   October Revolution and, 125–127
   Russian government by, 127–131
   Stalin and, 318
Bombers (airplanes), in Second World War, 410, 413
Bombs and bombings. *See also* Atomic bomb
   of Germany, 456
   of London, 420
   by plane, 84
   thermonuclear bomb, 514
Bonhoeffer, Dietrich, 442, 572
Boni de Castellane (Count), 14
Bonner, Elena, 611, 650
Bono, Emilio de, 207
Borders. *See also* Frontiers
   disputes over, 183
   German, 240
   opening to West, 652
   recognition of European, 603
   Soviet, 483
Boris III (Bulgaria), 250, 341
Bosnia, 45, 48
   Austria-Hungary and, 46
   crisis of 1908 in, 71
   EC and UN failures in, 671–676
   war in, 669–672
Bosnia-Herzegovina, annexation by Austria-Hungary, 48
Bosnian Serbs, 669–671
   Franz Ferdinand and, 45
Brandt, Willy, 567, 582, 601, 630
Braque, Georges, 35
Brasillach, Robert, 431
Brecht, Bertolt, 276, 284, 295

Brest-Litovsk, Treaty of, 128, 133, 135, 173
Breton, André, 114–115, 279–280
Bretton Woods Agreement (1944), 496–497. *See also* Gold standard
   breakdown of, 584, 597
Brezhnev, Leonid, 606
   Czechoslovak Springtime and, 614
   death of, 620
   de Gaulle and, 590
   Honecker and, 609
   legacy of, 618–620
   SALT I and, 600
   Soviet bloc under, 607–620
Brezhnev doctrine, 619, 651
Briand, Aristide, 187, 191, 194, 197, 239
   on United States of Europe, 544
Bright, John, 109
Britain. *See also* First World War; Second World War
   appeasement policy of, 394–397
   artillery in First World War, 79
   attitude toward First World War in, 72–73
   Battle of, 418–421
   Blair in, 678, 682
   coal industry in, 296–297
   consensus politics in, 566–567
   conservatives in, 539
   Council of Europe and, 549
   Defence of the Realm Act in, 111
   Depression politics in, 302–306
   dissidents in, 62
   Dunkirk and, 417, 418
   Easter Rebellion in, 109
   in EC, 594
   economy in First World War, 93–95
   empire of, 5, 543
   entry into First World War, 57–60

fascism in, 345–348
   after First World War, 146, 162, 231–236
   in First World War, 82, 84
   Gallipoli and, 77
   George V–Wilhelm II relationship, 57–59
   gold market in, 298
   gold standard and, 229
   Great Depression in, 294
   Greece and, 483
   immigrants in, 627
   inflation in, 107, 632
   Italy and, 85, 387, 388–389
   Korean War and, 537
   labor unions in, 105
   Labour government in (1945-1951), 497–500
   Labour Party in, 151, 567–568
   League of Nations and, 182
   mediation before First World War, 52–53
   middle class in, 15–16, 16–17
   missiles in, 619
   MLF and, 599
   monarchy in, 22
   Near East and, 160
   nuclear bombs of, 590
   oil in, 626
   "phony war" and, 415–416
   Poland supported by, 402–403
   police power in, 111
   Popular Front and, 360, 361–362
   postwar attitudes in, 559
   and postwar Germany, 479–480
   poverty in, 12, 13
   radio use in, 267
   Rhineland and, 169, 386
   Second World War strategy of, 452–453
   socialism in, 110
   Soviets as allies and, 401
   strikes in, 62, 108
   Suez and, 543
   Thatcher and conservatism in, 631–633
   three-way party system in, 231–232

   Tories (conservatives) in, 540
   universal manhood suffrage in, 230
   welfare state in, 498
   women's voting rights in, 21
   worker discontents in, 577–578
   Yalta Conference and, 467
British Army, 95
British Expeditionary Force, 94
   at Dunkirk, 417, 418
   First Battle of the Marne and, 74
British Union of Fascists (BUF), 346–348
Broadcasting. *See* Radio
Brooke, Rupert, 113, 114
Brown, Arthur, 273
Brown Shirts. *See* SA stormtroopers (Nazi Germany)
Broz, Josip. *See* Tito
Brücke school, 34
Bruckmann, Elsa, 213
Brüning, Heinrich, 310–311, 326, 327–328, 382
Brusilov, Alexei, 77
   offensive by (1917), 122, 124
Brussels, Treaty of, 545
Buchan, John, 92
Budapest, 144, 527–528. *See also* Hungary
   revolt in, 527–528
   Soviets and, 464–465
Buddenbrooks (Mann), 14–15
Bukharin, Nikolai, 127, 255, 256, 258, 316, 318, 650
Bukovina, 415
Bulgaria, 143, 178, 464, 618
   as Central Power, 84
   communism in, 516
   fascism in, 341
   First Balkan War and, 50
   First World War and, 77
   former communist leaders in, 666
   independence of, 46
   as parliamentary democracy, 246

revolt in, 652
Soviet control in, 519
Stamboliski in, 248
treaty with (1919), 164
Bulgarian Peasant Union, 248
Bulge, Battle of the, 457
Bülow, Bernhard von, 48–49,
194
Bultmann, Rudolf, 572
Bundesrat (Germany), 23
Buñuel, Luis, 571
Burgenland, 182
Bush, George H. W., nuclear
cuts by, 656
Bush, George W., 682
Business. *See also* Consumer
society; Prosperity
in Depression Scandi-
navia, 301–302
in fascist Italy, 254
Hitler and, 326
in Italy, 315
U.S. European subsidiaries
and branches, 597
Business cycle
depressions and, 294
prosperity and, 566
Butler, R. A., 568
Butler, Samuel, 15
Byelorussia, 467

Cabinet of Dr. Caligari, The
(movie), 278, 279
Caetano, Marcello, 637
Caillaux, Joseph, 111
Callaghan, James, 632
Camelots du roi, 31
Campbell, Roy, 376
Camping, 273
Camus, Albert, 566
Capitalism
communism and, 475–476
fascist roots and, 220–221
Habermas on, 644
and war, 61, 63
Caporetto, battle of, 134
Caribbean region, European
trade with, 596
Carol II (Romania), 250, 342
Carrillo, Santiago, 635, 636
Cartel des gauches (France),
236–238, 307
Cartels, 313, 314
Carter, Jimmy, 600
SALT agreements and, 619

Carvalho, Otelo de, 638
Casablanca Conference
(1943), 454, 462
"Cash and carry" policy, of
Roosevelt, Franklin
D., 412
Casualties
in First World War, 78,
105–106
in Second World War,
489–490
at Verdun, 80
Catalonia, social tensions in,
251
Catholic Church. *See also*
Center Party; Clerical
authoritarianism;
MRP; Papacy; *Popolari*
movement; specific
popes
in Austria, 339
authoritarianism of,
335–337
corporatist Italy and, 314
fascism and, 220
in France, 236
in Iberian Peninsula, 251
John Paul II and, 644
Mussolini accord with,
253
in Nazi Germany, 334
Opus dei and, 539
in Poland, 527
postwar, 571–572
and postwar political parties, 493
Salazar and, 337–338
in Spain, 369, 370, 636
Western European Com-
munists and, 535–536
Catholic Party, in Belgium,
348
Ceausescu, Nicolae, 589,
617–618, 654, 655
CEDA (Spain), 370
Center Party (Germany),
241, 242, 310, 328,
331–332
Central Europe, Soviets in,
458–459
Centralization, in Russia, 257
Central planning, in Soviet
Union, 609
Central Planning Commit-
tee, 426–427

Central Powers, 53n, 77
Bulgaria as, 84
after First World War,
159–160
in First World War, 84
Centrist parties, in Western
Europe, 538–540, 678
CERN (The European Cen-
ter for Nuclear
Research), 573, 678
World Wide Web and, 682
Ceuta, 4n
Cézanne, Paul, 34
Chagall, Marc, 282
Chamberlain, Austen, 188,
191
Chamberlain, Neville, 374,
394–397
Anglo-Polish guarantee
and, 405
appeasement and, 397
Munich settlement and,
398–400
"phony war" and, 415
Poland supported by, 402
on Soviets as allies, 401
Champagne region, in First
World War, 79
Chaplin, Charlie, 295
Charles of Hohenzollern-
Sigmaringen, 22.
See also Carol II
(Romania)
Charter 77 movement, 603,
653
Charterhouse of Parma, The
(Stendahl), 26
Chechnya, 663, 664
Cherbourg, 455
Chernenko, Konstantin,
620
Chernobyl, nuclear accident
in, 650
Chernomyrdin, Viktor, 662
Chetniks, 440
Chiang Kai-shek, 357, 472
Chicherin, George, 184,
196
"Chicken war" (1963),
595–596
Childbearing, 18–19
Children
family size and, 18
Russian famine and
(1921), 129

China
anti-colonial revolutions
and, 541
Mao Tse-tung in, 587
after Second World War,
475
Soviets and, 357, 466
Soviet split with, 583–584,
586–588
spheres of influence in, 5
China-India border war, 587
Chinese Wall, The (Frisch),
534
Chirac, Jacques, 640–641
Chlorine gas, 79
Christian Democrats, 493
European union and, 544
in France, 502
in Germany, 494, 539
in Italy, 504, 538, 634,
635, 678
in West Germany, 507
Christian Socialism, in Austria, 338–340
Church. *See also* Catholic
Church; Clerical
authoritarianism;
Protestantism; Reli-
gion
conservatism and, 31
in Nazi Germany, 334
resistance to Nazis by,
439, 441–442
Church and state, separation
of, 336
Churchill, Randolph, 14
Churchill, Winston, 14, 17,
64, 77, 86, 539
aid to Soviets, 460
Allied landings and,
455–456
appeasement and, 394
Arcadia meeting and,
451–452
Atlantic Charter and, 450
on Balkans, 465
Battle of Britain and,
418–421
exchange rates and, 234
on general strike of 1926,
236
on Germany, 479
on gold standard, 233
"iron curtain" speech of,
481

Churchill, Winston *(continued)*
after Second World War, 497
Second World War strategy and, 452–453
at Teheran, 463–464
at Yalta, 465–469
Ciano, Galeazzo, 389
Cinema. *See* Movies
CIS. *See* Commonwealth of Independent States (CIS)
Cities and towns, 7, 8–9. *See also* Urban living
interwar culture in, 282
Nazis in, 325
Citizenship, liberal concept of, 28
City, The (Léger), 262
Civil Guard (Spain), 637
Civilian economy, in First World War, 92–93
in Second World War, 412
Civilization and Its Discontents (Freud), 280
Civil liberties, suspension in Spain, 370
Civil wars
in Bosnia, 669–670
in Russia, 131–134
in Spain, 354, 372–374
in Yugoslavia, 668–673
Clair, René, 295
Class, 10–17. *See also* Elites; Workers
artists and, 283
in Britain, 305
clothing and, 274
father's authority and, 20
middle class, 14–17
poor, 12–13
upper class, xvi
upward mobility and, 17
wealthy, 13–14
"Class against class" policy, of Communist Party, 357–359
Class A mandates, 167
Class B mandates, 167
Class C mandates, 167
Classical economics, Great Depression and, 299

Classical education, 286
Classical-liberal economic system, 3, 299
Clay, Lucius, 480, 481
Clemenceau, Georges, 57n, 96–97, 111, 135, 161–162, 168, 179
Clercq, Staf de, 348
Clerical authoritarianism, 335–340
Clothing
First World War and, 103
homogeneity in, 274
social status and, 10–11
Club Méditerranée, 565
Coal and Steel Community. *See* European Coal and Steel Community (ECSC, 1951)
Coal industry. *See also* Coal miners' strike
Britain and, 234, 632
European Coal and Steel Community and, 550–551, 594
Great Depression and, 296–297
Ruhr region and, 184–185
Schuman Plan and, 550
Coalitions. *See also* Popular Front
in France, 307
in Italy, 539
Popular Front as, 308
in Weimar Germany, 241–243, 329
Coal miners' strike, in Britain (1972), 578
Codreanu, Corneliu, 217, 219, 341, 342
Cohn-Bendit, Daniel, 575
Cold War
in Asia, 535
capitalists vs. communists in, 475–476
colonial struggles and, 541
détente and, 583–604
end of, 656
Europe during (1947-1961), 533–553
Germany and, 478–481
in 1950s, 547 (map)
in 1985, 585 (map)

origins of, 470–476
Poland and, 476–478
Soviet Union and, 514
Teheran Conference and, 464
thaw in, 584–586
Versailles Treaty and, 163
Western Europe and, 535–543
Cole, G. D. H., 305
Collaboration with Nazis, 431–435
court hearings for, 492
ideological, 431–432
Jewish extermination and, 431
for national and economic interests, 432–433
passive, 433–435
by Soviets, 459
Collective bargaining, in France, 105, 366
in Germany, 105
Collective security, in 1930s, 193
Collectivization
doubts about, 566
in Eastern Europe, 521–522
in Hungary, 247
in Russia, 316
Cologne, 169
remilitarization of Rhineland and, 384, 385
Colonies and colonization, 5. *See also* Paris peace settlement (1919)
British, 543
European access to former, 596
after First World War, 159, 160
German, 540–541
postwar independence of, 540–543
pre-First World War I rivalries and, 61–62
COMECON (Council for Mutual Economic Assistance), 552 (map), 552–553, 588, 665
Cominform, 520

Comintern. *See* Third International (Comintern)
Commissariat du Plan, 502–503
Commission (EU), 592, 593, 674–675
Common Market, 551, 552 (map)
budget, 593
de Gaulle and, 592
European currency and, 598
redirection of, 592–595
Commonwealth (British), immigration within, 627
Commonwealth of Independent States (CIS), 658–659, 662
Communications
mass media and, 264–265
technology and, 558
Communist bloc
China-Soviet split in, 583–584
weakening of, 588–589
Communist China. *See* China
Communist (Third) International. *See* Third International (Comintern)
Communists and communism. *See also* Bolsheviks; Popular Front
aims of, 476
in Bulgaria, 248
capitalism and, 475–476
"class against class" policy of (1928-1934), 357–359
in Czechoslovakia, 484–485, 613
in Eastern Europe, 483, 516
end of Eastern European, 649
end of Soviet Union and, 649, 650–659
in France, 116, 377, 536, 538–539, 568, 635
in Germany, 140, 185, 242, 243, 324, 331
in Greece, 483
in Italy, 504, 538–539, 568, 633–635, 677
Jews under, 515, 521

in late 1980s, 645
National Front regimes
    replaced by, 520–521
in Poland, 519
polycentrism and,
    586–589
in Portugal, 635, 637
in Romania, 342
in Russia, 608, 662
after Second World War,
    492, 494
Socialists and, 361
and Soviet invasion of
    Czechoslovakia, 614
in Spain, 371, 373, 635,
    636
threat of, 196
treatment of, 666
in Vietnam, 542
in Western Europe,
    471–472, 535, 568
Computers, 558
Concentration camps. See
    also "Final Solution"
for German Jews, 334
Concerning the Spiritual in Art
    (Kandinsky), 34
Concert of Europe, 44
Conciliation, after First
    World War (1924-
    1929), 186–187
Condor Legion, 373, 374
Conference on Security and
    Cooperation in
    Europe (CSCE),
    602
Conflicts of interest, between
    U.S. and Western
    European democra-
    cies, 475
Congress of Berlin, 46
Conrad von Hötzendorf,
    Franz, 50, 77
Conscious. See Unconscious
Conscription
    in First World War
        Britain, 94
    in Germany, 98
Consensus politics, 566–568
Conservatism, 30–31
    in Britain, 304, 540
    consensus politics and,
        566–568
    fascist roots and, 220
    after First World War, 182

in Northern Europe,
    629–633
in Western Europe,
    538–540
Conservative Party (Tories,
    Britain), 231–232,
    233–236, 304, 500,
    540
    Thatcher and, 631–633
Constantinople, 159
    Straits at, 48
Constituent Assembly (Rus-
    sia), 130
Constitution(s)
    in Eastern Europe,
        245–246
    of East Germany, 506
    after First World War, 230
    monarchies and, 22
    in Russia, 661–662
    Weimar, 239–240
    of West Germany, 506
Constitutional liberals, 22
Consumer goods, in Nazi
    Germany, 426
Consumer society, 557–565
    distribution of wealth in,
        560–563
    goods in, 560
    politics in (1953-1968),
        565–568
    social mobility and,
        563–565
    student discontent in, 576
Continental Europe
    identity of, 543–544
    poverty of, 12–13
COPCON (Portugal), 638
Corbusier, Le (Charles-
    Édouard Jeanneret),
    276, 278, 571
Corfu incident, 209–210
Cornford, John, 376
Corporatism, 300–301, 336
    in France, 306–307
    in Italy, 314–315, 388
    in Portugal, 337–338
Cortes (Spain), 369
Coty, François, 344
Council of Europe, 548–549
Council of Four, 157n
Council of Permanent Rep-
    resentatives
    (COREPER), in Com-
    mon Market, 594

Counterrevolution, 133, 149
    in Hungary, 214–216
Coups
    against Mussolini, 454
    by Soviets in Czechoslova-
        kia, 521
    in Soviet Union, 657–658
    in Spain, 251, 636, 637
Court of Justice (EC), 594
Covenant. See League of
    Nations
Crankshaw, Edward, 523
Crash of 1929. See Great
    Depression; Stock
    market crash (1929)
Craxi, Bettino, 635, 677
Création du Monde, La (Mil-
    haud), 276
Creative Evolution (Bergson),
    36
Credit, Great Depression
    and, 297, 298
Credit-Anstalt (Vienna),
    297–298, 310, 339
Credit buying, 559
Creeds. See Political philoso-
    phy
Crematoria. See Extermina-
    tion camps
Crick, Francis, 573
Crime, in Russia, 660
    in Europe, 678
Cripps, Stafford, 499
Croatia, 179, 248, 668, 670
Croats, 46, 47, 141, 142, 178,
    181, 249
Croix de feu (France), 344
Cross-Channel invasion. See
    D-Day (1944)
Crowe, Eyre, 59
Cruise missiles, 619
Cruisers, in First World War,
    84
Cuban missile crisis,
    584–586, 599
Cubism, 35
Cult of action (Sorel), 203
Cultural pessimism, in Ger-
    many, 325–326
Culture. See also Art(s); Popu-
    lar culture
    clash of, 574
    high culture and, 276–282
    mass culture, 264–276
    in 1920s and 1930s, 263

revolution in, 32–38
setting of interwar,
    282–289
Cunhal, Alvaro, 635, 637, 638
Cuno, Wilhelm, 242, 243
Currency. See also specific
    currencies
    controls after Second
        World War, 475
    euro as, 674
    in France, 366
    gold standard and, 2–3
    Great Depression and,
        299
    in Nazi Germany, 312
    in unified Germany, 655,
        666–667
    U.S.-European values,
        597–598
    in Weimar Republic,
        244–245
Curzon, Lord and Lady, 4
Curzon Line, 476–477, 478
Customs duties, of EC, 594
Customs union
    Benelux as, 545n
    Germany-Austria, 310
Czech Charter 77 movement.
    See Charter 77 move-
    ment
Czechoslovakia, 150, 160,
    163, 180, 246, 250
    agrarian population of,
        247
    appeasement and,
        394–397
    Blum and, 397
    Communists in, 484–485,
        516
    German invasion of,
        393–394
    industry in, 517
    Klaus, Václav, and, 665
    Little Entente and, 183
    Marshall Plan and, 484
    Masaryk and, 179
    Munich settlement and,
        398–400
    rebellion in, 526
    Soviet invasion of (1968),
        566, 588, 589
    Soviet mutual security
        treaty with, 360
    Soviet Union and,
        519–520, 521

Czechoslovakia *(continued)*
  Sudetenland tensions
    and, 397–398
  "velvet revolution" in
    (1989), 653, 654
  West Germany and, 601
Czecho-Slovak National
  Council, 160
Czechoslovak Springtime
  (1968), 583, 586,
  612–614, 650
Czech Republic, 666
  in NATO, 546n, 676
Czechs, 46, 142, 143, 178
  Nazis and, 400

Dada movement, 114, 115
Daladier, Edouard, 345, 357,
  361, 363, 374
  Munich settlement and,
    398
  "phony war" and, 415
D'Alema, Massimo, 677
Dali, Salvador, 280
Daniel, Yuli, 610
D'Annunzio, Gabriele, 102,
  202, 205–206
Danube region, Allies and,
  464
Danzig, 177, 180, 187
  as free city, 179
  as Gdansk, 615
  Hitler and, 403
Dardanelles, 84
Dassault, Marcel, 561
Dawes, Charles G., 187–188
Dawes Plan, 188, 191, 297
  loans to Germany under,
    244–245
Dawson, Geoffrey, 396
Dayton Agreement (1995),
  671
D-Day (1944), 448, 454–457
Déat, Marcel, 300, 306, 344
Death penalty, 339, 370, 492,
  640
Death rate, 18
Debts
  in First World War, 171
  in France, 640
Declaration of General Secu-
  rity, 462
Decline of the West, The (Spen-
  gler), 275–276
Deconstructionism, 643

Defence of the Realm Act
  (Britain), 111
Defense
  common European sys-
    tem of, 545
  NATO and, 546
Defense treaty, Warsaw Pact
  as, 553
Deficit spending, 300, 625
Deflation, 299
  in France, 307
  in Germany, 310
De Gasperi, Alcide, 494, 504,
  536–537, 566
  Christian Democrats and,
    538–539
  European union and, 544
De Gaulle, Charles, 417, 434,
  492, 567
  Algeria and, 542–543
  Common Market and,
    592–593
  dollar and, 597
  Fifth Republic and, 539
  force de frappe of, 561
  as French leader, 500–502
  French resistance and,
    436, 438
  Gaullism and, 576,
    589–592
  student riots and, 575
  two-bloc system and,
    600–601
  U.S. nuclear strength
    and, 599
Degrelle, Léon, 348–349
Delors, Jacques, 673–674
Demilitarization, of Ger-
  many, 168–169
Demobilization, 228
  Italy and, 206
  Mussolini and, 203
Democracies
  in Eastern Europe,
    664–666
  after First World War, 230
  Portugal as, 637–639
  in Russia, 660–662
  Spain as, 635–637
Democratic Party (Ger-
  many), 241
Democritus, 32
Demographic transition, 18
Demonstrations. *See* Political
  demonstrations

Denazification, of Germany,
  480
Denikin, Anton, 133–134
Denmark, 631. *See also* Scandinavia
  birth rate in, 19
  collaboration with Nazis
    in, 432
  Depression politics in,
    301
  in EC, 594
  Nazi invasion of, 416
Depressions. *See also* Great
  Depression
  business cycle and, 294
  defined, 293–294
  in EC, 641–642
  in Italy, 206
  of 1970s-1980s, 625
  in Russia, 659
Derrida, Jacques, 643
De-Stalinization, 318,
  523–526
  ideology and, 566
  in Poland, 527–528
Détente
  end of, 620
  Helsinki Conference
    (1972-1975) and, 603
  movement toward,
    583–586
  rival versions of, 598–604
Devaluation
  of British pound, 304,
    306, 475
  in France, 366
  of U.S. dollar, 584, 598
Diaghilev, Sergei, 282
Dickens, Charles, 8
Dictatorship
  in Italy, 252–254
  in Portugal, 252, 635–
    636
  of the proletariat, 130,
    257
  in Russia, 256–257
  in Spain, 251–252, 340,
    635–636
Diet (nutrition). *See also* Food
  of workers, 12
Dinasos (organization), 348
Diplomacy
  of Great Powers, 52–53
  Italian conquest of
    Ethiopia and, 389

League of Nations and,
  196–197
  after peace settlement of
    1919, 193–197
  secret, 194
  before World War I, 44
Diplomatic corps, in Nazi
  Germany, 334–335
Dirigibles, 84
Disarmament
  failure of, 191–193
  League Covenant and,
    167
  movements, 619, 622
  naval, 193
  weapons cuts and, 656
Disarmament Conference,
  German withdrawal
  from, 382
Disarmament Preparatory
  Commission, 192–193
Discontent
  of students, 574–577
  terrorism and, 579
  of women, 578
  of workers, 577–578
Discrimination, among
  nationalities, 178–
  179
Disneyland (France), 644
Displaced persons (DPs),
  after Second World
  War, 491, 491 (map)
Dissent. *See* Dissidents; spe-
  cific individuals and
  movements
Dissidents, in Soviet Union,
  514, 610–611, 614
Distribution of wealth
  in postwar Europe,
    560–563
  in Russia, 659–660
Divorce
  rights to, 578
  in Spain, 370
Djilas, Milovan, 10
Djugashvili, Josef. *See* Stalin,
  Josef
DNA, 573
Dr. Zhivago (Pasternak), 525
Dodecanese Islands, 86
Dole, in Britain, 303
Dollar (U.S.), 496–497, 584
  de Gaulle, gold reserves,
    and, 597

speculation against, 597
supremacy of, 475
"Dollar gap," 595
Dollfuss, Engelbert, 339, 341, 382–383, 392
Domestic service, 15–16
Dopolavoro (Italy), 270
Doriot, Jacques, 344
Dorten, Hans Adam, 168
Douglas-Home, Alec, 540
Draft (military). *See* Conscription
Dreadnoughts, 57, 62, 86
Dresden (ship), 86
Dreyfus, Alfred, 237
"Dualist" period, of Soviet control, 519
Dubček, Alexander, 586, 653, 654
   Czechoslovak Springtime and, 612–614
Du Bois, W. E. B., 161
Duce, Il, Mussolini as, 315
Duchamp, Marcel, 114
Duclos, Jacques, 358
Dudintsev, Vladimir, 525
"Dulce et Decorum Est" (Owen), 114
Dulles, John Foster, 534
Duma (Russian parliament), 22, 25, 99, 121
Dunkirk, 452
   British evacuation from, 417, 418
Düsseldorf, remilitarization of Rhineland and, 384, 385
Duties (taxes)
   in Britain, 304
   in First World War Britain, 94
Dynasties, breakdown of, 142–143

EADS. *See* European Aeronautic, Defense and Space Co. (EADS)
East Berlin, 553. *See also* Berlin; Berlin Wall; East Germany
   revolt in, 526, 527, 535
Eastern Europe. *See also* specific countries
   agriculture in, 10

assessment of settlement in, 180–181
authoritarianism in, 323
collaboration with Nazis in, 432
cordon sanitaire in, 163
democracy and market economy in, 664–666
discontent in, 611–612
division of, 405
economies in, 558
end of communism in, 649
extermination of Jews in, 430–431
fascism in, 340–343
after First World War, 143–146, 245–250, 483
First World War settlement in, 172–181
German expansionism in, 390 (map), 390–393
national communism in, 588–589
National Front regimes in, 516–518
nationalism in, 26, 143–146, 150
from 1945 to 1953, 515–522
parliamentary democracies in, 245–246
peasant lifestyle in, 9–10
Peoples' Democracies in, 521–522
poverty in, 13
revolutions of 1989 in, 649, 650–658
Russian gains in, 414–415
Second World War in (1939-1940), 414–415
Second World War in (1941-1942), 421–424
Soviets and, 457–461, 471, 519–520
supranational organizations in, 552–553
thaw and rebellion in (1953-1956), 526–529
Western economic penetration of, 603
Eastern Front
   in First World War, 75–77, 131

in Second World War, 467 (map)
Easter Rebellion, 109, 111
East German Socialist Unity Party (SED), 602
East Germany, 481, 506–507. *See also* Germany; West Germany
   Berlin Wall destruction and, 652
   Brandt and, 601–602
   communism in, 516
   conditions in, 617
   disarmament movement in, 619
   Honecker and, 609
   missiles in, 619
   unification and, 654–656
   in United Nations, 584, 602
Ebert, Friedrich, 138, 139–140, 211, 230, 242, 245, 327
EC. *See* European Community (EC)
École des Beaux Arts, 37
Ecology, 579
   in Soviet Union, 610
Economic Consequences of the Peace, The (Keynes), 162, 186, 386
Economic union. *See also* European Community (EC); European Union (EU)
   in Europe, 549–551
Economy and economics. *See also* Consumer society; Great Depression; Inflation; specific systems and theories
   in Austria, 338–339
   in Britain, 93–95, 231, 302–306
   center of, 3
   classical, 299
   collaboration with Nazis and, 432–433
   corporatism and, 300–301
   of corporatist Italy, 314–315
   in Eastern Europe, 665
   fascism and, 218–219, 220

First World War and, 92, 106–108
   in France, 186, 238, 307, 640
   in Germany, 185, 241
   Hitler's expansionism and, 391
   imperialism and, 5
   inflation and, 106–107, 625
   international financial crisis and, 297–298
   in Italy, 206
   in late 1980s, 645
   liberalism in, 28–29
   "middle way" in, 300–301
   national boundaries and, 181
   in Nazi Germany, 311–313, 335, 425–426, 426–427
   neoliberal, 228–229
   oil crisis and, 624
   popes on, 336–337
   in postwar Britain, 499–500
   in postwar France, 502–503
   in postwar Germany, 480–481
   in postwar Italy, 505
   postwar prosperity and, 557–559
   in Russia, 254, 659–660
   after Second World War, 475, 495–497
   Second World War and, 406
   socialist, 299–300
   Soviet, 316–319, 508–509, 608–609
   stagflation and, 625
   U.S.-European rivalry and, 595–598
   in Weimar Germany, 244–245
   of West Germany, 507–508
ECSC. *See* European Coal and Steel Community (ECSC, 1951)
EDC. *See* European Defense Community (EDC)
Eddington, Arthur, 287

Eden, Anthony, 394, 539, 540, 543

Edison, Thomas, 558

Education
academic and scholarly worlds, 286
in arts, 37
egalitarianism and, 563–564
universal, 26

EFTA. *See* European Free Trade Association (EFTA)

Egalitarianism
distribution of wealth and, 562
education and, 563–564
homogeneity and, 274
social mobility and, 563–565

Egypt, 5
imperialism in, 6
Second World War and, 452
Suez Campaign and, 543

Eichmann, Adolf, 428–429, 430

Einstein, Albert, 33, 287

Eisenhower, Dwight D.
as Allied commander, 456–457
as Supreme Allied Commander-Europe, 546

Eisenstein, Sergei, 126, 285, 289
Alexander Nevsky and, 459, 514

Eisner, Kurt, 137, 140

Elbe River, U.S.-Soviet meeting at, 478

Elderly, inflation and, 107

ELDO (European Launch Development Organization), 573

Elections
in Britain (1931, 1935), 347
in Eastern Europe, 664
in Germany, 327
"khaki election" (1918), 170, 182
of 1924, 194
of 1936, 364

in Russia, 662
in Spain, 636

Electronic music, 571

Eliot, T. S., 115, 376

Elites
mass culture and, 275
Soviet, 525–526

Emancipated women, 103–104

Embargo, on Italy, 388

Empires, 5. *See also* Imperialism; Paris peace settlement (1919)
end of British, 419
after First World War, 157–161, 174–175 (maps)
multinational, 93
nationalism in, 26–27, 159
after Second World War, 540–543
Yalta Conference and, 467

Employment
in Britain, 497–498
in France, 640
in Nazi Germany, 313

Encirclement, German fears of, 51, 61
Soviet fears of, 475

Energy, 33
sources of, 626
in Soviet Union, 609

Engels, Friedrich, 16, 201–202

England. *See* Britain

English Channel, First World War and, 59

English Education Act (1944), 498

Entente Powers, 53n, 84. *See also* Allies (in First World War)
Italy and, 76

Entrepreneurs, postwar prosperity and, 561

Environment. *See also* Ecology
Soviet problems with, 610

Erhard, Ludwig, 507, 566, 630

Erhardt Brigade, 211, 212

Eritrea, 388

Erzberger, Matthias, 181, 241, 243

Escalator Clause, in London Naval Conference, 193

Esterházy family (Hungary), 9, 13

Estonia
independence of, 657
Soviets and, 405, 414

Ethiopia, 4n, 540
Italian conquest of, 384, 387–388, 541

Ethnic cleansing, Balkan Wars and, 50

Ethnic groups. *See also* Minorities; Nationalism; National minorities
in Austria-Hungary, 46–47, 47 (map), 100–101
in Balkans, 45–50
Eastern European fascism and, 340
Eastern European hatreds among, 666
after First World War, 141–146
in Soviet Union, 514, 610
Yugoslav civil war and, 668–673

Eton students, class and, 305

EU. *See* European Union (EU)

Euratom, 594

Euro, 674

Eurocommunists, 633
Berlinguer and, 633–635

Eurodollars, 597–598

Europe. *See also* Eastern Europe; Western Europe
Big Three and future of, 461–470
Cold War and (1947-1961), 533–553
Cold War and (1950s), 547 (map)
displaced persons in, 491, 491 (map)
First World War and, 44
Kellogg-Briand Pact and, 190
nationalities in, 176 (map)

in 1920s, 227–259
in 19th century, 2
peace settlements in (1919–1920), 165 (map)
reconstruction of, 489–509
recovery in, 495–497
settlement in Eastern, 172–181
settlement in Western, 167–172
unity movement in, 543–551
U.S. economic rivalry with, 595–598

European Advisory Commission, 462

European Aeronautic, Defense and Space Co. (EADS), 676

European Coal and Steel Community (ECSC, 1951), 550–551, 594

European Common Market, 551

European Community (EC), 594
as European Union (EU), 674
Portugal in, 639
in recession, 641–642
Single European Act and, 645
trade with former colonies, 596
U.S. subsidiaries and branches in, 597
wealth of, 583–584

European Convention on Human Rights (1950), 549

European Council, 674–675

European Court of Human Rights, 549

European Defense Community (EDC), 548

European Economic Sphere (Hitler), 544

European Free Trade Association (EFTA), 675

European Monetary System (EMS), 594, 598, 674

European Parliament, 594, 642

European Recovery Program, U.S. and, 484
European Single Act, 645, 673
European Union (EU), 673–677
  architects of, 544–545
  Council of Europe and, 548–549
  Eastern Europe and, 666
  economic union and, 549–551
  origins of, 543–544
  pressures for, 545–546
  problems of, 546–548
"Europe first" strategy, in Second World War, 452
Exchange rates
  Britain and, 234
  fixed, 584, 597
Existentialism, of Sartre, 442–443, 538
Expansionism
  of Hitler, 195, 313, 391
  of Italy, 387–388
Expatriate writers, from U.S., 282
Expenditures
  military, 64n
  in Nazi Germany, 312
  on social welfare, 629
Experimental arts, 277–278, 279
  opposition to, 288–289
Expressionism, 34, 278, 279
Extermination camps, for Jews, 429–431

Facta, Luigi, 208
Factory council movement, 205
Factory workers, 16
Faisal, 160
Faisceau (France), 217
Falange (Spain), 340, 371, 539
Falkenhayn, Erich von, 77, 79–80, 97
Falkland Islands, 86
  Britain and, 632
Fallada, Hans, 295, 325
Family size, 18–21
Famine, in Russia, 129, 254
Farben, I. G., 106, 245

Far East, Soviets in, 466
Farinacci, Roberto, 253
Farms and farming. *See also* Agrarian regions; Agriculture; Peasants
  discontents in, 578
  after First World War, 246–249
  Great Depression and, 296
  in Nazi Germany, 313
  in Russia, 316
Far Right
  in Austria, 676–677
  immigrants and, 628
  in Russia, 662
  in Western Europe, 676–678
Fascism, 148, 152, 200–224
  appeal of, 350
  in Belgium, 348–349
  Blum and, 366–367
  in Britain, 345–348
  in Bulgaria, 341
  Catholic Church and, 220
  early movement, 204
  in Eastern Europe, 340–343
  in France, 217, 343–345
  in Holland, 349
  in Hungary, 214–216, 341
  in Italy, 202–210, 252–254, 315
  in Low Countries, 348–349
  meaning of, 217–219
  Mussolini and, 202–203
  in 1930s, 323–324
  Popular Front and, 355–356
  power concentration and, 206
  in Romania, 341–343
  roots of, 219–224
  in Scandinavia, 349
  Spanish Civil War and, 372–373
  squadristi (direct-action bands) and, 205, 206
  in Western Europe, 343–349
  youth and, 219
Father, authority of, 19–20
Fatherland Party (Germany), 211
Fauves, 35, 277, 278

February Revolution (Russia), 120–121
Feder, Gottfried, 335
Federal Republic of Germany. *See* West Germany
Fellow travelers, 538
Feminism, 578
Ferdinand of Saxe-Coburg, 22
Ferenczi, Sandor, 288
Fertility transition, 18
FIAT, 505, 561
"fifth column," 372, 413
Fifth Republic (France), 492, 501
Figli della Lupa (Italy), 200
Films. *See* Movies
Final Act (1975), 603
"Final Solution," by Nazi Germany, 429–431
Financial crisis, international, 297–298
Financing, of First World War, 96
Fine arts, 569–571
Finland
  EFTA and, 675
  Soviets and, 405, 415, 416
First Balkan War, 50
First Battle of the Marne, 73–75, 78, 91, 96
First Five-Year Plan (Soviet Union), 316–317, 509
First World War. *See also* Allies (First World War); Central Powers; Entente Powers; Paris peace settlement (1919); Russia; Secret treaties; Treaties
  aims of, 134
  aircraft in, 272–273
  Allies in, 84–85
  Austria-Hungary and, 53, 100–102
  Austrian front in, 76–77
  Britain and, 57–60, 93–95, 499
  causes of, 60–65
  costs of, 170–171
  Eastern front in, 75–77
  escalation to continental war, 53–60
  events leading to, 43–53
  expectation of short war, 71

fascist roots and, 222
France and, 54–55, 95–97
fronts in, 85 (map)
Germany after, 167–172, 482 (map)
Germany and, 55–56, 68, 97–99, 134–136
government during, 93–102
Great Depression and, 296
Great Powers after, 161–163
inflation during, 106–107
intellectual thought during, 113–116
Italian neutrality and, 60
Italy and, 102
July crisis (1914) and, 44–45
liberal and social critiques of, 109–111
Marne battles and, 73–75, 78
nation-building after, 143–145
offensives in West, 79–82
peace settlement after, 157–197
police power during, 111–112
profiteers in, 106
public attitude toward, 69–73
public opinion controlled during, 111–113
Russia and, 53–54, 99–100, 127–128, 131
Russian Civil War and, 131–134
Schlieffen Plan and, 56–57
at sea, 86–87
self-determination after, 141–146
Serbia and, 53
social divisions in, 105–106
social peace and, 72–73
society during, 102–106
strikes during, 108–109
tactics in, 78–79
as total war, 87–88, 91–92
treaties in, 159–161

First World War (*continued*)
United States in, 87–88
as war of attrition, 92–93
weapons in, 82–84
Western front in, 77–84
widening of, 84–86
Fischer, Fritz, 61
Fiume, 148, 182, 202, 205
Five-year plans
in Eastern Europe, 522
in Russia, 316–317
Flame thrower, 83
Flanders, British in, 82
Flanner, Janet, 535, 548
Flemish, fascism and, 348, 349
Flemish National Union, 348
FLN (Front de Libération
Nationale), in Algeria,
541, 542
Foch, Ferdinand, 78,
135–136, 168
Fokker, A. G., airplane
machine guns and, 84
Food, after Second World
War, 490
Foot, Michael, 632
Football (soccer), 271–272
Force, levels in 1984, 602
Forced collectivization, in
Eastern Europe, 522
Force de frappe, 561
Forced labor camps, in
Soviet Union, 514
Force reduction talks
(MBFR). *See* Mutual
and Balanced Force
Reductions (MBFR)
talks
Ford, Gerald, 603
Foreign affairs
public knowledge of,
193–196
of Russia, 662–664
Foreign aid
end of, 595
to Europe, 495
Marshall Plan and, 484,
495–496
Foreign debt, of Eastern
bloc, 603
Foreign exchange. *See also*
Exchange rates
after First World War, 234
Foreign Legionnaires, in
Spain, 370, 371, 374

Forster, E. M., 17, 319
Fortress Europe, in Second
World War, 452
Forza italia, 677
Foucault, Michel, 643–644
Four-Power Pact (1933), 387
Fourteen Points, 136,
158–159, 162–163,
170, 193
Fourth Republic (France),
500–503, 540
collapse of, 539
Four-Year Plan (Germany),
312
Franc (France), 307, 640
France, 567. *See also* D-Day
(1944); De Gaulle,
Charles; First World
War; Marne; Second
World War; specific
leaders
Algeria and, 492, 540,
541, 542–543
alliance politics and,
183–184
Allied landing in south,
456
anti-Algerian feeling in,
628
aristocracy in, 14
artillery in First World
War, 79
British military planning
with, 57
Cartel des Gauches in,
236–238
Catholic Church and, 336
collaboration with Nazis
in, 431–433, 432, 492
Common Market and,
592–593
Communist Party in, 116,
535–536, 568, 635
conciliation with Ger-
many, 183
conservatism in, 182
Czech treaty with, 397
Depression politics in,
306–309
discrimination against
nationalities by,
178–179
economy in, 186, 640
education in, 286
elections of 1928 in, 358

empire of, 5
events leading to First
World War, 44
fall to Nazis, 416–418
Far Right in, 628, 676
fascism and, 217,
221–222, 343–345
Fifth Republic in, 492, 501
after First World War,
161–162, 236–239
First World War and, 73,
92, 95–97, 134–135
Fourth Republic in,
500–503, 540
Gaullism and, 589–592
German rearmament
and, 548
immigrants in, 627–628
independence of empire,
541–542
Indochina and, 541, 542
inflation in, 107
Italy and, 85, 387,
388–389
Jospin in, 678
labor unions in, 105
left wing after Popular
Front, 376–377
Locarno Agreements
and, 188–191
Maginot Line and, 192
maquis (resistance) in,
438
Mitterrand and, 639–641
MLF and, 599–600
mobilization by, 54–55
nationalization in,
502–503
NATO and, 548
Nazi labor from, 427
Nazi occupation of, 427
Near East and, 160
New Deal in, 364–368
normalcy under Poin-
caré, 238–239
nuclear power in, 626
occupation of Germany
and, 468
"phony war" and,
415–416
Poland supported by,
402–403
police power in, 111–112
Popular Front in,
356–357, 362–368

postwar attitudes in, 559
poverty in, 12
public attitude toward
First World War in, 70
readiness for war of, 51
remilitarization of
Rhineland and,
385–386
resistance movement in,
436
Rhineland and, 168–169
Ruhr region and, 171,
172, 184–185, 243
Saar region and, 168
Schlieffen Plan and,
56–57
security issues of (1920–
1940), 189 (map)
socialism in, 110
socialist rally in, 25
Soviet mutual security
treaty with, 360
Soviets as allies and, 401
Spanish Civil War and,
373
strikes in, 62, 108
student discontent in,
576
Suez and, 543
Third International and,
152
Third Republic in, 500
trade unions in, 72
unrest after First World
War, 146
U.S. peace aims for,
473–475
vacations in, 270
women's voting rights in,
21
worker protests in, 577
workweek in, 269–270
Yalta Conference and, 467
Franchet d',Esperey, Louis,
145
Franco, Francisco, 340, 370,
636
anti-Communist alliance
and, 539
Italian assistance to, 389
Nationalist Spain and,
371
recognition of, 373
Spanish Civil War and,
372–374

Franco-German agreement, for Rhine, 188
Franco-German frontier, 192
Franco-German War (1870-1871), 170
Franco-Russian Alliance, 51, 54, 183
    Schlieffen Plan and, 56
"Franglais," 591
Frankfurt School, 644
Franz Ferdinand (Austria-Hungary), 42, 141
    assassination of, 44, 45, 50
Franz Josef (Austria-Hungary), 27, 44–45, 51, 101
Free French, 422, 434
    de Gaulle and, 500, 501
    resistance to Nazis by, 436
Free market
    in Italy, 314
    in West Germany, 508
Free trade. *See also* European Community (EC); European Union (EU)
    Britain and, 232
    and First World War Britain, 94
    after Second World War, 475
    Single European Act and, 645
    Uruguay Round and, 645–646
Freikorps (Germany), 140, 211
    Czechoslovakia and, 398
    in Eastern Europe, 163
    Hitler and, 212
    Weimar Republic and, 240
French, John, 78
French Revolution, fascism and, 217–218
French Socialist Party (SFIO), 344
    Blum and, 308
Freud, Lucian, 570
Freud, Sigmund, 36, 280, 287
Frisch, Max, 534
Fritsch, Werner von, 335
Frontiers. *See also* Borders
    conflict over, 181–182

in Eastern Europe, after First World War, 173–178, 180–181
    Franco-German, 192
    German, 390 (map), 390–393
    of Poland, 476–477
    Polish-Soviet, 463
    Soviet-West German, 601
Front National, 628, 677
Fronts, in First World War, 85 (map)
    Eastern, 75–77
    Western, 77–84
Führer. *See* Hitler, Adolf
"Full employment in a Free Society" (Beveridge), 497
Functionalism, 278
Futurism, in arts, 35

Gaidar, Yegor, 659
Gaitskell, Hugh, 567
Galicia, 75, 76, 77, 158
Gallagher, John, 6
Gallipoli, 77, 84
Gandhi, Mohandas K., 540
Gas, in extermination camps, 429. *See* Poison Gas (First World War)
Gasparri (Cardinal), 253
GATT (General Agreement on Trade and Tariffs), 598, 645–646
Gauguin, Paul, 34, 35
Gaullism, 576, 589–592
Gdansk. *See also* Danzig
    demonstrations in, 615, 616
General Agreement on Trade and Tariffs. *See* GATT (General Agreement on Trade and Tariffs)
General Confederation of Italian Industry (CGII), 315
General Strike of 1926 (Britain), 234–235, 357
General Theory of Employment, Interest, and Money (Keynes), 305
generations, conflict between, 114, 575

Genetics, in Soviet Union, 514
Geneva Protocol (1924), 197
Genoa meeting (1922), 183
Gentry, 10
George V (England), 230
    Wilhelm II and, 57–59
George VI (England), 230
Georgia (Russia), 524, 663
German Coal Syndicate, 184
German Democratic Republic. *See* East Germany
German Evangelical Church, in Nazi Germany, 334
German National People's Party (DNVP), 241–242, 245, 326
German Peoples' Congress for Unity and a Just Peace, 481
German Social Democratic Party, 24–25
German Socialist Party (SPD), 137–138
German-speaking people
    in Austria, 46
    expulsion from Central Europe (1945-1947), 491, 491 (map)
German-speaking peoples, in Czechoslovakia, 397–398
German Workers' Party, 210–211
    Hitler and, 212
Germany. *See also* East Germany; First World War; Hitler, Adolf; Nazi Germany; Second World War; Weimar Republic (Germany); West Germany
    Adenauer and, 539
    Anschluß with Austria, 338, 382–384, 392–393
    anti-Soviet alliance and, 548
    attitudes toward, in First World War, 69–70
    "blank check" and, 50–51
    Bolshevism and, 164
    Christian Democrats in, 494

civil liberties in, 24
and coercion after First World War, 183–185
and conciliation after First World War, 186–187
demilitarization of, 168–169
denazification of, 480
economy of, 185
empire of, 5
encirclement fears of, 51, 61
end of Weimar Republic in, 327–331
events leading to First World War, 44, 50–51, 55–57
exchange rates and, 597–598
Far Right in, 676
fascism and, 221
financial crisis in, 298
after First World War, 161, 167, 168–172, 482 (map)
First World War and, 97–99, 134–136, 175 (map)
foreign policy of, 186–187
France and, 54, 367
frontiers of, 425
Great Depression in, 309–311
inflation in, 107, 224
interwar culture in, 282
knapsack travel in, 273
labor unions in, 105
in League of Nations, 188
Locarno Agreements and, 188–191
monarchy in, 22
national socialism in and Nazism in (1929-1932), 210–214, 324–326
New Center policy in, 678
occupation zones in, 468, 479–480
opposition to experimental arts in, 288–289
organized recreation in, 270–271
peace resolution in, 110

Germany (*continued*)
  postwar economic growth in, 558
  postwar leadership in, 494
  postwar Protestants and Catholics in, 493
  poverty in, 13
  radio and, 266, 267
  rearmament of, 192
  refusal to mediate, 52–53
  reparations after Second World War, 480–481, *See* Reparations
  resistance to Hitler within, 438–440
  revolution in (1918-1919), 136–140
  Rhineland and, 167
  Russian Civil War and, 133
  in Russian territories, 163
  after Second World War, 482 (map), 505–508
  security issues of (1920-1940), 189 (map)
  socialists in, 71–72, 110, 137–138, 151
  Soviet treaty with (1922), 183–184
  strategic position in 1914, 51
  strikes in, 108
  surrender in Second World War, 478–479
  theater in, 284
  Third International and, 152
  ultimatum to Belgium, 60
  unemployment in, 292, 294
  after unification, 666–668
  unification of, 26, 546n, 654–656
  war declared by (1914), 55–56
  Weimar Coalition in, 241–243
  Yalta Conference and, 468
Gheorghiu-Dej, Gheorghe, 588–589
Ghettos, for Jews, 429, 431
Giacometti, Alberto, 570
Gierek, Edward, 615
Gil Robles, José Maria, 370

Giolitti, Giovanni, 102, 147, 204, 205, 206
Giroud, Françoise, 639
Giscard d'Estaing, Valéry, 639
Glasnost (openness), 650
Gleichschaltung, 332–333, 335, 382
Glenn, John, 529n
Glistrup, Mogens, 630
Globalization, 678
Gneisenau (ship), 86
Godard, Jean-Luc, 571
Godesberg, 398
"God is dead" movement, 572
Goebbels, Joseph, 267, 330, 335, 432
Goldie, George, 5
Goldman, Marshall, 659
Gold reserves, of U.S., 597
Gold standard, 2–3
  Britain and, 233–234, 304
  after First World War, 229
  France and, 239, 306
  Great Depression and, 298
  U.S. removal of, 598
Goltz, Rüdiger von der, 163
Gömbös, Gyula [Julius], 215–217, 219, 339, 341
Gombrich, E. H., 569
Gomes, Costa, 638
Gomulka, Wladyslaw, 518, 527, 528, 614, 615
Gonçalves, Vasco, 638
Goncourt Prize, 490
Gonzáles, Felipe, 636–637
Gorazde, UN safe area in, 671
Gorbachev, Mikhail, 620
  collapse of Soviet Union and, 650–658, 656–659
  German unification and, 656
Gorbachev, Raisa, 648
Goremykin, Ivan, 99
Göring, Hermann, 213, 223, 312, 322
  on autarky, 391
  Battle of Britain and, 420
  Halifax and, 396
Gottwald, Klement, 612

"Goulash Communism," 589, 616–617
Gould, Jay, 14
Government. *See also* specific countries
  of Austria-Hungary, 100–102
  of Britain, 93–95
  dismantling of war governments, 228–229
  of fascist Italy, 315
  during First World War, 93–102
  of France, 95–97
  of Germany, 97–99
  of Gorbachev's Russia, 651
  of Italy, 102
  labor unions and, 105
  monarchy and, 21–22
  nationalism and, 26–27
  parliaments and, 22–24
  of Russia, 99–100, 129–130, 660–662
  socialism and, 24–26
  of Weimar Germany, 327–329
Graduated deterrence policy, 599
Grammar schools, 564
Grass, Günter, 490, 506
Graves, Robert, 69–70, 80, 376
Great Britain. *See* Britain
Great Coalition (Germany), 243–245, 309, 567
Great Depression, 292, 293–319
  arts in, 295
  in authoritarian states, 311–319
  Blum and, 366
  in Britain, 302–306
  domestic crises preceding, 296–297
  in France, 306–309
  international financial crisis preceding, 297–298
  in Italy, 314–315
  in Nazi Germany, 311–313
  origins of, 296–298
  politics in liberal states, 301–311
  remedies for, 298–301
  in Scandinavia, 301–302
  in Soviet Union, 316–319

in Weimar Germany, 309–311
Great Economic Unit, of Nazi Germany, 425
"Great leap forward" (China), 587
Great Patriotic War, 459, 513
Great Powers
  diplomacy of, 44, 52–53
  national interests after First World War, 161–163
  nationalism and, 26
  Ottoman breakup and, 46
  at Paris Peace Conference, 157n
  republics and monarchies among, 21–22
  Straits at Constantinople and, 48
Great War. *See* First World War
Greece
  Corfu and, 209–210
  in EC, 594
  First Balkan War and, 50
  independence of, 46
  Italian invasion of, 422
  mutiny in, 476
  PASOK in, 641
  as republic, 246
  after Second World War, 483
  Soviets and, 471
  Truman Doctrine and, 483–484
  war of independence, 27
Green activism, 579
Greenham Common, missile protest at, 619, 622
Green International, in Bulgaria, 248
Grenada, U.S. invasion of, 633
Grey, Edward, 59, 405
Grigorenko, Pyotr, 611
Groener, Wilhelm, 98, 105, 137, 139
Gropius, Walter, 276, 277, 282, 285
Grosz, George, 283, 284
Group Portrait with Lady (Böll), 571
Groza, Petru, 516

Grundig, Max, 561
Guérin, Daniel, 355
Guernica (Picasso), 375
Guerrillas, Chechen, 663
Guesde, Jules, 104
Guevara, Che, student discontent and, 574
Gulag Archipelago, The (Solzhenitsyn), 611
Guynemer, Georges, 84
Gypsies, Nazi extermination of, 431

Habermas, Jürgen, 644
Habsburg Empire. *See* Austria-Hungary
Hague Conferences
of 1899, 21, 110
of 1907, 110
Hahn, Otto, 413
Haider, Jörg, 677
Haig, Douglas, 78, 80
Haile Selassie, 388
Haldane, J. B. S., 376
Halévy, Elie, 112
Halifax, Lord (Edward Frederick Linley Wood), 396, 397, 401
Hall of Mirrors, Treaty of Versailles (1919) and, 164
Hallstein, Walter, 593, 673
Hamburg, social revolution in, 138–139
Hanfstaengl, Putzi, 213
Harding, Warren G., 182, 228
Harmsworth, Alfred (Lord Northcliffe), 265, 268
Hashemite family, 160
Havel, Václav, 653, 654, 664, 665
Heath, Edward, 577–578, 632
Hegemony
Soviet, in Eastern Europe, 457–461, 603
United States, in West, 450–457
Heidegger, Martin, 287–288, 443
Heisenberg, Werner, 33, 286–287
Helsinki Conference (1972-1975), 603

Helsinki Final Act. *See* Final Act (1975)
Hemingway, Ernest, 282
Henderson, Arthur, 94, 104–105
Henderson, Nevile, 397
Henlein, Konrad, 394, 398
Hereditary monarchies, after First World War, 229
Hermann Göring steel mill, 312, 313
Herriot, Edouard, 187, 197, 237–238, 307, 361, 501
on United States of Europe, 544
Hervé, Gustave, 73
Herzegovina, 45, 48
Austria-Hungary and, 46
Hess, Rudolf, 223
Heydrich, Reinhard, 430
High Authority, in ECSC, 550
High culture, in 1920s and 1930s, 276–282
Higher education, 563
Highways, in Germany, 312
Hiking, 273
Himmler, Heinrich, 428, 431
Hindenburg, Paul von, 75, 76, 81, 97, 98, 135, 245, 333, 334, 382
Great Depression and, 309, 310
presidential government by, 327–329
Hipper, Franz von, 86
Hiss, Alger, 465n
History of Bohemia (Palacký), 26
Hitler, Adolf, 31, 210–211, 219, 243. *See also* Beer Hall *Putsch;* Germany; *Mein Kampf* (Hitler); Nazi Germany; Second World War
aggression by, 381–384
Allied successes over, 449–450
on arts, 288–289
assassination attempt against, 440
British resistance and, 420–421
as chancellor, 330, 331–335

Communists and, 358–359
election poster for, 328
emergence of, 212
European Economic Sphere of, 544
expansionism of, 195, 411
expansion to east, 390 (map), 390–393
German resistance to, 438–440
Great Depression and, 311–313
Jews and, 428–431
Munich settlement and, 398–400
Mussolini and, 380
Nazism and, 325
"New Order" of, 424–431, 425 (map)
occupation policy of, 427–428
Papen and, 328
Poland attacked by, 402–406
Popular Front and, 378
radio use by, 267
Reichstag and, 322
remilitarization of Rhineland by, 384–387
resources of enemies, 412
suicide of, 469
support for, 223
two-front war and, 421
Versailles Treaty and, 384
Weimar Republic and, 241
World Disarmament Conference and, 193
Young Plan and, 324
Hlinka, Andrej, 179, 432
Hoare, Samuel, 388, 389
Hobsbawm, Eric, 569
Hobson, John A., 5
Ho Chi Minh, 475
Hoffman, Max, 76
Hoffmann, Stanley, 237
Hoggart, Richard, 275
Holland. *See also* Netherlands
collaboration cases in, 492
empire of, 5
fascism in, 349
Moluccan activists in, 628

natural gas in, 626
"Hollow Men, The" (Eliot), 115
Holy Alliance (1815), 544
Home Army (Poland), 478
Home Guard, in Austria, 338
Homogeneity of populations, 273–274
Honecker, Erich, 602, 609, 617, 651, 652
Honegger, Arthur, 278
Hoover, Calvin B., 480
Hoover, Herbert, 298
Horthy, Miklós, 146, 215, 216, 217, 341
Nazis and, 424, 431, 432
"Hot line," U.S.-Soviet, 586
Hottentot election (1907), 194
Household, women's roles in, 19–21
House of Commons (Britain), 23
House Un-American Activities Committee, Hiss and, 465n
Housing
in Austria, 338
in Britain, 304
Howard's End (Forster), 17
Hugenberg, Alfred, 326, 329
Hugo, Victor, 29
Hull, Cordell, 461, 462
Human Rights Code, of EC, 594
Human sexuality. *See* Sex and sexuality
Hundred Years' War, 44
Hungary, 9, 46, 526
borders to West opened, 652
communism in, 485, 516
counterrevolution in, 214–216
economy of, 666
fascism in, 214–216, 341
after First World War, 141, 144–146, 246
First World War and, 77
"Goulash Communism" in, 589, 616–617
Kun in, 145–146
in NATO, 546n
Nazis and, 432
reformist leaders in, 652

Hungary *(continued)*
    revolt in, 528–529, 535
    Second World War and,
        424
    Soviets and, 464–465,
        519, 566
    Transylvania and, 666
    treaty with (1919), 164
Hunger, after Second World
    War, 490
Hurricane fighter aircraft,
    420
Husband, authority of, 19–20
Husserl, Edmund, 287, 442
Huxley, Thomas Henry,
    31–32
Hypnosis, Freud and, 36

Iberian Peninsula, after First
    World War, 250–252
ICBMs (intercontinental bal-
    listic missiles), 606
    dismantling of, 656
    dismantling of installa-
        tion, 656
    U.S. installed in Europe,
        619
Ideological collaboration,
    with Nazis, 431–432
Ideology
    in Eastern Europe, 665
    "end of," 565–568
IMF. *See* International Mone-
    tary Fund (IMF)
Immigrants, Right wing and,
    626–628, 677
Immigration Acts (Britain),
    627
Imperialism, 4–6
    First World War and,
        61–62
*Imperialism: The Highest Stage
    of Capitalism* (Lenin),
    6, 61
Imperial Officer Corps. *See*
    Germany
Import Duties Act (1932),
    304
Improvisation No. 30. . . .
    (Kandinsky), 34
IMRO (nationalist-terrorist
    organization), 341
Income
    First World War and, 107
    in West Germany, 508

Income tax, in Britain, 96
Independence and indepen-
    dence movements
    in British colonies, 543
    in colonial empires,
        540–543
    in Eastern Europe, 483
    after First World War,
        160–161, 246
    in Ireland, 109
    in Ottoman Empire, 46
    among Soviet republics,
        657
Independent Labour Party
    (Britain), 232
Independent Social Demo-
    cratic Party (USPD),
    137–138
Indeterminacy theory
    (Heisenberg), 33,
    286–287
India, 6
    China and, 587
    independence movement
        in, 540
    independence of, 541
Indochina, 5
    independence movement
        in, 541, 542
    after Second World War,
        475
Indonesia, independence of,
    541
Industrialization, 7
    First World War and, 64
    in Russia, 255–256
Industrial production, in
    Great Depression, 294
Industrial Revolution, cities
    and, 8
Industrial tycoons, 14
Industry. *See also* Postindus-
    trial society
    in Britain, 94
    in Depression Scandi-
        navia, 301–302
    in Eastern Europe, 517
    in EC, 594–595
    First World War and, 107
    in Germany, 240,
        312–313, 425–426
    Great Depression and,
        296–297
    in Italy, 315
    non-European, 624–625

in postwar Germany, 480
    in Russia, 130–131,
        317–318, 459
    in Spain, 369
Inflation
    in Austria-Hungary, 223
    in Britain, 107, 632
    in Eastern Europe, 665
    fascism and, 218, 222–223
    and First World War,
        106–107, 229
    in France, 239, 307
    in Germany, 185, 223
    in Italy, 223, 577
    in 1970s and 1980s, 625
    after Second World War,
        490
    in United States, 597
    in Weimar Republic,
        244–245
Installment buying. *See*
    Credit buying
Institute for Industrial
    Reconstruction (IRI,
    Italy), 505
Integrated circuits, 558
Intellectuals and intellectual
    thought, 37. *See also*
    Art(s)
    academic and scholarly
        worlds, 286–288
    challenges to, 643–644
    Cold War and, 538
    First World War and,
        113–116
    Freud and, 280
    on mass homogeneity,
        274–276
    pessimism in Germany,
        325–326
    Popular Front and,
        374–376
    in postwar Europe, 558
    resistance to Nazis and,
        441–443
    revolution in, 35–36
Intercontinental ballistic mis-
    siles. *See* ICBMs (inter-
    continental ballistic
    missiles)
Interest rates, U.S. funds'
    transfers and,
    597–598
Intermediate-range ballistic
    missiles. *See* IRBMs

(intermediate-range
    ballistic missiles)
International arbitration, 21
International Brigade, in
    Spanish Civil War,
    376
International Court of Arbi-
    tration, 110
International Monetary
    Fund (IMF), 496, 597
    Portugal and, 638–639
    Russia and, 661
International payments sys-
    tem, after First World
    War, 229
Internationals. *See also* spe-
    cific Internationals
    socialist, 71, 110, 361
International trade, after
    First World War, 229
International War Crimes
    Tribunal, 470
Internet. *See* World Wide Web
Interpretation of Dreams, The
    (Freud), 36
Intervention squads *(Einsatz-
    gruppen)*, 429
Invergordon Mutiny
    (Britain), 303–304
Iran, 483
    overthrow of Shah,
        623–624
    Teheran Conference in,
        463
Iraq, 84, 160, 167, 540, 543
    nationalist rebellion in,
        422
    U.S. war in, 682
IRBMs (intermediate-range
    ballistic missiles)
    arms race and, 619
    in Italy, 539
    Soviet-U.S. dismantling
        of, 656
Ireland
    in EC, 594
    England and, 62–63,
        111
    independence movement
        in, 109
    strikes in, 108, 109
IRI (Institute for Industrial
    Reconstruction), in
    Italy, 315
Irish Home Rule, 63

Iron Curtain, 481–485, 583. *See also* Cold War

Iron Guard (Romania), 341, 342, 343, 432

Isolationism, in United States, 87
retreat from, 546

Israel
Six-Day War and, 623
Suez Campaign and, 543

Italian Socialist Party, 204

Italy, 556. *See also* Communists and communism; Fascism; First World War; Mussolini, Benito
African possessions in, 388
alliances of, 389
Allied invasion of, 454
anti-immigrant resentment in, 628
aristocracy in, 14
Austria-Germany *Anschluß* and, 383–384, 392
Berlinguer and, 633–635
Catholic Church and, 336
Christian Democrats in, 494, 539
consensus politics in, 566, 568
corporatist state in, 314–315
empire of, 5
Ethiopian conquest by, 384, 387–388
fascism in, 202–210, 222, 252–254
in First World War, 76, 84–85, 102, 134, 143, 159
Fiume and, 182
Franco and, 389
government crisis in, 205–206
monarchy in, 22
national recreation agency in, 270
neutrality of, 60
peasants in, 9
politics in, 677
postwar occupation of, 483

after Second World War, 503–505
seizure of territories by, 148
Socialists and Communists in, 536–537
Spanish Civil War and, 372–373
strikes in, 62, 108
unification of, 26
unrest after First World War, 146–147
withdrawal from Second World War, 462
women's voting rights in, 21
worker protests in, 577

Ivory Coast, 596

Izvolsky, Alexander, 48–49, 53, 55

James, Henry, 7
James, William, 7
Japan. *See also* First World War; Second World War
Allied strategy against, 452
atomic bombings of, 469–470
Balkan rivalries and, 62
empire of, 6
Kellogg-Briand Pact and, 190
Manchuria and, 197, 359
manufacturing in, 624
postwar occupation of, 483
in Second World War, 450
Soviets and, 463, 465–466
Uruguay Round and, 645–646

Jaruzelsky, Wojciech, 615–616, 651, 652

Jaurès, Jean, 25, 150, 363, 364

Jazz, 282, 284

Jeanneret, Charles-Édouard. *See* Corbusier, Le (Charles-Édouard Jeanneret)

Jellicoe, John, 86, 87

Jerome, Jennie, 14

Jessner, Leopold, 284

Jesuits, in Spain, 370

Jeunesses patriotes, 217

Jews and Judaism
Blum and, 308, 363
Brandt and, 582, 601
Einstein and, 37
emigration from Poland, 615
Freud and, 37
German atrocities against, 479
Hitler on role in arts, 288–289
in Hungary, 215, 216
Mosley and, 347
nationalism and, 222
Nazi "Final Solution" for, 428–431
Nazi Party and, 213
Palestine homeland for, 160
resistance to Nazis by, 431
in Romania, 341–342
in Russia, 123

Jobs. *See also* Employment; Labor; Unemployment; Workers
in 1970s-1980s, 625

Jodl, Alfred, 386

Joffre, Joseph, 55, 74–75, 77, 78, 80, 96

John XXIII (Pope), 571–572

John Paul II (Pope), 644

Jospin, Lionel, 678

Joyce, James, 280

Juan Carlos (Spain), 636

July crisis (1914), 44–45

July Days (Russia), 123, 125

Jutland, Battle of, 86

Kádár, János, 528, 589, 614, 616–617
ouster of, 652

Kahr, Gustav von, 211–212, 214

Kaiser. *See* Wilhelm II (Germany)

Kamenev, Lev, 125, 255–256
Stalin and, 258, 318

Kandinsky, Wassily, 34, 281, 282

Kapp, Wolfgang, 211

Kapp *Putsch* (1920), 211, 240, 243, 331

Karadžić, Radovan, 671

Karl (Austria-Hungary), 101–102, 142, 216

Karlsbad Program, 397

Károlyi, Mihály, 144–145, 150, 215

Katyn Forest Massacre, 477, 649

Kellogg-Briand Pact (1928), 190

Kemal, Mustafa (Atatürk), 164, 182

Kennan, George, 318, 453
on Second World War destruction, 490

Kennedy, John F., Cuban missile crisis and, 584–586, 599

Kerensky, Aleksandr, 22, 72, 118, 123, 124, 126
flight from Russia, 127
"Kornilov affair" and, 125

Kessler, Harry, 283

Keynes, John Maynard, 3, 162, 186, 304–305, 386
Great Depression and, 300

KGB, 620, 650, 657

"Khaki election" (1918), 170, 182, 231

Khrushchev, Nikita, 318, 319, 512, 608
Cuban missile crisis and, 584–586, 599
fall of (1964), 529–530, 607
as Soviet leader, 523

Kieffer, Anselm, 570

Kienthal, socialist conference at, 111

Kierkegaard, Sören, 32

Kimmochi Saïjonji, 157n

Kingdom of Serbs, Croats, and Slovenes (Yugoslavia). *See* Yugoslavia

Kipling, Rudyard, 6

Kirchner, Ludwig, 281

Kirov, Sergei, 318

Kissinger, Henry, 592
nuclear power and, 599

Kitchener, Horatio Herbert (Lord), 113

Klaus, Václav, 665

Klee, Paul, 276, 277, 282, 283, 286

Klossowski, Balthazar (Balthus), 570

Kluck, Alexander von, 74

"Knight of the long knives" (Nazi Germany), 335

Koblenz, 169

Koestler, Arthur, 375, 378

Kohl, Helmut, 620, 630, 645, 655, 674, 677
  after unification, 666–668, 677, 678

Korea, Soviets and, 466

Korean War, 535
  Britain and, 537
  West German rearmament and, 548

Kornilov, Lavr, 125

Kosova Polje, Battle of, 671

Kosovo, Milosevic and, 618, 668, 671–672

Kosovo Liberation Army (KLA), 671–672

Kostunica, Vojislavš, 672, 673

Kraft durch Freude (Germany), 270–271

Krajina. *See* Serbian Republic of Krajina

Kreisau Circle, 439

Kristallnacht, 334

Kronstadt naval base, uprising at, 126–127, 254–255

Krupp firm, 245, 561

Kulaks, 316, 317

Kun, Béla, 145–146, 150, 163, 215, 217, 247, 288

Kurds, 483

Kurile Islands, 466

Kursk-Orel, Battle of, 457

Kutuzov, Mikhail, 459

Labor. *See also* Workers
  in Eastern Europe, 522
  First World War and, 104–105
  General Strike (Britain) and, 234–235
  immigrants and, 626–627
  in Italy, 147–148
  migration of, 562
  militancy of, 146
  peasants and, 10
  in Portugal, 252
  in Second World War, 427
  strikes and, 108–109
  women in, 95, 103

Labor Office, League of Nations and, 167

Labor unions, 24
  in Britain, 236
  First World War and, 104–105
  in France, 365–366
  in Germany, 240, 312
  in Spain, 371

Labour Party (Britain), 25, 196, 230, 231, 232–233, 537, 567–568
  economics and, 305
  first government of (1924), 232–233
  Great Depression and, 302–303
  Mosley and, 345–346, 347
  from 1945-1951, 497–500
  Popular Front and, 361–362
  Thatcher and, 632

Laissez-faire economics
  Britain and, 231
  discrediting of, 566
  fascist roots and, 220
  after First World War, 228–229, 246
  in West Germany, 601

Lampedusa, Giuseppe de, 218

Land. *See also* Farms and farming; Peasants
  in Eastern Europe, 247, 516–517
  forced collectivization of, 522
  ownership of, 9–10
  in post-World War I Italy, 147–148
  in Russia, 127–128
  in Spain, 370

Landowners, 9–10, 13–14

Land Without Justice (Djilas), 10

Language
  Foucault on, 644
  Habermas and, 644

Laos, 541

Largo Caballero, Francisco, 372

Larina, Anna, 650

La Rochelle, Pierre Drieu, 273, 431

La Rocque, François de, 344, 363, 365

Lartigue, Jacques Henri, xvi

Laslett, Peter, 16

Lateran Pact (1929), 253

Latifundia, 9, 247, 251

Latin America, 5
  economic competition from, 624, 625
  investments and, 3–4

Latvia
  independence of, 657
  Soviets and, 405, 414

Laval, Pierre, 307, 360, 362, 367, 389

Law, The (Roger), 16

Lawrence, D. H., 38, 281, 283

Lawrence, T. E., 160–161

Leadership. *See also* specific individuals
  in France, 500–502
  in postwar Europe, 492–495

League of Nations, 110
  Covenant of, 163, 164–167
  Czechoslovakia and, 401
  diplomatic machinery of, 196–197
  Germany and, 188, 382
  Haile Selassie at, 388
  mandates under, 166 (map), 166–167
  minorities and, 167
  remilitarization of Rhineland and, 386
  Soviet Union in, 197, 359
  U.S. refusal to ratify, 182

Lebanon, 543

Lebensraum, 391

Left wing. *See also* Communist parties; Communists and communism; Liberalism; Socialist parties; Socialists and socialism
  division of European, 537–538
  in Italy, 677
  Mitterrand and, 639–641
  after Popular Front, 376–378
  Third International and, 150–152

Léger, Fernand, 262, 276, 278

Legionnaires. *See* Foreign Legionnaires

Legion of the Archangel Michael (Romania), 341

Legislatures, popular control over, 23

Lehideux, François, 433

Leighton, Frederick (Lord), Royal Academy of Arts and, 37

Leisure
  effects of, 273–276
  egalitarianism and, 564–565
  mass culture and, 269–273
  organized recreation and, 270–271
  sports and, 271–272
  travel and, 272–273
  of upper class, xvi

Le Monde (Paris), 682

Lend-lease, 450
  to Soviets, 460

Lenin, V. I., 110, 111, 122, 123. *See also* Bolsheviks; Russia
  Germany and, 138
  Hungary and, 146
  on imperialism, 6
  nationalization of land by, 150
  New Economic Policy of, 255
  on party rule, 130, 257
  "peace, land, and bread" policy of, 127–128
  in Petrograd, 128
  return to Russia, 123, 125
  on spread of revolutions, 150–151
  successor to, 255
  War Communism of, 254–255

Leningrad. *See also* Petrograd
  Nazis and, 423
  in Second World War, 458, 460

Leo XIII (Pope), 220, 314, 336

Leopard, The (Lampedusa), 218

Leopold of Saxe-Coburg, 22
Le Pen, Jean-Marie, 628, 677
Leroy-Beaulieu, Paul, 71
Les Champs Magnétiques (Breton), 115
Levi, Carlo, 10
Lévi-Strauss, Claude, 573–574, 643
Liberal economics
    after First World War, 230–231
    Great Depression and, 299
Liberal Party (Britain), 13, 231, 232, 302
    in Romania, 342
Liberal politics, after First World War, 230–231
Liberals and liberalism, 27–30, 201
    bankruptcy of, 375
    fascist roots and, 220, 221
    after First World War, 245–246
    First World War and, 109–110
    and Popular Front, 360–361
    in Russian provisional government, 121–122
Liberal states, Great Depression politics in, 301–311
Liberman, Yevsei, 609n
Libermanism, 609
Libya, 5, 453
    Hitler and, 422
Liddell-Hart, Basil H., 82, 192
Liebknecht, Karl, 108, 138, 140
Life expectancy
    poverty and, 13
    in Soviet Union, 610
Lifestyle
    family size and, 18
    middle-class, 14–17
    peasant, 9–10
    urban, 7, 8–9
Lightning war. *See Blitzkrieg* (lightning war)
Lip watch factory, 577
Literacy, in Italy, 102
Literature
    in First World War, 113–114, 115

novels and, 570–571
    in Russia, 525
    science fiction, 29
    unconscious in, 280
    urban immigrants in, 8
Lithuania, 182, 183
    independence of, 657
    Poles and, 179
    Soviets and, 405, 414–415
Little Entente, 183
Little Man, What Now? (Fallada), 325
Litvinov, Maxim, 359–360, 403
    Czechoslovakia and, 400–401
    firing of, 405
Litvinov, Pavel, 614
Living conditions, in Soviet Union, 618–619
Living standards
    in Britain, 234
    in Eastern Europe, 611–612
    in East Germany, 617
    in Europe, 678
    of workers, 12–13
    in Yugoslavia, 618
Living wage policy, in Britain, 304
Ljubljana Gap (Yugoslavia), 455–456, 464
Lloyd George, David, 13, 23, 94, 95, 103, 157n, 158, 162
    "khaki election" and, 170, 179, 196, 231
    on Mussolini, 350
    on postwar world, 229
Locarno Agreements (1925), 187–191
    Hitler's remilitarization of Rhineland and, 385–386
Logical positivists, 573
Lomé Convention (1975), 596
London, 8
    poverty in, 12
    world economy and, 3
London, Treaty of (1915), 159
London Naval Conference (1930), 193
London Poles, 477–478, 518

Longuet, Jean, 358
Lorraine, 54, 55
Lotta continua movement, 577
Low, David, 374
Low Countries. *See also* Belgium; Holland; Netherlands
    fascism in, 348–349
    Nazis and, 416, 426
    Popular Front and, 362
    poverty in, 12
Lower class. *See* Class; Poverty; Workers
Lubbe, Marinus van der, 331
Lublin Committee (Poland), 478
Ludendorff, Erich, 75, 76, 81, 91, 97, 98, 135, 214
    armed forces revolt and, 137
    First World War peace and, 136
    Hitler and, 244
Luftwaffe, Battle of Britain and, 420
Lukács, Georg, 145
Lunacharsky, Anatole, 259
Lusitania (ship), 86
Lutheran churches, in Nazi Germany, 334
Luxembourg, 457
Luxemburg, Rosa, 128, 138, 140, 150, 152
Lvov, George, 121, 123
Lycée system (France), 286
Lysenko, Trofim, 514

Maastricht Treaty, 674
MacDonald, Ramsay, 73, 187, 197, 232–233, 302, 303
Macedonia, 341
    First Balkan War and, 50
Machine, aesthetic uses of, 278
Machine gun, 78
    on airplanes, 84
Macmillan, Harold, 16, 539, 540
Madariaga, Salvador de, 193
Maginot Line, 192, 413
    Munich settlement and, 398
    Nazis and, 416

Magritte, René, 280
Magyars, 141, 142, 144–145
Mainz, 169
    remilitarization of Rhineland and, 384, 385
Malenkov, Georgi, 523, 526, 584
Malraux, André, 376
Malvy, Louis, 111
Man, Henri de, 300
Manchuria, 466
    Japan and, 197, 359
    Sino-Soviet rivalries and, 587
Mandarins, Les (Beauvoir), 568
Mandates (League of Nations), 166 (map), 166–167
    independence movements and, 541
Maniu, Iuliu, 520
Mann, Thomas, 14
Mannerheim, Karl Gustav, 424
Mannheim, bombing of, 456
Mansfield, Mike, 600
Man's Hope (Malraux), 376
Manstein, Fritz Erich von, 416, 417
Manufacturing
    costs of, 625
    in First World War, 106
Manuilski, Dimitri, 359
Maoism, 587
Mao Tse-tung, 587
    student discontent and, 574
Maquis (French resistance), 438, 501
"March 22 Movement" (France), 575
Marchais, Georges, 635
Marconi, Guglielmo, 264
Margueritte, Victor, 103
Marinetti, Filippo, 35, 102, 115, 221
Market(s)
    Great Depression and, 295, 299
    imperialism and, 5
Market economy
    in Eastern Europe, 666

Market economy (*continued*)
  in Germany, 312, 507
  in Russia, 661
Marketing, after Second
    World War, 490
Marks (Germany), 244
  exchange rates and,
    597–598
Marne
  First Battle of, 73–75, 78,
    91, 96
  Second Battle of, 136
Marriage
  birth control and, 19
  family size and, 18
Marshall, George C., 457,
    484
Marshall Plan, 484, 495–496
  and Italy, 505
Marx, Karl, 16, 24, 221
Marx, Wilhelm, 245
Marxism, 25. *See also* Social-
    ists and socialism
  of Bolsheviks, 122, 123
  critique of First World
    War and, 110
  after First World War, 196
  in France, 237, 344, 502,
    537
  in Italy, 148, 537
  liberals and, 360
  Nazism and, 325
  Popular Front and, 356,
    377
  in Spain, 373
  SPD and, 567
  successes and failures of,
    149–150
  in Western Europe, 494
Masaryk, Jan, 519, 521, 526
Masaryk, Thomas, 142, 179,
    250
Mass audiences
  creation of, 264, 265–266
  for newspapers, 265
  search for, 284–286
Mass communications. *See
    also* Movies; Radio
  advertising and, 268–269
  telegraph and, 264
Mass culture, 264–269. *See
    also* Culture; Popular
    culture
  effects of, 273–276
  fine arts and, 569–571

leisure and, 269–273
in "New Europe,"
    568–569
sciences and, 573–574
Massive retaliation policy
    (U.S.), 534, 599
Mass media, 264–265
  control of, 267–268
Mass politics, fascism and, 219
Mass society, warnings
    against, 275
"Master race," Nazi concept
    of, 427
Masurian Lakes, battle at, 75
Mater et Magistra (John
    XXIII), 572
Matignon Agreements,
    365–366
Matisse, Henri, 35, 277, 281
Matteotti, Giacomo, 210
Maurras, Charles, 31, 220,
    252, 337, 343, 348
Max of Baden (Germany),
    136, 137, 138, 167
Mayakovsky, Vladimir, 285,
    289
Mazowiecki, Tadeusz, 652
McDonald's, 681
McKenna, Reginald, 94
McNamara, Robert, 599
Mead, Margaret, 575
Mečiar, Vladimir, 665, 666
Media. *See* Mass media
Mediation efforts, before
    First World War,
    52–53, 59
Mediterranean region
  Allies and, 464
  Black Sea and, 483
  Churchill and, 452
  in First World War, 84
  Hitler and, 421
  Italian conflicts of inter-
    est in, 387
  peasants in, 10
  in Second World War,
    453–454
  social welfare and conser-
    vatism in, 633–641
Medvedev, Roy, 319, 611
Medvedev, Zhores, 611
Meinecke, Friedrich, 239
Meinhof, Ulrike, 579
Mein Kampf (Hitler), 212,
    245, 382

German *Lebensraum* and,
    391
Meitner, Lise, 413
Mensheviks, 122, 125
Mental illness, understand-
    ing of, 643–644
Mesopotamia, 84
Metaphysics, 287–288
Mexico, Spanish Civil War
    and, 372
Meyerhold, Vsevelod, 285, 289
Michael (Romania), 516,
    519, 520
Michaelis, Georg, 98, 135
Michel, Henri, 416
Middle class, 10, 14–17
  constraints on, 16
  fascism and, 217, 218, 221
  inflation and, 107
  upper, 13–14
  women and, 103–104
Middle East
  after First World War,
    160–161
  oil in, 59
Mies van der Rohe, Ludwig,
    277, 571
MIG-15 jet fighter, 514
Migration. *See also* Immigrants
  of workers, 562
Mikhailović, Drasa, 440–441
Mikolajczyk, Stanislaw, 518,
    519, 520
Milhaud, Darius, 276
Militant League for German
    Culture, 288
Militarization, of Rhineland,
    188
Military. *See also* Armed forces
  civilian relations in
    France and, 96
  compulsory service in, 95
  de Gaulle and, 590
  expenditures on, 64n
  Soviet officers and,
    459–460
  Stalin and, 464
Military dictatorship, in Rus-
    sia, 124–125
Military draft. *See* Conscrip-
    tion
Miliukov, Pavel, 22, 121
Mill, John Stuart, 28, 375
Milošević, Slobodan, 665
  Serbia and, 618, 664

Yugoslav civil war and,
    668, 669, 671–673
Miners, strike by (Britain,
    1926), 234, 235
Minorities. *See also* Ethnic
    groups
  in Austria-Hungary,
    100–101
  after First World War,
    141–146, 249–250
  in Russia, 222
Minorities Commission, of
    Paris Peace Confer-
    ence, 167
Mir, 529n
Mirage fighter bombers,
    561
MIRVs (Multiple Intertar-
    getable Reentry Vehi-
    cles), 600
Missiles. *See also* Cuban mis-
    sile crisis; Nuclear
    power; Weapons
  arms race and, 619
  in Germany, 413
  levels in 1984, 602
  MLF and, 599–600
  Soviet, 514, 600
  U.S. bases in Italy, 539
Mitchell, Wesley Clair, 294
Mitteleuropa, 98, 426
Mitterrand, François,
    639–641, 645, 673
Mladić, Ratko, 671
MLF. *See* Multilateral Nuclear
    Force (MLF)
Mobilization
  for First World War, 64
  of France, 54–55
  in Germany, 98
  in Nazi Germany, 426
  of Russia, 53–54
  Serbian, 52
Moch, Jules, 537
Modernism, in arts, 278
Moldavia, 46, 340
Mollet, Guy, 537, 540, 543
Molotov, V. M., 462, 519
Moltke, Helmut von, 51, 55,
    56, 73, 74, 77, 439
Monarchy
  conservatism and, 31
  constitutional limits on, 22
  after First World War, 229
  role of, 21–22

Monetary order, after Second World War, 496
Monnet, Jean, 503, 536, 593
  European union and, 545
Monroe Doctrine, 163
  Cuban missile crisis and, 584
Montagnier, Luc, 678
Montenegro, First Balkan War and, 50
  in Yugoslavia, 673
Montesquiou, Robert de, 13
Montgomery, Bernard Law, 456
Montreux, Treaty of, 483
Moog synthesizer, 571
Moore, Henry, 570
Morgan, J. P., 303
Morgenthau, Henry, 479
Moro, Aldo, 579
Morocco, 453
  crises in, 61–62, 71
  French and German conflict over, 44
Moscow
  Allied meeting in (1943), 462
  Nazi attack on, 423–424, 457
Moscow Art Theater, 285, 289
Moscow Declaration of Peaceful Co-existence, 587, 588
Moscow Treaty (1970), 601
Mosley, Oswald, 304, 306
  fascism and, 345–348
Movies, 265, 571
  commercial nature of, 268
  Eisenstein and, 285
  expressionism in, 278
  in Great Depression, 295
  mass audience for, 265–266
  political uses of, 266–267
  talkies, 268
Movimento sociale italiano (MSI), 628
Mozambique, Portugal and, 637, 638
MRP (Mouvement républicain populaire), 494, 502, 536, 544
"Mulberries," D-Day invasion and, 455

Müller, Hermann, 71, 309–310
Multilateral negotiations, over nuclear weapons, 602
Multilateral Nuclear Force (MLF), 599–600
Multinational empires. *See also* Empires
  First World War and, 93, 159–161
Munich
  Beer Hall *Putsch* in, 185, 186, 212–213
  Hitler in, 211–212
Munich settlement, 398–400. *See also* Appeasement
Munitions of War Act (Britain), 94
Murmansk, Russian Civil War and, 131–132
Museums, 37
Music
  Beatles and, 568–569
  experimental, 277–278
  jazz and, 282, 284
  postwar, 571
  primitivism and, 281–282
  between wars, 276, 282–284
Muslims
  in Bosnia, 670
  in France, 628
Mussert, Anton Adriaan, 349, 432, 492
Mussolini, Benito, 10, 73, 200, 455. *See also* Fascism; Italy
  Austria and, 339
  break with Britain and France, 388–389
  Corfu Incident and, 209–210
  corporatist state and, 314–315
  Ethiopia and, 384
  fascism and, 202–203, 204
  France and, 367
  government crisis and, 205–206
  Greece invaded by, 422
  as head of government, 208

  Hitler and, 380
  Italian dictatorship of, 252–254
  in Italian government, 205
  march on Rome by, 206–207
  Munich settlement and, 398–399
  overthrow of, 454
  personal rule of, 208–210
  radio use by, 267
Mutual and Balanced Force Reductions (MBFR) talks, 602
Mutual security treaties, Soviet Union and, 360

Nagy, Imre, 526, 528, 652
Napoleon III (France), 8, 219
Napoleonic Code, women's roles and, 19
Napoleonic wars, 44
Nasser, Gamal Abdel, 543
National-Christian Socialism (Romania), 217
National communism, in Eastern Europe, 588
National Democratic Party (Germany), 628
National Front regimes, 516–518
  Communist replacements for, 520–521
National Government (Britain), 303–304
National Health Service (Britain), 498
National Insurance Act (Britain), 93
Nationalism, 30
  of de Gaulle, 590
  in Eastern Europe, 26–27, 150, 173–181, 518, 611–618
  fascism and, 204
  after First World War, 141–146
  Flemish, 348
  in Germany, 240–241
  Hitler and, 326
  Jews and, 222
  in Soviet republics, 657
  in Ukraine, 133–134

Nationalist Spain, 354
  Franco and, 371
Nationalities. *See also* Ethnic groups; Minorities; National minorities
  in Balkans, 45–50
  collaboration with Nazis and, 432–433
  discrimination among, 178–179
  after First World War, 176 (map)
Nationalities Statute (1920, Czechoslovakia), 397
Nationalization
  in Britain, 500, 568
  disillusionment with, 566
  in Eastern Europe, 517
  in France, 502–503
  of land, 150
National League, in Norway, 349
National Liberals (Germany), 241
National minorities. *See also* Minorities
  in Czechoslovakia, 397–398
  after First World War, 249–250
National socialism. *See also* Nazi Germany; Nazi Party
  Déat and, 306
  fascism as, 218
  in Germany, 210–214
  in Hungary, 216
  Mosley and, 306
National Socialist German Workers' Party, 310. *See also* Nazi Germany
National-Socialist League (NSB), in Holland, 349
National strike, use of term, 235
National syndicalism
  fascism as, 218
  Mussolini and, 203
  in Portugal, 338
National Union of Writers (Russia), 289
Nation-building, after First World War, 143–145
Nation-states, 21
  after First World War, 173

NATO, 485, 539, 546–548, 675
  air strikes against Bosnian Serbs, 671, 672–673, 675
  Bosnia peacekeeping force and, 673
  de Gaulle and, 590, 592
  Final Act and, 603
  MLF and, 599–600
  Poland, Hungary, and Czech Republic in, 676
  Spain in, 636
  U.S. intermediate range missiles and, 619
Nature of the Physical Universe (Eddington), 287
Naumann, Friedrich, 24
Naval race, 62
Navies
  British, 57, 59
  in First World War, 86–87
  revolt of German, 137
  Washington Naval Conference and, 193
Nazi Germany, 212–213. *See also* Germany; Hitler, Adolf; Neo-Nazism; SA stormtrooper (Nazi Germany); SS (*Schutzstaffel*, Nazi Germany)
  appeasement and, 394–397
  arts and, 288
  Austria and, 339, 382–384
  Axis and, 389
  Blitzkrieg by, 410
  collaboration with, 431–435
  Czechoslovakia invaded by, 393–394
  D-Day invasion (1944) and, 454–457
  Denmark and Norway invaded by, 416
  empire of, 424
  excesses of, 395
  expansion in east, 390 (map), 390–393
  France conquered by, 416–418
  Great Depression and, 311–313

Hitler as chancellor of, 331–335
  Italy and, 387, 388–389
  Jews murdered by, 428–431
  Lebensraum and, 391
  from 1929 to 1932, 324–326
  occupied people and, 427–428
  Pius XI and, 336–337
  Poland attacked by, 402–406
  Quisling and, 349
  radio use by, 266
  resistance to, 435–443
  resistance to Hitler within, 438–440
  Soviet Union invaded by, 422–424
  Spanish Civil War and, 373
  speed as war tactic, 412–413
  war economy of, 426–427
  Young Plan and, 191
Nazi Party, in Austria, 383
Nazi Seizure of Power, The: . . . . (Allen), 326
Nazi-Soviet Pact (1939), 403–406, 415, 650, 657
Near East, after First World War, 160
Nenni, Pietro, 537, 539, 568
Neocapitalism, 558
Neoliberalism
  assessment of, 259
  in Britain, 233
  after First World War, 229–231
  war governments and, 228–229
Neo-Nazism, 628
Nervi, Pier Luigi, 571
Netherlands, OPEC boycott against, 641. *See also* Holland
Neurath, Konstantin von, 334–335, 382
Neutrality, of Italy, 60
Neutrality Acts (U.S.), 412
New Economic Policy (NEP), in Russia, 255, 256

New Middle, in Western Europe, 676–678
"New Order," of Hitler, 424–431, 425 (map)
"New poor," 107, 108, 659
New Right
  immigrants and, 626–628
  in late 1980s, 645
  Maurras and, 252
Newspapers
  advertising in, 269
  control of, 268
  mass audiences for, 265
Newton, Isaac, 28
  solar system of, 33
New Zealand, 21, 230
Nicholas II (Russia), 99, 100
  February Revolution and, 120–121
  murder of, 121n
  "Nicky"-"Willy" correspondence, 54
  "Nicky"-"Willy" correspondence, 54
Nicolson, Arthur, 53
Nicolson, Harold, 193
Niemöller, Martin, 439
Nietzsche, Friedrich, 32
Nigeria, 5
Nine, the, 641
1984 (Orwell), 499
Nivelle, Robert, 79, 80–81, 96
Nixon, Richard
  exchange system and, 598
  Romania and, 589
  SALT I and, 600
Nizan, Paul, 375
Nobel Prize
  to Böll, 571
  to Gorbachev, 651
  in Medicine and Physiology, 573
  to Pasternak, 525
Nobility, 14, 15
Nomenklatura, 608
Nonaggression pact, Germany-Poland, 382
Nono, Luigi, 571
Nonpartisan Bloc for Cooperation with the Government (Poland), 250
"Normalcy"
  in Britain, 233–236
  in fascist Italy, 253–254

in France, 238–239
  in 1920s, 228–231
Normandy. *See* D-Day (1944)
North Africa
  Churchill and, 452
  Hitler and, 422
  second front in, 453–454
North Atlantic, Allied shipping in, 454
North Atlantic Treaty Organization (NATO). *See* NATO
Northcliffe, Lord. *See* Harmsworth, Alfred (Lord Northcliffe)
Northern Europe, conservatism and welfare state in, 629–633
Northern Ireland, England and, 62–63
Northern League (Italy), 677
North Pole, 6
"North-South dialogue," 596
Norway. *See also* Scandinavia
  collaboration cases in, 492
  Depression politics in, 301
  German occupation of, 349
  Nazi invasion of, 416
  oil in, 626
  Third International and, 152
Noske, Gustav, 140, 211
Not by Bread Alone (Dudintsev), 525
Nouveau riche, 15
Novels, 570–571
Novotný, Antonín, 612
Nuclear physics, in Germany, 413. *See also* Atomic physics
Nuclear power, 558. *See also* Atomic bomb; Missiles; Weapons
  arms race and, 619
  Chernobyl accident and, 650
  Cuban missile crisis and, 584
  development of, 573
  as energy source, 626
  Europe under threat of, 534–535

in France, 590
graduated deterrence
policy and, 599
missile levels in 1984,
602
parity in, 619
protests against weapons
in Europe, 619
Soviet bomb and, 514
U.S. and, 599
weapons cuts, 656
Nuclear Test Ban Treaty
(1963), 586
Sino-Soviet disagreement
over, 587
Nuremberg
Nazi rally at (1934),
332–333
Party Rally (1938), 398
trials in, 386

Occupation policy, of Hitler,
427–428
Occupation zones, 553
in Germany, 468,
479–480, 505–508
after Second World War,
483
Ocean liners, 273
October Revolution (Rus-
sia), 125–127
Habsburgs and, 142
Oder-Neisse line, 477, 478
Odessa, 84
Russian Civil War and, 132
OEEC. *See* Organization for
European Economic
Cooperation (OEEC)
Oil
First World War and, 59
in Iran, 483
Oil crisis (1973), 579,
623–624, 641–642. *See
also* OPEC (Organiza-
tion of Petroleum-
Exporting Countries)
economy and, 624
Oligarchs, in Russia, 662, 664
Olive Tree Coalition, 677
Olivetti, Arrigo, 561
Olympics, in 1936 Berlin,
272
*One Day in the Life of Ivan
Denisovich* (Solzhenit-
syn), 525

On Liberty (Mill), 28
OPEC (Organization of
Petroleum-Exporting
Countries), 623–624,
641–642
Operation Barbarossa, 421,
422, 460
Operation OVERLORD, 464
Operation TORCH, 453
Opposition, to First World
War, 109–111
Opus dei movement, 539
Orban, Viktor, 666
Ordre nouveau, 628
Orff, Carl, 571
Organization for European
Economic Coopera-
tion (OEEC),
495–496, 545, 549
Organized labor. *See* Labor
unions
Organized recreation,
270–271
Organized religion. *See* Reli-
gion
Orlando, Vittorio Emanuele,
157n
Ortega y Gasset, José, 275
Orwell, George, 295, 499,
534
"Ossies" (East Germans),
666, 667
Osthilfe (relief fund), 309
Ostpolitik (eastern policy),
582, 601, 630
Ottoman Empire, 26–27
Balkans and, 46
First World War and, 93
Ottoman Turkey, after First
World War, 160
Otto of Bavaria, 22
OVERLORD. *See* Operation
OVERLORD
Owen, Wilfred, 114, 115

Pacem in Terris (John XXIII),
572
Pacific 231 (Honegger), 278
Pacific region, European
trade with, 596
Pacifism
appeasement of Hitler
and, 396
in Britain, 73
First World War and, 70

"Pact of Steel," between Italy
and Germany, 389
Painting, 276
abstract, 34
experimental, 277
primitivism and, 282
revolution in, 34–35
surrealist, 280
after World War II, 570
Pakistan, 541
Palacký, František, 26
Pale of Settlement, 123
Paléologue, Maurice, 55
Palestine
after First World War, 160
Jewish state in, 543
Palme, Olaf, 630
Pamyat movement, 662
Pan-African Congress, 161
Pan-Germans, 27, 393
Pankhurst, Emmeline, 21
Pan-Slavs, 27
Pan-Turanians, 27
Panzers, 410, 414
fall of France and, 416–418
Papacy. *See also* Catholic
Church; specific
popes
Italy and, 253, 314
postwar, 571–572
Papal States, 336
Papandreou, Andreas, 641
Papen, Franz von, 311, 326,
327, 328–329, 330,
331, 382
Paramilitary, in Austria, 338.
See also SA
Stormtroopers
Paris, 8
aesthetics in, 34
École des Beaux Arts in, 37
First Battle of the Marne
and, 74
interwar culture in, 282
Popular Front in, 357
World's Fair in (1900), 9
Paris Accords (1990), 656
Paris Commune (1871), 24
Paris May (1968), 575–576
Paris peace settlement
(1919), 148, 157–197
application of, 181–193
dismantlement of,
381–407
terms of, 164

Parliament(s). *See also* spe-
cific parliaments
Council of Europe as, 549
direct election of lower
houses, 23
in Eastern Europe, 664
role of, 22–24
in Russia, 661
Parliamentary democracies
in Eastern Europe, 246
after First World War, 230
Parti populaire Français, 344
Parti social Français, 345, 365
Party of Racial Defense
(Hungary), 216
Party of the Democratic Left
(PDS), in Italy, 677
Party system, three-way sys-
tem in Britain,
231–232
Pašić, Nicholas, 47
PASOK (Pan-Hellenic Social-
ist Movement), in
Greece, 641
Passchendaele, 452
battle at, 82
Pasternak, Boris, 514
Dr. Zhivago, 525
Patton, George S., 456
Pauker, Anna, 521
Paul VI (Pope), 572
Paulus, Friedrich, 458
Pavelič, Ante, 432
Peace. *See also* Paris peace
settlement (1919)
after First World War, 136
Lenin on, 127–128
Peace aims
of Soviet Union, 471–472
of United States, 472–475
Peaceful coexistence, 584–586
Peacekeeping force, in
Bosnia, 671, 673
Peace of Riga, 133
"Peace Resolution" (1917),
98–99, 135
Peary, Robert, 6
Peasant Party (Poland),
248
Peasants
in Bulgaria, 248
in Eastern Europe,
246–249
fascism and, 340–341
lifestyle of, 9–10

Peasants *(continued)*
  revolution and, 150
  in Romania, 247, 341,
    516–517
  in Russia, 128, 254, 256,
    316, 317
  Russian Civil War and,
    131
  in Spain, 251, 369, 371
Péguy, Charles, 113, 114
Peoples' Democracies, in
    Eastern Europe,
    521–522
People's Party (Germany),
    241, 243
Perestroika (restructuring),
    650–651
Pershing missiles, 619
Persian Gulf, in First World
    War, 84
Pessimism, and fascism, 221
  in Germany, 325–326
Pétain, Philippe, 80
    Vichy French government
      of, 418, 424, 431, 433
Petkov, Nikolaj, 520
Petőfi Circle (Budapest),
    527–528
Petrograd
    demonstrations in
      (1917), 118, 120, 123
    as Leningrad, 258
    Lenin in, 128
    soviets in, 121, 125, 126
Peugeot automobiles, 561
Philosophes, 28
Philosophy, between wars,
    287–288
  Postwar, 573
"Phony war," 415
Physics, 33, 573
    nuclear, in Germany, 413
    revolution in, 286–287
Picasso, Pablo, 35, 277, 281,
    282, 375
Pickles, Wilfrid, 549
"Pig War," 47
Pilsudski, Josef, 160, 178, 250
Pirelli, Alberto, 315
Pirelli tire factory, 577
Piscator, Erwin, 284–285
Pius X (Pope), 220
Pius XI (Pope), 336
Pius XII (Pope), 571
Pivert, Marceau, 368
Planck, Max, 33

Planned economies
  in Britain, 568
  confidence in, 565–566
  in France, 502–503
  in Italy, 314–315
Plebiscites, 180
  after First World War, 168
Pleven, René, 548
"Poem for Adults" (Wazyk),
    527
Poets and poetry
  in First World War,
    113–114, 115
  in Russia, 285
Poincaré, Raymond, 52, 53,
    54, 55, 56, 182,
    184–185, 186,
    238–239
Poison gas
  First World War, 78, 79,
    82, 83
  in Italian Empire, 169,
    388, 395, 413
Poland, 9, 150, 183. *See also*
    First World War; Sec-
    ond World War
  Blitzkrieg and, 414
  Cold War and, 476–478
  communism in, 516, 589
  Czechoslovakia and, 401
  economy of, 665
  after First World War,
    160, 246
  in First World War, 75
  German invasion of,
    402–406
  German nonaggression
    pact with, 382
  in Italian campaign, 454
  Katyn Forest massacre
    and, 477, 650
  land and nationalism in,
    518
  nationalism in, 141–142,
    143
  in NATO, 546n
  Nazi occupation of, 427
  openness in, 526–527
  Pilsudski in, 250
  planning for postwar,
    463
  plans for dividing, 405
  Poles in exile and, 477
  postwar government of,
    477
  revolt in, 535

Russian Civil War and,
    133
Russian Provisional Gov-
    ernment and, 123
after Second World War,
    476–478
Solidarity movement in,
    615–616, 651–652
Soviet frontier with,
    476–477
Soviets and, 405, 458,
    464, 467, 518–519
surrender to Nazis, 414
Walesa and, 664, 666
West Germany and, 582
Poles, 46, 178, 179
Police power, in First World
    War, 111–112
Polish Corridor, 177 (map),
    179, 187
Polish-Russian War (1920),
    181
Political demonstrations
  right-wing, in France,
    344–345
  in Russia, 118, 120–121,
    123
Political parties. *See also* Party
    system; specific par-
    ties and leaders
  in Depression Scandi-
    navia, 301
  after Second World War,
    492–495
  in unified Germany, 668
  in Weimar Germany, 327
Political philosophy. *See also*
    Political systems; spe-
    cific philosophies
  conservatism, 30–31
  liberalism, 27–30
Political systems, 21–27. *See
    also* specific systems
  monarchy and, 21–22
  parliaments, 22–24
  socialist movement and,
    24–26
Politics. *See also* specific
    countries, parties, and
    groups
  in Britain, 302–306
  consensus in, 566–568
  after First World War,
    230–231
  in France, 306–309
  in Italy, 314–315, 503–505

in liberal states during
    Great Depression,
    301–311
popes and, 336–337
in Portugal (1975), 638
in present Western
    Europe, 676–678
radio, movies, and,
    266–267
in Scandinavia, 301–302
in Weimar Germany, 186
women and, 21, 230
Pollution. *See also* Ecology
  in Soviet Union, 610
Polycentrism, in Communist
    world, 586–589
Pompidou, Georges, 639
Popes
  Benedict XV, 134
  John XXIII, 571–572
  John Paul II, 644
  Leo XIII, 220, 314, 336
  Paul VI, 572
  Pius X, 220
  Pius XI, 336
  Pius XII, 571
Popolari movement, 147, 148,
    206
Popolo d'Italia, Il (newspa-
    per), 203, 204
Popular culture. *See also* Cul-
    ture; Mass culture
  arts and, 284
  Beatles and, 568–569
  education and, 286
  homogeneity and,
    274–275
  in "New Europe," 568–569
Popular Front. *See also* Blum,
    Léon
  as anti-fascist alliance,
    356
  era of (1934-1939),
    355–378
  in France, 308, 344, 345,
    356–357, 362–368
  intellectual thought and,
    374–376
  left wing after, 376–378
  liberal reaction to,
    360–361
  Socialists and, 361–362
  in Spain, 367–368, 369,
    371–372, 372, 373
Popular press. *See*
    Newspapers

Popular sovereignty, nationalism and, 26
Population(s), 450
  demography and, 18
  European, 1–2
  of European cities, 7
  homogeneity of, 273–274
  of Soviet Union, 459
Porsche, Ferdinand, 313
Portugal. *See also* specific leaders
  in anti-Communist alliance, 539
  colonies of, 540
  communism and, 635
  democracy in, 637–639
  dictatorship in, 635–636
  in EC, 594, 639
  fascism in, 337–338
  after First World War, 250–251, 252
  military junta in, 224
  neutrality of, 424
  western alliance and, 539
  women's suffrage in, 21, 230
Positivism, 31
Postal service, airmail, 273
Postindustrial society, 623–624, 626
Poststructuralists, 643, 644
Postwar Europe. *See also* Europe; First World War; Second World War
  Allied planning for, 461–470
Potsdam Conference (1945), 463, 469–470
  German reparations and, 480
Poulenc, Francis, 284
POUM, in Spain, 373
Pound (Britain), 499
  devaluation of, 304, 306, 475
Pound, Ezra, 376
Poverty, 12–13
  After First World War, 195
  after Second World War, 558, 562
  First World War and, 107, 108
  in Great Depression, 295
Powell, Enoch, 627

Prague, Nazi occupation of, 400
Presidium, 524, 604
Press. *See* Newspapers
Prester John, 4n
Preuss, Hugo, 230, 241
Prices. *See also* Inflation
  Hitler and, 312
  labor-management relations and, 577–578
  in Russia, 659
Price supports, U.S.-European rivalry and, 596
Pride and Prejudice (Austen), 19
Primary education, 563
Primitive instincts, arts and, 281–282
Primitive peoples, Lévi-Strauss on, 573–574
Primo de Rivera, José Antonio, 224, 340, 371
Primo de Rivera, Miguel, 251–252, 368–369
Princip, Gavrilo, 44, 45, 50
Prisoners of war, as Nazi labor, 427
Privatization
  in Russia, 659
  in former Soviet areas, 659, 664, 665
Prodi, Romano, 675, 677
Production, 317
  in Austria-Hungary, 101
  in Britain, 94, 632
  in France, 95
  in Germany, 97
  national, 560
  after Second World War, 490
Profiteers, in First World War, 106
Prokofiev, Sergei, 514
Proletarian hundreds (Germany), 243
Proletariat, in Russia, 130
Pronunciamientos (coups), in Iberian Peninsula, 251
Propaganda
  in European blocs, 553
  by Nazi Germany, 432
Prosperity. *See also* Consumer society
  consumer societies and, 559–565
  in Europe (1920s), 229

after Second World War, 557–559
  in Western Europe, 227
Protective tariffs. *See also* Tariffs
  in Britain, 304
"Protectorate of Bohemia-Moravia," 400
Protestantism
  in Nazi Germany, 334
  postwar, 572
Protest movements. *See also* Discontent; Revolt(s)
  in Italy, 147
Proust, Marcel, 13, 36, 280
Provisional Government, in Russia, 121–125
Prussia, 177. *See also* Germany
  aristocracy in, 13–14
Prussian wars, 44
Psychoanalysis, 280, 287
  Freud and, 36
Psychological warfare, in Second World War, 413
Public education, 28, 286
Public involvement, in foreign affairs, 193–196
Public opinion, First World War control of, 111–113
Purchasing power, First World War and, 107
Purges
  Communist, 151, 318, 514–515, 521
  of Nazi collaborators, 435, 492
Putin, Vladimir, 664
Pygmalion (Shaw), 11

Quadragesimo Anno, 336, 339
Quantum theory, 33
Quisling, Vidkun, 349, 432, 492

Race and racism, immigration and, 628
Radić, Stjepan, 179, 248, 249
Radical Catholics. *See Popolari* movement
Radicalism
  fascism and, 204
  terrorism and, 579
Radical parties
  in France, 236, 237–238, 306–307

in Spain, 370
  Popular front and, 360–361, 370
Radio, 558
  advertising on, 269
  control of, 267–268
  Grundig and, 561
  homogeneity of populations and, 274
  impact of, 264–265
  mass audience for, 265–266
  politicians and, 233, 266–267
Radio Free Europe, 553
Radziwill family (Poland), 9
Railroads, First World War, 64, 93–94
Rajk, László, 521
Rákosi, Mátyás, 526
Ramadier, Paul, 536
Rapacki Plan, 553
Rapallo, Treaty of, 184, 196, 359
Rasputin, Grigori, 99, 100
Rathenau, Walther, 97, 106, 172, 183–184, 241, 243
Rationing
  in World War I, 94, 95
  in World War II, 412, 490, 499
Rauschning, Hermann, 218
Reagan, Ronald
  Cold War and, 620
  Gorbachev and, 656
  Thatcher, Margaret, and, 632–633
Rearmament
  in Germany, 192, 312
  of West Germany, 548
Reason, 28
  irrationality and, 36
Recession
  of 1966 and 1967, 557, 558
  in 1970s, 641–642, 645
Reconstruction of Europe (1945–1953), 489–509
  loan for France, 536
  of postwar Italy, 505
  in Soviet Union, 508–509
Recovery (after Second World War), 475
  Marshall Plan and, 484

Recovery *(continued)*
  postwar prosperity and,
    557–559
Recreation. *See also* Leisure
  organized, 270–271
Red and the Black, The (Stend-
  hal), 8
Red Army, 150, 468
  communism imposed by,
    476
  in Poland, 478
  Russian Civil War and,
    131, 133
Red Army Faction, 579
Red Baron. *See* Richthofen,
  Manfred von ("Red
  Baron")
Red Brigades (Italy), 579
"Red Front" (Aragon), 358
Red Guards, 125
Red Terror, of Szamuelly,
  145
"Red Week" (Italy), 62
Reforms. *See also* specific
  reforms and countries
  in Spain, 370
Regional separatism, Ger-
  many and, 140
  Spain and, 369
Reich. *See* Nazi Germany
Reich, Wilhelm, 280
Reichsmark, 245
Reichsrat, 230
Reichstag (Germany), 22, 25,
  230
  burning of (1933), 331
  election of 1930 and, 324
  elections between 1930
    and 1933, 327, 328
  Hitler addressing, 322
Reinhardt, Max, 284
Reith, John, 268
Relativity theory (Einstein),
  33, 287
Relief fund, in Germany, 309
Religion. *See also* specific religions
  in Balkans, 49
  decline in, 644–645
  in Eastern Europe, 249
  organized, 31–32
  postwar revival in,
    571–572
  resistance to Nazis and,
    441–442

Remagen, 457
Remarque, Erich Maria, 79,
  106, 114, 288
Remembrance of Things Past
  (Proust), 13, 36, 280
Remilitarization, of
  Rhineland, 384–387
Renault, Louis, 433
Rent controls, in First World
  War Britain, 94
Rentenmark, 244
Reparations, 186
  Dawes Plan and, 188
  after First World War,
    170–172
  Great Depression and,
    297
  moratorium on, 298
  for postwar Germany,
    480–481
  after Second World War,
    508
  Stresemann and, 187
  Young Plan and, 191
Reparations Commission,
  U.S. and, 171
Republic(s). *See also* specific
  republics
  after First World War,
    229–230
  in former Soviet Union,
    662–663
  among Great Powers,
    21–22
  Greece as, 246
  in Portugal, 252
Republicanism, 22
Republicans, in Spain, 354
Republic of Carnaro, 148
Republic of Salò, Mussolini
  and, 455
Republikaner (Germany), 677
Rerum Novarum, 314, 336
Resettlement, of Jews,
  428–429
Resistance to Nazis, 435–443
  French *maquis* and, 438,
    501
  intellectual impact of,
    441–443
  military impact of,
    440–441
  Tito and, 492, 493
Resorts, leisure travel and,
  273

Resources, in Depression
  Scandinavia, 301
Revisionist historians, on Second World War, 406
Revolt(s). *See also* Revolu-
  tion(s)
  in Eastern Europe, 535
Revolt of the Masses, The
  (Ortega y Gasset), 275
Revolution(s)
  communism and, 196
  cultural, 32–38
  of 1848, 24
  fascism as counterrevolu-
    tion, 201–202
  in Germany (1918-1919),
    136–140
  of 1989, 649–664
  in Russia (1917), 119,
    120–127
  successes and failures of,
    149–152
  in western Europe
    (1917), 134–136
Rexist movement (Belgium),
  348–349
Reynaud, Paul, 418
Rhineland, 162
  demilitarization of,
    168–169
  after First World War, 167
  Franco-German relations
    over, 188–190
  remilitarization of,
    384–387
Ribbentrop, Joachim von,
  335, 403, 404
Richthofen, Manfred von
  ("Red Baron"), 84
Riefenstahl, Leni, 267, 332
Right wing. *See also* Conser-
  vatism; Fascism
  anti-immigrant resent-
    ment in, 628
  in Spain, 370
Rijeka. *See* Fiume
Riots
  by students, 575
  during World War I, 134
*Rise and Fall of the City of
  Mahagonny, The*
  (Weill), 284
Ritter von Epp, Franz X.,
  211, 213
Robbe-Grillet, Alain, 570

Robinson, John, 572
Robinson, Ronald, 6
Rockets
  postwar development of,
    573
  V2's, 464
Röhm, Ernst, 213, 214, 223,
  335
Rokossovsky, Konstantin, 519
Rolland, Romain, 70
Romains, Jules, 70, 80, 106
Romania, 50, 150, 159, 179,
  462, 464
  Bessarabia and, 43, 163,
    179, 342, 415
  Ceausescu in, 617–618,
    654
  communism in, 516
  Czechoslovakia and, 401
  economy of, 665
  fascism in, 217, 341–343
  First World War and, 86
  formation of, 46
  land redistribution in,
    516–517
  Little Entente and, 183
  Nazis and, 432
  neighbors of, 342
  as parliamentary democ-
    racy, 246
  partial independence of,
    588–589
  peasant uprising in, 247
  Second World War and,
    424
  Soviet control in, 519
Rome, 8
  Mussolini's march on,
    206–207
  Treaty of, 593
Rome-Berlin "Axis," 389
Rommel, Erwin, 422, 453
Röntgen, Wilhelm, 32
Roosevelt, Franklin D., 461
  Arcadia meeting and,
    451–452
  Atlantic Charter and, 450
  "cash and carry" policy
    of, 412
  Second World War and,
    450
  Stalin and, 463
  at Teheran, 463–464
  at Yalta, 465–469
Rosenberg, Alfred, 213, 288

Rosenkavalier, Der (Strauss), 37
Rossoni, Edmondo, 315
Rostov-on-Don, 423
Rousseau, Henri, 35
Rowntree, Seebohm, 12, 562
Royal Academy of Arts
  (England), 37
Royal Air Force, Battle of
  Britain and, 418, 420
Royalty
  after First World War, 229
  relationships in Europe,
    54n
Ruhr region, French occupa-
  tion of, 171, 172,
  184–185, 243
Runciman (Lord), 93
Rural areas, 9–10. *See also*
  Agrarian regions
  discontents in, 578
  after First World War,
    246–249
Russell, Bertrand, 30, 573
Russia, 47. *See also* First World
  War; Russian Repub-
  lic; Soviet Union
  Allied intervention in,
    128, 131–133
  arts in, 289
  attitude toward First
    World War in, 70, 73
  Austria, Serbia, and, 51
  Austria-Hungary and, 48
  autocracy in, 22, 129–130
  Balkans and, 46
  Britain and, 59
  civil war in, 131–134
  as counterweight to Ger-
    many, 367
  economy of, 254,
    659–660
  empire of, 5
  exiles in arts, 281–282
  famine in (1921), 129;
    (1930–33), 316
  before and after First
    World War, 161, 174
    (map)
  First World War and, 75,
    76–77, 84, 93, 99–100,
    124, 128, 131
  foreign relations of,
    662–664
  France and, 54
  German ultimatum to, 56

Germany and, 55, 56
  government of, 660–662
  imperial family murdered
    in, 121n
  Japan and, 6
  military dictatorship in,
    124–125
  minorities in, 222
  mobilization of, 53–54, 64
  monarchy in, 22
  nationalism in, 46
  nationalization of land
    in, 150
  October Revolution in,
    125–127
  Ottoman Empire and, 46
  peasants in, 9, 10
  Provisional Government
    in, 121–125
  rearmament program of,
    51
  reforms in, 24
  revolutionary arts in, 285
  Romania and, 342
  separate peace and, 159
  Serbia and, 664
  socialist opposition to war
    in, 110
  socialists in, 72
  after Soviet collapse,
    658–664, 659–664
  strikes in, 108
  in 20th century, 472–473
    (map)
Russian Federation, 664
Russian Republic, 658
Russian Revolution (1905), 62
Russian Revolutions (1917),
  111, 115–116, 119,
  120–127
  anniversary of, 606
  Austria-Hungary and,
    142, 143
  First World War peace
    settlement and, 158
Russians, in Soviet Union, 610
Russo-Finnish "winter war,"
  415, 416
Russo-Japanese War, 48
Russo-Polish War (1920), 163
Ruthenian people, 163, 520
Rutherford, Ernest, 33

Saar region, 168
  Hitler and, 382, 386

Saint-Cyr military school
  (France), 73, 74, 106
Saint Germain, Treaty of,
  164, 338
St. Petersburg. *See also* Petro-
  grad
  as Petrograd, 120n
Saint-Pierre, Abbé de, 544
Sakhalin, 466
Sakharov, Andrei, 610–611,
  650
Salandra, Antonio, 102,
  146–147, 208, 209
Salazar, Antonio Oliveira,
  252, 337–338
  western alliance and,
    539
Salome (Strauss), 37
Salon (Society of French
  Artists), 37
Salonika, 77
SALT agreements, 586, 600,
  602
  Brezhnev and, 619
Samizdat, 610
Samuel, Herbert, 234
Sanctions
  after First World War,
    164–166
  against Germany,
    400–401
  against Italy, 417
Santos, Antonio dos, 638
Sarajevo
  Franz Ferdinand mur-
    dered in, 44
  war in, 670
Sarrault, Albert, 386
Sarraute, Natalie, 570
Sartre, Jean-Paul, 30, 275,
  442–443, 538, 568
Sassoon, Siegfried, 115
SA stormtroopers (Nazi Ger-
  many), 212, 213, 326,
  328, 335
  Kristallnacht and, 334
Satellite states, in Eastern
  Europe, 515–522, 649,
  651
Satie, Eric, 283
Saudi Arabia, 160
Savage Mind, The (Lévi-
  Strauss), 574
Sazonov, Sergei, 53, 54, 55,
  56, 63

Scala mobile, 577
Scandinavia
  fascism in, 349
  Great Depression politics
    in, 301–302
  Popular Front and, 362
  prosperity in, 558
  welfare system and con-
    servatism in, 629–630
Scapa Flow, 86
Schacht, Hjalmar, 243, 244,
  312, 391
Scharnhorst (ship), 86
Scheer, Reinhard, 86
Scheidemann, Philip, 138,
  181
Schlageter, Leo, 243
Schleicher, Kurt von, 327,
  329, 335
Schleswig, 177 (map)
Schleswig-Holstein, Nazis in,
  324–325
Schleyer, Hanns-Martin, 579
Schlieffen, Alfred von, 56, 71
Schlieffen Plan, 56–57, 57
  (map), 64, 73
  First Battle of the Marne
    and, 74
  Second World War and,
    416
Schmidt, Helmut, 619, 630
Schoenberg, Arnold, 277–278
Schönerer, Georg von, 31,
  221, 393
Schorske, Carl, 38
Schroeder, Gerhard, 668, 678
Schubert, Karl von, 191
  (illus.)
Schumacher, Kurt, 567
Schuman, Robert, 550
  European union and, 544
Schuman Plan, 550
Schuschnigg, Kurt, 339–340,
  383, 384
  Anschluß and, 392
Science and scientists, 7. *See
  also* Nuclear power;
  Physics; Technology;
  specific scientists
  postwar achievements,
    573–574
  revolution in, 32–33
  in Second World War,
    413
  between wars, 286–287

Science fiction, 29
Scotland, Clydeside area of, 119, 146
Scouting, 273
Secondary education, 286, 563–564
Second Balkan War, 50
Second Battle of the Marne, 136
Second Front (Second World War), 451–453
  in North Africa and Italy, 453–454
Second (Socialist) International, 110, 361
Second Republic (Spain), 368–372
  political phases of, 369–372
Second Sex, The (Beauvoir), 495
Second World War. *See also*
    Cold War; Eastern
    Europe; Hitler, Adolf;
    Nazi Germany; West-
    ern Europe; specific
    leaders and battles
  Allies in, 412–413
  Axis defeat in, 451 (map)
  Big Three planning for
    Europe, 461–470
  blocs after, 481–485
  British economy and, 499
  casualties in, 489–490
  Cold War and, 470–476
  collaboration with Nazis
    in, 431–435
  D-Day invasion (1944)
    and, 454–457
  in East (1939-1940), 414–415
  in East (1941-1942), 421–424
  Eastern and Western
    fronts in, 467 (map)
  end of British empire
    and, 419
  Germany after, 478–481, 482 (map)
  Hitler's "New Order" and, 424–431, 425 (map)
  Italy after, 503–505
  Jews and, 428–431
  in 1939, 412–413
  origins of, 406–407

reconstruction after, 492–497
resistance to Nazis in, 435–443
Second Front in, 451–453
Spanish Civil War and, 374
Stalingrad as turning
    point, 458
strategies in, 411, 450–451
territorial adjustments
    after (1945), 474 (map)
United States hegemony
    in West and, 450–457
  in West (1940), 415–421
Secret police, in Soviet
    Union, 514–515, 620, 650
  in East Germany, 617
Secret treaties, in First World
    War, 134, 158, 159, 161
Security. *See also* Mutual secu-
    rity treaties
  of France, 161–162
  Franco-German issues
    (1920-1940), 189 (map)
Sedan, size of force at, 78
Seeckt, Hans von, 211, 212, 243, 244
Seipel, Ignaz, 338
Selassie. *See* Haile Selassie
Self-determination, 181. *See
    also* Nationalism
  colonial independence
    movements and, 540
  in Danube region, 141
  in Eastern Europe, 172–181
  in Ukraine, 133–134
Sembat, Marcel, 104
Senegal, 596
Serbia, 178
  Austria-Hungary and, 46, 52–53
  First Balkan War and, 50
  First World War and, 77
  Franz Ferdinand and, 45
  Germany and, 55
  as Great Power threat, 47
  independence of, 46
  Milošević and, 618, 664, 668

Russian mobilization and, 53–54
  socialists in, 72
  war declaration against, 53
Serbian Republic of Krajina, 669, 671
Serbs, 47, 668–673
Serrati, Giacinto, 148n, 151
Servan-Schreiber, Jean-
    Jacques, 597
Servants, middle class and, 15–16
Settlement, imperialism
    and, 5
Sevastopol, 84
Seven Provinces (ship), mutiny
    on, 349
Seventeenth Communist
    Party Congress
    (1934), 359
Seventh World Congress of
    the Communist
    International
    (Comintern), 360
Sèvres, Treaty of, 164
Sex and sexuality
  artistic treatments of, 280–281
  Freud and, 36, 280
Seyss-Inquart, Arthur, 392
Shah of Iran, overthrow of, 623–624
Shaw, George Bernard, 11
Ships and shipping. *See also*
    Navies
  Dreadnoughts and, 57
  in First World War, 84, 86–87
  limitations on, 193
Shonfield, Andrew, 558
Show trials, in Soviet Union, 318
Siberia, 466
  Russian Civil War in, 132
Sicily, missiles in, 619
"Sick man of Europe." *See
    also* Ottoman Empire
  Ottoman Empire as, 46
Sikorski, Wladyslaw, 477
Silesia, 175–177, 177 (map), 179, 180
Sima, Horia, 343
Single European Act (1986), 645, 673

Sinkiang frontier, 587
Sino-Soviet split, 586–588
Sinyavsky, Andrei, 610
Six, the (Common Market), 551, 593
  U.S. and, 596–597
"Six, The" (French com-
    posers), 282–283, 284
Six-Day War (1973), 623
Sixth Comintern Congress, 357
Skinheads, 628
Slade School of Fine Arts
    (England), 37
Slanský, Rudolph, 521
Slavic peoples
  after First World War, 160
  nationalism among, 27
  Nazi treatment of, 427
  self-determination and, 141
  as *Untermenschen*, 459
Slovakia, 179, 665
Slovaks, 46, 178, 180–181
  collaboration with Nazis
    by, 432
  in Czechoslovakia, 145, 400
  secession from Czecho-
    slovakia, 665
Slovenia, 668
Slums, 8, 12
  slum clearance in Britain, 304
Smallholders' Party (Hun-
    gary), 248
Smart missiles, 676
Smith, Adam, 29
Snowden, Philip, 73, 302, 303, 304
Soares, Mario, 638
Soccer, 271–272
Social art, 278
Social change, after Second
    World War, 495–497
Social class. *See* Class
Social Democrats
  in Austria, 25, 338, 339
  Czech, 517
  in East Germany, 507
  in Germany, 62, 71, 211, 241, 331–332
  in Russia, 122
  in Scandinavia, 301

Stalin and, 358
in Sweden, 629–630
in West Germany (SPD),
538, 567, 601, 630
Socialist economics, 299–300
Socialist International. *See*
Second (Socialist)
International
Socialist parties. *See also* Popular Front
after First World War,
230
in France, 237–238, 308,
344, 540, 635,
639–641
in Italy, 204, 568, 635
in Norway, 349
in Spain, 372
Socialist Revolutionaries (SRs)
in Russia, 122, 130
Socialist Unity Party (East
Germany), 506–507
Socialists and socialism,
24–26, 201–202. *See
also* Communists and
communism; Marxism
attitude toward First
World War and, 71–72
in Britain, 146
European union and, 545
in France, 25, 306–307
in Germany, 137–140
in Hungary, 145–146
industry and, 256
in Italy, 539
opposition to First World
War and, 110–111
Papandreou and, 641
in Poland, 143
Popular Front and,
361–362
after Second World War,
492
in soviets, 121–122
successes and failures of,
149–150
war socialism, 97
in Western Europe, 535
Zimmerwald Conference
of, 110–111
Social market economy, 558
in West Germany,
507–508
Social mobility, 563–565
Social rank, 10–17

Social sciences, postwar
development of, 573
Social security
in Britain, 498
in France, 502
Social services, 562
Social welfare. *See also* Welfare state(s); specific
countries
in Russia, 660
Society
conservatives on, 30–31
First World War impact
on, 102–106
liberals on, 27–30
social change through
arts, 284–285
stratification of, 10–17
students in, 575–576
Sociology, 287
Solano, Javier, 676
Solar system, Newtonian, 33
Solidarity movement
(Poland), 615–616,
651, 652
Solzhenitsyn, Aleksandr, 318,
514, 611
Gulag Archipelago, The,
611, 643
*One Day in the Life of Ivan
Denisovich,* 525
Somaliland, 388
Sombart, Werner, 70
Somme, Battle of, 79
Sonnino, Sidney, 85
Sorbonne, 575, 576
Sorel, Georges, 203
South Africa, 5
Southern Europe, 633–641
agriculture in, 10
peasants in, 9
poverty in, 13
South Pole, 6
South Slavs, 47, 179
Milosevic and, 618
state of, 173
South Vietnam, 541
Souvarov, Alexander, 459
Sovereignty, First World War
and, 21, 61
Soviet bloc
in Brezhnev era, 607–620
from Stalin to
Khrushchev,
513–530

Soviet-Polish War (1920), 477
Soviets
in Budapest, 247
in Germany, 138
meaning of term, 121
Provisional Government
and, 125
in Russia, 121–125
Soviet Union, 183. *See also*
First World War;
Lenin, V. I.; Russia;
Second World War;
Stalin, Josef
anti-colonial revolutions
and, 541
arms race and, 619
in Balkans, 464–465
Brandt and, 601
British-U.S. policy and,
452–453
challenges to Bolsheviks
in, 254–255
China split with, 583–584,
586–588
Churchill and, 457
collapse of, 656–659
Cuban missile crisis and,
584
Czechoslovakia and,
400–401
Czechoslovakia invasion
by (1968), 566, 588,
589, 614
Czech treaty with, 397
degrees of Eastern European control by,
518–520
De-Stalinization and
"thaw" in, 523–526
diplomacy of, 196
disarmament and, 192
Eastern European gains
by, 414–415
Eastern Europe crackdown by, 519–520
economic growth in,
317–318
end of, 649
European union against,
545–546
in Far East, 466
forced labor in, 514
France and, 389, 590
German industry and,
480

German occupation of,
459
German treaty with
(1922), 183–184
Germany and anti-Soviet
alliance, 548
in Great Depression,
316–319
hegemony in Eastern
Europe, 457–461
industrialization in,
255–256
Jews in, 429, 515
Katyn Forest massacre
and, 650
in League of Nations,
197, 359
Marshall Plan and, 484
military officers in,
459–460
Nazi invasion of, 421,
422–424, 436
Nazi-Soviet Pact and,
403–406
organization of, 134
organized recreation in,
270–271
peace aims of, 471–472
peace treaty with Austria,
553
Polish frontier with,
476–477
Popular Front and,
357–358
power struggle in (1953-
1957), 522–526
problems under Brezhnev, 608–611
purges in, 318
reconstruction in,
508–509
revolution and, 494–495
satellite states of, 515–522
as source of Nazi labor,
427
Spanish Civil War and,
372
supranational organizations in Eastern
Europe, 552–553
survival of (1941-1943),
457–461
at Torgau, 468
in 20th century, 472–473
(map)

Soviet Union *(continued)*
  U.S. nuclear power and,
    599
  western advances by, 461
Spaak, Paul-Henri, 535, 545,
    549
Space exploration
  by Soviets, 529n
  Soviet-U.S. link-up, 586
  Sputnik and, 514
Spadolini, Giovanni, 635
Spain. *See also* Spanish Civil
    War
  in anti-Communist
    alliance, 539
  communism in, 371, 635
  democracy in, 635–637
  in EC, 594
  after First World War,
    250–252
  Franco and Falange in,
    340
  Juan Carlos in, 636
  in NATO, 546n, 636
  peasants in, 9–10
  Primo de Rivera in, 224
  Second Republic in,
    368–372
  women's suffrage in, 21,
    230
Spanish Civil War, 354,
    372–374
  France and, 389
  intellectuals and, 376
  Italian assistance in, 389
  Popular Front and, 367
Spare Rib (periodical), 578
Spartacists (Germany), 138,
    139–140, 164
SPD. *See* Social Democrats
Special Drawing Rights, 597
Spectator sports. *See also*
    Leisure
  soccer as, 272
Speculation, against U.S. dol-
    lar, 597
Speer, Albert, 426–427, 433
Speidel, Hans, 548
Spender, Stephen, 107, 375
Spengler, Oswald, 8–9, 275
Spheres of influence
  in China, 5
  after First World War, 160
  after Second World War,
    464–465, 471–472

Spitfire fighter aircraft, 420
Sports, 271–272
Springer, Axel, 561
Sputnik, 514
Squadristi (direct-action
    bands), 205, 206, 208,
    210
Srebrenica, 671
SS (*Schutzstaffel*, Nazi Ger-
    many), 428
  "Final Solution" and,
    429–431
Stadium-building, for sports,
    272
Stagflation, 625
Stakhanov, Aleksei, 317–318
Stakhanovites, 318
Stalin, Josef, 257–259, 459.
    See also Purges; Russia;
    Second World War;
    Soviet Union
  arts and, 289
  death of, 515
  de-Stalinization and,
    523–526
  in Great Depression,
    316–319
  Nazi-Soviet Pact and,
    403–405
  peace aims of, 471–472
  Poland and, 477–478
  Popular Front and,
    357–359, 377
  postwar Europe and, 463
  at Potsdam, 469
  power struggle after,
    522–526
  Second Front and, 453
  at Teheran, 463–464
  transfer of body, 524
  two-front war and, 359
  at Yalta, 465–469
Stalingrad, Battle of, 458
Stamboliski, Alexander, 248
Standard of living. *See* Living
    standards
Stanislavsky, Konstantin, 285,
    289
START agreements, 656
STASI, 617
Stauffenberg, Klaus Schenk
    von, 440
Stavisky affair, 344–345
Steel industry and
    production

  in Britain, 561
  in EC, 642
  European Coal and Steel
    Community and,
    550–551
  in Nazi Germany, 312
  Soviet, 608
  Western European vs.
    U.S. production, 595
Stendhal (Marie-Henri
    Beyle), 8, 26
Stimson, Henry, 452
Stockhausen, Karl-Heinz,
    571
Stock market crash (1929),
    294, 296. *See also*
    Great Depression
Stopes, Marie, 103
Stoph, Willi, 601–602
Stormtroopers. *See* SA
    stormtroopers (Nazi
    Germany)
Strachey, Lytton, 114
Straits, between Mediter-
    ranean and Black
    seas, 48, 159, 483
Strasser, Gregor, 329, 335
Strategic Arms Limitation
    Treaties (SALT). *See*
    SALT agreements
Strategic consideration,
    imperialism and, 6
Strauss, Richard, 37
Stravinsky, Igor, 277, 281–282
Stravinsky, Igor (Picasso), 281
Strength through Joy. *See*
    Kraft durch Freude
    (Germany)
Stresa Front, 384, 387, 389
Stresemann, Gustav,
    186–187, 190–191,
    241, 243, 382
Strikes, 62
  in Britain, 62, 578
  fascist, 206
  after First World War, 146
  during First World War,
    108–109
  in France, 365–366
  General Strike (Britain)
    and, 234–235
  in Portugal, 252
  in postwar Britain, 499
  in Vienna, 339
Stroop, Jürgen, 431

Structuralism, 643
Student discontent, 574–577
Stuka bombers, 410, 413, 414
Sturgkh, Karl (Count), 101
Sturzo, Luigi, 206
Suarez, Adolfo, 636
Submarine warfare
  in First World War, 86, 87
  in Second World War,
    412, 454
Subsistence economy, 9–10
Sudetenland
  Germans in, 180
  invasion of, 393–394
  tensions in, 397–398
  transfer to Germany,
    398–399
Suez Canal, 84
  crisis over (1956), 528,
    543, 584
  Rommel and, 453
  Second World War and,
    452
Suffrage. *See also* Women's
    suffrage
  in Britain, 62
  after First World War, 230
  in Romania, 342
  in rural Eastern Europe,
    247–248
  in Russia, 130
  universal male, 23
Suffragettes, 20
Summit diplomacy, of Cham-
    berlin, Neville, 394
"Supergrowth," economic,
    558–559
Superhighways, in Germany
    (*Autobahnen*), 312
Superpowers. *See also* Soviet
    Union; United States
  Cold War and (1947-
    1961), 533–553
Supreme Allied
    Commander-Europe
    (SACEUR), 546
Supreme Council of
    National Economy
    (Russia), 131
Supreme Revolutionary
    Council (Portugal),
    637–638
Supreme Soviet, 607
Surrealism, 115–116,
    279–280

Svoboda, Ludvík, 614
Swastika symbol, 211
Sweden, 629–630. *See also*
  Scandinavia
  conservatism in, 678
  Depression politics in,
    301
  EFTA and, 675
  Popular Front and, 362
  Social Democrats in, 151
Switzerland, neutrality of,
  424
  women's suffrage in, 21,
    230
Sykes-Picot Agreement
  (1916), 160, 167
Syndicalism, 146
  fascism and, 203
  First World War and, 73,
    102
  Italy and, 314
  in Spain, 371
Synthesizer. *See* Moog synthe-
  sizer
Synthetics, in Nazi Germany,
  312
Syria, 543
  Second World War and,
    422
Szálasi, Ferenc, 431–432
Szamuelly, Tibor, 145
Szczecin (Stettin), 615

Tactics
  in First World War, 78–79
  at Verdun, 80
Taittinger, Pierre, 217
Tanks, 83. *See also* Panzers
Tannenberg, battle at, 75, 76
Tariffs. *See also* Duties (taxes)
  Common Market and,
    551
  protective, 304
  U.S.-European, 596–597
Tatlin, Vladimir, 285
Taxation. *See also* Duties
  (taxes); Tariffs
  in Britain, 498
  in EC, 594
  income tax, 96
Taylor, A. J. P., 75, 215, 259
Tear gas, 83n
Technology. *See also* Science
  and scientists
  education and, 564

First World War weapons
    and, 82–84
  mass media and, 264–265
  prosperity and, 558
  in Second World War, 413
  student discontent and,
    575
Teheran Conference (1943),
  463–464
Telegraph, 264
Television, 560, 571
Ten, the, 594
Territorial changes
  in Eastern Europe after
    First World War,
    172–173
  after First World War, 168
  after Second World War,
    474 (map)
Territorial expansion. *See*
  Expansionism
Terrorism, 579
Teschen, 173–175, 179, 182,
  183, 402
Thälmann, Ernst, 245
Thatcher, Margaret, 540,
  620, 631–633, 665
"Thaw" (Soviet Union),
  523–526
  rebellion and, 526–529
Theater
  in Germany, 284–285
  in Russia, 285
Theology. *See also* Religion
  postwar, 572
Theory of relativity (Ein-
  stein), 287
Theresienstadt, 429
Thermonuclear bomb. *See
  also* Atomic bomb;
    Bombs and bombings;
    Nuclear power
  Soviets and, 514
Third Force, Europe as, 592
Third International (Com-
  intern), 150–152, 196,
    237, 520
  Italy and, 148n
  Norwegian Socialists in,
    349
  Popular Front and,
    357–358
  Radic and, 249
  reversal of policy (1934),
    359–360

Seventh Congress of,
    360
  Sixth Congress of, 357
Third Reich. *See* Nazi
  Germany
Third Republic (France),
  220, 236–239, 307,
    433–434, 500
Third World
  anticolonialism in, 541
  Catholic Church in, 572
  de Gaulle and, 591
  European trade with, 596
  "North-South dialogue"
    and, 596
  population and, 18
  Sino-Soviet relations and,
    587
  Soviet Union and, 526,
    619
Thirty Years' War, 44
Thomson, J. J., 32
Thorez, Maurice, 357, 363
Three-dimensional (3-D)
  movies, 266
Threepenny Opera, The (Brecht
  and Weill), 276, 284,
    295
Three White Bellflowers (Klee),
  283
Thyssen, Fritz, 326
Tildy, Zoltán, 520
Time Machine, The (Wells),
  29
Tin Drum, The (Grass), 490,
  506
Tirol, 85–86
Tito, 492, 493, 516n, 618
  resistance to Nazis by,
    440–441
Todt, Fritz, 426
Togliatti, Palmiro, 504, 603
Toller, Ernst, 140
Torgau, Germany, Soviet-
  U.S. armies at, 468,
    478
Tories (Britain). *See* Conserv-
  ative Party (Tories,
    Britain)
Totalitarian regimes. *See also*
  Dictatorship; specific
    regimes
  Nazi Germany and, 313
  organized recreation
    and, 270–271

Total war. *See also* First World
  War
  First World War as, 87–88
Touraine, Alain, 626n
Tour de France, 272
Town and Country Planning
  Act (Britain, 1943),
    498
Trade, 2–4. *See also* Duties
  (taxes); Free trade;
    Tariffs
  British, 499
  Common Market and,
    551
  European-U.S. rivalry
    and, 596
  after First World War, 229
  imperialism and, 5
  of Nazi Germany, 312
  after Second World War,
    475
Trade Act (1974, U.S.), 642
Trade Union Congress
  (TUC, Britain), 235,
    236
Trade unions. *See also* Labor;
  Labor unions
  in France, 72, 537
  in Germany, 240,
    309–310
  in Italy, 537
Transistors, 558
Trans-Siberian Railroad, 5
Transylvania, 46, 86, 150,
  159, 163, 179, 342,
    519, 666
Travel, 2–4, 272–273
  airplanes and, 272–273
  German knapsack travel,
    273
  as leisure activity,
    564–565
  ocean liners and, 273
  sea bathing and, 273
Treaties. *See also* Paris peace
  settlement (1919)
  of Amsterdam, 675
  Belgian Neutrality, 59–60
  of Brest-Litovsk, 128, 133,
    135, 173
  of Brussels, 545
  in First World War,
    159–161
  Locarno Agreements
    and, 188–190

Treaties *(continued)*
of London (1915), 85,
159
Maastricht, 674
of Montreux, 483
Moscow (1970), 601
of mutual assistance, 183
mutual security, 360
of Neuilly, 164
Nuclear Test Ban, 586
Peace of Riga and, 133
of Rapallo, 184, 196, 359
of Rome (1958), 593
of Saint Germain, 164,
338
secret treaties in World
War I, 134, 158, 159,
161
of Sèvres, 164
of Trianon, 164, 215
of Versailles, 156, 162,
164, 182, 382–383,
384
Trench warfare, 78, 79, 82,
83
at Verdun, 81
Trentino, 77, 85
Treuhandanstalt, 667
Trianon, Treaty of, 164, 215
Tripartisme, 503
Triple Alliance, 53n
Tristes Tropiques (Lévi-
Strauss), 574
Triumph of the Will, The
(Riefenstahl), 267,
332
Trotsky, Leon, 110, 125–126,
127, 128, 150, 158,
255–256, 538
on culture, 285
on France, 365
Russian Civil War and,
133
Stalin and, 258
Truman, Harry S *See also*
Truman Doctrine
on Poland, 478
at Potsdam, 469–470
Truman Doctrine, 483–484
Tsar. *See* Alexander I
(Russia); Nicholas II
(Russia)
Tudjman, Franjo, 665, 670, 671

Tukhachevsky, Mikhail, 133,
318
Tunisia, 5, 453
Turkey, 50. *See also* Ottoman
Empire
First World War and, 77,
84, 86
Greek independence
from, 27
after Second World War,
483
treaty with (1919), 164
Truman Doctrine and,
483–484
Turks, in Bulgaria, 618
Twentieth Party Congress
(Soviet Union), 319
Twenty-Five Points (Nazi
Party), 213
Twenty-One Points (Lenin),
151
Twenty-third Party Congress
(Soviet Union), 608
Twittering Machine (Klee),
282
Two Cheers for Democracy
(Forster), 319
Tzara, Tristan, 114

Ukraine, 46, 467, 658
Germans welcomed in,
422–423
nationalism in, 133–
134
Poles and, 179
Russian Provisional Gov-
ernment and, 123
Ulbricht, Walter, 508, 602,
612
Ulianov, Vladimir. *See* Lenin,
V. I.
Ulster, 62–63
Ulysses (Joyce), 280
Unconscious
in arts, 279–280
Freud and, 36, 280
in literature, 280
Underground, resistance to
Nazis and, 437–438
Unemployment
in Britain, 294, 303,
497–498, 632
in France, 306

in Germany, 292, 309,
310
in Great Depression, 294
in Italy, 206
Keynes on, 305
in Nazi Germany, 312
in 1970s-1980s, 625
Unification
of Germany, 26, 654–656
of Italy, 26
Union movement, in Poland,
615–616
Union of Soviet Socialist
Republics (USSR). *See*
Soviet Union
Union of Zemstvos and
Towns, 99, 121
Unions. *See* Labor unions
Union Treaties, in Soviet federation, 657, 658
United African Company, 5
United Nations, 462, 464,
465n
Germanies in, 584
Khrushchev at, 512,
523
United Nations Declaration
(1942), 452
United States. *See also* Dollar
(U.S.); Stock market
crash (1929); specific
countries
air strikes against Bosnian
Serbs and, 671, 672,
675
arms race and, 619
business subsidiaries and
branches in Europe,
597
Cold War, Europe, and,
583–584
de Gaulle and, 592
empire of, 6
European economic
rivalry with, 595–598
European investments in,
3–4
expatriate writers from,
282
in First World War, 87–88,
135
First World War repara-
tions and, 171

French nuclear weapons
and, 590
Great Depression and, 297
hegemony in Western
Europe, 450–457
investments in Common
Market countries,
596–597
Iran and, 483
Kellogg-Briand Pact and,
190
labor militancy in, 146
peace aims of, 472–475
peacekeeping force to
Bosnia, 671
rivalry with Europe over
agriculture, 595–596
in Second World War,
426, 450–457
intervention in Russia by,
132
Second World War strat-
egy and, 452–453
steel imports in, 642
Suez Campaign and, 543
at Torgau, 468
Trade Act (1974) in, 642
Treaty of Versailles and,
182
unemployment in, 294
Uruguay Round and,
645–646
Yalta Conference and,
466–467
United States of Europe,
544
United Steel (Germany),
245
Universal manhood suffrage,
23, 230
Universal suffrage. *See* Suffrage; Universal man-
hood suffrage;
Women's suffrage
Universities, student discontent and, 574–577
University education, 563, 564
UNRRA (United Nations
Relief and Rehabilita-
tion Agency), 491
Untermenschen (subhumans),
459
Upper class, leisure of, xvi

Upper middle class, 13–14
Upper Silesia, 177 (map), 182, 187
Uprooted, The (Barrès), 8
Upward mobility, 17
Urban living, 7, 8–9. *See also* Cities and towns
Uruguay Round, 645–646
USSR. *See* Soviet Union
Ustasha, 432, 670

Vacations, 564–565
in France, 270
Vacuum tube, 264
Vailland, Roger, 16
Valéry, Paul, 2
Valois, Georges, 217
Value-added tax, in EC, 594
Vandenberg, Arthur, 546
Van Gogh, Vincent, 34, 282
Van Severen, Joris, 348
Van Zeeland, Paul, 349
Varèse, Edgard, 571
"Varieties of Religious Experience, The" (James), 7
Vatican II, 572
Vatican City, papal sovereignty in, 253
Vecchi, Cesare de, 207
"Velvet revolution," in Czechoslovakia, 653, 654
Venice, 8
Verdinasos, 348
Verdun, 79, 80, 81, 90 (illus.)
flame thrower at, 83
Verdun (Romains), 70, 80, 106
Versailles Treaty (1919), 156, 162, 164. *See also* Paris peace settlement (1919)
dismantlement of, 187
first violations of, 384
German-Austrian *Anschluß* and, 382–384
Weimar Republic and, 240
Veterans
fascist roots and, 222
Mussolini and, 204
Vichy France, 421, 500. *See also* France; Pétain, Philippe

collaboration in killings of Jews, 431
collaboration with Nazis, 433–434
in North Africa, 453–454
Syria and, 422
Victor Emmanuel III (Italy), 102, 207, 208, 388, 455, 503–504
Vienna, 8. *See also* Austria
bank failure in, 297
Black Friday in, 338
Vienna Conference (1815), 173
Vietminh, 542. *See also* Vietnam War
independence movement of, 541
Vietnam War, 597
dollar and, 584
Vilna, 181–182, 183
Violence
in British general strike of 1926, 235–236
by Mussolini's *squadristi,* 205
by Nazis, 214, 326
Visconti, Luchino, 571
Vittorio Veneto, battle at, 143
Viviani, René, 52, 54, 56, 104
Vladivostok, Russian Civil War and, 132
Vlasov, Andrei, 459
Volk (Germany), 212, 391
Volkswagen, "Beetle" of 313, 594–595
Vollmar, Georg von, 150
Voltaire (François-Marie Arouet), 28
Volunteers, in British Army, 95
Voting and voting rights. *See also* Suffrage
after First World War, 230
parliaments and, 23
after Second World War, 493
socialist parties and, 24
for women, 21, 104
V2's, 464
Vyborg, destruction of, 490

Waffen-SS, 432. *See also* SS (*Schutzstaffel,* Nazi Germany)
Wages
in Britain, 304
in France, 309
in Italy, 315
Hitler and, 313
labor-management relations and, 577–578
Waiting for Godot (Beckett), 538
Walesa, Lech, 615–616, 652, 664, 666
Wallachia, independence of, 46
Walloons, 348
Walwal, 388
War aims, in First World War, 134, 135, 158
War and warfare. *See also* specific wars
appeasement and, 394–397, 400–402
before First World War, 43–44
in postwar colonial empires, 540–543
renunciation of, 190
War Communism, in Russia, 254
War Crimes Tribunal, 470
War debts
in First World War, 171, 450
moratorium on, 298
War economy, of Nazi Germany, 426–427
War governments, dismantling, 228–229
War of the Worlds, The (Wells), 29
War Industries Committee (Russia), 99, 121
War Raw Materials Corporations, 106
Warsaw, after Second World War, 488
Warsaw ghetto, resistance in, 431
Warsaw Pact, 485, 553, 652
abolition of, 656
Final Act and, 603

War socialism, 97
"War to end wars," 157
Washington Naval Conference (1921, 1922), 193
Waterloo, size of force at, 78
Watson, James, 573
Waugh, Evelyn, 376
Way of All Flesh, The (Butler), 15
Wazyk, Adam, 526–527
Wealth
disposable, 561–562
distribution of, 560–563, 659–660
of European Community, 583–584
national, 560
Wealthy people, 13–14
Weapons. *See also* Artillery; Atomic bomb; Disarmament; Nuclear power; specific wars; specific weapons
expenditures on, 600n
in First World War, 78, 82–84
Germany and, 310
missile levels in 1984, 602
of Nazi Germany, 412
in unified Germany, 655
U.S. production of, 450
V2's, 464
Web. *See* World Wide Web
Webb, Beatrice and Sidney, 319
Weber, Max, 19, 230, 287
Webern, Anton, 278
Weddings (Stravinsky), 282
Weill, Kurt, 276, 284, 295
Weimar Coalition, 241–243
Weimar Constitution, 230, 239–240
government by decree under, 310
Hitler and, 332–333
Weimar Republic (Germany), 140, 183, 186, 239–245
arts in, 282
"autonomy" in, 211–212
chancellors in, 327–331
enemies of, 211

Weimar Republic *(continued)*
  Great Coalition in,
    243–245
  Great Depression and,
    309–311
  Nazi Party and, 213
  presidential government
    and end of, 327–331
  Soviet Union and, 196
Weizmann, Chaim, 161
Welfare state(s)
  in Britain, 498
  confidence in, 565–566
  conservatism in, 629–633
  in Depression era Scandi-
    navia, 302
  in France, 502
  in Germany, 507
  stress in, 629–641
Wells, H. G., 29, 157
Werfel, Alma Mahler, 282
"Wessies" (West Germans),
    666, 668
West. *See also* Western
    Europe
  German occupying pow-
    ers in, 481
Western Europe
  Allied invasion of, 464
  centrist and conservative
    governments in,
    538–540
  Cold War politics in,
    535–543
  de Gaulle and, 592
  distribution of wealth in,
    560–563
  division of left wing in,
    537–538
  Far Right in, 628, 676–678
  fascism in, 343–349
  immigration restrictions
    in, 627
  intermediate range mis-
    siles in, 619
  in late 1980s, 645–646
  New Middle in, 676–678
  nuclear weapons, MLF,
    and, 599–600
  Paris Peace Conference
    settlement in,
    167–172
  postindustrial society in,
    623–624, 626

revolutionary movements
    in (1917), 134–136
  revolution of 1989 and,
    673–678
  after Second World War,
    471–472
  Second World War in
    (1940), 415–421
  structural problems in,
    624–625
  U.S. hegemony in,
    450–457
Western European Union
    (WEU), 676
Western front
  in First World War, 77–84
  in Second World War,
    467 (map)
West Germany, 481, 506–507
  consensus politics in, 566
  disarmament movement
    in, 619
  East German negotia-
    tions with, 601–602
  economic miracle in,
    507–508
  Far Right in, 628
  missiles in, 619
  in NATO, 548
  neo-Nazism in, 628
  Poland and, 582
  recession in, 642
  Social Democratic Party
    (SPD) in, 567, 601
  social welfare and conser-
    vatism in, 630–631
  unification and, 654–656
  in United Nations, 584,
    602
Weygand, Maxime, 418
Wheatley, John, 232
Wheatley Housing Act
    (Britain, 1924), 232,
    304
White-collar workers, 16,
    565
Whiteley, William, 549
Whites, in Russian Civil War,
    133, 147
White Terror, in Hungary,
    146, 217
Wife, role of, 19–21
Wilberforce, Samuel,
    31–32

Wilhelm II (Germany), 51,
    55, 98
  abdication of, 137
  domestic peace
    announcement by, 73
  First World War peace
    and, 136
  George V (Britain) and,
    57–59
  museums and, 37
William Tell (Schiller), 284
Wilson, Harold, 537, 568,
    632
Wilson, Horace, 396
Wilson, Woodrow, 101, 135,
    157n, 162
  diplomacy and, 193
  First World War and, 87
  Fourteen Points of,
    158–159
  peace settlement and,
    136, 162–163
Winter war, between Rus-
    sians and Finns, 415,
    416
"Wireless" radio. *See* Tele-
    graph
Witos, Wincenty, 248, 250
Wittgenstein, Ludwig, 287,
    573
Women
  churches and, 572
  employment of, 95, 426,
    564
  family life and, 18–21
  First World War and,
    103–104
  roles of, 19–21, 28, 495,
    564
  in Russian Revolution,
    120, 127
  status of, 639
Women's liberation, 578
Women's suffrage, 20–21,
    230, 493, 495
  in Britain, 62, 230
  in Finland, 21, 230
  in France and Italy, 230,
    493
  in Germany, 230
  in Norway, 21, 230
  outside Europe, 21
  in Portugal, 21, 230, 495
  in Spain, 230, 369, 370

in Switzerland, 21, 230,
    495
Woolf, Leonard, 30, 43
Workday, length of, 269
Workers, 16. *See also* Labor;
    Labor unions; Revolu-
    tion(s); Socialists and
    socialism
  in Britain, 234
  discontents of, 577–578
  First World War and,
    72–73
  inflation and, 107
  leisure and, 269–273,
    564–565
  living standards of,
    12–13, 624
  Marxism and, 377
  movement of, 562
  Mussolini and, 204
  occupation of Italian fac-
    tories by, 204–205
  resistance to Nazis by, 436
  in Russia, 256–257
  social services for, 562
  Solidarity in Poland and,
    615–616
  white- and blue-collar,
    565
Workers' Truth Movement
    (Russia), 255
Working class. *See* Workers
Working-class culture, Beat-
    les and, 568–569
Workweek
  in France, 366
  length of, 269–270, 309
World Cup contests (soccer),
    272
World Disarmament Confer-
    ence (1932), 192–193
World Trade Organization
    (WTO), 682
World War I. *See* First World
    War
World War II. *See* Second
    World War
World Wide Web, 682
Wozzeck (Berg), 276, 278, 282
Wright brothers, 272
Writers. *See also* Literature;
    specific writers and
    works
  in Soviet Union, 610

X-rays, 32

Yalta Conference (1945),
     461, 465–469
   concessions at, 478
Yaoundé Convention (1963),
     596
Yeltsin, Boris
   health of, 662
   after Soviet collapse,
     659–664
   Soviet collapse and,
     657–659
York, England, poverty in,
     12, 562
Young, Owen D., 191

Young Plan, 169, 191
   Hitler and, 324
Young Turk movement, 48
Youth culture, worldwide,
     574
Ypres, 79
   battle at, 82
   poison gas at, 83
Yugo (car), 618
Yugoslav Committee, 142
Yugoslav Federation, 668
Yugoslavia, 145, 150, 173,
     179, 246, 248. *See also*
     Croatia; Montenegro;
     Serbia; Slovenia; Milo-
     sevic, Slobodan
   China and, 587

civil war in, 668–673
communism in, 516,
     589
conflicts in former,
     668–673, 669 (map)
Fiume and, 182
Hitler and, 181
Little Entente and, 183
monarchy in, 229
national minorities and,
     249
resistance to Nazis in,
     440–441
in Second World War,
     422
after Tito, 618
Tito in, 492

Zhdanov, Andrei, 513–514,
     520
Zhirinovsky, Vladimir, 662
Zhivkov, Todor, 618, 652
Zhukov, Georgi, 423, 461
Zimmermann Note, 87
Zimmerwald Conference,
     110–111
Zinoviev, Grigori, 125, 196,
     233, 255–256
   Stalin and, 258
Zionism, 161, 543
Zola, Émile, 280
Zones. *See* Occupation zones
Zyklon-B gas, in extermina-
     tion camps, 429
Zyuganov, Gennady, 662